W9-CJZ-347

DIRECTORY OF RESEARCH GRANTS 2008

32nd Edition, Volume 1

Schoolhouse Partners LLC
Nashville, Indiana

authorHOUSE®

AuthorHouse™
1663 Liberty Drive, Suite 200
Bloomington, IN 47403
www.authorhouse.com
Phone: 1-800-839-8640

AuthorHouse™ UK Ltd.
500 Avebury Boulevard
Central Milton Keynes, MK9 2BE
www.authorhouse.co.uk
Phone: 08001974150

© 2007, 2008 by Schoolhouse Partners LLC
Schoolhouse Partners, Post Office Box 2059, Nashville, Indiana 47448
www.schoolhousepartners.net
Published 1975, 32nd edition 2008

No part of this book may be reproduced, stored in a retrieval system, or transmitted by any means without the written permission of the author.

ISBN: 978-1-4343-8448-5 (sc)

First published by AuthorHouse 04/30/2008

Printed in the United States of America
Bloomington, Indiana

This book is printed on acid-free paper.

Editorial Staff

Managing Editor
Louis S. Schafer

Associate Editor
Anita Schafer

Data Manager
Doug Springer

Other Contributors
Norman Crampton
Clara Gunter
Tammy McKee

Table of Contents

Introduction

For over three decades the GRANTS Database and its print complements, including the annual *Directory of Research Grants*, have provided the research community with current, accurate information regarding funding for research-related programs and projects, scholarships, fellowships, conferences, and internships. To meet the increased information needs of professionals, the GRANTS Database, researched and edited by members of the Schoolhouse Partners editorial staff, has grown significantly. This 32nd edition of the annual *Directory of Research Grants* offers factual and concise descriptions of more than 4,100 research funding programs. With this new edition both experienced and novice grantseekers will be better able to target only the most applicable programs for their research needs.

Directory of Research Grants 2008

The *Directory of Research Grants 2008* features listings of programs that offer non-repayable research funding for projects in medicine, the physical and social sciences, the arts and humanities, education, community and economic development, and children and youth programs. Listings in the main section of the *Directory* contain annotations describing each program's focuses and goals, program requirements explaining eligibility, funding amounts, deadlines, *Catalog of Federal Domestic Assistance* program number (for U.S. government programs only), sponsor name and address, contact information, and the sponsor's Internet Web address. Grantseekers with access to the Internet can use the addresses to locate further information about the organizations and their application procedures. Internet addresses are also provided, when available, within listings. Some of the grant programs listed in the main section have geographic restrictions for applicants.

Indexes. The Subject Index of this *Directory* lists all program titles—with accession numbers—under their applicable subject terms. Other indexes follow, including the Sponsoring Organizations Index, which lists program sponsors alphabetically along with their programs; the Grants by Program Type Index, which lists 38 program categories, such as Basic Research, Fellowships, Travel Grants, etc., with the grants that fall within their scope; and the Geographic Index, which lists programs that have state, regional, or international focus. See How to Use This Directory on pages v-vii for sample index entries.

Using the *Directory* for Grantseeking

By using the *Directory of Research Grants*, grantseekers can match the needs of their particular programs with those sponsors offering funding in the researchers' area of interest. The information listed here is meant to eliminate the costs incurred by both grantseekers and grantmakers when inappropriate proposals are submitted for a sponsor's funding program. However, because the GRANTS Database is updated daily basis, with program listings continually added, deleted, and revised, grantseekers using this *Directory* may also search the GRANTS database online through *GrantSelect* (www.grantselect.com).

All new and revised information has been taken from (1) the sponsor's updated of previously published program statements included in earlier editions of GRANTS publications, (2) questionnaires sent to sponsors whose programs were not listed in previous editions, or (3) other materials published by the sponsor and furnished to Schoolhouse Partners. Updated information for U.S. government programs includes new and revised program information published in the *Federal Register*; the latest edition of the *Catalog of Federal Domestic Assistance*; the *NIH Guide*, published weekly by the National Institutes of Health; and the *NSF E-Bulletin*, a monthly publication of the National Science Foundation. Included in this edition are identifying document numbers from the NIH and NSF publications. Located at the ends of the program descriptions in certain entries, the numbers indicated the ongoing NIH program number (PA) or the request for applications number (RFA). For programs of the National Science Foundation, the *NSF Bulletin* number appears. This information will help users identify the programs when seeking additional information from program staff.

While Schoolhouse Partners has made every effort to verify that all information is both accurate and current within the confines of format and scope, the publisher does not assume and hereby disclaims any liability to any party for loss or damages caused by errors or omissions in this *Directory*, whether such errors or missions result from accident, negligence, or any other cause. Anyone having questions regarding the content, format, or any other aspect of the *Directory of Research Grants 2008*, GrantSelect, or the GRANTS Database should contact the Editors, GRANTS, Schoolhouse Partners or editor@schoolhousepartners.net.

How to Use This Directory

The *Directory of Research Grants 2008* is designed to allow the user quick and easy access to information regarding funding programs in a researcher's specific area of interest. This *Directory* is composed of a main section, Grant Programs, which lists grant programs in alphabetical order, and three indexes: the Subject Index, the Grants by Program Type Index, and the Geographic Index.

GRANT PROGRAMS

Each listing in this section consists of the following elements: an annotation describing each program's focus and goals, requirements explaining eligibility, funding amounts, application and renewal dates, the *Catalog of Federal Domestic Assistance* program number (for U.S. government programs only), sponsor information, contact information, and Internet address.

GRANT TITLE — **Paul G. Allen Family Foundation Grants** **4298** — ACCESSION NUMBER

The single foundation, created through the consolidation of Allen's six previous foundations (The Allen Foundation for the Arts, The Paul G. Allen Charitable Foundation, The Paul G. Allen Foundation for Medical Research, The Paul G. Allen Forest Protection Foundation, The Allen Foundation for Music, and The Paul G. Allen Virtual Education Foundation), will continue to focus on the Allen family's philanthropic interests in the areas of arts and culture, youth engagement, community development and social change, and scientific and technological innovation. The Arts and Culture Program fosters creativity and promotes critical thinking by helping strong arts organizations become sustainable and supporting projects that feature innovative and diverse artistic forms. The Youth Engagement Program — GRANT DESCRIPTION — improves the way young people learn by supporting organizations that use innovative teaching strategies and provide opportunities for children to address issues relevant to their lives. The Community Development and Social Change Program promotes individual and community development by supporting initiatives and organizations that provide access to resources and opportunities. The Scientific and Technological Innovation Program advances promising scientific and technology research that has the potential to enhance understanding and stewardship of the world in which we live. Organizations may only receive one grant per year. Organizations must not have any delinquent final reports due to any of the Paul G. Allen Foundations for previous grants. Grantseekers are encouraged to apply through the online application process, where basic organizational and project information will be requested. Guidelines are available online.

REQUIREMENTS — *Requirements* 501(c)3 tax-exempt organizations, status from the Internal Revenue government entities, and IRS-recognized tribes are eligible. Eligible organizations must be located in, or serving populations of, the Pacific Northwest, which includes Alaska, Idaho, Montana, Oregon, and Washington.

RESTRICTIONS — *Restrictions* In general, the foundation will not consider requests for general fund drives, annual appeals, or federated campaigns; special events or sponsorships; direct grants, scholarships, or loans for the benefit of specific individuals; projects of organizations whose policies or practices discriminate on the basis of race, ethnic origin, sex, creed, or sexual orientation; contributions to sectarian or religious organizations whose principle activity is for the benefit of their own members or adherents; loans or debt retirement; projects that will benefit the students of a single school; general operating support for ongoing activities; or projects not aligned with the foundation's specified program areas. 509(a) private foundations are ineligible.

APPLICATION/ RENEWAL DATE — *Date(s) Application Is Due* Mar 31; Sep 30.

Contact Grants Administrator, (206) 342-2030; fax: (206) 342-3030; email: info@pgafamilyfoundation.org — CONTACT

INTERNET ADDRESS — *Internet* http://www.pgafamilyfoundation.org

Sponsor Paul G. Allen Family Foundation — SPONSOR INFORMATION
505 Fifth Ave S, Ste 900
Seattle, WA 98104

SUBJECT INDEX

The most effective way to access specific funding programs is through the Subject Index. This index lists the subject terms with applicable grants program titles – and their accession numbers – alphabetically under each term. Terms were assigned to target the specific area of research designated in the description of each program. Cross-references are used to link subjects and assist the user in finding specific grant information.

Following are general guidelines that can make your search of this index more successful. First, check under the specific topic of interest rather than a more general term. For instance, if you are interested in chemical engineering, look under "Chemical Engineering" rather than "Engineering." Items indexed under "Engineering" indicate funding in broad areas of engineering.

Use general headings when you want grants covering broader areas or if you can't find a specific topic. For example, many grants list funding for humanities research, health programs, or science and technology. To find these grants use such headings as "Humanities," "Medical Programs," "Science," or "Technology." For additional grant information on more specific humanities research opportunities, such as in American History or Cultural Anthropology, also check under the topics "United States History" and "Anthropology, Cultural."

Many of the grant programs provide funding for research-related scholarships, faculty fellowships, dissertations, undergraduate education, conferences, or internships. If grant funds are designated for specific disciplines, you will find the items under the specific subject. Scholarships and fellowships are also listed under the terms "Native American Education," "African Americans (Student Support)," "Hispanic Education," "Minority Education," and "Women's Education."

Grants concerning study of a particular country are listed under the name of the country. Grants concerning the history, literature, art and language of a country are listed under the name of the country also, e.g., "Chinese Art" and "Chinese Language/Literature."

SUBJECT TERM ——— **Education**

A.L. Mailman Family Foundation Grants, 5
AAAS Science & Technology Policy Fellowships - Health, Education & Human Services, 22
AARP Andrus Foundation Grants, 104
Abbott Laboratories Fund Grants, 125
ACIE Host University Edmund S. Muskie/Freedom Support Act Graduate Fellowships, 156
ACT Awards, 189
Akonadi Foundation Anti-Racism Grants, 351 ——— **PROGRAM TITLE**
Akron Community Foundation Grants, 352
Albert and Margaret Alkek Foundation Grants, 370
Albuquerque Community Foundation Grants, 379
Alcoa Foundation Grants, 380
Alcon Foundation Grants Program, 382

GEOGRAPHIC INDEX

This index lists programs that have state, regional, or international geographic focus. The Geographic Index is arranged by state, followed by Canadian programs, then by international programs by country, and lists grant program titles and their corresponding accession numbers.

COUNTRY ——— **United States**

Alabama ——— **STATE**

3M Fndn Grants, 2
Alabama Humanities Fndn Grants Program, 368
Arkema Inc. Fndn Science Teachers Program, 705
CDC Injury Control Research Centers Grants, 1198
DOE Experimental Program to Stimulate Competitive Research (EPSCoR), 1653
PROGRAM TITLE ——— Hill Crest Fndn Grants, 2293
Linn-Henley Charitable Trust Grants, 2777
NOAA Community-Based Restoration Program (CRP) Grants, 3843
Southern Company's Longleaf Pine Reforestation Fund, 4726

PROGRAM TYPE INDEX

This index is broken into 38 categories according to the type of program funded:

- Adult Basic Education
- Adult/Family Literacy Training
- Awards/Prizes
- Basic Research
- Building Construction and/or Renovation
- Capital Campaigns
- Centers: Research/Demonstration/Service
- Citizenship Instruction
- Community Development
- Consulting/Visiting Personnel
- Cultural Outreach
- Curriculum Development/Teacher Training
- Demonstration Grants
- Development (Institutional/Departmental)
- Dissertation/Thesis Research Support
- Educational Programs
- Environmental Programs
- Exhibitions, Collections, Performances, Video/ Film Production
- Faculty/Professional Development
- Fellowships
- General Operating Support
- Graduate Assistantships
- International Exchange Programs
- International Grants
- Job Training/Adult Vocational Programs
- Matching/Challenge Funds
- Materials/Equipment Acquisition (Computers, Books, Tapes, etc.)
- Preservation/Restoration
- Publishing/Editing/Translating
- Religious Programs
- Scholarships
- Seed Grants
- Service Delivery Programs
- Symposia, Conferences, Workshops, Seminars
- Technical Assistance
- Training Programs/Internships
- Travel Grants
- Vocational Education

Government and Organization Acronyms

AAAAI	American Academy of Allergy Asthma and Immunology
AAAS	American Association for the Advancement of Science
AACAP	American Academy of Child and Adolescent Psychiatry
AACN	American Association of Critical Care Nurses
AACR	American Association of Cancer Research
AAFCS	American Association of Family and Consumer Sciences
AAFP	American Academy of Family Physicians Foundation
AAFPRS	American Academy of Facial Plastic and Reconstructive Surgery
AAR	American Academy in Rome
AAS	American Antiquarian Society
AASL	American Association of School Libraries
AAUW	American Association of University Women
ACC	Asian Cultural Council
ACLS	American Council of Learned Societies
ACM	Association for Computing Machinery
ACS	American Cancer Society
ADA	American Diabetes Association
ADHF	American Digestive Health Foundation
AF	Arthritis Foundation
AFAR	American Federation for Aging Research
AFOSR	Air Force Office of Scientific Research
AFUD	American Foundation for Urologic Disease
AFUW	Australian Federation of University Women
AGS	American Geriatrics Society
AHA	American Heart Association
AHAF	American Health Assistance Foundation
AFHMR	Alberta Heritage Foundation for Medical Research
AHRQ	Agency for Healthcare Research and Quality
AICR	American Institute for Cancer Research
AIIS	American Institute for Indian Studies
AJA	American Jewish Archives
ALA	American Library Association
ALISE	Association for Library and Information Science Education
AMNH	American Museum of Natural History
AMS	American Musicological Society
ANL	Argonne National Library
ANS	American Numismatic Society
AOA	American Osteopathic Association
APA	American Psychological Association
APSA	American Political Science Association
ARIT	American Research Institute in Turkey
ARO	Army Research Office
ASA	American Statistical Association
ASCSA	American School of Classical Studies at Athens
ASECS	American Society for Eighteenth-Century Studies
ASF	American-Scandinavian Foundation
ASHRAE	American Society of Heating, Refrigerating, and Air Conditioning Engineers
ASME	American Society of Mechanical Engineers
ASNS	American Society for Nutritional Sciences
ASPRS	American Society of Photogrammetry and Remote Sensing
AWU	Associated Western Universities
AWWA	American Water Works Association
BA	British Academy
BWF	Burroughs Wellcome Fund
CBIE	Canadian Bureau for International Education
CCFF	Canadian Cystic Fibrosis Foundation
CDC	Centers for Disease Control and Prevention
CES	Council for European Studies
CF	The Commonwealth Fund
CFF	Cystic Fibrosis Foundation
CFPC	College of Family Physicians of Canada
CFUW	Canadian Federation of University Women
CHEA	Canadian Home Economics Association
CIES	Council for International Exchange of Scholars
CIUS	Canadian Institute of Ukrainian Studies
CLA	Canadian Lung Association
CLF	Canadian Liver Foundation
CRI	Cancer Research Institute
DAAD	Deutscher Akademische Austauschdienst (German Academic Exchange Service)
DHHS	Department of Health and Human Services
DOA	Department of Agriculture
DOC	Department of Commerce
DOD	Department of Defense
DOE	Department of Energy
DOI	Department of the Interior
DOJ	Department of Justice
DOL	Department of Labor
DOS	Department of State
DOT	Department of Transportation
EFA	Epilepsy Foundation of America
EPA	Environmental Protection Agency
ESF	European Science Foundation
ETS	Educational Testing Service
FCAR	Formation de Chercheurs et L'Aide a la Recherche
FDA	Food and Drug Administration
FIC	Fogarty International Center
GAAC	German American Academic Council
GCA	Garden Club of America

HHMI Howard Hughes Medical Institute
HRSA Health Resources and Services Administration
HUD Department of Housing and Urban Development
IRA International Reading Association
IREX International Research and Exchanges Board
IUCP Indiana University Center on Philanthropy
JDF Juvenile Diabetes Foundation International
JMO John M. Olin Foundation
JSPS Japan Society for the Promotion of Science
KFC Kidney Foundation of Canada
LSA Leukemia Society of America
MHRC Manitoba Health Research Council
MLA Medical Library Association
MMA Metropolitan Museum of Art
MSSC Multiple Sclerosis Society of Canada
NAACP National Association for the Advancement of Colored People
NARSAD National Alliance for Research on Schizophrenia and Depression
NASM National Air and Space Museum
NATO North Atlantic Treaty Organization
NCCAM National Center for Complementary and Alternative Medicine
NCI National Cancer Institute
NCIC National Cancer Institute of Canada
NCRR National Center for Research Resources
NEH National Endowment for the Humanities
NEI National Eye Institute
NFID National Foundation for Infectious Diseases
NFWF National Fish and Wildlife Foundation
NHGRI National Human Genome Research Institute
NHLBI National Heart, Lung and Blood Institute
NIA National Institute on Aging
NIAAA National Institute on Alcohol Abuse and Alcoholism
NIAF National Italian American Foundation
NIAID National Institute of Allergy and Infectious Diseases
NIAMS National Institute of Arthritis and Musculoskeletal Skin Diseases
NICHD National Institute of Child Health and Human Development
NIDA National Institute on Drug Abuse
NIDCD National Institute on Deafness and Other Communication Disorders
NIDCR National Institute of Dental and Craniofacial Research
NIDDK National Institute of Diabetes, and Digestive and Kidney Diseases
NIDRR National Institute on Disability and Rehabilitation Research
NIEHS National Institute of Environmental Health Sciences
NIGMS National Institute of General Medical Sciences
NIH National Institutes of Health
NIJ National Institute of Justice
NIMH National Institute of Mental Health
NINDS National Institute of Neurological Disorders and Stroke
NINR National Institute of Nursing Research
NIOSH National Institute for Occupational Safety and Health
NIST National Institute of Standards and Technology
NKF National Kidney Foundation
NL Newberry Library
NLM National Library of Medicine
NMF National Medical Fellowships, Inc.
NMSS National Multiple Sclerosis Society
NOAA National Oceanic and Atmospheric Administration
NRC National Research Council
NSERC Natural Sciences and Engineering Research Council of Canada
NSF National Science Foundation
OAH Organization of American Historians
ONF Oncology Nursing Foundation
ONR Office of Naval Research
OREF Orthopaedic Research and Education Foundation
ORISE Oak Ridge Institute for Science and Education
OSI Open Society Institute
PDF Parkinson's Disease Foundation
PhRMA Pharmaceutical Research and Manufacturers of American Foundation
PHSC The Photographic Historical Society of Canada
RCPSC Royal College of Physicians and Surgeons of Canada
RSC Royal Society of Canada
RWJF Robert Wood Johnson Foundation
SLA Special Libraries Association
SSHRC Social Sciences and Humanities Research Council of Canada
SSRC Social Science Research Council
STTI Sigma Theta Tau International
USHMM United States Holocaust Memorial Museum Research Institute
USIA United States Information Agency
USIP United States Institute of Peace
WAWH Western Association of Woman Historians

Grant Programs

3M Canada Teaching Fellowships 1

Nominations of faculty members teaching at Canadian universities for one-year teaching fellowships are invited. The program embodies the highest ideals of teaching excellence and scholarship with a commitment to enhance the educational experience of every learner. Up to 10 awards, presented annually at the STLHE conference in June, recognize exemplary contributions to educational and teaching excellence in Canadian universities. The award includes lifetime membership in the Society. 3M Fellowship winners will attend an all expense paid 3-day retreat at the Fairmont Le Chateau Montebello, to celebrate and share exceptional achievements in teaching and provide an opportunity for outstanding teachers to share experiences and ideas.
Requirements Awards are open to all individuals currently teaching at a Canadian university, regardless of discipline or level of appointment.
Date(s) Application Is Due Nov 17.
Contact Dr. Arshad Ahmad, Program Coordinator, c/o Centre for Leadership in Learning, (514) 848-2424 ext 2928 or 2793; email: arshad@jmsb.concordia.ca
Internet http://www.mcmaster.ca/3Mteachingfellowships/nom_info.html#3
Sponsor Society for Teaching and Learning in Higher Education (STLHE)
1280 Main Street West
Hamilton, ON L8S 4K1 Canada

3M Foundation Grants 2

The foundation supports organizat ions involved with arts and culture, education, the environment, and human services. Special emphasis is directed toward programs designed to help prepare individuals and families for success. Types of support include: building construction and renovation, capital campaigns, curriculum development, employee matching gifts, general operating support, inkind gifts, program development, and scholarship funds.
Requirements Established 501(c)3 organizations in 3M communities are eligible.
Restrictions No support for religious organizations, conduit agencies, political groups, fraternal organizations, social groups, or veteran organizations. No funding for hospitals, K12 schools, military organizations, animal related organizations, or disease specific organizations. No grants to individuals, or for endowments, emergency operating support, advocacy and lobbying efforts, fundraising events and associated advertising, travel, publications, startup needs, non 3M equipment, debt reduction, conferences, athletic events, or film or video production; no loans or investments.
Amount $47.1 million total
Contact Cynthia F. Kleven, Secretary, (651) 733-0144; fax: (651) 737-3061; email: cfkleven@mmm.com
Internet http://solutions.3m.com/wps/portal/3M/en_US/CommunityAffairs/CommunityGiving/US/K12/
Sponsor 3M Foundation
3M Ctr, Bldg 225-01-S-23
Saint Paul, MN 55144-1000

A-T Medical Research Foundation Grants 3

The foundation awards grants on a worldwide basis to individuals for medical research relating to ataxia-telangiectasia. Seed grants and research grants are available. Send two copies of application to Richard A. Gatti, MD, Professor, UCLA School of Medicine, Department of Pathology, 675 Young Drive South, Macdonald Research Laboratories, Los Angeles, CA 90095-1732.
Amount $35,000-$255,000
Contact Pamela Smith, Vice President, (818) 704-8146; fax: (818) 704-8310; email: becca4435@aol.com
Sponsor Ataxia Telangiectasia Medical Research Foundation
5241 Round Meadow Road
Hidden Hills, CA 91302

A.E. Bennett Basic and Clinical Science Research Award 4

The awards, supported by the A.E. Bennett Neuropsychiatric Research Foundation, are in recognition of basic science and clinical science research in biological psychiatry by young investigators. Candidates must be actively engaged in the research for which the award is sought. Applicants need only write a brief description of their research, submit 2-3 published or submitted papers and arrange for two letters of support (at least one of the letters needs to be from a member of the Society).
Requirements Submissions are welcomed from laboratory researchers in any country who have not passed their 45th birthday or have not been engaged in research for greater than 10 years following award of their terminal degree or the end of formal clinical/fellowship training, whichever is later by deadline date; candidates need not be current members of the society.
Amount $2000 each
Date(s) Application Is Due Jan 26.
Contact Maggie Peterson, c/o Society of Biological Psychiatry, (904) 953-2842; fax: (904) 953-7117; email: maggie@mayo.edu
Internet http://www.sobp.org/aebaward.asp
Sponsor A.E. Bennett Neuropsychiatric Research Foundation
4500 San Pablo Road
Jacksonville, FL 32224

A.L. Mailman Family Foundation Grants 5

The foundation awards grants on the state, regional, and national levels with a focus on childcare, especially on issues of quality, caregiver training, teacher/student ratios, and connecting quality childcare to later achievements. The foundation also supports efforts to stimulate moral growth and the development of social responsibility and for research in and refinement of developmental, individualized education of young children. Types of support include curriculum development, matching/challenge grants, program development, publication, research grants, seed grants, and technical assistance. Prospective aplicants should rite a letter describing the proposed project. The letter should include a project summary, contact information, fit with Foundation objectives, and an estimated budget and timeframe. The Foundation board meets in April and October to authorize grants. Proposals should be sent to the foundation by June 15 for fall review and by January 15 for spring review. Letters of inquiry should be submitted by May 1 for fall proposals and by December 1 for spring proposals.
Restrictions Grants do not support direct service organizations, childcare centers and schools, locally focused organizations, individuals, capital campaigns and endowments, scholarships, general operating expenses or deficit reduction, or organizations or projects outside of the United States.
Amount $25,000 average
Date(s) Application Is Due Jan 15; May 15; Jun 15; Dec 1.
Contact Luba Lynch, Executive Director, (914) 683-8089; fax: (914) 686-5519; email: info@mailman.org
Internet http://www.mailman.org/index.html
Sponsor A.L. Mailman Family Foundation
707 Westchester Ave
White Plains, NY 10604

A.O. Smith Community Grants 6

The foundation supports nonprofit organizations in communities where A.O. Smith Corporation has facilities. The foundation supports elementary and secondary school projects that focus on the quality of educational programs and curriculum development; civic, cultural, and social welfare of communities; and medical research and improved local health services. Types of support include continuing support, annual campaigns, building/renovation, scholarship funds, and employee matching gifts. Proposals should describe the project's benefits and constituency, budget information including other sources of funding, and how results will be reported. There is no deadline for applications, although proposals to be considered for the following years foundation budget must be received by October 30.
Requirements Nonprofit organizations in company areas may apply.
Restrictions Grants do not support political organizations or organizations whose chief purpose is to influence legislation.
Amount $500-$20,000 typically; $2000 average
Date(s) Application Is Due Oct 30.
Contact Program Contact, (414) 359-4000; fax: (414) 359-4064
Internet http://www.aosmith.com/about/aosfoundation/foundationindex.htm
Sponsor A.O. Smith Foundation
P.O. Box 245010
Milwaukee, WI 53224

AAA Foundation for Traffic Safety Grants 7

The foundation sponsors research that not only identifies critical traffic safety problems, but also searches for underlying causes and possible solutions, as well as identifying early trends and offering solutions before the general public is aware of the problem. The foundation continues research into ways to help the growing numbers of teen drivers and older drivers evaluate and improve their driving performance. A sampling of recent research includes drunk driving, seeking additional solutions; seated for safety; headlight glare countermeasures; supplemental transportation programs for seniors; distracted driving, phase I; and longer combination vehicle safety study. Prior to submitting unsolicited proposals, applicants may email a one-page preproposal to gauge the foundation's general interest in the proposed topic.
Requirements Research institutions and nonprofit organizations with 501(c)3 status are eligible.
Restrictions The foundation does not fund research to develop new devices. No grants are made for community action initiatives or other purely local traffic safety programs.
Contact Betty Barksdale, Foundation Office Manager, (202) 638-5944; fax: (202) 638-5943; email: info@aaafoundation.org
Internet http://www.aaafoundation.org/about_us/index.cfm
Sponsor AAA Foundation for Traffic Safety
607 14th Street NW, Suite 201
Washington, DC 20005

AAA Minority Dissertation Fellowship Program 8

The association invites minority doctoral candidates in anthropology to apply for a nonrenewable dissertation writing fellowship. Students of any subfield or specialty in anthropology will receive equal consideration. Dissertation topics in all areas of the discipline are welcome. Doctoral students who require financial assistance to complete the write-up phase of the dissertation are urged to apply. The dissertation proposal must be approved by the applicant's committee prior to application.
Requirements An applicant must be a US citizen; a member of an historically underrepresented ethnic minority group; enrolled in a full-time academic program

leading to a doctoral degree in anthropology at the time of application; admitted to degree candidacy before the dissertation fellowship is awarded; and a member of the American Anthropological Association.
Amount $10,000
Date(s) Application Is Due Feb 15.
Contact Kathleen Terry-Sharp, Director, (703) 528-1902; email: academic@aaanet.org
Internet http://www.aaanet.org/committees/minority/minordis.htm
Sponsor American Anthropological Association
2200 Wilson Blvd, Suite 600
Arlington, VA 22201-3357

AAAAI Asthma Research Award 9
Training program directors, deans, department chairpersons, and sponsors are invited to nominate promising investigators involved in research dealing with asthma for this award, which is cosponsored by Abbott Laboratories and AAAAI. The award is a grant in aid provided to the program sponsoring the applicant and is intended to provide salary support. The award is funded quarterly beginning July 1. Application should include a biographical sketch, including a curriculum vita, an outline of past accomplishments, a summary of a current research project, and plans for future research.
Requirements Applicants must be MDs or PhDs who are fellows in training or residents associated with an approved allergy and immunology program and are AAAAI members (or individuals who have submitted applications for membership by September 1).
Restrictions Individuals with a faculty appointment and past AAAAI research award recipients will not be considered.
Amount $25,000 for one year
Contact Angela Gade, Program Contact, (414) 272-6071; fax: (414) 276-6070; email: agade@aaaai.org. or info@aaaai.org
Internet http://www.aaaai.org/members/grants_awards
Sponsor American Academy of Allergy, Asthma, and Immunology
555 E Wells St, Ste 1100
Milwaukee, WI 53202-3823

AAAAI Education and Research Trust Faculty Development Award 10
The award offers an individual three years of financial support to concentrate his/her research efforts in either basic or clinical allergy and immunology. The objectives of this award are to recognize and support young researchers and promote the specialty of allergy/immunology. The recipient is expected to participate in a seminar at the AAAAI annual meeting, where awardees present their research.
Requirements The award is open to researchers of junior faculty status--either instructor, assistant professor, or the equivalent grade. This award is directed toward MDs, but in unusual circumstances PhDs will be considered. Applicants must be US or Canadian citizens or permanent residents who are AAAAI members (or have applied for membership by September 1).
Restrictions Past recipients are ineligible.
Amount $100,000 per year for three years
Date(s) Application Is Due Nov 15.
Contact Angela Gade, Program Manager, (414) 272-6071; fax: (414) 276-6070; email: agade@aaaai.org or info@aaaai.org
Internet http://www.aaaai.org/members/ert/default.stm
Sponsor American Academy of Allergy, Asthma, and Immunology
555 E Wells St, Ste 1100
Milwaukee, WI 53202-3823

AAAAI Research Awards 11
The goal of the program is to support the research by a fellow-in-training, resident, and post-doctoral scholar at an allergy and immunology or a clinical and laboratory immunology training program.
Requirements Fellow-in-training, resident, or post-doctoral scholar affiliated with an allergy and immunology or clinical and laboratory immunology training program that is in good standing with Residency Review Committee and is fully-accredited by the Accreditation Council of Graduate Medical Education may apply. Applicants must be an AAAAI member or must submit a membership application with the award application.
Restrictions Applicants with faculty status will not be considered. Past AAAAI research award recipients are not eligible.
Amount $25,000 for one year
Contact Angela Gade, (414) 272-6071; fax: (414) 276-6070; email: agade@aaaai.org or info@aaaai.org
Internet http://www.aaaai.org/members/grants_awards
Sponsor American Academy of Allergy, Asthma, and Immunology
555 E Wells St, Ste 1100
Milwaukee, WI 53202-3823

AAAAI Summer Fellowships 12
Fellowships are awarded on an annual basis to assist medical students interested in pursuing research in allergy and immunology during their summer recess. The fellowships will be awarded to outstanding individuals who wish to pursue research in the following areas: physiology of allergic diseases, pharmacology of allergy and inflammation, basic cellular and molecular immunology, AIDS, and other topics pertinent to the understanding of allergic and immune mechanisms of disease.
Requirements Applicant must be a full time medical student residing in the US or Canada and must have successfully completed at least eight months of medical school by May 15, 2006.
Restrictions Past recipients are ineligible.
Amount $2000
Date(s) Application Is Due Apr 1.
Contact Undergraduate and Graduate Education Committee, (414) 272-6071; fax: (414) 276-6070; email: info@aaaai.org
Internet http://www.aaaai.org/members/grants_awards/aaaaigrantsawards/aaaai_summer_fellowship_medical_student_grant.stm
Sponsor American Academy of Allergy, Asthma, and Immunology
555 E Wells St, Ste 1100
Milwaukee, WI 53202-3889

AAAS Award for International Scientific Cooperation 13
AAAS, in collaboration with its affiliated organizations, seeks to recognize an individual or a limited number of individuals working together in the scientific or engineering community for making an outstanding contribution to furthering international cooperation in science and engineering. Nominations for the award may be originated by anyone. CAIP administers the screening and selection process for the awarding of the AAAS Award for International Scientific Cooperation (ISC). The ISC award is presented each February at the AAAS Annual Meeting. A monetary prize of $5,000, a commemorative plaque, complimentary registration, and reimbursement for reasonable travel and hotel expenses to attend the AAAS annual meeting are given to the recipient.
Requirements Nominations should be typed and should include the following information: the nominator's name, address, and phone number; the nominee's name and title, institutional affiliation, and address; a summary of the actions that form the basis for the nomination (about 250 words); a longer statement (no more than three pages) providing additional details of the actions for which the candidate is nominated; at least two letters of support with addresses and phone numbers; and the candidate's vita (no more than three pages) containing professional positions held. Any documentation--books, articles, etc.--that illuminates the significance of the nominee's achievements may also be submitted.
Restrictions The award is open to all regardless of nationality or citizenship. Nominees must be living at the time of their nomination. Any individual or small group in the scientific and engineering community that has contributed substantially to the understanding or development of science or engineering across national boundaries is eligible for this award.
Amount $5000
Date(s) Application Is Due Aug 1.
Contact Linda Stroud, CAIP Coordinator, (202) 326-6659; fax: 202-289-4958; email: lstroud@aaas.org
Internet http://www.aaas.org/programs/international/caip/isc
Sponsor American Association for the Advancement of Science
1200 New York Ave NW
Washington, DC 20005

AAAS Award for Public Understanding of Science and Technology 14
AAAS invites nominations for this annual award, which honors working scientists and engineers who make outstanding contributions to the 'popularization of science'. It is intended to encourage technical professionals to communicate with the public by popularizing their own work. Such efforts can include publications or broadcasts, lectures, museum presentations or exhibit designs, or any other outreach project. The Award shall be given annually to scientists or engineers who, while working in their fields, have also contributed substantially to public understanding of science and technology. A monetary prize of $5,000, a commemorative plaque, complimentary registration, and reimbursement for reasonable travel and hotel expenses to attend the AAAS Annual Meeting to receive the prize are given to the recipient. Nominators are encouraged to identify candidates whose contributions reach broad audiences that include women, minorities, disabled persons, and senior citizens.
Requirements Eligible individuals include scientists and engineers (individual or a small group) from all disciplines (including social sciences and medicine) engaged in research, teaching, and related activities that have contributed substantially to the public's understanding of science or technology. Nominations should include name, position, institution, professional address and phone, and home address and phone of the candidate; name, position, institution, and professional address and phone of the nominator; a summary of the action or actions that form the basis for the nomination (about 250 words); a longer statement (no more than three pages) providing additional details of the actions for which the candidate is nominated, including one paragraph that describes the nominee's impact on the general public; the candidate's vita (three-page maximum); two letters of support; and at least one representative sample that illustrates the nominee's contribution. Books, videotapes, brochures, magazine articles, or other materials are welcome.
Restrictions Only materials produced for general audiences, as opposed to professional or trade audiences, will be considered. Employees of the AAAS are not eligible. All materials become the property of AAAS.
Amount $5000
Date(s) Application Is Due Aug 1.
Contact Public Understanding Awards Coordinator, (202) 326-6670; fax: (202) 371-9849; email: jkass@aaas.org

Internet http://www.aaas.org/aboutaaas/awards/public/index.shtml
Sponsor American Association for the Advancement of Science
Education & Human Resources Directorate, 1200 New York Ave NW, Rm 608
Washington, DC 20005

AAAS Mentor Award **15**

The two categories of the AAAS Mentor Awards (Lifetime Mentor Award and Mentor Award) both honor individuals who during their careers demonstrate extraordinary leadership to increase the participation of underrepresented groups in science and engineering fields and careers. These groups include: women of all racial or ethnic groups; African American, Native American, and Hispanic men; and people with disabilities. Both awards recognize an individual who has mentored and guided significant numbers of students from underrepresented groups to the completion of doctoral studies or who has impacted the climate of a department, college, or institution to significantly increase the diversity of students pursuing and completing doctoral studies. Nominations should include name, position, institution, professional address and phone, and home address and phone of the candidate; name, position, institution, and professional address and phone of the nominator; a summary of the actions that form the basis for the nomination (about 250 words); a letter of nomination that enumerates the ways in which the person reflects the purpose of this award; the candidate's vita (three-page maximum); the total number of students the candidate mentored at the bachelor's or master's level who went on to the doctoral level at other institutions, and the total number of underrepresented students the candidate mentored at the doctoral level; a maximum of five supporting letters from students and three supporting letters from colleagues representative of the different spheres in which the candidate has demonstrated effort, results, and commitment.
Requirements The award is open to all regardless of nationality or citizenship. Nominees must be living at the time of their nomination. Commitment and extraordinary effort may be demonstrated by the number and diversity of students mentored; assisting students to present and publish their work, to find financial aid, and to provide career guidance; providing psychological support, encouragement, and essential strategies for life in the scholarly community; and continued interest in the individual's professional advancement. The Lifetime Mentor award winner will have served in the role of mentor for 25 or more years. The Mentor Award winner will have served in the role of mentor for less than 25 years.
Amount Both award category recipients receive: A monetary prize ($5000), a commemorative plaque, complimentary registration, and reimbursement for reasonable travel and hotel expenses to attend the AAAS Annual Meeting.
Date(s) Application Is Due Jul 31.
Contact Mentor Awards Coordinator, (202) 326-6670; fax: (202) 371-9849; email: ygeorge@aaas.org
Internet http://www.aaas.org/aboutaaas/awards/mentor/index.shtml
Sponsor American Association for the Advancement of Science
AAS Education & Human Resources Programs, 1200 New York Ave NW
Washington, DC 20005

AAAS Newcomb Cleveland Prize **16**

The association's oldest award, funded by Newcomb Cleveland of New York City, is given to the author or authors of an outstanding paper published in the Research Articles or Reports sections of Science. Each annual contest starts with the first issue of June and ends with the last issue of the following May.
Requirements An eligible paper is one that includes original research data, theory, or synthesis; is a fundamental contribution to basic knowledge or is a technical achievement of far-reaching consequence; and is a first-time publication of the author's own work. Reference to pertinent earlier work by the author may be included to give perspective. Readers of 'Science' are invited to nominate papers appearing in the Articles, Research Articles, or Reports sections. Nominations must be typed and provide the following information: title of paper, author's name, date of issue in which it was published, page number, and a brief statement of justification for nomination.
Restrictions Self-nominations will not be accepted.
Amount $25,000. The winner also receives a bronze medal, complimentary registration and reimbursement for reasonable travel and hotel expenses to attend the AAAS Annual Meeting.
Date(s) Application Is Due Jun 30.
Contact Sylvia Kihara, Newcomb Cleveland Prize Coordinator, (202) 326-6507; fax: (202) 289-7562; email: skihara@aaas.org
Internet http://www.aaas.org/aboutaaas/awards/newcomb/index.shtml
Sponsor American Association for the Advancement of Science
'Science' Editorial Office, 1200 New York Ave NW, Room 1044
Washington, DC 20005

AAAS Philip Hauge Abelson Prize **17**

The prize was established by the AAAS Board of Directors and is presented at the AAAS Annual Meeting. It is awarded annually to either a public servant, in recognition of sustained exceptional contributions to advancing science, or to a scientist whose career has been distinguished both for scientific achievement and for other notable services to the scientific community.
Requirements The award is open to all regardless of nationality or citizenship. Nominees must be living at the time of their nomination. Any individual or small group in the scientific and engineering community that has contributed substantially to the understanding or development of science or engineering across national boundaries is eligible for this award.
Restrictions Each nomination must be seconded by at least two other AAAS members. The winner will be selected by a five-member judging panel.
Amount A monetary prize of $5,000, a commemorative plaque, complimentary registration, and reimbursement for reasonable travel and hotel expenses to attend the AAAS Annual Meeting are given to the recipient.
Date(s) Application Is Due Aug 1.
Contact Abelson Award Coordinator, (202) 326-6600; fax: (202) 289-4950; email: snelsond@aaas.org
Internet http://www.aaas.org/aboutaaas/awards/abelson/index.shtml
Sponsor American Association for the Advancement of Science
1200 New York Ave NW
Washington, DC 20005

AAAS Roger Revelle Fellowship in Global Stewardship **18**

The Fellowship is designed to provide a unique opportunity for an accomplished scientist to address global stewardship issues by applying his or her broad, multidisciplinary background toward solutions to these important societal problems. The Revelle Fellow will engage with professionals in the public policy arena to strengthen his or her understanding of the intricacies of environmental policymaking and make practical contributions to the more effective use of scientific and technical knowledge in federal decision-making. The fellowship provides the unique opportunity to address sustainability challenges across multiple disciplines. The focus will be on human interaction with ecosystems, which includes, but is not limited to, population, sustainable development, food, oceans, global climate change, and related environmental concerns.
Requirements Applications are invited from candidates in any physical, biological, or social science; any field of engineering; or any relevant interdisciplinary field. All applicants must have a PhD or an equivalent doctoral-level degree and at least three years of post-degree professional experience by the application deadline. Individuals with a master's degree in engineering and six years of post-degree, professional experience may apply. All applicants must be US citizens.
Restrictions Federal employees are not eligible.
Amount $64,000 stipend
Date(s) Application Is Due Dec 20.
Contact Program Director, (202) 326-6700; fax: (202) 289-4950; email: fellowships@aaas.org
Internet http://fellowships.aaas.org/02_Areas/02_Global_Stewardship.shtml
Sponsor American Association for the Advancement of Science
1200 New York Avenue, NW
Washington, DC 20005

AAAS Science & Technology Policy Fellowships - Congressional **19**

Fellows spend one year working as special legislative assistants on the staffs of members of Congress or congressional committees, beginning in September. The program includes an orientation on congressional and executive branch operations, and a year-long seminar program on issues involving science and public policy. The fellowships are designed to provide a unique public policy learning experience, to demonstrate the value of science-government interaction, and to bring technical backgrounds and external perspectives to the decision-making process in government. AAAS will select and sponsor two Congressional Fellows.
Requirements Prospective Fellows must demonstrate exceptional competence in some area of science or engineering; have a good scientific and technical background; be cognizant of and demonstrate sensitivity toward political and social issues; and, perhaps most importantly, have a strong interest and some experience in applying personal knowledge toward the solution of societal problems. Applications are invited from individuals in any physical, biological, or social science, any field of engineering, or any relevant interdisciplinary field. All applicants must have a Ph.D. or an equivalent doctoral-level degree by the application deadline (December 10). Individuals with a master's degree in engineering and at least three years of post-degree professional experience may apply. Persons from underrepresented minority groups and persons with disabilities are encouraged to apply.
Restrictions Applicants must be US citizens. Federal employees are not eligible. Will accept only online application submissions. Applications with fewer than three recommendation letters will not be considered.
Amount Annual stipends are $67,000 for the 2008-2009 fellowship year, with allowances for health insurance and relocation.
Date(s) Application Is Due Dec 10.
Contact Program Director, AAAS Science and Technology Policy Fellowships Program, (202) 326-6700; fax: (202) 289-4950; email: fellowships@aaas.org
Internet http://fellowships.aaas.org/02_Areas/02_Congressional.shtml
Sponsor American Association for the Advancement of Science
1200 New York Ave. NW
Washington, DC 20005

AAAS Science & Technology Policy Fellowships - Diplomacy **20**

Selected fellows apply their scientific and technical background to foreign policy, international affairs and development, and advancing research, programs, and treaties through international cooperation. Placement opportunities are available at Fogerty International Center, National Institutes of Health; Foreign Agriculture Service, U.S.

Department of Agriculture; U.S. Agency for International Development; or U.S. Department of State
Requirements Applicants must have a PhD or equivalent doctoral level degree at the time of application. Persons with a master's degree in engineering and at least three years of postdegree professional experience will also be considered. All applicants must be US citizens. Prospective fellows must demonstrate exceptional competence in some area of science and engineering (multidisciplinary expertise is especially valued); be cognizant of the ways in which science and technology affect a broad range of international development and foreign policy issues; communicate and work effectively with decision makers and others outside of the scientific and engineering communities; exhibit a willingness and flexibility to tackle problems in a number of nonscientific areas; demonstrate sensitivity toward political, economic, and social issues; and have some experience and/or strong interest in applying knowledge toward the solution of problems in the area of foreign affairs or international development. Applications are invited from individuals in any physical, biological, or social science; any field of engineering; or any relevant interdisciplinary field. Some program areas and agencies seek additional qualifications. See the website for more specific guidelines.
Restrictions Federal employees are not eligible.
Amount $67,000-$87,000
Contact Sage Russell, Associate Director; (202) 326-6700; fax: (202) 289-4950; email: fellowships@aaas.org
Internet http://fellowships.aaas.org/02_Areas/02_index.shtml#2
Sponsor American Association for the Advancement of Science
1200 New York Ave. NW
Washington, DC 20005

AAAS Science & Technology Policy Fellowships - Energy, Environment, Agriculture & Natural Resources 21

Fellows chosen for this program engage in projects, programs, policies and outreach initiatives to protect environmental and human health, tackle energy challenges and opportunities, and to safeguard our air, water, land, and natural resources. Placement opportunities are available with the national Oceanic Atmospheric Association, National Science Foundation, U.S. Department of Agriculture, USDA Forest Service, U.S. Department of Energy, and U.S. Environmental Protection Agency. Fellowships are awarded to highly qualified individuals interested in learning about the science-policy interface while applying their scientific and technical knowledge and analytical skills to the federal policy realm.
Requirements Prospective fellows must have a PhD or equivalent doctoral level degree. Persons with a master's degree in engineering and at least three years of postdegree professional experience may apply. Candidates must demonstrate exceptional competence in some area of science or engineering, and an interest in applying their expertise to the economic and technical assessment of problems relating to human health, agriculture, and the environment. Applications are invited from individuals in any physical, biological, or social science; any field of engineering; or any relevant interdisciplinary field. Persons with a DVM, MD, or a PhD in the natural sciences or economics are especially encouraged to apply. Applicants must be US citizens.
Restrictions Federal employees are ineligible.
Amount $67,000-$87,000
Date(s) Application Is Due Dec 20.
Contact Emily MacGillivray, Fellowships Program Coordinator; (202) 326-6700; fax: (202) 289-4950; email: fellowships@aaas.org
Internet http://fellowships.aaas.org/02_Areas/02_index.shtml
Sponsor American Association for the Advancement of Science
1200 New York Ave. NW
Washington, DC 20005

AAAS Science & Technology Policy Fellowships - Health, Education & Human Services 22

Fellows chosen for this program focus their experience to support improved programs, policies, planning, and risk analysis for initiatives in human and environmental health, biological threats, food safety, education and research, and to aid in developing and implementing regulations and providing oversight. Placement opportunities are available with the National Institutes of Health, National Science Foundation, USDA Food Safety Inspection Services and U.S. Department of Health & Human Services. Fellowships are awarded to highly qualified individuals interested in learning about the science-policy interface while applying their scientific and technical knowledge and analytical skills to the federal policy realm.
Requirements Prospective fellows must have a PhD or equivalent doctoral level degree. Persons with a master's degree in engineering and at least three years of postdegree professional experience may apply. Candidates must demonstrate exceptional competence in some area of science or engineering, and an interest in applying their expertise to the economic and technical assessment of problems relating to human health, agriculture, and the environment. Applications are invited from individuals in any physical, biological, or social science; any field of engineering; or any relevant interdisciplinary field. Persons with a DVM, MD, or a PhD in the natural sciences or economics are especially encouraged to apply. Applicants must be US citizens.
Restrictions Federal employees are not eligible.
Amount $67,000 - $87,000
Date(s) Application Is Due Dec 20.
Contact Emily MacGillivray, Program Coordinator, Science & Technology Policy Fellowships; (202) 326-6700; fax: (202) 289-4950; email: fellowships@aaas.org
Internet http://fellowships.aaas.org/02_Areas/02_index.shtml
Sponsor American Association for the Advancement of Science
1200 New York Ave. NW
Washington, DC 20005

AAAS Science & Technology Policy Fellowships - National Defense & Global Security 23

Fellows spend one year contributing external perspective and expertise on technology in defense policy, national and international security and systems analysis, and assisting with project and program oversight. Fellows will be placed in one of the following: Federal Bureau of Investigation (FBI), Nuclear Regulatory Commission, U.S. Department of Defense or U.S. Department of Homeland Security. Fellows will work on a variety of issues related to defense policy, national security, weapons of mass destruction, technology applications, defense systems analysis and support, and program oversight and management. Assignments may involve significant interagency, congressional or international activity. The program includes an orientation on international affairs and executive branch and congressional operations, and a year-long seminar series on issues involving science, technology and public policy. Fellows should not expect to work specifically on technical issues related to their dissertations or previous post-doctoral appointments, but rather to apply their technical, organizational, and communication skills to technical and policy issues in the placement agency. Additionally, Fellows help increase the awareness of the placement agency and its departments as a challenging and rewarding career environment for scientists and engineers.
Requirements All applicants must have a doctoral-level degree (PhD, MD, DVM, DSc, PharmD, and other terminal degrees), in any physical, biological, health/medical or social science, any field of engineering, or any relevant interdisciplinary field (individuals with a master's degree in engineering and at least three years of post-degree professional experience also may apply). Note: All requirements for the degree must be completed by the application deadline. A prospective fellow must demonstrate exceptional competence in their specialty appropriate to their career stage, and have the strong endorsement of three references. Show an understanding of the opportunities for science and engineering to support a broad range of non-scientific issues, and display a commitment to apply their scientific or technical expertise to serve society; Exhibit awareness and sensitivity to the political, economic and social issues that influence policy; Be articulate communicators, both verbally and in writing, to decision-makers and non-scientific audiences, and have the ability to work effectively with individuals and groups outside the scientific community; Demonstrate integrity and good judgment, and the flexibility and willingness to address policy issues outside their scientific realm.
Restrictions Federal employees are ineligible. All applicants must be US citizens (dual citizenship from the United States and another country is acceptable). Some program areas and host agencies seek additional qualifications. Holding a Title 42 position is considered federal employment and therefore renders an applicant ineligible for a AAAS Science & Technology Policy Fellowship. Individuals working in postdoctoral positions at government labs or agencies, for private contractors, and in state government posts are not federal employees and therefore are eligible for the AAAS Fellowships.
Amount Stipend: (depending on degree level and post-degree experience) $67,000-$87,000. Plus professional development, travel and relocation reimbursement and health insurance
Date(s) Application Is Due Dec 20.
Contact Program Director; (202) 326-6700; fax: (202) 289-4950; email: fellowships@aaas.org
Internet http://fellowships.aaas.org/02_Areas/02_index.shtml#3
Sponsor American Association for the Advancement of Science
1200 New York Ave. NW
Washington, DC 20005

AAAS Science Journalism Awards 24

The awards, which are cosponsored by AAAS and Johnson & Johnson Pharmaceutical Research & Development, recognize outstanding reporting for a general audience and honor individuals (rather than institutions, publishers or employers) for their coverage of the sciences, engineering and mathematics. The winning journalists have helped to foster the public's understanding and appreciation of science. Independent screening and judging committees select the winning journalists and their entries based on scientific accuracy, initiative, originality, clarity of interpretation and value in fostering a better understanding of science by the public. One award in each of six categories is given annually: newspapers with daily circulation more than 100,000, newspapers with circulation of less than 100,000, general circulation magazines, radio, and television, and online. Additional International category - Children's Science News (Provide English translations of foreign-language entries whenever possible).
Requirements Persons other than the author may submit entries in accordance with the rules of the competition. The contest is open to journalists who have published or broadcast in media outlets accessible to the general public. Except for the Children's Science News award, which is open to international media outlets, the submitted materials must have been published, broadcast or posted online within the United States by a U.S.-based news organization. Print articles must be available to the public by subscription or newsstand sales.
Restrictions Items exclusively concerning health or medical treatment; Items published originally in AAAS publicaitons or produced by AAAS; Items by employees of AAAS

or Johnson & Johnson Pharmaceutical Research Development, LLC. Winners from the previous year are not eligible. Individuals winning three times are no longer eligible.
Amount $3000 each + reimbursement for reasonable travel and hotel expenses. In cases of multiple authors or producers, only one person's travel expenses will be covered.
Date(s) Application Is Due Aug 1.
Contact Awards Coordinator, (202) 326-6781; fax: (202) 789-0455; email: media@aaas.org
Internet http://www.aaas.org/aboutaaas/awards/sja/index.shtml
Sponsor American Association for the Advancement of Science
1200 New York Ave NW
Washington, DC 20005

AAAS Scientific Freedom and Responsibility Award 25
The award is presented to honor scientists and engineers whose exemplary actions have served to foster scientific freedom and responsibility and recognizes scientists and engineers who have: acted to protect the public's health, safety, or welfare; or focused public attention on important potential impacts of science and technology on society by their responsible participation in public policy debates; or established important new precedents in carrying out the social responsibilities or in defending the professional freedom of scientists and engineers. Nominations should include nominator's name, address, and phone number; and the name and address of the nominee; a summary of the action or actions that form the basis for the nomination (about 250 words); a longer statement (no more than three pages) providing additional details of the actions for which the candidate is nominated; at least two letters of support with addresses and phone numbers; and the candidate's vita (no more than three pages). Any documentation--books, articles, etc.--that illuminates the significance of the nominee's achievements may also be submitted.
Requirements The award is open to all regardless of nationality or citizenship. Eligible nominees are scientists and engineers who have acted to protect the public's health, safety, or welfare; or to focus public attention on potentially serious impacts of science and technology on society by their responsible participation in public policy debates; or to establish important new precedents in social responsibility or in defending the professional freedom of scientists and engineers.
Restrictions All materials become the property of AAAS.
Amount Prize of $5,000, a commemorative plaque, complimentary registration, and reimbursement for travel and hotel expenses to attend the AAAS Annual Meeting.
Date(s) Application Is Due Aug 1.
Contact Deborah Runkle, (202) 326-6794; fax: (202) 289-4950; email: drunkle@aaas.org
Internet http://www.aaas.org/aboutaaas/awards/freedom/index.shtml
Sponsor American Association for the Advancement of Science
1200 New York Ave NW
Washington, DC 20005

AAB Berlin Prize Fellowships 26
The academy welcomes younger as well as established scholars, artists, and professionals who wish to engage in independent study in Berlin for an academic semester or, in special cases, for an entire academic year. Fellowships have been awarded to scholars working in a variety of disciplines, including history, political science, economics, German studies, art history, musicology, anthropology, law, and linguistics, as well as to writers and poets, public policy experts, journalists, composers, and artists. Fellows are encouraged to work in association with a Berlin institution such as a museum, library, archive, university, government agency, studio, or media organization. Guidelines and application are available online.
Requirements All candidates should be permanently based in the United States and must be either US citizens or permanent residents. They must have completed their doctorate or equivalent professional degree. Candidates need not work on German topics, but their project descriptions should explain how a residency in Berlin will contribute to further professional development.
Restrictions Applications are accepted from all fields except for the visual arts, music composition, and music performance.
Amount $3,500-$5,000 per month
Date(s) Application Is Due Oct 25.
Contact Fellowship Administrator, (212) 588-1755; fax: (212) 588-1758; email: nyoffice@americanacademy.de
Internet http://www.americanacademy.de/index.php?id=316
Sponsor American Academy in Berlin
14 E. 60th Street, Suite 604
New York, NY 10022

AAB Public Policy Fellowships 27
Short term fellowships of six to eight weeks are available for the Bosch Fellows in Public Policy. Fellows are sought from the fine arts including painting, sculpture, music, film, and drama; scholarly disciplines such as art history, history, philosophy, sociology, political science, and public policy; as well as from professional fields including architecture, law, business, economics, and journalism. Fellows are encouraged to take up an association with a Berlin institution such as a museum, library, archive, university, government agency, film studio, or media organization. Specialists on German topics as well as other persons for whom the cultural opportunities or political setting of Berlin offers an advantageous professional venue are encouraged to apply. Completed applications, with the exception of visual art and music applications, should be received by October 25 by the Berlin office only (ATTN: Application for Fellowship, Am Sandwerder 17-19, D-14109 Berlin, Germany; +49 30 804 83 0; fax: +49 30 804 83 111; email: applications@americanacademy.de).
Requirements Candidates must be either American citizens or permanent residents and in both cases should be permanently living and working in the United States.
Amount $3,000-$5,000 monthly
Date(s) Application Is Due Oct 25.
Contact Fellowship Administrator, (212) 588-1755; fax: (212) 588-1758; email: nyoffice@americanacademy.de
Internet http://www.americanacademy.de/index.php?id=6
Sponsor American Academy in Berlin
14 E. 60th Street, Suite 604
New York, NY 10022

AACAP Beatrix A. Hamburg Award for the Best New Research Poster by a Child and Adolescent Psychiatry Resident 28
This award recognizes the author of the best new research poster presented at the AACAP Annual Meeting. The award provides a $1,000 honorarium. The recipient will receive a plaque at the Young Leader Awards Ceremony during the AACAP Annual Meeting. There is no application process for this award. The AACAP Program Committee will review all new research poster submissions by child and adolescent psychiatry residents to determine the recipient of this award. The recipient will be notified through an acceptance letter. Non-recipients will not be notified.
Requirements The author must be a child and adolescent psychiatry resident at an accredited institution and AACAP member. Applicants must: be a child and adolescent psychiatry resident; attend an accredited institution; be an AACAP member; and attend and present a new research poster at the AACAP Annual Meeting.
Amount $1,000
Date(s) Application Is Due Jun 15.
Contact Stacie Hall, (202) 966-7300, ext. 113; fax: (202) 966-2891; email: shall@aacap.org
Internet http://www.aacap.org/page.ww?section=Research+and+Training+Awards&name=AACAP+Beatrix+A.+Hamburg+Award+for+the+Best+New+Research+Poster+by+a+Child+and+Adolescent+Psychiatry+Resident+at+the+AACAP+Annual+Meeting
Sponsor American Academy of Child and Adolescent Psychiatry
3615 Wisconsin Avenue, NW
Washington, DC 20016

AACAP Charlotte and Norbert Rieger Award for Scientific Achievement 29
This award is given annually for the most significant article published in the Journal of the American Academy of Child and Adolescent Psychiatry (JAACAP) in the past year (July-May). The article must be written by a psychiatrist specializing in child and/or adolescent psychiatry and cannot be a review.
Requirements The only submissions accepted are papers from child and adolescent psychiatrists that have been published in the Journal during the past year.
Amount $4,500 maximum
Date(s) Application Is Due May 1.
Contact Gabe Robbins, (202) 966-7300, ext. 117; fax: (202) 966-2891; email: grobbins@aacap.org
Internet http://www.aacap.org/page.ww?section=Research+and+Training+Awards&name=AACAP+Journal+Awards
Sponsor American Academy of Child and Adolescent Psychiatry
3615 Wisconsin Avenue, NW
Washington, DC 20016

AACAP Educational Outreach Program for Child and Adolescent Psychiatry Residents (former Travel Grant Program) 30
The Educational Outreach Program (EOP) funding provides the opportunity for up to 50 child and adolescent psychiatry residents to receive a formal overview to the field of child and adolescent psychiatry, establish child and adolescent psychiatrists as mentors and experience the AACAP Annual Meeting in Boston, MA. Participants will be exposed to the breadth and depth of the field of child and adolescent psychiatry, including research opportunities, access to mentors, and various networking opportunities. Participation in this program provides up to $750 for travel expenses.
Requirements Applicants must: be child and adolescent psychiatry residents at the time of the AACAP Annual Meeting; be currently enrolled in a residency program in the United States; be residents in their first or second year of child fellowship training are eligible (Triple Boarders in their fourth or fifth year of training in their triple board programs are eligible); either be members of the AACAP or have a membership application pending at the time of application; and attend all AACAP Annual Meeting events specified by AACAP.
Amount $750 maximum
Date(s) Application Is Due Jul 13.
Contact Gabe Robbins, (202) 966-7300, ext. 117; fax: (202) 966-2891; email: grobbins@aacap.org
Internet http://www.aacap.org/page.ww?section=Research+and+Training+Awards&name=AACAP+Educational+Outreach+Program+for+Child+and+Adolescent+Psychiatry+Residents+%28former+Travel+Grant+Program%29

Sponsor American Academy of Child and Adolescent Psychiatry
3615 Wisconsin Avenue, NW
Washington, DC 20009

AACAP Educational Outreach Program for General Psychiatry Residents (former Travel Grant Program) 31

The Educational Outreach Program (EOP) for General Psychiatry residents provides the opportunity for up to 20 general psychiatry residents to receive a formal overview to the field of child and adolescent psychiatry, establish child and adolescent psychiatrists as mentors and experience the AACAP Annual Meeting. Participants will be exposed to the breadth and depth of the field of child and adolescent psychiatry, including research opportunities, access to mentors, and various networking opportunities. Participation in this program provides up to $1,500 for travel expenses to the AACAP Annual Meeting.
Requirements Applicants must: be general psychiatry residents at the time of the AACAP Annual Meeting; be currently enrolled in a residency program in the United States; be residents in their first, second or third year of general psychiatry training (Triple Boarders in their first, second or third year of training in their triple board programs are eligible); either be members of the AACAP or have a membership application pending at the time of application; and attend all AACAP Annual Meeting events specified by AACAP.
Amount $1,500 maximum
Date(s) Application Is Due Jul 13.
Contact Camille Jackson, Training and Education Coordinator, (202) 966-7300, ext. 117; email: cjackson@aacap.org
Internet http://aacap.browsermedia.com/cs/root/research_and_training_awards/aacap_educational_outreach_program_for_general_psychiatry_residents_former_travel_grant_program
Sponsor American Academy of Child and Adolescent Psychiatry
3615 Wisconsin Avenue, NW
Washington, DC 20009

AACAP Elaine Schlosser Lewis Award for Research on Attention-Deficit Disorder 32

This annual award acknowledges outstanding leadership and continuous contributions in the field of research by giving $5,000 for the best paper published in the Journal on attention-deficit disorder written by a child and adolescent psychiatrist. The award winner will be recognized at a Distinguished Awards Luncheon and make an Honors Presentation about his or her work during the AACAP Annual Meeting.
Requirements Nomination letters must be accompanied by a CV for the individual nominated.
Amount $5,000
Date(s) Application Is Due May 4.
Contact Gabe Robbins, (202) 966-7300, ext. 117; fax: (202) 966-2891; email: grobbins@aacap.org
Internet http://www.aacap.org/page.ww?section=Research+and+Training+Awards&name=AACAP+Journal+Awards
Sponsor American Academy of Child and Adolescent Psychiatry
3615 Wisconsin Avenue, NW
Washington, DC 20016

AACAP Eli Lilly Pilot Research Awards 33

Six awards are available each year to junior faculty and child psychiatry fellows for pilot research with child and adolescent psychiatric researchers. Award recipients will be matched with child and adolescent psychiatric investigators working in their particular area of interest to act as consultants or mentors during the course of the award. Work must be completed within one year of receipt of the award.
Requirements Candidates must be board eligible, certified in child and adolescent psychiatry, or enrolled in a child psychiatry residency or fellowship program. Candidates must have a faculty appointment in an accredited medical school or be in a fully accredited child and adolescent psychiatry clinical research or training program.
Restrictions At the time of application, candidates may not have more than two years experience following graduation from residency/fellowship training. Candidates must not have any previous significant, individual research funding in the field of child and adolescent mental health. These include the following: NIMH/NIH Funding (Small Grants, T Award or R-01) or similar foundation or industry research funding.
Amount $9,000
Date(s) Application Is Due May 4.
Contact Stacie Hall, (202) 966-7300, ext. 113; fax: (202) 966-2891; email: shall@aacap.org
Internet http://www.aacap.org/cs/root/research_and_training_awards/aacap_pilot_research_award_for_junior_faculty_and_child_psychiatry_fellows_supported_by_eli_lilly_and_company
Sponsor American Academy of Child and Adolescent Psychiatry
3615 Wisconsin Avenue, NW
Washington, DC 20016

AACAP George Tarjan Award for Contributions in Developmental Disabilities 34

This award recognizes a child and adolescent psychiatrist and Academy member who has made significant contributions in a lifetime career or single seminal work to the understanding or care of those with mental retardation and developmental disabilities. These contributions must have national and/or international stature and clearly demonstrate lasting effects. The contributions may be in areas of teaching, research, program development, direct clinical service, advocacy or administrative commitment. A cash prize of up to $1,000 will be awarded. The award winner will be recognized at a Distinguished Awards Luncheon and make an Honors Presentation about his or her work during the AACAP Annual Meeting.
Requirements Nomination letters must be accompanied by a CV for the individual nominated.
Amount $1,000
Date(s) Application Is Due May 4.
Contact Gabe Robbins, (202) 966-7300, ext. 117; fax: (202) 966-2891; email: grobbins@aacap.org
Internet http://www.aacap.org/page.ww?section=Research+and+Training+Awards&name=AACAP+Distinguished+Member+and+Service+Awards
Sponsor American Academy of Child and Adolescent Psychiatry
3615 Wisconsin Avenue, NW
Washington, DC 20016

AACAP Irving Philips Award for Prevention 35

This award recognizes a child and adolescent psychiatrist and Academy member who has made significant contributions in a lifetime career or single seminal work to the prevention of mental illness in children and adolescents. These contributions must have national and/or international stature and clearly demonstrate lasting effects. The contributions may be in the areas of teaching, research, program development, direct clinical service, advocacy or administrative commitment. The award pays $2,500 to the winner and a $2,000 donation to a prevention program or center of the awardee's choice. The award winner will be recognized at a Distinguished Awards Luncheon and make an Honors Presentation about his or her work during the AACAP Annual Meeting.
Requirements Nomination letters must be accompanied by a CV for the individual nominated.
Amount $2,500 to winner plus $2,000 donation
Date(s) Application Is Due May 4.
Contact Gabe Robbins, (202) 966-7300, ext. 117; fax: (202) 966-2891; email: grobbins@aacap.org
Internet http://www.aacap.org/page.ww?section=Research+and+Training+Awards&name=AACAP+Distinguished+Member+and+Service+Awards
Sponsor American Academy of Child and Adolescent Psychiatry
3615 Wisconsin Avenue, NW
Washington, DC 20016

AACAP Jeanne Spurlock Lecture and Award on Diversity and Culture 36

The lecture and award reflects the spirit of the nomination for outstanding contributions to diversity and culture and in some way encourages individuals from diverse cultural backgrounds to become child and adolescent psychiatrists. Nominees should be individuals who have made contributions in the areas of social awareness including: civil rights; spirituality and/or religion; social welfare; public information; scientific research; education and mentoring; and the arts (literature, theatre, music, painting, sculpture or photography). The award includes an honorarium of $2,500, with the award winner being recognized at a Distinguished Awards Luncheon where he or she will make an honors award presentation about his or her work during the AACAP Annual Meeting.
Amount $2,500
Date(s) Application Is Due May 4.
Contact Jennifer Mecidus, Clinical Practice Manager, (202) 966-7300, ext. 137; fax: (202) 966-9518; email: jmedicus@aacap.org
Internet http://www.aacap.org/page.ww?name=Research+and+Training+Awards§ion=Research+and+Training+Awards
Sponsor American Academy of Child and Adolescent Psychiatry
3615 Wisconsin Avenue, NW
Washington, DC 20016

AACAP Jeanne Spurlock Minority Medical Student Clinical Fellowship in Child and Adolescent Psychiatry 37

Up to fourteen (14) fellowships are available each year for minority medical students to explore a career in child and adolescent psychiatry, gain valuable work experience, and meet leaders in the child and adolescent psychiatry field. The fellowship opportunity provides up to $3,500 for 12 weeks of clinical training under a child and adolescent psychiatrist mentor. Research assignments may include responsibility for part of the observation or evaluation, developing specific aspects of the research mechanisms, conducting interviews or tests, use of rating scales, and psychological or cognitive testing of subjects. Contact AACAP for applications.
Requirements African American, Asian American, Native American, Alaskan Native, Mexican American, Hispanic, and Pacific Islander students in accredited U.S. medical schools are eligible.
Amount $3,500 each, plus expenses to attend the annual meeting
Date(s) Application Is Due Mar 2.
Contact Stacie Hall, (202) 966-7300, ext. 113; fax: (202) 966-2891; email: shall@aacap.org

Internet http://www.aacap.org/cs/root/research_and_training_awards/jeanne_spurlock_minority_medical_student_clinical_fellowship_in_child_and_adolescent_psychiatry
Sponsor American Academy of Child and Adolescent Psychiatry
3615 Wisconsin Avenue, NW
Washington, DC 20016

AACAP Jeanne Spurlock Minority Medical Student Research Fellowship in Drug Abuse and Addiction 38

The Fellowship offers a unique opportunity for minority medical students to explore a research career in substance abuse in relation to child and adolescent psychiatry, gain valuable work experience, and meet leaders in the child and adolescent psychiatry field. The fellowship opportunity provides up to $3,500 for 12 weeks of summer research under a child and adolescent psychiatrist researcher/mentor. The research training plan must provide for significant contact between the student and the mentor and for exposure to state-of-the-art drug abuse and addiction research. The plan should include program planning discussions, instruction in research planning and implementation, regular meetings with the mentor, laboratory director, and the research group, and assigned readings. Research assignments may include responsibility for part of the observation or evaluation, developing specific aspects of the research mechanisms, conducting interviews or tests, use of rating scales, and psychological or cognitive testing of subjects.
Requirements All fellowship participants must attend the AACAP Annual Meeting. Applications are considered from African-American, Native American, Alaskan Native, Mexican American, Hispanic, Asian, and Pacific Islander students in accredited U.S. medical schools.
Amount $3,500 maximum
Date(s) Application Is Due Mar 2.
Contact Stacie Hall, (202) 7300 ext 113; fax: (202) 966-2891; email: shall@aacap.org
Internet http://www.aacap.org/cs/root/research_and_training_awards/jeanne_spurlock_research_fellowship_in_drug_abuse_and_addiction_for_minority_medical_students
Sponsor American Academy of Child and Adolescent Psychiatry
3615 Wisconsin Avenue, NW
Washington, DC 20016

AACAP Klingenstein Third Generation Foundation Award for Research in Depression or Suicide 39

This annual award acknowledges outstanding leadership and continuous contributions in the field of research by giving $5,000 for the best paper on suicide and/or depression published in the Journal during the past year. The award winner will be recognized at a Distinguished Awards Luncheon and make an Honors Presentation about his or her work during the AACAP Annual Meeting.
Requirements Nomination letters must be accompanied by a CV for the individual nominated.
Amount $5,000
Date(s) Application Is Due May 4.
Contact Gabe Robbins, (202) 966-7300, ext. 117; fax: (202) 966-2891; email: grobbins@aacap.org
Internet http://www.aacap.org/page.ww?section=Research+and+Training+Awards&name=AACAP+Journal+Awards
Sponsor American Academy of Child and Adolescent Psychiatry
3615 Wisconsin Avenue, NW
Washington, DC 20016

AACAP Norbert and Charlotte Rieger Psychodynamic Psychotherapy Award 40

The Award recognizes the best published or unpublished paper, written by an AACAP member that addresses the use of psychodynamic psychotherapy in clinical practice and fosters development, teaching, and practice of psychodynamic psychotherapy within child and adolescent psychiatry. Papers that express a novel hypothesis, raise questions about existing theory, or integrate new neuroscience and developmental psychotherapy research with psychodynamic principles may be nominated. Unpublished, new papers and papers published within the last three years may be submitted by their authors. Published papers may be nominated by any member of the AACAP. Authors may be senior or junior faculty members or residents. Delivery of the winning paper will be made at the AACAP Annual Meeting Honors Presentation.
Amount $4,500
Date(s) Application Is Due May 4.
Contact Gabe Robbins, (202) 966-7300, ext. 117; fax: (202) 966-2891; email: grobbins@aacap.org
Internet http://www.aacap.org/page.ww?section=Research+and+Training+Awards&name=The+Norbert+and+Charlotte+Rieger+Psychodynamic+Psychotherapy+Award
Sponsor American Academy of Child and Adolescent Psychiatry
3615 Wisconsin Avenue, NW
Washington, DC 20016

AACAP Pilot Research Award for Attention Disorder 41

The Award for Attention Disorder is available for a junior faculty or child psychiatry resident, and is supported by the Elaine Schlosser Lewis Fund. The award recipient will be encouraged to work with a child and adolescent psychiatric investigator with expertise in his or her particular area of interest. Work must be completed within one year of receipt of the award.
Requirements Candidates must be board eligible, certified in child and adolescent psychiatry, or enrolled in a child psychiatry residency or fellowship program. Candidates must also have a faculty appointment in an accredited medical school or be in a fully accredited child and adolescent psychiatry clinical research or training program.
Restrictions At the time of application, candidates may not have more than two years experience following graduation from residency/fellowship training. Candidates must not have any previous significant, individual research funding in the field of child and adolescent mental health. These include the following: NIMH/NIH Funding (Small Grants, T Award or R-01) or similar foundation or industry research funding.
Amount $9,000
Date(s) Application Is Due Jun 15.
Contact Stacie Hall, (202) 966-7300, ext. 113; fax: (202) 966-2891; email: shall@aacap.org
Internet http://www.aacap.org/page.ww?section=Research+and+Training+Awards&name=Pilot+Research+Award+for+Attention+Disorder+for+a+Junior+Faculty+or+Child+Psychiatry+Resident%2C+Supported+by+the+Elaine+Schlosser+Lewis++Fund
Sponsor American Academy of Child and Adolescent Psychiatry
3615 Wisconsin Avenue, NW
Washington, DC 20016

AACAP Pilot Research Award for Learning Disabilities for a Junior Faculty or Child Psychiatry Resident 42

The award encourages work with a child and adolescent psychiatric investigator with expertise in his or her particular area of interest. Work must be completed within one year of receipt of the award. The award will be disbursed as follows: $4,000 upon acceptance, $4,000 after the awardee submits a final report that includes all research outcomes and budget expenditures, $500 after he/she presents at the AACAP Annual Meeting, and $500 after presenting at the annual ESL Research Update Luncheon. Please note that travel to both the Annual Meeting and the Research Update Luncheon is not included in the award and is the responsibility of the recipient.
Requirements Candidates must be board eligible, certified in child and adolescent psychiatry, or enrolled in a child psychiatry residency or fellowship program. Candidates must also have a faculty appointment in an accredited medical school or be in a fully accredited child and adolescent psychiatry clinical research or training program.
Restrictions Candidates must not have any previous significant, individual research funding in the field of child and adolescent mental health. These include the following: NIMH/NIH Funding (Small Grants, T Award or R-01) or similar foundation or industry research funding. The recipient must be an AACAP member at the time of application and agree to present his or her research.
Amount $9,000
Date(s) Application Is Due Jun 15.
Contact Stacie Hall, (202) 966-7300, ext. 113; fax: (202) 966-2891; email: shall@aacap.org
Internet http://www.aacap.org/page.ww?section=Research+and+Training+Awards&name=Pilot+Research+Award+for+Learning+Disabilities+for+a+Junior+Faculty+or+Child+Psychiatry+Resident%2C+Supported+by+the+Elaine+Schlosser+Lewis+Fund
Sponsor American Academy of Child and Adolescent Psychiatry
3615 Wisconsin Avenue, NW
Washington, DC 20016

AACAP Rieger Service Program Award for Excellence 43

This award recognizes innovative programs that address prevention, diagnosis, or treatment of mental illnesses in children and adolescents, and serve as model programs to the community. This award of $3,500 is shared among the awardee and his or her service program. The award winner will be recognized at a Distinguished Awards Luncheon and make an Honors Presentation about his or her work during the AACAP Annual Meeting.
Requirements Nomination letters must be accompanied by a CV and any support materials for the individual or organization nominated.
Amount $3,500
Date(s) Application Is Due May 4.
Contact Gabe Robbins, (202) 966-7300, ext. 117; fax: (202) 966-2891; email: grobbins@aacap.org
Internet http://www.aacap.org/page.ww?section=Research+and+Training+Awards&name=AACAP+Distinguished+Member+and+Service+Awards
Sponsor American Academy of Child and Adolescent Psychiatry
3615 Wisconsin Avenue, NW
Washington, DC 20016

AACAP Robert Cancro Academic Leadership Award 44

This award recognizes a currently serving General Psychiatry Training Director, Medical School Dean, CEO of a Training Institution, Chair of a Department of Pediatrics or Chair of a Department of Psychiatry for his or her contributions to the promotion of child and adolescent psychiatry. Named in honor of Robert Cancro, M.D., Chairman at New York University, this award offers $1,500 to the awardee. Nominations for the award may be made by Child and Adolescent Training Directors or Division Directors. The recipient of this award will receive a plaque and be recognized at the AACAP Annual Meeting in

Boston, MA. The award recipient will be honored at the Distinguished Awards Luncheon, Training Directors Dinner, and will provide an Honors Presentation on his or her work during the Annual Meeting.
Requirements Nominations must include a CV for the individual nominated
Amount $1,500
Date(s) Application Is Due May 4.
Contact Gabe Robbins, (202) 966-7300, ext. 117; fax: (202) 966-2891; email: grobbins@aacap.org
Internet http://www.aacap.org/page.ww?section=Research+and+Training+Awards&name=AACAP+Distinguished+Member+and+Service+Awards
Sponsor American Academy of Child and Adolescent Psychiatry
3615 Wisconsin Avenue, NW
Washington, DC 20016

AACAP Robinson-Cunningham Award 45
The Award is given for the best manuscript written by a child and adolescent psychiatrist during residency training. The paper must involve children, adolescents, or their families and be published in a professional, peer-reviewed journal within 3-5 years of graduation from a residency training program. The recipient will receive a $100 honorarium and a plaque at the Young Leaders Awards Ceremony during the AACAP Annual Meeting.
Amount $100
Date(s) Application Is Due May 4.
Contact Stacie Hall, (202) 966-7300, ext. 113; fax: (202) 966-2891; email: shall@aacap.org
Internet http://www.aacap.org/page.ww?section=Research+and+Training+Awards&name=The+Robinson-Cunningham+Award
Sponsor American Academy of Child and Adolescent Psychiatry
3615 Wisconsin Avenue, NW
Washington, DC 20016

AACAP Sidney Berman Award for the School-Based Study and Intervention for Learning Disorders and Mental Ilness 46
This award recognizes an individual or program that has shown outstanding achievement in the school-based study or delivery of intervention for learning disorders and mental illness. A cash prize of $4,500 will be awarded. The award winner will be recognized at a Distinguished Awards Luncheon and make an Honors Presentation about his or her work during the AACAP Annual Meeting.
Requirements Nomination letters must be accompanied by a CV for the individual nominated or program information.
Amount $4,500
Date(s) Application Is Due May 4.
Contact Gabe Robbins, (202) 966-7300, ext. 117; fax: (202) 966-2891; email: grobbins@aacap.org
Internet http://www.aacap.org/page.ww?section=Research+and+Training+Awards&name=AACAP+Distinguished+Member+and+Service+Awards
Sponsor American Academy of Child and Adolescent Psychiatry
3615 Wisconsin Avenue, NW
Washington, DC 20016

AACAP Simon Wile Leadership in Consultation Award 47
This annual award acknowledges outstanding leadership and continuous contributions in the field of liaison child and adolescent psychiatry. Nomination letters must be accompanied by a CV for the individual nominated. The award winner will be recognized at a Distinguished Awards Luncheon and make an Honors Presentation about his or her work during the AACAP Annual Meeting.
Requirements Practicing child and adolescent psychiatrists are eligible for nomination.
Amount $500 honorarium and duty of presentation at annual meeting
Date(s) Application Is Due May 4.
Contact Gabe Robbins, (202) 966-7300, ext. 117; fax: (202) 966-2891; email: grobbins@aacap.org
Internet http://www.aacap.org/page.ww?section=Research+and+Training+Awards&name=AACAP+Distinguished+Member+and+Service+Awards
Sponsor American Academy of Child and Adolescent Psychiatry
3615 Wisconsin Avenue, NW
Washington, DC 20016

AACC International Alsberg-French-Schoch Memorial Lectureship Awards 48
This award, sponsored by the Corn Refiners Association, is the organization's highest award given every two to four years in recognition of scientists who have made significant and superior contributions to fundamental starch science. The award is given every two to four years and includes a $2,000 honorarium and a plaque, as well as the opportunity to present a lecture on some phase of starch science before an annual meeting of the Association. To be nominated for an award, contact information for both the person suggesting the nominee and the individual being nominated, as well as a summary of the nominee's career, accomplishments, and contributions should be forwarded directly to AACC International headquarters. Nominations should address the activities most relevant to the award, with a clear statement of the impact the nominee has had in his/her specific area of expertise.
Requirements Nominee must be an AACC International member. All members are strongly encouraged to submit nominations for these awards at any time.
Amount $2,000
Date(s) Application Is Due Jan 1.
Contact Linda Schmitt, (651) 454-7250; fax: (651) 454-0766; email: lschmitt@scisoc.org or aacc@scisoc.org
Internet http://www.aaccnet.org/membership/awards.asp#ALSBERG
Sponsor American Association of Cereal Chemists International
3340 Pilot Knob Road
St. Paul, MN 55121

AACC International Applied Research Award 49
The Award is presented for a significant body of distinguished contributions to the application of science in the cereals area. Of primary interest is the development of novel machinery, processes, products, patents, tests, methodologies, or procedures taking advantage of the wealth of accumulated knowledge from basic research as available in the literature together with basic/applied research performed by the applicant in developing the product/patent. The methodologies, applications, products and processes must have a clear and sustained record of adoption and/or commercialization and must have contributed positively to the development of science and knowledge of relevance to the cereal/food industry. The award will consist of a $2,000 honorarium and a plaque and will be given to an individual scientist or a team of scientists. Recipients of the Award are also accorded the status of AACC International Fellow for their contributions leading to this award. Awardees will have the opportunity to present a lecture during an annual meeting of the Association.
Requirements Nominee must be an AACC International member. All members are strongly encouraged to submit nominations for these awards at any time.
Amount $2,000
Date(s) Application Is Due Jun 1.
Contact Linda Schmitt, (651) 454-7250; fax: (651) 454-0766; email: lschmitt@scisoc.org or aacc@scisoc.org
Internet http://www.aaccnet.org/membership/awards.asp#ALSBERG
Sponsor American Association of Cereal Chemists International
3340 Pilot Knob Road
St. Paul, MN 55121

AACC International Bruce Wasserman Young Investigator Award 50
The purpose of the Award is to recognize young scientists who have made outstanding contributions to the field of cereal biotechnology. The research recognized by this award should be relevant to the broad aims of the AACC International. The work can be either basic (e.g., improved understanding of structure-function relationships) or applied (e.g., new approaches for cereal production, breeding or utilization). For the purposes of this award, 'Cereal Biotechnology' is broadly defined, and encompasses any significant body of research using plants, microbes, genes, proteins or other biomolecules. Contributions in the disciplines of genetics, molecular biology, biochemistry, microbiology and fermentation engineering are all included. The research will be evaluated by its impact as measured as either enhanced knowledge of cereal functionality or improved cereal production or utilization. Achievements will be considered in relation to the age and experience of the nominee. AACC International membership is not required.
Requirements Nominees must be no older than 40 by 1st of July, but nominations of younger scientists are particularly encouraged.
Amount $1,000
Date(s) Application Is Due Jan 15.
Contact Linda Schmitt, (651) 454-7250; fax: (651) 454-0766; email: lschmitt@scisoc.org or aacc@scisoc.org
Internet http://www.aaccnet.org/membership/awards.asp#YoungScientist
Sponsor American Association of Cereal Chemists International
3340 Pilot Knob Road
St. Paul, MN 55121

AACC International Carl Wilhelm Brabender Award 51
The Award provides a plaque and a travel grant to enable the recipient to visit scientists and laboratories in other parts of the world to increase the awardee's knowledge and experience in the field. The only qualification is to be professionally active in rheology, specifically those engaged in the milling and baking industry. The Awardee shall present an award address at the AACC International Annual Meeting or at one of the three annual meetings of the AG at which the award is given.
Date(s) Application Is Due Jun 1.
Contact Linda Schmitt, (651) 454-7250; fax: (651) 454-0766; email: lschmitt@scisoc.org or aacc@scisoc.org
Internet http://www.aaccnet.org/membership/awards.asp#BRABENDER
Sponsor American Association of Cereal Chemists International
3340 Pilot Knob Road
St. Paul, MN 55121

AACC International Excellence in Teaching Award 52
The Award is to be presented to an AACC International member and current teacher who has made significant contributions through teaching in the broad field of Cereal Science and Technology. The award consists of an honorarium of $1,500 and a suitably inscribed plaque. Nominations for the Award are due January 1. To be nominated for an

award, contact information for both the person suggesting the nominee and the individual being nominated, as well as a summary of the nominee's career, accomplishments, and contributions should be forwarded directly to AACC International headquarters. Nominations should address the activities most relevant to the award, with a clear statement of the impact the nominee has had in his/her specific area of expertise.
Requirements Nominee must be an AACC International member. All members are strongly encouraged to submit nominations for these awards at any time.
Amount $1,500
Date(s) Application Is Due Jan 1.
Contact Mike Tilley, (785) 776-2759; fax: (785) 537-5534; email: michael.tilley@gmprc.ksu.edu
Internet http://www.aaccnet.org/membership/awards.asp#EXCELLENCE%20IN%20TEACHING
Sponsor American Association of Cereal Chemists International
3340 Pilot Knob Road
St. Paul, MN 55121

AACC International Manhattan Section Student Travel Awards **53**
All student members of the AACC International are encouraged to apply for the Travel Awards, which are specifically designed to help students pay for travel costs to the Annual Meeting. Complete information and application forms are available online. Applications are due August 1.
Date(s) Application Is Due Aug 1.
Contact Mike Tilley, (785) 776-2759; fax: (785) 537-5534; email: michael.tilley@gmprc.ksu.edu
Internet http://www.aaccnet.org/default.asp
Sponsor American Association of Cereal Chemists International
3340 Pilot Knob Road
St. Paul, MN 55121

AACC International Rheology Division Young Scientist Award **54**
Sponsored by the Rheology Division of AACC International, the purpose of the Award is to recognize scientists who have completed their academic studies within the past five years and have demonstrated outstanding ability in research in the area of rheology and texture as related to cereal-based products. The award consists of an engraved plaque, $500 honorarium, and travel expenses (if necessary) to attend the AACC International Annual Meeting
Amount $500 plus travel expenses
Date(s) Application Is Due Aug 1.
Contact Saljid Alavi, (785) 532-2403; fax: (785) 532-4017; email: salavi@ksu.edu
Internet http://www.aaccnet.org/divisions/youngscientistaward.asp
Sponsor American Association of Cereal Chemists International
3340 Pilot Knob Road
St. Paul, MN 55121

AACC International Thomas Burr Osborne Medal **55**
The Medal is awarded to an individual whose research in the field of cereal chemistry has contributed significantly to the progress of the science. The award consists of an honorarium of $2,000 and a suitably inscribed medal in the form of a plaque. The recipient shall present an address at the AACC International Annual Meeting at which the medal is presented. Recipients of the Medal are also accorded the status of AACC International Fellow.
Amount $2,000
Date(s) Application Is Due Jun 1.
Contact Linda Schmitt, (651) 454-7250; fax: (651) 454-0766; email: lschmitt@scisoc.org or aacc@scisoc.org
Internet http://www.aaccnet.org/membership/awards.asp#FELLOWS
Sponsor American Association of Cereal Chemists International
3340 Pilot Knob Road
St. Paul, MN 55121

AACC International Young Scientist Research Award **56**
The Award is presented to an individual for outstanding contributions in basic and applied research to cereal science with the expectation that contributions will continue. This award recognizes research relevant to the broad aims and interests of AACC International. The research can be either basic (such as improved understanding of structure-function relationships) or applied (such as development of new products, processes, or techniques) and nominees may be from government, academia or industry. Evidence of accomplishments can include awards, publications, invitations to lecture, patents and commercialized foods, processes and/or testing procedures. The research will be evaluated based on impact on advancing cereal science knowledge or improved production or utilization. Achievements will be considered in relation to the age and experience of the nominee. The recipient will receive a $1000 honorarium, a plaque, and will be encouraged to present a lecture at the AACC International meeting of the year in which the award is given.
Requirements Nominees must be no older than 40 years by June 1 of the year the award is sought, but nominations of younger scientists are particularly encouraged. AACC International membership is required.
Amount $1,000
Date(s) Application Is Due Jan 1.
Contact Linda Schmitt, (651) 454-7250; fax: (651) 454-0766; email: lschmitt@scisoc.org or aacc@scisoc.org
Internet http://www.aaccnet.org/membership/awards.asp#YoungScientist
Sponsor American Association of Cereal Chemists International
3340 Pilot Knob Road
St. Paul, MN 55121

AACN Clinical Inquiry Fund Grants **57**
The fund provides small awards to qualified individuals carrying out clinical research projects that directly benefit patients and/or families. Interdisciplinary projects are encouraged. Funds may be awarded for new projects, projects in progress, and projects required for an academic degree as long as all other project criteria are met. The funds may be used to cover direct project expenses--i.e., printed materials, small equipment, and supplies including computer software. Applications are reviewed and funded twice each year.
Requirements The principal investigator must be a regular or affiliate member of AACN, employed in a clinical setting, and directly involved in patient care.
Restrictions Funds may not be used to pay salaries or institutional overhead or augment funding from formal grants.
Amount $500
Date(s) Application Is Due Jan 1; Jul 1.
Contact Grants Administrator, (949) 362-2000 ext 268; fax: (949) 362-2020; email: info@aacn.org
Internet https://www.aacn.org/AACN/research.nsf/vwdoc/grantSupport?opendocument
Sponsor American Association of Critical-Care Nurses
101 Columbia
Aliso Viejo, CA 92656-1491

AACN Clinical Practice Grants **58**
The annual grant supports research in the area of AACN's clinical research priorities for critical care (list of priorities is available on the Web site). Research conducted in fulfillment of an academic degree is acceptable.
Requirements Investigator must be a registered nurse with a current AACN membership.
Restrictions Principal investigators who have received funding from AACN are ineligible to receive additional funding from AACN during the lifetime of the original award.
Amount $6000 maximum
Date(s) Application Is Due Oct 1.
Contact Grants Administrator, (949) 362-2000 ext 268; fax: (714) 362-2020; email: info@aacn.org
Internet https://www.aacn.org/AACN/research.nsf/vwdoc/grantSupport?opendocument
Sponsor American Association of Critical-Care Nurses
101 Columbia
Aliso Viejo, CA 92656-4109

AACN Mentorship Grant **59**
This award, cosponsored by Mallinckrodt Inc and AACN, facilitates critical care nursing practice research between a novice and an experienced researcher. The novice researcher is a beginning researcher with limited or no research experience in the area of the proposed investigation. The novice researcher is also a registered nurse with current AACN membership. The grant may be used to fund research for an academic degree. The mentor must show strong evidence of research expertise in the proposed area of research to be pursued by the novice investigator. The mentor may not be designated mentor in two consecutive years and may not be conducting research as part of an academic degree. Proposals must be received by the listed application deadline date.
Amount $10,000 maximum
Date(s) Application Is Due Feb 1.
Contact Grants Administrator, (949) 362-2000; fax: (949) 362-2020; email: info@aacn.org
Internet http://www.aacn.org/aacn/aacnsite.nsf/htmlmedia/search.html
Sponsor American Association of Critical-Care Nurses
101 Columbia
Aliso Viejo, CA 92656-1491

AACN Physio-Control Small Projects Grants **60**
The program provides awards to qualified individuals carrying out projects focusing on aspects of acute myocardial infarction or resuscitation, such as the use of defibrillation, synchronized cardioversion, noninvasive pacing, or interpretive 12-lead electrocardiogram. Eligible projects may include patient education programs, staff development programs, competency-based educational programs, continuous quality improvement projects, outcomes evaluation projects, or small clinical research studies. Funds may be awarded for new projects, projects in progress, and projects required for an academic degree as long as all other project criteria are met. Collaborative projects are encouraged and may involve interdisciplinary teams, multiple nursing units, home health, subacute and transitional care, other institutions, or community agencies. Funds may be used to cover direct project expenses, such as printed materials, small equipment, or supplies including computer software.

Requirements Applicants must be regular or affiliate members of AACN and not currently conducting a study funded by another AACN research grant.
Restrictions Funds may not be used for salaries or institutional overhead.
Amount $1500 maximum
Date(s) Application Is Due Jul 1.
Contact Grants Administrator, (949) 362-2000; fax: (949) 362-2020; email: info@aacn.org
Internet http://www.aacn.org/aacn/aacnsite.nsf/htmlmedia/awards.html
Sponsor American Association of Critical-Care Nurses
101 Columbia
Aliso Viejo, CA 92656-1491

AACN-Sigma Theta Tau Critical Care Grant 61
The grant, cosponsored by AACN and Sigma Theta Tau International, supports critical care nursing research and is awarded annually for a study relevant to critical care nursing practice. The proposed study may be used to meet requirements of an academic degree. Proposals must be received by the listed application deadline date. Annual deadline dates may vary; contact program staff for exact dates.
Requirements The principal investigator must be a registered nurse with current AACN membership.
Amount $10,000 maximum
Date(s) Application Is Due Oct 1.
Contact Grants Administrator, (800) 899-2226; fax: (714) 362-2020; email: aacninfo@iqnow.com
Internet http://www.aacn.org/aacn/aacnsite.nsf/htmlmedia/search.html
Sponsor American Association of Critical-Care Nurses
101 Columbia
Aliso Viejo, CA 92656-1491

AACR Brigid G. Leventhal Scholar in Cancer Research Awards 62
The purpose of this award program is to enhance the education and training of early career scientists by providing financial support for their participation in AACR Annual Meetings and Special Conferences. The AACR-WICR Brigid G. Leventhal Scholar Award Committee makes selection for these competitive awards after careful consideration of the candidate's application and accompanying materials.
Requirements Candidates must be: Women in Cancer Research members; full time scientists in training who are graduate students, medical students, residents, clinical fellows or equivalent, or postdoctoral fellows; and first authors on abstracts submitted for consideration for presentation at the AACR Annual Meeting or Special Conference which the applicant wants to attend.
Date(s) Application Is Due Sep 10.
Contact Program Administrator, (215) 440-9300; fax: (215) 440-9412; email: wicr@aacr.org
Internet http://www.aacr.org/home/scientists/travel-grants--research-funding/travel-grants/brigid-g-leventhal-scholar-awards.aspx
Sponsor American Association for Cancer Research
615 Chestnut Street, 17th Floor
Philadelphia, PA 19106-4404

AACR Career Development Awards 63
Career development awards are two-year awards that support research by scientists who are engaged in meritorious cancer research at academic institutions. These awards provide important transitional support for direct research expenses as researchers move from the ranks of early career scientists to faculty status. The Awards are open to junior faculty who completed postdoctoral studies or clinical fellowships between specified dates and who are at an academic or medical institution. Current guidelines pertain to the AACR-Aflac, Incorporated Career Development Award for Pediatric Cancer Research. Candidates may conduct research at any research institution in the world.
Requirements Candidates must have acquired a doctoral degree in a related field and may not currently be a candidate for a further doctoral or professional degree. If a candidate has obtained an equivalent degree at a foreign institution, information on the nature of the degree must be provided at the time of application.
Restrictions Employees of a national government and employees of private industry are ineligible.
Amount $50,000
Date(s) Application Is Due May 8.
Contact Julia Laurence, Staff Assistant, (267) 646-0655; fax: (215) 440-9372; email: awards@aacr.org
Internet http://www.aacr.org/home/scientists/travel-grants--research-funding/research-funding/career-development-awards.aspx
Sponsor American Association for Cancer Research
615 Chestnut Street, 17th Floor
Philadelphia, PA 19106-4404

AACR Fellows Grants 64
The Grant supports innovative research by a meritorious young investigator by presenting the Fellow with research funds to pursue an independent line of investigation within the context of his/her current Fellowship placement. By allowing a Fellow to acquire the equipment and supplies needed to pursue a new direction in his/her research program, the Fellows Grant assists the Fellow in developing preliminary data to support a future project or investigating a new technique that otherwise would not be possible in the absence of this funding. The Selection Committee favors proposals that provided evidence of an applicant's research initiative and creativity, and the support of a scientific mentor. The Committee also weighed the potential of the candidate to make meaningful contributions to the field, and promise of success as a cancer researcher in future years. Application availability opens October 1 and closes on December 1. The grant term begins July 1.
Requirements Candidates must be, at the start of the grant term, in their third, fourth, or fifth year of their fellowship status.
Amount $30,000-$40,000 per year
Date(s) Application Is Due Dec 1.
Contact Julia Laurence, Staff Assistant, (267) 646-0655; fax: (215) 440-9372; email: awards@aacr.org
Internet http://www.aacr.org/home/scientists/travel-grants--research-funding/research-funding/fellows-grants.aspx
Sponsor American Association for Cancer Research
615 Chestnut Street, 17th Floor
Philadelphia, PA 19106-4404

AACR Gertrude Elion Cancer Research Award 65
This prestigious award provides a one-year research grant to an assistant professor at an academic or nonprofit research institute worldwide for salary and benefits, laboratory supplies, and limited domestic travel to support research in cancer etiology, diagnosis, treatment, or prevention (basic, translational, or clinical cancer research). Guidelines and application forms are available upon request or may be downloaded from the AACR Web site.
Requirements Candidates must be nominated by an AACR member and submit a detailed application. Candidates must have completed postdoctoral studies or clinical fellowships no later than July 1 of the award year and ordinarily not more than five years earlier. Candidates must be tenure-tracked scientists at the level of assistant professor at an academic institution anywhere in the world.
Restrictions Tenured faculty in academia, employees of a national government, and employees of private industry are not eligible.
Amount $50,000
Date(s) Application Is Due Dec 1.
Contact Gina R. Barnes, Staff Associate, (215) 440-9300 ext 102; fax: (215) 440-9372; email: awards@aacr.org
Internet http://www.aacr.org/home/scientists/travel-grants--research-funding/research-funding/elion-award.aspx
Sponsor American Association for Cancer Research
615 Chestnut Street, 17th Floor
Philadelphia, PA 19106-4404

AACR International Award for Cancer Research 66
The prestigious Award for Cancer Research was established to annually recognize a scientist: who has made a major scientific discovery in basic cancer research or who has made significant contributions to translational cancer research; who continues to be active in cancer research and has a record of recent, noteworthy publications; and whose ongoing work holds promise for continued substantive contributions to progress in the field of cancer. The Award is intended to honor an individual scientist. However, more than one scientist may be co-nominated and selected to share the Award when their investigations are closely related in subject matter and have resulted in work that is worthy of the Award.
Requirements Eligible candidates are cancer researchers affiliated with institutions in academia, industry, or government that are involved in cancer research, cancer medicine, or cancer-related biomedical science anywhere in the world. No regard shall be given to race, gender, nationality, geographic location, or religious or political views.
Restrictions Institutions or organizations are not eligible for the Award. Receipt of other major awards does not preclude a candidate from eligibility for the Award.
Amount C75,000
Date(s) Application Is Due Sep 14.
Contact Program Administrator, (215) 440-9300, ext 1400; fax: (215) 440-9372; email: awards@aacr.org
Internet http://www.aacr.org/home/scientists/scientific-awards/pezcoller-aacr-international-award.aspx
Sponsor American Association of Cancer Research / Pezcoller Foundation
615 Chestnut Street, 17th Floor
Philadelphia, PA 19106-4404

AACR Kirk A. Landon and Dorothy P. Landon Foundation Prizes 67
These two major international awards recognize outstanding scientists who have made seminal basic and translational cancer research discoveries at the cutting edge of scientific novelty and significance, which have accelerated progress against cancer and have implications for future discoveries and contributions to cancer research. The Kirk A. Landon-AACR Prize for Basic Cancer Research recognizes significant, fundamental contributions to laboratory research. The Dorothy P. Landon-AACR Prize for Translational Cancer Research recognizes extraordinary achievement in translational cancer research--the interface between basic research and its application to the clinic in the areas of diagnosis, treatment, or the prevention of cancer. Both prizes bring heightened public attention to landmark achievements in the continuing effort to prevent

and cure cancer through the presentation of dynamic lectures during the AACR annual meeting; and promote and reward continued, productive cancer research.
Requirements The prizes are open to all cancer researchers who are affiliated with any institution involved in cancer research, cancer medicine, or cancer-related biomedical science anywhere in the world. Such institutions include those in academia, industry, or government. Candidates must be active researchers and have a record of recent publications.
Restrictions Institutions or organizations are ineligible.
Amount $200,000
Date(s) Application Is Due Aug 10.
Contact Landon-AACR Prize Selection Committees, (215) 440-9300, ext 1400; fax: (215) 440-9372; email: awards@aacr.org
Internet http://www.aacr.org/home/scientists/scientific-awards/landon-prizes.aspx#a
Sponsor American Association for Cancer Research
615 Chestnut Street, 17th Floor
Philadelphia, PA 19106-4404

AACR Minority Scholar in Cancer Research Awards **68**
The AACR administers this award program that is supported by a grant from the Comprehensive Minority Biomedical Branch of the National Cancer Institute to provide funds for participation of meritorious minority scientists in the AACR Special Conferences Series (U.S. domestic conferences only). These awards are intended to enhance the education and training of minority researchers and to increase the visibility and recognition of minorities involved in cancer research.
Requirements Candidates must be full-time graduate students, medical students, residents, clinical or postdoctoral fellows, or junior faculty members who are either engaged in cancer research or who have the training and potential to make contributions to this field. Candidates must also be citizens or permanent residents of the United States or Canada.
Restrictions This program applies only to racial/ethnic minority groups identified by the National Cancer Institute as being traditionally underrepresented in cancer and biomedical research. These groups include African Americans/Blacks, Alaskan Natives, Hispanic Americans, Native Americans, and Native Pacific Islanders. Only citizens of the United States or Canada or scientists who are permanent residents of these countries may receive one of these awards.
Date(s) Application Is Due Dec 14.
Contact Program Administrator; (215) 440-9300; fax: (215) 440-9412; email: micr@aacr.org
Internet http://www.aacr.org/home/scientists/travel-grants--research-funding/travel-grants/minority-scholar-awards.aspx
Sponsor American Association for Cancer Research
615 Chestnut Street, 17th Floor
Philadelphia, PA 19106-4404

AACR Minority-Serving Institution Faculty Scholar in Cancer Research Awards **69**
The AACR is pleased to announce the availability of Scholar Awards in Cancer Research for full-time faculty members of Minority-Serving Institutions [Historically Black Colleges and Universities (HBCUs), Hispanic Serving Institutions (HSIs), and Tribal Colleges and Universities and other post-secondary institutions as defined by the US Department of Education]. The purposes of this Award program is to increase the scientific knowledge base of faculty members at Minority-Serving Institutions, and to encourage them and their students to pursue careers in cancer research. AACR Minority-Serving Institution Faculty Scholar in Cancer Research Awards are presented by the American Association for Cancer Research to scientists at the level of Assistant Professor or above at a Minority-Serving Institution, who are engaged in meritorious basic, clinical, or translational cancer research.
Requirements Candidates must have completed doctoral studies or clinical fellowships and hold full-time faculty status at an institution designated as a Minority-Serving Institution. Candidates must have acquired doctoral degrees in fields relevant to cancer research. Candidates must be citizens or permanent residents of the United States or Canada.
Date(s) Application Is Due Nov 21.
Contact Gary Davidoff, Staff Assistant; (267) 646-0654; fax: (215) 440-9372; email: davidoff@aacr.org
Internet http://www.aacr.org/home/scientists/travel-grants--research-funding/travel-grants/minority-serving-institution-faculty-scholar-awards.aspx
Sponsor American Association for Cancer Research
615 Chestnut Street, 17th Floor
Philadelphia, PA 19106-4404

AACR Research Fellowships **70**
The association awards one-, two-, or three-year grants to support the salary and benefits of the Fellow. Named fellowships include the: AACR-Amgen Fellowship in Clinical/Translational Cancer Research; AACR-Anna D. Barker Fellowship in Basic Cancer Research; AACR-Bristol-Myers Squibb Oncology Fellowship in Clinical Cancer Research; AACR-AstraZeneca-Cancer Research and Prevention Foundation Fellowship in Translational Lung Cancer Research; AACR-Genentech BioOncology Fellowship for Cancer Research on the HER Family Pathway; AACR-MedImmune Fellowship for Research on Biologics-Based Therapies for Cancer; AACR-National Brain Tumor Foundation Fellowship, in memory of Bonnie Brooks; and AACR-PanCAN Fellowship for PancreaticCancer Research, in memory of Samuel Stroum.
Requirements Applications are open to Postdoctoral Fellows and Clinical Research Fellows at an academic facility, teaching hospital, or research institution who will be in the 1st, 2nd, or 3rd year of their postdoctoral training at the start of the fellowship term.
Restrictions Academic faculty holding the rank of assistant professor or higher, graduate or medical students, government employees, and employees of private industry are not eligible.
Amount $30,000-$40,000 per year
Date(s) Application Is Due Dec 1.
Contact Gina R. Barnes, Staff Associate, (215) 440-9300, ext. 102; fax: (215) 440-9372; email: awards@aacr.org
Internet http://www.aacr.org/home/scientists/travel-grants--research-funding/research-funding/research-fellowships.aspx
Sponsor American Association for Cancer Research
615 Chestnut Street, 17th Floor
Philadelphia, PA 19106-4404

AACR Scholar-in-Training Awards **71**
Scholar-in-Training Awards provide financial support for early-career scientists to attend the AACR Annual Meeting. Since its inception in 1986, the program has provided over 3,200 grants and has received support from more than 30 cancer research foundations, corporations, individuals, and other organizations dedicated to the fight against cancer. A stipend (from $400-$2,000 depending on the geographic location of the recipient or the type of award) will be presented to recipients on-site. Recipients may pick up their a check and welcome package at the Associate Member Resource and Career Center.
Requirements Eligible candidates are graduate students, medical students and residents, clinical fellows or equivalent, and postdoctoral fellows. Eligible candidates must be the presenter of a proffered paper. Eligible candidates may be traveling within the U.S. or from abroad. Some awards are specifically designated for those traveling from Asia, Europe, and countries with emerging economies.
Restrictions Employees or subcontractors of private industry are not eligible.
Amount $400-$2,000
Date(s) Application Is Due Nov 28.
Contact Gary Davidoff, Staff Assistant; (267) 646-0654; fax: (215) 440-9372; email: gary.davidoff@aacr.org
Internet http://www.aacr.org/home/scientists/travel-grants--research-funding/travel-grants/scholar-in-training-awards-annual-meeting.aspx
Sponsor American Association for Cancer Research
615 Chestnut Street, 17th Floor
Philadelphia, PA 19106-4404

AACR Team Science Award **72**
The Award has been established by the AACR and Eli Lilly and Company to acknowledge and catalyze the growing importance of interdisciplinary teams to the understanding of cancer and/or the translation of research discoveries into clinical cancer applications. In addition, through the presentation of this Award, the AACR and Eli Lilly seek to effect change within the traditional cancer research culture by recognizing those institutions that value and foster interdisciplinary team science. These institutions will have demonstrated their support of a team science environment by creating mechanisms to enhance the required infrastructure, such as through pilot funding, technology transfer offices, shared resources, etc., and by presenting awards, honors, appointments, and promotions to those who participate in interdisciplinary teams.
Requirements For the purpose of this Award, a team is defined as a group of individuals representing interdisciplinary expertise, each of whom have made substantive and quantifiable contributions to the research being recognized. Team members may be working within the same institution or at several institutions. Candidacy is open to all cancer researchers who are affiliated with any institution involved in cancer research, cancer medicine, or cancer-related biomedical science anywhere in the world. Such institutions include those in academia, industry, or government.
Amount $50,000
Date(s) Application Is Due Mar 19.
Contact Victoria A.M. Wolodzko, Assistant Director, (215) 440-9356; fax: (215) 440-9372; email: wolodzko@aacr.org
Internet http://www.aacr.org/home/scientists/scientific-awards/team-science-award.aspx
Sponsor American Association of Cancer Research
615 Chestnut Street, 17th Floor
Philadelphia, PA 19106-4404

AACR Thomas J. Bardos Science Education Awards **73**
AACR-Thomas J. Bardos Science Education Awards for Undergraduate Students are available to full-time third-year undergraduate students majoring in science. The purpose of these awards is to inspire young science students to enter the field of cancer research. The award consists of a waiver of registration fees for two annual AACR meetings and $1500/year for research and travel expenses. The award is for a two-year period.
Requirements Candidates must be full-time, third year undergraduate students majoring in science. Applications from students who are not yet committed to cancer research are welcome.

Amount $1,500 plus a wave of registration fee
Date(s) Application Is Due Nov 21.
Contact Program Administrator, (215) 440-9300; fax: (215) 440-9412; email: constituencies@aacr.org
Internet http://www.aacr.org/home/scientists/travel-grants--research-funding/travel-grants/aacr-thomas-j-bardos-science-education-awards-for-undergraduate-students-.aspx
Sponsor American Association for Cancer Research
615 Chestnut Street, 17th Floor
Philadelphia, PA 19106-4404

AACR-Barletta Foundation Fellows Grant for Translational Cancer Research 74
The AACR-Barletta Foundation provide a grant to be used for direct research expenses associated with a fellow's proposal in the area of translational cancer research with a focus on any individualized therapeutic area. Research proposals include the use of human tissue and have implications for therapeutic application and individualized medicine.
Requirements Candidates should be in the third, fourth, or fifth year of their fellowship status. They are required to submit, and have accepted for presentation, a highly-rated abstract for the AACR-NCI-EORTC International Conference on Molecular Targets and Cancer Therapeutics.
Amount $35,000
Date(s) Application Is Due Jun 12.
Contact Gary Davidoff, Staff Assistant; (267) 646-0654; fax: (215) 440-9372; email: gary.davidoff@aacr.org
Internet http://www.aacr.org/home/scientists/travel-grants--research-funding/research-funding/aacr-barletta-foundation-fellows-grant.aspx
Sponsor American Association for Cancer Research
615 Chestnut Street, 17th Floor
Philadelphia, PA 19106-4404

AACR-Cancer Research Foundation of America Award for Excellence in Cancer Prevention Research 75
The international award recognizes outstanding cancer prevention research; it will be given to a scientist residing in any country in the world for seminal contributions in basic, translational, clinical, epidemiological, or behavioral science investigations in cancer prevention research that have had a major impact on the field and stimulated new directions in this important field. The awardee will receive an honorarium and a commemorative plaque, as well as support for travel and subsistence expenses to attend the AACR meeting.
Requirements The award is open to all cancer researchers who are affiliated with any research institution anywhere in the world. Candidates must currently maintain an active research program, have a record of recent publications, and be in a position to present the award lecture at the meeting. Nominations may be made by any scientist who is affiliated with any research institution whose work relates to cancer research or cancer-related biomedical research.
Date(s) Application Is Due Jun 29.
Contact Julia Laurence, Staff Assistant, (267) 646-0655; fax: (215) 440-9372; email: awards@aacr.org
Internet http://www.aacr.org/home/scientists/scientific-awards/crpf-prevention-award.aspx
Sponsor American Association for Cancer Research
615 Chestnut Street, 17th Floor
Philadelphia, PA 19106-4404

AACR-GlaxoSmithKline Clinical Cancer Research Scholar Awards 76
These awards provide support of $4,000 which may be used by the recipient to support attendance at the Annual Meeting and any other AACR meeting within a two-year period. Up to $2,000 per meeting may be used, and reimbursement checks are provided after the meeting upon submission of proper documentation of travel, housing, registration, and/or subsistence expenses. Award recipients are still required to pay the Annual Meeting registration fee and make their own travel and housing arrangements. Selection is made by the Program Committee based upon the novelty, quality, and significance of the abstract submitted. Award recipients will receive notification separate from abstract acceptance and scheduling information.
Requirements Graduate students, medical students and residents, clinical fellows or equivalent, and postdoctoral fellows (AACR members and nonmembers) who are presenters of a meritorious abstract in clinical cancer research are eligible.
Restrictions Employees or subcontractors of private industry are not eligible.
Amount $2,000-$4,000
Date(s) Application Is Due Nov 28.
Contact Gary Davidoff, Staff Assistant; (267) 646-0654; fax: (215) 440-9372; email: gary.davidoff@aacr.org
Internet http://www.aacr.org/home/scientists/travel-grants--research-funding/travel-grants/aacr-glaxosmithkline-clinical-cancer-research-scholar-awards.aspx
Sponsor American Association for Cancer Research
615 Chestnut Street, 17th Floor
Philadelphia, PA 19106-4404

AACR-NCI International Investigator Opportunity Grants 77
Recognizing that there is no substitute for the collegial interaction and scholarly discussion that is a cornerstone of scientific advancement, these grants provide significant financial support for meeting registration, housing, travel, and incidentals to attend the annual American Association for Cancer Research Meeting. The event takes place in April each year. Grants are available for ten cancer researchers from countries where such opportunities are limited.
Requirements Applicants must be nationals or permanent residents of, and must reside and conduct cancer research within, low and middle-income countries as defined by the World Bank. Applicants should also hold an doctorate or equivalent degree and be actively engaged in a program of cancer research with a record of cancer-focused publications in peer-reviewed scientific journals.
Restrictions Funds may not be used for entertainment expenses (such as for tours or in-room movies), meals for other individuals, souvenirs, and other non-meeting expenses.
Contact Gary Davidoff, Staff Assistant; (267) 646-0654; fax: (215) 440-9372; email: gary.davidoff@aacr.org
Internet http://www.aacr.org/home/scientists/travel-grants--research-funding/travel-grants/aacr-nci-international-investigator-opportunity-grants.aspx
Sponsor American Association for Cancer Research and the National Cancer Institute
615 Chestnut Street, 17th Floor
Philadelphia, PA 19106-4404

AAES Engineering Journalism Awards 78
The purpose of these American Association of Engineering Societies (AAES) awards is to recognize outstanding reporting of an event or issue that furthers public understanding of engineering and is given in one of these three categories: daily newspapers, general circulation print media, and broadcast radio or television. Nominations must be articles published or broadcast in English between January 1 and December 31. Nominations are welcome from reporters, editors, publishers, and members of the engineering community. Print entries must be easily reproducible; electronic entries must include both a VHS or audio cassette and a script. The nomination cycle runs from October 1 to December 31.
Amount $5000 maximum
Date(s) Application Is Due Dec 31.
Contact Awards Administrator, (202) 296-2237; fax: (202) 296-1151; email: info@aaes.org
Internet http://www.aaes.org
Sponsor American Association of Engineering Societies
1828 L St NW, Ste 906
Washington, DC 20036

AAF Richard Morris Hunt Architecture Fellowship 79
Cosponsored by the AAF and the French Heritage Society, this fellowship provides opportunities for French and American architects to learn and exchange information about their respective country's historic preservation process and techniques.
Amount $15,000
Date(s) Application Is Due Jan 31.
Contact Mary Felber, Director, Scholarship Program, (202) 626-7511; fax: (202) 626-7420; email: mfelber@archfoundation.org
Internet http://www.archfoundation.org/scholarships/index.htm
Sponsor American Architectural Foundation
1735 New York Ave NW
Washington, DC 20006

AAFA Investigator Research Grants 80
AAFA is dedicated to finding the causes, new treatments and cures for asthma and allergic diseases. AAFA offers a program that sponsors seed grants for investigators wishing to explore new areas of scientific merit related to asthma and allergic diseases. Support has enabled 80% of the researchers who have received the AAFA research grant to win additional research funding from other sources totaling more than $18 million. The Asthma and Allergy of Foundation of America is the only patient organization in the United States that funds research grants for both asthma and allergies. At this time, the application process for grants is through an NIH referral system.
Contact Mary Brasler, Director of Programs and Services, (202) 466-7643, ext. 238; email: mbrasler@aafa.org
Internet http://www.aafa.org/display.cfm?id=6
Sponsor Asthma and Allergy Foundation of America
1233 20th Street, NW, Suite 402
Washington, DC 20036

AAFCS National Fellowships 81
AAFCS annually awards national fellowships to support graduate study in areas such as family and consumer sciences, nutrition, textiles, and home economics. The fellowships are awarded to individuals who have exhibited the potential for making contributions to these professions. It is recommended that applicants first complete at least one year of professional family and consumer science experience by the time of application.
Requirements Applicants must be citizens or permanent residents of the United States. Applicant must show clearly defined plans for full-time graduate or undergraduate study during the time for which the fellowship is awarded. Each request for appropriate application form must be accompanied by an application fee of $40.
Amount $3500-$5000

Date(s) Application Is Due Jan 13.
Contact Fellowships and Awards Committee, (703) 706-4600; fax: (703) 706-4663; email: staff@aafcs.org
Internet http://www.aafcs.org/programs/fellowships.html
Sponsor American Association of Family and Consumer Sciences
400 N Columbus St, Ste 202
Alexandria, VA 22314

AAFP Pfizer Teacher Development Awards **82**
The purpose of the awards is to honor community-based physicians who give up time from their practice to teach family medicine students and/or residents part time. Eligible candidates may serve as preceptors or as volunteer teachers at other sites, including family medicine teaching centers. Guidelines are available online.
Requirements Applicant must have graduated from an ACGME-approved family practice residency program within the last seven years; have entered family medicine; be a member of the American Academy of Family Physicians; have entered or plan to enter part-time family medicine teaching (not less than four hours per month and no more than 32 hours per month--averaged over a year); and teach voluntarily or receive no more than $18,000 compensation for the educational time devoted to residents and/or students.
Amount $2000
Date(s) Application Is Due May 11.
Contact Sondra Goodman, (800) 274-2237 ext 4457; email: sgoodman@aafp.org
Internet http://www.aafpfoundation.org/x269.xml
Sponsor American Academy of Family Physicians Foundation
11400 Tomahawk Creek Pkwy
Leawood, KS 66211

AAFP Research Stimulation Grants **83**
Relatively small grants to stimulate research in family practice in the areas of preliminary efforts leading to a larger research project, pilot projects, and data collection for a larger research project are funded. The applicant must include a discussion of how the proposed project is anticipated to lead to a larger project. Applications may be submitted at any time.
Requirements Eligible to apply are individual family physicians, family practice/medicine organizations or associations, residents in family practice, departments of family medicine, and educational and health care institutions directly involved in family practice/medicine.
Amount $5000
Contact Susie Morantz, Senior Program Manager, (800) 274-2237 ext 4470; email: smorantz@aafp
Internet http://www.aafpfoundation.org/x446.xml
Sponsor American Academy of Family Physicians Foundation
11400 Tomahawk Creek Pkwy
Leawood, KS 66211

AAFPRS Ben Shuster Memorial Award **84**
This award is given annually for the best paper based on clinical work or research in the field of facial plastic surgery by a resident or fellow in training. The competitor must be the sole or senior author of the paper, which must have been delivered at a national meeting or its equivalent between March 1 of the previous year and the deadline date. Studies prepared during the first year after completion of residency training will be considered provided that the research was conducted during the author's residency training program or fellowship.
Requirements The competition is open to US or Canadian residents or fellows in otolaryngology who are members of AAFPRS.
Amount $1000
Date(s) Application Is Due Feb 28.
Contact Shuster Memorial Award, Educational and Research Foundation, (703) 299-9291; fax: (703) 299-8898
Internet http://www.aafprs.org/physician/awards_grants/awards.html
Sponsor American Academy of Facial, Plastic, and Reconstructive Surgery
310 S Henry St
Alexandria, VA 22314

AAFPRS Bernstein Award **85**
The purpose of the grant is to encourage original research projects that will advance facial plastic and reconstructive surgery. Grants may be used as seed money for research projects. Applicants are required to submit an application, a detailed proposal, the investigator's curriculum vita, and letters from the appropriate institutional review committees certifying institutional conformity to the US government guidelines for human and animal experiments. Annual deadline dates may vary; contact program.
Requirements Applicants should be US or Canadian AAFPRS fellow members. The primary criteria are that the research be original and have direct application to facial plastic and reconstructive surgery.
Amount $25,000
Date(s) Application Is Due Jan 15.
Contact Research Coordinator, Educational and Research Foundation, (703) 299-9291; fax: (703) 299-8898; email: lhacek@aafprs.org
Internet http://www.aafprs.org/physician/awards_grants/bernstein_grant.html
Sponsor American Academy of Facial, Plastic, and Reconstructive Surgery
310 S Henry St
Alexandria, VA 22314

AAFPRS Ira J. Tresley Research Award **86**
This annual award is given to a US or Canadian academy member for the best paper based on any research study in the field of facial plastic surgery. The competition is open to any US or Canadian physician who is an AAFPRS member and who has been board certified for at least three years. The paper must have been presented at a national meeting or its equivalent between March 1 of the previous year and the deadline date of the current year.
Amount $1000
Date(s) Application Is Due Feb 28.
Contact Tresley Research Award, Educational and Research Foundation, (703) 299-9291; fax: (703) 299-8898
Internet http://www.aafprs.org/physician/awards_grants/awards.html
Sponsor American Academy of Facial, Plastic, and Reconstructive Surgery
310 S Henry St
Alexandria, VA 22314

AAFPRS Surgery Resident Research Awards **87**
Two resident research grants, tenable in the United States or Canada, may be awarded each year to stimulate resident research in facial plastic surgery on projects that are well conceived and scientifically valid. Residents are encouraged to enter early in their training so that their applications may be revised and resubmitted if not accepted the first time. This award may be integrated with other funding to complete a project. Interested residents should write for entry guidelines.
Requirements US and Canadian residents at any level who are AAFPRS members are eligible to apply, even if the research work will be done during their fellowship year.
Amount $5000
Date(s) Application Is Due Jan 15.
Contact Resident Research Awards, Educational and Research Foundation, (703) 299-9291; fax: (703) 299-8898
Internet http://www.aafprs.org/physician/awards_grants/research_grant.html
Sponsor American Academy of Facial, Plastic, and Reconstructive Surgery
310 S Henry St
Alexandria, VA 22314

AAG Dissertation Research Grants **88**
The following funds provide financial assistance to PhD candidates preparing dissertations in geography. The Robert D. Hodgson Fund gives preference to those topics that best reflect Dr. Hodgson's belief that the pursuit and understanding of geographic knowledge may lead to international cooperation. The Paul Vouras Fund gives preference to minority applicants for support of dissertation work. The Otis Paul Starkey Fund gives preference to regional study or significant problem areas in the United States or its possessions. Funds are to be used for direct research expenses and may not be used to cover overhead costs. Applicants may obtain application forms from the association.
Requirements Any person is eligible to apply for a grant who has been a member of AAG for at least a year at the time of submitting the application, does not have a PhD degree at the time of the award, and has completed all PhD requirements except for the dissertation research.
Amount $500 maximum
Date(s) Application Is Due Dec 31.
Contact Ehsan Khater, (202) 234-1450; fax: (202) 234-2744; email: ekhater@aag.org
Internet http://www.aag.org/Grantsawards/Dissertationresearch.html
Sponsor Association of American Geographers
1710 16th St NW
Washington, DC 20009-3198

AAG John Brinkerhoff Jackson Prize **89**
The association offers this award for the best nonfiction book about the human geography of the United States. The prize will go to the writer who can best interpret geographical research in language that lay readers can understand. Publishers are invited to submit entries for the Jackson Prize competition, and should forward one copy of the published book to each of the four committee members: Michael P. Conzen (chair), Committee on Geographical Studies, University of Chicago, 5828 S. University Avenue, Chicago, IL 60637'1583; Karl B. Raitz, Department of Geography, University of Kentucky, Lexington, KY 40506'0027; Richard Francaviglia, Center for Southwest Studies, Box 19497'Central Library, University of Texas at Arlington, Arlington, TX 76019'0497; and Susan Hardwick, Department of Geography, University of Oregon, Eugene, OR 97403'1251.
Requirements The prize is restricted to books written by geographers, with preference given to those by US citizens or permanent residents.
Restrictions Textbooks, dissertations, and scholarly articles will not be considered.
Amount $1000
Date(s) Application Is Due Dec 31.
Contact Michael Conzen, Chair, (312) 702-8308; email: m-conzen@uchicago.edu
Internet http://www.aag.org/Grantsawards/jackson_prize.cfm
Sponsor Association of American Geographers
1710 16th St NW
Washington, DC 20009-3198

AAG Research Grants **90**

Grants are given to support research and fieldwork done by AAG members. Preference will be given to projects that may generate substantial support from private or federal granting agencies; may be pertinent to questions affecting important gaps in the spectrum of geographic knowledge and research; or will open up new areas, topics, or techniques for geographic research. Applicants should obtain forms from AAG.
Requirements Any person is eligible to apply for a grant who has been a member of the association for at least two years at the time of submitting an application.
Restrictions This grant will not be made to support doctoral dissertations.
Amount $1000 maximum
Date(s) Application Is Due Dec 31.
Contact Ehsan Khater, (202) 234-1450; fax: (202) 234-2744; email: ekhater@aag.org
Internet http://www.aag.org/Grantsawards/Generalresearch.html
Sponsor Association of American Geographers
1710 16th St NW
Washington, DC 20009-3198

AAHN Competitive Student Research Award **91**

The grant supports thesis-dissertation research and is designed to encourage and support graduate training in historical research at the master's and doctoral levels. One proposal will be funded.
Requirements Applications will be accepted from AAHN members enrolled in NLN-accredited master's or doctoral programs in regionally accredited universities.
Amount $1000
Date(s) Application Is Due May 15.
Contact Grants Administrator, (609) 693-7250; fax: (609) 693-1037; email: aahn@aahn.org
Internet http://www.aahn.org/awards.html#student
Sponsor American Association for the History of Nursing
P.O. Box 175
Lanoka Harbor, NJ 08734-0175

AAHPM Palliative Medicine Fellowships **92**

The program offers training programs to prepare physicians for careers in academic or community-based palliative medicine. Fellowships provide clinical experience and supervision for palliative medicine in hospitals, homes, hospices, chronic care institutions, and outpatient settings, and include consultational and longitudinal care exposure, as well as training in bereavement care. Some programs also provide opportunities for mentored research or teaching. Most programs being in July, and clinical training generally lasts one year, allowing for board eligibility upon successful completion. For a complete list of US palliative medicine fellowship training programs, visit www.aahpm.org/fellowship/directory.html.
Requirements Trainees must have already completed residency training in a primary specialty, such as internal or family medicine, or have similar clinical training and experience.
Contact Fellowships Administrator, (847) 375-4712; fax: (877) 734-8671; email: info@aahpm.org
Internet http://www.aahpm.org
Sponsor American Academy of Hospice and Palliative Medicine
4700 W Lake Ave
Glenview, IL 60025

AAJA Fellowship **93**

The fellowships are designed to enable members of the association to attend short-term professional training and skills development programs. These fellowships can be used to defray tuition, travel, food, lodging, and other related costs. News organizations of the recipients must grant them a leave of absence to attend the program. Fellowships must be used within 12 months of the award date. Applications are accepted on a case-by-case basis year-round. Grants will be awarded contingent upon proof of registration at, or acceptance to, the training program. Applications are accepted on a case-by-case basis throughout the year.
Requirements Applicants must be AAJA members with at least three years of professional journalism experience.
Amount $1000 maximum
Contact Albert Lee, Professional Programs Coordinator, (415) 346-2051 ext 107; fax: (415) 346-6343; email: albertl@aaja.org
Internet http://www.aaja.org/programs/professional/fellowships
Sponsor Asian American Journalists Association
1765 Sutter St, Rm 1000
San Francisco, CA 94115

AALAS Foundation Grants **94**

The foundation educational grants have a twofold purpose: to attract talented people to the field of laboratory animal science and to develop new training materials that promote the continuing education of AALAS members. The foundation awards grants for student clerkships to enhance the training of future laboratory animal personnel. The head of the training and/or research program sponsoring the clerkship should submit the application, not the student who will receive the education. Applications are judged on the strength of the training program, not the credentials of the students. Three aspects are considered--clinical experience, teaching experience, and research experience--in evaluating student training programs. The foundation also supports the development of training materials that address the continuing educational needs of AALAS members. After completion, AALAS will have unrestricted use of these materials and will make them available to the members. Interested persons should write for the brochure containing information required to apply for either type of grant.
Requirements Persons currently in the field of laboratory animal science and those persons who are considering the field as a career are eligible. Applications for student clerkship programs must be submitted by the program sponsor.
Amount $5000 maximum
Date(s) Application Is Due Apr 15; Sep 15.
Contact John McCutchen, (901) 754-8620; email: john.mccutchen@aalas.org
Internet http://foundation.aalas.org/index.htm
Sponsor American Association for Laboratory Animal Science
9190 Crestwyn Hills Dr
Memphis, TN 38125

AAMC Award for Distinguished Research **95**

The award honors outstanding biomedical research related to health and disease. The research recognized should have contributed to the substance of medicine. Presentation of the award and a prize will be made at the association's annual meeting. Nomination guidelines are available online.
Requirements Nominations may be made by anyone on the faculty or staff of a medical school or teaching hospital or by a member of an academic society. The nominee must be an individual who serves on the faculty of an AAMC member medical school or teaching hospital.
Amount $5000
Date(s) Application Is Due May 4.
Contact Sandra D. Gordon, (202) 828-0472; fax: (202) 828-1125; email: sgordon@aamc.org
Internet http://www.aamc.org/about/awards/research.htm
Sponsor Association of American Medical Colleges
2450 N Street NW
Washington DC 20037-1127

AANS Research Foundation Young Clinician Investigator Award **96**

This one-year, renewable award is available to North American neurosurgeons who are full-time faculty in teaching institutions and are in the early years of their careers. The purpose of the program is to fund pilot studies that could provide preliminary data to be used for strengthening applications for more permanent funding from other sources.
Restrictions Applicant may not accept another award for the same project during the same time period. No more than one award per year will be awarded to the same institution.
Amount $40,000
Date(s) Application Is Due Oct 31.
Contact Development Coordinator, (847) 378-0500; email: info@aans.org
Internet http://www.aans.org/research/fellowship/nref_y.asp
Sponsor Research Foundation of the American Association of Neurological Surgeons
22 S Washington St
Park Ridge, IL 60068

AAP International Travel Grants **97**

The AAP has set aside twelve (12) five-hundred dollar ($500.00) grants to be awarded to categorical pediatric or combined-training pediatric residents who wish to complete a clinical pediatric elective in the developing world during residency. The selection committee is composed of members from the AAP Section on International Child Health and the Section on Residents. After the selection committee reviews the applications the recipients will be notified mid-January.
Requirements Must be a categorical pediatric or combined-training pediatric resident at a U.S. or Canadian university.
Amount $500
Contact Kimberley VandenBrook, Grants Administrator, (800) 433-9016 ext 7134; email: kvandenbrook@core.com
Internet http://www.aap.org/sections/ypn/r/funding_awards/international_travel.html
Sponsor American Academy of Pediatrics
P.O. Box 927, 141 Northwest Point Blvd.
Elk Grove Village, IL 60007-1098

AAP Nutrition Award **98**

One award is given annually for outstanding achievements in research relating to nutrition of infants and children. The award is made to an individual or for one project. There is no age restriction for the award; however, it is hoped that younger persons will be considered. The award is made possible by a grant from the Infant Formula Council. In addition to the honorarium, the award includes round-trip airfare and two days' lodging for the recipient and a guest to attend the annual meeting and receive the award.
Requirements The competition is open to residents of the United States or Canada whose research has been completed and publicly reported. Separate letters should be written for each individual nominated; a letter should contain a description of the nominee's achievements, stating clearly the basis for the recommendation, including references to the literature that describes her/his work. Nominee's bibliography is to be submitted with the nominating letter together with copies of available reprints. Letters supporting the nomination are to be screened by the nominator and forwarded with the nomination.

Restrictions An individual may not submit more than five letters supporting the nomination. Current members of the AAP Committee on Nutrition are not eligible for this award.
Amount $3000 plus round-trip tourist class airfare and lodging for two days
Date(s) Application Is Due Mar 1.
Contact Debra Burrows, Manager, (847) 434-4000; fax: (847) 434-8000; email: research@aap.org
Internet http://www.aap.org/visit/nutrannouncemts.htm
Sponsor American Academy of Pediatrics
P.O. Box 927, 141 Northwest Point Blvd.
Elk Grove Village, IL 60009-0927

AAP Resident Research Grants **99**
The Program is designed to give pediatric residents with limited research experience an opportunity to initiate and complete research projects related to their professional interests. Projects may be related to the full spectrum of child health research, such as behavioral sciences, biomedical sciences, epidemiology, health services, perinatal/neonatal health, prevention, public health, quality improvement, quality measurement, or basic laboratory-based science. Research projects can be conducted for a maximum of 2 years and should be completed during the residency program.
Requirements Applicants must be legal residents of the United States or Canada. Although awards are primarily intended for support of first- and second-year pediatric residents, individuals who have secured a position for a third or fourth year of residency beginning in July may also apply.
Amount $2000 maximum
Date(s) Application Is Due Feb 28.
Contact Kimberley VandenBrook, Grants Administrator, (800) 433-9016 ext 7134; email: kvandenbrook@core.com
Internet https://www.aap.org/sections/ypn/r/research2007-view.htm
Sponsor American Academy of Pediatrics
P.O. Box 927, 141 Northwest Point Blvd
Elk Grove Village, IL 60007-1098

AAR Classical Society of the American Academy in Rome Summer Scholarships **100**
The Classical Society of the American Academy in Rome offers two scholarships, one to a graduate student and one to a secondary school teacher of classical languages and/or classical civilization. The scholarships are awarded on a competitive basis and are to be used to enable the recipients to attend the summer session of the American Academy in Rome. Contact the director for applications.
Requirements High school teachers and graduate students of Latin, ancient history, and the classics are eligible to apply.
Restrictions High school students and college undergraduates are not eligible.
Date(s) Application Is Due Mar 1.
Contact Myles McDonnell, Director, (212) 751-7200 ext 41; email: catulussr@aol.com
Internet http://www.aarome.org/summer/css
Sponsor American Academy in Rome
7 E 60th St
New York, NY 10022-1001

AAR Postdoctoral Fellowships **101**
The Academy offers 11-month postdoctoral fellowships in the following areas: architecture, design, historic preservation and conservation, landscape architecture, literature, musical composition, visual arts, ancient studies, medieval studies, Renaissance and early modern studies, and modern Italian studies. Applications may be downloaded from the Web site or obtained by contacting the office.
Requirements All applicants for postdoctoral fellowships must have received the PhD at the time of application. US citizens and those foreign nationals who have lived in the US for the three years immediately preceding the application deadline are eligible to apply for the NEH postdoctoral fellowships and are not required to submit the application fee. Applicants for academy postdoctoral awards must be assistant professors, associate professors appointed within the prior two years, or independent scholars who have received the PhD within the prior seven years.
Amount $21,000 maximum
Date(s) Application Is Due Nov 1.
Contact Shawn Miller, Programs Director, (212) 751-7200; fax: (212) 751-7220; email: info@aarome.org
Internet http://www.aarome.org/rome_prize/index.htm
Sponsor American Academy in Rome
7 E 60th St
New York, NY 10022-1001

AAR Predoctoral Fellowships **102**
The academy offers both 11-month and two-year predoctoral fellowships. Eleven-month awards are available in the following fields: architecture, design, historic preservation and conservation, landscape architecture, literature, musical composition, visual arts, ancient studies, medieval studies, Renaissance and early modern studies, and modern Italian studies. Two-year awards are limited to projects in the history of art and architecture of any period and to projects whose disciplinary focus is in ancient studies. Predoctoral fellowships are meant to provide scholars with the necessary time to research and complete their doctoral dissertations.
Requirements Applicants must have fulfilled all predissertation requirements by the application deadline. A nonrefundable fee of $40 must accompany each application. Applicants must include the following materials in support of their applications: six copies of the completed and signed application form; six copies of a current curriculum vitae, which includes languages read or spoken and level of fluency; Six copies of a project proposal (on 8.5 x 11 paper), not to exceed four pages, describing the nature of the work you plan to undertake in Rome and identifying the special resources in Italy that will be important to your work (please include bibliographical notes for any sources cited [not counted towards the four-page proposal statement limit]); and six copies of a supporting paper in the proposed field of study, not to exceed 20 pages, excluding bibliography and footnotes.
Amount $15,750
Date(s) Application Is Due Nov 1.
Contact Programs Department, (212) 751-7200; fax: (212) 751-7220; email: info@aarome.org
Internet http://www.aarome.org/rome_prize/index.htm
Sponsor American Academy in Rome
7 E 60th St
New York, NY 10022-1001

AAR Rome Prize Fellowships **103**
At its principal site in Rome, the academy operates a program of fellowships and residencies that has at its core the development of gifted American artists and scholars. Each year, through a national competition, the academy awards fellowships in the fine arts and pre- and postdoctoral fellowships in the humanities. Rome Prize winners pursue independent projects, which vary in content and scope, for periods ranging from six months to two years at the academy. To complement their work, a series of walks, talks and tours in and around Rome, Italy, and the Mediterranean is offered during the year. The academy's Rome Prize winners are part of a residential community of 65 to 70 people each year. The artists and scholars who make up this multidisciplinary community also have the opportunity to foster their work through exchanges with members of the Italian and newly-united European artistic and scholarly communities.
Requirements Applicants for the Rome Prize fellowships must be US citizens at the time of application, with the exception of those competing for postdoctoral fellowships sponsored by the National Endowment for the Humanities. US citizens and those foreign nationals who have lived in the United States for the three years immediately preceding the application deadline may apply for the NEH postdoctoral fellowships. Graduate students in the humanities may apply only for predoctoral fellowships.
Restrictions Previous winners of the predoctoral Rome Prize are not eligible to apply for the Academy's postdoctoral fellowships. Undergraduate students are not eligible for Rome Prize fellowships. There is an application fee based upon the postmark date and the number of disciplines in which you are applying. Those applicants applying solely for NEH post-doctoral fellowships are not required to submit application fees.
Amount $11,500-$23,000
Date(s) Application Is Due Nov 1.
Contact Programs Department, (212) 751-7200; fax: (212) 751-7220; email: info@aarome.org
Internet http://www.aarome.org/rome_prize/index.htm
Sponsor American Academy in Rome
7 E. 60th St.
New York, NY 10022-1001

AARP Andrus Foundation Grants **104**
The foundation actively seeks new approaches to maximizing the independence of older persons. Grants are awarded under two initiatives: living with chronic health conditions, and aging and living environments. Three types of grants are awarded. Research grants support cutting-edge, applied psychosocial, behavioral, health, and policy research and the dissemination of research findings. Dissemination grants support translating research information into language and materials useful to older adults and the practitioners, service providers, and others who work on their behalf. Grants generally are awarded for projects with the potential for national impact and high visibility, and may include public education programs, major media events, and the production of consumer or practitioner-oriented materials. Funding will also be allocated for the packaging and dissemination of research results and products related to aging and financial security, but not for conferences or the publication of conference proceedings. Education and training grants support graduate students engaged in aging-related research. National programs that provide leadership development, professional development, and research training to students and young professionals receive preference. Grants are awarded only to national organizations, not to individuals or individual educational institutions. Submit a letter of inquiry by the listed deadline dates; full proposals are by invitation.
Requirements Grants are awarded only to colleges, universities, and 501(c)(3) non-profit organizations.
Restrictions Grants do not fund capital campaigns, organizational infrastructure (bricks and mortar), or vehicle purchases; individuals; biomedical or basic (bench) research; programs and services for older adults; education and training programs for professionals; pilot or preliminary research studies; or organizational overhead expenses.
Date(s) Application Is Due Mar 1; Jul 1; Nov 1.

Contact Grants Administrator, (800) 775-6776 or (202) 434-6190; fax: (202) 434-6458; email: andrus@aarp.org
Internet http://www.aarp.org/about_aarp/nrta/nrta_past_present_and_future.html#top
Sponsor American Association of Retired Persons
601 E St NW
Washington, DC 20049

AARP Foundation Gerontology Grad Scholarships and Fellowships **105**
The association awards graduate scholarships and fellowships for research on aging. Gerontology and aging studies faculty are invited to nominate qualified students. This program is funded by the AARP Andrus Foundation. Faculty nomination and student application forms are available online. Annual deadline dates may vary; contact program staff for exact dates.
Requirements Gerontology and aging studies faculty are invited to nominate qualified students for these awards.
Amount $15,000; $7000 graduate scholarships
Contact Derek Stepp, Director, (202) 289-9806 ext 122; fax: (202) 289-9824; email: dstepp@aghe.org
Internet http://www.aghe.org/site/aghewebsite/section.php?id=8183
Sponsor Association for Gerontology in Higher Education
1030 15th St NW, Ste 240
Washington, DC 20005

AAS American Historical Print Collectors Society Fellowship **106**
This fellowship for research on American prints of the 18th and 19th centuries or for projects using prints as primary documentation is funded by the American Historical Print Collectors Society and AAS. Fellows are selected on the basis of the applicant's scholarly qualifications, the scholarly significance or importance of the project, and the appropriateness of the proposed study to the society's collections.
Requirements Doctoral candidates may apply.
Amount $1000 per month
Date(s) Application Is Due Jan 15.
Contact Grants Administrator, (508) 755-5221; fax: (508) 754-9069; email: academicfellowships@mwa.org
Internet http://www.americanantiquarian.org/ahpcs.htm
Sponsor American Antiquarian Society
185 Salisbury St
Worcester, MA 01609-1634

AAS Fellowships for Creative and Performing Artists and Writers **107**
The program supports visiting fellowships for historical research by creative and performing artists, writers, film makers, journalists, and other persons whose goals are to produce imaginative, non-formulaic works dealing with pre-20th-century American history. The fellowships provide the time for uninterrupted research, reading, and collegial discussion at the society, between January 1 and December 31. Fellows receive a stipend plus an allowance for travel expenses.
Requirements Successful applicants are those whose work is for the general public rather than for academic or educational audiences.
Amount $1200 stipend
Date(s) Application Is Due Oct 5.
Contact Fellowships Administrator, (508) 755-5221; fax: (508) 753-3311
Internet http://www.americanantiquarian.org/artistfellowship.htm
Sponsor American Antiquarian Society
185 Salisbury St
Worcester, MA 01609-1634

AAS Historic Research Fellowships **108**
AAS accepts applications for fellowships for historical research by creative and performing artists, writers, filmmakers, and journalists. Fellowships are for individuals whose research objectives are to produce works dealing with pre-20th century American history designed for the public rather than for the academic/educational community. Fellowship projects may include (but are not limited to): historical novels, performance of historical music or drama, poetry, documentary films, television programs, radio broadcasts, plays, libretti, screenplays, magazine or newspaper articles, costume designs, set designs, illustrations and other graphic arts, book designs, sculpture, paintings, other works of fine and applied art, and nonfiction works of history designed for general audiences of adults or children. Fellowships will allow recipients to conduct uninterrupted research, reading, and collegial discussion at AAS.
Amount $1200 per month, plus travel expense allowance
Date(s) Application Is Due Oct 5.
Contact James David Moran, Director of Outreach, (508) 471-2131; email: JMoran@mwa.org
Internet http://www.americanantiquarian.org/artistfellowship.htm
Sponsor American Antiquarian Society
185 Salisbury St
Worcester, MA 01609-1634

AAS/Mellon Post-Dissertation Fellowships **109**
The purpose of the 12-month fellowship is to provide the recipient with time and resources to extend research and/or to revise the dissertation for publication. Any topic relevant to the society's library collections and programmatic scope--American history and culture through 1876--is eligible. Applicants may come from such fields as history, literature, American studies, political science, art history, music history, and others relating to America in the period of the society's coverage. The society welcomes applicants who have already been in contact with potential publishers and will assist the successful candidate in finding a publisher. An application packet, including full details, must be requested before application is made.
Requirements Scholars who are no more than three years beyond receipt of the doctorate are eligible. Graduate students may apply if they expect to have the doctorate in hand by June 15.
Amount $30,000 stipend
Date(s) Application Is Due Oct 15.
Contact Fellowship Administrator, (508) 755-5221; fax: (508) 754-9069; email: academicfellowships@mwa.org
Internet http://www.americanantiquarian.org/mellon.htm
Sponsor American Antiquarian Society
185 Salisbury St
Worcester, MA 01609

AAS/NEH Long-Term/Short-Term Visiting Research Fellowships **110**
The society awards long-term fellowships to qualified scholars, tenable for four to 12 months under a grant from NEH, and also short-term fellowships for one to three months. Fellowships are awarded not only on the basis of the applicant's scholarly qualifications and the general interest of his/her project, but also on the appropriateness of the inquiry to the society's holdings--early US history and culture through 1876. Recipients are expected to be in regular residence at the society's library during the period of the grant. NEH fellows must devote full time to their study and may not accept teaching assignments nor undertake any other major activities during the tenure of the award. Recipients may not hold any other major fellowships, except sabbaticals or other grants from their own institutions.
Requirements Long-term awards are intended for scholars beyond the doctorate; senior and midcareer scholars are particularly encouraged to apply. Short-term fellowships are available for scholars holding the PhD and for doctoral candidates engaged in dissertation research.
Restrictions The NEH fellowships may not be awarded to degree candidates or for study leading to advanced degrees, nor may they be granted to foreign nationals unless they have been residents of the United States for at least three years preceding their award.
Amount $40,000 maximum for long-term fellowships; $1000 per month for short-term fellowships
Date(s) Application Is Due Jan 15.
Contact Caroline Sloat, Director of Scholarly Programs, (508) 755-5221 or (508) 754-9069; fax: (508) 753-3311; email: csloat@mwa.org
Internet http://www.americanantiquarian.org/acafellowship.htm
Sponsor American Antiquarian Society
185 Salisbury St
Worcester, MA 01609-1634

AASA Educational Administration Scholarships **111**
Scholarships are available for outstanding graduate students who intend to pursue the public school superintendency as a career. Applications are available online in the spring or from chairs of educational administration departments at universities that have such a program.
Requirements Only one candidate may be submitted by each university, and they must be recommended by a dean and at least one faculty member, with supporting statements.
Amount $2000
Date(s) Application Is Due Sep 30.
Contact Scholarships Administrator, (703) 875-0729; email: awards@aasa.org
Internet http://www.aasa.org/awards_and_scholarships/scholarships/Graduate_Student.htm
Sponsor American Association of School Administrators
801 N Quincy St, Ste 700
Arlington, VA 22203-1730

AASF Lydia Donaldson Tutt-Jones Memorial Research Grants **112**
The grant supports research that identifies attitudinal and behavioral contributors to African American academic success. The interest is to increase the body of knowledge about African American students who are excelling in school to aid in the replication of that success for others. Focus may be upon student or parental variables, or both. Recipients must prepare a publishable caliber paper upon completion of the project and provide a copy to the foundation. There is no special application form, recommended format, or length of material required. Interested individuals should submit a letter of interest, curriculum vita, a description of the proposed research project (including a timeline, plus a letter of recommendation from their faculty mentor, if students, or from their department chairperson, agency head, or officer of their professional association, if professionals). An original and five copies of the application materials should be submitted, along with a stamped, self-addressed postcard that will be used to acknowledge receipt of the application. Deadlines may vary. See website for more information.

Requirements Graduate students and professionals are eligible. Students must be recommended by a faculty mentor who agrees to oversee the project and the submission of a publishable paper upon its completion.
Amount $2000
Contact Award Administrator, (954) 792-1117; fax: (954) 792-9191; email: info@blacksuccessfoundation.org
Internet http://www.blacksuccessfoundation.org/lcdtj%20research%20grant.htm
Sponsor African American Success Foundation
4330 W Broward Blvd, Ste H
Fort Lauderdale, FL 33317-3753

AASL Collaborative School Library Media Award 113
The award recognizes and encourages collaboration and partnerships between school library media specialists and teachers through joint planning of a program, unit, or event in support of the curriculum and that uses media center resources. The award is given to the recipient's school library media center. The application must address the degree to which the project meets the standards outlined in Information Power: Building Partnerships for Learning. Application forms are available on the Web site. Annual deadline dates may vary; contact program staff for exact dates.
Requirements School library media specialist and teacher(s) who have worked together to execute a project, event, or program to further information literacy, independent learning, and social responsibility using resources of the school library media center may apply.
Amount $2500
Date(s) Application Is Due Feb 1.
Contact AASL Awards Program, (800) 545-2433 ext 4383; fax: (312) 664-7459; email: aasl@ala.org or kchaney@ala.org
Internet http://www.ala.org/ala/aasl/aaslawards/collaborativeslm/aaslcollaborative.htm
Sponsor American Association of School Librarians
50 E Huron St
Chicago, IL 60611-2795

AASL Distinguished School Administrator Award 114
This award, donated by Social Issues Resources Series Inc, is given annually to an administrator of a school or group of schools for developing an exemplary school library media program and for having made an outstanding and sustained contribution toward expanding the role of the school library media center as an agency for the improvement of education. Nomination forms are available on the Web site. Annual deadline dates may vary; contact program staff for exact dates.
Requirements State, county, or district school superintendents and building principals, currently in administrative office and directly responsible for a school or group of schools at any level, are eligible for nomination. District administrators responsible for broad instructional leadership, such as assistant superintendents, directors of curriculum and instruction, and directors of elementary and/or secondary education, are also eligible.
Amount $2000
Date(s) Application Is Due Feb 1.
Contact AASL Awards Program, (800) 545-2433; fax: (312) 664-7459; email: aasl@ala.org
Internet http://www.ala.org/ala/aasl/aaslawards/distinguishedsch/aasldistinguished.htm
Sponsor American Association of School Librarians
50 E Huron St
Chicago, IL 60611-2795

AASL/Highsmith Research Grant 115
Cosponsored by the AASL and the Highsmith Co Inc, this annual grant is presented to one or more AASL members who are school library media specialists, library educators, or library information science/education professors to conduct innovative research aimed at measuring and evaluating the impact of school library media programs on learning and education. Application forms are available on the Web site. Annual deadline dates may vary; contact program staff for exact dates.
Restrictions Applicants must be AASL personal members.
Amount $5000 maximum
Date(s) Application Is Due Feb 1.
Contact AASL Awards Program, (800) 545-2433; fax: (312) 664-7459; email: aasl@ala.org
Internet http://www.ala.org/ala/aasl/aaslawards/highsmithgrant/aaslhighsmith.htm
Sponsor American Association of School Librarians
50 E Huron St
Chicago, IL 60611-2795

AAUW American Fellowships 116
Fellowships support women doctoral candidates writing their dissertations and scholars seeking postdoctoral/research leave funds. Short-term publication grants also are available. One-year postdoctoral/research leave fellowships are for women who will have earned a doctorate by November 15. Fellowships are available in the arts and humanities, social sciences, and natural sciences, and one designated specifically for a woman of color. Dissertation fellowships are for women who will complete the writing of their dissertations between July 1 of the upcoming year and June 30 of the following year. Applicants are expected to receive a doctoral degree by the end of the fellowship year. Summer fellowships for postdoctoral/research leave are for women faculty at colleges and universities who are excellent teachers and whose teaching loads limit active research. Time must be available for eight weeks of summer research. Six summer fellowships are available. Short-term publication grants are available to college/university faculty or independent researchers to prepare completed research for publication.
Requirements Applicants must be US citizens or permanent residents by the application postmark deadline. When comparing proposals of equal merit, special consideration will be given to women holding junior academic appointments who are seeking research leave, women who have held the doctorate for at least three years, and women whose educational careers have been interrupted.
Amount $20,000 dissertation fellowships; $30,000 postdoctoral research fellowships, plus $5000 maximum matching funds; $6000 short-term publication grants
Date(s) Application Is Due Nov 15.
Contact Fellowships Officer, (800) 326-2289; fax: (202) 872-1425; email: info@aauw.org
Internet http://www.aauw.org/fga/fellowships_grants/american.cfm
Sponsor American Association of University Women Educational Foundation
1111 16th St NW
Washington DC 20036

AAUW Career Development Grants 117
Grants support women currently holding a bachelor's degree who are preparing to advance their careers, change careers, or re-enter the work force. Special consideration is given to AAUW members, women of color, and women pursuing their first advanced degree or credentials in nontraditional fields. Funds are available for tuition, fees, books, supplies, local transportation, and dependent care. Grants are awarded in two categories. Academic grants provide support for coursework toward a master's degree or specialized training in technical or professional fields. Coursework must be undertaken at a fully accredited two- or four-year college, university, or technical school. Professional development institute grants support women's participation in professional institutes that are academically based and have a focused and specific program of study with identified faculty; fixed schedules and short-term duration; and selection/enrollment processes with baseline eligibility criteria. Applicants for institute grants must also apply directly to the institute. Applications are available between August 1 and December 15 on the Web site and from the customer service center at AAUW Educational Foundation, Department 60, 2201 North Dodge Street, Iowa City, IA 52243-4030.
Requirements Applicants must be women who are US citizens or permanent residents of the United States who hold at least a baccalaureate degree and who have completed their most recent degree at least five years before the July 1 effective date of the award. Preference is given to AAUW members. Applicants must have applied or been accepted at a two- or four-year accredited college or university; technical schools must be licensed or accredited by an agency recognized by the US Department of Education. Coursework must be a prerequisite for a professional employment plan.
Restrictions Academic grants are not available for doctoral level work. Institute grants may not be used for internships, research, or independent study.
Amount $2000-$8000
Date(s) Application Is Due Dec 15.
Contact Educational Foundation, (319) 377-1716 ext 60; email: aauw@act.org
Internet http://www.aauw.org/3000/fdnfelgra/career.html
Sponsor American Association of University Women Educational Foundation
1111 16th St NW
Washington, DC 20036

AAUW Community Action Grants 118
One-year grants provide seed money for new projects. Topic areas are unrestricted, but should include a clearly defined activity that promotes education and equity for women and girls. Two-year Community Action Grants provide seed money to individual women, AAUW branches, AAUW state organizations, and community-based nonprofit organizations. These grants provide start-up funds for longer-term programs that address the particular needs of the community and develop girls sense of efficacy through leadership or advocacy opportunities. Topic areas are unrestricted, but should include a clearly defined activity that promotes education and equity for women and girls. Funds support planning activities, coalition building, program implementation, and evaluation. Guidelines are available online.
Requirements Applicants must be women who are US citizens or permanent residents. Grant projects must have direct public impact, be nonpartisan, and take place within the US or its territories.
Amount $2000-$7000 one-year grants; $5000-$10,000 two-year projects
Date(s) Application Is Due Jan 15.
Contact Fellowships Officer, (800) 326-2289; or (319) 337-1716 ext 60; fax: (202) 872-1425; email: foundation@aauw.org
Internet http://www.aauw.org/fga/fellowships_grants/community_action.cfm
Sponsor American Association of University Women Educational Foundation
301 ACT Dr
Iowa City, IA 52243-4030

AAUW International Fellowships 119
Funds are for one year of graduate and postgraduate study or research at an approved institution in the United States and are given to women of outstanding ability who are citizens of countries other than the United States. Strong preference will be given

to women whose credentials prove prior commitment to the amelioration of the lives of other women and girls through civic, community, or professional work and whose research proposals show a continued interest in the advancement of women. Applicants are judged on their professional potential and on the importance of their projects to their country of origin. The Foundation also awards several annual Home Country Project grants to support community-based projects designed to improve the lives of women and girls in the fellows' home country. Applications are available from August 1 to December 1.
Requirements Candidates must have an academic degree equivalent to the US bachelor's degree; must have a specific plan of study or research that will advance the applicant's professional competence; must intend to return home to pursue a professional career; must devote full time to graduate work; and must have satisfactory English proficiency. Applicants whose native language is not English must submit up-to-date scores on one of four language proficiency examinations. Preference will be given to applicants who have specific positions to return to in their own countries.
Restrictions Previous and current recipients of AAUW fellowships cannot apply.
Amount $18,000 master's, $20,000 doctoral, $30,000 postdoctoral; $5000-$7000 home country grants
Date(s) Application Is Due Dec 1.
Contact Fellowships Officer, (319) 337-1716 ext 60; email: aauw@act.org
Internet http://www.aauw.org/fga/fellowships_grants/international.cfm
Sponsor American Association of University Women Foundation
1111 16th St NW
Washington, DC 20036

AAUW Scholar in Residence Grants **120**
Colleges and universities in the United States may apply for funding for the University Scholar-in-Residence award to support a woman scholar to undertake and disseminate research on gender and equity for women and girls. Institutions may use the funds to bring a qualified scholar to the institution for a fixed period or to designate a scholar currently at the institution to undertake research activities that would not occur without such support. Preference will be given to proposals from institutions that demonstrate significant matching funds by all institutions involved. Preference also will be given to proposals for research and activities likely to continue after the funding period, as opposed to single events or one-time initiatives. Letters of intent are due by the December deadline; full proposals are due by the February deadline.
Amount $100,000 maximum for a two-year project
Date(s) Application Is Due Feb 1; Dec 1.
Contact Fellowships Officer, (202) 728-7602; email: foundation@aauw.org
Internet http://www.aauw.org/fga/fellowships_grants/university_scholar.cfm
Sponsor American Association of University Women Educational Foundation
1111 16th St NW
Washington, DC 20036

AAUW Selected Professions Fellowships **121**
Fellowships are awarded in designated fields where female participation has been low. Women in engineering master's programs are eligible to apply for either the first or final year of study. All women are eligible to apply for fellowships in the following degree programs: architecture (M.Arch), computer/information sciences (MS), engineering (ME, MS, PhD), and mathematics/statistics (MS). Fellowships in the following degree programs are restricted to women of color to increase their participation and access in these historically underrepresented fields: business administration (MBA, EMBA), law (JD), and medicine (MD, DO). Deadlines are January 10 for master's and first professional awards, and December 15 for engineering.
Requirements Applicants must be US citizens or permanent residents of the United States. Special consideration is given to applicants who show professional promise in innovative or neglected areas of research and/or practice in public interest concerns.
Amount $5000-$12,000
Date(s) Application Is Due Jan 10; Dec 15.
Contact Fellowships Officer, (319) 337-1716 ext 60; email: aauw@act.org
Internet http://www.aauw.org/3000/fdnfelgra/selectprof.html
Sponsor American Association of University Women Educational Foundation
1111 16th St NW
Washington, DC 20036

AAUW Selected Professions--Dissertation Fellowships in Engineering **122**
Fellowships program offers dissertation fellowships for doctoral candidates in engineering who will complete all required coursework and will have passed all preliminary exams by the deadline date. It is expected that the degree will be received at the end of the fellowship year. There are no restrictions as to place of study. Applications are available from August 1 through December 15 on the Web site and from the customer service center at AAUW Educational Foundation, Department 60, 2201 North Dodge Street, Iowa City, IA 52243-4030.
Requirements Applicants must be women who are citizens or permanent residents of the United States and who expect to receive their doctoral degree in engineering at the end of the fellowship year.
Restrictions Students holding any fellowship for the purpose of writing the dissertation in the year prior to the AAUW fellowship year are not eligible to apply.
Amount $20,000
Date(s) Application Is Due Dec 15.
Contact Fellowships Officer, (319) 337-1716 ext 60; email: foundation@aauw.org
Internet http://www.aauw.org/3000/fdnfelgra/selectprof.html
Sponsor American Association of University Women Educational Foundation
1111 16th St NW
Washington, DC 20036

AAUW University Scholar in Residence Grants **123**
Colleges and universities may apply for support for a woman scholar to undertake and disseminate research on gender and equity for women and girls. Institutions may use the funds either to bring a qualified scholar to the institution for a fixed period or to designate a scholar currently at the institution to undertake research activities that would not occur without such support. Proposals should strive to achieve impact nationally. Priority will be given to proposals that provide matching funds. Proposals for two-year projects will be considered depending on the nature of the project and cost sharing provided by the institution. Institutions must submit a three- to five-page letter of intent describing the research project and its intended outcomes. Letters of intent must be received by December 1; full proposals are due February 1.
Amount $100,000 maximum for a two-year project
Date(s) Application Is Due Feb 1; Dec 1.
Contact Fellowships Officer, (202) 728-7647; email: foundation@aauw.org
Internet http://www.aauw.org/3000/fdnfelgra/univsir.html
Sponsor American Association of University Women Educational Foundation
1111 16th St NW
Washington, DC 20036

ABA Minority Legal Opportunity Scholarships **124**
Each year, the program awards scholarships, which are renewable for two additional years, to minority first-year law students attending an ABA-accredited law school. Selected applicants are required to demonstrate admission to and plans to enroll at an ABA-accredited law school before receiving scholarship funds.
Requirements US students who are members of racial/ethnic minorities that have been underrepresented in the legal profession, who have achieved a minimum cumulative 2.5 grade-point average, are eligible.
Restrictions Law students who have completed one or more semesters or years of law school are not eligible.
Amount $5000 annually; $15,000 total
Date(s) Application Is Due Mar 1.
Contact Scholarship Administrator, (312) 988-5415; email: mastronardi@staff.abanet.org
Internet http://www.abanet.org/fje/losfpage.html
Sponsor American Bar Association
750 N Lake Shore Dr
Chicago, IL 60611

Abbott Laboratories Fund Grants **125**
The fund awards grants in its areas of interest, including human health and welfare, education, civic and culture, and employee-matching gifts. In the area of human health and welfare, the fund supports federated or community drives in Abbott communities. Selective support may be given to national agencies for specific and well-defined programs. Support of individual hospitals and other health care institutions is primarily to improve the services and facilities of those used most frequently by Abbott employees and their families. Educational support focuses on institutions whose programs and services have the potential to provide short- to long-term benefits to the health care industry and its employees. Priority is given to programs related to science and innovation. The fund also makes contributions to institutions of higher learning that are potential sources of professional, managerial, and technical personnel for the health care industry. In the areas of culture, art, and civic activities, the fund considers support for specific projects that are related to Abbott's overall interests and activities, including community improvement projects and organizations providing cultural enrichment in Abbott communities. Support is also considered for agencies involved in social policy and the environment. Applications are accepted throughout the year.
Requirements Grants are made to tax-exempt organizations in company operating areas in Arizona, California, Illinois, Kansas, Massachusetts, Michigan, New Jersey, New York, North Carolina, Ohio, Puerto Rico, Texas, and Virginia, and Utah.
Restrictions Contributions will not be made to individuals; for-profit entities; purely social organizations; political parties or candidates; sectarian religious organizations; advertising; symposia, conferences, and meetings; ticket purchases; memberships; business-related purposes; volunteer efforts of non-Abbott employees; or marketing sponsorships.
Amount $1000-$50,000 average
Contact Cindy Schwab, Vice President, (847) 937-7075; fax: (847) 935-5051
Internet http://www.abbottfund.org/default-2.html
Sponsor Abbott Laboratories Fund
100 Abbott Park Rd
Abbott Park, IL 60064-3500

Abbott Payson Usher Prize **126**
This prize was established to encourage the publication of original research of the highest standard. It is awarded annually to the author of the best scholarly work published during

the preceding three years under the auspices of the Society for the History of Technology. A certificate is included with the prize.
Amount $400
Contact Program Contact, (410) 516-8349; fax: (410) 516-7502
Internet http://shot.jhu.edu/Awards/usher.htm
Sponsor Society for the History of Technology
216B Ames Hall, Dept of the History of Science
Johns Hopkins University, MD 21218

Abbott-ASM Lifetime Achievement Award **127**
The award, sponsored by Abbott Laboratories, is given to honor a distinguished scientist for a lifetime of outstanding contributions in fundamental biomedical research in any of the microbiological sciences. The award consists of a cash prize, framed certificate, medallion, and national or international travel expenses incidental to receiving the award at the ASM general meeting. Guidelines and nomination form are available online.
Requirements Mature scientists, both active and retired, from all areas of microbiology are eligible.
Restrictions Self-nominations are not be accepted.
Amount $20,000 maximum
Date(s) Application Is Due Oct 1.
Contact Awards Committee, (202) 942-9226; fax: (202) 942-9380; email: awards@asmusa.org
Internet http://www.asm.org/Academy/index.asp?bid=2587
Sponsor American Society for Microbiology
1752 N St NW
Washington, DC 20036-2804

Abe Schecter Graduate Scholarship in Electronic News **128**
Any continuing or incoming graduate student whose career objective is electronic news or electronic news teaching or research may apply for this scholarship. The winner also receives an expense-paid trip to the RTNDF annual conference. Scholarships will be awarded on an international basis. Applications are available on the Web site.
Requirements Applicants must be currently enrolled in school, be in good standing, and have at least one full year of school remaining.
Restrictions Applicants may apply in more than one category but are restricted to one award. Previous winners are not eligible.
Amount $2000
Date(s) Application Is Due May 9.
Contact Irving Washington, (202) 467-5218; fax: (202) 223-4007; email: irvingw@rtndf.org
Internet http://www.rtnda.org/asfi/scholarships/graduate.shtml
Sponsor Radio and Television News Directors Foundation
1000 Connecticut Ave NW, Ste 615
Washington, DC 20036

Abraham Lincoln Fellowships in Constitutional Government **129**
The fellowship is awarded to bright, ambitious Americans who want to reclaim limited constitutional government. Each fellow will attend a one-week seminar in constitutional theory and practice led by eminent scholars. Fellows also will be invited to attend occasional weekend seminars in and around the nation's capital and will be honored at the institute's annual Lincoln Day Colloquium and Dinner. Fellowships include a stipend, all travel and lodging expenses, and most meals. Up to 10 fellowships will be awarded this year. Guidelines and application are available online.
Requirements Participation is open to young patriots working on matters of national public policy and politics. This includes, but is not limited to, US government employees, public policy research institutions, and print and broadcast media.
Amount $1500 stipend
Date(s) Application Is Due May 6.
Contact Thomas Krannawitter, Vice President, (909) 621-6825; fax: (909) 626-8724; email: tkrannawitter@claremont.org
Internet http://www.claremont.org/projects/lincoln/index.html
Sponsor Claremont Institute for the Study of Statesmanship and Political Philosophy
937 W Foothill Blvd, Ste E
Claremont, CA 91711

ACAAI Foundation Research Grants **130**
The Foundation develops, promotes and funds clinical research and educational programs related to allergy, asthma & immunology. It is dedicated to: strengthening, supporting and funding allergy/immunology training programs; heightening awareness of the critical role of the allergist in cost-effective treatment of asthma and other allergic and immunologic diseases; and supporting asthma camp programs. Programs include clinical fellowship stipends, fellow-in-training research grants, young faculty support awards, scholar's return awards, and support for asthma camps.
Amount $250,000 maximum
Contact Program Administrator, (847) 427-1200; fax: (847) 427-1294; email: mail@acaai.org
Internet http://www.acaai.org/Member/ACAAI_Foundation/ACAAI_Foundation.htm
Sponsor American College of Allergy, Asthma & Immunology Foundation
85 West Algonquin Road, Suite 550
Arlington Heights, IL 60005

Academic and Research Librarian of the Year Award **131**
This award is presented by the Association of College and Research Libraries and funded by the Baker & Taylor Company to recognize an individual member of the library profession who is making an outstanding national or international contribution to academic or research librarianship and library development. Individuals nominated should have demonstrated achievements in such areas as service to the organized profession through ACRL and related organizations, significant and influential research on academic or research library service, publication of a body of scholarly and/or theoretical writing contributing to academic or research library development, or planning and implementing a library program of such exemplary quality that it has served as a model for others.
Requirements Individuals may nominate themselves or others.
Amount $3000
Date(s) Application Is Due Dec 1.
Contact Megan Bielefeld, ACRL Program Coordinator, (800) 545-2433 ext 2514 or (312) 280-2514; email: mbielefeld@ala.org
Internet http://www.ala.org/Template.cfm?Section=Awards17&template=/ContentManagement/ContentDisplay.cfm&ContentID=93938
Sponsor Association of College and Research Libraries
50 E Huron St
Chicago, IL 60611-2795

Academy for International and Area Studies Fellowships Program **132**
The Academy Scholars Program has been established by the Harvard Academy for International and Area Studies to assist young scholars who are preparing for an academic career involving both a social science discipline and a particular area of the world. Those selected as academy scholars are given time, guidance, access to Harvard facilities, health insurance, and substantial financial assistance as they work for two years conducting either dissertation or postdoctoral research in their chosen fields and areas. The senior scholars, a distinguished group of senior Harvard faculty members, act as mentors to the academy scholars to help them achieve their intellectual potential. The fellowships are offered for research conducted while in residence at the Center for International Affairs, although travel for research is allowed.
Requirements Predoctoral applicants must have completed all coursework and general examinations by the beginning of the first year for which they seek support. Competitive candidates must have already made some significant progress on their dissertations.
Amount $25,000 for predoctoral students; $40,000 for postdoctoral scholars
Contact Beth Baiter, Fellowship Coordinator, (617) 495-4432; fax: (617) 384-9259; email: bbaiter@wcfia.harvard.edu
Internet http://www.wcfia.harvard.edu/progdetail.asp?ID=18
Sponsor Harvard University Weatherhead Center for International Affairs
1737 Cambridge St, Coolidge Hall
Cambridge, MA 02138

ACC Asian Art and Religion Fellowships **133**
Asian individuals in the visual and performing arts seeking grant assistance to conduct research, study, receive specialized training, undertake observation tours, or pursue creative activity in the United States are eligible to apply for fellowship support from the Council. Americans seeking aid to undertake activities in Asia are also eligible to apply. This Fellowship program focusing on the relationship between the artistic and religious traditions of Asia enables American scholars, specialists, and artists to conduct research and undertake projects in Asia involving the interdisciplinary analysis of religion and the arts. The Council awards up to five research fellowships or travel grants each year through this program. Asian Art and Religion Fellowships have supported research in India on the iconography of Hindu deities, in Indonesia on the relationship between tantric religious thought and masked performance, and in Thailand on Buddhist architecture of northern Thailand.
Requirements Completed applications must be submitted at least six months prior to the planned date of project implementation. There are two deadline dates for this award. Applicants should send a brief description of the activity for which assistance is sought. If the proposed activity falls within the council's guidelines, additional application materials will be provided.
Restrictions The Council is unable to consider proposals for the following: personal exhibitions; individual performance tours; undergraduate study; or activities conducted by individuals in their home countries.
Date(s) Application Is Due Jan 15; Aug 1.
Contact Program Director, (212) 812-4300; fax: (212) 812-4299; email: acc@accny.org
Internet http://www.asianculturalcouncil.org/programs.html
Sponsor Asian Cultural Council
437 Madison Avenue, 37th Floor
New York, NY 10022

ACC China Onsite Seminar Program in Art History **134**
The program awards one grant each year to an American university to provide special opportunities for American graduate students of Chinese art history to enlarge their understanding of Chinese art in its cultural context. At the same time, the program introduces art history students in China to American theoretical approaches to studies in this field. There are two deadline dates for this award.
Requirements Arts organizations and educational and cultural institutions are eligible to apply.

Date(s) Application Is Due Feb 1; Aug 1.
Contact Director, (212) 812-4300; fax: (212) 812-4299; email: acc@accny.org
Internet http://www.asianculturalcouncil.org/programs.html
Sponsor Asian Cultural Council
437 Madison Ave, 37th Fl
New York, NY 10022

ACC Ford Foundation Fellowships **135**
This fellowship program provides support for training, travel, and research in the United States by individuals from Asia engaged in the study, documentation, and preservation of Asian traditional arts. Funded by an endowment grant from the Ford Foundation, this program offers awards in archaeology, art history, conservation, dance ethnology, ethnomusicology, museology, and other disciplines involving traditional Asian culture. Fellowships are generally awarded for periods ranging from three to 12 months. Completed applications must be submitted at least six months prior to the planned date of project implementation.
Requirements Applicants should send a short description of the activity for which assistance is being requested. If the proposed activity falls within the council's guidelines, application materials will be provided by ACC.
Restrictions The Council is unable to consider proposals for the following: personal exhibitions; individual performance tours; undergraduate study; or activities conducted by individuals in their home countries.
Date(s) Application Is Due Jan 15; Aug 1.
Contact Program Director, (212) 812-4300; fax: (212) 812-4299; email: acc@accny.org
Internet http://www.asianculturalcouncil.org/programs.html#4
Sponsor Asian Cultural Council
437 Madison Avenue, 37th Floor
New York, NY 10022

ACC Hong Kong Arts Program Fellowships **136**
The Program, made possible by donations from a broad group of donors in Hong Kong, provides fellowships to especially promising artists, students, and scholars from Hong Kong and other parts of China for research, study, and creative work in the United States. Limited support is also available for projects sponsored by Hong Kong institutions that involve Hong Kong-United States or Hong Kong-Asia cultural exchange. The ACC is able to award grant support to approximately ten individual and institutional applicants each year.
Requirements Applicants should send a short description of the activity for which assistance is being requested. If the proposed activity falls within the council's guidelines, further application materials will be provided.
Restrictions The Council is unable to consider proposals for the following: personal exhibitions; individual performance tours; undergraduate study; or activities conducted by individuals in their home countries.
Date(s) Application Is Due Jan 15; Aug 1.
Contact Program Director, (212) 812-4300; fax: (212) 812-4299; email: acc@accny.org
Internet http://www.asianculturalcouncil.org/programs.html#5
Sponsor Asian Cultural Council
437 Madison Avenue, 37th Floor
New York, NY 10022

ACC Humanities Fellowship Program **137**
The program assists American scholars, doctoral students, and specialists in the humanities to undertake research, training, and study in Asia in the following fields: archaeology; conservation; museology; and the theory, history, and criticism of architecture, art, dance, film, music, photography, and theater. Fellowship grants range in duration from one to nine months. The program also supports American and Asian scholars participating in international conferences, exhibitions, visiting professorships, and similar projects. Funding includes international travel, maintenance, per diem, and related research expenses. Completed applications must be submitted at least six months prior to the planned date of implementation.
Requirements American scholars, doctoral students, and specialists in the humanities are eligible to apply. Applicants should send a short description of the activity for which assistance is being sought. If the proposed activity falls within the council's guidelines, application materials will be provided.
Restrictions The Council is unable to consider proposals for the following: personal exhibitions; individual performance tours; undergraduate study; or activities conducted by individuals in their home countries.
Date(s) Application Is Due Jan 15; Aug 1.
Contact Program Director, (212) 812-4300; fax: (212) 812-4299; email: acc@accny.org
Internet http://www.asianculturalcouncil.org/programs.html#6
Sponsor Asian Cultural Council
437 Madison Avenue, 37th Floor
New York, NY 10022

ACC Japan-US Arts Program Fellowships **138**
The Program provides grant fellowships to individuals and institutions in Japan and the United States for exchange activities that encourage the study and understanding of Japanese art and culture. The individual fellowships enable Japanese artists, scholars, and specialists to visit the United States for research, observation, and creative work and allow their American counterparts to visit Japan for similar purposes. The council also provides assistance for performances, exhibitions, and other projects of unusual importance for the development of Japanese-American cultural exchange. The program is administered with the assistance of the ACC's office in Tokyo. Annually, the program supports approximately thirteen individuals and seven institutional projects.
Requirements Applicants should send a short description of the activity for which assistance is being requested. If the proposed activity falls within the council's guidelines, application materials will be provided by the ACC.
Restrictions The Council is unable to consider proposals for the following: personal exhibitions; individual performance tours; undergraduate study; or activities conducted by individuals in their home countries.
Date(s) Application Is Due Jan 15; Aug 1.
Contact Program Director, (212) 812-4300; fax: (212) 812-4299; email: acc@accny.org
Internet http://www.asianculturalcouncil.org/programs.html#7
Sponsor Asian Cultural Council
437 Madison Avenue, 37th Floor
New York, NY 10022

ACC John D. Rockefeller III Award **139**
This annual award is presented to an individual from Asia or the United States who has made an especially significant contribution to the understanding, practice, or study of the visual or performing arts of Asia. The award will enable recipients to pursue work in some aspect of the arts of Asia through international travel and research. Applications are accepted anytime.
Requirements Individuals from Asia and the United States who are active in any field of the visual or performing arts of Asia, whether affiliated with an institution or working independently, are eligible for award consideration. Candidates are nominated by artists, scholars, and others professionally involved in Asian art and culture.
Amount $30,000
Contact Program Director, (212) 812-4300; fax: (212) 812-4299; email: acc@accny.org
Internet http://www.asianculturalcouncil.org/programs.html#12
Sponsor Asian Cultural Council
437 Madison Avenue, 37th Floor
New York, NY 10022

ACC Ock Rang Cultural Foundation Fellowship Program **140**
The Ock Rang Cultural Foundation in Seoul, Korea, which operates the Dongsung Art Center, provides funding to the ACC that supports one to four fellowships each year. The program funds artists and specialists from Korea pursuing research, study, and creative work in the United States, primarily in the technical theater arts. The program also funds American specialists traveling to Korea and Asian artists presenting workshops and surveying arts activities in Korea. There are two deadline dates for this award.
Date(s) Application Is Due Feb 1; Aug 1.
Contact Director, (212) 812-4300; fax: (212) 812-4299; email: acc@accny.org
Internet http://www.asianculturalcouncil.org/programs.html#1
Sponsor Asian Cultural Council
437 Madison Ave, 37th Fl
New York, NY 10022

ACC Philippines Fellowship Program **141**
The Program was formally inaugurated in 2000 in association with the ACC Philippines Foundation, a foundation established in Manila to collaborate with the ACC in raising funds and making grants for Philippines-U.S. cultural exchange. Through the ACC Philippines Foundation a range of donors in both countries are contributing to the Program, which emphasizes support for artists, scholars, and specialists from the Philippines undertaking research, study, and creative work in the United States. Some grants are also made to Americans pursuing similar activities in the Philippines and to institutions engaged in Philippines-U.S. or Philippines-Asia exchange projects.
Requirements Applicants should send a short description of the activity for which assistance is being requested. If the proposed activity falls within the council's guidelines, application materials will be provided by the ACC.
Restrictions The Council is unable to consider proposals for the following: personal exhibitions; individual performance tours; undergraduate study; or activities conducted by individuals in their home countries.
Date(s) Application Is Due Jan 15; Aug 1.
Contact Program Director, (212) 812-4300; fax: (212) 812-4299; email: acc@accny.org
Internet http://www.asianculturalcouncil.org/programs.html#8
Sponsor Asian Cultural Council
437 Madison Avenue, 37th Floor
New York, NY 10022

ACC Residency Program in Asia **142**
The program in Asia assists individual American artists, scholars, and professionals undertaking research, teaching, and creative residencies at cultural and educational institutions in East and Southeast Asia. Projects supported in the Program demonstrate close collaboration in design and execution between the visiting American specialist and the host organization and produce tangible results such as publication, course development, or the creation of new artistic work. The program helps to foster the growth of Asian cultural studies in the U.S. and of American cultural studies in Asia, as well as to stimulate long-term relationships in the arts and humanities between American individuals and institutions and their colleagues in Asia. Eligible fields for consideration

include archaeology, architecture (design, history, and theory), art history, conservation, crafts, dance, film, museology, music, painting, photography, printmaking, sculpture, theater, and video.
Requirements Applications may be submitted by the participating American specialist or by the host institution in Asia.
Restrictions The Council is unable to consider proposals for the following: personal exhibitions; individual performance tours; undergraduate study; or activities conducted by individuals in their home countries.
Date(s) Application Is Due Jan 15; Aug 1.
Contact Program Director, (212) 812-4300; fax: (212) 812-4299; email: acc@accny.org
Internet http://www.asianculturalcouncil.org/programs.html#1
Sponsor Asian Cultural Council
437 Madison Avenue, 37th Floor
New York, NY 10022

ACC Starr Foundation Fellowship Program 143
The contemporary visual arts of Asia are the focus of this fellowship program, established with an endowment grant from the Starr Foundation. Assistance is provided to artists and arts specialists from Asia for creative activity, research, training, and observation in the United States in the fields of art criticism, crafts, design, film, museology, painting, photography, printmaking, and sculpture. Assistance is provided for periods ranging from one month to one year. Approximately seventeen Fellowship grants are given annually supporting artists, curators, and critics from Asia traveling to the United States.
Requirements Asian artists and arts specialists are eligible to apply. Completed applications must be submitted at least six months prior to the planned date of project implementation.
Restrictions The Council is unable to consider proposals for the following: personal exhibitions; individual performance tours; undergraduate study; or activities conducted by individuals in their home countries.
Date(s) Application Is Due Jan 15; Aug 1.
Contact Program Director, (212) 812-4300; fax: (212) 812-4299; email: acc@accny.org
Internet http://www.asianculturalcouncil.org/programs.html#10
Sponsor Asian Cultural Council
437 Madison Avenue, 37th Floor
New York, NY 10022

ACC Taiwan Fellowship Program 144
The program makes grants to artists, scholars, and specialists from Taiwan for research, study, and creative work in the United States. The program also supports American and Asian arts specialists visiting Taiwan to participate in cultural exchange projects organized by local arts institutions. Application procedures and grantee programming are administered with the assistance of the ACC-SAACF office in Taipei. The program supports up to eight grant recipients each year.
Requirements Applicants should send a short description of the activity for which assistance is being sought. If the proposed activity falls within the council's guidelines, application materials will be provided.
Restrictions The Council is unable to consider proposals for the following: personal exhibitions; individual performance tours; undergraduate study; or activities conducted by individuals in their home countries.
Date(s) Application Is Due Jan 15; Aug 1.
Contact Program Director, (212) 812-4300; fax: (212) 812-4299; email: acc@accny.org
Internet http://www.asianculturalcouncil.org/programs.html#11
Sponsor Asian Cultural Council
437 Madison Avenue, 37th Floor
New York, NY 10022

Access Fund Climbing Preservation Grants 145
The program awards grants to projects that preserve and enhance climbing opportunities and conserve the climbing environment throughout the United States. Grants support projects that encourage access to or enhance opportunities for climbing; be supported by the climbing community; raise awareness about climber responsibilities through stewardship projects; develop or support partnerships with resource management agencies, conservation organizations, land trusts, and local climbing groups; reduce climber impacts on natural and cultural resources; develop knowledge about natural and cultural resource values where the information is used to open climbing areas or mitigate climbing impacts; include volunteer labor and/or pro bono services; use some matching funds; and be located within the United States. Requests over $10,000 are considered if the project has national significance and offers a high percentage of matching funds. Contact the office before submitting an application for a large grant.
Requirements Applications may be submitted by local climbing groups or organizations; governmental agencies that wish to sponsor or organize a local project; and research groups, conservation organizations, and land trusts. 501(c)3 status is not necessary.
Amount $500-$10,000
Date(s) Application Is Due Feb 15; Jun 15; Sep 15.
Contact Shawn Tierney, (303) 545-6772 ext 105; email: shawn@accessfund.org
Internet http://www.accessfund.org/programs/programs_prog.html
Sponsor Access Fund
207 Canyon, Ste 201
South Boulder, CO 80302

ACCP Frontiers Career Development Research Awards 146
Support previously unmet or under served areas of Pharmacy-Based Health Services Research, Clinical Research, or Translational Research. Through its awards, the Institute is especially interested in supporting: research that helps to pursue one or more of the priority areas outlined in the Research Agenda of the American College of Clinical Pharmacy (see below); the career development of clinical pharmacy investigators; health services research that assesses the impact of clinical pharmacy services on the use, costs, quality, accessibility, delivery, organization, financing, and outcomes of health care, including the development of payment models for clinical pharmacists' services; and clinical and translational research, including areas that extend beyond those funded by other ACCP awards and grants.
Requirements Any ACCP Full Member, Associate Member, or Affiliate Member is eligible to apply.
Restrictions Proposals submitted concurrently with an application for membership will not be considered.
Amount $10,000-$30,000
Date(s) Application Is Due Jun 1.
Contact Cathy Englund, Executive Secretary; (913) 492-3311; fax: (913) 492-0088; email: cenglund@accp.com
Internet http://www.accp.com/frontiers/research.php#resfel
Sponsor American College of Clinical Pharmacy
13000 W. 87th Street Parkway
Lenexa, KS 66215-4530

ACCP Hematology/Oncology PRN Minisabbatical Program 147
The Minisabbatical Program is an opportunity for members of the Hematology/Oncology PRN exclusively to gain or expand their skills in practice or research under the guidance of experts in oncology pharmacotherapy. The major purposes are: to learn new clinical skills or approaches to patient care that will enhance the applicant's practice in oncology pharmacotherapy (e.g., patient management, clinic development, payment for services); and to learn new research skills that will enhance or expand the applicant's research program in oncology pharmacotherapy (e.g., laboratory techniques, pharmacokinetic modeling).
Requirements The applicant for the program must be a current member of the Hematology/Oncology PRN.
Restrictions The following individuals will not be considered as candidates: current residents or fellows; members of the Minisabbatical Awards Committee; or persons in receipt of a minisabbatical award in the past 5 years.
Amount $2,750 for recipient; $750 for mentor
Date(s) Application Is Due May 1.
Contact Cathy Englund, Executive Secretary; (913) 492-3311; fax: (913) 492-0088; email: cenglund@accp.com
Internet http://www.accp.com/frontiers/rihmonmini.php
Sponsor American College of Clinical Pharmacy
13000 W. 87th Street Parkway
Lenexa, KS 66215-4530

ACCP Infectious Diseases PRN Minisabbatical Program 148
The minisabbatical program is an opportunity for members of the ID PRN exclusively to gain or expand their skills in practice or research under the guidance of experts in infectious diseases pharmacotherapy. The major purposes are: to learn new clinical skills or approaches to patient care that will enhance the applicant's practice in infectious diseases (e.g., patient evaluation techniques, practice management, antimicrobial surveillance, etc.); and to learn new research skills that will enhance or expand the applicant's research program in infectious diseases (e.g., laboratory techniques, pharmacokinetic and pharmacodynamic modeling, epidemiology, ID outcomes research).
Requirements The applicant for the ID PRN Minisabbatical Program must be a current member and maintain membership with the ID PRN for the duration of project.
Restrictions The following individuals will not be considered as candidates: current students, residents or fellows at time of application; members of the Minisabbatical Awards Committee; if currently funded by the NIH or have other multi-year peer reviewed funding; or persons in receipt of a minisabbatical award in the past 5 years.
Amount $,3000 for recipient; $1,000 for mentor
Date(s) Application Is Due May 1.
Contact Cathy Englund, Executive Secretary; (913) 492-3311; fax: (913) 492-0088; email: cenglund@accp.com
Internet http://www.accp.com/frontiers/riinfdmini.php
Sponsor American College of Clinical Pharmacy
13000 W. 87th Street Parkway
Lenexa, KS 66215-4530

ACCP Infectious Diseases Research Fellowships 149
The purpose of ACCP fellowships is to support the development of Clinical Scientists through postgraduate fellowship experiences, or through the support of graduate students who have at least completed their qualifying examinations. Research activities must relate directly to the stated areas of emphasis. Fellowships support a research training experience and not a clinical pharmacy residency program. A pharmacy fellowship is a directed, highly individualized postgraduate program designed to prepare the participant to become an independent researcher. Fellowships exist primarily to develop

competency in the scientific research process. The ACCP Research Institute believes that clinical pharmacy fellowships should be at least two years in length, and will give strong preference to funding applications that describe a multiyear training program. This grant will provide the fellow's stipend for either the first, second, or third year. Preceptors will have the option to receive the fellowship's entire funding over one year, or half funding for each of two years.
Requirements Preceptor: An ACCP Full Member at the time application is made. Fellowship applications submitted concurrently with an application for Full Membership will not be considered. Fellow: An ACCP Member, Associate Member, or applicant for member. If a graduate student, (a) preference will be given to supporting students who have received or are concurrently enrolled in a Pharm.D. degree program; and (b) the Fellow must at least have completed his/her qualifying examinations.
Restrictions Ineligible applicants include: ACCP Board of Regent members; ACCP Research Institute Board of Trustee members; Grants and Fellowship Selection Committee members; preceptor of an ACCP Research Institute fellowship within the previous year.
Amount $40,500
Date(s) Application Is Due Apr 3.
Contact Cathy Englund, Executive Secretary; (913) 492-3311; fax: (913) 492-0088; email: cenglund@accp.com
Internet http://www.accp.com/frontiers/research.php#resfel
Sponsor American College of Clinical Pharmacy
13000 W. 87th Street Parkway
Lenexa, KS 66215-4530

ACCP Investigator Development Research Awards **150**
The purpose of these awards is to provide funding for research projects that will: help pursue one or more of the priority areas outlined in the Research Agenda of the American College of Clinical Pharmacy; contribute to the development of the principal investigator's research career; promote the safe, effective, and cost-effective use of medications; and advance the practice of clinical pharmacy. This includes, but is not limited to, investigations aimed at generating preliminary data or seed money for pilot projects. The award may serve as the total support for a project or supplement an existing research effort as long as a specific portion of the research is identified as being made possible by this award, and provided that the investigator states specifically how the balance will be funded and provides evidence of its guaranteed availability. The overall goal of the awards is to assist developing researchers in improving their competitiveness for extramural funding and to support their evolving research careers. In this context, projects that involve the use of animals or in vitro models will be considered as long as the applicant adequately justifies the request.
Requirements The principal investigator of the award application must: be an ACCP member; be ten or fewer years since completion of his/her formal training or first academic appointment; not be currently funded by the NIH or have other multi-year peer reviewed funding; or not be a student, resident, or fellow.
Restrictions The award must not duplicate funding for another research project.
Amount $20,000
Date(s) Application Is Due Jul 16.
Contact Cathy Englund, Executive Secretary; (913) 492-3311; fax: (913) 492-0088; email: cenglund@accp.com
Internet http://www.accp.com/frontiers/research.php#resfel
Sponsor American College of Clinical Pharmacy
13000 W. 87th Street Parkway
Lenexa, KS 66215-4530

ACCP Nephrology PRN Minisabbatical Program **151**
The minisabbatical program is an opportunity for members of the Nephrology PRN exclusively to gain or expand their skills in practice or research under the guidance of experts in nephrology pharmacotherapy. The major purposes are: to learn new clinical skills or approaches to patient care that will enhance the applicant's practice in nephrology pharmacotherapy; and to learn new research skills that will enhance or expand the applicant's research program in nephrology pharmacotherapy.
Requirements The applicant for the minisabbatical program must be a current member of the Nephrology PRN.
Restrictions The following individuals will not be considered as candidates: current residents or fellows; members of the Minisabbatical Awards Committee; or persons in receipt of a minisabbatical award in the past 5 years.
Amount $2,750 for recipient; $750 for mentor
Date(s) Application Is Due May 1.
Contact Cathy Englund, Executive Secretary; (913) 492-3311; fax: (913) 492-0088; email: cenglund@accp.com
Internet http://www.accp.com/frontiers/rinephmini.php
Sponsor American College of Clinical Pharmacy
13000 W. 87th Street Parkway
Lenexa, KS 66215-4530

ACE Fellows Program **152**
The program supports leadership development program in higher education. Fellows spend an extended period of time on another campus, working directly with presidents and other senior leaders, observing firsthand how the institution and its leaders address strategic planning, resource allocation, development, policy, and other issues and challenges. Fellows observe and participate in key meetings and events, and take on special projects and/or assignments while under the mentorship of a team of experienced administrators. The program also includes participation in three week-long national seminars, visits to other campuses, attendance at national meetings, and contact with a national network of higher education leaders. Guidelines and application are available online.
Requirements Candidates must have demonstrated records of leadership in institutionwide contexts and must be nominated by the institution's president or other senior officer who agrees to pay the candidate's salary and benefits.
Date(s) Application Is Due Nov 1.
Contact Marlene Ross, Director, (202) 939-9420; fax: (202) 785-8056; email: fellows@ace.nche.edu
Internet http://www.acenet.edu/programs/fellows
Sponsor American Council on Education
1 Dupont Circle
Washington, DC 20036-1193

ACGT Young Investigator Grants **153**
The alliance funds research aimed at furthering the development of gene therapy approaches to the treatment of cancer. The overall objectives of this grant are to advance gene therapy into the causes, treatment, and prevention of all types of cancer by promoting development of novel and innovative studies by young investigators. The emphasis of this initiative is to promote basic, and preclinical research approaches utilizing cells and genes as medicine. The six main areas of research ACGT will support are: tumor-specific replicating viruses and bacteria, anti-angiogenesis, immune-mediated gene therapy and cancer vaccines, oncogenes/suppressor oncogenes/apoptosis, tumor targeting and vector development, and other cancer gene therapy research. The three-year grant may be used at the recipient's discretion for salary, technical assistance, supplies, animals or capital equipment, but may not support staff not directly related to the project, e.g. secretaries or administrative assistants. Purchase of equipment is not allowed in the third year of the grant. Continued support is contingent upon submission and approval of a noncompetitive renewal application each year. Guideline and applications are available online.
Requirements Candidates must hold an MD, MPH, PhD, or equivalent degree and be a tenure-track assistant professor within five years of their initial appointment to this rank, at the time of award activation. The investigator must be conducting original research as an independent faculty member. ACGT has no citizenship restrictions, and research supported by the award must be conducted at medical schools and research centers only in the United States.
Amount $500,000 maximum over three years
Date(s) Application Is Due Sep 21.
Contact Grace Pedersen, (203) 358-8000 ext 495; email: aneslage@acgtfoundation.org
Internet http://www.acgtfoundation.org/research.html
Sponsor Alliance for Cancer Gene Therapy
96 Cummings Point Rd
Stamford, CT 06902

ACHE Foster G. McGaw Student Scholarship **154**
The scholarship is designated for students enrolled in their final year of a healthcare management graduate program. One scholarship is awarded per candidate. Application is available online in the Fall.
Requirements Applicant must be a student associate in good standing of the American College of Healthcare Executives; enrolled in full-time study for the upcoming fall term, which is the student's final year of didactic work in a healthcare management graduate program; demonstrate financial need; and a US or Canadian citizen.
Restrictions Previous recipients of this scholarship and the Albert W. Dent Graduate Student Scholarship are ineligible.
Amount $3500
Date(s) Application Is Due Mar 31.
Contact Thomas Killam, (312) 424-9400; fax: (312) 424-0023; email: tkillam@ache.org
Internet http://www.ache.org/Faculty_Students/mcgaw_scholarship.cfm
Sponsor American College of Healthcare Executives
1 N Franklin St, Ste 1700
Chicago, IL 60606-3491

ACICS Dissertation Research Fellowship **155**
ACICS supports an annual competitive fellowship to support dissertation research in the realm of private career school accreditation. The fellowship will be awarded to the winner of a competition for the most promising 400-word dissertation proposal abstract. The applicant with the winning proposal will receive $1000, $3000 upon approval of the research proposal by the student's graduate committee; and $4000 after the fellow passes the final oral dissertation defense and submits a copy of the dissertation. Applicants must submit a 400-word research proposal abstract, evidence that the applicant has reached the dissertation stage of a doctoral program in an accredited doctoral degree-granting institution, curriculum vita, and three letters of reference (two from faculty at the individual's current institution and one from a professional, work-related contact).
Amount $8000
Date(s) Application Is Due May 1.
Contact Dr. Kathleen Prince, Director of Quality Enhancement, (202) 336-6775; fax: (202) 842-2593; email: kprince@acics.org

Internet http://www.acics.org/applications/fellowship.asp
Sponsor Accrediting Council for Independent Colleges and Schools
750 First St NE, Ste 980
Washington, DC 20002-4241

ACIE Host University Edmund S. Muskie/Freedom Support Act Graduate Fellowships **156**

The program is accepting applications from universities to host scholars from the New Independent States for the academic year. The Open Society Institute sponsors professors in the fields of education, environmental management, law, and public health. The American Councils for International Education sponsors professors in the fields of business administration, economics, international affairs, journalism and mass communications, library and information science, public administration, and public policy. Host institutions are selected on the basis of their academic strength, experience working with international students, ability to facilitate internships, ability to assign faculty advisors as well as a program coordinator, ability to contribute financially toward tuition in the form of cost-share, and ability to mentor and evaluate the academic progress and cultural adaptation of the fellow(s).
Requirements Applicants must be a citizen of one of the 12 participating countries, under the age of 40, with an undergraduate degree. Applicants must also currently reside in one of the 12 participating countries, have a professional aptitude and leadership potential, and must be committed to returning to their home country after fellowship. The participating countries are Armenia, Azerbaijan, Belarus, Georgia, Kazakhstan, Kyrgyzstan, Moldova, Russia, Tajikistan, Turkmenistan, Ukraine, and Uzbekistan.
Contact Susan Frarie, (202) 833-7522; fax: (202) 833-7523; email: frarie@actr.org or general@americancouncils.org
Internet http://www.americancouncils.org/program.asp?PageID=121&ProgramID=22
Sponsor American Councils for International Education
1776 Massachusetts Ave NW, Ste 700
Washington, DC 20036

ACIE Title VIII Research Scholar Program **157**

Funded by the US Department of State, Program for the Study of Eastern Europe and The Independent States of the Former Soviet Union (Title VIII), the American Councils Research Scholar program provides full support for graduate students, faculty, and independent scholars seeking to conduct research for three months to nine months in Belarus, Central Asia, Russia, the South Caucasus, Ukraine, and Moldova. Scholars may apply for support for research in more than one country during a single trip, provided they intend to work in the field for a total of three to nine months. Participants in the program will receive international airfare from the scholar's home to his/her host city overseas; academic affiliation at a leading local university; visa(s) arranged by American Councils in direct collaboration with academic host institutions in order to facilitate archive access and guarantee timely visa registration; housing in a university dormitory or with a local host family (American Councils also provides informal assistance in locating apartments in some cities); a monthly living stipend; financial and logistical support for travel within the region as required by research. Health insurance of up to $50,000 per accident or illness; ongoing logistical support from American Councils offices throughout the region, including in-country orientation programs and 24-hour emergency aid. Proposals will be reviewed by an independent selection committee of leading US scholars in the social sciences and the humanities. Award deadlines are twice per year. Applications for summer, fall, and academic year programs are due on January 15; applications for spring programs are due October 1.
Requirements US graduate students, faculty, and post-doctoral researchers are eligible to apply.
Amount $5000-$25,000
Date(s) Application Is Due Jan 15; Oct 1.
Contact Research Scholar Program Manager, (202) 833-7522; email: outbound@americancouncils.org
Internet http://www.americancouncils.org/program.asp?PageID=121&ProgramID=15
Sponsor American Councils for International Education
1776 Massachusetts Ave NW, Ste 700
Washington, DC 20036

ACIE US-Eurasia Awards for Excellence in Teaching (TEA) **158**

The program provides a professional development opportunity for award-winning US teachers to utilize their talents and expertise to improve the quality of secondary education in Russia and to create linkages and learning partnerships between US and Russian schools. Participants will take part in a three-day cross-cultural symposium, Celebrating Teaching Excellence Across Cultures, and a three-week exchange program with teachers from Armenia, Azerbaijan, Georgia, Kazakhstan, Kyrgyzstan, Russia, Tajikistan, Turkmenistan, Ukraine and Uzbekistan who have won the equivalent program in their country. Application and guidelines are available online.
Requirements US middle school and high school teachers of the English, English as a Foreign Language (EFL), social studies, history, math, science, or information technology who have been recognized for excellence in teaching at the national, state, or local level.
Restrictions Applicant must be a U.S. citizen or permanent resident.
Date(s) Application Is Due Feb 28.
Contact Ben Dunbar, TEA Program, (202) 833-7522; email: teachers@americancouncils.org
Internet http://www.americancouncils.org/newsDetail.php?news_id=NjY=
Sponsor American Councils for International Education
1776 Massachusetts Ave NW, Ste 700
Washington, DC 20036

ACLS Charles A. Ryskamp Research Fellowships **159**

These fellowships support advanced assistant professors and untenured associate professors in the humanities and related social sciences whose scholarly contributions have advanced their fields and who have well designed and carefully developed plans for new research. Appropriate fields of specialization include but are not limited to: anthropology, archeology, art history, economics, geography, history, languages and literatures, law, linguistics, musicology, philosophy, political science, psychology, religion, and sociology. Proposals in the social science fields listed are eligible only if they employ predominantly humanistic approaches (e.g., economic history, law and literature, political philosophy). Proposals in interdisciplinary and cross-disciplinary studies are welcome, as are proposals focused on any geographic region or on any cultural or linguistic group. The ultimate goal of the project should be a major piece of scholarly work by the applicant that will take the form of a monograph or other equally substantial form of scholarship. The fellowships support an academic year of research (nine months), plus an additional summer's research (two months) if justified. Fellows have three years to use the funds awarded them. Completed applications must be submitted through the ACLS Online Fellowship Application system.
Requirements The program is open to tenure-track assistant professors and untenured associate professors who by September 30 will have successfully completed their institution's last reappointment review before tenure review (if the institution does not have multi-year contracts, the guideline will mean having passed three annual reappointment reviews), and whose tenure review will not be complete before February 1. Applicants must hold the PhD or equivalent and be employed at academic institutions in the United States, remaining so for the duration of the fellowship.
Restrictions ACLS does not fund creative work (e.g., novels or films), textbooks, straightforward translation, or pedagogical projects.
Amount $64,000, plus $2500 for research and travel
Date(s) Application Is Due Oct 3.
Contact Office of Fellowships and Grants, (212) 697-1505; fax: (212) 949-8058; email: fellows@acls.org
Internet http://www.acls.org/rysguide.htm
Sponsor American Council of Learned Societies
633 Third Ave
New York, NY 10017-6795

ACLS Chinese Fellowships for Scholarly Development **160**

This program is for scholars in the humanities to do research in the People's Republic of China on China or the Chinese portion of a comparative study. Grants are offered for four to 12 months of research in China. Applicants should demonstrate that they have fully utilized the available resources in the United States and are prepared by virtue of study, training, and planning to take full advantage of an opportunity to do research in China. The fellowship includes a monthly stipend and travel allowance.
Requirements This program supports individuals with the MA, PhD, or equivalent. Scholars must be US citizens and permanent residents who have lived in the United States continuously for at least three years by the application deadline.
Restrictions Chinese scholars may not apply directly. Scholars who have previously visited the United States for five months or more, or who are enrolled in degree programs, are not eligible.
Date(s) Application Is Due Nov 14.
Contact Cynthia Mueller, Manager, Office of Fellowships and Grants, (212) 697-1505 ext 136; fax: (212) 949-8058; email: cmueller@acls.org
Internet http://www.acls.org/csccguid.htm
Sponsor American Council of Learned Societies
633 Third Ave
New York, NY 10017-6795

ACLS Digital Innovation Fellowships **161**

This program invites applications to pursue digitally based research projects in all disciplines of the humanities and humanities-related social sciences. It is hoped that projects of successful applicants will help advance digital humanistic scholarship by broadening understanding of its nature and exemplifying the robust infrastructure necessary for creating further such works. The fellowships are intended to support an academic year dedicated to work on a major scholarly project that takes a digital form. Projects might include but are not limited to digital research archives, new media representations of extant data, innovative databases, and digital tools that further humanistic research. The fellowships are intended as salary replacement and may be held concurrently with other fellowships and grants and any sabbatical pay up to an amount equal to the candidate's current academic year salary. All applications must include the endorsement of a senior administrator of the applicant's stitution. This endorsement should include discussion of how the institution's existing cyberinfrastructure complements and supports the technologies to be developed for the specified project. Completed applications must be submitted through the ACLS online application system (ofa.acls.org). Guidelines are available online.
Requirements This program is open to scholars in all fields of the humanities and the humanistic social sciences. Applicants must have a PhD degree conferred prior to the

application deadline. (An established scholar who can demonstrate the equivalent of the Ph.D. in publications and professional experience may also qualify.) US citizenship or permanent resident status is required as of application deadline.
Restrictions ACLS does not support creative works (e.g., novels or films), textbooks, straightforward translations, or purely pedagogical projects.
Amount $55,000 maximum stipend; $25,000 maximum project costs
Date(s) Application Is Due Oct 3.
Contact Grants Administrator, (212) 697-1505; fax: (212) 949-8058
Internet http://www.acls.org/difguide.htm
Sponsor American Council of Learned Societies
633 Third Ave
New York, NY 10017-6795

ACLS Dissertation Fellowships in East European Studies **162**
Dissertation fellowships are offered in the social sciences and humanities relating to Albania, Bulgaria, Czech Republic, Estonia, Slovakia, Hungary, Latvia, Lithuania, Poland, Romania, and the former Yugoslavia. Doctoral candidates may apply for support of dissertation research or writing to be undertaken at any university or institution outside of East Europe, although short visits to the area may be proposed as part of a coherent program primarily based elsewhere. Fellowships require an academic year of nine to 12 months devoted solely to work on the dissertation.
Requirements Currently enrolled graduate students who will have completed all requirements for the doctorate except the dissertation by June may apply for one-year, non-renewable support to complete the dissertation.
Amount $17,000 maximum
Date(s) Application Is Due Nov 9.
Contact Saul Fisher, Director of Fellowship Programs, (212) 697-1505 ext 124; fax: (212) 949-8058; email: sfisher@acls.org
Internet http://www.acls.org/eeguide.htm
Sponsor American Council of Learned Societies
228 E 45th St
New York, NY 10017-3398

ACLS East European Language Training Grants **163**
Individuals may apply for grants for summer study of Albanian, Bosnian-Croatian-Serbian, Bulgarian, Czech, Hungarian, Macedonian, Polish, Romanian, Slovak, or Slovene. Applicants should present proposals for attendance at intensive courses offered by institutions of higher education in the US, or, in exceptional cases, for study at the advanced level in courses in Eastern Europe. These grants are intended for people who will use the East European languages in academic research or teaching. In addition, grants will be available to US institutions to support intensive summer 2005 course instruction in Albanian, Bosnian-Croatian-Serbian, Bulgarian, Czech, Estonian, Hungarian, Latvian, Lithuanian, Macedonian, Polish, Romanian, Slovak, or Slovene. See the ACLS Web
Requirements Applicants must be citizens or permanent residents of the United States, and must have completed, at minimum, a four-year college degree. They may request support for beginning, intermediate, or advanced language study, and the application will request the name of the institution they wish to attend, along with a statement of the significance of this training for their career plans.
Amount $2000 maximum, individuals; $10,000 maximum, organizations
Date(s) Application Is Due Jan 13.
Contact Cynthia Mueller, Manager, Office of Fellowships and Grants , (212) 697-1505 ext 136; fax: (212) 949-8058; email: cmueller@acls.org
Internet http://www.acls.org/eeguide.htm
Sponsor American Council of Learned Societies
633 Third Ave
New York, NY 10017-6795

ACLS Eastern European Postdoctoral Research Fellowships **164**
Support is provided for six to 12 months of postdoctoral research and training in the social sciences and humanities relating to Albania, Bulgaria, Czech Republic, Estonia, Hungary, Latvia, Lithuania, Poland, Romania, Slovakia, and the successor states of Yugoslavia. Scholars may apply for fellowships for periods of six to 12 consecutive months of full-time research and writing between July 1 and September 1 of the following year. The fellowships are intended primarily as salary replacement to provide free time for research; the funds may be used to supplement sabbatical salaries or awards from other sources, provided they intensify or extend the contemplated research. Five to seven fellowships are awarded each year.
Requirements Applicants must be US citizens or permanent residents and must have obtained the PhD degree or its equivalent.
Restrictions These fellowships are to be used for work outside East Europe, although short visits to the area may be proposed as part of a coherent program primarily based elsewhere.
Amount $25,000 maximum
Contact Saul Fisher, Director of Fellowship Programs, (212) 697-1505 ext 124; fax: (212) 949-8058; email: sfisher@acls.org
Internet http://www.acls.org/eeguide.htm
Sponsor American Council of Learned Societies
633 Third Ave
New York, NY 10017-6795

ACLS Fellowships **165**
The program invites research applications in all disciplines of the humanities and humanities-related social sciences. Appropriate fields of specialization include but are not limited to: anthropology, archeology, art history, economics, geography, history, languages and literatures, law, linguistics, musicology, philosophy, political science, psychology, religion, and sociology. Proposals in the social science fields listed are eligible only if they employ predominantly humanistic approaches (e.g., economic history, law and literature, political philosophy). Proposals in interdisciplinary and cross-disciplinary studies are welcome, as are proposals focused on any geographic region or on any cultural or linguistic group. The fellowships are intended as salary replacement and may be held concurrently with other fellowships and grants and any sabbatical pay to reach that goal.
Requirements The applicant must have had a PhD degree conferred two years prior to the listed application deadline. An established scholar who can demonstrate the equivalent of the PhD in publications and professional experience may also qualify. The applicant must have U.S. citizenship or permanent resident status as of the application deadline. The most recent supported research leave must have concluded two years prior to July 1. (Supported research leave is defined as the equivalent of one semester or more of time free from teaching or other employment to pursue scholarly research or writing supported by sabbatical pay or other institutional funding, fellowships and grants, or a combination of these.) This definition will apply to independent scholars as well as those with institutional affiliations.
Restrictions ACLS does not fund creative work (e.g., novels or films), textbooks, straightforward translation, or pedagogical projects.
Amount $60,000 maximum, full professor and career equivalent; $40,000 maximum, associate professor and career equivalent; $30,000 maximum, assistant professor and equivalent
Date(s) Application Is Due Oct 3.
Contact Ruth Waters, Consultant, Fellowships and Grants, (212) 697-1505; fax: (212) 949-8058; email: ruth@acls.org
Internet http://www.acls.org/felguide.htm
Sponsor American Council of Learned Societies
633 Third Ave
New York, NY 10017-6795

ACLS Frederick Burkhardt Residential Fellowships for Recently Tenured Scholars **166**
The objectives of this program are to encourage more adventurous, more wide-ranging, and longer term patterns of research than are current in these disciplines; to link a small number of outstanding scholars and their projects to one of a limited number of residential study centers with an established record of advancing multi-disciplinary scholarship; and to sustain the scholarly momentum of the emerging intellectual leaders in fields of the humanities and related social sciences. Appropriate fields of specialization include but are not limited to: anthropology, archaeology, art history, economics, geography, history, languages and literatures, law, linguistics, musicology, philosophy, political science, psychology, religion, and sociology. Proposals in the social science fields listed above are eligible only if they employ predominantly humanistic approaches (e.g., economic history, law and literature, political philosophy). Proposals in interdisciplinary and cross-disciplinary studies are welcome, as are proposals focused on any geographic region or on any cultural or linguistic group. Fellowships are intended to support an academic year (normally nine months) of residence at any one of nine national residential research centers. Applications must be submitted online; guidelines also are available online.
Requirements The Burkhardt Fellowship Program is open to recently tenured humanists—scholars who will have begun their first tenured contracts by the application deadline but began their first tenured contracts no earlier than the fall 2002 semester or quarter. An applicant must be employed in a tenured position at a degree-granting academic institution in the US, remaining so for the duration of the fellowship. US citizenship or permanent residency is not required, and previous supported research leaves do not affect eligibility for the Burkhardt Fellowship.
Restrictions ACLS does not fund creative work (e.g., novels or films), textbooks, straightforward translation, or pedagogical projects.
Amount $75,000
Date(s) Application Is Due Oct 3.
Contact Cynthia Mueller, Manager, Fellowships and Grants, (212) 697-1505 ext 136; email: cmueller@acls.org
Internet http://www.acls.org/burkguid.htm
Sponsor American Council of Learned Societies
633 Third Ave
New York, NY 10017-6795

ACLS New Perspectives on Chinese Culture and Society Grants **167**
This program is intended to support projects that bridge disciplinary or geographic boundaries, engage new kinds of information, develop fresh approaches to traditional materials and issues, or otherwise bring innovative perspectives to the study of Chinese culture and society. The program awards funds in support of planning meetings, workshops, and/or conferences leading to publication of scholarly volumes. Proposals are expected to be empirically grounded, theoretically informed, and methodologically explicit. The program will support collaborative work of three types: formal research conferences intended to produce significant new research published in a conference volume; workshops or seminars designed to less formally facilitate new research on newly

available or inadequately researched problems, data, or texts; and planning meetings to organizers of the above-described types of projects. There are no application forms.
Requirements The program aims to provide opportunities for interchange among scholars who may not otherwise have chances to work with one another.
Restrictions Proposals for activities that involve scholars primarily from one institution and that fall within an institution's normal range of colloquia, symposia, or seminar series will not be supported. In addition, the program does not normally support regular scheduled meetings, conventions, or parts thereof. Funds cannot be used to cover the following expenses: direct research expenses, such as those of field work, obtaining research materials, or analysis of data; salaries or released time for organizers or participants; honoraria or speaker's fees for organizers or US participants; purchase of equipment; or institutional overhead (direct administrative costs are allowed).
Amount $25,000 maximum for formal research conferences; $15,000 maximum for workshops or seminars; $6000 for planning meetings
Date(s) Application Is Due Aug 15.
Contact Cynthia Mueller, Office of Fellowships and Grants, (212) 697-1505 ext 136; fax: (212) 949-8058; email: cmueller@acls.org
Internet http://www.acls.org/cck.htm#guide
Sponsor American Council of Learned Societies
633 Third Ave
New York, NY 10017-6795

ACM A.M. Turing Award **168**
This award is the association's most prestigious technical award and is given to an individual selected for contributions of a technical nature made to the computing community. The contributions should be of lasting importance to the computer field. Nomination forms should be obtained from ACM headquarters.
Requirements Each nomination should consist of name, address, and phone number of person making the suggestion; name and address of candidate; statement of 200 to 500 words explaining why the candidate deserves the award; and if possible, names and addresses or telephone numbers of others who agree with the recommendation.
Amount $100,000
Contact Rosemary McGuinness, Headquarters Liaison, (212) 626-0561; email: mcguinness@acm.org
Internet http://www.acm.org/awards/taward.html
Sponsor Association for Computing Machinery
2 Penn Plaza, Suite 701
New York, NY 10121-0701

ACM Doctoral Dissertation Award **169**
This award is given to the individual who has been judged to have prepared the most outstanding doctoral dissertation on computer science and engineering during the previous year. Dissertations will be reviewed for technical depth and significance of the research contribution, potential impact on theory and practice, and quality of presentation. A committee of five individuals serving staggered five-year terms performs an initial screening to generate a short list, followed by an in-depth evaluation to determine the winning dissertation. Nomination forms are available from ACM headquarters. The winning dissertation is published by Springer.
Requirements Each nominated dissertation must have been accepted by the department within a 12-month period prior to August 31. Exceptional dissertations completed in August, but too late for submission last year will be considered. Only English language versions will be accepted.
Restrictions Nominations are limited to one per university or college, from any country, unless more than 10 Ph.D.s are granted in one year.
Amount $5000
Date(s) Application Is Due Aug 31.
Contact Priya Narasimhan, (412) 268-8801; fax: (412) 268-1194; email: Priya@cs.cmu.edu
Internet http://awards.acm.org/homepage.cfm?awd=146
Sponsor Association for Computing Machinery
2 Penn Plaza, Suite 701
New York, NY 10121-0701

ACM Eckert-Mauchly Award **170**
This award is given for contributions to computer and digital systems architecture where the field of computer architecture is considered at present to encompass the combined hardware-software design and analysis of computing and of digital systems. The award is administered jointly by ACM and the IEEE Computer Society.
Requirements Nomination should consist of name, address, and phone number of person making the suggestion; name and address of candidate; a statement of 200-500 words explaining why the candidate deserves the award; and, if possible, the names and addresses or telephone numbers of others who agree with the recommendation.
Amount $5000
Date(s) Application Is Due Oct 31.
Contact Alan Berenbaum, (631) 435-6480; email: aberenbaum@acm.org
Internet http://awards.acm.org/homepage.cfm?awd=148
Sponsor Association for Computing Machinery
2 Penn Plaza, Suite 701
New York, NY 10121-0701

ACM Grace Murray Hopper Award **171**
This award is given to the outstanding young computer professional of the year, selected on the basis of a single recent major technical or service contribution. This candidate must have been 35 years of age or less at the time the qualifying contribution was made. Nominating forms should be obtained from ACM headquarters. This award is provided by Google.
Requirements Each nomination submitted should consist of name, address, and phone number of person making the nomination; name and address of candidate; a statement of 200-500 words explaining why the candidate deserves the award; and if possible, the names and addresses or telephone numbers of others who agree with the recommendation.
Amount $15,000
Date(s) Application Is Due Oct 31.
Contact Gabriel (Gabby) Silberman, (212) 415-6908; fax: (631) 342-5013; email: Gabby.Silberman@ca.com
Internet http://awards.acm.org/homepage.cfm?awd=145
Sponsor Association for Computing Machinery
2 Penn Plaza, Suite 701
New York, NY 10121-0701

ACM Karl V. Karlstrom Outstanding Educator Award **172**
This award is presented annually to an outstanding educator who is appointed to a recognized educational baccalaureate institution, recognized for advancing new teaching methodologies or effecting new curriculum development or expansion in computer science and engineering, or making a significant contribution to the educational mission of the ACM. Those who have been teaching for 10 years or less will be given special consideration. The prize is supplied by Prentice-Hall Publishing Company.
Requirements Each nomination should consist of name, address, and phone number of person making the suggestion; name and address of candidate; statement of 200 to 500 words explaining why the candidate deserves the award; and if possible, names and addresses or telephone numbers of others who agree with the recommendation.
Amount $5,000
Date(s) Application Is Due Oct 31.
Contact Jeffrey Ullman, (650) 494-8016; email: ullman@gmail.com
Internet http://awards.acm.org/homepage.cfm?awd=147
Sponsor Association for Computing Machinery
2 Penn Plaza, Suite 701
New York, NY 10121-0701

ACM Paris Kanellakis Theory and Practice Award **173**
The award honors specific theoretical accomplishments that have had a significant and demonstrable effect on the practice of computing. This award is endowed by contributions from the Kanellakis family, with additional financial support provided by ACM's Special Interest Groups on Algorithms and Computational Theory (SIGACT), Design Automaton (SIGDA), Management of Data (SIGMOD), and Programming Languages (SIGPLAN), the ACM SIG Projects Fund, and individual contributions.
Requirements Each nomination should consist of name, address, and phone number of person making the suggestion; name and address of candidate; statement of 200 to 500 words explaining why the candidate deserves the award; and if possible, names and addresses or telephone numbers of others who agree with the recommendation.
Amount $5,000
Date(s) Application Is Due Oct 31.
Contact Anna Karlin, (206) 543-9344; email: karlin@cs.washington.edu
Internet http://awards.acm.org/homepage.cfm?awd=147
Sponsor Association for Computing Machinery
2 Penn Plaza, Suite 701
New York, NY 10121-0701

ACM Software System Award **174**
Provided by IBM, this award goes to an institution or individual(s) recognized for developing a software system that has had a lasting influence, reflected in contributions to concepts, in commercial acceptance, or both.
Requirements Each nomination should consist of name, address, and phone number of person making the suggestion; name and address of candidate; statement of 200 to 500 words explaining why the candidate deserves the award; and if possible, names and addresses or telephone numbers of others who agree with the recommendation.
Amount $10,000
Date(s) Application Is Due Oct 31.
Contact Frank Tompa, (519) 888-4567; email: fwtompa@uwaterloo.ca
Internet http://awards.acm.org/homepage.cfm?awd=149
Sponsor Association for Computing Machinery
2 Penn Plaza, Suite 701
New York, NY 10121-0701

ACOG History of American Obstetrics and Gynecology Fellowship **175**
ACOG and Ortho-McNeil Pharmaceutical Corporation jointly sponsor the fellowship in the History of American Obstetrics and Gynecology each year. The recipient of the fellowship spends one month in the Washington, DC, area working full-time to complete their specific historical research project. Although the fellowship will be based in the ACOG History Library, the fellow is encouraged to use other national, historical, and

medical collections in the Washington, DC, area. The results of this research must be disseminated through either publication or presentation at a professional meeting.
Requirements ACOG junior fellows and fellows are encouraged to apply.
Amount $5000
Date(s) Application Is Due Oct 1.
Contact Debra Scarborough, (202) 863-2578; fax: (202) 484-1595; email: history@acog.org
Internet http://www.acog.org/from_home/departments/dept_notice.cfm?recno=21&bulletin=254
Sponsor American College of Obstetricians and Gynecologists
409 12th St SW
Washington DC 20024-2588

ACRL Doctoral Dissertation Fellowship **176**
This fellowship, sponsored by the Thomsn Scientific, is intended to foster research in academic librarianship by encouraging and assisting doctoral students in the field with their dissertation research. Qualified students who wish to be considered for the fellowship may apply by submitting a brief proposal that includes the following: a description of the research, including significance and methodology; a schedule; a budget; the name of dissertation advisor and committee members; a cover letter from dissertation advisor endorsing the proposal; and an up-to-date curriculum vita.
Requirements An applicant must be an active doctoral student in the academic librarianship area in a degree-granting institution, have completed all coursework, and have had a dissertation proposal accepted by the institution. The applicant need not be an ACRL member.
Restrictions Recipients of the fellowship may not receive it a second time.
Amount $1500
Date(s) Application Is Due Dec 1.
Contact Megan Bielefeld, (312) 280-2514; email: mbielefeld@ala.org
Internet http://www.ala.org/Template.cfm?Section=Grants_and_Fellowships&template=/ContentManagement/ContentDisplay.cfm&ContentID=29778
Sponsor Association of College and Research Libraries
50 E. Huron Street
Chicago, IL 60611

ACRL Miriam Dudley Librarian Instruction Award **177**
This grant recognizes a significant contribution by a librarian to the advancement of instruction in a college or research library environment. Nominees should have achieved distinction in one or more of the following areas: planning and implementation of an academic instruction program in a library environment that has served as a model for other programs nationally or regionally; production of a body of research and publication that has a demonstrable impact on the concepts and methods of teaching and information-seeking strategies in a college or research institution; sustained participation in organizations, at the national or regional level, devoted to the promotion and enhancement of academic instruction in a library environment; or promotion, development, and integration of education for instruction in ALA-accredited library schools or professional continuing education programs that have served as models for other courses and programs. Nominations must include a letter including the name, address, and phone number of the nominator and the nominee; a narrative statement supporting the nomination and addressing how the nominee meets the criteria for the award; and nominee's current vita. Send nominating package to: IS Miriam Dudley Award chair, Lisa J. Hinchliffe, Coordinator for Information Literacy, University of Illinois, 1408 W. Gregory Drive, Library 434, Urbana, IL 61801.
Restrictions Nominees will be judged on an individual basis; this award cannot be given to a pair or group of persons.
Amount $1000
Date(s) Application Is Due Dec 1.
Contact Megan Bielefeld, Program Officer, (800) 545-2433 ext. 2514; email: mbielefeld@ala.org
Internet http://www.ala.org/ala/acrl/acrlawards/miriamdudley.htm
Sponsor Association of College and Research Libraries
50 E Huron Street
Chicago, IL 60611-2795

ACS Master's Training Grants in Clinical Oncology Social Work **178**
These grants are awarded annually to qualifying institutions that train clinical oncology social workers to provide cancer patients and their families with psychosocial services. Grants are available to second-year students in a master's program and post-master's social workers within five years of graduation. The master's training must introduce social workers to the special needs of cancer patients and their families. Contact the society for application forms.
Requirements Applications will be considered from institutions that identify clinical oncology social work training activities, cancer programs with defined psychosocial support services, and relationships with schools accredited by the Council on Social Work Education.
Amount $12,000 maximum
Date(s) Application Is Due Oct 15.
Contact Extramural Grants Department, (404) 329-7558; fax: (404) 321-4669; email: grants@cancer.org
Internet http://www.cancer.org/docroot/RES/content/RES_5_2x_Masters_Training_Grants_in_Clinical_Oncology_Social_Work.asp?sitearea=RES
Sponsor American Cancer Society
1599 Clifton Rd NE
Atlanta, GA 30329-4251

ACS Audrey Meyer Mars International Fellowships in Clinical Oncology **179**
The purpose of the fellowships is to provide one year of advanced training in clinical oncology at participating cancer centers in the United States to qualified physicians and surgeons from other countries, particularly countries where advanced training is not readily available. Training will be conducted at one of the United States cancer centers participating in the program; a list of these centers is available on the Web site.
Requirements Eligible applicants must be qualified physicians or surgeons who have demonstrated an interest in clinical cancer management and who desire advanced training in clinical oncology; be accepted for training by one of the participating institutions and must have fulfilled all requirements of the institution and of the state in which the institution is located; and must have passed the ECFMG or the Test of English as a Foreign Language (TOEFL). Institutions should review applications to determine whether the applicant meets all institutional requirements and would be accepted for training; forward the completed nomination form to ACS by January 15 of the year in which the fellowship is to begin.
Restrictions Applications for training in basic cancer research will not be accepted for the award. Institutions should not submit applications for candidates they would not accept for training and must agree not to recruit fellows sponsored by the program for permanent positions.
Amount $45,000 maximum
Date(s) Application Is Due Dec 1.
Contact Extramural Grants Program, (404) 329-7558; fax: (404) 321-4669; email: grants@cancer.org
Internet http://www.cancer.org/docroot/res/content/res_5_2x_audrey_meyer_mars_international_fellowships_in_clinical_oncology.asp?sitearea=res
Sponsor American Cancer Society
1599 Clifton Rd NE
Atlanta, GA 30329-4251

ACS Cancer Control Career Development Awards for Primary Care Physicians **180**
ACS annually awards three three-year career development awards to physicians specializing in primary care (e.g., family practice, internal medicine, pediatrics, and obstetrics and gynecology). These awards are intended to encourage and assist in the development of promising candidates who will pursue academic careers in primary care specialties. It is anticipated that physicians trained under these awards will improve cancer control through involvement in primary care practice, education, and research activities related to cancer control. Awards are made for three years with progressive stipends.
Requirements Candidates must be US citizens or permanent residents; must hold an MD, DO, or equivalent degree; and must have completed residency requirements of the appropriate primary care specialty board. Candidate must hold academic rank from instructor to assistant professor and must not be more than 10 years out of training.
Restrictions Applicants may not have academic rank above that of assistant professor and must not be tenured or be the section head (or equivalent) in his/her discipline. Additionally, the applicant may not be training as a fellow at the time of the award.
Amount $50,000 first year, $55,000 second year, $60,000 third year; stipends paid in monthly installments
Date(s) Application Is Due Oct 15.
Contact Extramural Grants Department, (404) 329-7558 or (800) 875-2562; fax: (404) 321-4669; email: grants@cancer.org
Internet http://www.cancer.org/docroot/RES/content/RES_5_2x_Cancer_Control_Career_Development_Awards_for_Primary_Care_Physicians.asp?sitearea=RES
Sponsor American Cancer Society
1599 Clifton Rd NE
Atlanta, GA 30329-4251

ACS Doctoral Scholarships in Cancer Nursing **181**
Doctoral degree scholarships in cancer nursing are awarded to graduate students pursuing doctoral study in the following cancer nursing fields: research, education, administration, or clinical practice. Awards are made for up to four years.
Requirements Applicants must be currently enrolled in or applying to a doctoral degree program and have current licensure to practice as a registered nurse. American citizens or permanent residents are eligible.
Amount $15,000 per year
Date(s) Application Is Due Dec 1.
Contact Extramural Grants Department, (404) 329-7558; fax: (404) 321-4669; email: grants@cancer.org
Internet http://www.cancer.org/docroot/RES/content/RES_5_2x_Doctoral_Degree_Scholarships_in_Cancer_Nursing.asp?sitearea=RES
Sponsor American Cancer Society
1599 Clifton Rd NE
Atlanta, GA 30329-4251

ACS Institutional Research Grants 182
The IRG program provides seed money for the initiation of promising new projects by independent junior investigators so they may obtain preliminary results that will enable them to compete successfully for national research grants.
Requirements Only full-time, tenure-track JHU faculty members at the ranks of Instructor or Assistant Professor or equivalent who are within the first six years of their first independent research or faculty appointment may apply. Relevance to the cancer problem is important and must be well documented. Within this research scope, a wide breadth of research approaches will be considered; these include basic laboratory studies and clinical research.
Restrictions Senior investigators, postdoctoral fellows and junior investigators who have competitive national research grants or who have received prior support form the IRG are not eligible.
Amount $30,000 per year
Date(s) Application Is Due Mar 1.
Contact Grace Bigelow, Research Projects Administration, (410) 516-5256; fax: (410) 516-7775; email: graceb@jhu.edu
Internet http://www.cancer.org/docroot/RES/content/RES_5_2x_Institutional_Research_Grants.asp?sitearea=RES
Sponsor American Cancer Society
3100 Wyman Park Drive, Suite W400
Baltimore, MD 21211

ACS Postdoctoral Fellowships 183
Fellowships are designed to enable a new investigator to qualify for an independent career in cancer research. Postdoctoral fellowships may be made for one, two, or three years. Stipend payments are made directly to the individual, or the institution if requested, at the beginning of each month. Travel funds are paid to the individual. Institutional allowances are paid annually at the start of the grant and on the anniversary date thereafter. Awards are made for one to three years with progressive stipends. Application forms are available upon request; call (404) 329-7558.
Requirements Applicants must be citizens or permanent residents of the United States (the latter must provide notarized evidence of their legal resident alien status) and shall have been awarded a doctoral degree prior to the activation date of the grant. Application must be endorsed by applicant's mentor and the head of the department in which the training will be received. A plan of training must be formulated and agreed upon by the mentor and the applicant and described in detail in the application.
Restrictions Awards will not be made to applicants who have completed five or more years of postdoctoral training prior to the start date of the fellowship.
Amount $40,000, $42,000, and $44,000 for the first, second, and third years, respectively, and $4000 maximum per year institutional allowance
Date(s) Application Is Due Apr 1; Oct 15.
Contact Extramural Grants Department, (404) 329-7558; fax: (404) 321-4669; email: grants@cancer.org
Internet http://www.cancer.org/docroot/RES/content/RES_5_2x_Postdoctoral_Fellowships.asp?sitearea=RES
Sponsor American Cancer Society
1599 Clifton Rd NE
Atlanta, GA 30329-4251

ACS Research Scholar Grants for Beginning Investigators 184
The grants support basic, preclinical, or epidemiologic research projects initiated by investigators in the first eight years of independent cancer research careers. There is no deadline; however, a letter of intent is required to obtain applications and instructions.
Amount $72,000 maximum
Contact Research Scholar Grants for Beginning Investigators, (404) 329-7558; fax: (404) 321-4669; email: grants@cancer.org
Internet http://www.cancer.org/docroot/RES/RES_0.asp
Sponsor American Cancer Society
1599 Clifton Rd NE
Atlanta, GA 30329

ACS Research Grants for Health Services and Health Policy 185
The grants support research projects centered on health services and health policy initiated by investigators at any stage in their careers. The initial award includes 20 percent for indirect costs for up to four years, and may be renewed once for up to four years.
Amount $200,000 maximum per year
Date(s) Application Is Due Apr 1; Oct 15.
Contact Extramural Grants Department, (404) 329-7558; fax: (404) 321-4669; email: grants@cancer.org
Internet http://www.cancer.org/docroot/RES/content/RES_5_2x_Research_Scholar_Grants_For_Health_Services_and_Health_Policy_and_Outcomes_Research.asp?sitearea=RES
Sponsor American Cancer Society
1599 Clifton Rd NE
Atlanta, GA 30329-4251

ACS Research Grants in Psychosocial, Behavioral and Cancer 186
The grants support research projects focusing on the psychosocial and behavioral aspects of cancer by independent investigators at any stage in their careers. Applications are encouraged in which an individual at an early career stage is coprincipal investigator with an established researcher. The initial award supports four years of research and may be renewed once for four additional years.
Requirements Individuals must not have held an independent position for more than six years at the time the application is submitted.
Amount $400,000 maximum
Date(s) Application Is Due Apr 1; Oct 15.
Contact Extramural Grants Department, (404) 329-7558; fax: (404) 321-4669; email: grants@cancer.org
Internet http://www.cancer.org/docroot/RES/content/RES_5_2x_Research_Scholar_Grants_in_Psychological_and_Behavioral_Research_for_Beginning_and_Senior_Investigators.asp?sitearea=RES
Sponsor American Cancer Society
1599 Clifton Rd NE
Atlanta, GA 30329-4251

ACS Resident Research Scholarships 187
ACS scholarships will be awarded each year to encourage residents to pursue careers in academic surgery. Priority will be given to residents beginning full-time investigative activities, with no clinical responsibilities, for the two-year period of the scholarship. Study outside the United States or Canada is permissible. The scholarship is for the personal use of the recipient and is not to diminish or replace the usual or expected compensation; award is made directly to the scholar and not to the institution. Renewal for the second year is contingent upon acceptable progress and study protocol for the second year. Requests for application forms will not be accepted after July 1.
Requirements The applicant must have completed two postdoctoral years in an accredited surgical training program in the United States or Canada at the time the scholarship is awarded and shall not complete formal residency training before the end of the scholarship. Approval of the application is required from the administration (dean or fiscal officer) and the head of the department under whom the recipient will be studying.
Restrictions Only in exceptional circumstances will more than one ACS scholarship be granted in a single year to applicants from the same institution.
Amount $30,000 per year
Date(s) Application Is Due Sep 1.
Contact Administrator, Scholarships Division, (800) 621-4111 or (312) 202-5000; fax: (312) 202-5001
Internet http://www.facs.org/memberservices/acsresident.html
Sponsor American College of Surgeons
633 N Saint Clair St
Chicago, IL 60611-3211

ACSV Artist Fellowships 188
Artist fellowships are available in the categories of visual arts and literary arts. The deadline for visual arts is November 8 and the deadline for literary arts is November 15. Annual deadline dates may vary; contact program staff for exact dates.
Requirements Applicants must be a resident of Santa Clara County for at least one year prior to the application deadline; OR be a resident of an immediately bordering county for at least one year who can demonstrate through professional history that artistic activity has had signficant impact on residents of Santa Clara County.
Amount $4000
Date(s) Application Is Due Nov 8; Nov 15.
Contact Diem Jones, Director of Grants Program, (408) 998-2787 ext 207; fax: (408) 971-9458; email: djones@artscouncil.org
Internet http://www.artscouncil.org/af.htm
Sponsor Arts Council of Silicon Valley
4 N Second St, Ste 210
San Jose, CA 95113-1305

ACT Awards 189
The program is designed to benefit programs that aim to help middle and high school students reach their career and educational goals. The awards target programs that work with students whose circumstances and environments could keep them from continuing their education or career training. Winners receive awards in the form of ACT programs, services, consultation and resources. Awards are provided based on the benefit a program is likely to offer its defined at-risk population; overall program design; how readily it could be replicated elsewhere; and how much support a program has.
Requirements Proposed projects may be programs or studies undertaken with at-risk students in grades eight through 12 or in two- and four-year colleges and universities.
Restrictions Awards do not include salaries or stipends for recipients or other personnel, travel expenses, conference fees, tuition costs, or any types of direct expenses.
Amount $6000-$8000
Date(s) Application Is Due May 15.
Contact Director of Policy Research, (319) 337-1293; email: noethr@act.org
Internet http://www.act.org
Sponsor ACT Inc
P.O. Box 168, 500 ACT Dr
Iowa City, IA 52243-0168

ACT Summer Internship Program 190

The summer internship program is offered annually to outstanding graduate students interested in careers in testing and measurement. The eight-week program, which runs from early June through the end of July at ACT's national headquarters in Iowa City, IA, will provide interns with practical experience through direct interaction with professional and administrative staff responsible for research and development of ACT's testing programs. Internships will be offered in five categories including test development, I/O psychology, sychometric and statistical analysis, vocational psychology, and market research. Candidates may apply for more than one category, if interested and qualified. Interns selected to participate will be paid a stipend plus round-trip transportation costs. A supplemental living allowance for accompanying spouse and/or dependents is also available. Application forms are available on the Web site.
Requirements Graduate students enrolled in master's or doctoral programs in educational measurement, evaluation, mathematical and applied statistics, research, industrial/organizational psychology, and related fields are eligible. To apply, applicants must submit a completed application form, resume, a clear copy of graduate and undergraduate transcripts, and two letters of recommendation from persons who are familiar with the applicant's academic work and professional background.
Amount $5000 stipend
Date(s) Application Is Due Feb 13.
Contact Human Resources Dept, (319) 337-1763; email: working@act.org
Internet http://www.act.org/humanresources/jobs/intern.html
Sponsor American College Testing
P.O. Box 168, 500 ACT Dr
Iowa City, IA 52243-0168

ACTR/ACCELS Combined Research and Training Program 191

The program allows faculty and graduate students to conduct research in the New Independent States (NIS) in the humanities or social sciences. Awards are available for research projects lasting three to nine months. Combined research and language training programs also are available. The January deadline is for the summer, fall and academic year; the October deadline is for spring programs. Applications are available on the Web site as soon as they are available or may be obtained by contacting the program directly.
Requirements US citizens (graduate students, postdoctoral scholars, and faculty) who have the necessary background to conduct advanced research in the NIS are eligible.
Amount $5000-$25,000
Date(s) Application Is Due Jan 15; Oct 1.
Contact Research Grants Administrator, (202) 833-7522; fax: (202) 833-7523; email: general@actr.org
Internet http://www.americancouncils.org/program.asp?PageID=121&ProgramID=13
Sponsor American Council of Teachers of Russian/American Council for Collaboration in Education and Language Study
1776 Massachusetts Ave NW, Ste 700
Washington, DC 20036

Actuarial Foundation Research Grants 192

The foundation supports research that is of significant value to future endeavors of the actuarial profession. New knowledge and techniques developed in other fields, as well as enhanced applications of existing actuarial principles and techniques, that can be applied by actuaries are given priority, including those of a multidisciplinary nature. Jointly sponsored seminars and call for paper projects with or without linked symposia that promote research, as well as individual research papers, books and other projects will be considered. The Foundation is particularly interested in partnering with other organizations to promote research. The foundation does not require use of a standard proposal. Proposals are accepted at any time. Interested individuals or organizations should begin the process with a brief letter of interest.
Date(s) Application Is Due Oct 1.
Contact Grants Administrator, (847) 706-3535; fax: (847) 706-3599
Internet http://www.actuarialfoundation.org/research_edu/research.htm
Sponsor Actuarial Foundation
475 N Martingale Rd, Ste 600
Schaumburg, IL 60173-2226

ADA Career Development Awards 193

The awards assist exceptionally promising new investigators in their transition to the level of established investigators. The awards support such individuals' salary and research program for five years to enable the investigators to initiate an independent research effort that would result in sufficient accomplishments that in turn would qualify the investigators for long-term research funding. Application request forms are available on the Web site.
Requirements Applicants must hold full-time or clinical faculty positions or the equivalent at university-affiliated institutions within the United States or one of its possessions; have an MD or PhD degree, or in the case of other health professions, an appropriate advanced degree; and have only two to five years postdoctoral/postfellowship research experience. Applicants must be US citizens or permanent residents or have applied for permanent resident status and must be members of ADA's professional section.
Restrictions Time spent in residency training is not considered equivalent to research experience.
Amount $200,000 maximum per year for salary and expenses
Date(s) Application Is Due Jan 15.
Contact Research Department, (703) 299-2071; fax: (703) 549-1715; email: research@diabetes.org
Internet http://www.diabetes.org/diabetes-research/research-grant-application-forms/development-awards.jsp
Sponsor American Diabetes Association
1701 N Beauregard St
Alexandria, VA 22311

ADA Clinical Research Awards 194

The grants provide a stipend for three years for studies undertaken that involve humans directly. In vitro research on human blood or tissue samples does not qualify under this program unless there has been a major in vivo intervention (i.e., diet, drugs, exercise, etc.) and the study protocol is designed specifically to quantitate the effect of this manipulation on the tissue being examined in vitro. The funds may be used for equipment, supplies, and/or technician support. Up to $20,000 of the funds may be used as salary support for the principal investigator. Awards are made for up to three years. Application request forms are available on the Web site.
Requirements Applicants must be US citizens or permanent residents or have applied for permanent resident status, hold an MD or PhD degree (for other health professionals, an appropriate health- or science-related degree), and hold a faculty-level appointment at a university-affiliated institution within the United States or US possessions. Award recipients must be members of the ADA's professional section.
Amount $20,000-$100,000
Date(s) Application Is Due Jan 15; Jul 15.
Contact Research Department, (703) 299-2071 or (703) 549-1500; fax: (703) 549-1715; email: research@diabetes.org
Internet http://www.diabetes.org/diabetes-research/research-grant-application-forms/nationwide-research-awards.jsp
Sponsor American Diabetes Association
1701 N Beauregard St
Alexandria, VA 22311

ADA Foundation Dental Literature Grants 195

The foundation will award grants to applicants who submit competitive proposals to complete a systematic literature review on a high-priority research topic supporting evidence-based dentistry. The program focuses on available dental literature addressing four specific clinical questions. Applicants are asked to choose one of the following questions for a systematic literature review. At what frequency is dental prophylaxis effective in preventing periodontitis in individuals with and without known risk factors? Does correcting malocclusion in children and adults reduce the risk of periodontal disease? What are the clinical, biological, psychosocial, and/or economic outcomes of treating a pulpally involved (periodontally sound) single tooth through: endodontic care, extraction and implant placement, fixed partial denture, and/or extraction without implant placement? What are the longitudinal beneficial and harmful effects of endodontic services compared to extraction and implant placement? Proposals must be submitted in hard copy. Guidelines are available online.
Requirements Applicants must be affiliated with a dental school or advanced education program accredited by the Commission on Dental Accreditation, a dental specialty organization or a national dental related organization; should be knowledgeable and experienced in systematic review; have a demonstrated track record in research; and have published studies in clinical dental research.
Amount $50,000 maximum
Date(s) Application Is Due Jan 30.
Contact Lisa Barron, at (312) 440-4639; email: barronl@ada.org
Internet http://www.adafoundation.org/prof/resources/pubs/adanews/adanewsarticle.asp?articleid=1640
Sponsor American Dental Association Foundation
211 E Chicago Ave
Chicago, IL 60611-2616

ADA Medical Scholars and Physician-Scientist Training Awards 196

The goal of the program is to produce new leaders in diabetes research. The medical scholars program provides one year of research support to students in medical school; the physician-scientist award provides three years of support for the doctoral portion of an MD/PhD degree. Applications may be requested from the Web site.
Amount $30,000 Medical Scholars; $30,000 per year Physician-Scientist
Date(s) Application Is Due Jan 15.
Contact Research Department, (703) 299-2071 or (703) 549-1500; fax: (703) 549-1715; email: research@diabetes.org
Internet http://www.diabetes.org/diabetes-research/research-grant-application-forms/ADA-grant-opportunities/ADA-current-grant-opportunities.jsp
Sponsor American Diabetes Association
1701 N Beauregard St
Alexandria, VA 22311

ADA Mentor-Based Postdoctoral Fellowships 197

The purpose of this program is to support the training of scientists in an environment most conducive to beginning a career in diabetes research. An award is given to an established and active investigator in diabetes re-search for the annual stipend support

of a postdoctoral fellow to work closely with the mentor. The applicant investigator will be responsible for the selection of the qualified fellow. The term of the award is 4 years. Funding for each year will be contingent upon submission of the name and CV of a fellow by June 1 each year.
Requirements The postdoctoral fellow must have an MD or PhD degree, no more than three years of postdoctoral research experience, and cannot serve an internship or residency during the award period. There are no citizenship requirements for the fellow. The investigator must meet citizenship and employment eligibility requirements. Award recipients must be members of ADA's professional section.
Amount $45,000 maximum per year; $3000 maximum per year for laboratory supply costs; $1000 maximum for travel
Date(s) Application Is Due Jul 15.
Contact Research Department, (703) 299-2071 or (703) 549-1500; fax: (703) 549-1715; email: research@diabetes.org
Internet http://www.diabetes.org/diabetes-research/research-grant-application-forms/training-awards.jsp#medical
Sponsor American Diabetes Association
1701 N Beauregard St
Alexandria, VA 22311

ADA Minority Dental Student Scholarships **198**
Scholarships are awarded to minority students who are entering their second year of dental school. The number of scholarships awarded is dependent on funds available. Application forms are available at accredited dental schools.
Requirements Applicants must be citizens of the United States from one of the following minority groups currently underrepresented in the dental profession: Native American, African American, or Hispanic. Students selected must have been accepted by a dental school in the United States that is accredited by the Commission on Dental Accreditation. Applicants must demonstrate a minimum need of $2500 and maintain a 3.0 grade point average on a 4.0 scale.
Amount $2500 maximum per year
Date(s) Application Is Due Jul 31.
Contact Health Foundation, (312) 440-2547; fax: (312) 440-3526; email: adaf@ada.org
Internet http://www.ada.org/ada/prod/adaf/prog_scholarship_prog.asp
Sponsor ADA Endowment and Assistance Fund Inc
211 E Chicago Ave
Chicago, IL 60611

ADA Research Awards **199**
This program provides grant support to both new and established investigators. Applications will be considered in any area that is relevant to the etiology or pathophysiology of diabetes and its complications. Awards are made for up to three years for the purchase of equipment, supplies, and salary for technical assistance. Up to $20,000 may be used for the investigator's salary. Up to 15 percent of the award may be used for indirect costs.
Requirements Applicants must hold MD or PhD degrees or, in the case of other health professions, an appropriate advanced degree; must be US citizens or permanent residents or have applied for permanent resident status; and must hold full-time or clinical faculty positions or the equivalent at university-affiliated institutions within the United States or US possessions. Award recipients must be members of the ADA's professional section.
Amount $20,000-$100,000 per year for two years
Date(s) Application Is Due Jan 15; Jul 15.
Contact Magda Galindo, Research Program Manager, (703) 299-2071 or (703) 549-1500; fax: (703) 549-1715; email: mgalindo@diabetes.org. or research@diabetes.org
Internet http://www.diabetes.org/diabetes-research/research-grant-application-forms/ADA-grant-opportunities/ADA-current-grant-opportunities.jsp
Sponsor American Diabetes Association
1701 N Beauregard St
Alexandria, VA 22311

Adaptec Corporate Giving Grants **200**
The corporate contributions program is primarily directed, although not exclusively, to organizations and programs serving the communities where its employees work and live, with special emphasis in the Silicon Valley area. Funding priorities include education and research--programs that lower the drop-out rate of youth in accredited schools and colleges, address career development and preparation, job training and placement, educational scholarship assistance, and investment in higher education (primarily in engineering-related university programs); health and human services--research cures for devastating diseases, emergency shelter and subsistence for the homeless, treatment and assistance for abused spouses and children, drug and alcohol rehabilitation, and supporting organizations that strengthen youths and families; helping people enjoy life more fully through music, dance, art museums, opera, theater, and performing arts groups; and $25-$500 employee matching gifts. The Corporate Contributions Committee meets quarterly to consider requests.
Restrictions In general, Adaptec does not make contributions to any organization that does not have 501(c)3 or comparable status; individuals, except through the Adaptec Scholarship program; churches, synagogues, and other religious groups. (Requests are considered from religious-sponsored and other groups whose activities do not support any specific religious doctrine or ethnic/cultural group.); political or fraternal organizations; underwrite or assist with the development of films, television, or video/radio productions, whether for commercial, independent, or nonprofit ventures, unless such activity is in support of the computer I/O software/hardware industry and is directly related to the business of the company; tickets for raffles, contests, or other fundraising activities (except requests from major fundraising organizations that meet the defined objectives of the contribution program, such as United Way, the Silicon Valley Charity Ball and the San Jose Symphony); organizations whose primary objective is to assist, benefit, and address animal welfare or environmental issues, such as the preservation of endangered species and plants or conservation efforts to preserve the quality of wildlife, water, soil, or air; reduce debts, fund general operating expenses or capital improvement projects, or retroactively fund activities or programs that are already completed; and school sports leagues and events, and other non-educational related activities such as band, debate teams, and goodwill trips.
Amount $250-$2500
Contact Corporate Contributions, (408) 945-8600; fax: (408) 262-2533
Internet http://www.adaptec.com/en-US/company/about/_corporate/adaptec_corpcontributions.htm
Sponsor Adaptec Corporation
691 S Milpitas Blvd, MS-15
Milpitas, CA 95035

ADC Telecommunications STEM Education Grants **201**
The corporation supports science, math, technology, economic and business education, with a focus on K-12 public, charter, alternative, and culturally specific schools. Also of interest are industrial arts programs in public and private schools, public colleges, and graduate and postgraduate programs at public and private institutions.
Requirements Grants are awarded to MN nonprofits in Twin Cities Metro Area. Grants are also awarded in Marietta, Georgia, Santa Teresa, New Mexico, Raleigh, North Carolina, and Sidney, Nebraska. There is also some grantmaking outside of the United States.
Restrictions Requests for in-kind giving, general operating grants, capital grants or fundraisers including customer-sponsored charity benefit events are not considered.
Contact Bill Linder-Scholer, Executive Director ADC Foundation; (952)917-0580; email: bill.linder-scholer@adc.com
Internet http://www.adc.com/aboutadc/adcfoundation
Sponsor ADC Telecommunications
P.O. Box 1101
Minneapolis, MN 55440-1101

ADEC Agricultural Telecommunications Grants **202**
Grants will be awarded competitively to encourage the development and utilization of an agricultural communications network to facilitate and to strengthen agricultural extension, resident education, and research, and domestic and international marketing of United States agricultural commodities and products through a partnership between eligible institutions and the Department of Agriculture. The network will employ satellite and other telecommunications technology to disseminate and to share academic instruction, cooperative extension programming, agricultural research, and marketing information. Proposals will be accepted from new applicants (lead institutions) and repeat applicants (lead institutions). Proposals may be submitted electronically via the Web site, or applicants may contact the office for application materials.
Requirements Proposals are invited from accredited institutions of higher education.
Amount $50,000 maximum
Date(s) Application Is Due July 15.
Contact Dr. Janet Poley, President, (402) 472-7000; fax: (402) 472-9060; email: jpoley@unl.edu
Internet http://www.adec.edu/fed-pgms.html
Sponsor American Distance Education Consortium
P.O. Box 830952
Lincoln, NE 68583-0952

Adelle and Erwin Tomash Fellowship in the History of Information Processing **203**
The Charles Babbage Institute at the University of Minnesota is accepting applications for this fellowship to be awarded for the academic year to a graduate student whose dissertation will address some aspect of the history of computers and information processing. Topics may be chosen from the technical history of hardware or software; economic or business aspects of the information processing industry; or other topics in the social, institutional, or legal history of computing. Theses that consider technical issues in their socioeconomic context are especially encouraged. The fellowship may be held at the home academic institution, the Babbage Institute, or any other location where there are appropriate research facilities.
Requirements Priority will be given to students who have completed all requirements for the doctoral degree except the research and writing of the dissertation. Applicants should send biographical data and a research plan containing a statement and justification of the research problem, a discussion of procedure for research and writing, information on availability of research materials, and evidence of faculty support for the project. Applicants should also arrange for three letters of reference and certified transcripts of college credits to be sent directly to the institute. This fellowship has no geographical restrictions, and students from any country are eligible to apply.
Amount $10,000; $2000 maximum for tuition, fees, travel to Babbage Institute and relevant archives, and other approved research expenses

Date(s) Application Is Due Jan 15.
Contact Jeffrey Yost, Associate Director, (612) 642-5050; fax: (612) 625-8054; email: yostx003@tc..umn.edu
Internet http://www.cbi.umn.edu/research/tomash.html
Sponsor Charles Babbage Institute, University of Minnesota
211 Anderson Library
Minneapolis, MN 55455

ADHF Miles and Shirley Fiterman Basic Research Awards **204**
Two awards are offered: Hugh R. Butt Award in Hepatology or Nutrition, and the Joseph B. Kirsner Award in Gastroenterology. The awards are funded by the Miles and Shirley Fiterman Foundation and recognize excellence in clinical research in hepatology or nutrition and enterology and help support the clinical research efforts of the recipients. Each award, given annually, is provided to the awardee's institution to support his or her research. There are no application forms. A nominating letter, curriculum vita, bibliography, and five reprints of the candidate's most important work should be received by the listed deadline date for applications.
Requirements Young to midlevel investigators will be ranked above senior people whose contributions, although substantive, may have been accomplished in the distant past and whose major current activities do not include active, cutting-edge research activities.
Amount $35,000
Date(s) Application Is Due Jan 14.
Contact Grants Administrator, (301) 222-4005; fax: (301) 222-4010; email: info@fdhn.org
Internet http://www.fdhn.org/html/awards/elect_app.html
Sponsor American Digestive Health Foundation
4930 Del Ray Ave
Bethesda, MD 20814

ADHF/Elsevier Research Initiative Grant **205**
This research initiative grant is offered to investigators for support of pilot research projects in gastroenterology-related areas. The objectives of the program are to provide funds for new investigators to help them establish their research careers and to support pilot projects that represent new research directions for established investigators. The intent is to stimulate research in gastroenterology-related areas by permitting investigators to obtain new data that can ultimately provide the basis for subsequent grant applications of more substantial funding and duration. The awards may be used for salary, supplies, or equipment.
Requirements Investigators must possess an MD or PhD degree (or equivalent) and must hold faculty positions at an accredited North American institution.
Restrictions Applicants may not hold awards on a similar topic from other agencies.
Amount $25,000 per year
Date(s) Application Is Due Jan 14.
Contact Grants Administrator, (301) 222-4005; fax: (301) 222-4010; email: awards@fdhn.org
Internet http://www.fdhn.org/html/awards/elect_app.html
Sponsor American Digestive Health Foundation
4930 Del Ray Ave
Bethesda, MD 20814

Administration on Aging Alzheimer's Disease Demonstration Grants to States **206**
The purpose of this program is to develop models of assistance for persons with Alzheimer's disease and their families, and improve the responsiveness of existing home- and community-based care systems for persons with Alzheimer's disease and related disorders and their families. HHS-2005-AoA-AZ-0502
Requirements Eligibility for grant awards is limited to state agencies. Only one application per state will be accepted.
Amount $250,000-$325,000
Date(s) Application Is Due May 27.
Contact Margaret Tolson, Program Officer, (202) 357-3440; fax (202) 401-7620; email: Margaret.Tolson@aoa.hhs.gov
Internet http://www.aoa.dhhs.gov/doingbus/fundopp/fundopp.asp
Sponsor Administration on Aging
200 Independence Ave SW
Washington, DC 20201

Adoption Opportunities Project Grants and Contracts **207**
The program is intended to provide financial support for demonstration projects to improve adoption practices, eliminate barriers to adoption, and find permanent homes for children. Priority may be given to projects that are innovative, involve volunteers, demonstrate substantial private sector involvement, or serve children most in need. All projects may require a nonfederal match of at least 10 percent of total costs. The match may be contributed in cash or in-kind. Contact the agency for current priority funding areas and deadlines.
Requirements State or local agencies, public or private nonprofit organizations, child welfare or adoption agencies, universities, and child care providers are eligible for funding.
Amount $200,000-$700,000; $250,000 average
Contact Children's Bureau, Administration for Children and Families, (202) 205-8354
Internet http://www.acf.hhs.gov/programs/cb
Sponsor Administration for Children and Families
330 C Street, SW
Washington, DC 20447

Advancing Newborn Medicine Fellowship Grants **208**
The program's objectives are to promote research in the area of neonatal cardiorespiratory medicine, support the professional growth of neonatology fellows, and contribute to improvements in the medical care of hospitalized newborns. Fellows are invited to submit proposals stating a specific question to be answered, methods to be used, and type of analysis to be performed.
Requirements Proposals are accepted from individuals in accredited neonatal-perinatal medicine training programs in the United States.
Amount $7500 each
Date(s) Application Is Due Nov 30.
Contact Glen Santiago, Phase Five Communications, (888) 706-3899
Internet http://www.forestpharm.com
Sponsor Forest Pharmaceuticals Inc
909 Third Ave
New York, NY 10022

AED New Voices Fellowships **209**
The program seeks to strengthen small nonprofit organizations by supporting resident fellows who can bring a new voice to an organization and its field of work. Applications are reviewed under one of the following categories: foreign policy, peace and security; HIV/AIDS; international economic policy international human rights; migrant and refugee rights; racial justice and civil rights; and women's and reproductive rights. Awards include support for fellow's salary, fringe benefits, and to purchase a computer. Preference is given to nonprofits with budgets between $100,000 and $2 million. Applications are prepared jointly by an organization and its proposed fellow.
Requirements 501(c)3 nonprofit organizations that reflect diverse educational, cultural, and experiential backgrounds are eligible. Potential fellows should have completed an undergraduate or graduate degree or have comparable education, skills, and relevant experience.
Restrictions Groups with budgets of more than $5 million are not eligible.
Amount $100,000 average salary over two years
Date(s) Application Is Due Jan 10.
Contact Program Officer, (202) 884-8607; fax: (202) 884-8400; email: newvoice@aed.org
Internet http://www.aed.org/newvoices
Sponsor Academy for Educational Development
1825 Connecticut Ave NW, Ste 744
Washington, DC 20009-5721

AERA Dissertation Grants **210**
AERA invites education policy- and practice-related dissertation proposals using NCES, NSF, and other national data bases. Dissertation grants are available for advanced doctoral students and are intended to support the student while writing the doctoral dissertation. Dissertation topics may cover a wide range of policy- or practice-related issues. Researchers must include the analysis of data from at least one NSF or NCES data set in the dissertation. Additional large-scale nationally representative data sets may be used in conjunction with the obligatory NSF or NCES data set. If international data sets are used, the study must include US education. Minority researchers are strongly encouraged to apply. A total of two hard copies of all required materials must be submitted and received by the deadline above. Guidelines are available online.
Requirements Applicants may be US citizens, US permanent residents, or non-US citizens.
Amount $15,000 maximum
Date(s) Application Is Due Mar 1; Sep 1.
Contact Jeanie Murdock, (805) 964-5264; email: jmurdock@aera.net
Internet http://www.aera.net/grantsprogram/res_training/diss_grants/DGFly.html
Sponsor American Educational Research Association
5662 Calle Real, No 254
Goleta, CA 93117-2317

AERA Research Grants **211**
AERA invites education policy- and practice-related research proposals using NCES, NSF, and other national databases. One- and two-year research grants are available for faculty at institutions of higher education, postdoctoral researchers, and other doctoral-level researchers. Research topics may cover a wide range of policy- or practice-related issues. Researchers must include the analysis of data from at least one NSF or NCES data set in the proposed study. Successful principal investigators will consult with NCES or NSF staff regarding their proposed research projects and the handling of NCES, NSF, and other federal agency data sets pertinent to their projects. Guidelines are available online.
Requirements Applicants for may be US citizens, US permanent residents, or non-US citizens. Applicants must have received the doctoral degree by the start date of the grant.
Restrictions Institutions may not charge indirect costs on these awards.
Amount $20,000 maximum one-year projects; $35,000 maximum two-year projects

Date(s) Application Is Due Mar 1; Sep 1; Jan 8.
Contact Jeanie Murdock, (805) 964-5264; email: jmurdock@aera.net
Internet http://www.aera.net/grantsprogram/res_training/res_grants/RGFly.html
Sponsor American Educational Research Association
5662 Calle Real, No 254
Goleta, CA 93117-2317

Aerospace Postdoctoral Fellowships 212
Under this program, fellows conduct research at the NASA-Johnson Space Center and then work at the University of Houston and the University of Houston Clear Lake, where they transfer their research expertise and experiences to the academic community. Each research project is directed by a team consisting of at least one UH and/or UHCL faculty member and at least one senior research staff member of JSC. The fellowship program will enable UH/UHCL faculty to organize far stronger proposals for external support through stand alone proposals and for proposals in association with NASA-JSC area organizations. In addition, the program will stimulate publications, new intellectual property, new graduate courses, and several graduate fellowships.
Requirements Applicants must have PhD degrees and up to three years relevant experience. The program is open to US citizens and foreign nationals.
Amount $50,000 per year
Contact Aerospace Postdoctoral Fellowships, (713) 743-3524; fax: (713) 743-3589; email: dcriswell@uh.edu
Internet http://www.isso.uh.edu
Sponsor University of Houston
617 Science and Research 1, MC 5005
Houston, TX 77204

AF Doctoral Dissertation Award for Arthritis Health Professionals 213
The award provides one or two years of salary and/or research support to projects related to arthritis management and/or comprehensive patient care in rheumatology practice, research, or education. A dissertation project is preferred. Suitable studies include, but are not limited to, functional, behavioral, nutritional, occupational, or epidemiological aspects of patient care and management. Drug studies and laboratory in vitro studies are not appropriate. Application and guidelines are available online. Annual deadline dates may vary; contact program staff for exact dates.
Requirements The awards are designed for predoctoral students entering the research phase of their programs. The doctoral chairperson must approve the project. A candidate must have membership or eligibility for membership in his/her professional organization. Applicants must be US citizens or have permanent residence.
Restrictions The award does not support laboratory research.
Amount $30,000 per year
Date(s) Application Is Due Sep 1.
Contact Research Department, (404) 965-7537
Internet http://www.arthritis.org/research/ProposalCentral.asp
Sponsor Arthritis Foundation
1330 W Peachtree St, Ste 100
Atlanta, GA 30309

AF Investigator Awards 214
The purpose of the award is to provide support to physicians and scientists in research fields broadly related to arthritis for the period between completion of postdoctoral fellowship training and establishment as an independent investigator. A senior scientist familiar with the applicant's area of research should be designated as the sponsor. The sponsor and the chairperson of the relevant academic department are responsible for stating the role of the applicant within the department, promising protection of time for research activities related to the award, guaranteeing space for the investigative work, and outlining future opportunities for the applicant. Each investigator is expected to devote at least 80 percent of his/her professional time to laboratory research. Permission for US applicants to work abroad may be granted but the award may not be used for sabbatical leave. Awards will begin July 1 and will be renewed each year for a period of three years pending receipt of satisfactory evidence of progress. The awards will be paid to the sponsoring institution for stipend only, stipend plus research expenses, or research expenses only; the budget should indicate how the grant will be allocated.
Requirements Applicants must be US citizens or have permanent residence. Applicants must have completed a minimum of three and a maximum of six years postdoctoral research experience, and must hold an MD, PhD, or equivalent degree, and have demonstrated distinction and productivity in research.
Restrictions The applicant may not hold an NIH R01, NSF Grant, FIRST, Howard Hughes, Pew, VA Merit, Wellcome, Searle, Arthritis Foundation Biomedical Science Grant or Clinical Science Grant or equivalent award at the time of application. If such an award is made for a different project after the start date of the Arthritis Investigator Award, the individual may retain his/her Arthritis Foundation award. Individuals at the NIH and CDC are not eligible to apply.
Amount $75,000 annually plus $1000 institutional grant
Date(s) Application Is Due Sep 1.
Contact Research Department, (404) 965-7537; email: grantsupport@arthritis.org
Internet http://www.arthritis.org/research/ProposalCentral.asp#career
Sponsor Arthritis Foundation
1330 W Peachtree St
Atlanta, GA 30309

AF New Investigator Research for Arthritis Health Professionals 215
These research grants are to encourage PhD level health professionals who have research expertise to design and carry out innovative research projects related to the rheumatic diseases. The grant is intended to provide support for the period between completion of doctorate work and establishment as an independent investigator. The research project must be related to arthritis management and/or comprehensive patient care in rheumatology practice, research, or education. Suitable studies include, but are not limited to, functional, behavioral, nutritional, occupational, or epidemiological aspects of patient care and management. Individuals with limited research experience must apply in conjunction with a supervisor or co-investigator with demonstrated research expertise in the applicant's area of study. Awards are made for three years. Application and guidelines are available online.
Requirements Grants are designed for applicants with a PhD or equivalent doctoral degree and demonstrated research experience. These awards are meant to encourage investigators who have received a doctoral degree within the last five years. A candidate must have membership or eligibility for membership in her/his professional organization.
Restrictions Drug studies and laboratory in vitro studies are not appropriate. Individuals at the NIH and CDC are not eligible to apply. Not for laboratory research. MDs are not eligible.
Amount $50,000 annually
Date(s) Application Is Due Sep 1.
Contact Research Department, (404) 965-7636; email: grantsupport@arthritis.org
Internet http://www.arthritis.org/research/ProposalCentral.asp#grants
Sponsor Arthritis Foundation
1330 W Peachtree St
Atlanta, GA 30309

AF Physician Scientist Development Award 216
The award, which is cosponsored by the Scleroderma Foundation, is designed to enable MDs and those with an equivalent medical degree with no more than 1-1/4 years of research experience at the time of application to embark on careers in biomedical and/or clinical research related to the understanding of arthritis and the rheumatic diseases. Candidates with more than 1-1/2 years of postdegree laboratory experience must apply to the foundation's postdoctoral fellowship program. This is a two-year award that may be renewed for a third year. The stipend includes salary and fringe benefits. Application and guidelines are available online.
Requirements Only physicians with no more than 1-1/4 years of research training at the time of application are eligible. Individuals must have received an MD, DO, or equivalent medical degree from an accredited institution within the past seven years; completed training in internal medicine or pediatrics; and will have completed at least one year of specialty training as of the start date of the award. For those awards funded by the Scleroderma Foundation, applicants will have completed at least one year of specialty training in rheumatology. Applicants must be US citizens or have permanent residence.
Restrictions MD/PhDs, DO/PhDs, and PhDs are not eligible.
Amount $50,000 per year
Date(s) Application Is Due Sep 1.
Contact Research Department, (404) 965-7537; email: grantsupport@arthritis.org
Internet http://www.arthritisfoundation.org/research/ProposalCentral.asp
Sponsor Arthritis Foundation
1330 W Peachtree St
Atlanta, GA 30309

AF Postdoctoral Research Fellowships 217
The grant provides a salary stipend for MDs, DOs, PhDs, or equivalent for a three-year period. Ninety percent time must be devoted to arthritis-related research. A stipend and institutional grant are awarded. There are no citizenship requirements for this award. Application and guidelines are available online.
Requirements MDs are not eligible after six years of postdoctoral research training (or seven years in the case of a clinical training program, which includes one year in the laboratory).
Restrictions MDs are not eligible after six years of laboratory training or seven years in the case of a clinical training program that includes one year in the laboratory. PhDs are not eligible after four years of postdegree laboratory experience. Individuals at or above the assistant professor level, or those who have tenured positions, are ineligible; however, if one is promoted or establishes tenure after receiving an award, he/she may continue to receive the award for the remainder of the fellowship period.
Amount $50,000 stipend plus $500 institutional grant
Date(s) Application Is Due Sep 1.
Contact Research Department, (404) 965-7537; email: grantsupport@arthritis.org
Internet http://www.arthritis.org/research/proposalcentral.asp
Sponsor Arthritis Foundation
1330 W Peachtree St
Atlanta, GA 30309

AF Target Identifications in Lupus Grants 218
The purpose of the grants program is to fund highly meritorious and innovative research directed to the identification of targets for new therapies in the treatment of lupus. This award is open to nonprofit and industry applications from anywhere in the world. Grants

are made for two years with a possibility of renewal. Application and guidelines are available online.
Requirements Individuals with doctoral degrees (MD, PhD, DO, or equivalent) are eligible to apply. Scientific independence as evidenced by direction of a research program or a publication record or other experience that establishes scientific leadership is necessary to apply.
Amount $250,000 per year
Date(s) Application Is Due Sep 1.
Contact Research Department, (404) 965-7537; email: grantsupport@arthritis.org
Internet http://www.arthritis.org/research/ProposalCentral.asp
Sponsor Arthritis Foundation
1330 W Peachtree St
Atlanta, GA 30309

AFAR Medical Student Summer Research Training in Aging 219
The program provides eight- to 12-week scholarships for clinical geriatrics and aging research. Scholars receive training from top experts in geriatrics and/or gerontology and other disciplines such as physiology, molecular biology, neurology, and epidemiology at one of four national training centers or, for a limited number of medical schools, at their own institutions. Scholars also participate in research initiatives in basic, clinical, or health services research relevant to care of the elderly. Following the scholarship, scholars participate in aging research and/or related activities under the supervision of their home-site sponsor. Most scholars will conduct training and research during the summer months. Application and guidelines are available online.
Requirements Any allopathic or osteopathic medical student in good standing who has completed at least one year of medical school and is a US citizen or permanent resident may apply. Each student submits an application, which must be accompanied by a letter of support from an individual who knows the candidate and by a biographical sketch from the home school faculty member who has agreed to nurture the work of the scholar's geriatric career development.
Amount $1731 monthly stipend
Date(s) Application Is Due Feb 7.
Contact Grants Manager, (212) 703-9977; fax: (212) 997-0330; email: amfedaging@aol.com
Internet http://www.afar.org/grants.html
Sponsor American Federation for Aging Research
70 W 40th St
New York, NY 10018

AFAR Research Grants 220
The major goal of this program is to assist in the development of the careers of junior investigators committed to pursuing careers in the field of aging research. Of particular interest are research projects concerned with understanding the basic mechanisms of aging; projects investigating age-related diseases, especially if approached from the point of view of how basic aging processes may lead to these outcomes; and projects concerning mechanisms underlying common geriatric functional disorders, as long as these include connections to fundamental problems in the biology of aging. Examples of promising areas of research include: aging and immune function; genetic control of longevity; neurobiology and neuropathology of aging; invertebrate or vertebrate animal models; cardiovascular aging; aging and cellular stress resistance; metabolic and endocrine changes; age-related changes in cell proliferation; caloric restriction and aging; DNA repair and control of gene expression; biology of the menopause; and aging and apoptosis. Application and instruction sheet are available online.
Requirements US junior faculty, including individuals with the MD and PhD degrees, are eligible for research grant support. A typical successful applicant will be serving in his or her first or second year of a junior faculty appointment. The proposed research must be conducted at any type of nonprofit setting in the United States.
Restrictions The program does not provide support for postdoctoral fellows in the laboratory of a senior investigator; investigators who have already received major independent funding for research on aging, such as an R01 grant or a grant of equal to or greater than $100,000 from another private funding source; senior faculty, i.e., at the rank of associate professor level or higher; and projects that deal strictly with clinical problems, such as the diagnosis and treatment of disease, health outcomes, or the social context of aging. Former AFAR grant recipients are not eligible to reapply. Applicants for the Glenn/AFAR Breakthroughs in Gerontology (BIG) program cannot also submit an application for this research grant.
Amount $60,000
Date(s) Application Is Due Dec 15.
Contact Grants Manager, (212) 703-9977; fax: (212) 997-0330; email: grants@afar.org
Internet http://www.afar.org/grants.html
Sponsor American Federation for Aging Research
70 W 40th St
New York, NY 10018

AFAR/Merck Junior Investigators In Geriatric Clinical Pharmacology 221
The training program provides the opportunity for two fellows to acquire competency in clinical pharmacology, geriatrics/gerontology, and research in geriatric clinical pharmacology. Applications must be submitted by an institution on behalf of an individual candidate for the fellowship.
Requirements The candidate must be board certified or eligible in a primary specialty by July 1. Proof of board eligibility must be submitted. At the time of application, the candidate must be within three years of having completed postdoctoral or fellowship training. Previous training in geriatrics or clinical pharmacology is not required, but one or the other is highly desirable. Candidate must be a citizen or a permanent resident of the United States.
Amount $60,000 annually for two years, average
Date(s) Application Is Due Nov 3.
Contact Grants Manager, (212) 703-9977; fax: (212) 997-0330; email: grants@afar.org
Internet http://www.afar.org/grants.html
Sponsor American Federation for Aging Research
70 W 40th St
New York, NY 10018

AFAR/Paul Beeson Career Development Award 222
The award is aimed at bolstering the current and severe shortage of academic physicians who have the combination of medical, academic, and scientific training relative to caring for older people. The award provides support that can be used for the scholar's salary, additional limited support for mentors, and research expenses. Support may also be used for training expenses that will strengthen the scholar's ability to establish an independent research program. Up to 12 grants will be awarded. Guidelines are available online.
Requirements To be eligible, a candidate must have a clinical doctoral degree or its equivalent and have completed clinical training; commit at least 75 percent of his/her full-time professional effort to the goals of this award; be a US citizen, noncitizen national, or a permanent resident; and be a for-profit organization, public or private institution, unit of state and local governments, or eligible agency of the federation government.
Restrictions Ineligible individuals include current and former principal investigators on NIH research projects (R01), FIRST awards (R29), subprojects of program projects (P.O.1), or center grants (P50). Former K awardees who have completed their period of K support also are not eligible.
Amount $600,000-$800,000
Contact Grants Manager, (212) 703-9977; fax: (212) 997-0330; email: grants@afar.org
Internet http://www.afar.org/grants.html
Sponsor American Federation for Aging Research
70 W 40th St, 11th Fl
New York, NY 10018

AFB Ferdinand Torres Scholarship 223
The scholarship is awarded to a legally blind full-time undergraduate or graduate student who presents evidence of economic need. US citizens are eligible. Preference will be given to applicants residing in the New York City metropolitan area and new immigrants to the United States. Guidelines are available online.
Requirements Applicants must submit proof of legal blindess; proof of acceptance in an accredited undergraduate or graduate program; evidence of economic need; proof of US residence (e.g., telephone bill, lease, utility bill); and, for new immigrants, a description of country of origin and reason for coming to the United States.
Amount $1500
Date(s) Application Is Due Apr 30.
Contact Julie Tucker, (212) 502-7661; fax: (212) 502-7771; email: juliet@afb.net
Internet http://www.afb.org/section.asp?Documentid=1842
Sponsor American Foundation for the Blind
11 Penn Plz, Ste 300
New York, NY 10001

AFB Karen D. Carsel Memorial Scholarship 224
This scholarship is given annually to a legally blind full-time graduate student who presents evidence of economic need. Contact the foundation for an application packet. Annual deadline dates may vary; contact program staff for exact dates.
Requirements Applicant must submit application and the following information: proof of US citizenship; evidence of legal blindness; certified transcripts of grades; proof of acceptance into a full-time graduate program; evidence of economic need; three letters of reference; and a typewritten statement of no more than two double-spaced pages describing educational and personal goals, strengths, weaknesses, hobbies, achievements, information on any college financial assistance received, and how scholarship monies will be used.
Amount $500
Date(s) Application Is Due Apr 30.
Contact Julie Tucker, Executive Secretary, Information Center, (212) 502-7661; fax: (212) 502-7771; email: juliet@afb.net
Internet http://www.afb.org/info_document_view.asp?documentid=1842
Sponsor American Foundation for the Blind
11 Penn Plz, Ste 300
New York, NY 10011

AFB Rudolph Dillman Memorial Scholarship 225
Scholarships are offered to undergraduate or graduate students who are studying in the field of rehabilitation and/or education of persons who are blind or visually impaired. One of these grants is specifically for a student who meets all requirements and submits evidence of economic need.

Requirements Legally blind students are eligible. Applicants must submit proof of acceptance in an accredited undergraduate or graduate program studying in the field of rehabilitation and/or education of persons who are blind or visually impaired.
Restrictions Previous recipients are ineligible.
Amount $2500
Date(s) Application Is Due Apr 30.
Contact Brent Hopkins, Program Contact, (212) 502-7676; fax: (212) 502-7777; email: bhopkins@afb.net
Internet http://www.afb.org/info_document_view.asp?documentid=1907
Sponsor American Foundation for the Blind
11 Penn Plz, Ste 300
New York, NY 10011

AFCEA Educational Foundation Postgraduate Fellowships **226**
Fellowships of $15,000 will be awarded to full-time postgraduate students who have earned Master's degrees or the equivalent and who are currently enrolled in a doctoral degree program in electrical, electronic, chemical or communications engineering, physics, math, or computer science. The dissertation title or abstract of the specific area of research is required. The intent of the AFCEA Fellowship is to reward excellence of demonstrated effort at the doctoral level of study, rather than the potential of such excellence. Please read the requirements carefully to determine specific eligibility before submitting an application. Applications are available November through January 1.
Requirements Candidates must be US citizens and nominated by the dean of the college of engineering at any accredited university in the United States.
Amount $15,000
Date(s) Application Is Due Feb 1.
Contact Norma Corrales, Scholarships and Awards, (703) 631-6149 or (800) 336-4583 ext 6149; email: scholarship@afcea.org.
Internet http://www.afcea.org/scholarships/scholarships_details.asp?ID=7
Sponsor Armed Forces Communications and Electronics Association Educational Foundation
4400 Fair Lakes Ct
Fairfax, VA 22033

Affymetrix Corporate Contributions Grants **227**
Affymetrix makes charitable donations to nonprofit organizations through its corporate philanthropy program. The company focuses its giving in three main areas: education--programs that support science and math education, focusing on K-12 students and their teachers; ethics--organizations that help foster an ongoing public dialog about genetic-related ethics; and cancer research and advocacy--nonprofit organizations working in the areas of disease research and advocacy, with a specific emphasis on cancer. Requests are reviewed four times per year. The average grant size is approximately $2500.
Requirements 501(c)3 nonprofit organizations are eligible.
Restrictions The corporation does not provide funding for advertising journals or booklets; fundraising events such as telethons, walkathons, and races; specific performances or concerts; sporting events; endowment campaigns; film, video, television, or radio projects; grants to individuals; political causes or candidates; or organizations that practice discrimination or limit membership on the basis of race, creed, gender, age, sexual orientation, or national origin.
Contact Contributions Manager, email: outreach@affymetrix.com
Internet http://www.affymetrix.com/corporate/outreach/corporate.affx
Sponsor Affymetrix
3420 Central Expwy
Santa Clara, CA 95051

AFLAC Inc Grants **228**
The company awards grants to nonprofit organizations for cancer research, health-related projects, and community services. International contributions are determined by the company's senior officers. Submit a letter of inquiry that includes an organization description, amount requested, purpose of request, recently audited financial statement, and proof of tax-exempt status.
Requirements Nonprofit organizations are eligible.
Restrictions Grants are not made to individuals.
Contact Patsy Thomas, (706) 317-6109; fax: (706) 320-2288; email: pthomas3@aflac.com
Internet http://www.aflac.com
Sponsor AFLAC Inc
1932 Wynnton Rd
Columbus, GA 31999

AFOSR Artificial Intelligence Research Grants **229**
This program sponsors research into ways to make the best use of uncertain information; share and disseminate information; increase the accuracy, speed, and economy of the recognition and identification process; and aid the intelligence analyst. The program concentrates on research needed to develop large-scale intelligent systems that can address practical Air Force needs. To that end, means are sought to scale up those methods that work for small knowledge-based systems. To aid the information analyst in fusing information from diverse modalities, the program seeks means to combine numeric and symbolic inference methods. Research could also focus on integrating probabilistic reasoning methods with traditional formal logic methods, and perhaps with other forms of computation. Qualitative methods that will drastically simplify computation and increase performance robustness are also of interest. The program seeks to develop technology that will support decision making. To that end, research is needed to develop intelligent agents capable of gathering information, reducing data to a manageable amount of essential information, and cooperating with other agents to solve problems. Research is also needed to combine artificial intelligence methods with operations research tools to overcome inefficiencies in solving some mission-critical Air Force problems (e.g., scheduling in a distributed, dynamic environment). Intelligent tutoring is an area of increased interest to the Air Force. The focus of this effort is to develop efficient computer-mediated tools for instructional delivery both for training and tutoring, with the objective of reducing personnel needs and optimizing tutoring and training. Adaptive teaching systems that model the trainee and attempt to understand his or her responses by simulating these models is one area supported within this program. Research tasks in intelligent tutoring are linked to the Human Resource Laboratory of the Air Force Armstrong Laboratory, where the evaluation and experimentation with actual trainees occurs. Proposals are accepted at any time.
Requirements Prior to submitting an informal or formal proposal, investigators are encouraged to explore, with the program manager AFOSR's possible interest in their research ideas.
Contact Dr. Robert L. Herklotz, AFOSR/NM, (703) 696-6565; DSN: (703) 426-6565; fax: (703) 696-8450; email: robert.herklotz@afosr.af.mil
Internet http://www.afosr.af.mil/pdfs/BAA2005-1.pdf
Sponsor Air Force Office of Scientific Research
4015 Wilson Blvd, Rm 713
Arlington, VA 22203-1954

AFOSR Atomic and Molecular Physics Research Grants **230**
This program involves experimental and theoretical research on the properties and interactions of atoms and molecules and forms the basic underpinning of a large range of technological applications in navigation, guidance, communications, low- and high-altitude nuclear weapons effects phenomenology, directed energy weaponry, and lasing mechanisms. Among the topics of interest are the following: apply cooling and trapping techniques to a broad range of problems, including high-resolution spectroscopy and cold atom collisions'particularly between atoms in excited quantum states; develop high-precision techniques for navigation, guidance, and remote sensing'particularly those suited to use in an orbital environment; study and understand the evolution of cold atomic systems into ultralow-density condensed matter systems; study the formation and evolution of cold (<1 K) plasmas; study the dynamics of single, large molecules in complex systems; Study antiproton capture, confinement, transport, injection, and annihilation processes'particularly those leading to the formation and storage of anti-hydrogen; develop novel techniques for production of high-power microwaves, X-rays, and gamma rays; understand the interaction of atoms and molecules with strong fields; and study cross-sections of atmospheric species. Proposals are accepted at any time.
Requirements Scientists are encouraged to contact the program manager before submitting a formal proposal to determine whether their research interests would match existing programs.
Contact Dr. Anne Matsuura, Physics and Electronics, AFOSR/NE, (703) 696-6204; DSN: (703) 426-6204; fax: (703) 696-8481; email: anne.matsuura@afosr.af.mil
Internet http://www.afosr.af.mil/pdfs/BAA2005-1.pdf
Sponsor Air Force Office of Scientific Research
4015 Wilson Blvd, Rm 713
Arlington, VA 22203-1954

AFOSR Combustion and Diagnostic Research Grants **231**
Fundamental understanding of the physics and chemistry of multiphase turbulent reacting flows is essential for improving performance of air-breathing propulsion systems. The program is interested in innovative research proposals that use simplified configurations for experimental and theoretical investigations. Highest priority is assigned to studies of supersonic combustion, atomization and spray behavior of slurries and liquids, fuel combustion chemistry, supercritical fuel behavior in precombustion and combustion environments, and novel diagnostic methods for experimental measurements. Other topics of interest include turbulent combustion, soot formation, and interactive control. The program also seeks innovative approaches to produce reduced models of turbulent combustion. These models would improve upon current capability by producing prediction methods that are both quantitatively accurate and computationally tractable. They would address all aspects of multiphase turbulent reacting flow, including such challenging objectives as predicting the concentrations of trace pollutant and signature producing species as products of combustion. Approaches such as novel subgrid-scale models for application to large eddy simulations of subsonic and supersonic combustion are of interest. Proposals are accepted at any time.
Requirements Prior to submitting an informal or formal proposal, investigators are encouraged to explore, with the program manager, AFOSR's possible interest in their research ideas.
Contact Dr. Julian M. Tishkoff, AFOSR/NA, (703) 696-8478; DSN: 426-8478; fax: (703) 696-8451; email: julian.tishkoff@afosr.af. mil
Internet http://www.afosr.af.mil/pdfs/BAA2005-1.pdf
Sponsor Air Force Office of Scientific Research
4015 Wilson Blvd, Rm 713
Arlington, VA 22203-1954

AFOSR Defense University Research Instrumentation Program 232

This program is designed to improve the capabilities of US universities to conduct research and to educate scientists and engineers in areas important to national defense by providing funds for the acquisition of research equipment. AFOSR BAA 05-4

Requirements US higher education institutions with degree-granting programs in science, math, and engineering are eligible to apply.

Amount $60,000-$990,000 range; $207,000 average

Date(s) Application Is Due Aug 25.

Contact Douglas Glenn Holloway, (703) 696-5944; fax: (703) 696-7320; email: glenn.holloway@afosr.af.mil

Internet http://www.afosr.af.mil/docs/DURIP06BAA19May05.pdf

Sponsor Air Force Office of Scientific Research
PIE/DURIP, 875 N Randolph St, Ste 325, Rm 3112
Arlington, VA 22203

AFOSR Electromagnetics Research Grants 233

Conduct research in electromagnetics to produce conceptual descriptions of electromagnetic properties of novel materials/composites (such as photonic band gap media) and simulate their uses in various operational settings. Evaluate methods to recognize and track targets and to penetrate tree cover or other dispersive media with wide band radar (propagation of precursors for example) and design switches/transmitters to produce such pulses. Develop computational electromagnetic simulation codes that are rapid and accompanied by rigorous error estimates/controls. Proposals are accepted at any time.

Requirements Investigators are encouraged to discuss their projects with the program manager prior to submission of a proposal.

Contact Dr. Arje Nachman, Mathematics and Space Sciences, AFOSR/NM, (703) 696-8427; DSN: (703) 426-8427; fax: (703) 696-8450; email: arje.nachman@afosr.af.mil

Internet http://www.afosr.af.mil/pdfs/BAA2005-1.pdf

Sponsor Air Force Office of Scientific Research
4015 Wilson Blvd, Rm 713
Arlington, VA 22203-1954

AFOSR Metallic Materials Research Grants 234

The goal of research in metallic materials is to provide the fundamental knowledge required to develop metallic alloys for aerospace applications. Potential applications of these materials include turbine airfoils and disks, engine casings and nozzle components, rocket propulsion components, airframe and spacecraft structural components, and hypersonic vehicle skins. Research on improved metallic structural materials capable of operating with higher specific mechanical properties is encouraged. Research on new actuation/sensing alloys are also of interest. This goal will be accomplished by understanding the relationships between processing, chemistry, and structure on the one hand and properties of metallic and metallic composite materials on the other. Specific scientific topics include the development and experimental verification of theoretical and computational (atomistic) models, processing science, phase transformations, interfacial phenomena, strengthening mechanisms, plasticity, creep, fatigue, environmental effects, and fracture of structural metallic materials. Materials currently under research include lightweight structural metals, refractory metals, intermetallic alloys, amorphous alloys and their composites, and microlaminated materials. Proposals are accepted at any time.

Requirements Prior to submitting an informal or formal proposal, investigators are encouraged to explore, with the program manager, AFOSR's possible interest in their research ideas.

Contact Dr. Craig S. Hartley, AFOSR/NA, (703) 696-8523; DSN: (703) 426-8523; fax: (703) 696-8451; email: craig.hartley@afosr.af.mil

Internet http://www.afosr.af.mil/pdfs/BAA2005-1.pdf

Sponsor Air Force Office of Scientific Research
4015 Wilson Blvd, Rm 713
Arlington, VA 22203-1954

AFOSR Molecular Dynamics Research Grants 235

The objectives of this program are to understand, predict, and control the reactivity and flow of energy in molecules. This knowledge will be used in atmospheric chemistry, high-energy density material research, chemical laser research, and other chemical systems where predictive capabilities and control of chemical reactivity and energy flow at a detailed molecular level will be of importance. Areas of interest in atmospheric chemistry include the dynamics of ion-molecule reactions relevant to processes in weakly ionized plasmas in the ionosphere, gas-surface interactions in space, and reactive energy transfer processes that produce and affect radiant emissions in the upper atmosphere. Research on high-energy density matter for propulsion applications investigates novel concepts for storing chemical energy in low-molecular-weight systems, the stability of energetic molecular systems, and the storage of energetic species in cryogenic solids. Research in energy transfer and energy storage in metastable states of molecules supports an interest in new concepts for chemical lasers. Also of interest is the study of the structure, stability, and growth of metal/ceramic interfaces. Fundamental studies aimed at developing predictive capabilities for and control of chemical reactivity, bonding, and energy transfer processes are encouraged. Unsolicited proposals are welcomed at any time.

Requirements Prior to submitting an informal or formal proposal, investigators are encouraged to explore, with the program manager, AFOSR's possible interest in their research ideas.

Contact Dr. Michael R. Berman, AFOSR/NL, (703) 696-7781; DSN: (703) 426-7781; fax: (703) 696-8449; email: michael.berman@afosr.af.mil

Internet http://www.afosr.af.mil/pdfs/BAA2005-1.pdf

Sponsor Air Force Office of Scientific Research
4015 Wilson Blvd, Rm 713
Arlington, VA 22203-1954

AFOSR Optimization and Discrete Mathematics Research Grants 236

The goal of this program is to develop mathematical methods for solving large or complex problems, such as those occurring in logistics, engineering design, or strategic planning. These problems can often be formulated as mathematical programs. Therefore, research is directed at linear and nonlinear programming methods, especially when formulated for the solution of selected Air Force problems. In addition to the evolution of traditional solution methods, the program supports new algorithmic paradigms (e.g., simulated annealing, genetic algorithms). It supports research in discrete event systems, especially as it relates to Air Force transportation, manufacturing, command and control systems, and battlefield management. The program is particularly interested in the control of discrete event systems through models that combine simulation and optimization. Proposals are accepted at any time.

Requirements Prior to submitting an informal or formal proposal, investigators are encouraged to explore, with the program manager, AFOSR's possible interest in their research ideas.

Contact Dr. Neal Glassman, Mathematics and Space Sciences, AFOSR/NM, (703) 696-9548; DSN: (703) 426-9548; fax: (703) 696-8450; email: neal.glassman@afosr.af.mil

Internet http://www.afosr.af.mil/pdfs/BAA2005-1.pdf

Sponsor Air Force Office of Scientific Research
4015 Wilson Blvd, Rm 713
Arlington, VA 22203-1954

AFOSR Organic Matrix Composites Research Grants 237

This program addresses the materials science issues relating to the use of polymers in aerospace and space structures such as airframes, engine components, rocket, launch vehicles and satellites. The goal is to provide the scientific base that will lead to higher performance, more durable, and more affordable structures for Air Force applications. The approach is to address issues relating to the development of improved performance or lower cost polymer-matrix composite (PMC) systems and the processing and the utilization of these structures during deployment. Chemistry and processing of structural adhesives and polymeric precursors for ceramic and carbon-carbon structures are also within the scope of this program. Materials issues relating to all material preforms and processing leading to the end components are of interest. Examples of these include resin chemistry and formulations, prepregs processing, dry preforms, layups, and cure processes. The emphasis of the current program is to study the environmental effects on the long-term properties of polymer matrix composites. These environmental effects include a harsh processing environment (e.g., high-temperature processing), application environments (e.g., high- temperature exposure under pressurized conditions), and service environments (e.g., moisture, solvents). Research will address the chemistry and physics of the degradation mechanisms that lead to deterioration of the performance of the PMC structures. The scope will cover the matrix, reinforcement, interphase, and composite as a whole. The results of this research will lead to accurate prediction of PMC structures' service life and to alternative material systems, processing procedures, and service practices that can increase the service life of these structures. Proposals are accepted at any time.

Requirements Investigators are encouraged to discuss their projects with the program manager prior to submission of a proposal.

Contact Dr. Charles Y-C Lee, AFOSR/NL, (703) 696-7779; DSN: (703) 426-7779; fax: (703) 696-8449; email: charles.lee@afosr.af.mil

Internet http://www.afosr.af.mil/pdfs/BAA2005-1.pdf

Sponsor Air Force Office of Scientific Research
4015 Wilson Blvd, Rm 713
Arlington, VA 22203-1954

AFOSR Physical Mathematics and Applied Analysis Research Grants 238

Conduct research in physical mathematics and applied analysis to develop accurate models of physical phenomena to enhance the fidelity of simulation. Investigate the properties of coherently propagating ultrashort laser pulses (both the currently examined IR frequencies and possible extension to UV frequencies) through the air and their exploitation in areas such as electronic warfare (ancillary production of HPM), laser-guided munitions (possible propagation through obscurants), and irradiation of chem/bio clouds. Develop algorithms to simulate nonlinear optical effects within fiber lasers (with weaponization in mind) and nonlinear optical media. Study feasibility of designing reconfigureable warheads by suitable placement/timing of microdetonators as well as the operation of pulsed detonation engines. Pursue description of dynamics of internal stores released from transonic/supersonic platforms as well as the fluid dynamics accompanying curved, rotating jet turbine blades. Also the dynamics of the atmosphere near and above the tropopause with an emphasis on the understanding of turbulence and its production by topography and storms is of interest. Other areas of interest include the understanding

of chaos in circuitry such as missile guidance systems, prediction of effective properties of various composite media, advanced fracture mechanics theories, which also include thermal loading such as might be produced by exposure to a strong laser.
Requirements Prior to submitting an informal or formal proposal, investigators are encouraged to explore, with the program manager, AFOSR's possible interest in their research ideas.
Contact Dr. Arje Nachman, Mathematics and Space Sciences, AFOSR/NM, (703) 696-8427; DSN: (703) 426-8427; fax: (703) 696-8450; email: arje.nachman@afosr.af.mil
Internet http://www.afosr.af.mil/pdfs/BAA2005-1.pdf
Sponsor Air Force Office of Scientific Research
4015 Wilson Blvd, Rm 713
Arlington, VA 22203-1954

AFOSR Polymer Chemistry Research Grants **239**
The goal of this research area is to gain a better understanding of the influence of chemical structures and processing conditions on the properties and behaviors of polymeric and organic materials. Research interests include photonic polymers, polymers with interesting electronic properties, polymer blends, liquid crystals and liquid crystalline polymers, and durable coatings for aircraft and nanostructures. Proposals with innovative material concepts that will extend our understanding of the structure-property relationship of these materials and achieve significant property improvement over current state-of-the-art knowledge are sought. Research interests include creating new and improved properties, achieving reproducible properties, and addressing durability of properties during the life cycle of Air Force systems. Material concepts that can improve on the above-mentioned optical, electronic, and mechanical properties of polymers are sought. These concepts include, but are not limited to, polymer blends, liquid crystals and liquid crystalline polymers, and nanostructures. Proposals are accepted at any time.
Requirements Prior to submitting an informal or formal proposal, investigators are encouraged to explore, with the program manager, AFOSR's possible interest in their research ideas.
Contact Dr. Charles Lee, Chemistry and Life Sciences, AFOSR/NL, (703) 696-7779; DSN: (703) 426-7779; fax: (703) 696-8449; email: charles.lee@afosr.af.mil
Internet http://www.afosr.af.mil/pdfs/BAA2005-1.pdf
Sponsor Air Force Office of Scientific Research
4015 Wilson Blvd, Rm 713
Arlington, VA 22203-1954

AFOSR Quantum Electronic Solids Research Grants **240**
This program focuses on materials that exhibit cooperative quantum electronic behavior, with the primary emphasis on superconductors--and any conducting materials with surfaces that can be modified and observed through the use of scanning tunneling--and related atomic-force microscopies. The program also focuses on device concepts using these materials for electromagnetic detection and signal processing in Air Force systems. The long-standing materials aspects of the program are based on the fabrication, characterization, and electronic behavior of superconducting thin films, which ultimately can lead to the discovery of new and improved electronic circuit elements. Two main objectives are to understand the mechanisms that give rise to superconductivity in selected ceramics and to produce high-quality Josephson tunneling structures. Recently the program has been expanded to include bulk superconducting materials that can be useful in producing current-carrying wires in power applications. A continuing interest in this program is the search for new electronic device concepts that involve superconductive elements, either alone or in concert with semiconductors and normal metals; there is also interest in understanding high-power absorption in high-temperature superconducting materials at microwave frequencies. A minor aspect of this program is the inclusion of scanning probe techniques to fabricate, characterize, and manipulate atomic-, molecular-, and nanometer-scale structures, with the goal of producing a new generation of improved sensors, resulting in the ultimate miniaturization of analog and digital circuitry. Proposals are accepted at any time.
Requirements Investigators are encouraged to discuss their projects with the program manager prior to submission of a proposal.
Contact Dr. Harold Weinstock, Physics and Electronics, AFOSR/NE, (703) 696-8572; DSN: 426-8572; fax: (703) 696-8481; email: harold.weinstock@afosr.af.mil
Internet http://www.afosr.af.mil/pdfs/BAA2005-1.pdf
Sponsor Air Force Office of Scientific Research
4015 Wilson Blvd, Rm 713
Arlington, VA 22203-1954

AFOSR Semiconductor Materials Research Grants **241**
This research area is directed toward developing advanced optoelectronic and electronic materials and structures to provide improvements required for future Air Force systems. The focus is currently on growth and use of semiconductors in bulk structures, single heterostructures, quantum wells, superlattices, quantum wires, and quantum dots. Proposals are sought for significant advances in these areas, or expansion to novel application of materials such as organic polymers, amorphous, and polycrystalline materials, with estimates comparing potential improvements to present capabilities and the impact on Air Force capabilities. Wavelength ranges of interest span the spectrum from UV, visible, NIR, MWIR, FIR, and extending into the terahertz range. Also of interest are the semiconductor systems that exhibit ferromagnetism, which may lead to semiconductor spintronic devices. An understanding of these materials is important to device development. Proposals area accepted at any time.
Contact Dr. Anne Matsuura, AFOSR/NE, (703) 696-6204; DSN: (703) 426-6204; fax: (703) 696-8481; email: anne.matsuura@afosr.af.mil
Internet http://www.afosr.af.mil/pdfs/BAA2005-1.pdf
Sponsor Air Force Office of Scientific Research
4015 Wilson Blvd, Rm 713
Arlington, VA 22203-1954

AFOSR Sensory Systems Research Grants **242**
The sensory systems program pursues an understanding of biological sensing mechanisms and investigates the integration of multiple sensory systems in human perception. Emphasis is on studies that can contribute the basic science foundation needed to inform new approaches to enhance human performance. This program supports research that coordinates empirical studies with mathematical or computational modeling. The development of theoretical models is desired, in part, for their eventual application to human factors problems, such as those that arise in the design of human systems to, for example, assist spatial orientation or navigation, find, track, and manipulate objects, or respond to acoustic information from multiple, simultaneous sources. The current emphasis of this program is on the dynamic integration of multiple sensory inputs in human performance. One ongoing effort deals with the integration of auditory, visual, vestibular, and somatosensory inputs in response to non-standard gravito-inertial forces. Another deals with the coordination of head and eyes in tracking moving targets. A third effort studies several aspects of spatial audition, including sound localization, distance perception, and auditory cueing of visual search. The program is multi-disciplinary, drawing upon expertise in areas such as neurophysiology, computer and electrical engineering, biology, mathematics, and experimental psychology. Applicants are encouraged to develop collaborative relationships with scientists in the Air Force Research Laboratory. Proposals are accepted at any time.
Requirements Prior to submitting an informal or formal proposal, investigators are encouraged to explore, with the program manager, AFOSR's possible interest in their research ideas.
Contact Dr. Willard Larkin, Chemistry and Life Sciences, AFOSR/NL (703) 696-7793; DSN: (703) 426-7793; fax: (703) 696-8449; email: willard.larkin@afosr.af.mil
Internet http://www.afosr.af.mil/pdfs/BAA2005-1.pdf
Sponsor Air Force Office of Scientific Research
4015 Wilson Blvd, Rm 713
Arlington, VA 22203-1954

AFOSR Signals Communication and Surveillance Research Grants **243**
This research activity is concerned with the systematic analysis and interpretation of variable quantities in media that are intended to convey information. Communications signals and surveillance images are of special importance. Signals are physically generated, propagated through electromagnetic or other media, and recaptured for use at a receiving mechanism. Modern radar, infrared, and electro-optical sensing systems produce large quantities of raw signaling that exhibit hidden correlations, are vulnerable to distortion by noise, and retain features tied to a particular physical origin. Statistical research that treats spatial and temporal dependencies in such data is necessary to exploit the usable information within. An outstanding need in the treatment of signals is to develop resilient algorithms for data representation in fewer bits (compression), image reconstruction/enhancement, and spectral/frequency estimation in the presence of external corrupting factors. These factors can involve deliberate interference, noise, ground clutter, and multipath effects. Proposals are accepted at any time.
Requirements Prior to submitting an informal or formal proposal, investigators are encouraged to explore, with the program manager, AFOSR's possible interest in their research ideas.
Contact Dr. Jon Sjogren, AFOSR/NM, (703) 696-6564; DSN: (703) 426-6564; fax: (703) 696-8540; email: jon.sjogren@afosr.af.mil
Internet http://www.afosr.af.mil/pdfs/BAA2005-1.pdf
Sponsor Air Force Office of Scientific Research
4015 Wilson Blvd, Rm 713
Arlington, VA 22203-1954

AFOSR Software and Systems Research Grants **244**
The goal of this research program is to develop advanced computing technology to support future Air Force needs in battlespace information management. Computing research is sought to meet several challenges: control and integration of the vast amounts of information flowing through battlespace computer networks, protection of friendly information resources, and complexities in software and algorithm development in support of dynamic planning and execution control. Basic research is needed in a number of areas to build battlespace information systems of the future. For example, mathematical foundations of information fusion must be established--robust, integrated fusion architectures for handling increasing diversity of input sources are especially important. The program also is interested in foundational approaches to the specification and design of agents for network management, for information retrieval, filtering, summarizing, and for planning. For network protection, researchers will focus on determining and analyzing network security properties at all network layers and examining how to ensure that a network possesses these properties. New approaches to intrusion detection and attack recovery are also needed. Basic research that anticipates the nature of future information system attacks is critical to the survivability of these systems. In the area of software and algorithm development, we seek mathematical approaches for the specification, design, and analysis of distributed software systems. Rigorous mathematical methods,

especially those that involve aspects of timing, control, dependability, and security, will be crucial to development of future battlespace information systems. New approaches for overcoming the increasing computational complexity of these systems are essential. Proposals are accepted at any time.
Requirements Prior to submitting an informal or formal proposal, investigators are encouraged to explore, with the program manager, AFOSR's possible interest in their research ideas.
Contact Dr. Robert L. Herklotz, Mathematics and Space Sciences, AFOSR/NM, (703) 696-6565; DSN: (703) 426-6565; fax: (703) 696-8450; email: robert.herklotz@afosr.af.mil
Internet http://www.afosr.af.mil/pdfs/BAA2005-1.pdf
Sponsor Air Force Office of Scientific Research
4015 Wilson Blvd, Rm 713
Arlington, VA 22203-1954

AFOSR Space Electronics Research Grants **245**
This research program addresses Air Force requirements for advanced high-performance electronic devices. Depending upon the specific requirement, this calls for high-efficiency, greater-speed, higher-power, lower-noise, low-voltage/low-power performance, etc. Greater emphasis is given to analog devices than to digital and optoelectronic structures. Emphasis is shifting away from more traditional compound semiconductor materials, such as GaAs and InP, to emerging materials such as the wide bandgap GaN family. There is also interest in the understanding and electronic applications of so-called 'wet Al-oxides' formed by the oxidation of AlAs and related materials. The effects of radiation (natural and man made) on these and other electronic devices are important concerns. Proposals are accepted at any time.
Requirements Prior to submitting an informal or formal proposal, investigators are encouraged to explore, with the program manager, AFOSR's possible interest in their research ideas.
Contact Dr. Gerald Witt, Physics and Electronics, AFOSR/NE, (703) 696-8571; DSN: (703) 426-8571; fax: (703) 696-8481; email: gerald.witt@afosr.af.mil
Internet http://www.afosr.af.mil/pdfs/BAA2005-1.pdf
Sponsor Air Force Office of Scientific Research
4015 Wilson Blvd, Rm 713
Arlington, VA 22203-1954

AFOSR Space Power and Propulsion Research Grants **246**
Research activities fall into three areas: nonchemical orbit-raising propulsion, chemical propulsion, and plume signatures/contamination resulting from both chemical and nonchemical propulsion. Research in the first area is directed primarily at advanced space propulsion and is stimulated by the need to transfer payloads between orbits, station-keeping, and pointing. It includes studies of the sources of physical (nonchemical) energy and the mechanisms of release. Emphasis is on understanding electrically conductive flowing gases (plasmas) that serve to convert beamed or electrical energy into kinetic form. Theoretical and experimental investigations are being conducted on the phenomenon of energy coupling and the transfer of plasma flows in electrode and electrodeless systems under plasma dynamic environments. Topics of interest include characteristics of pulsed and steady-state plasmas; scaling physics; characteristics of equilibrium and non-equilibrium flowing plasma; characteristics of electrical and hydrodynamic flows; instabilities of plasma bulk and wall layers; interactions of plasma-surface, plasma-electrode, plasma-magnetic, and plasma-electric fields; losses to inert parts; characteristics of plasmas in high-magnetic fields and pressures; and plasma diagnostics (new and unique noninterfering measuring techniques). Research is sought on chemical propulsion to predict and suppress combustion instabilities in liquid rocket systems and pulsed detonation rocket engines. Topics of interest include the modeling of the coupling among unsteady flows, combustion, acoustic fields, and chemical kinetics, detonation phenomenon, modeling using novel tools such as molecular dynamics, direct simulation Monte Carlo, and hybrid approach. Proposals are accepted at any time.
Requirements Prior to submitting an informal or formal proposal, investigators are encouraged to explore, with the program manager, AFOSR's possible interest in their research ideas.
Contact Dr. Mitat Birkan, Aerospace and Materials Sciences, AFOSR/NA, (703) 696-7234; DSN: (703) 426-7234; fax: (703) 696-8451; email: mitat.birkan@afosr.af.mil
Internet Space Electronics
Sponsor Air Force Office of Scientific Research
4015 Wilson Blvd, Rm 713
Arlington, VA 22203-1954

AFOSR Space Sciences Research Grants **247**
The program's research interests include, but are not limited to, the hazards to spacecraft caused by space debris, interplanetary dust, asteroids, and comets; the structure and dynamics of the solar interior and their role in driving solar activity; the mechanism(s) responsible for heating the solar corona and accelerating it outward as the solar wind; coronal mass ejections (CMEs) and solar flares; the coupling between the solar wind, the magnetosphere, and the ionosphere; the origin and energization of magnetospheric plasma; and the triggering and temporal evolution of geomagnetic storms. By specifying the flow of mass, momentum, and energy from the sun to the earth, and by forecasting the plasma phenomena that mediate the flow of energy through space, the program's goal is to develop a global, coupled solar-terrestrial model that connects solar activity with the deposition of energy in the earth's upper atmosphere. The program also is strongly interested in advanced deep space surveillance techniques to observe and track Near Earth Objects and other physical threats to Air Force systems. In this regard, we are looking for innovative astronomical observation techniques that involve advanced image processing and/or sensor technology. Astrophysical or astronomical research and observations that investigate stellar-planetary interactions in general and physical processes occurring in the sun in particular are also of interest. Proposals are accepted at any time.
Requirements Investigators are encouraged to explore their projects with the program manager prior to submitting the proposal.
Contact Major David Byers, AFOSR/NM, (703) 696-8411; DSN: (703) 426-8411; fax: (703) 696-8450; email: david.byers@afosr.af.mil
Internet http://www.afosr.af.mil/pdfs/BAA2005-1.pdf
Sponsor Air Force Office of Scientific Research
4015 Wilson Blvd, Rm 713
Arlington, VA 22203-1954

AFOSR Structural Mechanics Research Grants **248**
The objective of this research program is to study solid mechanics fundamentals and structural principles that are necessary to ensure the integrity of current and future aerospace structures, including aircraft, missiles, and spacecraft. Proposals are sought that will lead to a fundamental understanding of the behavior of structures that are composed of current metallic materials as well as advanced composite materials. Proposals are also sought that will develop principles to predict nonlinear aerospace structural characteristics under coupled fluid, thermal, and mechanical loads. We are interested in solid mechanics principles that govern nonlinear coupled deformation and damage mechanisms that dictate anisotropic and heterogeneous medium response and structural performance. Topics such as damage localization, instability formation, homogenization, energy dissipation, and local and global response correlation are of interest. Structural nonlinear behavior and control owing to coupled mechanical, fluid, acoustic, and thermal loads are important to the design and performance prediction of aerospace systems. Fluid-structure interaction, aerothermoelasticity, and the development of intelligent materials and structures are of interest to this program. The degradation of materials and structures over long periods of service is also of interest, since current Air Force weapon systems will remain in service much longer than originally anticipated. This research includes the prediction of material degradation under combined mechanical and environmental loads, as well as the nondestructive detection and quantification of internal damage (e.g., corrosion, fatigue cracking). Proposals are accepted at any time.
Requirements Prior to submitting an informal or formal proposal, investigators are encouraged to explore, with the program manager, AFOSR's possible interest in their research ideas.
Contact Captain Clark Allred, Aerospace and Materials Sciences, AFOSR/NA (703) 696-7259; DSN: (703) 426-7259; fax: (703) 696-8451; email: clark.allred@afosr.af.mil
Internet http://www.afosr.af.mil/pdfs/BAA2005-1.pdf
Sponsor Air Force Office of Scientific Research
4015 Wilson Blvd, Rm 713
Arlington, VA 22203-1954

AFOSR Theoretical Chemistry Research Grants **249**
The major objective of the theoretical chemistry program is to develop new methods that can be utilized as predictive tools for designing new materials and improving processes important to the Air Force. These new methods can be applied to areas of interest to the Air Force including the structure and stability of molecular systems that can be used as advanced propellants; molecular reaction dynamics; and the structure and properties nanostructures and interfaces. Interest in advanced propellants is concentrated in the High Energy Density Matter (HEDM) Program, which aims to develop new propellant systems that can double the current payload capacity that can be put into orbit. Theoretical chemistry is used to predict promising energetic systems, to assess their stability, and to guide the efficient synthesis of selected candidates. These tools will help identify the most promising synthetic reaction pathways and predict the effects of condensed media effects on synthesis. This program is also seeking to identify novel energetic molecules and investigating the interactions that control or limit the stability of these systems. Particular interests in reaction dynamics include developing methods to seamlessly link electronic structure calculations with reaction dynamics, and using theory to describe and predict the details of ion-molecule reactions and electron-ion dissociative recombination processes relevant to ionospheric and space effects on Air Force systems. Interest in nanostructures and materials includes work on catalysis, surface-enhanced processes mediated by plasmon resonances, and bonding at metal-ceramic interfaces. This program also encourages the development of new methods and algorithms that take advantage of parallel computing architectures to predict properties with chemical accuracy for systems having a very large number of atoms that span multiple time and length scales. Proposals are accepted throughout the year.
Requirements Investigators are encouraged to discuss their projects with the program manager prior to submitting a proposal.
Contact Dr. Michael Berman, Chemistry and Life Sciences, AFOSR/NL, (703) 696-7781; DSN: (703) 426-7781; fax: (703) 696-8449; email: michael.berman@afosr.af.mil
Internet http://www.afosr.af.mil/pdfs/BAA2005-1.pdf
Sponsor Air Force Office of Scientific Research
4015 Wilson Blvd, Rm 713
Arlington, VA 22203-1954

AFOSR Turbulence and Rotating Flows Research Grants 250

This program seeks to advance fundamental understanding of the complex, unsteady flows occurring in gas turbine engines and to apply that understanding to the development of physically based predictive models and innovative concepts for controlling complex internal flows. The program also addresses a broader class of flow-control problems related to generic technologies such as fluid thrust vectoring, internal flow tailoring, high lift, enhanced mixing, noise and signature reduction, aero-optics, aeroacoustics, drag reduction, electronic cooling, compressor stability, heat transfer, and thermal management. Primary emphasis is placed on understanding and controlling fundamental flow processes using active flow control approaches, including the exploration of emerging microelectromechanical systems (MEMS) technology for aerodynamic measurement and control. A particular challenge is the exploration of innovative actuator concepts for fluids-based flow and flight control strategies. The program is also interested in ideas exploring frontiers in fluid mechanics relative to fundamental flow processes occurring in microscale devices and systems, and in the potential for MEMS-based approaches to the control of microscale flows relative to electronic cooling and materials-processing technology. Research contributing to the understanding of flow instabilities and the mechanisms of transition from laminar to turbulent flow in both bounded and free-shear flows is of interest--especially the receptivity of linear and nonlinear transition processes to background and imposed flow disturbances--as is the impact on flow controllability. Improved turbulence modeling approaches are sought for the prediction of flow and heat transfer in highly strained and unsteady turbulent environments (e.g., gas turbine engines). In this context, original ideas are sought for modeling turbulent transport, especially ideas for incorporating the physics of turbulence into predictive models. The program is also interested in improved subgrid models for LES methods, especially in the near-wall region. High-quality turbulent flow data relevant to the advancement of transport and subgrid models for high-Reynolds number turbulent flows are also of interest. Research that addresses fundamental flow phenomena occurring in gas turbine engines, emphasizing the roles of unsteadiness and three-dimensionality in determining the performance, stability, and heat-transfer characteristics of these internal flows, is encouraged. Active control strategies for rotating stall and surge instabilities in gas turbine engine compressors are of interest. Of particular concern is the phenomenon of unsteady flow-induced forced blade response and its impact on high-cycle fatigue of turbine engine components. Another principal concern is the prediction and control of heat transfer in gas turbines, including the effectiveness of both film-cooling and internal-cooling flows. The principal areas of interest include blade wake effects, shock impingement effects, high free-stream turbulence, stagnation-point heating, blade tip clearance flows, blade hub juncture flows, and transition heat transfer phenomena. Proposals are accepted at any time.

Requirements Prior to submitting an informal or formal proposal, investigators are encouraged to explore, with the program manager, AFOSR's possible interest in their research ideas.

Contact Dr. Thomas Beutner, AFOSR/NA, (703) 696-6961; DSN: (703) 426-6961; fax: (703) 696-8451; email: tom.beutner@afosr.af.mil

Internet http://www.afosr.af.mil/pdfs/BAA2005-1.pdf

Sponsor Air Force Office of Scientific Research
4015 Wilson Blvd, Rm 713
Arlington, VA 22203-1954

AFOSR Unsteady Aerodynamics and Hypersonics Research Grants 251

This program is focused on providing the fundamental fluid mechanics research base for future systems. Through a balance of experiments, analytical modeling approaches, and numerical simulations of the relevant flow physics, a fundamental understanding of the basic fluid flow fields associated with future complex configurations is achieved. This increased knowledge base will provide flow field prediction methods and flow control approaches that, in the short term, will reduce the weight and cost of future systems, and in the long term, will enable completely new, revolutionary vehicle designs that are unacceptable today due to aerodynamic performance constraints. Research areas of interest include understanding the basic mechanisms present in time-dependent aerodynamic flows of all types, separated flows, separation control, circulation control, and vortical flows. Low-order flow modeling approaches that lead to adaptive control methods are desired. Internal and external flow tailoring for aerodynamic shape change is of interest. Nonlinear aerostructure interaction research, including flow-control approaches for suppression of destructive flow-structure interactions, is also of interest. Aeroacoustics research, especially as it applies to airframe noise or sonic fatigue, would also be considered a part of the aerostructure interaction subthrust. A major research area of interest is high-speed boundary layers. Quiet wind tunnel research, cross-flow instability mechanisms, and the receptivity of high-speed boundary layers to external disturbances are all areas of interest. Weakly ionized flows used for high-speed vehicle drag reduction are of interest as well as secondary jet injection for high-speed flight control. Finally, the fundamental flow physics associated with the airframe integration of combined cycle propulsion systems of all types (ramjet, scramjet, PDEs) is of interest, particularly the time-dependent characteristics of the inlet and nozzle flow fields. Proposals are accepted at any time.

Requirements Prior to submitting an informal or formal proposal, investigators are encouraged to explore, with the program manager, AFOSR's possible interest in their research ideas.

Contact Dr. John Schmisseur, AFOSR/NA, (703) 696-6962; DSN: (703) 426-6962; fax: (703) 696-8451; email: john.schmisseur@afosr.af.mil

Internet http://www.afosr.af.mil/pdfs/BAA2005-1.pdf

Sponsor Air Force Office of Scientific Research
4015 Wilson Blvd, Rm 713
Arlington, VA 22203-1954

AFP Research Grants 252

The council awards annual research grants to individuals who wish to undertake research projects that enrich our knowledge of philanthropic fundraising and improve its practice. Preference will be given to research focused on Canada and the United States, regardless of where the research is based. Guidelines are available online.

Amount $10,000 maximum

Date(s) Application Is Due Mar 1; Sep 1.

Contact Awards Administrator, (703) 519-8469; fax: (703) 684-0540; email: cwilliams@afpnet.org

Internet http://www.afpnet.org/tier3_cd.cfm?folder_id=930&content_item_id=1531

Sponsor Association of Fundraising Professionals
1101 King St, Ste 700
Alexandria, VA 22314

AFP Skystone Ryan Prize for Research on Fundraising and Philanthropy 253

The award is made to the author of a published book or monograph of at least 50 pages that is based on applied or basic research in fundraising or philanthropy, and that was published by a commercial publishing house or a professional organizations during the 23 months preceding the November 1 deadline. Nominations are required by the listed application deadline.

Restrictions Articles, directories, op-ed pieces, and self-published or unpublished works will not be considered.

Amount $3000

Date(s) Application Is Due Nov 1.

Contact Prize Administrator, (800) 666-3863 or (703) 684-0410; fax: (703) 684-0540

Internet http://www.afpnet.org/tier3_cd.cfm?folder_id=891&content_item_id=1544

Sponsor Association of Fundraising Professionals
1101 King St, Ste 700
Alexandria, VA 22314

African American Heritage Grants 254

Grants are awarded to assist organizations in the preservation and promotion of historic African American properties and sites in Indiana. Awards are made on a four-to-one matching basis, funding 80% of the total project cost up to $2,500, whichever is less.

Requirements Civic groups, schools, libraries, historical societies, and other nonprofit agencies are eligible to apply for grants for organizational assistance, studies assisting in or leading to the preservation of a historic African American place, and programs promoting the preservation, interpretation, and/or visitation of a historic African American place. Contact the regional community preservation specialist that serves your community (see website for list of regional offices or contact the state headquarters office) for guidelines and forms.

Restrictions Properties must be located in Indiana.

Amount $500 - $2,500

Contact Carla Jones, Receptionist, State Headquarters; (317) 639-4534; fax: (317) 639-6734; email: info@historiclandmarks.org

Internet http://www.historiclandmarks.org/help/grants.html

Sponsor Historic Landmarks Foundation of Indiana
340 W. Michigan St.
Indianapolis, IN 46202

AFRL/NRC Resident Research Associateship (RRA) Program 255

The council administers postdoctoral and senior research awards through its associateship programs office, part of the Policy and Global Affairs Division. The programs are sponsored by 30 federal laboratories and NASA Research Centers at over 100 locations in the United States and overseas. Awards are made to doctoral level scientists and engineers who can apply their special knowledge and research talents to research areas that are of interest to them and to the host laboratories and centers. Each awardee works in collaboration with a research adviser, who is a staff member of the federal laboratory. In addition to traditional postdoctoral and senior awards, the associateship programs offer summer faculty awards, combined teaching and research awards, research management awards, opportunities in the NASA Astrobiology Institute, and international opportunities including a joint program with the Alexander von Humboldt Foundation.

Requirements Postdoctoral research associateships are awarded to US citizens and permanent residents who have held doctorates for less than five years at the time of application. Senior research associateships are awarded to individuals who have held doctorates for more than five years, have significant research experience, and are recognized internationally as experts in their specialized fields as evidenced by numerous publications in reviewed journals, invited presentations, authorship of books or book chapters, and professional society awards of international stature. US citizenship is not a requirement for senior research associateships.

Amount $36,000-$65,000 (higher for senior researchers)

Date(s) Application Is Due Feb 1; May 1; Aug 1; Nov 1.

Contact Associateship Programs, (202) 334-2760; fax: (202) 334-2759; email: rap@nas.edu

Internet http://www4.nationalacademies.org/pga/rap.nsf
Sponsor National Research Council
500 Fifth St NW
Washington, DC 20001

AFUD Student Summer Fellowships 256
Each year 10 fellowships are awarded to attract the best medical students to work in urology research laboratories. These fellowships are to be held in the summer months. A pre-approved study program and sponsor recommendation are required. Application forms may be obtained from the AFUD. Applications are available on the Web site.
Requirements Applicant must be a student at an accredited medical school in the U.S.
Amount $1000
Date(s) Application Is Due Sep 1.
Contact Anthony Caputi, Manager, Research Scholar Program, (410) 689-3990; fax: (410) 468-1808; email: anthony@afud.org
Internet http://www.afud.org/research/application/summerprogram.asp
Sponsor American Foundation for Urologic Disease
1128 N Charles St
Baltimore, MD 21201

AFUW South Australia Gilmore and Baddams Bursaries 257
The program offers a bursary to assist women to undertake and complete higher degrees at Australian universities and to encourage advanced scholarship and original research by university women. The bursary may be used for the purchase or hire of equipment, field trip or research expenses, thesis publication costs, fees, dependent care expenses incurred because of study commitments, or short-term assistance with living expenses. The bursary must be used within 12 months of the date of the award. Bursaries may be shared by two successful applicants.
Requirements Applications are invited from women who are enrolled in MA or PhD programs at Australian universities and who are Australian or overseas citizens.
Restrictions Applicants may not be in full-time paid employment or on fully paid study leave during the tenure of the bursary.
Amount $A6000 maximum each
Date(s) Application Is Due Mar 1.
Contact Suzette Jansen, Social Secretary, AFUW-SA, 08-8379-8552
Internet http://www.flinders.edu.au/womensinfo/AFUW/scholarships.html
Sponsor Australian Federation of University Women--South Australia Trust Fund
Box 16, University of Adelaide
Adelaide, South Austraila 5005 Australia

AFUW South Australia Trust Fund Coursework Bursaries 258
The program offers a bursary to assist women to undertake and complete higher degrees at Australian universities and to encourage advanced scholarship and original research by university women. The bursary may be used for the purchase or hire of equipment, field trip or research expenses, thesis publication costs, fees, dependent care expenses incurred because of study commitments, or short-term assistance with living expenses. The bursary must be used within 12 months of the date of the award. Bursaries may be shared by two successful applicants.
Requirements Applications are invited from women who are enrolled in MA programs at Australian universities and are Australian or overseas citizens.
Restrictions Applicants may not be in full-time paid employment or on fully paid study leave during the tenure of the bursary.
Amount $A3000
Date(s) Application Is Due Mar 1.
Contact Suzette Jansen, Social Secretary, AFUW-SA, 08-8379-8552
Internet http://www.flinders.edu.au/womensinfo/AFUW/scholarships.html
Sponsor Australian Federation of University Women--South Australia Trust Fund
Box 16, University of Adelaide
Adelaide, South Australia 5005 Australia

AFUW Winifred E Preedy Postgraduate Bursary 259
The program offers a bursary to assist women to undertake and complete higher degrees in dentistry or allied fields at Australian universities. The bursary may be used for the purchase or hire of equipment, field trip or research expenses, thesis publication costs, fees, dependent care expenses incurred because of study commitments, or short-term assistance with living expenses. The bursary must be used within 12 months of the date of the award. Bursaries may be shared by two successful applicants.
Requirements Applications are invited from women who are enrolled in MA or PhD programs in dentistry or a related field at Australian universities and have completed at least one year of a postgraduate degree.
Restrictions Applicants may not be in full-time paid employment or on fully paid study leave during the tenure of the bursary, nor be previous winners of the Bursary.
Amount $A5000
Date(s) Application Is Due Mar 1.
Contact Council Secretariat, 8 8303 4194; fax: 8 8303 4407
Internet http://www.adelaide.edu.au/prizes/health/dental/winifred_e_preedy_postgrad_bursary.html
Sponsor Australian Federation of University Women--South Australia Trust Fund
Box 16, University of Adelaide
Adelaide, South Austraila 5005 Australia

AGI Minority Participation Program 260
Scholarships are available for geoscience and geoscience education majors to assist with their graduate degrees. The term geoscience is used broadly to include major study in the fields of geology, geophysics, geochemistry, hydrology, meteorology, physical oceanography, planetary geology, and earth science education. Applications are available on the Web site.
Requirements Applicants must be US citizens and members of the following ethnic minority groups: African American, Hispanic, and Native American (American Indian, Eskimo, Samoan, or Hawaiian). Applicants must be enrolled in an accredited institution and must meet financial need criteria.
Amount $500-$3000
Date(s) Application Is Due Mar 1.
Contact Cindy Martinez, Project Manager, (703) 379-2480; fax: (703) 379-7563; email: cmm@agiweb.org
Internet http://www.agiweb.org/mpp/index.html
Sponsor American Geological Institute
4220 King St
Alexandria, VA 22302-1507

AGS Edward Henderson Student Award 261
The award is presented to a medical student interested in pursuing a career in geriatrics, who has demonstrated excellence in the field. The student must be nominated by one faculty member and have at least two supporting letters of nomination from other faculty. Annual deadline dates may vary; contact program staff for exact dates.
Requirements A student must have demonstrated a commitment to the field of geriatrics through leadership in areas pertinent to geriatrics; initiation of new information or programs in geriatrics; or scholarship in geriatrics through original research or reviews.
Amount $500 travel stipend to attend the annual meeting
Contact Dennise McAlpin, (212) 308-1414 ext 321; fax: (212) 832-8646; email: dmcalpin@americangeriatrics.org or info.amger@americangeriatrics.org
Internet http://www.americangeriatrics.org/news/meeting/awrdbroc.shtml#Henderson
Sponsor American Geriatrics Society
350 5th Ave, Ste 801
New York, NY 10018

AGS Foundation T. Franklin Williams Scholars Award 262
This program supports physician-scientists committed to improving the health care of older adults. The award is intended to allow individuals to initiate and ultimately sustain a career in research and education. Junior faculty members devoting 75 percent time to research are eligible to receive project support. The award must be matched. Guidelines and request for application are available online.
Requirements To be eligible, the applicant must have an MD or DO degree; and hold a full-time faculty appointment at a US academic medical institution at the level of assistant professor for no longer than four years at the time the grant becomes effective. The applicant must have at least two sponsors who are committed to providing guidance and collaboration throughout the course of the proposed project.
Amount $37,500 per year for two years
Date(s) Application Is Due Feb 28.
Contact Award Administrator, (800) 247-8779 or (212) 308-1414; fax: (212) 832-8646; email: sreinthaler@americangeriatrics.org
Internet http://www.frycomm.com/ags/Franklin_Williams/index.asp
Sponsor AGS Foundation for Health in Aging
350 Fifth Ave, Ste 801
New York, NY 10118

AGS John A. Hartford Foundation Geriatrics for Specialists Grants 263
AGS, through a program funded by the John A. Hartford Foundation, seeks proposals for specialty-specific initiatives from academic training centers to develop, initiate, and evaluate programs designed to increase education for residents in the geriatrics aspect of their disciplines. The overall project addresses the urgent need to create a structure for developing leaders in geriatrics in academic surgery and related medical specialties. The program was created to assure that specialty residency programs adopt specific learning objectives and curricula in geriatric care as part of a targeted effort to enhance residents' knowledge, skills, and attitudes relevant to care of the older patient, in order to improve dissemination of new clinical research findings in geriatrics into the surgical and medical specialties. Eight two-year grants will be awarded. Application and guidelines are available online.
Requirements Proposals must be from institutions that have well-developed academic programs in the applicant disciplines and in geriatrics. The proposal should be submitted by a member of the specialty department or division.
Amount $16,000 per year
Date(s) Application Is Due Apr 8.
Contact Grants Administrator, (212) 308-1414; fax: (212) 832-8646
Internet http://www.americangeriatrics.org/2005_GESR.shtml
Sponsor American Geriatrics Society
350 Fifth Ave, Ste 801
New York, NY 10118

AGS Student Research Award 264

An award will be given to the student presenting the most outstanding paper or poster at the AGS annual meeting. The awardee will be chosen based on originality, scientific merit, and relevance of the research. The awardee will present his/her research at the annual meeting. Annual deadline dates may vary; contact program staff for exact dates.

Requirements Students must submit an abstract of research or research in progress on the official AGS abstract form. In addition, the student's curriculum vita and a letter from the student's advisor verifying the student's contribution to the work must be provided.

Amount $500 travel stipend to attend the annual meeting

Contact Dennise McAlpin, Program Contact, (212) 308-1414 ext 321; fax: (212) 832-8646; email: dmcalpin@americangeriatrics.org or info@americangeriatrics.org

Internet http://www.americangeriatrics.org/education/geristudents/Scholarships_Awards

Sponsor American Geriatrics Society
350 Fifth Ave, Ste 801
New York, NY 10118

AGS/Merck New Investigator Awards 265

The awards, funded through an educational grant from Merck US Human Health, are given to individuals whose original research, as presented in a submitted abstract, reflects new and relevant research in geriatrics. Topics are invited in basic research, clinical investigation, clinical medicine, public health, and research in the fundamental neurosciences. Awards will be chosen based on originality, scientific merit, relevance of the research, and the applicant's overall academic accomplishments. The awards are intended, in part, to cover awardees' travel expenses to attend the AGS annual meeting. Annual deadline dates may vary; contact program staff for exact dates.

Requirements The awards are restricted to fellows in training and new and junior investigators holding an academic appointment not longer than five years postfellowship. The work reported must not have been published prior to the date of application.

Restrictions Materials presented at other national meetings will not be accepted.

Amount $1500

Contact Dennise McAlpin, (212) 308-1414; fax: (212) 832-8646; email: dmcalpin@americangeriatrics.org or info.amger@americangeriatrics.org

Internet http://www.americangeriatrics.org/news/meeting/am2004_newInvestAward.shtml

Sponsor American Geriatrics Society
350 Fifth Ave, Ste 801
New York, NY 10118

AHA Beginning Grants-in-Aid 266

Grants-in-aid promote the independent status of promising beginning scientists. Research areas broadly related to cardiovascular function and disease or stroke, or to related clinical, basic science, and public health problems are funded. All basic disciplines as well as epidemiological, community, and clinical investigations that bear on cardiovascular and stroke problems are eligible for funding. Awards are made for two years.

Requirements Applicants must have an MD, PhD, DO, or equivalent and be initiating an independent research career. Faculty up to and including assistant professor may apply. Applicants must have a full-time faculty/staff appointment at activation and must be US citizens, permanent residents, exchange visitors, temporary workers in a specialty occupation, Canadian or Mexican citizens engaging in professional activities, temporary workers with extraordinary abilities in the sciences, or students with student visas.

Amount $62,000 per year maximum

Date(s) Application Is Due Jan 5.

Contact Affiliate Research Services, (214) 706-1158; fax: (214) 706-1341; email: affil@heart.org

Internet http://www.americanheart.org/presenter.jhtml?identifier=2483

Sponsor American Heart Association--Desert Mountain Affiliate
7272 Greenville Ave
Dallas, TX 75231-4596

AHA Established Investigator Grants 267

The program supports the career development of highly promising clinician-scientists and PhDs who have recently acquired independent status by funding high quality, innovative research projects for which no previous financial support has been obtained from other granting agencies. Grants provide four-year project and salary support. At the time of award activation, the time period since applicant's first faculty appointment must be four to nine years. Approximately 50 grants will be awarded annually. Award amount includes salary/fringe and 10 percent indirect costs.

Requirements US citizens or permanent residents with the MD, PhD, DO, or equivalent doctoral degrees are eligible. Eligible applicants must have full-time faculty/staff appointment at application, up to and including Associate Professor (or equivalant). Applicant must have at least four years but no more than nine years since first full-time faculty/staff appointment.

Restrictions Current and past principal investigators are ineligible.

Amount $100,000 annually, including 10 percent indirect costs

Contact Division of Research Administration, National Center, (214) 706-1158; fax: (214) 706-1341; email: ncrp@heart.org

Internet http://www.americanheart.org/presenter.jhtml?identifier=9713

Sponsor American Heart Association
7272 Greenville Ave
Dallas, TX 75231-4596

AHA New York State Affiliate Postdoctoral Fellowships 268

Research fellowships are awarded for a two- to three-year period to help a trainee initiate a career in cardiovascular research while obtaining significant research results.

Requirements Applicants must be MDs, CVMs, PDs, or PhDs, no more than three years postdoctoral, who agree to commit full-time effort to research. US citizens, permanent residents, exchange visitors, temporary workers in specialty occupations, Canadian or Mexican citizens engaging in professional activities, temporary workers with extraordinary ability in the sciences, and those with student visas are eligible. Postdoctoral applicants who are outside the United States at time of application must provide visa documentation prior to award activation.

Restrictions The program is not intended for individuals of faculty rank.

Amount $38,000 maximum

Date(s) Application Is Due Jan 13; Nov 15.

Contact Grants Administrator, (214) 706-1158 or (214) 706-1744; fax: (214) 706-1341; email: ncrp@heart.org

Internet http://www.americanheart.org/presenter.jhtml?identifier=2402

Sponsor American Heart Association--New York State Affiliate
7272 Greenville Ave
Dallas, TX 75231-4596

AHA New York State Affiliate Scientist Development Grants 269

The purpose of the program is to help promising beginning scientists to move from completion of research training to the status of independent investigators. The focus of the research should be broadly related to CV function and disease, stroke, or to related clinical, basic science, and public health problems. The duration of the award is three years.

Requirements Eligible to apply are US citizens or permanent residents; individuals of up to and including assistant professor (or equivalent) rank at application; individuals holding MD, PhD, DO, or equivalent at application. At activation, no more than four years should have elapsed since first full-time faculty/staff appointment. At activation, applicant must have full-time faculty/staff appointment.

Restrictions At activation, applicants shall have received no prior national level grant. Awards are non-renewable.

Amount $66,000 maximum per year

Date(s) Application Is Due Jan 13.

Contact Grant Administrator, (214) 706-1158 or (214) 706-1744; fax: (214) 706-1341; email: ncrp@heart.org

Internet http://www.americanheart.org/presenter.jhtml?identifier=2402#sdg

Sponsor American Heart Association--New York State Affiliate
7272 Greenville Ave
Dallas, TX 75231-4596

AHA Postdoctoral Fellowship 270

The Pacific Mountain Affiliate focuses on services in its region, including Alaska, Arizona, Colorado, Hawaii, Idaho, Montana, New Mexico, Oregon, Washington and Wyoming. Fellowships assist postdoctoral trainees to initiate a career in cardiovascular research. Research funded is broadly related to cardiovascular function and disease, stroke, or to related clinical, basic science, and public health problems. All basic disciplines as well as epidemiological, community, and clinical investigations that bear on cardiovascular and stroke problems are funded. Awards are made for two to three years.

Requirements Applicants must be US citizens, permanent residents, exchange visitors, temporary workers in a specialty occupation, Canadian or Mexican citizens engaging in professional activities, temporary workers with extraordinary abilities in the sciences, or students with student visas. Applicants must have an MD, PhD, DO, or equivalent at the time the fellowship is activated.

Amount $40,568-$48,428

Date(s) Application Is Due Jan 10.

Contact Affiliate Research Services, (214) 706-1158, (214) 706-1744, (214) 706-1457; fax: (214) 706-1341; email: ncrp@heart.org

Internet http://www.americanheart.org/presenter.jhtml?identifier=2418

Sponsor American Heart Association--Pacific Mountain Affiliate
7272 Greenville Ave
Dallas, TX 75231-4596

AHA Predoctoral Fellowship 271

Fellowships help students initiate careers in cardiovascular research by providing research assistance and training. Research broadly related to cardiovascular function and disease, stroke or to related clinical, basic science, and public health problems will be funded. The fellowships are awarded in basic disciplines as well as epidemiological, community and clinical investigations that bear on cardiovascular and stroke problems. Awards are made for one or two years.

Requirements Predoctoral PhD, MD, DO (or equivalent) students seeking research training with a sponsor/mentor prior to embarking on a research career may apply. Applicants must be US citizens, permanent residents, exchange visitors, temporary workers in a specialty occupation, Canadian or Mexican citizens engaging in professional

activities, temporary workers with extraordinary abilities in the sciences, or students with student visas.
Restrictions An awardee may not hold another association award concurrently. No more than one fellow per sponsor will be funded. Funds may not be used to pay tuition.
Amount $24,000 maximum
Date(s) Application Is Due Jan 10.
Contact Affiliate Research Services, (214) 706-1457, (214) 706-1158, (214) 706-1744; fax: (214) 706-1341; email: ncrp@heart.org
Internet http://www.americanheart.org/presenter.jhtml?identifier=2418
Sponsor American Heart Association--Pacific Mountain Affiliate
7272 Greenville Ave
Dallas, TX 75231-4596

AHA Scientist Development Grants 272
The program supports highly promising beginning scientists in their progress toward independence and bridges the gap between completion of research training and readiness for competition as independent investigators. Grants provide four-year project and salary support. Applications may be submitted for review in the final year of a postdoctoral research fellowship or in the first four years of a faculty appointment. Peer review criteria will include originality and scientific merit of the proposed project (which cannot overlap with other funded work), prior productivity of the applicant, and evidence that the award will promote independent status for the applicant. Approximately 70 grants will be made annually. The award includes salary/fringe, project support, and 10 percent for indirect costs. The award is not renewable.
Requirements US citizens or permanent residents with the MD, PhD, DO, or equivalent doctoral degrees are eligible. Eligible applicants must have full-time faculty/staff appointment at activation, up to and including associate professor or equivalent.
Restrictions Applicants cannot hold or have held any other national award. Applicant must have no more than four years since first full-time faculty/staff appointment at activation.
Amount $65,000 maximumannually
Date(s) Application Is Due Jan 9.
Contact Division of Research Administration, National Center, (214) 706-1158, (214) 706-1744; fax: (214) 706-1341; email: ncrp@heart.org
Internet http://www.americanheart.org/presenter.jhtml?identifier=3004142
Sponsor American Heart Association
7272 Greenville Ave
Dallas, TX 75231-4596

AHAF Alzheimer's Disease Research Grants 273
AHAF funds outstanding scientists and physicians in neurobiology, physiology, pathology, molecular and developmental biology, chemistry, pharmacology, epidemiology, and surgery who are conducting research to better understand and/or treat Alzheimer's disease. Junior or senior investigators will be considered. Grants are awarded for up to two years and are renewable. Grant applications are reviewed by a scientific review committee on a competitive peer-review system.
Requirements Grants are awarded to universities, medical centers, and independent research institutions. AHAF funds grants for research at nonprofit organizations only. The principal investigator must hold the academic rank of assistant professor (or equivalent) or higher.
Restrictions Funding is not provided for overhead costs, construction, or building expenses.
Amount $300,000 maximum per year
Date(s) Application Is Due Oct 13.
Contact Sarah Barnhouse, Grants Administrator, (800) 437-2423 or (301) 948-3244; fax: (301) 258-9454; email: sbarnhouse@ahaf.org
Internet http://www.ahaf.org/alzdis/research/grants.htm
Sponsor American Health Assistance Foundation
22512 Gateway Center Drive
Clarksburg, MD 20871

AHAF Macular Degeneration Research Grants 274
The foundation awards research grants to advance study of macular degeneration. Applications are evaluated based on the scientific merit of the proposal, the feasibility of the proposed research, the potential of the research to lead to better understanding and treatment of eye diseases, and the demonstrated ability of the investigator to complete the research. Application materials are available on the Web site.
Amount $50,000 maximum per year
Date(s) Application Is Due Oct 27.
Contact Sarah Barnhouse, (800) 437-2423 or (301) 948-3244; fax: (301) 258-9454; email: sbarnhouse@ahaf.org
Internet http://www.ahaf.org/macular/research/grants.htm
Sponsor American Health Assistance Foundation
22512 Gateway Center Drive
Clarksburg, MD 20871

AHAF National Glaucoma Research Grants 275
AHAF funds outstanding scientists and physicians with expertise in cell and molecular biology, physiology, biochemistry, endocrinology, and pharmacology. Grants are awarded on the basis of scientific merit of the proposal, the relevance of the research, and the potential impact of the proposed study on better understanding and/or treatment of glaucoma. Applications are reviewed by a scientific review committee on a competitive peer-review system. AHAF is interested in receiving focused research grant applications from investigators at all stages of their careers. AHAF is particularly interested in new investigators with little or no previous grant support and established investigators with new ideas or directions for their research.
Requirements AHAF grants are awarded to universities, medical centers, and independent research institutions. AHAF provides grants for research at nonprofit organizations only.
Restrictions Grants are not made to individuals. Funding is not provided for overhead costs, construction, or building expenses.
Amount $45,000 maximum per year for up to two years
Date(s) Application Is Due Oct 11.
Contact Sarah Barnhouse, Grants Administrator, (301) 948-3244; fax: (301) 258-9454; email: sbarnhouse@ahaf.org
Internet http://www.ahaf.org/glaucoma/research/glresrch.htm
Sponsor American Health Assistance Foundation
22512 Gateway Center Drive
Clarksburg, MD 20871

AHAF National Heart Foundation Starter Grants 276
This program funds biomedical research aimed at improving the understanding and therapy of the disease process in cardiovascular diseases and stroke. Grants are intended to assist young investigators who are beginning independent research careers. Applications from investigators who are establishing careers as independent investigators in the field will be given the highest priority. Funds are awarded solely for research.
Requirements Applicants must be at the assistant professor level or its equivalent.
Restrictions Applications from senior investigators or investigators with substantial grant support will not be reviewed. AHAF funds grants for research at nonprofit organizations only.
Amount $25,000 maximum
Date(s) Application Is Due Nov 2.
Contact Sarah Barnhouse, Grants Administrator, (301) 948-3244; fax: (301) 258-9454; email: sbarnhouse@ahaf.org
Internet http://www.ahaf.org/hrtstrok/research/hsresrch.htm
Sponsor American Health Assistance Foundation
22512 Gateway Ctr Dr
Clarksburg, MD 20871

AHEPA Educational Foundation Scholarships 277
The AHEPA Educational Foundation's scholarship programs promote, encourage, induce, and advance education at the college, university, and graduate school level. A number of named undergraduate and graduate scholarships are available. Application and guidelines are available online. Annual deadline dates may vary; contact program staff for exact dates.
Amount $3000 - $5000
Date(s) Application Is Due Jun 1.
Contact AHEPA Headquarters, (202) 232-6300; fax: (202) 232-2140; email: ahepa@ahepa.org
Internet http://www.ahepa.org/educ_foundation/index.html
Sponsor American Hellenic Educational Progressive Association
1909 Q St NW, Ste 500
Washington, DC 20009

AHFMR Clinical Fellowships 278
The program is designed for highly qualified individuals who hold an M.D. or D.D.S. degree, and who anticipate undertaking a career in health related or clinical research in Alberta. The awards consist of a stipend and a research allowance. A Clinical Fellowship award is normally tenable for a maximum of 3 years. However, if the trainee is registered in a graduate program, the term may be extended.
Requirements Normally, an award will be held within the Province of Alberta; however, candidates who are Canadian citizens or permanent residents with records of outstanding performance in postgraduate training may seek research training elsewhere, if sponsored by an Alberta faculty with an expressed interest in future recruitment of the candidate. Candidates must hold an MD or DDS degree and have received a significant portion of their postgraduate training in Alberta.
Amount $20,000-$50,000
Date(s) Application Is Due Mar 1; Oct 1.
Contact Mark Taylor, Director of Grants and Awards, (780) 423-5727; fax: (780) 429-3509; email: mark.taylor@ahfmr.ab.ca
Internet http://www.ahfmr.ab.ca/grants/Clin-fellow.php
Sponsor Alberta Heritage Foundation for Medical Research
10104-103 Avenue, Suite 1500
Edmonton, Alberta T5J 4A7 Canada

AHFMR Clinical Investigators Awards 279
The Heritage Clinical Investigator Award allows highly qualified clinicians in the early stages of their careers in health research to commit the majority of their time (greater than 75%) to research. This award includes a contribution toward salary and benefits, and may also include a research allowance and funds for renovations, and relocation. In

all cases, the relevance of the applicant's proposed research to human health should be apparent. All applicants must name a mentor or group of mentors who will foster their early career development.
Requirements Canadian citizens or permanent residents of Canada who hold an MD or DDS degree, have completed all requirements for clinical specialty recognition, and qualify to hold a full-time position in a clinical department of the sponsoring institution are eligible to apply.
Amount $10,000
Date(s) Application Is Due Sep 15.
Contact Mark Taylor, Director of Grants and Awards, (780) 423-5727; fax: (780) 429-3509; email: mark.taylor@ahfmr.ab.ca
Internet http://www.ahfmr.ab.ca/grants/ClinInvest.php
Sponsor Alberta Heritage Foundation for Medical Research
10104-103 Avenue, Suite 1500
Edmonton, Alberta T5J 4A7 Canada

AHFMR Community Support Program Grants **280**
Community support program grants will provide two types of awards: Community Health Research Visiting Lecturer Awards and Community Health Research Travel Grants. The former (Community Health Research Visiting Lecturer Awards) are intended to assist Alberta's non-profit organizations in attracting outstanding health researchers to the province. The latter (Community Health Research Travel Grants) facilitate contact among health researchers in Alberta, as well as with national and international colleagues. Candidates from a wide variety of disciplines may apply as long as the purpose of the travel is to promote community health research.
Requirements The Community Health Research Visiting Lecturer Awards program is open to community organizations that are directly involved in health research. The Universities of Alberta, Calgary and Lethbridge are not eligible to apply to this program but must submit requests to the AHFMR Visiting Lecturer Program. The Community Health Research Travel Grants program is open to individuals (independent investigators) actively engaged in health research in a non-profit organization in Alberta are eligible to apply.
Restrictions University faculty are not eligible to apply for these awards.
Contact Mark Taylor, Director, (780) 423-5727; fax: (780) 429-3509; email: mark.taylor@ahfmr.ab.ca
Internet http://www.ahfmr.ab.ca/grants/commsupp.php
Sponsor Alberta Heritage Foundation for Medical Research
10104-103 Avenue, Suite 1500
Edmonton, Alberta T5J 4A7 Canada

AHFMR Dr. Lionel E. McLeod Health Research Scholarship **281**
The award enables academically superior graduate students to undertake full-time training in medical or health research. The Scholarship is tenable through the Faculty of Medicine in any area related to health including: medicine; health services research; social and behavioral sciences (sociology, anthropology, psychology, economics, or political science); quantitative and population sciences (epidemiology and biostatistics, operations research, decision sciences, or computer sciences); and the humanities (philosophy, history, or theology).
Requirements Candidates must be students at the University of Alberta, the University of Calgary, or the University of British Columbia and sponsored by Faculty of Medicine.
Amount $21,500
Contact Mark Taylor, Director of Grants and Awards, (780) 423-5727; fax: (780) 429-3509; email: mark.taylor@ahfmr.ab.ca
Internet http://www.ahfmr.ab.ca/grants/mcleod.php
Sponsor Alberta Heritage Foundation for Medical Research
10104-103 Avenue, Suite 1500
Edmonton, Alberta T5J 4A7 Canada

AHFMR Establishment and Independent Establishment Grants **282**
The two types of grants available include: Establishment Grants--AHFMR provides funds to assist reseachers (newly recruited to Alberta) in the start-up of their laboratories and/or research projects; and Independent Establishment Grants--open to new Alberta Investigators who are not candidates for Heritage personnel awards (it is understood that these investigators will commit much of their time to medical or health research). Those sponsoring investigators for these awards must notify the Foundation of their intent to do so at least four months in advance of the application deadline, and request a determination of the eligibility of the candidate. The Foundation will not accept applications for which advanced notice has not been received. There are two categories of grant funding: Operating Funds and Major Equipment Funds.
Requirements Eligibility to apply for these grants is restricted to applicants recruited to leadership positions (such as Department Head or Director of a centre, institute or division), where the recruitment is expected to stimulate the development of research in a field or discipline of interest to the Foundation.
Date(s) Application Is Due Sep 15.
Contact Mark Taylor, Director, (780) 423-5727; fax: (780) 429-3509; email: mark.taylor@ahfmr.ab.ca
Internet http://www.ahfmr.ab.ca/grants/EstabIndep.php
Sponsor Alberta Heritage Foundation for Medical Research
10104-103 Avenue, Suite 1500
Edmonton, Alberta T5J 4A7 Canada

AHFMR Fast-Track Studentships and Fellowships **283**
AHFMR will accept, at any time, applications from Alberta-based institutions for full-time Studentship or Fellowship awards for outstanding candidates currently training outside of Alberta. The fast-track program is intended to assist these institutions in recruiting highly qualified trainees to the province. Up to a maximum of 10 awards per calendar year will be awarded through the fast-track review process in each category. Applications to the program will be reviewed on a first come-first serve basis.
Requirements Applications must include a letter from the Dean/designate of the faculty indicating that the proposal for a fast-track award has been reviewed and stating why a fast-track application should be considered for the candidate in question. Please refer to the sections on Full-Time Fellowships or Full-Time Studentships for further details regarding eligibility for training awards.
Amount $20,000-$23,000 for studentships; $35,000-$50,000 for fellowships
Contact Mark Taylor, Director of Grants and Awards, (780) 423-5727; fax: (780) 429-3509; email: mark.taylor@ahfmr.ab.ca
Internet http://www.ahfmr.ab.ca/grants/fasttrack.php
Sponsor Alberta Heritage Foundation for Medical Research
10104-103 Avenue, Suite 1500
Edmonton, Alberta T5J 4A7 Canada

AHFMR Full-Time Fellowships **284**
The program is designed to enable highly qualified doctoral graduates to prepare for careers in medical or health research as independent investigators. A fellowship award will provide to the host institution funding for one year's stipend, its associated benefits, and a research allowance. Fellows may engage in teaching activities related to their research discipline a maximum of 20 percent of their time.
Requirements Candidates must have a Ph.D., M.D., D.D.S., D.V.M. or D.Pharm. degree. Normally, support will not be provided beyond 6 years after receipt of the Ph.D. degree, or beyond 8 years after receipt of the M.D., D.D.S., D.V.M. or D.Pharm. degrees.
Amount $35,000-$50,000
Date(s) Application Is Due Mar 1; Oct 1.
Contact Mark Taylor, Director of Grants and Awards, (780) 423-5727; fax: (780) 429-3509; email: mark.taylor@ahfmr.ab.ca
Internet http://www.ahfmr.ab.ca/grants/FT-fellow.php
Sponsor Alberta Heritage Foundation for Medical Research
10104-103 Avenue, Suite 1500
Edmonton, Alberta T5J 4A7 Canada

AHFMR Full-Time M.D./Ph.D. Studentships **285**
Full-Time M.D./Ph.D. Studentships are intended to provide an opportunity for exceptional candidates, who wish to pursue careers as Clinical Investigators, to study for the M.D. and the Ph.D. degrees simultaneously. AHFMR support is complementary to the formal M.D./Ph.D. programs at the University of Alberta and the University of Calgary. M.D./Ph.D. studentship awards are tenable only at an Alberta-based university.
Requirements Applicants are limited to those students that formally enter the MD/PhD program not later than the start of their second year of PhD studies at either the University of Alberta or the University of Calgary. AHFMR's offer of support is contingent on the granting of complementary stipend support from the Faculty of not less than 15% of the value of the AHFMR award, for the duration of the award. Furthermore, it is expected that the universities will undertake to provide administrative support to the offices of the coordinators of the M.D./Ph.D. programs.
Amount $20,000
Date(s) Application Is Due Mar 1; Oct 1.
Contact Mark Taylor, Director of Grants and Awards, (780) 423-5727; fax: (780) 429-3509; email: mark.taylor@ahfmr.ab.ca
Internet http://www.ahfmr.ab.ca/grants/FT-student.php#MPS
Sponsor Alberta Heritage Foundation for Medical Research
10104-103 Avenue, Suite 1500
Edmonton, Alberta T5J 4A7 Canada

AHFMR Full-Time Studentships **286**
These Studentships enable academically superior students to undertake full-time research training in the basic biomedical sciences or in clinical research. The award consists of a stipend and a research allowance. Approved uses of the research allowance include: the purchase of scientific materials, supplies and expendables; the purchase of minor equipment; computer software programs; costs for the use of libraries, or computers; costs associated with the publication of research results; travel expenses to attend scientific meetings; and purchase of books, periodicals and journals.
Requirements Candidates must have been accepted into, or be currently engaged in, a full-time, thesis-based, graduate program at an Alberta-based university in a health-related discipline leading to a Master's or doctoral degree. This award is not available to students registered in a course-based program. Normally, support will not be provided beyond 6 years of enrollment in graduate school. Candidates who have interrupted their training for parenting or other reasons and who have consequently exceeded this time limit, may apply for studentship support. In such cases, however, the candidate is advised to clearly explain the nature of his/her particular circumstances at the time of application.
Amount $20,000 plus research allowance
Date(s) Application Is Due Mar 1; Oct 1.

Contact Mark Taylor, Director of Grants and Awards, (780) 423-5727; fax: (780) 429-3509; email: mark.taylor@ahfmr.ab.ca
Internet http://www.ahfmr.ab.ca/grants/FT-student.php
Sponsor Alberta Heritage Foundation for Medical Research
10104-103 Avenue, Suite 1500
Edmonton, Alberta T5J 4A7 Canada

AHFMR Health Research Career Renewal Awards **287**
Research Career Renewal Awards allow qualified Alberta-based faculty members to obtain rigorous training in any of the following disciplines: epidemiology; biostatistics; psychosocial sciences; and clinical experimental method and design. Training must be undertaken in a center that is renowned for the quality of research and training in the particular area of study. The Career Renewal award will provide a contribution to stipend and/or a research allowance (which can be applied toward offsetting tuition costs, for example).
Requirements An Alberta-based institution must propose and sponsor the candidate (who must be a full-time faculty member) in addition to committing to provide an adequate research environment upon the trainee's return.
Date(s) Application Is Due Mar 1; Oct 1.
Contact Mark Taylor, Director of Grants and Awards, (780) 423-5727; fax: (780) 429-3509; email: mark.taylor@ahfmr.ab.ca
Internet http://www.ahfmr.ab.ca/grants/CareerAward.php
Sponsor Alberta Heritage Foundation for Medical Research
10104-103 Avenue, Suite 1500
Edmonton, Alberta T5J 4A7 Canada

AHFMR Health Research Full-Time Studentships **288**
The Full-Time Health Research Studentship program enables academically superior students to undertake full-time training in health research. The award supports training in: research on the organization and delivery of health care; technology assessment; community health; health promotion; disease prevention; and related disciplines. The Health Research Studentship consists of a stipend and a research allowance.
Requirements Candidates must have been accepted into, or be currently studying in, a full-time, thesis-based, graduate program at an Alberta-based university in a health-related discipline leading to a Master's or doctoral degree. This award is not available to students registered in a course-based program. Normally, support will not be provided beyond 6 years of enrollment in graduate school. Candidates who have interrupted their training for parenting or other reasons and who have consequently exceeded this time limit, may apply for studentship support. In such cases, the candidate is advised to clearly explain the nature of his/her particular circumstances at the time of application.
Amount $20,000 plus research allowance
Date(s) Application Is Due Mar 1; Oct 1.
Contact Mark Taylor, Director of Grants and Awards, (780) 423-5727; fax: (780) 429-3509; email: mark.taylor@ahfmr.ab.ca
Internet http://www.ahfmr.ab.ca/grants/FT-student.php#HRS
Sponsor Alberta Heritage Foundation for Medical Research
10104-103 Avenue, Suite 1500
Edmonton, Alberta T5J 4A7 Canada

AHFMR Institutional Support Program Grants **289**
AHFMR offers a variety of programs to help the members of the research community in Alberta access the most up-to-date information and technical developments in medical and health-related research. Funding for visiting scientists includes: visiting lecturer awards; Heritage visiting professorships; and Heritage visiting scientists (to or from Alberta). Funding for conferences and meetings includes: conferences and symposia; and local workshops, retreats or planning sessions.
Requirements Faculty members working in health research at the Alberta-based universities may apply. In the case of a visting professorship or scientist, the sponsoring institution must identify the candidate's special expertise, as well as the expected long-term research benefits of the visit.
Contact Mark Taylor, Director, (780) 423-5727; fax: (780) 429-3509; email: mark.taylor@ahfmr.ab.ca
Internet http://www.ahfmr.ab.ca/grants/institutional.php
Sponsor Alberta Heritage Foundation for Medical Research
10104-103 Avenue, Suite 1500
Edmonton, Alberta T5J 4A7 Canada

AHFMR Interdisciplinary Team Grants **290**
The Alberta Heritage Foundation for Medical Research (AHFMR) Interdisciplinary Team Grants Program provides opportunities for high-quality, internationally recognized teams of investigators to complete research initiatives with defined health outcomes. Funds available in this competition are to support collaborative, interdisciplinary and multi-institutional teams that address important research questions, health problems or issues in defined areas of research that are aligned with strategic research priorities of the Foundation and Alberta. The Program will provide up to $1 million per year per team for up to five years. Funding can be used for a broad range of research-related costs including research infrastructure, research operating costs, core administrative/management costs, scientific support for the team (including the costs associated with the recruitment of new investigators to the team), collaborative/linkage activity and knowledge exchange/translation activity.
Requirements Each eligible AHFMR Interdisciplinary Team Grant application will include: A Team Leader--the Team Leader must be an established researcher with proven leadership skills and experience who will act as research program director and who will assume administrative responsibility for the grant. It is expected that the Team Leader will devote a significant and appropriate portion of her/his time to these tasks. The Team Leader will have their primary academic appointment at an Alberta-based university; at least two additional independent investigators with established research track records. Teams with a nucleus of experienced investigators are encouraged to include promising new investigators as part of their group; team members who collectively have an extensive record of success, are creative and original in their approach to research and its translation, and who have experience working in research teams. The specific contribution of each team member and end-user partner, where applicable, must be described; representation from more than one research discipline and from more than one "research pillar" (i.e. biomedical; clinical science; health systems and services; and the social, cultural and other factors that affect the health of populations.); and representation from more than one Alberta-based university. Multi-institutional collaboration is strongly encouraged in this Program.
Amount $1,000,000 maximum
Date(s) Application Is Due Oct 1.
Contact Mark Taylor, Director, (780) 423-5727; fax: (780) 429-3509; email: mark.taylor@ahfmr.ab.ca
Internet http://www.ahfmr.ab.ca/grants/team_guidelines.php
Sponsor Alberta Heritage Foundation for Medical Research
10104-103 Avenue, Suite 1500
Edmonton, Alberta T5J 4A7 Canada

AHFMR Major Equipment Grants **291**
AHFMR holds an annual competition to assist Alberta's medical or health researchers in obtaining major scientific equipment (defined as equipment costing more than $10,000 per unit or setup). It is AHFMR's expectation that large requests (e.g. greater than $100,000) will include contribution from other sources. Major equipment funds may be applied toward the purchase of the equipment, as well as toward the following expenses: installation; freight; transportation; duty; sales tax; and GST.
Requirements An Alberta-based institution must sponsor applications on behalf of full-time, competitively-funded, productive faculty members.
Amount $10,000-$100,000 per unit
Date(s) Application Is Due Mar 1.
Contact Mark Taylor, Director, (780) 423-5727; fax: (780) 429-3509; email: mark.taylor@ahfmr.ab.ca
Internet http://www.ahfmr.ab.ca/grants/equipment.php
Sponsor Alberta Heritage Foundation for Medical Research
10104-103 Avenue, Suite 1500
Edmonton, Alberta T5J 4A7 Canada

AHFMR Medical or Health Scholars Investigator Grants **292**
Heritage Medical or Health Scholars are investigators who have recently completed their postdoctoral research training, and are currently seeking their first faculty-level appointments, or who are at the Heritage Population Heath Investigator or Heritage Clinical Investigator levels. Candidates must demonstrate an ability to initiate and conduct independent and collaborative research, as well as an interest and ability, or potential ability, to train future investigators. The Scholarship award includes a contribution toward salary and benefits, and may also include a research allowance and funds for renovations, and relocation.
Requirements Candidates for the Heritage Scholar award must possess a M.D., D.D.S., D.V.M., Ph.D. or equivalent qualification. Furthermore, they must be eligible to hold a full-time appointment with the sponsoring institution.
Amount $20,000
Date(s) Application Is Due Sep 15.
Contact Mark Taylor, Director, (780) 423-5727; fax: (780) 429-3509; email: mark.taylor@ahfmr.ab.ca
Internet http://www.ahfmr.ab.ca/grants/scholars.php
Sponsor Alberta Heritage Foundation for Medical Research
10104-103 Avenue, Suite 1500
Edmonton, Alberta T5J 4A7 Canada

AHFMR Medical or Health Scientist Awards **293**
The Heritage Medical or Health Scientist Award is the most senior personnel award offered by AHFMR. Heritage Scientists must be established, internationally recognized scientific leaders in their fields of study. Their stature should be apparent by: the quality of their publication records; the originality and vision of their research proposals; the quality and number of their trainees; their ability to attract and retain research grants; and the leadership qualities they exhibit locally, nationally, and internationally. The Scientist award includes a contribution toward salary and benefits, and may also include a research allowance and funds for renovations, and relocation.
Requirements Candidates for the Heritage Scientist award must possess a M.D., D.D.S., D.V.M., Ph.D. or equivalent qualification. Furthermore, they must be eligible to hold a full-time appointment with the sponsoring institution. AHFMR expects a time commitment of not less than 75% to health research activities. The department chair and the dean will designate the time expected for teaching, clinical duties, examining, and other activities.

Amount $10,000-$40,000
Date(s) Application Is Due Sep 15.
Contact Mark Taylor, Director, (780) 423-5727; fax: (780) 429-3509; email: mark.taylor@ahfmr.ab.ca
Internet http://www.ahfmr.ab.ca/grants/scientists.php
Sponsor Alberta Heritage Foundation for Medical Research
10104-103 Avenue, Suite 1500
Edmonton, Alberta T5J 4A7 Canada

AHFMR Part-Time Fellowships **294**
AHFMR Part-Time Fellowships enable highly qualified doctoral graduates to prepare for careers in medical or health research as independent investigators doing part-time research training during the regular academic year while enrolled in a full-time professional degree program in Alberta. Part-time awards will consist of a stipend only and will be pro-rated to the amount of time the candidate is prepared to commit to research. The full-time fellowship rate will be used as the basis for this calculation.
Requirements Candidates must hold a PhD and must be engaged in a professional degree program (usually the MD program).
Restrictions Part-time fellowship awards are tenable only at an Alberta-based university.
Amount $5,000-$30,000
Date(s) Application Is Due Mar 1; Oct 1.
Contact Mark Taylor, Director of Grants and Awards, (780) 423-5727; fax: (780) 429-3509; email: mark.taylor@ahfmr.ab.ca
Internet http://www.ahfmr.ab.ca/grants/PT-fellow.php
Sponsor Alberta Heritage Foundation for Medical Research
10104-103 Avenue, Suite 1500
Edmonton, Alberta T5J 4A7 Canada

AHFMR Part-Time Studentships **295**
AHFMR Part-Time Studentships enable students enrolled in a full-time professional degree program (usually the M.D. program) in Alberta to engage in part-time research training during the regular academic year. The award consists of a stipend only. Part-time students may elect to engage in full-time research during the summer; these students should contact AHFMR to request that full-time summer trainee status be implemented.
Requirements Candidates must normally have been accepted into, or be currently engaged in, a full-time graduate program at an Alberta-based university in a health-related discipline leading to a Master's or doctoral degree. It is expected that the amount of time the candidate will commit to research will not be less than the equivalent of 1 day per week, taken either as 1 full day or 2 half days.
Restrictions The award is tenable at an Alberta-based university only.
Date(s) Application Is Due Mar 1; Oct 1.
Contact Mark Taylor, Director of Grants and Awards, (780) 423-5727; fax: (780) 429-3509; email: mark.taylor@ahfmr.ab.ca
Internet http://www.ahfmr.ab.ca/grants/PT-student.php
Sponsor Alberta Heritage Foundation for Medical Research
10104-103 Avenue, Suite 1500
Edmonton, Alberta T5J 4A7 Canada

AHFMR Polaris Awards **296**
The Alberta Heritage Foundation for Medical Research (AHFMR) Polaris Award was established as a means to help Alberta universities recruit outstanding mid-career health researchers of exceptional international calibre to the province. Individuals supported via this program will be known as AHFMR Polaris Investigators. The goal of this Award is to accelerate research activity in key areas that are priorities for Albertans. AHFMR will provide up to $1 million per year per award for up to ten years. This funding is to be at least matched by the institution nominating the AHFMR Polaris Investigator. The institutional support can include funding provided from other partners including government, the private sector and non-profit agencies. It generally cannot include funding originating from standard grants and awards programs of research organizations such as CFI, CIHR, and NSERC. The first AHFMR Polaris Award will be made in 2008. It is anticipated that initially up to three awards will be available.
Requirements AHFMR Polaris Investigators must meet a number of eligibility criteria, including being: mid-career investigators with outstanding records of accomplishments in health research. Investigators active in any one (or more) of the four pillars of health research (basic, clinical, health services research, population health) are eligible for consideration; leaders who have histories of accomplishment in science and research demonstrated via executive positions in scientific societies, editorship of a prestigious journal, and invitations to speak at international conferences (they would be recognized as candidates for, or would have recently received, a major international recognition award); nominated by the University of Alberta, the University of Calgary, or the University of Lethbridge. Nominations may also be considered for individuals to be based within an Alberta Regional or Provincial Health Authority, but it is anticipated that they will have academic appointments at one of the universities as well; currently based outside Alberta and prepared to relocate to Alberta full-time for the duration of the AHFMR Polaris Award; and prepared to commit a majority of their time to research.
Amount $1,000,000
Contact Dr. Jacques Magnan, Vice President of Programs, (780) 423-5727; fax: (780) 429-3509; email: jacques.magnan@ahfmr.ab.ca
Internet http://www.ahfmr.ab.ca/grants/polaris.php
Sponsor Alberta Heritage Foundation for Medical Research
10104-103 Avenue, Suite 1500
Edmonton, Alberta T5J 4A7 Canada

AHFMR Population Health Investigator (PHI) Awards **297**
The Heritage Population Health Investigator (PHI) Award allows independent investigators in the early stages of their careers in health research to commit the majority of their time (greater than 75%) to research. This award includes a contribution toward salary and benefits, and may also include a research allowance and funds for renovations, and relocation. Potential areas of research are: quantitative and population sciences (epidemiology and biostatistics, operations research, decision sciences, and computer sciences); health services research; social and behavioural sciences (sociology, anthropology, psychology, economics, and political science); and the humanities (law, philosophy, history, and theology). In all cases, the relevance of the applicant's proposed research to human health should be apparent.
Requirements Canadian citizens or permanent residents of Canada who hold an MD or DDS degree, have completed all requirements for clinical specialty recognition, and qualify to hold a full-time position in a clinical department of the sponsoring institution are eligible to apply.
Amount $10,000
Date(s) Application Is Due Sep 15.
Contact Mark Taylor, Director of Grants and Awards, (780) 423-5727; fax: (780) 429-3509; email: mark.taylor@ahfmr.ab.ca
Internet http://www.ahfmr.ab.ca/grants/PopHealthInvest.php
Sponsor Alberta Heritage Foundation for Medical Research
10104-103 Avenue, Suite 1500
Edmonton, Alberta T5J 4A7 Canada

AHFMR Proposals for Special Initiatives **298**
AHFMR welcomes proposals for innovative initiatives that accelerate the achievement of its overall objectives. Institutions recruiting internationally-recognized researchers to lead new initiatives should consult AHFMR, if current programs are inappropriate. AHFMR will also consider proposals for pilot projects in patient or population-based research. These projects must have the potential to develop information, and the investigators must have the expertise to attract grants from other agencies. The review process and financial support for special initiatives may be shared by AHFMR and other agencies.
Restrictions Applications that are normally eligible for regular operating grants from other agencies will NOT be considered under this program.
Contact Dr. Jacques Magnan, Vice President of Programs, (780) 423-5727; fax: (780) 429-3509; email: jacques.magnan@ahfmr.ab.ca
Internet http://www.ahfmr.ab.ca/grants/initiatives.php
Sponsor Alberta Heritage Foundation for Medical Research
10104-103 Avenue, Suite 1500
Edmonton, Alberta T5J 4A7 Canada

AHFMR Research Prize **299**
The AHFMR Research Prize is intended to maintain and improve AHFMR Personnel Awards as a potent vehicle for the recruitment and retention of highly qualified, internationally competitive investigators at Alberta institutions. The Prize will be made to every eligible investigator supported by AHFMR through the AHFMR Personnel Support Programs (Population Health Investigator, Clinical Investigator, Scholar, Senior Scholar, Scientist).
Requirements To be eligible, the investigator must be currently supported by an unconditional AHFMR investigator award. Investigators receiving AHFMR Terminal support or those on Leaves of Absence are not eligible to receive the Research Prize. The Research Prize is not determined by institutional rank and salary scale. It is provided in recognition of the individual investigator's research accomplishments, and of his/her success in obtaining an AHFMR Independent Investigator award. The Research Prize is a personal prize to the recipient.
Restrictions Successful applicants for an Independent Establishment Grant are not eligible to receive the AHFMR Research Prize.
Amount $10,000-$20,000
Contact Mark Taylor, Director, (780) 423-5727; fax: (780) 429-3509; email: mark.taylor@ahfmr.ab.ca
Internet http://www.ahfmr.ab.ca/grants/resprize.php
Sponsor Alberta Heritage Foundation for Medical Research
10104-103 Avenue, Suite 1500
Edmonton, Alberta T5J 4A7 Canada

AHFMR Senior Medical or Health Scholars Investigator Grants **300**
Heritage Senior Medical or Health Scholars must have an excellent track record of independent research over several years. They are more senior than Heritage Scholars and have usually been previously supported via an external salary support award (e.g. as an AHFMR Scholar, CIHR New Investigator, or equivalent). At the time of application, candidates for a Senior Scholar Award will typically have four to six years as an independent investigator and will be appointed at either the Assistant Professor or Associate Professor level. The Senior Scholarship award includes a contribution toward

salary and benefits, and may also include a research allowance and funds for renovations, and relocation.
Requirements Candidates for the Heritage Senior Scholar award must possess a M.D., D.D.S., D.V.M., Ph.D. or equivalent qualification. Furthermore, they must be eligible to hold a full-time appointment with the sponsoring institution. AHFMR expects a time commitment of not less than 75% to health research activities. The department chair and the dean will designate the time expected for teaching, clinical duties, examining, and other activities.
Amount $30,000 maximum
Date(s) Application Is Due Sep 15.
Contact Mark Taylor, Director, (780) 423-5727; fax: (780) 429-3509; email: mark.taylor@ahfmr.ab.ca
Internet http://www.ahfmr.ab.ca/grants/seniorscholars.php
Sponsor Alberta Heritage Foundation for Medical Research
10104-103 Avenue, Suite 1500
Edmonton, Alberta T5J 4A7 Canada

Ahmanson and Getty Postdoctoral Fellowships **301**
Theme-based, residential fellowships are awarded for periods of two consecutive academic quarters for participation in the interdisciplinary, cross-cultural programs of the Center for 17th- & 18th-Century Studies/William Andrews Clark Memorial Library. The theme for each academic year is announced the preceding fall. An organized research unit of the University of California, the center provides a forum for the discussion of central issues in the study of the 17th and 18th centuries, facilitates research and publication, and encourages the creation of programs that advance understanding of this time period. The William Andrews Clark Memorial Library, which is administered by the center, is known for its collections on 17th- and 18th-century Britain, Oscar Wilde and the 1890s, the history of printing, and certain aspects of Western Americana. Application materials are available upon request.
Requirements Scholars who have received a Ph.D. in the last six years and are engaged in research pertaining to the announced theme are eligible to apply. Fellows are expected to make a substantive contribution to the Center's workshops and seminars. Awards are for one full academic year in residence at the Clark Library.
Amount $35,000 stipend
Date(s) Application Is Due Feb 1.
Contact Fellowship Coordinator, (310) 206-8552; fax: (310) 206-8577; email: c1718cs@humnet.ucla.edu
Internet http://www.humnet.ucla.edu/humnet/c1718cs/Postd.htm#AhmGet
Sponsor Center for 17th- & 18th-Century Studies
310 Royce Hall, UCLA
Los Angeles, CA 90095-1404

AHRQ Assessment of Quality Improvement Strategies in Health Care **302**
The projects undertaken as a result of this RFA will analyze the relative utility and costs of various approaches to health care quality improvement. The fundamental long-term goal of this effort is to strengthen the evidence base underlying the choice of strategies to employ when attempting to improve the quality of clinical care. Studies should focus on comparing improvement efforts that target those areas where the greatest improvements in health and functional status can occur, reliable and valid quality measures exist, and a variety of strategies are being employed. Partnerships between academic and other research organizations with existing health care quality improvement efforts through established mechanisms such as Peer Review Organizations (PROs), Quality Improvement Organizations (QIOs), purchaser groups, health plans, and accrediting bodies are required under this RFA. Special preference will be accorded to applications from investigators not recently or currently funded as principal investigators of an AHCPR grant for research on quality improvement strategies. RFA: HS-99-002
Requirements Applications may be submitted by public or private nonprofit organizations. For-profit entities may participate as members of consortia or subcontractors if the applicant is nonprofit.
Restrictions Organizations described in section 501(c)4 of the Internal Revenue Code that engage in lobbying are not eligible.
Amount $5000-$2.8 million; $310,000 average
Contact Mable Lam, Grants Management Officer, (301) 427-1448
Internet http://www.grants.nih.gov/grants/guide/rfa-files/RFA-HS-99-002.html
Sponsor Agency for Healthcare Research and Quality
2101 E Jefferson St
Rockville, MD 20852

AHRQ Centers for Education and Research on Therapeutics (CERTS) Grants **303**
CERTs is a three-year program that will support demonstration centers. These centers will evaluate and develop options and methods, and conduct and perform pilot studies. Studies will consist of state-of-the-art clinical, health services, or laboratory research to increase awareness of the benefits, risks and effectiveness of new uses, existing uses, or combined uses of therapeutics. This demonstration program seeks new and more effective ways to develop, translate, and disseminate objective information on therapeutics to health care providers and other decision makers to improve practice. In addition, CERTs may selectively develop protocols and possibly undertake pilot studies on the comparative cost effectiveness and safety of medical products. This will be accomplished with data on appropriate therapeutic usage and outcomes; and the identification and prevention of medical errors and adverse effects. The long-term goal of the program will be to improve the quality of care while reducing costs. RFA: HS-99-004
Requirements Applications may be submitted by public or private nonprofit organizations. For-profit organizations may participate as members of consortia or subcontractors if the applicant is nonprofit.
Restrictions Organizations described in section 501(c)4 of the Internal Revenue Code that engage in lobbying are not eligible.
Amount $5000-$2.8 million; $310,000 average
Contact Mable Lam, Grants Management Officer, (301) 427-1447
Internet http://www.grants.nih.gov/grants/guide/rfa-files/RFA-HS-99-004.html
Sponsor Agency for Healthcare Research and Quality
2101 E Jefferson St, Executive Office Ctr
Rockville, MD 20852

AHRQ Centers of Excellence for Patient Safety Research and Practice **304**
The purpose of this program is to support the development of multidisciplinary research teams to build the knowledge base on the scope and impact of medical errors; identify the root causes of threats to patient safety and effective system approaches to prevent the occurrence of errors; study the effectiveness of various interventions to capture information on medical errors; and evaluate the outcomes of promising interventions in a variety of healthcare settings. A letter of intent is requested by January 3; full application is due January 24. Annual deadlines may vary; contact program staff for exact dates.
Requirements Applications may be submitted by domestic, both public and private, nonprofit organizations; units of state and local governments; and eligible agencies of the federal government.
Restrictions Foreign institutions are not eligible to apply.
Amount $5000-$2.8 million; $310,000 average
Date(s) Application Is Due Jan 3; Jan 24.
Contact Mable Lam, Grants Management Officer, (301) 427-1447
Internet http://grants.nih.gov/grants/guide/rfa-files/RFA-HS-01-002.html
Sponsor Agency for Healthcare Research and Quality
2101 E Jefferson St
Rockville, MD 20852

AHRQ Health Care Access, Quality, and Insurance for Low-Income Children Grants **305**
AHCPR and the David and Lucile Packard Foundation invite applications for cooperative agreements to conduct research that will generate information useful to purchasers and designers of health insurance and health care delivery systems for low-income children. Specifically, answers are sought to the policy question: How do features of US health care insurance and delivery systems improve health care access and quality for low-income children, particularly racial and ethnic minority children or those with special health care needs? Studies will examine how the features of US insurance programs and the organization of the health care delivery systems associated with these programs affect access to services and the quality of care received by low-income children. Studies will fall into one of two categories: those examining the impact on low-income children enrolled in these insurance programs (enrollee impact), and those examining the impact on a low-income community's health care delivery system and all the children that it serves (community impact). Applicants may propose research that falls into one or both of these categories. Care should be taken not to replicate the work of other major health care studies. Application kits are available at most institutional offices of sponsored research and may be obtained from the Division of Extramural Outreach and Information Resources, Office of Extramural Research, National Institutes of Health, 6701 Rockledge Drive, MSC 7910, Bethesda, MD 20892-7910, telephone (301) 435-0714, email: Grantsinfo@nih.gov. RFA: HS-99-005
Requirements Applications may be submitted by domestic and foreign, public and private nonprofit organizations.
Restrictions For-profit organizations are not eligible as applicants, but may participate as members of consortia or as subcontractors. Organizations described in section 501(c)4 of the Internal Revenue Code that engage in lobbying are not eligible to receive grant/cooperative agreement awards.
Amount $5000-$2.8 million; $310,000 average
Contact Mable Lam, Grants Management Officer, (301) 427-1447
Internet http://www.grants.nih.gov/grants/guide/rfa-files/RFA-HS-99-005.html
Sponsor Agency for Healthcare Research and Quality
2101 E Jefferson St, Executive Office Ctr
Rockville, MD 20852

AHRQ Independent Scientist Award **306**
This program provides support for newly independent scientists who can demonstrate a need for a period of intensive research focus. This award is intended to foster the development of outstanding scientists and enable them to expand their potential to make significant contributions to their field of research. Applications that focus on developing the careers of investigators who will study minority, child, and older adult health services research with the above interests are strongly encouraged. PA: PAR-99-164
Requirements The candidate must have a clinical or research doctoral degree and must be no more than five years out of the latest research training experience. In addition,

at the time of award, the candidate will preferably either be playing a key role on a major ongoing peer-reviewed research project or be receiving independent peer-reviewed research support. Alternatively, the candidate can demonstrate potential excellence by having completed a research training experience through a nationally recognized, peer-reviewed, postdoctoral research program or individual grant. The candidate must also be willing to spend a minimum of 75 percent effort conducting research and research career development during the award, and institutional support for this time allocation must be clear. Lastly, the candidate must demonstrate that the requested period of research focus will foster his/her career as a highly productive investigator in the indicated field of research.
Amount Up to $75,000 annually, plus associated fringe benefits.
Contact Grants Administrator, Division of Research Education, (301) 594-1449; email: Training@ahcpr.gov
Internet http://grants.nih.gov/grants/guide/pa-files/PAR-99-164.html
Sponsor Agency for Healthcare Research and Quality
2101 E Jefferson St
Rockville, MD 20852

AHRQ Mentored Clinical Scientist Development Award **307**
This award provides support for the development of outstanding research scientists and specialized study support for trained professionals who are committed to a career in research and have the potential to develop into independent investigators. Because of the focus on progression to independence, the prospective candidate should propose a period of study and development consistent with his/her needs, and previous research or clinical experience. PA: PA-00-010
Requirements Candidates must have a clinical doctoral degree, have identified a mentor with extensive research experience, and be willing to spend a minimum of 75 percent of full-time professional effort conducting research and developing a research career during the award. The candidate must demonstrate that the requested period of research focus will foster his/her career as a highly productive scientist in the indicated field of research. Applications may be submitted on behalf of candidates by domestic, nonfederal public or private nonprofit organizations, including medical, dental, public health, or nursing schools or other institutions of higher education. Candidates must be US citizens or noncitizen nationals, or must have been lawfully admitted for permanent residence and possess an Alien Registration Receipt Card (I-151 or I-551) or some other verification of legal admission as a permanent resident.
Restrictions Individuals on temporary or student visas and organizations described in section 501(c)4 of the Internal Revenue Code that engage in lobbying are not eligible.
Amount Up to $75,000 annually plus associated fringe benefits.
Contact Office of Research Review, Education, and Policy, (301) 594-1452; email: Training@ahcpr.gov
Internet http://grants.nih.gov/grants/guide/pa-files/PA-00-010.html
Sponsor Agency for Healthcare Research and Quality
2101 East Jefferson St
Rockville, MD 20852

AHRQ Translating Research into Practice Grants **308**
AHCPR invites applications to conduct research related to implementing evidence-based tools and information in diverse health care settings among practitioners caring for diverse populations. Applications are sought for studies that apply innovative strategies for implementing evidence-based tools and information and demonstrate improved clinical practice and sustained practitioner behavior change. Evidence-based tools and information include findings from rigorously conducted research and from clinical practice guidelines, algorithms, treatment protocols, practice parameters, quality indicators, and continuous quality improvement initiatives that are developed using a systematic approach to evidence synthesis. AHCPR is especially interested in studies that implement AHCPR-supported, evidence-based tools and information, including Patient Outcome Research Team (P.O.RT) and other research findings; AHCPR-supported clinical practice guideline recommendations; and evidence reports and technology assessments produced by the AHCPR Evidence-based Practice Centers. The goal of this RFA is to improve the translation and use of research findings and evidence-based tools by developing and validating innovative principles, methods, and tools that work in diverse settings, populations, and payment systems. Applicants are encouraged to form public-private partnerships or consortia, such as between academic and other research organizations and health plans and purchasers, to perform this research. Such partnerships may help to more quickly translate research findings into actual practice settings.
Requirements Applications may be submitted by public or private nonprofit organizations. For-profit organizations may participate as members of consortia or subcontractors if the applicant is nonprofit.
Restrictions Organizations described in section 501(c)4 of the Internal Revenue Code that engage in lobbying are not eligible.
Amount $2 million maximum total for the first year for four to six grants
Contact Dr. Harold Goldstein, Division of Services and Intervention Research, NIMH (6001 Executive Blvd, Bethesda, MD 20892), (301) 443-3747; fax: (301) 443-4045; email: goharold@nih.gov; Joan Metcalfe, Grants Management Specialist, (301) 594-1841
Internet http://www.grants.nih.gov/grants/guide/rfa-files/RFA-HS-99-003.html
Sponsor Agency for Healthcare Research and Quality
2101 E Jefferson St, Executive Office Ctr
Rockville, MD 20852

AHRQ Understanding and Eliminating Minority Health Disparities **309**
The purpose of this program is to conduct research on racial and ethnic disparities in health that are amenable to improvements in health services. Projects funded under this RFA will build on previous research that has identified disparities in access to, and utilization, quality and outcomes of health care services and the excess burdens of illness and death for African Americans, Hispanic Americans, American Indians, Alaska Natives, Asian Americans and Pacific Islanders compared to the United States nonminority population. Projects funded by AHCPR will analyze causes and contributing factors for the inequalities that are related to the delivery and practice of health care, and identify and implement strategies to eliminate them. A letter of intent is requested by December 22; full application is due January 21. Annual deadline dates may vary; contact program staff for exact dates. RFA: HS-00-003
Requirements Applications may be submitted by domestic or foreign, public or private nonprofit organizations, including American Indian/Alaska Native organizations, universities, clinics, units of state, tribal and local governments, and eligible agencies of the federal government. AHCPR, by statute, can make grants only to nonprofit organizations; however, for-profit organizations may participate in grant projects as members of consortia or as subcontractors.
Restrictions 501(c)4 organizations that engage in lobbying are not eligible.
Amount $4.35 million total
Date(s) Application Is Due Jan 21; Dec 22.
Contact Joan Metcalfe, Grants Management Specialist, (301) 594-1841; fax: (301) 594-3210; email: jmetcalf@ahcpr.gov
Internet http://grants.nih.gov/grants/guide/rfa-files/RFA-HS-00-003.html
Sponsor Agency for Healthcare Research and Quality
2101 E Jefferson St
Rockville, MD 20852

AIA Latrobe Fellowship **310**
The purpose of the fellowship is to support research that will increase the knowledge base of the architecture profession. The fellow will receive a stipend for research, findings, and recommendations documented in publications, exhibitions, or educational programming that will inform, educate, and provide new insights for the architecture profession. The goal is to engage education and practice in the pursuit of knowledge. It is expected that the research and conclusions/recommendations will be completed within two years of the awarding of the grant. Guidelines are available online.
Requirements The college seeks applications from individuals with a proven track record of scholarly research. Applicants must demonstrate that they have successfully completed research leading to reasoned conclusions and/or recommendations.
Amount $100,000
Date(s) Application Is Due Feb 4.
Contact Pauline Porter, College of Fellows, (202) 626-7521; fax: (202) 626-7527; email: pporter@aia.org
Internet http://www.aia.org/aiarchitect/thisweek04/tw0924/0924nycu_latrobe.htm
Sponsor American Institute of Architects
1735 New York Ave NW
Washington, DC 20006-5292

AIA/AAF Scholarship for Advanced Study and Research **311**
This award supports projects by those who have already earned a professional degree. Scholarships are not given for tuition assistance for an advanced degree, but are based on the merits of a project proposal. Awards are issued to the individual and the US university under whose direction the project will be carried out. Deadline is mid-February. Application and guidelines are available online.
Amount $1000-$2500
Date(s) Application Is Due Feb 15.
Contact Mary Felber, Director, Scholarship Program, (202) 626-7511; fax: (202) 626-7420; email: mfelber@archfoundation.org
Internet http://www.archfoundation.org/scholarships/index.htm
Sponsor American Architectural Foundation
1735 New York Ave NW
Washington, DC 20006

AIA/AAF Scholarships for Advanced Degree/Research Candidates **312**
This program, supported through a combination of AIA and AAF funds, provides scholarship opportunities to practitioners, interns, educators, or others who have received a professional degree in architecture and who wish to pursue an advanced degree in architecture or a closely related field of study. Awards will be based on the merits of the proposed program of study or research. Applications are available on the Web site and must be submitted to the American Architectural Foundation.
Requirements Eligible to apply are candidates who are students at US, Canadian or Mexico universities in the final year of a first professional degree program resulting in a B.Arch, M.Arch, or equivalent; or practitioners, interns, educators, or others who have received the first professional degree in architecture. Apply by writing directly to the Scholarship Programs office at AIA in Washington, DC.
Restrictions Scholarship awards are not transferable, may not be deferred for use in a later year, and may not be used for a partial year of study. Awards are tenable only for the current full academic year.
Amount $1000-$2500
Date(s) Application Is Due Feb 15.

Contact Mary Felber, Director of Scholarships, (202) 626-7318; fax: (202) 626-7420; email: mfelber@archfoundation.org or info@archfoundation.org
Internet http://www.archfoundation.org/scholarships/index.htm
Sponsor American Institute of Architects/American Architectural Foundation
1799 New York Ave NW
Washington, DC 20006

AIA/AAF Scholarships for First Professional Degree Candidates 313
This program, supported through a combination of AIA and AAF funds, provides scholarship opportunities to students in one of the final two years of a professional degree program. All candidates must be students in schools accredited by the National Architectural Accrediting Board or recognized by the Royal Architectural Institute of Canada. Candidates must apply through the office of the head of an accredited school or through its scholarship committee. To equalize the opportunity for all students, a limited number of applications are sent to each school. Awards are based on strong academic performance, recommendations, and need.
Requirements Eligible to apply are students in US or Canadian universities who are currently in the third or fourth year of a five-year program that results in a B.Arch or equivalent; who are in the fourth or fifth year of a six-year program that results in an M.Arch or equivalent; or who are in the second or third year of a three- to four-year program that results in an M.Arch and whose undergraduate degrees are in a discipline other than architecture.
Restrictions Scholarships are awarded to individuals for the current full academic year, may not be deferred for use in a later year, and may not be used for a partial year of study.
Amount $500-$2500
Contact Mary Felber, Director of Scholarships, (202) 626-7511; fax: (202) 626-7420; email: mfelber@archfoundation.org
Internet http://www.archfoundation.org/scholarships/index.htm
Sponsor American Institute of Architects/American Architectural Foundation
1799 New York Ave NW
Washington, DC 20006

AIAR Andrew W. Mellon Foundation Fellowships 314
Fellowships are open to those in ancient Near Eastern studies, including the fields of archaeology, anthropology, art history, Bible, epigraphy, historical geography, history, language, literature, philology, and religion or related disciplines from Pre-history, through the early Islamic period. The program is open to Bulgarian, Czech, Estonian, Hungarian, Latvian, Lithuanian, Polish, Romanian, and Slovak scholars. Guidelines are available online.
Requirements Fellowships are available to Bulgarian, Czech, Estonian, Hungarian, Latvian, Lithuanian, Polish, Romanian, and Slovak scholars. Candidates should not be permanently resident outside the nine countries concerned, and should have obtained a doctorate by the time the fellowship is awarded.
Amount $34,500 for three awards ($11,500 each)
Date(s) Application Is Due Apr 2.
Contact Dr. Joan Branham, (401) 865-1789; fax: (401) 865-1036; email: jbranham@providence.edu
Internet http://www.aiar.org/deadlines.html
Sponsor W.F. Albright Institute
Providence College
Providence, RI 02918

AIAR Annual Professorships 315
Open to postdoctoral scholars in Near Eastern archaeology, geography, history, and Biblical studies. Residence at the institute is required. Period of appointment is 10 months. The professorship period should be continuous, without frequent trips outside the country. The professorship carries a stipend plus room and half-board for appointee and spouse. Annual deadline dates may vary; contact program staff for exact dates.
Requirements Postdoctoral scholars may apply. US citizens are eligible for the entire award. Non-US citizens may apply but are only eligible for nongovernmental funds. Residence at the institute is required.
Amount $30,000
Date(s) Application Is Due Oct 1.
Contact Dr. Joan Branham, Department of Art and Art History, (401) 865-1789; fax: (401) 865-1036; email: jbranham@providence.edu
Internet http://www.aiar.org/deadlines.html
Sponsor W.F. Albright Institute of Archaeological Research (AIAR) Jerusalem
Providence College
Providence, RI 02918

AIAR Educational and Cultural Affairs Fellowships 316
Junior Research Fellowships are open to those in ancient Near Eastern studies, including the fields of archaeology, anthropology, art history, Bible, epigraphy, historical geography, history, language, literature, philology and religion or related disciplines from Pre-history, through the early Islamic period. The research period should be continuous, without frequent trips outside the country. Fellowships support 10 months of research. Residence at the Albright is required. Guidelines are available online.
Requirements Doctoral students and recent PhD recipients who are US citizens are eligible.
Amount $16,000
Date(s) Application Is Due Oct 15.
Contact Dr. Joan Branham, (401) 865-1789; fax: (401) 865-1036; email: jbranham@providence.edu
Internet http://www.aiar.org/deadlines.html
Sponsor W.F. Albright Institute of Archaeological Research (AIAR) Jerusalem
Providence College
Providence, RI 02918

AIAR Ernest S. Frerichs Fellow and Program Coordinator Grant 317
The program supports predoctoral students and postdoctoral scholars specializing in near Eastern archaeology, geography, history, and biblical studies. The recipient is expected to assist the Albright's director in planning and implementing the Ernest S. Frerichs Program for Albright Fellows. Residence at the institute for the 10-month research period is required. The research period should be continuous, without frequent trips outside the country. The award covers stipend, room, and one-half board at the institute. Annual deadline dates may vary; contact program staff for exact dates.
Amount $19,000 ($10,900 stipend; $8100 room and half-board)
Date(s) Application Is Due Oct 1.
Contact Dr. Joan Branham, Department of Art and Art History, (401) 865-1789; fax: (401) 865-1036; email: jbranham@providence.edu
Internet http://www.aiar.org/deadlines.html
Sponsor W.F. Albright Institute of Archaeological Research (AIAR) Jerusalem
Providence College
Providence, RI 02918

AIAR George A. Barton Fellowships 318
This fellowship is open to seminarians, predoctoral students, and recent PhD recipients specializing in Near Eastern archaeology, geography, history, and biblical studies. Research period is for five months. Awards consist of a stipend plus room and half-board at the institute. The research period should be continuous, without frequent trips outside the country.
Amount $7000
Date(s) Application Is Due Oct 1.
Contact Dr. Joan Branham, Department of Art and Art History, (401) 865-1789; fax: (401) 865-1036; email: jbranham@providence.edu
Internet http://www.aiar.org/deadlines.html
Sponsor W.F. Albright Institute of Archaeological Research (AIAR) Jerusalem
Providence College
Providence, RI 02918

AIAR Samuel H. Kress Fellowship 319
The dissertation research fellowship supports students specializing in architecture, art history and archaeology. The research project must have a clear focus on art history or architecture. The 10-month research period should be continuous, without frequent trips outside the country. Guidelines are available online.
Requirements Applicants must be US citizens, or North American citizens studying at US universities.
Amount $18,500
Date(s) Application Is Due Oct 15.
Contact Dr. Joan Branham, Department of Religious Studies, Department of Art and Art History, (401) 865-1789; fax: (401) 865-1036; email: jbranham@providence.edu
Internet http://www.aiar.org/deadlines.html
Sponsor W.F. Albright Institute of Archaeological Research (AIAR) Jerusalem
Providence College
Providence, RI 02918

AIAR Samuel H. Kress Traveling Fellowship 320
The program awards a doctoral dissertation research fellowship for students specializing in architecture, art history, archaeology and classical studies. The fellowship supports travel for 10 months of research, including five months at the Albright, and five months at the American Center of Oriental Research in Amman, the Cyprus American Archaeological Research Institute in Nicosia, or the American School of Classical Studies at Athens. Applicants must demonstrate the necessity of being resident at the Albright and at one of the other three institutions mentioned above in order to complete their research. Guidelines are available online.
Requirements Applicants must be US citizens or students studying at US universities.
Amount $18,500
Contact Dr. Joan Branham, Department of Art and Art History, (401) 865-1789; fax: (401) 865-1036; email: jbranham@providence.edu
Internet http://www.aiar.org/deadlines.html
Sponsor W.F. Albright Institute of Archaeological Research (AIAR) Jerusalem
Providence College
Providence, RI 02918

AIAR/Council of American Overseas Research Centers 321
Fellowships for Advanced Multi-Country Research
The fellowships support scholars pursuing research on broad questions of multicountry significance in the fields of humanities, social sciences, and related natural sciences in

countries in the Near and Middle East and South Asia. For information and application, contact CAORC, (202) 842-8636; email: caorc@caorc.si.edu; web: www.caorc.org.
Requirements Doctoral candidates and established scholars with US citizenship, as individuals or as teams, are eligible.
Amount $9000 maximum
Date(s) Application Is Due Oct 1.
Contact 202-633-1599
Internet http://www.caorc.org/fellowships/multi/index.html, fellowships@caorc.org, 202-633-1599.
Sponsor W.F. Albright Institute of Archaeological Research (AIAR) Jerusalem
Council of American Overseas Research Centers (CAORC)
P.O. Box 37012, NHB, CE-123, MRC 178, Washington, DC 20013-7012

AICF Mellon Faculty Career Enhancement Fellowships **322**
The three-year program offers doctoral fellowships to current faculty of tribal colleges and universities (TCU) who are already in pursuit of a terminal degree and will benefit most if given the time and support to complete degree requirements, unfettered by financial considerations and professional demands. Fellows may use stipends to meet living expenses, tuition, and other expenses that enable dissertation research to be carried out. Additionally, each fellow will be provided an annual travel allowance to aid in travel expenses relating to research. Fellows will be expected to complete their terminal degree within a reasonable time upon receiving the award. Guidelines and application are available online.
Requirements Applicant must be/will: a current TCU member; considered all-but-dissertation in an accredited terminal degree program (or within one year of attaining an MFA degree); possess a demonstrated commitment to American Indian education and scholarship; agree to continue serving as faculty for at least two years at a TCU after completion of his/her degree; submit an approved dissertation prospectus from her/his institution, which will aid the selection process; work throughout the year with selected senior faculty member, who will serve as mentor; participate in an expense- paid annual fellow/mentor retreat in Arpil of the following year; complete the terminal degree within a reasonable time upon receiving this award; and be able to document that he/she is within one year of completing his/her terminal degree or MFA (all fields of study eligible).
Amount $30,000 stipend; $2250 travel allowance
Date(s) Application Is Due May 2.
Contact Kara Anderson, (800) 776-3863 or (303) 426-8900; fax: (303) 426-1200; email: kanderson@collegefund.org
Internet http://www.raconline.org/funding/funding_details.php?funding_id=519
Sponsor American Indian College Fund
8333 Greenwood Blvd
Denver, CO 80221

AIChE Computing Practice Award **323**
The award, which is sponsored by Aspen Technology, Inc., and ExxonMobil Chemical Company, recognizes outstanding contributions in the application of chemical engineering to computing and systems technology. All members as well as other interested persons are urged to nominate deserving candidates. All information and supporting documentation are to be included with completed forms; nominating forms and instructions may be obtained from the institute. Nominations will remain active for three years. The award is presented at a CAST Division luncheon or dinner at the AIChE annual meeting.
Amount $3000
Date(s) Application Is Due Apr 15.
Contact AIChE Awards Programs, (212) 591-7107; fax: (212) 591-8890; email: awards@aiche.org
Internet http://www.aiche.org/awards/awarddtl.asp?AwardID=29
Sponsor American Institute of Chemical Engineers
3 Park Ave
New York, NY 10016-5901

AIChE Environmental Division Graduate Student Paper Award **324**
The Environmental Division of AIChE awards outstanding graduate student papers contributing to environmental protection through chemical engineering. Student must be a member of AIChE, must have carried out the work while a graduate or undergraduate student at a university with an accredited chemical engineering program, and must be the primary author of the paper. The paper must describe original research or design and be suitable for publication in a refereed journal.
Requirements All members as well as other interested persons are urged to nominate deserving candidates. All information and supporting documentation are to be included with completed forms; nominating forms and instructions may be obtained from the institute.
Amount Plaques and $450, $300, and $150 for first, second and third place, respectively
Date(s) Application Is Due Oct 15.
Contact AIChE Awards Programs, (212) 591-7107; fax: (212) 591-8890; email: awards@aiche.org
Internet http://www.aiche.org/awards/awarddtl.asp?AwardID=33
Sponsor American Institute of Chemical Engineers
3 Park Ave
New York, NY 10016-5910

AICPA Fellowships for Minority Doctoral Students **325**
The primary objective of the fellowships is to enable more minorities to enter and move ahead in the accounting profession and academe. Recognizing the fact that professors serve as role models, a second objective is to increase the number of CPA role models who can positively influence the career decisions of a college student. These competitive fellowships are available to minority candidates who have been accepted into a doctoral accounting program. Fellowships are awarded once a year to full-time minority accounting scholars who show significant potential to become accounting educators. Renewals will be considered based on satisfactory progress, as a full-time student, toward completion of the degree requirements, up to a total of five years.
Requirements The applicant must be a minority student (African American, Native American, Pacific Island races, or of Hispanic ethnic origin) who has applied to or has been accepted into an accounting doctoral program; have earned a masters degree and/or completed a minimum of three years full-time experience in the practice of accounting; be attending or planning to attend school on a full-time basis and, once admitted, work consistently and forthrightly to attain the doctoral degree; agree not to work full time in a paid position or accept responsibility for teaching more than one course per semester as a teaching assistant or, dedicate more than one quarter of the time as a research assistant; and be a US citizen.
Amount $12,000 maximum per year
Date(s) Application Is Due Apr 1.
Contact Fellowship Administrator, (212) 596-6270; fax: (212) 596-6213
Internet http://www.aicpa.org/members/div/career/mini/fmds.htm
Sponsor American Institute of Certified Public Accountants
1211 Avenue of the Americas
New York, NY 10036-8775

AICPA John L. Carey Scholarships in Accounting **326**
This program is designed to encourage liberal arts undergraduates to consider professional accounting careers by providing scholarships for graduate accounting study to liberal arts undergraduates who plan to work toward a career in professional accounting. The recipients may attend US graduate schools only.
Requirements Applicants must be liberal arts degree holders of a regionally accredited institution in the United States.
Amount $5000 per year, renewable for a second year
Date(s) Application Is Due Apr 1.
Contact Academic and Career Developments, (212) 596-6221; fax: (212) 596-6292; email: educat@aicpa.org
Internet http://www.aicpa.org/members/div/career/mini/jlcs.htm
Sponsor American Institute of Certified Public Accountants
1211 Avenue of the Americas
New York, NY 10036

AICPA Minority Accounting Scholarships **327**
Scholarships are awarded to minority-group students who are US citizens majoring in accounting in graduate or undergraduate courses of study. Students should contact the institute for definitive application instructions. Both completed application form and transcripts must be received by deadline date.
Amount $5000 maximum
Date(s) Application Is Due Jun 1.
Contact Academic and Career Developments, (212) 596-6221; fax: (212) 596-6292; email: info@aicpa.org
Internet http://www.aicpa.org/members/div/career/mini/smas.htm
Sponsor American Institute of Certified Public Accountants
1211 Avenue of the Americas
New York, NY 10036-8775

AICR Investigator-Initiated Research Grants **328**
Grants are awarded to nonprofit institutions for research relevant to understanding the effects of dietary and nutritional practices on the etiology, pathogenesis, and treatment of cancer. Applications for this program should fall within the scope of diet and prevention of cancer and diet and treatment of cancer. New ideas in research that focus on dietary and nutritional means of preventing and treating cancer or improving the quality of life of the cancer patient are encouraged. Funded organizations receive two years of support with possible renewal for two additional years. Preproposal letters of intent are encouraged but are not required. Application forms, instructions, and policy information may be obtained from the institute.
Restrictions Indirect costs cannot exceed 10 percent of direct cost budget.
Amount $75,000 per year (plus 10% for indirect costs)
Date(s) Application Is Due Jul 1; Dec 16.
Contact Research Department, (202) 328-7744 or (800) 843-8114; fax: (202) 328-7226; email: research@aicr.org
Internet http://www.aicr.org/research/investigator.lasso
Sponsor American Institute for Cancer Research
1759 R St NW
Washington, DC 20009

AICR Postdoctoral Award **329**
These international fellowships are awarded to beginning investigators to stimulate innovative and new research on the prevention, etiology, or treatment of cancer by

dietary or nutritional methods. Applications should propose relevant feasibility studies to obtain data in support of a new hypothesis that then could be expanded to increase understanding of the role of dietary and nutritional factors in the etiology, pathogenesis, or treatment of cancer.
Requirements The principal investigator must have a PhD or MD degree that was awarded no more than three years prior to the date of the application and must hold an academic appointment no higher than assistant professor. The applicant must be sponsored by a professor in whose laboratory the applicant is to perform his or her research.
Amount $25,000 plus 10 percent of annual indirect costs
Date(s) Application Is Due Jul 1; Dec 16.
Contact Research Department, (202) 328-7744 or (800) 843-8114; fax: (202) 328-7226; email: research@aicr.org
Internet http://www.aicr.org/research/post_doc.lasso
Sponsor American Institute for Cancer Research
1759 R St NW
Washington, DC 20009

Aid to Scholarly Publications Programme 330
The program is designed to assist in the publication of works of advanced scholarly research that make an important contribution to the advancement of knowledge but that are unlikely to be published without assistance. Manuscripts in all disciplines of the humanities and social sciences are considered.
Requirements Candidates must be Canadian citizens or landed immigrants residing in Canada, must complete a registration form, and must provide two copies of the final manuscript for evaluation.
Restrictions The program does not provide grants for the publication of theses, original works of poetry, fiction, and drama or for journal articles; nor do they normally provide grants for manuscripts consisting, for the most part, of previously published material.
Amount $C7000
Contact Kel Morin Parsons, Program Manager, (613) 238-6112 ext 352; fax: (613) 238-6114; email: kmorin@fedcan.ca
Internet http://www.fedcan.ca/english/pdf/aspp/guidelines_e.pdf
Sponsor Canadian Federation for the Humanities and Social Sciences
151 Slater St, Ste 415
Ottawa, ON K1P 5H3 Canada

AIEA Honors Scholarships 331
These scholarships are intended to encourage and support self-supporting students who have achieved high academic standing to continue their studies in Japan. Grantees are selected on the basis of the recommendations of their Japanese universities' scholarship committees. Each year approximately 4400 scholarships are offered for the 12-month academic year. Application form is obtained from the university which forwards the completed form to the association. Each university has its own deadline date for receipt of the completed application form.
Requirements These scholarships are open to non-Japanese students who are under 30 years of age and in their junior or senior year at a Japanese university or college. Application should be made through the school the student is attending in Japan.
Amount @Y52,000 per month undergraduate students; @Y70,000 graduate students
Contact Student Affairs Division, 03 6407-7454; fax: 03 6407-7459
Internet http://www2.jasso.go.jp/study_j/scholarships_e.html
Sponsor Association of International Education, Japan
4-5-29 Komaba, Meguro-ku
Tokyo 153-8503
Japan

AIEA Research Grants 332
The association sponsors grants to encourage research projects that address the priorities of its international research agenda. Projects that include statewide, regional, or national frameworks, control groups, or comparative analyses are strongly recommended.
Requirements Applications are welcome from US and international researchers at higher education institutions or nonprofit educational associations.
Amount $20,000 maximum
Contact Stephen Dunnett, President, State University of New York at Buffalo, (716) 645-2368; fax: (716) 645-2528; email: aiea@buffalo.edu
Internet http://wings.buffalo.edu/intled/aiea
Sponsor Association of International Education
411 Capen Hall, Box 601604
Buffalo, NY 14260-1604

AIIS Junior Fellowships 333
Fellowships are awarded to graduate students from all academic disciplines whose dissertation research requires study in India. Awards are for up to 11 months. Fellowships for four months or less have significant travel restrictions. Fellowships for six months or more may include limited dependent coverage if funds are available. Junior fellows will have formal affiliation with Indian universities and Indian research supervisors. Awards are announced by the beginning of October; the earliest possible departure date for India by awardees is eleven (11) months following the date of application submission.
Requirements The fellowships are open to US citizens and noncitizen residents at American colleges and universities who are studying in the humanities, social sciences, or natural sciences. All AIIS-sponsored research projects and programs must receive the approval of the government of India.
Date(s) Application Is Due Jul 1.
Contact Fellowship Coordinator, (773) 702-8638; fax: (773) 702-6636; email: aiis@uchicago.edu
Internet http://www.indiastudies.org/fellow.htm
Sponsor American Institute of Indian Studies
1130 E 59th St, Foster Hall
Chicago, IL 60637

AIIS Performing and Creative Arts Fellowships 334
A limited number of fellowships are available each year to accomplished practitioners of the performing and creative arts of India who demonstrate that studying in India will enhance their skills, develop their capabilities to teach or perform in the United States, enhance American involvement with India's artistic traditions, and strengthen their links with peers in India. These fellowships can be either short-term (up to four months) or long-term (six to nine months).
Requirements US citizens and noncitizen residents who are engaged in research or teaching at American colleges and universities are eligible. All AIIS-sponsored research projects and programs must receive the approval of the government of India.
Restrictions Graduate students are ineligible.
Date(s) Application Is Due Jul 1.
Contact Fellowship Coordinator, (773) 702-8638; fax: (773) 702-6636; email: aiis@uchicago.edu
Internet http://www.indiastudies.org/fellow.htm
Sponsor American Institute of Indian Studies
1130 E 59th St, Foster Hall
Chicago, IL 60637

AIIS Professional Development Fellowships 335
A few fellowships are awarded to established scholars who have not previously specialized in Indian studies, and to established professionals who have not previously worked or studied in India. Proposals should have a substantial research or project component, and the anticipated results should be clearly defined. Awards are available for six to nine months. While in India, each fellow will be formally affiliated with an Indian university.
Requirements Eligible to apply are US citizens and resident aliens who are engaged in research or teaching at American colleges or universities. All AIIS-sponsored research projects and programs must receive the approval of the government of India.
Date(s) Application Is Due Jul 1.
Contact Fellowship Coordinator, (773) 702-8638; fax: (773) 702-6636; email: aiis@uchicago.edu
Internet http://www.indiastudies.org/fellow.htm
Sponsor American Institute of Indian Studies
1130 E 59th St, Foster Hall
Chicago, IL 60637

AIIS Senior Research Fellowships 336
Fellowships are awarded to academic specialists in Indian studies possessing the PhD or its equivalent. The fellowships are designed to enable scholars specializing in South Asian studies to pursue further research in India. Each senior fellow will be formally affiliated with an Indian university for the period of the award, ranging from four to nine months.
Requirements US citizens who hold the PhD or its equivalent and noncitizen residents who are engaged in research or teaching full time at American colleges or universities are eligible. All AIIS-sponsored research projects and programs must receive the approval of the government of India.
Date(s) Application Is Due Jul 1.
Contact Fellowship Coordinator, (773) 702-8638; fax: (773) 702-6636; email: aiis@uchicago.edu
Internet http://www.indiastudies.org/fellow.htm
Sponsor American Institute of Indian Studies
1130 E 59th St, Foster Hall
Chicago, IL 60637

AIIS Short-Term Senior Fellowships 337
A few fellowships are awarded to academic specialists in Indian studies who have a PhD or the equivalent. Formal affiliation is established for the fellow with an Indian university. Fellowships are offered for up to four months.
Requirements Eligible to apply are US citizens and permanent residents who are engaged in research or teaching at American colleges or universities. Selection is made without regard to race, color, national origin, sex, or religion of applicants. All AIIS-sponsored research projects and programs must receive the approval of the government of India.
Date(s) Application Is Due Jul 1.
Contact Fellowship Coordinator, (312) 702-8638; fax: (312) 702-6636; email: aiis@uchicago.edu
Internet http://www.indiastudies.org/fellow.htm
Sponsor American Institute of Indian Studies
1130 E 59th St, Foster Hall
Chicago, IL 60637

AINSE Postgraduate Research Awards 338

AINSE awards postgraduate studentships and research grants. The institute is a consortium of Australian universities and the University of Auckland, New Zealand, in partnership with the Australian Nuclear Science and Technology Organization (ANSTO). The consortium assists research and training in nuclear science and engineering and makes the facilities at the Lucas Heights Research Laboratories available to research staff and students from its member institutions. Projects in almost every discipline in the physical sciences are supported, particularly in the ANSTO program areas of advanced materials; biomedicine and health; environmental sciences; applications of nuclear physics, including neutron scattering, accelerator science, and radiation technology; nuclear technology and engineering; and supercomputing and Australian Isotope services.
Amount $7500
Date(s) Application Is Due Apr 15.
Contact Dr. Dennis Mather, Scientific Secretary, (61) 02 9717 3388; fax: (61) 02 9717 9268; email: d.mather@ainse.edu.au; Irene Parker, (61) 02 9717 3436; email: ainse@ainse.edu.au
Internet http://www.ansto.gov.au/ainse/01post.html
Sponsor Australian Institute of Nuclear Science and Engineering
Private Mail Bag 1
Menai, NSW 2234 Australia

AIR Improving Institutional Research in Postsecondary Education Institutions Grants 339

The program is supported by the Association for Institutional Research with support from the National Center for Education Statistics (NCES) and the National Science Foundation (NSF). The program includes research grants, dissertation grants, senior fellowships, and a focused grant program supported by the National Postsecondary Education Cooperative (NPEC). Research grants are made for conducting research on postsecondary education using the NCES and NSF national databases; conducting other research that promises a significant contribution to the national knowledge of the nature and operation of postsecondary education; or conducting research activities that will contribute to the professional development of professional personnel working in postsecondary education. Dissertation grant support is available to assist students in the acquisition, analysis, and reporting of data from the NCES and NSF data sets. The Senior Fellow program seeks proposals from senior institutional research officers for a fellowship to work with NCES staff on the organization and collection of postsecondary institutional data. Proposals must be submitted electronically, as a Word or PDF email attachment to the listed office email address. Guidelines and form are available online.
Requirements Research grant proposals are accepted from education administrators, professional staff, and faculty affiliated with US postsecondary institutions or governance agencies. Dissertation grants are solicited from doctoral students beginning their dissertation work.
Amount $30,000 maximum for research grants; $15,000 maximum for dissertation grants; $110,000 senior fellowships
Date(s) Application Is Due Jan 15.
Contact Dr. Anthony Bichel, (850) 644-4470; fax: (850) 644-8824; email:abichel@mailer.fsu.edu
Internet http://www.airweb.org/page.asp?page=40
Sponsor Association for Institutional Research
P.O. Box 2314
Tallahassee, FL 32316-2314

Air Transportation Centers of Excellence Grants 340

The program supports long-term, continuing research in specific areas of aviation-related technology. Responsibilities of centers include, but are not limited to, the conduct of research concerning catastrophic failure of aircraft, airspace and airport planning and design, airport capacity enhancement techniques, human performance in the air transportation environment, aviation safety and security, the supply of trained air transportation personnel including pilots and mechanics, and other aviation issues pertinent to developing and maintaining a safe and efficient air transportation system, and the interpretation, publication, and dissemination of the results of such research. FAA intends to support a center in three-year increments; each center will undergo a reassessment every three years. Contact the office for application deadlines.
Requirements Applicants are limited to colleges and universities with the financial resources to meet statutory requirements for matching federal funds and maintenance of effort. Locations shall be geographically equitable.
Amount $500,000 average per year, per center
Contact Dr. Patricia Watts, Program Director, FAA Technical Center, (609) 485-5043; fax: (609) 485-9430; email: patricia.watts@faa.gov
Internet http://www.dot.gov
Sponsor Department of Transportation
AAR-201, FAA Technical Ctr
Atlantic City International Airport, NJ 08405

AIR/National Postsecondary Education Cooperative Focused Grant 341

AIR and the National Postsecondary Education Cooperative (NPEC) support research to increase the understanding and knowledge of a specific issue area identified by the NPEC executive committee as critically important to the postsecondary education community. This year the focus is student success at all levels of postsecondary education. Focused grants support dissertation and research projects covering a variety of research activities that focus on student success, including: data synthesis or meta analysis of research studies that address a specific question regarding student success; new analyses of data using national, regional, state, or institutional databases; assessments of research and practices that have been initiated in the area of student success; models of student success that can be supported by research and/or that detail new data collection needs; case studies of activities that focus on student success; collections of best practices promoting student success; and other creative strategies. Proposals must be submitted electronically, as a Word or PDF email attachment, to the listed office email address. Guidelines and forms are available online. It is anticipated that five to 10 one-year grants will be made.
Requirements Dissertation grant proposals may be submitted by doctoral students affiliated with a US postsecondary institution. A letter of support from the faculty dissertation director is required. Research grant proposals usually are submitted by institutional researchers, faculty, and other higher education professionals.
Amount $30,000 maximum research grants; $15,000 maximum dissertation fellowships
Date(s) Application Is Due Jan 15.
Contact Program Contact, (850) 644-4470; fax: (850) 644-8824; email: atrexler@mailer.fsu.edu
Internet http://www.airweb.org/page.asp?page=10
Sponsor Association for Institutional Research
P.O. Box 2314
Tallahassee, FL 32316-2314

AJA Bernard and Audre Rapoport Fellowships in American Jewish Studies 342

Fellowships are available to postdoctoral candidates for research and writing at the American Jewish Archives for a one-month period. Annual deadline dates may vary; contact the program office for exact dates.
Requirements Applicant must provide an up-to-date curriculum vita, a research proposal (not more than five typewritten pages, double-spaced), evidence of published research, and two recommendations from academic colleagues. Typically, Marcus Center fellowships will be awarded to postdoctoral candidates, PhD candidates who are completing dissertations, and senior or independent scholars.
Date(s) Application Is Due Mar 18.
Contact Kevin Proffitt, Program Contact, (513) 221-7444 ext 304; fax: (513) 221-7812; email: kproffitt@huc.edu or aja@huc.edu
Internet http://www.americanjewisharchives.org/aja/programs/index.html
Sponsor American Jewish Archives
3101 Clifton Ave
Cincinnati, OH 45220-2408

AJA Ethel Marcus Memorial Fellowship in American Jewish Studies 343

The Marcus Center's Fellowship Program was founded with the intent of creating a forum where students and scholars of the American Jewish experience could gather together to research, discuss, and study their chosen topics. Under the auspices of this unique program scholars come to Cincinnati to conduct in-depth research at the American Jewish Archives and to take part in the academic community of the Hebrew Union College-Jewish Institute of Religion. The program provides fellows with an opportunity not only to pursue their own research, but also to interact and exchange ideas with research peers as well as with the faculty and students of HUC-JIR.
Requirements This fellowship is available to ABDs for one month of research or writing at the American Jewish Archives. Applicant must provide an up-to-date curriculum vita, a research proposal, and two faculty recommendations (including one from the dissertation supervisor). Typically, Marcus Center fellowships will be awarded to postdoctoral candidates, PhD candidates who are completing dissertations, and senior or independent scholars.
Date(s) Application Is Due Mar 18.
Contact Kevin Proffitt, Program Contact, The Jacob Rader Marcus Center, (513) 221-7444 ext 304; fax: (513) 221-7812; email: kproffitt@huc.edu or aja@huc.edu
Internet http://www.americanjewisharchives.org/aja/programs/index.html
Sponsor American Jewish Archives
3101 Clifton Ave
Cincinnati, OH 45220-2408

AJA Lowenstein-Wiener Summer Fellowship Awards in American Jewish Studies 344

Fellowships are available to ABDs or postdoctoral candidates for one month of research or writing at the American Jewish Archives during the stipend year. Applicant must provide an up-to-date curriculum vita, a research proposal, and evidence of published research, where possible. ABDs must provide three faculty recommendations (including one from the dissertation supervisor), and postdoctoral candidates must provide two recommendations from academic colleagues.
Requirements Typically, fellowships will be awarded to postdoctoral candidates, PhD candidates who are completing dissertations, and senior or independent scholars.
Date(s) Application Is Due Mar 18.
Contact Kevin Proffitt, Fellowship Director, (513) 221-7444 ext 304; fax: (513) 221-7812; email: kproffitt@huc.edu
Internet http://www.americanjewisharchives.org/aja/programs/index.html

Sponsor American Jewish Archives
3101 Clifton Ave
Cincinnati, OH 45220-2408

AJA Marguerite R. Jacobs Memorial Postdoctoral Award in American Jewish Studies 345

This award is made to postdoctoral candidates for one month of active research or writing at the American Jewish Archives. Applicant must provide an up-to-date curriculum vita; a research proposal; evidence of published research, where possible; and two recommendations from academic colleagues.
Requirements Typically, fellowships will be awarded to postdoctoral candidates, PhD candidates who are completing dissertations, and senior or independent scholars.
Amount $2000
Date(s) Application Is Due Mar 18.
Contact Kevin Proffitt, Director of the Fellowships Program, (513) 221-7444 ext 304; fax: (513) 221-7812; email: AJA@cn.huc.edu
Internet http://www.americanjewisharchives.org/aja/programs/index.html
Sponsor American Jewish Archives
3101 Clifton Ave
Cincinnati, OH 45220-2408

AJA Rabbi Frederic A. Doppelt Memorial Fellowship in American Jewish Studies 346

This award is available to ABDs for one month of research or writing at the American Jewish Archives during the stipend year. Applicant must provide an up-to-date curriculum vita, a research proposal, and two faculty recommendations (including one from the dissertation supervisor).
Requirements Typically, fellowships will be awarded to postdoctoral candidates, PhD candidates who are completing dissertations, and senior or independent scholars.
Amount $1000
Date(s) Application Is Due Mar 18.
Contact Kevin Proffitt, Director of the Fellowship Program, (513) 221-7444 ext 304; fax: (513) 221-7812; email: AJA@cn.huc.edu
Internet http://www.americanjewisharchives.org/aja/programs/index.html
Sponsor American Jewish Archives
3101 Clifton Ave
Cincinnati, OH 45220-2408

AJA Rabbi Levi A. Olan Memorial Fellowship in American Jewish Studies 347

Fellowships are available to postdoctoral candidates for research and writing at the American Jewish Archives for a one-month period. Applicant must provide an up-to-date curriculum vita, a research proposal (not more than five typewritten pages, double-spaced), evidence of published research, and two recommendations from academic colleagues.
Requirements Typically, fellowships will be awarded to postdoctoral candidates, PhD candidates who are completing dissertations, and senior or independent scholars.
Date(s) Application Is Due Mar 18.
Contact Kevin Proffitt, Director of the Fellowship Program, The Jacob Rader Marcus Center, (513) 221-7444 ext 304; fax: (513) 221-7812; email: kproffitt@huc.edu or aja@huc.edu
Internet http://www.americanjewisharchives.org/aja/programs/index.html
Sponsor American Jewish Archives
3101 Clifton Ave
Cincinnati, OH 45220-2408

AJA Rabbi Theodore S. Levy Tribute Fellowship in American Jewish Studies 348

Fellowships are available to postdoctoral candidates for research and writing at the American Jewish Archives for a one-month period. Applicant must provide an up-to-date curriculum vita, a research proposal (not more than five typewritten pages, evidence of published research, and two recommendations from academic colleagues.
Requirements Typically, fellowships will be awarded to postdoctoral candidates, PhD candidates who are completing dissertations, and senior or independent scholars.
Date(s) Application Is Due Mar 18.
Contact Kevin Proffitt, Director of the Fellowship Program, The Jacob Rader Marcus Center, (513) 221-7444 ext 304; fax: (513) 221-7812; email: AJA@cn.huc.edu
Internet http://www.americanjewisharchives.org/aja/programs/index.html
Sponsor American Jewish Archives
3101 Clifton Ave
Cincinnati, OH 45220-2408

AJA Starkoff Fellowship in American Jewish Studies 349

This fellowship is available to ABDs for one month of research or writing at the American Jewish Archives. Applicant must provide an up-to-date curriculum vita, a research proposal, and two faculty recommendations.
Requirements Typically, fellowships will be awarded to postdoctoral candidates, PhD candidates who are completing dissertations, and senior or independent scholars.
Amount $1000
Date(s) Application Is Due Mar 18.
Contact Kevin Proffitt, Director of the Fellowship Program, The Jacob Rader Marcus Center, (513) 221-7444 ext 304; fax: (513) 221-7812; email: AJA@cn.huc.edu
Internet http://www.americanjewisharchives.org/aja/programs/index.html
Sponsor American Jewish Archives
3101 Clifton Ave
Cincinnati, OH 45220-2408

AJCC Cancer Staging Grants 350

AJCC seeks proposals to develop and evaluate improved staging algorithms for specific cancer sites and types. Successful proposals will present new approaches and utilize data sets available to the applicant to test and validate current or revised staging algorithms. Applicants may use elements currently used for AJCC/UICC TNM staging, additional or modified anatomic and non-anatomic factors to define prognosis, and incorporate validated factors that identify response to treatment. Proposals that address and validate the use of non-anatomic factors to improve the utility of staging and define the response to therapy are encouraged. The AJCC will provide funding to a number of groups for a variety of disease sites to promote innovative strategies for enhancing the clinical utility of staging while maintaining compatibility with current staging data collection systems. The listed application deadline is for letters of intent. Guidelines are available online.
Requirements Eligible institutions include for-profit and nonprofit organizations; public or private institutions, such as universities, colleges, laboratories, and hospitals; units of state and local government; eligible agencies of the federal government; and domestic or foreign institutions/organizations.
Amount $150,000 maximum
Date(s) Application Is Due Dec 15.
Contact Valerie Vesich, (312) 202-5420; fax: (312) 202-5009; email: AJCC@facs.org
Internet http://www.cancerstaging.org/initiatives/rfp.html#
Sponsor American Joint Committee on Cancer
633 N Saint Clair St
Chicago, IL 60611

Akonadi Foundation Anti-Racism Grants 351

The foundation's mission is to work with others to eliminate racism, with a particular focus on structural and institutional racism. Grants have supported programmatic approaches including research, policy work, advocacy, litigation, organizing, media, arts, diversity training, education, and other tools in their anti-racism work. The foundation awards general operating grants and project grants. Grants are made to organizations in the San Francisco Bay area and to national organizations with national reach. Letters of interest will be accepted year round. Full proposals should be submitted upon request.
Amount $10,000-$50,000
Date(s) Application Is Due Feb 18.
Contact Grants Administrator, (510) 663-3867; email: info@akonadi.org
Internet http://www.akonadi.org/application_guidelines.html
Sponsor Akonadi Foundation
469 9th St, Ste 210
Oakland, CA 94607

Akron Community Foundation Grants 352

The foundation supports Summit County, OH, nonprofit organizations providing services in four categories. Culture/humanities grants are awarded to performing arts groups and humanities groups. Education grants are awarded for preschool through higher education programs, as well as vocational education, adult/continuing education, and enrichment and literacy programs. Health and human services grants encompass all aspects of health, including research, public health, substance abuse, mental health, and social service programs. Civic affairs grants are awarded to programs relating to business and employment, civic affairs and community service, consumer interests, crime and law enforcement as well as crime prevention, environment and energy programs, equal rights programs, and recreation. Types of support include general operating support, program development, seed funds, research, capital grants, and matching funds. The foundation looks favorably on requests that offer new approaches to solving problems or creating opportunities for organizations that collaborate. The board meets quarterly. Application deadlines are by category: education (January 2); arts and culture (April 1); civic affairs (July 1); and health and human services (October 1).
Requirements IRS 501(c)3 nonprofit Summit County, OH, organizations are eligible.
Restrictions The foundation generally does not consider requests for general operating support, computers, office equipment, or travel expenses. Grants may not be used for endowments, scholarships, religious purposes, capital campaigns, or deficit expenses. Organizations that do not operate programs in Summit County are not eligible for grants. Grants are not made to individuals.
Amount $100-$100,000 average
Date(s) Application Is Due Jan 2; Apr 1; Jul 1; Oct 1.
Contact Donae Eckert, Vice President of Programs, (330) 376-8522
Internet http://www.akroncommunityfdn.org/grants
Sponsor Akron Community Foundation
345 W Cedar St
Akron, OH 44307-2407

ALA Bogle Pratt International Library Travel Fund 353

Awards are granted to ALA members to travel abroad to attend their first international conference. An international conference may be defined as a conference sponsored by

an international organization or a conference held in a country other than your home country.
Requirements Applicants must be members of ALA.
Amount $1000
Date(s) Application Is Due Jan 1.
Contact Director, Office of International Relations, (312) 280-3200; fax: (312) 280-3256; email: intl@ala.org
Internet http://www.ala.org/ala/iro/awardsactivities/bogleprattaward.htm
Sponsor Bogle Memorial Fund and the Pratt Institute School of Information and Library Science
50 E Huron Street
Chicago, IL 60611

ALA Carnegie-Whitney Awards **354**
This award has been established to provide grants for the preparation and publication of popular or scholarly reading lists, indexes, and other guides to library resources that will be useful to users of all types of libraries. The grants may be used for print and electronic projects of varying lengths.
Requirements Grants are awarded to individuals, official units of the American Library Association (including committees), and other groups affiliated with the American Library Association.
Amount $5000 maximum
Date(s) Application Is Due Nov 6.
Contact ALA Awards Staff Liaison, (800) 545-2433 ext 5416 or (312) 280-3247; email: rtolere@ala.org
Internet http://www.ala.org/Template.cfm?Section=grantfellowship&template=/ContentManagement/ContentDisplay.cfm&ContentID=87437
Sponsor American Library Association
50 E Huron St
Chicago, IL 60611-2795

ALA Carroll Preston Baber Research Grant **355**
This grant is given annually to one or more librarians or library educators who will conduct innovative research that could lead to an improvement in services to any specified group(s) of people. The project should have the potential to serve as a model for the library community. Attention to the uses of technology will be given preference, and efforts involving cooperation between libraries, between libraries and other agencies, or between librarians and persons in other disciplines will also receive special consideration.
Requirements Any ALA member may apply. Preferential consideration will be given to projects that involve a practicing librarian.
Amount $3000
Date(s) Application Is Due Dec 10.
Contact Letitia Earvin, ALA Awards Staff Liaison, (800) 545-2433, ext 1-4274; fax: (312) 280-4393; email: learvin@ala.org or awards@ala.org
Internet http://www.ala.org/ala/ors/orsawards/baberresearchgrant/babercarroll.htm
Sponsor American Library Association
50 E Huron Street
Chicago, IL 60611

ALA Christopher Hoy/ERT Scholarship **356**
One or more scholarships are awarded annually to worthy students to begin their library education at the graduate level in an ALA-accredited master's program. The association advises interested parties to request application forms in the fall for the next academic year (number of scholarships granted depends on funds available). Annual deadline dates may vary; contact program staff for exact dates.
Requirements Applicants must be US or Canadian citizens, or permanent residents and attend ALA accredited Master's Program. Candidates must have no more than 12 semester hours towards MLS/MLIS/MIS prior to June 1 of year awarded.
Amount $5000
Date(s) Application Is Due Mar 1.
Contact ALA Scholarship Clearinghouse, (800) 545-2433 ext 4277; email: scholarships@ala.org
Internet http://www.ala.org/Template.cfm?Section=Scholarships&template=/ContentManagement/ContentDisplay.cfm&ContentID=142124
Sponsor American Library Association
50 E Huron Street
Chicago, IL 60611

ALA Coutts Nijhoff International West European Specialist Study Grant **357**
This grant is funded by Martinus Nijhoff International, a subscription agent and book dealer with headquarters in the Netherlands, and supports research pertaining to Western European studies, librarianship, or the book trade. The primary criterion for awarding the grant is the significance and utility of the proposed project as a contribution to the study of the acquisition, organization, or use of library materials from, or relating to, Western Europe. Current or historical subjects may be treated.
Requirements The nominee must be a librarian employed in a university, college, or community college library in the year prior to application for the award and must have a minimum of five years of professional experience in an academic library. Six copies of the application must be submitted and must contain a detailed description of the proposed project and an explanation of the value of the project to the library community.
Restrictions Funds may not be used for salaries, research-related supplies, publication costs, conference fees, or equipment purchases.
Amount 4500 Euros maximum
Date(s) Application Is Due Dec 1.
Contact Megan Bielefeld, ACRL Awards Program Assistant, (800) 545-2433 ext 2514 or (312) 280-2514; email: mbielefeld@ala.org
Internet http://www.ala.org/ala/acrl/acrlawards/nijhoffstudy.htm
Sponsor Association of College and Research Libraries
50 E Huron Street
Chicago, IL 60611-2795

ALA David H. Clift Scholarships **358**
One or more scholarships are awarded annually to worthy students to begin their library education at the graduate level in an ALA-accredited master's program. The association advises interested parties to request application forms in the fall for the next academic year (number of scholarships granted depends on funds available). Annual deadline dates may vary; contact program staff for exact dates.
Requirements Applicants must be US or Canadian citizens, or permanent residents and attend ALA accredited Master's Program. Candidates must have no more than 12 semester hours towards MLS/MLIS/MIS prior to June 1 of year awarded.
Amount $3000
Date(s) Application Is Due Mar 1.
Contact ALA Scholarship Clearinghouse, (800) 545-2433 ext 4277; email: scholarships@ala.org
Internet http://www.ala.org/Template.cfm?Section=scholarships&template=/ContentManagement/ContentDisplay.cfm&ContentID=16497
Sponsor American Library Association
50 E Huron Street
Chicago, IL 60611-2795

ALA Frances Henne YALSA/VOYA Research Grant **359**
This grant, donated by Voice of Youth Advocates, is given annually to provide seed money for small-scale projects that encourage significant research that will have an influence on library service to young adults. Only proposed research projects judged significant to the objectives of YALSA and the general area of young adult services will be considered. Applications are available on the Web site.
Requirements Applicants must be personal members of YALSA, although the research project may be undertaken by an individual, an institution, or a group. Grants will not be given for research leading to a degree.
Restrictions Previous winners are not eligible.
Amount $500
Date(s) Application Is Due Dec 1.
Contact ALA Awards Staff Liaison, (312) 545-2433 ext 4387; email: yalsa@ala.org
Internet http://www.ala.org/ala/yalsa/awardsandgrants/franceshenne.htm
Sponsor American Library Association
50 E Huron Street
Chicago, IL 60611

ALA Information Today Library of the Future Award **360**
The purpose of the award is to honor an individual library, library consortium, group of librarians, or support organization for innovative planning for, applications of, or development of patron training programs about information technology in a library setting. Selection criteria should include the benefit to clients served; benefit to the technology information community; impact on library operations; public relations value; and impact on the perception of the library or librarian in the work setting and to the specialized and/or general public. Applications are available on the Web site.
Amount $1500
Date(s) Application Is Due Dec 1.
Contact ALA Awards Staff Liaison, (312) 280-3247; fax: (312) 280-3257; email: awards@ala.org
Internet http://www.ala.org/work/awards/appls/lofappl.html
Sponsor American Library Association
50 E Huron St
Chicago, IL 60611-2795

ALA Jesse H. Shera Award for Published Research **361**
This award is given annually for an outstanding and original paper reporting the results of research related to libraries. All nominated articles must relate in at least a general way to library and information studies. Any research method is acceptable. Authors of nominated articles need not be Library Research Round Table members. Guidelines are available online.
Requirements All entries must be research articles published in English during the previous calendar year. Articles may be nominated by any member of LRRT or by the editors of research journals in the field of library and information studies. Articles by joint investigators are eligible, as are articles generated as a result of a research grant or other source of funding.
Restrictions No one may nominate more than two articles.
Amount $500

Date(s) Application Is Due Jan 31.
Contact Neal K. Kaske, (202) 606-9200; fax: (202) 606-9203; email: nkaske@nclis.gov
Internet http://www.ala.org/ala/ors/orsawards/sherajesseh/sherajesseh.htm
Sponsor American Library Association
50 E Huron Steet
Chicago, IL 60611

ALA Jesse H. Shera Award for Support of Dissertation Research 362
This award is intended to provide recognition and monetary support for dissertation research employing exemplary research design and methods. The award is restricted to research designs that have been approved by the doctoral candidate's dissertation committee and that are to be employed or are in the initial stage of use. Completed research is not eligible for consideration.
Requirements Any research design is acceptable, but the topic of the research must relate in at least a general way to library and information studies. Guidelines are available online.
Restrictions Eligibility is not limited to LRRT members.
Amount $500
Date(s) Application Is Due Jan 31.
Contact Neal K. Kaske, (202) 606-9200; fax: (202) 606-9203; email: nkaske@nclis.gov
Internet http://www.ala.org/Template.cfm?Section=awards&template=/ContentManagement/ContentDisplay.cfm&ContentID=138982
Sponsor ALA
50 E Huron Street
Chicago, IL 60611

ALA Marshall Cavendish Scholarship 363
The scholarship is awarded to a US or Canadian citizen to begin an MLS degree in an ALA-accredited program. Application forms are available on the Web site. Annual deadline dates may vary; contact program staff for exact dates.
Requirements Applicants must be US or Canadian Citizens or permanent residents and attend ALA accredited Master's Program. Candidates must have no more than 12 semester hours towards MLS/MLIS/MIS prior to June 1 of year awarded.
Amount $3000
Date(s) Application Is Due Mar 1.
Contact ALA Scholarship Clearinghouse, (800) 545-2433 ext 4277; email: scholarships@ala.org
Internet http://www.ala.org/ala/hrdr/scholarshipprgm/alageneralscholarships.htm
Sponsor American Library Association
50 E Huron Street
Chicago, IL 60611

ALA Spectrum Initiative Scholarship 364
The scholarship is awarded to minority college graduates planning to enter ALA-accredited master's programs. Spectrum provides a one-year scholarship and professional development opportunities to eligible students planning to attend an ALA-accredited graduate program in library and information studies or an ALA-recognized NCATE School Library Media program. This scholarship is a one-time, non-renewable $5000 award paid in two installments directly to the recipient. Application forms may be obtained from the Web site or by contacting the office.
Requirements Applicants must be citizens or permanent residents of the United States or Canada. Applicants can not have completed more than 12 semester hours (or its equivalent) toward a master's degree in library and information studies or school library media. Applicant must be a member of one of the four largest underrepresented groups in the library profession: African American/Canadian, Asian/Pacific Islander, Latino/Hispanic, or native people of the United States or Canada.
Amount $5000; $1500 professional development
Date(s) Application Is Due Mar 1.
Contact Program Contact, Office for Library Personnel Resources, (312) 280-4281 or (800) 545-2433 ext 4281; fax: (312) 280-3256; email: spectrum@ala.org or scholarships@ala.org
Internet http://www.ala.org/ala/diversity/spectrum/spectruminitiative.htm
Sponsor American Library Association
50 E Huron Street
Chicago, IL 60611-2795

ALA Tony B. Leisner Scholarship 365
The scholarship is open to library support staff currently working in a library. The scholarship is awarded to a US or Canadian citizen to begin an MLS degree in an ALA-accredited program. Application forms are available on the Web site and must be submitted online. Annual deadline dates may vary; contact program staff for exact dates. Factors considered in making the awards include academic excellence, leadership, and evidence of commitment to a career in librarianship.
Requirements Applicants must be US or Canadian Citizens or permanent resident and attend ALA accredited Master's Program. Candidates must have no more than 12 semester hours towards MLS/MLIS/MIS prior to June 1 of year awarded. A Personal statement is also required.
Amount $3000
Date(s) Application Is Due Mar 1.
Contact ALA Scholarship Clearinghouse, (800) 545-2433 ext 4277; email: scholarships@ala.org
Internet http://www.ala.org/Template.cfm?Section=scholarships&template=/ContentManagement/ContentDisplay.cfm&ContentID=107776
Sponsor American Library Association
50 E Huron Street
Chicago, IL 60611

ALA/LAM Foundation Career Investigator Award 366
The award supports research directly related to lymphangioleiomyomatosis (LAM) and is targeted at junior- to mid-level faculty who focus on the abnormal proliferation of smooth muscle that occurs in the disease. Awardees are expected to devote full time or at least 75 percent of their time to research. Awardees may undertake limited administrative, teaching, and clinical responsibilities if they are directly related to the nature of the research supported by the award. Up to three years of support will be awarded.
Requirements US citizens and foreign nationals with appropriate immigrant visa status are eligible. At the time of application, an applicant must hold a doctoral degree and faculty appointment at the level of assistant or associate professor and be undertaking a project related to LAM.
Restrictions Individuals who have attained the rank of full professor or who have more than eight years of faculty experience at the time of application are ineligible.
Amount $60,000 maximum
Date(s) Application Is Due Sep 1.
Contact Evita Mendoza, Grants Administrator, (212) 315-8793; email: emendoza@lungusa.org or info@lungusa.org
Internet http://www.lungusa.org/site/apps/s/content.asp?c=dvLUK9O0E&b=34706&ct=67676
Sponsor American Lung Association
1740 Broadway
New York, NY 10019

ALA/LAM Foundation Research Grants 367
The program provides seed money to investigators seeking to understand the abnormal smooth muscle proliferation that occurs in lymphangioleiomyomatosis (LAM). The grant supports clinical, laboratory, epidemiological, or any other kind of research that directly relates to LAM. Grants are subject to annual review and may be granted for up to two years.
Requirements US citizens and foreign nationals with appropriate immigrant visa status are eligible. At the time of application, an applicant must hold a doctoral degree and faculty appointment with an academic institution and have completed two years of research training.
Restrictions Residents, interns, postdoctoral fellows, students enrolled in degree-granting programs, and established investigators are ineligible.
Amount $40,000 maximum per year
Date(s) Application Is Due Sep 1.
Contact Evita Mendoza, Grants Administrator, (212) 315-8793; email: emendoza@lungusa.org or info@lungusa.org
Internet http://www.lungusa.org/site/apps/s/content.asp?c=dvLUK9O0E&b=34706&ct=67676
Sponsor American Lung Association
1740 Broadway
New York, NY 10019

Alabama Humanities Foundation Grants 368
Grants are awarded to Alabama nonprofit community organizations with program proposals focused on languages; literature; philosophy; history; jurisprudence; religious studies; archaeology; ethics; linguistics; folklore; history; criticism and theory of the arts; social sciences employing historical or philosophical approaches; and interdisciplinary areas such as women's studies, African American studies, and American studies. The study should concentrate on a book, film, play, or idea. Active public participation and strong humanities content are the two essential ingredients of the funded project. Mini-grant proposals should be postmarked by the first day of alternating months, beginning with January, for immediate consideration; major grant proposals should be received by deadline dates. Application forms may be obtained from the foundation. Deadline for grants over $2000 is March 1 and September 1. Deadlines for grants under $2000 is the first working day of every other month.
Requirements Grants are made to nonprofit public or private organizations. Funds are to be used in state only.
Restrictions Grants are not made to individuals.
Amount $1000 for planning/consultant mini-grants; $2000 maximum for all others; major grants: $8500 maximum for public discussion and $10,000 matching; $17,500 for teacher seminar and $5000 matching; $10,000 for exhibition and $5000 matching; $20,000 maximum
Date(s) Application Is Due Mar 1; Sep 1.
Contact Susan Perry, Grants Director, (205) 930-0540; email: sperry@ahf.net
Internet http://www.ahf.net/grants.htm
Sponsor Alabama Humanities Foundation
1100 Ireland Wy, Ste 101
Birmingham, AL 35205

Albany Medical Center Prize in Medicine and Biomedical Research 369
The prize recognizes a physician or biomedical scientist (or group of physicians or scientists) who has made extraordinary and sustained leadership contributions to improving healthcare and patient care; or who has successfully pursued innovative biomedical research with demonstrated translational benefits applied to improved patient care. Each year's prize winner will have demonstrated significant outcomes that offer medical value of national or international importance. Prize winner activities will include but not be limited to disease and injury management, clinical research, and basic science investigations of diseases and injuries, leading to new discoveries and improved clinical outcomes. Nomination guidelines are available online.
Requirements Any physician or scientist or group whose work has led to significant advances in the fields of health care and scientific research with demonstrated translational benefits applied to improved patient care may be nominated. Those honored will be practitioners and/or scientists whose accomplishments and outcomes have been demonstrated in the past quarter century, with preference to demonstrated accomplishments in the past decade.
Amount $500,000
Date(s) Application Is Due Jan 5.
Contact Fardin Sanai, Secretary, (518) 262-8043; fax: (518) 262-4769; email: AMCprize@mail.amc.edu
Internet http://www.amc.edu/Academic/AlbanyPrize/prize_criteria.html
Sponsor Albany Medical Center
Center Building, 628 Madison Avenue - 1st Floor
Albany, NY 12208

Albert and Margaret Alkek Foundation Grants 370
The foundation awards grants to Texas nonprofit organizations to support charitable, religious, scientific (primarily medical), literary, cultural and educational organizations and programs. Preference will be given to research and education-related projects that will pay lasting dividends in terms of new discoveries and improved quality of life. One application per 12-month period will be considered. There are no application deadlines or forms. Applicants should submit a one- to two-page letter of inquiry that includes a brief description of the organization and the project for which funds are being considered, and the amount of funding need in total as well as the amount being requested. Inquiries should be sent via US postal mail; fax or email applications are not accepted.
Requirements Texas nonprofit organizations are eligible.
Restrictions The foundation does not make grants to individuals or loans of any type. The foundation does not make direct scholarships to students. All scholarship programs are administered through educational institutions. The foundation prefers not to fund: organizations that in turn make grants to others; grants intended to influence legislation or to support candidates for political office; fund-raising events such as luncheons, dinners, galas, advertising in programs, or other similar activities; charities operated by service clubs; memorials for individuals; student organizations; or purchase of uniforms, equipment, or trips for school-related organizations or sports teams.
Contact Grants Administrator, (713) 951-0019; fax: (713) 951-0043; email: info@alkek.org
Internet http://www.alkek.org/grantguidelines.htm
Sponsor Albert and Margaret Alkek Foundation
1221 McKinney, Ste 4525
Houston, TX 77010-2023

Albert and Mary Lasker Foundation Awards 371
The major purpose of the awards is to honor the individual(s) who have made significant contributions in basic or clinical research in diseases that are the main cause of death and disability. Three categories of awards are made. The Basic Medical Research Award honors the scientist or scientists who have made fundamental investigations that open new areas of biomedical science. The Clinical Medical Research Award honors the scientist(s) whose contributions, directly or indirectly, have led to the improvement of the clinical management or treatment of patients and to the alleviation or elimination or one of the major medical causes of disability or death. The Special Achievement Award in Medical Science honors a scientist whose contributions to research are of unique magnitude and immeasurable influence on the course of science, health, or medicine, and whose professional career has engendered extreme respect within the biomedical community. Nomination forms are available online. Nominations must be received by the listed application deadline.
Amount $50,000 medical research award; $50,000 clinical medical research award; $25,000 special achievement award
Date(s) Application Is Due Feb 1.
Contact David Keegan, (212) 286-0222; fax: (212) 286-0924; email: dkeegan@laskerfoundation.org
Internet http://www.laskerfoundation.org/awards/awards.html
Sponsor Albert and Mary Lasker Foundation
110 E 42nd St, Ste 1300
New York, NY 10017

Albert Ellis Institute Clinical Fellowships 372
This fellowship program is a unique one- to two-year part-time course of study intended to help the therapist develop clinical proficiency in an active psychotherapy approach emphasizing rational emotive behavior psychotherapy and allied cognitive behavioral techniques. Fellows receive highly diversified training in clinical experience, supervision, workshop experience, and research. By special arrangement, persons on sabbatical or from out of town may complete the program in one year. Contact the institute for applications and deadline dates.
Requirements The fellowship is open to those who hold doctorates in psychology or counseling (or near completion of PhD); to MSWs, RNs, and MDs; and to licensed mental health counselors. All candidates must be licensed or license-eligible. Predoctoral interns pursue the same program as postdoctoral fellows and receive the same stipend.
Amount $6000 per year for two-year fellowships
Contact Dr. Kristene Doyle, Program Contact, (212) 535-0822 or (800) 323-4738; fax: (212) 249-3582; email: krisdoyle@albertellis.com or info@albertellis.org
Internet http://www.rebt.org/titlepages/professionals.asp
Sponsor Albert Ellis Institute
45 E 65th St
New York, NY 10021

Alberta Heritage Preservation Heritage Awareness Grants 373
Grants support tangible initiatives that promote awareness of Alberta's history and pre-history and have a lasting impact. Contact the foundation for application materials.
Requirements Applicants must be resident Albertans or have a permanent address in Alberta.
Restrictions Provincial government departments and their employees are not eligible to apply.
Amount $C5000 maximum
Date(s) Application Is Due Feb 1; Sep 1.
Contact Monika McNabb, Coordinator, Heritage Preservation Partnership Program, (780) 431-2305; fax: (780) 427-5598; email: monika.mcnabb@gov.ab.ca
Internet http://www.cd.gov.ab.ca/preserving/heritage/ahrf/partnership/HeritageAwareness/index.asp
Sponsor Alberta Historical Resources Foundation
8820-112 St
Edmonton, AB T6G 2P8 Canada

Alberta Historical Publications Grants 374
Grants are awarded to support the printing or reprinting of historical publications dealing with Alberta's human history or prehistory or the printing of brochures, pamphlets, or other materials of a commemorative or informative nature.
Requirements Applicants must be resident Albertans or have a permanent address in Alberta.
Restrictions Provincial government departments and their employees are not eligible to apply. Publisher/printers are not eligible to apply; and personal family histories are ineligible for funding.
Amount $C3000 maximum for brochures and pamphlets; $C5000 maximum for books
Date(s) Application Is Due Feb 1; Sep 1.
Contact Program Contact, (780) 431-2305; fax: (780) 427-5598; email: monika.mcnabb@gov.ab.ca
Internet http://www.cd.gov.ab.ca/preserving/heritage/ahrf/partnership/publications/index.asp
Sponsor Alberta Historical Resources Foundation
8820 112 St
Edmonton, AB T6G 2P8 Canada

Alberta Historical Resources Foundation Research Grants 375
Grants support research that will produce new understandings or add to the knowledge base of Alberta's history and pre-history. Projects such as oral histories and historic site inventories may be considered in this category. Contact the foundation for application materials.
Requirements Applicants must be resident Albertans or have a permanent address in Alberta.
Restrictions Provincial government departments and their employees are not eligible to apply.
Amount $C15,000 maximum
Date(s) Application Is Due Feb 1; Sep 1.
Contact Community Resources Officer, (780) 431-2305; email: monika.mcnabb@gov.ab.ca
Internet http://www.cd.gov.ab.ca/preserving/heritage/ahrf/partnership/research/index.asp
Sponsor Alberta Historical Resources Foundation
8820 112 St
Edmonton, AB T6G 2P8 Canada

Alberta Historical Resources Foundation Roger Soderstrom Scholarship 376
Scholarships are awarded to encourage research that will increase the knowledge of Alberta's history and historic resources. Applicable fields of study include anthropology, archaeology, history, historical geography, architectural history and preservation, and restoration architecture. One scholarship per Alberta university is awarded annually for the duration of one year, renewable for one year. Further information may be obtained through an Alberta university or from the foundation.
Requirements Applicants must be resident Albertans or have a permanent address in Alberta.

Restrictions Provincial government departments and their employees are not eligible to apply.
Amount $C3000
Date(s) Application Is Due Feb 1; Sep 1.
Contact Heritage Preservation Partnership Program, (780) 431-2305
Internet http://www.cd.gov.ab.ca/preserving/heritage/ahrf/partnership/rogerscholarship/index.asp
Sponsor Alberta Historical Resources Foundation
8820-112 St
Edmonton, AB T6G 2P8 Canada

Alberta Law Foundation Grants 377
The objectives of the foundation are to conduct research into and recommend reform of law and the administration of justice; establish, maintain, and operate law libraries; contribute to the legal education and knowledge of the people of Alberta and provide programs and facilities for those purposes; provide assistance to native people's legal programs, student legal aid programs, and programs of like nature; and contribute to the costs incurred by the Legal Aid Society of Alberta to administer a plan to provide legal aid. To be considered for funding, programs or projects must fall within these objectives. Operating grants and project grants are awarded. The application process begins with a discussing the program or project idea with the executive director. This will be followed by an exchange of drafts during the development of the application.
Restrictions Grants will not be made to an individual or for the support of a commercial venture. Funds are not available for bursaries, fellowships, sabbatical leave support, endowments, building funds, etc.
Contact David Aucoin, Executive Director, (403) 264-4701; fax: (403) 294-9238; email: contact@albertalawfoundation.org
Internet http://www.albertalawfoundation.org/Apply/general.html
Sponsor Alberta Law Foundation
407 8th Ave SW, Ste 300
Calgary, AB T2P 1E5 Canada

Alberta Research Council Scholarship 378
One scholarship is offered annually in open competition to a graduate student for research in areas of interest to the Alberta Research Council, such as agriculture, biotechnology, energy, forestry, environment, information technology, and manufacturing. The scholarship is awarded for 12 months duration; a student may apply in open competition for a subsequent year's award.
Requirements Applicants must be graduate students engaged in thesis research at the master's or doctoral level who are (or will be) registered full-time in a thesis-based graduate program in the Faculty of Graduate Studies at the University of Calgary.
Amount $C17,300
Contact Connie Busch, Faculty of Graduate Studies, (403) 220-5690; fax: (403) 289-7635; email: cbusch@.ucalgary.ca
Internet http://www.grad.ucalgary.ca/funding/internal_scholarships/lev_4/ab_research.htm
Sponsor University of Calgary
2500 University Dr NW, Earth Sciences Bldg, Rm 720
Calgary, AB T2N 1N4 Canada

Albuquerque Community Foundation Grants 379
The foundation seeks to improve the quality of life in the greater Albuquerque, NM, area by providing support for projects and organizations that serve the community in arts and culture, education, environmental and historic preservation, children and youth, and health and human services. Through its grant program, the foundation supports projects that are innovative, meet the needs of underserved segments of the community, encourage matching funds or additional gifts, promote cooperation among agencies, empower the disadvantaged and disabled, and enhance the effectiveness of local charitable organizations. Types of support include continuing support, general operating support, program development, publication, seed grants, scholarships funds and scholarships to individuals, and technical assistance.
Requirements IRS 501(c)3 organizations based in Albuquerque, NM, are eligible. Proposals are reviewed on the basis of the following priorities: impact, innovation, leverage, management, and nonduplication.
Restrictions Grants are generally not made to or for individuals, political or religious purposes, debt retirement, payment of interest or taxes, annual campaigns, endowments, emergency funding, to influence legislation or elections, scholarships, awards, or to private foundations and other grantmaking organizations.
Amount $10,000 maximum
Date(s) Application Is Due Apr 16, Aug 15.
Contact Grant Review Committee, (505) 883-6240; email: foundation@albuquerquefoundation.org
Internet http://www.albuquerquefoundation.org
Sponsor Albuquerque Community Foundation
P.O. Box 36960
Albuquerque, NM 87176-6960

Alcoa Foundation Grants 380
General priorities of the foundation include safe and healthy children and families--ensuring that children and their families have the tools, the knowledge and the services to remain healthy and safe at home, in the community and in the workplace; conservation and sustainability--educating young leaders on conservation issues, protecting forests, promoting sound public policy research, and understanding the linkages between business and the environment; skills today for tomorrow--providing individuals with critical skills and services to be economically connected, workplace-ready, and productive in a changing economy; business and community partnerships--strengthening the nonprofit sector and developing meaningful partnerships among nonprofits, the private sector, and local government; and global education in science, engineering, technology and business--broadening student participation in areas central to Alcoa to prepare a diverse cross-section of our communities for a global workplace. Types of support include capital grants, building funds, challenge grants, matching gifts, general support, research grants, scholarships, and seed money. Initial contact should be a letter of inquiry.
Requirements The foundation awards grants to nonprofit public charities in communities where Alcoa has a presence. Local Alcoans work within their communities to evaluate organizations and make recommendations for funding to Alcoa Foundation. Nonprofit organizations that serve localized communities should find the Alcoa facility nearest to them and write a one-page letter describing their mission, nature of request, connection to the areas of excellence and offering contact information. If interested, the Alcoa location contact will notify the requesting organization and invite them to submit more information. Areas of operation include western Pennsylvania; Davenport, IA; Evansville, IN; Massena, NY; New Jersey; Cleveland, OH; Knoxville, TN; and Rockdale, TX.
Restrictions The foundation does not make gifts to local projects other than those near Alcoa plant or office locations; endowment funds, deficit reduction, or operating reserves; hospital capital campaign programs unless the hospital presents a comprehensive area analysis that justifies, on a regional rather than an individual institutional basis, the need for the capital improvement; individuals, except for the scholarship program for children of Alcoa employees; tickets and other promotional activities; trips, tours, or student exchange programs; or documentaries and videos.
Amount $1000-$50,000 average
Contact Program Contact, (412) 553-2348; fax: (412) 553-4498
Internet http://www.alcoa.com/global/en/community/foundation.asp
Sponsor Alcoa Foundation
201 Isabella St
Pittsburgh, PA 15212-5858

Alcohol Misuse and Alcoholism Research Grants 381
The foundation's research interests include factors influencing transitions in drinking patterns and behavior, effects of moderate use of alcohol on health and well-being, mechanisms underlying the behavioral and biomedical effects of alcohol, biobehavioral/interdisciplinary research on the etiology of alcohol misuse. Applications may be obtained from the Web site or by contacting the office. Grantees are notified within two weeks following the advisory council meetings, which are held in April and November.
Requirements Applications may be submitted by public or private nonprofit organizations such as universities, colleges, hospitals, research institutes and organizations, and governmental research agencies and laboratories in the United States and Canada.
Restrictions Non-research activities such as education projects, public awareness efforts and treatment or referral services are not eligible for support. The Foundation also does not support the training of pre- and post-doctoral fellows, undergraduates, graduate students, medical students, interns or residents. It does not fund thesis or dissertation research. The Foundation does not encourage applications on treatment of the complications of advanced alcoholism. However, research involving treatment intended to elucidate the pathogenesis of alcohol-related problems will be considered.
Amount $100,000 maximum over two years
Date(s) Application Is Due Feb 1; Sep 1.
Contact Research Grants Administrator, (410) 821-7066; fax: (410) 821-7065; email: info@abmrf.org
Internet http://www.abmrf.org/grants.htm
Sponsor Alcoholic Beverage Medical Research Foundation (ABMRF)
1122 Kenilworth Dr, Ste 407
Baltimore, MD 21204

Alcon Foundation Grants Program 382
The foundation supports organizations in the fields of health care, leadership programs, research, education and community responsibility. Programs that advance the education and skill levels of eye care professionals are given special consideration. General operating grants to organizations and institutions improving education and research in the areas of specialization of Alcon Laboratories--ophthalmology and vision care. Grants are also awarded to community activities that benefit company employees. Applications may be submitted at any time.
Requirements Grants are not made for building programs.
Restrictions Non 501(c)(3)organizations, individuals and scholarship programs, religious, veterans or fraternal organizations, political causes, capital campaigns, matching gifts, trips, tournaments and tours, and endowments are not supported.
Amount $100-$50,000 average
Contact Mary Dulle, Chair, (817) 293-0450; email: Mary.Dulle@Alconlabs.com
Internet http://www.alconlabs.com/corporate-responsibility/alcon-foundation.asp
Sponsor Alcon Foundation
6201 S Freeway
Fort Worth, TX 76134

ALCTS Bowker-Ulrich's Serials Librarianship Award 383

This award, donated by the CSA/Ulrich Company, is given for contributions to serials librarianship in areas of professional association participation, library education, serials literature, research, or development of tools leading to better understanding of the field of serials.

Requirements Applications or nominations are invited; appropriate forms may be obtained through ALCTS. The award may be divided among two or more individuals who have participated jointly in the achievement for which it is granted.

Restrictions Employees of the CSA/Ulrich Company are not eligible to receive the award.

Amount $1500

Date(s) Application Is Due Dec 1.

Contact Mary Page, Chair, CSA/Ulrich's Serials Librarianship Award Committee, (732) 445-5894; fax: (732) 445-5888; email: mspage@rcirutgers.edu

Internet http://www.ala.org/Template.cfm?Section=awards&template=/ContentManagement/ContentDisplay.cfm&ContentID=48736

Sponsor Association for Library Collections and Technical Services
50 E. Huron Street
Chicago, IL 60611-2795

Alex C. Walker Educational and Charitable Foundation Grants 384

The foundation awards grants to investigate the causes of economic imbalances; investigate the effect of the monetary system in fostering a sustainable economy; investigate causes tending to destroy or impair the free-market system; explore and develop free-market solutions; and disseminate information on these issues. The foundation funds projects dealing with the research and development of innovative ideas, education of market principles, the application of ideas developed through seed grants and research, and ecological economics with a free-market orientation. Projects with the following qualities are favored: innovation, impact, longevity, collaboration, solution oriented, trackability, objectivity, and sustainability. Grant requests must be submitted on a formal application form through this website. Guidelines are available online.

Requirements US 501(c)3 tax-exempt organizations are eligible.

Restrictions Ideological or political activities and general educational programs are not funded. Grants do not support endowment, building funds, or individuals.

Amount $5000-$89,500

Date(s) Application Is Due Apr 1; Oct 1.

Contact Grants Administrator, c/o Barret P. Walker, (404) 378-2752

Internet http://walker-foundation.org/page.aspx?s=5534.0.69.5316

Sponsor Alex C. Walker Educational and Charitable Foundation
1729 Coventry Pl
Decatur, GA 30030

Alex Stern Family Foundation Grants 385

The foundation awards grants to North Dakota and Minnesota nonprofits in its areas of interest, including arts and culture, child welfare, the elderly, alcohol abuse, community funds, family and social services, education, minorities, hospices, and cancer research. Types of support include general operating support, continuing support, annual campaigns, building construction/renovation, equipment acquisition, emergency funds, program development, scholarship funds, research, and matching funds. Applications are reviewed in June and November.

Requirements Moorhead, MN, and Fargo, ND, nonprofit organizations are eligible.

Restrictions Grants are not awarded to individuals or for endowments.

Amount $1000-$50,000 range

Date(s) Application Is Due Mar 31; Aug 31.

Contact Donald Scott, Executive Director, (701) 237-0170

Sponsor Alex Stern Family Foundation
609 1/2 1st Avenue N., Ste 205
Fargo, ND 58102

Alexander and Margaret Stewart Trust Grants 386

The trust awards grants in the greater Washington, DC, area for cancer treatment, especially equipment used in diagnosis and treatment; and caring for children who are physically ill, mentally ill, or disabled. Grants also support research, education, and prevention of common childhood diseases, including negative societal behavioral patterns that impact children. Proposals for projects aiding the economically deprived receive preference. The trust awards start-up funding. Applications may be submitted at any time; requests received by the listed deadline date are reviewed by the end of the year.

Requirements Nonprofits in the greater District of Columbia area are eligible.

Restrictions Requests for support of endowments, buildings, or capital campaigns are denied.

Amount $50,000-$150,000 average

Date(s) Application Is Due Sep 15.

Contact Grants Administrator, (202) 785-9892; fax (202) 785-0918; email: wbierbower@stewart-trust.org

Internet http://www.stewart-trust.org/guidelines.htm

Sponsor Alexander and Margaret Stewart Trust
888 17th St NW, Brawner Bldg, Ste 610
Washington, DC 20006-3313

Alexander von Humboldt Foundation Feodor-Lynen Research Fellowships 387

Fellowships are offered to highly qualified German scholars from all disciplines for long-term research projects (one to four years) at foreign institutes. The host must be a foreign scholar formerly sponsored by the foundation (research fellow or research award winner). Guidelines and application are available online.

Requirements Applicants must be less than 38 years old; have successfully completed their doctorate with very good or good ratings; furnish proof of work published in recognized academic journals; submit a research plan agreed with the foreign host, including confirmation that research facilities can be made available; and possess a good knowledge of the host country's language or at least a very good knowledge of English, provided they can carry out their research project in that language. Nominating form is available on the Web site http://www.avh.de/en/programme/preise/pt_01.htm.

Date(s) Application Is Due Feb 10; Jun 10; Oct 10.

Contact Alexander von Humboldt-US Liaison Office, (202) 783-1907; fax: (202) 783-1908; email: lynen.select@avh.de

Internet http://www.avh.de/en/programme/stip_deu/flf.htm

Sponsor Alexander von Humboldt Foundation
1012 14th St NW, Ste 1015
Washington, DC 20005

Alexander von Humboldt Foundation Georg Forster Research Fellowships 388

Fellowships are available to scholars from developing countries in humanities and social sciences; political science and economics; projects in the public health sector and in the fields of agriculture, forestry, and geosciences; and interdisciplinary projects relating to environmental and resource protection. Fellowships are designed to promote the transfer of knowledge and methods and to contribute to further development in fellows' home countries. Applications may be submitted for long-term research stays of between six and 12 months. Applications forms are available on the Web site and may be submitted at any time.

Requirements Scholars from developing countries (excluding Egypt, Korea, Turkey, India, and the Peoples' Republic of China) may apply. Applicants must be less than 45 years old and hold doctorate degrees. Nominating forms are available on the Web site http://www.avh.de/en/programme/preise/pt_01.htm.

Restrictions Short-term study tours, participation in conferences, or educational visits cannot be funded. Applications for extension of research stays already commenced in Germany cannot be considered.

Contact Petra Marzouk, (+49) 0228-833-0; fax: (+49) 0228-833-199; email: forster.select@avh.de

Internet http://www.avh.de/en/programme/stip_aus/gf.htm

Sponsor Alexander von Humboldt Foundation
Jean-Paul-St 12
D-53173 Bonn Germany

Alexander von Humboldt Foundation Research Fellowships 389

The foundation offers research fellowships annually to enable highly qualified non-German postdoctoral scholars to pursue research of their own choice at universities or research institutes in Germany. Travel relocation allowance for fellow only and monthly allowance for accompanying spouse are provided. The research fellowships are provided on a long-term basis and usually cover a period of six to 12 months. Grant decisions are made in March, July, and November of each year. Applications are available on the Web site and are accepted at any time. The nomination form is available on the Web site http://www.avh.de/en/programme/preise/pt_01.htm.

Requirements Fellowships are open to non-Germans under age 40, who have an academic degree comparable to the doctorate (PhD, DSc, etc.), who can present evidence of independent research at universities and other research institutions, and whose research has been published. A good working knowledge of German is required of the candidates in the humanities, law, or the social sciences; scholars of natural, medical, and engineering sciences must have a good command of English.

Amount 75,000 Euro maximum

Contact Alexander von Humboldt-US Liaison Office, (202) 783-1907; fax: (202) 783-1908; email: avh@bellatlantic.net

Internet http://www.humboldt-foundation.de/en/programme/stip_aus/stp.htm

Sponsor Alexander von Humboldt Foundation
1012 14th St NW, Ste 301
Washington, DC 20005

Alexander von Humboldt Foundation Transatlantic Research Collaboration Awards 390

The program supports collaborative research among American, Canadian, and German scholars in the humanities, social sciences, economics, and law. Grants may be used to finance short-term research visits and travel, organize conferences and workshops, purchase materials and equipment, and cover costs for research assistants and printing. Funds must be matched by US or Canadian sources. Guidelines and application are available online.

Requirements Applications should be submitted jointly by at least one German and one US or Canadian scholar. The PhD degree is required.

Amount 45,000 Euro maximum ($54,000 approximately)

Date(s) Application Is Due Apr 30; Oct 31.

Contact Alexander von Humboldt-US Liaison Office, (202) 783-1907; fax: (202) 783-1908; email: avh@verizon.net
Internet http://www.humboldt-foundation.de/en/programme/stip_aus/transcoop.htm
Sponsor Alexander von Humboldt Foundation
1012 14th St NW, Ste 301
Washington, DC 20005

Alf Heggoy Memorial Book Award **391**
This award is given annually in recognition for the best book published during the previous year dealing with the French colonial experience from the 16th to the 20th century. Books from any academic discipline will be considered but they must approach the consideration of the French colonial experience from an historical perspective. Applicants or their publishers should submit three copies of books published (date of publication is determined by the copyright page of the book), one to each of the book prize committee members: Prof Sue Peabody, Heggoy Prize Committee Chair, Washington State University VMMC 202D, 14204 NE Salmon Creek Ave, Vancouver, WA, USA 98686, email: peabody@vancouver.wsu.edu; Prof Peter Moogk, Department of History, University of British Columbia, Buchanan Tower 1121, 1873 East Mall, Vancouver, BC V6T 1Z1, Canada; and Prof Eric Jennings, Department of History, University of Toronto, 100 Saint George St, Toronto, Ontario M5S 3G3, Canada. Annual deadline dates may vary; contact program staff for exact dates.
Amount $350
Date(s) Application Is Due Mar 1.
Contact Bill Shorrock, Chair, Alf Heggoy Book Prize Committee; email: w.shorrock@csuohio.edu
Internet http://www.frenchcolonial.org/Heggoy.html
Sponsor French Colonial Historical Society
Department of History, Cleveland State University, Euclid Ave/24th St
Cleveland, OH 44115

Alfred Bader Award in Bio-Inorganic or Bio-Organic Chemistry **392**
This award is given annually to recognize outstanding contributions to bio-organic or bio-inorganic chemistry. The award shall be for outstanding research and accomplishments without regard to age or nationality. The award is intended to recognize significant accomplishments that are at the interface between biology and organic or inorganic chemistry. Special consideration will be given to applications of the fundamental principles and experimental methodology of chemistry to areas of biological significance. The recipient's award address will be reprinted in Aldrichimica Acta. Annual deadline dates may vary; contact program staff for exact dates.
Requirements Any individual, except a member of the awards committee, may submit one nomination or seconding letter for the award in any given year. The nominating documents consist of a letter of not more than 1000 words containing an evaluation of the nominee's accomplishments and a specific identification of the work to be recognized, a biographical sketch including date of birth, and a list of publications and patents authored by the nominee. Six copies of all items to be included in the nomination must be submitted.
Restrictions Self-nominations are not accepted.
Amount $5000 and reimbursement of travel expenses to award meeting
Date(s) Application Is Due Feb 1.
Contact Awards Administrator, (202) 227-5558; fax: (202) 776-8211; email: awards@acs.org
Internet http://www.chemistry.org/portal/a/c/s/1/acsdisplay.html?DOC=awards%5Cbader.html
Sponsor American Chemical Society
1155 16th St NW
Washington, DC 20036

Alfred Burger Award in Medicinal Chemistry **393**
This award, sponsored by GlaxoSmithKline and administered by the American Chemical Society, is awarded biennially in even-numbered years to recognize outstanding contributions to research in medicinal chemistry. The award shall be granted without regard to age or nationality. Applications are accepted in odd-numbered years. Annual deadline dates may vary; contact program staff for exact dates.
Requirements Any individual, except a member of the award committee, may submit one nomination or seconding letter for the award in any given year. The nominating documents consist of a letter of not more than 1000 words containing an evaluation of the nominee's accomplishments and a specific identification of the work to be recognized, a biographical sketch including date of birth, and a list of publications and patents authored by the nominee. Six copies of all items to be included in the nomination must be submitted.
Restrictions Self-nominations are not accepted.
Amount $3000 and travel to award meeting
Date(s) Application Is Due Feb 1.
Contact Awards Administrator, (800) 227-5558; fax: (202) 872-6317; email: awards@acs.org
Internet http://www.chemistry.org/portal/a/c/s/1/acsdisplay.html?DOC=awards%5Cburger.html
Sponsor American Chemical Society
1155 16th St NW
Washington, DC 20036

Alfred D. Bell, Travel Grants **394**
The mission of the society is to advance understanding of the historical interaction of people with the forest environment. To this end, an average of six travel grants are awarded annually to researchers wishing to study at the society's library and archives. Research topics should be in the areas of forest or conservation history. Applications may be submitted at any time as grants are awarded year-round.
Requirements Preference is given to graduate students, but grants also are awarded to postgraduates and professionals pursuing career advancement.
Amount $950 maximum
Contact Grants Administrator, (919) 682-9319; fax: (919) 682-2349
Internet http://www.lib.duke.edu/forest/Research/bellgnt.html
Sponsor Forest History Society
701 Vickers Ave
Durham, NC 27701-3162

Alfred E. Driscoll Publication Prize **395**
This prize is awarded in even-numbered years for an outstanding doctoral dissertation on any aspect of New Jersey history. Unsuccessful applicants may resubmit their dissertations for consideration for the prize. One award is given each year. To apply, submit one copy of the dissertation by deadline date. Use the prize nomination form in the guidelines booklet.
Restrictions An applicant may not apply for a publication grant and the Driscoll Prize for the same work. Dissertations that have already been accepted for publication are ineligible.
Amount $1000
Date(s) Application Is Due Jan 2.
Contact Mary Murrin, Director Grants Program, (609) 984-0954; email: mary.murrin@sos.state.nj.us
Internet http://www.state.nj.us/state/history/grants_t.html
Sponsor New Jersey Historical Commission
225 W State St, 4th Fl, P.O. Box 305
Trenton, NJ 08625-0305

Alfred Hodder Fellowship **396**
The fellowship was established for the promotion of independent work in the humanities and is awarded to humanists of exceptional talent. The award is designed to offer one year of independent study in residence at Princeton University. The appointment of the Hodder Fellow is made each February on the recommendation of the Committee on Humanistic Studies at which time an announcement is sent to all applicants.
Requirements Preference is given to candidates outside of academia. Applicant must submit a resume, a sample of previous work (10-page maximum, nonreturnable), and a project proposal of two to three pages along with a self-addressed, stamped envelope.
Restrictions Funds are not to be used to pursue a PhD degree.
Amount $55,000 approximately for academic year
Date(s) Application Is Due Nov 1.
Contact Hodder Fellowship, Council of the Humanities, (609) 258-4717; fax: (609) 258-2783; email: dsteidl@princeton.edu
Internet http://www.princeton.edu/~humcounc/hodderfellows.shtml
Sponsor Princeton University
122 E Pyne
Princeton, NJ 08544

Alfred I. DuPont Foundation Grants **397**
Grants are awarded primarily to elderly adults requiring health, economic, or educational assistance. Support is also given for higher education and medical research. All grants to the elderly are made to individuals in the southeastern United States. General operating support and grants to individuals are awarded. An application form is required. Applications are accepted at any time and are dealt with promptly.
Requirements Nonprofit organizations in the southeastern US are eligible. Preference is given to those in Florida.
Amount $1000-$35,000 average for general operating support; $1000-$2000 average for individuals
Contact Rosemary Cusimano Wills, Secretary, (904) 232-4123
Sponsor Alfred I. DuPont Foundation Inc
4600 Touchton Rd E, Bldg 200, Ste 120
Jacksonville, FL 32246

Alfred P. Sloan Foundation Business Organizations Grants **398**
This program (formerly "Role of the Corporation") supports academic research and scholarship aimed at painting a realistic picture of how corporations and other business organizations function, with special emphasis on how the people in them actually behave, how they are motivated, and how they are rewarded. The Foundation has sought to increase understanding of these organizations because of the enormous effect they have on the standard of living and quality of life for most people in the United States and around the world. Grant requests can be made at any time for support of activities related to Foundation program areas and interests. The Foundation is generally limited to supporting tax-exempt organizations. The Foundation has no deadlines or standard forms. The Foundation accepts proposals sent by email. A brief letter of inquiry, rather than a fully developed proposal, is an advisable first step for an applicant, conserving

his or her time and allowing for a preliminary response regarding the possibility of support.
Requirements Concise, well-organized proposals are preferred. In no case should the body of the proposal exceed 20 double-spaced pages.
Restrictions The Foundation's activities do not normally extend to religion, the creative or performing arts, elementary or secondary education, medical research or health care, the humanities or to activities outside the United States. Grants are not made for endowments or for buildings or equipment.
Contact Gail M. Pesyna, Program Director; (212) 649-1649; fax: (212) 757-5117; email: pesyna@sloan.org
Internet http://sloan.org/programs/stndrd_role.shtml
Sponsor Alfred P. Sloan Foundation
630 Fifth Avenue, Suite 2550
New York, NY 10111

Alfred P. Sloan Foundation Census of Marine Life Research Grants 399
The goal of this project is to advance a major new international observational program to be completed by 2010 to assess and explain the diversity, distribution, and abundance of marine life. An international Scientific Steering Committee and Secretariat based at the Consortium for Oceanographic Research and Education in Washington DC now guide the program. Grant-making occurs in conjunction with the National Ocean Partnership Program. The Foundation seeks opportunities to work with the institutions and media that can build public interest and with maritime industries and environmentalists to assure their meaningful participation. Grant requests can be made at any time for support of activities related to Foundation program areas and interests. The Foundation is generally limited to supporting tax-exempt organizations. The Foundation has no deadlines or standard forms. The Foundation accepts proposals sent by email. A brief letter of inquiry, rather than a fully developed proposal, is an advisable first step for an applicant, conserving his or her time and allowing for a preliminary response regarding the possibility of support.
Requirements Concise, well-organized proposals are preferred. In no case should the body of the proposal exceed 20 double-spaced pages.
Restrictions The Foundation's activities do not normally extend to religion, the creative or performing arts, elementary or secondary education, medical research or health care, the humanities or to activities outside the United States. Grants are not made for endowments or for buildings or equipment.
Contact Jesse H. Ausubel, Program Director; (212) 649-1649; fax: (212) 757-5117; email: ausubel@sloan.org
Internet http://sloan.org/programs/scitech_supresearch.shtml
Sponsor Alfred P. Sloan Foundation
630 Fifth Avenue, Suite 2550
New York, NY 10111

Alfred P. Sloan Foundation Civic Program Grants 400
The goal of the Program is to make a contribution to the Foundation's home area, New York City. There are two directions to the Program: to respond to special opportunities in New York City; and to fund high-leverage projects in New York City that are related to other parts of our program. Interested readers should refer to the descriptions of other program areas in the Foundation website. Grant requests can be made at any time for support of activities related to Foundation program areas and interests. The Foundation is generally limited to supporting tax-exempt organizations. The Foundation has no deadlines or standard forms. The Foundation accepts proposals sent by email. A brief letter of inquiry, rather than a fully developed proposal, is an advisable first step for an applicant, conserving his or her time and allowing for a preliminary response regarding the possibility of support.
Requirements Concise, well-organized proposals are preferred. In no case should the body of the proposal exceed 20 double-spaced pages.
Restrictions The Foundation's activities do not normally extend to religion, the creative or performing arts, elementary or secondary education, medical research or health care, the humanities or to activities outside the United States. Grants are not made for endowments or for buildings or equipment.
Contact Ted Greenwood, Program Director; (212) 649-1649; fax: (212) 757-5117; email: greenwood@sloan.org
Internet http://sloan.org/programs/pg_civic.shtml
Sponsor Alfred P. Sloan Foundation
630 Fifth Avenue, Suite 2550
New York, NY 10111

Alfred P. Sloan Foundation Education and Careers in Science and Technology Grants 401
Programs to strengthen education in science and technology, to increase interest in these fields, and to understand and communicate to others the nature of careers in these fields have long been supported by the Foundation. Increasingly important are opportunities presented by electronic technologies for learning outside the classroom. This program is divided into the following sections: anytime, anyplace learning; information about careers; professional science master's degrees; the science and engineering workforce; increasing Ph.D.s for underrepresented minorities; education for underrepresented groups; retention of students in higher education; and public understanding of science and technology. Grant requests can be made at any time for support of activities related to Foundation program areas and interests. The Foundation is generally limited to supporting tax-exempt organizations. The Foundation has no deadlines or standard forms. The Foundation accepts proposals sent by email. A brief letter of inquiry, rather than a fully developed proposal, is an advisable first step for an applicant, conserving his or her time and allowing for a preliminary response regarding the possibility of support.
Requirements Concise, well-organized proposals are preferred. In no case should the body of the proposal exceed 20 double-spaced pages.
Restrictions The Foundation's activities do not normally extend to religion, the creative or performing arts, elementary or secondary education, medical research or health care, the humanities or to activities outside the United States. Grants are not made for endowments or for buildings or equipment.
Contact Jesse H. Ausubel, Program Director; (212) 649-1649; fax: (212) 757-5117; email: ausubel@sloan.org
Internet http://sloan.org/programs/pg_education.shtml
Sponsor Alfred P. Sloan Foundation
630 Fifth Avenue, Suite 2550
New York, NY 10111

Alfred P. Sloan Foundation Higher Education as an Industry Grants 402
The goal of this program is to produce understanding of how institutions of higher education actually work and how the set of institutions functions together as an industry. Grant requests can be made at any time for support of activities related to Foundation program areas and interests. The Foundation is generally limited to supporting tax-exempt organizations. The Foundation has no deadlines or standard forms. The Foundation accepts proposals sent by email. A brief letter of inquiry, rather than a fully developed proposal, is an advisable first step for an applicant, conserving his or her time and allowing for a preliminary response regarding the possibility of support.
Requirements Concise, well-organized proposals are preferred. In no case should the body of the proposal exceed 20 double-spaced pages.
Restrictions The Foundation's activities do not normally extend to religion, the creative or performing arts, elementary or secondary education, medical research or health care, the humanities or to activities outside the United States. Grants are not made for endowments or for buildings or equipment.
Contact Jesse H. Ausubel, Program Director; (212) 649-1649; fax: (212) 757-5117; email: ausubel@sloan.org
Internet http://sloan.org/programs/stndrd_universi.shtml
Sponsor Alfred P. Sloan Foundation
630 Fifth Avenue, Suite 2550
New York, NY 10111

Alfred P. Sloan Foundation History of Science and Technology Grants 403
The goal of this program is to preserve the raw material of history by supporting archival projects now centered on Charles Darwin, Thomas A. Edison, and Kurt G?'del, and via new projects based on the World Wide Web. Two specific areas are of interest: the archival program; and recent history of science and engineering on the web. Grant requests can be made at any time for support of activities related to Foundation program areas and interests. The Foundation is generally limited to supporting tax-exempt organizations. The Foundation has no deadlines or standard forms. The Foundation accepts proposals sent by email. A brief letter of inquiry, rather than a fully developed proposal, is an advisable first step for an applicant, conserving his or her time and allowing for a preliminary response regarding the possibility of support.
Requirements Concise, well-organized proposals are preferred. In no case should the body of the proposal exceed 20 double-spaced pages.
Restrictions The Foundation's activities do not normally extend to religion, the creative or performing arts, elementary or secondary education, medical research or health care, the humanities or to activities outside the United States. Grants are not made for endowments or for buildings or equipment.
Contact Doron Weber, Program Director; (212) 649-1649; fax: (212) 757-5117; email: weber@sloan.org; ; Jesse H. Ausubel, Program Director; (212) 649-1649; fax: (212) 757-5117; email: ausubel@sloan.org
Internet http://sloan.org/programs/scitech_historysci.shtml
Sponsor Alfred P. Sloan Foundation
630 Fifth Avenue, Suite 2550
New York, NY 10111

Alfred P. Sloan Foundation Indoor Environment Research Grants 404
The goal of this program is to understand the human indoor environment at the microbial level. The Foundation believes that this understanding may ultimately help to make this artificial environment more hospitable to human life or resistant to biological attacks. Their plan has three parts. First, the Foundation wants to establish a basic understanding of the indoor microbial environment. Second, it wants to help develop tools for understanding and probing the indoor environment. And lastly, it wants to apply the knowledge and tools to various human indoor environments, such as hospitals. Grant requests can be made at any time for support of activities related to Foundation program areas and interests. The Foundation is generally limited to supporting tax-exempt organizations. The Foundation has no deadlines or standard forms. The Foundation accepts proposals sent by email. A brief letter of inquiry, rather than a fully developed proposal, is an advisable first step for an applicant, conserving his or her time and allowing for a preliminary response regarding the possibility of support.

Requirements Concise, well-organized proposals are preferred. In no case should the body of the proposal exceed 20 double-spaced pages.
Restrictions The Foundation's activities do not normally extend to religion, the creative or performing arts, elementary or secondary education, medical research or health care, the humanities or to activities outside the United States. Grants are not made for endowments or for buildings or equipment.
Contact Paula J. Olsiewski, Program Director; (212) 649-1649; fax: (212) 757-5117; email: olsiewski@sloan.org
Internet http://sloan.org/programs/scitech_supresearch.shtml
Sponsor Alfred P. Sloan Foundation
630 Fifth Avenue, Suite 2550
New York, NY 10111

Alfred P. Sloan Foundation Industry Studies Fellowships 405

These Fellowships are intended to recognize and support junior faculty members in a wide range of academic disciplines. Awards are made to scholars who show the most outstanding promise of making important contributions to understanding the complex systems of companies, product and labor markets, institutions and their interactions that shape the multifaceted environment of modern industrial enterprises. Fellowships will be awarded to up to five (5) junior faculty members who are conducting such research on a topic important to a specific industry. At its discretion, the Foundation may choose to award more than five fellowships in a given year. Fellowships are awarded for a two-year period, with possible extension for another two years.
Requirements Candidates must hold a PhD or equivalent in chemistry, physics, mathematics, computer science, economics, neuroscience or computational and evolutionary molecular biology, or in a related interdisciplinary field, and must also be a faculty member at a U.S. or Canadian university. Candidates must be no more than six years from the completion of the most recent PhD or equivalent as of the year of their nomination.
Restrictions Direct applications are not accepted. Candidates must be nominated by department heads or other senior scholars.
Amount $45,000 for two years
Date(s) Application Is Due Oct 15.
Contact Gail M. Pesyna, Program Director; (212) 649-1649; fax: (212) 757-5117; email: pesyna@sloan.org
Internet http://sloan.org/programs/fellow_announ.shtml
Sponsor Alfred P. Sloan Foundation
630 Fifth Avenue, Suite 2550
New York, NY 10111

Alfred P. Sloan Foundation Industry Studies Grants 406

The primary missions of this Program are to encourage research cooperation between academics and industry, and to support the integration of observation-based research with appropriate theory and analysis among a growing community of industry studies scholars. Grant requests can be made at any time for support of activities related to Foundation program areas and interests. The Foundation is generally limited to supporting tax-exempt organizations. The Foundation has no deadlines or standard forms. The Foundation accepts proposals sent by email. A brief letter of inquiry, rather than a fully developed proposal, is an advisable first step for an applicant, conserving his or her time and allowing for a preliminary response regarding the possibility of support.
Requirements Concise, well-organized proposals are preferred. In no case should the body of the proposal exceed 20 double-spaced pages.
Restrictions The Foundation's activities do not normally extend to religion, the creative or performing arts, elementary or secondary education, medical research or health care, the humanities or to activities outside the United States. Grants are not made for endowments or for buildings or equipment.
Contact Gail Pesyna, Program Director; (212) 649-1649; fax: (212) 757-5117; email: pesyna@sloan.org
Internet http://sloan.org/programs/IndustryStudies.shtml
Sponsor Alfred P. Sloan Foundation
630 Fifth Avenue, Suite 2550
New York, NY 10111

Alfred P. Sloan Foundation Known, Unknown, and Unknowable Research Grants 407

The goal of this program is the exploration of what is known, unknown, and unknowable in a variety of fields. It is very valuable to know what you do not know and why. Research has been funded on limits to knowledge in a broad spectrum of academic areas. Grants have supported such studies in plant molecular biology and genetics, ecology, computational economics, history of science, and prehistoric linguistics. The Foundation would like to explore limits to knowledge in fields with obvious practical implications, such as health or finance, where it is important for knowledge consumers, such as regulators or investors, to know what can or cannot be known about therapies or market movements. Grant requests can be made at any time for support of activities related to Foundation program areas and interests. The Foundation is generally limited to supporting tax-exempt organizations. The Foundation has no deadlines or standard forms. The Foundation accepts proposals sent by email. A brief letter of inquiry, rather than a fully developed proposal, is an advisable first step for an applicant, conserving his or her time and allowing for a preliminary response regarding the possibility of support.
Requirements Concise, well-organized proposals are preferred. In no case should the body of the proposal exceed 20 double-spaced pages.
Restrictions The Foundation's activities do not normally extend to religion, the creative or performing arts, elementary or secondary education, medical research or health care, the humanities or to activities outside the United States. Grants are not made for endowments or for buildings or equipment.
Contact Jesse H. Ausubel; (212) 649-1649; fax: (212) 757-5117; email: ausubel@sloan.org
Internet http://sloan.org/programs/scitech_supresearch.shtml
Sponsor Alfred P. Sloan Foundation
630 Fifth Avenue, Suite 2550
New York, NY 10111

Alfred P. Sloan Foundation Making Municipal Governments More Responsive to Their Citizens Grants 408

The program to make municipal governments more responsive to their citizens has two components: promoting performance measurement and reporting; and enabling direct service requests. Grant requests can be made at any time for support of activities related to Foundation program areas and interests. The Foundation is generally limited to supporting tax-exempt organizations. The Foundation has no deadlines or standard forms. The Foundation accepts proposals sent by email. A brief letter of inquiry, rather than a fully developed proposal, is an advisable first step for an applicant, conserving his or her time and allowing for a preliminary response regarding the possibility of support.
Requirements Concise, well-organized proposals are preferred. In no case should the body of the proposal exceed 20 double-spaced pages.
Restrictions The Foundation's activities do not normally extend to religion, the creative or performing arts, elementary or secondary education, medical research or health care, the humanities or to activities outside the United States. Grants are not made for endowments or for buildings or equipment.
Contact Ted Greenwood, Program Director; (212) 649-1649; fax: (212) 757-5117; email: greenwood@sloan.org
Internet http://sloan.org/programs/stndrd_performance.shtml
Sponsor Alfred P. Sloan Foundation
630 Fifth Avenue, Suite 2550
New York, NY 10111

Alfred P. Sloan Foundation Research Fellowships 409

Fellowships stimulate fundamental research by young scholars of outstanding promise at a time in their careers when their creative abilities are especially high and when government or other support is difficult to obtain. Fellows are free to pursue whatever lines of inquiry that are of the most compelling interest to them. Funds are awarded directly to the fellow's institution and may be used by the fellow for such purposes as equipment, technical assistance, professional travel, trainee support, or activities directly related to the fellow's research. The foundation welcomes nominations of all candidates who meet the traditional high standards of this program and strongly encourages the participation of women and members of underrepresented minority groups. Awards are made in the fields of physics, chemistry, neuroscience, economics, pure mathematics, applied mathematics, computer science, and computational and evolutionary molecular biology. Fellowships are awarded for a two-year period, with possible extension for another two years. Each year 118 fellows are selected from the nominations received. Nominations are due September 15 for awards to begin the following September. Nomination forms are available upon request.
Requirements Candidates must hold a PhD or equivalent in chemistry, physics, mathematics, computer science, economics, neuroscience or computational and evolutionary molecular biology, or in a related interdisciplinary field, and must also be a faculty member at a U.S. or Canadian university. Candidates must be no more than six years from the completion of the most recent PhD or equivalent as of the year of their nomination.
Restrictions Direct applications are not accepted. Candidates must be nominated by department heads or other senior scholars.
Amount $45,000 for two years
Date(s) Application Is Due Sep 15.
Contact Michael Teitelbaum, Program Director; (212) 649-1649; fax: (212) 757-5117; email: teitelbaum@sloan.org
Internet http://sloan.org/programs/scitech_fellowships.shtml
Sponsor Alfred P. Sloan Foundation
630 Fifth Avenue, Suite 2550
New York, NY 10111

Alfred P. Sloan Foundation Selected National Issues Grants 410

The foundation attempts to contribute to studies of major issues of our time in a way appropriate to its expertise and size. A special approach to the study and understanding of broadly recognized problems is a requirement for foundation support. Grant requests can be made at any time for support of activities related to Foundation program areas and interests. The Foundation is generally limited to supporting tax-exempt organizations. The Foundation has no deadlines or standard forms. The Foundation accepts proposals sent by email. A brief letter of inquiry, rather than a fully developed proposal, is an advisable first step for an applicant, conserving his or her time and allowing for a preliminary response regarding the possibility of support.

Requirements Concise, well-organized proposals are preferred. In no case should the body of the proposal exceed 20 double-spaced pages.
Restrictions The Foundation's activities do not normally extend to religion, the creative or performing arts, elementary or secondary education, medical research or health care, the humanities or to activities outside the United States. Grants are not made for endowments or for buildings or equipment.
Contact Ted Greenwood, Program Director; (212) 649-1649; fax: (212) 757-5117; email: greenwood@sloan.org
Internet http://sloan.org/programs/pg_national.shtml
Sponsor Alfred P. Sloan Foundation
630 Fifth Avenue, Suite 2550
New York, NY 10111

Alfred P. Sloan Foundation Workplace, Work Force and Working Families Grants 411
The Foundation plays a vital role in developing work-family scholarship and supporting effective workplaces that meet the needs of working parents and older workers. The foundation awards grants for research into conflicts between job and home responsibilities. It will support studies on balancing parental responsibilities, as well as improving access to child care and elderly care. Grant requests can be made at any time for support of activities related to Foundation program areas and interests. The Foundation is generally limited to supporting tax-exempt organizations. The Foundation has no deadlines or standard forms. The Foundation accepts proposals sent by email. A brief letter of inquiry, rather than a fully developed proposal, is an advisable first step.
Requirements Concise, well-organized proposals are preferred. In no case should the body of the proposal exceed 20 double-spaced pages.
Restrictions The Foundation's activities do not normally extend to religion, the creative or performing arts, elementary or secondary education, medical research or health care, the humanities or to activities outside the United States. Grants are not made for endowments or for buildings or equipment.
Contact Kathleen Christensen, Program Director; (212) 649-1649; fax: (212) 757-5117; email: christensen@sloan.org
Internet http://sloan.org/programs/stndrd_dualcareer.shtml
Sponsor Alfred P. Sloan Foundation
630 Fifth Avenue, Suite 2550
New York, NY 10111

Alfred W. Bressler Prize in Vision Science 412
The Prize recognizes a professional in the field of vision science whose leadership, research and service have resulted in important advancements in the treatment of eye disease or rehabilitation of persons with vision loss. A panel of distinguished vision science professionals will select the winner who receives a prize of $35,000.
Requirements The application process is open to established professionals in the field of vision science whose contributions have advanced vision care, the treatment of eye disease, or the rehabilitation of persons with visual disabilities or blindness and whose further work is expected to contribute significantly. Candidates from the United States and countries around the world are eligible for the award.
Amount $35,000
Date(s) Application Is Due Dec 31.
Contact Program Administrator, (212) 769-7801; email: bressler@jgb.org
Internet http://www.jgb.org/programs_bressler.asp
Sponsor Jewish Guild for the Blind
15 West 65th Street
New York, NY 10023

Alice Fisher Society Historical Scholarship 413
The Center for the Study of the History of Nursing at the university sponsors four to six weeks of residential study using the center's collections. Selection of scholars will be based on evidence of interest in and aptitude for historical research related to nursing. Scholars will work under the general direction of nurse historians associated with the center and may participate in center activities. It is expected that the research and new materials produced by scholars will help ensure the growth of scholarly work focused on the history of nursing. Scholars may be asked to present their work before a meeting of the Philadelphia General Hospital School of Nursing Alumni--the founders of the scholarship. Annual deadline dates may vary; contact program staff for exact dates.
Requirements Open to those with master's and doctoral level preparation.
Amount $2500
Date(s) Application Is Due Dec 31.
Contact Dr. Karen Buhler-Wilkerson, Director, Center for the Study of the History of Nursing, School of Nursing, (215) 898-4725; fax: (215) 573-2168; email: karenwil@nursing.upenn.edu
Internet http://www.nursing.upenn.edu/history/research/fisher.htm
Sponsor University of Pennsylvania
307 Nursing Education Bldg, 420 Guardian Dr
Philadelphia, PA 19104-6906

Alice Tweed Tuohy Foundation Grants Program 414
The foundation promotes organizations that promote young people; that provide outstanding opportunities for performance, growth, and creativity; that nurture personal integrity and ambition; and that reward high achievement. The foundation assists organizations offering services to children whose choices might otherwise be unfairly restricted by need; supported are activities both academic and extracurricular that challenge young people while encouraging the growth of responsibility and personal integrity. Organizations dedicated to improving the quality of life by meeting the vital needs of the community are also supported. Types of support include building construction/ renovation, scholarship funds, and matching funds. Financing priority is accorded those organizations with the least in-house capacity to raise capital, assisting these groups to surmount critical monetary obstacles and continue productive service to the community. Proposals may be submitted annually between July 1 and September 15.
Requirements Applications are considered only from Santa Barbara, CA public, tax-exempt organizations. Priority consideration is given to applications from organizations serving young people, education, health and medicine, community affairs, and the arts.
Restrictions Excluded from consideration are applications for the benefit of specific individuals, organizations outside the Santa Barbara area, organizations in overpopulated nonprofit areas, national campaigns, fund-raising normally carried out by the organization, operating expenses, or budgetary support.
Amount $750-$98,000 range
Date(s) Application Is Due Sep 15.
Contact Program Contact, (805) 962-6430; fax: (805) 962-7135; email: ATuohyfdn@aol.com
Sponsor Alice Tweed Tuohy Foundation
P.O. Box 1328, 205 E Carrillo St, Rm 219
Santa Barbara, CA 93102-1328

ALISE Doctoral Students' Dissertation Competition Awards 415
Awards provide an opportunity for the exchange of research ideas between established researchers and doctoral students who have recently graduated in the field of education for library and information science. Doctoral students who have recently graduated, or who are about to finish their dissertations, are invited to submit papers summarizing their dissertation research in areas dealing with substantive issues in library and information science. Guidelines are available upon request.
Amount $400
Date(s) Application Is Due Sep 22.
Contact Deborah York, Executive Director, (865) 425-0155; fax: (865) 481-0390; email: dyork@infointl.com
Internet http://www.alise.org/awards/doctoralstudents.html
Sponsor ALISE National Office
P.O. Box 4219, 1009 Commerce Park Dr, Ste 150
Oak Ridge, TN 37839

ALISE Research Grants 416
ALISE accepts proposals for grants to support research broadly related to education for library and information science. Proposals should include an abstract of the project; a problem statement and literature review; project objectives and description; research design, methodology, and analysis techniques; detailed budget; expected benefits and impact from the research; and vita of project investigators.
Requirements Applicants must be personal members of ALISE.
Restrictions Grants will not be given to support doctoral dissertations.
Amount $5000
Date(s) Application Is Due Oct 3.
Contact Program Contact, (865) 425-0155 ; fax: (865) 481-0390; email: contact@alise.org
Internet http://www.alise.org/awards/researchgrants.html
Sponsor Association for Library and Information Science Education
P.O. Box 4219, 1009 Commerce Park Dr, Ste 150
Oak Ridge, TN 37839

ALISE Research Paper Competition Awards 417
Research papers concerning any aspect of librarianship or information studies are eligible for this award. Competition is not limited to research regarding education for librarianship and information studies. Any research mode is acceptable. All research papers submitted must represent completed research not previously published, though manuscript may have been submitted and be in the process of publication. Papers generated as a result of a research grant or some other source of funding are eligible. The same author may submit for both the research grant award and the research paper competition, but the same work cannot be submitted for both categories. In case of joint authorship, one honorarium will be awarded. Annual deadline dates may vary; contact program staff for exact dates.
Requirements Authors must be members of ALISE as of deadline date. Papers prepared by joint investigators are eligible, but at least one author must be a member of the association. Only one research paper per entrant will be considered.
Restrictions Research papers completed in the pursuit of master's or doctoral studies are not eligible for entry, but research utilizing data gathered by a master's or doctoral student is eligible unless the research report is taken directly from a paper submitted for degree requirements. Papers that are spinoffs of such research are eligible.
Amount $500
Date(s) Application Is Due Oct 3.
Contact Program Contact, (865) 425-0155 ; fax: (865) 481-0390; email: contact@alise.org

Internet http://www.alise.org/awards/methodology.html
Sponsor ALISE National Office
P.O. Box 4219, 1009 Commerce Park Dr, Ste 150
Oak Ridge, TN 37839

All Saints Educational Trust Grants 418

The main purposes of the trust is to help increase the number of qualified teachers, improve the skills and qualifications of teachers, encourage research that would assist teachers in their work, and support specifically the teaching of Religious Studies and Home Economics and related areas. There is no deadline date for the preliminary questionnaire form but there is a deadline for the full application form. Annual deadline dates may vary; contact program staff for exact dates. The Trustees normally only give financial assistance when the course of study is undertaken at recognised educational establishments within the United Kingdom.
Requirements Applicants must be over 18 years of age when they begin their studies.
Restrictions Applications are not accepted from people outside the U.K. except residents of Commonwealth nations. The trust cannot support general or core funds of any organization, public appeals, school buildings, equipment or supplies, the establishment of courses or departments in universities and colleges, and general Bursary funds of other organizations.
Contact Program Contact, 020-7283-4485; fax: 020-7621-9758; email: aset@aset.org.uk
Internet http://www.aset.org.uk
Sponsor All Saints Educational Trust
St Katharine Cree Church, 86 Leadenhall St
London EC3A 3DH United Kingdom

All Souls College Senior Research Fellowships 419

The college supports senior research fellowships, one in Classical Studies, and one in Literature in the English Language (both subjects broadly conceived). The fellowship program is of comparable academic standing to an Oxford University professorship, and applicants are expected to have a correspondingly distinguished record of achievement in research. The primary duty of a fellow is to pursue a program of advanced study and research in Oxford, approved by the college and at a level acceptable to it. The college will renew the fellowship only on evidence of satisfactory achievement and on presentation of a satisfactory program of research for the following seven years (or until retirement). Candidates should submit as part of their application a full curriculum vita with a list of published work. Application and guidelines are available online.
Amount 55,713 pounds-60,699 pounds
Date(s) Application Is Due Sep 12.
Contact Warden's Secretary
Internet http://www.all-souls.ox.ac.uk
Sponsor All Souls College
Oxford OX1 4AL United Kingdom

Allen Foundation Educational Nutrition Grants 420

The foundation supports projects that benefit human nutrition in the areas of education, training, and research. Priorities include training programs for children and young adults to improve their health and development; training programs for educators and demonstrators concerned with good nutritional practices; programs for the education and training of mothers during pregnancy and after the birth of their children, so that good nutritional habits can be formed at an early age; and programs that aid in the dissemination of information regarding healthful nutrition practices. Applications are available by fax or mail. There are no application deadlines; proposals are reviewed throughout the year.
Requirements 501(c)3 tax-exempt organizations nationwide may apply. In certain circumstances, the foundation will consider requests from the following: hospitals or medical clinics; social, religious, fraternal, or community organizations; private foundations; and K-12 public, parochial, or private schools.
Amount $5000-$250,000
Date(s) Application Is Due Dec 31.
Contact Dr. Dale Baum, Secretary, (989) 832-5678 or (979) 695-1132; fax:(989) 832-8842; email: d-baum@tamu.edu
Internet http://www.allenfoundation.org/commoninfo/aboutus.asp
Sponsor Allen Foundation
P.O. Box 1606
Midland, MI 48641-1606

Allen Lane Foundation Grants 421

The foundation operates in the United Kingdom and Ireland in the field of social welfare and awards grants to institutions at the local, regional, and national levels. Areas of interest include projects in Scotland, Northern Ireland, Wales, and regions outside the London area; groups supporting refugees and asylum-seekers; advisory and information services; and the coordination of small groups. The broad areas of work which are priorities for the foundation include the provision of advice, information, and advocacy; community development; employment and training; mediation, conflict resolution, and alternatives to violence; research and education aimed at changing public attitudes or policy; and social welfare.
Requirements Grants may be made for project costs or revenue costs. The foundation no longer has closing dates.
Restrictions The foundation only very rarely makes grants to national organizations with an income of more than $500,000 per annum or to local organizations with an income of more than about $150,000. Grants are not made to individuals.
Amount L500-L15,000 range
Contact Gill Aconley, Grants Officer, 01-904-613-223; fax: 01-904-613-133; email: info@allenlane.org.uk
Internet http://www.allenlane.org.uk
Sponsor Allen Lane Foundation
90 The Mount
York YO24 1AR United Kingdom

Alliance for Justice Internship Program 422

The program awards year-round, semester, winter-term, and summer internships. The organization's work consists of promoting reform of the legal system to ensure access to the courts. Projects include extensive legal, legislative, and policy research; special projects, such as helping to organize symposia and producing user-friendly legal publications for nonprofit organizations; attending congressional committee meetings on nonprofit advocacy, tax reform, takings, and judicial selection; contributing to the Alliance's newsletter, Justice First; and attending relevant public interest events around Washington, DC. Applications are accepted at any time.
Requirements Internships are available to law students and graduate and undergraduate students.
Contact Marissa Brown, (202) 822-6070; fax: (202) 822-6068; email: marissa@afj.org
Internet http://www.allianceforjustice.org/about_AFJ/jobs/index.html
Sponsor Alliance for Justice
11 Dupont Circle NW, 2nd Fl
Washington, DC 20036

Allstate Foundation Grants 423

The foundation awards grants to nonprofit organizations in the categories of Safe and Vital Communities, Economic Empowerment, and Tolerance, Inclusion and Diversity. In the area of Tolerance, Inclusion and Diversity, the foundation seeks to support programs that address teaching tolerance to youth, ending hate crimes, and alleviating discrimination. Programs with a focus on Safe and Vital Communities should address catastrophe response, youth anti-violence, neighborhood revitalization, and teen safe driving. Economic Empowerment programs should address financial and economic literacy, insurance education, and empowerment for victims of domestic violence. Programs should focus on teaching tolerance to youth, alleviating discrimination, and ending hate crimes. There are no application deadlines. Proposals are accepted throughout the year. Contact local branch offices or the foundation. Grant committees usually meet in March, June, September, and December.
Requirements 501(c)3 nonprofit organizations are eligible. Application guidelines are available. The initial contact should be by letter.
Restrictions The foundation does not support the following: individuals; fundraising events, sponsorships; capital and endowment campaigns; equipment purchase unless part of a community outreach program; athletic events; memorial grants; athletic teams, bands, and choirs; organizations that advocate religious beliefs or restrict participation on the basis of religion; groups or organizations that will re-grant the foundation's gift to other organizations or individuals; scouting groups; private secondary schools; requests to support travel; grant requests for production of audio, film, or video; multiyear pledge requests; or nondomestic (international) causes.
Amount $7 million total; $5000-$10,000 typically
Contact Program Contact, (847) 402-5502; fax: (847) 326-7517; email: allfound@allstate.com
Internet http://www.allstate.com/foundation
Sponsor Allstate Foundation
2775 Sanders Rd., Ste. F4
Northbrook, IL 60062

Allyn Foundation Grants 424

The foundation places emphasis on higher and other education, including adult basic education/literacy; and support for charitable purposes, including youth and social service agencies, hospitals, medical research, and community development in the central New York area. Types of support include capital campaigns, building and equipment, seed money, scholarship funds, and matching funds. There are no application deadlines. The board meets four times annually.
Requirements Nonprofit organizations in Onondaga and Cayuga Counties, NY, may submit grant applications.
Restrictions Grants are not awarded for religious purposes, endowment funds, loans, or to individuals.
Amount $500-$27,000 range
Contact Margaret O'Connell, Executive Director, (315) 685-5059
Sponsor Allyn Foundation
P.O. Box 22
Skaneateles, NY 13152

ALO Promoting Higher Education Partnerships for Global Development Grants 425

The program invites applications for the US-Middle East University Partnerships Program. ALO will award up to five grants, with funding over a three-year period,

to implement cooperative partnerships between higher education institutions in the United States and Arab universities located in Algeria, Bahrain, Egypt, Jordan, Kuwait, Lebanon, Morocco, Oman, Qatar, Saudi Arabia, Tunisia, the United Arab Emirates, the West Bank and Gaza, and Yemen. ALO seeks applications for higher education partnerships to strengthen Arab universities' programs in one of the following disciplines: business administration and economics; gender studies; government; information and communication technologies; legal studies; and teacher education. Application and guidelines are available online.
Amount $200,000 maximum over three years
Date(s) Application Is Due Aug 10.
Contact Tony Wagner, (202) 478-4704; email: wagner@aascu.org
Internet http://www.aascu.org/alo/RFPs/mepi05/mepi05.htm
Sponsor Association Liaison Office for University Cooperation in Development
1307 New York Ave NW, Ste 500
Washington, DC 20005-4701

ALO US-Japan Trilateral Program for Basic Education in Africa **426**
ALO, with funding support from USAID, is issuing this call for concept papers for institutional partnerships in basic education involving a US college or university (or a group of colleges and universities), public and private sector partners, Japanese universities, and institutions in Africa. Five countries have been identified as potential locations for program implementation: Ethiopia, Ghana, South Africa, Tanzania, and Uganda. Concept papers should indicate the specific results and impacts that will follow from the proposed activities, including the projected impact of the activity on basic education and basic education capacity in the target country. Evidence that such matters have received rigorous consideration will increase the competitiveness of the concept paper. The full Call for Concept Papers, with complete information, is available online.
Requirements ALO welcomes concept papers from the member institutions of ACE, AACC, AASCU, AAU, NAICU, and NASULGC; and from other regionally accredited, degree-granting, US higher education institutions. US colleges and universities may respond individually or in partnership with other institutions. Minority serving institutions are encouraged to submit papers.
Restrictions faxed and electronic submissions are not accepted.
Date(s) Application Is Due Mar 31.
Contact Tony Wagner, (202) 478-4700; fax: (202) 478-4715; email: wagner@aascu.org
Internet http://www.aascu.org/alo/RFPs/RFPMain.htm
Sponsor Association Liaison Office for University Cooperation in Development
1307 New York Ave NW, Ste 500
Washington, DC 20005-4701

Alpha Chi Sigma Award for Chemical Engineering Research **427**
This award, sponsored by the Alpha Chi Sigma fraternity and administered by AIChE, recognizes outstanding recent accomplishments by an individual in fundamental or applied research in the field of chemical engineering. Research awarded must have been carried out during the 10 years preceding the award year. The recipient need not be a member of AIChE or Alpha Chi Sigma.
Requirements All members of AIChE as well as other interested persons in North America are urged to nominate deserving candidates. All information and supporting documents are to be included with the completed form; nomination forms and instructions may be obtained from the institute.
Amount $5000
Date(s) Application Is Due Feb 15.
Contact AIChE Awards Programs, (212) 591-7107; fax: (212) 591-8890; email: awards@aiche.org
Internet http://www.aiche.org/awards/awarddtl.asp?AwardID=55
Sponsor American Institute of Chemical Engineers
3 Park Ave
New York, NY 10016-5991

Alpha Sigma Nu Book Award Competition **428**
The book awards operate on a three-year cycle. The category for 2007 is "The Professional Studies", and includes the following disciplines: Architecture, Business and Administration, Communication, Education, Engineering, Foreign Service, Law, and Social Work. Four prizes will be awarded. The category for 2008, will be "The Humanities" with one award each for Theology, Philosophy/Ethics, Literature/Fine Arts, and History. In 2009, the category will be "The Sciences" with one award for Social Sciences, Natural Sciences, Mathematics/Computer Science, and Health Sciences. Information and application forms are available from academic vice presidents and deans of the Jesuit colleges and universities, or from the Association of Jesuit Colleges and Universities.
Requirements Candidates must be full- or part-time staff or faculty or anyone who has emeritus status at a Jesuit college or university in the United States.
Amount $1000
Date(s) Application Is Due Mar 1.
Contact Program Contact, (202) 862-9893; email: agarner@ajcunet.edu
Internet http://www.marquette.edu/dept/ASN/book_award_competition.html
Sponsor Alpha Sigma Nu
One Dupont Cir, Ste 405
Washington, DC 20036

ALS Clinical Management Research Grants **429**
The mission of the association is to find a cure for and improve living with amyotrophic lateral sclerosis (often called Lou Gehrig's disease). Through this program, the association is encouraging new research, the results of which will build an evidence base and demonstrate measurable, positive effects on the clinical management and lives of patients with ALS. Clinical problems relating to the following priority areas for clinical management research include breathing; swallowing/ nutrition and PEG issues/ choking/excess saliva; speech/communication; musculoskeletal symptoms/treatment; mobility/ activities of daily living; and psychosocial/mental health. The association also will consider abstracts on other clinical management topics.
Requirements Applicants must be faculty members or scientists at reputable scientific institutions.
Amount $30,000 maximum
Date(s) Application Is Due Jan 7.
Contact Dr. Mary Lyon, Grants Administrator, (818) 880-9007 ext 217; fax: (818) 880-9006; email: mary@alsa-national.org
Internet http://www.alsa.org/patient/research.cfm?CFID=102432&CFTOKEN=86382360
Sponsor Amyotrophic Lateral Sclerosis Association
27001 Agoura Rd, Ste 150
Calabasas Hills, CA 9136491301

ALS Research Grants **430**
Research into the cause, means of prevention and possible cure of ALS is the driving priority of the ALS Association. The ALS Association annually awards $2 million or more in new research grants and currently holds two calls for abstracts each year. After review of the abstracts, selected investigators are asked to submit full applications which are also peer reviewed by ALSA's scientific review committee. Annual deadline dates may vary; contact program staff for exact dates.
Requirements Applicants must be faculty members or scientists at reputable scientific institutions.
Amount $80,000 maximum; $40,000 maximum for starter grants
Contact Grants Administrator, (888) 949-2577 or (818) 880-9007; email: researchgrants@alsa-national.org
Internet http://www.alsa.org/research/process.cfm?CFID=102432&CFTOKEN=86382360
Sponsor Amyotrophic Lateral Sclerosis Association
27001 Agoura Rd, Ste 150
Calabasas Hills, CA 91301

ALSAM Foundation Grants **431**
The foundation awards grants in its areas of interest, including agriculture, Christian agencies and churches, higher education, health care and medical research, human services, minorities, and the economically disadvantaged. Types of support include building construction/renovation, general operating costs, and scholarships. The board meets in January and October. Contact the office for application forms.
Requirements Higher education institutions, nonprofit organizations, religious organizations, and research institutions are eligible.
Restrictions No grants to individuals.
Amount $5000-$50,000 average
Contact Ron Cutshall, Chair, (801) 266-4950
Sponsor ALSAM Foundation
6190 Moffat Farm Lane
Salt Lake City, UT 84121

ALSC Bound to Stay Bound Books Scholarship **432**
Four annual scholarships assist individuals who wish to work in the field of library service to children. The scholarships may be used for study toward the MLS or graduate study beyond the MLS degree at an ALA-accredited library school. The scholarships are sponsored by Bound to Stay Bound Books Inc, and administered by the Association for Library Service to Children.
Requirements Only online applications will be accepted (there will be no exceptions). Online application forms are available on the Web site.
Amount $6500
Date(s) Application Is Due Mar 1.
Contact Linda Mays, Program Officer, (800) 545-2433 ext 1398; fax: (312) 944-7671; email: lmays@ala.org
Internet http://www.ala.org/ala/alsc/awardsscholarships/alscschol/alscscholarship.htm
Sponsor American Library Association
50 E Huron Street
Chicago, IL 60611-2795

ALSC Frederic G. Melcher Scholarships **433**
Two annual scholarships assist individuals in the field of library service to children. They are awarded to qualified candidates who have been accepted for admission to a graduate library school program accredited by the ALA but who have not yet begun the program. Application and additional information are available from the ALSC office, which administers the scholarships.
Requirements Only online applications will be accepted. Online applications are available on the Web site.

Amount $6000 each (2)
Date(s) Application Is Due Mar 1.
Contact ALA Awards Staff Liaison, (800) 545-2433 ext 3247; fax: (312) 944-6131; email: alsc@ala.org or lmays@ala.org
Internet http://www.ala.org/alsc/scholars.html
Sponsor American Library Association
50 E Huron Street
Chicago, IL 60611-2795

ALSC/Louise Seaman Bechtel Children's Library Collection Fellowships 434
The fellowship enables librarians with at least eight years of work at a professional level in a children's library collection to read and study at the Baldwin Library of the George Smathers Libraries, University of Florida. Applicants must be ALSC members in possession of the MLS degree from an ALA-accredited program. The program is administered by the Association for Library Service to Children of ALA.
Amount $4000
Date(s) Application Is Due Dec 1.
Contact ALA Awards Staff Liaison, (312) 280-3247; fax: (312) 280-3257; email: alsc@ala.org
Internet http://www.ala.org/Template.cfm?Section=Grants_and_Fellowships&template=/ContentManagement/ContentDisplay.cfm&ContentID=22345
Sponsor American Library Association
50 E Huron Street
Chicago, IL 60611

Alternatives Research and Development Foundation Grants 435
The foundation awards grants to research centers, educational institutions, and other nonprofit organizations exploring non-animal testing. Grants will be awarded for research projects that use human, rather than nonhuman, vertebrae tissue; do not use intact, vertebrae animals; and can be completed within one year. Multiyear projects are considered on a case-by-case basis. The foundation often provides partial grants to initiate projects, with continuation funding available at a later date. The foundation will not consider proposals if program staff uses animals acquired from a shelter, or if individuals are employed who use such animals in their personal research programs. Winners are announced on July 15. Telephone inquiries are discouraged.
Requirements Individuals attending or employed by US universities and research institutions may apply. Applications from non-US institutions or investigators may be considered.
Restrictions The foundation does not make grants for in vitro projects that use nonhuman animal serum, indirect costs, purchase of personal computers, salary supplements, fringe benefits, travel expenses, or publication costs for the principal investigators. Phone calls to the foundation are discouraged. Guidelines and application are available online.
Amount $40,000 maximum
Date(s) Application Is Due Apr 30.
Contact Dr. John McArdle, Director, (215) 887-8076; fax: (215) 887-0771; email: grants@ardf-online.org
Internet http://www.ardf-online.org
Sponsor Alternatives Research and Development Foundation
801 Old York Rd, Ste 316
Jenkintown, PA 19046

Alton E. Bailey Award 436
This award is given annually for research and/or service in the fields of oils, fats, and related disciplines by the North Central Section of AOCS.
Date(s) Application Is Due Nov 1.
Contact Kathleen Atchley, Awards, (217) 359-2344; fax: (217) 351-8091; email: awards@aocs.org
Internet http://www.aocs.org/member/awards/awd-bailey.asp
Sponsor American Oil Chemists' Society
P.O. Box 3489
Champaign, IL 61826-3489

Alton Ochsner Award 437
The Award is presented to one or more clinical or basic science investigators, for outstanding and exemplary original scientific investigations that relate tobacco consumption and health. This scientific work may be clinical, fundamental, epidemiological or preventive in scope. The prime criterion for award selection is its scientific impact on this major health threat. The $15,000 award is presented at the Annual Convocation of the American College of Chest Physicians.
Requirements All nominations, whatever the category of scientific inquiry, must be supported by letters and copies of peer-reviewed scientific publications.
Amount $15,000
Date(s) Application Is Due Mar 31.
Contact Edward D. Frohlich, Alton Ochsner Distinguished Scientist, (504) 842-3000; fax: (504) 842-3258
Internet http://www.ochsner.org/homepage.cfm
Sponsor Ochsner Clinic Foundation
1514 Jefferson Highway
New Orleans, LA 70121

Altria Group Contributions Grants 438
The corporation awards grants to local, national, and international nonprofit organizations in the areas of hunger relief, domestic violence prevention and art. Humanitarian aid is also supported. Guidelines and deadlines by program area are available online.
Requirements Grants are made through an invitation only application process. IRS 501(c)3 organizations are eligible.
Restrictions Generally, support will not be provided to/for fund-raising benefits; capital campaigns, endowments, or building fund drives; film, video, or television projects; one-time or annual events; individuals; political or lobbying organizations; religious, fraternal, or veterans groups; research or other activities related to specific diseases or disease-prevention (with the exception of AIDS); athletic or sports-related activities; travel funds; organizations that discriminate on the basis of race, creed, gender, sexual preference, or national origin; or organizations already supported through United Way contributions.
Amount $138 million in cash and products
Contact Manager, Corporate Contributions (program areas other than arts), or Manager, Cultural Program (arts), (212) 880-3366 or (800) 883-2422
Internet http://www.altria.com/responsibility/4_9_1_2_whowefund.asp
Sponsor Altria Group, Inc
120 Park Ave
New York, NY 10017

Alvin H. Johnson 50 Dissertation Fellowships 439
The society supports research in the various fields of music. Dissertation fellowships support full-time study and completion of the dissertation within the fellowship year. Preliminary application forms are sent to directors of graduate study at all North American doctorate-granting institutions. Applications should be sent to Kern Holoman, AHJ-AMS 50 Chair, Department of Music, University of California, One Shields Ave., Davis, CA 95616-5271. Applications are available on the Web site or from the AMS office.
Requirements Applicants must be registered for doctoral degrees at a North American university and have completed all formal degree requirements except the dissertation.
Amount $15,000
Date(s) Application Is Due Jan 15.
Contact Program Contact, (215) 898-8698; fax: (215) 573-3673; email: ams@sas.upenn.edu
Internet http://www.ams-net.org/awards.html
Sponsor American Musicological Society
201 S 34th St
Philadelphia, PA 19104-6313

ALZA Corporate Contributions Grants 440
The corporation awards grants to eligible California nonprofit organizations in four areas of interest: education--K-12 after school programs, professional development for teachers, and health care workers, nonprofit educational outreach programs; health and human services--projects that particularly access to healthcare for underserved and underrepresented members of our community; arts & culture--arts programs that have an education component or art related to health and healing are of particular interest; and environment--projects that focus on sustainable solutions, stewardship, & education.
Requirements Nonprofit organizations in ALZA's California operating areas are eligible.
Restrictions Grants will not be made to individuals, or to organizations whose activities or policies include sectarian or denominational religious activities, political campaigns, or organizations that discriminate on the basis of religion, race, nationality, sexual preference, or gender.
Amount $10,000 maximum
Contact Ellen Rose, Director, Corporate Communications, (650) 564-5000; fax: (650) 564-7070
Internet http://www.alza.com/alza/community
Sponsor ALZA Corporation
P.O. Box 7210, 1900 Charleston Rd
Mountain View, CA 94043

Alzheimer's Association Investigator-Initiated Research Grants 441
The program is structured to provide one to three years of sustained project support for independent, ongoing research. Proposals are solicited for basic, clinical, and social/behavioral research relevant to degenerative brain diseases such as Alzheimer's disease. Allowable costs for this award include the purchase and care of laboratory animals; small pieces of laboratory equipment and laboratory supplies; and salary for the principal investigator, scientific (including postdoctoral fellows) and technical staff (including laboratory technicians and modest secretarial support). It is required that most of the funds awarded under this program be used for direct research support.
Requirements Public, private, domestic and foreign research laboratories, medical centers and hospitals, and universities are eligible to apply. Investigators from all stages of their research career development are encouraged to apply.
Restrictions This program does not support travel to scientific and professional meetings, computer hardware or software, or construction or renovation costs.
Amount $240,000 total for up to three years; $100,000 maximum per year
Date(s) Application Is Due Jan 6.

Contact Grants Administrator, (800) 272-3900 or (312) 335-5747 fax: (312) 335-5729; email: grantsapp@alz.org or info@alz.org
Internet http://www.alz.org/Research/RGP/Investigator.asp
Sponsor Alzheimer's Association
225 N Michigan Ave, Ste 1700
Chicago, IL 60601-7633

Alzheimer's Association New Investigator Research Grants **442**
The purpose of this program is to provide new investigators with funding that will allow them to develop preliminary or pilot data, to test procedures, and develop hypotheses which will then underpin the preparation of research grant applications to NIH, NSF, and other funding agencies and groups, including the Alzheimer's Association. All applications submitted to the program must focus on a question or questions in interventions for Alzheimer's disease to be considered responsive to the program announcement. Twenty-five awards will be made under this program.
Requirements Public, private, domestic and foreign research laboratories, medical centers and hospitals, and universities are eligible to apply. Eligibility is restricted to investigators who have less than 10 years of research experience, including postdoctoral fellowships or residencies, after receipt of the doctoral degree. Applications from graduate and doctoral students for research projects, which will be used for the thesis or dissertation, will be accepted.
Amount $100,000 maximum for two years; $60,000 maximum per year
Date(s) Application Is Due Jan 6.
Contact Grants Administrator, (800) 272-3900 or (312) 335-5747 ; fax: (312) 335-1110; email: grantsapp@alz.org or info@alz.org
Internet http://www.alz.org/Research/RGP/NewRG.asp
Sponsor Alzheimer's Association
225 N Michigan Ave, Ste 1700
Chicago, IL 60601-7633

Alzheimer's Association Zenith Fellows Awards **443**
Five awards will be granted to talented scientists who have already contributed substantially to the advancement of Alzheimer's research and who are likely to continue to make significant contributions for many years. Proposals are solicited for basic, biomedical research only, and research should address fundamental problems related to early detection, etiology, pathogenesis, treatment, and prevention of Alzheimer's disease. Awardees receive a two-year grant, with a provision for possible competitive renewal upon review of research progress. Applications will be evaluated by an expert panel of senior scientists, already well recognized for their own accomplishments in Alzheimer's research. Annual deadline dates may vary; contact program staff for exact dates.
Requirements Only established independent investigators are eligible as evidenced by (examples are for illustrative purposes only) academic appointment; major, peer-reviewed, external multi-year grant support on which the applicant is the principal investigator (PI); independent laboratory operation; and quality and independence of publication record.
Restrictions Previous recipients of Zenith Awards, Alzheimer's Disease Center Directors (P50 and P30), Medical and Scientific Advisory Council, and members of the National Board of the Alzheimer's Association are not eligible to apply.
Amount $250,000 maximum for two years; $150,000 maximum for a single year
Date(s) Application Is Due Jan 6.
Contact Research Grants Office, (312) 335-5747 or (312) 335-5729; fax: (312) 335-1110; email: grantsapp@alz.org or info@alz.org
Internet http://www.alz.org/Research/RGP/Zenith.asp
Sponsor Alzheimer's Association
225 N Michigan Ave, Ste 1700
Chicago, IL 60601-7633

AMA Foundation Seed Grant Research Program **444**
Grants are awarded to medical students and residents to conduct small projects. Grants will be awarded in arthritis/rheumatism, cardiovascular/pulmonary diseases, HIV/AIDS, leukemia, neoplastic diseases, and neurological disorders. These funds will round out new project budgets, rather than sustain current initiatives.
Restrictions Grants cannot be used for salary or stipend.
Amount $1500-$2500
Date(s) Application Is Due Dec 15.
Contact Seed Grants Program, (312) 464-4200; fax: (312) 464-5973; email: seedgrants@ama-assn.org
Internet http://www.ama-assn.org/ama/pub/category/7785.html
Sponsor American Medical Association Foundation
515 N State St
Chicago, IL 60610

Amarillo Area/Harrington Foundations Grants **445**
The community foundation seeks to improve the quality of life in the 26 northernmost counties of the Texas Panhandle. Grants are awarded to nonprofits in support of arts and culture, education, health care, and social services. Types of support include research, building construction/renovation, equipment acquisition, program development, seed grants, scholarship funds, and matching funds.
Requirements Nonprofit 501(c)3 organizations located in the northernmost 26 counties of the Texas Panhandle, including Dallam, Sherman, Hansford, Ochiltree, Lipscomb, Hartley, Moore, Hutchinson, Roberts, Hemphill, Oldham, Potter, Carson, Gray, Wheeler, Deaf Smith, Randall, Armstrong, Donley, Collingsworth, Parmer, Castro, Swisher, Briscoe, Hall, and Childress, are eligible.
Restrictions The foundation does not make grants to or for religious activities; political lobbying or legislative activities; endowments; debt retirement; deficit financing, reduction of operating deficit, etc.; private or parochial schools; national, state, or local fund-raising activities; general operating expenses for United Way agencies; or umbrella funding organizations that would distribute requested funds at their own discretion.
Date(s) Application Is Due Jan 5; Jul 6.
Contact Kathy Grant, (806) 376-4521; email: kathie@aaf-hf.org
Internet http://aaf-hf.org/grants/guidelines.htm
Sponsor Amarillo Area/Harrington Foundations
801 S Fillmore St, Ste 700
Amarillo, TX 79101

Amazon Basin Scholarships **446**
Affiliated with Harvard University, LASPAU administers scholarships for 24 graduate students seeking to complete a master's degree or a one-year graduate certificate program. The purpose of the program is to develop a well-prepared cadre of professionals from the Amazon Basin countries who will return to their home institutions on completion of their studies and share their expertise with colleagues to foster research collaboration between countries.
Requirements Eligible applicants must be citizens and residents of Brazil, Bolivia, Colombia, Ecuador, Peru, or Venezuela; have a bachelor's degree in any natural science, social studies, or public policy relating to environmental issues; and have field experience in the Amazon region.
Restrictions Candidates must be nominated by a university, research institution, nongovernmental organization, or government agency in their home country.
Contact Fay Henderson de Diaz, Director, Program Relations and Management, (617) 495-0511; fax: (617) 495-8990; email: fay_henderson@harvard.edu
Internet http://www.laspau.harvard.edu/fb-oas.htm
Sponsor LASPAU: Academic and Professional Programs for the Americas
25 Mount Auburn St
Cambridge, MA 02138-6095

Amelia Peabody Charitable Fund Grants **447**
This fund gives grants for higher education, hospitals and health services, the environment, and culture primarily in Massachusetts and New England. Types of support include capital campaigns, building construction/renovation, equipment acquisition, endowment funds, and research. Initial approach should be a proposal giving pertinent information concerning the structure of the requesting organization, amount requested, purpose of the project, budget, personnel involved, and other foundations with whom proposals have been filed for this project. Application guidelines are available upon request.
Requirements Nonprofit organizations operating in Massachusetts are eligible to apply.
Restrictions Awards will not be made to individuals, for films, or for periods of more than one year, nor will grants be awarded to religious or political organizations or organizations maintained by local, state, or federal governments. Salaries will not be supported and very seldom will operating grants be awarded.
Amount $10,000-$100,000 average
Date(s) Application Is Due Feb 1; Jun 1; Oct 1.
Contact Cheryl Gideon, Program Contact, (617) 451-6178
Sponsor Amelia Peabody Charitable Fund
10 P.O. Sq, North Ste 995
Boston, MA 02109-4603

America-Norway Heritage Fund Grants **448**
The fund provides honorariums and travel expenses to Americans of Norwegian descent who have made significant contributions to American culture, enabling them to visit Norway to share the results of their work--through lectures, exhibitions, and/or performances--with the people of Norway. The program's goal is to acquaint Norwegians with the cultural, economic, political, and religious contributions made by Norwegian Americans in the building of America. The preferred length of stay in Norway is one to two weeks. There is no application form. Interested candidates are requested to submit curriculum vita, concrete proposal, estimated budget, and three letters of recommendation mailed directly to Nordmanns-Forbundet, Raadhusgata 23 B, N-0158 Oslo, Norway. Applications for the grant are no longer being accepted. However, the Board of Directors appreciate receiving proposals for possible candidates.
Requirements Americans of Norwegian descent who have made significant contributions to American culture are eligible to apply.
Contact America-Norway Heritage Fund, (212) 421-7333; fax: (212) 754-0583; email: norseman@online.no
Internet http://www.norway.org/education/frontpage.htm
Sponsor Norwegian Information Service in the 825 Third Ave, 38th Fl
New York, NY 10022-7584

American Academy of Arts and Sciences Visiting Scholars Program **449**
The program supports research fellowships at the academy's visiting scholars center. Fellowships will be awarded to individuals who can demonstrate that their work will make a substantial contribution in one or more of the academy's four major research

areas: science and global security; social policy and American institutions; humanities and culture; and education. The academy also welcomes proposals that explore the impact of scientific and technological advances over the past two centuries on American institutions, humanities and culture in America, American foreign policy, and global security. Proposals should take into account the academy's emphasis on interdisciplinary work, as well as its interest in broadening public understanding of important intellectual trends and contemporary policy choices. In addition to pursuing individual projects, scholars participate in activities of the academy; collaboration with academy fellows is encouraged. Visiting scholars remain in residence at the academy throughout the academic year (September-May), with some fellowships eligible for a one-year renewal. Faculty remain in residence for one academic year, although one-semester fellowships may be considered. Scholars receive office space, computer services, library privileges, and assistance in locating housing. Health benefits can be arranged. Applicants are responsible for contacting three references and ensuring that their letters are mailed to the academy by the postmark deadline. For details, contact the academy.
Requirements Fellowships are open to US citizens and permanent residents. The PhD, JD, or equivalent professional training (e.g., public policy) should have been completed within the last 10 years (although exceptional circumstances will be taken into consideration). Graduate student applicants must complete all degree requirements by August 1.
Restrictions Applications may not be submitted electronically.
Amount $35,000 for postdocs; $50,000 for faculty
Date(s) Application Is Due Oct 14.
Contact Alexandra Oleson, (617) 576-5014; fax: (617) 576-5050; email: aoleson@amacad.org
Internet http://www.amacad.org/visiting.aspx
Sponsor American Academy of Arts and Sciences
136 Irving St
Cambridge, MA 02138-1996

American Academy of Neurology Clinical Research Training Fellowship 450
This fellowship is a two-year award to support research in clinical neurosciences. The award supplies a stipend plus tuition coverage of formal education in clinical research methodology at the institution or elsewhere. Supplementation of the stipend by other grants is allowable.
Requirements The fellowship is open to non-US neurologists with interest in an academic career in clinical research who have completed residency training less than five years prior to application. Preference will be given to applicants who have completed one or two years subspecialty training in an area of clinical research interest. Only one application per department will be considered. *Amount* $50,000 per year for two years plus $7000 tuition
Date(s) Application Is Due Oct 3.
Contact Martin Schaefer, Executive Director, (651) 695-2759; fax: (651) 695-2791; email: foundation@aan.com or mschaefer@aan.com
Internet http://www.neurofoundation.org/research/research.cfm
Sponsor American Academy of Neurology
1080 Montreal Ave
St Paul, MN 55116

American Academy of Neurology International Scholarship Program 451
The purpose of this scholarship is to enable a young investigator to attend the academy's annual meeting to deliver a platform or poster presentation at the scientific sessions. A stipend, travel and lodging expenses, and program admission fees are provided. Application forms are available on the Web site. Annual deadline dates may vary; contact program staff for exact dates.
Requirements This scholarship is available to residents of countries other than the United States or Canada who are investigators in the field of neurology. Applications are especially welcome from qualified individuals in underdeveloped countries.
Restrictions Foreign residents living in the United States or Canada are not eligible.
Amount Up to $2500 toward hotel accommodations and a round-trip coach airfare to the American Academy of Neurology Annual Meeting.
Date(s) Application Is Due Dec 1.
Contact Cheryl Alementi, (651) 695-2737; email: calementi@aan.com
Internet http://www.aan.com/professionals/awards/award/awa_res_scho.cfm
Sponsor American Academy of Neurology
1080 Montreal Ave
Saint Paul, MN 55116

American Academy of Nursing Building Academic Geriatric Nursing Capacity (BAGNC) Scholarships 452
The Foundation's overall goal is to increase the nation's capacity to provide effective and affordable care to its rapidly increasing older population. Specifically, the Foundation seeks to enhance the training of physicians, nurses, social workers and other health professionals who care for older adults, and promote innovations in the integration and delivery of services. The goal of the Scholarship program is to increase academic geriatric nursing capacity in the United States. BAGNC focuses on the development of academic leadership in gerontological nursing through strong mentorship in the components of academic geriatric nursing (research, teaching and community service); leadership development, a national network of scholars and academic geriatric nurses; and exposure to a wide range of experts in gerontology and geriatrics. Scholars in collaboration with their identified mentor will design and implement a tailored professional development plan designed to support development of new competencies and enhanced effectiveness as an academic leader.
Requirements Registered nurses who are US citizens or US permanent residents and who hold a degree(s) in nursing are eligible. Predoctoral applicants must: be registered nurses; hold degree(s) in nursing; be United States citizens or permanent U.S. residents; plan an academic and research career; and demonstrate potential for long-term contributions to geriatric nursing.
Amount $50,000 maximum per annum for two years
Date(s) Application Is Due Jan 15.
Contact Pamela Dudzik, Program Administrator; (202) 777-1171; fax: (202) 777-0107; email: pdudzik@aannet.org
Internet http://www.geriatricnursing.org/applications/predoc-scholarship.asp
Sponsor American Academy of Nursing / John A. Hartford Foundation
888 17th Street, NW Suite 800
Washington, DC 20006

American Academy of Nursing Claire M. Fagin Fellowships 453
The Fellowship supports two years of full time advanced research and leadership training for doctorally prepared faculty committed to careers in academic geriatric nursing by providing $120,000 for the 2-year fellowship ($60,000 per annum). Program focuses on the development of academic leadership in gerontological nursing through such activities as: research; focused study; networking among scholars, mentors and colleagues in other fields; demonstration of growth in ability to transform self and organizations by moving outside of traditional modes of success; completion and write-up of a significant research project; and by success in achieving funding from other sources. Selected fellows, in collaboration with their mentor, will design and implement an individual professional development plan that will support them in developing new competencies and enhanced effectiveness as an academic leader and researcher. Award programs must begin between July 1st and September 1st of the award year. The program is committed to advancing well-qualified applicants from under-represented minority groups to improve the nation's ability to provide culturally competent care to its increasingly diverse aging population.
Requirements Applicants must: be doctorally-prepared registered nurses; hold degree(s) in nursing; be United States citizens or permanent U.S. residents; be doctorally-prepared registered nurses,; have the potential to develop into independent investigators; and demonstrate potential for long-term contributions to geriatric nursing. Applications will be accepted from doctoral students who will complete their doctoral program prior to the award. Faculty members in accredited Schools of Nursing who hold the rank of assistant professor or associate professor may apply for fellowships.
Amount $120,000 for the 2-year fellowship ($60,000 per annum)
Date(s) Application Is Due Jan 15.
Contact Pamela Dudzik, Program Administrator; (202) 777-1171; fax: (202) 777-0107; email: pdudzik@aannet.org
Internet http://www.geriatricnursing.org/applications/cmf-fellowship.asp
Sponsor American Academy of Nursing / John A. Hartford Foundation
888 17th Street, NW Suite 800
Washington, DC 20006

American Academy of Nursing Mayday Fund Grants 454
The Foundation's overall goal is to increase the nation's capacity to provide effective and affordable care to its rapidly increasing older population. Specifically, the Foundation seeks to enhance the training of physicians, nurses, social workers and other health professionals who care for older adults, and promote innovations in the integration and delivery of services. This program is aimed at candidates whose research includes the study of pain in the elderly. Award programs must begin between July 1st and September 1st.
Requirements Predoctoral applicants must: be registered nurses; hold degree(s) in nursing; be United States citizens or permanent U.S. residents; plan an academic and research career; and demonstrate potential for long-term contributions to geriatric nursing.
Amount $5,000 maximum
Date(s) Application Is Due Jan 9.
Contact Pamela Dudzik, Program Administrator; (202) 777-1171; fax: (202) 777-0107; email: pdudzik@aannet.org
Internet http://www.geriatricnursing.org/applications/applications.asp
Sponsor American Academy of Nursing / John A. Hartford Foundation
888 17th Street, NW Suite 800
Washington, DC 20006

American Academy of Religion Collaborative Research Grants 455
These grants are intended to stimulate cooperative research among scholars in different institutions, with a focus on a clearly identified research project. They may also be used for interdisciplinary work with scholars outside the field of religion, especially when such work shows promise of continuing beyond the year funded. Grants can provide funds for networking and communication. In addition, grants may be used to support small research conferences. Conference proposals will be considered only if they are designed primarily to advance research. Conferences presenting papers that report on previous research will not be considered. Award notification letters will be sent by the end of October. There are no application forms; guidelines are available online.

Requirements Applicants must be current AAR members who have been in good standing for the previous three years. In the case of proposals involving scholars from other disciplines, not all participants need to hold AAR membership.
Restrictions Applicants will not be considered who have received an AAR research grant in the previous five years.
Amount $500-$5000
Date(s) Application Is Due Aug 1.
Contact Grants Administrator, (404) 727-4707; fax: (404) 727-7959; email: info@aarweb.org
Internet http://www.aarweb.org/grants/collaborative.asp
Sponsor American Academy of Religion
825 Houston Mill Rd, Ste 300
Atlanta, GA 30329-4246

American Academy of Religion Individual Research Grants **456**
The grants provide support to academy members for important aspects of research, such as travel to archives and libraries, research assistance, field work, and release times. Proposals are judged on the project's contribution to scholarship in religious studies and on the significance of that contribution for advancing the understanding of religion or for advancing discussion between religion and other humanistic and social science disciplines. Scholars in small institutions, departments, or programs without research support and unaffiliated scholars are encouraged to apply.
Requirements Applicants: must be current AAR members who have been in good standing for the previous three years; will not be considered if they have received an AAR Research Award in the previous five years; must have completed the doctorate.
Restrictions Funds are not provided for dissertation research, nor for travel to attend the AAR annual meeting.
Amount $500-$5000
Date(s) Application Is Due Aug 1.
Contact Research Grants Program, (404) 727-4707; fax: (404) 727-7959; email: info@aarweb.org
Internet http://www.aarweb.org/grants/individual.asp
Sponsor American Academy of Religion
825 Houston Mill Rd, Ste 300
Atlanta, GA 30329

American Academy of Underwater Science Student Scholarship **457**
The AAUS awards scholarships to graduate students engaged in, or planning to begin, a research project in which diving will be used as a principal research tool. One scholarship will be awarded to a masters program student and the other to a PhD candidate.
Requirements Applicant must be a member of AAUS and submit a three- to five-page proposal and a statement of support from a faculty member.
Amount $2500
Date(s) Application Is Due Jun 30.
Contact Roy Houston, AAUS Scholarship Committee Chair, (310) 338-7343; email: rhouston@lmu.edu
Internet http://www.aaus.org/scholarshipweb.cfm
Sponsor American Academy of Underwater Sciences
430 Nahant Rd
Nahant, MA 01908

American Association of Petroleum Geologists Foundation Grants in Aid **458**
The purpose of the program is to support graduate students in the earth sciences whose research has application to the search for and development of petroleum and energy-minerals resources and to related environmental geology issues. Eighteen special grants named in recognition of individuals or entities that have made substantial contributions to the foundation, petroleum and energy-mineral sciences, and teaching are awarded each year. Grants are to be applied to expenses directly related to the student's thesis work, such as summer fieldwork, analytical analyses, etc.
Requirements The program focuses on support of qualified candidates for master's and equivalent degrees. Qualified doctoral candidates with expenses outside the usual scope of funding by other agencies are also encouraged to apply.
Amount $500-$2000
Date(s) Application Is Due Jan 31.
Contact Rebecca Griffin, Grants Coordinator, (888) 945-2274 ext 409 or (918) 560-9409; fax: (918) 560-2642; email: rgriffin@aapg.org
Internet http://www.aapg.org/foundation/gia/index.cfm
Sponsor American Association of Petroleum Geologists Foundation
P.O. Box 979
Tulsa, OK 74101

American Astonomical Society Chretien International Research Grants **459**
AAS administers this award in honor of the late Henri Chretien to further international collaborative projects in observational astronomy with emphasis upon long-term international visits and the development of close working relationships with astronomers in other countries. Awards are open to astronomers throughout the world and may be used to cover any reasonable costs associated with astronomical observational research including travel costs, salary, publication costs, and small pieces of research equipment. If appropriate, the recipient's family is encouraged to accompany him/her. Preference will be given to individuals of high promise who are otherwise unfunded. Innovative technical approaches including the development and use of new optics, new devices, and new techniques will count heavily in the applicant's favor.
Requirements Astronomers with a Ph.D or equivalent. Applications should A description of the research project (less than three pages in length) including an assessment of its importance to that particular subfield of astronomy and a statement enumerating all the aspects of international collaboration. A statement of the candidate's ability to do the proposed research. Special emphasis should be placed on international collaboration and foreign visits which have been arranged. Include facilities available and observing time allocations, if any. A proposed budget with brief justification for the amount requested. A description of other financial resources available. The candidate's curriculum vitae and bibliography of recent papers. Two letters of reference from astronomers who know the candidate's work. The candidate is responsible for ensuring that these letters reach the Committee by the application deadline. Any special circumstances which might help in the decision process.
Restrictions These awards will normally not be given to supplement a major research project that is funded elsewhere. There is no institutional overhead included in this award. Graduate students are not eligible.
Amount $20,000 maximum for one or more individuals or groups
Date(s) Application Is Due Apr 1.
Contact Grants Manager, (202) 328-2010; fax: (202) 234-2560; email: aas@aas.org
Internet http://www.aas.org/grants/chretien.html
Sponsor American Astronomical Society
2000 Florida Ave NW, Ste 400
Washington, DC 20009-1231

American Astronomical Society Small Research Grants **460**
These small research grants, sponsored jointly by the American Astronomical Society and NASA and administered by AAS, are awarded to postdoctoral astronomers to cover costs associated with any type of astronomical research. Eligible costs include page charges, computing costs, equipment, shipping of equipment, and travel to some observatories.
Requirements Applicants must be astronomers with a PhD or equivalent degree. Astronomers from smaller, less well-endowed institutions will be given priority. Proposals will be accepted from individuals not associated with an institution. Proposals are reviewed at January and June AAS meetings.
Restrictions Graduate students are ineligible. No salaries or overhead will be paid.
Amount $1000-$7000
Date(s) Application Is Due May 6; Dec 2.
Contact Susana Deustua, Grant Administrator, (202) 328-2010; fax: (202) 234-2560; email: deustua@aas.org
Internet http://www.aas.org/grants/smrg.html
Sponsor American Astronomical Society
2000 Florida Ave NW, Ste 400
Washington, DC 20009

American Australian Association Australia To USA Fellowships **461**
The fellowships are available for Australian scholars doing advanced research or study in the fields of business, science, technology, medicine or engineering in the United States. In return, the fellows are expected to add to Australia's intellectual capital as well as contribute to the country's overall social and economic well-being upon their return. The Fellowships will support part of the costs of one year of research or study in the United States. Applicants must submit a complete budget. The Association's budget form lists acceptable expenses.
Requirements Applicants must: be Australian citizens doing research or study at the graduate level. Applicants may already be in the U.S.; conduct a well-defined research project or study in one of the following fields--business, science, technology, medicine or engineering; demonstrate why travel to the United States is important to their research or study; demonstrate how their research or study will benefit Australia and intend to return to work in Australia; show proof of the arrangements made at a United States university or institution where the research or study will be conducted for the academic year beginning in September of that year; are expected to devote full time to their research or study; and be fluent in English.
Amount $25,000 maximum
Date(s) Application Is Due Mar 15.
Contact Diane Sinclair, Director, (212) 338-6860; email: diane.sinclair@aaanyc.org
Internet http://www.americanaustralian.org/Educational/australia-usa.php
Sponsor American Australian Association
599 Lexington Avenue, 18th Floor
New York, NY 10022

American Australian Association USA to Australia Fellowships **462**
Fellowships are available for Americans who will benefit from doing advanced research or study in the fields of life sciences, engineering, medicine, or mining; there will be particular interest in the fields of oceanography/marine sciences and stem cell research. In return, the fellows are expected to add to the United States and Australia's intellectual capital as well as contribute to those countries' overall social and economic well-being upon their return.

Requirements Applicants must: be American citizens or permanent residents of the USA doing research or study at the graduate level (applicants may already be in Australia); conduct a well-defined research project or study in one of the following fields: life sciences, engineering, medicine or mining. There will be particular interest in the fields of oceanography/marine sciences and stem cell research; demonstrate how their research or study will benefit the United States and Australia and that they intend to return to work in the United States; demonstrate why travel to Australia is important to their research or study; show proof of the arrangements made at an Australian university or institution where the research or study will be conducted for the next academic year; devote full time to their research or study; and be fluent in English.
Amount $20,000 maximum
Date(s) Application Is Due Oct 31.
Contact Diane Sinclair, Director, (212) 338-6860; email: diane.sinclair@aaanyc.org
Internet http://www.americanaustralian.org/Educational/usa-australia.php
Sponsor American Australian Association
599 Lexington Avenue, 18th Floor
New York, NY 10022

American Automatic Control Council John R. Ragazzini Award **463**
The award is made for outstanding contributions to automatic control education in any form. The awardee normally is a teacher, but there is no formal requirement that nominees be members of a university faculty. Nomination forms are available on the Web site.
Requirements Nomination packages should consist of a letter of nomination, three to five reference letters, current resume, current list of publications and patents, any other supporting material, and a nomination form. The nomination letter should clearly identify the primary reason that the nominee should receive the award, as well as four ancillary reasons. All materials should be submitted in a single package.
Date(s) Application Is Due Dec 1.
Contact Professor Pradeep Misra, Electrical Engineering Department, Wright State University, (937) 775-5062; fax: (937) 775-3936; email: pmisra@cs.wright.edu
Internet http://www.a2c2.org/awards/ragazzini/nomination.php
Sponsor American Automatic Control Council
3640 Col Glenn Hwy
Dayton, OH 45435

American College of Bankruptcy Grants **464**
The college awards grants for existing bankruptcy or consumer-debtor programs, programs in development, and research projects to improve the delivery of pro bono bankruptcy services. Grants also support organizations for broad educational purposes. There are no application guidelines. Submit inquiries to George Cauthen, c/o Nelson Mullins Riley and Scarborough, LLP, (803) 255-9425, email: george.cauthen@nelsonmullins.com; P.O. Box 11070; Columbia, SC 29211. Guidelines and application are available online.
Amount $1000-$10,000
Date(s) Application Is Due Mar 1.
Contact American College of Bankruptcy, (703) 934-6154; fax: (703) 802-0207; email: college@amercol.org
Internet http://www.amercol.com/index.html
Sponsor American College of Bankruptcy
PMB 626A, 11350 Random Hills Rd, Ste 800
Fairfax, VA 22030-6044

American College of Surgeons Faculty Career Development Award for Oncology of the Head And Neck **465**
The program was developed through Clowes Fund Inc and provides two years of support for promising young surgical investigators. Funds may be used for salary support or other purposes at the discretion of the awardee and the institution. ACS will look favorably upon applicants who have received investigator-initiated, peer-reviewed research awards. Applicants must submit a detailed research plan and propose a budget for the two-year period of the award.
Requirements Application is open to surgeons who have completed their specialty training in a residency or an accredited fellowship in general surgery or a surgical specialty within the preceding five years and have received full-time faculty appointments at medical schools accredited by the Liaison Committee on Medical Education in the United States or by the Committee for Accreditation of Canadian Medical Schools in Canada. Applicants should provide evidence of productive initial efforts in laboratory research.
Restrictions The committee will not consider applicants who have received research career development awards from NIH, AHA, or other funding agencies. Also, awardees may not receive other career development awards during the two-year period of support.
Amount $40,000 per year for two years
Date(s) Application Is Due Nov 1.
Contact Administrator, Scholarships Division, (312) 664-4050
Internet http://www.facs.org/memberservices/headandneck.html
Sponsor American College of Surgeons
633 N Saint Clair St
Chicago, IL 60611-3211

American College of Surgeons Faculty Research Fellowships **466**
ACS offers two-year fellowships to surgeons entering academic careers in surgery or a surgical specialty to assist in the establishment of a new and independent research program by surgeons who, during their residencies, have demonstrated their potential to begin work as independent investigators. The fellowship grant is to be used by the recipient and is not to diminish or replace the usual expected compensation; the award is made to the fellow, not the institution. Preference will be given to applicants who are not current recipients of major research grants. The fellow's institution must make a commitment to continue the academic position and availability of facilities for research. The applicant must submit a research plan and budget for the two-year period of the fellowship. A minimum of 50 percent of the fellow's time is to be spent in research. Requests for application forms will not be accepted after October 1.
Requirements The fellowship is restricted to surgeons who have recently (usually within three years) completed formal surgical education and entered the field of full-time academic surgery and received a faculty appointment in a department of surgery, or one of the surgical specialties, at an approved medical school in the United States or Canada. Preference will be given to applicants who directly enter academic surgery following residency or fellowships. Approval of the application is required from the administration (dean or fiscal officer) and the head of the department under whom the recipient will be studying during the fellowship.
Amount $40,000 per year
Date(s) Application Is Due Nov 1.
Contact Administrator, Scholarships Division, (312) 202-5000; fax: (312) 202-5001; email: postmaster@facs.org
Internet http://www.facs.org/memberservices/acsfaculty.html
Sponsor American College of Surgeons
633 N Saint Clair St
Chicago, IL 60611-3211

American Council of the Blind Scholarships **467**
The council funds scholarships to assist outstanding blind and visually impaired students to continue their education at the postsecondary level. Education may be contemplated in an academic, technical, vocational, or professional training program. These scholarships are one-time awards with no renewal. Contact office for availability.
Requirements Applicant must be legally blind in both eyes; must be a US citizen or resident alien; and must be enrolled in or under consideration for admission at the postsecondary level.
Date(s) Application Is Due Mar 1.
Contact Terry Pacheco, (800) 424-8666 or (202) 467-5081 ext 19; fax: (202) 467-5085; email: TerryPach@aol.com or info@acb.org
Internet http://www.acb.org/magazine/2005/bf022005-5.html
Sponsor American Council of the Blind
1155 15th St NW, Ste 1004
Washington, DC 20005

American Council on Germany Journalism Fellowship **468**
The fellowship enables recipients to conduct research in Germany on current political, economic, and social issues. Proposed research projects should address topics with current political or policy significance in Germany's relations with the United States or within the European Union. The program seeks to create a better understanding of transatlantic matters among American journalists and to enable fellows to gain new perspectives on such topics. While applicants should demonstrate an interest in German and European issues, no prior experience in Germany or Europe is required. ACG will make travel arrangements and develop research itineraries in consultation with the fellows. If desired, the fellows may consult with the German Information Center in New York to help implement their projects. Following the completion of the trip, fellows will submit a report summarizing their findings. Fellows are also encouraged to publish articles on their findings. The fellowship award covers the costs of pre-approved international and domestic travel and a per diem allowance for 14 to 28 days in Germany. Applications are reviewed on a rolling basis. Guidelines are available online.
Requirements The fellowship program aims to serve American print or broadcast journalists who are in relatively early stages of their careers, including those with only limited exposure to Europe. Knowledge of the German language is not a prerequisite for the program.
Amount $150 per diem allowance
Contact Emily Gildersleeve, Fellowship Coordinator, (212) 826-3636; email: egildersleeve@acgusa.org
Internet http://acgusa.org/acg_journalism_fellowships.htm
Sponsor American Council on Germany
14 E 60th St, Ste 606
New York, NY 10022

American Dietetic Association Foundation Scholarships **469**
As the largest provider of dietetic scholarships, the program awards funds to deserving students at all levels of study. Additional funds are granted in the form of continuing education stipends, research grants, and recognition awards to practicing dietitians and nutritionists. Additional program information is available online. Application deadlines vary, and applications are typically made available four to six months before the deadline. To receive an application for a particular award or for more information contact the office.

Requirements Applicant must be a US citizen. Scholarships are awarded in the field of dietetics at all levels: undergraduate, graduate, internship, technician, and for preprofessional practice programs.
Amount $500-$5000
Contact Grants Administrator, (800) 877-1600 ext 5400; email: education@eatright.org.
Internet http://www.eatright.org/Public/7772.cfm
Sponsor American Dietetic Association Foundation
120 S Riverside Plz, Ste 2000
Chicago, IL 60606

American Education Research Association Grants **470**
The American Educational Research Association, with support from the National Science Foundation (NSF), and the National Center for Education Statistics (NCES), award grants to stimulate quantitative policy- and practice-related research using nationally representative NCES and NSF data sets, improve knowledge of the range of data available at the two agencies and how to use them, and increase the number of educational researchers using the data sets. Research topics include school persistence and career entry, policies and practices related to achievement, policies and practices influencing student and parental attitudes, middle school education, educational finance, and the quality of educational institutions. One- and two-year projects will be funded, excluding indirect costs. Minorities are encouraged to apply.
Requirements Grants are available for faculty and postdoctoral researchers.
Amount $20,000 maximum for one-year projects; $35,000 maximum for two-year projects
Date(s) Application Is Due Jan 3; Mar 1; Sep 1.
Contact Jeanie Murdock, (805) 964-5264; email: jmurdock@aera.net
Internet http://www.aera.net/grantsprogram/res_training/res_grants/RGFly.html
Sponsor University of California, Santa Barbara
1190 Phelps Hall
Santa Barbara, CA 93106-9490

American Family Insurance Corporate Giving Program Grants **471**
The corporation awards grants to nonprofits in its areas of interest, including education and youth, arts and culture, health, and human services.
Requirements Nonprofit organizations and K-12 and higher education institutions located in the companies area of interest.
Restrictions Individuals or teams and organizations outside the 18-state operating territory will not be supported.
Amount $2 million total
Contact Community Relations, (608) 249-2111; email: info@amfam.com
Internet http://www.amfam.com/company/commitment_contribution.asp
Sponsor American Family Insurance Corporation
6000 American Pkwy
Madison, WI 53783

American Foundation for Aging Research Fellowhips **472**
AFAR awards fellowships to undergraduate, graduate and pre-doctoral (MD, PhD, DDS, etc.) students who are actively involved or are planning active involvement in a biomedical age-related research project. Awards are to alleviate the costs of tuition and fees at a United States degree granting institution. If such costs are already covered by another source of funds, other than personal funds, the awards are to be used for research purposes. Awards are made each semester and are renewable once. Preapplications may be submitted at any time; renewal requests should be made at least 30 days before the next semester.
Requirements Applicants must be undergraduate, graduate and pre-doctoral (MD, PhD, DDS, etc.) students who are enrolled at degree programs at colleges or universitites in the United States.
Restrictions Sociology, psychology, and health-professional related research such as physical therapy and exercise physiology are not currently being funded.
Amount $1000 graduate fellowships; $500 undergraduate scholarships
Contact Executive Secretary, (919) 515-5679; fax: (919) 515-2047; email: afar_office@ncsu.edu
Internet http://www4.ncsu.edu/unity/users/a/agris/afar/afar.htm
Sponsor American Foundation for Aging Research
Campus Box 7622, North Carolina State University
Raleigh, NC 27695-7622

American Foundation for Suicide Prevention Grants **473**
The research grants are awarded to investigators conducting clinical, biological, or psychosocial research on the problem of suicide, for one- or two-year periods, and for up to three years for research fellowships. Grant applicants compete in five categories: Pilot Grants provide seed money for new projects and are awarded to individual investigators without regard to academic rank or pervious research experience with suicide; Young Investigator Grants are awarded for two years of support to investigators at the level of assistant professor or lower; Standard Research Grants are awarded to individual investigators for a two-year period; Distinguished Researcher Awards are awarded to investigators at the level of associate professor or higher with a proven history of research in the area of suicide (to fund new directions and initiatives in suicidology); Postdoctoral Research Fellowships are awarded for full-time training projects by investigators who have received a PhD degree within the preceding three years and have not had more than three years of fellowship support. Application deadlines are December 15 for Young Investigator Grants, Standard Research Grants, Distinguished Researcher Awards, and Postdoctoral Fellowships; and April 15, August 15, and December 15 for Pilot Grants. Guidelines and application forms are available online.
Amount $20,000 maximum Pilot Grants; $70,000 maximum Young Investigator Grants; $60,000 maximum Standard Research Grants; $100,000 maximum Distinguished Researcher Awards
Date(s) Application Is Due Apr 15; Aug 15; Dec 15.
Contact Grants Administrator, (888) 333-2377 or (212) 363-3500; fax: (212) 363-6237; email: bkoestner@afsp.org
Internet http://www.afsp.org/research/grants.htm
Sponsor American Foundation for Suicide Prevention
120 Wall St, 22nd Fl
New York, NY 10005

American Historical Association Albert B. Corey Prize in Canadian-American Relations **474**
The prize is awarded biennially in even-numbered years to an American or Canadian resident for the best book on the history of Canadian-American relations or on the history of both countries. The prize is awarded jointly by the Canadian Historical Association and the American Historical Association.
Requirements Books bearing an imprint of the previous two years are eligible for the prize.
Date(s) Application Is Due Jan 15.
Contact Book Prize Administrator, (202) 544-2422; fax: (202) 544-8307; email: aha@theaha.org
Internet http://www.historians.org/prizes/index.cfm?PrizeAbbrev=COREY
Sponsor American Historical Association
400 A Street, SE
Washington, DC 20003

American Historical Association Albert J. Beveridge Award **475**
The Award is given annually for the best book in English on the history of the United States, Latin America, or Canada from 1492 to the present. Books that employ new methodological or conceptual tools or that constitute a significant reinterpretation of an important historical problem are given preference in the awarding of this prize. Biographies, monographs, and works of synthesis or interpretation are eligible.
Requirements U.S. and Canadian citizens and permanent residents are eligible. Books published after May 1 of the previous year and before April 30 of the award year are eligible.
Restrictions Translations, anthologies, and collections of documents are not eligible.
Date(s) Application Is Due May 15.
Contact Book Prize Administrator, (202) 544-2422; fax: (202) 544-8307; email: aha@theaha.org
Internet http://www.historians.org/prizes/AWARDED/BeveridgeWinner.htm
Sponsor American Historical Association
400 A Street, SE
Washington, DC 20003

American Historical Association Albert J. Beveridge Grants for Research in the History of the Western Hemisphere **476**
The grants support research in the history of the Western hemisphere (United States, Canada, and Latin America). The funds for this program come from the earnings of the Albert J. Beveridge Memorial Fund. Only members of the Association are eligible. The grants are intended to further research in progress and may be used for travel to a library or archive, for microfilms, photographs, or photocopying-a list of purposes that is meant to be merely illustrative, not exhaustive. Preference will be given to those with specific research needs, such as the completion of a project or completion of a discrete segment thereof. Preference will be given to Ph.D. candidates and junior scholars.
Restrictions Within a five-year period, no individual is eligible to receive more than a combined total of $1,000 from the Beveridge, Kraus, and Littleton-Griswold grant programs.
Amount $1,000 maximum
Date(s) Application Is Due Feb 15.
Contact Research Grant Administrator, (202) 544-2422; fax: (202) 544-8307; email: aha@theaha.org
Internet http://www.historians.org/prizes/BeveridgeGrantInfo.htm
Sponsor American Historical Association
400 A Street, SE
Washington, DC 20003

American Historical Association Award for Scholarly Distinction **477**
According to the selection criteria of this Award, recipients must be senior historians of the highest distinction who have spent the bulk of their professional careers in the United States. Generally, they must also be of emeritus rank, if from academic life, or equivalent standing otherwise. Under normal circumstances the award is not intended to go to former presidents of the Association; rather, the intent is to honor persons not otherwise recognized by the profession to an extent commensurate with their contributions.
Date(s) Application Is Due Apr 30.

Contact Sharon K. Tune, Assistant Director, (202) 544-2422; fax: (202) 544-8307; email: aha@theaha.org
Internet http://www.historians.org/prizes/ScholarlyDistinction.htm
Sponsor American Historical Association
400 A Street, SE
Washington, DC 20003-3889

American Historical Association Bernadotte E. Schmitt Research Grants 478

Modest grants support research in the history of Europe, Africa, and Asia. The grants are intended to further research in progress and may be used for travel to a library or archive; for microfilms, photographs, or photocopying; or for coding and keypunching; and other approved research-related activities.
Requirements Preference will be given to those with specific research needs, such as the completion of a project or completion of a discrete segment thereof. Preference will be given to Ph.D. candidates and junior scholars.
Restrictions Only members of the Association are eligible to apply.
Amount $1,000 maximum
Date(s) Application Is Due Feb 15.
Contact Research Grant Administrator, (202) 544-2422; fax: (202) 544-8307; email: aha@theaha.org
Internet http://www.historians.org/prizes/SchmittGrantInfo.htm
Sponsor American Historical Association
400 A Street, SE
Washington, DC 20003

American Historical Association Clarence H. Haring Prize 479

This prize is awarded every five years to a Latin American who, in the opinion of the committee, has published the most outstanding book on Latin American history during the preceding five years ending June 1 of the award year. Books published between May 1, 2006, and April 30, 2011, will be eligible for the prize in 2011. There is no language limitation on works submitted. Authors should obtain guidelines from the association.
Requirements Books published between May 1, 2006, and April 30, 2011, will be eligible for the prize in 2011.
Date(s) Application Is Due May 15.
Contact Book Prize Administrator, (202) 544-2422; fax: (202) 544-8307; email: aha@theaha.org
Internet http://www.historians.org/prizes/index.cfm?PrizeAbbrev=HARING
Sponsor American Historical Association
400 A Street, SE
Washington, DC 20003

American Historical Association George L. Mosse Prize 480

The prize is designated for an outstanding major work of extraordinary scholarly distinction, creativity, and originality in the intellectual and cultural history of Europe since the Renaissance. This prize was established with funds donated by former students, colleagues, and friends of Dr. Mosse. Only books of a high scholarly distinction should be submitted. Research accuracy, originality, and literary merit are important factors.
Requirements Books published after May 1 of the previous year and before April 30 of the award year are eligible.
Date(s) Application Is Due May 15.
Contact Book Prize Administrator, (202) 544-2422; fax: (202) 544-8307; email: aha@theaha.org
Internet http://www.historians.org/prizes/index.cfm?PrizeAbbrev=MOSSE
Sponsor American Historical Association
400 A Street, SE
Washington, DC 20003

American Historical Association George Louis Beer Prize 481

The prize is awarded in recognition of outstanding historical writing in European international history since the year 1895 that is submitted by a scholar who is a United States citizen or permanent resident. The phrase - European international history since the year 1895 - may be understood to mean any study of international history since the year 1895 with a significant European dimension. Research accuracy, originality, and literary merit are important factors.
Requirements Books published after May 1 of the previous year and before April 30 of the award year are eligible. Only books of a high scholarly historical nature should be submitted.
Date(s) Application Is Due May 15.
Contact Book Prize Administrator, (202) 544-2422; fax: (202) 544-8307; email: aha@theaha.org
Internet http://www.historians.org/prizes/index.cfm?PrizeAbbrev=BEER
Sponsor American Historical Association
400 A Street, SE
Washington, DC 20003

American Historical Association Helen and Howard R Marraro Prizes 482

The prizes are given annually by the American Historical Association, the American Catholic Historical Association, and the Society for Italian Historical Studies for the best works on any epoch of Italian cultural history or on Italian-American relations written by American and Canadian resident citizens. The associations appoint a joint selection committee. One copy of each work, together with a brief curriculum vita and bibliography of the author, must be submitted to designated committee members. The American Historical Association will send instructions upon request.
Requirements Books published after May 1 of the previous year and before April 30 of the award year are eligible. Entries must first have been published in English by a historian whose usual residence is North America.
Date(s) Application Is Due May 15.
Contact Book Prize Administrator, (202) 544-2422; fax: (202) 544-8307; email: aha@theaha.org
Internet http://www.historians.org/prizes/index.cfm?PrizeAbbrev=MARRARO
Sponsor American Historical Association
400 A Street, SE
Washington, DC 20003

American Historical Association Herbert Baxter Adams Prize 483

The association annually awards this prize for an author's first book in the field of European history. Chronological coverage follows a two-year cycle: in even-numbered years, subject matter includes ancient, medieval, or early modern European history through 1815; in odd-numbered years, the subject matter should deal with 1816 through the 20th century. The submission of an entry may be made by an author, a third party, or a publisher. Annual deadline dates may vary; contact the association or visit the Web site for exact dates.
Requirements US and Canadian citizens and permanent residents are eligible. Books published after May 1 of the previous year and before April 30 of the award year are eligible.
Restrictions Textbooks in the strict sense of the word are not eligible, but a work of wide scope that interprets a major period or area qualifies. Pamphlets, anthologies, edited works, and other small-scale efforts do not qualify.
Date(s) Application Is Due May 15.
Contact Book Prize Administrator, (202) 544-2422; fax: (202) 544-8307; email: aha@theaha.org
Internet http://www.historians.org/prizes/index.cfm?PrizeAbbrev=ADAMS
Sponsor American Historical Association
400 A Street, SE
Washington, DC 20003

American Historical Association Herbert Feis Award 484

This prize is offered annually to recognize the scholarly interests of historians outside academe and the importance of the work of independent scholars in the United States. The terms of the award define both □contribution□ and □public history□ broadly. Contributions could include work as the administrator of a public history group or agency (such as a historical society, a historic site, or a community history project) or as the creator or producer of a public history product or products (such as a museum exhibit, radio script, web site, oral history collection, or film). The contribution may be the result of years of effort in the field, but the prize might also recognize a singular contribution of major importance such as a path breaking museum exhibit. Public history is defined as work primarily directed at non-academic, non-school-based audiences. Those audiences could be very broad (e.g., television viewers) or highly specialized (e.g., policymakers). Although the audience should be primarily outside of academia, the recipient of the award could be employed at a university.
Requirements Works published or issued in-house between May 1 of the previous year and April 30 of the upcoming year are eligible.
Date(s) Application Is Due May 15.
Contact Book Prize Administrator, (202) 544-2422; fax: (202) 544-8307; email: aha@theaha.org
Internet http://www.historians.org/prizes/index.cfm?PrizeAbbrev=FEIS
Sponsor American Historical Association
400 A Street, SE
Washington, DC 20003

American Historical Association J. Franklin Jameson Fellowship 485

This fellowship is offered collaboratively each year by the Library of Congress and the Association to support significant scholarly research by young historians for one semester in the collections of the Library of Congress. The applicant's project in American history must be one for which the general and special collections of the Library of Congress offer unique research support. The fellowship will be awarded for one semester or as much of an academic year (September-May) as the fellow desires to spend in residence at the Library of Congress, but the fellow is required to spend at least three months. Working space will be provided by the Library of Congress. Fellows are not required to complete their projects during tenure, nor need they necessarily publish the results as a discrete work.
Requirements Applicants must hold the PhD degree or equivalent, must have received this degree within the last seven years, and must not have published or had accepted for publication a book-length historical work. Letters of application should include a vita, a statement concerning the proposed project and its relationship to the Library of Congress holdings, a tentative schedule for tenure of the fellowship, and the names and addresses of three persons qualified to judge the project and the applicant's fitness to undertake it.

Restrictions The fellowship will not be awarded to permit completion of a doctoral dissertation.
Amount $5,000
Date(s) Application Is Due Mar 15.
Contact Arnita A. Jones, Executive Director, (202) 544-2422, ext. 100; fax: (202) 544-8307; email: ajones@theaha.org or aha@theaha.org
Internet http://www.historians.org/prizes/Jameson_fellowship.htm
Sponsor American Historical Association
400 A Street, SE
Washington, DC 20003

American Historical Association J. Russell Major Prize 486
The Prize will be awarded annually for the best work in English on any aspect of French history. The prize was established in memory of J. Russell Major, the distinguished scholar of French history who died on December 12, 1998 at the age of 77. One copy of each entry must be received by each of the following committee members.
Requirements Books published after May 1 of the previous year and before April 30 of the award year are eligible.
Date(s) Application Is Due May 15.
Contact Book Prize Administrator, (202) 544-2422; fax: (202) 544-8307; email: aha@theaha.org
Internet http://www.historians.org/prizes/index.cfm?PrizeAbbrev=MAJOR
Sponsor American Historical Association
400 A Street, SE
Washington, DC 20003

American Historical Association James A. Rawley Prize in Atlantic History 487
This AHA Prize is intended to recognize outstanding historical writing that explores aspects of integration of Atlantic worlds before the twentieth century. The prize was established in accordance with the terms of a gift from James A. Rawley, Carl Adolph Happold Professor of History Emeritus at the University of Nebraska at Lincoln. Only books of high scholarly and literary merit will be considered. Research accuracy and originality also will be important factors in the evaluation of the books. Books published between May 1 of the previous year and April 30 of the current year are eligible.
Date(s) Application Is Due May 15.
Contact Book Prize Administrator, (202) 544-2422; fax: (202) 544-8307; email: aha@theaha.org
Internet http://www.historians.org/prizes/index.cfm?PrizeAbbrev=ATLANTIC
Sponsor American Historical Association
400 A Street, SE
Washington, DC 20003

American Historical Association James Harvey Robinson Prize 488
The Prize is awarded biennially for the teaching aid which has made the most outstanding contribution to the teaching and learning of history in any field for public or educational purposes. Teaching aid encompasses textbooks, source and reference materials, audiovisuals, computer-assisted instruction, and public history or museum materials. Monographs and revisions will not be considered. The winner will receive a one-year membership in the Association. The work should: have the potential to influence history education (this influence could be in the form of a model that would have wide adaptability and/or could affect teachers and students through widely taught courses; demonstrate recent and good historical scholarship; and be well written and attractively presented.
Requirements Monographs and revisions will not be considered. Books published after May 1 two years prior and before April 30 of the award year are eligible.
Date(s) Application Is Due May 15.
Contact Book Prize Administrator, (202) 544-2422; fax: (202) 544-8307; email: aha@theaha.org
Internet http://www.historians.org/prizes/index.cfm?PrizeAbbrev=ROBINSON
Sponsor American Historical Association
400 A Street, SE
Washington, DC 20003

American Historical Association James Henry Breasted Prize 489
The prize is offered for the best book in English in any field of history prior to 1000 AD and rotates annually among the following geographical areas: Near East and Egypt; Far East and South Asia; Africa, North America, and Latin America; and Europe. Only works of high scholarly and literary merit will be considered. One copy of each entry must be submitted to designated committee members.
Requirements Books published after May 1 of the previous year and before April 30 of the award year are eligible.
Date(s) Application Is Due May 15.
Contact Book Prize Administrator, (202) 544-2422; fax: (202) 544-8307; email: aha@theaha.org
Internet http://www.historians.org/prizes/index.cfm?PrizeAbbrev=BREASTED
Sponsor American Historical Association
400 A Street, SE
Washington, DC 20003

American Historical Association Joan Kelly Memorial Prize in Women's History 490
This prize is awarded annually for the book in women's history and/or feminist theory that best reflects the high intellectual and scholarly ideals exemplified by the life and work of the late Joan Kelly. Books should demonstrate originality of research, creativity of insight, graceful stylistic presentation, analytical skills, and a recognition of the important role of sex and gender in the historical process. The inter-relationship between women and the historical process should be addressed. Authors must obtain application forms and guidelines for submission from the association.
Requirements Books in any chronological period, any geographical location, or in an area of feminist theory that incorporates a historical perspective are eligible for consideration. Books published after May 1 of the previous year and before April 30 of the award year are eligible.
Date(s) Application Is Due May 15.
Contact Book Prize Administrator, (202) 544-2422; fax: (202) 544-8307; email: aschulkin@theaha.org or aha@theaha.org
Internet http://www.historians.org/prizes/index.cfm?PrizeAbbrev=KELLY
Sponsor American Historical Association
400 A Street, SE
Washington, DC 20003-3889

American Historical Association John E. Fagg Prize 491
The Prize is conferred annually for the best publication in the history of Spain, Portugal, or Latin America. The prize will be awarded annually for a period of 10 years beginning in 2001 and ending in 2011. Only works of high scholarly and literary merit will be considered. One copy of each entry must be submitted to designated committee members.
Requirements Applicant must be a published author. To be eligible, a book must be published after May 1 of the previous year and before April 30 of the current year.
Date(s) Application Is Due May 15.
Contact Book Prize Administrator, (202) 544-2422; fax: (202) 544-8307; email: aha@theaha.org
Internet http://www.historians.org/prizes/index.cfm?PrizeAbbrev=FAGG
Sponsor American Historical Association
400 A Street, SE
Washington, DC 20003

American Historical Association John H. Dunning Prize 492
The prize is awarded in odd-numbered years by the association to a young scholar for an outstanding monograph in manuscript or in print on any subject relating to United States history. Research accuracy, originality, and literary merit are important factors. One copy of each entry must be submitted to each committee member.
Requirements An entry must be the author's first or second book published or completed. Books published after May 1 of the previous year and before April 30 of the deadline year are eligible.
Date(s) Application Is Due May 15.
Contact Book Prize Administrator, (202) 544-2422; fax: (202) 544-8307; email: aha@theaha.org
Internet http://www.historians.org/prizes/index.cfm?PrizeAbbrev=DUNNING
Sponsor American Historical Association
400 A Street, SE
Washington, DC 20003

American Historical Association John K. Fairbank Prize in East Asian History 493
The prize is awarded annually for an outstanding book on the history of China proper, Vietnam, Chinese Central Asia, Mongolia, Manchuria, Korea, or Japan substantially since the year 1800. Only books of high scholarly and literary merit will be considered. One copy of each entry must be submitted to each committee member. Application forms are available from the association.
Requirements Books published after May 1 of the previous year and before April 30 of the award year are eligible.
Restrictions Anthologies, edited works, and pamphlets are ineligible for the competition.
Date(s) Application Is Due May 15.
Contact Book Prize Administrator, (202) 544-2422; fax: (202) 544-8307; email: aha@theaha.org
Internet http://www.historians.org/prizes/index.cfm?PrizeAbbrev=FAIRBANK
Sponsor American Historical Association
400 A Street, SE
Washington, DC 20003

American Historical Association Leo Gershoy Award 494
The award is given annually by the association to the author of the most outstanding work in English on any aspect of the field of 17th- and 18th-century western European history. Only books of high scholarly and literary merit will be considered. One copy of each entry must be submitted to designated committee members.
Requirements Books published after May 1 of the previous year and before April 30 of the award year are eligible.
Date(s) Application Is Due May 15.

Contact Book Prize Administrator, (202) 544-2422; fax: (202) 544-8307; email: aha@theaha.org
Internet http://www.historians.org/prizes/index.cfm?PrizeAbbrev=GERSHOY
Sponsor American Historical Association
400 A Street, SE
Washington, DC 20003

American Historical Association Littleton-Griswold Prize in American Law and Society 495

This prize is offered annually for the best book in any subject on the history of American law and society. The $1,000 prize is administered by a joint committee of the American Historical Association and the American Society for Legal History. Only books of high scholarly and literary merit will be considered. Recipients are announced at the association's annual meeting. *Requirements* Books published between May 1 of the previous year and April 30 of the award year are eligible.
Amount $1,000
Date(s) Application Is Due May 15.
Contact Book Prize Administrator, (202) 544-2422; fax: (202) 544-8307; email: aha@theaha.org
Internet http://www.historians.org/prizes/index.cfm?PrizeAbbrev=LITTLETON%2DGRISWOLD
Sponsor American Historical Association
400 A Street, SE
Washington, DC 20003

American Historical Association Littleton-Griswold Research Grants 496

Grants are given annually for research in U.S. legal history and in the general field of law and society. The funds for this program come from the earnings of the Littleton-Griswold Fund. Only members of the Association are eligible to apply. The grants are intended to further research in progress and may be used for travel to a library or archive, for microfilms, photographs, or photocopying-a list of purposes that is meant to be merely illustrative, not exhaustive.
Requirements Preference will be given to those with specific research needs, such as the completion of a project or completion of a discrete segment thereof. Preference will be given to Ph.D. candidates and junior scholars.
Restrictions Specifically excluded from funding are use of research assistants except in cases of technical skills such as data entry, coding of data, and other procedures relating to the preparation of data for machine computation; help with typing except for typing of camera-ready copy for an article, dissertation, or book, which would qualify as a technical expense; and use of funds for partial salary replacement.
Amount $1,000 maximum
Date(s) Application Is Due Feb 15.
Contact Research Grant Administrator, (202) 544-2422; fax: (202) 544-8307; email: aha@theaha.org
Internet http://www.historians.org/prizes/Littleton-GriswaldGrantInfo.htm
Sponsor American Historical Association
400 A Street, SE
Washington, DC 20003

American Historical Association Michael Kraus Research Grant in American Colonial History 497

This annual grant seeks to recognize the most deserving proposal relating to work in progress on a research project in American colonial history, with particular reference to the inter-cultural aspects of American and European relations. Only members of the Association are eligible. The grants are intended to further research in progress and may be used for travel to a library or archive, for microfilms, photographs, or photocopying--a list of purposes that is meant to be merely illustrative, not exhaustive.
Requirements Applicants must be members of the association. Preference will be given to those with specific research needs such as the completion of a project or a discrete segment thereof. Preference will be given to Ph.D. candidates and junior scholars.
Restrictions Specifically excluded from funding are use of research assistants except in cases of technical skills such as keypunching, coding of data, and other procedures relating to the preparation of data for machine computation; help with typing except for typing of camera-ready copy for an article, dissertation, or book, which would qualify as a technical expense; and use of funds for partial salary replacements. Within a five-year period, no individual is eligible to receive more than a combined total of $1,000 from the Beveridge, Kraus, and Littleton-Griswold grant programs.
Amount $800 maximum
Date(s) Application Is Due Feb 15.
Contact Research Grant Administrator, (202) 544-2422; fax: (202) 544-8307; email: aha@theaha.org
Internet http://www.historians.org/prizes/KrausGrantInfo.htm
Sponsor American Historical Association
400 A Street, SE
Washington, DC 20003

American Historical Association Morris D. Forkosch Prize 498

The prize is awarded annually in recognition of the best book in English in the field of British, British Imperial, or British Commonwealth history. Submission of books relating to the shared common law heritage of the English-speaking world is particularly encouraged. One copy of each entry must be submitted to designated committee members. Prize recipients are announced at the association's annual meeting.
Requirements Books published after May 1 of the previous year and before April 30 of the award year are eligible.
Date(s) Application Is Due May 16.
Contact Book Prize Administrator, (202) 544-2422; fax: (202) 544-8307; email: aha@theaha.org
Internet http://www.historians.org/prizes/index.cfm?PrizeAbbrev=FORKOSCH
Sponsor American Historical Association
400 A Street, SE
Washington, DC 20003-3889

American Historical Association NASA Research Fellowship in Aerospace History 499

The fellowship, supported by NASA, annually funds one or more research projects for six to nine months. Proposals of advanced research in history related to all aspects of aerospace, from the earliest human interest in flight to the present, are eligible, including cultural and intellectual history, economic history, history of law and public policy, and history of science, engineering, and management. The Fellowship term is for a period of at least six months, but not more than one year. The Fellow will be expected to devote the term entirely to the proposed research project.
Requirements The fellowship is open to any US citizen who holds a doctoral degree in history or a closely related field, or who is enrolled in and has completed all course work for a doctoral degree-granting program.
Restrictions Funds may not be used to support tuition or fees. A Fellow may not hold other major fellowships or grants during the fellowship term, except sabbatical and supplemental grants from their own institutions, and small grants from other sources for specific research expenses.
Amount $20,000
Date(s) Application Is Due Mar 1.
Contact Arnita A. Jones, Executive Director, (202) 544-2422, ext. 100; fax: (202) 544-8307; email: ajones@theaha.org or
Internet http://www.historians.org/prizes/NASA.htm
Sponsor American Historical Association
400 A Street, SE
Washington, DC 20003

American Historical Association Paul Birdsall Prize in European Military and Strategic History 500

The prize is offered biennially in even-numbered years for a major work in European military and strategic history since 1870. Preference will be given to the international aspects of military history (military/diplomatic), but the political, economic, and social impact of technological developments, strategic planning, and military events on society will also qualify.
Requirements Authors must be citizens of the United States or Canada; preference will be given to younger academics, but older scholars and nonacademic candidates will not be excluded. Books published after May 1 of the previous year and before April 30 of the award year are eligible.
Date(s) Application Is Due May 15.
Contact Book Prize Administrator, (202) 544-2422; fax: (202) 544-8307; email: aha@theaha.org
Internet http://www.historians.org/prizes/index.cfm?PrizeAbbrev=BIRDSALL
Sponsor American Historical Association
400 A Street, SE
Washington, DC 20003

American Historical Association Premio Del Rey 501

The prize is awarded biennially for a distinguished book in English in the field of early Spanish history. It was endowed by a gift of Robert I. Burns S.J., from his Llull and Catalonia prizes and covers the medieval period in Spain's history and culture CE 500-1516. The terms of the prize include works on Hispanic history and culture, including the Islamic and Jewish communities of Medieval Spain as well as early New World topics prior to 1516. Only books of a high scholarly historical nature should be submitted. Research accuracy, originality and literary merit are important factors. One copy of each entry must be received by each of the committee members.
Requirements Books published after May 1 of the previous year and before April 30 of the award year are eligible.
Date(s) Application Is Due May 15.
Contact Book Prize Administrator, (202) 544-2422; fax: (202) 544-8307; email: aha@theaha.org
Internet http://www.historians.org/prizes/index.cfm?PrizeAbbrev=DEL%2DREY
Sponsor American Historical Association
400 A Street, SE
Washington, DC 20003

American Historical Association Waldo J. Leland Prize 502

The prize is awarded every five years (next in 2011) by the American Historical Association to an American resident for the most outstanding reference tool in the field of history. The award is honorific. The term reference tool encompasses bibliographies,

indexes, encyclopedias, and other scholarly apparatus. Guidelines must be obtained from the association.
Requirements Books published after May 1 of the previous award year and before April 30 of the current award year are eligible.
Date(s) Application Is Due May 16.
Contact Book Prize Administrator, (202) 544-2422; fax: (202) 544-8307; email: aha@theaha.org
Internet http://www.historians.org/prizes/index.cfm?PrizeAbbrev=LELAND
Sponsor American Historical Association
400 A Street, SE
Washington, DC 20003

American Historical Association Wesley-Logan Prize **503**
The prize is jointly sponsored by the association and the Association for the Study of Afro-American Life and History. The prize is offered for a book on some aspect of the history of the dispersion, settlement, adjustment, and/or return of peoples originally from Africa. Eligible for consideration are books in any chronological period and any geographical location. Only books of high scholarly and literary merit will be considered. One copy of each entry must be submitted to designated committee members. Recipients will be announced at the association's annual meeting.
Requirements Books published between May 1 of the previous year and April 30 of the current year are eligible.
Date(s) Application Is Due May 15.
Contact Book Prize Administrator, (202) 544-2422; fax: (202) 544-8307; email: aha@theaha.org
Internet http://www.historians.org/prizes/index.cfm?PrizeAbbrev=WESLEY%2DLOGAN
Sponsor American Historical Association
400 A Street, SE
Washington, DC 20003

American Historical Association William Gilbert Award **504**
The Award recognizes outstanding contributions to the teaching of history through the publication of journal articles. Eligible for consideration in a given year are articles by members of the AHA, published in the United States between June 1 and May 31 of the award year. Journals and individual members may submit nominations on the teaching of history (including scholarship of teaching and learning, methodology and theory of pedagogy) for each biennial cycle of this award. Journals, magazines, and other serials can submit up to two articles for each award cycle. Each nominator is required to provide a brief letter of support (no more than two pages) with the article.
Date(s) Application Is Due Jul 16.
Contact Program Administrator, (202) 544-2422; fax: (202) 544-8307; email: aha@theaha.org
Internet http://www.historians.org/prizes/Gilbert.htm
Sponsor American Historical Association
400 A Street, SE
Washington, DC 20003-3889

American Honda Foundation Grants **505**
American Honda Foundation seek out those programs and organizations with a well-defined sense of purpose, demonstrated commitment to making the best use of available resources and a reputation for accomplishing their objectives. Grants are provided in the fields of youth education and science education to the following: educational institutions, K-12; accredited higher education institutions (colleges and universities); community colleges and vocational or trade schools; scholarship and fellowship programs at selected colleges and/or universities or through selected non-profit organizations; other scientific and education-related, non-profit, tax-exempt organizations; gifted student programs; media concerning youth education and/or scientific education; private, non-profit scientific and/or youth education projects; other non-profit, tax-exempt, institutions in the fields of youth education and scientific education; and programs pertaining to academic or curriculum development that emphasize innovative educational methods and techniques.
Requirements An applicant must be a nonprofit, tax-exempt educational organization.
Restrictions The foundation does not consider proposals for service clubs, arts and culture, health and welfare issues, research papers, social issues, medical or educational research, trips, attempts to influence legislation, advocacy, annual funds, hospital operating funds, student exchanges, marathons, sponsorships, political activities, conferences, or fundraising events. An organization may submit only one proposal per year.
Amount $10,000-$100,000; $40,000-$80,000 average
Date(s) Application Is Due Feb 1, May 1, Aug 1, Nov 1.
Contact Program Director; (310) 781-4090; fax: (310) 781-4270
Internet http://corporate.honda.com/america/philanthropy.aspx?id=ahf
Sponsor American Honda Foundation
1919 Torrence Blvd., P.O. Box 2205
Torrance, CA 90509-2205

American Horticultural Society Internship Program **506**
Interns spend from three to nine months at River Farm, a 25-acre estate in Virginia, learning about horticulture and gardening. The program is designed to expose interns to a wide range of horticultural practices, activities, and experiences, thereby allowing them the opportunity to integrate academic theories with practical, real-world experiences. Interns also become involved in society programs and projects such as an annual seed program and catalog, open house events, and lectures and seminars. Applications are accepted at any time, but must be received at least two months before the internship is to begin. Applications are available at the Web site.
Requirements Interns must be undergraduate or graduate students majoring in horticulture or a related field, or an adult making a career change into horticulture. The application includes a completed application form; resume; the name, address, and phone number of three references; and a copy of applicant's college transcript (an official original is not required).
Date(s) Application Is Due Mar 1; Jul 1; Nov 1.
Contact Tom Underwood, Director and Curator of Gardens and Buildings, (703) 768-5700 ext 112; fax: (703) 765-6032; email: tunderwood@ahs.org
Internet http://www.ahs.org/river_farm/internships_employment.htm
Sponsor American Horticultural Society
7931 E Boulevard Dr
Alexandria, VA 22308-1300

American Indian Graduate Center Scholarships **507**
Scholarships are available each year to American Indian students meeting the following qualifications: a member of a federally recognized American Indian tribe or Alaska Native group, or possess one-fourth degree federally recognized Indian blood; demonstrate financial need after exhausting available aid at the college financial aid office; and attending an accredited graduate school in the United States. The April deadline is for summer enrollment; the June deadline is for fall enrollment. Applications are available upon request.
Amount $250-$10,000
Date(s) Application Is Due Apr 15; Jun 1.
Contact Scholarship Administrator, (800) 628-1920 or (505) 881-4584; fax: (505) 884-0427; email: aigc@aigc.com
Internet http://www.aigc.com
Sponsor American Indian Graduate Center
4520 Montgomery Blvd NE, Ste 1B
Albuquerque, NM 87109

American Indian Science and Engineering Scholarships **508**
The A.T. Anderson Memorial Scholarship is awarded to Native American/Alaskan Native graduate or undergraduate students pursuing programs in the sciences, engineering, health-related fields, business, natural resources, and math and science secondary education. Awards are made for one academic year. Deadlines, guidelines, and application forms are available on the Web site.
Requirements Applicants must be society members who are at least one-quarter Native American or recognized as a member of a tribe and full-time students at the undergraduate or graduate level.
Amount $5000 per academic year
Date(s) Application Is Due Jun 15.
Contact Scholarship Department, (505) 765-1052 ext 105; fax: (505) 765-5608; email: scholarship@aises.org
Internet http://www.aises.org/highered/scholarships/index.html
Sponsor American Indian Science and Engineering Society
P.O. Box 9828
Albuquerque, NM 87119-9828

American Institute for Economic Research Summer Fellowships **509**
These fellowships are awarded to further the development of economic scientists. Fellows participate in an four-week program and are provided with room and board. They attend seminars that primarily focus on scientific procedures of inquiry and on monetary economics. Attention also is given to business cycle analysis and forecasting. Assigned readings provide the basis for written assignments and seminar discussions. Applications may be downloaded from the Web site.
Requirements Graduating seniors applying to doctoral programs in economics and students already enrolled in such programs are eligible to apply. (Preference is given to graduate students.) US citizens are given first priority; foreign students must be able to speak and write in English with native fluency.
Restrictions The program is not designed for students wishing to pursue graduate work in a business school program (e.g. MBA.).
Amount $250 per week basic stipend, plus room and board
Date(s) Application Is Due Mar 31.
Contact Susan Gillette, Assistant to the President, (413) 528-1216; fax: (413) 528-0103; email: fellowship@aier.org
Internet http://www.aier.org/summer.html
Sponsor American Institute for Economic Research
P.O. Box 1000
Great Barrington, MA 01230

American Institute of Bangladesh Studies (AIBS) Postdoctoral Research and Dissertation Research Grants **510**
The institute awards stipends of two to 12 months duration for postdoctoral research and six to 12 months for dissertation research in Bangladesh. The award includes round-

trip transportation and a small cash supplement. Applications must be received by the deadline for study beginning in the summer or fall.
Requirements Applicants must have completed at least one year of graduate study in a recognized Ph.D. granting institution in either the social sciences or the humanities. Grantees must be US citizens or permanent residents of the United States.
Contact Grants Administrator, (814) 865-0436; fax: (814) 865-8299; email: sxr17@psu.edu
Internet http://www.aibs.net/aibsfellowship.htm
Sponsor American Institute of Bangladesh Studies
111 Sowers St, Ste 501
State College, PA 16801

American Institute of Physics Science-Writing Awards in Physics and Astronomy 511
Four awards are given to professional writers or to scientists to stimulate and recognize distinguished writing that improves public understanding of physics and astronomy. The Journalist Award is for professional writers writing for the general public; the Scientists Award is for the work of a physicist or astronomer writing for the general public as opposed to writing for strictly scientific, technical, or trade publications; the Children's Books Award is for physics and astronomy writing aimed at children up to 15 years of age; and the Broadcast Media Award is for journalists of scripted radio or television programming aimed at the general public. Entry forms are available on the Web site.
Requirements Articles or books must have been published within the last year. Entries must be in English or English translations.
Amount $3000
Date(s) Application Is Due Mar 1.
Contact Marc Brodsky, Executive Director, (301) 209-3131; fax: (301) 209-0846; email: brodsky@aip.org
Internet http://www.aip.org/aip/writing
Sponsor American Institute of Physics
1 Physics Ellipse
College Park, MD 20740-3843

American Jewish Historical Society Awards and Prizes 512
In cooperation with the Jewish Historical Society of New York, the society grants awards and prizes to assist researchers to carry on projects in the area of American Jewish history, including immigration, economic, social, political, and religious history. For current awards, details, and deadlines, see the AJHS website (above).
Contact David Solomon, Executive Director, (212) 294-6160; fax (212) 294-6161; email: dsolomon@ajhs.cjh.org
Internet http://www.ajhs.org/academic/Awards.cfm
Sponsor American Jewish Historical Society
15 W 16th St
New York, NY 10011

American Legacy Foundation National Calls for Proposals Grants 513
The American Legacy Foundation provides grants to support innovations in tobacco control. National calls for proposals, such as the Priority Populations Initiative, are issued annually to address a variety of tobacco prevention and control issues. Comprehensive assistance and training are provided to the foundation's grantees as well as to state and local tobacco programs. Application forms, guidelines, and procedures are available online. There are no application deadlines.
Requirements Funding is available only to state or local political subdivisions and legally constituted tax-exempt 501(c)3 organizations based in the 46 states, the District of Columbia, and five territories (American Samoa, Guam, Northern Mariana Islands, Puerto Rico, and the Virgin Islands) identified in the MSA with tobacco product manufacturers (http://www.naag.org/tobaccopublic/library.cfm). An Indian reservation, Indian tribe, or tribal organization located within the 46 settling states or a non-governmental entity that serves such a reservation may also apply for funding.
Restrictions The foundation will not award grants to applicants that are in current receipt of grant monies or in-kind contributions from any tobacco manufacturer, distributor, or other tobacco-related entity.
Contact Grants Administrator, (202) 454-5555; fax: (202) 454-5599; email: grantsinfo@americanlegacy.org
Internet http://www.americanlegacy.org/146.htm
Sponsor American Legacy Foundation
2030 M Street, NW, Sixth Floor
Washington, DC 20036

American Legacy Foundation Small Innovative Grants 514
The program supports projects that advance creative, promising solutions based on sound principles of tobacco control to remedy the harm caused by tobacco use in America. The program was created to seed new projects or enable an organization to pilot a new idea or approach.
Requirements The proposed project must demonstrate an element of creativity, ingenuity or innovation and must distinguish itself from the large number of solid programs proposed to the foundation in each grant round. Funding is available only to state or local political subdivisions and legally constituted tax-exempt 501(c)3 organizations based in the 46 states, the District of Columbia, and five territories (American Samoa, Guam, Northern Mariana Islands, Puerto Rico, and the Virgin Islands) identified in the MSA with tobacco product manufacturers. An Indian reservation, Indian tribe, or tribal organization located within the 46 settling states or a nongovernmental entity that serves such a reservation may also apply for funding. Successful applications submitted under the Small Innovative Grants Program must: Address one or both of Legacy's goals; Demonstrate innovative or new tobacco prevention or cessation efforts; Demonstrate a strong likelihood for a sustainable effort after the grant period; Demonstrate that the project may be replicated; Address the Healthy People 2010 risk reduction objectives related to tobacco use, and; Incorporate the CDC's Best Practices for Comprehensive Tobacco Control Programs as appropriate. The foundation will give special consideration to applications addressing these current areas of interest (see website and guidelines for current listing).
Restrictions The foundation will not award a grant to any applicant that is in current receipt of any grant monies or in-kind contribution from any tobacco manufacturer, distributor, or other tobacco-related entity. In addition, the foundation expects that a grantee will not accept any grant monies or in-kind contribution from any tobacco manufacturer, distributor, or other tobacco-related entity over the duration of the grant. Additionally, will not consider applications for: Projects focusing on youth prevention, cessation, activism, or education (up to 18 years old) ; Nicotine replacement therapy (NRT) and pharmaceuticals (as the sole or primary focus of the grant); Conference support (as the sole or primary focus of the grant); Media or marketing campaigns (as the sole or primary focus of the grant); Research projects EXCEPT community-based participatory research, which is allowed ; Projects focusing on substances other than tobacco; Replication of an existing program; Expansion of an existing program; and Replacement funds; Grants to individuals, for religious activities, to build endowments, to support operating deficits, to retire debt, for capital purchases for building improvements, for construction, for lobbying, or for real estate purchase or development.
Amount $20,000-$100,000 annually
Date(s) Application Is Due Feb 27; Jul 27.
Contact Grants Administrator, (202) 454-5555; fax: (202) 454-5599; email: info@americanlegacy.org
Internet http://www.americanlegacy.org/707.htm
Sponsor American Legacy Foundation
2030 M St. NW, 6th Floor
Washington, DC 20036

American Liver Foundation Innovative Hepatology Seed Grant 515
The goal of this program is to foster development of an imaginative research program in Alpha 1 Antitrypsin Deficiency and/or directly related areas of scientific investigation.
Requirements To be eligible candidates must be a faculty member in an academic institution in the United States or its possessions. Applicants who hold research awards directed at salary support, such as Veterans Administration, Research Associates, Clinical Investigator, AGA Industry Research Awards, Glaxo Institute Awards, and ALF Liver Scholar Awards are also eligible.
Restrictions Individuals with an RO1, Merit Review, or NIH FIRST Award are ineligible if their grant overlaps with the present application.
Amount $100,000 over two years
Date(s) Application Is Due Oct 1.
Contact Joan Gallagher, Program Director, (973) 256-2550 ext 224 or (800) 465-4837; email: jgallagher@liverfoundation
Internet http://www.liverfoundation.org/db/grants/114
Sponsor American Liver Foundation
1425 Pompton Ave, Ste 3
Cedar Grove, NJ 07009

American Liver Foundation Liver Scholar Awards Program 516
The goal of the program is to permit scientists with liver research training to bridge the gap between completion of research training and attainment of status as independent research scientists. This additional research experience should enable scientists to compete for research grants from national sources, particularly NIH. The program aims to attract well-trained, basic scientists, who hold MD, PhD, or MD/PhD degrees, to a career in liver disease research. These awards are for the purpose of encouraging research into liver physiology and disease research and developing the potential of young, outstanding scientists; therefore, individuals who already are well established in the fields are not considered eligible. The awards will be made to eligible institutions and are for salary only. Each awardee must continue to hold a full-time faculty appointment in the sponsoring institution; devote at least 75 percent of time to their research project; attend the annual meeting of the American Association for the Study of Liver Diseases; acknowledge support by the ALF in any publications resulting from research performed during the tenure of the award; and submit an annual progress report describing results, their significance, and pending or planned applications for research support.
Requirements Candidates must be sponsored by a nonfederal public or private nonprofit institution engaged in health care and health-related research within the United States and its possessions. Applicants must have had three to four years of relevant postdoctoral experience prior to the beginning date of the award; have obtained their doctorate degree within the last 10 years; and have institutional confirmation of a faculty appointment at the time the award commences and throughout its duration. Applicants who hold or have applied for nonfederal research awards must provide the title and specific aims of the awards with their application.
Restrictions At the time of application, the applicant cannot hold or have held any of the following awards: NIH R01, R29, K11, K08; Veterans Administration Merit Review;

Associate Investigation; Research Associate; Clinical Investigator; or AGA Industry Award.
Amount $75,000 per year over three years
Date(s) Application Is Due Oct 1.
Contact Joan Gallagher, (973) 256-2550 ext 224; fax: (973) 256-3214; email: jgallagher@liverfoundation.org
Internet http://www.liverfoundation.org/db/grants/113
Sponsor American Liver Foundation
1425 Pompton Ave, Ste 3
Cedar Grove, NJ 07009

American Liver Foundation Physician Research Development Award 517
The purpose of this award is to support and develop clinical research training of fellows seeking junior faculty appointment (or in their first years as a junior faculty member). Preference is given to translational research in pathobiology and treatment of viral hepatitis toward developing preclinical and clinical applications as well as addressing natural history, prevention, and epidemiology of viral hepatitis.
Amount $225,000-$270,000 over three or four years
Date(s) Application Is Due Oct 1.
Contact Joan Gallagher, (973) 256-2550 ext 224; fax: (973) 256-3214; email: jgallagher@liverfoundation.org
Internet http://www.liverfoundation.org/db-list/grants/0/descend/ID/Validated
Sponsor American Liver Foundation
1425 Pompton Ave, Ste 3
Cedar Grove, NJ 07009

American Liver Foundation Postdoctoral Research Fellowships 518
The foundation offers postdoctoral research fellowships to encourage the development of individuals with research potential who require additional research training and experience, specifically in investigational work relating to liver physiology and disease, in preparation for careers of independent research in this field. The goal of the program is to encourage MD, PhD, and MD/PhD postdoctoral fellows to enter an academic career in liver disease research. Fellows are expected to devote at least 75 percent of time to their specific research project, attend the annual meeting of the American Association for the Study of Liver Diseases, acknowledge support by the ALF in any publications resulting from the research performed during the tenure of the award, and submit a progress report describing results obtained and their significance. The application must be written by the applicant.
Requirements Candidates must be sponsored by a nonfederal public or private nonprofit institute engaged in health care and health-related research within the United States and its possessions. Physician applicants (MD and MD/PhD) must submit documentation that all clinical training has been completed. All applicants must be in the first year of appointment as a postdoctoral research fellow or trainee.
Restrictions Individuals with more than two years of postdoctoral research training or those already well established in the field of hepatology are ineligible. In addition, the fellowship is designed as a supplement to augment NIH or nonfederal fellowship stipends and will not be awarded to an applicant who has no other source of research salary support.
Amount $12,500 for one year
Date(s) Application Is Due Oct 1.
Contact Joan Gallagher, (973) 256-2550 ext 224; fax: (973) 256-3214; email: jgallagher@liverfoundation.org
Internet http://www.liverfoundation.org/db/grants/131
Sponsor American Liver Foundation
1425 Pompton Ave, Ste 3
Cedar Grove, NJ 07009

American Liver Foundation Student Research Fellowship Award 519
The foundation offers awards to MD and PhD students to encourage them to gain exposure to the research laboratory, and possibly consider liver research as a career option. Each fellowship is for a three-month period. The candidate must be in full-time research for a period of 10-12 weeks under the supervision of a preceptor in hepatic physiology or disease.
Requirements Full-time students of US undergraduate, graduate, or medical school programs are eligible to apply.
Amount $2500
Date(s) Application Is Due Oct 1.
Contact Joan Gallagher, (973) 256-2550 ext 224; fax: (973) 256-3214; email: jgallagher@liverfoundation.org
Internet http://www.liverfoundation.org/db-list/grants/0/descend/ID/Validated
Sponsor American Liver Foundation
1425 Pompton Ave, Ste 3
Cedar Grove, NJ 07009

American Lung Association Career Investigator Award 520
The award supports individuals who have demonstrated success in research and who show great promise for a career in investigation. Awards are subject to annual review and may be granted for up to three years. Awardees are expected to devote full time, and in no case less than 75 percent of their time, to research. Awardees may undertake limited administrative, teaching, and clinical responsibilities if they are directly related to the nature of the research supported by this award.
Requirements US citizens and foreign nationals with appropriate visa immigration status are eligible. At the time of application, an applicant must hold a doctoral degree and faculty appointment at the level of assistant or associate professor and be undertaking a project related to lung disease.
Restrictions Individuals who have attained the rank of full professor or who have more than eight years of faculty experience at the time of application are ineligible.
Amount $60,000 maximum per year
Date(s) Application Is Due Sep 1.
Contact Evita Mendoza, Grants Administrator, (212) 315-8793; email: emendoza@lungusa.org or info@lungusa.org
Internet http://www.lungusa.org/site/apps/s/content.asp?c=dvLUK9O0E&b=34706&ct=67676
Sponsor American Lung Association
1740 Broadway
New York, NY 10019

American Lung Association Clinical Patient Care Research Grants 521
The objective of the grant is to support investigators working in patient-focused research. The areas of research may include the disciplines of health services research, behavioral research, epidemiology, pharmacology, and medical ethics. The outcome of these research activities is to develop new insights into clinical, social, behavioral, and biological factors that affect the manifestation of lung health and disease. Grants are subject to annual review and may be granted for up to two years.
Requirements US citizens and foreign nationals with appropriate visa immigration status are eligible. At the time of application, an applicant must hold a doctoral degree and faculty appointment with an academic institution and have completed two years of postdoctoral research training.
Restrictions Residents, interns, postdoctoral fellows, graduate students, and established investigators are ineligible.
Amount $40,000 maximum per year
Date(s) Application Is Due Sep 1.
Contact Evita Mendoza, Grants Administrator, (212) 315-8793; email: emendoza@lungusa.org or info@lungusa.org
Internet http://www.lungusa.org/site/apps/s/content.asp?c=dvLUK9O0E&b=34706&ct=67676
Sponsor American Lung Association
1740 Broadway
New York, NY 10019-4374

American Lung Association Dalsemar Research Grant 522
The grant supports up to two years of research in interstitial lung disease. Grants are subject to annual review and may be granted for up to two years. The second year of support is based on demonstrating satisfactory progress as well as the availability of American Lung Association funding.
Requirements US citizens and foreign nationals with appropriate immigration visa status are eligible. At the time of application, an applicant must hold a doctoral degree and a faculty appointment with an academic institution and have completed two years of research training.
Restrictions Residents, interns, postdoctoral fellows, students enrolled in degree-granting programs, and established investigators are not eligible.
Amount $40,000 maximum per year
Date(s) Application Is Due Sep 1.
Contact Evita Mendoza, Grants Administrator, (212) 315-8793; email: emendoza@lungusa.org or info@lungusa.org
Internet http://www.lungusa.org/site/apps/s/content.asp?c=dvLUK9O0E&b=34706&ct=67676
Sponsor American Lung Association
1740 Broadway
New York, NY 10019

American Lung Association Research Grants 523
The grants provide starter or seed money to new investigators working in areas relevant to the prevention of lung disease and the promotion of lung health. The research supported may be clinical, laboratory, epidemiologic, social, environmental, or any other kind as long as it is relevant to lung biology. Six individuals will be designated Edward Livingston Trudeau Scholars. Awards are for one year and may be renewed for an additional year, depending on the availability of funds.
Requirements At the time of application, an applicant must hold a doctoral degree, faculty appointment with an academic institution, and have completed two years of research training. US citizens, Canadian citizens, and permanent residents of the United States training in US institutions are eligible.
Restrictions An American Lung Association grantee cannot simultaneously hold any other national ALA award. An investigator who has previously received a research grant or a Dalsemer Award is not eligible for additional national research grant support. An ALA research grant awardee may not hold an award of established investigatorship or large grant during the tenure of her or his ALA award.
Amount $35,000 maximum
Date(s) Application Is Due Sep 1.

Contact Evita Mendoza, Grants Administrator, (212) 315-8793; email: emendoza@lungusa.org or info@lungusa.org
Internet http://www.lungusa.org/site/apps/s/content.asp?c=dvLUK9O0E&b=34706&ct=67676
Sponsor American Lung Association
1740 Broadway
New York, NY 10019-4374

American Lung Association Senior Research Training Fellowship 524
The fellowship supports the training of scientific investigators in the fields of adult and pediatric pulmonary medicine and lung biology. Preference is given to applicants who demonstrate a program of training that will enable them to pursue academic careers. Fellows are expected to devote full time or at least 75 percent of their time to research training. Fellowships may be renewed for an additional year.
Requirements US citizens and foreign nationals with appropriate immigration visa status are eligible. At the time of application, an applicant must hold a doctoral degree or have comparable qualifications. MD applicants must have completed their clinical training, have some research experience, and be entering the third or fourth year of research fellowship training. PhD applicants must not be beyond the third postdoctoral year at the time of application.
Amount $32,500 maximum per year
Date(s) Application Is Due Sep 1.
Contact Evita Mendoza, Grants Administrator, (212) 315-8793; email: emendoza@lungusa.org
Internet http://www.lungusa.org/site/apps/s/content.asp?c=dvLUK9O0E&b=34706&ct=67676
Sponsor American Lung Association
61 Broadway, 6th Fl
New York, NY 10006

American Mathematical Society Centennial Fellowships 525
The program makes awards annually to outstanding mathematicians to help further their careers in research. Fellowship holders may use their stipend as full support for a year or may combine it with half-time teaching and use it as half support over a two-year period. Fellows are expected to spend some of the fellowship period at another institution that has a stimulating research environment suited to the candidates' research development. Preference will be given to candidates who have not had extensive fellowship support in the past. Applications should include a short research plan describing both an outline of the research to be pursued and a program for using the fellowship, including the institutions at which it will be used and reasons for the choices. Completed applications and references should not be sent to this address but to the address given on the application form. Applications are available on the Web site.
Requirements A recipient of the fellowship will have held his or her doctoral degree for at least three years and not more than 12 years at the inception of the award (that is, received between September 1, 1994, and September 1, 2003). Applications will be accepted from those currently holding a tenured, tenure track, postdoctoral, or comparable (at the discretion of the selection committee) position at an institution in North America.
Restrictions Recipients may not hold the fellowship concurrently with other research fellowships (e.g., Sloan Foundation fellowships or NSF postdoctoral fellowships), and they may not use the stipend solely to reduce teaching at the home institution.
Amount $64,000 and $3250 (approximately) expense allowance
Date(s) Application Is Due Dec 1.
Contact Executive Director, (401) 455-4107; fax: (401) 331-3842; email: ams@ams.org
Internet http://www.ams.org/employment/centflyer.html
Sponsor American Mathematical Society
201 Charles St
Providence, RI 02940-3842

American Nurses Foundation Nursing Research Grants 526
The program is designed to award grants for nursing research conducted by registered nurses who are either beginning nurse researchers or experienced nurse researchers entering a new field of investigation. Priority is based upon the scientific merit of the proposal, with consideration given to the investigator's ability to conduct the study.
Requirements Principal investigators must be baccalaureate-prepared registered nurses; however, the coinvestigator does not have to be a nurse as long as the proposal is for a nursing research project.
Restrictions Some ANF grants are restricted as to their use by corporations and organizations that have contributed the funds.
Amount $2700
Date(s) Application Is Due May 3.
Contact Leo Schargorodski, Executive Director, (301) 628-5230; email: anf@ana.org or lschargo@ana.org
Internet http://www.nursingworld.org/anf/nrggrant.htm
Sponsor American Nurses Foundation
8515 Georgia Ave, Ste 400 W
Silver Spring, MD 20910

American Oil Chemists' Society Honored Student Award 527
This international award is given annually to a graduate student in fats and lipid chemistry who is currently attending a college or university. An applicant must submit a research paper for presentation at the annual meeting of the society. The awards provide funds equal to travel costs, complementary registration, and hotel accommodations, plus an additional stipend to permit attendance at the AOCS annual meeting. Application forms and guidelines are available upon request.
Date(s) Application Is Due Oct 15.
Contact Membership Department, (217) 359-2344; fax: (217) 351-8091; email: awards@aocs.org
Internet http://www.aocs.org/member/awards/awd-honstud.asp
Sponsor American Oil Chemists' Society
P.O. Box 3489
Champaign, IL 61826-3489

American Otological Society Research Fund Fellowhips and Grants 528
Research grants and fellowships are awarded to US and Canadian physicians and doctoral-level investigators in all aspects of otosclerosis, Meniere's disease, and related ear disorders. The one-year grants, which begin July 1, are renewable for a second year and are tenable at US and Canadian institutions. Awards are made to an institution on behalf of a candidate. Appropriate areas of research include diagnosis, management, and pathogenesis of otosclerosis and Meniere's disease as well as underlying processes. The applicant should describe correlations between proposed research with the clinical pathological entities of otosclerosis and Meniere's disease.
Requirements Physician and nonphysician investigators are eligible for research grants. Fellowships are open to physicians (residents and medical students).
Restrictions Research grants do not support funding for investigator's salary.
Amount $40,000
Date(s) Application Is Due Jan 31.
Contact Dr. Jeffrey Harris, Otolaryngology--Head and Neck Surgery, (619) 543-7896; fax:(619) 543-5521; email: jpharris@ucsd.edu
Internet http://itsa.ucsf.edu/~ajo/AOS/SchGra.html
Sponsor American Otological Society
200 W Arbor Dr, 8895
San Diego, CA 92103-8895

American Parkinson's Disease Association Cotzias Fellowships 529
This three-year fellowship is intended to recruit and assist young neurologists in establishing careers in research, teaching, and patient service relevant to the problems, causes, prevention, diagnosis, and treatment of Parkinson's disease and other neurological movement disorders.
Requirements An applicant must be a US citizen, have an MD degree obtained within 10 years of application, and must have training in a clinical discipline concerned with disorders of the nervous system. Rank of assistant professor is required. The applicant must be sponsored by a nonprofit institution in the United States or its territories.
Amount $80,000 per year for three years
Date(s) Application Is Due Mar 1.
Contact Grants Administrator, (718) 981-8001 or (800) 223-2732; fax: (718) 981-4399; email: apda@apdaparkinson.org
Internet http://www.apdaparkinson.org/user/ViewFellowshipAndGrants.asp
Sponsor American Parkinson's Disease Association
1250 Hylan Blvd, Ste 4B
Staten Island, NY 10305-1946

American Parkinson's Disease Association Research Grants 530
Qualified scientists may apply for grants for research in the area of Parkinson's disease. Grants are awarded for one year for direct costs of the research project; indirect costs, salary for the principal investigator, travel expenses, and institutional overhead are not covered. Grants may be renewed for a second year on deadline date, but reapplication must be made. Description of the research proposal should not exceed two pages and should include a statement of how research is related to Parkinson's disease.
Requirements Scientists affiliated with US institutions are eligible.
Restrictions Publication costs may not exceed $300, and equipment budget may not exceed $5000.
Amount $50,000
Date(s) Application Is Due Mar 1.
Contact Grants Administrator, (718) 981-8001 or (800) 223-2732; fax: (718) 981-4399; email: apda@apdaparkinson.org
Internet http://www.apdaparkinson.org/user/ViewFellowshipAndGrants.asp
Sponsor American Parkinson's Disease Association
1250 Hylan Blvd, Ste 4B
Staten Island, NY 10305-1946

American Press Institute Seminar Fellowships 531
The institute conducts seminars on all phases of newspaper operation at announced times and locations. In conjunction with these seminars, the API offers a few fellowships for attendance by faculty members in good standing in journalism departments at four-year colleges and universities. API also offers a few fellowships to newspaper employees; marketing or general management executive, city editor, female reporter, or editor with a daily circulation below 25,000. Periodically, announcements are made through departments of journalism; information also is available from the institute. The listed deadline is for seminars in the following calendar year. Some fellowships will be awarded

to journalism faculty members who belong to a minority group. Funding includes tuition, room and board, and a travel subsidy if funds permit.
Requirements Applicants must be US citizens.
Amount $650-$1175
Date(s) Application Is Due Nov 18.
Contact Linda Kepner, Fellowship Coordinator, (703) 620-3611; fax: (703) 620-5814; email: lkepner@americanpressinstitute.org
Internet http://www.americanpressinstitute.org/fellowships
Sponsor American Press Institute
11690 Sunrise Valley Dr
Reston, VA 22091

American Psychiatric Association Award for Research in Psychiatry 532
The Award is given in recognition of a single distinguished contribution, a body of work, or a lifetime contribution that has had a major impact on the field and/or altered the practice of psychiatry. The Award is intended to cover the full spectrum of psychiatric research. The Award consists of a $5,000 prize and an honorary plaque to be presented at APA's Annual Meeting in May. The Award also includes an honorary lecture by the awardee.
Requirements Candidates for the Award must be citizens of the United States or Canada and be nominated by a sponsor. Sponsors must be members of the American Psychiatric Association.
Restrictions Members of the Award Committee are excluded from submitting nominations.
Amount $5,000
Date(s) Application Is Due Aug 28.
Contact Harold Goldstein, (703) 907-8623; email: goharold@psych.org
Internet http://www.psych.org/research/apire/training_fund/psychaward.cfm
Sponsor American Psychiatric Association
1000 Wilson Blvd, Suite 1825
Arlington, VA 22209-3901

American Psychiatric Association Early Career Award 533
APA's early career award recognizes the best nominated paper published during the past year by an early career psychiatrist (defined by the APA as under 40 years of age or within five years of training). Nominations can be either from the individual or a colleague in the field, such as a department chairperson, division chief, or other health services researcher. While the proposed applicant must be an APA member, the nominating individual need not be a member and may be from any discipline. The award will be presented at the Health Services Research Breakfast which is held in conjunction with APA's Institute for Psychiatric Services (IPS) meeting.
Requirements Nomination letters should succinctly indicate the contributions that are the basis for the nomination and the nature of the relationship of the nominator and nominee. A curriculum vita of the nominee should accompany the letter, along with the nominated paper (in the case of early career award) or one to two papers of greatest significance (for senior scholar award).
Amount $1,000
Date(s) Application Is Due Aug 29.
Contact Harold Goldstein, (703) 907-8623; email: goharold@psych.org
Internet http://www.psych.org/research/apire/res_careerdev/ecpsscholaraward.cfm
Sponsor American Psychiatric Association
1000 Wilson Blvd, Suite 1825
Arlington, VA 22209-3901

American Psychiatric Association Minority Fellowships Program 534
The APA offers psychiatric residents one-year fellowships in the APA organization to increase the knowledge of cultural factors influencing psychiatric diagnosis and treatment, provide opportunities for these residents to participate in the deliberations and decision-making processes, and provide role models for the fellows. Each fellow is appointed to a component of the APA's organizational structure and attends the association's annual meeting as an observer and active participant. Fellows are selected on the basis of their commitment to serving underrepresented populations, demonstrated leadership abilities, and interest in the interrelationship between mental health/illness and transcultural factors.
Requirements Psychiatric residents who are starting their second year of psychiatric training, or third year if they are in a four-year residency program, are eligible to apply.
Contact Marilyn King, Fellowship Coordinator, (703) 907-8653; fax: (703) 907-7849; email: mking@psych.org
Internet http://www.psych.org/edu/other_res/apa_fellowship/cmhs_index.cfm
Sponsor American Psychiatric Association
1000 Wilson Blvd, Suite 1825
Arlington, VA 22209-3901

American Psychiatric Association Minority Medical Student Fellowship in HIV Psychiatry 535
The APA invites ethnic minority medical students who have an interest in psychiatric issues to apply. The program is intended to identify minority medical students who have primary interests in services related to HIV/AIDS and substance abuse and its relationship to the mental health or psychological well being of ethnic minorities.
Requirements These programs are open to ethnic minority medical students who are U.S. citizens or permanent residents currently enrolled in a U.S. medical school.
Date(s) Application Is Due Mar 31.
Contact Carol Svoboda, (703) 907-8642; email: csvoboda@psych.org; Diane Pennessi, (703) 907-8668; email: dpennessi@psych.org
Internet http://www.psych.org/edu/other_res/apa_fellowship/cmhs_index.cfm
Sponsor American Psychiatric Association
1000 Wilson Blvd, Suite 1825
Arlington, VA 22209-3901

American Psychiatric Association Minority Medical Student Summer Externship in Addiction Psychiatry 536
The APA invites ethnic minority medical students who have an interest in psychiatric issues to apply. This clinical shadowing program identifies minority medical students who may have a specific interest in services related to substance abuse treatment/prevention and provide a setting where the student can work closely with a mentor who specializes in addiction psychiatry for one month.
Requirements These programs are open to ethnic minority medical students who are U.S. citizens or permanent residents currently enrolled in a U.S. medical school.
Date(s) Application Is Due Feb 28.
Contact Marilyn King, (703) 907-8653; fax: (703) 907-7849; email: mking@psych.org; Rosa Bracey, (703) 907-8539; email: rbracey@psych.org
Internet http://www.psych.org/edu/other_res/apa_fellowship/cmhs_index.cfm
Sponsor American Psychiatric Association
1000 Wilson Blvd, Suite 1825
Arlington, VA 22209-3901

American Psychiatric Association Minority Medical Student Summer Mentoring Program 537
The APA invites ethnic minority medical students who have an interest in psychiatric issues to apply. This program is intended to identify ethnic minority medical students who have an interest in psychiatric issues and expose students to a setting where they can work closely with a psychiatrist mentor for one month.
Requirements These programs are open to ethnic minority medical students who are U.S. citizens or permanent residents currently enrolled in a U.S. medical school.
Date(s) Application Is Due Feb 28.
Contact Marilyn King, (703) 907-8653; fax: (703) 907-7849; email: mking@psych.org; Rosa Bracey, (703) 907-8539; email: rbracey@psych.org
Internet http://www.psych.org/edu/other_res/apa_fellowship/cmhs_index.cfm
Sponsor American Psychiatric Association
1000 Wilson Blvd, Suite 1825
Arlington, VA 22209-3901

American Psychiatric Association Program for Minority Research Training in Psychiatry (PMRTP) 538
The program is designed to increase the number of underrepresented minority men and women in the field of psychiatric research. Research training offers the opportunity to engage in scientific investigation across the full array of disciplines, from basic neuroscience, genetics, and pharmacology to the cognitive behavioral, and social sciences, clinical psychiatry, and mental health services research. Research exposure can help students and trainees develop sound skills for clinical assessment and treatment planning. The program provides funding for short and long-term training opportunities at three levels: Medical School, Residency and Post-residency. National competitions also enable qualified mini-fellows to attend research-oriented meetings of psychiatric organizations. For medical students and residents, the duration can be two months to one year. For post-residency fellows, the duration is generally two years. A third year of fellowship support may be available if appropriate to a trainee's career development. Support from PMRTP falls into three categories: stipends, travel, and tuition and fees. Stipends are based on the trainee's years of relevant experience and the length of the research training experience.
Requirements Preference in selection is given to underrepresented minorities such as American Indians, Asian-Americans, Blacks/African-Americans, Hispanics, Pacific Islanders, or other ethnic or racial group members found to be underrepresented in biomedical or behavioral research.
Amount $19,968-$51,036
Contact Ernesto Guerra, (703) 907-7300; fax: (703) 907-1085; email: eguerra@psych.org or apa@psych.org
Internet http://www.psych.org/research/APIRE/pmrtp5302.cfm
Sponsor American Psychiatric Association
1000 Wilson Blvd, Suite 1825
Arlington, VA 22209-3901

American Psychiatric Association Research Colloquium for Junior Investigators 539
The purpose of the colloquium is to provide guidance, mentorship and encouragement to young investigators in the early phases of their training. Junior investigators will have an opportunity to obtain feedback about their past, present, and future research interests from mentors who are tops in their field in a small group setting as well as

general information about research career development and grantsmanship. Candidates whose research interests are similar to those listed below are also encouraged to apply. An all-day workshop for junior psychiatric investigators will focus on these three areas: childhood disorders including autism, ADHD, conduct, eating, and mood disorders; genomics, epigenetics, and proteomics; and treatment of major psychiatric disorders: from substance abuse to schizophrenia.
Requirements Psychiatrists who are senior residents, fellows, or junior faculty, and who have an interest and potential in developing research careers in the areas of research listed above. Participants should hold a medical degree or be a member of the APA; or be eligible to become members of the APA.
Restrictions Those with individual federal research awards are not eligible.
Amount $1,000
Date(s) Application Is Due Nov 15.
Contact Ernesto Guerra, (703) 907-7300; fax: (703) 907-1085; email: eguerra@psych.org or apa@psych.org
Internet http://www.psych.org/research/APIRE/researchtrainfund.cfm
Sponsor American Psychiatric Association
1000 Wilson Blvd, Suite 1825
Arlington, VA 22209-3901

American Psychiatric Association Senior Scholar Award 540

The Award recognizes singular or sustained research accomplishments by a researcher beyond early career status which have made an important contribution to the field of mental health services research. Nominations can be either from the individual or a colleague in the field, such as a department chairperson, division chief, or other health services researcher. While the proposed applicant must be an APA member, the nominating individual need not be a member and may be from any discipline. The award will be presented at the Health Services Research Breakfast which is held in conjunction with APA's Institute for Psychiatric Services (IPS) meeting.
Requirements Nomination letters should succinctly indicate the contributions that are the basis for the nomination and the nature of the relationship of the nominator and nominee. A curriculum vita of the nominee should accompany the letter, along with the nominated paper (in the case of early career award) or one to two papers of greatest significance (for senior scholar award).
Amount $1,000
Date(s) Application Is Due Aug 29.
Contact Harold Goldstein, (703) 907-8623; email: goharold@psych.org
Internet http://www.psych.org/research/apire/res_careerdev/ecpsscholaraward.cfm
Sponsor American Psychiatric Association
1000 Wilson Blvd, Suite 1825
Arlington, VA 22209-3901

American Psychiatric Association Travel Scholarships for Minority Medical Students 541

The APA invites ethnic minority medical students who have an interest in psychiatric issues to apply. The program supports travel and related costs for approximately 10 minority medical students interested in psychiatric to attend either the APA annual meeting in May or the Institute on Psychiatric Services (IPS) meeting in October. This program is a way for medical students to witness organized psychiatry at work and to learn more about the field. Not only will students attend sessions for experts and trainees alike, but they will be assigned to a mentor who will help them maximize their annual meeting or IPS experience and discuss career plans and resident training programs.
Requirements These programs are open to ethnic minority medical students who are U.S. citizens or permanent residents currently enrolled in a U.S. medical school.
Date(s) Application Is Due Jan 26.
Contact Marilyn King, (703) 907-8653; fax: (703) 907-7849; email: mking@psych.org; Rosa Bracey, (703) 907-8539; email: rbracey@psych.org
Internet http://www.psych.org/edu/other_res/apa_fellowship/cmhs_index.cfm
Sponsor American Psychiatric Association
1000 Wilson Blvd, Suite 1825
Arlington, VA 22209-3901

American Psychiatric Association/AstraZeneca Young Minds in Psychiatry International Awards 542

The program recognizes and supports promising international young psychiatrists within five years of completing a psychiatric residency. Four unrestricted career development awards of $45,000 (USD) will be available. Awards will be made to two promising physicians from the U.S. with one in Bipolar Disorder research and one on research in Schizophrenia. An additional two awards will be made to promising physicians from countries outside the U.S., with one in Bipolar Disorder research and one on research in Schizophrenia. Three other awards of $30,000 (USD) in either Bipolar Disorder or Schizophrenia research will specifically focus on applicants from developing countries whose economies are classified as low income or lower middle income.
Requirements The U.S. applicants must be citizens or permanent residents of the United States. Applications are evaluated based on evidence of academic promise; how the proposal will advance the applicant's career; and innovative or original concepts, approaches, or methods for developing the applicant's career.
Amount $45,000
Date(s) Application Is Due Oct 31.
Contact Ernesto Guerra, (703) 907-7300; fax: (703) 907-1085; email: eguerra@psych.org or apa@psych.org
Internet http://www.psych.org/research/apire/res_careerdev/youngminds_announce.cfm
Sponsor American Psychiatric Association
1000 Wilson Blvd, Suite 1825
Arlington, VA 22209-3901

American Psychiatric Association/Janssen Resident Psychiatric Rsch Scholars 543

The program is intended to identify promising PGY-1, PGY-2, and PGY-3 psychiatric residents with the potential to become leaders in clinical and health services research in all areas of psychiatric research. Emphasis will be placed on special mentoring and career enrichment programs both at the APA Annual Meeting and throughout the year. An individual research mentor will be assigned to oversee the resident's fellowship. The mentors will be chosen among nationally known leaders in clinical and health services research. The mentor will advise and encourage the Scholar during the two-year fellowship. The scholar will receive $2,500 during the second year of the fellowship, to assist in their research career development (e.g., for use in developing a pilot research project, obtaining statistical consultation, or visiting potential research training programs). The program also provides funding for travel to the American Psychiatric Association (APA) Annual Meeting during both years of the fellowship.
Amount $2,500
Date(s) Application Is Due Jan 15.
Contact Ernesto Guerra, (703) 907-7300; fax: (703) 907-1085; email: eguerra@psych.org or apa@psych.org
Internet http://www.psych.org/edu/res_fellows/res_training/janssen.cfm
Sponsor American Psychiatric Association
1000 Wilson Blvd, Suite 1825
Arlington, VA 22209-3901

American Psychiatric Association/Kempf Fund Award for Research Development in Psychobiological Psychiatry 544

This award recognizes a senior researcher who has made a significant contribution to research on the causes and treatment of schizophrenia as both a researcher and a mentor. A stipend will support the research career development of a young research psychiatrist working in a mentor-trainee relationship with the award winner on further research in this field. Submissions will be judged on the excellence of the nominee's overall contribution to the body of research in schizophrenia, including submission of the nominee's most significant paper or book; a description of the nominee's role as a mentor to younger colleagues; and a description of the qualifications of the young research psychiatrist, as well as a detailed description of his or her career development plan.
Amount $1,500 to senior researcher; $20,000 to young research psychiatrist
Date(s) Application Is Due Oct 14.
Contact APA/Kempt Fund Award, (202) 682-6316 or (800) 852-1390; email: apa@psych.org
Internet http://www.psych.org/research/apire/res_careerdev/kempf.cfm
Sponsor American Psychiatric Association
1000 Wilson Blvd, Suite 1825
Arlington, VA 22209-3901

American Psychiatric Association/Lilly Psychiatric Research Fellowship 545

This one-year fellowship is awarded to two postgraduate psychiatry trainees specifically to focus on research and personal scholarship. Minimal time will be devoted to teaching, patient care, consultation, or other duties. The fellowship is designed for a resident who demonstrates significant research potential, has not had extensive research training prior to residency, and is not already an established investigator. Each chairman of a department of psychiatry is invited to nominate one outstanding eligible resident.
Requirements Individuals who have their MD or DO degree and who have completed residency training in general psychiatry or child psychiatry immediately prior to the time the fellowship commences are eligible. The individual must also be a member of APA.
Amount $45,000
Date(s) Application Is Due Oct 14.
Contact Darrel A. Regier, (202) 682-6316 or (800) 852-1390; email: apa@psych.org
Internet http://www.psych.org/research/apire/training_fund/fellow/lilly.cfm
Sponsor American Psychiatric Association
1000 Wilson Blvd, Suite 1825
Arlington, VA 22209-3901

American Psychiatric Association/Merck Co., Inc. Early Academics Career Research Award 546

The Award is intended to help support the research of a junior faculty member with an interest in sleep disorders or schizophrenia. Two separate awards will be made to candidates who have completed a psychiatry residency, at least one year of a psychiatry research fellowship, and are seeking to make a commitment to a research career with the end goal of successfully transitioning to that of an independent investigator. The Award is intended to assist in this key transition period by providing one year of funding of $45,000. Salary support provided by this award will allow junior faculty in departments of psychiatry at U.S. academic institutions to devote more time to research.
Requirements Candidates must be citizens or permanent residents of the U.S. and should also be APA members. Eligible candidates will be trained psychiatrists with an MD,

MD/Ph.D. or DO degree who have completed residency training in general psychiatry or child psychiatry in the U.S. Candidates also should have completed at least one year of a psychiatry research fellowship but are not 3 or more years post fellowship completion, and do not currently hold an academic rank higher than Assistant Professor.
Restrictions Individuals who have obtained K-awards or are considered an independent Principal Investigator on R-01 or R-21 research grants from NIH are not eligible.
Amount $45,000
Date(s) Application Is Due Oct 14.
Contact Ernesto Guerra, (703) 907-7300; fax: (703) 907-1085; email: eguerra@psych.org or apa@psych.org
Internet http://www.psych.org/research/apire/res_careerdev/apamerck.cfm
Sponsor American Psychiatric Association
1000 Wilson Blvd, Suite 1825
Arlington, VA 22209-3901

American Psychiatric Association/SmithKline Beecham Young Faculty Award for Research Development in Biological Psychiatry **547**
This award is designed to support research by a junior faculty member in the biology and psychopharmacology of mood disorders and/or anxiety disorders. Applicants must hold a tenure track position as an assistant professor in the psychiatry department at a school of medicine in the United States.
Requirements APA members with a MD or DO degree who have completed residency training in general or child psychiatry are eligible for this award.
Amount $45,000
Date(s) Application Is Due Oct 14.
Contact Darrel A. Regier, (202) 682-6316 or (800) 852-1390; email: apa@psych.org
Internet http://www.psych.org/research/apire/training_fund/beecham.cfm
Sponsor American Psychiatric Association
1000 Wilson Blvd, Suite 1825
Arlington, VA 22209-3901

American Psychiatric Association/Wyeth Pharmaceuticals M.D./Ph.D. Psychiatric Research Fellowships **548**
The Fellowship provides one year of funding and is designed to support two post-graduate psychiatry trainees with research experience, specifically to focus on research and personal scholarship. Minimal time will be devoted to teaching, patient care, consultation, or other duties. The protection of time for research should be assured by the department chairman.
Requirements Individuals who have received their MD or DO and a PhD degree and who have completed residency training in general psychiatry or child psychiatry immediately prior to the time the fellowship commences are encouraged to apply. The Fellowship is designed for residents who: (a) have demonstrated significant research potential, (b) have had research training (i.e. as part of their work towards their PhD), and (c) are not already an established investigators. These individuals must also be members of the APA.
Amount $45,000
Date(s) Application Is Due Oct 14.
Contact Darrel A. Regier, (202) 682-6316 or (800) 852-1390; email: apa@psych.org
Internet http://www.psych.org/research/apire/training_fund/fellow/wyeth.cfm
Sponsor American Psychiatric Association
1000 Wilson Blvd, Suite 1825
Arlington, VA 22209-3901

American Psychoanalytic Association Fellowships **549**
The fellowship provides outstanding early-career psychiatrists, psychologists, social workers, and academics additional knowledge of psychoanalysis. All qualified applicants receive a psychoanalyst mentor with whom they meet to discuss their interest in psychoanalysis, a free subscription to the newsletter of the association, and complimentary registration at the annual meetings of the association. The fellowship term is July 1 through June 30. Seventeen fellowships are awarded. Applicants need not be planning to become psychoanalysts. Application guidelines are available online.
Requirements Psychiatrists, psychologists, social workers, and academics who meet the specific eligibility requirements (available online) are eligible. Applicants may be nominated by their department chairs or program directors if applicable. When not applicable, self-nominations are encouraged. Applicants must be training or working in the United States during the fellowship year. All applicants should have demonstrated leadership ability in their discipline, or have special aptitude in research, teaching, and/or clinical endeavors; and have special interest in psychodynamics, psychoanalysis, or applied psychoanalysis.
Date(s) Application Is Due Feb 14.
Contact Carolyn Gatto, (212) 752-0450; email: cgatto@apsa.org
Internet http://www.apsa.org/ctf/fellowship/index.htm
Sponsor American Psychoanalytic Association
309 E 49th St
New York, NY 10007

American Psychological Foundation F. J. McGuigan Young Investigator Prize **550**
The American Psychological Foundation awards this biennial prize to recognize the efforts of a young psychological science investigator in the areas of research consistent with those pursued by Frank Joseph McGuigan, PhD. The prize is focused to support research to explicate the concept of the human mind. The approach must be a materialistic one fostering both empirical and theoretical research. Empirical research would primarily be psychophysiological, but physiological and behavioral research may also qualify for support. The recipient will be selected based on the excellence of the full breadth of research conducted and published to date, as well as the promise of research planned for five years. The prize will be awarded to the recipient's institution for the benefit of his or her research. Nomination guidelines are available online.
Requirements Nominees must have earned a doctoral degree in psychology or a related field, and be nine or fewer years post doctoral degree at the time of the nomination deadline. Nominees must have an affiliation with an accredited college, university, or other research institution.
Restrictions Faculty salaries and indirect costs (i.e., overhead) may not be requested. Dualistic approaches such as espoused by many contemporary cognitive psychologists do not qualify for support.
Amount $25,000
Date(s) Application Is Due Mar 1.
Contact Science Directorate, (202) 336-6000; fax: (202) 336-5953; email: science@apa.org
Internet http://www.apa.org/science/mcguigan.html
Sponsor American Psychological Association
750 First St NE
Washington, DC 20002-4242

American Psychological Foundation Todd E. Husted Memorial Award **551**
This award supports dissertation research that indicates the most potential to contribute toward the development and improvement of mental illness services for those with severe and persistent mental illness. Relevant topics include those that foster the development of a more comprehensive, humane, and responsive system of mental health care; develop a protective and humane sequencing of interventions that prevents the deterioration, homelessness, and premature deaths of those with serious mental illness; develop effective methods of improving patient compliance with medication and treatment for those having impaired insight as a result of schizophrenia and bipolar affective disorder; demonstrate practical methods of improved identification, diversion, and treatment of persons with mental illness who, as a result of that illness, enter the criminal justice system; foster methods to improve training and social attitudes of professionals in the criminal justice system (attorneys, public defenders, judges) regarding the role of serious mental illness in the behaviors of mentally ill offenders; and increase access to and utilization of appropriate services and supports for the most treatment-resistant and severely mentally ill persons. Application and guidelines are available online.
Requirements APA student affiliates enrolled in a psychology graduate program are eligible to apply.
Amount $1000
Date(s) Application Is Due Sep 15.
Contact Science Directorate, (202) 336-6000; fax: (202) 336-5953; email: science@apa.org
Internet http://www.apa.org/science/dissinfo.html
Sponsor American Psychological Association
750 First St NE
Washington, DC 20002-4242

American Psychosomatic Society Herbert Weiner Early Career Awards **552**
These annual awards honor individuals early in their career who have contributed significantly to the field of psychosomatic medicine and show substantial promise of continued meritorious academic accomplishments in the field. Recipients have the opportunity to present their research findings during the annual meeting of the society. A plaque is included with the award.
Requirements Nominees of any nationality must be fewer than 10 years past their final academic degree and must be members of the society.
Amount $1000
Date(s) Application Is Due Nov 1.
Contact Program Contact, (703) 556-9222; fax: (703) 556-8729; email: info@psychosomatic.org
Internet http://www.psychosomatic.org/awards/index.htm
Sponsor American Psychosomatic Society
6728 Old McLean Village Dr
McLean, VA 22101

American Schlafhorst Foundation Grants **553**
The foundation awards grants to eligible North Carolina nonprofit organizations in its areas of interest, including arts, children and youth, elderly, education, health care, science, and social services delivery. Types of support include building construction/renovation, equipment acquisition, general operating grants, research grants, scholarships, and seed money grants.
Requirements 501(c)3 organizations serving the greater Charlotte, NC, area are eligible.
Restrictions Individuals are not eligible.
Amount $1000-$40,000
Contact Grants Administrator, (704) 554-0800; email: info@schlafhorst.com

Sponsor American Schlafhorst Foundation
8801 South Blvd
Charlotte, NC 28224

American Society for Dermatologic Surgery Cutting Edge Research Program Grants 554

The goal of the program is to encourage research in areas of specific relevance to dermatologic surgery and/or cutaneous oncology. It is the hope of the ASDS Research Grant Committee to encourage well-conceived basic and clinical research projects to stimulate the transfer of new technologies from the clinical setting or laboratory to dermatologic surgery practice.
Restrictions Only one application for an ASDS grant award will be considered from an institution or practice.
Amount $5000-$15,000
Date(s) Application Is Due Jul 15.
Contact Dermatology Foundation, Medical and Scientific Committee, (847) 956-0900; fax: (847) 956-0999
Internet http://www.asds-net.org/education/ResearchGrant/education-research.html
Sponsor American Society for Dermatologic Surgery
5550 Meadowbrook Dr. Ste 120
Rolling Meadows, IL 60008

American Society for Enology and Viticulture Scholarships 555

Numerous scholarships are awarded annually to undergraduate and graduate students in North America pursuing a degree in enology, viticulture, or in a curriculum emphasizing a science basic to the wine and grape industry. Candidates are required to submit transcripts of previous education, information on financial need, and a written statement of intention to pursue a career in the wine or grape industry. Previous recipients are eligible each year in open competition with all other applicants.
Requirements Applicant must be a resident of a North American country and accepted in a full-time college or university degree program in the required fields at the junior unit level or higher. Undergraduates must have at least a 3.0 GPA; graduate students must have at least a 3.2 GPA.
Date(s) Application Is Due Mar 1.
Contact Executive Director, (530) 753-3142; fax: (530) 753-3318; email: society@asev.org
Internet http://www.asev.org
Sponsor American Society for Enology and Viticulture
P.O. Box 1855
Davis, CA 95617-1855

American Society for Surgery of the Hand Outcome Studies Grants 556

Outcome studies grants are awarded to encourage young investigators to initiate projects that will lead to additional funding from other sources. There are no specific eligibility requirements, although the society encourages applications from surgeons and other allied health personnel who have a primary interest in hand surgery. All proposals must make use of a recognized and well-documented outcomes instrument, such as the SF-36, Sickness Impact Profile, Arthritis Impact Measurement Scale, etc., and must address an issue of importance to hand surgery. The society encourages applications from surgeons and other allied health personnel who have a primary interest in hand surgery.
Restrictions Grants may not be used for the personal compensation of investigators, travel or conferences, publication costs, the payment of hospital care for patients under study, or the purchase of major pieces of equipment.
Amount $10,000 per year
Date(s) Application Is Due Jul 11.
Contact Julie Quinn, (847) 384-9250; fax: (847) 384-1435; email: jquinn@assh.org
Internet http://www.assh.org/Content/NavigationMenu/Hand_Surgery_Professionals/Outcome_Studies/Translational_and_Clinical_Research.htm
Sponsor American Society for Surgery of the Hand
6300 N River Rd, Ste 600
Rosemont, IL 60018-4256

American Society for Surgery of the Hand Research Grants 557

The society has established grant funding of research projects to encourage young investigators. It is anticipated that the funding will enable investigators to initiate projects that will lead to additional funding from other sources. Submission of proposals intended for NIH or OREF is discouraged. There are no specific guidelines within the framework of hand surgery; in the past, funding has been provided for a range of subjects, including microvascular, tendons, nerves, artificial joints, biochemical, biomechanical, rehabilitation, and other subjects.
Requirements Awards are made to universities, medical schools, research institutions, or individuals. Grants may be used for salaries of technical and professional assistants, purchase of supplies, or minor pieces of equipment.
Restrictions Grants may not be used for the personal compensation of investigators, travel or conferences, publication costs, the payment of hospital care for patients under study, or the purchase of major pieces of equipment. No overhead or indirect costs may be imposed by the recipient institution.
Amount $16,000 maximum
Date(s) Application Is Due May 2.
Contact Julie Quinn, (847) 384-9250; fax: (847) 384-1435; email: jquinn@assh.org
Internet http://www.assh.org/Content/NavigationMenu/Hand_Surgery_Professionals/Research/Basic_Science_Research.htm
Sponsor American Society for Surgery of the Hand
6300 N River Rd, Ste 600
Rosemont, IL 60018-4256

American Society of Criminology Gene Carte Student Paper Competition 558

This competition is held to recognize outstanding scholarly work done by students in the field of criminology. To enter the competition, students must submit papers, conceptual and/or empirical, directly related to criminology. Papers must be 7500 words or less, typewritten double-spaced, on standard-size white paper using standard format for the organization of text, citations, and references. Submissions must be accompanied by a letter indicating the author(s) enrollment status and cosigned by the dean, department chair, or program director. Author name(s), department(s), and advisor(s) must appear only on the title page since papers will be evaluated by blind review. Eight copies of the paper must be provided. Papers should be submitted to the office.
Requirements Any student currently enrolled on a full-time basis in an academic program at either the undergraduate or graduate level may apply.
Amount $500 first prize plus a travel award to annual meeting; $300 second prize; $200 third prize
Date(s) Application Is Due Apr 15.
Contact Crystal Garcia, (317) 274-7006; fax: (317) 274-7860; Awards Committee, (614) 292-9207; fax: (614) 292-6767
Internet http://www.asc41.com/cartesp.html
Sponsor American Society of Criminology
1314 Kinnear Rd, Ste 212
Columbus, OH 43212

American Society of Naval Engineers Scholarship Program 559

This scholarship program is intended to encourage college students to enter into the field of naval engineering and to seek advanced education in this field. Programs of study that are supported include naval architecture; marine, mechanical, civil, aeronautical, ocean, electrical, and electronic engineering; and the physical sciences. Naval engineering includes the design, construction, and repair of ships and their installed systems and equipment, as well as research, logistic support, and the management of acquisition and maintenance. Candidates may apply for support for either the last year of a full-time or co-op undergraduate program or for one year of full-time graduate study leading to a designated engineering or physical science degree in an accredited college or university of the student's choice. Application forms are available on the Web site.
Requirements This scholarship program is open to US citizens who have expressed an interest in a career in naval engineering.
Restrictions Doctoral candidates or those who have an advanced degree are ineligible for this scholarship. A scholarship leading to an undergraduate degree will not be continued for enrollment in a graduate program; however, a student may apply for a new award for a graduate scholarship.
Amount $3500 for graduate students; $2500 for undergraduate students
Date(s) Application Is Due Feb 15.
Contact Dennis Pignotti, Operations Manager, (703) 836-6727; fax: (703) 836-7491; email: dpignotti@navalengineers.org
Internet http://www.navalengineers.org/Programs/Scholarships/sc_info.htm
Sponsor American Society of Naval Engineers
1452 Duke St
Alexandria, VA 22314-3458

American Studies in Japan Research Grants 560

Through their public school system and media, the Japanese people have achieved a level of general knowledge about and interest in the United States. Nevertheless, the formal or integrated study of US history and civilization, and of the economic, social, and political institutions of the United States, has been a relatively recent development in Japanese universities. Moreover, opportunities for Japanese scholars to track major developments and changes in contemporary US society need to be expanded. The commission, therefore, has committed itself to the long-term development of both institutional and individual expertise in the Japanese academic world in US studies, as well as to curriculum development at the more general undergraduate level. The commission will give high priority to research projects that investigate the study of the United States itself, particularly on how the Japanese acquire basic knowledge about the United States (its politics, society, and economy) through both formal and informal channels, such as classroom instruction and media, and how to increase that knowledge and make it more accurate. The following project areas are of interest: research center development, research projects in and about US studies, faculty development, curriculum development, and conferences and seminars. Projects receiving matching grants from other appropriate US or Japanese sources will be given high priority.
Requirements Citizens and permanent residents of the United States and Japan are eligible. Grants may be made to individual universities or local organizations. Awards made to individuals under all programs normally will be made through academic, professional, artistic, or other appropriate organizations that will examine, recommend, and, in most instances, select the individuals to be supported financially by the commission.
Restrictions Japanese institutions and US academic organizations only may apply. This award is granted twice a year.

Date(s) Application Is Due Mar 1; Aug 1.
Contact Grant Administrator, (202) 418-9800; fax: (202) 418-9802; email: grants@jusfc.gov
Internet http://www.jusfc.gov/commissn/BrochureJan03.htm#_The_Study_of
Sponsor Japan-United States Friendship Commission
1201 15th St NW, Ste 330
Washington, DC 20005

American Translators Association German Prize **561**
The prize is awarded biennially in odd-numbered years for works translated from German and published in the United States during the preceding two years. The award includes a monetary prize, certificate of recognition, and travel allowance to attend the annual meeting. Ten pages from the original and two copies of the published translation must be submitted for consideration along with any other documentation.
Amount $1000 and $500 maximum toward travel expenses
Date(s) Application Is Due May 15.
Contact Walter Bacak, Honors and Awards Committee, (703) 683-6100 ext. 3006; fax: (703) 683-6122 ext 3066; email: Walter@atanet.org or ata@atanet.org
Internet http://www.atanet.org/News_Award_German.htm
Sponsor American Translators Association
225 Reinekers Ln, Ste 590
Alexandria, VA 22314

American Wine Society Educational Foundation Scholarship Program **562**
The foundation provides academic scholarships and research grants to graduate students based on academic excellence and genuine interest in pursuing a career in enology, viticulture, or the responsible use and health aspects of wine.
Requirements Awards are made to North American (US, Canada, Mexico, and islands of Caribbean) citizens who have been accepted into a graduate program in enology, viticulture, or a wine-related area. Applicants must complete the undergraduate degree with a 2.8 overall academic average and a 3.0 in their major area of study.
Amount $2500
Date(s) Application Is Due Mar 31.
Contact Dr. Les Sperling, (610) 758-3845 or 865-2401 (7-9 pm Eastern time preferred); fax: (610) 758-3526; email: lhs0@lehigh.edu or Sperling@AmericanWineSociety.com
Internet http://www.americanwinesociety.com/web/scholarship_eligibility.htm
Sponsor American Wine Society Educational Foundation
1134 Prospect Ave
Bethlehem, PA 18018-4914

American-Italian Cancer Foundation Fellowships **563**
The mission of the program is to further the advancement of cancer research by sponsoring the research and training of promising young scientists in Italy and in the United States. A major activity is the award of fellowships to Italian and American scientists so that they might spend a period of research and advanced training in preclinical or clinical research centers in the United States or Italy. The fellowships are intended to augment the training of motivated scientists who have the potential to conduct path-breaking original research upon the return to their respective countries. The one-year fellowships are renewable for an additional year.
Requirements Individuals in the United States and Italy who have been awarded the degrees of PhD, MD, DSc, or DVM may apply in conjunction with a host institution. Candidates must have received their degree no more than three years prior to the date of application.
Amount $25,000 Italian fellowships; $30,000 US fellowships
Date(s) Application Is Due Mar 1.
Contact Franca Gaudio, (212) 628-9090; fax: (212) 517-6089; email: fgaudio@aicfonline.org
Internet http://www.aicfonline.org
Sponsor American-Italian Cancer Foundation
112 E 71st St, Ste 2B
New York, NY 10021

American-Italian Cancer Foundation Prize for Scientific Excellence **564**
The prize recognizes a major scientific discovery in basic or translational cancer research advances that emanate from outstanding scientific work that has reached the early stages of clinical trials and shows real promise. The foundation is keenly interested in research that promises to make a difference in the quality of life for cancer patients. Prize winners will have made a significant contribution to understanding cancer, continue to be active in research, and their work holds promise for future outstanding contributions to the field. Each year two awards will be presented to one US and one European scientist. Nomination guidelines are available online.
Requirements Nominations may be made by any scientist currently or previously affiliated with a cancer research institution or an advocacy organization.
Restrictions Institutions or organizations are not eligible for this award, and candidates may not nominate themselves.
Amount $50,000
Contact Dr. Esther Dyer, Executive Director, (212) 628-9090; fax: (212) 517-6089; email: aicf@aicfonline.org
Internet http://www.aicfonline.org
Sponsor American-Italian Cancer Foundation
112 E 71st St, Ste 2B
New York, NY 10021

Ametek Foundation Grants **565**
Corporate contributions are made through the foundation to nonprofit organizations in company-operating areas. The foundation supports programs and projects in the categories of health, education, and social services, with education being the largest area of support. Under the category of health, grants are awarded to hospitals, health care facilities, and for medical research. Support for education is given to colleges and universities and technical schools, as well as scholarship funds. Welfare funding supports philanthropic organizations, including the United Way. Arts groups, museums, and civic groups also receive support. Types of support include general operating support, annual campaigns, building construction/renovation, equipment acquisition, endowment funds, scholarship funds, research, technical assistance, and matching funds. Annual application deadline dates may vary; contact the office for specific dates. The board meets in November and May to consider requests.
Requirements IRS 501(c)3 organizations are eligible.
Restrictions Individuals, political, fraternal, or veterans organizations are not eligible.
Amount $1000-$25,000 average
Date(s) Application Is Due Feb 28; Sep 1.
Contact Kathryn Londra, (610) 647-2121; fax: (610) 296-3412
Sponsor Ametek Foundation
P.O. Box 1764, 37 N Valley Rd, Bldg 4
Paoli, PA 19301-0801

AmFAR Research Grants and Fellowships **566**
Grants are awarded to support basic and clinical research projects in biomedical, humanistic, and social sciences research relevant to AIDS. Three types of awards are made: basic research grants, postdoctoral fellowships, and short-term travel grants for postdocs to train at another institution. The listed application deadline is for letters of intent; full proposals are by invitation.
Requirements Applicants for research grants must be faculty members at nonprofit institutions. Applicants for fellowships must have an MD, PhD, or equivalent degree and must conduct their projects at nonprofit institutions. Applicants for short-term travel grants must be postdoctoral scientists affiliated with nonprofit institutions.
Amount $90,000 research grants; $99,000 two-year fellowships; $5000 travel grants
Contact Grant Administrator, (212) 806-1696; fax: (212) 806-1601; email: grants@amfar.org
Internet http://www.amfar.org/cgi-bin/iowa/grants/index.html
Sponsor American Foundation for AIDS Research
120 Wall St, 13th Fl
New York, NY 10005-3902

Amgen Foundation Grants **567**
Amgen seeks to: advance science education, improve quality of care and access for patients, and support resources that create sound communities where Amgen staff members live and work. Requests must be received at least 90 days in advance of the desired contribution date. Guidelines are available online.
Requirements 501(c)3 tax-exempt organizations located in Amgen communities are eligible. Eligible grantees may include public elementary and secondary schools, as well as public colleges and universities, public libraries and public hospitals.
Restrictions In general, Amgen does not consider requests for the following: support to individuals, fundraising or sports-related events, corporate sponsorship requests, religious organizations unless the program is secular in nature and benefits a broad range of the community, political organization or lobbying activity, labor unions, fraternal, service or veterans' organizations, private foundations, or organizations that are discriminatory.
Contact Program Contact, (805) 447-4056 or (805) 447-1000; fax: (805) 447-1010
Internet http://wwwext.amgen.com/citizenship/apply_for_grant.html
Sponsor Amgen Foundation
1 Amgen Center Dr, MS 38-3-B
Thousand Oaks, CA 91320

AMI Semiconductors Corporate Grants **568**
The company makes grants to nonprofit organizations in support of the performing arts, economic development, business education, health cost containment, and social services for senior citizens. Types of support include conferences and seminars, general operating support, matching grants, multiyear grants, professorships, research, and scholarships. There are no application deadlines. Submit a letter of inquiry that includes a description of the organization and program, amount of funds requested, purpose of the request, recently audited financial statement, and proof of tax-exempt status.
Restrictions The company does not support political or lobbying groups.
Amount $1000-$2500
Contact TAMERA DRAKE, (208) 234-6890 ; fax: (208) 234-6795 email: tamera_Drake@amis.com
Internet http://www.amis.com/about
Sponsor AMI Semiconductors
2300 Buckskin Rd
Pocatello, ID 83201

AMNH Collection Study Grants 569

These grants provide financial assistance to enable predoctoral and recent postdoctoral investigators to study any of the scientific collections at the American Museum in the departments of anthropology, earth and planetary sciences, entomology, herpetology, ichthyology, invertebrates, mammalogy, ornithology, and vertebrate paleontology. The awards partially support travel and subsistence; visits are arranged through and approved by the appropriate scientific department of the museum and are expected to be four days or longer in duration. Applicants should first contact the staff to discuss the feasibility of the proposed visit prior to requesting the special application form. Applications may be submitted any time during the year.

Requirements Predoctoral and recent postdoctoral investigators are eligible to apply. Only one collection study grant will be awarded to an individual.

Restrictions Grants are not available to investigators residing within daily commuting distance of the American Museum.

Amount $500-$1500 range

Date(s) Application Is Due May 1; Nov 1.

Contact Grants Administrator, Office of Grants and Fellowships, (212) 769-5467; fax: (212) 769-5495; email: grants@amnh.org

Internet http://research.amnh.org/grants/grantsprog.html

Sponsor American Museum of Natural History
Central Park W at 79th St
New York, NY 10024

AMNH Frank M. Chapman Memorial Fellowships 570

These fellowships are intended for postdoctoral scientists to support one year of ornithological research, both neontological and paleontological, with the possibility of renewal for a second year. These are salaried positions and have a benefits package. Fellows are expected to do the majority of their work at the museum.

Requirements Graduate students and established ornithologists are eligible to apply for grants. Recent postdoctoral scholars and distinguished ornithologists may apply for fellowships to support a year of research at the museum or one of its field stations.

Amount $500-$2000; $1000 average

Date(s) Application Is Due Nov 15.

Contact Grants Administrator, Office of Grants and Fellowships, (212) 769-5467; fax: (212) 769-5495; email: grants@amnh.org

Internet http://research.amnh.org/ornithology/grants.htm

Sponsor American Museum of Natural History
Central Park W at 79th St
New York, NY 10024-5192

AMNH Graduate Student Fellowships 571

The program is an educational partnership with selected universities and is dedicated to the training of PhD candidates in those scientific disciplines practiced at the Museum. The university exercises educational jurisdiction over the program and awards the degree. The museum curator serves as a graduate advisor, co-major professor, or major professor. Joint programs are with Columbia University, providing students opportunities in vertebrate and invertebrate paleontology, astrophysics, earth and planetary sciences, and evolutionary biology; Cornell University in entomology; City University of New York in the Evolutionary Biology Program; Yale University in molecular biology/systematics. Fellowships cover stipend and health insurance, and awards are for one year, renewable annually for up to a maximum of four years.

Requirements US and non-US citizens are eligible. Students in developing nations are particularly encouraged to apply. Applicants must have bachelors' degrees and be able to fulfill university admission requirements, which include TOEFL and Graduate Record Examinations.

Restrictions Candidates for the master's degree are ineligible.

Date(s) Application Is Due Nov 30.

Contact Grants Administrator, Office of Grants and Fellowships, (212) 769-5467; fax: (212) 769-5495; email: grants@amnh.org

Internet http://research.amnh.org/grants/gradprog.html

Sponsor American Museum of Natural History
Central Park W at 79th St
New York, NY 10024-5192

AMNH Lerner-Gray Grants for Marine Research 572

The grants provide financial assistance to highly qualified persons starting careers in marine zoology. Support is limited to projects dealing with systematics, evolution, ecology, and field-oriented behavioral studies of marine animals. Research projects need not be carried out at the American Museum. Application forms and guidelines are available from the museum. Awards are announced in May.

Requirements Eligible to apply are advanced graduate students and postdoctoral researchers at the beginning of their careers.

Amount $200-$2000; $1400 average

Date(s) Application Is Due Mar 15.

Contact Grants Administrator, Office of Grants and Fellowships, (212) 769-5467; fax: (212) 769-5495; email: grants@amnh.org

Internet http://research.amnh.org/grants/grantsprog.html

Sponsor American Museum of Natural History
Central Park W at 79th St
New York, NY 10024-5192

AMNH Research and Museum Fellowships 573

Fellowships provide support to recent postdoctoral investigators, established scientists, and other scholars to carry out a specific project within a limited time period. The project must fit into the areas of vertebrate zoology, invertebrate zoology, paleozoology, anthropology, mineral sciences, astronomy, or museum education. The program is designed to advance the training of the participant by having her/him pursue a project in association with museum professionals in a museum setting. Grants provide funds to be used for travel, expendable supplies, and living expenses. Appointment is usually made for a one-year term but may be for a longer or shorter period depending on the source of funds. Candidates are expected to be in residence at the museum or at one of its field stations. Limited relocation, research, and publication support is often available. Interested researchers should obtain a special application form from the Office of Grants and Fellowships. Appointments are effective between July 1 and September 1.

Requirements Graduate and undergraduate students and scientists who have recently received the doctorate are eligible.

Amount $500-$2000

Date(s) Application Is Due Nov 15.

Contact Grants Administrator, Office of Grants and Fellowships, (212) 769-5467; fax: (212) 769-5495; email: grants@amnh.org

Internet http://research.amnh.org/grants/resprog.html

Sponsor American Museum of Natural History
Central Park W at 79th St
New York, NY 10024

AMS Alfred Einstein Award 574

This award is given annually to the author of the article on a musicological subject selected by a committee of scholars to be the most significant published in a periodical during the preceding calendar year. Nominations should include the name of the author, the title of the article, and the name and year of the periodical or other collection in which it was published. Additionally, the award committee will solicit the curriculum vita of each nominee.

Requirements Must be Canadian or US scholar in the early stages of your careers.

Amount $400

Date(s) Application Is Due Jun 1.

Contact Arved Ashby, Committee Chair, email: ams@sas.upenn.edu

Internet http://www.ams-net.org/einstein.html

Sponsor American Musicological Society
201 S 34th St
Philadelphia, PA 19104-6313

AMS Howard Mayer Brown Fellowship 575

Intended to increase the presence of minority scholars and teachers in musicology, the fellowship will support one year of graduate work for a member of a group historically underrepresented in the discipline. Applications are encouraged from African Americans, Native Americans, Latinos/Hispanics, and Asian Americans. Nominations may come from a faculty member of the institution at which the student is enrolled, from a member of the AMS at another institution, or directly from the student. The fellowship is awarded in alternating years. Inquiries should be addressed to the chair of the committee.

Requirements The fellowship will be awarded to a student who has completed at least one year of academic work at an institution with a graduate program in musicology, and who intends to complete a PhD in the field.

Amount $14,000 stipend

Date(s) Application Is Due Jan 15.

Contact Ellen Harris, Massachusetts Institute of Technology; email: eharris@mit.edu

Internet http://www.ams-net.org/hmb.html

Sponsor American Musicological Society
201 S 34th St
Philadelphia, PA 19104-6313

AMS Noah Greenberg Award 576

The award is given annually for a distinguished contribution to the study and performance of early music, up to the end of the 17th century. The award is intended as a grant-in-aid to stimulate active cooperation between scholars and performers by recognizing and fostering outstanding contributions to historical performing practices. Both scholars and performers may apply, since the award may subsidize the publication costs of articles, monographs or editions, as well as performance, recordings, or other projects. Applicants must submit, in triplicate, a description of the project, a detailed budget, and relevant supporting materials to the committee chair.

Amount $2000 maximum

Date(s) Application Is Due Aug 15.

Contact Robert Judd, Executive Director, (215) 898-8698; fax: (215) 573-3673; email: ams@sas.upenn.edu

Internet http://www.ams-net.org/GreenbergGuidelines.html

Sponsor American Musicological Society
201 S 34th St
Philadelphia, PA 19104-6313

AMS Otto Kinkeldey Award 577

The award is given each year for a scholastic work in musicology that is judged by a committee of scholars to be the most distinguished of those published the previous year

in any language and in any country, by a citizen or permanent resident of Canada or the United States. Nominations may be submitted at any time.
Amount $400
Date(s) Application Is Due Jun 1.
Contact Robert Judd, Executive Director, (215) 898-8698; fax: (215) 573-3673; email: ams@sas.upenn.edu
Internet http://www.ams-net.org/kinkeldey.html
Sponsor American Musicological Society
201 S 34th St
Philadelphia, PA 19104-6313

AMS Paul A. Pisk Prize 578
This prize is awarded each year to a graduate music student for a scholarly paper, to be read at the annual meeting of the society. Any paper for which the abstract has been submitted to the program committee, and the paper accepted for inclusion in the annual meeting, is eligible. Five copies of the complete text of the paper together with supporting materials to be presented must be submitted to the Philadelphia AMS office by the listed application deadline. The submission must be accompanied by a statement from the student's academic advisor affirming graduate-student status of the applicant as of the date of the paper's acceptance by the program committee.
Amount $1000
Date(s) Application Is Due Sep 25.
Contact Robert Judd, Executive Director, (215) 898-8698; fax: (215) 573-3673; email: ams@sas.upenn.edu
Internet http://www.ams-net.org/pisk.html
Sponsor American Musicological Society
201 S 34th St
Philadelphia, PA 19104-6313

AMS/Industry Government Graduate Fellowships 579
The graduate fellowships are sponsored by major high-technology firms and government agencies and are designed to attract promising young scientists to prepare for careers in the meteorological, oceanic, and hydrologic fields. Candidates currently studying chemistry, computer sciences, engineering, environmental sciences, mathematics, and physics who intend to pursue careers in the atmospheric, oceanic, or hydrologic sciences also are encouraged to apply. Awards are based on the applicant's performance as an undergraduate student and his or her qualifications to pursue a career in the atmospheric and related oceanic and hydrologic sciences. Applications may be downloaded from the Web site.
Requirements Students entering their first year of graduate study who wish to pursue advanced degrees in the atmospheric and related oceanic and hydrologic sciences are eligible.
Amount $22,000 nine-month stipend
Date(s) Application Is Due Feb 10.
Contact Donna Fernandez, Development Program Coordinator, (617) 227-2426 ext 246; fax: (617) 742-8718; email: dfernand@ametsoc.org
Internet http://www.ametsoc.org/amsstudentinfo/scholfeldocs
Sponsor American Meteorological Society
45 Beacon St
Boston, MA 02108

AMWA Anne C. Carter Student Leadership Award 580
AMWA honors the memory of Anne C. Carter, MD, with an annual award for outstanding student leadership. Nominees must meet the following criteria: national AMWA medical student member; demonstrated exceptional leadership skills through vision, inspiration, innovation, and coordination of local projects that further the mission of AMWA by improving women's health and/or supporting women in medicine; and must be nominated by an AMWA student chapter. Awardees will be honored during AMWA's annual meeting. Nomination guidelines are available online.
Amount $1500 ($750 to awardee, $750 to nominating chapter)
Date(s) Application Is Due Oct 31.
Contact Award Administrator, (703) 838-0500; fax: (703) 549-3864; email info@amwa-doc.org
Internet http://www.amwa-doc.org/index.cfm?objectId=855A0811-D567-0B25-5094E9176D8FFF58
Sponsor American Medical Women's Association Foundation
801 N Fairfax St, Ste 400
Alexandria, VA 22314

AMWA Carroll L. Birch Award 581
The annual award, sponsored by the Chicago Branch of AMWA, is presented for the best original research paper written by an AMWA student member. Award criteria include: original research paper written by a national AMWA medical student member; and applicant must attend an accredited US allopathic or osteopathic medical school. The paper may have been previously published. The recipient receives a cash award, a plaque presented at AMWA's annual meeting, and an article noting the award winner will appear in one of the association's publications. The award recipient is strongly encouraged to attend AMWA's annual meeting. Submit the following materials to the office: cover letter stating applicant's medical school, graduation date, and permanent mailing address; an abstract of 250 words or less; four copies of the manuscript; and a letter from the faculty research sponsor.
Amount $1000
Date(s) Application Is Due Jun 30.
Contact Award Administrator, (703) 838-0500; fax: (703) 549-3864; email info@amwa-doc.org
Internet http://www.amwa-doc.org/index.cfm?objectId=E5F39C87-D567-0B25-5377ABBB15148B2E
Sponsor American Medical Women's Association Foundation
801 N Fairfax St, Ste 400
Alexandria, VA 22314

AMWA Glasgow-Rubin Essay Award 582
The annual award is presented to a medical student for the best essay about a mentor. Award criteria include: AMWA national student member; attends an accredited US allopathic or osteopathic medical school; original research paper written about a personal relationship with a woman physician mentor; and essay must be approximately 1000 words. Submitted essays should be of publishable quality; typed, double-spaced; and title page to include title, author's name, address and phone number, email address, and name medical school.
Amount $1000
Date(s) Application Is Due May 31.
Contact Award Administrator, (703) 838-0500; fax: (703) 549-3864; email: info@amwa-doc.org
Internet http://www.amwa-doc.org/index.cfm?objectId=288C83B1-D567-0B25-539772C31D5C35EC
Sponsor American Medical Women's Association Foundation
801 N Fairfax St, Ste 400
Alexandria, VA 22314

AMWA Kathryn C. Bemmann New Investigator Grant on Violence against Women 583
The grant supports a physician early in his or her career to pursue research on violence against women. The candidate should be a recent graduated physician; have a serious interest in research on violence against women; and have the ability to pursue an independent career in research. Proposals will be judged on scientific quality, research facility, and significance to the field. The grant recipient will be recognized at the annual meeting. Transportation, one-night's hotel accommodation, and complimentary meeting registration will be provided. Guidelines and application are available online.
Requirements Physicians who have received their medical degree within the last five years are eligible.
Amount $3000-$5000
Date(s) Application Is Due Apr 30.
Contact Julie Dogil, (703) 838-0500; fax: (703) 549-3864; email: jdogil@amwa-doc.org
Internet http://www.amwa-doc.org/index.cfm?objectId=E22EC179-D567-0B25-5D6E0F68BB316ECB
Sponsor American Medical Women's Association Foundation
801 N Fairfax St, Ste 400
Alexandria, VA 22314

Andrew W. Mellon Curatorial Fellowships 584
These two-year fellowships, renewable for a third year, will provide curatorial training and support scholarly research related to the gallery's collections of European and American art. Fellows will be fully integrated into a specific curatorial department with duties, privileges, and status equivalent to an assistant curator; divide their time between specific research projects and more general curatorial work within the department, including research on the collection and new acquisitions, work on the presentation of the collection, participation in aspects of special exhibition projects, and opportunities to give public lectures and gallery talks; and, in consultation with the supervising curator, develop a concrete project intended to complement their own research interests. Fellowships include stipend, annual travel allowance, and eligibility for medical and term life insurance through the federal government. Guidelines are available online.
Requirements Consideration will be given to candidates in the fields of European, American, and British paintings, drawings, prints, photographs, and sculpture from the 13th century to the present. Applicants must have completed a PhD before beginning a fellowship and within the last five years.
Amount $41,815 annually approximately
Date(s) Application Is Due Jan 14.
Contact Grants Administrator, (202) 842-6257; email: intern@nga.gov
Internet http://www.nga.gov/education/fellowed.htm
Sponsor National Gallery of Art
2000B S Club Dr
Landover, MD 20785

Andrew W. Mellon Fellowships in Humanistic Studies 585
The fellowships are issued to attract especially promising students into the humanities and to support students while preparing for teaching and other scholarly careers in humanistic disciplines. Selection procedures include review by regional and national

committees. Winners of fellowships may take their awards to graduate schools of their choice in the United States and Canada. Fellowships are not renewable.
Requirements College seniors or recent graduates with outstanding academic records and plans to enter PhD programs in the humanities are eligible, providing that they are US citizens or permanent residents. PhD programs should begin in September.
Restrictions Individuals who have been candidates in a previous year are not eligible. Applicants must not be already enrolled in graduate or professional study or hold the MA degree. Ineligible fields of study include archaeology (except within art history), education (or any studies leading to the EdD), fine arts, performing arts, international studies, law, political science, psychology, public policy, science and medicine, sociology, or theology for pastoral ministry (or any DDiv).
Amount $17,500 plus tuition and fees for the first year
Date(s) Application Is Due Dec 1.
Contact Robert Weisbuch, Program Director, Mellon Fellowships in Humanistic Studies, (800) 899-9963 ext 127 or (609) 452-7007; fax: (609) 452-0066; email: bobweis@woodrow.org or mellon@woodrow.org
Internet http://www.woodrow.org/mellon
Sponsor Woodrow Wilson National Fellowship Foundation
P.O. Box 5329
Princeton, NJ 08543-5329

Andrew W. Mellon Postdoctoral Fellowship in American Cultures **586**
The college invites applications for a two-year Mellon Postdoctoral Fellowship in Native American Studies, to begin in the fall. The program seeks scholars who have an interest in teaching in an undergraduate liberal arts college and who would welcome the opportunity to participate in the development of a multidisciplinary concentration in Native American Studies within the college's American Culture Program. The fellow will teach or team-teach one course in the fall semester entitled Introduction to Native American Studies, and will help facilitate a monthly faculty seminar throughout the academic year intended to extend and deepen the interests in Native American Studies of faculty from several disciplines. The fellowship includes salary plus benefits, as well as support for research, professional travel, and relocation expenses. Application guidelines are available online.
Requirements Candidates should be relatively new PhDs with training in Native American Studies or any relevant discipline.
Amount $44,000 stipend
Date(s) Application Is Due Feb 15.
Contact Ron Sharp, Dean of the Faculty, (845) 437-7485; fax: (845) 437-7204
Internet http://americanculture.vassar.edu/index.html?posting=39
Sponsor Vassar College
Box 746, 124 Raymond Ave
Poughkeepsie, NY 12604-0739

Andrew W. Mellon Postdoctoral Fellowship in Medieval Studies **587**
The Mellon Fellow's principal obligation will be to pursue his or her research. Though the fellowship carries no teaching responsibilities, it is expected that the Fellow will take advantage of the opportunity to participate in the intellectual life of the institute and the multidisiciplinary activities that it sponsors for the medievalist community at Notre Dame. The Fellow will be provided an office in the Medieval Institute, full library and computer privileges, and access to the Institute's research tools.
Requirements Mellon scholars must hold a regular appointment at a US institution and plan to return to their institution following their fellowship year. Applicants must have the PhD in hand as of the application date and must not be more than five years beyond the PhD. The fellow will be expected to live in South Bend, IN.
Amount $37,500
Date(s) Application Is Due Jan 15.
Contact Roberta Baranowski, (574) 631-8304; email: Roberta.Baranowski.7@nd.edu
Internet http://www.nd.edu/~medinst/funding/funding.html#mellon
Sponsor University of Notre Dame
715 Hesburgh Library
Notre Dame, IN 46556-5629

Andrew W. Mellon Postdoctoral Fellowships at UCLA Humanities Consortium **588**
These fellowships are devoted to the theme Nations and Identities. The topic for the current year is The Secularization Thesis. Fellows are required to be in residence and to participate in the consortium's Mellon Seminar and Conference. Fellows also will teach, through relevant departments or programs, one course in their first year and two courses in their second, and will be expected to participate in the intellectual life of these programs. One fellow will be appointed in each of three historical periods: AD 600 to 1600, 1600 to 1800, and 1800 to present.
Requirements Fellows must have earned their doctorates after September 1, and must have the doctorate in hand by September 1.
Amount $35,000 stipend
Date(s) Application Is Due Mar 1.
Contact Mark Pokorski, (310) 206-0559; email: mpok@humnet.ucla.edu
Internet http://www.humnet.ucla.edu/humnet/consortium/fships.html
Sponsor UCLA Humanities Consortium
310 Royce Hall
Los Angeles, CA 90095-1461

Andrew W. Mellon Postdoctoral Fellowships at Washington University **589**
The program encourages interdisciplinary scholarship and teaching across the humanities and social sciences. It supports new and recent PhDs who wish to strengthen their own advanced training and to participate in the university's ongoing interdisciplinary programs and seminars. Fellows receive a two-year appointment with stipends. Fellows will outline a plan for their own continuing research in association with a senior faculty member at the university. Over the course of the two-year appointment, fellows will teach three undergraduate courses in their home discipline and collaborate each spring semester in leading a seminar in theory and methods of interdisciplinary research. There is no application form. Submit a cover letter, a description of the research program (three-page maximum, single spaced), a brief proposal for the seminar and theory and methods, a curriculum vita, and three letters of recommendation.
Amount $40,700 minimum
Date(s) Application Is Due Dec 1.
Contact Steven Zwicker, Department of English, (314) 935-5190; email: szwicker@artsi.wustl.edu
Internet http://www.artsci.wustl.edu/~szwicker/Mellon_Postdoctoral_Program.html
Sponsor Washington University
Campus Box 1122, 1 Brookings Dr
Saint Louis, MO 63130

Andrew W. Mellon Postdoctoral Fellowships in the Humanities at Stanford University **590**
The fellowship is designed to give the best recent PhD recipients in the humanities a unique opportunity to develop as scholars and teachers. Each year, up to six fellowships are awarded for a two-year term. Fellows teach one course and contribute a second course-equivalent per year in one of Stanford's 15 humanities departments. In addition, fellows participate in the intellectual life of the program by sharing work in progress, meeting regularly as a group and with faculty, and generally contributing to the community of humanists at Stanford. It is expected that fellows are in residence during the term of their appointment. The total number of fellows in the program will typically be between 12 and 15. In addition to the stipend, the fellowship includes additional support for computer assistance, research, and relocation expenses. Application and guidelines are available online.
Requirements Candidates must have received their PhD degree between January 1, 2002, and June 30, 2005.
Amount $50,000 annual stipend plus benefits
Date(s) Application Is Due Nov 28.
Contact Dr. Seth Lerer, (650) 723-3054; fax: (650) 725-0755; email: lerer@stanford.edu
Internet http://fellows.stanford.edu
Sponsor Stanford University
Stanford University, 450 Serra Mall, Bldg 460, Rm 201
Stanford, CA 94305-2070

Andrew W. Mellon Predoctoral Fellowship **591**
The fellowship is for research in fields other than Western art, to be held partly in residence at the National Gallery of Art, Center for Advanced Study in the Visual Arts, and partly elsewhere in the United States or abroad. The fellow is expected to spend the second year of the fellowship at the center to complete the dissertation. Application may be made only through the chairs of the graduate departments of art history or other appropriate departments, who should act as sponsors for applicants from their respective schools. Departments should limit nominations to one candidate. Fellowships begin September 1 and are not renewable.
Requirements Applicants must have completed their residence requirements and coursework for the PhD and general or preliminary examinations before the date of application and know two foreign languages related to the topic of the dissertation. Applicants must be either US citizens or enrolled in a university in the United States.
Amount $20,000 per year; $4000 housing subsidy
Date(s) Application Is Due Nov 15.
Contact Grants Administrator, Fellowships Program, Center for Advanced Study in Visual Arts, (202) 842-6482; fax: (202) 789-3026; email: advstudy@nga.gov
Internet http://www.nga.gov/resources/casvapre.htm
Sponsor National Gallery of Art
Fourth St and Constitution Ave NW
Washington, DC 20565

Andrew W. Mellon Predoctoral Fellowships at the University of Pittsburgh **592**
Fellowships are awarded to students of exceptional ability and promise who wish to enroll, or are enrolled, at the University of Pittsburgh in programs leading to the PhD in various fields of the humanities, the natural sciences, and the social sciences. Awards are made on an annual basis but may be renewed; fellows who wish to renew must file new applications. Annual deadline dates may vary; contact the office listed for exact dates.
Requirements Applicant must submit the formal application form supported by transcripts of all previous academic work, three letters of recommendation from persons able to judge the applicant's qualification for graduate study, a three-page summary describing the applicant's proposed research or study program, and any other materials that would show promise of distinguished achievement.

Restrictions Individuals holding the fellowships are expected to engage in full-time study during the periods of their fellowships; no additional duties will be required or permitted.
Amount $15,000 for 12 months plus tuition
Date(s) Application Is Due Jan 15.
Contact Financial Aid Office, (412) 624-7488
Internet http://www.fas.pitt.edu/financial.htm#apply
Sponsor University of Pittsburgh
2604 Cathedral of Learning
Pittsburgh, PA 15260

Anesthesia Clinical Research Starter Grants 593
The grants offer start-up money to institutions on behalf of faculty members who seek to obtain further funding for continuation of their anesthesiology-related projects that focus on scholarly, hypothesis-based clinical studies. Institutional matching funds are required.
Requirements Faculty members may be at the associate, instructor, or assistant professor level.
Amount $35,000 first year; $50,000 second year
Date(s) Application Is Due Feb 15; Aug 15.
Contact Thomas Bruckman, Executive Director, (507) 266-6866; fax: (507) 284-0120; email: grunewald.nathan@mayo.edu
Internet http://www.faer.org/grants.php
Sponsor Foundation for Anesthesia Education and Research
200 First St SW, Charlton Bldg, Mayo Clinic
Rochester, MN 55905

Animal Behavior Society Developing Nations Research Grants 594
Awards provide financial support for scientific studies of animal behavior conducted by current members of the Animal Behavior Society. Applications are invited from student members as well as more established members of the research community. Electronic application forms are available on the Web site. Grants are awarded for research to be conducted within a one-year period from the date of award.
Requirements Only members of the Animal Behavior Society who are residents of a developing nation and are conducting research at an institution in a developing nation are eligible to apply. The following nations shall not be considered as developing nations: the United States, Canada, Israel, Japan, Australia, New Zealand, Iceland, Norway, Sweden, Finland, Denmark, Germany, the Netherlands, Belgium, Luxembourg, Ireland, Switzerland, Austria, Italy, France, the United Kingdom, Spain, and Portugal.
Amount $700 maximum
Date(s) Application Is Due Jan 12.
Contact Stephen Nowicki, Department of Biology, Duke University, (919) 684-6950; email: snowicki@duke.edu
Internet http://www.animalbehavior.org/ABS/Grants/DNG/dng_info2005.html
Sponsor Animal Behavior Society
Box 90325
Durham, NC 27708-0325

Animal Behavior Society Student Research Grants 595
The program provides financial support for scientific studies of animal behavior. Grants are ordinarily awarded for research to be conducted within a one-year period from the date of award. An electronic submission form is available on the Web site. Annual deadline dates may vary; contact program staff for exact dates.
Requirements Society members who are currently enrolled in graduate programs may apply.
Amount $1000 maximum
Date(s) Application Is Due Jan 28.
Contact Dr. Stephen Nowicki, (919) 684-6950; email: snowicki@duke.edu or plsch@ou.edu
Internet http://www.animalbehavior.org/ABS/Grants/SRG/ABSSRG_announcement_2004_2005.html
Sponsor Animal Behavior Society
700 College St
Beloit, WI 53511

ANL Faculty Research Leave Program 596
Argonne National Laboratory, one of DOE's major research centers, offers faculty research leave appointments (FRLA) to college and university faculty members. Faculty members spend their sabbatical leave, typically 9-12 months, at the Argonne Laboratory. The purpose of the program is to involve college/university faculty in DOE research programs conducted at Argonne, and stimulate continuing research collaboration between faculty and Argonne scientists. Participation takes the form of individual collaboration with an Argonne staff member in some part of an ongoing project of interest to the faculty participant. The research experience is augmented by seminars, independent study, and other appropriate activities. Faculty research projects are available in the basic physical and life sciences, mathematics, computer science, and in engineering, as well as in a variety of applied research programs. Interaction of faculty with students in the research programs is strongly encouraged. Typically, Argonne reimburses the university for 50 percent of salary and fringe benefits for the academic year (9 months) and full salary and fringe benefits for the summer (three months). In addition, the laboratory may negotiate reimbursement for certain travel, moving, and housing expenses. Applications are accepted at any time. Write for additional information and application forms.
Requirements An appointee must be a full-time faculty member of an accredited US college or university and must have a commitment to continue in teaching and research as a career. The applicant's objectives for the Argonne tour should be clearly specified, and these objectives must be endorsed by the department head or dean. The expression of interest in participation by an individual faculty member, along with university endorsement of such participation, should be transmitted to the Cross Division Program Leader, Division of Educational Programs. Initial expressions of interest should include a curriculum vita, a publication list, and a brief statement of the research interests of the faculty member.
Contact Carol Przyzycki, Faculty Research Leave (Sabbatical), Division of Educational Programs, (630) 252-5448; email: cprzyzy@dep.anl.gov
Internet http://www.dep.anl.gov/crossdiv/frl.htm
Sponsor Argonne National Laboratory
9700 S Cass Ave, DEP 223
Argonne, IL 60439-4845

ANL Faculty Research Participation Program 597
Faculty participants in the program spend 10-12 weeks collaborating with an Argonne staff scientist or engineer on an existing project of interest to the faculty member. Argonne research falls into four broad categories: engineering research (including advanced nuclear reactors, batteries, and fuel cells); physical research (materials science, physics, chemistry, mathematics, and computer science); energy and environmental science and technology research (biology, alternate energy systems, and environmental and economic impact assessments); and technology transfer (moving the benefits of Argonne's publicly funded research to the marketplace). Appointments are made principally for the summer; however, similar arrangements can be made during the academic year. Stipends are based on academic-year salary and round-trip travel is provided. Additional information and application forms are available upon request.
Requirements An appointee must be a US citizen or permanent resident who is a full-time faculty member of an accredited US college or university and must have a commitment to continue in teaching and research as a career. The applicant's objectives for the Argonne tour should be clearly specified, and these objectives must be endorsed by the department head or dean.
Date(s) Application Is Due Jan 13.
Contact Carol Przyzycki , Faculty Research Participation (Short-Term), Division of Educational Programs, (630) 252-5448; email: cprzyzy@dep.anl.gov
Internet http://www.dep.anl.gov/p_faculty/frp.htm
Sponsor Argonne National Laboratory
9700 S Cass Ave, DEP 223
Argonne, IL 60439

ANL Graduate Thesis Parts Research Appointments 598
Thesis Parts appointments support qualified graduate students who wish to visit Argonne for periods from a few days to a few months so that they may utilize special laboratory facilities or capabilities during the course of their thesis research. Research areas include physical and life sciences, mathematics, computer science, engineering, conservation, environment, fission and fusion energy, and other energy technologies. Application is best made through an Argonne staff member or research division appropriate to the proposed activity.
Requirements Qualified graduate students in US universities who wish to carry out some thesis research at Argonne are eligible to apply.
Contact Lisa Reed, Lab-Grad Research Appointments, Division of Educational Programs, (630) 252-3366; email: Lreed@dep.anl.gov
Internet http://www.dep.anl.gov/p_graduate/thesispa.htm
Sponsor Argonne National Laboratory
9700 S Cass Ave, DEP 223
Argonne, IL 60439

ANL Laboratory-Graduate Research Appointments 599
Laboratory graduate research appointments are available for qualified graduate students at US universities who wish to carry out their thesis research at Argonne National Laboratory under the cosponsorship of an Argonne staff member and a faculty member. Research may be conducted in the basic physical and life sciences, mathematics, computer science, and engineering, as well as in a variety of applied areas relating to conservation, environment, fission and fusion energy, and other energy technologies. Lab-grad appointments are for a one-year term with annual renewals being contingent upon satisfactory performance by the appointee. Applications may be submitted at any time, and appointments may commence any time during the year. Completed application should be submitted at least one month prior to proposed starting date. Temporary appointments are available to qualified graduate students so they may work with an Argonne staff member and become familiar with his/her work prior to application for a year-long research appointment. The student's faculty sponsor may also receive payment for limited travel expenses.
Requirements An applicant must currently be a full-time graduate student in a recognized graduate program in a US university and must be a US citizen or permanent resident alien.
Amount $5000 maximum tuition payment, stipend, and travel expenses

Contact Lisa Reed, Lab-Grad Research Appointments, Division of Educational Programs, (630) 252-3366; email: Lreed@dep.anl.gov
Internet http://www.dep.anl.gov/p_graduate/labgrad.htm
Sponsor Argonne National Laboratory
9700 S Cass Ave, DEP 223
Argonne, IL 60439

Ann Arbor Area Community Foundation Grants **600**
The foundation is interested in funding projects that will improve the quality of life for citizens of the Ann Arbor, MI, area. Eligible projects generally fall within the categories of education, culture, social service, community development, environmental awareness, health and wellness, and youth and senior citizens. Types of support include emergency funds, program development, conferences and seminars, publication, seed grants, scholarship funds, research, and matching funds. Higher priority is given to programs that are preventive rather than remedial, increase individual access to community resources, examine and address the underlying causes of local problems, promote independence and personal achievement, attract volunteer resources and support, strengthen the private nonprofit sector, encourage collaboration with other organizations, and build the capacity of the applying organization. Organizations interested in applying are strongly encouraged to discuss their project with the program director prior to submitting an application.
Requirements 501(c)3 nonprofit organizations in the Ann Arbor, MI, area, which is the area that falls within the boundaries of the Ann Arbor public schools district, are eligible.
Restrictions The foundation usually does not make grants for construction projects, annual giving campaigns or capital campaigns, normal operating expenses (except for start-up purposes), religious or sectarian purposes, computer hardware equipment, individuals, advocacy or political purposes, multiyear funding, or regranting.
Date(s) Application Is Due Feb 14, Oct 3.
Contact Phil D'Anieri, (734) 663-2173; email: pdanieri@aaacf.org
Internet http://www.aaacf.org/grants.asp
Sponsor Ann Arbor Area Community Foundation
201 S Main St, Ste 501
Ann Arbor, MI 48104

Ann Peppers Foundation Grants **601**
The foundation awards grants to eligible California nonprofit organizations in its areas of interest, including arts and cultural programs, disabled, elderly, health care, private education, and social services. Types of support include capital grants, general operating grants on a temporary basis, matching grants, scholarships, and research grants. Grants are initiated by the foundation manager. There are no application deadlines; the board meets quarterly to consider requests.
Requirements Southern California 501(c)3 nonprofits, colleges, and universities are eligible. Preference is given to requests from Los Angeles County.
Amount $2000-$50,000 range
Contact Jack Alexander, Secretary, (626) 449-0793
Sponsor Ann Peppers Foundation
625 S Fair Oaks Ave
South Pasadena, CA 91030

Anna C. and Oliver C. Colburn Fellowship **602**
One fellowship will be awarded every other year for an academic year of study and research to an applicant contingent upon his or her acceptance as an incoming associate member or student associate member of the American School of Classical Studies at Athens. Candidates for the fellowship must apply concurrently to the American School for associate membership or student associate membership. Application forms are available from the institute.
Requirements This competition is open to US or Canadian citizens or permanent US residents who are at the predoctoral stage or who have received the PhD degree within the last five years.
Restrictions Applicants may not be members of the American School during the year of application. The fellowship may be held for a maximum of one year. Other major fellowships may not be held during the requested tenure of the award.
Amount $11,000
Date(s) Application Is Due Jan 15.
Contact Elizabeth Gilgan, AIA Programs Administrator, (617) 353-9361; fax: (617) 353-6550; email: egilgan@aia.bu.edu or aia@aia.bu.edu
Internet http://www.archaeological.org/webinfo.php?page=10007
Sponsor Archaeological Institute of America
656 Beacon St
Boston, MA 02215-2010

Anna Louise Hoffman Award for Outstanding Achievement in Graduate Chemistry Research **603**
At the time of nomination, the candidate must be a full-time female graduate student who is a candidate for a graduate degree at an accredited institution. Research presented by the candidate must be original and of one of the main chemical divisions--analytical, biochemical, inorganic, organic, physical, and/or ancillary. The nominee may be, but need not be, a member of Iota Sigma Pi.
Requirements Nomination must be made by members of the institution's graduate faculty. Dossier must contain an academic history, including all transcripts; candidate's permanent and school addresses; two letters of recommendation; the nomination; a brief description of the candidate's research; and a list of publications and talks or papers presented outside of degree requirements. Description of the research should be no more than 1000 words and prepared by the candidate.
Amount $500
Date(s) Application Is Due Feb 15.
Contact Vicki Grassian, (319) 335-1392; fax: (319) 353-1115; email: vicki-grassian@uiowa.edu
Internet http://www.iotasigmapi.info//studentAwards.htm
Sponsor Iota Sigma Pi National Honor Society for Women in Chemistry
Euclid Ave at East 24th St
Cleveland, OH 44115

Anna-Greta and Holger Crafoords Foundation Grants **604**
The foundation operates in Sweden and the grants promote international basic research within the following subject areas: mathematics and astronomy; geosciences; biosciences, with particular emphasis on ecology; and polyarthritis. In addition to the Crafoord Prize, research grants are awarded within the relevant disciplines to individual persons or researchers in Sweden. Award of a research grant within polyarthritis takes place every third year, but a prize within polyarthritis is only awarded when a specific enquiry has demonstrated that such scientific progress has been made that a prize is warranted.
Contact Grants Administrator, 046-38 58 80; fax: 046-38 58 85; email: crafoord@crafoord.se
Internet http://www.crafoord.se/index-e.htm
Sponsor Anna-Greta and Holger Crafoords Foundation
P.O. Box 137, Malmovagen 8
Lund 22100 Sweden

Anne Louise Barrett Fellowship **605**
This fellowship is awarded in music, preferably and primarily for study or research in musical theory, composition, or the history of music. The fellowship may be used abroad or in the United States. Awards are usually made to applicants who plan full-time graduate study for the coming year. Preference will be given to applicants who have not previously held one of Wellesley College's awards. Awards will be based on merit and need. One fellowship is awarded annually; application form must be used. Annual deadline dates may vary; contact program officer for exact dates.
Requirements The fellowship is open to graduating seniors and graduates of Wellesley College to be used for study at institutions other than Wellesley.
Amount $15,000 maximum
Contact Secretary to the Committee on Graduate Fellowships, Center for Work and Service, (781) 283-3525; email: cws-fellowships@wellesley.edu
Internet http://www.wellesley.edu/CWS/alumnae/wellfs.html
Sponsor Wellesley College
106 Central St
Wellesley, MA 02181-8200

Annenberg Foundation Grants **606**
The foundation provides support for projects within its grantmaking interests of education and youth development, arts and culture, civic, community and the environment, and health and human services. It encourages the development of more effective ways to share ideas and knowledge. Letters of inquiry may be submitted at all times during the year and there are no deadlines. Please review the grants database for additional types of grants given.
Requirements 501(c)3 tax-exempt organizations are eligible.
Restrictions Full proposals are not accepted unless requested by a Foundation representative. The foundation is not presently considering inquiries for: individuals, individual K-12 schools, for-profit organizations, political activities or attempts to influence specific legislation, individual scholarships, projects focused exclusively on research, or programs outside of its grant-making interests.
Contact Program Contact, (610) 341-9066; fax: (610) 964-8688; email: info@annenbergfoundation.org
Internet http://www.annenbergfoundation.org/grants
Sponsor Annenberg Foundation
150 N. Radnor-Chester Road, Suite A-200
Radnor, PA 19087-5252

ANS Dissertation Fellowships **607**
The society will award a fellowship to a university graduate student in the United States or Canada in the fields of the humanities or the social sciences who will be writing a dissertation during the academic year on a topic in which the use of numismatic evidence plays a significant part.
Requirements Candidates must have completed the general examinations or the equivalent for the doctorate and must have attended the society's graduate seminar.
Amount $2000
Date(s) Application Is Due Mar 1.
Contact Ute Wartenberg Kagan, Executive Director, (212) 571-4470 ext 1307; fax: (212) 571-4479; email: wartenberg@amnumsoc.org
Internet http://www.amnumsoc.org/about/study.html

Sponsor American Numismatic Society
Broadway at 155th St
New York, NY 10032

ANS Donald Groves Numismatic Research Grants **608**
The fund supports research and publication in the field of early US numismatics involving material dated no later than 1800. Funds are available for travel and other expenses in association with research, as well as for publication costs. Applications in letter form are welcome at any time, setting forth the proposed research project, the method of accomplishing the research, and a budget supporting the funding requested.
Contact Program Contact, (212) 571-4470; fax: (212) 571-4479; email: info@amnumsoc.org
Internet http://www.amnumsoc.org/about/grove.html
Sponsor American Numismatic Society
96 Fulton St
New York, NY 10038

ANS Frances M. Schwartz Fellowship **609**
The fellowship supports the work and study of numismatic and museum methodology at the society. The purpose of establishing the fellowship was so that the funds would be used to educate qualified students in museum practice and to train them in numismatics, as well as to provide for curatorial assistance in the Greek, Roman, and Byzantine departments.
Requirements Candidates must have completed the BA or the equivalent.
Amount $2000 maximum
Date(s) Application Is Due Mar 1.
Contact Program Contact, (212) 571-4470; fax: (212) 571-4479; email: info@amnumsoc.org
Internet http://www.amnumsoc.org/about/study.html
Sponsor American Numismatic Society
96 Fulton St
New York, NY 10038

ANS Graduate Seminar Grants **610**
The program provides graduate students and university instructors in the United States and Canada with a deeper understanding of the indispensable contributions numismatics makes to other fields of study. The program includes attendance at lectures and research on individual topics at museum headquarters, culminating in oral and written presentations.
Requirements Applicants must have completed at least one year of graduate study at a US or Canadian university in classics, archaeology, history, art history, or related disciplines. Applications will also be accepted from junior college or university instructors with a degree in one of those fields.
Amount $3000
Date(s) Application Is Due Feb 15.
Contact Dr. Peter van Alfen, Seminar Director, (212) 571-4470; fax: (212) 571-4479; email: vanalfen@numismatics.org or info@amnumsoc.org
Internet http://www.amnumsoc.org/about/study.html
Sponsor American Numismatic Society
96 Fulton St
New York, NY 10038

Anthem Blue Cross and Blue Shield School Nurse Grants **611**
The mission of the project is to promote cardiovascular health among school-age children. Anthem's goals are to assist school nurses in initiating programs that may encourage a healthy lifestyle, reduce cardiovascular risk factors, promote physical activity, and encourage healthy eating behaviors; and facilitate the development of innovative school health programs that are based on research. No awards will be made to individuals, but will be awarded to the school. To apply, the school nurse representing the school must submit a completed application form with the appropriate attachments by the listed application deadline. Guidelines, including program contacts in Kentucky and Indiana, and application are available online.
Requirements Eligible applicants include school nurses who are licensed in the state in which they practice and who represent a public or private school (elementary, junior high, middle, or high school) in Ohio, Kentucky, or Indiana.
Restrictions Funds cannot be used for the salary or wages of any staff or employee.
Amount $500-$1000
Date(s) Application Is Due Feb 1.
Contact Gabrielle Karpowicz, (614) 529-5068; email: gkarpowicz@aol.com
Internet http://oasn.org/Awards_Grants/awards.htm
Sponsor Ohio Association of School Nurses
6167 Heritage Point Ct
Hilliard, OH 43026

Anthony R. Abraham Foundation Grants **612**
The foundation awards general operating grants to Roman Catholic organizations, including churches, hospitals, missions, schools, and community groups. The foundation also supports human service organizations, youth agencies, and medical research. Giving is primarily in Miami, Florida. Applicants should submit a brief letter of inquiry describing the program/project and include proof of tax-exempt status. There are no application deadlines.
Requirements Florida nonprofit organizations are eligible.
Restrictions Grants are not made to individuals.
Amount $100-$50,000 average
Contact Anthony Abraham, Chair, (305) 665-2222
Sponsor Anthony R. Abraham Foundation
6600 SW 57th Avenue
Miami, FL 33143

AO North America Grants **613**
Support is given to trauma research projects, training in the management and care of teachers, and to visiting professors in the teaching of orthopedic, maxillofacial, spine, or veterinary trauma treatment.
Contact Grants Administrator, (610) 251-9007; fax: (610) 251-9059; email: ellisa@aona.com
Internet http://www.aona.org/fellow_preceptor.asp
Sponsor AO North America Inc
P.O. Box 308
Devon, PA 19333-0308

AOA Clinical Investigator Development Award **614**
This program recruits and supports osteopathic physicians for research and teaching careers in the medical sciences. Support is given for three years. Contact program staff for availability.
Amount $50,000
Contact Elizabeth Freeman, (800) 621-1773 ext 8006; email: research@osteopathic.org
Internet http://do-online.osteotech.org/index.cfm?PageID=res_main
Sponsor American Osteopathic Association
142 E Ontario St
Chicago, IL 60611-2864

AOA Gutensohn-Denslow Award **615**
The award recognizes and rewards a person who has made an outstanding contribution to the osteopathic profession in the areas of research and education. AOA and the National Osteopathic Foundation administer this program, which is funded by Glaxo Wellcome Inc.
Requirements A nominee must be either an osteopathic physician or hold a doctoral level degree and be on the faculty or staff of an osteopathic institution. Nominations may come from anyone in the osteopathic profession and from colleagues of osteopathic physicians. Individuals nominated previously must be renominated for consideration. Initial nominations must include a current curriculum vita of the nominee and a detailed account of his/her contributions to research.
Amount $5000, consisting of $4250 stipend and $750 travel allowance
Date(s) Application Is Due Mar 15.
Contact Elizabeth Freeman, Division of Research Development, (800) 621-1773 ext 8006; fax: (312) 280-3860; email: research@osteopathic.org
Internet http://www.osteopathic.org/index.cfm?PageID=ost_resoverview
Sponsor American Osteopathic Association
142 E Ontario St
Chicago, IL 60611-2864

AOA Osteopathic Research Fellowships **616**
These research fellowships are designed to enable the applicant to conduct a basic science or clinical research project that will make a significant contribution to osteopathic medicine. The fellowship also serves as seed funding to encourage an osteopathic physician to contribute to research throughout his/her career in osteopathic medicine.
Requirements Applicant must be either a postdoctoral osteopathic medical student, possessing an earned DO degree awarded by an AOA-accredited institution and be enrolled in an internship, residency, or research fellowship; or an undergraduate osteopathic medical student enrolled in an AOA-accredited institution.
Amount $5000 stipend
Date(s) Application Is Due Mar 15.
Contact Elizabeth Freeman, Division of Research Develoopment, (800) 621-1773 ext 8006; fax: (312) 202-8200; email: research@osteopathic.org
Internet http://www.do-online.osteotech.org/index.cfm?PageID=res_grant
Sponsor American Osteopathic Association
142 E Ontario St
Chicago, IL 60611-2864

AOA Osteopathic Research Grants **617**
Grants support projects investigating problems of a biological nature that will lead to a better understanding and a more effective application of the principles and concepts of osteopathic medicine. Grants are supported by AOA and the A.T. Still Osteopathic Foundation and Research Institute and administered by the foundation at the same address.
Requirements Grants are made to qualified AOA-accredited, -affiliated, or -approved osteopathic institutions, not to individuals. Osteopathic physicians having the DO degree who are at non-osteopathic-accredited, -affiliated, or -approved institutions are also

eligible to apply. Grantee must operate within an established institutional research program.
Amount $25,000-$50,000 average per year
Date(s) Application Is Due Dec 1.
Contact Elizabeth Freeman, Division of Research Development, (800) 621-1773 ext 8006; email: research@osteopathic.org
Internet http://www.do-online.osteotech.org/index.cfm?PageID=res_grant
Sponsor American Osteopathic Association
142 E Ontario St
Chicago, IL 60611-2864

AOA-Burnett Osteopathic Student Research Award 618
AOA offers this annual award in recognition of a student of osteopathic medicine for the most outstanding concept paper pertaining to an osteopathic-oriented research proposal. The award consists of an all-expense paid trip to the association's research conference plus a cash award and submittal of the paper to the Journal of the American Osteopathic Association for possible publication.
Requirements Eligibility is limited to students enrolled in AOA-accredited colleges of osteopathic medicine.
Amount $100 plus all-expense paid trip to research conference
Date(s) Application Is Due Apr 1.
Contact Elizabeth Freeman, Division of Research Development, (800) 621-1773 ext 8006; fax: (312) 202-8200; email: research@osteopathic.org
Internet http://www.do-online.osteotech.org/index.cfm?PageID=res_grant
Sponsor American Osteopathic Association
142 E Ontario St
Chicago, IL 60611-2864

AORN Foundation Scholarships 619
AORN scholarships provide funds for tuition and registration fees to members enrolled in baccalaureate, master's, and doctoral degree programs. Payment is made directly to the educational institution. The scholarships are granted for a one-year period; reapplication for funds is required annually through a new application and all supporting documents. An applicant must submit evidence of acceptance or enrollment in the particular program with specific information in support of accreditation status and a school catalog description of course of study; a personal statement reflecting contributions in nursing practice, research, and/or education; an official AORN scholarship application; official school transcripts; and three personal reference letters.
Requirements Applicants must be RNs and currently active or associate members of AORN in good standing; membership must have been maintained continuously for 12 months prior to application deadline. Applicants must maintain a cumulative GPA of 3.0.
Restrictions Members of the national board of directors during their elected terms, the scholarship board, and AORN headquarters personnel are ineligible. It is not possible to combine an AORN scholarship with a federal nurse traineeship or other total funding awards; other nonconflicting one-time only scholarships received by an applicant will not affect the funds of an AORN scholarship.
Amount $500 minimum
Date(s) Application Is Due May 1.
Contact Ingrid Bendzsa, (800) 755-2676 ext 328; fax: (303) 755-4219; email: ibendzsa@aorn.org
Internet http://www.aorn.org/foundation/scholarship.htm
Sponsor Association of Operating Room Nurses Foundation
2170 S Parker Rd, Ste 300
Denver, CO 80231-5711

AOS Research Grants 620
Research grants are awarded for experimental projects and applied and fundamental research pertaining to orchids. Support is given in biological research including taxonomy, genetics, cytogenetics, physiology, and pathology as well as in conservation and education. The society wishes to further the study of orchids in every aspect including their classification, evolution, conservation, propagation, culture, care, and development. As a first step, prospective applicants should submit a brief letter requesting an application form and instructions for requesting a grant. Grants are usually awarded for one year, possibly renewable, but not to exceed a maximum of three years. Grants received by January 1 are reviewed at the Spring Trustees Meeting and those grants received by July 1 are reviewed at the Fall Trustees Meeting
Requirements Graduate students or other qualified research personnel associated with accredited institutions of higher learning or appropriate research institutes may apply.
Amount $500-$12,000
Date(s) Application Is Due Jan 1; Jul 1.
Contact Pamela Giust, (561) 404-2000; fax (561) 404-2045; email: pgiust@aos.org
Internet http://www.theaos.org/aos/research/research.aspx?sec=2
Sponsor American Orchid Society
16700 AOS Ln
Delray Beach, FL 33446-4351

APA Congressional Fellowships 621
The fellowships afford an opportunity for the recipient psychologists to participate in the policy-making process of the US Congress. Trained scientists and practitioners work with the staff members of Congress or congressional committees and are involved in the process of relating social and behavioral science to public policy. The fellowships are sponsored by APA in cooperation with American Association for the Advancement of Science (AAAS). The fellowship is for a period of one year beginning in September. Application consists of curriculum vita, statement of interest, and three letters of reference.
Requirements Applicants must have a doctorate in psychology and be members of APA. Persons who are receiving sabbatical funds are also eligible to apply.
Amount $55,000-$70,000 plus up to $3500 toward relocation expenses
Date(s) Application Is Due Jan 2.
Contact APA Public Policy Office, (202) 336-6062; email: ppo@apa.org
Internet http://www.apa.org/ppo/funding/congfell.html
Sponsor American Psychological Association
750 First St NE
Washington, DC 20002-4242

APA Culture of Service in the Psychological Sciences Award 622
The Award recognizes departments that demonstrate a commitment to service in the psychological sciences. Departments selected for this award will show a pattern of support for service from faculty at all levels, including a demonstration that service to the discipline is rewarded in faculty tenure and promotion. Successful Departments will also demonstrate that service to the profession is an integral part of training and mentoring. Service to the discipline includes such activities as departmental release time for serving on boards and committees of psychological associations; editing journals; serving on a review panel; or chairing an IRB. Other culture of service activities that a department would encourage include mentoring students and colleagues; advocating for psychological science's best interests with state and federal lawmakers; and promoting the value of psychological science in the public eye. The focus of this award is a department's faculty service to the discipline and not their scholarly achievements. Both Undergraduate and Graduate Departments of Psychology are eligible. Self-nominations are encouraged.
Amount $5,000
Date(s) Application Is Due May 20.
Contact Suzanne Wandersman, Director for Governance Affairs, (202) 336-6000; fax: (202) 336-5953; email: swandersman@apa.org
Internet http://www.apa.org/science/dept_award.html
Sponsor American Psychological Association
750 First Street, NE
Washington, DC 20002-4242

APA Dissertation Research Awards 623
Dissertation awards are granted to graduate students in psychology programs to help offset the costs associated with dissertation research. The research may be done in any area of psychology. Applicants who have already defended their dissertations are eligible to apply for these funds, as long as they have not yet received doctoral degrees as of the application deadline. APA provides dissertation research awards to approximately 50 students annually. Dissertations must be approved by the students' committees before application. The application deadline falls in mid-September of each year. Awards are announced in late December.
Requirements APA student affiliates enrolled in a psychology graduate program are eligible to apply.
Restrictions Departments may not nominate more than three students per year for dissertation awards.
Amount $1000, $3000, $5000
Date(s) Application Is Due Sep 15.
Contact APA Science Directorate, (202) 336-6000; fax: (202) 336-5953; email: science@apa.org
Internet http://www.apa.org/science/dissinfo.html
Sponsor American Psychological Association
750 First St NE
Washington, DC 20002-4242

APA Distinguished Scientific Award for Early Career Contribution to Psychology 624
The Distinguished Scientific Award for Early Career Contribution to Psychology recognizes excellent young psychologists. Nominations of persons who received doctoral degrees during and since 1998 are being sought in these five areas: animal learning and behavior, comparative; cognition/human learning; developmental psychology; health; and psychopathology. These categories should be interpreted broadly and are not meant to be exclusive; all of psychology is of sufficient merit to be considered for awards. The Award consists of a citation and a cash prize, which are presented at the APA Annual Convention.
Date(s) Application Is Due Jun 1.
Contact Suzanne Wandersman, Director for Governance Affairs, (202) 336-6000; fax: (202) 336-5953; email: swandersman@apa.org
Internet http://www.apa.org/science/sciaward.html
Sponsor American Psychological Association
750 First Street, NE
Washington, DC 20002-4242

APA Distinguished Scientific Award for the Applications of Psychology 625

The Distinguished Scientific Award for the Applications of Psychology honors psychologists who have made distinguished theoretical or empirical advances in psychology leading to the understanding or amelioration of important practical problems. The Award consists of a citation and a cash prize, which are presented at the APA Annual Convention.
Date(s) Application Is Due Jun 1.
Contact Suzanne Wandersman, Director for Governance Affairs, (202) 336-6000; fax: (202) 336-5953; email: swandersman@apa.org
Internet http://www.apa.org/science/sciaward.html
Sponsor American Psychological Association
750 First Street, NE
Washington, DC 20002-4242

APA Distinguished Scientific Contribution Award 626

The Distinguished Scientific Contribution Award honors psychologists who have made distinguished theoretical or empirical contributions to basic research in psychology. The Award consists of a citation and a cash prize, which are presented at the APA Annual Convention.
Date(s) Application Is Due Jun 1.
Contact Suzanne Wandersman, Director for Governance Affairs, (202) 336-6000; fax: (202) 336-5953; email: swandersman@apa.org
Internet http://www.apa.org/science/sciaward.html
Sponsor American Psychological Association
750 First Street, NE
Washington, DC 20002-4242

APA Distinguished Service to Psychological Science Award 627

This Award recognizes individuals who have made outstanding contributions to psychological science through their commitment to a culture of service. Award recipients will receive an honorarium of $1,000. Nominees will have demonstrated their service to the discipline by aiding in association governance; serving on boards, committees and various psychological associations; editing journals; reviewing grant proposals; mentoring students and colleagues; advocating for psychological science's best interests with state and federal lawmakers; and promoting the value of psychological science in the public eye. Nominees may be involved in one service area, many of the areas, or all of the service areas noted above. An individual's service to the discipline and not a person's scholarly achievements are the focus of this award.
Amount $1,000
Date(s) Application Is Due May 20.
Contact Suzanne Wandersman, Director for Governance Affairs, (202) 336-6000; fax: (202) 336-5953; email: swandersman@apa.org
Internet http://www.apa.org/science/serv_award.html
Sponsor American Psychological Association
750 First Street, NE
Washington, DC 20002-4242

APA Minority Predoctoral and Postdoctoral Fellowship Programs in Neuroscience 628

The pre- and postdoctoral fellowship programs in neuroscience are designed to increase the number of ethnic and racial minorities who complete the doctorate in neuroscience. Benefits for the predoctoral program include: financial support for a period of up to three years; travel funds to visit universities being considered for graduate training and to attend the Society for Neuroscience annual meeting; summer training at the Marine Biological Laboratory in Woods Hole, MA. Benefits for the postdoctoral program include: financial support for up to two years; travel funds to visit laboratories being considered for postdoctoral research and to attend the Society for Neuroscience annual meeting; summer training at the Marine Biological Laboratory in Woods Hole, MA, and also at the McDonnell Foundation Summer Institute in Cognitive Neuroscience at Dartmouth College. Training for both programs includes: behavioral neurobiology, cellular neurobiology, developmental neurobiology, membrane biophysics, molecular neurobiology, neuroanatomy, neurobiology of aging, neuroimmunology, neuropathology, neuropharmacology, neurophysiology, and neurotoxicology. Postdoctoral training also includes neurochemistry and neurogenetics.
Requirements Eligible for fellowships are US citizens and permanent visa residents including, but not limited to, those who are African American, Hispanic, Native American, Alaskan Native, Asian American, and Pacific Islander and those who show an interest in and commitment to careers in neuroscience research. For the predoctoral program, applicants must be enrolled in a full-time doctoral program. For the postdoctoral program, applicants must hold a PhD or MD degree, and have prior graduate training either in neuroscience or in other basic science disciplines.
Date(s) Application Is Due Jan 15.
Contact Dr. James Jones, Director, Minority Fellowship Program, (202) 336-6127; fax: (202) 336-6012; email: jjones@apa.org
Internet http://www.apa.org/mfp/pdprogram.html
Sponsor American Psychological Association
750 First St NE
Washington, DC 20002-4242

APA Minority Research Training Fellowships in Psychology 629

The APA minority research training fellowships, funded by the National Institutes of Mental Health and administered by APA, are geared to those pursuing careers as research scientists on mental health issues related to minority populations. Students specializing in such research areas as developmental, physiological, experimental, social, industrial/organizational, quantitative, and educational psychology are encouraged to apply, as are students of any other specialty in psychology if they plan careers in research.
Requirements Applicants must be US citizens or permanent visa residents; be enrolled in a full-time academic program leading to a doctoral degree by the time the fellowship is awarded; and be members of an ethnic minority group, including, but not limited to, Hispanics, Native Americans, Alaskan Natives, African Americans, Asian Americans, Pacific Islanders, and/or demonstrate a commitment to careers in psychology related to ethnic minority mental health.
Restrictions Students of clinical and counseling psychology are ineligible.
Date(s) Application Is Due Jan 15.
Contact Dr. James Jones, Program Director, (202) 336-6127; fax: (202) 336-6012; email: jjones@apa.org
Internet http://www.apa.org/mfp/rprogram.html
Sponsor American Psychological Association
750 First St NE
Washington, DC 20002-4242

APA Planning Fellowships 630

The goals of this program are both to encourage students of certain minority backgrounds to enter the planning profession and to help such students who would otherwise be unable to continue their studies in planning. The exact amount of the awards offered is contingent upon the number and qualifications of the applicants. The program is open to first- and second-year students; first-year students who receive fellowships are eligible to compete for an award the following year as well.
Requirements Eligible to apply are US or Canadian citizens who are African Americans, Hispanics, or Native Americans currently enrolled or accepted for enrollment in a PAB-accredited graduate planning program. Applicants must document their need for financial assistance.
Amount $1000-$5000
Date(s) Application Is Due Apr 30.
Contact Kriss Blank, Leadership Affairs Associate, Scholarships and Fellowships, (312) 786-6722 or (312) 431-9100; fax: (312) 431-9985; email: kblank@planning.org or fellowship@planning.org
Internet http://www.planning.org/institutions/scholarship.htm
Sponsor American Planning Association
122 S Michigan Ave, Ste 1600
Chicago, IL 60603

APA Scientific Conferences Grants 631

The program seeks proposals for research conferences in psychology. The purpose of this program is to promote the exchange of important new contributions and approaches in scientific psychology. Conference formats include festschrifts--conferences organized as tributes to distinguished scholars; stand-alone conferences--usually two days long, involves psychologists as the primary organizers; and add-a-day conference--meetings that occur at the beginning or end of a scientific conference other than APA (e.g., Society for Ingestive Behavior or Psychonomics Society). The conference must also be supported by the host institution with direct funds, in-kind support, or a combination of the two.
Requirements One of the primary organizers must be a member of APA. Only academic institutions accredited by a regional body may apply. Independent research institutions must provide evidence of affiliation with such an accredited institution. Joint proposals from cooperating institutions are encouraged. Conferences may be held only in the United States, its possessions, or Canada.
Restrictions APA governance groups, APA divisions, and related entities are not eligible for funding under this program.
Amount $500-$20,000
Date(s) Application Is Due Jun 1; Dec 1.
Contact Deborah McCall, Science Directorate, (202) 336-6000; fax: (202) 336-5953; email: dmccall@apa.org
Internet http://www.apa.org/science/confer2.html
Sponsor American Psychological Association
750 First St NE
Washington, DC 20002-4242

APA Young Investigator Grant Program 632

The program provides financial support to teaching, research, and health care delivery projects in general pediatrics. The number of awards is dependent on available funds and the size of grant requests of selected projects. Proposals should address the goal of the association: to encourage, promote, and facilitate improved patient care, teaching, and research in general pediatrics.
Requirements The principal investigator must be a member of the APA or have submitted an application for membership. Preference will be given to new investigators, including those in training.
Restrictions Multiple year funding requests will not be considered.
Amount $10,000 maximum
Date(s) Application Is Due Jan 30; Nov 15.

Contact Grants Administrator, (703) 556-9222; fax: (703)556-8729; email: info@ambpeds.org
Internet http://www.ambpeds.org/youn-invest-grant.cfm
Sponsor Ambulatory Pediatric Association
6728 Old McLean Village Dr
McLean, VA 22101

APF Call for Proposals **633**
The program is intended to fund public education programs, as well as information and outreach initiatives that promote the early recognition and treatment of mental illness. Up to $750,000 in grant funds are available over the course of three years. Average grants are in the $50,000 range. Grant making under this program has been temporarily suspended while a new Call for Proposals is being developed. Please check back in mid-July 2007 for more details.
Requirements Organizations that have been in existence for at least two years and currently maintain a 501(c)3 charitable status and American Psychiatric Association District Branches and subsidiaries. Organizations need not be mental health programs.
Amount $50,000 average
Contact Barbara Matos, (703) 907-8517; email: bmatos@psych.org
Internet http://www.psychfoundation.org/call_for_proposals.cfm
Sponsor American Psychiatric Foundation
1000 Wilson Blvd., Suite 1825
Arlington, VA 22209-3901

APF James H. Scully Jr., M.D., Educational Fund Grants **634**
The fund supports education and research within the APA, its subsidiary organizations, or affiliated organizations, including district branches, state associations, or other psychiatric organizations that are in partnership with the APA. The fund can be used to support education and research activities that improve the quality of care for patients with mental illness, advance the prevention of mental illness, raise awareness of mental illness and its treatments, and increase access to mental health services. The fund will not support public policy or lobbying activities. Requests for funding should be sent in writing to the foundation and include the following: identification and significance of need; description of program/activity to address that need; expected outcomes and evaluation process; budget and timeline; and background of key project personnel. Funding decisions are made by the foundation's board of directors.
Contact Barbara Matos, (703) 907-8517; email: bmatos@psych.org
Internet http://www.psychfoundation.org/scully.cfm
Sponsor American Psychiatric Foundation
1000 Wilson Blvd., Suite 1825
Arlington, VA 22209-3901

APF Jeanne Spurlock Congressional Fellowship **635**
The fellowship provides general psychiatry and child psychiatry residents an opportunity to work in a congressional office or committee on federal health policy, particularly policy related to child and minority issues. The recipient will serve a six-month fellowship starting January 1 and ending June 30. The fellow will be introduced to the structure and development of federal and congressional health policy, with a focus on mental health issues affecting children and minorities. Fellows traditionally help develop legislative proposals, track and analyze legislative initiatives, arrange hearings, brief congressmen or congresswomen and staff, and interact with constituents. During the fellowship, recipients have opportunities to interact with health policymakers and advocacy/professional groups, including the American Psychiatric Association. The recipient will be required to submit a written summary of her or his experience at the end of the fellowship and provide recommendations or suggestions for improving the fellowship. Applications must include a current curriculum vita; three letters of recommendation; one- or two-page essay giving the reasons for applying for this fellowship, including any past educational and/or political experience that would enhance performance as a fellow; and a detailed letter (no more than two typed pages) from the department chairperson or training director delineating the candidate's qualifications and describing any plans the institution may have for using the experience to be gained. Each fellow will receive a stipend, which may be supplemented by the fellow's institution, and reimbursement for moving expenses to and from Washington, DC. Guidelines are available online. Annual deadline dates may vary; contact program staff for exact dates.
Requirements PGY-II and III general psychiatry residents, child psychiatry residents, or child psychiatrists who will be out of training for less than one year at the time of the fellowship may apply. Applicants must be US citizens or permanent residents. Applications, in the form of a letter to the APA, must be received by March 9 in order to be considered.
Amount $35,000 stipend; $2500 maximum moving expenses
Date(s) Application Is Due Mar 9.
Contact Marilyn King, (703) 907-8653; email: mking@psych.org
Internet http://www.psychfoundation.org/spurlock.cfm
Sponsor American Psychiatric Foundation
1000 Wilson Blvd, Suite 1825
Arlington,VA 22209-3901

APHA Fellowship in Printing History **636**
The fellowship is awarded for research in any area of the history of printing in all its forms, including all the arts and technologies relevant to printing, the book arts, and letter forms. The subject of research has no geographical or chronological limitations, and may be national or regional in scope, biographical, analytical, technical, or bibliographical in nature. Printing history-related study with a recognized printer or book artist may also be supported. The fellowship can be used to pay for travel, living, and other expenses.
Amount $2000 maximum
Date(s) Application Is Due Dec 10.
Contact Stephen Crook, Executive Secretary, email: sgcrook@printinghistory.org
Internet http://printinghistory.org/htm/fellowship/2005.html
Sponsor American Printing History Association
P.O. Box 4519, Grand Central Sta
New York, NY 10163-4519

APhA Foundation Incentive Grants **637**
The incentive grants provide seed funding to help pharmacists in all practice settings explore new methods and services that enhance their role as pharmaceutical care providers, and to encourage them to share their experiences with other pharmacists. This year, the incentive grants program will continue to expand to include project proposals specifically for pharmacists interested in establishing or supporting an already existing practice model in the area of pain management. Projects should concentrate on new, innovative patient care service that is of significance to pharmacy care settings and that can be evaluated for its relevance. Application and guidelines are available online.
Requirements Applicants must be members of APhA, currently licensed, and actively engaged in ambulatory pharmacy practice. Recipients are encouraged to attend the APhA annual meeting and submit present findings, if applicable.
Restrictions Indirect costs will not be funded. Salaries for recipients are not funded; however, consultant fees, fees for reseach/technician services, and expenses for adminsitrative services may be allowable if essential if essential to development/implementation of the project.
Amount $1000
Date(s) Application Is Due Oct 3.
Contact Grants Administrator, email: info@aphafoundation.org
Internet http://www.aphafoundation.org/IncentiveGrants/incentive.htm
Sponsor American Pharmacists Association
2215 Constitution Ave NW
Washington, DC 20037-2985

APHA Youth Development Foundation Grants **638**
The Youth Development Foundation is a nonprofit corporation established in 1980 by the American Paint Horse Association (APHA). The YDF provides grants for equine research on topics such as the lethal white syndrome in foals and the genetic basis of Paint Horse coat patterns. YDF also annually presents scholarships of up to $1000 per year to young horsemen and women who are pursuing their educational goals at a college or university. Deadline listed is for scholarships. Guidelines and application are available online.
Requirements Scholarship applicants must be participants in the American Junior Paint Horse Association, demonstrate potential for continued achievement, and excel academically. Heavy consideration is also given to students with financial need. Contact the foundation for requirements for research grant applicants.
Restrictions Children of the YDF board or the executive committee board are ineligible.
Amount $1000 scholarships
Date(s) Application Is Due Mar 1.
Contact Program Contact, (817) 834-2742; fax: (817) 834-3152; email: askapha@apha.com
Internet http://www.apha.com/ydf/ydfscholarships.html
Sponsor American Paint Horse Association
P.O. Box 961023
Fort Worth, TX 76161-0023

Appalachian Regional Development Program and Research Grants **639**
Program grants and research grants are funded to stimulate substantial public investments in public services and facilities that will attract private sector investments and start the region on its way toward accelerated social and economic development; to help establish a set of institutions in Appalachia capable of permanently directing the long-term development of the region; and on a joint federal-state-local basis, to develop comprehensive plans and programs to help accomplish overall objectives of Appalachian development, including meeting the special demands created by the nation's energy needs and policies.
Requirements States, and through states, public bodies and private nonprofit organizations are eligible to apply.
Contact Executive Director, (202) 884-7700
Internet http://www.arc.gov/index.do?nodeId=101
Sponsor Appalachian Regional Commission
1666 Connecticut Ave NW
Washington, DC 20235

Applied Biosystems Grants **640**
The company is committed to the communities where its employees live and work. Financial contributions as well as in-kind and product donations are awarded to nonprofit organizations. The focus is on education, health and human services, community outreach

programs, environment, arts & culture, and civic. Precollege, college, graduate, and other unique programs that use technology to improve science, math, and engineering education are education programs supported. Organizations providing access to quality health care facilities and innovative solutions to chronic problems through disease and therapeutic research are supported. Outreach programs and civic groups that improve communities with innovative science, technology, and education are supported. Programs maintaining a healthy environment, arts and culture, and civic programs are also supported. Requests are accepted at any time.
Requirements Nonprofit organizations in communities where Applied Biosystems has operations are eligible.
Contact Applied Biosystems, (800) 327-3002 or (650) 638-5800; fax: (650) 638-5998
Internet http://www.appliedbiosystems.com/about/community.cfm
Sponsor Applied Biosystems
850 Lincoln Centre Dr
Foster City, CA 94404

Appraisal Institute Education Trust Scholarships **641**
Graduate and undergraduate scholarships are offered to students majoring in programs in land economics, real estate, real estate appraising, or allied fields. The scholarships are awarded on the basis of scholarly qualities and are intended to help finance the cost of college work leading to a degree in one of the aforementioned professional fields. The institute also awards scholarships to minority and women college students pursuing academic degrees in real estate appraisal or related fields. Application forms must be obtained from the institute.
Requirements Applicants must be sophomores, juniors, seniors, or graduates, as well as US citizens.
Amount $2000 undergraduate; $3000 graduate
Date(s) Application Is Due Mar 15.
Contact Olivia Carreon, Project Coordinator, (312) 335-4100; fax: (312) 335-4400; email: ocarreon@appraisalinstitute.org
Internet http://www.appraisalinstitute.org/education/scolarshp.asp
Sponsor Appraisal Institute Education Trust
550 W Van Buren St., Ste 1000
Chicago, IL 60607

APS Andreas Acrivos Dissertation Award in Fluid Dynamics **642**
The program provides recognition to exceptional young scientists who have performed original doctoral thesis work of outstanding scientific quality and achievement in the area of fluid dynamics. The annual award consists of monetary prize, a certificate citing the accomplishments of the recipient, and an allowance for travel to attend the annual meeting of the Division of Fluid Dynamics at which the award will be presented. Each nominee will be considered in not more than two consecutive cycles. Nomination guidelines are available online.
Requirements Nominations will be accepted for any doctoral student studying at a college or university in the United States or in a education abroad program of a college or university in the United States. The work to be considered must have been accomplished as part of the requirements for a doctoral degree. Nominees must have completed their dissertations during the previous calendar year, or by March 31 of the year of the award, at a university within the United States.
Amount $1000 award; $1500 maximum travel allowance
Date(s) Application Is Due May 1.
Contact Dissertation Administrator, (301) 209-3200; fax: (301) 209-0865; email: honors@aps.org
Internet http://www.aps.org/praw/acrivos/index.cfm
Sponsor American Physical Society
One Physics Ellipse
College Park, MD 20740-3844

APS Aneesur Rahman Prize for Computational Physics **643**
The annual prize recognizes and encourages outstanding achievement in computational physics research. The award consists of a monetary prize, an allowance for travel to the meeting of the society at which the prize is awarded and at which the recipient will deliver the Rahman Lecture, and a certificate citing the contributions made by the recipient. The prize ordinarily is awarded to one person, but a prize may be shared when all recipients have contributed to the same accomplishments. Nominations are active for three years. Nomination guidelines are available online.
Requirements Nominations are open to scientists of all nationalities regardless of the geographical site at which the work was done.
Amount $5000
Date(s) Application Is Due Jul 1.
Contact Prize Administrator, (301) 209-3200; fax: (301) 209-0865; email: honors@aps.org
Internet http://www.aps.org/praw/rahman/index.cfm
Sponsor American Physical Society
One Physics Ellipse
College Park, MD 20740-3844

APS Arthur L. Schawlow Prize in Laser Science **644**
The prize recognizes outstanding contributions to basic research that uses lasers to advance knowledge of the fundamental physical properties of materials and their interaction with light. Some examples of relevant areas of research are: nonlinear optics, ultrafast phenomena, laser spectroscopy, squeezed states, quantum optics, multiphoton physics, laser cooling and trapping, physics of lasers, particle acceleration by lasers, and short wavelength lasers. The award consists of a monetary prize plus an allowance for travel to the meeting at which the prize is awarded and a certificate citing the contributions made by the recipient. Nominations are active for three years. Nomination guidelines are available online.
Requirements Nominations are open to candidates who have made outstanding contributions to basic research using lasers.
Amount $10,000
Date(s) Application Is Due Jul 1.
Contact Prize Administrator, (301) 209-3200; fax: (301) 209-0865; email: honors@aps.org
Internet http://www.aps.org/praw/schawlow/index.cfm
Sponsor American Physical Society
One Physics Ellipse
College Park, MD 20740-3844

APS Biological Physics Prize **645**
The prize recognizes and encourages outstanding achievement in biological physics research. The prize consists of a monetary prize, an allowance for travel to attend the meeting at which the prize is awarded, and a certificate citing the contributions made by the recipient or recipients. It will be presented biennially in even-numbered years. The prize may be awarded to more than one investigator on a shared basis. Nominations are active for three years. Nomination guidelines are available online.
Requirements Nominations are open to scientists of all nationalities regardless of the geographical site at which the work was done.
Amount $5000
Date(s) Application Is Due Jul 1.
Contact Prize Administrator, (301) 209-3200; fax: (301) 209-0865; email: honors@aps.org
Internet http://www.aps.org/praw/biologic/index.cfm
Sponsor American Physical Society
One Physics Ellipse
College Park, MD 20740-3844

APS Daland Fellowships in Clinical Investigation **646**
A limited number of fellowships are awarded annually for research in clinical medicine including the fields of internal medicine, neurology, psychiatry, pediatrics, and surgery. Patient-oriented research is emphasized. Essentially 100 percent of the fellow's time will be devoted to research. Teaching or clinical service of a limited amount is permitted. Additional salary may be granted by the institution at which the fellow is located, from another fellowship, or from a similar award during the tenure of the fellowship. The term of the fellowship is one year, with possible renewal for another year. Applications are available on the Web site, or may be obtained by written request, stating when the MD or MD/PhD degree was awarded; include a self-addressed mailing label. Telephone requests for forms cannot be honored.
Requirements These fellowships are designed for qualified persons who have held an MD, or MD/PhD degree for less than eight years. The fellowship is generally intended to be the first post-clinical fellowship; but each case will be decided on its merits. Preference is generally given to candidates who have not more than two years of post-doctoral training and research. Applicants must expect to perform their research at an institution in the United States, under the supervision of a scientific adviser. Candidates are to be nominated by their department chairman, in a letter providing assurance that the nominee will work with the guidance of a scientific adviser of established reputation who has guaranteed adequate space, supplies, etc. for the Fellow. The adviser need not be a member of the department nominating the Fellow, nor need the activities of the Fellow be limited to the nominating department. As a general rule, no more than one fellowship will be awarded to a given institution in the same year of competition.
Restrictions The society does not provide funds for institutional overhead.
Amount $50,000 per year for up to two years
Date(s) Application Is Due Sep 1.
Contact Fellowships Administrator, (215) 440-3429; email: eroach@amphilsoc.org
Internet http://www.amphilsoc.org/grants/daland.htm
Sponsor American Philosophical Society
104 S Fifth St
Philadelphia, PA 19106-3387

APS Dannie Heineman Prize for Mathematical Physics **647**
The annual prize recognizes outstanding publications in the field of mathematical physics. The award consists of a monetary prize and a certificate citing the contributions made by the recipient plus travel expenses to attend the meeting at which the prize is bestowed. The prize may be awarded to more than one person on a shared basis when all recipients have contributed to the same accomplishments. Nominations are active for three years. Nomination guidelines are available online.
Requirements This prize is awarded solely for valuable published contributions made in the field of mathematical physics with no restrictions placed on a candidate's citizenship or country of residence. Publication is defined as either a single paper, a series of papers, a book, or any other communication that can be considered a publication.
Amount $7500

Date(s) Application Is Due Jul 1.
Contact Prize Administrator, (301) 209-3200; fax: (301) 209-0865; email: honors@aps.org
Internet http://www.aps.org/praw/heineman/index.cfm
Sponsor American Physical Society
One Physics Ellipse
College Park, MD 20740-3844

APS Davisson-Germer Prize in Atomic or Surface Physics 648
The prize recognizes and encourages outstanding work in atomic physics or surface physics. The award consists of a monetary prize and a certificate citing the contributions made by the recipient or recipients. This prize will normally be awarded in even-numbered years for outstanding work in atomic physics and odd-numbered years for outstanding work in surface physics. The prize ordinarily is awarded to one person but may be shared when all recipients have contributed to the same accomplishments. Nominations are active for three cycles. Nomination guidelines are available online.
Requirements Nominations are open to scientists of all nationalities regardless of the geographical site at which the work was done.
Amount $5000
Date(s) Application Is Due Jul 1.
Contact Prize Administrator, (301) 209-3200; fax: (301) 209-0865; email: honors@aps.org
Internet http://www.aps.org/praw/davisson/index.cfm
Sponsor American Physical Society
One Physics Ellipse
College Park, MD 20740-3844

APS Dissertation Award in Nuclear Physics 649
The program recognizes a recent PhD in nuclear physics. The annual award consists of a monetary stipend and an allowance for travel to the annual Spring Meeting of the Division of Nuclear Physics of the American Physical Society, where the award will be presented. Nomination guidelines are available online.
Requirements Nominations are open to any person who has received a PhD degree in experimental or theoretical nuclear physics from a North American university within the two-year period preceding September 1 of the current year.
Amount $2000
Date(s) Application Is Due Jul 1.
Contact Program Administrator, (301) 209-3200; fax: (301) 209-0865; email: honors@apes.org
Internet http://www.aps.org/praw/dissnucl/index.cfm
Sponsor American Physical Society
One Physics Ellipse
College Park, MD 20740-3844

APS Earle K. Plyler Prize for Molecular Spectroscopy 650
The annual prize recognizes and encourages notable contributions to the field of molecular spectroscopy. The prize may be given for experimental or theoretical achievements, for a single dramatic innovation, or for a series of research contributions which, when integrated, amounts to a major contribution to the field of molecular spectroscopy. The award consists of a monetary prize, an allowance for travel expenses to attend the meeting at which the prize is to be presented, and a certificate citing the contributions made by the recipient. The prize ordinarily is awarded to one person, but a prize may be shared when all the recipients have contributed to the same accomplishments. Nominations are active for three years. Nomination guidelines are available online.
Requirements Nominations are open to scientists in North America.
Amount $10,000
Date(s) Application Is Due Jul 1.
Contact Prize Administrator, (301) 209-3200; fax: (301) 209-0865; email: honors@aps.org
Internet http://www.aps.org/praw/plyler/index.cfm
Sponsor American Physical Society
One Physics Ellipse
College Park, MD 20740-3844

APS Einstein Prize 651
The prize recognizes outstanding accomplishments in the field of gravitational physics. The award consists of a monetary prize and a certificate citing the contributions of the recipient. It also includes an allowance for the recipient to travel to a meeting of the society to receive the award and deliver a lecture. It will be awarded biennially. The award, usually to a single individual, is for outstanding achievement in theory, experiment, or observation in the area of gravitational physics. Nominations will remain active for three years. Nomination guidelines are available online.
Requirements Scientists worldwide are eligible for nomination.
Restrictions Members of the Topical Group on Gravitation Executive Committee are not eligible for nomination while sitting on the committee.
Amount $10,000
Date(s) Application Is Due Jul 1.
Contact Prize Administrator, (301) 209-3200; fax: (301) 209-0865; email: honors@aps.org
Internet http://www.aps.org/praw/einstein/index.cfm
Sponsor American Physical Society
One Physics Ellipse
College Park, MD 20740-3844

APS Fluid Dynamics Prize 652
The annual prize recognizes and encourages outstanding achievement in fluid dynamics research. The award consists of an allowance for travel to the meeting at which the prize is awarded, and a certificate citing the contributions made by the recipient. This prize is awarded for outstanding contributions to fundamental fluid dynamics research. The prize ordinarily is awarded to one person but may be shared when all the recipients have contributed to the same achievement. Nominations are active for three years. Nomination guidelines are available online.
Amount $10,000
Date(s) Application Is Due Mar 31.
Contact Prize Administrator, (301) 209-3200; fax: (301) 209-0865; email: honors@aps.org
Internet http://www.aps.org/praw/fluid/index.cfm
Sponsor American Physical Society
One Physics Ellipse
College Park, MD 20740-3844

APS Foundation Grants 653
Grants are awarded to support Arizona nonprofit organizations in the areas of health and human services, community development, arts and culture, education, and environment. The foundation awards support for project grants, capital building funds, research, employee matching gifts, in-kind services, conferences and seminars, and operating support. Applications are accepted on an ongoing basis and are reviewed monthly.
Requirements Arizona 501(c)3 nonprofits are eligible.
Restrictions The foundation does not fund individuals or individual scholarships; religious, political, fraternal, legislative, or lobbying efforts; or travel or hotel expenses.
Contact Sandie Jones, Corporate Contributions, (602) 250-2257; fax: (602) 250-2113; email: sandie.jones@aps.com
Internet http://www.aps.com/general_info/aboutaps_14.html
Sponsor Arizona Public Service Foundation
P.O. Box 53999, MS 8510
Phoenix, AZ 85072-3999

APS Frank Isakson Prize for Optical Effects in Solids 654
The prize recognizes outstanding optical research that leads to breakthroughs in the condensed matter sciences. The award consists of a monetary prize, an allowance for travel to the meeting of the society at which the prize is being presented, and a certificate citing the contributions made by the recipient. The prize is awarded biennially in even-numbered years as a memorial to Frank Isakson. The prize ordinarily is awarded to one person, but the prize may be shared among recipients when all recipients have contributed to the same accomplishment. Preference will be given to work that has been published within the past 10 years. Nominations are active for three years. Nomination guidelines are available online.
Requirements Nominations are open to scientists of all nations regardless of the geographical site at which the work was done.
Amount $5000
Date(s) Application Is Due Jul 1.
Contact Prize Administrator, (301) 209-3200; fax: (301) 209-0865; email: honors@aps.org
Internet http://www.aps.org/praw/isakson/index.cfm
Sponsor American Physical Society
One Physics Ellipse
College Park, MD 20740-3844

APS Franklin Research Grants 655
The society awards small grants to scholars to support the cost of research leading to publication in all areas of knowledge. The program is particularly designed to help meet the costs of travel to libraries and archives for research purposes; the purchase of microfilm, photocopies, or equivalent research materials; the costs associated with fieldwork; or laboratory research expenses. Franklin grants are made for noncommercial research. They are not intended to meet the expenses of attending conferences or the costs of publication. The society is particularly interested in supporting the work of young scholars who have recently received their PhDs. Applicants who have received Franklin grants may reapply after an interval of two years. Applications and guidelines are available online.
Requirements Applicants are expected to have a doctorate, or to have published work of doctoral character and quality. American citizens and residents of the United States may use their Franklin awards at home or abroad. Foreign nationals must use their Franklin awards for research in the United States.
Restrictions Predoctoral graduate students are not eligible. The society does not pay overhead or indirect costs to any institution. Grants will not be made to replace salary during a leave of absence or earnings from summer teaching; pay living expenses while working at home; cover the costs of consultants or research assistants; or purchase permanent equipment such as computers, cameras, tape recorders, or laboratory apparatus.
Amount $6000 maximum

Date(s) Application Is Due Oct 1; Dec 1.
Contact Linda Musumeci, (215) 440-3429; email: LMusumeci@amphilsoc.org or
Internet http://www.amphilsoc.org/grants/franklin.htm
Sponsor American Philosophical Society
104 S Fifth St
Philadelphia, PA 19106-3387

APS George E. Pake Prize 656

The annual prize recognizes and encourages outstanding work by physicists combining original research accomplishments with leadership in the management of research or development in industry. The award consists of a monetary prize, an allowance for travel to the meeting at which the prize is to be awarded, and a certificate recognizing the contribution of the recipient. Nominations are active for three years. Nomination guidelines are available online.
Requirements This prize will be awarded to one individual for outstanding achievements in physics research combined with major success as a manager of research or development in industry.
Amount $5000
Date(s) Application Is Due Jul 1.
Contact Prize Administrator, (301) 209-3200; fax: (301) 209-0865; email: honors@aps.org
Internet http://www.aps.org/praw/pake/index.cfm
Sponsor American Physical Society
One Physics Ellipse
College Park, MD 20740-3844

APS George E. Valley, Jr., Prize 657

The prize recognizes one individual in the early stages of his or her career for an outstanding scientific contribution to physics that is deemed to have significant potential for a dramatic impact on the field. The award consists of a monetary award and a certificate citing the contribution made by the recipient. Nomination documents must include a statement from the nominator or from the candidate's department certifying the date of the candidate's PhD. The prize is awarded biennially. Nomination guidelines are available online.
Requirements The nominee must have received his/her PhD no earlier than five years before April 1 of the year of the nomination deadline. Work done by a graduate student for his/her thesis is eligible for consideration if it is demonstrated that the student's contributions have been crucial to an important piece of research.
Amount $20,000
Date(s) Application Is Due Jul 1.
Contact Prize Administrator, (301) 209-3200; fax: (301) 209-0865; email: honors@aps.org
Internet http://www.aps.org/praw/valley/index.cfm
Sponsor American Physical Society
One Physics Ellipse
College Park, MD 20740-3844

APS Hans A. Bethe Prize 658

To prize recognizes outstanding work in theory, experiment, or observation in the areas of astrophysics, nuclear physics, nuclear astrophysics, or closely related fields. The prize consists of a monetary prize and a certificate citing the contributions made by the recipient. It is presented annually. Nominations are active for three years. Nomination guidelines are available online.
Requirements This award is made annually to one individual for outstanding accomplishments in the areas of astrophysics, nuclear physics, nuclear astrophysics, or closely related fields. It is open to any scientist working in these areas, worldwide.
Amount $7500
Date(s) Application Is Due Jul 1.
Contact Prize Administrator, (301) 209-3200; fax: (301) 209-0865; email: honors@aps.org
Internet http://www.aps.org/praw/bethe/index.cfm
Sponsor American Physical Society
One Physics Ellipse
College Park, MD 20740-3844

APS Herbert P. Broida Prize 659

The prize recognizes and enhances outstanding experimental advancements in the fields of atomic and molecular spectroscopy or chemical physics. The prize consists of a monetary prize, an allowance for travel to the award ceremony, and a certificate citing the contributions made by the recipient. Preference will be granted to an individual whose contributions have displayed a high degree of breadth, originality, and creativity. Nominations are active for three years. Nomination guidelines are available online.
Requirements The prize is awarded to one individual in recognition of an outstanding contribution to the field of atomic and molecular spectroscopy or chemical physics. Emphasis will be given to work done within the five years prior to the awarding of the prize.
Amount $5000
Date(s) Application Is Due Jul 1.
Contact Prize Administrator, (301) 209-3200; fax: (301) 209-0865; email: honors@aps.org
Internet http://www.aps.org/praw/broida/index.cfm
Sponsor American Physical Society
One Physics Ellipse
College Park, MD 20740-3844

APS I.I. Rabi Prize in Atomic, Molecular, and Optical Physics 660

The prize recognizes and encourages outstanding research in atomic, molecular, and optical physics. It will be awarded in odd-numbered years. The award consists of a monetary prize and a certificate citing the contributions made by the recipient. An allowance will be provided for travel expenses of the recipient to the society meeting at which the prize is presented. The prize ordinarily is awarded to one person but may be shared when all recipients have contributed to the same accomplishment. Nominations are active for three years. Nomination guidelines are available online.
Requirements Nominations are open to scientists of all nationalities regardless of the geographical location at which the work was done. Investigators who have held a PhD for 10 years or less are eligible.
Amount $7500
Date(s) Application Is Due Jul 1.
Contact Prize Administrator, (301) 209-3200; fax: (301) 209-0865; email: honors@aps.org
Internet http://www.aps.org/praw/rabi/index.cfm
Sponsor American Physical Society
One Physics Ellipse
College Park, MD 20740-3844

APS Irving Langmuir Prize in Chemical Physics 661

The prize recognizes and encourages outstanding interdisciplinary research in chemistry and physics. This biennial prize consists of a monetary award and a certificate citing the contributions made by the recipient. In even-numbered years, the American Chemical Society selects the prize recipient and presents the prize. In odd-numbered years, the American Physical Society selects the prize recipient and presents the prize. An allowance is provided for travel expenses of the recipient to the meeting of the society at which the prize is to be bestowed. The prize is made to one person who has made an outstanding contribution in the field of chemical physics or physical chemistry within the 10 years prior to the prize. Nominations are active for three years. Nomination guidelines are available online.
Requirements The prize is granted without restriction, except that the recipient must be a resident of the United States at the time of selection and the prize funds must be used in the United States or its possessions.
Amount $10,000
Date(s) Application Is Due Jul 2.
Contact Prize Administrator, (301) 209-3200; fax: (301) 209-0865; email: honors@aps.org
Internet http://www.aps.org/praw/langmuir/index.cfm
Sponsor American Physical Society
One Physics Ellipse
College Park, MD 20740-3844

APS J. J. Sakurai Prize for Theoretical Particle Physics 662

The annual prize recognizes and encourages outstanding achievement in particle theory. The award consists of a monetary prize, an allowance for travel to the meeting of the society at which the prize is to be awarded, and a certificate citing the contributions made by the recipient. The prize may be awarded to more than one person on a shared basis. Nominations are active for three years. Nomination guidelines are available online.
Requirements Nominations are open to scientists of all nationalities regardless of the geographical site at which the work was done. The prize will normally be awarded for theoretical contributions made at an early stage of the recipients research career.
Amount $5000
Date(s) Application Is Due May 1.
Contact Prize Administrator, (301) 209-3200; fax: (301) 209-0865; email: honors@aps.org
Internet http://www.aps.org/praw/sakurai/index.cfm
Sponsor American Physical Society
One Physics Ellipse
College Park, MD 20740-3844

APS James C. McGroddy Prize for New Materials 663

To annual prize recognizes and encourages outstanding achievement in the science and application of new materials, including the discovery of new classes of materials, the observation of novel phenomena in known materials leading to both fundamentally new applications and scientific insights, as well as theoretical and experimental work contributing significantly to the understanding of such phenomena. The award consists of a monetary prize plus a certificate citing the contribution of the recipient and an allowance for travel to the meeting of the society at which the award is presented. Nominations are active for three years. Nomination guidelines are available online.
Requirements The prize is open to scientists of all nationalities irrespective of where their work has been carried out.
Amount $5000
Date(s) Application Is Due Jul 1.

Contact Prize Administrator, (301) 209-3200; fax: (301) 209-0865; email: honors@aps.org
Internet http://www.aps.org/praw/mcgroddy/index.cfm
Sponsor American Physical Society
One Physics Ellipse
College Park, MD 20740-3844

APS James Clerk Maxwell Prize for Plasma Physics **664**
The annual prize recognizes outstanding contributions to the field of plasma physics. The prize is made for outstanding contributions to the advancement and diffusion of the knowledge of properties of highly ionized gases of natural or laboratory origin. The award consists of a monetary prize and a certificate citing the contributions made by the recipient. A travel allowance to attend the meeting at which the prize is to be presented is also provided. The prize ordinarily is awarded to one person, but a prize may be shared when all the recipients have contributed to the same accomplishments. Nominations are active for three years. Nomination guidelines are available online
Amount $5000
Date(s) Application Is Due Apr 1.
Contact Prize Administrator, (301) 209-3200; fax: (301) 209-0865; email: honors@aps.org
Internet http://www.aps.org/praw/maxwell/index.cfm
Sponsor American Physical Society
One Physics Ellipse
College Park, MD 20740-3844

APS John Hope Franklin Dissertation Fellowship **665**
The fellowship is designed to support an outstanding African-American graduate student attending any PhD- granting institution in the United States, in any field of knowledge. There is no residential requirement. The fellowship stipend is for a 12-month award period, and the 12-month period is flexible.
Requirements Candidates must have completed all course work and examinations preliminary to the doctoral dissertation and be prepared to devote full time for 12 months--with no teaching obligations--to research on their dissertation projects or the writing of their dissertations.
Amount $25,000
Date(s) Application Is Due Apr 1.
Contact Linda Musumeci, (215) 440-3429; email: LMusumeci@amphilsoc.org
Internet http://www.amphilsoc.org/grants/johnhopefranklin.htm
Sponsor American Philosophical Society
104 S Fifth St
Philadelphia, PA 19106-3387

APS Julius Edgar Lilienfeld Prize **666**
The annual prize recognizes a most outstanding contribution to physics. The award consists of a monetary prize, a certificate citing the contributions made by the recipient, plus expenses for the three lectures by the recipient given at an APS meeting, a research university, and a predominantly undergraduate institution. Nominations are active for three years. Nomination guidelines are available online.
Requirements The prize is awarded for outstanding contributions to physics by a single individual who also has exceptional skills in lecturing to diverse audiences.
Amount $10,000
Date(s) Application Is Due Jul 1.
Contact Prize Administrator, (301) 209-3200; fax: (301) 209-0865; email: honors@aps.org
Internet http://www.aps.org/praw/lilienfe/index.cfm
Sponsor American Physical Society
One Physics Ellipse
College Park, MD 20740-3844

APS Lars Onsager Prize **667**
The prize recognizes outstanding research in theoretical statistical physics including the quantum fluids. The prize is open to researchers in statistical physics covering a wide range of physical phenomena, as long as the nominee is active at the time of the award. The award consists of a monetary prize as well as a certificate citing the contribution made by the recipient. Nominations are active for three years. Nomination guidelines are available online.
Requirements Nominations are accepted from all scientists of all nations regardless of geographical location.
Amount $15,000
Date(s) Application Is Due Jul 1.
Contact Prize Administrator, (301) 209-3200; fax: (301) 209-0865; email: honors@aps.org
Internet http://www.aps.org/praw/onsager/index.cfm
Sponsor American Physical Society
One Physics Ellipse
College Park, MD 20740-3844

APS Lewis and Clark Fund for Exploration and Field Research **668**
The program encourages exploratory field studies for the collection of specimens and data and to provide the imaginative stimulus that accompanies direct observation. Applications are invited from disciplines with a large dependence on field studies, such as archeology, anthropology, astrobiology and space science, biology, ecology, geography, geology, and paleontology, but grants will not be restricted to these fields. Budgets should be limited to travel and related expenses, including personal field equipment. Application and guidelines are available online.
Requirements Grants are available to graduate students, postdoctoral students, junior and senior scientists, and social scientists who wish to participate in field studies for their theses or for other purposes. A graduate student applicant should ask his or her academic supervisor or field trip leader to write one of the two letters of recommendation, specifying the role of the student in the field trip and the educational contribution of the trip. The competition is open to US residents wishing to carry out research anywhere in the world. Foreign applicants must either be based at a US institution or plan to carry out their work in the United States.
Restrictions Undergraduates are not eligible.
Amount $5000 maximum
Date(s) Application Is Due Mar 15.
Contact Linda Musumeci, Research Administrator, (215) 440-3429; email: LMusumeci@amphilsoc.org
Internet http://www.amphilsoc.org/grants/lewisandclark.htm
Sponsor American Philosophical Society
104 S Fifth St
Philadelphia, PA 19106-3387

APS Library Resident Research Fellowships **669**
Short-term residential fellowships encourage research in the library's collections. Outstanding historical collections and subject areas include the papers of Benjamin Franklin; the American Revolution; 18th- and 19th-century natural history; western scientific expeditions and travel including the journals of Lewis and Clark; polar exploration; the papers of Charles Wilson Peale, including family and descendants; history of genetics, eugenics, and evolution; history of biochemistry, physiology, and biophysics; 20th-century medical research; and history of physics. There is no special application form. Applicant should submit a letter (not to exceed three single-spaced pages) that briefly describes the project, states its specific relevance to the library's collections, and indicates the expected dates of residence. Also required are curriculum vita and one letter of reference (doctoral candidates must use their dissertation advisors). The term of the fellowship must be at least one month and no more than three months, taken between June 1 and May 31. Recipients are expected to be in residence during the period of their awards.
Requirements US citizens and foreign nationals who hold the PhD or the equivalent, PhD candidates who have passed their preliminary exams, and independent scholars are eligible to apply. The fellowships are intended to encourage research in the library collections by scholars who reside beyond a 75-mile radius of Philadelphia.
Amount $2000 per month
Date(s) Application Is Due Mar 1.
Contact Library Resident Research Fellowships, (215) 440-3443; fax: (215) 440-3423; email: jjahern@amphilsoc.org
Internet http://www.amphilsoc.org/grants/resident.htm
Sponsor American Philosophical Society Library
105 S Fifth St
Philadelphia, PA 19106-3386

APS Marshall N. Rosenbluth Outstanding Doctoral Thesis Award **670**
The program recognizes exceptional young scientists who have performed original thesis work of outstanding scientific quality and achievement in the area of plasma physics. The award consists of a stipend, a certificate to be presented during the award ceremony at the banquet for the Division of Plasma Physics Annual Meeting, and a travel allowance to the meeting. Nomination guidelines are available online.
Requirements Nominations will be accepted for any doctoral student of a college or university in the United States or for a United States student abroad who has successfully passed his/her final thesis defense within the preceding 24 months of the current nomination deadline. The work to be considered must have been performed as part of the requirements for a doctoral degree.
Amount $2000; $500 maximum travel allowance
Date(s) Application Is Due Apr 1.
Contact Program Administrator, (301) 209-3200; fax: (301) 209-0865; email: honors@apes.org
Internet http://www.aps.org/praw/ramo/index.cfm
Sponsor American Physical Society
One Physics Ellipse
College Park, MD 20740-3844

APS Mitsuyoshi Tanaka Dissertation Award in Experimental Particle Physics **671**
The award provides recognition to exceptional young scientists who have performed original doctoral thesis work of outstanding scientific quality and achievement in the area of experimental particle physics. The annual award consists of a monetary award, a certificate citing the accomplishments of the recipient, and an allowance for travel to attend the annual meeting of the Division of Particles and Fields, at which the award will be presented. Each nominee will be considered in not more than two consecutive cycles. Nomination guidelines are available online.

Requirements Nominations will be accepted for any doctoral student studying at a college or university in the United States or in an education abroad program of a college or university in the United States for dissertation research carried out at a US laboratory. The work to be considered must have been accomplished as part of the requirements for a doctoral degree. Nominees must pass their thesis defense 12 months or less from the nomination deadline, for the selection cycle in which the nomination is to be considered.
Amount $1500; $1000 maximum travel allowance
Date(s) Application Is Due Jun 30.
Contact Program Administrator, (301) 209-3200; fax: (301) 209-0865; email: honors@apes.org
Internet http://www.aps.org/praw/tanaka/index.cfm
Sponsor American Physical Society
One Physics Ellipse
College Park, MD 20740-3844

APS Nicholas Metropolis Award for Outstanding Doctoral Thesis Work in Computational Physics **672**
The purpose of the annual award is to recognize doctoral thesis research of outstanding quality and achievement in computational physics and to encourage effective written and oral presentation of research results. The award consists of a monetary prize and a certificate to be presented at an awards ceremony at the Division of Computational Physics annual meeting and an additional allowance to travel to the meeting. The recipient will be invited to present his or her work in an appropriate session of the meeting. An individual can be nominated only once; however, an unsuccessful candidate will be carried over for one year. Nomination guidelines are available online.
Requirements Nominations will be accepted for any doctoral student (present or past) in any country for work performed as part of the requirements for a doctoral degree. Nominees must pass their thesis defense not more than 18 months before the nomination deadline.
Amount $1500; $500 maximum travel allowance
Date(s) Application Is Due Sep 1.
Contact Program Administrator, (301) 209-3200; fax: (301) 209-0865; email: honors@apes.org
Internet http://www.aps.org/praw/metropol/index.cfm
Sponsor American Physical Society
One Physics Ellipse
College Park, MD 20740-3844

APS Oliver E. Buckley Condensed Matter Prize **673**
The annual prize recognizes and encourages outstanding theoretical or experimental contributions to condensed matter physics. The prize ordinarily is awarded to one person but may be shared when all the recipients have contributed to the same accomplishments. The award consists of a monetary prize and a certificate citing the contributions made by the recipient or recipients. Nominations are active for three years.
Amount $10,000
Date(s) Application Is Due Jul 1.
Contact Prize Administrator, (301) 209-3200; fax: (301) 209-0865; email: honors@aps.org
Internet http://www.aps.org/praw/buckley/index.cfm
Sponsor American Physical Society
One Physics Ellipse
College Park, MD 20740-3844

APS Outstanding Doctoral Thesis Research in Atomic, Molecular, or Optical Physics **674**
The annual award recognizes doctoral thesis research of outstanding quality and achievement in atomic, molecular, or optical physics and encourages effective written and oral presentation of research results. The award consists of a monetary prize and a certificate citing the contribution made by the recipient. All finalists will receive a travel stipend. A student may be a finalist in the competition only once. Eligible nonfinalists may only be renominated by submitting an entirely new package, even if it is the same as the original package. Nomination guidelines are available online.
Requirements Doctoral students at any university in the United States or abroad who have passed their thesis defense for the PhD in the disciplines of atomic, molecular, or optical physics any time during the prior two calendar years are eligible for the award, except for those whose thesis advisors serve on the current selection committee.
Amount $2500 award; $500 travel allowance
Date(s) Application Is Due Dec 1.
Contact Program Administrator, (301) 209-3200; fax: (301) 209-0865; email: honors@apes.org
Internet http://www.aps.org/praw/dissdamo/index.cfm
Sponsor American Physical Society
One Physics Ellipse
College Park, MD 20740-3844

APS Phillips Fund Grants for Research in North American Indian Linguistics and Ethnohistory **675**
Grants are given for research in North American (United States and Canada) Indian anthropological linguistics and ethnohistory. Preference is given to young scholars, including graduate students. Grants are intended for such extra costs as travel, tapes or films, informant's fees, etc., but not for general maintenance or permanent equipment, and are ordinarily given for the 12 months following the date of the award. Telephone requests for forms cannot be honored, but programmatic inquiries may be made by telephone. For applications, write to address listed, specifying the field of research; include a self-addressed mailing label. Applications are also available on the Web site.
Requirements Applicants may be graduate students who have passed their qualifying examinations for either the master's or doctorate degrees; postdoctoral applicants are eligible.
Restrictions Grants are not made for projects in archaeology, ethnography, or psycholinguistics, nor for the preparation of pedagogical materials.
Amount $3000 maximum
Date(s) Application Is Due Mar 1.
Contact Linda Musumeci, Research Administrator, (215) 440-3429; email: LMusumeci@amphilsoc.org
Internet http://www.amphilsoc.org/grants/phillips.htm
Sponsor American Philosophical Society
104 S Fifth St
Philadelphia, PA 19106-3387

APS Polymer Physics Prize **676**
The annual prize recognizes outstanding accomplishment and excellence of contributions in polymer physics research. The award consists of a monetary prize and a certificate citing the contributions made by the recipient. The prize ordinarily is awarded to one person, but a prize may be shared when all the recipients have contributed to the same accomplishments. Nominations are active for three years. Nomination guidelines are available online.
Requirements Nominations are open to all scientists of all nations regardless of membership in the society or the geographical location in which the work was carried out.
Amount $10,000
Date(s) Application Is Due Jul 1.
Contact Prize Administrator, (301) 209-3200; fax: (301) 209-0865; email: honors@aps.org
Internet http://www.aps.org/praw/polymer/index.cfm
Sponsor American Physical Society
One Physics Ellipse
College Park, MD 20740-3844

APS Prize for a Faculty Member for Research in an Undergraduate Institution **677**
The annual prize honors a physicist whose research in an undergraduate setting has achieved wide recognition and contributed significantly to physics and who has contributed substantially to the professional development of undergraduate physics students. The award consists of a stipend to the prize recipient and a separate unrestricted grant for the research to the prize recipient's institution. An additional allowance will be provided for travel expenses to the APS meeting at which the prize ceremony will take place, and a certificate citing the contributions by the recipient. Nominations are active for three years. Nomination guidelines are available online.
Requirements The prize will be given to a physics faculty member at a US undergraduate institution. The recipient will have been recognized as contributing substantially to physics research and providing inspirational guidance and encouragement of undergraduate students participating in this research. Nominations also should include a publication list that highlights student co-authors, including whether these students are high school, undergraduate, or graduate students.
Restrictions The nominee's department may offer a program leading to a masters degree but must not have a doctoral program in physics.
Amount $5000 stipend; $5000 unrestricted grant
Date(s) Application Is Due Jul 1.
Contact Prize Administrator, (301) 209-3200; fax: (301) 209-0865; email: honors@aps.org
Internet http://www.aps.org/praw/undergrad/index.cfm
Sponsor American Physical Society
One Physics Ellipse
College Park, MD 20740-3844

APS Research Grants **678**
Grants are made toward the cost of scholarly research in all areas of knowledge except those in which support by government or corporate enterprise is more appropriate. Grants contribute toward expenses such as living costs while away from home, some special scientific supplies, microfilms, photostats, photographs, and necessary foreign and domestic travel at the lowest rates available. It is the society's practice to encourage research by younger and less well-established scholars. Application and three letters of reference must be made on APS forms. Send a brief letter describing project and proposed budget to receive application forms. Telephone requests for forms will not be honored; write for application materials, and include a self-addressed mailing label. Application forms are also available on the Web site. Deadlines vary from program to program; contact program staff for exact dates.
Requirements Applicants are expected to have held the doctorate for at least one year. Applications may be made by residents of the United States, by American citizens on the

staffs of foreign institutions, and by foreign nationals whose research can only be carried out in the United States. Applicants expecting to use materials or conduct interviews in foreign languages must possess the necessary competence in the language or languages involved. Submit three letters of support.
Restrictions Grants will not be made for journalistic or other writing for general readership; the preparation of textbooks, casebooks, anthologies, or other materials for classroom use by students; nor for the work of creative and performing artists. Grants are rarely made to persons who have had the doctorate less than a year and never for predoctoral study or research. The committee will seldom approve more than two grants for the same project within any five-year period.
Amount $6000 maximum
Date(s) Application Is Due Oct 1; Dec 1.
Contact Committee for Research, (215) 440-3429; email: eroach@amphilsoc.org
Internet http://www.amphilsoc.org/grants
Sponsor American Philosophical Society
104 S Fifth St
Philadelphia, PA 19106-3387

APS Robert R. Wilson Prize **679**
The annual prize recognizes and encourages outstanding achievement in the physics of particle accelerators. The award consists of a monetary prize, an allowance for travel to the meeting at which the prize is awarded, and a certificate citing the contributions made by the recipient. The prize ordinarily is awarded to one person but may be shared when all recipients have contributed to the same accomplishment. Nominations are active for three years. Nomination guidelines are available online.
Requirements Nominations are open to scientists of all nations regardless of the geographical site at which the work was done. The prize will normally be awarded for contributions made at an early stage of the recipient's career.
Amount $5000
Date(s) Application Is Due Jul 1.
Contact Prize Administrator, (301) 209-3200; fax: (301) 209-0865; email: honors@aps.org
Internet http://www.aps.org/praw/wilson/index.cfm
Sponsor American Physical Society
One Physics Ellipse
College Park, MD 20740-3844

APS Sabbatical Fellowship for the Humanities and Social Sciences **680**
The society supports fellowships in the humanities and the social sciences for faculty of US universities and four-year colleges. The awards are intended for those, usually in midcareer, who have been granted a sabbatical year/research leave by the university or college, but for whom full financial support from the parent institution is available for only half an academic year. The fellowship helps defray expenses for the second half of an awarded sabbatical year. There is no restriction on where the fellow resides during the fellowship year, but an indication of the appropriateness of the available library resources should be given. The application requires a form for the cover sheet and three letters of support; details are available on the Web site.
Requirements Applicants should be based in the United States, but need not be US citizens, and must not have had a financially supported leave during the past three years.
Restrictions The fellowship cannot be used to supplement external awards of similar purposes. Institutions are not eligible to apply.
Amount $30,000-$40,000 for second half of awarded sabbatical year
Date(s) Application Is Due Oct 15.
Contact Sabbatical Fellowships, (215) 440-3429; email: eroach@amphilsoc.org
Internet http://www.amphilsoc.org/grants/#details
Sponsor American Philosophical Society
104 S Fifth St
Philadelphia, PA 19106

APS Tom W. Bonner Prize in Nuclear Physics **681**
The prize recognizes and encourages outstanding experimental research in nuclear physics, including the development of a method, technique, or device that significantly contributes in a general way to nuclear physics research. The prize consists of monetary prize and a certificate citing the contributions made by the recipient. It is presented annually. The prize ordinarily is awarded to one person but may be shared when all the recipients have contributed to the same accomplishment. Nominations are active for three years. Nomination guidelines are available online.
Requirements Nominations are open to physicists whose work in nuclear physics is primarily experimental or a particularly outstanding piece of theoretical work. There is no time limitations on work described.
Amount $7500
Date(s) Application Is Due Jul 1.
Contact Prize Administrator, (301) 209-3200; fax: (301) 209-0865; email: honors@aps.org
Internet http://www.aps.org/praw/bonner/index.cfm
Sponsor American Physical Society
One Physics Ellipse
College Park, MD 20740-3844

APS W.K.H. Panofsky Prize in Experimental Particle Physics **682**
The annual prize recognizes and encourages outstanding achievements in experimental particle physics. The award consists of a monetary prize, an allowance for travel to the meeting at which the prize is to be awarded, and a certificate citing the contributions made by the recipient. The prize ordinarily is awarded to one person, but the prize may be shared when all recipients have contributed to the same accomplishment. Nominations are active for three years. Nomination guidelines are available online.
Requirements Nominations are open to scientists of all nations regardless of the geographical site at which the work was accomplished. The prize will normally be awarded for contributions made at an early stage of the recipient's career.
Amount $5000
Date(s) Application Is Due May 1.
Contact Prize Administrator, (301) 209-3200; fax: (301) 209-0865; email: honors@aps.org
Internet http://www.aps.org/praw/panofsky/index.cfm
Sponsor American Physical Society
One Physics Ellipse
College Park, MD 20740-3844

APS Will Allis Prize for the Study of Ionized Gases **683**
The prize was established in 1989 by contributions from American Telephone and Telegraph, General Electric, General Telephone and Electronics, International Business Machines, and Xerox Corporations in recognition of the outstanding contributions of Will Allis to the study of ionized gases. The prize ordinarily is awarded to one person, but the prize may be shared when all recipients have contributed to the same accomplishment. The prize consists of a monetary award and a certificate citing the contributions made by the recipient. An allowance will be provided for travel expenses of the recipient to the society's meeting, where the prize is bestowed. The prize is awarded in even-numbered years. Nominations are active for three years. Nomination guidelines are available online.
Requirements Nominations are open to scientists of all nations regardless of the geographical location at which the work was done.
Amount $5000
Date(s) Application Is Due Jul 1.
Contact Prize Administrator, (301) 209-3200; fax: (301) 209-0865; email: honors@aps.org
Internet http://www.aps.org/praw/allis/index.cfm
Sponsor American Physical Society
One Physics Ellipse
College Park, MD 20740-3844

APS/Phoenix Suns Energy and Environmental Minigrants **684**
The program supports innovative, student-based educational projects that enhance learning with the objective of improving student achievement. Projects should have the ability of being replicated or adapted by other schools. Projects addressing energy, the environment, reading, mathematics or character education will be considered. Annual deadline dates may vary; contact program staff for exact dates.
Requirements The program is open to educators who teach in public schools in the Arizona Public Service territory. Funds may be applied to equipment, materials and field trips that would not normally be provided by the school or school district.
Amount $500
Date(s) Application Is Due Jan 31.
Contact Louise Moskowitz, (602) 250-2291; email: Louise.Moskowitz@aps.com
Internet http://www.aps.com/my_community/LearningCenter/LearningCenter_1.html
Sponsor Arizona Public Service
P.O. Box 53999 MS 8010
Phoenix, AZ 85072-3999

APSA Minority Fellows Program **685**
The program is designed primarily for minority students applying to enter a doctoral program in political science for the first time. The association has refocused and increased its efforts to assist minority students in completing their doctorates by concentrating not only on the recruitment of minorities, but also on the retention of these groups within the profession. The program designates six stipend minority fellows each year. Additional applicants who do not receive funds from the association may also be recognized and recommended for admission and financial support to graduate political science programs. Fellows with stipends receive a fellowship that is disbursed in two payments--one at the end of their first graduate year and one at the end of their second--provided that they remain in good academic standing. Awards are based on students' undergraduate course work, GPA, extracurricular activities, GRE scores, and recommendations from faculty. Guidelines are available online.
Requirements Applicants must: be members of one of the following racial/ethnic minority groups: African Americans, Latinos/as, and Native Americans (federal and state recognized tribes); demonstrate an interest in teaching and potential for research in political science; be a US citizen at time of award; and demonstrate financial need.
Amount $4000
Date(s) Application Is Due Oct 25.
Contact Graduate Fellowships, (202) 483-2512; fax: (202) 483-2657; email: apsa@apsanet.org
Internet http://www.apsanet.org/content_11666.cfm

Sponsor American Political Science Association
1527 New Hampshire Avenue NW
Washington, DC 20036

APSA Political Science Doctoral Dissertation Awards 686

There are eight named prize awards given annually for specific doctoral dissertations. The Almond Award is for the best doctoral dissertation in the field of comparative politics; the Anderson Award, in the general field of state and local politics, federalism, or intergovernmental relations; the Corwin Award, in the field of public law broadly defined to include the judicial process, judicial biography, judicial behavior, courts, law, legal systems, the American constitutional system, civil liberties, or any other substantive area, or any work that deals in a significant fashion with a topic related to or having substantial impact on the American Constitution; the Lasswell Award, in the field of policy studies; the Reid Award, in the field of international relations, law, and politics; the Schattschneider Award, in the general field of American government and politics; the Strauss Award, in political philosophy; and the White Award, within the general field of public administration including broadly related problems of policy formation and administrative theory.
Requirements Political science departments are invited to nominate not more than one doctoral dissertation per award. The dissertations must have been completed and accepted during the two calendar years preceding the date of the prize.
Amount $750-$1,000
Date(s) Application Is Due Jan 15.
Contact Doctoral Dissertation Awards, (202) 483-2512; fax: (202) 483-2657; email: apsa@apsanet.org
Internet http://www.apsanet.org/section_260.cfm
Sponsor American Political Science Association
1527 New Hampshire Ave NW
Washington, DC 20036-1206

APSA Small Research Grants 687

The APSA Small Research Grant Program supports research in all fields of political science. The intent of these grants is to support the research of political scientists who are not employed at PhD granting department in the field and to help further the careers of these scholars. Grant recipients in the last five years have published over 12 books, 16 refereed articles, 8 book chapters, many working papers, and a large number of conference presentations. Others are still working on book, article, and conference projects and many recipients report great benefits for their students. Students have co-authored projects, worked as research assistants, and benefited through the professors' classroom use of their research. Many recipients also were able to use the APSA grant as seed money to get additional funding.
Requirements Applicants must be APSA members at the time of application and at the time funds are dispersed. In addition, the principal investigator and any co-author must be one of the following: a faculty member at a college or university that does not award a PhD in Political Science, Public Administration, Public Policy, International Relations, Government, or Politics and whose primary appointment is in one of these departments; or a political scientist not affiliated with an academic institution and is either (a) unemployed or (b) working in a research organization such as a think tank.
Restrictions This grant does not provide support for dissertation research or writing and graduate students are not eligible to apply.
Amount $2,500
Date(s) Application Is Due Feb 1.
Contact Bahram Rajaee, (202) 483-2512, ext. 130; fax: (202) 483-2657; email: brajaee@apsanet.org
Internet http://www.apsanet.org/section_509.cfm
Sponsor American Political Science Association
1527 New Hampshire Avenue, NW
Washington, DC 20036

APSA Travel Grants 688

APSA provides travel grants to assist some members in attending the Annual Meeting. U.S. graduate students, international graduate students studying in the U.S., unemployed APSA members, and international scholars are encouraged to apply. Priority will be given to presenters at the Annual Meeting, first-time applicants, or those who have not received a travel grant since 2005. Application forms are available upon request.
Requirements Only applicants who are APSA members and pre-registered for the APSA Annual Meeting are eligible to receive travel grants.
Amount $700 maximum
Date(s) Application Is Due May 24.
Contact Program Coordinator, (202) 483-2512; fax: (202) 483-2657; email: travelgrants@apsanet.org
Internet http://www.apsanet.org/section_542.cfm
Sponsor American Political Science Association
1527 New Hampshire Ave NW
Washington, DC 20036-1206

Aratani Foundation Grants 689

The foundation awards grants to nonprofits in its areas of interest, including education, health care, museums, recreation, and religion. Preference is given to Japanese-American cultural organizations. Types of support include annual campaigns, building construction/renovation, capital campaigns, conferences and seminars, continuing support, curriculum development, endowments, exchange programs, fellowships, general operating support, program development, scholarship funds, and seed grants. Application forms are not required, but application outlines are available.
Requirements Giving primarily in California.
Restrictions Grants are not made to individuals.
Amount $100-$150,000 average range
Contact George Aratani, President
Sponsor Aratani Foundation
23505 Crenshaw Blvd, No 230
Hollywood, CA 90505

Arca Foundation Grants 690

The foundation is dedicated to the pursuit of social equity and justice, particularly given the growing disparities in our world. The foundation's specific program focus may change from time to time but the fundamental purpose is always supported through efforts that can affect public policy.
Requirements The foundation accepts proposals from 501(c)3 and 509(a) tax-exempt organizations.
Restrictions The foundation does not fund organizations that provide direct social services, scholarship funds or scholarly research, capital projects or endowments, individuals, or government programs. Proposals received via fax or email will not be considered.
Amount $50,000 average
Date(s) Application Is Due Mar 1; Sep 1.
Contact Donna Edwards, Executive Director, (202) 822-9193; fax: (202) 785-1446; email: grants@arcafoundation.org
Internet http://www.arcafoundation.org
Sponsor Arca Foundation
1308 19th St, NW
Washington, DC 20036

Arcadia Foundation Grants 691

The foundation awards grants to Pennsylvania nonprofit organizations to improve the quality of life. Areas of interest include hospitals and hospital building funds, health agencies and services, nursing, hospices, early childhood, adult and higher education, libraries, child development and welfare agencies, youth organizations, and social service and general welfare agencies, including care of the handicapped, aged, and hungry. Also supported are family services, environment and conservation, wildlife and animal welfare, religious organizations, historical preservation, and music organizations. Types of support include general operating support, continuing support, annual campaigns, capital campaigns, building construction/renovation, equipment acquisition, endowment funds, program development, scholarship funds, and research. Applications are accepted between September 1 and November 1.
Requirements Eastern Pennsylvania organizations whose addresses have zip codes of 18000-19000 are eligible. Application form not required. The initial approach should be a letter or proposal--not exceeding two pages.
Restrictions Grants are not awarded to support individuals, deficit financing, land acquisition, fellowships, demonstration projects, publications, or conferences.
Date(s) Application Is Due Nov 1.
Contact Marilyn Lee Steinbright, President, fax: (610) 275-8460
Sponsor Arcadia Foundation
105 E Logan St
Norristown, PA 19401

Archaeological and Pre-Colonial History in Eastern Africa Research Grants 692

The institute occasionally offers limited support to qualified scholars undertaking field research in eastern African history, later archaeology, or related studies. The Institute intends to give priority to research in relevant fields which focuses on at least one of the following themes: Histories of Environmental Change; Colonial Encounters; Sacred Space in Eastern Africa; Maritime Heritage of the Western Indian Ocean; or Migrations in Cultural and Historical Perspective.
Requirements Graduate background or comparable experience in the subject and the relevant research methods are required.
Amount @L1000 sterling or its equivalent in local currency
Date(s) Application Is Due May 30; Oct 31.
Contact Paul Lane, Director, 254 2 4343190; fax: 254 2 4343365; email: pjlane@africaonline.co.ke
Internet http://www.britac.ac.uk/institutes/eafrica
Sponsor British Institute in Eastern Africa
P.O. Box 30710
Nairobi GP.O. 00100
Kenya

Archer Daniels Midland Foundation Grants Program 693

The foundation prefers to fund programs that will directly impact the communities where operating units are located. Nearly a third of the funding is directed toward educational institutions, including elementary, secondary, and higher education. The advocacy category covers world affairs and foreign relations groups that deal with

international trade; also supported are projects stressing free enterprise and assistance for women. Support of social services goes to minority group development, cultural activities, and hospital and youth agencies. Health service funding supports hospital and disease association programs. Conservation funding supports programs for protecting the environment and beautification as well as conservation. Religion grants support Christian, Jewish, and Roman Catholic organizations, such as churches, colleges and universities, international ministries/missions, Jewish welfare, and the Salvation Army. Applications are accepted at any time.
Requirements Tax-exempt organizations are eligible. Current United Way recipients and national organizations are also eligible.
Restrictions Grants are restricted to public, religious, charitable, philanthropic, benevolent, scientific, literary, artistic, educational, or for the prevention of cruelty to children and animals.
Amount $10,000 per award
Contact Brian Peterson, Program Contact, (217) 424-5413
Internet http://www.admworld.com/naen/
Sponsor Archer Daniels Midland Foundation
P.O. Box 1470
Decatur, IL 62526

Archibald Waynne Dingman Memorial Graduate Scholarship 694
This scholarship is for four months of study related to the petroleum industry, awarded annually to qualified graduates of any recognized university registered in or admissible to a program leading to a master's or doctoral degree at the University of Calgary.
Requirements To be eligible, applicants must be graduate students that are Canadian citizens or permanent residents.
Amount $C3000
Date(s) Application Is Due Feb 1.
Contact Connie Busch, Faculty of Graduate Studies, (403) 220-5690; email: cbusch@ucalgary.ca
Internet http://www.grad.ucalgary.ca/funding/internal_scholarships/lev_4/dingman.htm
Sponsor University of Calgary
2500 University Dr NW, Earth Sciences Bldg, Rm 720
Calgary, AB T2N 1N4 Canada

Arie and Ida Crown Memorial Grants 695
The program supports programs that offer opportunities to the disadvantaged, strengthens the bond of families, and improves the quality of people's lives. As a general rule, the Foundation funds organizations that serve the greater Chicago area as well as organizations that serve the broader Jewish community. Most grants are awarded to organizations within the city of Chicago. Organizations are supported in the areas of arts and culture (concentrating on educational and enrichment programs for youth), civic affairs, education, health (stressing access to services, hospice and health promotion), and human service (focusing on programs which offer assistance for children and families).
Requirements Nonprofit organizations in Chicago and Cook County, IL, may apply for grant support.
Restrictions Grants are not made to support individuals, conference expenses, film projects, government programs (50 percent government funded), or research projects.
Amount $1000-$200,000 average
Date(s) Application Is Due Jan 31; Jul 31.
Contact Susan Crown, President, (312) 236-6300; fax: (312) 984-1499; email: AICM@crown-Chicago.com
Internet http://www.crownmemorial.org/
Sponsor Arie and Ida Crown Memorial
222 N LaSalle St, Ste 2000
Chicago, IL 60601

ARIT Andrew W. Mellon Foundation Postdoctorals Fellowships for Central and East European Scholar 696
The postdoctoral fellowships are intended to bring scholars from Central and Eastern Europe into the broader research community, specifically into Turkey. Fellowships, offered in all areas of the humanities and social sciences, have a tenure of two to three months for research to be carried out in Turkey. Preference will be given to scholars in the early stages of their careers. Fellows are expected to devote full time to their projects and to participate in the activities of the institute. Turkish law requires all foreign scholars, prior to entering the country, to obtain formal permission for any research to be carried out. Fellowship recipients are personally responsible for obtaining their own research permission and may acquire forms and procedures through the Turkish diplomatic office within each country included in the competition. Replies for permission may take six months or more. Applicants may contact the office for advice about research permission.
Requirements The fellowships are available to Czech, Hungarian, Polish, Slovak, Bulgarian, and Romanian scholars holding the PhD or its equivalent who are engaged in advanced research in any field of the social sciences or the humanities involving Turkey. Scholars must be permanent residents of one of the included countries.
Restrictions Applicants may not have held a prior fellowship under this program.
Amount $11,500 maximum stipend for two to three months of research
Date(s) Application Is Due Mar 6.
Contact G. Kenneth Sams, President, (215) 898-3474; fax: (215) 898-0657; email: leinwand@sas.upenn.edu
Internet http://ccat.sas.upenn.edu/ARIT/MellonFellowships.htm
Sponsor American Research Institute in Turkey
3260 South St
Philadelphia, PA 19104-6324

ARIT Fellowships 697
Fellowships support research in ancient, medieval, or modern times, in any field of the humanities and social sciences. Postdoctoral and dissertation research fellowships may be held for terms of two months to one year. Grants for tenures up to one year will be considered, but preference will be given to projects of shorter duration. ARIT maintains two research institutes in Turkey. ARIT-Istanbul has a research library focused on Byzantine, Ottoman, and modern studies of Turkey. ARIT-Ankara focuses on art, archaeology, and ancient history in its library and serves Turkish and American archaeologists through its programs. Both institutes have residential facilities for fellows and provide general assistance as well as introductions to colleagues, institutions, and authorities in Turkey. Predoctoral applicants also may qualify for ARIT's Kress fellowship, and postdoctoral scholars also may qualify for ARIT's NEH fellowships. Applicants will be notified of the fellowship committee's decision by January 25.
Requirements Applicants must be US citizens or permanent residents affiliated with US or Canadian institutions. Scholars and advanced graduate students engaged in research on ancient, medieval, or modern times in Turkey, in any field of the humanities and social sciences, are eligible. Student applicants must have fulfilled all preliminary requirements for the doctorate except the dissertation. Turkish law requires all foreign scholars, prior to entering the country, to obtain formal permission for any research to be carried out in Turkey.
Date(s) Application Is Due Nov 1.
Contact ARIT Fellowships, (215) 898-3474; fax: (215) 898-0657; email: leinwand@sas.upenn.edu
Internet http://ccat.sas.upenn.edu/ARIT/ARITFellowships.htm
Sponsor American Research Institute in Turkey
3260 South St
Philadelphia, PA 19104-6324

ARIT Fellowships for Intensive Advanced Turkish Language Study 698
ARIT offers fellowships for 10 advanced students for participation in the summer program in intensive advanced Turkish language at Bogazici University in Istanbul. This intensive program offers the equivalent of one full academic year of study in Turkish at the college level. ARIT fellowship- supported courses are offered at the advanced level. Classes are conducted in Turkish, with informal and formal styles introduced and reviewed through instruction, language laboratory work, and open conversations with teaching assistants. Students meet with teaching assistants on an informal basis for additional instruction and free conversation. Participants also attend extracurricular activities including films, lectures, and cultural events both on- and off-campus. The fellowships cover round-trip airfare to Istanbul, application and tuition fees, and a maintenance stipend. Full-time students and scholars affiliated at academic institutions are eligible to apply. Guidelines and application are available online.
Requirements Applicant must be a US citizen, national, or permanent resident; be currently enrolled in an undergraduate or graduate-level academic program, or be faculty; have a minimum B average, if still a student; and perform at the high-intermediate level on a proficiency-based admissions examination.
Date(s) Application Is Due Feb 15.
Contact Erika Gilson, Director, email: leinwand@sas.upenn.edu
Internet http://ccat.sas.upenn.edu/ARIT/ARITSummerLanguageProgram.htm
Sponsor American Research Institute inTurkey
33rd and Spruce Sts
Philadelphia, PA 19104-6324

ARIT Kenan T. Erim Fellowship for Research at Aphrodisias 699
The institute invites applications for a fellowship to support excavation and/or research in art history and archaeology to be carried out at the site of Aphrodisias in Turkey during the summer. Applicants must submit an application, a letter of acceptance from a director of the excavations at Aphrodisias, and two letters of reference by the listed application deadline. Graduate students should supply a copy of their graduate transcript. Guidelines are available online.
Requirements Scholars or advanced graduate students engaged in excavation at the site of Aphrodisias or research on material from that site are eligible to apply. Fields of study include the history of art and architecture from antiquity to the present, and archaeology. Graduate student applicants must have fulfilled all preliminary requirements for the doctorate except the dissertation by June, and before beginning any ARIT-sponsored research.
Amount $2375 maximum
Date(s) Application Is Due Nov 1.
Contact ARIT Fellowships, (215) 898-3474; fax: (215) 898-0657; email: leinwand@sas.upenn.edu
Internet http://ccat.sas.upenn.edu/ARIT/ErimFellowship.htm
Sponsor American Research Institute in Turkey
3260 South St
Philadelphia, PA 19104-6324

ARIT/NEH Fellowships for Research in Turkey **700**

ARIT invites applications for two or three postdoctoral fellowships made possible by support from NEH. The fields of study cover all periods in the general range of the humanities, including humanistically oriented aspects of social sciences, prehistory, history, art, archaeology, literature, and linguistics, as well as interdisciplinary aspects of cultural history. The fellowships for research in Turkey can be held for four to 12 months. ARIT maintains two research institutes in Turkey: ARIT-Istanbul, with a research library focused on Byzantine, Ottoman, and modern studies of Turkey; and ARIT-Ankara, which focuses on art, archaeology, and ancient history in its library and serves Turkish and American archaeologists through its programs. Both institutes have residential facilities for fellows and provide general assistance as well as introductions to colleagues, institutions, and authorities in Turkey.
Amount $13,335-$40,000
Date(s) Application Is Due Nov 1.
Contact Fellowship Administrator, (215) 898-3474; fax: (215) 898-0657; email: leinwand@sas.upenn.edu
Internet http://ccat.sas.upenn.edu/ARIT/NEHFellowships.htm
Sponsor American Research Institute in Turkey
3260 South St
Philadelphia, PA 19104-6324

Arizona Cardinals Grants **701**

The National Football League franchise supports programs designed to improve the quality of life and enhance opportunities for children, women, and minorities in the state of Arizona. Specific areas of interest include arts and culture, civic affairs, education, health, science, and social services. The foundation is interested in expanding its giving and looks for new charities to fund. First-time applicant organizations generally will receive grants of $5000 or less.
Requirements Applicants must be exempt under 501(c)(3) of the Internal Revenue Service code.
Amount $2000-$5000
Date(s) Application Is Due Aug 1.
Contact Pat Tankersley, (602) 379-0101; fax: (480) 785-7327
Internet http://www.azcardinals.com/community/charities.php
Sponsor Arizona Cardinals
P.O. Box 888
Phoenix, AZ 85001-0888

Arizona Commission on the Arts Education Projects Grants **702**

The Arizona Commission on the Arts is committed to making the arts fundamental to education, particularly in programs that serve Pre-K-12 students, classroom teachers, teaching artists, arts specialists and administrators in school, after-school and summer/inter-session programs. Our goal is that applicants present a plan that creatively stimulates arts education in their school/community organizations.
Requirements An applicant organization must be a 501(c)3 Arizona nonprofit organization or school, or a unit of government. An unincorporated Arizona organization may apply through a fiscal agent, providing that the fiscal agent is an Arizona 501(c)3 or a governmental organization. Grant applications must be submitted online.
Restrictions No more than one Arts Learning project per individual site is funded per year. Support for staff salaries, funding for insurance or supplies are not provided through this grant.
Date(s) Application Is Due Mar 22.
Contact Alison Marshall, Arts Learning Director, (602) 771-6523; email: amarshall@azarts.gov
Internet http://www.azarts.gov/index.htm
Sponsor Arizona Commission on the Arts
417 W Roosevelt
Phoenix, AZ 85003

Arizona Commission on the Arts Folklorist Residencies **703**

In this residency program, folklorists guide students and teachers in the process of researching, identifying, and documenting traditional art forms in their community. Students develop a new sense of community as they learn and experience the significance of family, community, and cultural traditions directly from parents and family members, employers and workers, senior citizens, public officials, and other community members. Residency lengths are variable and are built around a combination of services: training for students and teachers in research methodology; fieldwork conducted by the folklorist with participating students and teachers; classroom workshops; lecture-demonstrations on traditional art forms; interviews with local traditional artists; and presentation of traditional artists/art forms in school or community settings. A travel, lodging, and meal subsidy is provided for artists funded for out-of-town residencies in addition to their payment for services.
Requirements 501(c)3 tax-exempt Arizona nonprofit organizations, schools, or units of government are eligible. Schools must select an individual artist, performing company, folklorists, or interdisciplinary artists from the Arizona Artist Roster.
Amount $3500 minimum: $3000 for folklorist services; $500 for services by local traditional artists
Contact Robert Booker, Executive Director, (602) 771-6501; fax: (602) 256-0282; email: rbooker@azarts.gov
Internet http://www.azarts.gov/localarts/index.htm#
Sponsor Arizona Commission on the Arts
417 W Roosevelt St
Phoenix, AZ 85003

Arizona Commission on the Arts Planning and Development Grants **704**

Planning grants aid in the thoughtful development of artistic projects. The grants do not have to result in a final artistic product, but can be used in an early phase of a project. Examples of projects are: rehearsals with a guest choreographer/composer/playwright in the gradual development of a new work that may not necessarily be ready for production during the grant period; research toward a specific project; identification of guest artists for a specific project; bringing guest artists/collaborators/community partners on-site for planning meetings; and identification of curators for the development of an exhibition. Funding may be requested for the project director, guest artist, consultant, curator and/or collaborator fees; travel, lodging, and meals for planning activities; company/ensemble members' pay involved in the development and rehearsal of work involving a guest artist; and prospectus printing and mailing. Applicants who have received planning grants can apply to the arts commission the following year or in subsequent years to complete the project.
Requirements An applicant organization must be a 501(c)3 Arizona nonprofit organization or school, or a unit of government. An unincorporated Arizona organization may apply through a fiscal agent, providing that the fiscal agent is an Arizona 501(c)3 or a governmental organization.
Restrictions Funding may not be requested for attendance at booking conferences, company/ensemble rehearsal fees for projects that do not involve guest artists, artistic director fees for the development of new work, or purchase of materials during the development of a work.
Amount $500 maximum
Contact Jo Kobert, (602) 255-5882; email: jkobert@ArizonaArts.org
Internet http://www.arizonaarts.org/organizations/planning_development.htm
Sponsor Arizona Commission on the Arts
417 W Roosevelt St
Phoenix, AZ 85003

Arkema Inc. Foundation Science Teachers Program **705**

This program is an intensive week-long session for elementary and secondary school teachers. Armed with innovative science experiment kits and the guidance of chemical engineers and scientists, teachers learn new and fascinating ways to illustrate scientific concepts. Scientific topics explored include life, earth and physical science and technology. School principals are asked to nominate two teachers in grades three through six, who are then chosen by the corporate committee to participate in the program. Application forms and contact information are available on the Web site.
Requirements Teachers in the following geographic areas may participate: Alabama (Mobile county); Kentucky (Graves, Livingston, Lyon, Marshall, McCracken, Carroll, Gallatin, Trimble, Jefferson counties); Michigan (Wayne county); Minnesota (Didge, Mower, Steele counties); New Jersey (Burlington, Camden, Gloucester, and Salem counties); New York (Genesee, Livingston counties); Pennsylvania (Berks, Bucks, Chester, Delaware, Montgomery, and Philadelphia counties); Tennessee (Shelby county); Texas (Jasper, Newton, Jefferson, Orange, Harris, and Brazos counties).
Amount $500
Contact Jane Crawford, (215) 419-7614; email: jane.crawford@arkemagroup.com
Internet http://www.products.arkemagroup.com/index.cfm?pag=190
Sponsor Arkema Inc. Foundation
2000 Market St
Philadelphia, PA 19103-3222

ARM Faculty Fellowships **706**

The fellowships provide opportunities for college and university faculty members in science and engineering to participate in research and collaborative activities at government and industrial research facilities. Sabbatical and travel awards also are available. Fellowship duration varies with the research project needs and facility approval. Award funding may be allocated for a stipend up to the faculty member's certified college/university salary, travel expenses to and from the facility, and a modest relocation allowance. Award funding may also be allocated for research participation by undergraduate or graduate students. Applications may be submitted at any time.
Requirements The program is open to full-time faculty members at an accredited college or university. Citizenship restrictions may apply for some awards or facilities. Selection is based on applicant's professional qualifications, references, strength of the research proposal, and the expected benefit of the fellowship experience to the applicant, the applicant's home institution, and the host facility. Preference is given to faculty redirecting their research or establishing new collaborations with facility scientists.
Contact Mariann Bleazard, Faculty Fellowship Program, (801) 273-8911; fax: (801) 277-5632; email: mariann@armanagement.org
Internet http://www.awu.org/faculty_default.htm
Sponsor Academia Resource Management
535 E 4500 S, Ste D120
Salt Lake City, UT 84107

ARM Graduate Fellowships **707**

Graduate student fellowships provide master's and doctoral degree candidates in science and engineering the opportunity to conduct research toward their thesis or

dissertation at one of more than 50 cooperating government and industrial facilities. Institutional affiliation and citizenship restrictions may apply for some awards or facilities. The fellowship term ranges from one to 12 months. The award includes a monthly stipend, tuition assistance, and travel allowance.Renewals are competitive and require reapplication annually. Applications may be submitted at any time. To insure optimum consideration submit by February 22 for summer, by March 20 for fall, and by October 20 for spring.
Requirements The program is open to master's and doctoral degree candidates enrolled in an accredited graduate program. Institutional affiliation and citizenship restrictions may apply for some awards or facilities.
Amount $1300 minimum stipend per month
Contact Mariann Bleazard, Graduate Fellowship Program, (801) 273-8911; fax: (801) 277-5632; email: info@armanagement.org
Internet http://www.awu.org/appl_forms/descriptions/lg.htm
Sponsor Academia Resource Management
535 E 4500 S, Ste D120
Salt Lake City, UT 84107

ARM Postgraduate Fellowships **708**
The fellowships provide opportunities for post-master's and postdoctoral research associates to participate in research at national laboratories and other research facilities. Stipends are established by the host facility, and travel and relocation expenses may be available. The initial fellowship term is up to one year but may be renewed up to two additional years upon mutual agreement by the fellow and the facility and the availability of funds. Applicants must have identified a host scientist and a research project at a cooperating facility before sending their completed application to AWU. Applications may be submitted at any time but Applications may be submitted at any time, however, it is recommended that applications are submitted two to three months prior to the requested start date.
Requirements Candidates must have been awarded the master's or doctoral degree within four years of applying. A commitment to a professional career in science or engineering research is expected. US citizenship or permanent resident status is required. Exceptions to these requirements are subject to the approval of the host facility.
Contact Mariann Bleazard, Postgraduate Fellowship Program, (801) 273-8900; fax: (801) 277-5632; email: info@armanagement.org
Internet http://www.awu.org/appl_forms/descriptions/pd.htm
Sponsor Academia Resource Management
535 E 4500 S, Ste D120
Salt Lake City, UT 84107

ARM Visiting Scientist Awards **709**
AWU administers awards to Visiting Scientists who are industrial associates and collaborators in science, mathematics, engineering, and technology. They provide the opportunity to participate in and contribute to science and technology at sponsoring facilities and are designed to encourage professional development and provide special expertise to the host facility. Stipend is established by the host facility and varies by experience and discipline; usually, it is based on the applicant's current salary. Funds for relocation, supplemental travel, and professional expenses may be available. Applicants must have identified a host scientist and a project at a cooperating facility before sending their application to AWU. Applications may be submitted at any time.
Requirements Professionals with continued commitment to science and engineering. US citizenship or permanent resident status is required. Nonresident aliens require the approval of the host facility and an appropriate visa status.
Contact Mariann Bleazard, Postgraduate Fellowship Program, (801) 273-8900; fax: (801) 277-5632; email: info@awu.org
Internet http://www.awu.org/appl_forms/descriptions/vs.htm
Sponsor Academia Resource Management
535 E 4500 S, Ste D120
Salt Lake City, UT 84107

Armenian Students' Association Scholarships **710**
The association awards undergraduate and graduate scholarships to applicants of Armenian ancestry. Scholarship applications must be requested (obtain form from office or the Web site--application fee required) by February 15; applications must be received March 15. Guidelines and request form are available online.
Requirements Students must be enrolled full-time in four-year accredited colleges or universities in the United States and must be of Armenian descent. The student must be a sophomore or beyond in the current academic year.
Amount $500-$1500
Date(s) Application Is Due Feb 15; Mar 15.
Contact Scholarship Administrator, (401) 461-6114; email: headasa@aol.com
Internet http://www.asainc.org/national/scholarships.shtml
Sponsor Armenian Students' Association of America
333 Atlantic Ave
Warwick, RI 02888

Arnold Fund Grants **711**
The primary focus of the fund is to support charitable organizations located in Newton County, GA. Fields of interest include performing arts, music, higher education, library, education, biomedicine, and medical research. Grants are also made to institutions of higher education in which the founders had a special interest. Proposers are requested to write a brief letter explaining the project for which the funds are being requested. A formal application form is not required.
Restrictions Grants are not made to individuals.
Amount $500-$279,000 range
Contact John Sawyer, Executive Director, (404) 881-7886
Sponsor Arnold Fund
1201 W Peachtree St, Ste 4200
Atlanta, GA 30309-3400

ARO Atomic, Molecular, and Optical (AMO) Physics Research Contracts **712**
Research in atomic, molecular, and optical physics will create fundamentally new capabilities for the army, as well as providing the scientific underpinnings to enhance existing technologies. Topics of interest include unconventional optics for enhanced imaging and detection; atom optics and laser cooling and trapping for ultrasensitive detectors; nonlinear atomic and molecular processes for sensor protection and optical processing; and the investigation of plasmas for toxic gas destruction, pollution reduction, materials processing, and propellant ignition. Image science, automatic target recognition, and sensor fusion issues are also addressed in the AMO program. Proposals may be submitted at any time.
Requirements Organizations and individuals interested in submitting research proposals are strongly encouraged to make preliminary inquiries as to the general need for the type of research effort contemplated before expending extensive effort in preparing a detailed research proposal or submitting proprietary information.
Contact Dr. Richard Hammond, Physics Division, Army Research Office, (919) 549-4313; email: richard.hammond@us.army.mil
Internet http://www.arl.army.mil/main/main/default.cfm?Action=29&Page=203#atomic_molecular_physics
Sponsor Army Research Office
P.O. Box 12211
Research Triangle Park, NC 27709-2211

ARO Biomolecular and Cellular Materials and Processes Research Contracts **713**
The program supports Fundamental studies to define structure-function relationships and biochemical interactions for enzymes, receptors and other macromolecules exhibiting mechanisms and properties uniquely relevant to synthetic and degradative pathways of interest to the military, including establishment of the foundations for manipulation and exploitation of biocatalysis, ribosomal and non-ribosomal biosynthesis to enhance permissiveness toward elaboration of useful biomolecular structures and cellular systems designed with "metabolic engineering" in mind. Also, research to provide insight from nature on novel theoretical principles and mechanisms in sensory and motor function, as well as on materials with extraordinary properties, from biological sources. Includes not only initial molecular events, signal transduction pathways and integrated information processing for the powerful sensing capabilities exhibited in the biological world, but also self-assembly processes, hierarchical structure formation, and functional characterization of biomolecular materials such as those with potential biomimetic utility for nanometer scale fabrication or for energy and information transfer, among other possibilities. Proposals may be submitted at any time.
Requirements Organizations and individuals interested in submitting research proposals are strongly encouraged to make preliminary inquiries as to the general need for the type of research effort contemplated before expending extensive effort in preparing a detailed research proposal or submitting proprietary information.
Contact Dr. Robert Campbell, Biosciences, (919) 549-4230; email: bob.Campbell@us.army.mil
Internet http://www.aro.ncren.net
Sponsor Army Research Office
P.O. Box 12211
Research Triangle Park, NC 27709-2211

ARO Chemical Kinetics Research Contracts **714**
The army's program in ignition and combustion processes associated with energetic materials, explosives, detonation phenomena, the control of energy release and energy transfer processes will benefit from increased understanding of fast reactions of energetic species. The army is especially interested in the investigation of chemical reactions using time-resolved techniques to observe transient species and infer reaction pathways and other experiments and calculations that enable modeling of the time dependent processes of ignition and combustion. Research on controlled transformation of toxic materials to relatively benign products in chemical reactors is also of interest. Proposals are accepted at any time.
Requirements Organizations and individuals interested in submitting research proposals are strongly encouraged to make preliminary inquiries as to the general need for the type of research effort contemplated before expending extensive effort in preparing a detailed research proposal or submitting proprietary information.
Contact Dr. Robert Shaw, Chemistry Division, (919) 549-4293; email: Robert.Shaw@us.army.mil
Internet http://www.aro.ncren.net
Sponsor Army Research Office
P.O. Box 12211
Research Triangle Park, NC 27709-2211

ARO Computational Mathematics Research Contracts 715

The computational mathematics program supports army needs in producing faster, more stable and accurate solutions to relevant problems in the physical, biological and engineering sciences, and in operations. The areas of interest in numerical methods include methods for efficient numerical solution of nonlinear partial differential equations (both time-dependent and steady state), such as adaptive finite difference and finite element methods, high order methods, gridless methods and methods for computing interfaces, such as front tracking and level sets. In the field of optimization, specific topics currently supported include interior-point trust-region approaches to nonlinearly constrained optimization, limited-memory approaches for large-scale optimization, and convergence of optimization methods for singular problems. Proposals are accepted at any time.

Requirements Organizations and individuals interested in submitting research proposals are strongly encouraged to make preliminary inquiries as to the general need for the type of research effort contemplated before expending extensive effort in preparing a detailed research proposal or submitting proprietary information.

Contact Dr. Stephen Davis, Mathematics and Computer Science Division, (919) 549-4284; email: stephen.f.davis@arl.army.mil

Internet http://www.aro.ncren.net/research/index.htm

Sponsor Army Research Office
P.O. Box 12211
Research Triangle Park, NC 27709-2211

ARO Conference and Symposia Grants 716

ARO supports conferences and symposia in special areas of science that bring experts together to discuss recent research or education findings or to expose other researchers or advanced graduate students to new research and educational techniques. ARO encourages the convening in the United States of major international conferences and assemblies of international alliances.

Requirements Scientific, technical, or professional organizations that qualify for tax exemption under 501(c)3 may receive conference and symposia grants. Conference support proposals should be submitted a minimum of six months prior to the date of the conference.

Restrictions Cosponsorship of conferences and symposia with industrial concerns is not eligible. Funds provided by the ARO cannot be used to support participants from communist countries, nor can they be used for payment to any federal government employee for support, subsistence, or services in connection with the proposed conference or symposium.

Contact ARO Legal Office, (919) 549-4292; email: Mark.rutter@us.army.mil

Internet http://www.aro.army.mil

Sponsor Army Research Office
P.O. Box 12211
Research Triangle Park, NC 27709-2211

ARO Degradation, Reactivity, and Protection of Materials Research Contracts 717

The program in degradation, reactivity, and protection of materials investigates the metastable behavior of materials prepared by nonequilibrium surface processing approaches, including high-pressure, shock, plasma, beam, and self-assembling techniques. The principal objective is to discover new nonequilibrium structural materials and novel smart materials, which will enhance the reliability of Army systems in service. This research includes nondestructive characterization of smart and ultra-hard/superstrong materials and in-situ process monitoring. Principal emphasis is on surface or interface control during processing of these materials, characterization of their near-surface transport behavior and surface properties, and modeling or theoretical predictions of their properties. The synthesis of novel degradation-resistant, ultra-high strength nanolaminates and other refractory materials is also of interest. Experimental and theoretical approaches are sought that provide for characterization of surfaces and interfaces, modification of surface and near-surface regions, and processing and materials characterization as this relates to the structure, wear, and environmental resistance of smart materials and ultrahard/superstrong structural materials. Other phenomena including spectroscopic and chemical analysis of low level hydrogen and hydrocarbons, where these are important for understanding the properties of such new materials during processing and in-service life assessment, are also of interest. Proposals may be submitted at any time.

Requirements Organizations and individuals interested in submitting research proposals are strongly encouraged to make preliminary inquiries as to the general need for the type of research effort contemplated before expending extensive effort in preparing a detailed research proposal or submitting proprietary information.

Contact Dr. John Prater, Materials Science Research, (919) 549-4259; email: John.T.Prater@us.army.mil

Internet http://www.aro.ncren.net/research/index.htm

Sponsor Army Research Office
P.O. Box 12211
Research Triangle Park, NC 27709-2211

ARO Discrete Mathematics and Computer Science Research Contracts 718

The interests in discrete mathematics are the development and analysis of solution procedures for discrete problems in computational geometry, computational algebra, logic, network flows, graph theory and combinatorics. Specific areas of emphasis include robust geometric computation, solid modeling, multiresolution methods, parallel and distributed computing and dynamic interactive visualization techniques. Other areas of interest include distributed algorithms for network flows, randomization in computing, computational algebraic geometry techniques for solution of polynomial systems, discrete methods for combinatorial optimization, symbolic methods for differential equations, mixed symbolic-numerical methods for applied problems, parallel symbolic sparse matrix methods, and algorithmic methods in symbolic mathematics arising in, for example, automated reasoning systems, mathematical logic and formal language theory. The interests in theoretical computer science include fundamental issues in parallel computing such as advanced data structures for parallel architectures, parallel algorithms, graph theoretic methods applied to a parallel and distributed computation and models and algorithms for the control of heterogeneous concurrent computing. Also of interest is research on tools for the development of parallel algorithms and expert systems for computation and visualization of solutions to partial differential equations. Exploring fundamental techniques that optimize I/O communication is a research area of great strategic importance. Proposals are accepted at any time.

Requirements Organizations and individuals interested in submitting research proposals are strongly encouraged to make preliminary inquiries as to the general need for the type of research effort contemplated before expending extensive effort in preparing a detailed research proposal or submitting proprietary information.

Contact Michael Coyle, Mathematics and Computer Science Division, (919) 549-4256.; email: joseph.michael.Coyle@us.army.mil

Internet http://www.aro.ncren.net

Sponsor Army Research Office
P.O. Box 12211
Research Triangle Park, NC 27709-2211

ARO Electrochemistry and Advanced Energy Conversion Research Contracts 719

Army relies on compact power sources to support many different weapons systems, communications, and other devices. Power sources under development include batteries and fuel cells, microturbines, thermophotovoltaics, alkali metal thermal to electric converters. This program supports fundamental chemical studies of materials and processes that limit the performance of current or enable future power sources. Topics include ionic conduction in electrolytes, electro catalysis, fuel processing (particularly hydrogen), interfacial electron transfer, transport through coatings, surface films and polymer electrolytes, and activation of carbon-hydrogen bonds. Novel electrochemical synthesis, investigations into the effect of microenvironment on chemical reactivity, and quantitative models of electrochemical systems are also encouraged. Proposals are accepted at any time.

Requirements Organizations and individuals interested in submitting research proposals are strongly encouraged to make preliminary inquiries as to the general need for the type of research effort contemplated before expending extensive effort in preparing a detailed research proposal or submitting proprietary information.

Contact Dr. Richard Paur, Chemistry Division, (919) 549-4208; email: Richard.Paur@us.army.mil

Internet http://www.aro.ncren.net

Sponsor Army Research Office
P.O. Box 12211
Research Triangle Park, NC 27709-2211

ARO Fluid Dynamics Research Contracts 720

Research in fluid dynamics supports the development of improved or new technology for advanced helicopters, small gas turbine engines, improved airdrop (parachute) systems, maneuverable high-speed missiles and high performance gun-launched projectiles. While basic research studies that address the fundamental flow physics underlying these devices are solicited, innovative research in the specific topical thrust areas of vortex-dominated flows, unsteady aerodynamics, and thermal science of micro-/mesoscale devices are especially encouraged. Proposals may be submitted at any time.

Requirements Organizations and individuals interested in submitting research proposals are strongly encouraged to make preliminary inquiries as to the general need for the type of research effort contemplated before expending extensive effort in preparing a detailed research proposal or submitting proprietary information.

Contact Dr. Thomas Doligalski, Engineering Sciences Division, (919) 549-4251; email: Thomas.Doligalski@us.army.mil

Internet http://www.aro.ncren.net

Sponsor Army Research Office
P.O. Box 12211
Research Triangle Park, NC 27709-2211

ARO Information Processing and Fusion and Circuits Research Contracts 721

This program sponsors research the understanding of image background, including target-competitive clutter, and of how image background compounds the difficulty of target detection and recognition. Available models for background and clutter are currently inadequate. Objective measures of clutter and modeling paradigms that enable the quantification of image properties are needed for effective comparison of scenes, evaluation of algorithm performance, validation of synthetic imagery, and strategies for data fusion. Research is needed which addresses: (i) modeling of background and

clutter, (ii) definition and assessment of clutter metrics, (iii) the manner in which clutter degrades the discrimination processes, and (iv) interaction between image background and targets. Proposals may be submitted at any time.
Requirements Organizations and individuals interested in submitting research proposals are strongly encouraged to make preliminary inquiries as to the general need for the type of research effort contemplated before expending extensive effort in preparing a detailed research proposal or submitting proprietary information.
Contact Dr. William Sander, Electronics Division, (919) 549-4241; email: william.sander@us.army.mil
Internet http://www.aro.ncren.net
Sponsor Army Research Office
P.O. Box 12211
Research Triangle Park, NC 27709-2211

ARO Mechanical Behavior of Materials Research Contracts 722
The program on Mechanical Behavior of Materials addresses the fundamental relationships between the structure of materials and their mechanical properties as influenced by composition, processing, environment, stress state, and loading rate. The objectives of the subfield are to provide structural materials with improved mechanical properties and quantitative models for predicting both the response and the remaining useful life of a material. Major thrusts include the development of new strengthening, plasticity and toughening mechanisms for preventing or retarding fracture; especially at large strains (1000%) and high strain rates (to 10 6/sec). New knowledge is sought concerning fundamental deformation processes in materials including: load transfer, fatigue, creep, transformation toughening, super plasticity, and shear localization. New processing procedures are required for optimizing the mechanical properties of a material and reducing the inherent variations in the mechanical properties of materials. Additional thrusts include fundamental investigations on biomimetic and hierarchical materials to afford improved mechanical behavior and reliability. A fundamental understanding of the role of grain boundaries and interphases in composites and their hierarchical relationship to the overall mechanical behavior of the material system is desired. Proposals may be submitted at any time.
Requirements Organizations and individuals interested in submitting research proposals are strongly encouraged to make preliminary inquiries as to the general need for the type of research effort contemplated before expending extensive effort in preparing a detailed research proposal or submitting proprietary information.
Contact Dr. David Stepp, Materials Science Research, (919) 549-4329; email: David.M.Stepp@us.army.mil
Internet http://www.aro.ncren.net
Sponsor Army Research Office
P.O. Box 12211
Research Triangle Park, NC 27709-2211

ARO Microbiology and Biodegradation Research Contracts 723
This program supports basic research on the biochemical and physiological mechanisms underlying the biodegradative processes in normal, extreme, and engineered environments; basic studies on organisms from extreme environments; the properties of materials that make them susceptible or resistant to biological attack; basic concepts for antifungals; mechanisms for the remediation of contaminated sites; analytical microbiology, including microbial signatures; and general microbial mechanisms with relevance to Army problems. Research into microbial communities and how to study organisms that cannot be grown in the lab. Research into methods to enhance the stabilization of military materiel that would include methods to prevent microbial growth is also sought. Proposals may be submitted at any time.
Requirements Organizations and individuals interested in submitting research proposals are strongly encouraged to make preliminary inquiries as to the general need for the type of research effort contemplated before expending extensive effort in preparing a detailed research proposal or submitting proprietary information.
Contact Dr. Shirley Tove, Biosciences, (919) 549-4344; email: sherry.tove@us.army.mil
Internet http://www.aro.army.mil/research/index.htm
Sponsor Army Research Office
P.O. Box 12211
Research Triangle Park, NC 27709-2211

ARO Minimum Energy Low Power Electronics Research Contracts 724
The future army communications, information processing, imaging, and other systems must be portable, functional, versatile, and highly reliable. In addition, the systems will require ultra-high speed capability for handling complex voice, data, and video multimedia signal formats. Many of the new systems will find application in wireless communications, infrared imaging, and portable diagnostic and computational equipment. As these systems become more sophisticated, the necessary electronic circuitry becomes more complex, with increased prime power requirements. Currently, and in the near future, prime power for mobile and light weight system utilization is limited. It is necessary, therefore, to develop a new generation of electronic and other systems that can operate under minimum energy constraints with very low direct current (DC) power dissipation. This research topic goes beyond the simple desirability of efficient devices and circuits. It is aimed at new concepts resulting from considering the multilevel problem; materials, devices, circuits, coding, networking, and an overarching system of systems considerations, in order to reduce overall power dissipation in RF systems. Research can be approached from the component level or the overall design level. Proposals may be submitted at any time.
Requirements Organizations and individuals interested in submitting research proposals are strongly encouraged to make preliminary inquiries as to the general need for the type of research effort contemplated before expending extensive effort in preparing a detailed research proposal or submitting proprietary information.
Contact Dr. William Clark, Associate Director, Electronics Division, (919) 549-4314; email: William.W.Clark@us.army.mil
Internet http://www.aro.ncren.net
Sponsor Army Research Office
P.O. Box 12211
Research Triangle Park, NC 27709-2211

ARO Mobile, Wireless Communications and Networks Research Contracts 725
The mobile, wireless communications and networks research program is concerned primarily with establishing the fundamental understanding necessary to support the Army's future mobile, wireless tactical battlefield communications needs. The research in this program primarily targets the tactical battlefield at brigade and below. The Army is interested in communication systems operating in frequency bands traditionally occupied by narrowband radios high frequency (HF), very high frequency (VHF), and ultrahigh frequency (UHF) as well as systems operating in frequencies extending into the millimeter wave region. These systems must support broad-based and highly mobile communications and must perform in environments of impressive diversity, from dense foliage to dense urban obstructions, and unintentional and intentional jamming. Future Army tactical communication systems for the digital battlefield will consist of many different types of networks and must be capable of communicating on the move. These systems will be highly mobile creating highly dynamic network topologies (mobile ad-hoc networks) and routing multimedia (voice, data and video) data. Unlike commercial systems, the communications infrastructure must be mobile. In addition to the highly mobile communications, there is interest in algorithms for small, very energy-limited, stationary, unattended ground sensors. Proposals may be submitted at any time.
Requirements Organizations and individuals interested in submitting research proposals are strongly encouraged to make preliminary inquiries as to the general need for the type of research effort contemplated before expending extensive effort in preparing a detailed research proposal or submitting proprietary information.
Contact Dr. Robert Ulman, Electronics Division, (919) 549-4330; email: Robert.Ulman@us.army.mil
Internet http://www.aro.ncren.net
Sponsor Army Research Office
P.O. Box 12211
Research Triangle Park, NC 27709-2211

ARO Organic Chemistry Research Contracts 726
Molecules targeted for special attention include pigments and dyes with emission and reflectance characteristics useful for camouflage and controlled signature applications, potentially important monomers, especially for preparation of elastomer barrier materials and polymer electrolytes. New, more efficient, and environmentally benign organic reactions, both stoichiometric and catalytic, are of interest, especially nitration, and oxidative and nucleophilic displacements of phosphorus and sulfur for destruction of toxic organic compounds. Selected mechanistic studies that promise new insights to the pathways of the above reactions are encouraged as are new synthetic pathways with reduced production of waste byproducts. Proposals may be submitted at any time.
Requirements Organizations and individuals interested in submitting research proposals are strongly encouraged to make preliminary inquiries as to the general need for the type of research effort contemplated before expending extensive effort in preparing a detailed research proposal or submitting proprietary information.
Contact Dr. Stephen Lee, Chemistry Division, (919) 549-4365; email: Stephen.Lee2@us.army.mil
Internet http://www.aro.ncren.net
Sponsor Army Research Office
P.O. Box 12211
Research Triangle Park, NC 27709-2211

ARO Physical Behavior of Materials Research Contracts 727
The program of Physical Behavior of Materials seeks research directed at providing an improved understanding of the fundamental mechanisms and key materials and processing variables that determine the electronic, magnetic and optical (EMO) properties of materials and affect the reliability of EMO devices. Emphasis is on research that will facilitate the nanostructuring of materials to realize the materials-by-design concept where new and unique materials are constructed on the atomic scale with application-specific properties. This includes research on understanding the underlying thermodynamic and kinetic principles that control the evolution of microstructures; understanding the mechanisms whereby the microstructure affects the physical properties of materials; and developing insight and methodologies for the beneficial utilization and manipulation of defects and microstructure to improve material performance. Major trends in this subfield include: (i) electronic materials - materials for microelectronics and packaging; fabrication and processing of semi-conductors, interconnects and device structures, and the characterization and control of trace impurities, defects and interfaces in semiconductors, (ii) magnetic materials--bulk and thin-film processing of magnetic

materials for electronic and high frequency communications; and fundamental studies on magnetic coercivity and spin dynamics, and (iii) optical materials - materials and processing methods for detectors, lasers, nonlinear optical materials, refractive and diffractive optics, and optical windows and coatings. Research to improve the long-term stability of EMO materials, develop multifunctional or smart EMO materials, and develop low observable materials is also being sought. Other important areas of interest include new approaches for materials processing, new composite formulations, and surface treatments that minimize environmental impacts; and novel composite concepts, including multifunctional and hierarchical materials. Finally, there is general interest in identifying basic research in the area of manufacturing science, which will address fundamental issues related to the reliability and cost (including environmental) associated with the production and long-term operation of Army systems. Proposals may be submitted at any time.
Requirements Organizations and individuals interested in submitting research proposals are strongly encouraged to make preliminary inquiries as to the general need for the type of research effort contemplated before expending extensive effort in preparing a detailed research proposal or submitting proprietary information.
Contact Dr. John Prater, Materials Science Research, (919) 549-4259; email: John.T.Prater@us.army.mil
Internet http://www.aro.ncren.net
Sponsor Army Research Office
P.O. Box 12211
Research Triangle Park, NC 27709-2211

ARO Polymer Chemistry Research Contracts **728**
The Polymer Chemistry Program seeks novel, fundamental polymer research that may lead to new materials that provide the soldier with critical protection and required materiel. Research of interest may be related to chemical and biological agent protective materials, ballistic protection, transparent materials for eye protection and sensors, including laser protection, materials that have tunable optical properties, and lightweight super-strong materials. Research areas of interest that may be relevant include synthesis of polymers, including polymers with novel architectures and compositions, new approaches to synthesizing polymers, organic/inorganic hybrid polymeric materials, creating light-weight polymeric materials with enhanced strength, and the design and synthesis of environmentally benign polymeric materials that may benefit the soldier. Also of potential interest is characterization of structure/property relationships, diffusion and transport, and fiber properties related to polymer chemistry. Proposals may be submitted at any time.
Requirements Organizations and individuals interested in submitting research proposals are strongly encouraged to make preliminary inquiries as to the general need for the type of research effort contemplated before expending extensive effort in preparing a detailed research proposal or submitting proprietary information.
Contact Dr. Douglas Kiserow, Chemistry Division, (919) 549-4213; email: Douglas.Kiserow@.us.army.mil
Internet http://www.aro.ncren.net
Sponsor Army Research Office
P.O. Box 12211
Research Triangle Park, NC 27709-2211

ARO Quantum Information Science Research Contracts **729**
Quantum mechanics provides the opportunity to perform highly nonclassical operations that can result in exponential speed ups in computation or ultra-secure transmittal of information. This workpackage seeks to understand, control, and exploit such nonclassical phenomena for revolutionary advances in computation and secure communication. Major areas of interest are fundamental studies, quantum computation, and quantum communication. Proposals may be submitted at any time.
Requirements Organizations and individuals interested in submitting research proposals are strongly encouraged to make preliminary inquiries as to the general need for the type of research effort contemplated before expending extensive effort in preparing a detailed research proposal or submitting proprietary information.
Contact Dr. Henry Everitt, Physics Division, (919) 549-4369; email: henry.o.everitt@us.army.mil
Internet http://www.aro.ncren.net/research/index.htm
Sponsor Army Research Office
P.O. Box 12211
Research Triangle Park, NC 27709-2211

ARO Short-Term Innovation Research Program (STIR) **730**
The objectives of the STIR program are to fund innovative ideas in basic research. Proposed research may be for the continuation of or the natural outgrowth of experimental or theoretical explorations.
Requirements Research proposals are sought from educational institutions, nonprofit organizations, and private industry. Prospective offerors of a STIR proposal are encouraged to contact the ARO program manager in their area of interest to ascertain the extent of interest in the specific research project. Research must be completed within six months of award of the agreement.
Restrictions No capital equipment may be purchased. Travel costs must not exceed $500. Report preparation costs must not exceed $100. The assessment of indirect costs or fee is unallowable.
Amount $50,000 maximum
Contact Dr. Jim Chang, Director, (919) 549-4201; email: jim.chang@us.army.mil
Internet http://www.aro.army.mil/research
Sponsor Army Research Office
P.O. Box 12211
Research Triangle Park, NC 27709-2211

ARO Software and Knowledge-Based Systems Research Contracts **731**
The program in software and knowledge-based systems (SKBS) addresses the theoretical bases for the analysis, design, development, and evolution of advanced information-based systems that enable significant improvements in state-of-the-art engineering for software, software-based applications (including modeling and simulation), machine learning, knowledge/acquisition/representation/synthesis, and knowledgebases/databases. Currently, the research supported by the program is in software prototyping, development and evolution, formal methods for software engineering, and knowledgebase/database sciences. Proposals may be submitted at any time.
Requirements Organizations and individuals interested in submitting research proposals are strongly encouraged to make preliminary inquiries as to the general need for the type of research effort contemplated before expending extensive effort in preparing a detailed research proposal or submitting proprietary information.
Contact Dr. David Hislop, Mathematics and Computer Science Division, (919) 549-4255; email: David.W.Hislop@us.army.mil
Internet http://www.aro.ncren.net
Sponsor Army Research Office
P.O. Box 12211
Research Triangle Park, NC 27709-2211

ARO Solid Mechanics Research Contracts **732**
Solid mechanics provides the link between optimized material properties on the one hand and the desired structural behavior in terms of changes in shapes under a specific set of constraints on the other. Complete understanding of the behavior of structures made of advanced materials and quantitative description of their behavior allow predictive capability so necessary for design methodology. In situations that are described as ballistic in nature, the army faces unique constraints of very high strain rates, large deformations, high pressures, and rapid changes in temperature. Analytical, experimental, and computational techniques are integrated to solve well-formulated problems. Predictive models, validated by well-characterized experiments, are needed to identify controlling parameters at every scale. These models must be implementable in codes for the analysis of the efficiency of the designed hardware in the performance of military missions. Proposals may be submitted at any time.
Requirements Organizations and individuals interested in submitting research proposals are strongly encouraged to make preliminary inquiries as to the general need for the type of research effort contemplated before expending extensive effort in preparing a detailed research proposal or submitting proprietary information.
Date(s) Application Is Due Oct 15.
Contact Dr. Bruce LaMattina, (919) 549-4379; email: Bruce.LaMattina@us.army.mil
Internet http://www.aro.army.mil/research/index.htm
Sponsor Army Research Office
P.O. Box 12211
Research Triangle Park, NC 27709-2211

ARO Solid State Devices Research Contracts **733**
research area emphasizes efforts to establish a new and comprehensive base of knowledge for the electronic, photonic, acoustic and magnetic properties of solid-state materials, structures and devices. Functions such as very intelligent surveillance and target acquisition; command, control, and communications; electronic warfare; and reconnaissance, must be accomplished with the high data rates and real-time capability that are essential for these applications. To support the U.S. Army vision of Objective Force and Future Combat System of Systems (FCSS), these systems will need to operate at much higher speeds and frequencies, have greatly increased functionality, and have much higher levels of integration than present day technology provides. Therefore, fundamental research in the area of Solid State Devices is the corner stone and an essential requirement in the development of these future systems for military defense. Proposals may be submitted at any time.
Requirements Organizations and individuals interested in submitting research proposals are strongly encouraged to make preliminary inquiries as to the general need for the type of research effort contemplated before expending extensive effort in preparing a detailed research proposal or submitting proprietary information.
Contact Dr. Dwight Woolard, Electronics Division, (919) 549-4297; email: Dwight.Woolard@us.army.mil
Internet http://www.aro.ncren.net
Sponsor Army Research Office
P.O. Box 12211
Research Triangle Park, NC 27709-2211

ARO Stochastic Analysis, Applied Probability, and Statistics Research Contracts **734**
Army R&D programs directed toward system design, development, testing and evaluation problems generate a need for research in the field of stochastic processes, including stochastic differential equations. Under the stochastic analysis and applied probability subarea, special emphasis is placed on research into methods for the analysis

of observations from phenomena modeled by such processes and to numerical methods for stochastic partial differential equations. Research areas of importance to the army in probability and its applications include stochastic optimization and approximation, stochastic control, large deviations, simulation methodology, spatial processes, and image analysis. Ideas are needed from Markov random fields, renormalization of the state space, scaling of time, nonlinear stochastic analysis, and infinite-dimensional stochastic differential equations. The techniques required include Brownian flows, infinite-dimensional stochastic processes driven by Poisson noise, and Levy noise. Under the statistical methods subarea, the army has great interest in statistical methods for very large data sets or very small data sets, sampled from nonstandard, poorly understood distributions. The extraction of more information from small data sets requires improved methods for combining information from disparate sets, as in meta-analysis. Useful statistical models should be based on a thorough understanding of physical processes combined with sound statistical theory. Thus, it is important to integrate statistical procedures with scientific and engineering information about mechanisms as exemplified by a probabilistic methodology that describes the nature of the growth of cracks in different media and the associated statistical analysis. More research is required in several statistical areas including Bayesian methods, Markov random fields, cluster analysis, change point methods, and Markov chain Monte Carlo methods.
Requirements Organizations and individuals interested in submitting research proposals are strongly encouraged to make preliminary inquiries as to the general need for the type of research effort contemplated before expending extensive effort in preparing a detailed research proposal or submitting proprietary information.
Contact Dr. Mou-Hsiung Harry, (919) 549-4229; email: mouhsiung.chang@us.army.mil
Internet http://www.aro.ncren.net
Sponsor Army Research Office
P.O. Box 12211
Research Triangle Park, NC 27709-2211

ARO Structures and Dynamics Research Contracts **735**
A significant challenge facing Army laboratory engineers is the determination of the influence of inertial, thermal, electrical, magnetic, impact, damping, and aerodynamic forces on the dynamic response of adaptive armament systems, ground vehicles, rotorcraft, missiles, projectiles, gears, parachutes, and shelters. Its resolution is of fundamental importance to the design and construction of affordable, reliable, durable, and maintainable Army equipment with acceptable levels of personnel safety and comfort. Consequently, the ARO is supporting basic research in these areas, with emphasis on air vehicle dynamics, including missile and rotorcraft dynamics; the dynamics, non-linear vibrations, structural control, and simulation of land vehicles and weapon systems; and the dynamic response of structural components and systems fabricated from advanced composite materials, with or without embedded actuators and sensors. Submittal of fundamental research proposals on the general topics described above is encouraged, keeping in view the paramount importance of Army relevance.
Requirements Organizations and individuals interested in submitting research proposals are strongly encouraged to make preliminary inquiries as to the general need for the type of research effort contemplated before expending extensive effort in preparing a detailed research proposal or submitting proprietary information.
Contact Dr. Gary Anderson, Engineering Sciences Division, (919) 549-4317; email: Gary.L.Anderson@us.army.mil
Internet http://www.aro.ncren.net
Sponsor Army Research Office
P.O. Box 12211
Research Triangle Park, NC 27709-2211

ARO Synthesis and Processing of Materials Research Contracts **736**
The program on synthesis and processing of materials focuses on the use of innovative approaches for processing high-performance structural materials reliably and at lower costs. Emphasis is placed on the design and fabrication of new materials with specific microstructure, constitution, and properties. Research interests include experimental and theoretical modeling studies to understand the influence of fundamental parameters on phase formation, microstructural evolution, and the resulting properties, in order to predict and control materials structures at all scales ranging from atomic dimensions to macroscopic levels. Trends in this subfield include nonequilibrium materials processing (e.g., rapid solidification); powder synthesis and consolidation; novel processing of ceramics, polymers, metals and composites; welding and joining including composite materials; elastomers; fibers and fabrics; and utilization of microstructural, compositional, or other unique signatures which may provide non-destructive in situ feedback process control to enhance product reproducibility and quality. Supercritical fluid, shock-induced chemical processing and other innovative approaches for processing materials are also of interest. Proposals may be submitted at any time.
Requirements Organizations and individuals interested in submitting research proposals are strongly encouraged to make preliminary inquiries as to the general need for the type of research effort contemplated before expending extensive effort in preparing a detailed research proposal or submitting proprietary information.
Contact Dr. William Mullins, (919) 549-4286; email: William.Mullins@us.army.mil
Internet http://www.aro.army.mil/matsc/matsc.htm
Sponsor Army Research Office
P.O. Box 12211
Research Triangle Park, NC 27709-2211

ARO Terrestrial Sciences Research Contracts **737**
In general, the terrestrial sciences program is concerned with the impact of the earth's surficial environment on army activities. Program interests cover a broad spectrum, ranging from terrain characterization and analysis, military engineering, and mobility considerations under combat conditions, to the management and stewardship of its installations as regards the impact of army activities on the natural environment. Primary emphasis is directed toward understanding the behavior of the land surface and the near-surface environments, understanding the natural processes operating upon and within these domains, and modeling these environments for predictive and simulation purposes. Special emphasis is given to the need to better understand, model/simulate, and predict those environments/conditions that are most extreme, dynamic, or restrictive to systems performance or military operations. Proposals may be submitted at any time.
Requirements Organizations and individuals interested in submitting research proposals are strongly encouraged to make preliminary inquiries as to the general need for the type of research effort contemplated before expending extensive effort in preparing a detailed research proposal or submitting proprietary information.
Contact Dr. Russell Harmon, Environmental Sciences Division, (919) 549-4326; email: Russell.Harmon@us.army.mil
Internet http://www.aro.ncren.net
Sponsor Army Research Office
P.O. Box 12211
Research Triangle Park, NC 20779-2211

ARO Theoretical Physics and Nonlinear Phenomena Research Contracts **738**
The theoretical physics and nonlinear phenomena program is very closely coupled to experimental science as well as to ARO's programs in mathematics, chemistry, biological chemistry, materials science, and engineering sciences. The program thus encompasses a broad base including research in electron physics, photon physics, and classical and quantum mechanical systems, and statistical physics. It includes first-principles derivations of thermomechanical strengths of alloys for armor and armor penetrators; and electronic band structure calculations of materials for electronic, magnetic, optical, and optoelectronics applications, including those that result from quantum well and multiquantum well structures for signal generation, signal processing, and propagation and detection of signals. Also of interest are many-body theoretic approaches that address the electron correlation problem in extended molecular and condensed matter systems to provide the means to predict reaction kinetics, nonequilibrium dynamics, and application to the "alloy problem. There is interest in quantum optics research to explore the role of coherent states, squeezed states, etc. which may provide new tools for improved information processing and means to control information. Statistical physics interests go beyond thermodynamics, into nonequilibrium structures and their metastability, into information theoretic formulations, and into decision algorithms to connect the underlying physics to real world applications via proper modeling, instrumentation, and data analysis. Subtopics of interest include theoretical condensed matter physics, nonlinear dynamics, and nonequilibrium dynamics.
Requirements Organizations and individuals interested in submitting research proposals are strongly encouraged to make preliminary inquiries as to the general need for the type of research effort contemplated before expending extensive effort in preparing a detailed research proposal or submitting proprietary information.
Contact Dr. Mikael Ciftan, Physics Division, (919) 549-4236; email: Mikael.Ciftan@us.army.mil
Internet http://www.aro.army.mil
Sponsor Army Research Office
P.O. Box 12211
Research Triangle Park, NC 27709-2211

ARO Young Investigator Program/Presidential Early Career Awards **739**
The objective of the Young Investigator Program (YIP) is to attract to army research outstanding young university faculty members, to support their research and to encourage their teaching and research careers. Outstanding YIP projects may be considered for a Presidential Early Career Award for Scientists and Engineers (PECASE). PECASE awards are the highest honor bestowed by the Army on outstanding scientists and engineers beginning their independent careers. Awards are granted in all research topic areas in the army Research Office. Support for the YIP is limited to three years; PECASE support is limited to five years. Proposals may be submitted at any time.
Requirements This program is open to US citizens holding tenure-track positions at US universities and colleges who have held their graduate degrees (PhD or equivalent) for fewer than five years at the time of application. ARO strongly encourages informal discussions with the cognizant ARO technical program manager before submission of a formal proposal.
Amount $50,000 maximum for three years
Contact Kurt Preston, (919) 549-4234; email: Kurt.Preston@us.army.mil
Internet http://www.aro.ncren.net
Sponsor Army Research Office
P.O. Box 12211
Research Triangle Park, NC 27709-2211

Arronson Foundation Grants **740**
The foundation supports nonprofit organizations in the areas of religion, including churches (Baptist, Christian, Jewish, Roman Catholic, and Salvation Army) and religious education, higher education, health care, hospices, Jewish welfare, international

ministries/missions, and youth. The foundation awards grants primarily in New York, NY; Philadelphia, PA; and Israel. Types of support include endowment funds, general operating support grants, research, scholarships, and seed money grants. Applicants should submit a brief letter of inquiry and include information on the organization and its work. There are no application deadlines.
Requirements Nonprofit organizations in Pennsylvania, with emphasis on the Philadelphia area, are eligible to apply.
Amount $200-$25,000 range
Contact Joseph Kohn, President & Secretary, (215) 238-1700 or (215) 238-1968; email: jkohn@kohnswift.com
Sponsor Arronson Foundation
1 S Broad St, Ste 2100
Philadelphia, PA 19107

Art Conservation Advanced Training Fellowships 741
The fellowships are awarded to encourage qualified individuals to prepare for careers as conservators and curators in museums of art. Conservation fellowships support one-year internships in advanced fine arts conservation at a museum or conservation research facility. Curatorial fellowships support one-year internships for curatorial training in European art at an American museum. Fellowship stipends support travel, administrative costs, benefits for the fellow, and other direct costs of the fellowship. Deadlines are January 15 for curatorial fellowships and March 1 for conservation fellowships.
Requirements Individuals who have completed an MA degree in art conservation are eligible for conservation fellowships. Application must be made by the museum or conservation research facility at which the internship will be based. Individuals who have completed a PhD in the history of European art are eligible for curatorial fellowships.
Restrictions Fellowships will not be awarded to complete a degree program.
Amount $30,000
Date(s) Application Is Due Jan 15; Mar 1.
Contact Lisa Ackerman, Executive Vice President, (212) 861-4993; fax: (212) 628-3146
Internet http://www.kressfoundation.org/kressorg/advafell.html
Sponsor Samuel H. Kress Foundation
174 E 80th St
New York, NY 10021

Arthritis Foundation of Australia Grants 742
The foundation awards grants in the fields of medicine and health, with emphasis on arthritis research and education. Types of awards include grants-in-aid, fellowships, and scholarships. Grants are awarded in Australia, the United Kingdom, and the United States. Annual deadline dates may vary; contact program staff for exact dates.
Requirements Awards are available to clinical, scientific, and allied health professionals who are Australian citizens or permanent residents. Scholarships, fellowships, and grants may only be held in universities, hospitals, or recognized research institutes.
Amount $A10,000-$A15,000 grants-in-aid
Date(s) Application Is Due Jun 30.
Contact Grant Coordinator, 61 (0)2 9552 6085; fax: 61 (0)2 9552 6078; email: info@arthritisaustralia.com.au
Internet http://arthritisaustralia.com.au/Research%20Grants
Sponsor Arthritis Foundation of Australia
P.O. Box 121
Sydney 2001 Australia

Arthritis Medical Research Grants 743
The foundation's primary purpose is to provide financial support to research studies aimed at discovering new knowledge for the prevention, treatment, and cure of arthritis and other rheumatic diseases. Both clinical and basic studies will be considered. The focus of proposals should be on high-incidence diseases. Grants are awarded for one year; projects requiring multiyear funding must reapply each year. Partial funding may be awarded if the grantee has documentation that the remainder of the funding for proposed research has been acquired. Grants support salaries, supplies, and equipment directly related to the proposed studies. Overhead or indirect costs will not be funded.
Requirements Priority will be given to newer investigators possessing either a MD and/or PhD degree who are associated with qualified institutions.
Amount $20,000-$50,000
Date(s) Application Is Due Jan 15.
Contact Helene Belisle, Executive Director, (800) 588-2873; fax: (562) 983-1410; email: anrf@ix.netcom.com
Internet http://www.curearthritis.org/grant.htm
Sponsor Arthritis National Research Foundation
200 Oceangate, Ste 400
Long Beach, CA 90802

Arthritis Society Investigator Awards 744
A limited number of grants are offered to individuals who have demonstrated their ability as independent research scientists with international impact and are pursuing a full-time academic career in medical science. Candidates will only be considered between three and eight years after receiving their first academic appointment. Registration deadline is August 15; full application is due by September 15.
Requirements Application is made on behalf of candidates by the chair of the department or director of the research institute in which the scholar will be appointed. Application should be submitted on form NF-109A.
Restrictions Grants will not be made to replace faculty salary support for well-established investigators who have held faculty appointment for longer than five years at the applying institution.
Amount $C70,000
Contact Medical and Scientific Program, (416) 967-3353 ext 311 or 979-7228; fax: (416) 979-8366; email: can@mtsinai.on.ca
Internet http://www.arthritis.ca/look%20at%20research/awards/investigators/default.asp?s=1
Sponsor The Arthritis Society (Canada)
393 University Ave, Ste 1700
Toronto, ON M5G 1E6 Canada

Arthritis Society Multicenter Grants 745
Multicenter grants are designed to foster collaboration of individuals, working at different geographic locations, on a research project deemed relevant to the rheumatic diseases. Grants are usually made for a period of three years and are intended to cover the costs of the research for which they are provided. Appropriate space and basic facilities at the institutions concerned are prerequisite to an application. Registration deadline is November 15; full application is due by December 15.
Requirements Completed applications for grants or renewals must be submitted on form NF-107A; obtain detailed instructions from the society.
Amount $C60,000 average
Date(s) Application Is Due Nov 15; Dec 15.
Contact Medical and Scientific Program, (416) 967-3353 ext 311 or 979-7228; fax: (416) 979-8366; email: can@mtsinai.on.ca
Internet http://www.arthritis.ca/look%20at%20research/awards/default.asp?s=1
Sponsor The Arthritis Society (Canada)
393 University Ave, Ste 1700
Toronto, ON M5G 1E6 Canada

Arthritis Society New Investigator Award 746
The awards are intended to support newly appointed junior faculty members (within three years of appointment) who are planning to pursue a career in basic or clinical research related to arthritis. The scholarships assist individuals with the PhD or MD degree who have received extensive postdoctoral research training in their chosen area and who have clearly demonstrated their potential as independent research scientists to establish themselves. Scholarships are not renewable; prior recipients may apply for research scientist grants. Registration deadline is November 15; full application is due by December 15.
Requirements Application is made on behalf of candidates by the chair of the department or director of the research institute in which the scholar will be appointed. Application should be submitted on form NF-110A.
Restrictions Awards are not intended to replace faculty salary for well-established investigators who have been on duty for a number of years at the applying institution.
Amount $C50,000
Date(s) Application Is Due Nov 15; Dec 15.
Contact Medical and Scientific Program, (416) 967-3353 ext 311 or 979-7228; fax: (416) 979-8366; email: can@mtsinai.on.ca
Internet http://www.arthritis.ca/look%20at%20research/awards/new%20investigators/default.asp?s=1
Sponsor The Arthritis Society (Canada)
393 University Ave, Ste 1700
Toronto, ON M5G 1E6 Canada

Arthritis Society Research Grants 747
Grants in aid of research are designed to promote and support research proposed by investigators holding staff appointments at Canadian universities or other recognized Canadian institutions where the research is deemed relevant to the rheumatic diseases. Grants are usually made for a period of three years and are intended to cover the costs of the research for which they are provided. Appropriate space and basic facilities at the institution concerned are prerequisite to an application. Requests for all funds on grant applications must be carefully and fully justified.
Requirements Completed applications for grants or renewals must be submitted on form NF-104A; obtain detailed instructions from the society.
Amount $C60,000 average
Date(s) Application Is Due Dec 15.
Contact Medical and Scientific Program, (416) 967-3353 ext 311 or 979-7228; fax: (416) 979-8366; email: can@mtsinai.on.ca
Internet http://www.arthritis.ca/look%20at%20research/awards/d9/default.asp?s=1
Sponsor The Arthritis Society (Canada)
393 University Ave, Ste 1700
Toronto, ON M5G 1E6 Canada

Arthur and Rochelle Belfer Foundation Grants 748
The foundation awards grants to nonprofit organizations of the Jewish faith, with a focus on New York. Grants are targeted toward programs supporting the elderly and women; education/higher education; institutions such as seminaries, synagogues, and temples;

hospitals; Jewish welfare; and medical centers. Types of support include general support grants and fellowships. There are no application deadlines. Applicants should send a brief letter of inquiry describing the program.
Restrictions Grants are not made to individuals.
Amount $1000-$100,000 average
Contact Robert Belfer, President; 212-508-6020
Sponsor Arthur and Rochelle Belfer Foundation, Inc
767 Fifth Ave, 46th Fl
New York, NY 10153-0002

Arthur C. Cope Award in Organic Chemistry 749
The award is given to recognize outstanding achievement in the field of organic chemistry, the significance of which has become apparent within the five years preceding the year in which the award will be considered. In addition to the award to the recipient, an unrestricted grant in aid for $150,000 for research in organic chemistry, under the direction of the recipient, will be made to any university or nonprofit institution selected by the recipient. The recipient may choose to assign the Arthur C. Cope Fund Grant to an institution for use by others than the recipient for research or education in organic chemistry.
Requirements Any individual, except a member of the award committee, may submit one nomination or seconding letter for the award in any given year. The nominating documents consist of a letter of not more than 1000 words containing an evaluation of the nominee's accomplishments and a specific identification of the work to be recognized, a biographical sketch including date of birth, and a list of publications and patents authored by the nominee.
Restrictions Self-nominations are not accepted.
Amount $25,000 plus travel to award meeting for recipient
Date(s) Application Is Due Feb 1.
Contact Awards Administrator, (800) 227-5558 or (202) 872-4600; fax: (202) 872-4615; email: awards@acs.org or help@acs.org
Internet http://www.chemistry.org/portal/a/c/s/1/acsdisplay.html?DOC=awards%5Cc opeaward.html
Sponsor American Chemical Society
1155 16th St NW
Washington, DC 20036

Arthur C. Cope Scholar Awards 750
These awards are given to recognize and encourage excellence in organic chemistry. Ten (10) Arthur C. Cope Scholars will be named annually: Four (4) between the ages of thirty-six and forty-nine, four (4) age fifty or older, and two (2) thirty-five and younger all inclusive before April 30, of the year in which the award is presented. The award consists of a certificate and an unrestricted research grant to be assigned by the recipient to any university or nonprofit institution. The recipient is required to deliver a lecture at the annual Arthur C. Cope Symposium; traveling expenses incidental to participation in the symposium will be paid.
Requirements Any individual qualified to evaluate the nominee's accomplishments may submit one nomination for the award in any year; nomination should include a letter containing an evaluation of the nominee's contributions to organic chemistry with identification of the work to be recognized including literature and/or patent references; a biographical sketch of the nominee including date of birth and record of employment; and a list of publications and patents authored by the nominee. Mail six copies of all items to the awards office.
Restrictions Self-nominations are not accepted. An individual may not receive the award a second time. Recipients of the Arthur C. Cope Award are ineligible to be named Arthur C. Cope Scholars.
Amount $5000 plus $40,000 for unrestricted research to a named institution
Date(s) Application Is Due Feb 1.
Contact Awards Administrator, (800) 227-5558 or (202) 872-4600; fax: (202) 872-4615; email: awards@acs.org or help@acs.org
Internet http://www.chemistry.org/portal/a/c/s/1/acsdisplay.html?DOC=awards%5Cc opescholar.html
Sponsor American Chemical Society
1155 16th St NW
Washington, DC 20036

Arthur H. Cole Grants in Aid for Research in Economic History 751
These grants in aid are designed to be supplemental to other grants or income, and support research in economic history regardless of time or geographic area. Applicants should supply seven copies of a presentation of not more than five pages that includes a description of the project, a curriculum vita, and a brief budget for the project. Annual deadline dates may vary; contact program staff for exact dates.
Requirements Preference is given to recent PhD recipients.
Amount $1500 typically
Date(s) Application Is Due Apr 1.
Contact The Committee on Research in Economic History, (785) 864-2847; fax: (785) 864-5270; email: eha@falcon.cc.ukans.edu
Internet http://www.eh.net/EHA
Sponsor Economic History Association
213 Summerfield Hall, University of Kansas, Dept of Economics
Lawrence, KS 66045

Arthur L. Williston Medal 752
This award is given annually for the best paper or thesis submitted in the Williston Award Contest by an undergraduate or junior engineer fostering a spirit of civil service. Candidates must be student members or associate members with an ASME sponsor for the award. In addition to the Williston Medal, second and third prizes are awarded.
Requirements Applicant must be a student member or an associate member of ASME who has not graduated more than two years prior.
Amount $1000 first prize; $500 second prize; $250 third prize
Date(s) Application Is Due Mar 1.
Contact Grants Administrator, (212) 591-7735; email: persaudl@asme.org
Internet http://www.asme.org/honors/ms71/list.html
Sponsor American Society of Mechanical Engineers
3 Park Ave
New York, NY 10016

Arthur S. Tuttle Memorial Scholarships 753
Scholarships are for tuition assistance to students during their first year of graduate studies in civil engineering. Any student in good standing who is also a national student member of the society may apply; the funds may be applied only for tuition expenses during the first year of formal graduate civil engineering education in an accredited educational institution. Financial need and educational standing will be considered in selecting recipients. The total sum for awards available will be determined annually based on earnings available from the endowment.
Requirements Application consists of a completed application form; applicant's justification for applying; plans for continuing formal education; official transcripts, recommendation forms, and supporting statements from the student chapter faculty advisor and two other members of the engineering school faculty; and a detailed financial plan outlining both income and expenses anticipated for the award year. Applicants must be a member of the society, in any grade, and must be in good standing at the time of application and award. Membership applications may be submitted with scholarship application.
Amount $2000-$5000
Date(s) Application Is Due Feb 9.
Contact Grants Coordinator, (800) 548-2723; fax: (703) 295-6132; email: student@ asce.org
Internet http://www.asce.org/inside/stud_tuttle.cfm
Sponsor American Society of Civil Engineers
1801 Alexander Bell Dr
Reston, VA 20191-4400

Arthur W. Adamson Award for Distinguished Service in the Advancement of Surface Chemistry 754
This annual award, sponsored by Occidental Petroleum Corporation and administered by the American Chemical Society, recognizes distinguished services in the advancement of surface chemistry. Activities recognized by the award may include such fields as teaching, writing, research, and administration. A gold medal and a bronze replica of the medal are also provided.
Requirements Any individual, except a member of the award committee, may submit one nomination or seconding letter for each award in any given year. The letter of nomination should contain an evaluation of the nominee's accomplishments and a specific identification of the work to be recognized, and may not exceed 1000 words in length. Six copies of all items to be included in the nomination should be submitted.
Restrictions Self-nominations are not accepted.
Amount $5000 and up to $1000 travel allowance to the award meeting
Date(s) Application Is Due Feb 1.
Contact Awards Administrator, (202) 872-4408; fax: (202) 776-8211; email: awards@ acs.org
Internet http://www.chemistry.org/portal/a/c/s/1/acsdisplay.html?DOC=awards%5Ca damson.html
Sponsor American Chemical Society
1155 16th St NW
Washington, DC 20036

Artists's Exploration Fund Travel Grants 755
The grants enable individual performing artists to pursue opportunities abroad that further their artistic development. Grants support a variety of activities, including development of relationships with artists and arts organizations, research of significant artistic expression, participation in international conferences and seminars, or creation of new work. Eligible expenses include international and in-country travel, food and lodging, and other essential costs. The Explorations Fund will reimburse up to $2,000 to cover the real cost of one international airfare (based on a 14-day advance fare) and per diem, not to exceed $35 per day for up to 10 days. Per diems will be based on the total amount of days traveled.
Requirements US citizens and permanent residents are eligible for travel to any country outside the United States and its protectorates.
Restrictions The fund will not support travel costs related to touring. Applications will not be accepted from students, scholars, curators, presenters, administrators, and critics.
Amount $1000-$3000
Date(s) Application Is Due Apr 7; Sep 23.

Contact Olga Martins, Program Coordinator, (212) 924-0771 ext 101; fax: (212) 924-0773; email: omartins@artsinternational.org.
Internet http://www.performingartsregister.com/opportunities.phtml
Sponsor Arts International
770 Broadway, 2nd Fl
New York, NY 10003

ASA and USDA/NASS Research Fellow Program 756
ASA, in cooperation with the National Agricultural Statistics Service (NASS) of the Department of Agriculture, sponsors this program to supplement graduate education and research in statistics with experience in residence at NASS. The program provides selected fellows with research opportunities or experience in the application of statistical theory in all phases of large-scale agricultural survey operations, including design, collection, quality control, forecasting, estimation, and analysis. Positions are typically an academic year for nine to 12 months. They may be extended up to one additional year under special circumstances. Special appointments covering one or several periods of two to three months also will be considered. The program year normally begins in January or September, but it is possible for an applicant to begin at another date. Applications for positions for the year beginning September should be received by March 1. For a starting date of January, applications should arrive at the ASA office approximately six months in advance. Questions about the NASS program can be directed to Dr. Phillip Kott, Chief, Survey Research Branch, (703) 235-5211 ext 102. Applications should be sent to the address shown.
Requirements Applicants for the fellowship program should have a PhD, an established recognized research record, and considerable expertise in their area of proposed research.
Date(s) Application Is Due Mar 1.
Contact Fellowship Programs Director, (703) 684-1221; fax: (703) 684-2037; email: asainfo@amstat.org
Internet http://www.nass.usda.gov/research/ASA-NASS.html
Sponsor American Statistical Association
1429 Duke St
Alexandria, VA 22314-3402

ASA Bureau of Justice Statistics Data Analysis Small Grants 757
The ASA Committee on Law and Justice Statistics supports a program of small grants for the analysis of Bureau of Justice Statistics (BJS) data. The program is designed to encourage the creative and appropriate use of these data to inform substantive and methodological issues. An illustrative list of of BJS data sources for potential research topics includes national crime victimization survey, federal justice data, law enforcement data, and national prisoner statistics. These grants are also available to support dissertation research for up to two years. Proposals should be no more than eight double-spaced pages (excluding bibliography, tables, budgets, and appendices) and describe the research question, indicate its substantive or methodological importance, describe the analysis to be done, outline the specific tasks to be done and who is to do them, and identify any unique problems that may be encountered in conducting this research.
Amount $25,000
Date(s) Application Is Due Dec 1.
Contact Carolyn Kesner, (703) 684-1221; fax: (703) 684-3410; email: carolyn@amstat.org
Internet http://www.amstat.org/research_grants/BJSsolicitation.PDF
Sponsor American Statistical Association
1429 Duke St
Alexandria, VA 22314-3402

ASA Graduate Student Research Award 758
The award is presented annually to a graduate student for research relevant to aging and applicable to practice. The winner will be expected to attend the joint conference of the ASA and the National Council on the Aging to present the winning paper. The award comprises a certificate, complimentary registration and one-night's lodging for the conference, presentation of research findings at a highlighted session at the conference, and complimentary one-year membership in ASA. Submission guidelines and application are available online.
Requirements Only graduate-level research will be considered. Findings must be from completed research; submission of the conceptual framework alone is not sufficient. Applicants must either be currently enrolled in a graduate degree program or must have completed their studies no more than one year before the time of submission. Applicants must be sponsored by a faculty member. Applicants and faculty sponsors need not be ASA members.
Restrictions Papers that have been published are not eligible for submission.
Amount $500 cash prize
Date(s) Application Is Due Oct 14.
Contact Valerie Jones, Award Coordinator, (415) 974-9602; fax: (415) 974-0300; email: vjones@asaging.org
Internet http://www.asaging.org/awards/students.cfm
Sponsor American Society on Aging
833 Market St, Ste 511
San Francisco, CA 94103-1824

ASA Minority Fellowship Program 759
The fellowships are awarded to contribute to the development of sociology by recruiting persons who will add differing orientations and creativity to the field. Prospective and current graduate students who can approach research on mental health issues relating to minorities from an indigenous perspective will be selected for these awards. Dependent upon the availability of funds, approximately 10 fellowships will be awarded annually.
Requirements American citizens and permanent visa residents including, but not limited to, persons who are African American, Latino/Hispanic (e.g., Chicano, Cuban, Puerto Rican), Native American, and Asian American (e.g., Chinese, Japanese, Korean), and Pacific Islanders (e.g., Hawaiian, Guamanian, Samoan, Filipino) are eligible. The program is open to students beginning or continuing study in graduate sociology departments. New students must qualify for acceptance at accredited institutions of higher learning and express a commitment to sociological research on mental health. Upon completion of their support, recipients are expected to engage in behavioral research or teaching, or a combination thereof, for a period equal to the period of support beyond 12 months.
Amount $20,772 stipend
Date(s) Application Is Due Jan 31.
Contact Minority Affairs Manager, (202) 383-9005; fax: (202) 638-0882; email: minority.affairs@asanet.org
Internet http://www.asanet.org/page.ww?section=Funding&name=Minority+Fellowship+Program
Sponsor American Sociological Association
1307 New York Ave NW, Ste 700
Washington, DC 20005

ASA Small Grants Program--Teaching Enhancement Fund 760
The goal of this program is to support projects that extend the quality of teaching in the United States and Canada. Proposals limited to a maximum of five pages should describe the project and the intended audience or beneficiaries, explain how the financial support would be used, describe the expected benefits of the project including systemic impacts, and indicate how the project might have a lasting benefit.
Requirements An individual, department, program, or committee of a state/regional association may apply. Individuals applying for the award must be members of ASA.
Amount $1000 maximum
Date(s) Application Is Due Feb 1.
Contact Program Officer, (202) 383-9005; fax: (202) 638-0882; TDD (202) 872-0486; email: asanet@asanet.org
Internet http://www.asanet.org/page.ww?section=Funding&name=Teaching+Enhancement+Fund
Sponsor American Sociological Association
1307 New York Ave NW, Ste 700
Washington, DC 20005

ASA/NCHS Research Fellowships 761
The program is designed to bridge the gap between academic scholars and the federal government's health research programs. Fellowship recipients conduct research in Washington, DC, at the National Center for Health Statistics (NCHS), where they may use NCHS data and interact with NCHS staff. The 12-month fellowship may be extended one additional year under special circumstances. The stipend received is commensurate with current faculty salaries plus moving expenses and a travel allowance. Each applicant is required to submit a curriculum vita; the names and addresses of three references who may be contacted; and two copies of a detailed research proposal that includes a one-half page abstract, statement of relevant work already accomplished, statement citing the significance of the expected results to NCHS, and resource requirements.
Requirements Applicants must be US citizens.
Restrictions US government employees are ineligible.
Date(s) Application Is Due Oct 7.
Contact Carolyn Kesner, (703) 684-1221; fax: (703) 684-2037; email: carolyn@amstat.org
Internet http://www.amstat.org/research_grants/index.cfm?fuseaction=main
Sponsor American Statistical Association
1429 Duke St
Alexandria, VA 22314-3402

ASA/NSF/BLS Senior Research Fellow Program 762
ASA, under a grant from the National Science Foundation and with cosponsorship by the Bureau of Labor Statistics (BLS), seeks senior researchers for this program. Fellows conduct research in residence at BLS, gaining unique opportunities for use of BLS data and interaction with bureau staff. Fellows may pursue research in any area related to BLS data or methodology. Possible areas for research include, but are not limited to, areas under the fields of economic and social measurement and research, and statistical methodology and computing. Any proposed project should have the potential of encouraging further significant, broadly based research and should require hands-on access to BLS data and/or have direct application to BLS programs. Salary is commensurate with qualifications; fringe benefits and a travel allowance are included. A program brochure is available.
Requirements Applicants for fellowships should have recognized research records and considerable expertise in their area of proposed research. Qualified women and members of minority groups are encouraged to apply for fellowships and associateships.
Date(s) Application Is Due Dec 10.

Contact Carol Kesner, Fellowship Programs Director, (888) 231-3473 or (703) 684-1221; fax: (703) 684-2037; email: carolyn@amstat.org
Internet http://www.amstat.org/research_grants/ASANSFBLSSeniorResearchFellowbrochure.pdf
Sponsor American Statistical Association
1429 Duke St
Alexandria, VA 22314-3415

ASA/NSF/Census Research Fellowships **763**
ASA, under a grant from the National Science Foundation, administers the research fellowship program, in cooperation with the Bureau of the Census. The fellows conduct research in residence at the US Bureau of Census. Fellows may pursue research in any area related to Census Bureau data or methodology. Possible areas for research include, but are not limited to, social and demographic studies, statistical methodology and computing, and economic measurement and analysis. Qualified women and members of minority groups are encouraged to apply for these fellowships. A program brochure is available.
Requirements Applicants should have recognized research records and considerable expertise in their areas of proposed research. They must submit detailed research proposals for competitive evaluation.
Date(s) Application Is Due Dec 10.
Contact Carolyn Kesner, (888) 231-3473 or (703) 684-1221; fax: (703) 684-2037; email: carolyn@amstat.org
Internet http://www.amstat.org/research_grants
Sponsor American Statistical Association
1429 Duke St
Alexandria, VA 22314-3402

ASCE Samuel Fletcher Tapman Scholarships **764**
These scholarships are awarded for undergraduate tuition assistance to ASCE Student Chapter members in good standing who will employ them to continue their formal undergraduate education in a recognized educational institution.
Requirements Any undergraduate freshman, sophomore, or junior of an ASCE Student Chapter may apply; previous holders of this scholarship may also apply. Application consists of brief application form; statement of applicant's justification for receiving the award; applicant's plans for continuing his/her formal education; official transcript; and applicant appraisals from student chapter faculty advisor and not less than two other faculty members.
Restrictions Each student chapter may submit only one application from its membership; three applicants in each society zone (total of 12) are selected each year.
Amount $2000
Date(s) Application Is Due Feb 9.
Contact Grants Coordinator, (800) 548-2723; fax: (703) 295-6132; email: student@asce.org
Internet http://www.asce.org/inside/stud_tin-tap.cfm
Sponsor American Society of Civil Engineers
1801 Alexander Bell Dr
Reston, VA 20191-4400

ASCO Advanced Clinical Research Awards in Breast Cancer **765**
The ASCO Foundation and Genentech BioOncology invite physicians with full-time faculty appointments to apply for a clinical oncology research award in Breast Cancer. The program funds clinical investigators who are committed to clinical cancer research. Their research must have a direct patient-oriented focus including clinical trials and/or translational research involving human subjects. The Advanced Clinical Research Award is designed to provide funding beyond the Clinical Research Career Development Award (CDA). By continuing to support proven clinical researchers who are post-CDA but at a critical stage in their early career, the foundation hopes to expand the cadre of expert clinical oncology researchers who are developing promising research initiatives.
Requirements The applicant must meet the following criteria at the time of grant award: be a physician (MD or DO) who is 5-10 years post final sub-specialty training; have a full-time faculty appointment in a clinical department at an academic medical center; have completed productive postdoctoral/post-fellowship research and demonstrated the ability to undertake independent investigator-initiated clinical research; be an active member of the American Society of Clinical Oncology (ASCO); and expect to spend 75% of time during the award period dedicated to research.
Amount $450,000
Date(s) Application Is Due Feb 14.
Contact Julia McCormack, Executive Director, (703) 299-0150; fax: (703) 299-1044; email: McCormaj@asco.org
Internet http://www.asco.org/portal/site/ASCO/menuitem.c543a013502b2a89de912310320041a0/ ?vgnextoid=8d2a61439056d010VgnVCM100000ed730ad1RCRD&vgnextfmt=default
Sponsor American Society of Clinical Oncology
1900 Duke Street, Suite 200
Alexandria, VA 22303

ASCO Advanced Clinical Research Awards in Hematologic Makignancies **766**
The ASCO Foundation and Genentech BioOncology invite physicians with full-time faculty appointments to apply for a clinical oncology research award in Hematologic Malignancies. The program funds clinical investigators who are committed to clinical cancer research. Their research must have a direct patient-oriented focus including clinical trials and/or translational research involving human subjects. The Advanced Clinical Research Award is designed to provide funding beyond the Clinical Research Career Development Award (CDA). By continuing to support proven clinical researchers who are post-CDA but at a critical stage in their early career, the foundation hopes to expand the cadre of expert clinical oncology researchers who are developing promising research initiatives.
Requirements The applicant must meet the following criteria at the time of grant award: be a physician (MD or DO) who is 5-10 years post final sub-specialty training; have a full-time faculty appointment in a clinical department at an academic medical center; have completed productive postdoctoral/post-fellowship research and demonstrated the ability to undertake independent investigator-initiated clinical research; be an active member of the American Society of Clinical Oncology (ASCO); and expect to spend 75% of time during the award period dedicated to research.
Amount $450,000 (paid over three years)
Date(s) Application Is Due Aug 15.
Contact Julia McCormack, Executive Director, (703) 299-0150; fax: (703) 299-1044; email: McCormaj@asco.org
*Internet*http://www.asco.org/portal/site/ASCO/menuitem.c543a013502b2a89de912310320041a0/ ?vgnextoid=91de00b9851e1110VgnVCM100000ed730ad1RCRD&vgnextfmt=default
Sponsor American Society of Clinical Oncology
1900 Duke Street, Suite 200
Alexandria, VA 22303

ASCO Advanced Clinical Research Awards in Lung Cancer **767**
The ASCO Foundation and Genentech BioOncology invite physicians with full-time faculty appointments to apply for a clinical oncology research award in lung cancer. The program funds clinical investigators who are committed to clinical cancer research. Their research must have a direct patient-oriented focus including clinical trials and/or translational research involving human subjects. The Advanced Clinical Research Award is designed to provide funding beyond the Clinical Research Career Development Award (CDA). By continuing to support proven clinical researchers who are post-CDA but at a critical stage in their early career, the foundation hopes to expand the cadre of expert clinical oncology researchers who are developing promising research initiatives.
Requirements The applicant must meet the following criteria at the time of grant award: be a physician (MD or DO) who is 5-10 years post final sub-specialty training; have a full-time faculty appointment in a clinical department at an academic medical center; have completed productive postdoctoral/post-fellowship research and demonstrated the ability to undertake independent investigator-initiated clinical research; be an active member of the American Society of Clinical Oncology (ASCO); and expect to spend 75% of time during the award period dedicated to research.
Amount $450,000 (paid over three years)
Date(s) Application Is Due Aug 8.
Contact Julia McCormack, Executive Director, (703) 299-0150; fax: (703) 299-1044; email: McCormaj@asco.org
*Internet*http://www.asco.org/portal/site/ASCO/menuitem.c543a013502b2a89de912310320041a0/ ?vgnextoid=fa8c66da0d06d010VgnVCM100000ed730ad1RCRD&vgnextfmt=default
Sponsor American Society of Clinical Oncology
1900 Duke Street, Suite 200
Alexandria, VA 22303

ASCO Career Development Award **768**
The program provides funds to clinical investigators who have received their initial faculty appointment to establish an independent clinical cancer research program. Since many awards are supported with restricted grants from outside organizations, the ASCO is particularly interested in identifying young researchers working in the following sub-specialties and emerging disciplines: breast cancer; cancer survivorship; geriatric oncology; health disparities; kidney cancer; multiple myeloma; ovarian cancer; pancreatic cancer; sarcoma; survivorship; and young adult cancer. However, The ASCO Foundation welcomes application submissions in all oncology sub-specialties.
Requirements Clinical investigators who have received their initial faculty appointment to establish an independent clinical cancer research program are eligible.
Amount $200,000 (paid over three years)
Date(s) Application Is Due Nov 8.
Contact Julia McCormack, Executive Director, (703) 299-0150; fax: (703) 299-1044; email: McCormaj@asco.org
Internet http://www.asco.org/portal/site/ASCO/menuitem.509189bfd2c2bf5ca7ffa807320041a0/ ?vgnextoid=d140e30e7208e010VgnVCM100000ed730ad 1RCRD
Sponsor American Society of Clinical Oncology
1900 Duke Street, Suite 200
Alexandria, VA 22314

ASCO Geriatrics/Oncology Training Program Development Grant **769**
The grant is designed to aid institutions in developing three-year fellowship training programs in geriatric medicine and medical oncology. The goal of these grants is to produce academicians who will be teachers of geriatric issues in medical oncology and lead research efforts in geriatric oncology. Grants support fellow stipends, faculty

development support (to support investigators who would be mentors to geriatric oncology fellows; to develop geriatric oncology curricula; and/or to lead advancements in clinical care); and support for ongoing geriatric oncology research projects. Up to seven grants will be awarded over three years.
Requirements Applying institutions must have in place the elements necessary for a geriatrics/medical oncology training program.
Amount $100,000 year one, $75,000 year two, and $50,000 year three; plus $75,000 institutional matching funds
Contact ASCO Training Division, (703) 299-1076; fax: (703) 299-1044; email: driscolh@asco.org
Internet http://www.asco.org/portal/site/ASCO/menuitem.509189bfd2c2bf5ca7ffa8073 20041a0/? vgnextoid=b4b5e30e7208e010VgnVCM100000ed730ad1RCRD
Sponsor American Society of Clinical Oncology
1900 Duke Street, Suite 200
Alexandria, VA 22314

ASCO International Development and Education Award (IDEA) 770
The award provides support for oncologists in developing countries to attend the ASCO annual meeting and spend additional time at a comprehensive cancer center. The grants are designed to provide continuing medical education, assist in career development, and help establish strong relationships with leading ASCO members who serve as scientific mentors to each recipient. The strongest consideration will be given to candidates who: have submitted an abstract for the most recent Annual Meeting; and have less than 10 years of experience in the field of oncology. Guidelines are available online.
Requirements Applicants must: complete an application, which includes a 250-word essay, letter of recommendation, and submission of the applicant's CV; be able to travel to the United States and have no visa restrictions or anticipate having any difficulty obtaining a US visa; be citizens of a country identified by ASCO as one of greatest need or with limited resources; and either be or meet the requirements of being either an ASCO Active Member, Active-Junior Member, or an Associate Member.
Restrictions Applicants cannot: have received one year or more of formal training (for instance, attended medical school, participated in internships, fellowships, or residency programs) in the United States, Western Europe, Australia, New Zealand, Canada, or the United Kingdom; be a previous recipient of the IDEA (formally known as ITG) program; or have previously attended more that one (1) ASCO Annual Meeting.
Contact Amanda Woodell, (703) 519-1448; fax: (703) 518-5046; email: idea@asco.org
Internet http://www.asco.org/portal/site/ASCO/menuitem.56bbfed7341ace64e7cba5b4 320041a0/? vgnextoid=e2e4e30e7208e010VgnVCM100000ed730ad1RCRD
Sponsor American Society of Clinical Oncology
330 John Carlyle Street, Suite 300
Alexandria, VA 22314

ASCO Merit Awards 771
The Merit Awards are designed to further promote clinical research by young scientists and to provide fellows with an opportunity to present their research and interact with other clinical cancer investigators at ASCO scientific meetings. A select number of Merit Awards are given annually to recognize outstanding abstracts submitted for consideration for presentation at an ASCO scientific meeting. The awards are given to oncology fellows who are first authors on selected abstracts.
Requirements The first author of an abstract must meet the following requirements to be considered for an Award: be a physician (MD or DO) in an oncology fellowship training program or a doctoral degree candidate (such as PharmD or PhD) enrolled in an approved oncology specialty training program at the time of abstract submission; work in an oncology laboratory or clinical research setting; agree to present the abstract at the ASCO scientific meeting; check the Merit Award consideration box on the online abstract submitter; provide a letter of support from the Training Program Director indicating eligibility for the award; and submit a two-page curriculum vitae.
Date(s) Application Is Due Jan 9.
Contact Julia McCormack, Executive Director, (703) 299-0150; fax: (703) 299-1044; email: McCormaj@asco.org
Internet http://www.asco.org/portal/site/ASCO/menuitem.509189bfd2c2bf5ca7ffa8073 20041a0/? vgnextoid=0904e30e7208e010VgnVCM100000ed730ad1RCRD
Sponsor American Society of Clinical Oncology
1900 Duke Street, Suite 200
Alexandria, VA 22314

ASCO Young Investigator Award 772
This grant provides funding to promising investigators to encourage and promote quality research in clinical oncology. The purpose of this award is to fund physicians during the transition from a fellowship program to a faculty appointment. Priority consideration will be given to proposals that include patient-oriented and, ultimately, clinical research. Since many awards are supported with restricted grants from outside organizations, the ASCO is particularly interested in identifying young researchers working in the following sub-specialties and emerging disciplines: breast cancer; cancer survivorship; geriatric oncology; health disparities; kidney cancer; multiple myeloma; ovarian cancer; pancreatic cancer; sarcoma; survivorship; and young adult cancer. However, The ASCO Foundation welcomes application submissions in all oncology subspecialties.
Requirements The recipient must be a physician (MD or DO) who, at the time of grant award is in the final year of his/her final sub-specialty training program or in the first year post his/her final sub-specialty training. The sponsoring facility must be an academic medical institution. The primary mentor must be in the candidate's proposed research field, must assume responsibility, and provide guidance for the research. The applicant must either be a member of ASCO or submit a membership application with the grant application. The applicant should spend at least 60 to 75% of his or her time in research during the award period.
Amount $40,000
Date(s) Application Is Due Nov 8.
Contact Julia McCormack, Executive Director, (703) 299-0150; fax: (703) 299-1044; email: McCormaj@asco.org
Internet http://www.asco.org/portal/site/ASCO/menuitem.509189bfd2c2bf5ca7ffa8073 20041a0/? vgnextoid=56efe30e7208e010VgnVCM100000ed730ad1RCRD
Sponsor American Society of Clinical Oncology
1900 Duke Street, Suite 200
Alexandria, VA 22314

ASCO/UICC International Cancer Technology Transfer Fellowships 773
The scholarships are intended primarily for researchers in the early stages of their career as well as for experienced clinical oncologists. The ICRETT objective is to facilitate rapid international transfer of cancer research and clinical technology, and it allows fellows to exchange knowledge and enhance skills in basic, clinical, behavioral and epidemiological areas of cancer research, and cancer control and prevention. Through the program fellows also acquire appropriate clinical management, diagnostic and therapeutic expertise for effective application and use in home organizations upon return. The UICC has also developed the ICRETT for teaching faculty which funds experts to teach at host institutions throughout the world for a duration of 1 week to 1 month.
Requirements The candidate must possess the appropriate professional qualifications and experience according to the specifications of each fellowship described on the website and must currently be engaged in cancer research, clinical oncology practice, or cancer society work. To permit effective communication at the host institute, the candidate must have adequate fluency in a common language. The candidate must also be on the staff payroll of a university, research laboratory or institute, hospital, oncology unit, or voluntary cancer society (or be accredited volunteers of such societies) to where they will return at the end of a fellowship.
Restrictions Candidates attached to commercial entities, going to a profit organization or have associations with the tobacco industry not eligible.
Amount $3,000
Contact Julia McCormack, Executive Director, (703) 299-0150; fax: (703) 299-1044; email: McCormaj@asco.org
Internet http://www.ascofoundation.org/portal/site/
ASCO/menuitem.5d1b4bae73a9104ce277e89a320041a0/
?vgnextoid=5e55e30e7208e010VgnVCM100000ed730ad1RCRD
Sponsor American Society of Clinical Oncology
1900 Duke Street, Suite 200
Alexandria, VA 22314

ASCSA Alison M. Frantz Fellowship 774
The fellowship supports research in postclassical studies at the Gennadius Library in Greece. Fields of study include late antiquity, Byzantine studies, and modern Greek studies. A limited number of research associateships are awarded for well-defined projects (deadlines April 1, September 1, and December 1). Travel grants for graduate students or postdoctoral scholars from North American institutions working on projects in archeological science in Greece also are awarded. Guidelines and application are available online.
Requirements PhD candidates and recent PhDs from US or Canadian institutions are eligible. Fellows are expected to be in residence at the school for the full term of the fellowship.
Amount $10,000 stipend
Date(s) Application Is Due Jan 15.
Contact Program Contact, (609) 683-0800; fax: (609) 924-0578; email: ascsa@ascsa.org
Internet http://www.ascsa.edu.gr/fellowship/fellowships.htm
Sponsor American School of Classical Studies at Athens
6-8 Charlton St
Princeton, NJ 08540-5232

ASCSA Fellowships 775
Fellowships awarded include the Heinrich Schliemann and John Williams White Fellowships in archaeology; the Thomas Day Seymour Fellowship in history and literature; two Brunilde Ridgway Fellowships in art history; and seven Fellowships unrestricted as to field--the Virginia Grace, the Michael Jameson, the Philip Lockhart, the Lucy Shoe Meritt, the Martin Ostwald, the James and Mary Ottaway Jr., and the James Rignall Wheeler fellowships. The Bert Hodge Hill fellowship is unrestricted, but with a preference for a student in art history. Fellowships are awarded on the basis of examinations and recommendations to students of classical archaeology, ancient history, and classical languages and literature.
Requirements Applicants must be students in an American or Canadian university and will, preferably, have taken at least one year of graduate work but will not have completed the PhD before the term of fellowship starts.
Amount $10,000
Date(s) Application Is Due Jan 15.

Contact Carolyn Snively, Program Officer, (609) 683-0800; fax: (609) 924-0578 ; email: ascsa@ascsa.org
Internet http://www.ascsa.edu.gr/fellowship/fellowships.htm#regular
Sponsor American School of Classical Studies at Athens
6-8 Charlton St
Princeton, NJ 08540

ASCSA Harry Bikakis Fellowship **776**
The fellowship is available to graduate students attending North American institutions or Greek graduate students whose research subject is ancient Greek law; or Greek graduate students working on a school excavation. The fellowship is awarded periodically, but not more frequently than once a year. An outline of the proposed project should be sent to Professor Stephen V. Tracy, Director of the School, c/o the office in Athens: 54 Solidias St; Athens, Greece 106 76; 011-30-210-723-6313, fax: 011-30-210-725-0584.
Amount $1875
Date(s) Application Is Due Jan 15.
Contact Fellowship Administrator, (609) 683-0800; fax: (609) 924-0578; email: asca@ascsa.org
Internet http://www.ascsa.edu.gr/Forms/bikakis.pdf
Sponsor American School of Classical Studies at Athens
6-8 Charlton St
Princeton, NJ 08648-5232

ASCSA Jacob Hirsch Fellowship **777**
ASCSA offers this annual fellowship in preclassical, classical, or postclassical archaeology to US or Israeli graduate students who are at the dissertation-writing stage, or to recent recipients of the PhD who are completing the dissertation program with dissertation publication. Project requires substantial residence in Greece. The fellowship is nonrenewable. Requests for applications should be forwarded to the Committee on Admissions and Fellowships at the school.
Requirements Students in the United States or Israel who are PhD candidates writing their dissertations in archaeology or recent PhD's completing a project are eligible to apply.
Amount $10,000 stipend plus room and board
Date(s) Application Is Due Jan 15.
Contact Jacob Hirsch Fellowship Program, (609) 683-0800; fax: (609) 924-0578; email: ascsa@ascsa.org
Internet http://www.ascsa.edu.gr/fellowship/fellowships.htm
Sponsor American School of Classical Studies at Athens
6-8 Charlton St
Princeton, NJ 08540

ASCSA NEH Fellowships **778**
The school is the most significant resource on Greece for American scholars in the fields of ancient and postclassical studies in Greek language, literature, history, archeology, philosophy, and art, from pre-Hellenic times to the present. The fellowships support scholars with distinguished research and teaching careers in the humanities. Fellows will be expected to reside primarily in Athens, contribute to and enhance the scholarly dialog, as well as contribute to and expand scholarly horizons at the school. Guidelines and application are available online.
Requirements Postdoctoral scholars and professionals in relevant fields who are US citizens or foreign nationals who have lived in the United States for the three years immediately preceding the application deadline are eligible. Applicants must have completed their professional training but do not have to hold the PhD.
Amount $17,500 five-month tenure; $35,000 10-month tenure
Date(s) Application Is Due Nov 15.
Contact NEH Fellowship, (609) 683-0800; fax: (609) 924-0578; email: asca@ascsa.org
Internet http://www.ascsa.edu.gr/fellowship/fellowships.htm
Sponsor American School of Classical Studies at Athens
6-8 Charlton St
Princeton, NJ 08648-5232

ASCSA Summer Sessions Scholarships **779**
Scholarships are awarded annually for six-week summer sessions of study and research emphasizing the topography and antiquities of Greece. Graduate and advanced undergraduate students and high school and college teachers may apply. Application information is available on the Web site.
Date(s) Application Is Due Jan 15.
Contact Summer Sessions Committee, (609) 683-0800; fax: (609) 924-0578; email: ascsa@ascsa.org
Internet http://www.ascsa.edu.gr/fellowship/fellowships.htm#SummerSession
Sponsor American School of Classical Studies at Athens
6-8 Charlton St
Princeton, NJ 08540

ASCSA Weiner Laboratory Faunal Studies Research Fellowship **780**
This is a one-year fellowship at the Wiener Laboratory for graduate students or postdoctoral scholars working on projects in skeletal, faunal, geoarcheological, or environmental studies in Greece. Applicants must have a well-defined project that can be undertaken within the given time in the laboratory or in collaboration with local research institutions. In addition to the proposed research, the fellow will be expected to develop and curate the lab's comparative collection, contribute to the development of the lab, assist with queries from excavators, offer a lecture on the work undertaken while at the lab, participate in one regular member school trip, and contribute to seminars on aspects of archaeological science as part of the school's annual curriculum. Applications can be downloaded from the Web site. Athens Office address is 54 Souidias Street, GR-106 76 Athens Greece; phone: 30-1-723-6313; fax: 30-1-725-0584; email: info@ascsa.edu.gr; Web site: www.ascsa.edu.gr.
Requirements The fellowship is open to scholars with PhDs and those working on doctoral dissertations.
Amount $15,500-$25,000
Date(s) Application Is Due Jan 15.
Contact Director, Wiener Laboratory, (609) 683-0800; fax: (609) 924-0578; email: ascsa@ascsa.org
Internet http://www.ascsa.edu.gr/Wiener/fellowship.htm
Sponsor American School of Classical Studies at Athens
6-8 Charlton St
Princeton, NJ 08540-5232

ASECS Aubrey Williams Research Travel Fellowship **781**
The fellowship is awarded annually to support documentary research in 18th-century English literature by US-based scholars. The fellowship is restricted to doctoral students working on the dissertation in the field of 18th-century English literature. Applicants must be members of the society at the time of the award and residents of North America.
Requirements The fellowship is restricted to doctoral students at work on a dissertation in the field of eighteenth-century English literature.
Amount $1000
Date(s) Application Is Due Jan 1.
Contact Program Director, (336) 727-4694; fax: (336) 727-4697; email: ASECS@wfu.edu
Internet http://asecs.press.jhu.edu/travelgr.html
Sponsor American Society for Eighteenth-Century Studies
P.O. Box 7867, Wake Forest University
Winston-Salem, NC 27109

ASECS Cooperative Fellowships **782**
The society participates in eight fellowship programs to promote and sustain the study of the 18th century, funded jointly by the society and some of North America's leading research institutions: the Folger Shakespeare Library and the Folger Institute of Renaissance and Eighteenth Century Studies; the Newberry Library; the William Andrews Clark Memorial Library of the University of California, Los Angeles; McMaster University Library; Yale Center for British Art; the Houghton Library of Harvard University; the Harry Ransom Center of the University of Texas at Austin; and the American Antiquarian Society. Fellowships will generally be limited to one month's support, although individual institutions may make adjustments depending on the quality of applications and the availability of funds. Evaluation and selection will be by each institution in accordance with its established procedures. Applications are available from ASECS or the participating institutions.
Requirements An applicant must be a member in good standing of ASECS, be a postdoctoral scholar no more than 10 years beyond receipt of the PhD or equivalent degree at the time of application, and be working on a project concerning the 18th century. Contact should be made to the specific library of interest; complete contact information for each library is available on the ASECS Web site.
Contact ASECS Fellowship Program, (336) 727-4694; fax: (336) 727-4697; email: ASECS@wfu.edu
Internet http://asecs.press.jhu.edu/aboutus.html
Sponsor American Society for Eighteenth-Century Studies
P.O. Box 7867, Wake Forest University
Winston-Salem, NC 27109

ASECS Gwin J. and Ruth Kolb Research Travel Fellowship **783**
The fellowship is awarded annually to supplement costs for 18th-century scholars to travel to distant collections in North America and abroad. There are no restrictions based on applicants' age, sex, race, religion, or academic rank or discipline. Advanced doctoral candidates with demonstrable need for specific collections necessary for their dissertations also are encouraged to apply.
Requirements Applicants must be members of ASECS at the time of application and faculty or independent scholars within the first five years of receipt of their PhD.
Amount $500
Date(s) Application Is Due Jan 1.
Contact Program Director, (336) 727-4694; fax: (336) 727-4697; email: ASECS@wfu.edu
Internet http://asecs.press.jhu.edu/travelgr.html
Sponsor American Society for Eighteenth-Century Studies
P.O. Box 7867, Wake Forest University
Winston-Salem, NC 27109

ASECS Irish-American Research Travel Fellowship **784**
The award is given annually to support documentary research in Irish repositories, both in the Republic of Ireland and the North, by US-based scholars of Ireland in the period

between the Treaty of Limerick (1691) and the Act of Union (1800). In alternate years, the award will go to Irish-based scholars seeking to travel to North America. The fellowship is restricted to documentary scholars whose research centers on primary sources from the 18th century (printed matter, manuscripts, buildings, works of art, or other artifacts), rather than on extant secondary literature. Applications are available on the Web site.
Requirements Applicants must be members of the society at the time of the award and must be residents of North America. The fellowship is restricted to documentary scholars, whose research centers on primary sources from the 18th century (printed matter, manuscripts, buildings, works of art, or other artifacts), rather than on the secondary literature already extant.
Amount $1500
Date(s) Application Is Due Nov 1.
Contact Program Director, (336) 727-4694; fax: (336) 727-4697; email: ASECS@wfu.edu
Internet http://asecs.press.jhu.edu/travelgr.html
Sponsor American Society for Eighteenth-Century Studies
P.O. Box 7867, Wake Forest University
Winston-Salem, NC 27109

ASECS James L. Clifford Prize **785**
The prize is awarded annually for an outstanding article appearing in a journal, festschrift, or other serial publication; the article must be an outstanding study of some aspect of 18th-century culture interesting to any 18th-century specialist, regardless of discipline, and no longer than 15,000 words. Nominations must be accompanied by eight copies of the article.
Requirements The article may be nominated by any member of the society, by its author, or by an editor of the publishing journal. The author must be a member of the society at the time of presentation of the award.
Amount $500
Date(s) Application Is Due Jan 1.
Contact Clifford Prize Committee, (336) 727-4694; fax: (336) 727-4697; email: ASECS@wfu.edu
Internet http://asecs.press.jhu.edu/awards.html
Sponsor American Society for Eighteenth-Century Studies
P.O. Box 7867, Wake Forest University
Winston-Salem, NC 27109

ASECS Louis Gottschalk Prize **786**
The prize is awarded annually for an outstanding historical or critical study on a subject of 18th-century interest. Books, which may be written in any modern language, may be commentaries, critical studies, biographies, or critical editions.
Requirements Applicants must be members of the society at the time of the award. Submission must be made by the publisher and received at ASECS by the listed application deadline.
Restrictions Books that are primarily translations are ineligible.
Amount $1000
Date(s) Application Is Due Nov 15.
Contact Gottschalk Prize Committee, (336) 727-4694; fax: (336) 727-4697; email: asecs@wfu.edu
Internet http://asecs.press.jhu.edu/awards.html
Sponsor American Society for Eighteenth-Century Studies
P.O. Box 7867, Wake Forest University
Winston-Salem, NC 27109

ASECS Robert R. Palmer Research Travel Fellowship **787**
The travel fellowship is awarded annually to support documentary research related primarily to the history and culture of France. Applicants must be members of the society at the time of application. There are no restrictions based on age, sex, race, religion, or academic rank. Applications are available on the Web site.
Requirements All members of ASECS are eligible to apply.
Amount $500
Date(s) Application Is Due Jan 1.
Contact Program Director, (336) 727-4694; fax: (336) 727-4697; email: ASECS@wfu.edu
Internet http://asecs.press.jhu.edu/travelgr.html
Sponsor American Society for Eighteenth-Century Studies
P.O. Box 7867, Wake Forest University
Winston-Salem, NC 27109

ASECS/Clark Fellowships **788**
One-month resident fellowships at the William Andrews Clark Memorial Library are available to postdoctoral scholars with projects in the Restoration or the 18th century. The library, which is administered by the Center for 17th- and 18th-Century Studies, is known for its collections on 17th- and 18th-century Britain, Oscar Wilde and the 1890s, the history of printing, and certain aspects of the American West. The application deadline is for fellowships to be held between July 1 of the current year and June 30 of the next. Applications are available on the Web site.
Requirements Scholars who have received a PhD in the last six years and are engaged in research pertaining to the announced theme are eligible to apply.
Amount $2000
Date(s) Application Is Due Feb 1.
Contact Program Contact, fax: (310) 206-8577
Internet http://www.humnet.ucla.edu/humnet/c1718cs/applic3.htm
Sponsor William Andrews Clark Memorial Library
310 Royce Hall, 405 Hilgard Ave
Los Angeles, CA 90095-1404

ASEE Army Research Laboratory Postdoctoral Fellowships **789**
The program is designed to significantly increase the involvement of creative and highly trained scientists and engineers from academia and industry in scientific and technical areas of interest and relevance to the Army. Scientists and engineers at the Army Research Laboratory (ARL) help shape and execute the Army's program for meeting the challenge of developing technologies that will support Army forces in meeting future operational needs by pursuing scientific research and technological developments in such diverse fields as applied mathematics, atmospheric characterization, simulation and human modeling, digital/optical signal processing, material science and technology, multifunctional technology, combustion processes, propulsion, and flight physics. Before writing a proposal, applicants are advised to communicate directly with an ARL advisor, who can provide more specific information on the current research and available technical facilities and offer scientific support of proposal development. Applications are available on the Web site.
Requirements Before appointment, participants must present evidence of having received the PhD, ScD, or other earned research doctoral degree recognized in US academic circles as equivalent to the PhD within seven years of the date of application, or must present evidence of having completed all formal academic requirements for one of these degrees.
Contact Rick Kempinski, (202) 331-3525; email: r.kempinski@asee.org
Internet http://www.asee.org/arl
Sponsor American Society for Engineering Education
1818 N St NW, Ste 600
Washington, DC 20036-2479

ASEE Naval Research Laboratory Postdoctoral Fellowships **790**
The purpose of this program is to increase the involvement of highly trained US scientists and engineers in disciplines to meet the evolving needs of naval technology. To this goal, the ASEE, as the agent for the Naval Research Laboratory, will award approximately 40 postdoctoral appointments per year for research at 15 participating navy laboratories. Appointments are for one year and renewable for a second. At the discretion of the laboratory, third-year appointments may be arranged if warranted. A person who has received a prior postdoctoral appointment at a navy laboratory under any program may not be eligible to participate in this postdoctoral program. Applications may be downloaded from the Web site. Applications are accepted on an ongoing basis.
Requirements Before appointment, participants must present evidence of having received the PhD, ScD, or other earned research doctoral degree recognized in US academic circles as equivalent to the PhD within seven years of the date of application, or must present evidence of having completed all formal academic requirements for one of these degrees. Participants must be US citizens.
Amount $65,000 maximum stipend, depending on qualifications and experience
Contact Program Manager, (202) 331-3525; fax: (202) 265-8504; email: r.kempinski@asee.org
Internet http://www.asee.org/resources/fellowships/nrl/about.cfm
Sponsor American Society for Engineering Education
1818 N St NW, Ste 600
Washington, DC 20036

ASF Awards for Advanced Study or Research in the United States **791**
ASF offers a limited number of awards, usually at the graduate level, for Scandinavians wishing to undertake research or studies in the United States. The program also is designed to foster understanding and further cooperation between the nations. Candidates are recommended by cooperating Scandinavian organizations such as the Denmark-America Foundation, the League of Finnish-American Societies, the Icelandic-American Society, the Norway-America Association, and the Sweden-America Foundation.
Requirements Applicants must be citizens of a Scandinavian country (Denmark, Finland, Iceland, Norway, or Sweden).
Contact Administrator, Fellowships and Grants, (212) 879-9779; fax: (212) 249-3444; email: grants@amscan.org
Internet http://www.amscan.org/fellowship.html
Sponsor American-Scandinavian Foundation
58 Park Ave
New York, NY 10016

ASF Fellowship for Study in Scandinavia **792**
ASF encourages a full academic year of advanced study and research in the Scandinavian countries (Denmark, Norway, Finland, Sweden, and Iceland). Outstanding proposals from all sources are invited; priority for fellowships is given to candidates at the dissertation level. It is desirable that all candidates have at least some ability in the language of the country in which they plan to study. These awards may require supplementation from other sources, but benefits cannot be duplicated. ASF usually will not provide funds if the project can be followed without its assistance.

Requirements Awards are open to US citizens and permanent residents of the United States who are in good health and who will have completed their undergraduate education at the time their overseas program begins. A nonrefundable $10 fee must accompany the application.
Restrictions Application may be made for either an ASF fellowship or a grant, not for both. Funds will not be provided for research assistants, dependent support, loan obligations, publication costs, equipment purchase, institutional overhead charges, study at English-language institutions, beginning studies of any subject matter, conference attendance, foregone salary, or supplementation of substantial sabbatical support.
Amount $20,000
Date(s) Application Is Due Nov 1.
Contact Administrator, Fellowships and Grants, (212) 879-9779; fax: (212) 249-3444; email: grants@amscan.org
Internet http://www.amscan.org/fellowship.html
Sponsor American-Scandinavian Foundation
58 Park Ave
New York, NY 10016

ASF Grant for Study in Scandinavia 793
ASF encourages advanced study and research in Scandinavian countries. Grants are considered especially suitable for postgraduate scholars, professionals, and candidates in the arts to carry out research or study visits of one to three months. Outstanding proposals from all sources are invited. ASF desires that all candidates have at least some ability in the language of the country in which they plan to study.
Requirements Awards are open to US citizens and permanent residents who are in good health and who will have completed their undergraduate education at the time their overseas program begins. A nonrefundable fee of $10 must accompany the application.
Restrictions Application may be made for either an ASF grant or a fellowship, not for both.
Amount $3000 maximum
Date(s) Application Is Due Nov 1.
Contact Administrator, Fellowships and Grants, (212) 879-9779; fax: (212) 249-3444; email: grants@amscan.org
Internet http://www.amscan.org/fellowship.html
Sponsor American-Scandinavian Foundation
58 Park Ave
New York, NY 10016

ASF Short-Term Training Program 794
Grants enable US citizens and permanent residents who are at least 20 years of age to live, work, and train in Scandinavia on a temporary basis. Work assignments of eight to 12 weeks or longer (from spring through fall), are available to US students in certain fields, principally engineering, chemistry, and agriculture. The emphasis of the program is the cultural and educational experience rather than financial gain.
Requirements An applicant should be a full-time student majoring in the field in which training is sought; have at least three years of undergraduate studies completed; and have some previous related work experience. Knowledge of a Scandinavian language is not necessary.
Restrictions Applications are not accepted in the medically related professions involving patient care.
Contact Fellowships and Grants Office, (212) 879-9779; fax: (212) 249-3444; email: training@amscan.org or info@amscan.org
Internet http://www.amscan.org/training.html
Sponsor American-Scandinavian Foundation
58 Park Ave
New York, NY 10016

ASGE/ConMed Award for Outstanding Manuscript by a Fellow/Resident 795
The American Society for Gastrointestinal Endoscopy and ConMed Endoscopic Technologies sponsor the annual ASGE/ConMed Outstanding Manuscript Award. The prize consists of $10,000 cash award to the Fellow or Resident in training in a gastroenterology or a surgical gastrointestinal endoscopic program whose manuscript is accepted in for publication in Gastrointestinal Endoscopy. The award is presented during Digestive Disease Week, the largest and most prestigious meeting in the world for the GI professional.
Amount $10,000
Contact Chair, ASGE Research Committee, (630) 573-0600; fax: (630) 573-0691; email: grants@asge.org
Internet http://www.asge.org/nspages/about/center/factsheet.cfm#conMed
Sponsor American Society for Gastrointestinal Endoscopy and ConMed Endoscopic Technologies
1520 Kensington Road, Suite 202
Oak Brook, IL 60523

ASGE Don Wilson Award 796
The Award provides Advanced Fellows or Junior Faculty with the opportunity to train outside of their home country with a premier GI endoscopist or group in order to advance their training. The award assists in underwriting reasonable and customary travel and living expenses for a period of one to three months. The award includes a $7,500 cash stipend prior to the recipient's travel. In addition, a 20% disbursement will be made to the host institution. A total of three awards will be available annually for North American and International ASGE members. Note: One training must take place in the United States.
Requirements Applicants must be the equivalent of Junior Faculty or Advanced Fellows and be proficient in the English Language. Applicants must also: be a current ASGE Member; be a Junior Faculty or Advanced Fellow (3rd or 4th year or international equivalent); have permission from their own institution to undertake the travel; and have permission from an ASGE member at the host institution to accept the application for training.
Restrictions Individuals applying for 1-2 year advanced fellowships do not qualify for this award.
Amount $7,500
Date(s) Application Is Due Sep 1.
Contact Chair, ASGE International Committee, (630) 573-0600; fax: (630) 573-0691; email: membership@asge.org
Internet http://www.asge.org/nspages/research/applications/donWilson.cfm
Sponsor American Society for Gastrointestinal Endoscopy
1520 Kensington Road, Suite 202
Oak Brook, IL 60523

ASGE Endoscopic Research Awards 797
These research awards are offered to physicians for projects in basic and clinical endoscopic technology research, outcomes and effectiveness of endoscopy research. The primary objective is to foster research in gastrointestinal endoscopy both within and outside of academic centers. Two categories of grants may be used for up to two years of study: grants of $1-15,000 (category A) and grants of $15,001 - 50,000 (category B). Requests for funding seed projects that will lead to further research as well as larger requests for definitive clinical trials will be considered. Funding requests may also include: personnel expenses for research assistant and/or faculty salary support (percentage of time for study should be specified and appropriately justified); study supplies; and equipment essential for study.
Requirements Candidate must be: an ASGE member; an MD (or have equivalent degree); and current in a gastroenterology-related and endoscopic practice in academic institutions or private practice in North America.
Restrictions Funding will not be provided for: salary support for trainees; computer purchases (unless a unique application is proposed); standard equipment and supplies needed for appropriate patient care (for example, sclerotherapy needles); travel to meetings; or indirect costs.
Amount $50,000 maximum per year for ywo years
Date(s) Application Is Due Sep 15.
Contact Chair, ASGE Research Committee, (630) 573-0600; fax: (630) 573-0691; email: grants@asge.org
Internet http://www.asge.org/nspages/research/applications/roeapp.cfm
Sponsor American Society for Gastrointestinal Endoscopy
1520 Kensington Road, Suite 202
Oak Brook, IL 60523

ASGE Endoscopic Research Career Development Awards 798
These awards provide the salary and/or research support necessary for the investigator to enhance his/her career development. The award must be used to acquire new skills for furthering a career in endoscopic research. Examples of such skills include advanced training in endoscopic procedures, training in outcomes research relevant to endoscopy, training in use of large databases such as CORI, and new endoscopic research techniques, including animal models.
Requirements Applicants must be ASGE members and hold full-time faculty positions at North American (U.S., Canada, or Mexico) universities or professional institutions at the time of application. The award is intended for faculty who have demonstrated promise and have some record of accomplishment in research. Candidates must devote at least 30 percent of their effort to research related to gastrointestinal endoscopy during the period of the award.
Restrictions The award is not available for fellows. Faculty with principle investigator current federal funding or other concurrent career development support still active at the time of this award are not eligible. Recipients of the ASGE Career Development Awards may not be granted an ASGE Research & Outcomes & Effectiveness Award during their two-year award period.
Amount $75,000 per year for two years
Date(s) Application Is Due Dec 14.
Contact Chair, ASGE Research Committee, (630) 573-0600; fax: (630) 573-0691; email: grants@asge.org
Internet http://www.asge.org/nspages/research/applications/careerapp.cfm
Sponsor American Society for Gastrointestinal Endoscopy
1520 Kensington Road, Suite 202
Oak Brook, IL 60523

ASGE Given Capsule Endoscopy Research Award 799
These research awards are offered to physicians for projects specific to capsule endoscopy both within and outside of academic centers. The award must be used for projects directly relating to capsule endoscopy. Requests for funding seed projects that will lead to further research as well as requests for definitive clinical trials will be considered. Funding requests may include: personnel (research assistant and/or faculty salary support--

percentage of time for study should be specified and appropriately justified); study supplies; and equipment essential for study.
Requirements Candidate must be an ASGE member, be an MD (or have equivalent degree), and be current in a gastroenterology-related and endoscopic practice in academic institutions or private practice in North America.
Restrictions Funding will not be provided for: salary support for trainees; computer purchases (unless a unique application is proposed); standard equipment and supplies needed for appropriate patient care (for example, sclerotherapy needles); travel to meetings; publication costs; or indirect costs.
Amount $25,000 maximum
Date(s) Application Is Due Dec 7.
Contact Chair, ASGE Research Committee, (630) 573-0600; fax: (630) 573-0691; email: grants@asge.org
Internet http://www.asge.org/nspages/research/applications/ceapp.cfm
Sponsor American Society for Gastrointestinal Endoscopy
1520 Kensington Road, Suite 202
Oak Brook, IL 60523

ASHE/Lumina Foundation Dissertation Fellowship **800**
With support of the Lumina Foundation, the association awards fellowships to support dissertation research on the broad topics of financial aid, student retention and success, and adult learners and learning. The fellowships will support up to one year of activity that will be conducted through the students' home universities and can be used to support costs of supplying data, dissemination of project results, travel, tuition, and salary for the fellows. Eight one-year fellowships will be awarded over a three-year period.
Requirements Doctoral students affiliated with any accredited doctoral program may submit a proposal. Students in doctoral programs outside the United States may apply if their study is about student financial assistance, student retention and success, and/or adult learning and learners in the United States.
Amount $12,500
Date(s) Application Is Due Apr 1.
Contact Dennis Brown, Executive Director, Michigan State University, (517) 432-8805; fax: (517) 432-8806; email: browndf@msu.edu
Internet http://www.ashe.ws/fellowship/aboutfellowship.htm
Sponsor Association for the Study of Higher Education
424 Erickson Hall
East Lansing, MI 48824

ASHFoundation Graduate Student Scholarships **801**
The foundation invites full-time graduate students to submit applications in competition for one of seven scholarships. Full-time master's or doctoral students in communication sciences and disorders programs demonstrating outstanding academic achievement are eligible to compete for these $4,000 awards. Supported in part by Psi Iota Xi National Philanthropic Organization and the Marni Reisberg Memorial Fund. All scholarship recipients will be announced and recognized at the annual convention held in November.
Requirements Applicants must be accepted for graduate study in a communication sciences and disorders program (master's degree candidates must be in an ASHA Educational Standards Board accredited program; this is not mandatory for doctoral degree candidates); be enrolled for full-time study (12 or more credit hours or the full-time standard); submit official university transcripts of academic coursework, credits, and grades; and be recommended by a committee of two or more past or present college faculty and colleagues (at least one supervisor) at the student's current place of employment. Annual deadline dates may vary; contact program staff for exact dates.
Restrictions Applicants must not have received a prior scholarship from the foundation.
Amount $4,000
Date(s) Application Is Due Jun 11.
Contact Emily Diaz, (301) 897-5700, ext. 4314; fax: (301) 571-0457; email: ediaz@asha.org
Internet http://www.ashfoundation.org/Foundation/grants/GraduateScholarships.htm#gss
Sponsor American Speech-Language-Hearing Foundation
10801 Rockville Pike
Rockville, MD 20852

ASHFoundation Graduate Student Scholarships for Minority Students **802**
Racial/ethnic minority students who are U.S. citizens, who are accepted for graduate study in speech-language pathology or audiology, and who demonstrate outstanding academic achievement are eligible to compete for this scholarship. Applicants should submit a formal paper, such as a term paper, in competition for this award. The paper must be either an integrative literature review or an opinion paper on a current professional issue. All scholarship recipients will be announced and recognized at the ASHA convention.
Requirements Candidates must be US citizens and members of a racial/ethnic minority, including Native American and Alaska Native, Asian and Pacific Islander, African American, and Hispanic. Applicants must be accepted for master's or doctoral study in a speech-language pathology or audiology program for the upcoming academic year. The student must be enrolled for full-time (12 or more credit hours) study.
Restrictions Applicants may not have received a prior scholarship from the foundation.
Amount $2,000-$4,000
Date(s) Application Is Due Jun 4.
Contact Emily Diaz, Project Assistant, (301) 897-5700, ext. 4314; fax: (301) 571-0457; email: ediaz@asha.org
Internet http://www.ashfoundation.org/Foundation/recipients/Minority-Student-Scholarship.htm
Sponsor American Speech-Language-Hearing Foundation
10801 Rockville Pike
Rockville, MD 20852

ASHFoundation Graduate Student with a Disability Scholarship **803**
Full-time graduate students with a disability who are enrolled in a communication sciences and disorders program and demonstrate outstanding academic achievement are eligible to compete for a $4,000 scholarship. Applicants must demonstrate superior academic achievement and submit transcripts, essay and references with official application. The Award is intended for the blind, hearing impaired, physically handicapped, or learning impaired. Master's, but not doctoral, students must be enrolled in an ASHA Council on Academic Accreditation approved program.
Requirements Candidates must be U.S. citizens and either blind, hearing impaired, physically handicapped, or learning impaired. Applicants must be accepted for master's study in a speech-language pathology or audiology program for the upcoming academic year. The student must be enrolled for full-time (12 or more credit hours) study.
Amount $4,000
Date(s) Application Is Due Apr 4.
Contact Emily Diaz, Project Assistant, (301) 897-5700, ext. 4314; fax: (301) 571-0457; email: ediaz@asha.org
Internet http://www.ashfoundation.org/Foundation/recipients/Student-With-a-Disability-Scholarship.htm
Sponsor American Speech-Language-Hearing Foundation
10801 Rockville Pike
Rockville, MD 20852

ASHFoundation New Century Scholars Program Doctoral Scholarships **804**
The Program is a special funding initiative resulting from the ASHFoundation's Dreams and Possibilities Campaign. The Award is for students accepted or currently enrolled in a research doctoral program in communications sciences and disorders. Full-time study will be given priority; part-time status will be considered. Students should be committed to a teacher-investigator career in communication sciences and disorders in the United States.
Requirements The Award is available to U.S. citizens only. Applicants must be accepted or currently enrolled in a research doctoral program.
Amount $10,000 minimum
Contact Emily Diaz, Project Assistant, (301) 897-5700 ext. 4314; fax: (301) 571-0457; email: ediaz@asha.org
Internet http://www.ashfoundation.org/Foundation/recipients/NCS-Doctoral-Scholarship.htm
Sponsor American Speech-Language-Hearing Foundation
10801 Rockville Pike
Rockville, MD 20852

ASHFoundation New Century Scholars Research Grant **805**
The Program is a special funding initiative resulting from the ASHFoundation's Dreams and Possibilities Campaign. The Grant is a one-time award intended to advance the knowledge base in communication sciences and disorders. Applicants must have a PhD or equivalent research doctorate within the discipline. Priority will be given to studies that are innovative, groundbreaking, or that meet research needs not yet addressed.
Restrictions Students enrolled in a degree program or working on dissertation research are not eligible.
Amount $10,000
Date(s) Application Is Due Apr 1.
Contact Emily Diaz, Project Assistant, (301) 897-5700 ext. 4314; fax: (301) 571-0457; email: ediaz@asha.org
Internet http://www.ashfoundation.org/Foundation/recipients/NCS-Research-Grant.htm
Sponsor American Speech-Language-Hearing Foundation
10801 Rockville Pike
Rockville, MD 20852

ASHFoundation Research Grant for New Investigators **806**
The grants are designed to help further research activities of new investigators and should have particular clinical relevance to speech-language pathology and audiology. The awards are designed to encourage research activities of new scientists who earned their latest degree within the last five years. Proposals, while not limited in topic, are encouraged in the area of treatment research, particularly efficacy and outcome studies. Include abstract, research plan, bibliography, management plan, and budget with application. Grant recipients will be announced and recognized at the ASHA convention in Seattle, WA.

Requirements The individual must have received the master's or doctoral level degree in the last five years; must not have received prior funding for research, with the exception of internal university funding; and the proposal must be for research to be initiated.
Restrictions Open to individuals with a Master's degree or doctoral degree who are not currently enrolled in a degree program.
Amount $5,000
Date(s) Application Is Due May 21.
Contact Emily Diaz, Project Assistant, (301) 897-5700 ext. 4314; email: ediaz@asha.org
Internet http://www.ashfoundation.org/Foundation/recipients/Research-Grant-for-New-Investigators.htm
Sponsor American Speech-Language-Hearing Foundation
10801 Rockville Pike
Rockville, MD 20852

ASHFoundation Research Grant in Speech Science **807**
ASLH, in conjunction with the Acoustical Society of America, invites new researchers to submit proposals in competition for one grant every other year. The grant is designed to further research activities of new investigators and promulgate the work of the late Dennis Klatt, a noted researcher and scientist in the area of speech communication. Priority will be given to areas reflecting Dr. Klatt's broad interests, such as proposals studying speech perception, synthesis, and acoustics, with an emphasis on an interdisciplinary research approach. The grant can be used to initiate new research or supplement an existing research project. Funds may be requested for a variety of purposes, i.e., equipment, subjects, research assistants, or research-related travel. The grant recipient will be announced at the ASHA convention.
Requirements Individuals having received a doctoral degree within the last five years and who wish to further research activities in the areas of speech communication are eligible to compete for the grant.
Amount $4,000
Contact Emily Diaz, Project Assistant, (301) 897-5700, ext. 4314; fax: (301) 571-0457; email: ediaz@asha.org
Internet http://www.ashfoundation.org/Foundation/recipients/Research-Grant-in-Speech-Science.htm
Sponsor American Speech-Language-Hearing Foundation
10801 Rockville Pike
Rockville, MD 20853

ASHFoundation Student Research Grants in Audiology **808**
Each year the foundation awards one grant for support of research to be initiated in the area of clinical and/or rehabilitative audiology. One $2,000 award to a master's or doctoral student for research to be initiated in the area of audiology. Applicants must submit up to a ten-page research plan, one-page abstract, two-page management plan and budget, and letter of support. All study must be done in the United States.
Requirements The competition open to master's or doctoral degree students enrolled in, or accepted for, graduate study in a communication sciences and disorders program in the United States. Master's degree candidates must be in a program accredited by the Council on Academic Accreditation in Audiology and Speech-Language Pathology (CAA); this is not mandatory for doctoral degree candidates. Applicants must be enrolled for full-time study for the full academic year.
Amount $2,000
Date(s) Application Is Due Jun 4.
Contact Emily Diaz, Project Assistant, (301) 897-5700, ext. 4314; fax: (301) 571-0457; email: ediaz@asha.org
Internet http://www.ashfoundation.org/Foundation/grants/research_grants.htm
Sponsor American Speech-Language-Hearing Foundation
10801 Rockville Pike
Rockville, MD 20852

ASHFoundation Student Research Grants in Early Childhood Language Development **809**
One $2,000 grant per year is awarded to a graduate or postgraduate student to support research in early childhood language development. The applicant must submit up to a ten-page research plan, one-page abstract, two-page management plan and budget, and letter of support. All study must be done in the United States. The recipient and the recipient's mentor will be announced and recognized at the ASHA Convention.
Requirements The competition is open to graduate or postgraduate students in the area of communication sciences and disorders. Applicants must submit a proposal according to foundation guidelines, to be received by the indicated deadline date for applications.
Amount $2,000
Date(s) Application Is Due Jun 4.
Contact Emily Diaz, (301) 897-5700, ext. 4314; fax: (301) 571-0457; email: ediaz@asha.org
Internet http://www.ashfoundation.org/Foundation/recipients/Student-Research-Grant-in-Early-Childhood-Language.htm
Sponsor American Speech-Language-Hearing Foundation
10801 Rockville Pike
Rockville, MD 20852

Ashland Corporate Contributions Grants **810**
The foundation awards grants to eligible Kentucky, Ohio, and West Virginia nonprofit organizations in its areas of interest, including education, arts, communities/civic, disaster relief, environment, and health and human services. Types of support include seed money grants, project grants, endowments, matching gifts, and employee volunteers. The foundation does not provide an application. Most giving is centered on programs that best address the needs of Ashland's employees, stockholders, customers, and other constituencies, and the communities in which they live. Funding requests are not solicited but will be considered. The primary focus is on education, with an emphasis on mentoring, literacy and/or diversity.
Requirements 501(c)3 tax-exempt organizations in Boyd and Greenup Counties, KY; Lawrence County, OH; and Cabell and Wayne Counties, WV; are eligible. Charitable groups within church or religious organizations are eligible.
Restrictions The foundation does not support individuals, capital campaigns for building or equipment, endowments, travel, film or video production, tickets, religious or political activities, or goodwill advertising.
Contact Program Contact, (859) 815-3333; email: community@ashland.com
Internet http://www.ashland.com/commitments/contributions.asp
Sponsor Ashland Inc
P.O. Box 391, 50 E Rivercenter Blvd
Covington, KY 41012-0391

ASHP Research and Education Foundation Research Grants **811**
The ASHP offers grants in three different categories. Medication Safety Research grants give priority to projects that study medication-use design in hospitals and health systems and result in promotion of safety initiatives in medication use. Junior Investigator Research Grants support health services research in medication use that is conducted by pharmacist junior investigators; and strengthen the skills of newer pharmacist investigators while fostering development of mentoring relationships with more experienced senior investigators. The Pharmacy Resident Medication Safety Grant program is intended to support a worthy research project devoted to improving medication safety. Projects that demonstrate the role of the pharmacist in safe medication use, enhance medication-use systems, and can be duplicated in other health systems will be given high priority. Annual deadline dates may vary.
Requirements Eligibility requirements vary by program; contact program staff for eligibility.
Contact Daniel Cobaugh, Director of Research, (301) 664-8767; fax: (301) 664-8872; email: foundation@ashp.org
Internet http://www.ashpfoundation.org/Research/fundingOpps.cfm
Sponsor American Society of Health-System Pharmacists Research and Education Foundation
7272 Wisconsin Ave
Bethesda, MD 20814

ASHRAE Graduate Student Grant-in-Aid Program **812**
The Grant is intended to encourage the student to continue his or her preparation for service in the HVAC&R industry. The relevance of the research proposed by the candidate is a consideration for awarding the grant. The Grant-in-Aid is made through the university solely for the support of the student in an amount not to exceed US $10,000.00 per school year per student and is not renewable. Typical expenditures include living expenses, tuition, travel to ASHRAE meetings, experimental equipment, and supplies. The basis for scoring heavily emphasizes ASHRAE involvement and is intended to stimulate advisor activity in ASHRAE and associate societies.
Requirements Qualified graduate engineering students capable of carrying out appropriate and scholarly research are eligible to apply.
Amount $10,000 maximum per year
Date(s) Application Is Due Dec 15.
Contact Manager of Research, (404) 636-8400; fax: (404) 321-5478; email: mvaughn@ashrae.org
Internet http://www.ashrae.org/template/AssetDetail/assetid/23027
Sponsor American Society of Heating, Refrigerating, and Air Conditioning Engineers
1791 Tullie Cir NE
Atlanta, GA 30329-2305

ASHRAE Willis H. Carrier Graduate Research Fellowship **813**
This fellowship is awarded for graduate research at Purdue University. The fellowship is for one year with monies dispersed by the University to the student. Completed applications must be mailed to the ASHRAE. Application forms are available on the Web site.
Requirements Applicants should have a cumulative college grade point average of at least 3.0 (where 4.0 is the highest); current full-time enrollment with at least one full year of studies remaining; potential service to the HVAC and/or refrigeration profession; need for financial assistance; leadership ability; and recommendations from instructors.
Amount $21,000
Contact Graduate Administrator, (765) 494-6900; fax: (765) 494-0539; email: PurdueME@ecn.purdue.edu
Internet http://www.ashrae.org/template/AssetDetail/assetid/23628
Sponsor American Society of Heating, Refrigerating, and Air Conditioning Engineers
1791 Tullie Cir NE
Atlanta, GA 30329

Asia Foundation Exchange Programs 814

The foundation seeks to encourage greater understanding between Asians and Americans with the ultimate aim of contributing towards strengthened US-Asia relations. Exchange programs administered by the San Francisco-based Asian-American Exchange (AAX) unit help shape the perceptions of the Asians and Americans who take part in academic studies, conferences, special programs, and study tours tailored to particular needs that address U.S.-Asia interests. The foundation also sponsors the following special exchange programs: the William P. Fuller Fellowship in Conflict Resolution; the Chang-Lin Tien Distinguished Fellowship Program; the L.Z. Yuan Fellowship in Media and International Affairs; India Regional Security Studies Fellowship; and the Freeman Program for Broadening American Engagement with Southeast Asia. Guidelines are available online.
Contact Grants Administrator, (415) 982-4640; fax: (415) 392-8863; email: info@asiafound.org
Internet http://www.asiafoundation.org
Sponsor Asia Foundation
465 California St, 9th Fl
San Francisco, CA 94104

ASID Educational Foundation Joel Polsky Academic Achievement Award 815

This prize is given annually to recognize an outstanding interior design research or thesis project by an undergraduate or graduate student. Entries should address the needs of the public, designers, and students on such topics as educational research, behavioral science, business practice, design process, theory, or other technical subjects. Material will be judged on bibliography/references, breadth of material, comprehensive coverage of topic, graphic presentation and organization, and innovative subject matter. Entries will be returned upon request with a $10 postage and handling fee. Annual deadline dates may vary; contact program staff for exact dates.
Amount $1000
Date(s) Application Is Due Mar 28.
Contact Program Contact, (202) 546-3480; fax: (202) 546-3240; email: education@asid.org
Internet http://www.asid.org/learning/asid_ed_foundation/awards_ed.asp
Sponsor American Society of Interior Designers Educational Foundation Inc
608 Massachusetts Ave NE
Washington, DC 20002-6006

ASID Educational Foundation Mabelle Wilhelmina Boldt Memorial Scholarship 816

One scholarship will be awarded to a student who is enrolled in or has applied for admission to a graduate-level interior design program at a degree-granting institution. Applicants must have been practicing designers for a period of at least five years prior to returning to graduate study. The scholarship will be awarded on the basis of academic/creative accomplishment, as demonstrated by school transcripts and a letter of recommendation. Preference will be given to students with a focus on design research. Annual deadline dates may vary; contact program staff for exact dates.
Amount $2000
Date(s) Application Is Due Mar 28.
Contact Program Contact, (202) 546-3480; fax: (202) 546-3240; email: education@asid.org
Internet http://www.asid.org/learning/asid_ed_foundation/awards_ed.asp
Sponsor American Society of Interior Designers Educational Foundation Inc
608 Massachusetts Ave NE
Washington, DC 20002-6006

ASM International Fellowships 817

The program encourages research and training collaborations in the microbiological sciences internationally. ASM is currently focusing on Latin American partnerships. A visiting scientist will collaborate with an ASM member who is permanently employed at an accredited institution. Fellowships include: ASM International Fellowship for Latin America--available to young scientists from any Latin American country working in any of the microbiology disciplines to visit a host scientist in the United States or Canada; ASM-Antorchas Fellowship for Argentina--available to young scientists from Argentina working on nonmedically related research to visit a host scientist in the United States or Canada; Alfredo Sordelli Fellowship for Argentina--available to young scientists from Argentina working in any of the microbiology disciplines to visit a host scientist in the United States or Canada; and ASM-PAHO Fellowship for Latin America--available to young scientists from Bolivia, Colombia, Costa Rica, Dominican Republic, Ecuador, El Salvador, Guatemala, Honduras, Nicaragua, Panama, Paraguay, or Peru, working in the field of antimicrobial resistance to visit a host scientist in the United States or Canada. Preference will be given to applications that have additional sources of funding which would enable the applicants to maximize their collaborations. A minimum of six weeks is required for participation in the fellowship program. The applicant is allowed to extend his/her stay with the host scientist for up to a maximum of six months if other sources of support are available.
Requirements The program requires a joint application from two partners, the visiting scientist and the ASM host scientist.
Amount $4000 maximum
Contact International Fellowship Program, (202) 942-9368; fax: (202) 942-9328; email: international@asmusa.org
Internet http://www.asm.org/International/index.asp?bid=2778
Sponsor American Society for Microbiology
1752 N St NW
Washington, DC 20036

ASM International Professorships 818

International professorships are intended to provide microbiological expertise and resources to faculty and students throughout the world. The program offers ASM International Professorship for Latin America--professorships to Latin American institution/North American ASM member partnerships; ASM-PAHO Professorship for Latin America--one professorship per year to a North American ASM member who partners with an institution in Bolivia, Colombia, Costa Rica, Dominican Republic, Ecuador, El Salvador, Guatemala, Honduras, Nicaragua, Panama, Paraguay, or Peru, to present a course in the field of bacterial resistance to antimicrobials; and Indo-US Professorships in Microbiology--microbiologists in India and the United States visit institutions in the other country to teach an interactive short course on a topic in any of the microbiological disciplines. Open to ASM members and non-members alike. The program enables an institution of higher learning the resources to bring an ASM member who is scientifically recognized in his/her area to teach a hands-on, highly interactive short course on a single topic in the microbiological sciences. Preference will be given to applicants who will be able to make maximal use of the course, as demonstrated by the applicability of the course's contents to existing programs at the institution. Funds from ASM must be matched by the hosting institution.
Restrictions No amount of the award may be used for housing and board by either the visiting professor or co-professor at the host institution.
Date(s) Application Is Due Apr 15; Oct 15.
Contact International Professorship Program, (202) 942-9368; fax: (202) 942-9328; email: international@asmusa.org
Internet http://www.asm.org/International/index.asp?bid=2781
Sponsor American Society for Microbiology
1752 N St NW
Washington, DC 20036

ASM Postdoctoral Research Associates Program in Infectious Diseases and Public Health Microbiology 819

The purpose of this program is to support the development of new approaches, methodologies, and knowledge in infectious disease prevention and control in areas within the public health mission of the CDC. Eligible fields of study include bacterial and mycotic diseases, viral and rickettsial infections, nosocomial infections, HIV/AIDS, vector-borne infectious diseases, sexually transmitted diseases, and parasitic diseases.
Requirements The program is intended for individuals who either earned their doctorate degree or completed a primary residency within three years of their proposed start date. Consideration is given to individuals with more experience if there are compelling reasons. Qualified applicants will receive consideration without regard to race, creed, color, age, sex, or national origin.
Restrictions Applicants may not have a faculty position or be enrolled in a graduate degree program during the fellowship.
Amount $37,300 maximum annual stipend; $3500 maximum in health benefits; $2000 maximum for professional development
Date(s) Application Is Due Nov 15.
Contact Grants Administrator, Office of Education and Training, (202) 942-9295; email: Fellowhips-CareerInformation@asmusa.org
Internet http://www.asm.org/Education/index.asp?bid=15497
Sponsor American Society for Microbiology
1325 Massachusetts Ave NW
Washington, DC 20005-4171

ASME Gas Turbine Award 820

The award is given annually in recognition of an outstanding individual or multiple-author contribution to the literature of combustion gas turbines or gas turbines thermally combined with nuclear or steam power plants. The paper may be devoted to the design aspects of overall gas turbines or individual components and/or systems such as compressors, combustion systems, turbines, controls and accessories, bearings, regenerators, inlet air filters, silencers, etc. It may cover topics specifically related to gas turbines, such as high-temperature materials or fuel considerations including erosion and corrosion complications. It also can be devoted to application or operational aspects of gas turbines for aircraft propulsion and ground power units, or automotive, electric utility, gas pipeline pumping, locomotive, marine, oil field pumping, petrochemical, space power, steel, and similar uses.
Requirements Papers published anywhere in the world are eligible; authors are not restricted by nationality, age, profession, or membership in any engineering society or other organizations.
Amount $1000
Date(s) Application Is Due Jan 1.
Contact Honors Department, (800) 843-2763 or (212) 591-7722; fax: (212) 591-7674; email: infocentral@asme.org
Internet http://www.asme.org/honors/ms71/sla/turbine.html
Sponsor American Society of Mechanical Engineers
3 Park Ave
New York, NY 10016-5990

ASME Heat Transfer Memorial Award **821**
This award is bestowed on individuals who have made outstanding contributions to the field of heat transfer through teaching, research, design, or publications. Each award is based on papers in an area of heat transfer or on a paper dealing with the science or art of heat transfer. Awards are made annually in each of the three following categories: the science of heat transfer, the art of heat transfer, and the general subject of heat transfer.
Requirements There are no restrictions by age, nationality, or society membership.
Amount $1000
Date(s) Application Is Due Oct 1.
Contact Gilda DiTullio, Manager, (212) 591-7736; fax: (212) 705-7739; email: ditulliog@asme.org
Internet http://www.asme.org/honors/ms71/saa/heat.html
Sponsor American Society of Mechanical Engineers
3 Park Ave
New York, NY 10016

ASME Internal Combustion Engine Award **822**
This award is given in recognition of eminent achievement or distinguished contribution over a substantial period of time, which may result from research, innovation, or education in advancing the art of engineering in the field of internal combustion engines or in directing the efforts and accomplishments of those engaged in engineering practice in the design, development, application, and operation of internal combustion engines.
Amount $1000
Date(s) Application Is Due Feb 1.
Contact Gilda DiTullio, Manager, (212) 591-7736; fax: (212) 705-7739; email: ditulliog@asme.org
Internet http://www.asme.org/honors/ms71/saa/ice.html
Sponsor American Society of Mechanical Engineers
3 Park Ave
New York, NY 10016

ASME Machine Design Award **823**
The award is made to recognize eminent achievement or distinguished service in the field of machine design, which includes application, research, development, or teaching of machine design.
Requirements Any individual member, group of members, or committee may nominate candidates for this award.
Amount $1000
Date(s) Application Is Due Feb 1.
Contact Gilda DiTullio, Manager, (212) 591-7736; fax: (212) 705-7739; email: ditulliog@asme.org
Internet http://www.asme.org/honors/ms71/saa/md.html
Sponsor American Society of Mechanical Engineers
3 Park Ave
New York, NY 10016

ASME Medal **824**
One medal may be awarded annually to an individual of any age or nationality for a lifetime of service in engineering or related fields. Any individual member, group of members, or committee may nominate candidates. Application available online.
Amount $10,000
Date(s) Application Is Due Mar 1.
Contact Gilda DiTullio, Manager, (212) 591-7736; fax: (212) 705-7739; email: ditulliog@asme.org
Internet http://www.asme.org/honors/ms71/daa/asme.html
Sponsor American Society of Mechanical Engineers
3 Park Ave
New York, NY 10016

ASME Melvin R. Green Codes and Standards Medal **825**
This award is given annually for outstanding contribution to codification, standardization, and certification for service on ASME, ANSC, or ISO/TAC Committee administered by ASME.
Requirements The recipient may be from industry, government, education, or private professional practice, and need not be an ASME member.
Amount $1500
Date(s) Application Is Due Jan 1.
Contact Gilda DiTullio, Manager, (212) 591-7736; fax: (212) 705-7739; email: ditulliog@asme.org
Internet http://www.asme.org/honors/ms71/saa/green.html
Sponsor American Society of Mechanical Engineers
3 Park Ave
New York, NY 10016

ASME Performance Test Codes Medal **826**
This medal is awarded to an individual (or individuals in exceptional circumstances) who has made an outstanding contribution to the development and promotion of ASME performance test codes including the supplements on instruments and apparatus.
Requirements Any individual member, group of members, or committee may nominate candidates for this award.
Amount $1000
Date(s) Application Is Due Jan 1.
Contact Gilda DiTullio, Manager, (212) 591-7736; fax: (212) 705-7739; email: ditulliog@asme.org
Internet http://www.asme.org/honors/ms71/saa/ptc.html
Sponsor American Society of Mechanical Engineers
3 Park Ave
New York, NY 10016

ASNS Bio-Serv Award in Experimental Animal Nutrition **827**
The award is given for meritorious research in nutrition by an investigator who received the doctoral degree in the 10 years preceding the month the award is presented. The work recognized must involve the nutrition of experimental animals used as models. The award and an engraved plaque are made available by Bio-Serv Inc. Nominations should include a letter stating the basis for the nomination, a selected bibliography that supports the nomination, and the reprint or series of reprints on which the nomination is based.
Requirements Nominations may be made by anyone, including members of the respective nominating committees and nonmembers of the institute. Nominations will be retained for two years. Candidates may be renominated. Candidates need not be members of the institute. However, the awards are usually given to professionally active nutrition scientists.
Restrictions An individual who has received one AIN award is not eligible to receive another award unless it is for accomplishments not covered by the first award.
Amount $1000
Date(s) Application Is Due Sep 1.
Contact Secretariat, (301) 530-7051; fax: (301) 571-1892; email: nnotes@asns.faseb.org
Internet http://www.asns.org/invitation.html
Sponsor American Society for Nutritional Sciences
9650 Rockville Pike, Ste L-4500
Bethesda, MD 20814

ASNS Centrum Center for Nutrition Science Award **828**
The award is given for recent investigative contributions of contemporary significance to the understanding of human nutrition. The contributions need not be restricted to investigative work with humans as long as they have relevance to human nutrition and health. Preference is usually given to scientists in the Western Hemisphere. The award and an engraved plaque are made available by Wyeth Consumer Healthcare. Nomination should include a letter stating the significance of the work, a selected bibliography that supports the nomination, and a reprint or series of reprints reporting such research.
Requirements Nominations may be made by anyone, including members of the respective nominating committees and nonmembers of the institute. Nominations will be retained for two years. Candidates may be renominated. Candidates need not be members of the institute. However, the awards are usually given to professionally active nutrition scientists.
Restrictions An individual who has received one ASNS award is not eligible to receive another award unless it is for accomplishments not covered by the first award.
Amount $1500
Date(s) Application Is Due Sep 1.
Contact Program Officer, (301) 530-7050; fax: (301) 634-7892; email: sec@asns.org
Internet http://www.asns.org/awards.html
Sponsor American Society for Nutritional Sciences
9650 Rockville Pike, Ste L-4500
Bethesda, MD 20814

ASNS Conrad A. Elvehjem Award for Public Service in Nutrition **829**
The award is given for specific and distinguished service to the public through the science of nutrition. Such service could be rendered through governmental, industrial, private, or international institutions, but contributions of an investigative character are not excluded. The award and an engraved plaque are made available by Kraft Foods. Nominations should include a letter stating the basis for the nomination, a selected bibliography indicating the candidate's contributions to public service, and the candidate's curriculum vita.
Requirements Nominations may be made by anyone, including members of the respective nominating committees and nonmembers of the institute. Nominations will be retained for two years. Candidates may be renominated. Candidates need not be members of the institute. However, the awards are usually given to professionally active nutrition scientists.
Restrictions An individual who has received one ASNS award is not eligible to receive another award unless it is for accomplishments not covered by the first award.
Amount $1500
Date(s) Application Is Due Oct 1.
Contact Secretariat, (301) 530-7050; fax: (301) 637-7892; email: sec@asns.org
Internet http://www.asns.org/awards.html
Sponsor American Society for Nutritional Sciences
9650 Rockville Pike, Ste L-4500
Bethesda, MD 20814

ASNS Mead Johnson Nutrition Award **830**
The award is given to an investigator for a single outstanding piece of nutrition research or a series of papers on the same subject completed within 10 years of postgraduate

training. The award and an inscribed scroll are made available by Mead Johnson Nutritionals. Nominations should include a letter stating the significance of the work, a selected bibliography that supports the nomination, and a reprint or series of reprints reporting such research.
Requirements Nominations may be made by anyone, including members of the respective nominating committees and nonmembers of the institute. Nominations will be retained for two years. Candidates may be renominated, and need not be members of the institute. However, the awards are usually given to professionally active nutrition scientists.
Restrictions An individual who has received one ASNS award is not eligible to receive another award unless it is for accomplishments not covered by the first award.
Amount $2500
Date(s) Application Is Due Sep 1.
Contact Program Officer, (301) 530-7050; fax: (301) 634-7892; email: sec@asns.org
Internet http://www.asns.org/awards.html
Sponsor American Society for Nutritional Sciences
9650 Rockville Pike, Ste L-4500
Bethesda, MD 20814

ASNS Osborne and Mendel Nutrition Award **831**
The award is given for outstanding recent basic research accomplishments in nutrition. Nominations should include a letter stating the significance of the work, a selected bibliography of all papers relating to the research on which the nomination is based, and a reprint or series of reprints reporting this research.
Requirements Nominations may be made by anyone, including members of the respective nominating committees and nonmembers of the institute. Nominations will be retained for two years. Candidates may be renominated, and need not be members of the institute. However, awards are usually given to professionally active nutrition scientists.
Restrictions An individual who has received one ASNS award is not eligible to receive another award unless it is for accomplishments not covered by the first award.
Amount $2500
Date(s) Application Is Due Sep 1.
Contact Program Officer, (301) 530-7050; fax: (301) 634-7892; email: sec@asns.org
Internet http://www.asns.org/awards.html
Sponsor American Society for Nutritional Sciences
9650 Rockville Pike, Ste L-4500
Bethesda, MD 20814

ASNS Predoctoral Fellowship Program **832**
This fellowship is designed to support research in human and clinical nutrition. Preference will be given to work of immediate relevance to human nutrition information and human nutrition status. Contact the institute for application materials.
Requirements Applicants must be enrolled in a graduate program registered in the AIN Directory of Graduate Programs in Nutritional Sciences.
Amount $5000
Date(s) Application Is Due Dec 1.
Contact Secretariat, (301) 530-7052; fax: (301) 364-7892; email: sec@asns.org
Internet http://www.asns.org/winners.html
Sponsor American Society for Nutritional Sciences
9650 Rockville Pike, Ste L-4500
Bethesda, MD 20814

ASOR Fellowships at Cyprus American Archaeological Research Institute **833**
ASOR offers opportunities for study at CAARI in humanistic disciplines in studies of the Middle East from prehistoric times to the modern era. One Stuart Swiny fellowship is available to support participation in any phase or aspect of a project in Cyprus that has been approved by ASOR's Committee on Archaeological Policy (CAP). A $750 stipend is included to help cover room and board at CAARI. This program is open to scholars of any nationality (application deadline February 1). One Anita Cecil O'Donovan fellowship ($750 maximum) is available for a one- to three-month period to assist in partial payment of essential expenses for an undergraduate or graduate student to conduct research in Cyprus. Residence at CAARI is mandatory (application deadline February 1). A number of Fulbright fellowships are also available. Interested persons should contact the Fulbright program advisors at the Council for International Exchange of Scholars, 3007 Tilden St NW, Ste 5M, Box GP.O.S, Washington, DC 20008-3009, (202) 686-7877 (application deadline August 1).
Requirements All eligible persons are encouraged to apply for as many fellowships and professorships as they wish, but a person may hold only one award at a time. Persons who receive awards in one year can reapply for the same or other awards the following year, but new applicants will have priority.
Amount $750
Date(s) Application Is Due Feb 1.
Contact Program Contact, (617) 353-6574; fax: (617) 353-6575; email: caari@bu.edu
Internet http://www.caari.org/fellow.html
Sponsor American Schools of Oriental Research
656 Beacon St, 5th Fl
Boston, MA 02215-2010

ASOR Mesopotamian Fellowship **834**
The Mesopotamian Fellowship provides support for one three-to-six month period of research. This fellowship is primarily intended to support field research in ancient Mesopotamian civilization carried out in the Middle East, but other research projects such as museum or archival research, related to ancient Mesopotamian studies may be considered. The Mesopotamian Fellowship is based on a 1 July 2005 to 30 June 2006 fiscal year. A recipient who does not use the fellowship for at least three months must forfeit and return a prorated amount of the stipend. Fellowship time should be continuous, without frequent trips outside the Middle East. It is open to qualified predoctoral students and postdoctoral students and scholars from any country. Prospective applicants are encouraged to consult with the ASOR coordinator of academic programs for inquiries.
Requirements Fellowship is open to predoctoral students or postdoctoral scholars for research on a project dealing with ancient Mesopotamian civilization. Applicants must become professional members of ASOR and be either affiliated with an institution that is a corporate member of ASOR or have been an individual professional member for more than two years. Priority is given to applicants whose projects are affiliated with ASOR.
Amount $7000
Date(s) Application Is Due Apr 1.
Contact Director, Mesopotamian Fellowship, (617) 353-6570; fax: (617) 353-6575; email: asor@bu.edu
Internet http://www.asor.org/bagdam.html
Sponsor American Schools of Oriental Research
656 Beacon St, 5th Fl
Boston, MA 02215-2010

ASPEN C. Richard Fleming Grant **835**
The Foundation provides annual grant support to nutrition researchers at all stages of their careers. This grant, funded by the donations of ASPEN members, is intended to assist a nutrition investigator by providing preliminary funding for promising new research in the field of nutrition and metabolic support and related areas of clinical nutrition. Applicants still in training positions may apply. Corporate employees are eligible to receive grants if the research project is not part of their normal duties and they have at least a part-time academic appointment or are associated with a professional institute that conducts nutrition research. In making choices among otherwise high-quality applicants, the reviewers will take into account the geographic distribution of grant winners; their ethnic background and gender, should the applicant choose to supply such information; their professional discipline; and other criteria as appropriate to ensure an equitable system. Funds may be used only for technician salary, equipment, supplies, animals, clinical research costs or other expenses directly related to the conduct of the proposed research.
Requirements Applicants must submit a letter from their supervisor or department head at the institution confirming his/her commitment to the project. If the project involves human subjects, a letter pledging support in recruiting patients from the primary care provider and the institutional review board overseeing human studies is required. For junior faculty and applicants who do not hold faculty positions, three letters of reference are required.
Restrictions This grant is not intended to support pursuit of an additional degree. Grant funds may not be used for: comparison of commercial products; indirect costs or overhead; costs of patient care; constructing or renovating facilities; furniture or office equipment; secretarial services; honoraria or membership dues; textbooks or periodicals; repair or service contract costs on institutional equipment; entertainment; travel; or salary support for the Principal Investigator.
Amount $5,000
Date(s) Application Is Due Oct 15.
Contact Kandra Strauss-Riggs, Program Director, (301) 920-9145 or (301) 587-6315; email: kandras@aspen.nutr.org or aspen@nutr.org
Internet http://www.nutritioncare.org/
Sponsor American Society for Parenteral and Enteral Nutrition (ASPEN) Rhoads Research Foundation
8630 Fenton Street, Suite 412
Silver Spring, MD 20910

ASPEN Douglas Wilmore Grant **836**
The Foundation provides annual grant support to nutrition researchers at all stages of their careers. The grant is intended to assist a nutrition investigator by providing preliminary funding for promising new research in the field of nutrition and metabolic support and related areas of clinical nutrition. Priority consideration is given to applications that involve a multidisciplinary team or that investigate the efficacy of parenteral or enteral nutrition. Applicants still in training positions may apply for the Fleming Grant. Corporate employees are eligible to receive grants if the research project is not part of their normal duties and they have at least a part-time academic appointment or are associated with a professional institute that conducts nutrition research. In making choices among otherwise high-quality applicants, the reviewers will take into account the geographic distribution of grant winners; their ethnic background and gender, should the applicant choose to supply such information; their professional discipline; and other criteria as appropriate to ensure an equitable system. Funds may be used only for technician salary, equipment, supplies, animals, clinical research costs or other expenses directly related to the conduct of the proposed research. The grant can be renewed for a second year of funding, assuming satisfactory progress.
Requirements Applicants must submit a letter from their supervisor or department head at the institution confirming his/her commitment to the project. If the project involves human subjects, a letter pledging support in recruiting patients from the primary care provider and the institutional review board overseeing human studies is required.

Requirements Applicants must be 501(c)3 nonprofits with a three-year operating history providing microenterprise services to a significant number of low-income clients.
Amount $100,000 maximum over two years
Date(s) Application Is Due Jan 15.
Contact Program Coordinator, (202) 736-1071; fax: (202) 467-0790; email: fieldus@aspeninst.org
Internet http://www.fieldus.org
Sponsor Aspen Institute
1 Dupont Cir NW, Ste 700
Washington, DC 20036

ASPEN Maurice Shils Grant **841**
The Foundation provides annual grant support to nutrition researchers at all stages of their careers. This grant, funded by a donation from Baxter Health Care and Nestle Clinical Nutrition, is intended to assist a nutrition investigator by providing preliminary funding for promising new research in the field of nutrition and metabolic support and related areas of clinical nutrition. Persons applying for the grant must be in a post-training position and commit at least 20% of their time to research. Corporate employees are eligible to receive grants if the research project is not part of their normal duties and they have at least a part-time academic appointment or are associated with a professional institute that conducts nutrition research. In making choices among otherwise high-quality applicants, the reviewers will take into account the geographic distribution of grant winners; their ethnic background and gender, should the applicant choose to supply such information; their professional discipline; and other criteria as appropriate to ensure an equitable system. Funds may be used only for technician salary, equipment, supplies, animals, clinical research costs or other expenses directly related to the conduct of the proposed research. Grants can be renewed for a second year of funding, assuming satisfactory progress.
Requirements Applicants must submit a letter from their supervisor or department head at the institution confirming his/her commitment to the project. If the project involves human subjects, a letter pledging support in recruiting patients from the primary care provider and the institutional review board overseeing human studies is required. For junior faculty and applicants who do not hold faculty positions, three letters of reference are required.
Restrictions Individuals who have received other research grants in excess of $25,000 are ineligible to apply, as are those who completed training more than 5 years prior to the start of the grant period. This grant is not intended to support pursuit of an additional degree. Grant funds may not be used for: comparison of commercial products; indirect costs or overhead; costs of patient care; constructing or renovating facilities; furniture or office equipment; secretarial services; honoraria or membership dues; textbooks or periodicals; repair or service contract costs on institutional equipment; entertainment; travel; or salary support for the Principal Investigator.
Amount $25,000
Date(s) Application Is Due Oct 15.
Contact Kandra Strauss-Riggs, Program Director, (301) 920-9145 or (301) 587-6315; email: kandras@aspen.nutr.org or aspen@nutr.org
Internet http://www.nutritioncare.org/
Sponsor American Society for Parenteral and Enteral Nutrition (ASPEN) Rhoads Research Foundation
8630 Fenton Street, Suite 412
Silver Spring, MD 20910

ASPEN Norman Yoshimura Grant **842**
The Foundation provides annual grant support to nutrition researchers at all stages of their careers. This grant, supported by B. Braun Medical, Inc. funding, is intended to assist a nutrition investigator by providing preliminary funding for promising new research in the field of nutrition and metabolic support and related areas of clinical nutrition. Applicants still in training positions may apply. Corporate employees are eligible to receive grants if the research project is not part of their normal duties and they have at least a part-time academic appointment or are associated with a professional institute that conducts nutrition research. In making choices among otherwise high-quality applicants, the reviewers will take into account the geographic distribution of grant winners; their ethnic background and gender, should the applicant choose to supply such information; their professional discipline; and other criteria as appropriate to ensure an equitable system. Funds may be used only for technician salary, equipment, supplies, animals, clinical research costs or other expenses directly related to the conduct of the proposed research.
Requirements Applicants must submit a letter from their supervisor or department head at the institution confirming his/her commitment to the project. If the project involves human subjects, a letter pledging support in recruiting patients from the primary care provider and the institutional review board overseeing human studies is required. For junior faculty and applicants who do not hold faculty positions, three letters of reference are required.
Restrictions This grant is not intended to support pursuit of an additional degree. Grant funds may not be used for: comparison of commercial products; indirect costs or overhead; costs of patient care; constructing or renovating facilities; furniture or office equipment; secretarial services; honoraria or membership dues; textbooks or periodicals; repair or service contract costs on institutional equipment; entertainment; travel; or salary support for the Principal Investigator.
Amount $5,000
Date(s) Application Is Due Oct 15.
Contact Kandra Strauss-Riggs, Program Director, (301) 920-9145 or (301) 587-6315; email: kandras@aspen.nutr.org or aspen@nutr.org
Internet http://www.nutritioncare.org/
Sponsor American Society for Parenteral and Enteral Nutrition (ASPEN) Rhoads Research Foundation
8630 Fenton Street, Suite 412
Silver Spring, MD 20910

ASPEN Nutrition Research Grants **843**
The Foundation provides annual grant support to nutrition researchers at all stages of their careers. This grant, funded by a donation from the Abbott Foundation, is intended to assist a nutrition investigator by providing preliminary funding for promising new research in the field of nutrition and metabolic support and related areas of clinical nutrition. Persons applying for the grant must be in a post-training position and commit at least 20% of their time to research. Corporate employees are eligible to receive grants if the research project is not part of their normal duties and they have at least a part-time academic appointment or are associated with a professional institute that conducts nutrition research. In making choices among otherwise high-quality applicants, the reviewers will take into account the geographic distribution of grant winners; their ethnic background and gender, should the applicant choose to supply such information; their professional discipline; and other criteria as appropriate to ensure an equitable system. Funds may be used only for technician salary, equipment, supplies, animals, clinical research costs or other expenses directly related to the conduct of the proposed research. Grants can be renewed for a second year of funding, assuming satisfactory progress.
Requirements Applicants must submit a letter from their supervisor or department head at the institution confirming his/her commitment to the project. If the project involves human subjects, a letter pledging support in recruiting patients from the primary care provider and the institutional review board overseeing human studies is required. For junior faculty and applicants who do not hold faculty positions, three letters of reference are required.
Restrictions Individuals who have received other research grants in excess of $25,000 are ineligible to apply, as are those who completed training more than 5 years prior to the start of the grant period. This grant is not intended to support pursuit of an additional degree. Grant funds may not be used for: comparison of commercial products; indirect costs or overhead; costs of patient care; constructing or renovating facilities; furniture or office equipment; secretarial services; honoraria or membership dues; textbooks or periodicals; repair or service contract costs on institutional equipment; entertainment; travel; or salary support for the Principal Investigator.
Amount $25,000 maximum
Date(s) Application Is Due Oct 15.
Contact Kandra Strauss-Riggs, Program Director, (301) 920-9145 or (301) 587-6315; email: kandras@aspen.nutr.org or aspen@nutr.org
Internet http://www.nutritioncare.org/
Sponsor American Society for Parenteral and Enteral Nutrition (ASPEN) Rhoads Research Foundation
8630 Fenton Street, Suite 412
Silver Spring, MD 20910

ASPEN Scientific Abstracts Awards for Papers or Posters **844**
ASPEN will consider all Scientific Abstract submissions for awards. Applicants will be notified if their abstract is a candidate. The first authors of the three highest ranked abstracts from this category (paper or poster) will receive travel grants to attend the Research Workshop, and to present their work at Clinical Nutrition Week. In addition, cash awards in the amounts of $750, $500 and $250 will be offered to the presenters of the three best papers. Awards are presented during the Rhoads Lecture and Research Awards Ceremony at Clinical Nutrition Week.
Amount $250-$750 plus travel expenses
Contact Jewel Saunders, (301) 587-6315, ext. 150; email: jewels@aspen.nutr.org
Internet http://208.126.13.55/scientific_abstracts05.html#Awards%20for%20Scientific%20Abstracts
Sponsor American Society for Parenteral and Enteral Nutrition
8630 Fenton Street, Suite 412
Silver Spring, MD 20910

ASPEN Scientific Abstracts Promising Investigator Awards **845**
ASPEN will consider all Scientific Abstract submissions for awards. Applicants will be notified if their abstract is a candidate. These awards are presented to the top three Scientific Abstract authors, who are also in the early stages of their careers. Winners receive $750 in travel funds to offset their travel expenses to and from Clinical Nutrition Week. Vars Award winners are eligible for these awards if they are in the early stages of their careers.
Amount $750 in travel funds
Contact Jewel Saunders, (301) 587-6315, ext. 150; email: jewels@aspen.nutr.org
Internet http://208.126.13.55/scientific_abstracts05.html#Awards%20for%20Scientific%20Abstracts
Sponsor American Society for Parenteral and Enteral Nutrition
8630 Fenton Street, Suite 412
Silver Spring, MD 20910

ASPET Award for Experimental Therapeutics 846

This award is given annually to recognize outstanding research in pharmacology and experimental therapeutics (either basic laboratory or clinical research) that has had or potentially will have a major impact on the pharmacological treatment of disease.
Requirements Nominations must be made by ASPET members; however, the nominee need not be a member. No restrictions exist as to age or institutional affiliation of nominee.
Amount $2500
Date(s) Application Is Due Sep 15.
Contact Dr. Christine Carrico, Executive Officer, (301) 530-7060; fax: (301) 530-7061; email: ccarrico@aspet.org or info@aspet.org
Internet http://www.aspet.org/public/awards/exp_ther_award.html
Sponsor American Society for Pharmacology and Experimental Therapeutics
9650 Rockville Pike
Bethesda, MD 20814-3995

ASPET Harry Gold Award in Clinical Pharmacology 847

The Harry Gold Award is given biennially (odd-numbered years) to honor excellence in research and/or teaching in clinical pharmacology.
Requirements There are no restrictions as to age, institutional affiliation, or membership in ASPET; however, nominations must be made by ASPET members.
Amount $2000
Date(s) Application Is Due Sep 15.
Contact Dr. Christine Carrico, Executive Officer, (301) 530-7060; fax: (301) 530-7061; email: ccarrico@aspet.faseb.org
Internet http://www.aspet.org/public/awards/gold_award.html
Sponsor American Society for Pharmacology and Experimental Therapeutics
9650 Rockville Pike
Bethesda, MD 20814-3995

ASPET John J. Abel Award in Pharmacology 848

This award, sponsored by Eli Lilly and Company and administered by ASPET, is given annually to stimulate original and outstanding fundamental research in pharmacology and experimental therapeutics by young investigators. Candidates may not have passed their 39th birthday as of April 30 of the year of the award, or previously received an award from the sponsor for the same technical accomplishment.
Requirements Candidates need not be members of the society; however, nominations must be made by ASPET members.
Amount $2500
Date(s) Application Is Due Sep 15.
Contact Dr. Christine Carrico, Executive Officer, (301) 530-7060; fax: (301) 530-7061; email: ccarrico@aspet.faseb.org
Internet http://www.aspet.org/public/awards/abel_award.html
Sponsor American Society for Pharmacology and Experimental Therapeutics
9650 Rockville Pike
Bethesda, MD 20814-3995

ASPRS Leica Geosystems Internship 849

The award is an eight-week internship for graduate students in photogrammetry. The selected intern will work with LH Systems personnel at its facilities in San Diego, Denver, Heerbrugg, or elsewhere. The internship provides the award winner with an opportunity to carry out a small research project of his or her own choice or to work on an existing LH Systems project as part of a team. Application form is available on the Web site. The intern will provide ASPRS with a final report of his or her research accomplishments during the period of the internship.
Requirements The internship is open to graduate students of photogrammetry and remote sensing who are also members of ASPRS.
Amount $2500 stipend plus expenses
Date(s) Application Is Due Dec 1.
Contact ASPRS Awards Director, (301) 493-0290; fax: (301) 493-0208; email: scholarships@asprs.org
Internet http://www.asprs.org/membership/scholar.html#LH
Sponsor American Society for Photogrammetry and Remote Sensing
5410 Grosvenor Ln, Ste 210
Bethesda, MD 20814

ASPRS Robert E. Altenhofen Memorial Scholarship 850

This award, given in memory of Robert E. Altenhofen, who was an outstanding practitioner of photogrammetry and who made notable contributions to the mathematical aspects of the science, is to encourage and commend college students who display exceptional interest and ability in the theoretical aspects of photogrammetry.
Requirements Application may be made by an undergraduate or graduate student in a recognized college or university in the United States or elsewhere, who is either a student member or active member of the ASPRS. The recipient is obligated to provide a final report to ASPRS of his or her scholastic accomplishments during the period for which the award is granted.
Amount $2000
Date(s) Application Is Due Dec 1.
Contact ASPRS Awards Director, (301) 493-0290 ext 101; fax: (301) 493-0208; email: scholarships@asprs.org
Internet http://www.asprs.org/membership/scholar.html#altenhofen
Sponsor American Society for Photogrammetry and Remote Sensing
5410 Grosvenor Ln, Ste 210
Bethesda, MD 20814

ASPRS Ta Liang Memorial Award 851

This award is given annually to one graduate student in remote sensing. The award is to be used for research-related travel. Application forms are available on the Web site.
Requirements The award is restricted to student members of the society who are currently pursuing graduate-level studies at an accredited college or university. The recipient is obligated to provide ASPRS and Ta Liang's family, a report of his or her accomplishments during the travel for which the award is granted.
Amount $500
Date(s) Application Is Due Dec 1.
Contact Award Administrator, (301) 493-0290 ext 101; fax: (301) 493-0208; email: scholarships@asprs.org
Internet http://www.asprs.org/membership/scholar.html#ta%20liang
Sponsor American Society for Photogrammetry and Remote Sensing
5410 Grosvenor Ln, Ste 210
Bethesda, MD 20814

ASPRS William A. Fischer Memorial Scholarship 852

This scholarship, created in memory of William A. Fischer, a pioneer in the use of remote sensing from space for the study of the earth, is presented annually to a worthy student from the United States or another country to facilitate graduate studies and career goals judged to address new and innovative uses of remote sensing that relate to the natural, cultural, or agricultural resources of the earth.
Requirements The award is restricted to society members. It is intended for a student who is currently pursuing graduate-level studies or who plans to enroll in a graduate program in an accredited college or university in the United States or elsewhere. The recipient is obligated to provide ASPRS with a final report of his/her scholastic accomplishments during the period for which the award is granted.
Amount $2000
Date(s) Application Is Due Dec 1.
Contact ASPRS Awards Director, (301) 493-0290; fax: (301) 493-0208; email: scholarships@asprs.org
Internet http://www.asprs.org/membership/scholar.html#fischer
Sponsor American Society for Photogrammetry and Remote Sensing
5410 Grosvenor Ln, Ste 210
Bethesda, MD 20814

ASR Fichter Research Grant 853

Applications are invited from scholars involved in promising research on women and religion, gender issues, feminist perspectives on religion, and new religious movements. Dissertation research qualifies for funding. Scholars at the beginning of their careers are particularly encouraged to apply. Send four copies of the proposal, budget, and curriculum vita to the address listed.
Requirements Applicants must be members of the Association for the Sociology of Religion at the time of submission. A membership form is available online.
Amount $12,500 total
Date(s) Application Is Due Mar 1.
Contact William Swatos, Jr., Executive Director, (309) 932-2727; fax: (309) 932-2282
Internet http://www.sociologyofreligion.com/FICHEXLP2004.html
Sponsor Association for the Sociology of Religion
618 SW 2nd Ave
Galva, IL 61434-1912

ASR Robert J. McNamara Student Award 854

The annual competition recognizes an outstanding student paper in the sociology of religion. The paper must not have appeared in print prior to receiving the award. Students who wish their papers considered for the program must submit paper abstracts to the program chair following the guidelines of all standard paper submissions. Submissions should be by one of the following methods: IBM-formatted, virus-free disk, with the text in WordPerfect, Microsoft Word, or plain ASCII; or four paper copies, typed double spaced, and single sided. Submission should be in the form of articles with a maximum length of 40 single-sided pages inclusive of all material. The title page should include an abstract of no more than 200 words. Text should not exceed 12,000 words, i.e., approximately 36 double-spaced pages of 12 point (or 10 cpi) type. Sociology of Religion has the right of first review of award-winning papers.
Requirements Authors must be currently enrolled students who have not defended the PhD when the paper is submitted. Membership in the Association for the Sociology of Religion is required either at the time of application or previously (membership form available online).
Amount $500
Date(s) Application Is Due Jun 1.
Contact Prof. Lutz Kaelber, email: lkaelber@zoo.uvm.edu
Internet http://www.sociologyofreligion.com/MCNAMARA2004.html
Sponsor Association for the Sociology of Religion
1291 University of Oregon
Eugene, OR 97403-1291

ASSE Liberty Mutual Safety Research Fellowship 855

The program supports two four- to six-week summer research fellowships at the Liberty Mutual Research Center for Safety and Health, in Massachusetts. The goals of the program are to encourage research activity in the field of safety; familiarize graduate students and faculty members with current research projects for application in teaching situations; provide a forum for linking safety professionals, industry needs, and quality research programs; and lay the groundwork for graduate students and faculty members to pursue safety/health applied research projects of their choice. Fellows receive a weekly stipend to cover transportation to and from the fellow's home to Hopkinton, MA; room and board; and rental car as needed. Members of the society receive special consideration.

Requirements Application is open to US citizens or permanent residents who possess the PhD degree or are working toward a master's or PhD degree and are enrolled or teaching at an accredited US college or university in a safety or safety related field. Preference will be given to applicants holding appointments or enrolled in a department with an ABET accredited program.

Amount $2000 maximum for the first week; $1000 maximum per week thereafter; $8000 total

Date(s) Application Is Due Mar 1.

Contact Mary Goranson, (847) 699-2929; fax: (847) 296-3769; email: mgoranson@asse.org

Internet www.asse.org/foundat.htm

Sponsor American Society of Safety Engineers
1800 E Oakton St
Des Plaines, IL 60018-2187

ASSE Safety Research Grants 856

The foundation supports safety and health research projects, particularly in the following areas: effective interventions for prevention of traumatic injuries; effectiveness of incentive programs; developing management commitment to safety/risk control; criteria to measure risk control effectiveness; effective safety programs for temporary workers; proactive incorporation of risk control principles in early design of facilities, processes, and management systems; study cultures within organizations with outstanding safety records; and safety in public places.

Amount $20,000

Date(s) Application Is Due Oct 1.

Contact Mary Goranson, Foundation Manager, (847) 768-3412; fax: (847) 296-3769; email: mgoranson@asse.org

Internet http://www.asse.org/foundat.htm

Sponsor American Society of Safety Engineers
1800 E Oakton St
Des Plaines, IL 60018-2187

ASSE Scholarships 857

The foundation's mission is to promote the advancement of the safety, health, and environmental professions engaged in protecting people, property, and the environment by providing the necessary resources. The program supports a variety of undergraduate and graduate scholarships. Applications are available September 1. Winners names are posted on the foundation's website on or around April 1.

Amount $1000-$5000

Date(s) Application Is Due Dec 1.

Contact Grants Administrator, (847) 699-2929; fax: (847) 768-3434

Internet http://www.asse.org/foundat.htm

Sponsor American Society of Safety Engineers
1800 E Oakton St
Des Plaines, IL 60018-2187

Assisi Foundation Grants 858

The foundation supports organizations in its areas of interest, including health and human services--promote the health and well-being of the Mid-South community and help the healthcare system respond more effectively to community needs; education and literacy--projects/programs that build organizational capacity of provider agencies, provide professional development to service providers, promote collaboration among provider agencies, and leverage resources (local, state, and federal); social justice/ethics--projects/programs that strengthen ethical values among Mid-South citizens and promote social justice leading to a better understanding of and a more effective response to economic or social threats to the community; and cultural enrichment and the arts--projects/programs that foster an appreciation of the arts in the Greater Memphis community. Religious organizations seeking funding for religious programs also are eligible. Types of support include general grants, mini grants, and capital project grants. Deadlines are set to coordinate with quarterly meetings of the Board of Directors of the Foundation. Information and application are available online.

Requirements Memphis-area and Shelby, Fayette, and Tipton Counties, TN, Crittenden County, AK, and Desota County, Mississippi nonprofit organizations are eligible.

Restrictions Grants are not made for individuals, national fundraising drives, projects that address the needs of only one congregation, tickets for benefits, political organizations or candidates for public office, lobbying activities, recurring budget deficits, or tournament fees and/or travel for athletic competitions.

Amount $20,000 maximum

Contact Jan Young, Executive Director, (901) 684-1564; email: joung@assisifoundation.org

Internet http://www.assisifoundation.org/generalgrants.html

Sponsor Assisi Foundation
515 Erin Drive
Memphis, TN 38117

Association for Research on Nonprofit Organizations and Voluntary Action Awards 859

ARNOVA invites nominations for the current year's awards, to be presented at the annual conference in Los Angeles, CA. The following awards will be presented: Award for Outstanding Book in Nonprofit and Voluntary Action Research--books published in the three calendar years preceding the award that contribute to the advancement of theory, conceptualization, research, or practice; Award for Distinguished Achievement and Leadership in Nonprofit and Voluntary Action--for significant contributions to the field through research and leadership; and the Gabriel G. Rudney Memorial Award for an Outstanding Dissertation in Nonprofit and Voluntary Action Research--for a PhD dissertation completed and/or defended in the three calendar years preceding the award that contributes to the advancement of theory, conceptualization, research, or practice. Guidelines and nominating form are available online.

Amount $1000

Date(s) Application Is Due Mar 17.

Contact Katherine Finley, Executive Director, (317) 684-2120; fax: (317) 684-2128; email: kmfinley@arnova.org

Internet http://www.arnova.org/award_nominations_news.php

Sponsor Association for Research on Nonprofit Organizations and Voluntary Action
550 W North St, Ste 301
Indianapolis, IN 46202-3162

Association for the Study of Higher Education Dissertation Fellowships 860

With support of the Lumina Foundation for Education, the association awards fellowships to support dissertation research on the broad topics of financial aid, student retention and success, and adult learners and learning. The fellowships will support up to one year of activity that will be conducted through the students' home universities and can be used to support costs of supplying data, dissemination of project results, travel, tuition, and salary for the fellows. Eight one-year fellowships will be awarded. Guidelines are available online.

Requirements Doctoral students affiliated with any accredited doctoral program may submit a proposal. Students in doctoral programs outside the United States may apply if their study is about student financial assistance, student retention and success, and/or adult learning and learners in the United States. Recipients of the fellowship must have completed their course work and any required qualifying examinations and have their dissertation proposal accepted by their institution.

Amount $12,500

Date(s) Application Is Due May 31.

Contact Dr. Dennis Brown, Executive Director, (517) 432-8805; fax: (573) 884-2197; email: ashemsu@msu.edu

Internet http://35.8.168.242/fellowship/aboutfellowship.htm

Sponsor Michigan State University
424 Erickson Hall
East Lansing, MI 48824

Association for Women in Mathematics Mentoring Travel Grants 861

The program helps junior women develop long-term working and mentoring relationships with senior mathematicians. The relationship should help the junior mathematician establish her research program and eventually receive tenure. The applicant's research may be conducted in any field funded by the NSF Division of Mathematical Sciences. Up to seven grants will be awarded, each to fund travel, subsistence, and other required costs for an untenured woman to travel to an institute and do research with a senior mentor for one month. Specific guidelines and instructions are available on the Web site.

Requirements Applicants holding a doctorate or equivalent experience are eligible.

Amount $4000

Date(s) Application Is Due Feb 1.

Contact Grants Administrator, (703) 934-0163; email: awm@awm-math.org

Internet http://www.awm-math.org/travelgrants.html#mentor

Sponsor University of Maryland
4114 Computer and Space Sciences Bldg
College Park, MD 20742-2461

Association of Teachers of Latin American Studies Grants 862

Grants are intended to improve the teaching about Latin America in US secondary schools by permitting high school social studies teachers and graduate students to participate in six-week summer seminars in a Latin American country. This program is sponsored by the Department of Education, and the number and amount of grants available each year varies according to program funding. A letter of application should include a self-addressed, stamped envelope for reply.

Requirements Applicants must be high school teachers, college faculty, supervisors, or curriculum developers. The grants are aimed at teachers from secondary level social studies and Spanish language who can enrich their programs through participation in an overseas experience.

Date(s) Application Is Due May 1.
Contact Dr. Daniel Mugan, President, (718) 428-1237; email: djmugan@aol.com
Sponsor Association of Teachers of Latin American Studies
P.O. Box 754
Flushing, NY 11362

ASTD Dissertation Award **863**
The award is given to foster and disseminate research in the practice of workplace learning and performance. It is presented annually to the person who has submitted the best dissertation completed during the previous academic year (September 21 through September 20). Illustrative areas of concentration include training and development, performance analysis, career development, organizational development/learning, workplace design, and human resource planning. All materials submitted must be in English and include the following: letter of application from candidate; recommendation from committee chair, on letterhead, with the dissertation completion date; abstract of dissertation (five to 15 pages, double-spaced) including summary of the problem addressed by the study, critique of relevant literature, synopsis of the findings, and implications for practice and research.
Requirements The candidate must be recommended and sponsored by his or her committee chair. A committee chair may nominate more than one candidate who meets the criteria.
Amount $500
Date(s) Application Is Due Sep 20.
Contact Ray Rivera , (703) 683-8144; email: rrivera@astd.org
Internet http://www.astd.org/astd/About_ASTD/Awards/dissertation.htm
Sponsor American Society for Training and Development
P.O. Box 1443, 1640 King St
Alexandria, VA 22313-2043

ASTD Research Award **864**
The award is given to encourage the publication of research with practical implications for practitioners of workplace learning and performance. It is presented annually to the author(s) of the best article published in a refereed journal during the calendar year. Illustrative areas of concentration include training and development, career development, work design, performance analysis, organizational development/learning, and human resource planning. Applications must include letter of application; proof of publication--either a galley proof or reprint of the article in its entirety or a copy of the article with its letter of acceptance; and supporting documents, including the name and issue of the refereed journal in which the article appeared or will appear and contact information for the editor of the journal (name, address, and telephone number). The award includes a cash prize, designated place on the international conference program to present the research, and a commemorative plaque(s) presented at the awards ceremony.
Requirements The article must have appeared, or will appear, in print in a refereed journal between January 1 and December 31 of the current year. All materials submitted, including the article, must be in English.
Amount $500
Date(s) Application Is Due Oct 31.
Contact Ray Rivera, ASTD Research Department, (703) 683-8144.; email: rrivera@astd
Internet http://www.astd.org/astd/About_ASTD/Awards/research_award.htm
Sponsor American Society for Training and Development
P.O. Box 1443, 1640 King St
Alexandria, VA 22313-2043

Astronomical Society of the Pacific Amateur Achievement Award **865**
The award and a plaque are given annually to recognize significant contributions to astronomy or amateur astronomy by those not employed in the field of astronomy in a professional capacity. Nominations may be submitted by any individual or group. All nominations will remain active for three years of competition; additional support letters or nomination updates will be accepted at any time.
Restrictions Self nominations or nomination by a family member will not be accepted.
Amount $500
Date(s) Application Is Due Dec 15.
Contact Marilyn Delgado, Program Contact, (415) 337-1100; fax: (415) 337-5205; email: mdelgado@astrosociety.org
Internet http://www.astrosociety.org/membership/awards/amateur.html
Sponsor Astronomical Society of the Pacific
390 Ashton Ave
San Francisco, CA 94112

ASU Graduate Scholar Awards **866**
The awards recognize outstanding students with high credentials such as GRE scores, GPA, publications, and prestigious awards. Students are nominated by the program areas to which they are applying. Three-year award packages include a stipend plus tuition and fees. A recruiting visit to ASU is available to finalists. Members of groups traditionally underrepresented in graduate education are strongly encouraged to apply.
Requirements Recipients of the award must be U.S. citizens or permanent residents.
Date(s) Application Is Due Nov 18.
Contact Dr. Marjorie Zatz, (480) 965-5906 or (480) 965-3521; email: marjorie.zatz@asu.edu
Internet http://www.asu.edu/graduate/generalinfo/UGS/index.html
Sponsor Arizona State University Graduate College
P.O. Box 871003
Tempe, AZ 85287-1003

ASU Institute for Humanities Research Visiting Fellowships **867**
The program is for scholars from other institutions of higher education in the United States and abroad to spend spring semester (January 15 through May 15) in residence at the Institute for Humanities Research (IHR), participating in the intellectual life of the IHR and the university community. The theme is broadly defined as Humanities in Times of Crises to encourage applications from a wide range of intellectual and scholarly approaches and chronological time frames within the humanities. Fellows will be provided a stipend, an office, and support services. The fellowship provides the opportunity to conduct research and write. Visiting fellows will participate in weekly meetings around the theme with the working groups of ASU fellows, and will give public lectures and seminars on their research topics while in residence. Application and guidelines are available online.
Amount $20,000 maximum stipend
Date(s) Application Is Due Feb 20.
Contact Rachel Fuchs, (480) 965-3000; email: ihr@asu.edu
Internet http://www.asu.edu/clas/ihr/faculty/fellows/index.html
Sponsor Arizona State University
P.O. Box 876505
Tempe, AZ 85287-6505

ASU SIRLS Scholarships and Grants **868**
A variety of grants and scholarships are awarded through the university's School of Information Resources and Library Science. Graduate aid is available to students enrolling in SIRLS based on financial need, individual accomplishments, prior experiences and expertise, academic record, and contributions to the diversity of the SIRLS student community. Application and guidelines are available online.
Requirements Eligible students must have been accepted for admission or be currently enrolled in a SIRLS graduate degree program. Students receiving financial aid are required to maintain full-time enrollment status (nine credits) and maintain successful progress toward their degree, defined at a minimum as a GPA of at least 3.0
Date(s) Application Is Due Apr 1; Sep 1.
Contact Scholarships Administrator, (520) 621-3565; email: sirls@email.arizona.edu
Internet http://www.sir.arizona.edu/program/admissions/financial.html
Sponsor Arizona State University
1515 E First St
Tucson, AZ 85719

AT&T Bell Labs Graduate Research Program **869**
The Graduate Research Program for Women (GRPW) is designed to increase the number of minorities and women in the fields of science, math, engineering and technology. Financial support is provided to outstanding women students from the beginning of their full-time graduate studies leading to a PhD. The program includes two types of financial awards, fellowships and grants, which may be renewed on a yearly basis for the normal duration of the graduate program, subject to the participant's satisfactory progress toward the doctoral degree. Employment at AT&T Bell Laboratories is offered to fellowship and grant holders for the summer preceding their entry into graduate school as well as for subsequent summers during graduate school. If a fellowship holder chooses to remain on campus for supervised university research or study during the summer, her fellowship support will be continued through the calendar year. Application forms must be obtained from AT&T Bell Laboratories. Applications and all supporting materials are due January 13.
Requirements Women who are applying to graduate school to eventually obtain a PhD in chemical engineering, chemistry, communications science, computer science/engineering, electrical engineering, information science, materials science, mathematics, mechanical engineering, operations research, physics, or statistics are eligible. Applicants must be US citizens or permanent residents and, by the time the award is made, be admitted to full-time study in a doctoral program approved by AT&T Bell Laboratories.
Amount $25,000
Date(s) Application Is Due Jan 13.
Contact Fellowship Program Manager, GRPW, (908) 582-4822; email: coopgraduate@lucent.com
Internet http://www.lucent.com/social/blgrfp
Sponsor AT&T Bell Laboratories
P.O. Box 297, 1505 Riverview Rd
St Peter, MN 56082

AT&T Education Grants **870**
The foundation supports initiatives that improve student achievement, teacher preparedness, minority student success and that increase the use of new technologies, from kindergarten to the university. The foundation also supports NCCEP and GEAR UP. Primary support is provided to projects in math, technology, science and reading that provide the skills and knowledge that students need in order to succeed in an ever-expanding global economy. The request for proposals process is invitational for some special grants programs and an open, competitive process for others. Those who wish to

submit an unsolicited proposal should send a brief letter of introduction and description of their organization and project to the office.
Requirements The foundation prefers to work with 501(c)(3) public charity or government instrumentalities that have clearly stated objectives, long-range planning, active participation of the governing board and strategies that incorporate diversified sources of support. The foundation also considers grants to organizations that qualify as government instrumentalities, including public libraries, police and fire departments and publicly funded social services agencies.
Contact Program Contact; (800) 591-9663
Internet http://www.att.com/foundation
Sponsor AT&T Foundation
32 Avenue of the Americas, 6th Fl
New York, NY 10013

AT&T Industrial Ecology Faculty Fellowships **871**
The foundation awards fellowships to academic researchers in the emerging, multidisciplinary field of industrial ecology. The program is intended to stimulate interdisciplinary research and curriculum development that involve social issues, engineering, the sciences, economics, management, business, law, and public policy issues. The overarching objectives of the program are (1) to produce university faculty and students who can contribute to solving global and regional environmental problems and help shape environmentally and economically efficient strategies that have a firm scientific and engineering basis and (2) to advance the theoretical basis for the field of industrial ecology and its application in service sectors, industrial activity, and regulatory arenas. Application guidelines are available online and applications are solicited electronically.
Requirements Individuals working independently or in collaboration at US universities in the following fields are eligible: business, economics, engineering, law, management, physical sciences, public policy, and social sciences.
Amount $25,000
Date(s) Application Is Due Nov 20.
Contact Michael Blazek, Fellowships Administrator, (908) 221-4191; email: mblazek@att.com
Internet http://www.corp.att.com/ehs/ind_ecology/fellow_guidelines.html
Sponsor AT&T Foundation
1 AT&T Way
Bedminster, NJ 07921

ATA Doctoral Fellowships in Education **872**
Each year, the Alberta Teachers Association awards two fellowships, to Alberta teachers entering the first year of a full-time, campus-based doctoral program in education. The fellowship program is intended to recognize academic excellence and to help defray the financial costs of university study.
Requirements Each applicant must be a current member and have a permanent Alberta teaching certificate.
Restrictions A teacher who is not an active ATA member at the time of application must be an associate member and either must have been an associate member for the last three consecutive years, or must have been an active member at some time within the three years preceding the deadline date for application.
Amount $15,000 annually each
Date(s) Application Is Due Mar 10.
Contact Corinne Anderson, Administrative Assistant, (800) 232-7208 or (780) 447-9470; email: corrine.anderson@ata.ab.ca
Internet http://www.teachers.ab.ca/Professional+Development/Grants+and+Scholarships/Fellowships+and+Scholarships.htm
Sponsor Alberta Teachers Association
11010 142 St NW
Edmonton, AB T5N 2R1 Canada

ATA Education Research Award **873**
The award is presented annually to a faculty member or sessional lecturer at an Alberta university who has undertaken high-quality research on classroom teaching and learning. Research must be directly related to school and classroom practice; be focused on school teaching and/or learning; be current (either ongoing or completed within the last two years); be related to critical issues; have involved classroom teachers and/or students; be applicable to the Alberta context and must be of practical benefit to teachers in improving their professional practice, and be of high quality in terms of purpose, approach, methodology, originality and clarity.
Requirements Applicant must be a faculty of education member or sessional lecturer at an Alberta university who has undertaken high quality research on classroom teaching and learning to be eligible.
Amount $5000 (Canadian)
Date(s) Application Is Due May 11.
Contact Corinne Anderson, Program Contact, (780) 447-9400 or (800) 232-7208; email: corrine.anderson@ata.ab.ca
Internet http://www.teachers.ab.ca/Professional+Development/Grants+and+Scholarships
Sponsor Alberta Teachers Association
11010 142nd St NW
Edmonton, AB T5N 2R1 Canada

ATA Nadene M. Thomas Graduate Research Bursary **874**
The research bursary is offered annually to current members of the association. The award is based on a research focus on challenges to public education and professional practice, the applicant's contribution to the association, the research proposal, a letter of support from the university advisor, and the applicant's commitment to public education. The recipient is required to submit a copy of the completed research to the association. The award is payable in two equal installments, half upon receipt of the award and half upon receipt of the completed research.
Requirements An applicant must hold a permanent Alberta teaching certificate and have completed at least five years of successful teaching in Alberta; be either an active or associate ATA member; state intention to continue a career in education in Alberta; and be registered as a graduate student in a specialty in education at an Alberta university.
Restrictions The applicant must not have received an ATA fellowship.
Amount $C5000
Date(s) Application Is Due Mar 10.
Contact Corinne Anderson, Administrative Assistant, (780) 447-9470 or (800) 232-7208; email: corrine.anderson@ata.ab.ca
Internet http://www.teachers.ab.ca/Professional+Development/Grants+and+Scholarships
Sponsor Alberta Teachers Association
11010 142nd St NW
Edmonton, AB T5N 2R1 Canada

Athenaeum of Philadelphia Senior Fellowships **875**
The fellowship trust supports the study, recording, and preservation of early American architecture and building technology and the teaching of conservation skills in American schools of architecture. Research is not subject to geographical restrictions, although preference is given to Delaware Valley topics. Applications are reviewed by a committee of architects, architectural historians, and educators appointed by the board of directors. Applications should be submitted in the form of a single-page letter setting forth a brief statement of the project, with attached budget, schedule for completion, and professional resume. Two letters of reference should be requested by the applicant and submitted directly to the committee. There are no application forms. A clear statement of objectives is necessary, and a final report is expected. Successful applicants may be invited to give a public lecture or participate in a seminar at the Athenaeum sharing the results of the project.
Requirements Senior fellows must hold a terminal degree and possess a distinguished record of accomplishment.
Restrictions Grants may not be used for international travel.
Amount $5000 maximum
Date(s) Application Is Due Mar 1.
Contact Eileen Magee, Assistant Director for Programs, (215) 925-2688; fax: (215) 925-3755; email: magee@PhilaAthenaeum.org
Internet http://www.philaathenaeum.org/grants.html
Sponsor Athenaeum of Philadelphia
219 S Sixth St
Philadelphia, PA 19106-3794

Athwin Foundation Grants **876**
Areas of interest include arts and humanities, education, human services, the natural environment, and organizational capacity building. General operating grants, capital grants, and special project grants will be awarded. Applications are accepted throughout the year.
Requirements Tax-exempt organizations in the Twin Cities area of Minnesota and Western Montana are eligible.
Restrictions Grants do not support individuals, scholarships, fellowships, or loans.
Amount $1000-$100,000 range
Date(s) Application Is Due Mar 1: Oct 1.
Contact Bruce Bean, Trustee, (952) 915-6165
Sponsor Athwin Foundation
5200 Wilson Rd, Ste 307
Minneapolis, MN 55424

ATLA Bibliography Grant **877**
The grant is awarded annually to one or more bibliographers or indexers to aid in the development of a work that provides access to a significant body of literature within the fields of theological and/or religious studies. The scope, subject matter, length, and format are broadly conceived, with the intent of encouraging bibliographical or indexing work at all levels, especially by persons undertaking their first major project in this area. The applicant(s) should complete and submit the application form (available online) along with the two requisite letters of reference by the specified due date.
Requirements This grant is open to applicants inside and outside of the association.
Amount $1500 maximum
Date(s) Application Is Due Jan 15.
Contact Publications Committee; (888) 665-2852.
Internet http://www.atla.com/pub_com/grant.html
Sponsor American Theological Library Association
300 S Wacker Dr, Ste 2100
Chicago, IL 60606-6701

Atlantic Fellowships in Public Policy 878
The fellowships provide an opportunity for outstanding mid-career professionals to study and gain practical experience in a variety of public policy areas in the United Kingdom, as well as a firsthand introduction to the European Union. Approximately 10 awards are made each year, and fellows spend between six and 10 months in the UK. Brochures and applications are available on the Web site.
Requirements Fellowships are open to US citizens with at least five years experience in their professions. Candidates should be between their late 20s and early 40s.
Restrictions Fellowships are not awarded to support basic research or to enable study for an academic degree.
Contact Scholarships and Exchanges Officer, (202) 588-7844; fax: (202) 588-7918; email: atlantic.fellow@us.britishcouncil.org
Internet http://www.britishcouncil-usa.org/learning/policy/atlantics.shtml
Sponsor The British Council
3100 Massachusetts Ave NW
Washington, DC 20008

ATS Lilly Theological Research Grants 879
The grants, supported by the Lilly Endowment, encourage scholarly research that contributes to theological education, informs the life of the church, develops a greater public voice for theology in society, collaborates with other academic disciplines, and offers new perspectives on Christianity in a pluralistic setting. The program has three components: faculty fellowships, theological research grants, and research expense grants. Faculty fellowships support five faculty members during a sabbatical or other leave. Research grants provide up to 10 grants for research apart from a formal research leave. Research expense grants support up to 10 scholars who are engaged in well-designed and significant research projects. Annual deadline dates may vary; contact the program officer for exact dates.
Requirements All full-time faculty members at ATS-accredited and candidate schools are eligible to apply. For faculty fellowships applicants must have a research leave of at least one term from all teaching and institutional responsibilities during the award year.
Restrictions Project proposals for less than six months will not be considered for faculty fellowships. No more than two applicants from a single institution may receive awards in any given competition.
Amount $25,000 maximum for faculty fellowships; $10,000 maximum for research grants; $5000 maximum for research expense grants
Date(s) Application Is Due Jan 4.
Contact William Myers, Program Contact, (412) 788-6505 ext 252; fax: (412) 788-6510; email: myers@ats.edu
Internet http://www.ats.edu/faculty/grants/granttoc.htm
Sponsor Association of Theological Schools
10 Summit Park Dr
Pittsburgh, PA 15275-1103

ATS Henry Luce III Fellowships 880
The grants, supported by the Henry Luce Foundation, are awarded to scholars of distinction for research and publication that offer an innovative and substantial contribution to theological scholarship. The foundation supports the research of junior and senior scholars whose projects offer significant and innovative contributions to theological studies; meet high scholarly standards; enhance the theological understanding of people of faith and enrich the experience of church life in North America; and develop ways for scholarship to inform contemporary culture. No more than one fellow will be selected per the following categories: bible and the church, Christianity and contemporary culture, constructive theology, history of Christianity and the church today, ministry and practice of communities of faith, plus topics that do not fall into the above categories. Applicants must specify the category in which they are requesting appointment. Fellows present their research at the annual conference, held in the fall. Annual deadline dates may vary; contact the program officer for exact dates.
Requirements The program is open to full-time faculty members of ATS-accredited and candidate schools who have an appropriate period of leave from all teaching and institutional responsibilities. Applicants also must be eligible to receive at least one-half salary support from their institutions.
Restrictions Fellows may not hold any other major fellowship or grant during the tenure of the award without express approval of the association.
Amount $75,000 maximum
Date(s) Application Is Due Nov 30.
Contact William Myers, Program Contact, (412) 788-6505 ext 252; fax: (412) 788-6510; email: myers@ats.edu
Internet http://www.ats.edu/faculty/external/spons/A0000010.HTM
Sponsor Association of Theological Schools in the United States and Canada
10 Summit Park Dr
Pittsburgh, PA 15275-1103

AUAF Health Services Research Scholar Grants in Urology 881
The program supports urology residents or trained urologists (MD/DO) within five years of residency who aspire to conduct research in health care services as it relates to urology. The candidate must be committed to a career in academic urology and able to provide evidence of current interest and/or accomplishments in matters relating to the delivery of health services and health economics and policy. The project should include didactic experience and may include plans for obtaining an advanced degree in public health, health policy, health financing and economics, or other relevant areas. In view of the multidisciplinary nature of health services research and health care policy, the proposal should include an explanation of how researchers from different clinical and nonclinical disciplines will be involved in the research project. The candidate must dedicate a minimum of 80 percent of his/her time to the research project. This experience should prepare the scholar for a subsequent career in academic urology as it relates to health care policy, health financing, and health economics. Applications are available on the Web site. Annual deadline dates may vary; contact program staff for exact dates.
Requirements An accredited medical education research institution and/or department within such an institution must sponsor the candidate. A preceptor, an established health services researcher in a urology department or a nonurology clinician/researcher in a school of public health/health policy, must have prior experience in health services research with funded grant support and must make a two-year commitment to sponsor the scholar.
Amount $44,000 per year
Date(s) Application Is Due Sep 1.
Contact Anthony Caputi, Manager, Research Scholar Program, (800) 828-7866; fax: (410) 468-1808; email: anthony@afud.org
Internet http://www.afud.org/research/index.asp
Sponsor American Urologic Association Foundation, Inc.
1128 N Charles St
Baltimore, MD 21201

AUAF PhD Research Scholars Program 882
These fellowships are offered to postdoctoral basic scientists with a research interest in urologic or related diseases and dysfunctions. Research projects focus on many different diseases including, but not limited to: prostate cancer, bladder cancer, kidney stones, incontinence, impotence, BPH, prostatitis, urinary tract infections, interstitial cystitis, and pediatric dysfunctions. A commitment to dedicate two years in the program as a full-time researcher is required. The sponsoring urology department is required to provide space, laboratory equipment, and supplies to enable the recipient to perform the proposed research. Continued support is subject to yearly review and evaluation by the scientific and education committee. Application forms are available on the Web site. Annual deadline dates may vary; contact program staff for exact dates.
Requirements An accredited medical education research institution or department within such an institution must sponsor the candidate by guaranteeing research time commitment and adequate financial support, including responsibility for the adequacy of the scientific environment, laboratory equipment, and supplies to perform the proposed research.
Amount $10,000-$60,000
Date(s) Application Is Due Sep 1.
Contact Anthony Caputi, Manager, Research Scholar Program, (410) 468-1803; fax: (410) 468-1808; email: anthony@afud.org
Internet http://www.afud.org/research/index.asp
Sponsor American Urologic Association Foundation, Inc.
1128 N Charles St
Baltimore, MD 21201

AUAF Practicing Urologist Research Awards 883
To aid and encourage practicing urologists with research ideas to undertake collaborative investigations at a urological research laboratory, the AUAF grants research awards to be matched by the sponsoring institution. Applications are available on the Web site. Annual deadline dates may vary; contact program staff for exact dates.
Requirements An accredited medical research institution or department must sponsor the candidate by guaranteeing adequate support, including responsibility for the adequacy of the environment, laboratory equipment, and supplies needed to perform the proposed research.
Amount $5000 matched by sponsoring institution
Date(s) Application Is Due Sep 1.
Contact Anthony Caputi, Manager, Research Scholar Program, (410) 468-1803; fax: (410) 468-1808; email: anthony@afud.org
Internet http://www.afud.org/research/index.asp
Sponsor American Urologic Association Foundation, Inc.
1128 N Charles St
Baltimore, MD 21201

AUAF Research Scholar Program 884
The fellowship program supports urology residents in training or post residency (not more than five years) for one year of full-time investigation in laboratory research of urologic diseases. An established basic science academician in either a basic science or clinical department with substantial experience in grant support and mentoring of scientific trainees must make a one-year commitment to sponsor the scholar. One-year awards can be renewed for a second year. Annual deadline dates may vary; contact program staff for exact dates.
Requirements An accredited medical education research institution or department within such an institution must sponsor the candidate by guaranteeing research time commitment and adequate financial support, including responsibility for the adequacy of the scientific environment, laboratory equipment, and supplies to perform the proposed research.
Amount $25,000 for one year

Date(s) Application Is Due Sep 1.
Contact Anthony Caputi, Manager, Research Scholar Program, (410) 468-1803; fax: (410) 468-1808; email: anthony@afud.org
Internet http://www.afud.org/research/scholars/current.asp
Sponsor American Urologic Association Foundation, Inc.
1128 N Charles St
Baltimore, MD 21201

AUAF/NIH Intramural Urology Research Training Grants 885
This intramural program, developed by NIDDK and NCI in collaboration with AFUD, provides an opportunity for selected individuals to complete a research project under the direction of a senior investigator at NIDDK or NCI. Two positions each are available in NIDDK and NCI for laboratory-based research. Up to two positions are available in the surgery branch of NCI, of which six months are dedicated to clinical training in urologic oncology. The program consists of a two-year fellowship with possible extension for a third year. Applications are available on the Web site. Annual deadline dates may vary; contact program staff for exact dates.
Requirements Eligibility is open to physicians in urology residency programs, or those who have recently completed a urology residency, who desire intensive exposure to research experience utilizing basic molecular and cellular biologic techniques in projects relevant to urology. Applicants must have less than five years of postdoctoral research experience (clinical residency training is not counted as postdoctoral research).
Amount $40,000-$44,000 per year, depending on experience
Date(s) Application Is Due Sep 1.
Contact Kym Liddick, Director, Research Scholar Program, (410) 468-1812; fax: (410) 468-1808; email: kym@afud.org
Internet http://www.afud.org/research/index.asp
Sponsor American Urologic Association Foundation, Inc.
1128 N Charles St
Baltimore, MD 21201

Auburn Foundation Grants 886
The purpose of the Foundation is to stimulate giving and cooperative leadership among the citizens of Auburn; help improve the lives of all community residents, especially those who are most vulnerable; and enrich the cultural environment and community life. Of special interest are projects that bring together all ages and sections of the town, or that contribute to healthy, active living. Application is available online.
Requirements Any nonprofit organization that serves residents of Auburn is invited to apply.
Restrictions Grants will not be awarded to for-profit businesses or expenses already incurred by the applicant.
Amount $5,000
Date(s) Application Is Due Oct 15.
Contact Lois Smith, (508) 755-0980, ext. 107; email: lsmith@greaterworcester.org
Internet http://www.greaterworcester.org/grants/Auburn.htm
Sponsor Auburn Foundation
370 Main Street, Suite 650
Worcester, MA 01608-1738

Auburn University President's Graduate Opportunities Program 887
The major purpose of the program is to recruit, retain, and support African-American students engaged in graduate study leading to a doctoral degree from Auburn University. Successful applicants will receive a fellowship in addition to a stipend provided by the department, school, or college in which recipients are enrolled. Both the fellowship and the departmental stipend are renewable for up to four years of doctoral study. Application and guidelines are available online.
Requirements Candidates must hold a degree from an accredited institution, meet admission standards of the graduate school and the doctoral program in which they seek to enroll, and be recommended for the award by that academic department or unit.
Amount $10,000 stipend plus $5000 minimum from recipients' department, school, or college
Date(s) Application Is Due Feb 1.
Contact Dr. Christine Curtis, Chair, (334) 844-5771; email: curticw@auburn.edu
Internet http://education.auburn.edu/files/file76.pdf
Sponsor Auburn University
2003 RBD Library, 231 Mell St
Auburn University, AL 36849-5168

AUCC Education Funding Programs 888
On behalf of governments, foundations, and private sector companies, the association administers Canadian and international scholarships, exchange programs, work placements, and research opportunities. With a focus on international opportunities that enhance other countries' resources and lead to improvements in their living standards, the association administers more than 150 scholarship, fellowship, and internship programs.
Requirements Canadian citizens and permanent residents of Canada can apply for AUCC-administered programs. Certain programs are also open to foreign professors.
Contact International and Canadian Programs Division, (613) 563-1236; fax: (613) 563-9745; email: awards@aucc.ca
Internet http://www.aucc.ca/programs/index_e.html
Sponsor Association of Universities and Colleges of Canada
350 Albert St, Ste 600
Ottawa, ON K1R 1B1 Canada

Audio Engineering Society Graduate Scholarships 889
Graduate students in audio engineering and related fields may apply for the scholarships, which will be awarded on the basis of demonstrated past interest and achievements in the field and on two faculty recommendations. Awards are made annually, in August, and each successful applicant may apply for a one-time renewal after the successful completion of at least one year of graduate studies. Payments for the original award or the renewal will be sent directly to the graduate school on behalf of the student's account. Completed applications including recommendations will be accepted from March 15 to the listed application deadline.
Requirements Applicants must have acceptance or pending application for graduate studies leading to a master's or higher degree or an internationally recognized equivalent. Applications are accepted from students worldwide.
Amount $3000
Date(s) Application Is Due May 15.
Contact Scholarship Coordinator, (212) 661-8528; fax: (203) 682-0477; email: HQ@aes.org
Internet http://www.aes.org/education/edu_foundation.html
Sponsor Audio Engineering Society Educational Foundation
60 E 42nd St
New York, NY 10165

Audubon Naturalist Society Research Grants 890
This program provides grants for either conservation-related field work or conservation and education projects. The project should be located outside the United States. One need not be affiliated with an institution or organization to apply. There are no restrictions on nationality. Preference given to start-up projects. Applied research projects are given preference over basic research projects.
Amount $500-$2000
Contact Education Program Coordinator, (301) 652-9188; fax: (301) 951-7179; email: Contact@audubonnaturalist.org
Internet http://www.audubonnaturalist.org
Sponsor Audubon Naturalist Society of the Central Atlantic States
8940 Jones Mill Rd
Chevy Chase, MD 20815

AUPHA Baxter International Foundation Prize for Health Service Research 891
The prize acknowledges national or international contributions of health services research, defined as a product of the application of analytic methods to the organization, financing, and/or delivery of health services. An individual's specific contribution or a career-long achievement may be recognized. The prize recognizes a person who has made significant and demonstrable contributions to the health of the public in three primary areas: health services management, health policy development, and health care delivery.
Requirements Nominations must include a letter of nomination, two letters of recommendation, and a current curriculum vita. Nominations should focus on the nominee's contribution in the areas of health services management, health policy development, and health care delivery. Nominations should be sent to and further information can be obtained from the Secretary, HSR Prize Committee, AUPHA, 2000 N. 14th Street, Suite 780, Arlington, VA 22201.
Amount $10,000 personal award and $15,000 to a nonprofit institution designated by the recipient, to support his or her work
Date(s) Application Is Due Dec 15.
Contact Lydia Reed, (703) 894-0940; email: lydia.reed@aupha.org
Internet http://www.e-guana.net/organizations.php3?action=printContentItem&orgid=75&typeID=506&itemID=3744
Sponsor Association of University Programs in Health Administration
2000 14th St N, Ste 780
Arlington, VA 22201

Australian Academy of Science Grants 892
The objectives of the Academy are to promote science through a range of activities. It has defined four major program areas as their focus. The Academy focus is on recognition of outstanding contributions to science, education and public awareness, science policy, and international relations. Guidelines are available online.
Contact Executive Secretary, 61-2-6201-9400; fax: 61-2-6201-9494; email: eb@science.org.au
Internet http://www.science.org.au
Sponsor Australian Academy of Science
GP.O. Box 783
Canberra, ACT 2601 Australia

Australian Cancer Foundation for Medical Research Grants 893
The foundation awards grants in Australia in the field of cancer research. This includes, but is not limited to, cell or molecular biology, epidemiology, prevention or drug development. Types of support include capital projects and equipment.
Amount $A2 million total

Date(s) Application Is Due May 12.
Contact Lorraine McNuff, (02) 9223 7833; fax: (02) 9223 1800; email: lmcnuff@acrf.com.au
Internet http://www.acrf.com.au/page/research_grants.html
Sponsor Australian Cancer Foundation for Medical Research
Strand Arcade, Ste 403
Sydney NSW 2000 Australia

Australian Department of Health and Aging Packer Policy Fellowships 894
This program offers a unique opportunity for US health policy researchers and practitioners to spend six to 10 months in Australia conducting original research and working with leading Australian health policy experts on issues relevant to both countries. The fellowships provide a stipend plus family allowance. Applicants must submit a formal application, including a project proposal that falls within an area of mutual policy interest, such as health care quality and safety, the private/public mix of insurance and providers, the fiscal sustainability of health systems, the health care workforce, and investment in preventive care strategies.
Requirements The fellowships are open to accomplished, midcareer health policy researchers and practitioners, including, academics, physicians, decisionmakers in managed care and other private organizations, federal and state health officials, and journalists. Applicants must be US citizens.
Amount $50,000 (Australian) maximum
Date(s) Application Is Due Aug 15.
Contact Robin Osborn, (212) 606-3809; email: ro@cmwf.org
Internet http://www.cmwf.org/fellowships/fellowships_list.htm?attrib_id=9158
Sponsor Commonwealth Fund
1 E 75th Street
New York, NY 10021-2692

Australian Institute of Aboriginal and Torres Strait Islander Studies--Research Grants 895
Grants cover costs associated with conduct of research for projects concerned with Australian Aboriginal and Torres Strait Island cultures in fields such as health, human biology, social anthropology, linguistics, ethnomusicology, material culture, rock art, archaeology, ethnobotany, psychology, education, and Aboriginal history including oral history. Annual deadline dates may vary; contact program staff for exact dates.
Requirements Nationals of any country are eligible for assistance.
Amount $A45,000 maximum generally
Date(s) Application Is Due Dec 21.
Contact Research Grants Administrator, 61 2 6246 1145; fax: 61 2 6249 7714; email: grants@aiatsis.gov.au
Internet http://www.aiatsis.gov.au/rsrch/rsrch_grnts/rg_abt.htm
Sponsor Australian Institute of Aboriginal and Torres Strait Islander Studies
GP.O. Box 553
Canberra, ACT 2601 Australia

Australian National University Humanities/Research Center Visiting Fellowships 896
The fellowships are awarded to established academics who wish to do research in the humanities worldwide. Each year a particular theme is announced for the next academic year, and most fellowships are awarded on some variation of that theme. Fellowships are awarded for the academic year and are not usually renewable. Approximately 20 awards are made annually.
Requirements Applicants must complete a formal application form and send it with curriculum vita and three references.
Restrictions Candidates currently working for an advanced degree in the humanities are not eligible.
Amount $A550 stipend per week and travel allowance
Date(s) Application Is Due Mar 31.
Contact Leena Messina, (02) 6125 4357; fax: (06) 248-0054; email: leena.messina@anu.edu.au
Internet http://www.anu.edu.au/hrc/grants/index.php
Sponsor Australian National University
Humanities Research Centre, Old Canberra House Bldg 73
Canberra, ACT 0200 Australia

Australian Postdoctoral Research Fellowships 897
The specific purpose of the fellowship is to strengthen Australia's national research and development capability by providing opportunities for postdoctoral level researchers to undertake research of national and international significance and to broaden their research experience.
Requirements Applicants must have submitted their PhD thesis before commencement of the fellowship. Candidates must obtain Australian citizenship or temporary residency status at the time of commencing the fellowship.
Contact Dr. Andrew Smith, Australian Postdoctoral Fellowships, 61 2 6284 6629; email: andrew.smith@arc.gov.au
Internet http://www.arc.gov.au/grant_programs/linkage_australian.htm
Sponsor Australian Research Council
GP.O. Box 2702
Canberra ACT 2601 Australia

Australian Postgraduate Research Fellowships 898
The program supports postgraduate training with stipends available through Linkage-Projects (APAIs), ARC Centres of Excellence (APACs), and Discovery-Projects. International opportunities for postgraduate researchers are also offered through Linkage-International awards, and project support is offered through Discovery-Indigenous Researchers Development. Guidelines are available online.
Requirements The applicant must have a PhD degree and at least three but no more than eight years of postdoctoral experience at the time of application.
Restrictions Postgraduate students are not normally eligible to apply for funding: applications seeking support for research training must be submitted by eligible researchers and research teams.
Contact Program Contact, Research Grant and Training Section, 61-2-6284-6600; fax: 61-2-6284-6601; email: info@arc.gov.au
Internet http://www.arc.gov.au/info_users/researcher_postgraduate.htm
Sponsor Australian Research Council
GP.O. Box 2702
Canberra, ACT 0200 Australia

Australian Research Fellowships/Queen Elizabeth II Fellowships 899
ARFs and QEIIs provide opportunities for established researchers to undertake research of national and international significance. QEIIs encourage research in Australia by postdoctoral graduates of exceptional promise and proven capacity for original work.
Requirements Australian Research Fellowships (ARF) and Queen Elizabeth II Fellowships (QEII) are available to researchers with three to eight years of research experience since the award of the PhD or equivalent research doctorate.
Contact Program Contact, Research Grant and Training Section, 61-2-6284-6600; fax: 61-2-6284-6601; email: info@arc.gov.au
Internet http://www.arc.gov.au/info_users/researcher_fellowships.htm
Sponsor Australian Research Council
GP.O. Box 2702
Canberra, ACT 2601 Australia

Australian Spinal Research Foundation Grants 900
The foundation invites applications for grants to support research concerning chiropractic. Priority will be given to projects that investigate the vertebral subluxation complex and how chiropractic contributes to wellness. In addition, priority will be given to chiropractic-based research projects that cover topics as diverse as those comparing the clinical outcome of various chiropractic techniques, or the effect of the chiropractic adjustment (e.g. sleep patterns, colic or immune function), or an analysis of how ergonomics may benefit posture, whether this be lying, sitting, or standing.
Amount $2000
Date(s) Application Is Due May 31.
Contact Grants Administrator, 61 (7) 3808 4098; fax: 61 (7) 3808 8109; email: asrf@spinalresearch.com.au
Internet http://www.spinalresearch.com.au/Research/research.html
Sponsor Australian Spinal Research Foundation
P.O.B 1047
Springwood, Queensland QLD 4127 Australia

Austro-American Association of Boston Scholarship 901
The scholarship is awarded to a student at any level (degree or nondegree) or to any other person demonstrating a capacity for scholarly research, creative work, or cultural mediatorship. The basic requirement is that the project relate to Austrian literature, music, art, history, or to other aspects of the Austrian culture. The grant may be used to travel to Europe or within the United States, to purchase books and other materials, or to facilitate publication. The scholarship also supports dissertation research and faculty/professional development. The award recipient will be announced by May 15.
Requirements Applicants should be Massachusetts residents and may be asked to appear for an interview. Application should include a curriculum vita, a detailed description of the proposed project, and two letters of recommendation from persons well acquainted with the applicant's background and potential.
Amount $1000 maximum
Date(s) Application Is Due Apr 15.
Contact Dr. George Hauser, Chairperson, Scholarship Committee, (617) 332-4055; email: george_hauser@hms.harvard.edu
Internet http://www.austria-boston.org/scholar.asp
Sponsor Austro-American Association of Boston
47 Windermere Rd
Newton, MA 02166-2521

AVDF Religion Grants 902
The foundations's principal commitment in the field of religion is to graduate theological education. All grants to institutions of graduate theological education will be to schools or seminaries that are fully accredited by the Association of Theological Schools; primarily produce persons prepared for ordination to pastoral or pulpit ministry; are known for academic excellence; and have solid records of continued alumni/trustee support and institutional financial stability. All denominations are eligible. Proposals from recognized consortia representing several seminaries of this type also will be considered. Similarly, joint proposals from two or more seminaries sharing programs or facilities are also of interest. No preference exists for any particular category or type of

project for which grants are requested. Grantees should wait at least four years from the time of an award before reapplying for a grant.
Requirements Proposals should be signed by the president or dean and should represent the leader's highest priority for reinforcing institutional excellence. The head of a seminary or divinity school should be in office for at least one year prior to submitting a grant request.
Restrictions Proposals normally will not be considered from institutions in transition.
Amount $100,000--$150,000 typically
Contact Dr. Jonathan Howe, Executive Director, (904) 359-0670; email: arthurvining@msn.com
Internet http://jvm.com/davis/PROGRAMS.HTM#religion
Sponsor Arthur Vining Davis Foundations
225 Water St, Ste 1510
Jacksonville, FL 32202-5185

AVDF Health Care Grants **903**
This program supports efforts to encourage caring attitudes in the delivery of patient care. Projects should have potential for widespread practical application and should be of interest to other groups. New ideas are encouraged, especially if they facilitate communication between patients (and their families) and doctors, nurses and other caregivers; ameliorate patient anxieties; strengthen trust and cooperation; and foster caring attitudes. Proposals, must have potential for wide application and not merely local improvement of requesting institutions or their communities.
Requirements Proposals should be submitted by the head of the institution under whose auspices the project would be accomplished.
Amount $100,000-$200,000
Contact Dr. Jonathan Howe, Executive Director, (904) 359-0670; email: arthurvining@msn.com
Internet http://jvm.com/davis/PROGRAMS.HTM#health
Sponsor Arthur Vining Davis Foundations
225 Water St, Ste 1510
Jacksonville, FL 32202-5185

AVDF Private Higher Education Grants **904**
The higher education program seeks to strengthen private four-year liberal arts institutions that place strong emphasis on teaching and whose students choose majors in the humanities, science, and math. Support generally will be reserved for schools of broadly acknowledged academic excellence in the liberal arts and sciences and a solid record of financial strength. A few grants are also made to larger teaching and research universities with a national reputation for excellence in graduate and undergraduate education. The foundations also have an interest in helping to improve programs at historically black colleges, those that primarily have a Native American student body, colleges in Appalachia, and similar schools that provide opportunities for traditionally underserved students. Joint proposals from two or more colleges that share a program or facilities are also of interest.
Requirements Successful applicants in higher education should have a recognized position of leadership in the liberal arts with emphasis on the humanities and science/math majors, rather than career or vocational studies; adequate financial resources; and a record of outstanding support from trustees and alumni/ae.
Amount $100,000-$200,000
Contact Dr. Jonathan Howe, Executive Director, (904) 359-0670; email: arthurvining@bellsouth.net
Internet http://jvm.com/davis/PROGRAMS.HTM#Private
Sponsor Arthur Vining Davis Foundations
225 Water St, Ste 1510
Jacksonville, FL 32202-5185

AVDF Secondary Education Grants **905**
The goal of the program is to strengthen teachers of grades nine through 12 and their teaching; examples are teacher professional development and use of new technologies. Collaboration between school districts and higher education institutions is encouraged. Special consideration will be given to projects addressing education issues on a national level.
Requirements Nonprofit organizations are eligible.
Restrictions Projects mainly benefiting a local school or district will not be approved, and only in rare situations are applications from individual schools and districts accepted.
Amount $100,000-$150,000 average
Contact Dr. Jonathan Howe, Executive Director, (904) 359-0670; email: arthurvining@bellsouth.net
Internet http://jvm.com/davis/PROGRAMS.HTM#secondary
Sponsor Arthur Vining Davis Foundations
225 Water St, Ste 1510
Jacksonville, FL 32202-5185

Aviation Research Grants **906**
The program objectives are to encourage and support innovative and advanced research in the areas of potential benefit to the long-term technical needs of the National Airspace System; areas related to research on the prevention of catastrophic failures; and areas related to research, development, and implementation of technologies and procedures to counteract terrorist acts against civil aviation. The grants may be used to support research and development projects in the following areas: communications, navigation, and surveillance; capacity and air traffic control technology; aviation weather; airport technology; aircraft safety technology; system security technology; human factors and aviation medicine; environment and energy; and operations research.
Requirements Colleges, universities, and nonprofit institutions are eligible. Profit-making organizations may be eligible in the area of aviation security.
Restrictions Discretionary funds are not currently available.
Amount $25,000-$5 million; $50,000-$150,000 average
Contact Aviation Research Grants Program, (609) 485-4424; fax: (609) 485-6509
Internet http://www.tc.faa.gov/logistics/grants
Sponsor Department of Transportation
800 Independence Ave SW
Washington, DC 20591

Avon Foundation Breast Care Fund Grants **907**
The fund awards grants for the development of breast cancer education and outreach activities, particularly breast health education and early detection services for underserved women. AFBCF supports programs that: recruit women for both first time screening and annual screening; develop partnerships between community-based outreach providers and local medical providers; work with health care providers to ensure proper clinical follow-up of abnormal screening results; and educate older women (65+ years old) about Medicare coverage of annual screening mammograms and assist them in obtaining the service from providers who accept Medicare.
Requirements Private, non-government, nonprofit organizations in the United States and Puerto Rico are eligible. Grants are awarded to community-based programs and/or health care agencies that provide medically under-served women aged 40 and older with direct access to breast cancer education, annual clinical screening services, and prompt follow-up care. All programs must utilize the three-part approach to breast cancer early detection including regular screening mammography, clinical breast examination, and monthly breast self-examination.
Amount $30,000-$50,000
Date(s) Application Is Due Aug 1.
Contact Coordinating Center; (212) 244-5368; fax: (212) 695-3081; email: admin@avonbreast care.org
Internet http://www.avonbreastcare.org/fundinginfo.htm
Sponsor Avon Foundation
505 Eighth Avenue, Suite 1601
New York, NY 10018-6505

Avon Foundation-AACR International Scholar Awards in Breast Cancer Research **908**
The awards have been established to enhance the quality of cancer research and clinical breast care for women in countries where opportunities for specialized scientific training and advancement for physicians and scientists are limited, including those in Asia, Latin America, and Eastern Europe. The program provides two-year career development awards for promising junior faculty members residing and conducting breast cancer research in those areas of the world, and allows principal investigators in the United States who are conducting breast cancer research to apply for the prestigious designation of an Avon Foundation-AACR Scholar host. Scholars and scholar hosts receive an annual salary and grant for research expenses. Potential candidates are also encouraged to consider the AACR-Gertrude B. Elion Cancer Research Award and the AACR Career Development Awards.
Requirements Eligible principal investigators include those working in a program of breast cancer research at all NCI-designated cancer centers and those institutions holding membership with the Association of American Cancer Institutes. Eligible applicants must be nationals or permanent residents currently residing and conducting research within the targeted regions. They must be at the level of instructor, acting assistant professor, or assistant professor at the start of the award term; currently hold a doctoral degree; and not currently be a candidate for a further doctoral or professional degree.
Restrictions Governmental institutions are not eligible. Employees and subcontractors of private industry are not eligible.
Amount $50,000 per year for scholar's salary; $25,000 grant for direct research expenses; $10,000 for administrative expenses
Contact Grants Administrator, (215) 440-9300; fax: (215) 440-9313; email: foundation@aacr.org
Internet http://www.aacr.org/home/scientists/travel-grants--research-funding/research-funding/avon-foundation-aacr-international-scholar-awards-in-breast-cancer-research.aspx
Sponsor American Association for Cancer Research
615 Chestnut Street, 17th Floor
Philadelphia, PA 19106-4404

Avon Products Foundation Grants **909**
The foundation's two-fold focus is to support education, community and social services, and arts organizations and programs that provide economic opportunities for women and girls; and to support breast cancer and other women's health organizations and programs. The foundation awards grants in cities and regions with a large concentration of representatives and business operations, with the majority of funds going to US-based institutions. National, international, and New York metropolitan area programs are administered through the foundation's headquarters in New York. For regional

funding support, contact the following locations and ask for the corporate contributions department: Atlanta, GA, (770) 271-6100; Morton Grove, IL, (847) 583-5169; Newark, DE, (302) 453-7700; Pasadena, CA, (626) 578-8000; Rye, NY, ((914) 935-2000; Suffern, NY, (845) 369-2000; Caguas, Puerto Rico, (787) 476-6161; and Springdale, OH, (513) 551-2000.
Requirements Applying organizations must be tax-exempt; national and municipal organizations are eligible. Request the guidelines brochure prior to submitting a formal proposal.
Restrictions Grants do not support individuals; memberships; lobbying organizations; political activities and organizations; religious, veteran, or fraternal organizations; fundraising events; and journal advertisements.
Amount $2.3 million total
Contact Grants Administrator, (866) 505-2866; email: info@avonfoundation.org
Internet http://www.avoncompany.com/women/avonfoundation
Sponsor Avon Products Foundation
1345 Avenue of the Americas
New York, NY 10105

Award for Computers in Chemical or Pharmaceutical Research and Development **910**
This award, sponsored by Accelrys Inc., is given annually and recognizes and encourages the use of computers in the advancement of chemical and biological science. The award was established as part of ACS's continuing effort to recognize the contributions of scientists and engineers in applying computers to the solution of problems in chemistry. The award will be granted to an individual without regard to age or nationality for outstanding achievement in the use of computers in research, development, or education in chemical science.
Requirements Any individual, except a member of the award committee, may submit one nomination or seconding letter for the award in any given year. The nominating documents consist of a letter of not more than 1000 words containing an evaluation of the nominee's accomplishments and a specific identification of the work to be recognized, a biographical sketch including date of birth, and a list of publications and patents authored by the nominee. Six copies of all items to be included in the nomination must be submitted.
Restrictions Self-nominations are not accepted.
Amount $5000 and travel expenses up to $1000
Date(s) Application Is Due Feb 1.
Contact Awards Administrator, (202) 872-4408; fax: (202) 872-6317; email: awards@acs.org
Internet http://www.chemistry.org/portal/a/c/s/1/acsdisplay.html?DOC=awards%5Ccomp.html
Sponsor American Chemical Society
1155 16th St NW
Washington, DC 20036

Award for Creative Advances in Environmental Science and Technology **911**
This award, sponsored by Air Products and Chemicals and administered by the American Chemical Society, is given annually to encourage creativity in research and technology or in methods of analysis to provide a scientific basis for informed environmental control decision-making processes or to provide practical technologies that will reduce health risk factors. The award is granted without regard to age or nationality. Annual deadline dates may vary; contact program staff for exact dates.
Requirements Any individual, except a member of the award committee, may submit one nomination or seconding letter for the award in any given year. The nominating documents consist of a letter of not more than 1000 words containing an evaluation of the nominee's accomplishments and a specific identification of the work to be recognized, a biographical sketch including date of birth, and a list of publications and patents authored by the nominee. Six copies of all items to be included in the nomination must be submitted.
Restrictions Self-nominations are not accepted.
Amount $5000 and allowance of up to $1000 for travel expenses to award meeting
Date(s) Application Is Due Feb 1.
Contact Awards Administrator, (202) 872-4408; fax: (202) 872-6317; email: awards@acs.org
Internet http://www.chemistry.org/portal/a/c/s/1/acsdisplay.html?DOC=awards%5Cest.html
Sponsor American Chemical Society
1155 16th St NW
Washington, DC 20036

Award for Creative Invention **912**
This award, sponsored by Corporation Associates and administered by the American Chemical Society, recognizes individual inventors for successful applications of research in chemistry and/or chemical engineering that contribute to the material prosperity and happiness of people. A gold medal is included with the award, and travel expenses up to $1000 to attend the award ceremony are provided. In cases of multiple inventors on a single patent, the award will be divided equally among the inventors; each inventor will receive a medal. A nominee must be a resident of the United States or Canada. A patent must have been granted for the work to be recognized, and it shall have been developed during the 17 years ending January 1 of the presentation year. A copy of the patent must be submitted with the nominating document.
Requirements Any individual, except a member of the award committee, may submit one nomination or seconding letter for the award in any given year. The nominating documents consist of a letter of not more than 1000 words containing an evaluation of the nominee's accomplishments and a specific identification of the work to be recognized, a biographical sketch including date of birth, and a list of publications and patents authored by the nominee. Six copies of all items to be included in the nomination must be submitted.
Restrictions Self-nominations are not accepted.
Amount $5000 and up to $1000 travel expenses
Date(s) Application Is Due Feb 1.
Contact Awards Administrator, (202) 872-4408; fax: (202) 872-6317; email: awards@acs.org
Internet http://www.chemistry.org/portal/a/c/s/1/acsdisplay.html?DOC=awards\quicklist.html
Sponsor American Chemical Society
1155 16th St NW
Washington, DC 20036

Award for Creative Work in Fluorine Chemistry **913**
This award, presented in odd-numbered years is sponsored by SynQuest Laboratories Inc. and Honeywell, and administered by the American Chemical Society, recognizes outstanding contributions to the advancement of the chemistry of fluorine. A nominee must have made an outstanding contribution or contributions to the field of fluorine chemistry. A certificate is included with the award.
Requirements Any individual, except a member of the award committee, may submit one nomination or seconding letter for each award in any given year. The nominating documents consist of a letter of not more than 1000 words containing an evaluation of the nominee's accomplishments and a specific identification of the work to be recognized, a biographical sketch including date of birth, and a list of publications and patents authored by the nominee. Six copies of all items to be included in the nomination must be submitted.
Restrictions Self-nominations are not accepted.
Amount $5000
Date(s) Application Is Due Feb 1.
Contact Awards Administrator, (202) 872-4408; fax: (202) 872-6317; email: awards@acs.org
Internet http://www.chemistry.org/portal/a/c/s/1/acsdisplay.html?DOC=awards\fluo.html
Sponsor American Chemical Society
1155 16th St NW
Washington, DC 20036

Award for Creative Work in Synthetic Organic Chemistry **914**
This award, sponsored by Aldrich Chemical Company and administered by the American Chemical Society, recognizes and encourages creative work in synthetic organic chemistry. A nominee must have accomplished outstanding creative work in synthetic organic chemistry that has been published during the five years ending January 1 of the presentation year. Some travel expenses for the awardee to attend the award ceremony and a certificate are provided.
Requirements Any individual, except a member of the award committee, may submit one nomination or seconding letter for the award in any given year. The nominating documents consist of a letter of not more than 1000 words containing an evaluation of the nominee's accomplishments and a specific identification of the work to be recognized, a biographical sketch including date of birth, and a list of publications and patents authored by the nominee. Six copies of all items to be included in the nomination must be submitted.
Restrictions Self-nominations are not accepted.
Amount $5000 and up to $1000 for travel
Date(s) Application Is Due Feb 1.
Contact Awards Administrator, (202) 872-4408; fax: (202) 872-6317; email: awards@acs.org
Internet http://www.chemistry.org/portal/a/c/s/1/acsdisplay.html?DOC=awards\synorgn.html
Sponsor American Chemical Society
1155 16th St NW
Washington, DC 20036

Award for Distinguished Service in the Advancement of Inorganic Chemistry **915**
This award, sponsored by Strem Chemicals Inc and administered by the American Chemical Society, is awarded on an annual basis to recognize distinguished service to the advancement of inorganic chemistry. A nominee must have demonstrated extensive contributions to the advancement of inorganic chemistry. Activities recognized by the award may include such fields as teaching, writing, research, and administration. A certificate is included with the award. A nominee must be a member of the American Chemical Society.
Requirements Any individual, except a member of the award committee, may submit one nomination or seconding letter for the award in any given year. The nominating documents consist of a letter of not more than 1000 words containing an evaluation of

the nominee's accomplishments and a specific identification of the work to be recognized, a biographical sketch including date of birth, and a list of publications and patents authored by the nominee. Six copies of all items to be included in the nomination must be submitted.
Restrictions Self-nominations are not accepted.
Amount $5000 and up to $1000 for travel expenses to award meeting
Date(s) Application Is Due Feb 1.
Contact Awards Administrator, (202) 872-4408; fax: (202) 872-6317; email: awards@acs.org
Internet http://www.chemistry.org/portal/a/c/s/1/acsdisplay.html?DOC=awards\advinor.html
Sponsor American Chemical Society
1155 16th St NW
Washington, DC 20036

Award for Encouraging Disadvantaged Students into Careers in the Chemical Sciences **916**
This award, sponsored by the Camille and Henry Dreyfus Foundation Inc and administered by ACS, is given annually to recognize individuals who have significantly stimulated or fostered the interest of students, especially minority and/or economically disadvantaged students, in chemistry, thereby promoting their professional development as chemists or chemical engineers. Included in the award is $10,000 to an academic institution, designated by the recipient, to strengthen that institution's activities in meeting the objective of the award.
Requirements Any individual, except a member of the award committee, may submit one nomination or seconding letter for the award in any given year. Nominating documents consist of a letter of not more than 1000 words containing an evaluation of the nominee's accomplishments and a specific identification of the work to be recognized, a biographical sketch including date of birth, and a list of publications and patents authored by the nominee. Six copies of all items to be included in the nomination must be submitted.
Restrictions Self-nominations are not accepted.
Amount $5000 personal prize and $1500 travel allowance to award meeting
Date(s) Application Is Due Feb 1.
Contact Awards Administrator, (202) 872-4600 or (800) 227-5558; fax: (202) 776-8211; email: awards@acs.org
Internet http://www.chemistry.org/portal/a/c/s/1/acsdisplay.html?DOC=awards%5Cdadvstudt.html
Sponsor American Chemical Society
1155 16th St NW
Washington, DC 20036

Award for Encouraging Women into Careers in the Chemical Sciences **917**
This award, sponsored by the Camille and Henry Dreyfus Foundation Inc and administered by ACS, is given annually and will recognize an individual who has significantly stimulated or fostered the interest of women in chemistry, thereby promoting their professional development as chemists or chemical engineers. The award is intended to recognize significant accomplishments by individuals in stimulating women to elect careers in the chemical sciences and engineering. Award is given to an academic institution designated by the recipient, to strengthen that institution's activities in meeting the objectives of the award.
Requirements Any individual, except a member of the award committee, may submit one nomination or seconding letter for the award in any given year. Nominating documents consist of a letter of not more than 1000 words containing an evaluation of the nominee's accomplishments and a specific identification of the work to be recognized, a biographical sketch including date of birth, and a list of publications and patents authored by the nominee. Six copies of all items to be included in the nomination must be submitted.
Restrictions Self-nominations are not accepted.
Amount $5000 and $1500 travel allowance to award meeting; $10,000 to an academic institution
Date(s) Application Is Due Feb 1.
Contact Awards Administrator, (202) 872-4408; fax: (202) 872-6317; email: awards@acs.org
Internet http://www.chemistry.org/portal/a/c/s/1/acsdisplay.html?DOC=awards\women.html
Sponsor American Chemical Society
1155 16th St NW
Washington, DC 20036

Award for Research at an Undergraduate Institution **918**
This award, sponsored by Research Corporation and administered by the American Chemical Society, is given annually to recognize the importance of research with undergraduates. The award will honor a chemistry faculty member whose research in an undergraduate setting has achieved wide recognition and contributed significantly to chemistry and to the professional development of undergraduate students. Nominees will be drawn from the tenured faculty of predominantly undergraduate institutions. The nominee's department may offer work leading to the master's degree but shall not have a doctoral program. Recognition will be given for successful research as evidenced by such factors as publications with undergraduate coauthors, external grant support, and the subsequent professional development of students who have participated in the research program. Generally, the award will be given for significant work over a long period of time rather than for a specific limited project.
Requirements Any individual, except a member of the award committee, may submit one nomination or seconding letter for the award in any given year. The nominating documents consist of a letter of not more than 1000 words containing an evaluation of the nominee's accomplishments and a specific identification of the work to be recognized, a biographical sketch including date of birth, and a list of publications and patents authored by the nominee. Six copies of all items to be included in the nomination must be submitted.
Restrictions Self-nominations are not accepted.
Amount $5000 plus travel expenses to award meeting
Date(s) Application Is Due Feb 1.
Contact Awards Administrator, (800) 227-5558 or (202) 872-4600; email: awards@acs.org
Internet http://www.chemistry.org/portal/a/c/s/1/acsdisplay.html?DOC=awards%5Cundergrad.html
Sponsor American Chemical Society
1155 16th St NW
Washington, DC 20036

Award in Analytical Chemistry **919**
This award, sponsored by Battelle Memorial Institute and administered by the American Chemical Society, is given annually to recognize and encourage outstanding contributions to the science of analytical chemistry, pure or applied, carried out in the United States or Canada. A nominee must be a resident of the United States or Canada and must have made an outstanding contribution to analytical chemistry. Special consideration will be given to the independence of thought and the originality shown, or to the importance of the work when applied to public welfare, economics, or the needs and desires of humanity.
Requirements Any individual, except a member of the award committee, may submit one nomination or seconding letter for the award in any given year. The nominating documents consist of a letter of not more than 1000 words containing an evaluation of the nominee's accomplishments and a specific identification of the work to be recognized, a biographical sketch including date of birth, and a list of publications and patents authored by the nominee. Six copies of all items to be included in the nomination must be submitted.
Restrictions Self-nominations are not accepted.
Amount $5000 and travel expenses to award meeting
Date(s) Application Is Due Feb 1.
Contact Awards Administrator, (202) 872-4408; fax: (202) 872-6317; email: awards@acs.org
Internet http://www.chemistry.org/portal/a/c/s/1/acsdisplay.html?DOC=awards\anyl.html
Sponsor American Chemical Society
1155 16th St NW
Washington, DC 20036

Award in Applied Polymer Science **920**
This award, sponsored by Eastman Chemical Company and administered by the American Chemical Society, is given annually to recognize and encourage outstanding achievements in the science or technology of plastics, coatings, polymer composites, adhesives, and related fields. The recipient will be selected primarily on the basis of scientific contributions made to the specified fields during the 10-year period preceding date of selection. To avoid repeating specific areas of technology, preference will be given whenever recognized by the granting of this award in the two preceding years.
Requirements Any individual, except a member of the award committee, may submit one nomination or seconding letter for the award in any given year. The nominating documents consist of a letter of not more than 1000 words containing an evaluation of the nominee's accomplishments and a specific identification of the work to be recognized, a biographical sketch including date of birth, and a list of publications and patents authored by the nominee. Six copies of all items to be included in the nomination must be submitted.
Restrictions Self-nominations are not accepted.
Amount $5000 and up to $1000 for travel to award meeting
Date(s) Application Is Due Feb 1.
Contact Awards Administrator, (202) 872-4408; fax: (202) 872-6317; email: awards@acs.org
Internet http://www.chemistry.org/portal/a/c/s/1/acsdisplay.html?DOC=awards\appoly.html
Sponsor American Chemical Society
1155 16th St NW
Washington, DC 20036

Award in Chromatography **921**
This award, sponsored by SUPELCO Inc and administered by the American Chemical Society, is given annually to recognize outstanding contributions to the field of chromatography. A nominee must have made an outstanding contribution to the field with particular consideration given to developments of new methods.
Requirements Any individual, except a member of the award committee, may submit one nomination or seconding letter for the award in any given year. The nominating

documents consist of a letter of not more than 1000 words containing an evaluation of the nominee's accomplishments and a specific identification of the work to be recognized, a biographical sketch including date of birth, and a list of publications and patents authored by the nominee. Six copies of all items to be included in the nomination must be submitted.
Restrictions Self-nominations are not accepted.
Amount \$5000 and travel expenses to award meeting
Date(s) Application Is Due Feb 1.
Contact Awards Administrator, (202) 872-4408; fax: (202) 872-6317; email: awards@acs.org
Internet http://www.chemistry.org/portal/a/c/s/1/acsdisplay.html?DOC=awards\chroma.html
Sponsor American Chemical Society
1155 16th St NW
Washington, DC 20036

Award in Colloid or Surface Chemistry **922**
The award, sponsored by Procter & Gamble Co, is given annually to recognize and encourage outstanding scientific contributions to colloid or surface chemistry in the United States or Canada. The nominee must be a resident of the United States or Canada and must have made outstanding scientific contributions to colloid or surface chemistry. Recognition will also be given to originality and independence of thought, and to the technological impact of the nominee's contribution. In odd-numbered years, awards are made for contributions in surface chemistry. In even-numbered years, awards are made for advances in colloid chemistry.
Requirements Any individual, except a member of the award committee, may submit one nomination or seconding letter for the award in any given year. The nominating documents consist of a letter of not more than 1000 words containing an evaluation of the nominee's accomplishments and a specific identification of the work to be recognized, a biographical sketch including date of birth, and a list of publications and patents authored by the nominee. Six copies of all items to be included in the nomination must be submitted.
Restrictions Self-nominations are not accepted.
Amount \$5000 and travel to award meeting
Date(s) Application Is Due Feb 1.
Contact Awards Administrator, (202) 872-4408; fax: (202) 872-6317; email: awards@acs.org
Internet http://www.chemistry.org/portal/a/c/s/1/acsdisplay.html?DOC=awards\colloid.html
Sponsor American Chemical Society
1155 16th St NW
Washington, DC 20036

Award in Industrial Chemistry **923**
The award, sponsored by ACS Division of Business Development and Management, is given annually to recognize outstanding contributions to industrial chemistry resulting in the commercialization of an economically significant new product or process. Any field of chemical, chemical engineering, or biochemical research is appropriate if it is of general interest and reflects the concerns of modern society. Any chemical research, whether industrial, governmental, or academic, is eligible, provided the work was done in North America and yielded significant commercial results for a period of more than one year.
Requirements Any individual, except a member of the award committee, may submit one nomination or seconding letter for the award in any given year. The nominating documents consist of a letter of not more than 1000 words containing an evaluation of the nominee's accomplishments and a specific identification of the work to be recognized, a biographical sketch including date of birth, and a list of publications and patents authored by the nominee. Six copies of all items to be included in the nomination must be submitted.
Restrictions Self-nominations are not accepted.
Amount \$5000 and travel to award meeting
Date(s) Application Is Due Feb 1.
Contact Awards Administrator, (202) 872-4408; fax: (202) 872-6317; email: awards@acs.org
Internet http://www.chemistry.org/portal/a/c/s/1/acsdisplay.html?DOC=awards\industry.html
Sponsor American Chemical Society
1155 16th St NW
Washington, DC 20036

Award in Inorganic Chemistry **924**
This award, sponsored by Aldrich Chemical Company Inc and administered by the American Chemical Society, is given annually to recognize and encourage fundamental research in the field of inorganic chemistry. A nominee must have accomplished outstanding research in the preparation, properties, reactions, or structure of inorganic substances. Special consideration shall be given to the independence of thought and originality shown. The award shall be granted without regard to age or nationality.
Requirements Any individual, except a member of the award committee, may submit one nomination or seconding letter for the award in any given year. The nominating documents consist of a letter of not more than 1000 words containing an evaluation of the nominee's accomplishments and a specific identification of the work to be recognized, a biographical sketch including date of birth, and a list of publications and patents authored by the nominee. Six copies of all items to be included in the nomination must be submitted.
Restrictions Self-nominations are not accepted.
Amount \$5000 and up to \$1000 for travel to award meeting
Date(s) Application Is Due Feb 1.
Contact Awards Administrator, (202) 872-4408; fax: (202) 872-6317; email: awards@acs.org
Internet http://www.chemistry.org/portal/a/c/s/1/acsdisplay.html?DOC=awards\inor.html
Sponsor American Chemical Society
1155 16th St NW
Washington, DC 20036

Award in Organometallic Chemistry **925**
This award, sponsored by the Dow Chemical Company Foundation and administered by the American Chemical Society, is given annually to recognize a recent advancement that is having a major impact on research in organometallic chemistry. A nominee must have shown outstanding research in the preparation, reactions, properties, or structure of organometallic substances. Special consideration will be given to demonstrated creativity and independence of thought. Preference will be given to US citizens.
Requirements Any individual, except a member of the award committee, may submit one nomination or seconding letter for the award in any given year. The nominating documents consist of a letter of not more than 1000 words containing an evaluation of the nominee's accomplishments and a specific identification of the work to be recognized, a biographical sketch including date of birth, and a list of publications and patents authored by the nominee. Six copies of all items to be included in the nomination must be submitted.
Restrictions Self-nominations are not accepted.
Amount \$5000 plus \$1000 toward travel to award meeting
Date(s) Application Is Due Feb 1.
Contact Awards Administrator, (202) 872-4408; fax: (202) 872-6317; email: awards@acs.org
Internet http://www.chemistry.org/portal/a/c/s/1/acsdisplay.html?DOC=awards\organomet.html
Sponsor American Chemical Society
1155 16th St NW
Washington, DC 20036

Award in Pure Chemistry **926**
This award, sponsored by Alpha Chi Sigma Fraternity and the Alpha Chi Sigma Educational Award Foundation, and administered by the American Chemical Society, is given annually to recognize and encourage fundamental research in pure chemistry carried out in North America by young individuals. Special consideration is given to independence of thought and the originality shown in the research.
Requirements Any individual except a member of the award committee may submit one nomination or seconding letter for the award in any given year. The nominating documents consist of a letter of not more than 1000 words containing an evaluation of the nominee's accomplishments and a specific identification of the work to be recognized, a biographical sketch including date of birth, and a list of publications and patents authored by the nominee. A nominee must not have passed his/her 36th birthday by April 30 of award year and must have accomplished research of unusual merit for an individual on the threshold of his/her career. Six copies of all items to be included in the nomination must be submitted.
Restrictions Self-nominations are not accepted.
Amount \$5000; \$1000 toward travel to awards meeting
Date(s) Application Is Due Feb 1.
Contact Awards Administrator, (800) 227-5558 or (202) 872-4600; email: awards@acs.org
Internet http://www.chemistry.org/portal/a/c/s/1/acsdisplay.html?DOC=awards%5Cpure.html
Sponsor American Chemical Society
1155 16th St NW
Washington, DC 20036

Award in Separations Science and Technology **927**
This award is given annually to recognize outstanding accomplishments in fundamental or applied research directed to separations science and technology. The award shall be granted to an individual without regard to age or nationality. The scope of the award is to be as broad as possible, covering all fields where separations science and technology is practiced, including but not limited to biology, chemistry, engineering, geology, and medicine. Annual deadline dates may vary; contact program staff for exact dates.
Requirements Any individual, except a member of the award committee, may submit one nomination or seconding letter for the award in any given year. The nominating documents consist of a letter of not more than 1000 words containing an evaluation of the nominee's accomplishments and a specific identification of the work to be recognized, a biographical sketch including date of birth, and a list of publications and patents authored by the nominee. Six copies of all items to be included in the nomination must be submitted.

Restrictions Self-nominations are not accepted.
Amount $5000 and reimbursement of travel expenses to award meeting
Date(s) Application Is Due Feb 1.
Contact Awards Administrator, (202) 227-5558; fax: (202) 776-8211; email: awards@acs.org
Internet http://www.chemistry.org/portal/a/c/s/1/acsdisplay.html?DOC=awards%5Cseparation.html
Sponsor American Chemical Society
1155 16th St NW
Washington, DC 20036

Award in the Chemistry of Materials 928
This award, sponsored by E.I. du Pont de Nemours & Company and administered by the American Chemical Society, is given annually to recognize and encourage creative work in the chemistry of materials. A nominee must have made outstanding contributions to the chemistry of materials. Particular emphasis will be placed on research relating to materials of actual or potential technological importance, where a fundamental understanding of the chemistry associated with materials preparation, processing, or use is critical. The award will be granted without regard to the nominee's age or nationality.
Requirements Any individual, except a member of the award committee, may submit one nomination or seconding letter for the award in any given year. The nominating documents consist of a letter of not more than 1000 words containing an evaluation of the nominee's accomplishments and a specific identification of the work to be recognized, a biographical sketch including date of birth, and a list of publications and patents authored by the nominee. Six copies of all items to be included in the nomination must be submitted.
Restrictions Self-nominations are not accepted.
Amount $5000 and reimbursement of travel expenses to award meeting
Date(s) Application Is Due Feb 1.
Contact Awards Administrator, (202) 872-4408; fax: (202) 872-6317; email: awards@acs.org
Internet http://www.chemistry.org/portal/a/c/s/1/acsdisplay.html?DOC=awards\materials.html
Sponsor American Chemical Society
1155 16th St NW
Washington, DC 20036

Award in Theoretical Chemistry 929
The purpose of this annual award, which is sponsored by IBM Corporation and administered by the American Chemical Society, is to recognize innovative research in theoretical chemistry that either advances theoretical methodology or contributes to new discoveries about chemical systems. Emphasis in the selection process will be on work characterized by depth, originality, and scientific significance. The award is given without regard to age or nationality.
Requirements Any individual, except a member of the award committee, may submit one nomination or seconding letter for each award in any given year. The letter of nomination may not exceed 1000 words and should contain an evaluation of the nominee's accomplishments and a specific identification of the work to be recognized. Six copies of all items to be included in the nomination must be submitted.
Restrictions Self-nominations are not accepted.
Amount $5000 plus travel to award meeting
Date(s) Application Is Due Feb 1.
Contact Awards Administrator, (202) 872-4408; fax: (202) 872-6317; email: awards@acs.org
Internet http://www.chemistry.org/portal/a/c/s/1/acsdisplay.html?DOC=awards\theoretical.html
Sponsor American Chemical Society
1155 16th St NW
Washington, DC 20036

AWHONN Research Grants 930
The AWHONN small grants program is designed primarily for novice researchers, serving first-time efforts or beginning development of a program of research. The purpose of the funding is to provide seed money, pilot funding, or total funding for small projects with promising contributions to nursing knowledge in clinical practice. The focus of the research is women's health, obstetric, or neonatal nursing phenomena.
Requirements Applicants must be members of the association. An application for membership may accompany the proposal.
Restrictions Primary investigators of current federally funded research and of previous AWHONN research are not eligible. Grant funds may not be used for indirect costs, tuition, computer hardware/printers.
Amount $2500-$10,000
Date(s) Application Is Due Nov 1.
Contact Daniella McCarthy, Research Program Manager, (202) 261-2434; fax: (202) 728-0575; email: ResearchPrograms@awhonn.org or daniellam@awhonn.org
Internet http://www.awhonn.org/awhonn/?pg=0-874-2240
Sponsor Association of Women's Health, Obstetric, and Neonatal Nurses
2000 L St NW, Ste 740
Washington, DC 20036

AWIS Educational Foundation Predoctoral Awards 931
Grants provide funds for women graduate students enrolled in a program in the life, physical, or social sciences or in an engineering program leading to a PhD degree. The award can be used for any aspect of education--tuition, books, housing, research, expenses, equipment, and so forth. US citizens may use the money for study in the United States or abroad; non-US citizens must be enrolled in a US institution of higher education. Each year regular awards and named awards are granted; at times, citations of merit also are awarded.
Requirements Women students enrolled in any life, physical, or social science or in an engineering program leading to a PhD degree are eligible. Candidates should have passed all qualifying exams and expect to complete the dissertation within two years.
Restrictions Students pursuing a professional doctorate other than the PhD are not eligible to apply.
Amount $1000 grant
Date(s) Application Is Due Jan 26.
Contact Dr. Barbara Filner, Foundation President, (202) 326-8940; fax: (202) 326-8960; email: awisedfd@awis.org
Internet http://www.awis.org/resource/edfoundation.html
Sponsor Association for Women in Science Educational Foundation
1200 New York Ave, Ste 650
Washington, DC 20005

AWM Mentoring Travel Grants for Women 932
The objective of the program is to help junior women develop a long-term working and mentoring relationship with a senior mathematician. This relationship should help the junior mathematician to establish her research program and eventually receive tenure. Grants support travel, subsistence, and other required expenses for an untenured woman mathematician to travel to an institute or a department to do research with a specified individual for one month. Any unexpended funds could be used for further travel to work with the same individual during the following year. Applicants may receive up to three grants through their careers, possibly in successive years. Submit five copies of the cover letter; curriculum vita; research proposal of approximately five pages in length that specifies why the proposed travel is particularly beneficial; supporting letter from the proposed mentor (who must promise to be available at the time of the proposed travel and may be either a man or a woman), together with the curriculum vita of the proposed mentor; approximate budget; and information about other sources of funding available.
Requirements Applicants must be women holding a doctorate or equivalent experience and with a work address in the United States (or home address in case of unemployed). The applicant's research may be in any field that is funded by the Division of Mathematical Sciences of NSF.
Amount $4000 maximum
Date(s) Application Is Due Feb 1.
Contact Association for Women in Mathematics, Travel Grant Selection Committee, (703) 934-0163; email: awm@awm-math.org
Internet http://awm-math.org/travelgrants.html
Sponsor University of Maryland
4114 Computer and Space Sciences Bldg
College Park, MD 20742-2461

AWM Travel Grants for Women Researchers 933
This program is supported by NSF and the Association for Women in Mathematics. Grants provide full or partial support to women researchers for travel to attend research conferences in their fields of specialization. An applicant should send five copies of a description of her current research and how the proposed travel will benefit her research program; curriculum vita; budget for the proposed travel; and information about all other sources of travel funding. In a cover letter, indicate the conference name, dates, and location (city/state/country). There are three award periods per year.
Requirements The research conference must be in an area supported by the Division of Mathematical Sciences of NSF. Applicants must be women holding a doctorate (or equivalent experience) and with a work address in the United States.
Restrictions Individuals who were awarded an AWM-NSF travel grant in the past two years, or who have other sources of external funding, such as any type of NSF grant, are ineligible. Partial support from the applicant's institution or from a nongovernmental agency does not make the applicant ineligible.
Amount $1500 maximum for domestic travel; $2000 maximum for foreign travel
Date(s) Application Is Due Feb 1; May 1; Oct 1.
Contact Association for Women in Mathematics, (703) 934-0163; email: awm@awm-math.org
Internet http://awm-math.org/travelgrants.html
Sponsor University of Maryland
4114 Computer and Space Sciences Bldg
College Park, MD 20742-2461

AWRA Richard A. Herbert Memorial Scholarship 934
This scholarship is to be used for the enhancement of education in water resources. One scholarship is awarded to a full-time undergraduate student working toward his/her first undergraduate degree and enrolled in a program related to water resources. The second scholarship is awarded to a full-time graduate student enrolled in a program related to water resources. In addition to the scholarships, each winner receives a complimentary membership in AWRA for the year.

Requirements Full-time graduate and undergraduate students enrolled in a program related to water resources are eligible to apply.
Amount $2000 maximum
Date(s) Application Is Due Apr 29.
Contact Harriette Bayse, (540) 687-8390; fax: (540) 687-8395; email: harriette@awra.org
Internet http://www.awra.org/student/herbert.html
Sponsor American Water Resources Association
P.O. Box 1626, 4 W Federal St
Middleburg, VA 20118

AWWA Abel Wolman Doctoral Fellowships **935**
The fellowships are designed to encourage promising students to pursue advanced training and research in the field of water supply and treatment. Applicants are evaluated on the basis of the quality of their academic record, the significance of the proposed research to water supply and treatment, and the applicant's potential to perform high-quality research.
Requirements Applicants must be citizens of Canada, Mexico, or the United States and anticipate completion of the requirements for the PhD degree within two years of the award.
Amount $20,000 maximum annually
Date(s) Application Is Due Jan 15.
Contact Stepanie Wheeler, Scholarship Coordinator, (303) 347-6206; email: swheeler@awwa.org
Internet http://www.awwa.org/About/scholars
Sponsor American Water Works Association
6666 W Quincy Ave
Denver, CO 80235

AWWA Academic Achievement Awards **936**
The awards recognize outstanding academic achievement on a graduate level through the selection of excellent master's theses and doctoral dissertations that relate to the field of potable water. First- and second-place awards are given for master's theses and also for doctoral dissertations. An announcement and form must be obtained from the training programs manager prior to submitting an application.
Requirements All master's theses and doctoral dissertations that are relevant to the water supply industry are eligible. Applicants must have completed their theses or dissertations within the specified year.
Amount $3000 each, doctoral dissertation and master's thesis; $1500 for second place in each category
Date(s) Application Is Due Oct 1.
Contact Linda Moody, Scholarship Coordinator, (303) 347-6201; fax: (303) 347-0804; email: swheeler@awwa.org
Internet http://www.awwa.org/About/scholarships.cfm
Sponsor American Water Works Association
6666 W Quincy Ave
Denver, CO 80235

AWWA Holly A. Cornell Scholarship **937**
The annual scholarship is made to encourage master's-level female and/or minority students to pursue advanced training and careers in the field of water supply and treatment. The recipient is expected to complete all requirements for the MS degree no sooner than December 1 of the year of the award.
Requirements Female and/or minority (as defined by the Equal Employment Opportunity Commission) US citizens who are currently master's degree students and anticipate completion of the requirements for a master's degree in engineering no sooner than December 1 of the year of the award are eligible to apply.
Amount $5000
Date(s) Application Is Due Jan 15.
Contact Linda Moody, Scholarship Coordinator, (303) 347-6201; email: swheeler@awwa.org
Internet http://www.awwa.org/About/scholarships.cfm
Sponsor American Water Works Association
6666 W Quincy Ave
Denver, CO 80235

AWWA Larson Aquatic Research Support (LARS) Scholarships **938**
These scholarships, given in honor of Dr. Thurston E. Larson, are intended to provide encouragement to outstanding graduate students in the fields of water treatment; aquatic, analytic, and environmental chemistry; and corrosion control. Guidelines and application are available online.
Requirements Applicant must be pursuing a degree (MS or PhD) at an institution of higher learning in the United States, Canada, Puerto Rico, or Mexico. MS candidates must complete the requirements of their degree sometime after August 1 of the year of the award, and PhD candidates must complete degree requirements sometime after December 1 of the year of the award.
Amount $5000 for MS candidates; $7000 for PhD candidates
Date(s) Application Is Due Jan 15.
Contact Linda Moody, Scholarship Coordinator, (303) 347-6201; email: swheeler@awwa.org
Internet http://www.awwa.org/About/scholarships.cfm
Sponsor American Water Works Association
6666 W Quincy Ave
Denver, CO 80235

AWWA Thomas R. Camp Scholarship **939**
The annual scholarship is presented to an outstanding graduate student doing applied research in the drinking water field and planning a career in this field. The scholarship is awarded to master's-level students in odd-numbered years and to doctoral-level students in even-numbered years. The recipient should not anticipate completion of his/her degree program before May of the year following the award.
Requirements Students pursuing a graduate degree at an institution of higher education located in Canada, Guam, Puerto Rico, Mexico, or the United States are eligible.
Amount $5000
Date(s) Application Is Due Jan 15.
Contact Linda Moody, Scholarship Coordinator, (303) 347-6201; email: swheeler@awwa.org
Internet http://www.awwa.org/About/scholarships.cfm
Sponsor American Water Works Association
6666 W Quincy Ave
Denver, CO 80235

Axe-Houghton Foundation Grants **940**
The foundation operates in the New York City metropolitan area exclusively for charitable, educational, and scientific purposes to foster and encourage an appreciation of the English language, with major emphasis on the spoken language. Priority is given to projects for the improvement of speech and its uses in the areas of public affairs, education, theater, poetry, debate, and the oral interpretation of literature. A portion of available funds is devoted to speech remediation and to scientific research pertaining to speech. Types of support include program grants and seed money grants.
Requirements Initial inquiries should be by full proposal and should contain a brief statement of objective, duration of time required to complete this objective, qualifications of personnel responsible for conducting the project, and the general amounts of funds needed. The proposal should also indicate the degree of internal support that would be committed.
Restrictions Grants are made only to tax-exempt institutions and not to individuals, private foundations or organizations outside of the United States. Grants are not made for scholarships, fellowships, capital, or general support programs.
Amount $1000-$7500
Date(s) Application Is Due Sep 1.
Contact Claire Brook, President, (212) 909-8304
Internet http://www.foundationcenter.org/grantmaker/axehoughton/index.html
Sponsor Axe-Houghton Foundation
919 3rd Ave, 2nd Fl
New York, NY 10022

BA British Conference Grants **941**
These awards are intended as contributions toward the expenses of conferences held in the United Kingdom. Awards may be used for any aspect of the conference costs, but the awarding committee, in reaching its decisions, will pay particular attention to the overall budget for the conference. Applications should be submitted on the British Conference Grant form, available from university research offices, or from the academy's Research Grants Department. Applications should not be submitted more than one year before the date of the conference. Annual deadline dates may vary; contact program staff for exact dates.
Requirements Applications may be submitted by British academics or organizations responsible for organizing conferences in Britain.
Restrictions Applications for support for one-day conferences will not normally be accepted. Applications on behalf of bilateral conferences between two institutions will not be considered unless it is shown that there will be open and widespread national participation.
Amount @L500-@L2000
Date(s) Application Is Due Jan 15; Apr 15; Oct 15.
Contact Research Grants Department, 020 7969 5217; fax: 020 7969 5414; email: grants@britac.ac.uk
Internet http://www.britac.ac.uk/funding/guide/bcg.html
Sponsor British Academy
10 Carlton House Terrace
London SW1Y 5AH United Kingdom

BA Central and Eastern Europe and the Former Soviet Union Exchange Grants **942**
The primary purpose of the exchange programs is to facilitate scholarly research in the humanities and social sciences with academies in Central and Eastern Europe and the former Soviet Union. The academy will meet the British scholar's travel expenses to the receiving country. The host institution will provide accommodation, a maintenance allowance, and local travel expenses. Applicants should bear in mind that the maintenance allowance may not cover all necessary expenses. The academy will not undertake to supplement the allowance, but applications may be made to other sources of support. No contribution can be made by either side towards the expenses of accompanying partners,

although host institutions may be asked to facilitate their visit. Application must be made on the East Europe Exchanges application form, available from the academy.
Requirements Applicants must be ordinarily resident in the United Kingdom, the Isle of Man, or the Channel Islands. Most awards are made to staff employed in universities and other institutions of higher education, but applicants are not restricted by either academic or employment status.
Restrictions Awards are not available for the completion of doctoral research projects, nor for the support of courses of study leading to professional qualifications.
Amount @L2500
Date(s) Application Is Due Apr 30; Sep 31; Dec 31.
Contact International Relations Department, 020 7969 5220; fax: 020 7969 5414; email: overseas@britac.ac.uk
Internet http://www.britac.ac.uk/funding/guide/intl/ceefsujp.html
Sponsor British Academy
10 Carlton House Terrace
London SW1Y 5AH United Kingdom

BA Elie Kedourie Memorial Fund Research Grants **943**
The object of this fund, established by the family of Elie Kedourie, FBA, is to promote the study of Middle Eastern and modern European history, and the history of political thought by recent postdoctoral scholars of any nationality. Applications should be submitted on the standard research grant application form, available from university research offices, or from the academy.
Restrictions Funds are not available to support travel to or attendance at conferences, workshops, or seminars, either in the United Kingdom or elsewhere.
Amount @L1000 maximum typically
Date(s) Application Is Due Apr 15.
Contact Research Grants Department, 020 7969 5217; fax: 020 7969 5414; email: grants@britac.ac.uk
Internet http://www.britac.ac.uk/funding/guide/ekmf.html
Sponsor British Academy
10 Carlton House Terrace
London SW1Y 5AH United Kingdom

BA Elisabeth Barker Fund **944**
The fund was established in memory of Elisabeth Barker (1910-1986), diplomatic correspondent and historian of modern Europe. It is intended to support studies in recent European history, particularly the history of central and eastern Europe. Grants may be made to support individual, collective, or institutional projects (including conferences). Awards to individuals may take the form of grants for private study and research in other European countries. British scholars and institutions may also apply for funds to assist scholars from other European countries to visit the United Kingdom, or to extend a stay arranged under other auspices. Application is made by letter, with appropriate supporting documentation, including a curriculum vita, a detailed research proposal describing the project and the scheme of research, a breakdown of the costs, and details of the plans for publication or dissemination of the research. Two referees, from outside the employing institution of the applicant, should be asked to submit references on the applicant and the project direct to the academy. Applicants will be notified of the outcome approximately three months after the closing date.
Requirements Applicants must be ordinarily resident in the United Kingdom, the Isle of Man, or the Channel Islands. Most awards are made to staff employed in universities and other institutions of higher education, but applicants are not restricted.
Restrictions PhD candidates are not eligible to apply, whether or not the project is related to the topic of their thesis. Awards are not available for the support of courses of study leading to professional qualifications.
Amount @L1000 maximum typically
Date(s) Application Is Due Jan 15; Apr 15; Oct 15.
Contact Research Grants Department, 020 7969 5217; fax: 020 7969 5414; email: grants@britac.ac.uk
Internet http://www.britac.ac.uk/funding/guide/intl/ebf.html
Sponsor British Academy
10 Carlton House Terrace
London SW1Y 5AH United Kingdom

BA Exchange Grants **945**
The academy provides opportunities, through exchange agreements, for British scholars to undertake approved programs of research in the humanities and social sciences in certain countries overseas. The programs vary in nature and structure, from formal agreements, mainly with the countries of Central and Eastern Europe, the former Soviet Union and China, to less formal arrangements with individual institutions in particular countries, including France, Israel, Japan, Korea, Sweden, Switzerland, and the U.S.
Requirements Applicants must be ordinarily resident in the United Kingdom, the Isle of Man, or the Channel Islands. Most awards are made to staff employed in universities and other institutions of higher education, but applicants are not restricted by either academic or employment status.
Restrictions Awards are not available for the completion of doctoral research projects, nor for the support of courses of study leading to professional qualifications.
Date(s) Application Is Due Jan 15; Apr 15; Oct 15.
Contact International Relations Department, 020 7969 5220; fax: 020 7969 5414; email: overseas@britac.ac.uk
Internet http://www.britac.ac.uk/funding/guide/research.html
Sponsor British Academy
10 Carlton House Terrace
London SW1Y 5AH United Kingdom

BA Larger Research Grants **946**
Grants are available for primary research in the humanities and social sciences for which support is not normally available from other funding agencies. Eligible costs include travel and maintenance, research assistance, workshops, consumables, specialist software, and costs of interpreters in the field. Applications for collaborative or individual research projects are equally welcome. Applications from international groups of scholars are welcome, provided there is a UK-based scholar as lead applicant. The maximum grant period is three years. Guidelines are available online.
Restrictions The following items are not eligible for support: institutional overheads; computer hardware; books and other permanent resources; the preparation of camera-ready copy; any editorial-related task; publication subventions; costs of publication in electronic media; payment to the principal researcher(s) in lieu of salary, or for personal maintenance at home; replacement teaching costs; travel and maintenance expenses for purposes such as lecture tours, or to write up the results of research; or attendance at conferences or organization of conferences either in the UK or abroad to disseminate the results of research.
Amount @L15,000-@L100,000
Date(s) Application Is Due Oct 15.
Contact Research Grants Department, 020-7969 5217; fax: 020-7969 5414; email: grants@britac.ac.uk
Internet http://www.britac.ac.uk/funding/guide/lrg.html
Sponsor British Academy
10 Carlton House Terrace
London SW1Y 5AH United Kingdom

BA Neil Ker Memorial Fund Research Grants **947**
The object of this fund, established by the family and friends of Neil Ker, FBA, is to promote the study of Western medieval manuscripts--and in particular, those of British interest--by means of awards in support of all aspects of research, including travel and publication, made to both younger and established scholars of any nationality. Applications should be submitted on the standard research grant application form, available from university research offices, or from the academy. Applicants will be notified approximately three months after the closing date.
Requirements Younger and established scholars of any nationality are eligible.
Restrictions The program does not fund travel to or attendance at conferences, workshops, or seminars, either in the United Kingdom or elsewhere.
Amount @L2000 maximum typically
Date(s) Application Is Due Apr 15.
Contact Research Grants Department, 020 7969 5217; fax: 020 7969 5414; email: grants@britac.ac.uk
Internet http://www.britac.ac.uk/funding/guide/nkmf.html
Sponsor British Academy
10 Carlton House Terrace
London SW1Y 5AH United Kingdom

BA Postdoctoral Fellowships **948**
This fellowship is designed to enable outstanding younger scholars to obtain experience of research and teaching in the university environment, which will strengthen their curriculum vita and improve their prospects of obtaining permanent posts by the end of the fellowship. Awards will be tenable for three years (not renewable) and are offered with a salary starting at spine point six on the University Lecturer's Grade A scale or equivalent scale. Applicants nominate the institution at which they wish to hold their award; that institution will be asked to give its consent before any award made by the academy is confirmed. Fellows will be employees of their host institution and will be subject to the terms and conditions of that institution. Applications should be made on the postdoctoral fellowship application form, available from the academy.
Requirements These awards are open to scholars in the humanities and social sciences. Eligible applicants must be ordinarily resident in the United Kingdom; must be under the age of 30 at time of award (but special factors may be taken into account and this discretionary criterion set aside); and must have obtained or expect to obtain their doctorate by the award year.
Restrictions Applicants must not have held an established teaching post in an institution of higher education.
Date(s) Application Is Due Feb 28.
Contact Dr. Ken Emond, Assistant Secretary (Research Appointments), 020 7969 5265; fax: 020 7969 5414; email: posts@britac.ac.uk if
Internet http://www.britac.ac.uk/funding/guide/pdfells.html
Sponsor British Academy
10 Carlton House Terrace
London SW1Y 5AH United Kingdom

BA Research Readerships **949**
These awards are aimed at established scholars in United Kingdom universities who are in midcareer, and are designed to allow the award holders to undertake or to complete an approved program of sustained research, while relieved of their normal teaching

and administrative commitments. The principal purpose of the awards is to enable the completion of a major piece of research which will not only be an important contribution to knowledge and understanding but also help to enhance the future career and career prospects of the award holder. Grants are made direct to the award holder's employing institution to cover the costs of replacement teaching. Readerships are tenable for two years.
Requirements Readerships are open to scholars in the humanities and social sciences. Applicants are expected normally to be aged 55 or under at time of application unless they can show that exceptional circumstances have delayed the advancement of their academic career. Awardees will be expected to be able to disseminate the results of their research not only through publications, but also through the teaching of future courses after the end of their awards.
Date(s) Application Is Due Sep 30.
Contact Research Appointments Department, 020 7969 5265; fax: 020 7969 5414; email: posts@britac.ac.uk
Internet http://www.britac.ac.uk/funding/guide/readfell.html
Sponsor British Academy
10 Carlton House Terrace
London SW1Y 5AH United Kingdom

BA Senior Research Fellowships **950**
These awards are aimed at established scholars in United Kingdom universities who are in midcareer, and are designed to allow the award holders to undertake or to complete an approved program of sustained research, while relieved of their normal teaching and administrative commitments. The principal purpose of the awards is to enable the completion of a major piece of research that will not only be an important contribution to knowledge and understanding but also help to enhance the future career and career prospects of the award holder. Grants are made direct to the award holder's employing institution to cover the costs of replacement teaching. Fellowships are tenable for one year.
Requirements Fellowships are open to scholars in the humanities and social sciences. Applicants are expected normally to be aged 55 or under at time of application unless they can show that exceptional circumstances have delayed the advancement of their academic career. Awardees will be expected to be able to disseminate the results of their research not only through publications, but also through the teaching of future courses after the end of their awards.
Date(s) Application Is Due Sep 30.
Contact Research Appointments Department, 020 7969 5265; fax: 020 7969 5414; email: posts@britac.ac.uk
Internet http://www.britac.ac.uk/funding/guide/readfell.html
Sponsor British Academy
10 Carlton House Terrace
London SW1Y 5AH United Kingdom

BA Sino-British Fellowship Trust **951**
The academy is able to bid for funds from the Sino-British Fellowship Trust (SBFT) to support individual or cooperative research projects, which may be conducted either in Britain or in China, or in both countries, and must involve person-to-person contacts. Applications should first be made to the academy; if approved, the bids will be submitted to the SBFT. Advice on the nature and structure of applications should be sought from the academy's International Relations Department. The academy will be unable to offer support should the SBFT decline to offer funding.
Amount @L10,000 maximum
Date(s) Application Is Due Jan 15; Apr 15; Oct 15.
Contact International Relations Department, 020 7969 5220; fax: 020 7969 5414; email: overseas@britac.ac.uk
Internet http://www.britac.ac.uk/funding/guide/intl/sbft.html
Sponsor British Academy
10 Carlton House Terrace
London SW1Y 5AH United Kingdom

BA Sir Ernest Cassel Educational Trust Fund Grants **952**
The academy administers funds on behalf of the Sir Ernest Cassel Educational Trust, to promote research in any field falling within the humanities or social sciences. Awards are offered to support travel costs relating to a research project, and are particularly aimed at recent postdoctoral scholars. Awards for travel costs rarely exceed @L1000; however, an application to this fund for travel costs may be combined with an application for a personal research grant for other costs, up to a total of @L7500. Applications should be submitted on the standard research grant application form, available from university research offices, or from the academy. In cases where an applicant seeks both travel and other costs, a single application form should be used. Applicants should not complete two separate forms when submitting a dual application to the Cassel fund for travel and to the research grants fund for other elements of a project. Applicants will be notified of the outcome approximately three months after the closing date.
Requirements Applicants must be ordinarily resident in the United Kingdom, the Isle of Man, or the Channel Islands. Most awards are made to staff employed in universities and other institutions of higher education, but applicants are not restricted by either academic or employment status. These awards are particularly at recent postdoctoral scholars.
Amount @L1000 maximum typically; @L7500 maximum for dual applications
Date(s) Application Is Due Apr 15.
Contact Research Grants Department, 020 7969 5217; fax: 020 7969 5414; email: grants@britac.ac.uk
Internet http://www.britac.ac.uk/funding/guide/cetf.html
Sponsor British Academy
10 Carlton House Terrace
London SW1Y 5AH United Kingdom

BA Small Research Grants **953**
Small research grants are available to support primary research in the humanities and social sciences. Eligible costs include travel and maintenance, research assistance, workshops, consumables, specialist software, and costs of interpreters in the field. Applications for collaborative or individual projects are equally welcome. Applications from international groups of scholars are welcome, provided there is a UK-based scholar as lead applicant. Grants are tenable for up to 24 months.
Amount @L500-@L7500
Date(s) Application Is Due Jan 15; Apr 15; Oct 15.
Contact Research Grants Department, 020-7969 5217; fax: 020-7969 5414; email: grants@britac.ac.uk
Internet http://www.britac.ac.uk/funding/guide/srg.html
Sponsor British Academy
10 Carlton House Terrace
London SW1Y 5AH United Kingdom

BA Stein-Arnold Exploration Fund Research Grants **954**
The fund was established according to the terms of the will of Sir Aurel Stein, FBA, to commemorate his friendship with Sir Thomas Arnold, FBA. Eligible projects include research on the antiquities, historical geography, early history, or arts of those parts of Asia that come within the sphere of the ancient civilizations of India, China, and Iran, including Central Asia, or of one or more of these. Special consideration shall be paid, if possible, to research of this character bearing upon the territories comprised in the present Kingdom of Afghanistan, including the region of ancient Bactria and in the northwestern frontier region of India. Research should be so far as possible by means of exploratory work.
Requirements Applicants should be British or Hungarian subjects.
Amount @L2500 maximum
Date(s) Application Is Due Apr 15.
Contact Research Grants Department, 020 7969 5217; fax: 020 7969 5414; email: grants@britac.ac.uk
Internet http://www.britac.ac.uk/funding/guide/saef.html
Sponsor British Academy
10 Carlton House Terrace
London SW1Y 5AH United Kingdom

BA Thank-Offering to Britain Fellowship **955**
The fellowship is funded by the Thank-Offering to Britain fund from part of a generous endowment arising from the proceeds of a Thank-You Britain Appeal, initiated by the Association of Jewish Refugees as a mark of gratitude for Britain's provision of a home for Jews persecuted by the Nazi regime. These awards are aimed at established scholars in United Kingdom universities who are in midcareer, and are designed to allow the award holders to undertake or to complete an approved program of sustained research, while relieved of their normal teaching and administrative commitments. The principal purpose of the awards is to enable the completion of a major piece of research which will not only be an important contribution to knowledge and understanding but also help to enhance the future career and career prospects of the award holder. Grants are made direct to the award holder's employing institution to cover the costs of replacement teaching. Appropriate subjects for research will be related to human studies widely interpreted and their bearing on the well-being of the inhabitants of the United Kingdom.
Requirements Fellowships are open to scholars in the humanities and social sciences. Applicants are expected normally to be aged 55 or under at time of application unless they can show that exceptional circumstances have delayed the advancement of their academic career. Awardees will be expected to be able to disseminate the results of their research not only through publications, but also through the teaching of future courses after the end of their awards.
Date(s) Application Is Due Sep 30.
Contact Research Grants Department, 020 7969 5265; fax: 020 7969 5414; email: posts@britac.ac.uk
Internet http://www.britac.ac.uk/funding/guide/readfell.html
Sponsor British Academy
10 Carlton House Terrace
London SW1Y 5AH United Kingdom

BA Visiting Professorships and Fellowships **956**
The program enables distinguished scholars from overseas to be invited to spend a minimum of two weeks in the United Kingdom. The academy grants the title of British Academy Visiting Professor or (for a more junior scholar) British Academy Visiting Fellow and awards a sum of money towards the estimated travel and maintenance costs. All arrangements are undertaken by the visitor's British sponsor. While the delivery of lectures and participation in seminars is not precluded, the main purpose of the visit should be to enable the visitor to pursue research. It is not intended that the fellowships and professorships should be used in conjunction with a nonstipendiary university

fellowship. The normal maximum length of visit will be one month, but applications for longer periods will be considered, although it will be expected that the weekly budget for longer visits will be set at a more moderate level.
Requirements Candidates for nominations must be from the United Kingdom and must be either established scholars of distinction or younger people who show great promise and who would benefit from time to pursue their research.
Amount @L700 per week, usually for one month; travel expenses to the UK
Date(s) Application Is Due Dec 15.
Contact International Relations Department, 020 7969 5220; fax: 020 7969 5414; email: overseas@britac.ac.uk
Internet http://www.britac.ac.uk/funding/guide/intl/visprof.html
Sponsor British Academy
10 Carlton House Terrace
London SW1Y 5AH United Kingdom

BA Worldwide Congress Grants 957
Grants are available for the congresses of major subject areas or disciplines, ordinarily occurring every three, four, or five years, and involving an extensive program and large attendance from all over the world. It should clearly be the British turn to host such a congress, and the event should not have been held in the UK for a considerable period. Typical examples would be the International Congress of Historical Sciences, or the Congress of the International Geographical Union. British scholars contemplating the possibility of extending an invitation for a worldwide congress to be held in Britain are invited to contact the academy to discuss possible support. Please note that it is expected that preliminary proposals should be submitted at least three years in advance of the date of the Congress.
Restrictions Applications from individual scholars for conferences supported by a block grant will not be accepted.
Amount @L15,000 maximum
Date(s) Application Is Due Jan 15; Apr 15; Oct 15.
Contact Research Grants Department, 020 7969 5217; fax: 020 7969 5414; email: grants@britac.ac.uk
Internet http://www.britac.ac.uk/funding/guide/wcg.html
Sponsor British Academy
10 Carlton House Terrace
London SW1Y 5AH United Kingdom

Bailey Family Foundation Grants 958
The foundation's primary mission is to expand the availability and enhance the quality of postsecondary education. The foundation also conducts research directed toward improving the state of higher education. Financial assistance in the form of scholarships is awarded to students based on their academic record, financial need, and level of community involvement. Scholarship programs include educational scholarships to high school seniors and college students.
Requirements Applicants must possess a minimum cumulative GPA of 2.5, demonstrate financial need, be a graduating senior from a participating high school/college listed on the application, be US residents, and be pursuing their undergraduate degree.
Amount $5000
Date(s) Application Is Due Mar 31; Sep 30.
Contact Grants Administrator, (703) 971-6203; fax: (703) 971-6205; email: Bailey@Bailey-Family.org
Internet http://www.bailey-family.org
Sponsor Bailey Family Foundation
P.O. Box 803
Newington, VA 22122-0803

Bailey Wildlife Foundation Grants 959
The foundation awards grants to support research projects in the natural sciences and arts and for wildlife and environmental conservation and protection in the eastern United States.
Restrictions Individuals are not eligible.
Amount $1890-$260,000
Contact H. Whitney Bailey, (978) 901-3471
Sponsor Bailey Wildlife Foundation
10223 Bushveld Ln
Raleigh, NC 27612-6149

Ball Brothers Foundation Grants 960
The foundation seeks to build and sustain a high quality of life in Indiana by awarding grants to nonprofit organizations in broad subject areas, including elementary, secondary, higher, and adult basic education and literacy skills; cultural activities; community betterment; and health and human services. Usually Muncie and Delaware Counties receive a higher priority for funding than requests from within East Central Indiana or across the state. Types of support include general operations, annual campaigns, capital campaigns, building construction/renovation, program development, conferences and seminars, professorships, publication, curriculum development, research, fellowships, matching funds, seed grants, and technical assistance. Preference will be given to catalytic grants that will stimulate others to participate in problem solving or in matching fund programs and to innovative approaches for addressing either traditional or emerging community needs. Applications are reviewed by the board of directors in January, May, and September of each calendar year. Proposals are encouraged to be submitted from February to May. Grant seekers may send a preliminary proposal, complete proposal, or ask for a personal visit to discuss a potential grant request.
Requirements Indiana nonprofit institutions and organizations are eligible.
Restrictions Grants will not support: Individuals; Booster organizations; Direct scholarships to individuals; Services that the community-at-large should normally underwrite (e.g., roads, bus transportation, etc.).
Contact Douglas Bakken, Executive Vice President, (765) 741-5500; fax: (765) 741-5518; email: doug.bakken@ballfdn.org
Internet http://www.ballfdn.org
Sponsor Ball Brothers Foundation
222 South Mulberr Street
Muncie, IN 47305

Bancroft Prizes 961
Two annual prizes are awarded to the authors of distinguished works in either or both of the following categories: American history (including biography) and diplomacy. The awards in any given year are for books first published in the previous year. The word American is interpreted to include all of the Americas--North, Central, and South; however, the award is confined to works originally written in English or where there is a translation published in English.
Amount $4000
Contact Bancroft Prizes Program Support, (212) 854-2271; fax: (212) 854-9099
Internet http://www.columbia.edu/cu/lweb/eguides/amerihist/bancroft.html
Sponsor Columbia University
517 Butler Library, 535 W 114th St
New York, NY 10027

Banfi Vintners Foundation Grants 962
The foundation awards general operating grants to nonprofits in its areas of interest, including higher education, civic and public affairs, arts and humanities, wildlife protection, health (hospitals and disease research/prevention), religion, science, social services, and international. Grants are made nationwide, with preference given to requests from Massachusetts and the New York, NY, area.
Amount $100-$465,000 range
Contact Philip Calderone, Executive Director, (516) 626-9200
Sponsor Banfi Vintners Foundation
1111 Cedar Swamp Rd
Glen Head, NY 11545

Banfield Charitable Trust Grants 963
This trust offers grants annually to nonprofit organizations and educational institutions that make life better for Pets and their families. Special considerations will be given to collaborative programs with Pet-related organizations and Banfield team members working together towards a shared goal. At this time, Banfield Charitable Trust is pursuing the following funding priorities: promotion of preventative healthcare for Pets; educating children about veterinary medicine and the Pets they love; programs based on the human-Pet bond and how this relates to longer, healthier lives for Pets and people; and veterinary education programs. The Trust does not generally fund an entire project, but expects to be one of multiple funding sources. Typically, the Trust will not fund more than 50% of the project's entire budget.
Requirements 501(c)3 organizations and educational institutions are eligible.
Restrictions Funding will not be considered for: spay and neuter or adoption programs; general operating expenses, deficit reduction, or general administrative overhead expenses; fundraising; individuals, or to provide support for business enterprise.
Date(s) Application Is Due Jun 30; Nov 30.
Contact Grants Administrator, (503) 922-5801 or (866) 802-0566; email: charitabletrust@banfield.net
Internet http://www.banfieldcharitabletrust.net/guidelines.html
Sponsor Banfield Charitable Trust
8000 NE Tillamook Sreet, P.O. Box 13998
Portland, OR 97213

Bank of Sweden Tercentenary Foundation Grants 964
The foundation focuses on research aimed at expanding knowledge of the effects of technical, economic, and social changes on Sweden and its people. The foundation awards project grants to individual scientists or groups of scientists. Grants generally support large, long-term projects.
Requirements Applicants outside of Sweden must work with Swedish researchers or research institutes.
Contact Dr. Dan Brandstrom, Director, 46-8-506 264 02; fax: 46-(0)8-506-264-30; email: rj@rj.se
Internet http://www.rj.se/default.asp?ItemID=22770
Sponsor Bank of Sweden Tercentenary Foundation
P.O. Box 5675
Stockholm 114 86 Sweden

Barbara Thom Postdoctoral Fellowships 965
The Huntington Library and Art Gallery is an independent research center with holdings in British and American history, literature, art history, the history of science, and

photography. The program awards fellowships to support nontenured faculty members pursuing scholarship in a field appropriate to the Huntington's collections while revising a manuscript for publication. Recipients are expected to be in continuous residence at the Huntington during the nine- to 12-month fellowship tenure and to participate in the intellectual life of the center. There is no application form. Applications consist of cover sheet, description of the project, curriculum vita, and three letters of recommendation.
Requirements Preference will be given to scholars who received the PhD three years prior to the fellowship.
Amount $40,000
Date(s) Application Is Due Dec 15.
Contact Robert Ritchie, Director of Research, (626) 405-2194; fax: (626) 449-5703; email: cpowell@hungtington.org
Internet http://www.huntington.org/ResearchDiv/Fellowships.html
Sponsor Huntington Library and Art Gallery
1151 Oxford Rd
San Marino, CA 91108

BARD Postdoctoral Fellowships **966**
The United States-Israel Binational Agricultural Research and Development Fund (BARD) was established to promote and support research and development in agriculture for the mutual benefit of both countries. The postdoctoral program was initiated to promote cooperative agricultural research between postdoctoral fellows from one country and senior scientists from the other; to assist young scientists to become professionally established in the scientific community; and to provide BARD with input into new research areas and to enhance scientific competence in these areas. The program emphasizes innovation in agriculture, particularly in the areas of cellular and molecular biology and the use and development of explanatory models in agriculture. Also included in the fellowship is a $5000 allowance for children, and, if necessary, a small allowance not to exceed $3000 to host institution for research-related expenses. The duration of the fellowship is one year. Requests for application kits and information may be obtained from the Maryland address or BARD, P.O. Box 6, Bet Dagan, Israel 50250; phone: 03-968-3230, fax: 03-966-2506, or email: bard@bard-isus.com.
Requirements Applicants must be US or Israeli citizens. Applicants should have fulfilled the requirements for a PhD degree within the last three years. Candidates must file an application with BARD in English naming only one senior scientist. Application kits may be obtained at either BARD office. Only one application per year for each candidate will be accepted.
Restrictions Israelis already in the United States and Americans already in Israel (for a period of six months or longer) are not eligible.
Amount $32,000 to cover travel and living expenses
Date(s) Application Is Due Jan 15.
Contact BARD, USDA-ARS-OIRP, (301) 504-4584; fax: (301) 504-4619; email: lea@bard-isus.com
Internet http://www.bard-isus.com
Sponsor United States-Israel Binational Agricultural Research and Development Fund
5601 Sunnyside Ave
Beltsville, MD 20705

BARD Research Grants **967**
The United States-Israel Binational Agricultural Research and Development Fund (BARD) was established by the governments of the United States and Israel for the purpose of promoting and supporting cooperative research and development projects in agriculture for the mutual benefit of both countries. Proposals may be unidisciplinary or interdisciplinary and may cover any or all phases of research and development. BARD will consider financing research and development projects, exploratory or basic research studies, and small initial feasibility studies and other closely related activities in the areas of soil and water conservation management and utilization; crop production including new technology; crop protection; animal production including aquaculture; veterinary medicine; crop and animal genetic improvement; recycling of wastes; postharvest sciences covering operations from production through processing; agricultural engineering; agricultural economics; and cellular and molecular biology in agriculture. Investigators of either country may request information or mail proposals to Lynn Gipe, USDA-ARS-BARD at the Maryland address, or BARD Executive Director, Volcani Center, P.O. Box 6, Bet Dagan, Israel 50250, 03-9683230. Guidelines and applications are also available on the Web site.
Requirements Affiliates of public or private nonprofit research institutions that demonstrate the necessary research and development capabilities are eligible to apply for funding. Scientists who wish to apply for grants should submit their proposals through such legally constituted institutions or agencies. The research proposal should be prepared jointly by at least one US and one Israeli investigator and should describe the areas of anticipated cooperative endeavor between them. BARD will assist scientists who are unable to find collaborators; the BARD office in Israel or its liaison office in the United States should be contacted if such assistance is necessary.
Restrictions BARD will not consider more than one application from the same investigator in a given year or fund the same investigator in more than one concurrent project.
Amount $100,000-$350,000; $300,000 average for three years
Date(s) Application Is Due Sep 1.
Contact Program Contact, BARD, c/o Department of Agriculture, (301) 504-4522; fax: (301) 504-4619; email: bard@bard-isus.com
Internet http://www.bard-isus.com
Sponsor United States-Israel Binational Agricultural Research and Development Fund
5601 Sunnyside Ave
Beltsville, MD 20705

Barker Award **968**
Open to qualified graduate students registered full-time in the Faculty of Graduate Studies at the University of Calgary.
Requirements Applicants must be studying in the fields of Business Administration with emphasis on Entrepreneurship, New Venture Development and Marketing. The award is tenable during a student's first year of the MBA program.
Amount $C1500
Date(s) Application Is Due May 30.
Contact Connie Baines, (403) 220-5690; email: cbaines@ucalgary.ca
Internet https://prlweb.ucalgary.ca/FGS_SAM/public/InternalSearchResults.aspx
Sponsor University of Calgary
2500 University Dr., NW, Earth Sciences Bldg., Room 720
Calgary, AB T2N 1N4 Canada

Barra Foundation Grants **969**
Project grants are one-time grants generally for amounts above $10,000. The Foundation considers grants for innovative projects that aid research in advancing the frontiers of human services, arts and culture, health and education. Grants are not made for ongoing or expanding programs where substantial initial support was previously provided from other sources. Three principal criteria are strictly adhered to in judging the merits of a proposed project. They are: Innovation; Evaluation; Dissemination. Community Fund Grants provide unrestricted contributions to qualified organizations primarily in the Greater Philadelphia area. These grants are generally in amounts between $1,000 and $10,000 per year. The Foundation's categories of funding for these grants are Human Services, Arts and Culture, Health and Education.
Requirements The foundation does not provide grants for: ongoing operating budgets, including staff salaries; budget deficits; endowments; capital campaigns and projects; international programs; environmental and religious organizations; scholarships and fellowships or audio/video projects, publications, catalogues, and exhibitions.
Restrictions In general, the foundation does not support ongoing operating expenses, budget deficits, publications unrelated to projects, international programs and institutions, or individual scholarships or fellowships.
Amount $1000-$500,000 range
Contact William Harrall, III, President, (215) 233-5115; fax: (215) 836-1033; email: william.harral@verizon.net
Internet http://www.barrafoundation.org/forms/index.html
Sponsor Barra Foundation
8200 Flourtown Avenue, Suite 12
Wyndmoor, PA 19038-7976

Barra Postdoctoral Fellowship **970**
Specialists working in any field of early American studies are encouraged to apply, though the center is particularly interested in projects that utilize Philadelphia-area libraries and archives. Appointment is for a nine-month term, beginning September 1. No teaching is required, but the recipient is expected to spend the appointment in residence and to participate in MCEAS seminars and other community activities. The fellow will receive a stipend and be provided with a private office and computer facilities two blocks from the University of Pennsylvania library.
Requirements The competition is open to both junior and senior scholars, but all candidates must have the PhD in hand by the deadline date.
Amount $32,000
Date(s) Application Is Due Nov 1.
Contact Postdoctoral Fellowship Program, (215) 898-9251 or 898-9251; fax (215) 573-3391; email: mceas@ccat.sas.upenn.edu
Internet http://www.mceas.org/postdoctoralfellowship.htm
Sponsor McNeil Center for Early American Studies
3619 Locsut Walk, 3rd Fl
Philadelphia, PA 19104-3325

Barth Syndrome Foundation Research Grants **971**
Barth syndrome is a serious X-linked recessive condition associated with cardiomyopathy, neutropenia, skeletal muscle weakness, exercise intolerance, growth delay, and diverse biochemical abnormalities (including defects in mitochondrial metabolism and phospholipid biosynthesis). Because many clinical and biochemical abnormalities of Barth syndrome remain poorly understood, the program is seeking proposals for research that will advance knowledge on any aspect of the syndrome. The foundation prefers to award seed grants to experienced investigators for testing of initial hypotheses and collection of preliminary data leading to successful long-term funding by NIH and other major granting institutions. The foundation also encourages investigators new to the field of Barth Syndrome research. Send an electronic version of the full application and all the attachments by the listed application deadline. Guidelines are available online.
Requirements Principal investigators who are affiliated with nonprofit institutions are eligible.
Amount $150,000 total; $10,000-$40,000
Date(s) Application Is Due Sep 30.

Contact Kate McCurdy, Science and Medicine, (914) 834-1771; email: kmccurdy@barthsyndrome.org
Internet http://www.barthsyndrome.org/Grants/grants.html
Sponsor Barth Syndrome Foundation
P.O. Box 618
Larchmont, NY 10538

Batchelor Foundation Grants **972**
The foundation awards grants to Florida nonprofits in its areas of interest, including medical research, childhood diseases, and natural resource conservation. There are no application forms. Initial approach should be a letter that details the grant proposal.
Requirements Florida area nonprofits are eligible.
Restrictions Individuals are not eligible.
Amount $5000-$3 million range
Contact Anne Batchelor-Robjohns, Treasurer, (305) 416-9066
Sponsor Batchelor Foundation Inc
111 NE 1st Street, Suite 820
Miami, FL 33132

Baxter International Foundation Grants **973**
The foundation supports the development of more accessible and affordable healthcare. The foundation funds initiatives that improve the access, quality and cost-effectiveness of healthcare. Focusing on these priorities, the foundation makes grants in and near communities throughout the world where significant numbers of Baxter employees live and work.
Requirements Nonprofits in the United States, Europe, Latin America, and Mexico, with some emphasis on Chicago and Puerto Rico, are eligible.
Restrictions In general, the foundation does not make grants to capital and endowment campaigns; disease-specific organizations; educational institutions (except in instances where a grant would help to achieve other goals, such as increasing the skills and availability of health care providers); hospitals; individuals; fraternal, veterans, or religious organizations; lobbying and political organizations; organizations soliciting contributions for advertising space, tickets to dinners, benefits, social and fund-raising events, sponsorships and promotional materials; organizations seeking travel support for individuals or groups, medical missions or conferences; magazines, professional journals, documentary, film, video or radio productions.
Amount $2.5 million total
Date(s) Application Is Due Jan 12; Apr 2; Jun 27; Sep 19.
Contact (847) 948-4605; email: fdninfo@baxter.com
Internet http://www.baxter.com/about_baxter/foundation/index.html
Sponsor Baxter International Foundation
Baxter International Foundation, One Baxter Parkway - DF2-2E
Deerfield, IL 60015-4625

Bay and Paul Foundations, Inc Grants **974**
General operating and project grants are awarded for support of children's services and precollege educational programs, with an emphasis on technology and enhancement of science, math, and writing curricula; preservation of cultural and natural history collections and collections care training in museums, zoos, libraries, and botanical gardens; advocacy and research programs for preserving biodiversity; and Native American cultural heritage preservation and economic development programs. There are no application forms. Proposals should be directed to the executive director and should include a brief description of the applicant organization and of the program for which funding is requested, including objectives and numbers served; a project budget or financials; other expected sources of support; qualifications of key personnel; and evidence of tax-exempt status. The foundation's directors meet three times a year, usually in January, May, and October, to consider grant proposals. Requests are not accepted via fax. Regular postal service delivery is the preferred method of proposal acceptance.
Requirements Nonprofits in Connecticut, Massachusetts, Maine, New Hampshire, New Jersey, New York, Rhode Island, and Vermont are eligible.
Restrictions Grants do not support requests for endowments, building campaigns, building construction or maintenance, sectarian religious programs, books or studies, individual scholarships or fellowships, loans, travel, film, television or video productions, programs consisting primarily of conferences, for annual fund appeals, or to other than publicly recognized charities. First time grants for K-12 arts-in-education programs and K-12 science and math programs are currently geographically restricted to the New York City metropolitan area.
Contact Frederick Bay, Executive Director, (212) 663-1115; fax: (212) 932-0316; info@bayandpaulfoundations.org
Internet http://www.bayandpaulfoundations.org/areas.html
Sponsor Bay and Paul Foundations, Inc
17 West 94th Street
New York, NY 10025

Bayer Clinical Scholarship Award **975**
This award is intended to facilitate the development of specific clinical expertise in the field of hemophilia for applicants who have completed medical training and have an interest in pursuing a career as a hemophilia treater/researcher. The award will support a mentored physician in training for two years. Clinical duties will encompass diagnosis, evaluation, and the planning of management strategies for patients with hereditary bleeding disorders. In addition to the clinical experience, the applicant may pursue a research project in the field of hemostasis. Clinical scholarships will provide funding for two years. Up to five new awards will be made each year. Guidelines and application are available online.
Requirements The applicant should have earned his/her medical degree within the previous eight years. The commitment of the mentor to the grantee and the research project (if applicable) is a vital element of the application, as is the quality of the clinical environment at which the applicant will undertake the scholarship.
Amount $70,000 annually for two years
Contact Program Administrator, email: programadministrator@bayer-hemophilia-awards.com
Internet http://www.bayer-hemophilia-awards.com/awards.cfm#clinical
Sponsor Bayer HealthCare Corporation
100 Bayer Road
Pittsburgh, PA 15205-9741

Bayer Foundation Grants **976**
The Bayer Foundation supports programs that enhance the quality of life, provide unique and enriching opportunities that connect diverse groups and ensure preparedness for tomorrow's leaders. The Foundation welcomes proposals from 501(c)(3) organizations whose programming matches at least one of the following areas: Civic and Social Service Programs; Education and Workforce Development; Arts and Culture and Health and Human Services.
Requirements 501(c)3 nonprofit organizations in Bayer operating communities are eligible. Submit proposals to regional offices in California, Connecticut, Georgia, Indiana, Kansas, Massachusetts, New Jersey, New York, North Carolina, Ohio, Pennsylvania, Texas and West Virginia.
Restrictions The Foundation will not fund: For-profit organizations or those without Internal Revenue Service code 501(c)(3) nonprofit, tax-exempt status; Organizations that discriminate on the basis of race, color, creed, gender, sexual orientation or national origin; General operating support for United Way affiliated agencies. Only support for special projects will be considered; Organizations or programs designed to influence legislation or elect candidates to public office; General endowment funds; Deficit reduction or operating reserves; Religious organizations; Charitable dinners, events or sponsorships; Community or event advertising; Individuals; Student trips or exchange programs; Athletic sponsorships or scholarships; Telephone solicitations; Organizations outside of the United States or its territories
Contact Bayer Foundation, (800) 422-9374
Internet http://www.bayerus.com/about/community/i_foundation.html
Sponsor Bayer Foundation
100 Bayer Road, Bldg. 4
Pittsburgh, PA 15205-9741

Bayer Hemophilia Early Career Investigator Award **977**
This award will fund salary support and research funds for a junior faculty member who wishes to undertake a mentored basic and/or clinical research project in the bleeding disorders field. The applicant would be expected to dedicate a significant amount of time to the project. Examples of topics for research projects that might be considered for these awards include, but are not limited to: clinical studies; properties and delivery of clotting factor proteins; assays and models; genetics and epidemiology; and molecular aspects and mechanisms of clotting factor inhibitor formation. Awards will provide funding for two years. Up to five new awards will be made each year. Part of the award may fund salary support. The candidate must spend at least 25 percent of his/her time on the project in order to request salary support. Applicants should submit a letter of intent via email describing the proposed project in 500 words or fewer; full proposals are by invitation. Guidelines are available online.
Requirements The applicant should have an entry-level academic or clinical appointment within his or her institution. This award is open to applicants with a medical degree and/or PhD. Applicants should have earned their terminal degree within the previous 10 years.
Amount $100,000 annually
Date(s) Application Is Due Oct 31.
Contact Corporate Communications, (412) 777-2000
Internet http://www.bayer-hemophilia-awards.com/awards.cfm#early
Sponsor Bayer HealthCare Corporation
100 Bayer Rd
Pittsburgh, PA 15205-9741

Bayer Hemophilia Special Project Award **978**
The award is designed to support a wide range of research projects in the field of hemophilia. Examples of the types of projects that might be considered for these awards include, but are not limited to, those related to: clinical research; basic research; assessment and intervention in psychosocial issues facing patients and their families; assessment of quality of life and other health economic outcomes in patients with bleeding disorders; and the effects of treatment modalities on such outcomes. The award is designed to encourage hypothesis-driven research, where the investigator is attempting to prove or disprove a set of assumptions. It is not designed to support studies such as the collection of epidemiological data. The funding will be awarded to allow the project to run for one or two years. Part of the award may fund salary support. The candidate must spend at least 25 percent of his/her time on the project in order to request salary support.

Applicants should submit a letter of intent via email describing the proposed project in 500 words or fewer; full proposals are by invitation.
Requirements Any individual affiliated with a facility that carries out research in inherited bleeding disorders, or provides care to patients with those disorders, may make a request for these grants. Such facilities may include medical universities, hospitals, treatment centers, blood centers, and other laboratories. All applications must be in English.
Amount $200,000 maximum
Date(s) Application Is Due Oct 31.
Contact Corporate Communications, (412) 777-2000
Internet http://www.bayer-hemophilia-awards.com/awards.cfm
Sponsor Bayer HealthCare Corporation
100 Bayer Rd
Pittsburgh, PA 15205-9741

Baylor Institute for Faith and Learning Visiting Fellows Program 979
The Institute for Faith and Learning sponsors a visiting fellows program that brings outstanding scholars to the university for one-year appointments. Fellows pursue research in their academic disciplines informed by Christian intellectual traditions. They serve as participants in the full life of the university, assisting the institute in its aim to encourage academic research that integrates faith and learning, and helping to cultivate a context conducive to the pursuit of such scholarship. Fellows may teach one course per term within a cohosting department, help lead institute-sponsored colloquia, and otherwise further the work of the institute. Applicants should submit a curriculum vita, three recommendation letters, a 750-word description of the project to be undertaken while at the institute, and a published paper.
Requirements Senior fellows typically hold senior faculty rank at their home institutions, possess records as accomplished, nationally recognized scholars, and pursue research programs of the highest caliber integrative of their academic discipline and the Christian faith. Junior fellows typically hold junior but tenure-track faculty rank at their home institutions, possess records showing clear promise commensurate with their time in rank, and also pursue research programs of the highest caliber integrative of the Christian faith and their area of expertise.
Amount $50,000 maximum for senior fellows; $40,000 maximum for junior fellows
Date(s) Application Is Due Nov 1.
Contact Dr. Douglas Henry, (254) 710-4805; fax: (254) 710-4813; email: IFL@baylor.edu
Internet http://www.baylor.edu/ifl
Sponsor Baylor University
P.O. Box 97270
Waco, TX 76798

BC Center for Retirement Research Dissertation Fellowships 980
The purpose of the program is to promote the next generation of retirement research scholars and to improve the quality of scholarship in Social Security and income studies. Applicants must demonstrate their dissertation focuses on the Social Security Administration research priorities including Social Security and retirement; macroeconomic analyses of Social Security; wealth and retirement income; program interactions; international research; and demographic research. Doctoral candidates from a wide variety of academic disciplines, including actuarial science, demography, economics, finance, gerontology, political science, public administration, public policy, sociology, social work, and statistics are encouraged to submit a proposal. Awards will be announced in March. Fellowships for successful applicants are renewable for a second-year based on adequate progress. Application and guidelines are available online.
Requirements Applicants are required to be enrolled in a qualified doctoral program at a US university; have completed all coursework for a PhD by the time funding would start; and have a dissertation advisor and/or committee.
Amount $20,000 ($16,000 stipend, $4000 tuition and summer support)
Date(s) Application Is Due Jan 31.
Contact Fellowship Administrator, (617) 552-1762; fax: (617) 552-0191; email: crr@bc.edu
Internet http://www.bc.edu/centers/crr/dissertation.shtml
Sponsor Boston College
140 Commonwealth Ave, Fulton Hall 550
Chestnut Hill, MA 02467-3808

BC Steven H. Sandell Grant Program 981
The program's purpose is to promote research on retirement issues including: Social Security and retirement; macroeconomic analyses of Social Security; wealth and retirement income; program interactions; international research; and demographic research. Within the six broad areas, four topics of particular interest include: retirement planning/risk management decisions of workers and retirees; measures of retirement well-being; trends in labor force participation and their implications for Social Security and for the well-being of the elderly; Social Security reform.
Requirements The principal investigator must have a PhD in a related discipline or a comparable professional certification; and must be a nontenured junior scholar or senior scholar working in a new area. All applicants must complete the online submission form.
Amount $40,000
Date(s) Application Is Due Mar 31.
Contact Paige Eppenstein, Center for Retirement Research, Sandell Grant Program, (617) 552-1092; email: eppenste@bc.edu
Internet http://www.bc.edu/centers/crr/sandellguidelines.shtml
Sponsor Boston College
140 Commonwealth Ave, Fulton Hall 550
Chestnut Hill, MA 02467-3808

BCBS Improving Men's Health Grants 982
The purpose of this initiative is to encourage research, as well as demonstration and evaluation projects, on improving men's health through the early detection and screening of disease. The foundation will focus on increasing screening and prevention for men in the following five clinical areas: diabetes, hypertension, coronary heart disease, colorectal cancer, and prostate cancer. Proposed projects should focus on one or more of three clinical areas: screen men for specific diseases and/or conditions; refer men with abnormal screens for diagnostic and treatment services in a timely and efficient manner; and follow-up on men for subsequent testing. Funds are available for salary support, supplies and office operations, as well as limited staff travel expenses and consultant fees for Michigan-based researchers working on initiative to improve men's health through the early detection of disease. The listed application deadline is for letters of intent; full proposals are by invitation.
Requirements Letters of interest are sought from Michigan-based physicians and doctoral-level researchers based at universities, academic medical settings, community hospitals, health systems, and community-based nonprofit organizations.
Amount $25,000-$50,000; $100,000 maximum over two years
Date(s) Application Is Due Jan 15.
Contact Grants Administrator, (313) 225-8706; fax: (313) 225-7730; email: foundation@bcbsm.com
Internet http://www.bcbsm.com/foundation/grant_programs.shtml
Sponsor Blue Cross Blue Shield of Michigan Foundation
600 E Lafayette, X520
Detroit, MI 48226-2998

BCBS of Massachusetts Foundation Grants 983
With a mission to expand access to health care, the foundation awards grants intended to make a significant impact on the health of Massachusetts's low income and uninsured residents. Grant programs include Innovation Fund for the Uninsured; Connecting Consumers with Care; Strengthening the Voice for Access; Pathways to Culturally Competent Health Care; Catalyst Fund; Building Bridges in Children's Mental Health; and Policy Research and Analysis. Grant awards in particular focus areas are made during specific grant cycles. Deadlines and additional information are available online.
Requirements Massachusetts 501(c)3 nonprofit organizations or government agencies with a mission that includes improving access and removing barriers to healthcare for low-income or uninsured Massachusetts's residents are eligible.
Restrictions The foundation will not fund individuals; for-profit organizations; capital campaigns, endowments, or building drives; fundraising drives and events; retiring debt or operating deficits; direct political or lobbying activity; projects outside of Massachusetts; or religious organizations for religious purposes (proposals for secular programs of faith-based organizations that meet funding criteria will be considered). Grants are rarely made for curriculum development, conferences, film or video production, or scholarships.
Date(s) Application Is Due Jan 20; Sep 7.
Contact Grant Requests, (617) 246-3744; fax: (617) 246-3992; email: grantinfo@bcbsmafoundation.org
Internet http://www.bcbsmafoundation.org/foundationroot/en_US/grants/focusArea.jsp#aInnovation%20Fund%20for%20the%20Uninsured
Sponsor Blue Cross Blue Shield of Massachusetts Foundation
401 Park Dr
Boston, MA 02215

BCBS of Minnesota Healthy Together Grants 984
Healthy Together: Creating Community with New Americans is a grantmaking initiative designed to reduce health disparities for immigrants and improve the health and vitality of the entire community. The foundation awards grants to projects that foster exchanges and interactions between newcomers and the receiving community, strengthen the capacity of immigrant-led organizations and their attention to health, and address social adjustment and mental health.
Requirements Eligible applicants include community- and faith-based organizations; state, county and municipal agencies; tribal governments and agencies; professional associations or collaboratives; and policy and research organizations. Applicants must be located in Minnesota or serve Minnesotans. Eligible applicants include units of government as well as organizations designated as nonprofit under section 501(c)(3) of the IRS code.
Amount $1200-$250,000
Date(s) Application Is Due Feb 1.
Contact Jocelyn Ancheta, program officer, (651) 662-2894; email, Jocelyn_L_Ancheta@bluecrossmn.com.
Internet http://www.bluecrossmn.com/public/foundation/index.html
Sponsor Blue Cross Blue Shield of Minnesota Foundation
3535 Blue Cross Rd, Rte M459
Eagan, MN 55122

BCBSM Domestic Abuse Research Grants **985**

The program supports grants to conduct research and to develop research, demonstration, and evaluation projects designed to prevent and treat domestic abuse in Michigan. The foundation seeks applications from a variety of disciplines and interdisciplinary efforts including but not limited to law enforcement, medicine, nursing, public health, economics, and social sciences. Funding will be available for salary support, supplies, and office operations, as well as limited staff travel expenses and consultant fees for Michigan-based researchers working on initiatives to address domestic abuse. Letters of interest are due by the listed application deadline; guidelines are available online.

Requirements The primary applicant must be based in Michigan and is expected to have medical or terminal research (e.g., PhD, DrPH) credentials.

Amount $25,000-$50,000 per year; $100,000 maximum

Date(s) Application Is Due Apr 4.

Contact Dr. Nora Maloy, (313) 225-8706; email: nmaloy@bcbsm.com

Internet http://www.bcbsm.com/foundation/grant_programs.shtml

Sponsor Blue Cross Blue Shield of Michigan Foundation
600 Lafayette E, Ste X520
Detroit, MI 48226

BCBSM Foundation Depression Research Grants **986**

The program awards grants to support programs that implement and evaluate creative interventions to screen for depression at established primary clinics; make appropriate clinical referrals or provide appropriate treatment; and/or longitudinal research and follow-up for patients under treatment for depression. All proposed efforts to increase appropriate screening, referral, and treatment for depression must include an evaluation of the effectiveness of the proposed intervention(s). Preference will be given to programs that rigorously assess new measures that integrate depression screening and care into routine practice, reduce the stigma associated with the condition, and are economically sustainable. Innovative collaborations are encouraged. Guidelines and application are available online.

Requirements Michigan-based 501(c)3 nonprofit healthcare providers, managed care networks, nonprofit primary care clinics, and academic institutions are eligible.

Restrictions Does not fund the purchase of equipment or support clinical drug trials.

Amount $50,000 per year for two years

Date(s) Application Is Due Mar 31.

Contact Elizabeth Greaves-Hoxsie, Program Officer, email: ehoxsie@bcbsm.com

Internet http://www.bcbsm.com/home/social_mission/depression.shtml

Sponsor Blue Cross Blue Shield of Michigan Foundation
600 E Lafayette, X520
Detroit, MI 48226-2998

BCBSM Foundation Student Award Program **987**

The program offers a one year stipend to fund a wide range of health care projects, including applied research, pilot programs, or demonstration and evaluation projects.

Requirements All doctoral and medical students enrolled in Michigan universities are eligible. For consideration, the proposed project must focus geographically on the state of Michigan and address the BCBSM Foundation's objectives.

Restrictions Completed or substantially completed dissertations or research projects are not eligible. Students who previously received this award are not eligible. Blue Cross and Blue Shield of Michigan affiliates and subsidiaries are not eligible. Investigation of pharmaceutical efficacy, basic research or research involving non-human subjects is not eligible. Grant monies are not intended to support field placements, practica or internships.

Amount $3000

Date(s) Application Is Due Apr 30.

Contact Program Officer, (313) 225-8706; email: foundation@bcbsm.com

Internet http://www.bcbsm.com/foundation/

Sponsor Blue Cross Blue Shield of Michigan Foundation
Program Officer, Student Award Program, BCBSM Foundation, 600 Lafayette East-X520
Detroit, MI 48226

BCBSM Grants **988**

The foundation is dedicated to improving individual and community health by offering grants that support Michigan-based research and innovative health programs. The focus is to enhance quality and appropriate use of health care services; improve access to appropriate health services; control healthcare costs; and support a socially responsible public health agenda. Approximately $3 million is available annually for grants to support the healthcare-related work of Michigan's researchers and nonprofit community organizations. The foundation supports research, fosters community solutions to critical health care problems, acknowledges excellence in research, and supports medical and doctoral students interested in health care.

Requirements Applicants must be based in Michigan.

Amount $3 million total

Contact Program Officer, (313) 225-8706; fax: (313) 225-7730; email: foundation@bcbsm.com

Internet http://www.bcbsm.com/foundation

Sponsor Blue Cross Blue Shield of Michigan
600 E Lafayette Blvd, MC X520
Detroit, MI 48226

BCBSM Investigator-Initiated Research Program Grants **989**

This program encourages Michigan-based research projects that focus on the cost of health care, quality of health care, and access to health care, including: organization and delivery of health care services; evaluation of new methods or approaches to containing health care costs; evaluation of new methods or approaches to providing access to high-quality health care; assessment and assurance of quality care; and identification and validation of clinical protocols and practice guidelines. Exceptional projects will be considered for multiyear funding or funding requests in excess of $75,000.

Amount $50,000-$75,000 per year

Contact Grants Administrator, (313) 225-8706; fax: (313) 225-7730; email: foundation@bcbsm.com

Internet http://www.bcbsm.com/foundation/gp_iip.shtml

Sponsor Blue Cross Blue Shield of Michigan Foundation
600 Lafayette East, X520
Detroit, MI 48226

BCBSM Physician-Investigator Research Awards **990**

This program is for physicians who have an interest in health and medical care research. The purpose is to provide seed money to physicians to explore the merits of a potential research idea. The proposed project might be in the form of a pilot study, feasibility study, or a small research study. Grants are available for research related to the quality of care, cost, and appropriate access to health and medical care.

Requirements The foundation seeks applications from physicians interested in research, who are licensed and domiciled in the state of Michigan. Applicants may include physicians working in research environments such as medical schools or university-affiliated hospitals, health care systems, as well as physicians working in nonprofit agencies or in private practice.

Restrictions The program does not support basic science, biomedical research including drug studies, or studies using animals

Amount $10,000

Contact Dr. Nora Maloy, Senior Program Officer, (313) 225-8706; email: foundation@bcbsm.com

Internet http://www.bcbsm.com/foundation/gp_pira.shtml

Sponsor Blue Cross Blue Shield of Michigan Foundation
600 Lafayette E, X520
Detroit, MI 48226

BCBSM Women's Health Early Detection Grants **991**

The goal of the initiative is to increase the early detection of disease among Michigan women through the support of research or demonstration/evaluation projects. Proposals must concentrate on increasing detection of breast and cervical cancer, hypertension and cardiovascular disease, diabetes, or sexually transmitted diseases. Proposed projects should be designed to increase appropriate screens, referrals, and follow-ups. The foundation encourages applicants to focus on low-income, uninsured women who live in geographically or culturally remote areas, older women, racial and ethnic minorities, and women with disabilities. Projects should be based on clinically accepted guidelines. The listed application deadline is for letters of intent.

Requirements Michigan 501(c)3 nonprofit or educational entities are eligible.

Amount $75,000-$100,000

Date(s) Application Is Due Apr 15.

Contact Dr. Nora Maloy, Senior Program Officer, (313) 225-8706; fax: (313) 225-7730; email: foundation@bcbsm.com

Internet http://www.bcbsm.com/foundation/grant_programs.shtml

Sponsor Blue Cross Blue Shield of Michigan
600 Lafayette East, X520
Detroit, MI 48226

BCBSNC Foundation Grants **992**

The foundation's primary objective is to fund clearly defined, innovative grants that further the foundation mission of improving the health and well-being of North Carolinians. The foundation typically funds: programs and/or services designed to produce measurable, long-term impact; programs that are sustainable and designed to be ongoing, rather than one-time or sporadic events; programs and/or services that are replicable. The three primary focus areas include health of vulnerable populations, healthy active communities and community impact through nonprofit excellence.

Requirements Applicants must meet the following criteria to be eligible for funding: organization is located within North Carolina; organization is a 501(c)(3) organization or an educational or governmental entity with tax-exempt status, that is not a private foundation or Type III supporting organization; organization must be able to provide its most recent IRS Form 990. Depending on the type of grant and the size of the organization, an audit may be required as part of the submitted proposal.

Restrictions The foundation will not provide funding for annual campaigns, political campaigns, religious purposes, individuals, endowments, purchase of advertisements, or for the sole purpose of receiving goods or entitlements from a charitable organization.

Contact Grant Review Committee, (919) 765-7347; email: foundation@bcbsnc.com

Internet http://www.bcbsnc.com/foundation/grants.html?previouslyOver=true¤tlyOver=true

Sponsor Blue Cross Blue Shield of North Carolina Foundation
P.O. Box 2291
Durham, NC 27702

BCRF Research Grants **993**
The goal of the grant process is a serious peer review of all proposals. Proposals are invited by the Medical Advisory Board, rather than accepted as unsolicited requests. The MAB generally reviews proposals in the late summer. There is no set format, but the BCRF requests a brief narrative (no more than 4-5 pages), lay language summary, annual budget (no more than $225,000 initially, with a maximum of 20% in indirect costs) and budget narrative. Considerable latitude is given to the investigators in terms of the work proposed. Both the Board of Directors and the Medical Advisory Board concur that some of the most important advances in understanding the disease will most likely occur by enabling brilliant minds to pursue some of their most creative theories.
Restrictions While most of the grants are unrestricted, the Foundation has donors requesting restricted grants for specific purposes. When this occurs, the Medical Advisory Board will meet to determine whether the area of interest merits further exploration. If so, they will identify various research projects meeting the donor's criteria.
Amount $225,000 maximum
Contact Program Administrator, (646) 497-2600; fax: (646) 497-0890; email: bcrf@bcrfcure.org
Internet http://www.bcrfcure.org/rese_meet_grantapp.html
Sponsor Breast Cancer Research Foundation
60 East 56th Street, 8th Floor
New York, NY 10022

BCRF-AACR Grants for Translational Breast Cancer Research **994**
The grants will provide direct support for innovative cancer research projects designed to accelerate the discovery, development, and application of new agents to treat breast cancer and/or for pre-clinical research with direct therapeutic intent. Special emphasis will be placed on research that holds promise for leading to individualized therapeutic options for treatment in the near future.
Requirements Researchers who are affiliated with any institution involved in cancer research, cancer medicine, or cancer-related biomedical science anywhere in the world may apply. There are no geographic, national, or residency status restrictions. Applicants must have acquired a doctoral degree in a related field. If an applicant has obtained an equivalent degree at a foreign institution, information on the nature of the degree must be provided at the time of application.
Restrictions Employees or subcontractors of a national government or the for-profit private industry are not eligible to serve as the Principal Investigator for the purpose of these grants. However, collaborations with such individuals are encouraged. Neither the members of the Scientific Review Committee nor the members of their individual laboratories are eligible for these grants.
Amount $225,000 maximum
Date(s) Application Is Due May 17.
Contact Julia Laurence, Staff Assistant, (267) 646-0655; fax: (215) 440-9372; email: laurence@aacr.org
Internet http://www.aacr.org/home/scientists/travel-grants--research-funding/research-funding/bcrf-aacr-grants.aspx
Sponsor Breast Cancer Research Foundation and the American Association for Cancer Research
615 Chestnut Street, 17th Floor
Philadelphia, PA 19106-4404

Beatrice Laing Trust Grants **995**
The trust was founded for the relief of poverty and for the advancement of the evangelical faith internationally. Grants are awarded for general charitable purposes at the discretion of the Trustees, with an emphasis on social services and relief, and medical aid and research. Grant recipients typically are charities working in deprived sections of the community in the United Kingdom, to missionary societies and, less frequently, to individuals working in the field of missions in United Kingdom and abroad.
Contact Trust Administrator, 020 8238 8890; fax: 020 8238 8897
Sponsor Beatrice Laing Trust
33 Bunns Ln
London NW7 2DX United Kingdom

Beckman Coulter Community Relations Grants **996**
The corporation funds nonprofit organizations, charities and educational institutions that support and promote progress and interest in the areas of science, research-related health care and science education in our plant and customer communities.
Requirements Organizations seeking funding should submit a letter of request providing the following information: full legal name of the organization; brief description of the organization, including a mission statement and services provided; amount requested; description of how the funds will be used. Additional attachments should include: history of previous support by Beckman Coulter; description of any involvement by Beckman Coulter employees; statement as to why you consider Beckman Coulter an appropriate donor; list of governing board members.
Restrictions Grants do not support golf tournaments, galas, or religious or political activities.
Contact Cathy Doherty, Community Relations, (714) 961-4478
Internet http://www.beckman.com/hr/ourcompany/oc_communityRelations.asp#
Sponsor Beckman Coulter Corporation
Community Relations, Beckman Coulter, Inc., 200 S. Kraemer Boulevard
Brea, CA 92821

Beckman Scholars Program Grants **997**
The Program is an invited program for accredited universities and four-year colleges in the United States. It provides scholarships that contribute significantly in advancing the education, research training and personal development of select students in chemistry, biochemistry, and the biological and medical sciences. The sustained, in-depth undergraduate research experiences and comprehensive faculty mentoring are unique in terms of program scope, content and level of scholarship awards. The amount given is $19,300 for two summers and one academic year.
Amount $19,300
Contact Program Administrator, (949) 721-2222; fax: (949) 721-2225; email: beckmanscholars@beckman-foundation.com or k.williams@beckman-foundation.com
Internet http://www.beckman-foundation.com/bsp.html
Sponsor Arnold and Mabel Beckman Foundation
100 Academy Drive
Irvine, CA 92617

Beckman Young Investigators Program Grants **998**
The foundation makes grants to nonprofit research institutions to promote research in chemistry and the life sciences, broadly interpreted, and particularly to foster the invention of methods, instruments, and materials that will open up new avenues of research in science. The program is intended to provide research support to the most promising young faculty members in the early stages of academic careers in the chemical and life sciences. The program is open to persons with tenure-track appointments in academic and nonprofit institutions that conduct fundamental research in the chemical and life sciences. The program is intended primarily for US institutions. Only proposals of exceptional merit from foreign institutions will receive consideration. Projects are normally funded for a period of two years. When extraordinary circumstances warrant, support may be provided over a one-year or three-year period. Application materials are available on the Web site.
Requirements To be eligible, an applicant should not have completed more than three full years in his or her tenure-track or other comparable independent research appointment on the anniversary date of initial appointment in the year in which application is to be made. Individuals may not apply more than three times.
Restrictions Funding will not be considered for general institutional expenses or general fund-raising campaign expenses such as dinners and mass mailings. The foundation does not provide funds for overhead or indirect costs.
Amount $264,000 average
Date(s) Application Is Due Sep 28.
Contact Program Administrator, (949) 721-2222; fax: (949) 721-2225; email: younginvestigators@beckman-foundation.com or k.williams@beckman-foundation.com
Internet http://www.beckman-foundation.com/byi_guides.html
Sponsor Arnold and Mabel Beckman Foundation
100 Academy Drive
Irvine, CA 92617

Becton Dickinson and Company Grants **999**
The company supports national and international activities in keeping with its commitment to advance the quality of medical practice and patient care in four areas: the global healthcare fund; the local initiatives fund; the matching gifts program; and the BD product donation program. Call for guidelines.
Contact Community Relations, (201) 847-6800
Internet http://www.bd.com/responsibility/contributions
Sponsor Becton Dickinson and Company
1 Becton Drive
Franklin Lakes, NJ 07417

Bedding Plants Foundation Horticulture Scholarships **1000**
Scholarships are available to graduate students in the following categories: majors in horticulture or related fields with a specific interest in bedding or flowering potted plants; students interested in international horticulture marketing; work/study abroad programs; students who intern or work for public gardens; and students in horticulture with a business emphasis or business with a horticulture emphasis. Application for all scholarships is available from the BPFI office, or students may apply via Fastweb.com.
Amount $500-$2000 range
Date(s) Application Is Due May 1.
Contact William Willbrandt, Executive Director, (517) 333-4617; fax: (517) 333-4494; email: first@firstinfloriculture.org
Internet http://www.firstinfloriculture.org/scholarships.htm
Sponsor Bedding Plants Foundation
P.O. Box 280
Lansing, MI 48826

Bedding Plants Foundation Research Grants **1001**
Grants provide funding for scientific research related to the production of bedding and potted plants. Topics include genetic engineering for diseases and insect resistance, management of greenhouse waste, increasing product shelf life and garden life, evaluation of biocontrol methods and techniques, water recirculation and reuse, water quality/alkalinity control, IPM in the greenhouse, insect problems (aphids, whitefly,

thrips, fungus gnats), disease problems (botrytis, damping off, root rot, tomato spotted wilt virus, pythium), energy efficient greenhouse designs, and evaluation of alternative media.
Requirements Work must be carried out by a nonprofit organization with IRS tax-exempt status.
Restrictions The foundation does not fund overhead or travel expenses.
Amount $100,000 average total
Date(s) Application Is Due Jan 15.
Contact Executive Director, (517) 333-4617; fax: (517) 333-4494; email: bpfi@aol.com
Sponsor Bedding Plants Foundation
P.O. Box 280
Lansing, MI 48826

Beez Foundation Grants **1002**
The foundation's mission is to raise money for pediatric brain cancer research and pediatric patient services. Research and/or support grants are awarded for brain cancer research projects or studies that are designed to advance the treatment, cure, outcome, and etiology of pediatric brain cancer; and any patient services that are focused on making the lives of children with cancer and their families a little easier. The foundation's particular interest is in the initial funding of projects that are likely to generate data that can be used in larger scale projects or studies. Preference is made to pediatric cancer-related requests. Applicants are requested to forward a one-page summary (in Microsoft Word or Adobe Acrobat format), the amount requested, and how the funds will be spent.
Amount $40,000 total
Date(s) Application Is Due Nov 20.
Contact Grants Administrator, (732) 563-1144; email: proposals@beezfoundation.org
Internet http://www.beezfoundation.org/Pages/Grants.html
Sponsor Beez Foundation
26 H Worlds Fair Dr
Somerset, NJ 08873

Beim Foundation Grants **1003**
The foundation awards grants to eligible nonprofit organizations in its areas of interest, including arts and culture, environmental conservation, education, and social services. Types of support include program grants, general operating grants, capital campaigns, building construction/renovation, land acquisition, equipment acquisition, and seed grants. High priority is given to the following types of projects: capital drives and equipment purchases; innovative start-up programs that require a moderate amount of grant money; intergenerational projects that involve community service; cooperative projects that involve several agencies or volunteers; on-going programs that have proven themselves unique and essential; matching funds drives. Low priority is given to the following types of projects: medical research, debt retirement, national fundraising programs, and requests from public schools and governmental agencies due to the lack of good financial data. Deadlines are February 3 for education, and human services; and July 3 for arts, arts small capital equipment, and environment.
Requirements 501(c)3 tax-exempt organizations located within Minnesota, as well as the city of Denver, CO; counties of Park and Gallatin in Montana; county of Santa Fe in New Mexico; and county of Cumberland in Maine are eligible.
Restrictions The foundation does not fund individuals; private foundations; political organizations or campaigns; religious organizations, including schools, except for secular human service activities; memberships, subscriptions, tickets for benefits, conferences, fundraising events, or annual campaigns; organizations that have as a substantial part of their purpose the influencing of legislation; endowment; multi-year commitments; or international efforts.
Amount $2000-$10,000 average
Date(s) Application Is Due Jan 17; Jul 18.
Contact Grants Administrator, (612) 605-8192; email: contact@beimfoundation.org
Internet http://www.beimfoundation.org/guide.html
Sponsor Beim Foundation
3109 W 50th St, Ste 120
Minneapolis, MN 55410-2102

Beinecke Library Resident Fellowships **1004**
The Beinecke Rare Book and Manuscript Library offers short-term fellowships to support visiting scholars pursuing postdoctoral or equivalent research in its collections. The library is Yale's principal repository for literary papers, and for early manuscripts and rare books in the fields of literature, theology, history, and the natural sciences. The fellowships, which pay for travel costs to and from New Haven and a living allowance, are designed to provide access to the library for scholars who live outside the greater New Haven area. Fellowships, normally granted for one month, must be taken up between September and May. Recipients are expected to be in residence during the period of their award and are encouraged to participate in the activities of Yale University. Successful applicants normally explain in extensive and specific detail the relationship of the Beinecke collections to the project and the significance of the project to its larger field of scholarly concern. Application form and guidelines are available online.
Restrictions Students enrolled in degree programs are ineligible.
Amount $3800 for one month plus travel
Date(s) Application Is Due Dec 15.
Contact Program Contact, Beinecke Rare Book and Manuscript Library, (203) 432-2956; fax: (203) 432-4047; email: beinecke.fellowships@yale.edu
Internet http://www.library.yale.edu/beinecke/brbleduc/brblapplyvisiting.html
Sponsor Yale University Library
Box 208240, Yale Station
New Haven, CT 06520-8240

Bell Labs Graduate Research Fellowship Program **1005**
The fellowship program is designed to increase the number of minorities and women in the fields of science, math, engineering, and technology. Students must be pursuing full-time doctoral studies in the following disciplines: chemical engineering, chemistry, communications science, computer science/engineering, electrical engineering, information science, materials science, mathematics, mechanical engineering, operations research, physics, and statistics. The fellowship provides an annual stipend, book allotment, and conference travel expenses. Fellowships will be renewed on a yearly basis for up to four years of graduate study, subject to the participant's satisfactory progress toward the doctoral degree.
Requirements Fellowships are awarded to women and members of a minority group currently underrepresented in the sciences who are US citizens or permanent residents. The program is primarily directed to graduating college seniors, but applications from first-year graduate students will be considered. Candidates are selected on the basis of scholastic attainment in their fields of specialization, and other evidence of their ability and potential as research scientists. Students are eligible when pursuing full-time doctoral studies in various mathematic and scientific fields. Fellowship recipients may not accept any other full fellowship support.
Amount $17,000 stipend; $250 book allowance; $1000 travel
Date(s) Application Is Due Jan 13.
Contact Lucent Fellowship Program, (908) 582-7906; email: coopgraduate@lucent.com
Internet http://www.lucent.com/news/foundation/blgrfp/index.html
Sponsor Lucent Technologies Foundation
600 Mountain Ave, Rm 6F4
Murray Hill, NJ 07974

Benign Essential Blepharospasm Research Grants **1006**
The foundation supports research to find the cause and cure for benign essential blepharospasm/meige and related disorders of the facial musculature. A number of grants are issued annually. Proposals detailing research projects to be considered for support are welcomed.
Amount $150,000 maximum
Date(s) Application Is Due Jul 1.
Contact Office Manager (409) 832-0788; fax: (409) 832-0890; email: bebrf@blepharospasm.org
Internet http://www.blepharospasm.org/res-prop.html
Sponsor Benign Essential Blepharospasm Research Foundation
P.O. Box 12468
Beaumont, TX 77726-2468

Berea College Appalachian Music Fellowships **1007**
The program is designed to support graduate students, faculty, public school teachers, and/or performers for a period of one to six months in order to conduct research in Berea's collection of noncommercial traditional music and to promote the preservation of and access to that music. Proposals should address the applicant's background and interest in Appalachian music, the reason(s) for seeking an opportunity for concentrated study in Berea's traditional music collections, anticipated contribution to the preservation or promotion of these musical resources (e.g., assistance with sound digitization; website development; writing contextual historical summaries, biographies, musical annotations; public performances, publications), and the length of time needed for the project (one month minimum, six months maximum). Contact information for three references should be included with proposals. Guidelines are available online. The fellowships must be taken up between January and August 2006. Fellows are expected to be in residence during the term of the fellowship.
Restrictions Berea College employees are ineligible.
Amount $5000
Date(s) Application Is Due Dec 5.
Contact Steve Gowler, (859) 985-3272; email: steve_gowler@berea.edu
Internet http://www.berea.edu/hutchinslibrary/specialcollections/MusicFellowship2006.asp
Sponsor Berea College
Berea, KY 40404

Berks County Community Foundation Grants **1008**
The foundation supports a broad range of community projects in this Pennsylvania county, including the arts and culture, economic development, education, the environment, and health and human services. Types of support include general operating grants, capital campaigns, demonstration grants, seed grants, and program grants. Although applicants do not have to be located in Berks County, they must provide programs and services within the county.
Requirements Tax exempt or public benefit organizations, individuals, associations and private or public agencies are eligible to apply. The grant must be used for charitable purposes only. Organizations are eligible to apply to more than one grant program in the same year.

Contact Richard Mappin, Vice President for Grantmaking, (610) 685-2223; fax: (610) 685-2240; email: info@bccf.org
Internet http://www.bccf.org
Sponsor Berks County Community Foundation
P.O. Box 212, 501 Washington Street, Suite 801
Reading, PA 19603-0212

Berlex Foundation Reproductive Scientist Development Program Grants 1009
The program supports the postdoctoral career development of young obstetrician-gynecologists who are committed to careers in academic medicine. Grants support two to three years of full-time research under the mentorship of internationally recognized senior scientists. Applicants should contact Dr. Robert Jaffee, University of California, San Francisco, Box 0922, San Francisco, CA 94145-0922, (415) 476-9047.
Amount $25,000 annually
Contact Grants Administrator, (201) 342-4441; email: llisanti@berlex-foundation.org
Internet http://www.berlex-foundation.org/aw04.asp
Sponsor Berlex Foundation
433 Hackensack Ave, 9th Fl
Hackensack, NJ 07601

Berlex Foundation Scholar Award in Basic Science Research 1010
The award provides the opportunity for clinician-investigators who wish to initiate new studies or who are currently conducting promising basic research in the area of reproductive medicine to continue work on their projects for an additional year. One or more awards may be made annually.
Requirements Candidates must have completed an approved residency or fellowship in the field of obstetrics/gynecology. The applicant should be junior faculty. If not yet faculty, the individual should have reasonable assurance of such a position within a department of obstetrics and gynecology as evidenced by a Letter of Endorsement from the department head.
Restrictions Candidates who are in an active training program as of January 1 are ineligible.
Amount $40,000 to the scholar; $10,000 for laboratory support
Date(s) Application Is Due Oct 1.
Contact Grants Administrator, (201) 342-4441; email: llisanti@berlex-foundation.org
Internet http://www.berlex-foundation.org/aw01.asp
Sponsor Berlex Foundation
433 Hackensack Ave, 9th Fl
Hackensack, NJ 07628

Berlex Foundation Scholar Award in Clinical Research 1011
The award is intended to support studies that are specifically focused on clinical research in obstetrics and gynecology. Its goal is to promote excellent clinical research by young investigators in the areas of diagnosis, treatment, and prognosis. The foundation plans to give more weight to proposals that incorporate more rigorous methods such as randomized controlled trials. Analytic studies, including cohort and case-control studies, also may be considered. One or more awards may be presented annually. Support is awarded to the institution in which the recipient will conduct the research. The recipient must identify the total amount required to complete the study and designate the specific allocation of funds. It is expected that the candidate devote a minimum of 50 percent of his/her time to the research activity.
Requirements Candidates must have full-time faculty appointments in schools of medicine or public health. Preference will be given to proposals by academicians who are early in their careers.
Restrictions Applicants should not currently be in training programs. The foundation is not seeking proposals for descriptive studies. This award is not intended for support of basic science research or animal studies.
Amount $50,000 maximum awarded to the institution
Date(s) Application Is Due Oct 1.
Contact Svetlana Lisanti, Administrator, (201) 342-4441; email: llisanti@berlex-foundation.org
Internet http://www.berlex-foundation.org/aw02.asp
Sponsor Berlex Foundation
433 Hackensack Ave, 9th Fl
Hackensack, NJ 07628

Bernard and Audre Rapoport Foundation Grants 1012
The mission of the foundation is to support programs that have the broadest possible impact in meeting important human needs and aspirations, with an emphasis on the needs of the least advantaged members of society. Preference is given to five primary areas: education, including early learning through the elementary years, adult education and training initiatives, and programs that enhance the capabilities of teachers and other professionals in public schools; arts and culture, especially activities that encourage the participation and enrich the lives of children and disadvantaged members of the community; healthcare-- especially services to women, children, and those who do not have access to conventional medical resources; community-based outreach initiatives such as immunization programs; community building and social services--i.e., programs that build grassroots neighborhood networks, provide job training and job opportunities for the unemployed and underemployed, or provide a comprehensive safety net of social services for the least advantaged citizens; democracy and civic participation--efforts to make government more responsive, encourage citizens to take an active interest and role in political life, encourage intergovernmental cooperation, broaden public awareness of public policy issues and alternatives, build skills necessary for political leadership, and provide opportunities for community service; and Rapoport Service Scholarships at the University of Texas at Austin. There are no deadlines for proposals.
Requirements Applicant must provide proof of tax exempt status.
Contact Carole Jones, (254) 741-0510; fax: (254) 741-0092; email: carole@rapoportfdn.org
Internet http://www.rapoportfdn.org/priorities.asp
Sponsor Bernard and Audre Rapoport Foundation
5400 Bosque Boulevard, Suite 245
Waco, TX 76710

Bernard B. Brodie Award in Drug Metabolism 1013
This biennial award (even-numbered years), established by CIBA-GEIGY Corporation to honor the fundamental contributions of Bernard B. Brodie, is presented to recognize outstanding original research contributions in drug metabolism and disposition, particularly those having a major impact on future research in the field. Only one nominator is necessary although more are acceptable. Nominations must be received by the deadline prior to the award year.
Requirements Nominees must be members of ASPET; nominators need not be members of ASPET.
Restrictions Supporting research accomplishments must not have been used to win any other major award.
Amount $2000
Date(s) Application Is Due Sep 15.
Contact Dr. Christine Carrico, Executive Officer, (301) 530-7060; fax: (301) 530-7061; email: ccarrico@aspet.faseb.org
Internet http://www.aspet.org/public/awards/brodie_award.html
Sponsor American Society for Pharmacology and Experimental Therapeutics
9650 Rockville Pike
Bethesda, MD 20814-3995

Bernard F. Langer Nuclear Codes and Standards Award 1014
Recognition of an individual(s) who has contributed to the nuclear power plant industry through the development and promotion of ASME nuclear codes and standards or the ASME nuclear certification program is made through the presentation of this award. The award includes a bronze plaque and certificate.
Requirements Any individual member, group of members, or committee may nominate candidates.
Amount $1000
Date(s) Application Is Due Feb 1.
Contact Award Administrator, (212) 591-7158; fax: (212) 591-7739; email: soukupd@asme.org
Internet http://www.asme.org/honors/ms71/saa/langer.html
Sponsor American Society of Mechanical Engineers
3 Park Ave
New York, NY 10016

Bernard L. Schwartz Fellows Program 1015
The foundation awards a number of fellowships to help individuals establish themselves as credible new voices in the country's public debate. Regular and senior fellowships are available. Fellowships are awarded for one year, subject to renewal. Fellows choosing to work out of the Washington, DC, office will receive fully equipped offices, health benefits, research and editorial assistance, and the opportunity to formulate their ideas in a well-knit community. Applications are available on the Web site.
Requirements Regular fellows show promise in writing for student, academic, or popular publications, but have yet to establish themselves as leading commentators. Senior fellows are generally established academics, policy analysts, or journalists wishing to make departures in their work.
Amount $25,000-$45,000 fellowships; $75,000 maximum stipend for senior fellows
Contact Sherle Schwenninger, Program Director, (202) 986-2700; fax: (202) 986-3696; email: schwenninger@newamerica.net
Internet http://www.newamerica.net/index.cfm?pg=fellows
Sponsor New America Foundation
1630 Connecticut Ave NW, 7th Fl
Washington, DC 20009

Bernard Lowy Fund for the Study of Tropical Botany in Latin America 1016
The Department of Plant Biology of Louisiana State University (LSU) and the family of the late mycologist, Bernard Lowy, established the Bernard Lowy Fund for the Study of Tropical Botany in Latin America. The fund is designed to provide much-needed additional funding for research travel by graduate students and postdoctoral researchers studying diverse aspects of tropical botany in Latin America.
Requirements Applicant either must be studying or working at a university or research organization in Latin America or be studying, working at, or have received the doctoral degree from LSU at Baton Rouge. Support for applicants from Latin American institutions is for travel and living expenses for research conducted at LSU. These applicants must seek sponsorship from a faculty member in the Plant Biology Department at LSU.
Amount $1000 maximum

Date(s) Application Is Due May 1.
Contact Dr. Meredith Blackwell, Lowy Fund Committee, (225) 388-1557; fax: (504) 388-8459; email: mblackwell@lsu.edu
Sponsor Bernard Lowy Fund
Dept of Plant Biology, Louisiana State University
Baton Rouge, LA 70803-1705

Bernard Van Leer Foundation Grants **1017**
The foundation operates in 34 countries in Europe, the Far East, Australia, Central and South America, the United States, and Africa to further the holistic development of young children. Grantmaking focuses on thematic initiatives, which may include partners from countries where the foundation does not otherwise have a grantmaking program. Current themes are: children affected by HIV/AIDS; respect for diversity; and growing up in indigenous societies. The foundation funds projects that promote a holistic approach to early childhood development; the enhancement of parental capacity to support their children's development; a development strategy that is rooted in the local context and is culturally, socially, and economically appropriate; and the building of capacity, local ownership, and working in partnership. Unsolicited proposals are rarely funded. To be considered, submit information about the organization; the project's objectives, strategies, beneficiaries, scope, location, and duration; and the overall budget and the amount required.
Requirements Grants are made to governmental and nongovernmental organizations located in the list of eligible countries, which include: Brazil, Colombia, the East Caribbean region, Germany, Greece, India, Indonesia, Israel, Kenya, Mexico, Morocco, the Netherlands, Peru, Poland, South Africa, Tanzania, Thailand, Turkey, Uganda, United States of America and Zimbabwe.
Restrictions The foundation does not fund applications for support to individual children; projects that concentrate solely on one aspect of children's development or learning; projects that specifically focus on children with special needs such as mental and/or physical handicap; proposals for the construction and maintenance of buildings, or the purchase of equipment and materials; isolated requests for scholarships, conferences, media or theatre events; or general support to organisations, recurrent costs or deficits
Contact Peter Laugharn, Executive Director, 31-70-351-20-40; fax: 31-70-350-23-73; email: proposal.administration@bvleerf.nl
Internet http://www.bernardvanleer.org/about/Applications_for_funding
Sponsor Bernard Van Leer Foundation
Eisenhowerlaan 156, P.O. Box 82334
The Hague 2508 EH
The Netherlands

Bersted Foundation Grants **1018**
The foundation awards grants to Illinois nonprofit organizations in response to changing community needs. Areas of interest include health care and mental health, social services, children and youth services, family services, the economically disadvantaged and homeless, community development, and environment. Types of support include scientific research, general operating support, continuing support, building construction/ renovation, and technical assistance. The board meets in January, April, July, and October. Submit a letter of request detailing the request and organization.
Requirements Illinois tax-exempt organizations in DeKalb, DuPage, Kane, and McHenry Counties are eligible.
Restrictions Grants do not support religious houses of worship, institutions of higher education, endowment funds, or deficit financing.
Amount $5000-$35,000 average
Contact M.Catherine Ryan, (312) 828-1785
Sponsor Bersted Foundation
231 S LaSalle St
Chicago, IL 60697

Bethesda Foundation Grants **1019**
The foundation awards grants to nonprofits in Hornell, NY, in its areas of interest, including education, hospitals, health care, substance abuse services, nutrition, AIDS research, and social services. Types of support include general operating support, equipment acquisition, program development, and scholarship funds. The board meets in March, June, September, and December.
Requirements Nonprofit organizations in Hornell, NY, are eligible.
Amount $1000-$24,000
Contact Grants Administrator, (513) 745-1616; fax: (513) 745-1623; email: bethesdafoundation@trihealth.com
Internet http://www.bethesdafoundation.com
Sponsor Bethesda Foundation
10506 Montgomery Rd, Ste 304
Cincinnati, OH 45242

Bettina Bahlsen Memorial Graduate Scholarship **1020**
The scholarship competition is open to full-time graduate students registered in or eligible to register in the Department of Biological Sciences at the university in the field of cellular, molecular, microbial, or biochemical biology. Selection will be based on academic excellence. Preference will be accorded to a foreign student and, if possible, to a student entering the first year of graduate studies. The scholarship is awarded annually for one-year duration with possibility of renewal in open competition.
Requirements To be eligible applicants must be graduate students in the department of biological sciences
Amount $C17,500 maximum
Date(s) Application Is Due Feb 1.
Contact Connie Baines, Faculty of Graduate Studies, (403) 220-5690; email: cbaines@ucalgary.ca
Internet http://www.grad.ucalgary.ca/funding/internal_scholarships/lev_4/bahlsen_bettina.htm
Sponsor University of Calgary
2500 University Dr NW, Earth Sciences Bldg, Rm 720
Calgary, AB T2N 1N4 Canada

Beverly Willis Architecture Foundation Grants and Fellowships **1021**
The foundation offers funding to individuals and institutions to support innovative projects that advance the study and expand the recognition of women in architecture and related professions, and that lead to the dissemination of this knowledge to professional and public audiences alike. Grant funding is divided into the following categories: fellowships for scholarly research, publication, exhibition, or documentary in film or other media; and grants for honoraria to plenary session speakers at professional meetings, conferences, or symposia whose focus matches the mission of BWAF; and travel grants for research trips or professional conferences at which the recipient will be making a presentation related to the purpose of the BWAF. Successful candidates receive their fellowship awards in two equal installments. Applicants are strongly encouraged to send a preliminary inquiry to the director regarding their proposal and its eligibility for funding. Application guidelines are available online. Although not mandatory, applicants are encouraged to send a preliminary inquiry to the Director of BWAF regarding their proposal and its eligibility for funding.
Requirements Applications should contain, as their cover page, a summary sheet that includes the following: project title; name, address, telephone number, and email address of the applicant; a concise abstract (150 words or less) of the proposed project; a specific amount (in US dollars) sought from the Foundation; a description of the anticipated final product(s) that would result from the proposed project, including plans for distribution of the completed work; names and contact information of the people from who letters of support have been requested. Tax-exempt organizations must include with their grant request a copy of the IRS Determination Letter, which indicates the particular paragraph of the Internal Revenue Code that governs their exempt activities.
Amount $10,000 maximum fellowships; $3000 maximum grants; $1500 maximum travel
Date(s) Application Is Due Mar 15.
Contact Director, (212) 577-1200; email: director@bwaf.org
Internet http://www.bwaf.org/grants.html
Sponsor Beverly Willis Architecture Foundation
2 Columbus Avenue, Suite 3A
New York, NY 10023

BFGoodrich Collegiate Inventors Prize **1022**
The national competition is designed to encourage undergraduate and graduate college students active in science, technology, and creative invention, while stimulating their problem-solving abilities. Prizes are awarded to recognize students and their faculty advisors for research and innovative discoveries that can be patented. Winners are honored alongside inductees of the National Inventors Hall of Fame in September.
Requirements Students enrolled full-time in any US college or university as of the date of entry submission are eligible to participate.
Amount $30,000 maximum total
Date(s) Application Is Due Sep 1.
Contact Ray DePuy, (330) 849-6887; email: rdepuy@invent.org
Internet http://www.invent.org/collegiate/overview.html
Sponsor BFGoodrich Collegiate Inventors Program
221 S Broadway St
Akron, OH 43308-1505

BIA Native American Graduate Student Fellowships **1023**
Graduate fellowship grants are provided to supplement financial assistance to eligible American Indian/Alaska Native students pursuing a postbaccalaureate degree. OIEP contracts with the American Indian Graduate Center (AIGC). Application requirements and time frames for submitting an application are available with the AIGC by calling (505) 881-4584, writing to 4520 Montgomery Blvd NE, Ste 1-B, Albuquerque, NM 87109, or visiting their web site at www.aigc.com.
Requirements Graduate fellowship grants are available to individuals who are pursuing a master's or doctorate degree as a full time student at a US accredited graduate school; able to demonstrate financial need; and an enrolled member of a federally recognized American Indian tribe or Alaskan Native group, or possess one- fourth degree federally recognized Indian blood.
Contact American Indian Higher Education Grant Program, (202) 208-3478; fax: (202) 208-3312
Internet http://www.aigc.com/fellowship-application/what-is-graduate-education.html
Sponsor Bureau of Indian Affairs
1849 C St NW, MS 3512 MIB
Washington, DC 20240

Bibliographical Society of America Fellowships 1024

Short-term (one- or two-month) fellowships are available in support of bibliographical inquiry as well as research in the history of the book trades and in publishing history. Topics may concentrate on books and documents in any field but should focus on the book or manuscript as historical evidence, whether for establishing a text or understanding the history of book production, publication, distribution, collection, or consumption. Stipends support travel, living, and research expenses.
Amount $2000 maximum per month
Date(s) Application Is Due Dec 1.
Contact Executive Secretary, (212) 452-2710; fax: (212) 452-2710
Internet http://www.bibsocamer.org
Sponsor Bibliographical Society of America
P.O. Box 1537, Lennox Hill Sta
New York, NY 10021

Bilateral Scholarships 1025

Scholarships are offered for three to nine months to foreign students, research workers, and specialists in various fields for studies and research in Finland on a reciprocal basis to nationals of the following countries: Australia, Austria, Belgium, Bulgaria, Canada, China, Cuba, Czech Republic, Denmark, Egypt, France, Germany, Great Britain, Greece, Hungary, Iceland, India, Ireland, Israel, Italy, Japan, Luxembourg, Mexico, Mongolia, the Netherlands, Norway, Poland, Portugal, Republic of Korea, Romania, Slovakia, Spain, Sweden, Switzerland, Turkey, and the United States. Application must be made on a form obtainable from the diplomatic representatives or directly from CIMO.
Requirements Applicant must have been awarded a degree at a university or institute of higher education in his/her own country; applicant must also have a working knowledge of Finnish, Swedish, English, or German. Selection of scholars is primarily in the hands of the relevant authorities in the candidate's own country who will make the selection and propose the candidates to the Ministry of Education for final approval.
Restrictions Scholars may not do full-time paid work during the scholarship period.
Contact Ulla-Maija Anttila, Exchanges Coordinator, 358-9-7747 7680; helpline: 358-1080-6767; email: cimoinfo@cimo.fi
Internet http://www.cimo.fi/Resource.phx/cimo/services/scholarships.htx
Sponsor Center for International Mobility (CIMO)
P.O. Box 343, Hakaniemenkatu 2
Helsinki 00531 Finland

Bill & Melinda Gates Foundation Grand Challenges in Global Health 1026

A grand challenge is a call for a specific scientific or technological innovation that removes a critical barrier to solving an important health problem in the developing world with a high likelihood of global impact and feasibility. Grand challenges address the diseases and health conditions that cause the greatest morbidity and mortality in the developing world, thus accounting for the enormous health disparities between the developing and the developed world, and that receive disproportionately less attention from the scientific and technical community than their consequences demand. The goals are broad, encompassing prevention, detection, diagnosis, treatment, rehabilitation, and surveillance and control of diseases. Challenges include to improve childhood vaccines; create new vaccines; control insects that transmit agents of disease; improve nutrition to promote health; improve drug treatment of infectious diseases; cure latent and chronic infections; and measure disease and health status accurately and economically in developing countries. Letters of intent are due by the listed application deadline; form and guidelines are available online.
Requirements For-profit, nonprofit, academic, domestic, and foreign institutions may submit letters of intent.
Restrictions Individuals not affiliated with an institution are ineligible.
Contact Program Administrator, (301) 402-4968; fax: (301) 480-1661; email: Grants@GrandChallengesGH.org
Internet http://www.grandchallengesgh.org/challenges.aspx?SecID=258
Sponsor Foundation for the National Institutes of Health
Natcher (Bldg 45), Rm 3AN-44
Bethesda, MD 20892-6300

Billie Jean King Foundation Grants 1027

The mission of the foundation is to inspire humankind in the pursuit of excellence, ensure equal opportunity, and enhance the quality of life for all individuals-'regardless of gender, race, religion, appearance, or sexual orientation. Areas of interest include health, education, and athletics. Programs eligible for support include public education, training, service provision, research, legal services, advocacy, and legislative reform. Priority will be given to projects focusing on women; multicultural, lesbian, gay, bisexual, and transgendered individuals; minorities; and youth. Innovative, entrepreneurial efforts where new funding is likely to have a broad and lasting impact receive preference. There are no application deadlines. Submit a brief letter of inquiry; full applications are by invitation.
Requirements 501(c)3 nonprofit organizations are eligible.
Amount $1000-$25,000
Contact Billie Jean King, President, (623) 362-7208
Internet http://vpr2.admin.arizona.edu/rso/02010411.htm
Sponsor Billie Jean King Foundation
P.O. Box 10777
Phoenix, AZ 85064-0777

Blackall Machine Tool Award 1028

This award is given annually for the best paper or papers clearly concerned with or related to the design or application of machine tools or dimensional measuring instruments, submitted to ASME for presentation and publication. Papers by multiple authors are eligible.
Requirements Authors are not restricted by nationality, age, or society membership.
Amount $1000
Date(s) Application Is Due Feb 1.
Contact Gilda DiTullio, Manager, (212) 591-7736; fax: (212) 705-7739; email: ditulliog@asme.org
Internet http://www.asme.org/honors/ms71/sla/bmtg.html
Sponsor American Society of Mechanical Engineers
3 Park Ave
New York, NY 10016

Blakemore Freeman Fellowships for Advanced Asian Language Study 1029

The fellowships are awarded for one year of advanced language study in East or Southeast Asia in structured language programs or private tutorial programs where the primary focus is on study of the modern language. Eligible languages include Chinese, Vietnamese, Tibetan, Japanese, Indonesian, Thai, Korean, Khmer, Burmese, and Malaysian. Consideration will be given to other East or Southeast Asian languages on an individual basis. The program also supports short-term refresher grants, which are awarded to college professors, postdoctoral professionals, and indiviudals who have previously completed certain designated advanced language study abroad. Application and guidelines are available online.
Requirements An applicant must be pursuing an academic, professional, or business career that involves the regular use of a modern East or Southeast Asian language; have a college undergraduate degree; be at or near an advanced level in the language (a minimum of three academic years of regular language study at the college level, or a minimum of one academic year of full-time intensive language study at the college-level, or proof of equivalent competency); be able to devote oneself exclusively to language study during the term of the grant (grants are not made for part-time study or research); and be a US citizen or permanent resident of the United States.
Restrictions Grants will not be made for the study of classical forms of Chinese, Japanese, Korean, Tibetan, or other languages not in current use in Asia that are studied primarily for academic purposes.
Date(s) Application Is Due Dec 30.
Contact Cathy Scheibner, Administrative Assistant, (206) 583-8778; fax: (206) 359-9778; email: blakemore@perkinscoie.com
Internet http://www.blakemorefoundation.org/language.htm
Sponsor Blakemore Foundation
1201 Third Ave, Ste 4800
Seattle, WA 98101-3266

Bliss Prize Fellowships in Byzantine Studies 1030

This award is intended to provide encouragement, assistance, and training to outstanding college seniors who plan to enter the field of Byzantine studies. The fellowship covers graduate school tuition and living expenses as estimated by the graduate school in which the successful candidate enrolls. In addition, it includes summer travel for the intervening summer to areas that are important for an understanding of Byzantine civilization and culture. Students must be nominated by their advisors by October 15 and must furnish an application stating their future plans by November 1. Official undergraduate transcripts as well as two letters of recommendation and a writing sample must also be received by November 1. Write to the office for application information.
Requirements The fellowship is normally restricted to candidates currently enrolled in US or Canadian universities or colleges. Applicants must be in their last year of undergraduate education or have a BA, must have completed at least one year of Greek by the end of the senior year, and must be applicants to graduate school in any field or area of Byzantine studies.
Amount $5000 maximum for summer travel, plus tuition and living expenses for two years
Date(s) Application Is Due Oct 15; Nov 1.
Contact Alice-Mary Talbot, Director's Office, (202) 339-6940; fax: (202) 339-6419; email: DumbartonOaks@doaks.org or Byzantine@doaks.org
Internet http://www.doaks.org/Blissprize.html
Sponsor Dumbarton Oaks
1703 32nd St NW
Washington, DC 20007

Blowitz-Ridgeway Foundation Early Childhood Development Research Award 1031

The foundation supports nonprofit organizations and programs in the areas of medicine, psychology, residential care, and education, and for research in medicine, psychology, social science, and education. Types of support include capital grants, endowments, program development grants, research grants, and scholarships. The Foundation prefers prospective grantees whose programs or services benefit persons who have not yet reached their majority and/or are for the care of individuals or elderly persons who lack sufficient resources to provide for themselves. Although grants may be made to

organizations outside the state of Illinois, preference will generally be given to applicants from Illinois. Application information is available on the Web site.
Requirements Applicants must be classified as 501(c)3 by the IRS.
Restrictions Grants will not be made for religious or political purposes, nor generally for the production or writing of audio-visual materials.
Contact Serena Moy, Administrator, (847) 330-1020; fax: (847) 330-1028; email: megan@blowitzridgeway.org
Internet http://www.blowitzridgeway.org/information/information.html
Sponsor Blowitz-Ridgeway Foundation
1701 E. Woodfield Road, Suite 201
Schaumburg, IL 60173

Blowitz-Ridgeway Foundation Grants **1032**
The foundation supports nonprofit agencies that provide medical, psychiatric, and psychological care to economically disadvantaged children and adolescents. Program and capital grants are awarded, primarily in Illinois, in support of medical, psychiatric, psychological, and/or residential care; and research programs in medicine, psychology, social science, and education. The foundation supports operating budgets, and applicants may request commitments that extend beyond one year, but requests for annual funding will not be considered. Applications are accepted throughout the year and are reviewed in the order in which they are received. Guidelines and applications are available online.
Requirements 501(c)3 nonprofit organizations that offer services to people who lack resources to provide for themselves may apply.
Restrictions Grants will not be awarded to government agencies or to organizations that subsist mainly on third-party funding and have demonstrated no ability or expended little effort to attract private funding. Grants will not be made for religious or political purposes or for the production or writing of audio-visual materials.
Amount $5000-30,000
Contact Serena Moy, Administrator, (847) 330-1020; fax: (847) 330-1028; email: serena@blowitzridgeway.org
Internet http://www.blowitzridgeway.org/information/information1.html
Sponsor Blowitz-Ridgeway Foundation
1701 E Woodfield Rd, Ste 201
Schaumburg, IL 60173

Blue Shield of California Grants **1033**
Consideration for funding will be given exclusively to organizations that pursue activities directly related to the foundation's program goals, including domestic violence prevention through service provision, education, and outreach; research and education regarding medical best practices and health technologies; and direct or indirect provision of medical insurance or health care to those populations that are uninsured or underinsured, and related policy development.
Requirements The Foundation funds organizations that are non-profit and tax-exempt under 501(c)(3) of the Internal Revenue Service Code (IRC) and defined as a public charity under 509(a)1, 2, or 3 (types I, II, or a functionally integrated type III); accredited schools; units of government/public agencies; tribal governments. The foundation will only support projects that meet the following criteria: the mission of the grantee organization is consistent with the goals and mission of the foundation; the grant is used primarily to serve Californians; the grant seeking organization has a reputation for credibility and integrity; the grant seeking organization is pursuing activities directly related to one of the Foundation's three Program Areas: Health Care and Coverage, Health and Technology and Blue Shield Against Violence.
Restrictions The foundation does not fund award dinners, athletic events, competitions, special events, or tournaments; conferences or seminars; capital construction; television/film/media production; religious organizations for religious purposes; political causes, candidates, organizations or campaigns; capital projects over $50,000; multi-year projects (generally); grants to individuals (with the exception of the regulated Blue Shield of California Employee Scholarship Program); grants to 509(a) 3, type III supporting organizations that are not "functionally integrated".
Contact Grants Administrator, (415) 229-5785; fax: (415) 229-6268
Internet http://blueshieldcafoundation.org/grant-center/index.cfm
Sponsor Blue Shield of California
50 Beale Street
San Francisco, CA 94105-1808

Blum-Kovler Foundation Grants **1034**
The foundation awards general operating grants to eligible Illinois nonprofit organizations in its areas of interest, including child welfare, civic affairs, cultural programs, health care, higher education, hospitals, medical research, and social services. Grants are awarded primarily in the Chicago metropolitan area. There are no application forms or deadlines. Submit a letter of request.
Requirements Illinois nonprofit organizations are eligible.
Amount $2500-$50,000 average
Contact Hymen Bregar, Secretary, (312) 664-5050
Sponsor Blum-Kovler Foundation
875 N. Michigan Avenue, Suite 3400
Chicago, IL 60611

BMI Woody Guthrie Fellowships **1035**
The foundation awards fellowships to support research on topics or themes related to the creative work and contribution to American music and culture made by Woody Guthrie. Disciplines may include, but are not limited to, American musicology, historical musicology, ethnomusicology, cultural studies, social sciences, humanities, and American history. Research proposals should indicate the work's contribution to Guthrie scholarship; and give promise of deliverable and publishable results. The award helps defray travel to New York City and residence expenses for the duration of the fellowship, which normally is from one to six months. An application cover sheet and guidelines are available online.
Amount $2500 maximum
Date(s) Application Is Due May 31.
Contact Fellowships Administrator, email: info@bmifoundation.org
Internet http://www.bmifoundation.org/pages/WGuthrie.asp
Sponsor BMI Foundation
320 W 57th St
New York, NY 10019

BMW of North America Charitable Contributions **1036**
The corporation funds charitable programs that seek to benefit society. Areas of interest include education, road traffic safety, and environment. Education--at all levels, from the very young to those pursuing advanced degrees; intercultural learning for K-12 students and their teachers; automotive technology, mechanics, and career and repair programs (in high schools, technical schools, and community colleges); research in the areas of safety design, ergonomics, and new materials. Road traffic safety--drivers' education programs geared at teenagers and new drivers; basic maintenance programs for women; consumer education on general road safety issues; and programs to promote the safety of children and young people on the road. Environment--conserve/preserve natural resources, in particular parklands and waterways; research/promote the use of alternative fuels; and provide environmental education for K-12 students. In general, grants are awarded for specific projects rather than for general operating support, although some operating and capital grants are given consideration. Applicants must submit an online application; guidelines are available online. Telephone solicitations are not considered.
Requirements Organizations that have been approved by the IRS as 501(c)(3) charities or 501(c)(9) organizations are eligible.
Restrictions Grants do not support non-tax-exempt organizations; individuals; religious organizations for religious purposes; political candidates or lobbying organizations; organizations with a limited constituency, such as fraternal, labor, or veterans groups; travel by groups or individuals; national or local chapters of disease-specific organizations; national conferences, sports events, and other one-time, short-term events; sponsorships or advertising; anti-business groups; team sponsorships or athletic scholarships; or organizations outside the United States or its territories.
Contact Corporate Contributions, (201) 307-4000
Internet http://www.bmwusa.com/About/philanthropy.htm
Sponsor BMW of North America, LLC
300 Chestnut Ridge Rd
Woodcliff Lake, NJ 07677-7731

Boat US Foundation Clean Water Grants **1037**
Grants are available for projects that encourage boaters to learn to love their waterways. Projects of interest are helping boaters understand and appreciate their local boating habitat, as well as learn hands-on boating strategies that will keep the water and local habitat healthy and accessible for future boaters. Topics can range from petroleum pollution prevention to pumpout education to keeping trash out of our waterways. Guidelines and application are available online.
Requirements The Foundation is interested in funding small, local, volunteer based nonprofits. The Foundation will fund volunteer boating groups, clubs, and associations, as well as local nonprofit organizations, including local chapters of national organizations.
Restrictions Government agencies, national or international organizations, for-profit businesses, individuals, and private clubs not open to the general public are not eligible.
Amount $4000 maximum
Date(s) Application Is Due Feb 1.
Contact Grants Administrator, (703) 823-9550; email: cleanwater@boatus.com
Internet http://www.boatus.com/cleanwater/grants
Sponsor Boat US Foundation for Boating Safety and Clean Water
147 Old Solomon's Island Road, Suite 513
Annapolis, MD 21401

Bodenwein Public Benevolent Foundation Grants **1038**
The foundation awards grants to Connecticut nonprofit organizations to support social service and health agencies, including AIDS support, mental health services, health associations, and cancer and AIDS research; arts and culture, including performing arts and fine arts; youth and child welfare agencies; community development; education, including early childhood education, adult basic education, and continuing education; libraries and literacy and reading programs; the environment; animal rights and welfare; legal services; children, youth, women, and family services; religion; and minority services. Types of support include capital campaigns, building/renovations, equipment, program/project development, conferences and seminars, publication, seed money,

scholarship funds, research, consulting services, and matching funds. The board meets in January and July of each year to consider requests. Applicants may submit one grant application per calendar year.
Requirements Nonprofit groups in Lyme, Old Lyme, East Lyme, Waterford, New London, Montville, Groton, Ledyard, Stonington, and North Stonington, CT, are eligible.
Date(s) Application Is Due May 15; Nov 15.
Contact Grants Administrator, c/o Bank of America (800) 841-4000
Sponsor Bodenwein Public Benevolent Foundation
777 Main Street, CTEH40222B
Hartford, CT 06115

Bodman Foundation Grants Program **1039**
The Foundation concentrates its programs in New York City, but also makes some grants in northern New Jersey. Funding is concentrated in six program areas: Arts and Culture, Education, Employment, Health, Public Policy, and Youth and Families. In both Health and Arts and Culture, the Foundation tends to focus its grants on leading institutions, generally where there is a longstanding relationship. In other areas, special consideration is given to competition, self-help, volunteerism, leadership and character development, parental involvement, consumer choice, economic empowerment, independent living, prevention and earlier intervention, independent research, faith-based programs, free markets, social entrepreneurship, advancing the state of the art, measuring participant outcomes and programs results, and strengthening traditional marriages and families.
Requirements Nonprofit organizations based in New York City and northern New Jersey tax-exempt under Section 501(c)3 and fall within the program areas of the Foundations are welcome to submit an inquiry or proposal letter. Initial contact should only include: an inquiry or proposal letter briefly summarizing the history of the project, need, research, objectives, time period, key staff, project budget, and evaluation plan emphasizing measurable outcomes and specific program results; latest annual report; current and complete audited financial statements; copy of IRS 501(c)(3) tax-exemption letter.
Restrictions The Foundations generally do not offer the following types of support, nor participate in the following program areas: nonprofit organizations outside of New York and New Jersey; annual appeals, dinner functions, and fundraising events; endowments and capital campaigns; loans and deficit financing; direct grants to individuals (such as scholarships and financial aid); individual day-care and after-school programs; housing; international; films and travel; projects for the elderly; small art, dance, music, and theater groups; independent or public K-12 schools (except charter schools); national health and mental health organizations; government agencies and nonprofit programs and services significantly funded or substantially reimbursed by government.
Amount $10,000-$100,000 average
Contact Joseph S. Dolan, Executive Director, (212) 644-0322; fax: (212) 759-6510; email: main@achelis-bodman-fnds.org
Internet http://fdncenter.org/grantmaker/achelis-bodman
Sponsor Bodman Foundation
767 Third Avenue, 4th Floor
New York, NY 10017-2023

Boeing Company Contributions Program Grants **1040**
The Boeing U.S. contributions program welcomes applications in five focus areas: education; health and human services; arts and culture; civic and the environment. Education is a priority for Boeing. The largest single block of charitable contributions goes toward supporting programs and projects related to education. Boeing also believes that the health of a community is measured by the well being of all its citizens. Boeing looks for innovative initiatives that promote the economic well-being of the community and neighborhood revitalization. Boeing invests in programs that promote participation in arts and cultural activities and experiences, programs that increase public understanding of and engagement in the processes and issues that affect communities and programs that protect and conserve the natural environment. Boeing accepts applications for cash grants, in-kind donations, and services.
Requirements To apply for support you must be a U.S. based IRS 501(c)(3) qualified charitable or educational organization or an accredited K-12 educational institution. U.S. grant guidelines and applications are available online.
Restrictions Grants do not support: an individual person or families; adoption services; political candidates or organizations; religious activities, in whole or in part, for the purpose of further religious doctrine; memorials and endowments; travel expenses; nonprofit and school sponsored walk-a-thons, athletic events and athletic group sponsorships other than Special Olympics; door prizes or raffles; U.S. hospitals and medical research; school-affiliated orchestras, bands, choirs, trips, athletic teams, drama groups, yearbooks and class parties; general operating expenses for programs within the U.S.; organizations that do not follow our application procedures; follow-on applications from past grantees that have not met our reporting requirements or satisfactorily completed the terms of past grants; fundraising events, annual funds, galas and other special-event fundraising activities; advertising, t-shirts, giveaways and promotional items; documentary films, books, etc.; debt reduction; dissertations and student research projects; loans, scholarships, fellowships and grants to individuals; for-profit businesses; gifts, honoraria, gratuities; capital improvements to rental properties.
Contact Corporate Contributions Manager, (312) 544-2000
Internet http://www.boeing.com/companyoffices/aboutus/community/charitable.htm
Sponsor Boeing Company Contributions Program
100 North Riverside
Chicago, IL 60606

Bogliasco Foundation Liguria Study Center Residencies **1041**
The fellowships are awarded, without regard to nationality, to qualified persons doing advanced creative work or scholarly research in the following disciplines: archaeology, architecture, classics, dance, film or video, history, landscape architecture, literature, music, philosophy, theater, and visual arts. Applicants are expected to demonstrate significant achievement in their disciplines, commensurate with their age and experience. In addition, they must submit descriptions of the projects that they intend to pursue in Bogliasco. An approved project is presumed to lead to the completion of an artistic, literary, or scholarly work, followed by publication, performance, exhibition, or other public presentation. Approximately 50 fellowships are awarded during two semesters each year--September 8 to December 13 (fall-winter), and February 9 to May 16 (winter-spring). Fellowships usually are for one month (31-32 days) or, in some cases, a half semester (48 days). Fellows may be accompanied by spouses (or spouse-equivalent companions) during their stay at the Liguria Study Center (separate application required). Information and application procedures are available online.
Date(s) Application Is Due Jan 15; Apr 15.
Contact Grants Administrator, email: info@bfny.org
Internet http://www.liguriastudycenter.org/english/home.htm
Sponsor Bogliasco Foundation
885 Second Ave, Rm 3100
New York, NY 10017

Booth-Bricker Fund Grants **1042**
The Foundation makes contributions for the purposes of promoting, developing and fostering religious, charitable, scientific, literary and educational programs. Requests are welcomed for capital needs, special projects and other one-time requirements. Applications should be made by letter. There are no forms or deadlines. Requests should include complete information about the applicant organization, including its history, purpose, finances, current operations, governing board and tax status. A detailed explanation of the proposed use of the funds must be provided.
Requirements Requests are accepted for the funding of projects within the state of Louisiana. Priority is given to the New Orleans area.
Restrictions The Foundation generally does not provide sustaining (operations and maintenance) funding. No grants are made to individuals.
Amount $5000-$50,000
Contact Gray S. Parker, Chairperson, (504) 581-2430
Sponsor Booth-Bricker Fund
826 Union Street, Suite 300
New Orleans, LA 70112

Bosque Foundation Grants **1043**
The foundation awards grants to support higher education and medical research in Texas. Types of support include capital grants and research grants. There are no application forms or deadlines. Applicants should submit a one-page letter of intent that describes the program and request.
Requirements Texas nonprofit and for-profit organizations are eligible.
Restrictions Individuals are not eligible.
Amount $5000-$20,000 average
Contact Grants Administrator, (214) 956-6732; fax: (214) 956-6733
Sponsor Bosque Foundation
5950 Cedar Springs Boulevard, Suite 210
Dallas, TX 75235

Boston Athenaeum Fellowships **1044**
The program supports up to seven short-term fellowships. One fellowship is available for research on topics concerning the confederate states and the Civil War, and one fellowship is offered through the American Society for Eighteenth-Century Studies. Grants will support use of the Athenaeum collections for research, publication, curriculum and program development, or other creative projects. Guidelines are available online.
Requirements Fellowships are open to advanced scholars, graduate students, independent scholars, teaching faculty, and professionals in the humanities, with applications encouraged from teachers and librarians in secondary public, private, and parochial schools.
Amount $1500
Date(s) Application Is Due Apr 1.
Contact Stephen Nonack, Head Reference Librarian, (617) 227-0270 ext 250; email: nonack@bostonathenaeum.org
Internet http://www.bostonathenaeum.org/fellowships.html
Sponsor Boston Athenaeum
10 1/2 Beacon St
Boston, MA 02108-3777

Boston Foundation Grants Program **1045**
The Boston Foundation has a particular concern for low income and disenfranchised communities and residents and supports organizations and programs whose work helps advance the Foundation's high priorities in a variety of subject areas: Arts and Culture; Civic Engagement; Community Safety, Economic Development; Education/ Out-of-School Time, Health and Human Services; Housing and Community Economic Development; the Nonprofit Sector, Urban Environment and Workforce Development. The Foundation generally makes the following types of grants: Project or program

support for community-based efforts that improve the quality of life in the community, test new models, and promote collaborative and innovative ventures; advocacy and public policy research that is linked to specific action; support for planning to enable organizations and residents to assess community needs, respond to new challenges and opportunities, and provide for the inclusion of new populations; organizational support to develop and build the capacity of nonprofit organizations - support that helps organizations keep pace with the changing requirements and demands of their communities and broader environments; small grants awarded on a rolling basis for one-time organizational development needs through the Vision Fund. In addition, on a very limited basis, the Foundation will consider development grants and strategic alliances.
Requirements Grants are made only to tax-exempt organizations in Massachusetts.
Restrictions The committee does not consider more than one proposal from the same organization within a 12-month period. Discretionary grants are generally not made to the following applicants: city or state government agencies or departments; individuals; medical research; endowments; equipment; replacement of lost/expired government funding or gap funding to cover the full cost of providing services; scholarships and fellowships; video and film production; construction and renovation projects and capital campaigns; programs with religious content; travel; summer camps and lobbying. Activities that are generally lower priorities for the Foundation are conferences, lectures, one-time events, programs benefiting only a small number of participants or routine service delivery and/or operating expenses.
Date(s) Application Is Due Jan 5; Jul 1.
Contact Corey Davis, Grants Manager, (617) 338-1700; fax: (617) 338-1604; email: info@tbf.org
Internet http://www.tbf.org/Fund/Fund-L1.asp
Sponsor Boston Foundation
75 Arlington Street, 10th Floor
Boston, MA 02116

Bower Award and Prize for Achievement in Science **1046**
The Award recognizes outstanding achievement in life, physical, and applied sciences; innovation in the sciences; and training of scientists. The award is given without regard for nationality and includes a gold medal and prize of $250,000. The theme for the 2008 Bower Award for Achievement in Science is Robotics. The Institute seeks to honor an individual who has played a seminal role in either the design and construction of robotic systems or the advancement of enabling technologies as related to robotics such as mechanical structure, sensors, and control algorithms.
Requirements This is an international competition for individuals whose work has had a significant impact on the field of Robotics. In cases of equal scientific merit, the factor of current economic value of the discovery or application will weigh favorably on behalf of the candidate. Candidates for the Award must be living, and the winner must participate in the April Awards Ceremony in Philadelphia.
Restrictions This award is for an individual rather than for a group.
Amount $250,000 cash prize
Date(s) Application Is Due May 31.
Contact Awards Program Director, (215) 448-1329; fax: (215) 448-1364; email: awards@fi.edu
Internet http://www.fi.edu/tfi/exhibits/bower/07/bscience_nominate.html
Sponsor The Franklin Institute
222 N. 20th Street
Philadelphia, PA 19103-1194

BP Conservation Programme Future Conservationist Awards **1047**
The aim of the awards is to develop leadership capacity for biodiversity conservation as a fundamental contribution to sustainable development. The program provides annual grants to passionate people developing innovative projects addressing biodiversity issues of global importance. Projects should address three key areas: development of team capabilities and skills; practical high-priority conservation projects combining research and action; and demonstrate long-term conservation benefits contributing to sustainable development. Application and guidelines are available online.
Requirements Teams must include only members less than 35 years of age with no more than two years professional conservation and include a minimum of three people.
Restrictions The program does not fund conference attendance, tuition fees or scholarships, salaries, costly laboratory analyses or gene storage, captive breeding projects, or high school level expeditions. Projects that are specifically for PhD research or master's dissertations will not be supported. Employees from any of the BPCP partner organizations are not eligible to apply.
Amount $12,500 maximum
Date(s) Application Is Due Dec 16.
Contact Marianne Dunn, Conservation Program Manager, (44 01223) 277318; fax: (44 01223) 277200; email: bp-conservation-programme@birdlife.org.uk
Internet http://conservation.bp.com/applications/default.asp
Sponsor BP Conservation Programme
Wellbrook Ct, Griton Rd
Cambridge CB3 ONA United Kingdom

BP Conservation Programme Grants **1048**
This initiative, which is the result of a collaboration between BirdLife International, Fauna and Flora International, the Wildlife Conservation Society, Conservation International, and BP, aims to support and encourage long-term conservation projects that address global conservation priorities at a local level. The program provides advice, training, and financial awards, primarily targeting university students. Each year, the program awards gold, silver, and bronze awards; follow-up awards, and consolidation awards. Eligible projects must take place in Africa, Asia, the Pacific Islands, the Middle East, Eastern Europe, or Latin America; address a globally recognized conservation priority; involve local people; be approved by the host government; and last for less than one year but show potential for follow-up work.
Requirements The program is open to teams for all over the world. Teams should include individuals from the host country and members from more than one country, and demonstrate collaboration with local and national conservationists. All applicant projects must address a wildlife conservation priority of global importance (preferably linking with established work-plans--e.g., national biodiversity action plan); have a strong link with the country where the project will take place (local people participating in all parts of project planning and implementation); and have a majority of team members in full- or part-time university education (undergraduate or postgraduate, and of any age).
Restrictions The program does not offer scholarships, pay for any salaries, or fund projects organized by other organizations.
Amount $17,500 Gold Awards; $12,500 Silver Awards; $7500 Bronze Awards; $20,000-$55,000 Follow-up Awards; $75,000 Consolidation Awards
Date(s) Application Is Due Oct 31.
Contact Marianne Dunn, Conservation Program Manager, (44 01223) 277318; fax: (44 01223) 277200; email: bp-conservation-programme@birdlife.org.uk
Internet http://conservation.bp.com/aboutus/default.asp
Sponsor BP Conservation Programme
Wellbrook Ct, Griton Rd
Cambridge CB3 ONA United Kingdom

BPW Career Advancement Scholarships **1049**
These scholarships assist mature women who need further education or training to reenter the workforce, enter a new career field, or to improve their chances for advancement. Applicants are strongly encouraged to seek training at the undergraduate or graduate level in computer science, education, science, engineering, paralegal studies, or professional (JD, MD, DDS) degrees. Scholarships are awarded for a one-year period to cover tuition, fees, and school-related expenses such as child care and transportation. Application requests must include a #10 self-addressed double-stamped (first-class) envelope. The listed application deadline date is to request an application.
Requirements The scholarships are open to women who are US citizens and 25 years of age or older; demonstrate financial need; are officially accepted into a program or course of study in an accredited institution in the United States, Puerto Rico, or the US Virgin Islands; and will graduate within 24 months from date of receipt of funds.
Restrictions Doctoral studies, study abroad, or correspondence courses are not supported.
Amount $750-$1000
Date(s) Application Is Due Apr 15.
Contact Tricia Dwyer-Morgan, (202) 777-8932; fax: (202) 861-0298; email: bpwfoundation@act.org or tdwyermorgan@bpwusa.org
Internet http://www.bpwusa.org/i4a/pages/index.cfm?pageid=4553
Sponsor Business and Professional Women's Foundation
1900 M St, NW, Ste 310
Washington, DC 20036

Bradley Faculty Fellowships **1050**
The institute offers partial fellowships to attend summer session in Santa Fe, NM. Study at the institute provides college faculty with an opportunity to explore and discuss issues raised by the great works of Western civilization and to participate in a well-known academic program. The fellowships will be of particular interest to faculty and institutions engaged in curricular reform and the revitalization of liberal arts education.
Requirements Faculty members must be sponsored by their institution.
Contact Graduate Institute, (505) 984-6082; fax: (505) 984-6003; email: gi@mail.sjcsf.edu
Internet http://www.stjohnscollege.edu/asp/main.aspx?page=3001#fellow
Sponsor Saint John's College
1160 Camino Cruz Blanca
Santa Fe, NM 87505

Brain Trust Translational Research Grants **1051**
The program, a collaborative effort of Accelerate Brain Cancer Cure, the Alzheimer's Association, the Michael J. Fox Foundation for Parkinson's Research, and the Robert Packard Center for ALS Research at Johns Hopkins University, seeks to identify common challenges, explore possible solutions, and fund development of new therapeutic approaches with application to diverse brain diseases. The program seeks applications focused on technologies that can achieve selective targeting and/or delivery of therapeutic agents to specific regions/cells in the brain, including overcoming the limitations imposed by the blood-brain barrier, which can be applied in the clinical setting in the next 24 months. Funding is for one year, and the funds can only be applied to direct costs of research.
Requirements For-profit and nonprofit organizations, individuals affiliated with nonprofit and for-profit organizations, and unaffiliated individuals are eligible.
Date(s) Application Is Due Jun 1.
Contact John Reher, (650) 685-2202; email: info@brain-trust.org

Internet http://www.brain-trust.org/html/rfa.html
Sponsor Brain Trust
800 Airport Blvd, Ste 508
Burlingame, CA 94010

Brain Tumor Research Grants **1052**
Grants support basic scientific research directed at finding a cure for brain tumors. Grants are awarded for up to a two-year period and may be used for start-up projects or supplementary funding. Research guidelines and application are available on the Web site.
Amount $100,000 maximum per year
Date(s) Application Is Due Mar 16.
Contact Carrie Treadwell, Research Manager, (800) 770-8287 ext 10 or (480) 575-8388; email: grants@tbts.org
Internet http://www.tbts.org/itemDetail.asp?categoryID=300&itemID=16402
Sponsor The Brain Tumor Society
124 Watertown St
Watertown, MA 02472-2500

Brainerd Foundation Grants **1053**
The foundation is dedicated to protecting the environmental quality of the Pacific Northwest, including Washington, Oregon, Idaho, Montana, Alaska, and British Columbia. Program grants are made in the following areas: endangered ecosystems--conservation biology, conservation assessment, and mining reform and roadless areas; and communications and capacity building--organizational development, and allied voices. Program grants are awarded to cover costs associated with activities such as public education and grassroots outreach, media strategies, litigation, scientific and economic studies, computer networking, and building organizational capacity. Opportunity Fund grants are awarded to organizations for support such as outreach, litigation, applied research, and other unexpected needs. Additional types of support include general operating support, continuing support, equipment acquisition, conferences and seminars, seed money, research, technical assistance, and employee matching gifts. Applications are available online.
Requirements Nonprofit organizations in the Pacific Northwest are eligible.
Restrictions The foundation does not favor proposals for school education programs, land acquisition, endowments, capital campaigns, projects sponsored by government agencies, basic research, fellowships, or books or videos that are not part of a broader strategy.
Amount $250-$25,000 range
Contact Ann Krumboltz, Executive Director, (206) 448-0676; fax: (206) 448-7222; email: annk@brainerd.org
Internet http://www.brainerd.org/grants/intro.php
Sponsor Brainerd Foundation
1601 Second Ave, Ste 610
Seattle, WA 98101-1541

Bread and Roses Community Fund Grants and Scholarships **1054**
The program awards grants to a broad spectrum of organizations and individuals working on social change. Programs include general fund grants--for organizations whose chief aim is to take collective action against a problem affecting the community, to work for social change, emergency/discretionary grants, Lax scholarships (graduate)--available to gay men, and the Phoebus Criminal Justice Initiative.
Requirements Pennsylvania nonprofit organizations in the Delaware Valley (Philadelphia, Chester, Montgomery, Bucks, and Delaware Counties) and Camden County, NJ, are eligible.
Amount $2000-$10,000
Contact Grants Administrator, (215) 731-1107; fax: (215) 731-0453; email: info@breadrosesfund.org
Internet http://www.breadrosesfund.org/grants/grants.html
Sponsor Bread and Roses Community Fund
1500 Walnut St, Ste 1305
Philadelphia, PA 19102

Brico Fund Grants **1055**
The mission of the fund is to effect systemic change--to change attitudes, policies and societal patterns. Grants are made to secure full participation in society for women and girls; restore and sustain the earth's natural systems; promote a just and equitable society; and nourish the creative spirit. Types of support include general operating, program, and rarely, capital and endowment grants. Applicants should complete the fund's preliminary application form and a two-page letter of intent, describing the organization's intended project or program.
Requirements The fund supports organizations with projects and programs within the Greater Milwaukee community. Some funding is done statewide or nationally for programs of broader scope.
Restrictions Grants do not support conferences and meetings, disease-specific programs, educational institutions, individuals, media projects, medical institutions, religions, or organizations with a focus on animals.
Amount $1000-$500,000 range
Date(s) Application Is Due Jan 15; Jul 15.
Contact Melissa Nimke, Grants Administrator, (414) 272-2747; fax: (414) 272-2036; email: mbn@bricofund.org or bricofund@bricofund.org
Internet http://www.bricofund.org
Sponsor Brico Fund
205 E Wisconsin Ave, Ste 200
Milwaukee, WI 53202

Bright Family Foundation Grants **1056**
The foundation awards grants to eligible California nonprofit organizations in its areas of interest, including children and youth, education (medical, business, and other), health, medical research, and religion. Types of support include general operating support, building construction/renovation, scholarship funds, and special projects. Grants are awarded for one year, with possible renewal.
Requirements Stanislaus County, CA, 501(c)3 tax-exempt organizations within 30 miles of Modesto, CA, are eligible.
Amount $377,500 total
Date(s) Application Is Due Dec 1.
Contact Calvin Bright, President, (209) 526-8242
Sponsor Bright Family Foundation
1620 N Carpenter Rd, Bldg B
Modesto, CA 95351

Brinson Foundation Grants **1057**
The foundation supports education, public health, and scientific research programs that engage, inform, and inspire committed citizens to confront the challenges that face humanity. Grantmaking priorities are education--awareness and outreach, democracy and citizenship, economically disadvantaged, and libraries and literacy; public health--awareness and outreach, and economically disadvantaged; and scientific research--astrophysics, cosmology, geophysics, medical research (i.e., Alzheimer's disease, cancer, Lou Gehrig's Disease (ALS), and stroke). Types of support include general operating grants and project grants. The foundation does not accept unsolicited grant applications. Grantseekers are asked to review the foundation's mission, vision, beliefs, priorities (accessed from the Who We Are link), and guidelines. If a grantseeker believes the request would match one or more of the foundation's grantmaking priorities, they can make an inquiry by completing the online Grantseeker Information Form. The completed form should be emailed to the office. Further application is by invitation.
Requirements The foundation will consider inviting grant applications from organizations: whose request matches one or more of the Foundation's grantmaking priorities; located in the United States of America that are exempt from tax under Section 501(c)(3) of the Internal Revenue Code and are defined as charitable organizations as described in Section 509(a)(1), (2) or (3) or 170(b)(1)(A); located outside the United States of America provided they produce a written legal opinion stating that they are a charitable equivalency to a qualifying U.S. organization and/or a written affidavit containing sufficient information for the Foundation to make a reasonable judgment that the organization is charitable.
Restrictions The Foundation will not consider grant inquiries from organizations that: discriminate on the basis of race, gender, religion, ethnicity or sexual orientation. The Foundation will not consider grant inquiries that request funding for: activities that attempt to influence public elections; voter registration; political activity; lobbying efforts; promotion of a specific religious faith; medical research involving human cloning. The Foundation discourages grant inquiries requesting funds for: capital improvements; endowments; fundraising events.
Contact Grants Administrator, (312) 799-4500; fax: (312) 799-4310; email: mail@brinsonfoundation.org
Internet http://www.brinsonfoundation.org/grants/index.html
Sponsor Brinson Foundation
737 North Michigan Avenue, Suite 1850
Chicago, IL 60611

Bristol-Myers Squibb Clinical Outcomes and Research Grants **1058**
Bristol-Myers Squibb's mission is to extend and enhance human life. To help achieve that mission, the Company has established programs to support Investigator Sponsored Trials (ISTs). ISTs must be medically appropriate and scientifically valid. While the Company will consider requests for clinical research trials in all clinical and therapeutic areas, it currently gives priority to proposals in the following therapeutic areas: Cardiovascular/Metabolics, Infectious Diseases, Neuroscience, Oncology, Immunology, and Virology. Bristol-Myers Squibb maintains a strict policy of not exercising any influence or control over the design of any investigator initiated clinical research trial supported by BMS.
Requirements Individuals in the following settings are eligible for support: private practice, hospitals, community health centers, cooperative groups, physician networks, and academic medical centers and universities.
Contact Amit Duggal; (212) 546-4000; fax: (212) 546-9574; email: amit.duggal@bms.com
Internet http://www.bms.com/sr/content/data/clinical.html
Sponsor Bristol-Myers Squibb Company
777 Scudders Mill Road
Plainsboro, NJ 08536

Bristol-Myers Squibb Foundation Global HIV/AIDS Initiative Grants **1059**
The intent of the Program is to develop new models in awareness, in medical care, in community development and in prevention and treatment in poor and resource-

limited areas of the world, where the need for all such efforts is greatest. Health care infrastructures must be developed and enhanced, stigmatization must be overcome, health care worker capacity must be built and preserved and local people must be empowered to generate and sustain local solutions to this global problem.
Requirements The Bristol-Myers Squibb Foundation considers requests for support only from tax-exempt organizations that satisfy the requirements of section 501(c)(3) of the U.S. Internal Revenue Code.
Restrictions The Foundation does not award funds to: individuals; political, fraternal, social or veterans' organizations; religious or sectarian organizations unless engaged in a significant project benefiting the entire community; organizations receiving support through United Way or other federated campaigns; endowments; courtesy advertising; or conferences/special events/videos.
Contact John Damonti, President; (212) 546-4000; fax: (212) 546-9574
Internet http://www.bms.com/sr/philanthropy/data/globhiv.html
Sponsor Bristol-Myers Squibb Foundation
345 Park Avenue, Suite 4364
New York, NY 10154-0037

Bristol-Myers Squibb Foundation Health Disparities Grants **1060**
One mission of the Foundation is to reduce health disparities by strengthening community-based health care worker capacity, integrating medical care and community-based supportive services, and mobilizing communities to fight disease. To this end, this Program attempts to address health disparities in four strategic disease areas representing major public health burdens and in four highly affected geographies: hepatitis in Asia, HIV/AIDS in Africa, serious mental illness in the U.S., and cancer in Europe. Additional areas of concern include: metabolic diseases, infectious diseases; rheumatoid arthritis; cardiovascular diseases; substance abuse; women's health issues; and overal health care giving.
Requirements Nonprofit organizations in communities where Bristol-Myers Squibb maintains a facility should submit their requests for company contributions directly to that location. Contact persons are listed at the company website.
Restrictions The foundation does not support individuals; conferences, special events, or videos; political, fraternal, social, or veterans organizations; religious or sectarian activities, unless they benefit the entire community; organizations funded through federated campaigns; endowments; or courtesy advertising.
Contact John Damonti, President, Bristol Myers Squibb Foundation, (212) 546-4000; fax: (212) 546-9574
Internet http://www.bms.com/sr/foundation/health_disparities/data/health_intro.html
Sponsor Bristol-Myers Squibb Foundation
345 Park Avenue, Suite 4364
New York, NY 10154-0037

Bristol-Myers Squibb Foundation Women's Health Grants **1061**
Bristol-Myers Squibb Women's Health Program supports projects that enhance women's health with strategies that improve education, prevention, diagnosis, treatment and access to care for women worldwide. Support has been given to projects that test innovative outreach programs, cultivate multi-sectoral partnerships and add new information to the existing body of knowledge to help define and achieve improved health for women around the world. The goal of the program is to generate initiatives that will help enhance women's health through novel interdisciplinary strategies that improve education, prevention, diagnosis, treatment and access to care for women worldwide. Since its inception, significant resources have been invested in programs that educate women about diseases and conditions that particularly threaten them as women.
Requirements The Bristol-Myers Squibb Foundation considers requests for support only from tax-exempt organizations that satisfy the requirements of section 501(c)(3) of the U.S. Internal Revenue Code.
Restrictions The Foundation does not award funds to: individuals; political, fraternal, social or veterans' organizations; religious or sectarian organizations unless engaged in a significant project benefiting the entire community; organizations receiving support through United Way or other federated campaigns; endowments; courtesy advertising; or conferences/special events/videos.
Contact John Damonti, President; (212) 546-4000; fax: (212) 546-9574
Internet http://www.bms.com/sr/philanthropy/data/global_keypast.html
Sponsor Bristol-Myers Squibb Foundation
345 Park Avenue, Suite 4364
New York, NY 10154-0037

Bristol-Myers Squibb Virology Research Fellowships **1062**
The Program provides support for fellows to gain experience in epidemiological and clinical research as it relates to the care of individuals infected with HIV/AIDS and/or HBV. Goals of the Program include: support of studies that will further strengthen the science and knowledge of HIV/AIDS and HBV; development of a foundation for future prospective and retrospective studies; to provide a forum to share research findings; and support of the development of future clinical researchers. Up to 18 fellows will be selected annually, with grant awards up to $15,000 to support research-related expenses for a one-year research period. Applications will be accepted online.
Requirements Candidates must: be an active Fellow in good standing in an ACGME-accredited Fellows training program; desire to enhance knowledge and skill development in the area of HIV/AIDS or HBV clinical research; desire to pursue clinical research related to optimal sequencing of agents, efficacy, epidemiology, resistance, or toxicity in HIV/AIDS and/or HBV treatment; and identify a faculty member to serve as the project mentor.
Restrictions Total grant amount is inclusive of indirect costs and associated IRB fees and is not permitted for use towards travel to conferences or for durable equipment.
Amount $15,000 maximum
Date(s) Application Is Due Jun 29.
Contact Amit Duggal; (212) 546-4000; fax: (212) 546-9574; email: amit.duggal@bms.com
Internet http://www.bms.com/sr/virologyfellows/data/index.html
Sponsor Bristol-Myers Squibb Company
777 Scudders Mill Road
Plainsboro, NJ 08536

British and American History, Literature, Art, and History of Science Fellowships **1063**
The Huntington Library has established a fellowship fund for graduate and postdoctoral scholars in British and American history, history of science, literature, and art. Special awards of three months or less are available for persons writing doctoral dissertations. Award holders are expected to be in continuous residence at the Huntington throughout their tenure. Applications are accepted from October 1 to December 15 of each year for awards within the 12-month period beginning on the following June 1; results are announced by April 1. Each fellowship will carry a stipend while the scholar is in residence at Huntington.
Requirements Scholars must possess the PhD or equivalent degree.
Amount $2000 per month for one to five months
Date(s) Application Is Due Dec 15.
Contact Robert Ritchie, Director of Research, (626) 405-2194; fax: (626) 449-5703; email: cpowell@hungtington.org
Internet http://www.huntington.org/ResearchDiv/Fellowships.html
Sponsor Huntington Library and Art Gallery
1151 Oxford Rd
San Marino, CA 91108

British-American Transnational History Fellowships **1064**
Central Michigan University has joined with the University of Strathclyde, Glasgow, Scotland, in establishing an innovative collaborative degree program that offers the master's and Ph.D. degrees through study under joint British-American faculty. The program provides international academic study and dialogue beyond ordinary student and faculty exchanges by pooling the faculty of two universities, thereby offering graduate students the opportunity of directed research and study in a truly comparative and transnational environment. Students in the joint history degree program benefit from a small program, in terms of the number of students, with a large combined faculty of 32 members who are able to give considerable attention to individual student coursework and research. The curriculum of the joint history program centers on traditional fields of historical concentration but is strongly international in emphasis, requiring a degree of coursework and research that is transnational and comparative. The joint faculty is strongly grounded in social, cultural and economic history.
Requirements Candidates are required to select two major fields or one major and two minor fields from the following: the United States, the British Isles, Modern Continental Europe, and the Atlantic World. Minor fields are the Ancient Near East and Mediterranean, Medieval Europe, Latin America, East Asia, and India. Topical fields such as women, ethnicity, race, and poverty are possible. See Web site for MA and PhD requirements.
Contact Annette Davis, Graduate Programs, (989) 774-3374; email: annette.davis@cmich.edu
Internet http://www.chsbs.cmich.edu/history/grad.htm
Sponsor Central Michigan University
History Department, Powers Hall 106
Mount Pleasant, MI 48859

Broad Foundation IBD Research Grants **1065**
The program seeks to stimulate innovative research that will lead to both the prevention and successful therapy of inflammatory bowel disease (IBD), including Chrohn's disease and ulcerative colitis. The foundation's goal is to fund basic or clinical research projects that are in the early stages of exploration; propose new directions or ideas; are creative, novel, cutting edge, and imaginative; and are not ready for funding by other more traditional granting agencies. All proposals must be based on sound scientific evidence and careful evaluation of current knowledge in IBD research. Requests must be preceded by a brief (one to three pages)letter of interest, which may be submitted at any time. Funding will be granted for one year; continued funding is based on progress reports and the perceived value of the findings.
Requirements Nonprofit institutions worldwide, such as universities, hospitals, and research institutes, are eligible.
Restrictions It is anticipated that the foundation will not fund projects after sufficient progress and maturity have made them fundable by other agencies.
Amount $100,000 average
Contact Dr. Daniel Hollander, (310) 954-5091; email: info@broadmedical.org
Internet http://www.broadmedical.org/funding.htm
Sponsor Broad Foundation
10900 Wilshire Blvd., 12th Floor
Los Angeles, CA 90024-6532

Broadcast Media Awards for Television **1066**
These awards recognize outstanding reporting and programming on television that deals with reading and literacy, recognizing the value of reading in today's society, or promoting literacy. Entries must be oriented toward the general public rather than reading education professionals and should be informational, critical, or motivational rather than instructional. Entries may include but are not limited to: journalism on reading in schools, the home, or the community, including accounts of research and educational practices, coverage of reading activities, or appraisals of school reading programs; interview programs on reading in schools or the community or on reading education in general; public service programming that informs about reading, seeks to instill a love of reading, and/or promotes literacy; entertainment programming that informs about reading, seeks to instill a love of reading, and/or promotes literacy.
Requirements Entries must have aired during the previous calendar year beginning January 1. Only one entry may be submitted per producer. Entries must be sent to Nancy E. Frey, San Diego State University - City Heights, Suite 100, 4283 El Cajon Boulevard, San Diego, CA 92105-1289.
Date(s) Application Is Due Jan 8.
Contact Program Contact, (302) 731-1600 ext 293; fax: (302) 731-1057; email: bcady@reading.org
Internet http://www.reading.org/association/awards/index.html
Sponsor International Reading Association
P.O. Box 8139, 800 Barksdale Road
Newark, DE 19714-8139

Broadhurst Foundation Grants **1067**
The foundation supports the arts and humanities, community development, and medical research. In addition to program support, funds are awarded for building programs and necessary equipment in these areas. Support for scholarship funds for students training for the Christian ministry at institutions selected by the foundation; grants also to educational and religious institutions, and to medical research institutions, especially those related to pediatric diseases.
Requirements Organizations in Oklahoma are eligible to apply.
Restrictions No grants to individuals or for scholarship funds.
Amount $100-$18,000
Contact Ann Cassidy Baker, Chair, (918) 584-0661; fax: (918) 584-5831
Sponsor Broadhurst Foundation
401 S Boston, Ste 100
Tulsa, OK 74103-4002

Brookhaven National Laboratory Sambamurti Memorial Lectureship **1068**
The lectureship is awarded yearly to a young (under 40) high-energy or heavy-ion experimentalist of outstanding achievement. The lecture, which should describe the work for which the lecturer is being honored, is to be delivered to students working at BNL during the summer.
Amount $500
Contact Laurence Littenberg, Department of Physics, (516) 344-3811; email: littenbe@bnl.gov
Internet http://www.phy.bnl.gov/edg/sambamurti.html
Sponsor Brookhaven National Laboratory
P.O. Box 5000
Upton, NY 11973-5000

Brookings Institution Predoctoral Research Fellowships in Foreign Policy Studies **1069**
A limited number of resident fellowships are awarded for policy-oriented predoctoral research in government studies. The fellowships are designed for doctoral candidates whose dissertation topics are directly related to public policy issues and thus to the major interests of the institution. Fellowships will be awarded to scholars whose research will benefit from access to the data, opportunities for interviewing, and consultation with senior staff members afforded by the institution and by residence in Washington, DC. Fellows may participate in appropriate staff conferences and seminars of the institution and have access to the research resources available to resident staff members. Outstanding dissertations will be considered for publication by Brookings. Computer facilities are provided. Stipend is payable on a 12-month basis, 11 months of research in residence and one month of vacation.
Requirements Candidates must be nominated by the graduate departments of their universities. Departments should nominate no more than two persons who should have completed the preliminary examinations for the doctorate no later than February 15. The institution particularly encourages the participation of women and members of minority groups.
Restrictions Individual applications are not accepted.
Amount $20,500 stipend, supplementary assistance not to exceed $750, and reimbursement for research-related travel up to $750
Date(s) Application Is Due Feb 15; Dec 15.
Contact Sarah Yerkes, (202) 797-6043; fax: (202) 797-2481; email: syerkes@brookings.edu
Internet http://www.brook.edu/admin/fellowships.htm
Sponsor Brookings Institution
1775 Massachusetts Ave NW
Washington, DC 20036

Brookings Institution Sakip Sabanci International Research Award **1070**
This annual award is designed to promote fresh thinking, new ideas, and original research relevant to Turkish studies conducted in any field of the humanities and social sciences. The competition calls for original, essay-length studies that address the key issues relating to the changes in Turkey's neighborhood and how Turkey might respond to these changes. Studies focusing on any one or several of the following themes are welcome: Turkey's relations with the European Union, Russia, the Balkans, the Caucasus, Middle Eastern neighbors, and Central Asia, as well as Turkey's potential role in transatlantic relations and democratization in the broader Middle East. The topic changes each year. Topic for the current year is Turkey's New Geopolitical Environment: Policy Challenges and Opportunities for Engagement. Guidelines are available online.
Requirements All entries must be new and original works, not published previously in any form. Essays must be approximately 5000 to 6000 words. Essays must be submitted in English only by means of email in the form of an attached Word document to the following two addresses simultaneously: sabanciaward@sabanciuniv.edu; acause@brookings.edu.
Amount $20,000 first prize; $10,000 second prize; $5000 third prize
Date(s) Application Is Due Jan 31.
Contact Amanda Cause, Center on the United States and Europe, (202) 797-6227; Katie Busch , Brookings Media Relations Officer, (202) 797-6467
Internet http://www.brookings.edu/comm/news/20050620sabanciaward.htm
Sponsor Brookings Institution
1775 Massachusetts Ave NW
Washington, DC 20036

Brucebo Fine Art Summer Scholarship **1071**
The annual, three-month summer scholarship supports a Canadian artist to be used during a three month summer term on the island of Gotland, Sweden. The program supports housing, research, travel, and work-study in the fine arts, handcrafts, and related fields. There are no application forms.
Amount $C5000 approximately
Contact Dr. Jan Lundgren, (514) 398-4111; fax: (514) 398-7437; email: lundgren@felix.geog.mcgill.ca
Internet http://www.canada-scandinavia.ca/CSFGrants.htm
Sponsor Canadian-Scandinavian Foundation
McGill University, 805 Sherbrooke St W
Montreal, PQ H3A 2K6 Canada

Brush Foundation Grants Program **1072**
The primary goal of the foundation is to ensure that family planning worldwide becomes acceptable, available, accessible, affordable, effective, and safe. It focuses on projects that protect and enhance people's ability to manage their reproductive health; carry out public policy analysis and public education in the areas related to reproductive behavior and its social implications; and advance the personal knowledge and purposeful behavior of young people with respect to sexuality within a broad social context. Letters on inquiry are requested by January 15 and June 15.
Requirements Grants are limited to 501(c)3 organizations.
Restrictions The foundation will not accept unsolicited proposals.
Amount $5000-$50,000
Date(s) Application Is Due Jan 15; Jun 15.
Contact Krystal Fletcher, Grants Administrator, (216) 881-5121; fax: (216) 881-1834; email: brushfoundation@hotmail.com
Sponsor Brush Foundation
3135 Euclid Ave, Ste 102
Cleveland, OH 44115

Buell Book Fellowship in American Architecture, Urbanism, or Landscape **1073**
These fellowships, sponsored by the Temple Hoyne Buell Center for the Study of American Architecture at Columbia University, offer promising writers and scholars working in an area of American architecture, urbanism, or landscape studies the opportunity to turn a completed book-length manuscript or doctoral dissertation into publishable form. The center will provide office space, library usage fees, and eligibility for housing at Columbia. Fellows will also have access to the resources of the Avery Architectural Library. Fellows are expected to be in residence at Columbia for a substantial part of their tenure, to teach a seminar related to their research, and to contribute to the intellectual life of the Buell Center. Note: Program may not be offered for the current year; contact the center for availability.
Requirements Applicants must submit a manuscript, accompanied by a summary of content, a project history, and proposed plan of development; a professional resume; and two letters of recommendation by the deadline date.
Amount $20,000 for one academic year
Date(s) Application Is Due May 9.
Contact Director, The Buell Center, (212) 854-8165; fax: (212) 854-2127; email: buellcenter@columbia.edu
Internet http://www.arch.columbia.edu/Buell
Sponsor Columbia University
400 Avery Hall, Columbia University
New York, NY 10027

Bullard Fellowship in Forest Research **1074**
These fellowships are offered annually to midcareer individuals in biological and physical sciences and social and political studies to promote the advanced study, research, or integration of subjects relating to forested ecosystems. The fellowships are designed to provide an opportunity for candidates to use the facilities at Harvard University and the Harvard Forest to further their scientific and professional growth.
Amount $40,000 maximum
Date(s) Application Is Due Feb 1.
Contact Fellowship Administrator, (978) 724-3302; fax: (978) 724-3595; email: hfapps@fas.harvard.edu
Internet http://harvardforest.fas.harvard.edu/education/bullard.html
Sponsor Harvard University
P.O. Box 68, 324 N Main St
Petersham, MA 01366

Bullitt Foundation Grants **1075**
The foundation functions to protect and restore the environment of the Pacific Northwest, including Washington, Oregon, Idaho, western Montana, coastal rainforests in Alaska, and British Columbia, Canada. Program priorities include aquatic ecosystems; terrestrial ecosystems; conservation and stewardship in agriculture; energy and climate change; growth management and transportation; toxic and radioactive substances; training, organizational development, and unique opportunities (including education and public outreach). Areas of interest include air pollution, climate change, endangered species, energy conservation, environmental education and justice, human health, transportation, and tribal communities. The foundation supports challenge/matching, general operating, project/program, seed money, demonstration, and development grants, as well as requests for conferences/seminars and technical assistance support. Grants will be awarded for one year with possible renewal.
Requirements Nonprofit organizations in the Pacific Northwest, including Washington, Oregon, Idaho, western Montana, coastal rainforests in Alaska, and British Columbia, Canada are eligible.
Date(s) Application Is Due May 1; Nov 1.
Contact Program Officer , (206) 343-0807; fax: (206) 343-0822; email: info@bullitt.org
Internet http://www.bullitt.org
Sponsor Bullitt Foundation
1212 Minor Avenue
Seattle, WA 98101-2825

Bunge y Born Foundation Grants **1076**
The foundation awards grants in Argentina in the fields of education, social welfare and studies, the arts and humanities, and science and medicine. Types of support include research prizes, research grants, research scholarships, and support to attend conferences.
Contact Grants Administrator, 011-4318-6600; fax: 011-4318-6610; email: info@fundacionbyb.org
Internet http://www.fundacionbyb.org.ar/ingles/index.htm
Sponsor Bunge y Born Foundation
25 de Mayo 565
Buenos Aires 1002
Argentina

Bunting Fellowship Program **1077**
The Mary Bunting Institute of Radcliffe College is a multidisciplinary research center for women scholars, scientists, artists, and writers and is one of the major centers for advanced study in the United States. One fellowship will be awarded to a professional woman in the field of infant and child development, who is conducting research within the framework of, or contributing to, psychoanalysis. Applications will be judged on the quality and significance of the proposed project, the applicant's record of accomplishment, and the stage in the applicant's career. Office or studio space, auditing privileges, and access to libraries and most other resources of Radcliffe College and Harvard University are provided. Residence in the Boston area and participation in the institute community are required during the one-year fellowship appointment. Fellows are expected to present their work-in-progress at public colloquia, performances, or exhibitions.
Amount $33,000 stipend
Date(s) Application Is Due Oct 1.
Contact Fellowship Coordinator, (617) 496-1324; fax: (617) 495-8136; email: fellowships@radcliffe.edu
Internet http://www.radcliffe.edu/fellowships/bunting.php
Sponsor Bunting Institute of Radcliffe College
34 Concord Ave
Cambridge, MA 02138

Burden Trust Grants **1078**
The trust supports international nonprofit organizations in the fields of medical research and hospitals; schools and training institutions; and care of and homes for the elderly, children, and other individuals in need. Preference will be given to organizations affiliated with the Anglican Church.
Date(s) Application Is Due Mar 31.
Contact Patrick O'Conor, 0117 9628611; email: p.oconor@netgates.co.uk
Sponsor Burden Trust
51 Downs Park W
Bristol BS6 7QL United Kingdom

Bureau of Broadcast Measurement Research Scholarship **1079**
This scholarship is awarded to a graduate student for research into the fields of communications or broadcast journalism as they relate to radio and television. Application materials are available upon request.
Requirements Applicants must be Canadian citizens who are enrolled in a recognized communications or broadcast journalism course at a Canadian university.
Amount $C4000
Date(s) Application Is Due Jun 30.
Contact Scholarships Administrator, (613) 233-4035; fax: (613) 233-6961; email: cab@cab-acr.ca
Internet http://www.cab-acr.ca/english/about/awards/scholarships/bbm.pdf
Sponsor Canadian Association of Broadcasters
P.O. Box 627, Sta B, 350 Sparks St
Ottawa, ON K1P 5S2 Canada

Burlington Northern Santa Fe Foundation Grants **1080**
The foundation is focused on the communities where the company operates and areas where its railways pass. The foundation supports education, including scholarships for Native Americans and scholarships for children of employees in conjunction with the National Merit Scholarships program; the arts, including museums, performing arts, and libraries; and civic and public affairs. Support goes to the Nature Conservancy and for local fire departments and law enforcement. Types of support include general operating support, continuing support, annual campaigns, capital campaigns, and program development. Health and human services funding concentrates on the United Way. Awards are made for a single year and for continuing support. The company also matches employee funds given to public and private colleges and universities, cultural organizations, and hospitals in the United States. Requests for applications should describe the purpose for the grant. Requests are reviewed every six weeks.
Requirements 501(c)3 organizations located in Schaumburg, IL, and communities where the corporation operates, including 28 states and two Canadian provinces, are eligible to apply.
Contact Richard Russack, President, (708) 924-5615; fax: (708) 924-5657
Sponsor Burlington Northern Santa Fe Foundation
5601 West 26th Street
Cicero, IL 60804

Burton G. Bettingen Grants **1081**
The fields of activity of the corporation are education at all levels, mental health, crime and abuse victims and public protection programs, religion (Christian, Roman Catholic, and Salvation Army), environment, and welfare. Top funding priority is children and youth. The current focus is on child prostitutes, runaways, and abandoned children. Nonprofits servicing the economically disadvantaged also may apply. The corporation provides broad types of support, including operating, capital, research, challenge/matching grants, and endowments. A letter of inquiry stating the applicant's background, goals and objectives, and the specific need for funding is welcome. Unsolicited submissions are considered but receive low priority.
Requirements IRS 501(c)3 organizations are eligible. Giving primarily, but not limited to, Southern California.
Restrictions The corporation does not award grants to individuals; for general fund-raising events, dinners, or mass mailings; or to grantmaking organizations.
Amount $5000-$200,000 average
Contact Patricia Brown, Executive Director, (323) 938-8478; fax: (323) 938-8479; email: burtonbet@aol.com
Sponsor Burton G. Bettingen Corporation
134 S Mansfield Ave
Los Angeles, CA 90036-3019

Bush Foundation Artist Fellowships **1082**
The fellowships enable artists to further their work and contribution to their communities. Fellows may decide to take time for solitary work or reflection, engage in collaborative community projects, embark on travel or research, or pursue any other activity that contributes to their lives as artists. Artists may use the fellowship in many ways--to explore new directions, continue work already in progress, or accomplish work not financially feasible otherwise. Grant categories rotate on a two-year cycle. Check the website for this year's categories, which could include: Literature (Fiction, Creative Nonfiction, Poetry); Scriptworks (for stage and screen); Film/Video; or, Music Composition. The program also supports visual artists, performance artists, storytellers and traditional folk artists. Fellowships may last from 12 to 24 months.
Requirements Applicants must be US citizens or permanent residents and residents of Minnesota, North Dakota, South Dakota, or one of the 26 counties of northwestern Wisconsin (Ashland, Barron, Bayfield, Buffalo, Burnett, Chippewa, Douglas, Dunn, Eau Claire, Florence, Forest, Iron, La Crosse, Lincoln, Oneida, Pepin, Pierce, Polk, Price, Rusk, Saint Croix, Sawyer, Taylor, Trempealeau, Vilas, and Washburn) and must have lived in this funding region for at least 12 of the 36 months preceding the application deadline. Applicants must be 25 years or older at the time of the application deadline.

Restrictions Artists are not eligible to apply if they are a student enrolled full- or part-time in a degree-granting program after July 1 of the program year; and a director or staff member of the Bush Foundation, or a spouse, parent, child, or grandchild of a director or staff member of the foundation.
Amount $48,000
Contact Julie Gordon Dalgleish, Program Director; (651) 227-0891; email: bafinfo@bushfoundation.org
Internet http://www.bushfoundation.org/fellowships/artists_overview.asp
Sponsor Bush Foundation
332 Minnesota Street, Suite E-900
Saint Paul, MN 55101

Bushrod H. Campbell and Adah F. Hall Charity Fund Grants **1083**
Grants are awarded to organizations in the Boston area devoted to basic needs for the elderly, projects relating to medicine and medical research, health care, hospitals, the blind and deaf, and certain discretionary projects. Grants are also awarded countrywide for projects addressing population control. Types of support include capital grants, general operating grants, program grants, and research grants.
Requirements Tax-exempt groups located within Boston and neighboring communities and US tax-exempt organizations devoted to population control are eligible.
Restrictions Grants are not awarded to individuals.
Amount $3000-$7500 average
Date(s) Application Is Due Jan 15; Apr 15; Aug 15; Oct 15.
Contact Brenda Taylor, c/o Palmer & Dodge, (617) 239-0556; fax: (617) 227-4420
Sponsor Bushrod H. Campbell and Adah F. Hall Charity Fund
111 Huntington Ave at Prudential Ctr
Boston, MA 02199-7613

Business and Society Foundation Grants **1084**
The foundation was established to encourage Spanish and foreign companies working in Spain to improve the quality of life in operating communities. Foundation activities are carried out through research, conferences, and training courses. Types of support include prizes and grants to organizations.
Contact Francisco Abad, Director, 34-91-4358997; fax: 34-91-4353974; email: fundacion@empresaysociedad.org
Internet http://www.empresaysociedad.org
Sponsor Business and Society Foundation
Goya 15, 2 derecha
Madrid 28001
Spain

BWF Career Awards at the Scientific Interface **1085**
This initiative supports the early career development of postdoctoral scientists in the physical and computational sciences, whose work addresses biological questions and who are dedicated to pursuing careers in academic research. Research methods may include any combination of experiment, computation, mathematical modeling, statistical analysis, or computer simulation. Areas of interest include chemistry, computer sciences, engineering, mathematics, and physics. Awards provide a stipend over five years to support up to two years of advanced postdoctoral training and the first three years of a faculty appointment. During both the postdoctoral and the faculty periods, grants must be made to degree-granting institutions in the United States or Canada on behalf of the award recipient. Award recipients must complete at least one year of postdoctoral training during the period of the award, usually at the institution that nominates the candidate.
Requirements US and Canadian academic institutions, including medical schools, graduate schools, affiliated hospitals, and research institutes are eligible. Candidates must hold a PhD degree in the fields of mathematics, physics, chemistry (physical, theoretical, or computational), computer science, statistics, or engineering. Exceptions will be made only if the applicant can demonstrate significant expertise in one of these areas, evidenced by publications or advanced course work. Candidates must have completed at least six months but not more than 48 months of postdoctoral training at the time of application.
Restrictions Candidates must not hold or have accepted a faculty appointment as a tenure-track assistant professor at the time of application.
Amount $500,000 total over five years
Date(s) Application Is Due May 1.
Contact Dr. Nancy Sung, Senior Program Officer, (919) 991-5100; fax: (919) 991-5160; email: info@bwfund.org
Internet http://www.bwfund.org/programs/interfaces/index.html
Sponsor Burroughs Wellcome Fund
P.O. Box 13901
Research Triangle Park, NC 27709-3901

BWF Career Awards in the Biomedical Sciences **1086**
The awards provide support over five years to bridge advanced postdoctoral training and the early years of faculty service. Researchers who are interested in applying may be working in any of the basic biomedical sciences. During the postdoctoral period, awardees may train at degree-granting institutions in the United States, Canada, or the United Kingdom. All faculty positions must be taken at US or Canadian degree-granting institutions. The aim of the program is to provide research training support and to assist individuals during their initial years of faculty service in making the critical transition to becoming independent investigators. It is expected that by the end of the award program, individuals will be engaged in productive research programs and better able to compete effectively for grant support from government and other extramural sources. Candidates must be nominated by their institution. A US or Canadian institution--including its medical school, graduate schools, and all affiliated hospitals and research institutes--may nominate up to six candidates. Institutions that nominate at least one candidate in the reproductive sciences may nominate an additional candidate.
Requirements candidates must have completed at least 12 months but not more than 48 months of postdoctoral research training by the application deadline. Candidates must be nominated by accredited, degree-granting institutions in the United States, Canada, or the United Kingdom; and be citizens or permanent residents of the United States or Canada at the time of application.
Restrictions Researchers who hold a faculty appointment as an assistant professor or the equivalent, or who know they will receive such an appointment within a year of the application deadline, are not eligible. Individuals who are working in intramural programs at governmental institutions such as the NIH are not eligible.
Amount $500,000 over five years
Date(s) Application Is Due Oct 3.
Contact Rolly Simpson, Program Associate, (919) 991-5100; fax: (919) 941-5884; email: mailback@bwfund.org
Internet http://www.bwfund.org/programs/biomedical_sciences/career_awards_main.html
Sponsor Burroughs Wellcome Fund
P.O. Box 13901
Research Triangle Park, NC 27709-3901

BWF Clinical Scientist Awards in Translational Research **1087**
The awards foster the development of outstanding physician-scientists who strengthen transitional research (the two-way transfer between basic research and patient care). Selection criteria include the candidate's qualifications, quality of the proposed activities, the ability to conduct innovative research, originality of the proposed research, and the potential to advance research in the scientific fields of study. Applications must be submitted electronically via proposalCENTRAL.
Requirements US or Canadian nonprofit hospitals and educational, scientific, research, or health institutions may submit applications. Candidates must have an MD or MD/PhD degree; hold an appointment or a joint appointment in a subspecialty of clinical medicine; present evidence of an established research career; and be investigators at the assistant-professor level, associate-professor level, or an equivalent tenure-track position. Institutions may nominate up to four candidates, as long as at least one of the candidates is female, and at least one of the candidates is a member of an underrepresented minority group (Hispanic-American, African-American, Native American).
Amount $750,000 average over five years ($150,000 per year)
Date(s) Application Is Due Sep 1.
Contact Debi Vought, (919) 991-5116; email: dvought@bwfund.org
Internet http://www.bwfund.org/programs/translational/index.html
Sponsor Burroughs Wellcome Fund
21 T.W. Alexander Dr
Research Triangle Park, NC 27703-8472

BWF Program in Pathogenesis of Infectious Disease **1088**
The goal of the program is to provide new opportunities for accomplished investigators still early in their careers to study pathogenesis, with a focus on the intersection of human and pathogen biology. The program is intended to shed light on the overarching issues of how human hosts handle infectious challenge. BWF is particularly interested in work focused on the host, as well as host-pathogen studies originating in viral, bacterial, fungal, or parasite systems. Studies in this area may have their root in the pathogen, but the focus of the work should be on the effects on the host at the cellular and/or systemic levels. Excellent animal models of human disease are within the scope of the program. The awards are intended to give recipients the freedom and flexibility to pursue new avenues of inquiry and higher-risk research projects that hold potential for advancing significantly the biochemical, pharmacological, immunological, and molecular biological understanding of how infectious agents and the human body interact.
Requirements Applications must be submitted by accredited degree-granting US or Canadian institutions on behalf of individual candidates. Candidates must have an MD or PhD degree, and they must hold a tenure-track faculty appointment or its equivalent. Candidates must be citizens or permanent residents of the United States or Canada at the time of application to be eligible.
Amount $400,000 over five years
Date(s) Application Is Due Nov 1.
Contact Jean Kramarik, Senior Program Associate, (919) 991-5122; fax: (919) 991-5160; email: jkramarik@bwfund.org
Internet http://www.bwfund.org/programs/infectious_disease/index.html
Sponsor Burroughs Wellcome Fund
P.O. Box 13901
Research Triangle Park, NC 27709-3901

Bydale Foundation Grants **1089**
The foundation emphasizes international understanding, public policy research, environmental quality, cultural programs, the law and civil rights, social services, higher education, and economics. Funding includes support for: conference/seminars,

continuing support, general operating support, matching/challenging support, program development, publication, research, and seed money. An application form is not required. Submit an initial approach in the form of a letter or proposal.
Requirements US 501(c)3 nonprofits are eligible.
Date(s) Application Is Due Nov 1.
Contact Milton Solomon, Vice President, (914) 428-3232; fax: (914) 428-1660
Sponsor Bydale Foundation
11 Martine Avenue
White Plains, NY 10606

Byron W. and Alice L. Lockwood Foundation Grants **1090**
The foundation awards grants to Washington nonprofit organizations in its areas of interest, including arts, biomedical research, higher education, hospitals and health care organizations, housing and homelessness, museums, religion and religious welfare programs, and social services. Types of support include capital improvements, continuing support, general operating grants, professorships, projects grants, and research grants. There are no application forms; submit a letter of request.
Requirements Washington nonprofit organizations are eligible. Grants are awarded primarily in Washington's Seattle and Puget Sound areas.
Amount $900-$56,000 range
Date(s) Application Is Due Oct 31.
Contact Lee Kraft, Executive Director, (206) 230-8489
Sponsor Byron W. and Alice L. Lockwood Foundation
P.O. Box 4
Mercer, WA 98040

BYU Religious Studies Center Research Grants **1091**
The mission of the BYU Religious Studies Center is to encourage and sponsor serious, faithful, gospel-related scholarship and the ensuing publication of that scholarship. The mission is accomplished by providing grants to assist worthwhile projects; encouraging faculty members to submit their manuscripts for publication; and publishing and marketing high-quality religious books and periodicals of a scholarly nature.
Contact Richard Neitzel Holzapfel, Managing Director (801) 422-2332; email: holzapfel@byu.edu
Internet http://religion.byu.edu/rsc_about.php
Sponsor Brigham Young University
Brigham Young University, 167 HGB
Provo, UT 84602

C. Alma Baker Trust Grants **1092**
The trust operates in the fields of agriculture and education and supports students studying for agricultural degrees at Massey University. Types of support include postgraduate scholarships for agricultural and horticultural research, grants for research to further the science of agriculture and horticulture, and travel grants for overseas trips of three to six weeks. Travel grant recipients are expected to contribute to the New Zealand horticultural or agricultural community upon return. Deadlines vary for each program; contact program staff for exact dates.
Amount $10,000 per year for Masters; $20,000 per year for PhD
Date(s) Application Is Due Feb 1.
Contact Trust Administrator, 01480 411331; fax: 01480 459012
Internet http://www.massey.ac.nz
Sponsor C. Alma Baker Trust
Private Bag, Massey University
Palmerston North
New Zealand

C. Wright Mills Award **1093**
The award is an annual prize for a book that best exemplifies social science research and scholarship. The books nominated must have been published in the year preceding the year of the award.
Amount $500
Date(s) Application Is Due Jan 15.
Contact Michele Koontz, Administrative Officer, (865) 689-1531; fax: (865) 689-1534; email: mkoontz3@utk.edu
Internet http://www.sssp1.org/index.cfm?contentID=566
Sponsor C. Wright Mills Award Committee
901 McClung Tower, SSSP, Univ of TN
Knoxville, TN 37996-0490

C.R. Bard Foundation Grants **1094**
The foundation's areas of interest are health care; arts, cultural, and community life; and education and research in company-operating areas. In the area of health care, the foundation supports organizations and programs specializing in vascular medicine, urology, and oncology. In the arts/cultural/community category, the foundation considers requests from local civic, recreational, youth, and art and cultural organizations. In the area of education and research, the foundation considers requests from institutions of higher education that offer medical and managerial curricula, as well as organizations whose programs and services benefit the health care industry. Types of support include program development, scholarship funds, and employee matching gifts. Requests for funding must be in writing. Contact the office for application requirements.
Requirements 501(c)3 organizations in primarily New Jersey, Massachusetts, and California may apply for grant support.
Amount $1.4 million total
Contact Program Contact, (908) 277-8182, (800) 367-2273; fax: (908) 277-8240
Internet http://www.crbard.com/about/com_relations/foundations/index.cfm
Sponsor C.R. Bard Foundation
730 Central Ave
Murray Hill, NJ 07974

Cabot Corporation Foundation Grants Program **1095**
The objective of the company's corporate giving is to support community outreach objectives, with priority given to science and technology education; safety health and environment (SH&E); and community and civic improvement efforts in the communities where the company has major facilities or operations. Types of support include capital grants, challenge grants, employee matching gifts, fellowships, general support, professorships, project support, research, scholarships, and seed money. The board meets in January, April, July, and October to consider requests. Applications must be received at least 30 days before a board meeting.
Requirements The foundation supports only nonprofit 501(c)3 tax-exempt organizations in Georgia, Illinois, Louisiana, Massachusetts, Pennsylvania, Texas, and West Virginia. Modest support is available for international organizations that qualify under US tax regulations.
Restrictions Contributions are not made to individuals; fraternal, political, athletic or veterans organizations; religious institutions (except for projects that are open to individuals without regard to religious preference); capital and endowment campaigns; sponsorships of local groups/individuals to participate in regional, national, or international competitions, conferences or events; advertising, dinner-table sponsorship, or fund-raising events.
Amount $1,000-$25,000; $5000 average
Contact Karen Morrissey, Executive Director, (617) 345-0100; fax: (617) 342-6312; email: Karen_Morrissey@cabot-corp.com
Internet http://w1.cabot-corp.com/controller.jsp?N=21+3030
Sponsor Cabot Corporation Foundation
Two Seaport Lane, Suite 1300
Boston, MA 02210

CALA C.C. Seetoo/CALA Conference Travel Scholarship **1096**
One scholarship is awarded each year to a student of Chinese nationality or Chinese descent currently enrolled in an ALA-accredited library and information science program in the United States to attend the ALA annual conference. The purpose of the award is to provide its recipient mentoring and networking opportunities and professional development at the annual conference. Selection will be based on academic achievement and leadership potential.
Requirements Students who are currently enrolled in ALA-accredited master's or doctoral programs of Library and Information Science in degree-granting institutions in North America are eligible to apply. Applicants must be of Chinese nationality or of Chinese descent.
Amount $500
Date(s) Application Is Due Apr 15.
Contact Y. Diana Wu, (408) 808-2087; email: dwu@sjsu.edu
Internet http://www.cala-web.org
Sponsor Chinese-American Librarians Association
One Washington Sq
San Jose, CA 95192-0028

Calgary CFUW Nursing Scholarships **1097**
This award has been made available through the Calgary Chapter of the Canadian Federation of University Women with a matching grant from the Province of Alberta's Advanced Education Endowment Fund. One award is given per year; selection is made by the Graduate Scholarship Committee.
Requirements Applicants must be Canadian citizens registered in or admissible to the first year of a program leading to a master's degree in nursing. Candidates must demonstrate both clinical and academic achievement, supported by three letters of reference.
Amount $C1000
Date(s) Application Is Due Feb 1.
Contact Scholarship Administrator, (403) 220-5690; email: gsaward@ucalgary.ca
Internet http://www.grad.ucalgary.ca/funding/internal_scholarships/lev_4/can_fed_nursing.htm
Sponsor University of Calgary
2500 University Dr NW, Earth Sciences Bldg, Rm 720
Calgary, AB T2N 1N4 Canada

California and Michigan Nonprofit Research Program Grants **1098**
The Nonprofit Sector Research Fund of the institute makes grants to expand understanding of nonprofit activities, including philanthropy. The fund encourages projects that will inform public policy toward nonprofits and invites proposals from scholars and practitioners. Nine priority areas for national and international grantmaking activity include the role of nonprofits in fostering democratic values, their role in society, advocacy issues, philanthropy, governance, public accountability, financing, workforce, and international nonprofit activities. The California and Michigan programs support

studies with the potential to inform public policy and benefit nonprofit practices in those states. The listed application deadline is for preproposals; full proposals are by invitation.
Amount $25,000 maximum
Date(s) Application Is Due Jul 15.
Contact Rachel Mosher-Williams, (202) 736-2501; fax: (202) 293-0525; email: rwilliams@aspeninstitute.org
Internet http://www.nonprofitresearch.org/newsletter1531/newsletter.htm
Sponsor Aspen Institute
One Dupont Circle NW, Ste 700
Washington, DC 20036

California Breast Cancer Research Program Grants **1099**
The state-funded breast cancer research effort supports a partnership comprising community members (such as a breast cancer advocacy organization, a community clinic or organization serving women with breast cancer, or a member of a California community affected by breast cancer) and experienced research scientists. Two funding mechanisms are available. The 18-month pilot award supports the initial phase of the project, including feasibility of methods, strengthening collaborations, development of tools and methods, and/or collecting pilot data. The three-year full award is for projects with a fully developed research plan with supporting preliminary data, carried out by a well integrated team of scientific and community members with a previous work relationship. The partnership works together to identify the research question, develop the research plan, carry out the research, interpret the results, and disseminate information to the community. The listed application deadline is for concept papers. Guidelines are available online.
Requirements A partnership consists of California community members (organization or individual) and experienced research scientists.
Amount $600,000 maximum, full award ; $150,000 maximum, pilot award
Date(s) Application Is Due Nov 3.
Contact Natalie Collins, MSW, (510) 987-0646; email: natalie.collins@ucop.edu
Internet http://www.cbcrp.org/apply/crcCall
Sponsor University of California
300 Lakeside Dr, 6th Fl
Oakland, CA 94612-3550

California Stories Grants **1100**
The fund is one of the components of California Stories, the California Council for the Humanities' statewide initiative that seeks to strengthen California communities through story-based public humanities projects. Through grants awarded quarterly through a competitive process, the fund supports public humanities programs that will bring to light compelling stories from California's diverse communities and provide opportunities for collective reflection and discussion. The current competition invites proposals for projects that document the stories of Gulf Coast residents evacuated to California in the aftermath of Hurricane Katrina and make use of the humanities in exploring those stories. Guidelines and application materials are available online.
Requirements Projects must strengthen communities through public sharing and discussion of stories; focus on California communities (defined as such on the basis of geography, ethnicity, culture, or shared experience); use grant funds to gather stories from community members, for archival research, or to provide a forum to share and discuss stories; use one or more formats to present and communicate these stories, including photography and interpretive exhibit, radio documentary, digital media, dramatic presentation, interpretive artwork, author/poetry readings, storytelling events, film festivals, and community conferences; include a community discussion component that engages people in discussion of the stories and their relevance to the community; involve at least one humanities expert in the design and implementation of the project; produce photos, transcripts of stories, or audio and video recordings that can be archived and shared with larger audiences through broadcast, publication, or website dissemination; have a total budget of no more than $30,000; and include plans for assessing project outcomes. Culminating events should be free and open to participation by the general public. Project activities should not start before October 1. 1.
Amount $7500; $15,000 maximum Hurricane Katrina evacuee stories
Date(s) Application Is Due Dec 1.
Contact Susana Loza, (415) 391-1474 ext 314; email: info@calhum.org
Internet http://www.californiastories.org/guidelines/guidelines_ca_story_intro.htm
Sponsor California Council for the Humanities
312 Sutter St, Ste 601
San Francisco, CA 94108-4371

California Teachers Association Scholarships **1101**
The CTA Scholarship gives support for study in higher education to active members and/or dependent children of active members and/or dependent children of deceased members. Twenty-five scholarships are awarded annually. Applications are available in October, and may be obtained by contacting the CTA Human Rights Department in Burlingame or any CTA Regional Resource Center office.
Requirements Applicant must be an active member of California Teachers Association or applicant must be the dependent child of an active, retired-life or deceased member of California Teachers Association depending on which program they are applying for.
Amount $2000
Date(s) Application Is Due Feb 15.
Contact Manuel Ayan, (650) 552-5204; fax: (650) 552-5002; email: scholarships@cta.org
Internet http://www.cta.org/InsideCTA/ScholarshipsWorkshops/ScholarshipsWorkshops.htm
Sponsor California Teachers Association
P.O. Box 921, 1705 Murchison Dr
Burlingame, CA 94011-0921

California Wellness Foundation Work and Health Program Grants **1102**
The foundation focuses its activities on specific priority areas where it has a significant, long-term commitment. Within each priority area, the foundation allocates the majority of its funds toward initiatives. Initiatives are targeted grantmaking programs with distinct objectives and are generally announced through requests for proposals. The foundation awards general grants and project grants. Under general grants, requests for core operating support for organizations that provide direct services to Californians for disease prevention or health promotion are of primary interest. Priority areas under general grants are diversity in the health professions, environmental health, healthy aging, mental health, teenage pregnancy prevention,, violence prevention, women's health, and work and health. Special projects grants are awarded to areas that fall outside the priority areas. Of particular interest are proposals to help California communities respond to cutbacks in federally funded programs. Activities commonly supported under special projects include strengthening traditional safety-net providers, educating consumers about changes in health care systems, advocating for underserved communities in health policy debates, and informing public decision making through policy analysis.
Requirements Eligible applicants are California 501(c)3 nonprofit organizations, or organizations with a preapproved fiscal sponsor. An organization should first write a succinct letter of interest (one to two pages) that describes the organization, its leadership, the region and population(s) served, and the activities for which funding is needed, including the amount requested.
Amount $5000-$200,000 over one to three years
Contact Grants Administrator, (818) 702-1900; fax: (818) 593-6614
Internet http://www.tcwf.org/grants_program/index.htm
Sponsor California Wellness Foundation
6320 Canoga Ave, Ste 1700
Woodland Hills, CA 91367-7111

Calvin Institute of Christian Worship Renewal Grants **1103**
The grants program is designed to foster well-grounded worship renewal in congregations throughout North America. Made possible through support of the Lilly Endowment, Inc., these grants are intended to serve a grass-roots constituency of those concerned for the vitality of the worship life in their local Christian communities in a variety of denominations. Through its grantmaking, the institute intends to stimulate thoughtful and energetic work that will result in worship services that exhibit renewed creativity, theological integrity, and relevance. The institute solicits proposals for grants to support a wide variety of projects. Grants will be awarded both to individuals and to nonprofit organizations, such as churches, colleges, seminaries, or other church-related organizations. Grants to individuals, however, will be awarded through the church or organization with which they are affiliated.
Requirements Any individual or team of people with leadership role(s) who are directly related to the worship life of a congregation, school, church-related organization, or other ministry is encouraged to apply. This includes pastors, educators, church staff persons, church musicians, directors of worship, liturgists, artists, architects, and scholars.
Amount $5000-$15,000 range
Date(s) Application Is Due Jan 10.
Contact Betty Grit, Grants Administrator, (616) 526-7168; fax: (616) 957-7168; email: worshipgrants@calvin.edu
Internet http://webapps.calvin.edu/worship/grants/wrgp.php
Sponsor Calvin Institute of Christian Worship
3201 Burton SE
Grand Rapids, MI 49546

Camargo Foundation Fellowships **1104**
The program provides, at no cost, furnished apartments and a reference library in the city of Cassis for scholars who wish to pursue projects in the humanities and social sciences related to French and francophone cultures. The foundation also sponsors creative projects by visual artists, photographers, composers, and writers. The term of residence is one semester (early September to mid-December or mid-January to May 31), precise dates being announced each year. An informational brochure and application form are available upon request.
Requirements Applicants may include members of university and college faculties, including professors emeriti; independent scholars working on specific projects; secondary school teachers; graduate students completing the dissertation required for their degree; and writers, photographers, visual artists, and composers.
Amount $3500 stipend
Date(s) Application Is Due Jan 15.
Contact Program Contact, (651) 238-8805
Internet http://www.camargofoundation.org/aboutus.asp
Sponsor Camargo Foundation
400 Sibley St, Ste 125
Saint Paul, MN 55101-1928

Cambridge Foundation For Peace Prize **1105**
The foundations announces a call for papers that explore the role of diasporas as transnational actors in preventing violence, crisis response, or postconflict peacebuilding. The prize will be awarded for the winning proposal, which will contribute to systematic research on diasporas. In particular, the paper should concentrate on identifying and specifying the mechanisms by which diasporas can be engaged in policy planning and implementation. The regional and/or country focus is open, but preference will be give to Southeastern Europe and/or the Eastern Mediterranean. The CFP will distribute the winning paper to its worldwide audience of policymakers, political leaders, academics, and journalists. The winning paper also will be posted as a working paper on CFP-web.
Requirements The competition is open to public policy professionals and academics (including graduate students).
Amount $3000
Date(s) Application Is Due Apr 1.
Contact Grants Administrator, (617) 254-5437; fax: (617) 254-5437; email: schmitz@cfp-web.org
Internet http://www.cfp-web.org
Sponsor Cambridge Foundation for Peace
1770 Massachusetts Ave, Box 303
Cambridge, MA 02140-2808

Camille Dreyfus Teacher-Scholar Awards Program **1106**
The purpose of this award is to support the teaching and research careers of talented young faculty in the chemical sciences. Based on institutional nominations, the program provides discretionary funding to faculty at early stages in their careers. This awards program is focused primarily on individual research accomplishments and promise, but evidence of excellence in teaching is also expected. The Award provides a $75,000 unrestricted research grant. Of the total amount, $7,500 is for departmental expenses associated with research and education. Guidelines and required information are available online.
Requirements Institutions that grant a bachelor's or higher degree in chemistry, chemical engineering, or biochemistry may submit nominations to the program. Nominees must hold a full-time tenure-track academic appointment, and are normally expected to be within the first five years of their independent academic careers.
Restrictions Defrayal of academic-year salary is not permitted.
Amount $75,000
Date(s) Application Is Due Jan 9.
Contact Mark Cordillo, Executive Director, (212) 753-1760; fax: (212) 593-2256; email: mcardillo@dreyfus.org
Internet http://www.dreyfus.org/tc.shtml
Sponsor Camille and Henry Dreyfus Foundation
555 Madison Ave, 20th Fl
New York, NY 10022-1301

Campaign for the Civic Mission of Schools Grants **1107**
The program is a long-term effort to renew and elevate civic education in the schools, based on recommendations in The Civic Mission of Schools report. The report identifies six promising approaches to good civic education: instruction in government, history, law, and democracy; class discussion of current local, national, and international issues and events; community service and service-learning linked to curriculum and class instruction; extracurricular opportunities to get involved in the school and community; participation in school governance; and simulations of democratic processes and procedures. A major component of the campaign focuses on education policy at the state and local level. The program seeks applications from state-level coalitions for grants in two categories: small grants--two-year grants to state coalitions that propose a specific project or activity that promotes policy-related work that is tied to one or more of the recommendations of the report (July 19 deadline); and large grants--two-year grants to state coalitions that have the capacity and will to implement several of the six recommended approaches (June 4 deadline). Guidelines are available online.
Requirements An applicant should represent a coalition of education and civic engagement stakeholders and other interested parties, including for example: government agencies, legislators, state and local school board members, student leaders, student associations, government relations and strategic communications firms, business alliances, colleges and universities, and philanthropic institutions.
Amount $150,000 over two years, large grants; $20,000 over two years, small grants
Date(s) Application Is Due Jun 4; Jul 19.
Contact Richard Russo, Center for Democracy and Citizenship, Council for Excellence in Government, (202) 530-3260; email: rrusso@excelgov.org
Internet http://www.civicmissionofschools.org
Sponsor Carnegie Corporation of New York
437 Madison Ave
New York, NY 10022

Campbell Foundation HIV/AIDS Research Grants **1108**
The foundation awards grants for research projects on ways to prevent and treat HIV, AIDS, and related conditions or illnesses. Proposals focusing on alternative, nontraditional avenues of study receive preference. Most grants support clinical research, although other types of work are considered. After initial screening, requests are reviewed by a peer review board of noted HIV/AIDS physicians and then sent to the board for final decisions. There are no application deadlines, but as all grants are handled chronologically, the foundation suggests submitting grant requests as early as possible.
Requirements US nonprofit organizations are eligible.
Amount $20,000-$80,000 average
Contact Program Contact, (954) 493-8822; fax: (954) 493-8801; email: campfound@aol.com
Internet http://members.aol.com/campfound
Sponsor Campbell Foundation
5975 N Federal Hwy, Ste 126
Fort Lauderdale, FL 33308

CampusRN/AACN Nursing Scholarship Fund **1109**
The scholarship program supports students who are seeking a baccalaureate, master's, or doctoral degree in nursing. Special consideration will be given to students enrolled in a master's or doctoral program with the goal of pursuing a nursing faculty career; completing an RN to baccalaureate program (BSN); or enrolled in an accelerated baccalaureate or master's degree nursing program. Applicants must submit an online application and create a complete profile on CampusRN. All applicants must already be enrolled (not just accepted) at an AACN member institution. Applications are accepted only by email.
Requirements Nursing students enrolled in a baccalaureate, master's or doctoral degree program in nursing are eligible.
Amount $2500
Date(s) Application Is Due Jan 1; Mar 1; May 1; Jul 1; Sep 1; Nov 1.
Contact Scholarship Administrator, (202) 463-6930; fax: (202) 785-8320; email: info@campuscareercenter.com
Internet http://aacn.campusrn.com/scholarships/scholarship_rn.asp
Sponsor American Association of Colleges of Nursing
One Dupont Circle NW, Ste 530
Washington, DC 20036

CAN Autism Treatment-Related Study Awards **1110**
The organization recognizes the urgent need to develop effective therapies to treat both core and domain specific features of autism. Research proposals focused on all aspects of treatment, from basic research models, to clinical trials, to biomarker identification, are acceptable for submission. Due to the current lack of effective treatment and absence of known biomarkers, applications are reviewed as they are received. Funding amount and duration is determined per individual proposal. Indirect costs are limited to 10 percent of the total amount. Letters of intent are required prior to invitation of full proposals.
Amount $60,000 per year for one, two, or three years
Date(s) Application Is Due Sep 1.
Contact Therese Finazzo, Grants Officer, (888) 828-8476 or (323) 549-0500 ext 18; fax: (323) 549-0500; email: therese@cureautismnow.org
Internet http://www.cureautismnow.org/research/funding/3523.jsp
Sponsor Cure Autism Now
5455 Wilshire Blvd, Ste 715
Los Angeles, CA 90036

CAN Pilot Research Projects **1111**
Pilot research programs will provide funding for investigators at any stage in their career to work on innovative pilot projects. The purpose of these awards is to encourage innovative approaches towards elucidating the causes, prevention, and appropriate therapy of autism. They are intended to provide support for innovative research that may not have reached a stage where funding can be obtained from federal sources. Annual deadline dates may vary; contact program staff for exact dates.
Requirements Investigators whose focus has been outside the field of autism as well as innovative investigators from within the field are encouraged to apply.
Restrictions Members of CAN's Board of Directors are not eligible as investigators in CAN supported research. Members of CAN's Scientific Advisory Committee are eligible, provided they comply with foundation policies regarding the avoidance of conflict of interest.
Amount $120,000 maximum two-year award
Date(s) Application Is Due Mar 3; Jun 9.
Contact Therese Finazzo, Grants Officer, (888) 828-8476 or (323) 549-0500 ext 18; fax: (323) 549-0500; fax: (323) 549-0547; email: therese@cureautismnow.org
Internet http://www.cureautismnow.org/research/funding/3522.jsp
Sponsor Cure Autism Now
5455 Wilshire Blvd, Ste 715
Los Angeles, CA 90036-4234

CAN Young Investigator Awards **1112**
The purpose of these awards is to encourage innovative approaches towards elucidating the causes, prevention, and appropriate therapy of autism. These awards are designed to support outstanding projects that involve innovative approaches and the application of cutting-edge technologies. All proposals must have direct and immediate relevance to autism and related disorders.
Requirements Awards provide for the work of outstanding candidates to be carried out under the supervision of a mentor who is an established investigator. The investigator need not be directly involved in autism research but must provide an environment in which the CAN fellow can pursue a project with relevance to autism or related disorders.

Restrictions Applicants should be no more than four years out of a MD or PhD program on the date the fellowship would begin.
Amount $40,000 and $1000 travel allowance per year for two years
Date(s) Application Is Due Mar 3; Jun 9.
Contact Therese Finazzo, Grants Officer, (323) 549-0500 ext 18 or (888) 828-8476; fax: (323) 549-0500; email: therese@cureautismnow.org
Internet http://www.cureautismnow.org/research/funding/3522.jsp
Sponsor Cure Autism Now
5455 Wilshire Blvd, Ste 715
Los Angeles, CA 90036-4234

Canada Council for the Arts Grants **1113**
The council awards a wide range of grants to professional Canadian artists and arts organizations in dance, interdisciplinary work and performance art, media arts, music, theater, writing, publishing, architecture, and the visual arts. The council also administers the Killam Program of prizes and fellowships to Canadian scholars of exceptional ability engaged in significant research projects.
Requirements Professional Canadian artists and arts organizations are eligible.
Contact Lise Rochon, Information Officer, (800) 263-5588 ext 4138 or (613) 566-4414 ext 4138; fax: (613) 566-4390; email: info@canadacouncil.ca
Internet http://www.canadacouncil.ca/grants/default.asp
Sponsor Canada Council for the Arts
P.O. Box 1047, 350 Albert St
Ottawa, ON K1P 5V8 Canada

Canada Council John G. Diefenbaker Award **1114**
This annual award enables a distinguished German scholar to spend up to 12 months in Canada, which may include brief periods in the United States. While research must be the primary activity during the tenure of the award, the recipient will also be encouraged to participate in the activities of the host institution and to interact more extensively with the research communities in Canada and the United States by visiting other institutions. Candidates may not apply for this award, but instead must be nominated by a host university department or research institute in Canada.
Requirements Candidates must be German citizens and must have a sound working knowledge of one of Canada's two official languages. German scholars who have demonstrated outstanding ability, especially through a substantial publication record over several years, are eligible to apply.
Amount $C75,000 maximum plus $C20,000 for travel expenses
Date(s) Application Is Due Dec 1.
Contact Nathalie Lauzon, Administrative Assistant, (800) 263-5588 or (613) 566-4414 ext 4083; fax: (613) 566-4430; TTY: (613) 565-5194; email: endowments.prizes@canadacouncil.ca
Internet http://www.canadacouncil.ca/prizes/john_g_diefenbaker/hn127223038493593750.htm
Sponsor Canada Council for the Arts
P.O. Box 1047, 350 Albert St
Ottawa, ON K1P 5V8 Canada

Canada-US Fulbright Program Grants **1115**
The Canada-U.S. Fulbright Program strengthens bi-national collaborative research and promotes thoughtful public debate on topics that reflect the broad range of contemporary issues relevant to Canada, the United States and the relationship between the two countries. The Program operates on the principle of reciprocal exchange and provides the opportunity for outstanding Canadian and American students and scholars to lecture, research and pursue graduate study in the United States and Canada, respectively. Award recipients include prominent and promising scholars, experienced and junior professionals and exceptional students.
Requirements Canadians applying to the United States must be Canadian citizens, and Americans applying to Canada must be American citizens. Faculty intending to lecture must possess a terminal degree and postdoctoral college or university experience; for research, faculty must possess a doctoral degree or, in some fields, have recognized professional standing. Students applying as formal enrollment awards candidates must be accepted, or anticipating acceptance, into a graduate program at the desired university in the other country. Research awards candidates must have completed at least an initial year of graduate work in their home country, but not completed the graduate thesis. Graduating senior awards candidates must concurrently apply for graduate school in the United States and show evidence of graduate program acceptance before receiving their Fulbright award.
Restrictions Applicants are not eligible for a Canada-U.S. Fulbright Award if he or she: currently holds permanent residency status in the intended host country; is currently residing in or enrolled at a university in the intended host country; has resided abroad for five or more consecutive years in the six year period immediately preceding the date of application; has received a Fulbright Award within the last five years; has had recent substantial experience in the intended host country (recent substantial experience is defined as study, teaching, research or employment for a period of more than an academic year (nine months) during the past five years); is a Canadian applicant and you are a dual citizen of Canada and the United States.
Amount $C15,000
Contact Dr. Michael K. Hawes, Executive Director, (613) 688-5540; fax: (613) 237-2029; email: mhawes@fulbright.ca
Internet http://www.fulbright.ca/en/award.asp
Sponsor The Foundation for Educational Exchange between Canada and the United States of America
350 Albert Street, Ste 2015
Ottawa, ON K1R 1A4 Canada

Canadian Dental Research Foundation Award **1116**
This award is offered biennially to encourage research related to dentistry conducted by graduate or postgraduate students in Canada. The monetary prize will be presented to the student who will have submitted the best report on a research project at the CDA annual meeting and the paper will be presented at the ACFD/CADR biennial meeting.
Requirements Research papers entered are limited to graduate or postgraduate students who have conducted their work in association with the dental faculty of a Canadian university.
Contact Richard Munro, Executive Director, (613) 236-4763; fax: (613) 236-3935; email: Information@dcf-fdc.ca
Internet http://www.dcf-fdc.ca
Sponsor Dentistry Canada Fund
427 Gilmour St
Ottawa, ON K2P OR5 Canada

Canadian Foundation for Dietetic Research Awards **1117**
Within the broad category of practice-based dietetic research, the foundation prefers to support research that is of direct relevance to the nutritional well-being of populations within Canada. Priority research directions are outcomes of intervention, new roles for dietitians in meeting the health needs of all Canadians, identification of vulnerable groups and their nutritional needs, and determinants of food choice. An active member of Dietitians of Canada must be a member, if not the leader, of the research team. Applications for projects extending beyond one year will not be considered. The researchers must be associated with an institution or agency with charitable status (such as a teaching hospital or university) that will administer the funds awarded. Grants are intended to finance the direct operating costs of dietetic practice-based research projects. Calls for proposals are posted on the Web site.
Requirements Applications will only be considered where a practicing dietitian who is an active member of Dietitians of Canada and who is delivering direct or indirect client/patient/public care of service is the principal investigator or a co-investigator.
Amount $C10,000 maximum for larger projects; $C5000 maximum for smaller projects
Date(s) Application Is Due Sep 30.
Contact Awards Manager, (416) 642-9307; fax: (416) 596-0603; email: cfdr@dietitians.ca
Internet http://www.dietitians.ca/cfdr/grants.htm
Sponsor Canadian Foundation for Dietetic Research
480 University Ave, Ste 604
Toronto, ON M5G 1V2 Canada

Canadian Friends of Hebrew University Research and Study Grants **1118**
Grants are awarded for one year of undergraduate or graduate study to Canadian citizens or residents of Canada who are able to fulfill the entrance requirements of the Hebrew University in Jerusalem in their chosen fields of study, which may include law, dentistry, social sciences and economics, humanities, arts, science, agriculture, pharmacy, and library science.
Amount $C1000-$C4000
Date(s) Application Is Due May 1.
Contact Dina Wachtel, National Director, (416) 485-8000; fax: (416) 485-8565; email: dwachtel@cfhu.org
Internet http://www.cfhu.org
Sponsor Canadian Friends of Hebrew University
3080 Yonge St, Ste 5024
Toronto, ON M4N 3P4 Canada

Canadian Library Association Dafoe Scholarship **1119**
This scholarship is awarded annually, when merited, to a student entering an accredited Canadian library school. Consideration is given to academic achievement, leadership potential, and demonstrated interest in the profession. Support is for one year.
Requirements Scholarship candidates must be commencing studies for their first professional library degree and must be Canadian citizens or possess landed immigrant status.
Amount $C5000
Date(s) Application Is Due May 1.
Contact Brenda Shields, Member Services Associate, (613) 232-9625 ext 318; fax: (613) 563-9895; email: bshields@cla.ca
Internet http://www.cla.ca/awards/dafoe.htm
Sponsor Canadian Library Association
328 Frank St
Ottawa, ON K2P 0X8 Canada

Canadian Library Association Library Research and Development Grants **1120**
Grants support theoretical and applied research that advances the fields of library and information science in their broadest context. Grants are meant to cover only the costs associated with the research, not the salary of the principals. Some examples of typical

costs that will be considered are travel, computer time, costs of hiring clerical support, or costs of purchasing supplies.
Requirements All personal members of the CLA, except current members of the R&D Committee, are eligible for the grants.
Amount $C1000 maximum
Date(s) Application Is Due Feb 28.
Contact Brenda Shields, Member Services Associate, (613) 232-9625 ext 318; fax: (613) 563-9895; email: bshields@cla.ca
Internet http://www.cla.ca/awards/grants.htm
Sponsor Canadian Library Association
328 Frank St
Ottawa, ON K2P 0X8 Canada

Canadian Liver Foundation Grants **1121**
The foundation awards organization grants, fellowships, and studentships to support research into nephrology, hepatic function or disease, and other related disciplines.
Requirements Canadian citizens and organizations are eligible.
Date(s) Application Is Due Mar 31.
Contact Billie Potkonjak, (800) 563-5483 ; fax: (416) 491-4952; email: bpotkonjak@liver.ca
Internet http://www.liver.ca/Research/Grant_Program
Sponsor Canadian Liver Foundation
2235 Sheppard Ave E, Ste 1500
Toronto, ON M2J 5B5 Canada

Canadian Nurses Foundation Study Awards **1122**
Grants provide funding for nurses undertaking university studies in nursing and health care and for research related to nursing practice and health care. Awards are given for university study at the baccalaureate, master's, and doctoral levels. Priority will be given to nurses studying in programs with a nursing focus. Once recipients have completed their degrees, they must return to nursing and assist in the development of improved nursing and health care in Canada.
Requirements Applicants must be members of the Canadian Nurses Foundation and must have gained acceptance into a university program of study; applicants must identify the practice area in which they plan to study and have definite career goals.
Amount $C3000-$C6000
Contact Linda Piazza, Executive Director, (613) 237-2159 ext 250; fax: (613) 237-3520; email: lpiazza@cna-aiic.ca orcnf@cnursesfdn.ca
Internet http://www.canadiannursesfoundation.com/welcome.htm
Sponsor Canadian Nurses Foundation
50 Driveway
Ottawa, ON K2P 1E2 Canada

Canadian Political Science Association Parliamentary Internships **1123**
The work-study program gives university graduates an opportunity to supplement their theoretical knowledge of Parliament with firsthand experience of the day-to-day work of the members and of Parliament. Following an orientation period, the interns' responsibilities include working with members of the House of Commons on both sides, conducting scholarly research dealing with Parliament, and undertaking study travel. Tenures begin in September for a period of 10 months. 10 internships will be awarded per year. Request application forms in writing. Application due the last friday in January.
Requirements The program is open to Canadian citizens who are recent graduates of a university and have an interest in Parliament.
Amount $C16,500 estimated plus travel subsidies
Contact Parliamentary Internship Program, (613) 995-0764; fax: (613) 995-5357; email: cartwj@parl.ga.ca
Internet http://www.pip-psp.org
Sponsor Canadian Political Science Association
151 Sparks St, House of Commons, Rm 1200
Ottawa, ON K1A 0A6 Canada

Canadian Science Writers Association Awards **1124**
The program comprises a handful of awards including the Canadian Forest Service-Ontario Journalism Award for accurate and informed reporting on research and/or its application to the aesthetics, recreation, timber, and wildlife habitat of Ontario's forests. This award is open to writers whose writings have been published in English or French in a news story, feature, or editorial of a daily or weekly magazine or periodical. The Science in Society Journalism Award considers books that deal with aspects of basic or applied science or technology, historical or current, in areas such as health, social or environmental issues, and regulatory trends. Books will be evaluated by their literary excellence and scientific content and accuracy. Applicants need not be members of the association. Entry forms are available on the Web site.
Requirements Canadian citizens and residents are eligible.
Amount $C1000 each Canadian Forest Service and Science in Society awards
Contact Program Contact, (800) 796-8595; fax: (416) 408-1044; email: awards@sciencewriters.ca
Internet http://www.sciencewriters.ca/awards/index.html
Sponsor Canadian Science Writers Association
P.O. Box 75, Station A
Toronto, ON M5W 1A2 Canada

Canadian Studies Conference Grants **1125**
This program has as its purpose the support of major conferences addressing important and timely Canadian or Canada-US issues. It is intended to secure a greater understanding of the background, complexity, and ramifications of these issues. The grants are designed to assist an institution in holding a conference and to publish the resultant papers and proceedings in a scholarly fashion. Application materials are available on the Web site.
Requirements This grant is intended for four-year US colleges and universities, research and policy-planning institutes, or other established research institutions that undertake a major conference on a Canadian or Canada-US issue.
Restrictions Provisions are not made for released time stipends nor for overhead costs to the institution.
Amount $5000-$15,000 per year
Date(s) Application Is Due Jun 15.
Contact Daniel Abele, Academic Relations Officer, (202) 682-7727; email: daniel.abele@international.gc.ca
Internet http://www.canadianembassy.org/education/grantguide-en.asp#conference
Sponsor Canadian Embassy
501 Pennsylvania Ave NW
Washington, DC 20001

Canadian Studies Faculty Enrichment Grants **1126**
The Faculty Enrichment Program (Course Development) provides faculty members an opportunity to develop or redevelop a course(s) with substantial Canadian content that will be offered as part of their regular teaching load, or as a special offering to select audiences in continuing and/or distance education. Priority topics include bilateral trade and economics, Canada-US border issues, cultural policy and values, environmental, natural resources, and energy issues, and security cooperation (in alphabetical order). In addition, projects that examine Canadian politics, economics, culture, and society as well as Canada's role in international affairs are welcome. We especially encourage the use of new internet technology to enhance existing courses, including the creation of instructional Web sites, interactive technologies, and distance learning links to Canadian universities. Applications on official forms must be accompanied by an institutional commitment that the department will offer the new course to be taught by the applicant at least two times during the four following years.
Requirements This program is intended for full-time, tenured or tenure-track faculty members at accredited four-year US colleges and universities. The candidates should be able to demonstrate that they are already teaching, or will be authorized to teach, courses with substantial Canadian content (33 percent or more). Team teaching applications are welcome. Applicants are required to conduct research in Canada for a minimum of three weeks during the award period.
Restrictions Provisions are not made for released time stipends nor for overhead costs to the institution. This award is not available two consecutive years to the same recipient.
Amount $US5000 maximum
Date(s) Application Is Due Oct 31.
Contact Academic Relations Office, (202) 682-7727; email: AcademicRelations@CanadianEmbassy.org
Internet http://www.canadianembassy.org/education/grantguide-e.asp#faculty
Sponsor Canadian Embassy
501 Pennsylvania Ave NW
Washington, DC 20001

Canadian Studies Graduate Student Fellowships **1127**
The Graduate Student Fellowship Program promotes research in the social sciences and humanities with a view to contributing to a better knowledge and understanding of Canada and its relationship with the United States and/or other countries of the world. Priority topics include bilateral trade and economics, Canada-US and values, environmental, natural resources, and energy issues, and security cooperation (in alphabetical order). In addition, projects that examine Canadian politics, economics, culture, and society as well as Canada's role in international affairs are welcome. The purpose of the fellowship is to offer graduate students an opportunity to conduct part of their doctoral research in Canada. Annual deadline dates may vary; contact the program office for exact dates.
Requirements This program is intended for full-time doctoral students at accredited four-year US and Canadian colleges and universities whose dissertations are related in substantial part to the study of Canada, Canada/United States or Canada/North America. Candidates must be citizens or permanent residents of the United States and should have completed all doctoral requirements other than the dissertation when they apply for a grant.
Amount $10,000 maximum
Date(s) Application Is Due Oct 31.
Contact Academic Relations Office, (202) 682-7727; email: AcademicRelations@CanadianEmbassy.org
Internet http://www.canadianembassy.org/education/grantguide-e.asp#graduate
Sponsor Canadian Embassy
501 Pennsylvania Ave NW
Washington, DC 20001

Canadian Studies Matching Grants **1128**
The Government of Canada, through the Canadian Embassy, Washington, DC, in cooperation with Canadian Consulates General throughout the United States, at its

discretion, may provide a matching grant to support Canadian Studies Programs and projects which have been funded by a major foundation or other funding institution. It is usually a partial match of a larger award (e.g., one to four ratio) provided for a specific project, e.g., the creation of a Canada/US trade institute, or the establishment of a permanent Canadian Studies professorship. Applications are accepted at any time.
Requirements Four-year, fully accredited US colleges and universities and research institutes which demonstrate a serious interest in Canada, Canada/United States or Canada/North America, are eligible. The institution must estimate the longevity of the program or project after Canadian government support is exhausted.
Contact Academic Relations Office, (202) 682-7727
Internet http://www.canadianembassy.org/education/grantguide-e.asp#matching
Sponsor Canadian Embassy
501 Pennsylvania Ave NW
Washington, DC 20001

Canadian Studies Program Enhancement Grants **1129**
This grant is designed to encourage scholarly inquiry and multidisciplinary professional academic activities that contribute to the development and/or expansion of a Canadian Studies Program. We are particularly interested in innovative projects that promote awareness among students and the public about Canadian society, culture, and values as well as Canada-US bilateral relations and Canada's role in international affairs. Linkages with Canadian institutions, such as student and faculty exchanges or joint academic programs, are especially welcome.
Requirements This grant is intended for four-year US colleges, universities, and research institutions, which undertake professional academic activities to further the development of a Canadian Studies Program at their institution. Long-term program development proposals spanning several years will be considered. The Canadian Government should be approached as a partial funder. Institutions must demonstrate that they are bringing new sources of funds and innovative ideas to the program.
Restrictions Provisions are not made for released time stipends nor for overhead costs to the institution.
Amount $18,000 maximum per year
Date(s) Application Is Due Jun 15.
Contact Dr. Daniel Abele, Academic Relations Office, (202) 682-7717; fax: (202) 682-7791; email: AcademicRelations@CanadianEmbassy.org
Internet http://www.canadianembassy.org/education/grantguide-en.asp#enhancement
Sponsor Canadian Embassy
501 Pennsylvania Ave NW
Washington, DC 20001

Canadian Studies Research Grants **1130**
The Research Grant Program promotes research in the social sciences and humanities with a view to contributing to a better knowledge and understanding of Canada and its relationship with the United States and/or other countries of the world. Priority topics include bilateral trade and economics, Canada-US border issues, cultural policy and values, environmental, natural resources, and energy issues, and security cooperation. In addition, projects that examine Canadian politics, economics, culture, and society as well as Canada's role in international affairs are welcome. The purpose of the grant is to assist individual scholars, or a team of scholars, in writing an article-length manuscript of publishable quality and reporting their findings in scholarly publications, with a view to contributing to the development of Canadian Studies in the United States. We welcome efforts to integrate the research findings into the applicant's teaching load. Annual deadline dates may vary; contact the program officer for exact dates.
Requirements This program is intended for full-time faculty members at accredited four-year US colleges and universities, as well as scholars at American research and policy-planning institutes who undertake significant Canada, Canada-United States or Canada/North America research projects. Recent PhD recipients who are citizens or permanent residents of the United States are also eligible to apply. Applicants are ineligible to receive the same grant in two consecutive years or to receive two individual category Canadian Studies grants in the same grant period.
Restrictions Provisions are not made for released time stipends nor for overhead costs to the institution.
Amount $15,000 maximum
Date(s) Application Is Due Sep 30.
Contact Dr. Daniel Abele, Academic Relations Office, (202) 682-7717; fax: (202) 682-7791; email: daniel.abele@international.gc.ca
Internet http://www.canadianembassy.org/education/grantguide-en.asp#research
Sponsor Canadian Embassy
501 Pennsylvania Ave NW
Washington, DC 20001

Canadian Studies Senior Fellowships **1131**
The Senior Fellowship (awarded every other year) provides senior scholars with an opportunity to complete and publish a major study which will significantly benefit the development of Canadian Studies in the United States. A limited number of fellowships are awarded to academics who have a lengthy track record in teaching, researching and publishing on Canada, Canada/United States or Canada/North America; and on the social, cultural, political and economic issues that impact on these relationships. Preference in such instances is to fund a book project after a publisher has indicated an interest.
Requirements This program is intended for full-time tenured faculty members at accredited four-year US colleges and universities who are fully involved in Canadian Studies. These Canadianists should be in the process of completing research for a book or major monograph. The study must be on a subject of widespread interest to the Canadian Studies community in the United States as well as in Canada. This fellowship is awarded only once to any one recipient and is in recognition of an academic career dedicated to the promotion of Canadian Studies. It is expected that a recipient will be granted a leave of absence or a sabbatical during the award period.
Restrictions This award is not available two consecutive years to the same recipient. An individual may not receive two individual category Canadian Studies grants during the same grant period.
Amount $3000 maximum monthly stipend for up to six months
Date(s) Application Is Due Jun 16.
Contact Dr. Daniel Abele, Academic Relations Office, (202) 682-7717; fax: (202) 682-7791; email: daniel.abele@dfait-maeci.gc.ca
Internet http://www.dfait-maeci.gc.ca/can-am/washington/studies/grantguide-en.asp
Sponsor Canadian Embassy
501 Pennsylvania Ave NW
Washington, DC 20001

Cancer Research Postdoctoral Fellowships for Basic and Physician Scientists **1132**
This program grants initial postdoctoral fellowships to support promising young investigators pursuing careers in cancer research. The fund encourages all theoretical and experimental research that is relevant to the study of cancer and the search for cancer causes, mechanisms, therapies, and prevention. Candidates must apply for the fellowships under the guidance of a sponsor--a senior member of the scientific research community. The sponsor should be actively engaged in the planning, execution, and supervision of the proposed research and should encourage the fellow to report the results of the research in scientific journals and meetings. Awards are made to institutions for the support of the fellow under direct supervision of the sponsor.
Requirements Candidates must have completed one or more of the following degrees or equivalent: MD, PhD, DDS, or DVM. For level one funding, basic and physician scientist applicants must have received their degrees no more than one year prior to the SAC meeting at which their applications are to be considered and DVM applicants no more than three years. For level two funding, physician scientists (MD, DDS, DVM, or the equivalent) must have completed their residencies and clinical training no more than three years prior to the SAC meeting at which their applications are to be considered.
Restrictions Only one application will be accepted from a given sponsor or fellow per review session; there is no limit, however, on the number of applications from an institution. No more than two Runyon-Winchell Fellows will be funded to work with the same sponsor at any time.
Amount $41,000 first year, $43,000 second year, $44,000 third year for level 1; $55,000 first year, $56,000 second year, $57,000 third year for level 2
Date(s) Application Is Due Mar 15; Aug 15.
Contact Lorraine Egan, Executive Director, (212) 455-0541; fax: (212) 697-4950; email: lorraine.egan@drcrf.org or fellowship@cancerresearchfund.org
Internet http://www.drcrf.org/apFellowship.html
Sponsor Cancer Research Fund of the Damon Runyon-Walter Winchell Foundation
675 Third Ave, 25th Fl
New York, NY 10017

Cancer Research Society Fellowships and Grants **1133**
Grants and fellowships are supported for projects researching the cause and cure of cancer. Recipients are selected annually by the society's medical advisory board on the basis of the scientific value of the research projects submitted.
Requirements Research projects supported must be carried out in Canada.
Date(s) Application Is Due Feb 15.
Contact Program Director, (514) 861-9227; fax: (514) 861-9220; email: grants@cancerresearchsociety.ca
Internet http://src-crs.ca/main.php?lang=2&id=305
Sponsor Cancer Research Society
402-625 Av Du President-Kennedy
Montreal, QC H3A 3S5 Canada

Cancer Research UK Fellowships **1134**
The fund operates in the United Kingdom and worldwide to investigate all matters connected with or bearing on the causes, prevention, treatment, and cure of cancer. Principal disciplines include cellular and molecular biology, clinical cancer research, and epidemiology. Types of support include research fellowships, visiting fellowships, clinical research fellowships, and graduate studentships.
Contact Grants Administrator, 020 7242 0200; fax: 020 7269 3100; email: research_enquiries@cancer.org.uk
Internet http://science.cancerresearchuk.org/fandm/grantapplications/?version=1
Sponsor Cancer Research UK
P.O. Box 123, Lincoln's Inn Fields
London WC2A 3PX United Kingdom

Cancer Research UK Grants **1135**
The organization supports cancer research throughout the United Kingdom. Grants are awarded to universities, medical schools, and hospitals in support of research projects.

Additional types of support include life fellowships, career development awards, clinical and nonclinical scientists fellowships, and capital grants for new research buildings and major items of equipment.
Contact Grants Administrator, 020 7242 0200; fax: 020 7269 3100; email: research_enquiries@cancer.org.uk
Internet http://science.cancerresearchuk.org/gapp/?version=3
Sponsor Cancer Research UK
P.O. Box 123, Lincoln's Inn Fields
London WC2A 3PX United Kingdom

Cancer Society of New Zealand Grants **1136**
The society supports cancer research through grants to individuals and organizations in New Zealand. Types of support include research grants and traveling fellowships to enable New Zealand graduates to travel abroad for study.
Date(s) Application Is Due Nov 1.
Contact Grants Administrator, (04) 494 7270; fax: (04) 494 7271; email: admin@cancernz.org.nz
Internet http://www.cancernz.org.nz
Sponsor Cancer Society of New Zealand
P.O. Box 10847
Wellington
New Zealand

Cancer Treatment Research Foundation Clinical Investigation Grants **1137**
The grants support new and pilot feasibility clinical projects in cancer therapy. Grants are intended to stimulate innovative research relevant to cancer therapy, such as new agents, innovative anticancer therapies, biological response modifiers, immunotherapy, and gene therapy; and quality of life, cancer education, and nutritional oncology. Funds may be used for salaries, supplies, and nonreimbursable research-related patient care costs, including extraordinary laboratory and imaging studies. There are no application deadlines. Preliminary grant request forms are available on the foundation's Web site. The foundation will invite a formal application.
Requirements New and established investigators are encouraged to apply: young investigators working in established research programs relevant to clinical research who are without support from NIH or other cancer research agencies; and established, clinical researchers who wish to embark on innovative studies directly relevant to the foundation's mission with novel, new, or pilot projects distinctly removed from their currently funded research projects.
Amount $25,000-$300,000 range
Date(s) Application Is Due Aug 15.
Contact Kristine Nelson, Grants Administrator, (847) 342-7450; email: grants@ctrf.org
Internet http://www.ctrf.org/grantapp.cfm
Sponsor Cancer Treatment Research Foundation
1336 Basswood Rd
Schaumburg, Illinois 60173

Canon Foundation Grants **1138**
The foundation functions to facilitate mutual understanding in all fields of interest and the development of scientific expertise, particularly between Europe and Japan. Types of support include visiting research fellowships and professorships to enable European students to visit Japan and Japanese students to visit Europe. Up to 15 fellowships are awarded each year.
Requirements Young, highly qualified postgraduate European and Japanese researchers, preferably holding a PhD and not older than 40 years, are eligible.
Amount 22,500-27,500 Euro per year
Date(s) Application Is Due Sep 15.
Contact Corrie Siahaya-Van Nierop, Director, 31-20-545-8934; fax: 31-20-712-8934; email: foundation@canon-europa.com
Internet http://www.canonfoundation.org/pages/main.htm
Sponsor Canon Foundation in Europe
P.O. Box 2262
Amstelveen 1180 EG The Netherlands

Canon National Parks Science Scholars Program Grants **1139**
The program is underwritten by Canon USA Inc and awards scholarships to eight doctoral students each year for up to three years of support to conduct research on critical problems facing national parks worldwide. Research projects in the biological sciences, physical sciences, social sciences, cultural sciences, and technology innovation in support of conservation science are eligible. National parks are those protected areas officially recognized and identified as national parks by the national government of a country in the Americas. Scholarship applicants must submit dissertation proposals that address these topics. The program will award eight scholarships based on two separate competitions: four scholars will be selected from students studying at US universities (one winner in each category) and four scholars will be selected from students studying at universities throughout the Americas, but outside the United States (one winner in each category).
Requirements Proposals can be considered only from currently enrolled PhD students at an accredited university within the Americas. The Americas include Canada, the United States, Mexico, the countries of Central and South America, and the Caribbean. At least some portion of the student's proposed research must take place in--or be significantly and specifically relevant to--one or more national parks in the student's country of citizenship. Students must have completed a majority of their coursework, and be able to complete the proposed dissertation research within three years of receiving an award.
Amount $80,000 scholarship; $1000 honorable mention scholarship
Date(s) Application Is Due May 3.
Contact Dr. Gary Machlis, Program Coordinator, (208) 885-7054; email: gmachlis@uidaho.edu
Internet http://www.nature.nps.gov/canonscholarships
Sponsor National Park Service
P.O. Box 441133
Moscow, ID 83844-1133

CAORC Andrew W. Mellon East-Central European Fellowships **1140**
The program of fellowships enables Bulgarian, Czech, Estonian, Hungarian, Latvian, Lithuanian, Polish, Romanian and Slovak scholars in the humanities and allied social sciences to carry out research at institutes of advanced study in other countries. Each cycle will fund short-term residencies for up to three Mellon Research Fellows at each of the 17 designated institutes in Austria, England, France, Germany, Greece, India, Israel, Italy, Jordan, the Netherlands, Norway, Scotland, Spain, Turkey, and Yemen. Each institute will issue its own announcement and will handle all matters concerning application and selection. Guidelines are available online.
Requirements The fellowships are intended to serve younger scholars who have already obtained a PhD or have equivalent experience and who wish to undertake a specific research project at one of the participating institutes. Bulgarian, Czech, Estonian, Hungarian, Latvian, Lithuanian, Polish, Romanian and Slovak scholars who wish to apply should contact the participating institute directly for an application.
Contact Grants Administrator, (202) 633-1599; fax: (202) 786-2430; email: fellowships@caorc.org
Internet http://www.caorc.org/fellowships
Sponsor Council of American Overseas Research Centers
P.O. Box 37012, NHB Rm CE-123, MRC 178
Washington, DC 20113-7012

CAORC Regional Research Fellowships **1141**
Fellowships are available to US doctoral and postdoctoral candidates researching in the fields of the humanities, social sciences, or allied natural sciences. The research will have regional significance and must be conducted in more than one country. At least one of the following countries must be included: Scholars must carry out research in at least one of the countries which host overseas research centers: Bangladesh, Cambodia, Cyprus, Egypt, Greece, India, Iran, Israel, Italy, Jordan, Mexico, Morocco, Pakistan, Senegal/West Africa, Sri Lanka, Tunisia, Turkey, West Bank/Gaza Strip and Yemen, as well as in other countries unless subject to official security and/or travel restrictions or warnings. Research in Nepal is possible via the Center for South Asia Libraries; contact CAORC for more information. Fellows are required to obtain their own research permissions in countries that do not host centers. Application forms are available on the Web site.
Requirements US doctoral candidates and postdoctoral scholars in the humanities, social sciences, or allied natural sciences are eligible. Candidates may apply either as individuals or in teams.
Amount $9000 maximum stipend
Date(s) Application Is Due Jan 13.
Contact Executive Director, (202) 633-1599; fax: (202) 786-2430; email: caorc@caorc.org
Internet http://www.caorc.org/fellowships
Sponsor Council of American Overseas Research Centers
1100 Jefferson Dr SW, NHB Rm CE-123, MRC 178
Washington, DC 20013-7012

CAPAA Mini Grant for Research Related to African Americans in Education **1142**
The program awards mini grants to support theoretical and empirical research that examines the current status of, challenges to, and strategies for improving African Americans' access to the University of California system. The College Access Project for African Americans (CAPAA)awards mini grants to support short-term (two years or less) research projects. CAPAA encourages researchers with diverse perspectives to develop ideas and approaches that extend the conventional boundaries of a research question, area, or method. Request for proposals to conduct specific projects are being supported. 1) Survey at the community level and in school districts with students, parents, and teachers designed to elicit perceptions on factors affecting access to and achievement in higher education by African American students. 2) The educational landscape in school districts and institutions of higher education in California, especially the UC and CSU systems, and the extent to which it creates an environment conducive to learning and achievement by African American students. 3) Studies that investigate the role of African American community resources (networks of support, educational enhancement activities/programs, family support) in determining students' choices, references, aspirations, and performance vis-a-vis higher education. Guidelines are available online.
Requirements Studies must relate to issues of access and equity for African Americans in California's secondary and higher education institutions. Individual as well as collaborative efforts will be considered.
Amount $15,000 maximum each

Date(s) Application Is Due Nov 12.
Contact Dr. Ana-Christina Famon, (310) 794-4997; email: acramon@bunche.ucla.edu
Internet http://www.bunche.ucla.edu/frames/index.html
Sponsor UCLA Ralph J. Bunche Center
160 Haines Hall, Box 951545
Los Angeles, CA 90095

Cape Branch Foundation Grants 1143
The foundation awards grants to New Jersey nonprofit organizations in its areas of interest, including education and secondary education, natural resource conservation, and museums. Types of support include general operating support, building construction/renovation, land acquisition, scholarship funds, and research grants. There are no application forms or deadlines. A letter should be submitted outlining purpose and amount of request.
Requirements New Jersey nonprofit organization are eligible.
Amount $1000-$329,268 range
Contact Dorothy Frank, c/o Danser, Balaam and Frank, (609) 987-0300; fax: (609) 452-1024
Sponsor Cape Branch Foundation
P.O. Box 86
Oldwick, NJ 08858

Cardiac Arrhythmias Research and Education Foundation Research Grants 1144
The foundation's two primary goals are to raise funds for clinical research of cardiac arrhythmias and to educate the public and the medical community about sudden death. Awards will be granted to promising young investigators working on the genetics, mechanisms, therapy, and prevention of sudden death due to cardiac arrhythmias. Two research grants are awarded each year.
Amount $50,000
Contact Grants Administrator, (800) 404-9500 or (425) 788-1987; fax: (425) 788-1927; email: care@longqt.org
Internet http://www.longqt.org/fundingmedical.html
Sponsor Cardiac Arrhythmias Research and Education Foundation
P.O. Box 369, 26425 NE Allen St, Ste 103
Duvall, WA 98019

Carl and Eloise Pohlad Family Foundation Grants 1145
The mission of the foundation is to improve the lives of economically disadvantaged children and youth and participate in projects that positively impact the quality of life in the Minneapolis/St.Paul area. The foundation awards grants to Minnesota nonprofits in its areas of interest, including arts and culture, economic development, education, environment, health care, housing, and social services. Types of support include general operating support, continuing support, capital campaigns, building construction/renovation, endowments, emergency funds, scholarship funds, and research.
Requirements Minnesota nonprofits are eligible.
Restrictions Individuals are not eligible. Capital request are considered only for physical plant improvements or significant technology investments. Capital requests for housing construction, endowment, program start-up or expansion or to establish operating reserves are not considered.
Amount $3.2 million total
Contact Rose Peterson, Program Manager, (612) 661-3903; fax: (612) 661-3715; email: rpeterson@pohladfamilygiving.org
Internet http://www.pohladfamilyfoundation.org/pff/pff_default.aspx
Sponsor Carl and Eloise Pohlad Family Foundation
60 S Sixth St, Ste 3900
Minneapolis, MN 55402

Carl and Lily Pforzheimer Foundation Grants 1146
The foundation awards grants to US nonprofit organizations in its areas of interest, including higher and secondary education, cultural activities and programs, public affairs, and healthcare. Types of support include capital campaigns, fellowships, internship funds, matching grants, professorships, program development, publication, scholarship funds, and seed grants. There are no application forms or deadlines. The board meets in April, June, October, and December to consider requests.
Restrictions Grants are not awarded to individuals or for building construction/renovation.
Amount $10,000-$150,000 average
Contact Grants Administrator, (212) 223-6500
Sponsor Carl and Lily Pforzheimer Foundation
950 Third Ave, 30th Fl
New York, NY 10022

Carl C. Icahn Foundation Grants 1147
The foundation awards grants to New York and New Jersey nonprofits in the areas of education, arts and culture, health care, child welfare, and Jewish temples and organizations. Types of support include general operating support, annual campaigns, building construction/renovation, and matching funds. There are no application deadlines or forms.
Requirements New York and New Jersey nonprofits are eligible to apply.
Restrictions No grants are provided to individuals.
Amount $1000-$500,000 range
Contact Gail Golden, Secretary-Treasurer, c/o Icahn Associates, (212) 702-4300
Sponsor Carl C. Icahn Foundation
767 5th Ave, 47th Fl
New York, NY 10153-0023

Carl Gellert and Celia Berta Gellert Foundation Grants 1148
The foundation funds religious, charitable, scientific, literary or educational purposes restricted in the nine counties of the greater San Francisco Bay Area (Alameda, Contra Costa, Marin, Napa, San Francisco, San Mateo, Santa Clara, Solano and Sonoma). No grants are made to individuals. Types of support include general operations, annual and capital campaigns, building construction/ renovation, equipment acquisition, debt reduction, program/project development, medical research, publication, and scholarships.
Requirements California 501(c)3 tax-exempt nonprofit organizations that are not private foundations are eligible.
Restrictions Grants are not awarded to individuals.
Amount $1000-$10,000 typically
Date(s) Application Is Due Aug 15 at noon.
Contact Jack Fitzpatrick, Executive Director, (415) 255-2829
Internet http://home.earthlink.net/~cgcbg
Sponsor Carl Gellert and Celia Berta Gellert Foundation
1169 Market St, Ste 808
San Francisco, CA 94103

Carl J. Herzog Foundation Grants 1149
The foundation awards grants, primarily in Connecticut, for research and general operating support in its areas of interest, including medical research, dermatology research, hospitals, and education. There are no application deadlines or forms.
Requirements 501(c)3 tax-exempt organizations are eligible.
Amount $1000-$200,000; $5000-$50,000 average
Contact David Babson, (203) 629-2424
Sponsor Carl J. Herzog Foundation
321 Railroad Ave
Greenwich, CT 06836-0788

Carlos and Marguerite Mason Trust Grants 1150
The trust awards grants in Georgia with a focus on organ transplants. The trust's interests are patient services--needs relating to the transplantation process for the patient and the immediate family members, as well as donor family members and living donors; donation and transplantation--related education (donor education, professional education, and technical education for transplantation providers; programs to improve consent rates; and programs to promote living organ donations); and research--medical research relating to the area of transplantation. Types of support include capital improvements, start-up grants for new projects, and challenge/matching grants. Grants will be awarded for up to three years. Applicants are encouraged to contact the trustee for an appointment prior to submitting a grant request.
Requirements Georgia nonprofit organizations are eligible.
Restrictions Requests for general operating or administrative funds are discouraged. The trust generally does not fund endowment, nor does it fund general goodwill advertising; make grants that would replace existing sources of funding; or pay indirect overhead expenses for projects at colleges, universities, governmental units, or other established organizations.
Amount $1.5 million maximum
Date(s) Application Is Due Jun 1.
Contact Randy Karesh, c/o Wachovia Bank of Georgia, (404) 332-6677; email: grantinquiriesga@wachovia.com
Internet http://www.wachovia.com/corp_inst/charitable_services/0,,4269_3300,00.html
Sponsor Carlos and Marguerite Mason Trust
3414 Peachtree Rd, 5th Fl, MC GA8023
Atlanta, GA 30326

Carnegie Corporation of New York Grant Programs 1151
The foundation provides research, study, and support for projects to improve government at all levels, to increase public understanding of social policy issues, to equalize opportunities for minorities and women, and to increase participation in political and civic life. Also supported are projects that promote electoral reform; education reform from early childhood through higher education; early childhood development; and urban school reform. The foundation will also fund research on the increasing availability and success of after-school and extended service programs for children and teenagers, particularly those in urban areas, that promote high academic achievement. Dissemination of best practices in teacher education will also be emphasized. There is no formal procedure for submitting a proposal. To apply under any of the corporation's grantmaking programs, applicants should submit a full proposal that describes the project's aims, duration, methods, amount of financial support required, and key personnel. The board meets four times a year, in October, February, April, and June.
Restrictions Grants are not made for construction or maintenance of facilities or endowments. The Corporation does not generally make grants to individuals except

through the Carnegie Scholars Program, that supports the work of select scholars and experts conducting research in the foundation's fields of interest.
Amount $80 million total approximately annually
Contact Grants Administrator, (212) 371-3200; fax: (212) 754-4073
Internet http://www.carnegie.org/sub/program/grant.html
Sponsor Carnegie Corporation of New York
437 Madison Ave
New York, NY 10022

Carnegie Developmental Biology Research Fellowships **1152**
Fellowships are awarded, primarily at the postdoctoral level, for research at the Carnegie Institution Department of Embryology, Baltimore, MD, under the guidance of the department's staff scientists. Topics include the expression of genes through development and growth, chromosome structure and function, and intracellular communication. Facilities include extensive laboratories for biochemistry and molecular biology. Applicants are encouraged to submit materials a year in advance of the proposed starting date. Fellowships are awarded for one year with possible renewal for a second year.
Requirements Applicant must be postdoctoral researcher. Predoctoral candidates must obtain special permission to apply. Applications should be sent to the director, Carnegie Institution Department of Embryology, 3520 San Martin Dr, Baltimore, MD 21218.
Contact Grants Administrator, (410) 246-3001; fax: (410) 243-6311; email: carnegiecollaborative@ciwemb.edu
Internet http://www.ciwemb.edu
Sponsor Carnegie Institution of Washington
1530 P St NW
Washington, DC 20005

Carnegie Endowment for International Peace Junior Fellows Program **1153**
Each year the endowment offers eight to 10 one-year fellowships to uniquely qualified graduating seniors and individuals who have graduated during the past academic year. They are selected from a pool of nominees from close to 300 colleges (list of participating colleges available online). Junior fellows provide research assistance to associates working on the Carnegie Endowment's projects such as nonproliferation, democracy building, trade, US leadership, China-related issues, and Russian/Eurasian studies. Junior fellows have the opportunity to conduct research for books, co-author journal articles and policy papers, participate in meetings with high-level officials, contribute to congressional testimony, and organize briefings attended by scholars, activists, journalists, and government officials. The endowment's annual nomination deadline is the listed application deadline; colleges generally set an earlier application deadline (contact the college's Career Services/Placement Office to learn more about the college application process). Information to participating universities generally is sent by the second week of October each year. All fellowships begin on August 1.
Requirements The Carnegie Endowment accepts applications only through participating universities via designated nominating officials. The program relies on participating universities to nominate uniquely qualified students. Students need not be US citizens; however, all applicants must be eligible to work in the United States from August 1 through July 31 following graduation.
Restrictions Students who have started graduate studies are not eligible for nomination.
Amount $2750 per month plus benefits
Date(s) Application Is Due Jan 15.
Contact Julia McElderry, Fellowship Administrator, (202) 483-7600; fax: (202) 483-1840; email: jrfellowinfo@ceip.org
Internet http://www.ceip.org/files/about/about_Junior.asp
Sponsor Carnegie Endowment for International Peace
1779 Massachusetts Ave. NW
Washington, D.C. 20036-2103

Carnegie Plant Biology Fellowships **1154**
Fellowships primarily at the postdoctoral level are available for research at the Carnegie Institution Department of Plant Biology in Stanford, CA, under the guidance of the department's staff scientists. Topics range from biochemical and molecular experiments to broad-ranging ecological research. Facilities include greenhouses, controlled-growth chambers, biochemical and molecular biology laboratories, and varied specialized apparatus. The period of appointment starts July 1. Fellowships are normally awarded for one year and may be renewed for up to two additional years.
Requirements The successful applicant must have completed, or nearly completed, requirements for the PhD prior to assuming the fellowship. Applications should include educational record, professional positions held, and a list of papers published and submitted. Applicants should write a brief essay describing their interests and what they hope to achieve during the tenure of the fellowship. Applicants should arrange for letters of recommendation from three professional scientists. Materials should be sent to the director, Carnegie Institution Department of Plant Biology, 260 Panama St, Stanford, CA 94305-4101.
Contact Tina McDowell, Publications Office, (202) 939-1120; fax: (202) 387-8092; email: tmcdowell@pst.ciw.edu
Internet http://www-ciwdpb.stanford.edu
Sponsor Carnegie Institution of Washington
1530 P St NW
Washington, DC 20005

Carnegie Postdoctoral Research Fellowships **1155**
Primarily at the postdoctoral level, fellowships support research at the Geophysical Laboratory and the Department of Terrestrial Magnetism, both in Washington, DC, under the guidance of staff scientists. The Geophysical Laboratory is a private research and educational institution emphasizing high pressure/high temperature research, metamorphic, igneous, and experimental petrology, stable isotope geochemistry, crystallography, mineral physics, theoretical and experimental condensed matter physics, materials research, organic geochemistry, and biogeochemistry. Fellowships are awarded for one year and may be renewed for one and occasionally two additional years.
Requirements The applicant must have completed, or nearly completed, requirements for the PhD prior to assuming the fellowship. Applications should include a curriculum vita, description of thesis research, a list of publications, transcript/grade report, a two- to three-page research proposal for the fellowship period, and three letters of recommendation.
Date(s) Application Is Due Dec 31.
Contact Dr. Wesley Huntress Jr., Director, Geophysical Laboratory, (202) 478-8900; fax: (202) 478-8901; email: w.huntress@gl.ciw.edu
Internet http://www.gl.ciw.edu/employment/postdoc1.php
Sponsor Carnegie Institution of Washington
5251 Broad Branch Rd, NW
Washington, DC 20015

Carnegie Postdoctoral Research Fellowships in Astronomy **1156**
Applications are invited for one or more fellowships at the Observatories of the Carnegie Institution for research in theoretical astronomy and/or instrumentation to begin annually in September. Fellows will have access to the observatories' research facilities in Pasadena and on Cerro Las Campanas, Chile. Fellows will be expected to devote a major portion of their time to astronomical research. Fellowships are awarded for one year and may be renewed for up to two additional years. Foreign applicants will be sponsored under the Carnegie Institution's visitor exchange program.
Requirements The successful applicant must have completed, or nearly completed, requirements for the PhD prior to assuming the fellowship. Persons who have received a PhD degree within the past three years are particularly urged to apply. Applications should include educational record, professional positions held, and a list of papers published and submitted. Applicants also should write a brief essay describing recent astronomical research and indicate what they would hope to accomplish during tenure of the fellowship. Applicants should arrange for separate transmittal of letters of recommendation from three professional scientists. Materials should be sent to The Chair, OCIW Fellowship Committee, The Observatories of the Carnegie Institution, 813 Santa Barbara St, Pasadena, CA 91101.
Date(s) Application Is Due Dec 1.
Contact Dr. John S. Mulchaey, email: cfellow@ociw.edu
Internet http://www.ociw.edu/ociw/fellow
Sponsor Carnegie Institution of Washington
1530 P St NW
Washington, DC 20005

Carole Fielding Film/Video Production or Research Grants **1157**
The program offers annual grants for film, video, or multimedia production, and for research projects in historical, critical, theoretical or experimental studies of film or video.
Requirements Applicant must be an undergraduate or graduate student at the time of application and must be sponsored by a faculty member who is an active member of the University Film and Video Association.
Amount $4000 maximum for film or video productions; $1000 maximum for research projects
Date(s) Application Is Due Jan 1.
Contact UFVA Contact, (866) 244-0626; fax: (217) 244-9910; email: berryks@gwm.sc.edu
Internet http://www.ufva.org/publication.php
Sponsor University Film and Video Association
University of Illinois Press, 1325 S Oak St
Champaign, IL 61820-6903

Carolina Minority Postdoctoral Scholars Program **1158**
University funds are available each year to award five or more postdoctoral research appointments for periods of up to two years on the UNC-CH campus. Postdoctoral scholars may teach not more than one course per year, and will spend essentially full-time in research. The stipend includes some funds available for research expenses, including travel. Applications may be for study in any discipline represented at Carolina, preference being given to applicants in the areas of the humanities, social sciences, and fine arts where postdoctoral opportunities are seldom available.
Requirements Minority students who will have completed the doctoral degree within last four years and by July 1st are eligible to apply. Preference will be given to US citizens and permanent residents. This program is funded by the University of North Carolina and places emphasis on underrepresented minorities. The primary criterion for selection is evidence of scholarship potentially competitive for tenure track appointments in research universities.
Amount $35,625 per calendar year with some funds available for research expenses, including travel

Date(s) Application Is Due Jan 6.
Contact Holli Wilson, Program Manager, (919) 962-1319; email: hjwilson@unc.edu
Internet http://research.unc.edu/red/postdoc.html
Sponsor University of North Carolina at Chapel Hill
CB 4000, South Bldg
Chapel Hill, NC 27599-4000

Carpenter Foundation Grants **1159**
The foundation's primary areas of interest include the arts, education, public interest, and human services. The foundation is deeply concerned with the well-being of children and families and their relationship to their neighborhoods and communities. Also of concern is the health of the web of agencies and organizations which serve them. Grants are awarded for general operating support, program development, capital campaigns, equipment acquisition, scholarship funds, seed money, matching funds, and technical support. Deadlines are generally about six weeks before the quarterly board meetings, held in January, March, June, and September.
Requirements Tax exempt agencies in the Jackson and Josephine Counties of Oregon may submit proposals.
Restrictions Grants are not made to individuals. The foundation rarely makes grants for historical applications, hospital construction or equipment, group or individual trips, or activities for religious purposes.
Amount $250-$25,000 range
Contact Polly Williams, Program Officer, (541) 772-5732; fax: (541) 773-3970; email: carpfdn@internetcds.com
Internet http://www.carpenter-foundation.org
Sponsor Carpenter Foundation
711 E Main St, Ste 10
Medford, OR 97504

Carr P. Collins Award **1160**
This award is given annually to honor a nonfiction book that, in the opinion of the judges, is considered the most outstanding of the previous year's output. Annual deadline dates may vary; contact program staff for exact dates.
Requirements The author must have lived in Texas for two years, or the book must be about a Texas subject. One copy of each entry must be mailed to each of the three judges. Names and addresses of the judges are available from the institute after October 15 each year.
Amount $5000
Date(s) Application Is Due Jan 7.
Contact Program Contact, (512) 245-2428; email: MB13@swt.edu.
Internet http://www.wtamu.edu/til/awards.htm
Sponsor Texas Institute of Letters
217 Wood St, Houston House
San Marcos, TX 78666

Carter G. Woodson Institute Research Fellowships **1161**
The Carter G. Woodson Institute for Afro-American and African Studies located at the University of Virginia sponsors residential pre- and postdoctoral research fellowships. All fellowships are for the completion of research on race, ethnicity, and society in Africa and the Atlantic world (broadly defined as the African diaspora). Preference will be given to applicants whose research is substantially complete. Tenure for the fellowships begins in August. Postdoctoral fellowships are for one year; predoctoral fellowships are for two years. Application guidelines are available on the Web site. Annual deadline dates may vary; contact program staff for exact dates.
Requirements Applicants for the fellowships must have been awarded their PhD by the time of application or must furnish proof that it will have been received prior to June 30. The competition is open to qualified candidates without restriction as to citizenship or current residence.
Restrictions Employees of the University of Virginia and former university employees whose termination dates are less than one year prior to the time of application are not eligible.
Amount $25,000 postdoctoral fellowships; $15,000 per year predoctoral fellowships
Date(s) Application Is Due Dec 1.
Contact William Jackson, Associate Director for Research, (434) 924-3109; fax: (434) 924-8820; email: woodson@gwis.virginia.edu
Internet http://www.virginia.edu/woodson/programs/fellowships.html
Sponsor Carter G. Woodson Institute for Afro-American and African Studies
P.O. Box 400162
Charlottesville, VA 22904-4162

Carthage Foundation Grants **1162**
The foundation awards grants to nonprofit organizations for programs that address public questions concerned with national and international issues, such as public policy, research, government, and international affairs. There are no application deadlines; proposals are reviewed at quarterly meetings.
Restrictions Proposals for the following are usually declined: event sponsorships, endowments, capital campaigns, renovations, or government agencies. Grants are not made to individuals.
Amount $50,000-$100,000 average
Contact Michael Gleba, Treasurer, (412) 392-2900
Internet http://www.scaife.com/carthage.html
Sponsor Carthage Foundation
301 Grant St, Ste 3900
Pittsburgh, PA 15219

Castle Rock Foundation Grants **1163**
The foundation's grants are awarded to promote a better understanding of the free-enterprise system; preserve principles on which democracy was founded, ensure a limited role for government, and protect individual rights; encourage personal leadership; and uphold traditional American values. Types of support include general operating grants and special project grants.
Requirements US 501(c)3 organizations are eligible.
Restrictions Grants requests from human service agencies, museums, organizations primarily supported by tax-derived funding, endowments, scientific or medical research, publications or media projects, churches, debt retirement, special events, or individuals will be denied.
Amount $25,000-$75,000 average
Date(s) Application Is Due Mar 15.
Contact Sally W. Rippey, Executive Director, (303) 388-1683; fax: (303) 388-1684; email: generalinfo@castlerockfdn.org
Internet http://www.castlerockfoundation.org
Sponsor Castle Rock Foundation
4100 E Mississippi Ave, Ste 1850
Denver, CO 80246

Catherine Holmes Wilkins Foundation Grants **1164**
The foundation awards grants in Washington's Puget Sound region to nonprofit organizations in its areas of interest. Funding priorities include medical research and education--medical and academic centers conducting research and training in areas such as cancer, heart disease, and mental illness; physically handicapped and mentally ill--community nonprofit agencies providing direct social services to people with physical disabilities or mental illness; services for the needy--community-based programs providing immediate support to the needy, with particular emphasis on services for abused women and children. Preference will be given to project support, rather than ongoing operating expenses. Proposals are accepted throughout the year. Grants are awarded quarterly.
Requirements 501(c)3 nonprofit organizations that operate within or significantly affect the residents of the greater Seattle region--Tacoma to Everett, Seattle, and the Eastside--are eligible.
Restrictions Grants are not made for multi-year projects, debt retirement, operational deficits, or to individuals or for scholarships.
Amount $3000-$10,000
Contact c/o Bank of America, Charitable Investment Services
Internet http://fdncenter.org/grantmaker/wilkins
Sponsor Catherine Holmes Wilkins Foundation
P.O. Box 24565
Seattle, WA 98124

Catholic University Academic Scholarships, Grants, and Awards **1165**
The university offers a wide range of scholarships that recognize and reward outstanding academic performance in high school, exceptional leadership, and service school, church, and the community. Awards include academic scholarships and grants--Archdiocesan/Trustees Scholarships, University Merit Scholarships, and CUA Incentive Grants; high school nominated scholarships--Award of Excellence, and Leadership/Service Scholarship; alumni grant--CU graduates may recommend new first-time, full-time freshmen for the grant, which is renewable for four years; parish scholarship--parishioners of Catholic churches who are admitted for full-time undergraduate study at CUA; scholarships with special eligibility requirements; and school and departmental scholarships. Deadlines and scholarship amounts vary. Guidelines are available online.
Amount $1000-$10,000
Contact Office of University Admissions, (800) 673-2772 or (202) 319-5305; fax: 202-319-6533; email: cua-admissions@cua.edu
Internet http://admissions.cua.edu/undergrad/finaid/
Sponsor Catholic University of America
620 Michigan Ave NE
Washington, DC 20064

Catholic University Life Cycle Institute Research Fellowship **1166**
The Life Cycle Institute, a multidisciplinary research center for social sciences at the university, offers facilities for visiting research fellows to work for a period of one semester to one year on research projects that develop wider dimensions of topics to which the institute is devoted. The institute is particularly interested in developing global, transnational, and comparative dimensions of current research interests in youth development, gender and education, social movements and civil society, volunteerism and NGO careers including religious vocations, the demographics of professions, and the social frontiers of the information revolution. The institute currently houses specialists in sociology, anthropology, politics, demography, developmental psychology, and religious studies who are on the CUA faculty or doing project-funded research. Fellows will be provided office space, secretarial and other services (including computer, Internet, and

library facilities and on-line databases), and administrative support for funded projects within the university's guidelines. Guidelines are available online.
Requirements Applicants with PhDs in the social sciences and related disciplines, including history and economics, should send a letter of intent outlining a proposed project.
Amount $6000
Date(s) Application Is Due Feb 15.
Contact Dr. John White, Director, (202) 319-5999; fax: (202) 319-6267; email: white@cua.edu
Internet http://lifecycle.cua.edu
Sponsor Catholic University of America
620 Michigan Ave NE
Washington, DC 20064

CBO Economic Policy Fellowships **1167**
The program provides experts in macroeconomics, health economics, financial economics, public finance, and other specialties with a unique opportunity to address complex budgetary and economic policy issues. While in residence, fellows will conduct research based on a submitted proposal, use the agency's data and facilities, and work daily with colleagues at CBO to contribute to analyses and publications. Fellows will also be able to participate in professional development opportunities and will be in an excellent position to draw on the resources of experts at CBO, at other federal agencies, and within the extended community of policy analysts in Washington, DC. Fellowship appointments typically last one year but may vary depending on the project and individual circumstances. Appointment terms are flexible and can be full-time or part-time, and fellows may be employees of CBO or may maintain employment with their permanent employer depending on the availability of such an agreement. Salaries will be commensurate with qualifications and experience. Applicants must submit application materials via email. Guidelines are available online.
Requirements In addition to expertise in macroeconomics, health economics, financial economics, or public finance, economists or budget policy analysts should have a PhD or equivalent schooling; considerable expertise in their area of proposed research; a commitment to analyze interesting real-world issues in economics and public policy; and a recognized record of research and publications.
Date(s) Application Is Due Mar 1.
Contact Nancy Fahey, (202) 226-2628; email: jobs@cbo.gov
Internet http://www.cbo.gov/employment/fellowships.shtml
Sponsor Congressional Budget Office
Second and D Sts SW, Ford House Office Bldg, 4th Fl
Washington, DC 20515-6925

CCA Visiting Scholars Grants **1168**
The Study Centre is an international institute for advanced research at the postdoctoral level on all aspects of architectural thought, promoting a broad range of inquiry spanning the boundaries of the field and related disciplines. The Visiting Scholar Program promotes research of very specialized as well as interdisciplinary kinds, offering a unique study environment and full access to the outstanding resources of the Collection and Library. Each year the program appoints seven to 15 scholars at various stages of their careers, with highly diverse academic and professional accomplishments. Visiting scholars are provided with generous stipends for periods of residency at the CCA ranging from three to eight months. Applicants are encouraged to apply on the basis of an independent research project based on or supported by the extensive holdings of the CCA library and collection. Submissions should be made in either English or French. Application is available online.
Date(s) Application Is Due Nov 1.
Contact 939-7000; fax: (514) 939-7020; email: studium@cca.qc.ca
Internet http://www.cca.qc.ca/pages/Niveau3.asp?page=application_details□=eng
Sponsor Canadian Centre for Architecture
1920 rue Baile
Memorial, Quebec H3H 256 Canada

CCCF Dora Macllelan Brown Seminary Scholarships **1169**
Scholarships are awarded to Christian men and women from the greater Chattanooga area who are theologically and biblically conservative, and are seeking a Masters of Divinity or Masters of Theology degree at a theological Seminary approved by the foundation. The scholarship committee's preference is for candidates for the pulpit ministry, although all applications will be considered. Scholarships are awarded based on merit and need. They are granted usually for three or four years depending on the duration of the degree program. Guidelines and application are available online.
Date(s) Application Is Due Feb 15.
Contact Henry Henegar, Scholarship Coordinator, (423) 266-5257 ext 101; fax: (423) 265-0949; email: henryhenegar@cccfdn.org
Internet http://www.cccfdn.org/page18325.cfm
Sponsor Chattanooga Christian Community Foundation
736 Market St, Ste 1706
Chattanooga, TN 37402

CCFF Clinic Incentive Grants **1170**
The grants are intended to enhance the standard of clinical care available to Canadians with cystic fibrosis by providing funds to initiate a comprehensive program for cystic fibrosis patient care, research, and teaching; or to strengthen an existing program. Clinic incentive grants are awarded for a term of one year, and are renewable on an annual basis. The grants provide an honorarium for the clinic director, as compensation for his or her administrative responsibilities. Requests may be made for salary support for other nonphysician clinic personnel. A component of the grants is allocated to travel.
Requirements Canadian hospitals and/or medical schools are eligible to apply for grants.
Date(s) Application Is Due Oct 3.
Contact Grants Administrator, (416) 485-9149; fax: (416) 485-0960; email: info@cysticfibrosis.ca
Internet http://www.ccff.ca/page.asp?id=87
Sponsor Canadian Cystic Fibrosis Foundation
2221 Yonge St, Ste 601
Toronto, ON M4S 2B4 Canada

CCFF Fellowships **1171**
A limited number of competitive fellowships are offered by the foundation each year for basic or clinical research training in areas of the biomedical or behavioral sciences pertinent to cystic fibrosis. Fellowships are tenable at approved universities, hospitals, and research institutes in Canada. Initial fellowships are awarded for a two-year period. Fellows may apply for a one-year renewal. No one may receive more than three years of support under a CCFF fellowship. Canadian fellowship applicants of exceptional quality requesting funding to study abroad will be considered. Applicants are expected to demonstrate that comparable training is not available in Canada. Equitable consideration is given to applicants from outside of Canada who intend to return to their own country on completion of the fellowship.
Requirements Individuals who hold MD or PhD degrees are eligible to apply.
Restrictions Applicants who have already completed six or more years of postgraduate study or training are not eligible.
Date(s) Application Is Due Oct 1.
Contact Grants Administrator, (416) 485-9149; fax: (416) 485-0960; email: info@cysticfibrosis.ca
Internet http://www.ccff.ca/page.asp?id=87
Sponsor Canadian Cystic Fibrosis Foundation
2221 Yonge St, Ste 601
Toronto, ON M4S 2B4 Canada

CCFF Research Grants **1172**
Research grants are intended to facilitate the scientific investigation of all aspects of cystic fibrosis. Applications may be submitted by groups of individuals who plan to collaborate. Grants are awarded for up to three years. Investigators are eligible to hold more than one research grant. Research grants may be allocated to personnel (research assistant(s), technicians, and specified other personnel); materials and supplies; equipment not in excess of $10,000; and travel.
Requirements A principal investigator should hold a recognized, full-time faculty appointment in a relevant discipline at a Canadian university or hospital.
Restrictions Research grants do not provide support for graduate students, postdoctoral fellows, or summer students; construction costs; institutional overheads for laboratory facilities; or purchase of equipment in excess of $10,000.
Date(s) Application Is Due Oct 1.
Contact Grants Administrator, (416) 485-9149; fax: (416) 485-0960; email: info@cysticfibrosis.ca
Internet http://www.ccff.ca/page.asp?id=87
Sponsor Canadian Cystic Fibrosis Foundation
2221 Yonge St, Ste 601
Toronto, ON M4S 2B4 Canada

CCFF Scholarships **1173**
Scholarships provide salary support to gifted investigators in CF research, offering them the opportunity to develop outstanding cystic fibrosis research programs. Scholarships are held in conjunction with a CCFF research grant. Applications are available online.
Requirements Applications are accepted from candidates who have received their first faculty appointment within the preceding five calendar years.
Date(s) Application Is Due Oct 1.
Contact Grants Administrator, (416) 485-9149; fax: (416) 485-0960; email: info@cysticfibrosis.ca
Internet http://www.ccff.ca/page.asp?id=87
Sponsor Canadian Cystic Fibrosis Foundation
2221 Yonge St, Ste 601
Toronto, ON M4S 2B4 Canada

CCFF Small Conference Grants **1174**
Small conference grants are offered to support medical/scientific conferences which focus on subjects of direct relevance to cystic fibrosis. Such grants will be up to a maximum of $C2500 and are intended to supplement other funding sources. The small conference grants will also support inter-clinic exchanges which are used to facilitate the exchange of special expertise between larger, university-based CF clinics and smaller, more remote clinics. Requests of this type will involve fewer individuals, and will not normally exceed $C1000. Applications may be submitted at any time, but the foundation should be consulted in advance with respect to the availability of funds.

Requirements CF clinic directors and CCFF-funded investigators are eligible to apply.
Amount $C2500 for medical/scientific conferences; $C1000 for inter-clinic exchanges
Contact Grants Administrator, (416) 485-9149; fax: (416) 485-0960; email: info@cysticfibrosis.ca
Internet http://www.ccff.ca/page.asp?id=87
Sponsor Canadian Cystic Fibrosis Foundation
2221 Yonge St, Ste 601
Toronto, ON M4S 2B4 Canada

CCFF Studentships **1175**
A limited number of competitive studentships are offered by the foundation each year to highly qualified graduate students who are registered for a higher degree and who are undertaking full-time research training in areas of the biomedical or behavioral sciences relevant to cystic fibrosis. Students are expected to spend at least 75 percent of their time on the research training described in their application.
Requirements Awards are tenable only at Canadian universities.
Date(s) Application Is Due Apr 1; Oct 1.
Contact Grants Administrator, (416) 485-9149; fax: (416) 485-0960; email: info@cysticfibrosis.ca
Internet http://www.ccff.ca/page.asp?id=87
Sponsor Canadian Cystic Fibrosis Foundation
2221 Yonge St, Ste 601
Toronto, ON M4S 2B4 Canada

CCFF Summer Studentship **1176**
Summer studentships are intended to provide support to students engaged in summer research projects in areas of the biomedical or behavioral sciences relevant to cystic fibrosis, under the direction of CF clinic directors or principal investigators. The research project should be attainable within the three-month term of the award.
Requirements Full-time students pursuing an undergraduate degree in an appropriate discipline are eligible to receive this award. Under certain circumstances, other special academic situations, may be considered for a summer studentship.
Restrictions Applications must be made by the proposed supervisor on behalf of a student. Applications directly from students cannot be accepted.
Date(s) Application Is Due Feb 1.
Contact Grants Administrator, (416) 485-9149; fax: (416) 485-0960; email: info@cysticfibrosis.ca
Internet http://www.ccff.ca/page.asp?id=87
Sponsor Canadian Cystic Fibrosis Foundation
2221 Yonge St, Ste 601
Toronto, ON M4S 2B4 Canada

CCFF Transplant Center Incentive Grants **1177**
The grants are intended to enhance the quality of care available to cystic fibrosis transplant candidates by providing eligible centers with supplementary funding for support of personnel directly involved in the provision of patient services; travel to the annual North American Cystic Fibrosis conference; and administrative costs associated with providing data to the Canadian Cystic Fibrosis Lung Transplant Registry. Grants are renewable on an annual basis.
Requirements Canadian lung transplant centers that currently have one or more individuals with cystic fibrosis listed for transplant may apply.
Date(s) Application Is Due Oct 1.
Contact Grants Administrator, (416) 485-9149; fax: (416) 485-0960; email: info@cysticfibrosis.ca
Internet http://www.ccff.ca/page.asp?id=87
Sponsor Canadian Cystic Fibrosis Foundation
2221 Yonge St, Ste 601
Toronto, ON M4S 2B4 Canada

CCFF Visiting Scientist Awards **1178**
Awards are made to senior investigators from abroad who are invited to engage in CF research at a Canadian institution; or junior and senior Canadian investigators who wish to work in another laboratory in Canada or abroad. It is intended that this experience as a CCFF visiting scientist will, in some way, benefit the Canadian CF research effort. Applications may be submitted at any time, but the foundation should be consulted in advance with respect to the availability of funds.
Requirements Senior investigators from abroad or junior/senior Canadian investigators who wish to work in another laboratory in Canada or abroad are eligible to apply.
Contact Grants Administrator, (416) 485-9149; fax: (416) 485-0960; email: info@cysticfibrosis.ca
Internet http://www.ccff.ca/page.asp?id=87
Sponsor Canadian Cystic Fibrosis Foundation
2221 Yonge St, Ste 601
Toronto, ON M4S 2B4 Canada

CCT Fellowships for Community Leaders **1179**
The program affords outstanding nonprofit and public sector leaders opportunities to expand their knowledge base through a self-directed course of learning, travel, observation, and reflection. The program gives professionals up to 15 months' time off from their day-to-day professional responsibilities. The fellowship includes a stipend covering current salary and benefits, and associated expenses. Once they return to their work, these leaders draw on new experiences to help improve the entire community. Individuals who want to apply must submit a letter of interest and a current resume. The letter and resume may be sent by email or by postal mail. Guidelines are available online.
Requirements The fellowship is open to applicants who currently are employed full-time in the not-for-profit or public sectors in metropolitan Chicago; have 10 years of professional experience in the sector; and have demonstrated leadership in the field.
Amount $150,000 maximum
Date(s) Application Is Due Jul 8.
Contact Anne Blanton, (312) 616-8000; email: fellowship@cct.org
Internet http://www.cct.org/grantsseekers/specialprogramsandawards/fcl_programinfo.html
Sponsor Chicago Community Trust
111 E Wacker Dr, Ste 1400
Chicago, IL 60601

CCWH Catherine Prelinger Award **1180**
The award is made to a scholar who has not followed a traditional academic path of uninterrupted and completed secondary, undergraduate, and graduate degrees leading into a tenured faculty position. Although the recipient's degrees do not have to be in history, the recipient's work should clearly be historical in nature. In accordance with the general goals of CCWH, the award is intended to recognize or to enhance the ability of the recipient to contribute significantly to women in history, whether in the profession in the present or in the study of women in the past. Candidates should submit the application package to Carol Gold, Department of History, University of Alaska Fairbanks, P.O. Box 756460, Fairbanks, AK 99775-6460. Telephone: 907-474-6509. Applications may be requested from the same address or on email at ffcg@uaf.edu. Application and guidelines also are available online. faxed or emailed applications will not be considered.
Requirements Application is open to scholars with a PhD or ABD degree.
Amount $20,000
Date(s) Application Is Due Mar 13.
Contact Carol Gold, Chair, Catherine Prelinger Award Committee, (907) 474-6509; email: ffcg@uaf.edu
Internet http://theccwh.org/preapp.htm
Sponsor Coordinating Council for Women in History
P.O. Box 9715
Portland, ME 04104-5015

CCWH Ida B. Wells Graduate Student Fellowship **1181**
The fellowship is awarded to an ABD woman graduate student working on a historical dissertation, not necessarily in a history department. History graduate students who apply for the award will automatically be considered for the CCWH/Ida B. Wells award. No additional application is necessary. Request applications from Dr. Ann Le Bar, Department of History, Eastern Washington University, Patterson Hall 200, Cheney, WA 99004; email: alebar@mail.ewu.edu. Application and information also are available online.
Requirements The applicant must be a woman graduate student in a US institution; must have passed to ABD status by the time of application; may specialize in any field, but must be working on an historical project; may hold this award and others simultaneously; and need not attend the award ceremony to receive the award.
Amount $500
Date(s) Application Is Due Sep 1.
Contact Ann Le Bar, Department of History, Eastern Washington University, email: alebar@mail.ewu.edu
Internet http://theccwh.org
Sponsor Coordinating Council for Women in History
P.O. Box 9715
Portland, ME 04104-5015

CCWH/Berkshire Conference of Women Historians Graduate Student Fellowship **1182**
The fellowship is awarded to a woman graduate student completing a dissertation in a history department. History graduate students who apply for the CCWH/Berkshire Award will automatically be considered for the CCWH/Ida B. Wells Award. No additional application is necessary. Request applications from Dr. Ann Le Bar, Department of History, Eastern Washington University, Patterson Hall 200, Cheney, WA 99004; email: alebar@mail.ewu.edu. Information and application form also are available online.
Requirements The applicant must be a woman graduate student historian in a history department in a US institution; must have passed to ABD status by the time of application; may specialize in any field of history; may hold this award and others simultaneously; and need not attend the award ceremony to receive the award.
Amount $500
Date(s) Application Is Due Sep 1.
Contact Ann Le Bar, Department of History, Eastern Washington University, email: alebar@mail.ewu.edu
Internet http://theccwh.org/awards.htm
Sponsor Coordinating Council for Women in History
P.O. Box 9715
Portland, ME 04104-5015

CDC Evidence-Based Laboratory Medicine: Quality/Performance Measure Evaluation 1183

The purpose of the program is to evaluate clinical laboratory practice by identifying evidence-based laboratory medicine quality/performance measures associated with the pre- and post-analytic stages of the total testing process, and to identify and address gaps and opportunities for improvement consistent with national health care priorities to improve public health. The primary objectives are to: provide an evidence base which systematically identifies and defines important gaps in laboratory medicine quality related to individuals or populations and/or patient safety health outcomes with demonstrated impacts (i.e., clinical and/or economic); identify, develop, and define laboratory medicine performance/quality measures that can be broadly implemented to evaluate performance associated with patient outcomes; and identify interventions effective in improving performance.
Requirements Eligible applicants include: public nonprofit organizations; private nonprofit organizations; small, minority, women-owned businesses; universities; colleges; research institutions; hospitals; community-based organizations; faith-based organizations; federally recognized Indian tribal governments; Indian tribes; Indian tribal organizations; state and local governments or their Bona Fide Agents (this includes the District of Columbia, the Commonwealth of Puerto Rico, the Virgin Islands, the Commonwealth of the Northern Marianna Islands, American Samoa, Guam, the Federated States of Micronesia, the Republic of the Marshall Islands, and the Republic of Palau); and political subdivisions of States (in consultation with States).
Restrictions Recipients may: not use funds for research; not use funds for clinical care; only expend funds for reasonable program purposes, including personnel, travel, supplies, and services, such as contractual. Awardees may not generally use HHS/CDC/ATSDR funding for the purchase of furniture or equipment (any such proposed spending must be identified in the budget). The direct and primary recipient in a cooperative agreement program must perform a substantial role in carrying out project objectives and not merely serve as a conduit for an award to another party or provider who is ineligible. Reimbursement of pre-award costs is not allowed.
Amount $100,000-$500,000
Date(s) Application Is Due Jul 17.
Contact Yolanda Sledge, Grants Management Specialist, (770) 488-2787; email: yiso@cdc.gov
Internet http://www.cdc.gov/od/pgo/funding/FOAs.htm
Sponsor Centers for Disease Control and Prevention
2920 Brandywine Road, Mail stop: E-14
Atlanta, GA 30341-3717

CDC Antimicrobial Resistance in Hospital-Acquired Infections Among Intensive Care Unit Patients 1184

CDC offers funds to conduct studies on antimicrobial resistance in hospital-acquired infections among intensive care unit patients. Grants will be awarded to conduct both economic and outcome evaluations on the extent of the problem, as well as on factors that lead to different outcomes.
Requirements Applications may be submitted by public and private nonprofit organizations and by governments and their agencies.
Amount $60,000-$100,000
Contact Nealean Austin, Centers for Disease Control and Prevention, (770) 488-2700
Internet http://edocket.access.gpo.gov/2004/04-9808.htm
Sponsor Centers for Disease Control and Prevention
2920 Brandywine Rd, Rm 3000
Atlanta, GA 30341

CDC Cancer Prevention and Control Programs 1185

The purpose of the program is to improve and to promote health among at-risk cancer populations and to reduce cancer morbidity and mortality.
Requirements Assistance will be provided only to the organizations listed. The Healthcare Association of New York to develop an integrated model for the delivery of comprehensive breast cancer services; the Health Choice Network, Miami/Dade County, Florida to administer the Jesse Trice Cancer Prevention Project; the East Tennessee State University, Cancer Prevention Research Center, James H. Quillen College of Medicine to address cancer care in the rural Appalachian region; the University of Rhode Island, Cancer Prevention Research Center to provide interactive interventions to at-risk populations; the Sisters of Charity Health Care System, to ensure that patients have access to early detection of gastrointestinal cancers; and Marin County, California to evaluate high incidence of breast cancer in the San Francisco Bay Area.
Amount $4.1million total
Contact Grants Administrator, (770) 488-4751; email: cancerinfo@cdc.gov
Internet http://www.cdc.gov/cancer
Sponsor Centers for Disease Control and Prevention
4770 Buford Hwy NE, MS K-64
Atlanta, GA 30341-3717

CDC Community Responses to Prevent Intimate Partner Violence 1186

The program's goals are to create and enhance community coalitions and responses for addressing intimate partner violence, to establish community programs for the primary prevention of intimate partner violence, and to evaluate the process and impact of using a coordinated community response to reduce this type of abuse. Officials are particularly interested in projects that focus on preventing violence against adolescents and women by people known to the victim. Other priorities are for projects that implement coalition-building and that expand existing coalitions and associated primary prevention activities. Two types of grants will be awarded: to organizations in rural or tribal areas that do not have intimate partner violence prevention coalitions or where those coalitions are in the early stages of development; and to urban or rural areas with established intimate partner violence prevention coalitions that have broad-based representation. An optional letter of intent is requested by March 13; full application is due April 12. Annual deadline dates may vary; contact the program officer to confirm exact dates.
Requirements Applications may be submitted by public and private nonprofit and for-profit organizations and by governments and their agencies.
Amount $300,000 maximum
Date(s) Application Is Due Mar 13; Apr 12.
Contact Ted Jones, Program Manager, (770) 488-4810; fax (770) 488-1011; email: FIVPINFO@cdc.gov
Internet http://www.cdc.gov/ncipc/factsheets/ipvfacts.htm
Sponsor Centers for Disease Control and Prevention
4770 Buford Hwy NE
Atlanta, GA 30341

CDC Cooperative Agreement for Continuing Enhanced National Surveillance for Prion Diseases in the United States 1187

The purpose of the funding is to continue an active surveillance program similar to that conducted by the National Prion Disease Pathology Surveillance Center since 1997 to monitor the occurrence of potentially emerging human TSEs in the United States. This program addresses the Healthy People 2010 focus area(s) of Immunizations and Infectious Diseases. Eligible applicants should have experience in conducting prion disease surveillance and must be capable of fulfilling the ongoing needs for enhancing such surveillance at the national level.
Requirements Eligible applicants include: public nonprofit organizations; private nonprofit organizations; small, minority, women-owned businesses; universities; colleges; research institutions; hospitals; community-based organizations; faith-based organizations; federally recognized Indian tribal governments; Indian tribes; Indian tribal organizations; state and local governments or their Bona Fide Agents (this includes the District of Columbia, the Commonwealth of Puerto Rico, the Virgin Islands, the Commonwealth of the Northern Marianna Islands, American Samoa, Guam, the Federated States of Micronesia, the Republic of the Marshall Islands, and the Republic of Palau); and political subdivisions of States (in consultation with States).
Restrictions Recipients may: not use funds for research; not use funds for clinical care; only expend funds for reasonable program purposes, including personnel, travel, supplies, and services, such as contractual. Awardees may not generally use HHS/CDC/ATSDR funding for the purchase of furniture or equipment (any such proposed spending must be identified in the budget). The direct and primary recipient in a cooperative agreement program must perform a substantial role in carrying out project objectives and not merely serve as a conduit for an award to another party or provider who is ineligible.
Amount $2,550,000.00 first year; $12,750,000.00 over five years
Date(s) Application Is Due Jun 30.
Contact Mattie Jackson, Grants Management Specialist, (770) 488-2696; email: MIJ3@cdc.gov
Internet http://www.cdc.gov/od/pgo/funding/FOAs.htm
Sponsor Centers for Disease Control and Prevention
2920 Brandywine Road, Mail stop: E-14
Atlanta, GA 30341-3717

CDC Cooperative Agreement for the Development, Operation, and Evaluation of an Entertainment Education Program 1188

The purpose of this program is raise awareness and behavioral change concerning public health issues through the use of the television media as means of accessing the television viewing public by providing: accurate public health information and public health issues, as well as accurate depictions of healthy living at all stages of life, to entertainment industry leadership for possible inclusion in television story lines; assistance with public health outreach, including providing additional information concerning public health topics depicted on television story lines, and assistance with public service announcements and informational short videos to be aired in conjunction with drama presentations; and evaluation of public health television story lines and the effect on the viewing public.
Requirements Eligible applicants include: public nonprofit organizations; private nonprofit organizations; universities; colleges; research institutions; federally recognized Indian tribal governments; Indian tribes; Indian tribal organizations; state and local governments or their Bona Fide Agents (this includes the District of Columbia, the Commonwealth of Puerto Rico, the Virgin Islands, the Commonwealth of the Northern Marianna Islands, American Samoa, Guam, the Federated States of Micronesia, the Republic of the Marshall Islands, and the Republic of Palau); and political subdivisions of States (in consultation with States).
Date(s) Application Is Due Jun 7.
Contact Sharon Robertson, Grants Management Officer, (770) 488-2748; email: SRobertson1@cdc.gov
Internet http://www.cdc.gov/od/pgo/funding/FOAs.htm
Sponsor Centers for Disease Control and Prevention
2920 Brandywine Road, Mail stop: E-14
Atlanta, GA 30341

CDC Core Capacity Program Grants 1189

This program seeks to develop basic cardiovascular health promotions and strategies at the state level. It should include statewide partnerships and program coordination among health agencies aimed at primary and secondary heart disease prevention.
Requirements State health agencies, the District of Columbia, Puerto Rico, and US territories are eligible to apply.
Restrictions Funds may not be used to supplant state or local funds, to provide inpatient care or personal health services, nor to support construction or renovation of facilities.
Amount $250,000-$500,000 range; $300,000 average
Contact Nealean Austin, Team Lead, Branch B, Procurement and Grants Office, Centers for Disease Control and Prevention, (770) 488-2754
Internet http://www.cdc.gov
Sponsor Centers for Disease Control and Prevention
2920 Brandywine Rd
Altanta, GA 30341

CDC Disabilities Prevention Demonstration-Epidemiology Project Grants 1190

The objectives of this program are to provide a national focus for the prevention of disabilities in targeted disability groups: developmental disabilities, injury disabilities from health and spinal cord trauma, selected adult chronic conditions, and secondary disabilities in persons with physical disabilities; to build capacity at the state and community level to coordinate disabilities prevention activities and establish surveillance; to employ epidemiological methods to set priorities and target interventions; and to quantify and conduct programs to prevent secondary conditions in persons with primary disabilities. For demonstration/epidemiology projects, grant support may be used to implement and evaluate specified project activities to identify and quantify preventable secondary disabilities and measure the effectiveness and costs of preventive interventions. Funds may be used to support personnel services, equipment, supplies, travel, and services directly related to project activities. Projects will be supported for two to three years depending on availability of funds. Contact the office for deadline dates.
Requirements Eligible applicants are public and private nonprofit entities, including disabilities services organizations (such as independent living centers), local health departments, other local governmental agencies including local organizations, units of state agencies, voluntary agencies, universities, colleges, medical facilities, research institutions, and federally recognized Native American tribal governments.
Restrictions Project funds may not be used to supplant state or local funds available for disabilities prevention or for construction costs, or to lease or purchase facilities or space.
Amount $130,000-$460,000 range; $310,000 average
Contact Donald Betts, Sr., Division of Human Development and Disability, (404) 498-3957; email: dib3@cdc.gov
Internet http://www.cdc.gov
Sponsor Centers for Disease Control and Prevention
255 E Paces Ferry Rd
Atlanta, GA 30305

CDC Evaluation of the Use of Rapid Testing For Influenza in Outpatient Medical Settings 1191

The purpose of this project is to evaluate how rapid tests for influenza are being implemented and used in clinical practice in outpatient medical settings such as community clinics, solo and group practice physician offices, and hospital emergency rooms across the United States. This evaluation will include a determination of the scope of rapid influenza test use, the types of tests in use and how they are selected, the personnel performing testing, the extent to which good laboratory practices and testing guidelines are being followed, how results are reported and interpreted, how results are used for patient care and antiviral and antibiotic prescribing practices, and the presence of linkages between these outpatient settings and the public health system. Additionally, this project may identify potential opportunities to provide guidance to assist sites in making decisions on the appropriate use of these tests and ways to enhance the connectivity with the public health system. Connectivity with public health is especially important in light of the possibility of an influenza pandemic. This project will identify and evaluate practices used in outpatient settings related to processes such as specimen collection, testing, reporting and referral for influenza.
Requirements Eligible applicants include: public nonprofit organizations; private nonprofit organizations; small, minority, women-owned businesses; universities; colleges; research institutions; hospitals; community-based organizations; faith-based organizations; federally recognized Indian tribal governments; Indian tribes; Indian tribal organizations; state and local governments or their Bona Fide Agents (this includes the District of Columbia, the Commonwealth of Puerto Rico, the Virgin Islands, the Commonwealth of the Northern Marianna Islands, American Samoa, Guam, the Federated States of Micronesia, the Republic of the Marshall Islands, and the Republic of Palau); and political subdivisions of States (in consultation with States).
Restrictions Recipients may: not use funds for research; not use funds for clinical care; only expend funds for reasonable program purposes, including personnel, travel, supplies, and services, such as contractual. Awardees may not generally use HHS/CDC/ATSDR funding for the purchase of furniture or equipment (any such proposed spending must be identified in the budget). The direct and primary recipient in a cooperative agreement program must perform a substantial role in carrying out project objectives and not merely serve as a conduit for an award to another party or provider who is ineligible. Reimbursement of pre-award costs is not allowed. Reimbursement of construction costs is not allowed.
Amount $200,000
Date(s) Application Is Due Aug 6.
Contact Yolanda Sledge, Grants Management Specialist, (770) 488-2787; email: yiso@cdc.gov
Internet http://www.cdc.gov/od/pgo/funding/FOAs.htm
Sponsor Centers for Disease Control and Prevention
2920 Brandywine Road, Mail stop: E-14
Atlanta, GA 30341-3717

CDC Foundation Applied Epidemiology Fellowship 1192

The fellowship provides medical students with an applied hands-on training experience in epidemiology and public health. Eight competitively selected third- and fourth-year medical students from around the country will spend up to one full year at the Centers for Disease Control and Prevention (CDC) in Atlanta, Georgia. While at CDC, they will participate in an orientation to CDC, applied epidemiology, the national public health system, and the role of physicians in that system. With the guidance of experienced CDC epidemiologists, they will perform epidemiologic analyses and research, design public health interventions, and assist in field investigations. Annual deadline dates may vary; contact program staff for exact dates.
Requirements US citizens currently enrolled in an allopathic or osteopathic school of medicine in the United States and would be in the third or fourth year of training are eligible.
Date(s) Application Is Due Dec 2.
Contact Karen Torghele, Program Contact, (404) 639-2696: email: ktorghele@cdc.com
Internet http://cdcfoundation.org/pages.html?page=303
Sponsor CDC Foundation
1600 Clifton Rd NE, Mailstop D-18
Atlanta, GA 30333

CDC Grants for Violence-Related Injury Prevention Research 1193

Funded projects should identify effective ways of preventing violence-related injuries and expand the use of new and current intervention methods for preventing these types of injuries. In the areas of suicide and assaultive behavior, projects may focus on understanding the factors that affect this behavior, such as the nature of suicide among gay and lesbian people as compared to the general population or how unequal access to criminal justice, health care, and education is related to violent behavior. Family and intimate violence prevention projects may examine the intervention strategies that are most effective in preventing injuries. CDC encourages projects to study the needs of mothers and children in families where intimate partner violence takes place and to use population-based research to quantify injury and disability among women as a result of partner violence. Officials are also interested in research that defines the cost of violent injuries and the cost effectiveness of prevention or intervention methods. Contact the program office for deadline dates.
Requirements Public and private nonprofit and for-profit agencies may apply for grants. This includes state and local agencies, hospitals, and universities.
Amount $300,000 maximum; $250,000 average
Contact Paul Smutz, Injury Prevention and Control Research Projects, (770) 488-1508
Internet http://www.cdc.gov/ncipc/res-opps/VIOLENCE_04045.htm
Sponsor Centers for Disease Control and Prevention
4770 Buford Hwy NE, MS K65
Atlanta, GA 30341-3724

CDC HIV Demonstration, Research, Public and Professional Education Project Grants 1194

Grants are awarded to states, political subdivisions of states, and other public and nonprofit entities for research on the prevention of HIV infection at the community level. Funds may be used to develop, implement and evaluate new intervention, including those targeting people who are infected with HIV. Applicants are encouraged to have research groups participate in the program. Contact the program office for exact deadline dates.
Requirements States, political subdivisions of states, other public and nonprofit private entities are eligible to apply.
Amount $50,000-$1 million; $293,253 average
Contact Allyn Nakashima, National Center for HIV, STD, and TB Prevention, (404) 639-0900; Cheryl Maddux, Grants Management Branch, (770) 498-1911
Internet http://www.cdc.gov
Sponsor Centers for Disease Control and Prevention
2920 Brandywine Rd
Atlanta, GA 30341

CDC HIV Prevention among Ethnic Minority Populations 1195

The purpose of this program is to create community-based organizations aimed at HIV prevention among ethnic minority populations.
Requirements State health departments and public and private institutions of higher education may apply, along with any community-based organization (CBO). Minority-oriented CBO's must have at least 50 percent of their governing board composed of the racial minority that will be served and at least 50 percent of the program's positions be held by persons who reflect the intended racial demographics.
Amount $6.45 million total

Date(s) Application Is Due Mar 7.
Contact Grant Administrator, (404) 639-2072
Internet http://www.cdc.gov/about/funding.htm
Sponsor Centers for Disease Control and Prevention
1600 Clifton Rd NE
Atlanta, GA 30333

CDC HIV Prevention Projects for Community-Based Organizations **1196**
CDC announces the availability of funds to support community-based organizations (CBOs) to develop, implement, and evaluate state-of-the-art, model community-based HIV prevention programs for populations at risk for HIV infection, especially racial/ethnic minority populations at risk. The goals of this program are to reduce the disproportionate impact of the HIV epidemic on racial/ethnic minority populations and other at-risk populations; to improve and expand community-based HIV prevention services by supporting community-based HIV prevention programs that address priorities described in applicable state and local comprehensive HIV prevention plans (that is, the plans developed by the official HIV prevention community planning groups for the jurisdiction in which the CBO is located) or that adequately justify addressing other priorities; enhance CBOs' incorporation of scientific theory and data, and validated program experience into the design, implementation, and evaluation of HIV prevention services; and support collaboration and coordination of HIV prevention efforts among CBOs, community planning groups, local organizations, local and state health departments, and managed care organizations serving populations at risk for HIV infection.
Requirements Applicant organization must have current, valid 501(c)3 tax-exempt status; must be located in the community; and have an established record of at least two years of service to the proposed target population. Contact program staff for a complete list of requirements.
Amount $225,000 maximum
Contact Allyn Nakashima, National Center for HIV, STD, and TB Prevention, (404) 639-0900; Chreyl Maddux, Grants Management Officer, (770) 498-1911
Internet http://www.cdc.gov/about/funding.htm
Sponsor Centers for Disease Control and Prevention
2920 Brandywine Rd
Atlanta, GA 30341

CDC HIV Prevention: Community-Based Organizations **1197**
CDC invites comments under a planned request for applications to support community-based organizations (CBO) to develop, implement, and evaluate effective community-based HIV prevention programs for at-risk populations, especially racial and ethnic minority populations.
Requirements Applicants must be tax-exempt. They may apply as minority organizations that intend to serve predominantly racial or ethnic minority populations at risk or as CBOs that will serve high-risk populations in general. Applicants must also have two years of service with the proposed target population.
Amount $17.6 million total
Date(s) Application Is Due Oct 29.
Contact Division of HIV/AIDS Prevention, Intervention, Research and Support, National Center for HIV, STD and TB Prevention, (404) 639-5230; fax: (404) 639-2072; email: hivmail@cdc.gov
Internet http://www.cdc.gov/od/pgo/funding/grantmain.htm
Sponsor Centers for Disease Control and Prevention
1600 Clifton Rd NE
Atlanta, GA 30333

CDC Injury Control Research Centers Grants **1198**
Grants are intended to support injury control research and demonstrations on priority issues; to integrate aspects of engineering, public health, behavioral sciences, medicine, and other disciplines to prevent and control injuries more effectively; to rigorously apply and evaluate current and new interventions, methods, and strategies that focus on the prevention and control of injuries; to stimulate and support injury control research centers in academic institutions that will develop a comprehensive and integrated approach to injury control research and training; and to bring the knowledge and expertise of injury control research centers to bear on the development of effective public health programs for injury control. Annual deadline dates may vary.
Requirements Any nonprofit or for-profit organization in eligible regions may apply. Eligible regions include 34 states as well as the District of Columbia, the Virgin Islands, and Puerto Rico. The 34 states are: Alabama, Alaska, Arizona, Arkansas, California, Delaware, Florida, Georgia, Hawaii, Idaho, Illinois, Indiana, Kentucky, Louisiana, Maryland, Michigan, Minnesota, Mississippi, Nevada, New Jersey, New Mexico, New York, North Carolina, Ohio, Oklahoma, Oregon, Pennsylvania, South Carolina, Tennessee, Texas, Virginia, Washington, West Virginia, and Wisconsin.
Restrictions Grantees may not award subgrants but may enter into contracts as necessary to achieve the aims of the program.
Amount $905,500 average
Contact Program Manager, National Center for Injury Prevention and Control, (770) 488-1506; email: OHCINFO@cdc.gov
Internet http://www.cdc.gov/ncipc/profiles/icrcs/default.htm
Sponsor Centers for Disease Control and Prevention
4770 Buford Hwy NE, MS K65
Atlanta, GA 30341-3724

CDC Injury Prevention and Control Research and State and Community Based Programs **1199**
Research grants support injury control research on priority issues; projects that integrate aspects of engineering, public health, behavioral sciences, medicine, and other disciplines in order to prevent and control injuries more effectively; projects that rigorously apply and evaluate current and new interventions, methods, and strategies that focus on the prevention and control of injuries; projects that stimulate and support Injury Control Research Centers (ICRC) in academic institutions which will develop a comprehensive and integrated approach to injury control research and training; and projects that bring the knowledge and expertise of ICRC's to bear on the development of effective public health programs for injury control. State and Community Program grants are to develop and evaluate new methods or to evaluate existing methods and techniques used in injury surveillance by public health agencies; and to develop, expand, or improve injury control programs to reduce morbidity, mortality, severity, disability, and cost from injuries.
Requirements Applications may be submitted by all public and private nonprofit and for-profit organizations and by governments and their agencies.
Contact Program Officer, Injury Prevention and Control Research Projects, (770) 488-1506; fax: (770) 488-1667; email: OHCINFO@cdc.gov
Internet http://www.cdc.gov/ncipc/profiles/icrcs/default.htm
Sponsor Centers for Disease Control and Prevention
4770 Buford Hwy NE, MS K65
Atlanta, GA 30341-3724

CDC Intervention Epidemiologic Research Studies of HIV/AIDS **1200**
CDC announces the availability of funds for a cooperative agreement program to support intervention epidemiologic research studies of AIDS and HIV infection. These awards will help support researchers in two areas: the development and evaluation of innovative interventions for preventing and reducing the transmission of HIV infection in young and recently initiated injection drug users (IDUs); and the development and evaluation of an intervention study to improve access to antiretroviral therapy in HIV-infected disadvantaged populations.
Requirements Applications may be submitted by public and private nonprofit organizations and by governments and their agencies.
Amount $5000-$270,000 range; $200,265 average
Contact Allyn Nakashima, Epidemiology Branch, Center for Disease Control and Prevention, (404) 639-0900
Internet http://www.cdc.gov/epo
Sponsor Centers for Disease Control and Prevention
1600 Clifton Rd NE, MS-E-45
Atlanta, GA 30333

CDC Minority Health Statistics Dissertation Research Grants **1201**
The purpose of the program is to make awards for the conduct of special surveys or studies on the health of racial and ethnic populations or subpopulations; analysis of data on ethnic and racial populations and subpopulations; and research on improving methods for developing statistics on ethnic and racial populations and subpopulations. The deadline date listed is for letters of intent. Annual dates may vary; contact the program office for exact dates.
Requirements Eligible applicants may be public or private nonprofit institutions that will administer the grant on behalf of the proposed principal investigator. The proposed principal investigator must be a registered doctoral candidate in resident or nonresident status. All requirements for the doctoral degree other than the dissertation must be completed by the time of the award. Students seeking a doctorate in any relevant research discipline are eligible. An applicant institution may be either the degree-granting institution or another nonprofit institution with which the proposed principal investigator is professionally affiliated.
Amount $15,000-$30,000; $20,000 average
Contact Program Contact, Minority Health Statistics Grants, National Center for Health Statistics (3311 Toledo Rd, Hyattsville, MD 20782); (301) 458-4000; email: MGP@cdc.gov
Internet http://www.cdc.gov/nchswww/about/grants/grants.htm
Sponsor Centers for Disease Control and Prevention
1600 Clifton Rd
Atlanta, GA 30333

CDC National Breast and Cervical Cancer Early Detection Program **1202**
The purpose of this program is to apply a state, territorial, or tribal public health approach to increase access to and use of screening services. Funded programs will establish a comprehensive breast and cervical cancer early detection screening program that includes breast and cervical cancer screening, tracking, follow-up and case management; public education and outreach; professional education; quality assurance and improvement; surveillance and evaluation; coalitions and partnerships; and management.
Requirements Assistance will be provided only to the official health departments of states or their bona fide agents, including the District of Columbia, the Commonwealth of Puerto Rico, the Virgin Islands, the Commonwealth of the Northern Mariana Islands, the Republic of Palau, and federally recognized Indian Tribal governments.
Restrictions Alaska, Arizona, Arkansas, American Samoa, California, Colorado, Connecticut, Florida, Georgia, Illinois, Iowa, Kansas, Louisiana, Maine, Maryland, Massachusetts, Michigan, Minnesota, Missouri, Nebraska, New Jersey, New Mexico,

New York, North Carolina, Ohio, Oklahoma, Oregon, Pennsylvania, Rhodes Island, South Carolina, Texas, Utah, Vermont, Washington, West Virginia, Wisconsin, Puerto Rico, and Guam are not eligible for funding. See announcement for complete listing.
Amount $145,000-$8.4 million; $2.1 million average
Contact Carlos Smiley, Grants Management Branch, Procurement and Grants Office, (770) 488-2754
Internet http://www.cdc.gov/cancer/nbccedp/index.htm
Sponsor Centers for Disease Control and Prevention
2920 Brandywine Rd
Atlanta, GA 30341-4146

CDC National Poison Prevention and Control Program Grants 1203
The purpose of the program is to support an integrated system of poison prevention and control services including: coordination of all poison control centers (PCCs) through development, implementation, and evaluation of standardized public education; and development of a plan to improve national toxicosurveillance and development of a single, nationwide toll-free telephone number and related public service media campaign.
Requirements Applications may be submitted by public and private nonprofit organizations, governments and their agencies, other public and private nonprofit organizations, state and local governments or their bona fide agents, and federally recognized American Indian tribal governments, American Indian tribes, or American Indian tribal organizations.
Contact Cheryl Maddux, Grants Management Officer, Centers for Disease Control and Prevention, (770) 488-2645
Internet http://www.cdc.gov
Sponsor Centers for Disease Control and Prevention
4770 Buford Hwy NE
Atlanta, GA 30341

CDC National Programs That Build the Capacity of Schools to Prevent Foodborne Illness Through Coordinated School Health 1204
The purpose of this program is to develop a national program to build the capacity of state and local education and health agencies, and others to prevent foodborne illness and other important health problems as part of a coordinated school health program.
Requirements Assistance will be provided to national organizations that are private health, education, or social service agencies (professional, or voluntary); qualify as a nonprofit 501(c)3 entity; have the capacity and experience to assist their local affiliates; and have affiliate offices or local, state, or regional membership constituencies in a minimum of ten states and territories.
Restrictions National organizations that are funded currently by CDC/Division of Adolescent and School Health (DASH) under program announcements 99023, 97065, 00026, 00081, 00109, 00719, 98885, 99072, 00079 or 00618 are not eligible for this program announcement.
Amount $299,000 average
Contact Nealean Austin, Grants Management Officer, (770) 488-2754
Internet http://www.cdc.gov/healthyyouth
Sponsor Centers for Disease Control and Prevention
2920 Brandywine Rd, MS E-18
Atlanta, GA 30341-4146

CDC National Training Information and Exchange Program 1205
The purpose of this program is to make data and information on trauma care in the United States more accessible to a broad spectrum of individuals and organizations, including trauma care professionals and professional associations, trauma centers and other acute care hospitals, trauma care systems, emergency medical services (EMS) systems, injury researchers and research organizations, public health agencies, health care payers, and the general public.
Requirements Applications may be submitted by public and private nonprofit organizations and by governments and their agencies.
Contact Cheryl Maddux, Grants Management Officer, (770) 488-2645
Internet http://www.cdc.gov
Sponsor Centers for Disease Control and Prevention
2920 Brandywine Rd, Ste 3000
Atlanta, GA 30341

CDC Public Health Conference Support Grant Program 1206
The purpose of the grants is to provide partial support for specific non-federal conferences in the areas of health promotion and disease prevention information/education programs. Funds may be used for direct cost expenditures, such as salaries, speaker fees, rental of necessary equipment, registration fees, and transportation costs (not to exceed economy-class fare) for non-federal individuals. The program continues through March 8, 2009.
Requirements Public and private organizations, including colleges and universities, and units of state and local government are eligible to apply. Applicants must provide a portion of the conference cost.
Restrictions Funds may not be used for indirect costs, equipment purchases, honoraria, entertainment, or personal expenses.
Contact Sharon Robertson, Grants Management Officer, (770) 488-2748; email: SRobertson1@cdc.gov
Internet http://www.cdc.gov/od/pgo/funding/FOAs.htm
Sponsor Centers for Disease Control and Prevention
2920 Brandywine Road, Room 3000
Atlanta, GA 30341

CDC Research, Treatment, and Education Programs on Lyme Disease in the United States Cooperative Agreements 1207
The objective of the program is to develop and implement practical and effective measures for the primary and secondary prevention of Lyme disease. Funds will be available to develop disease surveillance, conduct ecological and epidemiological studies, develop prevention and control activities, develop better diagnostic tests, and develop and disseminate educational materials and programs. Cooperative agreements are usually awarded for a three-year project period. Initial awards are made for a one-year budget period with continuation awards for up to an additional two years. Contact the office listed for application deadline dates. PA-04-008
Requirements Public and nonprofit organizations able to provide services to geographical areas where Lyme disease is endemic or found to be newly emerging are eligible to apply. Funding preference will be given to proposals that incorporate evaluation of effectiveness, cost, and acceptability of strategies, or combinations of strategies, for population-based control of tick-borne diseases.
Amount $100,000-$700,000; $350,000 average
Contact Dr. Brian Mahy, National Center for Infectious Diseases, (404) 639-0043; fax: (404) 639-2469; email: bxm1@cdc.gov
Internet http://www.cdc.gov/od/pgo/funding/Expired/04008.htm
Sponsor Centers for Disease Control and Prevention
P.O. Box 2087
Fort Collins, CO 80522

CDC Sexually Transmitted Diseases Research, Demonstration, Public Information, and Education Grants 1208
The grants are meant to develop, improve, apply, and evaluate methods for the prevention and control of syphilis, gonorrhea, and other sexually transmitted diseases through demonstration and applied research. Also, the grants are meant to develop, improve, apply, and evaluate methods and strategies for public information and education about these diseases; to support professional (including appropriate allied health personnel) education, training, and clinical skills improvement activities; and to support particularly deserving public information and education programs that cannot be supported through other grant programs. Grant funds may be used for the costs associated with planning, organizing, and conducting applied research, demonstrations and education programs, and to reimburse individuals asked to be participants in the applied research. Contact the program office for deadline dates.
Requirements Any state, political subdivision of a state, or any other public or private nonprofit institution may apply.
Amount $125,000-$450,000; $313,809 average
Contact Sevgi Aral, Director, Division of STD Prevention, (404) 639-8259; Gladys Gissentanna, Grants Management Officer, (770) 498-1912
Internet http://www.cdc.gov
Sponsor Centers for Disease Control and Prevention
255 E Paces Ferry Rd NE
Atlanta, GA 30305

CDC Using Genetic Information to Prevent Disease and Improve Health Research Grants 1209
The purpose of this program is to strengthen science for public health action, collaborate with health care partners for prevention, and promote healthy living at every stage of life. The program will provide funding for conducting population-based research to assess how risk for disease and disability in well-defined populations is influenced by the interaction of human genetic variation with modifiable risk factors, and ensure that genetic tests and services are incorporated in population-based interventions that promote health and prevent disease and disability. Annual deadline dates may vary; contact the program office for exact dates.
Requirements Applications may be submitted by public and private nonprofit organizations and by governments and their agencies, other public and private nonprofit organizations, state and local governments or their bona fide agents, and federally recognized American Indian tribal governments, American Indian tribes, or American Indian tribal organizations.
Contact Nealean Austin, Grants Management Branch, Centers for Disease Control and Prevention, (770) 488-2700
Internet http://www.cdc.gov
Sponsor Centers for Disease Control and Prevention
4770 Buford Hwy NE
Atlanta, GA 30341

Cen Cal Diving and Aquatic Studies Scholarship 1210
This scholarship is awarded annually to an outstanding individual who is engaging in studies of underwater habitats. Aquatic-related programs in the disciplines of biology, physical sciences, marine education, maritime archaeology, historical and social aspects of marine resources, or the science of diving are relevant for consideration. Application forms are available on the Web site. Annual deadline dates may vary; contact program staff for exact dates.
Requirements Applicants must be California residents enrolled in an undergraduate or graduate program at a California college or university, be over 18 years of age, maintain

a high academic standing with a minimum GPA of 3.0, and have a national/regional diver certification.
Amount $1000
Date(s) Application Is Due Apr 30.
Contact Jim Kaller, (415) 362-9134 ext 12; email: jameskaller@batnet.com
Internet http://www.cencal.org/requirements.html
Sponsor Central California Council of Diving Clubs
P.O. Box 779, Cen Cal
Daly City, CA 94017

Center for Advanced Judaic Studies Postdoctoral Fellowships **1211**
The program is designed to engage scholars from within Jewish studies, who specialize in Jewish life under Islamic rule, in fruitful conversation with scholars in Arabic, Syriac, Persian, and Ottoman studies. By bringing together experts from these disparate disciplines who deal with aspects of Jewish, Christian, and Muslim life within pre-modern Islamic polities, the program hopes to encourage a broad view of Islamic societies and to foster new approaches to their religious, ethnic, and linguistic diversity. Guidelines are available online. The 2006-2007 program is Jewish, Christian, and Muslim Life under Caliphs and Sultans. The 2007- 2008 program will be Jewish and Other Imperial Cultures in Late Antiquity: Literary, Social, and Material Histories
Requirements Any individual or group of scholars in the fields of Jewish studies may submit a proposal for an annual theme.
Amount $33,000
Date(s) Application Is Due Nov 1.
Contact David B. Ruderman, Director, (215) 238-1290; fax: (215) 238-1540; email: ruderman@sas.upenn.edu
Internet http://www.cjs.upenn.edu/program/fellowship.htm
Sponsor Center for Jewish Studies
Center for Advanced Judaic Studies, 420 Walnut St
Philadelphia, PA 19106

Center for Advanced Study in the Behavioral Sciences Postdoctoral Fellowships **1212**
The center offers nine- to 12-month residential postdoctoral fellowships for scientists and scholars of proven accomplishment or exceptional promise. Fellowships have been offered in psychology, sociology, anthropology, political science, history, economics, philosophy, psychiatry-psychoanalysis, linguistics, humanities, law, and education; and certain biomedical, mathematical, and statistical specialties. The selection process is started by nominations being received from well-known behavioral scientists, academic administrators, and former fellows. Nominees are screened by a review panel and the final selections are made by the center's board of trustees. The selection process normally takes several years, with the fellowship roster for any given year usually prepared more than a year in advance. Usually 45 to 50 fellowships are awarded annually. Nominations may be submitted at any time.
Requirements Qualified scholars in behavioral and biological sciences, humanities, and certain areas of statistics and computer science from any country are eligible. Resident participants usually have completed university training, hold university appointments, are engaged in research and research training, and are in the top 5 to 10 percent of the scholars in their field.
Contact Robert Scott, Associate Director, (650) 321-2052; fax: (650) 321-1192; email: info@casbs.org
Internet https://casbs.stanford.edu
Sponsor Center for Advanced Study in the Behavioral Sciences
75 Alta Rd
Stanford, CA 94305

Center for Advanced Study in the Visual Arts Senior Fellowships **1213**
Applications will be considered from scholars for study in the history, theory, and criticism of the visual arts (painting, sculpture, architecture, landscape architecture, urbanism, graphics, film, photography, decorative arts, industrial design, etc.) of any geographical area and of any period. Applications are also solicited from scholars in other disciplines whose work examines physical objects or has implications for the analysis and criticism of physical form. In addition, applications are solicited from scholars who are specifically interested in curatorial research related to objects in the painting, sculpture, graphics, and other collections of the gallery. One Paul Mellon Senior Fellowship and four to six Ailsa Mellon Bruce and Samuel H. Kress Senior Fellowships will normally be awarded for an academic year; applications for a single academic term or a quarter are also possible. In exceptional cases, application may be made for a period of two years. The Samuel H. Kress Senior Fellowships are intended to support primarily research related to objects in the collection of the gallery. Senior fellows receive a monthly stipend with additional allowances for research materials, round-trip travel, and local expenses.
Requirements Applicants must have held the PhD for five years or more or possess a record of professional accomplishment at the time of application. Senior fellowships are awarded without regard to the age or nationality of the applicant. Fellowships will normally be awarded for an academic year, early fall to late spring, but fellowships for a single term or quarter are also possible. Scholars are expected to reside in Washington, DC, throughout their fellowship and participate in the activities of the center.
Restrictions Fellowships may not be postponed or renewed.
Amount $50,000 maximum; $12,000 maximum housing allowance
Date(s) Application Is Due Oct 1.
Contact Fellowships Program, Center for Advanced Study in the Visual Arts, (202) 842-6482; fax: (202) 789-3026; email: advstudy@nga.gov
Internet http://www.nga.gov/resources/casvasen.htm
Sponsor National Gallery of Art
2000B S Club Dr
Landover, MD 20785

Center for Advanced Study in the Visual Arts Visiting Senior Fellowships **1214**
Applications will be considered from scholars for short-term fellowships (maximum of 60 days) for study in the history, theory, and criticism of the visual arts (painting, sculpture, architecture, landscape architecture, urbanism, graphics, film, photography, decorative arts, industrial design, etc.) of any geographical area and of any period. Applications are also solicited from scholars in other disciplines whose work examines physical objects or has implications for the analysis and criticism of physical form. In addition, applications are solicited from scholars who are specifically interested in curatorial research related to objects in the painting, sculpture, graphics, and other collections of the gallery. The notable resources represented by the collections of the National Gallery of Art, its library, photographic archives, the Library of Congress, and other specialized research libraries and collections in Washington will be available to the visiting senior fellows; lectures, colloquia, and informal discussions will complement the program. Fellows are provided with a monthly stipend that includes round-trip travel and local expenses. Fellows may be eligible for a $1500 per month housing allowance. Application forms must be obtained from the center. This award is granted twice per year.
Requirements Applicants must have held the PhD for five years or more or possess a record of professional accomplishment at the time of application. Fellowships are awarded without regard to age or nationality. All grants are based on individual need. Scholars are expected to reside in Washington, DC, throughout their fellowship and participate in the activities of the center.
Restrictions Fellowships may not be postponed or renewed.
Amount $6000-$8000
Date(s) Application Is Due Mar 21; Sep 21.
Contact Fellowships Program, Center for Advanced Study in the Visual Arts, (202) 842-6482; fax: (202) 789-3026; email: advstudy@nga.gov
Internet http://www.nga.gov/resources/casvavissen.htm
Sponsor National Gallery of Art
Fourth St and Constitution Ave NW
Washington, DC 20565

Center for African Studies Postdoctoral Fellowships **1215**
Funded by the Rockefeller Foundation, postdoctoral fellowships on the theme of Globalization and Higher Education in Africa are offered by the university's Center for African Studies and the College of Education. This three-year program offers fellows the opportunity to explore and interrogate, through interdisciplinary inquiries, the role of higher education in and on Africa. Applicants for the 10-month fellowships need not be US citizens. Interdisciplinary, comparative, and regional interests are especially welcome. All fellows will be based in Champaign-Urbana, IL, and some support for relocation expenses, housing, and benefits is also available.
Requirements Applications are welcome from the humanities, education, and social sciences fields, and applicants must have a PhD or its equivalent.
Amount $37,500-$40,000
Date(s) Application Is Due Jan 5.
Contact Rockefeller Postdoctoral Fellowships, (217) 333-6335; fax: (217) 244-2429; email: swisher@uiuc.edu
Internet http://www.afrst.uiuc.edu/postdoc04-05.htm
Sponsor University of Illinois at Urbana-Champaign
910 S Fifth St, 210 International Studies Bldg
Champaign, IL 61801

Center for Alternatives to Animal Testing Grants **1216**
The center seeks to develop innovative non-whole animal methods to evaluate fully commercial and/or therapeutic products to ensure the health and safety of the public. The program funds research that will lead to the refinement, replacement, or reduction of animals in toxicity testing and by disseminating scientifically correct information about these methods and their applications. The center encourages the development of in vitro approaches to toxicity evaluation including, but not limited to, methods using human cells/cell lines and studies in the areas of skin hypersensitivity/toxicity, phototoxicity, target organ toxicity, and structure-activity relationships. Grants support one year of research with possible renewal for another year. Preproposals must meet the application deadline; full proposals are invited.
Requirements Applicants must have an established mechanism for handling private funding.
Restrictions Projects focusing on mutagenicity or carcinogenicity are not funded.
Amount $25,000 maximum per year
Contact Alan Goldberg, Center Director, (410) 223-1692; fax: (410) 223-1603; email: caat@jhsph.edu or goldberg@jhsph.edu
Internet http://caat.jhsph.edu/programs/grants/grants.htm
Sponsor Johns Hopkins University
111 Market Pl, Ste 840
Baltimore, MD 21202-6709

Center for Black Music Research Rockefeller Fellowships 1217
Under the auspices of the Rockefeller Foundation, the Center for Black Music Research (CBMR) will offer a series of resident research fellowships under the theme of Researching the Circum-Caribbean. The CBMR will accept applications to pursue work on musico-cultural issues related to Latin-American and West Indian cultures in the circum-Caribbean region. Applications will be considered from scholars in the fields of music and music librarianship, history, Caribbean studies, and American cultural studies. Two fellowships will be offered. Fellows will spend half their time in residence at the AMRI in Saint Thomas, US Virgin Islands, from which they will do field or archival research, and the other half at the CBMR's Chicago site preparing for or writing the results of the work they performed while at the Caribbean site or other sites of field research. The fellows will present work-in-progress at colloquia and will have opportunities to interact with faculty, students, and members of the Chicago and Saint Thomas arts, cultural, and educational communities. Each fellowship includes a stipend ($25,000), an allowance ($4000 maximum) for moving to and from the fellow's home and the CBMR (or the Virgin Islands); an allowance $2000 maximum) for inter-island or intra-Caribbean research travel; and free housing in both locations.
Requirements Applicants must have completed work on their terminal degree (PhD degree or its equivalent) at the time of application and should be able to demonstrate their familiarity with the research of or related to the circum-Caribbean region.
Amount $37,750 total for stipend, travel allowances, and housing
Date(s) Application Is Due Feb 2.
Contact Linda Hunter, Fellowship Administrator, (312) 344-7559; fax: (312) 344-8029; email: lhunter@cbmr.colum.edu
Internet http://www.cbmr.org/fellows0405.htm
Sponsor Columbia College Chicago
600 S Michigan Ave
Chicago, IL 60605-1996

Center for Chicana/o Studies Rockefeller Fellowships 1218
The center seeks applicants for postdoctoral fellowships from scholars and artists conducting research on Chicana/o culture, and in particular, from scholars who focus on the interaction of hybridity, cultural mobility, and literacy in a transnational context. Projects on the ways Chicana/o culture responds to, as well as maps, the flows and conflicts among forms of cultural literacy are especially welcome, as are studies exploring the ways diverse global processes affect this cultural literacy. Fellows are expected to remain in residence at the center during the regular academic year (September-June), to participate in the ongoing activities of the center, and to live in the immediate area of the university. During the academic year, fellows will be required to present their research through lectures and workshops, to engage with faculty and students at colloquia and conferences, and to draw on the variety of resources available at the university. Fellows will also be expected to participate in a conference at the end of the four-year program.
Requirements Junior, senior and independent scholars and artists of any nationality who are conducting research on Chicana/o culture and the interplay of hybridity, cultural mobility and literacy are eligible.
Amount $35,000 stipend plus $1575 maximum toward moving allowance, benefits, and research assistance funds
Date(s) Application Is Due Feb 1.
Contact Carl Gutierrez-Jones, Center for Chicano Studies, (805) 893-3895; email: carlgj@english.ucsb.edu
Internet http://research.ucsb.edu/ccs/rockefeller.html
Sponsor University of California, Santa Barbara
125 Park Sq Crt, 400 Sibley St
Santa Barbara, CA 93106-6040

Center for Cultural Studies Resident Scholars Program Grants 1219
The center invites applications from postdoctoral scholars in the humanities, social sciences, and arts. Residencies vary from several months to a full academic year. Resident scholars are provided an office and have access to the UC library and other facilities. The center cannot provide a stipend. To apply, send a project statement, curriculum vita, two letters of recommendation, and a cover letter indicating the desired period of residency. Annual deadline dates may vary; contact program staff for exact dates.
Requirements Applicants should hold a doctorate or the equivalent.
Date(s) Application Is Due Apr 29.
Contact Resident Scholars Program, Center for Cultural Studies, (831) 459-4899; fax: (831) 459-1349; email: cult@ucsc.edu
Internet http://humwww.ucsc.edu/CultStudies/PROG/RSCHOL/residence.html
Sponsor Center for Cultural Studies
University of California, Oakes College
Santa Cruz, CA 95064

Center for Defense Information Internships 1220
The center offers an intern program to undergraduate and graduate students and recent graduates who have strong interests in US military issues and related public policy issues. Interns perform a variety of professional support functions but serve mainly as research and outreach assistants. Interns also assist with the production of CDI's weekly television show on military-related current affairs. They work closely with the center staff, usually with considerable responsibility. Intern projects have included such diverse research subjects as US military nuclear wastes, military spending, and US arms transfer policy, as well as media activities. There is no preferred academic background. Fields of study might encompass the social and policy sciences, physical sciences, and preprofessional curricula. Although prior coursework in US military issues and related public policy areas is not required, high academic achievements are important. Experience with video production is a plus. Writing skills are essential. Interns are expected to work on a full-time basis. Internships run from January through May, June through August, and September through December.
Requirements Internships are open to undergraduates, graduates, and graduate students with strong interests in military policy, national security, foreign affairs, and related public policy issues and/or interest in broadcast communications.
Amount $1000 monthly stipend
Date(s) Application Is Due Mar 1; Jul 1; Oct 1.
Contact Internship Coordinator, (202) 332-0600; fax: (202) 462-4559; email: internships@cdi.org
Internet http://www.cdi.org/about/internships.cfm
Sponsor Center for Defense Information
1779 Massachusetts Ave NW
Washington, DC 20036-2109

Center for East Asian Studies Fellowships 1221
The center was formed to increase interdisciplinary communication among linguists, historians, art historians, political scientists, anthropologists, and others whose research, teaching, or study focuses on China, Korea, or Japan. Some students accepted into the graduate program in East Asian studies at Stanford receive financial assistance through these fellowships. The center also offers a limited number of student awards to Stanford students for summer research and/or study. The most up-to-date information about fellowships is available in the CEAS newsletter which can be accessed on the Web site. Deadlines vary for individual programs; contact program staff for exact dates.
Requirements Graduate students at Stanford University specializing in East Asia may apply for fellowships at the time of initial application for admission.
Restrictions Students attending institutions other than Stanford are ineligible.
Contact Connie Chin, Program Administrator, (650) 723-3362; fax: (650) 725-3350; email: csquare@stanford.edu
Internet http://www.stanford.edu/dept/CEAS
Sponsor Stanford University
Rm 51-L, Bldg 50
Stanford, CA 94305-5013

Center for Education of Women Visiting Scholar Research Grants 1222
The Center for Education of Women (CEW) invites applications from scholars and practitioners interested in being in residence at the university for a period of one to 12 months to pursue research, writing, and publication interests. Applicants in the following general areas are invited to apply: Women in Higher Education, Women's Work, Women of Color in the Academy, Gender and Education, Career Development, Women in Non-Traditional Fields, Leadership, Gender Equity in Education and Employment, and Gender and Poverty. Other areas of research may also be considered. Scholars will have the opportunity to conduct their research and will be asked to prepare a working paper and/or give a seminar based on this work. CEW will provide office space, access to facilities and programs, modest stipends, and/or research support funds. Applicants should send letter of interest, a one- to two- page outline of proposed project, funding requirements, anticipated dates of stay, and a vita.
Requirements Applicants should hold an earned PhD, EdD, JD, etc., or have equivalent experience in a relevant field.
Amount $7500 maximum per scholar
Date(s) Application Is Due Mar 1; Jun 1.
Contact Beth Sullivan, (734) 998-7225; email: bsulliva@umich.edu
Internet http://www.umich.edu/~cew/faculty-staff/vs.htm
Sponsor University of Michigan
330 E Liberty St
Ann Arbor, MI 48104-2289

Center for Ethics and Public Affairs Faculty Fellowships 1223
The Center for Ethics and Public Affairs supports residential faculty fellowships to support outstanding faculty whose teaching and research focus on questions of ethics and moral choice in such areas as architecture, business, government, law, medicine, urban design and planning, and engineering. Fellows will participate in conferences and seminars and devote the majority of time to conducting their own research. The fellowships are open to all, regardless of citizenship.
Requirements Applicants should hold a doctorate in philosophy, political theory, or related disciplines; or a professional degree in architecture, business, engineering, law, medicine, urban design and planning, or public policy. Preference will be given to applicants at an early stage of their careers, normally no more than 10 years from the terminal degree in their field.
Amount $35,000 maximum
Date(s) Application Is Due Dec 8.
Contact Faculty Fellowships, (504) 862-3236; fax: (504) 862-8360; email: cepa@tulane.edu
Internet http://www.tulane.edu/~murphy/Faculty%20F.htm
Sponsor Tulane University
Murphy Institute, 108 Tilton Hall
New Orleans, LA 70118

Center for Hellenic Studies Fellowships 1224

Fellowships for research in ancient Greek history, philosophy, literature, language, and religion are offered at the center. Letters of recommendation are due separately at the Director's office by November 1. Application forms are available upon request.
Requirements Applicants must have PhDs or equivalent, be professionally competent in ancient Greek, and be published writers.
Amount $26,000 maximum stipend plus $1000 for travel and research assistance
Date(s) Application Is Due Oct 15.
Contact Program Contact, (202) 234-3738; fax: (202) 797-3745; email: chs@fas.harvard.edu
Internet http://www.chs.harvard.edu/fellowships.sec
Sponsor Center for Hellenic Studies
3100 Whitehaven St NW
Washington, DC 20008

Center for Inquiry Science and the Public Visiting Research Fellowships 1225

Each academic year, the center awards visiting research fellowships at the postdoctoral or senior level in the area of science and the public. All relevant disciplines are welcome. Fellowships include an appointment in the appropriate department at State University of New York-Buffalo and a stipend plus accommodations (optional). Candidates should send a research project proposal (1000 to 2000 words), curriculum vita, two references (for recent doctorates), and a writing sample. Guidelines and current research themes are available online.
Amount $15,000 per semester
Date(s) Application Is Due Mar 1.
Contact Austin Dacey, Fellowship Committee, fax: (716) 636-1733; email: adacey@centerforinquiry.net
Internet http://www.scienceandthepublic.org/programs.htm
Sponsor Center for Inquiry
P.O. Box 741
Amherst, NY 14226

Center for Italian Renaissance Studies Fellowships 1226

The center awards up to 15 fellowships for independent study on any aspect of the Italian Renaissance. Each fellow is given a place to study, use of the Biblioteca and Fototeca Berenson, weekday lunch, and an opportunity to meet scholars from various countries working in related fields. The selection committee looks for scholarly excellence and promise, requires a project of importance that is suitable to the resources of I Tatti and Florence, and assesses the candidate's ability to contribute to collegiality and the intellectual life of the other fellows. Projects do not have to be devoted to Florentine subjects, but it must be possible for the greater part of the project to be accomplished in Florence. Fellows will be in residence for a full academic year. Renewals are rarely granted. Applicants should send completed application form, curriculum vita, project description, and three letters of recommendation.
Requirements Fellowships are for scholars of any nationality, normally postdoctoral (or equivalent), and in the earlier stages of their careers. Preference is given to scholars beginning new research projects and to applicants who have not previously had residencies in Florence.
Restrictions faxed applications and letters of recommendation will not be accepted.
Amount $45,000-$50,000 range
Date(s) Application Is Due Oct 15.
Contact Amanda Smith, Villa I Tatti Fellowship Program, (617) 495-8042; fax: (617) 495-8041; email: amanda_smith@harvard.edu; Villa I Tatti (Italy), email: info@itatti.it
Internet http://www.itatti.it/fellow_home.html
Sponsor Harvard University Center for Italian Renaissance Studies
124 Mount Auburn St
Cambridge, MA 02138-5795

Center for Judaic Studies Fellowships 1227

The center invites applications from scholars engaged in all fields of Judaic studies and from scholars in other fields interested in approaching the general topic from a comparative and interdisciplinary perspective. Outstanding graduate students in the final stages of writing their dissertations also may apply. Fellowship recipients also may receive a contribution toward travel expenses. Annual research topics vary; contact the center for current topic. Application materials are available upon written request.
Amount $33,000 maximum for academic year
Date(s) Application Is Due Nov 15.
Contact Administrator, Fellowship Program, Center for Judaic Studies, (215) 238-1290; fax: (215) 238-1540; email: allenshe@sas.upenn.edu
Internet http://www.cjs.upenn.edu/program/fellowship.htm
Sponsor University of Pennsylvania
420 Walnut St
Philadelphia, PA 19104-6906

Center for Khmer Studies Fellowships 1228

The center invites applications from US scholars from all disciplines who wish to conduct their research in Cambodia. The program supports dissertation research fellowships and senior fellowships. Dissertation research fellowships enable doctoral candidates to pursue their dissertation research in Cambodia. Awards are available for periods of up to 11 months. Senior research fellowships enable scholars in all disciplines focusing on Southeast Asia to pursue further research in Cambodia. Short-term awards are available for up to four months. Long-term awards are available for six to nine months. Fellowships for four months or less have some travel restrictions.
Requirements Dissertation research fellowships are available to doctoral candidates at US colleges and universities in all fields of studies. Senior research fellowships are available to scholars who hold the PhD or its equivalent. Non-US citizens are welcome to apply if they are teaching full-time at US colleges and universities.
Date(s) Application Is Due Nov 1.
Contact Dr. Thak Chaloemtiarana, Southeast Asia Program, Cornell University, email: fellowships@khmerstudies.org
Internet http://www.khmerstudies.org/fellowships/fellows.htm
Sponsor Center for Khmer Studies
180 Uris Hall
Ithaca, NY 14853

Center for Medieval and Renaissance Studies Assistantships, Grants and Fellowships 1229

The center has six available programs. Research assistantships are awarded to four graduate students working in the field of medieval and Renaissance studies at UCLA. During the academic year, recipients work with several faculty members on research and publication projects. The summer fellowship is awarded each year to a scholar (holding a PhD or the equivalent) who wishes to pursue research within the Los Angeles area in the field of medieval and Renaissance studies; the Lynn White fellowship is awarded each year to an outstanding UCLA graduate student in medieval and Renaissance studies who has advanced to PhD candidacy; this one-year fellowship provides the recipient with support for research and related travel in order to complete the dissertation. The Portuguese Fellowship will be awarded annually on a competitive basis to one outstanding UCLA graduate student to support interdisciplinary research in any area pertaining to Portugal during the Middle Ages and Renaissance, that is, between AD 400 and 1650. Fredi Chiappelli travel fellowships provide a travel grant to assist the recipient with research in any area of medieval and Renaissance Italian studies; the fellowship is open to UCLA graduate students and travel is not restricted to Italy. Grants for interdisciplinary research are awarded to interdisciplinary teams of two or more CMRS faculty and/or graduate students to pursue collaborative research. These grants are not intended to replace Senate research grants or instructional resources grants, but may be used in conjunction with research support from other sources. Applicant teams may include faculty and/or graduate students but must represent more than one department. Annual deadline dates may vary; contact program staff for exact dates.
Amount $500 summer fellowships; $15,000 for the Lynn White fellowship; $1500 for the Fredi Chiappelli travel fellowships
Contact Program Contact, (310) 825-1880; email: cmrs@humnet.ucla.edu
Internet http://www.humnet.ucla.edu/humnet/CMRS/Awards/Awards_default.htm
Sponsor Center for Medieval and Renaissance Studies - RA Coordinator
10745 Dickson Plz, 302 Royce Hall
Los Angeles, CA 90095-1485

Center for National Policy Internships 1230

One intern per semester or summer is employed for a position dealing with the overall general operations of CNP. The program promotes practical opportunities to advance the public policy process, as experts and decisionmakers debate significant national objectives and determine how government can best serve American interests both at home and abroad. The intern will conduct research, write briefings, prepare press materials, participate in fund raising, and perform general office support work. Applications must be received two months prior to the semester.
Requirements Applicants must be undergraduate students.
Date(s) Application Is Due Apr 15; Aug 12 Nov 12.
Contact Alex Sunshine, Intern Coordinator, (202) 682-1800; fax: (202) 682-1818; email: asunshine@cnponline.org or thecenter@cnponline.org
Internet http://www.cnponline.org/employment.htm
Sponsor Center for National Policy
1 Massachusetts Ave NW, Ste 333
Washington, DC 20001

Center for Science in the Public Interest Internships 1231

The center is a national consumer organization that focuses on health and nutrition issues. CSPI offers internships for a small number of qualified students in undergraduate, graduate, law, and medical schools each summer and during the school year. Generally, an internship is for 10 weeks. The specific dates of internship are flexible and depend on the center's needs and the applicant's schedule. Application materials should include a cover letter indicating issues of interest, future plans, available dates; resume; writing sample; two letters of recommendation; and official transcript of courses and grades. Application materials should be submitted as early as possible.
Amount $6 per hour undergraduates; $7 per hour graduates
Contact Human Resources Manager, (202) 332-9110; fax: (202) 265-4954; email: cspi@cspinet.org
Internet http://www.cspinet.org/about/jobs_internship_2005_2006.html
Sponsor Center for Science in the Public Interest
1875 Connecticut Ave NW, Ste 300
Washington, DC 20009-5728

Center for the Critical Analysis of Contemporary Culture Faculty Fellowships 1232

The center, at Rutgers University, invites applications proposing studies of all kinds--empirical, analytical, theoretical, historical, literary, social, etc.--on the theme of the current year's seminar. Investigation of a range of topics connected to the overarching theme is encouraged. Each year the center brings together approximately 15 internal fellows (faculty and graduate students) and two external fellows from many of the established disciplines to study a single defined problem of large significance. The fellows will be expected to present their work in center seminars, to meet regularly with the center's internal fellows, and to teach one course on the subject in the department to which their work most closely relates. Applications must be requested in early December, with applications due in early January.
Amount $40,000
Date(s) Application Is Due Jan 7.
Contact External Fellowship Program, Center for the Critical Analysis of Contemporary Culture, (732) 932-8426; fax: (732) 932-8683; email: theccacc@aol.com
Internet http://www.criticalanalysis.rutgers.edu
Sponsor Rutgers, The State University of New Jersey
8 Bishop Pl
New Brunswick, NJ 08903

Center for the Humanities Andrew W. Mellon Postdoctoral Fellowship 1233

The purpose of this fellowship is to provide scholars who have lately completed their PhDs with free time to further their own work in a cross-disciplinary setting, and to associate them with a distinguished faculty. Current themes are The Natural, the Supernatural, and the Unnatural (fall); and Domesticity, Past, Present, and Future (spring). At least one and possibly two fellows will be appointed to the Center for the Humanities for the entire academic year, and each fellow will be awarded a stipend. He or she will teach a one-semester undergraduate course; participate in the collegial life of the Center for the Humanities, which sponsors conferences, lectures, and colloquia; and give one public lecture. The fellow will be provided with an office at the Center for the Humanities, and will be expected, during the term of the fellowship, to work there on weekdays while the university is in session, and also to reside in Middletown. Guidelines are available online.
Requirements Scholars who have received their PhD degree after June 2003 in any field of inquiry in the humanities or humanistic social sciences'broadly conceived'are invited to apply.
Amount $45,000 stipend
Date(s) Application Is Due Nov 10.
Contact Dr. Henry Abelove, Director
Internet http://www.wesleyan.edu/chum/mellon.html
Sponsor Wesleyan University
95 Pearl St
Middletown, CT 06459

Center for the Humanities Mellon Postdoctoral Fellowship 1234

The college's Center for the Humanities offers a two-year Mellon postdoctoral fellowship to candidates who have broad training in the humanities, which might include disciplines such as comparative literature or rhetoric, or interdisciplinary fields such as women's studies. The successful applicant will teach one course per semester and will be expected to participate in the annual fall faculty seminar, directed by the center's distinguished visiting professor. In addition to a salary, which is comparable to that of a new assistant professor, fellowships include benefits and support for research and travel. Fellows will be matched with an experienced faculty mentor.
Requirements Candidates should have received the PhD within the past three years.
Amount $45,000 stipend
Date(s) Application Is Due Nov 11.
Contact Alan Schrift, Director, (641) 269-3161; email: schrift@grinnell.edu
Internet http://www.grinnell.edu/offices/dean/supfac/oncampusopportunities/mellon/postdoc
Sponsor Grinnell College
Grinnell, IA 50112-1690

Center for the Study of Books and Media Visiting Research Fellowships 1235

The Center for the Study of Books and Media at the university invites applications for a visiting research fellowship in any field related to the history of books. The fellow is expected to pursue his or her research at Princeton throughout the academic year and is encouraged to participate in the activities of the center. The stipend depends on qualifications.
Requirements Candidates should have completed a dissertation in book history within the last three years and should propose a project involving research on subjects such as publishing, the book trade, and reading.
Date(s) Application Is Due Mar 1.
Contact John Hintermaier, (609) 258-8295; email: johnmh@princeton.edu; Thierry Rigogne, email: trigogne@princeton.edu
Internet http://web.princeton.edu/sites/english/csbm/postdoc_fellowship.htm
Sponsor Princeton University
129 Dickinson Hall
Princeton, NJ 08544

Center for the Study of Philanthropy International Fellowships 1236

The center provides leadership training through applied research and professional mentorships for young scholar-practitioners in the nonprofit sector. The program offers leadership training to scholar-practitioners outside the US as a means to help build Third-Sector capacity in the fellows' home countries. Specific topical areas are chosen each year. Special attention will also be given to diaspora philanthropy. Fellows participate in a three-month seminar on the US and international voluntary sectors. Fellows are expected to produce a 30-50 page paper on their findings to be presented in the seminar. They will learn about the work of key agencies and meet with foundation and nonprofit representatives. They may also have the opportunity to attend selected conferences. Fellowship includes tuition and monthly stipend, housing, and round-trip air travel to and from the US.
Requirements The program is open to practitioners and researchers under the age of 36 who are citizens of countries other than the US. Applicants must have a college or university degree and speak and write English fluently. Preference will be given to candidates with a strong institutional base and demonstrated research skills.
Amount $1300 monthly stipend
Date(s) Application Is Due Sep 13.
Contact Dr. Kathleen McCarthy, Director, (212) 817-2010; fax: (212) 817-1572; email: info@philanthropy.org
Internet http://www.philanthropy.org/programs/intnl_fellows_program.html
Sponsor City University of New York
365 Fifth Ave, Rm 5401
New York, NY 10016-4309

Center for the Study of Philanthropy Senior International Fellowships 1237

The center provides leadership training through applied research and professional mentorships for young scholar-practitioners in the nonprofit sector. The program offers leadership training to scholar-practitioners outside the United States as a means to help build Third-Sector capacity in the fellows' home countries. Specific topical areas are chosen each year. The current year's theme is community foundations. Fellows participate in a three-month seminar on the US and international voluntary sectors. Fellows attend weekly seminars, learn about the work of key agencies and foundations, meet with nonprofit representatives, and study US and international community foundation models. Fellowship includes tuition and monthly stipend, housing, and round-trip air travel to and from the United States.
Requirements The program is open to senior-level practitioners and researchers under the age of 36 who are citizens of countries other than the United States. Applicants must have a college or university degee and speak and write English fluently. Preference will be given to candidates with a strong institutional base and demonstrated research skills.
Amount $1300 monthly stipend
Date(s) Application Is Due Jun 15; Oct 15.
Contact Senior International Fellows Program, Graduate School and University Center, fax: (212) 817-1572; email: csp@gc.cuny.edu
Internet http://www.philanthropy.org/programs/intnl_fellows_program.html
Sponsor City University of New York
365 Fifth Ave, Rm 5116
New York, NY 10016-4309

Center for the Study of Professional Military Ethics Resident Fellowships 1238

The goal of this full-time, in-residence program is to help prepare select military officers, career civil servants, academics, and others to teach, apply, and practice ethics in a variety of professions and institutional settings. Each fellow will be required to complete a research project and to participate in a weekly fellows seminar; be encouraged to participate in other activities and programs of the center; and receive office space, computer facilities, library privileges, and a stipend. Applicants should send a letter describing their interests in ethics in the areas listed; a proposal for a research project to be undertaken during the fellowship; a curriculum vita; and copies of relevant publications. Two letters of reference also should be sent directly to the center. Recipients are announced by the end of April.
Requirements Ideal candidates from academia will have a background in ethics, international affairs, security studies, and/or public policy, with an interest in pursuing issues of ethics in military affairs, national defense, and international security in their teaching and research.
Amount $35,000 maximum
Date(s) Application Is Due Oct 14.
Contact Dr. Albert Pierce, Director, Center for the Study of Professional Military Ethics, (410) 293-6057; email: acpierce@gwmail.usna.edu
Internet http://www.usna.edu/Ethics/Programs/Residentfellowship/fellows.htm
Sponsor US Naval Academy
112 Cooper Rd
Annapolis, MD 21402

Center for the Study of Religion Fellowships 1239

The Center brings a select number of pre-tenure scholars and recent Ph.D. graduates to Princeton University to study religion and religious history. The fellows, who are appointed by the Dean of the Faculty, devote time to servicing the intellectual life of the Center and the University through mentoring graduate and undergraduate students and participating in one of the Center's weekly interdisciplinary seminar. For 2007-2008, fellows will be appointed in two areas: Christian Thought and Practice, special

emphasis on the religious life of American Christians, congregations, or clergy; and Public Theology: special emphasis on contemporary issues bridging theology and the social sciences, such as just war theory, pluralism, or social welfare.
Requirements To apply, submit CV, 3 letters of recommendation, a 5 page proposal, and published or unpublished paper demonstrating scholarly command of topic of one of the three themes. Applications available on Web site.
Restrictions Princeton University PhDs are not eligible.
Date(s) Application Is Due Jan 5.
Contact Anita Klein, Director, The Center for the Study of Religion, (609) 258-5545; fax: (609) 258-6940
Internet http://www.princeton.edu/~csrelig/opportunities/undergrad_ops.html
Sponsor Princeton University
5 Ivy Lane
Princeton, NJ 08544-1013

Center of Excellence (COE) in General Aviation Grants **1240**
The FAA has identified a need for a Center of Excellence in general aviation. The center will conduct research, which includes the entire spectrum (i.e., basic research through engineering development, prototyping, and testing) within the scope of general aviation. This scope includes, but is not limited to airport technology; propulsion and structures; aging aircraft; flight safety; fire safety; and training. The FAA intends to provide long-term funding to establish and operate a prestigious partnership with academia, industry, and government. To this end, the FAA encourages offerors to team with organizations that complement their expertise from academia, industry, state/local government, and other governmental agencies. The successful applicant is required to match FAA grant funds with nonfederal funding over the term of the cooperative agreement. Cost sharing (negotiated individually) also is required for any orders placed under the IDIQ contract.
Requirements Colleges and universities are eligible to apply.
Restrictions Individuals are not eligible for a COE designation and do not qualify for grants under this program.
Amount $300,000 minimun per year
Contact Pat Watts, Grants Manager, (609) 485-5043; email: patricia.watts@faa.gov
Internet http://www.cgar.org/about_program.asp
Sponsor Department of Transportation
William J Hughes Technical Ctr
Atlantic City International Airport, NJ 08405

Center on Philanthropy and Civil Society's Emerging Leaders International Fellows Program **1241**
The program provides leadership training through applied research and professional mentorships for young scholar-practitioners in the nonprofit sector. The program is open to scholars and practitioners interested in building Third-Sector capacity in the United States and overseas. This year's fellows will be selected from abroad and also from communities of color under-represented in the United States grantmaking sector. Fellows are based at the Graduate Center of The City University of New York, where they design and pursue an individualized research project and participate in a seminar with Third-Sector leaders. Specific topical areas are chosen each year.
Requirements The program is open to practitioners and researchers under the age of 36. Applicants must hold a college or university degree and speak and write English fluently. Preference will be given to candidates with strong ties to a Third-Sector institution and demonstrated research skills.
Amount $1300-per month stipend plus tuition
Date(s) Application Is Due Dec 7.
Contact Dr. Kathleen McCarthy, Director , (212) 817-2010; fax: (212) 817-1572; email: csp@gc.cuny.edu
Internet http://www.philanthropy.org/programs/ifp/application.html
Sponsor City University of New York
365 Fifth Ave, Ste 5401
New York, NY 10016-4309

Central European University Fellowships **1242**
The university offers full fellowships for master's, doctoral, and doctoral support programs in Budapest, Hungary and Warsaw, Poland. 625 fellowships covering tuition and living expenses are available to individuals from Central and Eastern Europe and the former Soviet Union. A wide variety of other financial aid programs are available to all students on a competitive basis.
Date(s) Application Is Due Jan 15.
Contact Grants Administrator, (36-1) 327-3000 ext 2311; email: finaid@ceu.hu
Internet http://www.ceu.hu/financial_forms.html
Sponsor Central European University
Nador u 9
Budapest 1051
Hungary

Century Foundation Grants **1243**
The foundation sponsors and supervises research on significant economic, social, and political issues. The foundation's research projects usually are designed to produce analytic, book-length manuscripts containing public policy recommendations. They are aimed at an audience that includes the informed public, the press, policymakers, and the academic community. The foundation commissions individuals (project directors) to carry out the projects, and the book-length manuscripts that result are edited and then published by the foundation's press or placed with commercial publishers or university presses. Proposals are welcome for reports and books. Preliminary proposals should summarize in no more than three pages the central argument of the proposed publication, the main themes that would be developed in support of the argument, and examples of evidence that would be explored in making the project director's case. A curriculum vita should be included with the proposal.
Restrictions The foundation does not award scholarships or support dissertation research, nor does it make grants to individuals or institutions.
Contact Carl Robichaud, Program Officer, (212) 452-7712; fax: (212)535-9803; email: robichaud@tcf.org
Internet http://www.tcf.org/about.asp
Sponsor Century Foundation
41 East 70th St
New York, NY 10021

CES Predissertation Fellowships **1244**
The fellowships enable graduate students in the social science disciplines to pursue two to three months of exploratory research in Europe to determine the viability and to better define the scope of their proposed dissertation projects. The geographic scope for these fellowships includes Western, Central and Eastern Europe, including Russia and Turkey as they relate to Europe. Recipients will test the research design of their dissertation, determine the availability of archival materials, and contact European scholars in the relevant field.
Requirements Applicants must be doctoral candidates at an American or Canadian university in anthropology (excluding archaeology), economics, history (post-1750), geography, political science, sociology, social psychology, or urban planning; must be citizens or permanent residents of the United States or citizens or landed immigrants of Canada; and should have completed at least two years of full-time graduate study prior to the beginning date of their proposed research.
Restrictions Funds may be expended only for research in Europe on the project detailed in the applicant's proposal. Students who are advanced in their dissertation research or whose dissertation prospectuses have received formal approval from their academic departments are ineligible, as are students already in Europe at the time of application.
Amount $4000 for travel and living expenses
Date(s) Application Is Due Feb 1.
Contact Fellowship Administrator, (212) 854-4172; fax: (212) 854-8808; email: ces@columbia.edu
Internet http://www.columbia.edu/cu/ces/frames/overall.html
Sponsor Council for European Studies
420 W 118th St, 1203 International Affairs Bldg, Columbia University, MC 3310
New York, NY 10027

CES Travel Subsidies for European Scholars **1245**
Under this program, the council subsidizes the travel of European social scientists who are temporarily in the United States and who have been invited to lecture at a university or college that is an institutional member of the council. Invitations are initiated by the council's institutional representative at the member university or by the faculty member responsible for arranging the European scholar's visit. The council should be contacted for the application form once details of the visit are completed. Except in unusual circumstances, the European scholar's visit should be scheduled during the academic year. The visit should include classroom or university-wide lectures and/or participation in graduate seminars. The council reimburses the European scholar's transportation expenses within North America; the balance of travel costs, if any, as well as lodging, meals, and honoraria, are to be provided by the host university. An application form is available on the Web site.
Amount $300 maximum per visit
Contact Executive Director, (212) 854-4172; fax: (212) 854-8808; email: ces@columbia.edu
Internet http://www.columbia.edu/cu/ces/frames/overall.html
Sponsor Council for European Studies
420 W 118th St, 1203 International Affairs Bldg, MC 3310
New York, NY 10027

Cesar Chavez Dissertation Fellowship for US Latina or Latino Scholars **1246**
The fellowship will support a US Latina or Latino scholar for a year-long residency (September 1 through August 31) at Dartmouth College. The fellowship offers an opportunity for scholars who plan a career in college teaching and who have completed all other PhD requirements to finish the dissertation with access to the outstanding library, computing facilities, and Dartmouth faculty members. In addition, the fellow may participate in classroom activities with scholars who are dedicated to undergraduate teaching. Each fellow will be affiliated with a department or program at the college. The fellow will be expected to complete the dissertation during the tenure of the fellowship, and will have the opportunity to participate in teaching, either as a primary instructor or as part of a team. Office space and library privileges are provided.
Requirements The fellow may be taking the PhD degree in any discipline or area taught in the Dartmouth undergraduate arts and sciences curriculum.
Amount $25,000 plus office space, library privileges, and a $2500 research assistance fund

Date(s) Application Is Due Feb 1.
Contact Sandy Spiegel, Director of Grad Recruiting and Diversity, (603) 646-6578; fax: (603) 646-3488; email: Sandra.J.Spiegel@Dartmouth.edu
Internet http://www.dartmouth.edu/~gradstdy/funding/fellowships/cem.html
Sponsor Dartmouth College
6062 Wentworth Hall, Rm 304
Hanover, NH 03755

CF Clinical Research Trainee Awards **1247**
This is a training program for physicians enrolled in a US or Canadian subspecialty training program. Ten awards will be granted for clinical research in thrombosis, asthma, critical care, lung cancer, and women's health. Applicants may apply for only one type of clinical research award, and each program director may support only one applicant for an award in each area. Requests should be written to include goals and objectives that may be accomplished within one year of the starting date (July 1) of the research project. Research funding may be used as the research mentor and program director deem appropriate (e.g., salary support and supplies directly related to the research project).
Requirements Applicants must be citizens of the United States or Canada or have a J-1 or H-1 visa and be working in a certified US or Canadian institution and enrolled in a subspecialty training program at the time of application; hold an MD degree or its equivalent; be enrolled in a US or Canadian subspecialty training program in allergy/ immunology, cardiac electrophysiology, critical care anesthesiology, critical care intensive care, critical care medicine, infectious disease, cardiology, pediatric critical care, pediatric pulmonary disease, pulmonary disease, surgical critical care, or thoracic surgery; be affiliate members of the American College of Chest Physicians (contact Angela Popa-Padilla at 847/ 498-1400 for an application); show promise of significant contribution to his/her specialty; and apply for only one type of award and be the sole applicant from the subspecialty program to apply for that type of award.
Restrictions Awards are to support clinical research and not basic or bench level research.
Amount $10,000
Date(s) Application Is Due Jun 30.
Contact Sue Ciezadlo, Grants Administrator, (847) 498-8363; fax: (847) 498-5460; email: sciezadlo@chestnet.org
Internet http://www.chestfoundation.org/researchAwards/index.php
Sponsor Chest Foundation
3300 Dundee Rd
Northbrook, IL 60062-2348

CF Eli Lilly and Company Distinguished Scholar in Critical Care Medicine Award **1248**
The goals of the program are to establish an identity for the diagnosis and management of diseases (e.g., sepsis) in a critical care environment; promote alternatives for the treatment of critical care diseases; educate patients about options for diagnosis and management; educate and disseminate new knowledge about diagnosis and treatment within a critical care environment; and address family, legislative, and regulatory issues, and define new funding mechanisms leading to innovation and improvement in critical care. Selected scholars will be expected to develop an original educational project that helps disseminate new knowledge about critical care medicine and advances the creation of best practices in patient care. Scholars will create, manage, and evaluate projects over the three-year term and serve in a mentorship capacity during the fourth year. Application materials are available online.
Requirements An applicant must be: an FCCP and hold the degree of MD, DO, MBChB, MBBCh, MBBS, DNSc, PharmD, PhD, or EdD; board-certified in critical care medicine; and a recognized clinician and/or scientist with a specialty in sepsis and/or critical care as evidenced by publications, presentations, and/or peers.
Amount $50,000 per year for first three years, $10,000 for fourth year
Date(s) Application Is Due Apr 30.
Contact Grants Administrator, CHEST Foundation, (847) 498-1400; fax: (847) 498-5460; email: chestfoundation@chestnet.org
Internet http://www.chestfoundation.org
Sponsor Chest Foundation
3300 Dundee Rd
Northbrook, IL 60062-2348

CF General Grants Program **1249**
The fund supports independent research on health and social issues and makes grants to improve healthcare practice and policy. The fund also supports efforts that help people live healthy and productive lives and assists specific groups with serious and neglected problems. The fund is dedicated to helping people become more informed about their healthcare and improving care for vulnerable populations such as children, the elderly, low-income families, minority Americans, and the uninsured. Types of support include program development, research, program evaluation, and employee matching gifts. Preference is given to proposals to clarify the scope of serious and neglected problems, especially those affecting vulnerable groups of Americans; to analyze the impact of policies and trends on well-defined issues; or to develop and test practical solutions. Special programs include minority medical fellowships and fellowships in patient-centered care research. More than 84 percent of all funds are devoted to national or international programs. The board considers requests in April, July, and November.
Requirements Nonprofit organizations are eligible.
Restrictions Grants do not support individuals, building or endowment funds, general support, capital funds, equipment acquisition, operating deficits of established organizations, matching gifts, or major media projects.
Contact Andrea Landes, Director of Grants Management, (212) 606-3800; fax: (212) 606-3508; email: grants@cmwf.org
Internet http://www.cmwf.org/programsgrants/programsgrants.htm
Sponsor The Commonwealth Fund
1 E 75th St
New York, NY 10021-2692

CF Geriatric Development Research Awards **1250**
The two-year award is intended to provide the impetus required for long-term career development focused on integrating geriatrics into the subspecialties of internal medicine. The program awards the grant to an academic internist to develop and implement a basic, clinical, or health services research project focused on a geriatric aspect of chest medicine. The funding can support the salary of the award recipient and/or the purchase of supplies, the salaries of technical personnel, and other resources necessary for the completion of the research project. The award also includes a one-time travel grant to attend the meetings of the American Geriatrics Society and the American College of Chest Physicians in the second year of the award.
Requirements To be eligible for the award, applicants must: have US citizenship or permanent resident status; hold a degree of MD or its equivalent; have completed a subspecialty internal medicine fellowship leading to certification in his/her subspecialty by the American Board of Internal Medicine and be within the first three years of his/her faculty appointment; possess a faculty appointment by July 1 (this faculty appointment should be documented in the required letters of recommendation from the applicant's department chair and division director); be a member of the American College of Chest Physicians (contact Angela Popa-Padilla at 847/498-1400 for a membership application); commit 75 percent of his/her professional effort to research activities; develop and implement a basic, clinical, or health services research project focused on a geriatric aspect of chest medicine; and generate and implement a career development plan focused on the geriatrics aspects of chest medicine. This plan must include organizing and interacting with a mentorship team made up of a minimum of four members--the applicant's research mentor as the leader of the research team, a subspecialist in the applicant's field of chest medicine, a geriatrician, and one other member at the applicant's descretion.
Restrictions The funding cannot be used to acquire administrative or clerical support. Funding is to cover total costs; no indirect cost funds will be provided.
Amount $50,000 per year for two years plus $3000 travel grant
Date(s) Application Is Due Mar 31.
Contact Sue Ciezadlo, Grants Administrator, (847) 498-8363; fax: (847) 498-5460; email: sciezadlo@chestnet.org
Internet http://www.chestfoundation.org/researchAwards/index.php
Sponsor Chest Foundation
3300 Dundee Rd
Northbrook, IL 60062-2348

CF Harkness Fellowships for British, Australian, and New Zealand Residents **1251**
The Harkness Fellowships in Health Care Policy provide an opportunity for professionals from the United Kingdom, Australia, and New Zealand to spend four to 12 months in the United States conducting a research study that is relevant to health care policy and practice in both the United States and the fellow's home country, and that is focused on the issues of greatest concern to the fund. The program provides an opportunity for fellows to conduct a policy-oriented research project in the United States, gain first-hand exposure to innovative practices and models of health care delivery, enhance their methodological skills, and work with leading health policy experts in the United States. Fellows must demonstrate a strong interest in health policy issues and propose a well-designed research study within the scope of the fund's national program areas: improving health care services; bettering the health of minorities; advancing the well-being of elderly people; and developing the capacities of children and young people. Studies that include comparisons between the United States and the applicant's home countries are encouraged. Up to 10 Harkness fellows are selected annually. Generally the fellowships provide round-trip airfare to the United States, a fixed monthly stipend for living expenses in the United States, support toward the portion of the project conducted in the home country, funds for project-related travel and other research expenses, tuition for related academic courses taken during the fellowship period, health insurance coverage while in the United States, and US taxes. A family supplement including round-trip airfare, living allowance, and health insurance is also available to fellows accompanied by a spouse and/or children.
Requirements Applicants must be citizens of Great Britain, Australia, or New Zealand in their late 20s to early 40s with broad educational backgrounds, not just those in research or academic careers. In order to apply, applicants must be nominated by their institution and submit a formal application, which is available from The Commonwealth Fund in New York City or its representatives in Australia and New Zealand.
Amount $95,000 maximum
Date(s) Application Is Due Sep 1.
Contact Robin Osborn, Director, International Program in Health Policy (UK), (212) 606-3809; fax: (212) 606-3875; email: cmwf@cmwf.org
Internet http://www.cmwf.org/fellowships/fellowships_list.htm?attrib_id=9157

Sponsor The Commonwealth Fund
Harkness House, 1 E 75th St
New York, NY 10021-2692

CF New Zealand Ian Axford Fellowships 1252
The fellowships are made to US citizens with leadership potential in any field of public policy to enable them to spend six to nine months in New Zealand. Fellows on paid leave who will be on full salary will receive a living allowance of NZ$500 per month on top of their salaries. Those on partial salary receive an allowance of NZ$1700 per month on top of their salaries and will be entitled to family and other allowances. Fellows unable to obtain paid leave receive a living allowance of NZ$4000 per month, intended to cover the basic expenses of residence in New Zealand. Annual deadline dates may vary; contact program staff for exact dates.
Restrictions Fellowships are not awarded to support basic research or to enable study for an academic degree.
Date(s) Application Is Due Mar 1.
Contact Program Contact, (212) 606-3800; fax: (212) 606-3500; email: info@cmwf.org
Internet http://www.cmwf.org/fellowships/fellowships_list.htm?attrib_id=9159
Sponsor The Commonwealth Fund
One E 75th St
New York, NY 10021-2692

CF Roger C. Bone Award for Advances in End-of-Life Care 1253
The award was created to annually recognize members of the American College of Chest Physicians who have demonstrated leadership in end-of-life care. Recipients of this award have shown substantial improvement in the care of patients as documented in the related sections of the application form. Application forms and guidelines are available online.
Requirements Applicants must be members of the American College of Chest Physicians and have the endorsement of another ACCP member.
Amount $10,000
Date(s) Application Is Due Apr 29.
Contact Sue Ciezadlo, Senior Project Coordinator, (847) 498-8363; fax: (847) 498-5460; email: sciezadlo@chestnet.org
Internet http://www.chestfoundation.org/criticalCare/index.php
Sponsor Chest Foundation
3300 Dundee Rd
Northbrook, IL 60062-2348

CFF Clinical Research Grants 1254
These awards offer support of clinical research projects directly related to cystic fibrosis. Projects may address diagnostic or therapeutic methods related to cystic fibrosis or the pathophysiology of cystic fibrosis. However, studies performed in animal models or cell/tissues removed from patients will not be supported under this award. Applicants must demonstrate access to a sufficient number of cystic fibrosis patients and appropriate controls. A letter of intent to apply must be submitted by June 1 with applications required by December 1.
Amount $80,000 maximum per year for single center; $150,000 maximum for multicenter
Date(s) Application Is Due Jun 1; Dec 1.
Contact Office of Grants Management, (800) 344-4823 or (301) 951-4422; fax: (301) 951-6378; email: grants@cff.org
Internet http://www.cff.org/research/cystic_fibrosis_foundation_grants/research_grants
Sponsor Cystic Fibrosis Foundation
6931 Arlington Rd, 2nd Fl
Bethesda, MD 20814

CFF First- and Second-Year Clinical Fellowships 1255
The foundation offers competitive clinical fellowships for up to three years for physicians interested in cystic fibrosis and other chronic pulmonary and gastrointestinal diseases of children and adolescents/adults. The intent of this award is to encourage specialized training early in a physician's career and to prepare well-qualified candidates for careers in academic medicine. Training must take place in one of the foundation's accredited centers and must provide thorough grounding in diagnostic and therapeutic procedures, comprehensive care, and cystic fibrosis-related research. All first- and second-year programs must commit a significant portion (at least 30 percent over two years) to research training. Fellows funded by other sources for their first year of training may apply to the foundation for subsequent training support. Third-year fellowships are available for additional basic and/or clinical research training. Research fellowships are also available from the foundation to support physicians beyond the fellowship experience; salary will be commensurate with experience.
Requirements Applicants must be US citizens or have permanent US resident visas, and must have completed pediatric training and be eligible for board certification in pediatrics by the time the fellowship begins. Candidates with prior training in internal medicine may also apply but must have completed at least two years of an approved adult pulmonary or GI fellowship; be jointly sponsored by the departments of medicine and pediatrics; and be willing to commit at least 75 percent of their time to cystic fibrosis and related problems of young adults.
Amount $42,000 stipends first year, $43,750 second year
Date(s) Application Is Due Oct 1.
Contact Office of Grants Management, (800) 344-4823 or (301) 951-4422; fax: (301) 951-6378; email: grants@cff.org
Internet http://www.cff.org/research/cystic_fibrosis_foundation_grants/training_grants
Sponsor Cystic Fibrosis Foundation
6931 Arlington Rd, 2nd Fl
Bethesda, MD 20814

CFF Leroy Matthews Physician-Scientist Awards 1256
This award will provide up to six years of support for outstanding newly trained pediatricians and internists (MDs and MD/PhDs) to complete subspecialty training, develop into independent investigators, and initiate research programs. Institutional and individual grants are available.
Requirements US citizenship or permanent resident status is required.
Amount $42,000 stipend plus $10,000 for research and development for years one through five; up to $70,000 stipend plus $15,000 for research and development for year six
Date(s) Application Is Due Sep 1.
Contact Office of Grants Management, (800) 344-4823 or (301) 951-4422; fax: (301) 951-6378; email: grants@cff.org
Internet http://www.cff.org/research/cystic_fibrosis_foundation_grants/research_grants
Sponsor Cystic Fibrosis Foundation
6931 Arlington Rd, 2nd Fl
Bethesda, MD 20814

CFF Pilot and Feasibility Awards 1257
These grants are for developing and testing new hypotheses and/or new methods, and to support promising new investigators as they establish themselves in research areas relevant to cystic fibrosis. Proposed work must be hypothesis driven and must reflect innovative approaches to critical questions in cystic fibrosis research. Two years of support may be requested.
Restrictions The award is not meant to support continuation of programs begun under other granting mechanisms. Electronic submission is required.
Amount $40,000 per year maximum
Date(s) Application Is Due Sep 1.
Contact Office of Grants Management, (800) 344-4823 or (301) 951-4422; fax: (301) 951-6378; email: grants@cff.org
Internet http://www.cff.org/research/cystic_fibrosis_foundation_grants/research_grants
Sponsor Cystic Fibrosis Foundation
6931 Arlington Rd, 2nd Fl
Bethesda, MD 20814

CFF Postdoctoral Research Fellowships 1258
Competitive postdoctoral fellowships in basic or clinical research are made on an annual basis, renewable for a second year. The fellowships are awarded in areas of basic cellular and metabolic research or in other problem areas pertinent to cystic fibrosis and related chronic and recurrent pulmonary and gastrointestinal diseases of childhood. Preference is shown to recent graduates or those just beginning their investigative careers. A third year is offered on a limited basis to highly qualified candidates. Interested individuals are encouraged to contact the foundation for application procedures and/or to discuss the potential relevance of their work to the objectives of the foundation.
Requirements These awards are offered to MDs, PhDs, and MD/PhDs interested in conducting basic or clinical research related to cystic fibrosis.
Restrictions Electronic submission only.
Amount $33,000 first year, $34,100 second year, $36,300 optional third year
Date(s) Application Is Due Sep 1.
Contact Office of Grants Management, (800) 344-4823 or (301) 951-4422; fax: (301) 951-6378; email: kcurley@cff.org
Internet http://www.cff.org/research/cystic_fibrosis_foundation_grants/training_grants
Sponsor Cystic Fibrosis Foundation
6931 Arlington Rd, 2nd Fl
Bethesda, MD 20814

CFF Research Grants 1259
Grants are offered in support of high-quality research projects ranging from basic cellular and metabolic mechanisms to therapy of cystic fibrosis and related chronic and recurrent pulmonary and gastrointestinal diseases of childhood. These grants are broadly oriented to the support of projects for developing and initially testing new hypotheses and/or new methods, or those being applied to problems of cystic fibrosis for the first time. The intent of this award is to enable the investigator to collect sufficient data to compete successfully for long-term support from NIH. Interested individuals are encouraged to contact the foundation for guidelines and/or to discuss the potential relevance of their work to the objectives of this program.
Requirements Applications may be submitted by established investigators or new investigators starting their independent research careers but may not represent support for continuation of a line of research already established by the applicant.
Amount $90,000 maximum per year for a two-year period

Date(s) Application Is Due Sep 1.
Contact Office of Grants Management, (800) 344-4823 or (301) 951-4422; fax: (301) 951-6378; email: grants@cff.org
Internet http://www.cff.org/research/cystic_fibrosis_foundation_grants/research_grants
Sponsor Cystic Fibrosis Foundation
6931 Arlington Rd, 2nd Fl
Bethesda, MD 20814

CFF Student Traineeships **1260**
The traineeships are offered to qualified students to introduce them to cystic fibrosis research. Each recipient must work with a faculty sponsor on a research project related to cystic fibrosis. Interested individuals are encouraged to contact the foundation for application procedures and/or to discuss the potential relevance of their work to the objectives of the program. Applications are accepted throughout the year. A maximum of $300 of the award may be used for laboratory expenses with the remainder used as a stipend for the trainee.
Requirements Applicants must be students in or about to enter a doctoral program (MD, PhD, or MD/PhD); senior-level undergraduates planning to pursue graduate training may also apply.
Amount $1500
Contact Office of Grants Management, (800) 344-4823 or (301) 951-4422; fax: (301) 951-6378; email: grants@cff.org
Internet http://www.cff.org/research/cystic_fibrosis_foundation_grants/training_grants
Sponsor Cystic Fibrosis Foundation
6931 Arlington Rd, 2nd Fl
Bethesda, MD 20814

CFF Therapeutics Development Program **1261**
The purpose of this program is to provide funds to businesses that will develop commercial products to benefit individuals with cystic fibrosis. Structured as a matching grants program, funds will be awarded only if they are matched by the recipient. First, the grantee will examine the scientific potential of new products under component 1. Component 2 studies will involve support for the continuation of component 1 developments and the initiation of patient clinical studies. Component 1 and component 2 awards each will receive a maximum of two years of support. Funds will be provided for research prior to, but not including, phase 3 clinical trials. Applications are accepted on an ongoing basis.
Amount $100,000 maximum per year for component I; up to $750,000 per year for component II
Contact Office of Grants Management, (800) 344-4823 or (301) 951-4422; fax: (301) 951-6378; email: grants@cff.org
Internet http://www.cff.org/research/cystic_fibrosis_foundation_therapeutics
Sponsor Cystic Fibrosis Foundation
6931 Arlington Rd, 2nd Fl
Bethesda, MD 20814

CFF Third-Year Clinical Fellowships **1262**
The foundation offers competitive clinical fellowships for up to three years for physicians interested in cystic fibrosis and other chronic pulmonary and gastrointestinal diseases of children and adolescents/adults to encourage specialized training early in a physician's career and to prepare well-qualified candidates for careers in academic medicine. The third-year fellowship award offers support for additional intense basic and/or clinical research training related to cystic fibrosis.
Requirements Applicants and sponsors must submit proposals of the research studies to be undertaken and other specialized training that will be offered during this year. Preference will be given to applicants whose training was supported by the foundation.
Restrictions Recipients who do not enter a career of academic medicine will be subject to payback provisions.
Amount $62,600 maximum; $52,600 stipend for fellow and up to $10,000 for research costs
Date(s) Application Is Due Oct 1.
Contact Office of Grants Management, (800) 344-4823 or (301) 951-4422; fax: (301) 951-6378; email: grants@cff.org
Internet http://www.cff.org/research/cystic_fibrosis_foundation_grants/training_grants
Sponsor Cystic Fibrosis Foundation
6931 Arlington Rd, 2nd Fl
Bethesda, MD 20814

CFF-NIH Funding Grants **1263**
The objective of this award is to support excellent cystic fibrosis-related research projects that have been submitted to and approved by NIH but cannot be supported by available NIH funds. Applications must fall within the upper 40th percentile with a priority score of 200 or better. Investigators will be required to resubmit applications to NIH. Interested individuals are encouraged to contact the foundation for application procedures and/or to discuss the potential relevance of their work to the objectives of this program. Applications may be submitted on an ongoing basis.
Amount $75,000-$125,000 per year for up to two years
Contact Office of Grants Management, (800) 344-4823 or (301) 951-4422; fax: (301) 951-6378; email: grants@cff.org
Internet http://www.cff.org/research
Sponsor Cystic Fibrosis Foundation
6931 Arlington Rd, 2nd Fl
Bethesda, MD 20814

CFPC Family Medicine Resident Leadership Awards **1264**
The CFPC Research and Education Foundation honors outstanding educational and research initiatives in the area of family medicine through conferral of Family Medicine Resident Awards. Canadian Research Awards for Family Medicine Residents provide national recognition for original research carried out by postgraduate trainees. The Murray Stalker Memorial Lecture Award is given to promote and recognize scholarly activities of family medicine residents. The Nadine St. Pierre Award recognizes the outstanding achievement of a francophone family practice resident. Award recipients receive return air fare, complimentary registration for the Section of Teachers Annual Workshop, and a stipend for expenses. Deadline dates vary between programs; contact program staff for exact dates.
Amount $C250-$C1000
Date(s) Application Is Due Jun 1.
Contact Kiki Ziten, Coordinator, (905) 629-0900 ext 432; fax: (905) 629-0893; email: kziten@cfpc.ca
Internet http://www.cfpc.ca/English/cfpc/programs/awards%20program/default.asp?s=1
Sponsor College of Family Physicians of Canada
2630 Skymark Ave
Mississauga, ON L4W 5A4 Canada

CFPC Family Physician of the Year Award **1265**
The annual award recognizes an individual for outstanding contribution to family medicine. Criteria for the award include excellence in family practice over time, community medical service, contribution to the community, and involvement with CFPC. The award is presented at the time of the CFPC Convocation in conjunction with the National Annual Scientific Assembly in Halifax, Nova Scotia. The recipient will present a short addresss at the time of convocation and will be involved as a spokesperson for Canadian family medicine throughout the year following receipt of the award. The recipient will receive return air fare, complimentary registration, and a stipend for expenses. The deadline for submission varies according to each Provincial Chapter. Please contact the Provincial Chapter of your nominee to confirm the deadline date.
Requirements Each provincial chapter may select a nominee for the award. Names must be submitted to the National Honours and Awards Committee.
Amount $C2000
Contact Kiki Ziten, Coordinator, Honours and Awards Program, (905) 629-0900 ext 432; fax: (905) 629-0893; email: kziten@cfpc.ca
Internet http://www.cfpc.ca/English/cfpc/programs/awards%20program/members%20can%20apply%20for/default.asp?s=1#Perkinawards
Sponsor College of Family Physicians of Canada
2630 Skymark Ave
Mississauga, ON L4W 5A4 Canada

CFPC Fellowships **1266**
The program awards fellowships to CFPC members to recognize achievement in the discipline of family medicine. The conferral of fellowships will take into consideration the nominee's exemplary performance as a family physician and exceptional contributions to community activities that enhance health in its broadest sense; outstanding leadership in the academic discipline of family medicine and major administrative responsibilities within a university department of family medicine; and significant elected or appointed executive positions at the national or chapter level of the CFPC or involvement in major committee or other college activities.
Requirements Nominees must hold certification in family medicine, have a minimum of 10 years continuous membership, and be members in good standing at the time of nomination.
Date(s) Application Is Due Feb 15.
Contact Kiki Ziten, Coordinator, (905) 629-0900 ext 432; fax: (905) 629-0893; email: kziten@cfpc.ca
Internet http://www.cfpc.ca/English/cfpc/research/section%20of%20researchers/home/default.asp?s=1
Sponsor College of Family Physicians of Canada
2630 Skymark Ave
Mississauga, ON L4W 5A4 Canada

CFPC Research and Education Foundation Grants **1267**
The program is supported by the CFPC Research and Education Foundation and industry partners and comprises research grants, scholarships, and training programs for educational and research initiatives in the area of family medicine. The Royal Canadian Legion One-Month Traineeship grants are awarded to improve the quality of medical education and the provision of care to elderly patients. The Hollister King grant provides an opportunity for a practicing family physician to attain or enhance special skills in the delivery of rural medical care. The Douglas M. Robb research grant is given to a community-based member who plans to conduct research on a topic relevant to

the practice of family medicine. Research/development grants provide seed money to members to initiate or complete research/development projects in family medicine. Practice Enrichment grants enable members in active practice to participate in a course of study under the direction of a Canadian university for a minimum of three months in fields related to family medicine. Traveling Scholarship grants enable members to pursue clinical studies for a minimum of three weeks under the direction of a clinical department at a Canadian university. Graduate Study grants enable members to pursue a course of study at a Canadian university for a period of at least six months on a part-time basis.
Amount $C1000-$C5000
Contact Kiki Ziten, Coordinator, (905) 629-0900 ext 432; fax: (905) 629-0893; email: kziten@cfpc.ca
Internet http://www.cfpc.ca/English/cfpc/programs/awards%20program/awardshome%20pdf/default.asp?s=1
Sponsor College of Family Physicians of Canada
2630 Skymark Ave
Mississauga, ON L4W 5A4 Canada

CFUW A. Vibert Douglas International Fellowship **1268**
The fellowship is donated by the CFUW to the IFUW. This competition is open to women graduates for research for a period of eight months abroad. Members of the IFUW should apply through their national affiliate (in the United States, the American Association of University Women, 1111 16th St NW, Washington, DC 20036). The competition is held in even-numbered years. The deadline for receipt of applications is determined by each affiliate but normally falls between early September and mid-October of the year preceding the competition; contact national headquarters for exact date.
Requirements An applicant must be a woman graduate and must be well started on the research program to which the application relates.
Restrictions A fellowship will not be awarded for the first year of a PhD program.
Amount $C12,000
Contact Fellowships Officer, 41-22-731-23-80; fax: 41-22-738-04-40; email: info@ifuw.org
Internet http://www.ifuw.org/i_fell.htm
Sponsor International Federation of University Women
8 rue de l'Ancien Port
Geneva CH 1201
Switzerland

CFUW Alice E. Wilson Grant **1269**
These grants are to assist women to do refresher work in their chosen field, to do specialized study, or to retrain in new techniques applicable to their field. Special consideration is given to candidates returning to studies after at least three years. Work may be undertaken at a Canadian institution or elsewhere. For guidelines and application forms, contact the federation in the spring.
Requirements Applicant must have a bachelor's degree or equivalent from a recognized university, must be a Canadian citizen or have held landed immigrant status for one year prior to submitting application and documentation, and must have been accepted at her place of study.
Amount $5000
Date(s) Application Is Due Nov 1.
Contact Fellowships Program Manager, (613) 234-2732; email: cfuwfls@rogers.com
Internet http://www.cfuw.org/index.php?option=com_content&task=view&id=75&Itemid=88□=eng
Sponsor Canadian Federation of University Women
251 Bank St, Ste 600
Ottawa, ON K2P 1X3 Canada

CFUW Beverley Jackson Fellowship **1270**
This fellowship is awarded annually to assist a Canadian woman to pursue graduate work at an Ontario university. The applicant must have been accepted into her place of study at time of application. Guidelines and application forms are available from the federation in the spring.
Requirements Applicant must be a woman over the age of 35 pursuing graduate work in an Ontario university, must hold at least a bachelor's degree or its equivalent from a recognized university, and must be a Canadian citizen or have held landed immigrant status for one year prior to submitting application.
Amount $2000
Date(s) Application Is Due Nov 1.
Contact Fellowships Program Manager, (613) 234-2732; email: cfuwfls@rogers.com
Internet http://www.cfuw.org/index.php?option=com_content&task=category§ionid=7&id=85&Itemid=88□=eng
Sponsor Canadian Federation of University Women
251 Bank St, Ste 600
Ottawa, ON K2P 1X3 Canada

CFUW Bourse Georgette LeMoyne Award **1271**
Grants awarded by the CFUW are for graduate study at a university where one of the languages of administration and instruction is French. Application forms are available from the federation in the spring.
Requirements At time of application, applicant must hold a bachelor's degree or its equivalent from a recognized university, must be a Canadian citizen or have held landed immigrant status for one year prior to submitting application, and must have been accepted at her place of study. A $C45 application fee is required.
Amount $7000
Date(s) Application Is Due Nov 1.
Contact Fellowships Program Manager, (613) 234-2732; email: cfuwfls@rogers.com
Internet http://www.cfuw.org/index.php?option=com_content&task=category§ionid=7&id=85&Itemid=88□=eng
Sponsor Canadian Federation of University Women
251 Bank St, Ste 600
Ottawa, ON K2P 1X3 Canada

CFUW Canadian Home Economics Association Fellowship **1272**
The candidate must be studying one or more aspects in the field of home economics, at the masters or doctoral level. She must be already accepted into or be enrolled in her postgraduate program in Canada.
Amount $C3000
Date(s) Application Is Due Nov 1.
Contact Fellowships Program Manager, (613) 234-2732; email: cfuwfls@rogers.com
Internet http://www.cfuw.org/index.php?option=com_content&task=category§ionid=7&id=85&Itemid=88□=eng
Sponsor Canadian Federation of University Women
251 Bank St, Ste 600
Ottawa, ON K2P 1X3 Canada

CFUW Margaret Dale Philp Award **1273**
This award, donated by the Kitchener-Waterloo Club of CFUW, is open to any woman who holds, at the time of application, a bachelor's degree or equivalent from a recognized university and who wishes to enter, or continue, a program leading to an advanced degree in the field of humanities or social sciences. Special consideration will be given to candidates who wish to specialize in Canadian history. Guidelines and application forms are available from the federation in August. These grants are not awarded every academic year. Check with the office or Web site for current offerings and deadlines.
Requirements Applicant must be a Canadian citizen or have held landed immigrant status for one year prior to submitting application and documentation, must reside in Canada, and must have been accepted at her place of study.
Amount $3000
Date(s) Application Is Due Nov 1.
Contact Fellowships Program Manager, (613) 234-2732; email: cfuwfls@rogers.com
Internet http://www.cfuw.org/index.php?option=com_content&task=category§ionid=7&id=85&Itemid=88□=eng
Sponsor Canadian Federation of University Women
251 Bank St, Ste 600
Ottawa, ON K2P 1X3 Canada

CFUW Margaret McWilliams Predoctoral Fellowship **1274**
This predoctoral fellowship is open to any woman who is a full-time student and has completed at least one full calendar year in doctoral studies at the time of application. An applicant may be studying abroad when applying; the fellowship may be used in Canada or elsewhere. Contact the federation for guidelines and application forms in the spring.
Requirements Applicant must be a Canadian citizen or have held landed immigrant status for one year prior to submitting application and documentation and must be enrolled in a master's degree program.
Amount $C12,000
Date(s) Application Is Due Nov 1.
Contact Fellowships Program Manager, (613) -234-2732; email: cfuwfls@rogers.com
Internet http://www.cfuw.org/index.php?option=com_content&task=category§ionid=7&id=85&Itemid=88□=eng
Sponsor Canadian Federation of University Women
251 Bank St, Ste 600
Ottawa, ON K2P 1X3 Canada

CFUW Marion Elder Grant Fellowship **1275**
This fellowship is open to any woman who is studying full-time at the master's or doctoral level, in Canada or abroad. All else being equal, preference will be given to the holder of an Acadia University degree.
Requirements Candidates must be studying full-time at the master's or doctoral level in Canada or abroad.
Amount $C10,000
Date(s) Application Is Due Nov 1.
Contact Fellowships Program Manager, (613) 234-2732; email: cfuwfls@rogers.com
Internet http://www.cfuw.org/index.php?option=com_content&task=category§ionid=7&id=85&Itemid=88□=eng
Sponsor Canadian Federation of University Women
251 Bank St, Ste 600
Ottawa, ON K2P 1X3 Canada

CFUW Polytechnique Commemorative Award **1276**
This award is made annually for graduate studies in any field, with special consideration given in the study of issues related particularly to women. Application forms are available in August.

Requirements At the time of application, an applicant must hold at least a bachelor's degree or equivalent from a recognized university, have been accepted into the proposed place of study, and be a Canadian citizen or have held landed immigrant status for at least one year.
Amount $5600
Date(s) Application Is Due Nov 1.
Contact Fellowships Program Manager, (613) 234-2732; email: cfuwfls@rogers.com
Internet http://www.cfuw.org/index.php?option=com_content&task=category§ionid=7&id=85&Itemid=88□=eng
Sponsor Canadian Federation of University Women
251 Bank St, Ste 600
Ottawa, ON K2P 1X3 Canada

Chancellor's Minority Postdoctoral Fellowship **1277**
Program assists underrepresented minority faculty members in developing their careers as scholars. For those members of underrepresented minorities committed to university teaching and research this fellowship program provides a stipend, close association with faculty at the university and assistance in furthering the fellow's development as a productive scholar. Application materials are available on the Web site.
Requirements An applicant must demonstrate promise for a tenure-track appointment at a research college or university, must be a US citizen or permanent resident, and must have received a doctorate or appropriate terminal degree within the past four years, or have completed this requirement by June of the fellowship year. Afro-American Studies must be the candidate's primary research focus. Contact Afro-American Studies and Research Program or check Web site for application deadline announcement.
Amount $42,000 stipend; $5000 maximum for travel and other research-related expenses
Date(s) Application Is Due Jan 15.
Contact Carla Bloom, Afro-American Studies, (217) 333-7781; fax: (217) 244-4809; email: c-bloom@uiuc.edu
Internet http://www.aasrp.uiuc.edu/education/postDoc.html
Sponsor University of Illinois at Urbana-Champaign
1201 W Nevada
Urbana, IL 61801

Changemakers Grants **1278**
Changemakers makes grants to the following types of community-based philanthropic organizations: local, regional, national, and international public foundations; alternative community foundations; affinity groups/networking organizations; groups that administer donor-advised funds; donor organizing/service providers; federations/alternative workplace giving programs; groups that recruit and train grassroots development staff; groups that provide research, media, education, or advocacy on philanthropy; and fundraising and grantmaking collaboratives. Types of support include capacity building grants, collaborative initiatives, general support grants, and technical assistance.
Requirements Community-based philanthropic organizations that are committed to the principles of community-based philanthropy, have a record of success or a potential for increased success, and demonstrate that they have a vision for the future are eligible.
Restrictions Grants do not support service providers.
Contact Grants Administrator, (415) 561-2363; fax: (415) 561-2366; email: grants@changemakers.org
Internet http://www.changemakersfund.org/grantsprograms.htm
Sponsor Changemakers
1550 Bryant St, Ste 850
San Francisco, CA 94103

Chapin Hall International Fellowships in Children's Policy Research **1279**
The program is designed to increase research and development capacity in the field of child and family policy and to develop leadership for this enterprise. Fellows will work on existing Chapin Hall projects in one of three broadly defined areas of research: developing conceptual bases for and evaluating implementation of community-based supports and services for all children; developing and using data to improve analysis, planning, and management of services for children; and developing and testing new ideas, policies, and programs for children. Some senior fellows may also work on projects of their own design that fit the Chapin Hall research agenda. The two- to 12-month appointments will provide competitive stipends and housing. A form for the fellowship letter of inquiry is available on the Web site.
Requirements The fellowships are open to individuals from any country with any of a wide range of disciplinary interests and training, including economics, education, history, human development, law, medicine, psychology, public policy, social work, and sociology. All fellows will be expected to conduct work in English.
Contact Christin Glodek, Fellowship Coordinator, (773) 256-5151; fax: (773) 256-5351; email: internationalprogramcoordinator@chapinhall.org
Internet http://www.about.chapinhall.org/intprograms/intprograms.html
Sponsor Chapin Hall Center for Children at the University of Chicago
1313 E 60th St
Chicago, IL 60637

Charitable Leadership Foundation Education Grants **1280**
The foundation supports educational programs and organizations that address long-term goals, including: improvement of early childhood literacy and improvement of children's ability to maintain grade level reading skills through eighth grade; improvement of science, technology, engineering and math (STEM) skills for K-12 students and the increase in the number of children who pursue these fields in college, and; improvement of management, involvement, and engagement in the public school system. Types of support include grants, loans, and technical assistance for projects, programs, and capacity building. Letters of inquiry and formal proposals are reviewed on an ongoing basis. Applicants are required to discuss formal proposals with the staff prior to submission. Preference will be given to projects in upstate New York; however, projects will be considered in any geographic area of the United States.
Requirements 501(c)3 charitable organizations are eligible.
Restrictions The foundation does not normally fund organizations with substantial amounts of other resources, or arts or cultural organizations, unless the proposed project presents a compelling need or opportunity and substantially matches the funding criteria described above. Any grants to religious organizations will be restricted to nonsectarian purposes. Grants are not awarded to individuals.
Amount $20,000 minimum
Contact Rosemary Weaver McKenna, Esq., General Counsel & Senior Program Officer, (518) 877-6701, ext. 309; fax: (518) 877-6260; email: rmckenna@charitableleadership.org
Internet http://www.charitableleadership.org/education.aspx?ID=13&subid=13
Sponsor Charitable Leadership Foundation
747 Pierce Road
Clifton Park, NY 12065

Charles A. Eastman Dissertation Fellowship for Native American Scholars **1281**
The immediate goal of the fellowship is to increase the number of Native American faculty in US higher education by supporting Native American scholars in completing the final academic requirement, the dissertation. The second goal is to bring to the college more role models for potential Native American graduate students among Dartmouth undergraduates. The one-year residential fellowship provides access to Dartmouth's outstanding library, computing facilities, and faculty. In addition, fellows will participate in classroom activities with scholars who are dedicated to undergraduate teaching. Fellows may be taking the PhD degree in any discipline or area taught in the undergraduate arts and sciences curriculum. Each fellow will be affiliated with a department or program at the college. The dissertation fellowship will generally run from September 1 through August 31. Each fellow will be expected to complete the dissertation during the tenure of the fellowship and will have the opportunity to participate in teaching either as a primary instructor or as part of a team.
Requirements The college invites applications from US citizens of Native American descent who plan careers in college or university teaching.
Amount $25,000 stipend, office space, library privileges, and $2500 research assistance fund
Date(s) Application Is Due Feb 1.
Contact Sandy Spiegel, Director of Grad Recruiting and Diversity, (603) 646-6578; fax: (603) 646-3488; email: Sandra.J.Spiegel@Dartmouth.edu
Internet http://www.dartmouth.edu/~gradstdy/funding/fellowships/index.html
Sponsor Dartmouth College
6062 Wentworth, Rm 304
Hanover, NH 03755-3526

Charles Abrams Scholarships **1282**
This scholarship is awarded annually to a student enrolled in a graduate planning program leading to a master's degree at one of the five schools at which Charles Abrams taught: Division of Urban Planning, Columbia University; Department of City and Regional Planning, Harvard University; Department of Urban Studies and Planning, Massachusetts Institute of Technology; Department for Urban Affairs and Policy Analysis, New School for Social Research; and Department of City and Regional Planning, University of Pennsylvania. The program is designed to aid students who will pursue careers as practicing planners.
Requirements Applicant must be a US citizen, must be enrolled in a graduate planning program at one of the five eligible schools, must be able to demonstrate a genuine financial need, and must be nominated by his/her school.
Amount $2000
Date(s) Application Is Due Apr 30.
Contact Kriss Blank, Scholarships and Fellowships, (312) 786-6722; email: kblank@planning.org
Internet http://www.planning.org/institutions/scholarship.htm
Sponsor American Planning Association
122 S Michigan Ave, Ste 1600
Chicago, IL 60603

Charles Edison Fund Grants **1283**
The fund's grants are equally divided among medical research projects, science education, and historic preservation. Science kits designed to experiment for classroom have been distributed. Additionally, but with some important and increasing exceptions, institutions and organizations assisted are based principally in the New York-New Jersey metropolitan area. Grant requests should be submitted on the requesting organization's letterhead and be signed by an official on behalf of the governing board. There are no application forms. The request should be detailed, complete and include background information about the organization, a full explanation of the project and its costs, and

a financial report, current budget and evidence of tax-exempt status of the requesting organization. The fund meets three times a year, usually in February or March, June and December at which time requests which have been submitted at least three weeks prior to the meeting will be considered. Progress reports and a final accounting of the use of grant funds will be required of all grant recipients.
Requirements Public and private schools, universities and colleges, and nonprofits are eligible.
Amount $2 million total
Contact Fund Administrator, (973) 648-0500; fax: (973) 648-0400; email: info@charlesedisonfund.org
Internet http://www.charlesedisonfund.org/thefund.html
Sponsor Charles Edison Fund
One Riverfront Plz, 4th Fl
Newark, NJ 07102

Charles G. Koch Charitable Foundation Grants **1284**
The foundation provides funding for academic and public policy research directed at solving social problems through voluntary action and free enterprise. In the area of research, the foundation primarily funds organizations working with doctorate-level investigators in disciplines such as economics, history, philosophy, political science, and organizational behavior. Types of support include general operating, scholarship funds, conferences and seminars, research, special projects, and seed money. There are no application deadlines. Submit preproposal letters (three-page limit).
Amount $25,000-$300,000 average
Contact Kelly Young, Vice President, (202) 393-2354; fax: (202) 393-2355; email: email@cgkfoundation.org
Internet http://www.cgkfoundation.org
Sponsor Charles G. Koch Charitable Foundation
655 15th St NW, Ste 445
Washington, DC 20005-2001

Charles H. Farnsworth Trust Grants **1285**
Grants are awarded to nonprofits whose programs and activities provide services to seniors in their residences for health care, homemaker services, nutrition, services to elderly persons in collective/supportive housing, and research and communication to better inform individuals and institutions of ways to improve the quality and quantity of housing and support services for the elderly. Types of support include equipment, general operating budgets, renovation projects, seed money, research, and building funds.
Requirements Only nonprofits in Massachusetts are eligible to apply.
Amount $80,000 maximum
Contact Grants Administrator, (617) 451-0049 ext 702; fax: (617) 423-4619; email: research@tmfnet.org
Sponsor Charles H. Farnsworth Trust
95 Berkeley St, Ste 201
Boston, MA 02116

Charles H. Hood Foundation Child Health Research Grants **1286**
The grants assist in the promotion of child health in New England. Interest areas include pediatrics, pediatric surgery, pediatric medical and surgical subspecialties, and perinatal obstetrics. Emphasis is on medical research contributing to a reduction of the health problems and health needs of large numbers of children. The foundation seeks innovative, start-up projects that are not yet candidates for government or large foundation support. Guidelines are published twice each year.
Requirements Applicants must have completed postdoctoral training and must not be receiving salary support from training funds, including fellowships, at the time of the grant award. Giving is limited to Connecticut, Massachusetts, Maine, New Hampshire, Rhode Island, and Vermont.
Restrictions Grants are not given for building funds, endowments, regular budgets, or public fund-raising campaigns. Grants are not awarded to individuals.
Amount $75,000 average
Contact Raymond Considine, Executive Director, (617) 695-9439; fax: (617) 423-4619; email: chhoodfdn@tmfnet.org
Sponsor Charles H. Hood Foundation
95 Berkeley St, Ste 201
Boston, MA 02116

Charles H. Revson Fellowships **1287**
The program awards fellowships to those who have made significant contributions to New York City or to another large metropolitan center and who can be expected to make even greater contributions in the future, after using Columbia University's instructional, research, and other resources for an academic year. Ten awards are given each year within this program. Award includes tuition.
Amount $23,000 stipend
Date(s) Application Is Due Feb 1.
Contact Coordinator, Revson Program, (212) 280-4023; fax: (212) 663-7537; email: revson@columbia.edu
Internet http://www.columbia.edu/cu/revson
Sponsor Columbia University
420 W 116th St, Office 1A
New York, NY 10027

Charles H. Revson Foundation Grants **1288**
The foundation awards grants nationwide in its areas of interest, including urban affairs and public policy, education and higher education, biomedical research policy, and Jewish education and philanthropy. Types of support include capital campaigns, continuing support, fellowships, internship funds, program development, and research. Preference is given to requests serving New York, NY. There are no application forms or deadlines. The board meets in April, June, October, and December.
Restrictions Grants do not support local or national health appeals or direct service programs, individuals, building construction/renovation, book projects, charity events, travel expenses, or budgetary support.
Contact Grants Administrator, (212) 935-3340; fax: (212) 688-0633; email: info@revsonfoundation.org
Internet http://www.revsonfoundation.org/guidelines.htm
Sponsor Charles H. Revson Foundation
55 E 59th St, 23rd Fl
New York, NY 10022

Charles Lafitte Foundation Grants **1289**
The foundation is committed to helping groups and individuals foster lasting improvement on the human condition by providing support to education, children's advocacy, medical research, and the arts. Children's advocacy grants support organizations working to improve the quality of life for children, particularly in relation to child abuse, literacy, foster housing, hunger, and after-school programs. Education grants support innovative programs that work to resolve social service issues, address the needs of students with learning disabilities, provide technology and computer-based education, offer leadership skills education, and support at-risk students. Colleges and universities also receive support for research and conferences. The foundation's medical issues and research grants support healthcare studies, with emphasis on cancer research and treatment, children's health, health education, and promoting healthy living and disease prevention. Art grants support emerging artists and educational art programs.
Requirements 501(c)3 tax-exempt organizations are eligible.
Contact Jennifer Vertetis, President, email: jennifer@charleslafitte.org
Internet http://www.charleslafitte.org
Sponsor Charles Lafitte Foundation
29520 2nd Ave SW
Federal Way, WA 98023

Charles Lathrop Parsons Award **1290**
This award is given to recognize outstanding public service by a member of the American Chemical Society. The award is normally given every two years; however, the board of directors may at its discretion reduce the interval to one year if in its judgment circumstances in a given year warrant such action. A nominee must be a member of ACS and a citizen of the United States, and must have performed outstanding public service. Neither the scientific reputation nor the record of scientific achievement of a member affects his or her eligibility for this award, which is not directed toward recognition of scientific accomplishment or stature. The public service to be recognized may be performed either as a part of or completely outside the regular duties and activities of the nominee's employment.
Requirements Any individual, except a member of the award committee, may submit one nomination or seconding letter for the award in any given year. Nominating document consists of a letter of not more than 1000 words containing an evaluation of the nominee's accomplishments and a specific identification of the public service to be recognized.
Restrictions Current members of the ACS board of directors are ineligible.
Amount $3000
Date(s) Application Is Due Feb 1.
Contact Awards Administrator, (202) 872-4600; fax: (202) 872-4615; email: awards@acs.org
Internet http://www.chemistry.org/portal/a/c/s/1/acsdisplay.html?DOC=awards%5cparsons.html
Sponsor American Chemical Society
1155 16th St NW
Washington, DC 20036

Charles Russ Richards Memorial Award **1291**
This award is given annually to the engineering graduate who has demonstrated outstanding achievement in mechanical engineering 20 years or more after graduation from the regular engineering course of a recognized college or university. Achievement shall be all or in part in any field including industrial, educational, political, research, civic, and artistic. The candidate's achievements will be examined for an application of basic engineering methods or principles. A special nomination form must be acquired from ASME. Award includes certificate and expense supplement.
Requirements Applicants must be engineering graduates.
Amount $1000
Date(s) Application Is Due Feb 1.
Contact Gilda DiTullio, Manager, (212) 591-7736; fax: (212) 705-7739; email: ditulliog@asme.org
Internet http://www.asme.org/honors/ms71/gaa/russ.html
Sponsor American Society of Mechanical Engineers
3 Park Ave
New York, NY 10016

Charles S. Sydnor Award 1292

The prize is given in even-numbered years for a distinguished book in southern history published in odd-numbered years. The application due date is March 1 of the year in which the prize is to be awarded. Books must be submitted by the publishers. Books should be sent directly to committee members listed on the Web site, not the national office.

Amount $1000

Date(s) Application Is Due Mar 1.

Contact Dr. John Inscoe , Secretary-Treasurer, (706) 542-8848; fax: (706) 542-2455; email: jinscoe@uga.edu

Internet http://www.uga.edu/%7Esha/charle~1.htm

Sponsor Southern Historical Association
Rm 111A , LeConte Hall
Athens, GA 30602

Charles Stewart Mott Foundation Anti-Poverty Program 1293

This program focuses on improving education, expanding economic opportunity, building organized communities, and special initiatives as pathways out of poverty. The overall goal is to help people vocalize and mobilize around local concerns, grow through participation in educational opportunities, and attain economic self-sufficiency by engaging more fully in the economy. Types of support include challenge/matching grants, conferences and seminars, demonstration grants, general operating grants, program grants, seed money grants, technical assistance, and training grants. The board meets in March, June, September, and December. Organizations should apply at least four months prior to the start date of the project for which they are seeking funds.

Requirements Nonprofits and K-12 organizations are eligible to apply. A proposal may be submitted by a church-based or similar organization if the project falls clearly within program guidelines and is intended to serve as broad a segment of the population as the program of a comparable nonreligious organization.

Amount $139.5 million total

Contact Office of Proposal Entry, (810) 238-5651; fax: (810) 766-1753; email: info@mott.org

Internet http://www.mott.org/programs/poverty.asp

Sponsor Charles Stewart Mott Foundation
503 S Saginaw St, Ste 1200
Flint, MI 48502-1851

Charles Stewart Mott Foundation Grants 1294

The focus of the foundation's grant making is organized in four programs: civil society; environment; Flint, MI; and poverty. Flexibility to investigate new opportunities is maintained through an exploratory and special projects program. The civil society program promotes and supports civil society in the United States; Central/Eastern Europe and South Africa. The environment program supports efforts to achieve a healthy global environment capable of sustaining all forms of life. The Flint program seeks to strengthen the capacity of local institutions, including schools and school districts, in the foundation's home community of Flint, MI, to respond to economic and social needs. The poverty program addresses issues that contribute to improved life outcomes for children, youth, and families in low-income communities. Programs in low-income communities that connect schools and communities through systemic reform, improved teaching, leadership development, networking, technical assistance, and advocacy are also applicable. In all grant making, particular interest will be given to fresh approaches to solving community problems in the defined program areas; approaches that can generate long-term support from other sources and/or can be replicated in other communities; public policy development and research and development activities to further existing programs as well as to explore new fields of interest; and approaches and activities that lead to systemic change. Although proposals may be submitted at any time, applicants are strongly encouraged to submit during the first quarter of the year for which funding is requested. Grant expenditures are determined by September 1 of each year. The review process takes up to four months from the time the proposal is received. Therefore, proposals should be submitted at least four months prior to the start of the proposed grant period. Funding for unsolicited proposals is limited. It is recommended that letters of inquiry be submitted instead of a full proposal.

Requirements Only 501(c)3 groups are eligible, including schools and school districts.

Restrictions Grants are not made to/for individuals; religious activities or programs that serve, or appear to serve, specific religious groups or denominations; or local projects outside the Flint area unless the projects are part of a national demonstration or foundation-planned network of grants that have clear and significant implications for replication in other communities.

Amount $139.5 million total

Contact Office of Proposal Entry, (810) 238-5651; fax: (810) 766-1753; email: info@mott.org

Internet http://www.mott.org/about/programs.aspx

Sponsor Charles Stewart Mott Foundation
503 S Saginaw St, Ste 1200
Flint, MI 48502-1851

Charles W. Finley Visiting Scholar Education Grant 1295

The American Academy of Periodontology Foundation established Finley Visiting Scholar Education Grants to honor the memory of Dr. Charles W. Finley and all of the great periodontal leaders of the past, present, and future. Grants are awarded to accredited periodontal programs to offset honoraria, travel, promotion, and seminars by speakers in periodontology. As required, the grants are being matched by funds from each department or institution. Though the speakers will spend the majority of their time with the periodontics department, both students and faculty, the grant requires that the speaker present a formal program to the faculty and students of the institution on a subject of interest to the entire dental institution. Applications are available on the Web site.

Requirements Accredited periodontal programs are eligible to apply.

Amount $1500

Date(s) Application Is Due Feb 14.

Contact Sharon Mellor, Executive Director, (800) 282-4867 ext 256; fax: (312) 573-3272; email: sharon@perio.org

Internet http://www.perio.org/foundation/research.html

Sponsor American Academy of Periodontology Foundation
737 N Michigan Ave, Ste 800
Chicago, IL 60611

Charlotte Geyer Foundation Cancer Research Grants 1296

The foundation supports research into the cause, prevention, and treatment of cancer. The purpose of the awards is to provide one year's funding to exceptional proposals to give investigators the opportunity of advancing and improving projects to the point where they are able to successfully compete for an NCI RO1 or other award. Proposals are reviewed three times per year. Application guidelines and procedures are available online.

Requirements The foundation will review recent proposals--either the original proposal, a revised proposal, or a portion of the original proposal deemed to have special merit--that were submitted to NCI; received a peer-review ranking in the 10 percentiles above the NCI payline; and did not receive funding.

Amount $100,000 maximum

Date(s) Application Is Due Feb 1; Jun 1; Oct 1.

Contact Nancy Falletta, Executive Director, (716) 632-6448; fax: (716) 632-6098

Internet http://www.charlottegeyer.org

Sponsor Charlotte Geyer Foundation
P.O. Box 1276
Williamsville, NY 14231-1276

Charlotte W. Newcombe Doctoral Dissertation Fellowships 1297

This program provides approximately 28 dissertation awards annually to encourage original and significant study of ethical and religious values in all fields. The selection process and all administration for this continuing fellowship program are handled by the Woodrow Wilson National Fellowship Foundation and is supported by the Charlotte W. Newcombe Foundation. The awards are intended to finance the last full year of dissertation writing. Annual deadline dates may vary; contact program staff for exact dates.

Requirements An applicant must be a candidate for a PhD or ThD degree in a doctoral program at a graduate school in the United States.

Amount $18,000

Date(s) Application Is Due Nov 1.

Contact Program Director, (609) 452-7007, ext 131; fax: (609) 452-7828; email: charlotte@woodrow.org

Internet http://www.woodrow.org/newcombe/

Sponsor Charlotte W. Newcombe Fellowships/Woodrow Wilson National Fellowship Foundation
P.O. Box 5281
Princeton, NJ 08543-5281

Chateaubriand Exact Sciences, Engineering, and Medicine Research Scholarships 1298

Individuals currently pursuing the PhD or who have completed it in the last three years may qualify for a scholarship from the French government to conduct research at a French university, school of engineering, or state-funded laboratory. Candidates must contact the host institution to secure a position before applying. Scholarships are available for periods of six to 18 months and carry a stipend, health insurance, and round-trip travel expenses. Application forms are available on the Web site.

Requirements Applicants must be US citizens and registered in a US university, and must be PhD candidates or recent PhD holders. Applicants must obtain written agreement from the French hosting institution before applying; an online registration form is available on the Web site.

Amount Ff8700 minimum per month

Date(s) Application Is Due Jan 15.

Contact Chateaubriand Fellowship Program, Mission pour la Science et la Technologie, Ambassade de France, (202) 944-6246; fax: (202) 944-6244; email: Chateaubriand@amb-wash.fr

Internet http://www.frenchculture.org/education/support/chateaubriand/

Sponsor French Embassy Cultural Services
4101 Reservoir Rd NW
Washington, DC 20007-2176

Chatham Valley Foundation Grants 1299

The foundation awards grants to nonprofits in the metropolitan Atlanta, GA, area in the areas of arts (performing arts and cultural programs), museums, education and

higher education, health care and health associations, medical research (cancer), crime prevention and law enforcement, Jewish services (nursing homes, religious welfare, and temples), and social services (homeless and economically disadvantaged). Types of support include general operating support, annual campaigns, capital campaigns, building construction/renovation, endowment funds, and program development. Application forms are not required.
Requirements Nonprofit organizations in the greater metropolitan Atlanta, GA, area are eligible.
Amount $1 million total
Contact Avery Tucker, c/o Wachovia Charitable Services, (404) 266-3081
Sponsor Chatham Valley Foundation
3414 Peachtree Rd
Atlanta, GA 30326

Chatlos Foundation Grants Program **1300**
The foundation gives consideration to requests for program support. Grants to bible colleges total 33 percent of the foundation distribution per year, and 30 percent is allowed to religious causes, 7 percent to liberal arts colleges, 26 percent for medical concerns with emphasis placed on the purchase of equipment, and 4 percent to social concerns. Types of support include operating budgets, emergency funds, equipment, land acquisition, matching funds, scholarship funds, special projects, publications, and renovation projects. Requests for funding must be submitted in writing. Although there is no deadline for receipt of requests, those received later than one month prior to board meetings may be carried forward. The preliminary review committee meets monthly. Organizations may submit proposals six months from date of denial but are limited to one grant award within any 12-month period.
Requirements Applicants must be US tax-exempt, nonprofit organizations that provide services in the following areas: bible colleges, religious causes, medical concerns, liberal arts colleges, and social concerns. Proposals must include cover letter, specific request, tax-exemption letter, and budget. If proposal is to be considered at board level, additional information will be requested.
Restrictions The foundation will not accept requests from individual church congregations, individuals, organizations in existence for less than two years as indicated by IRS tax-exempt letter of determination, for education below the college level, for medical research projects, or for support of the arts.
Amount $10,000 maximum for initial request
Contact Grants Administrator, (407) 862-5077; email: cj@chatlos.org
Internet http://www.chatlos.org/AppInfo.htm
Sponsor Chatlos Foundation
P.O. Box 915048
Longwood, FL 32791-5048

Chautauqua Region Community Foundation Grants **1301**
Grants support projects serving communities in Chautauqua County in its areas of interest, including arts and culture, libraries, education, housing and shelters, children and youth, human services and general charitable giving, and government and public administration. Types of support include general operating support, continuing support, building construction/renovation, equipment acquisition, conferences and seminars, publication, seed grants, emergency funds, and undergraduate and graduate scholarships to individuals.
Requirements Nonprofit organizations may apply for grants in support of projects serving communities in Chautauqua County, excluding the Fredonia/Dunkirk area, which is served by the Northern Chautauqua Community Foundation.
Amount $1.6 mil total
Date(s) Application Is Due Jan 31; Mar 1; Nov 1.
Contact June Diethrick, Grants Coordinator, (716) 661-3392; fax: (716) 488-0387; email: jdiethrick@crcfonline.org
Internet http://www.crcfonline.org/
Sponsor Chautauqua Region Community Foundation
418 Spring St
Jamestown, NY 14701

CHCF Grants **1302**
The foundation's mission is to expand access to affordable, quality health care for underserved individuals and communities in California and to promote fundamental improvements in the health status of Californians. The foundation has five funding areas: improving care delivery, business of healthcare, healthcare quality, California health policy, and California's uninsured. The one-year, renewable grants will focus on areas where the foundation's resources can initiate meaningful policy recommendations, innovative research, and the development of model programs. Philanthropic activities include foundation-initiated projects, requests for proposals, and unsolicited proposals. emailed letters of inquiry should include, in two to three pages, a brief description of the proposed project, along with an estimated time line and budget. A full proposal may be requested.
Requirements California 501(c)3 nonprofit organizations are eligible.
Restrictions The foundation does not generally support the cost of direct clinical care, ongoing general operating expenses, capital campaigns, annual appeals or other fund-raising events, construction, purchase or renovation of facilities, or purchase of equipment.
Date(s) Application Is Due Oct 14.
Contact Grants Administrator, (510) 238-1040; fax: (510) 238-1388; email: grants@chcf.org
Internet http://www.chcf.org/grantinfo
Sponsor California HealthCare Foundation
476 Ninth St
Oakland, CA 94607

Chestnut Hill Charitable Foundation, Inc Grants **1303**
The foundation awards grants to nonprofit organizations in the greater Boston, MA, area in support of medical research, children and youth, and arts and education. Specifically, the foundation's interests include visual arts, museums, humanities, arts and culture, early childhood education and development, education at all levels, hospitals and medical research (cancer, heart and lungs, AIDS, and diabetes), social services, and general charitable giving. Types of support include general operating support, annual campaigns, capital campaigns, building construction/renovations, programs and projects, seed grants, curriculum development, research, and matching funds. There are no application forms; submit a letter of request.
Requirements Nonprofit organizations in the greater Boston, MA, area may submit letters of request.
Restrictions Grants are not awarded to support individuals or political or religious organizations.
Amount $1000-$15,000 average
Contact Kay Kilpatrick, Director Corporate Giving, (617) 630-2415
Sponsor Chestnut Hill Charitable Foundation, Inc
27 Boylston St
Chestnut Hill, MA 02167-1700

CHF Academic-Year Fellowships **1304**
This program emphasizes basic research in the history of the chemical sciences, scholarly publications, and the building of a strong chemical presence in the world of academic and public history. The foundation offers a variety of fellowships. The Gordon Cain Fellowship in Technology, Policy, and Entrepreneurship is open to a scholar with a PhD who will carry out historical research on the development of the chemical industry. The Sidney M. Edelstein International Fellowship in the Chemical Sciences and Technologies is open to established scholars pursuing the history of science. The Sidney M. Edelstein International Studentship in the Chemical Sciences and Technologies is open to a student in the history of the chemical sciences and technology who has completed all the requirements for the PhD except the dissertation. The John C. Haas Fellowship is open to PhD scholars whose projects will enhance public understanding of the chemical industries in relation to environmental, health, and safety issues. The Charles C. Price Fellowship in Polymer History is open to established scholars pursuing the history of science. Preference will be given to those candidates whose projects deal with polymer history. The Chemical Heritage Foundation also offers small travel grants to enable interested individuals to make use of the research resources of the Beckman Center for the History of Chemistry, the Othmer Library of Chemical History, and its associated facilities.
Requirements Applications are encouraged from scholars, educators, and science writers.
Amount $16,000-$43,000
Date(s) Application Is Due Jan 15.
Contact Gabriella Petrick, Acting Fellowship Coordinator, (215) 873-8247; fax: (215) 925-1954; email: gpetrick@chemheritage.org
Internet http://www.chemheritage.org/research/research-nav1.html
Sponsor Chemical Heritage Foundation
315 Chestnut St
Philadelphia, PA 19106

CHF Summer Fellowships **1305**
CHF offers two summer fellowships for scholars in residence between June and August. The program offers the Soci't' de Chimie Industrielle (American Section) Fellowship, open to writers, journalists, educators, and historians of science, technology, or business whose projects will advance public understanding of the chemical industries. The Glenn E. and Barbara Hodsdon Ullyot Scholarship is open to scholars, graduate students, science writers, and journalists who plan to conduct historical research that will advance public understanding of the chemical sciences.
Amount $15,000 Societe de Chimie Industrielle (American Section) Fellowship; $4500 minimum, Glenn E. and Barbara Hodsdon Ullyot Scholarship
Date(s) Application Is Due Feb 15.
Contact Gabriella Petrick, (215) 873-8247; email: fellowships@chemheritage.org
Internet http://www.chemheritage.org/research/research-nav1.html
Sponsor Chemical Heritage Foundation
315 Chestnut St
Philadelphia, PA 19106

Chicago Reporter Minority Urban Journalism Fellowship **1306**
An experienced minority journalist will be selected for this year-long fellowship to work at the Chicago Reporter, an investigative monthly that covers issues of race and poverty in Chicago. Postgraduate coursework will be available through local colleges and universities. The award includes salary plus benefits and educational opportunities. Interested candidates should send a resume and five clips to the office listed.

Requirements Applicants must have a bachelor's degree, a minimum of three years reporting experience, excellent news judgment, and a strong interest in urban affairs and investigative reporting. Fluency in Spanish a plus.
Contact Rui Kaneya, Program Contact, (312) 427-4830 ext 3864; fax: (312) 427-6130; email: ruik@chicagoreporter.com
Internet http://chicagoreporter.com/Gizmos/Navigation/Aboutus/aboutus.htm
Sponsor Chicago Reporter
332 S Michigan Ave, Ste 500
Chicago, IL 60603

Chicago Tribune Heartland Prizes for Nonfiction and the Novel **1307**
Two annual prizes are awarded to honor a novel and a book of nonfiction written from or about the nation's heartland. Winners are notified in August.
Requirements Eligible books must be published between August 1 of the current year and July 31 of the next.
Amount $7500
Date(s) Application Is Due Jul 31.
Contact Literary Awards, (312) 222-4300; fax: (312) 222-3751; email: ctcommunityrelations@tribune.com
Internet http://about.chicagotribune.com/community/literaryawards.htm
Sponsor Chicago Tribune
435 N Michigan Ave
Chicago, IL 60611-4041

Chicano Dissertation Fellowships **1308**
The Chicano Studies Department offers two Chicano dissertation fellowships. Candidates must have been advanced to doctoral candidacy by the beginning of the fellowship term. Duties of fellows include working toward the completion of the dissertation and teaching one undergraduate course in areas of research expertise. In sponsoring these fellowships, the department hopes that it will assist promising scholars to complete their dissertations, prepare for university teaching and research, and achieve increased professional recognition and associations. The usual fellowship duration is nine months. Fellows are required to be in residence during the entire fellowship period.
Requirements To apply, submit a letter of application describing progress toward PhD including date of advancement to candidacy, a dissertation proposal, a curriculum vita, and a writing sample. Applicants must arrange to have two letters of recommendation sent by March 29.
Amount $20,000 for nine months plus benefits
Date(s) Application Is Due Mar 29.
Contact Program Contact, Department of Chicano Studies, (805) 893-5546; fax: (805) 893-4076
Internet http://www.chicst.ucsb.edu/jobs
Sponsor University of California, Santa Barbara
1713 S Hall
Santa Barbara, CA 93106

Child Abuse and Neglect Discretionary Activities Grants **1309**
The grants and contracts support projects intended to improve the national, state, community, and family activities for the prevention, identification, and treatment of child abuse and neglect through research, demonstration service improvement, information dissemination, and technical assistance. Grants or contracts are provided for technical assistance to public and private nonprofit agencies; demonstration, research, and service projects to identify, prevent, and treat child abuse and neglect; and research into the incidence, cause, and prevention of child abuse and neglect. Contact headquarters for annual deadline dates.
Requirements Grants are available to state or local governments or other nonprofit institutions and organizations engaged in activities related to the prevention, identification, or treatment of child abuse and neglect.
Amount $80,000-$1.9 million range; $300,000 average
Contact Jan Shafer, Director, Research and Innovation Division, Children's Bureau, (202) 205-8172
Internet http://www.acf.hhs.gov/programs/cb/programs/discretionary.htm#5
Sponsor Administration for Children and Families
330 C St SW
Washington, DC 20447

Child Abuse and Neglect Research Grants **1310**
The program's objectives are to improve the national, state, community and family activities for the prevention, assessment, identification, and treatment of child abuse and neglect through research, demonstration service improvement, information dissemination, and technical assistance. Grants are provided for technical assistance to public and private nonprofit agencies; research and service demonstration projects to identify, assess, prevent, and treat child abuse and neglect; research into the incidence, consequences, and prevalence of child abuse and neglect; and for the dissemination of information on the incidence, causes, prevention and treatment of child abuse and neglect. Deadlines are published in program announcements.
Requirements Applications may be submitted by states, local governments, tribes, nonprofit institutions, and organizations engaged in activities related to the prevention, identification, and treatment of child abuse and neglect.
Amount $80,000-$1.9 million; $300,000 average
Contact Jan Shafer, Director, Research and Innovation Division, Children's Bureau, (202) 205-8172
Internet http://www.acf.dhhs.gov/programs/cb
Sponsor Administration for Children and Families
330 C St SW
Washington, DC 20447

Children's Advocacy Center Grants **1311**
The program supports the establishment and expansion of children's advocacy centers, with the goal of helping to prevent child abuse. One-year grants are awarded in the following categories: program support, research, member training, prevention, associate member program development, nonmember training, and recognized chapters. Applicants must designate a steering committee that comprises child-welfare workers, law-enforcement officials, medical doctors, and mental-health professionals. Application and guidelines are available online.
Requirements 501(c)3 tax-exempt organizations are eligible.
Amount $4.989 million total; $5000-$50,000
Date(s) Application Is Due Sep 13.
Contact Grants Administrator, (800) 239-9950 ext 116
Internet http://www.nca-online.org
Sponsor National Children's Alliance
516 C St NE
Washington, DC 20002

Children's Brain Tumor Foundation Research Grants **1312**
Science grants are awarded for basic laboratory research on pediatric brain and central nervous system tumors. Priority will be given to research that relates to: priorities I and II of the Research and Scientific Priorities for Pediatric Brain Tumors, as listed in the Report of the Brain Tumor Progress Review Group, which can be found at: http://prg.nci.nih.gov/brain/pediatrics.Submission of a two-page, preapplication form, equivalent to a letter of intent, is required. An original, signed form must be submitted along with five copies. The listed deadline is for preapplication forms; full proposals are by invitation.
Requirements Funding is currently restricted to principal investigators at institutions within the United States.
Restrictions The foundation does not award grants to individuals or to private foundations, and does not fund debt reduction, capital improvements, or travel expenses. Overhead expenses are not to exceed 10 percent of the total project cost.
Amount $75,000 per year
Contact Judy Hurley, Executive Director, (212) 448-9494; fax: (212) 448-1022; email: JHurley@cbtf.org
Internet http://www.cbtf.org/grant_info.html
Sponsor Children's Brain Tumor Foundation
274 Madison Ave, Ste 1301
New York, NY 10016-0701

Children's Leukemia Research Association Research Grants **1313**
The association supports research efforts into the causes and cure of leukemia and gives patient aid to families in need while meeting the expenses incurred in leukemia treatment. A medical advisory committee consisting of prominent internationally known and respected hematologists reviews grant proposals submitted for consideration of projects that are not otherwise funded. Grants are available for start-up funding for laboratory or clinical investigations in leukemia. Although the association prefers to fund new investigators, applications from established investigators for new initiatives are also solicited. Renewal for a second year is considered if other funding for promising projects has not been obtained.
Restrictions Previously funded projects are not usually considered for additional funding.
Amount $20,000 maximum per year
Date(s) Application Is Due Jun 30.
Contact Executive Director, (516) 222-1944; fax (516) 222-0457; email: info@childrensleukemia.org
Internet http://www.childrensleukemia.org/ResearchPast%20Pres.htm
Sponsor Children's Leukemia Research Association Inc
585 Stewart Ave, Ste LL-18
Garden City, NY 11530

Children's Literature Association Research Fellowships **1314**
The association awards a number of fellowships and scholarships annually to support research and original scholarship associated with serious literary criticism of children's literature. In honor of the achievement and dedication of Dr. Margaret P. Esmonde, proposals that deal with critical or original work in the areas of fantasy or science fiction for adolescents or children will be awarded the Margaret P. Esmonde memorial scholarship. It is expected that the research undertaken will lead to publication and make a significant contribution to the field of children's literature. The award may be used for transportation, living expenses, materials, and supplies. Grant recipients should be prepared to submit either a progress report or a summary of the completed project to the Scholarship Committee in February of the year following the award.
Requirements Recipients must be members of the association. Application consists of a detailed description of the research proposal, a vita that includes a bibliography of major

publications and scholarly achievements, and three letters of reference. Applications and supporting materials should be written in or translated into English.
Restrictions Officers of the association may not apply. Recipients of a scholarship are not eligible to reapply until the third year from the date of the first award. The award may not be used for obtaining advanced degrees, for textbook writing, for pedagogical projects, or for researching or writing a thesis or dissertation.
Amount $500-$1000
Date(s) Application Is Due Feb 1.
Contact Scholarship Committee, (616) 965-8180; fax: (616) 965-3568
Internet http://ebbs.english.vt.edu/chla/
Sponsor Children's Literature Association
P.O. Box 138
Battle Creek, MI 49016-0138

Children's Medical Research Institute Grants **1315**
The program, designed to promote pediatric research as a career, supports summer scholarships for first- and second-year Oklahoma University College of Medicine students. Each year awardeds support their pediatric research interests as students assist OU Medical Center Department of Pediatrics physicians. The program also awards small research grants/short-term projects to individual scientists at the OU Medical Center, who often use the funds as seed money to finance pilot research projects.
Contact Sana Rettig, (405) 271-8001 option 1, ext 42389; fax: (405) 271-1175; email: sana-rettig@ouhsc.edu
Internet http://www.cmri.net/scholarships.html
Sponsor Children's Medical Research Institute
800 Research Pwy, Ste 150
Oklahoma City, OK 73104

Children's Cardiomyopathy Foundation Research Grants **1316**
The foundation awards funds to support research related to all forms of cardiomyopathy affecting children under the age of 18 years. The goal of CCF's research program is to advance medical knowledge on the disease and develop more accurate diagnostic methods, life-improving therapies and ultimately a cure. The grant program is designed to provide seed funding to investigators for the testing of initial hypotheses and collecting of preliminary data to help secure long-term funding by the National Institutes of Health and other major granting institutions.
Requirements Proposals will be accepted on an annual basis for innovative basic, clinical or translational research relevant to the cause or treatment of cardiomyopathy in children. Principal investigators must hold a MD, PhD or equivalent degree and reside in the United States or Canada. The investigator must have a faculty appointment at an accredited U.S. or Canadian institution and have the proven ability to pursue independent research as evidenced by original research in peer-reviewed journals.
Amount $25,000 - $50,000
Date(s) Application Is Due Oct 5.
Contact Grants Administrator; (866) 808-CURE (2873); email: info@childrenscardiomyopathy.org
Internet http://www.childrenscardiomyopathy.org/site/grants.php
Sponsor Children's Cardiomyopathy Foundation (CCF)
P.O. Box 547
Tenafly, NJ 07670

Chiles Foundation Grants **1317**
The foundation has a deep concern for and confidence in the future of Oregon and the Pacific Northwest. Although the foundation has made a steady commitment to the improvement of the quality of life for those who live and work in this area, it is not restricted in its grant making to the Pacific Northwest. The foundation has traditionally made grants to certain select institutions of higher education for business schools, scholarships, and athletics; supports basic research in certain select medical institutions; supports religion through divinity schools and religious education; and believes that the arts and cultural activities of a community are important and supports certain select, established institutions. Types of support include building construction/renovation, equipment acquisition, and scholarship funds. Annual deadline dates may vary.
Requirements The preferred initial method of contact is a phone call to determine whether a prospective proposal is within guidelines; if so, an applicant will be invited to submit a one-page written preliminary proposal. An application form will be sent after approval of the preliminary proposal by the executive committee.
Restrictions No support for projects involving litigation. Grants are not made to individuals, for deficit financing, mortgage retirement, or projects and conferences already completed.
Amount $1000-$10,000 average
Contact Grants Administrator, (503) 222-2143; email: cf@uswest.net
Sponsor Chiles Foundation
111 SW Fifth Ave, Ste 4050
Portland, OR 97204-3643

Chinese-American Librarians Association Sheila Suen Lai Scholarships **1318**
The Scholarship is designed to encourage the professional and leadership development in Chinese American librarianship. For more information about the application and the Scholarship, visit the CALA's Web page or contact Y. Diana Wu, Chair of the CALA Scholarship Committee.
Requirements Students of Chinese nationality or Chinese descent who are enrolled in ALA-accredited master's programs or in doctoral programs in Library and Information Science in degree-granting institutions in North America are eligible. The recipient must be enrolled as a full-time student at the time the scholarship is awarded.
Amount $500
Date(s) Application Is Due Apr 15.
Contact Y. Diana Wu, CALA Scholarship Committee, (408) 808-2087; email: dwu@sjsu.edu
Internet http://www.cala-web.org
Sponsor Chinese-American Librarians Association
P.O. Box 208240, Sterling Memorial Library
New Haven, CT 06520-8240

Chiron Foundation Community Grants **1319**
The foundation's focus areas are health and medicine, education, and community. Four imperatives guide health-care giving: accelerating progress toward the prevention and cure or successful management of cancer through research, education, early detection, and public-policy debate; combating infectious disease through prevention-related programs, educational efforts, and therapeutics targeting at-risk populations, with emphasis on the special needs of children and families; ensuring the availability and safety of the blood supply and promoting the highest standards of care for blood donors and recipients; and supporting initiatives in the international medical community to provide vaccines and immunization services to protect at-risk populations, especially children, against the devastation of crippling and lethal diseases. Four imperatives guide education giving: providing training and professional development opportunities to enable classroom teachers to teach science and math more effectively; increasing opportunities for economically disadvantaged students to continue on to postsecondary education; supporting community-based training programs to prepare underrepresented minorities and underprivileged groups for careers in the biosciences; and encouraging and assisting promising scholars to pursue advanced research in the biosciences and medicine. Four imperatives guide community giving: providing early diagnosis, intervention, and support for children with disabilities or other special physical or emotional needs; providing essential social services such as meals and housing to those in greatest need; empowering individuals to achieve self-sufficiency through employment training and job-skill development; and enriching the character and celebrating the distinctives of local communities. Requests are accepted at anytime, and proposals are reviewed quarterly.
Requirements 501(c)3 tax-exempt organizations in the San Francisco East Bay Area, including Alameda, Contra Costa, and Solano Counties; Seattle; and Philadelphia are eligible.
Restrictions In general, Chiron does not support organizations that do not have 501(c)3 tax status; religious, fraternal, service, or veterans' organizations; civic or cultural organizations that do not serve the areas in which Chiron is located; alumni drives and teacher organizations; memorials; municipal and for-profit hospitals; labor unions; city, municipal, or federal government departments; organizations or causes that do not support the company's commitment to non-discrimination and diversity; projects of national scope or from national organizations not related to health care; matching gifts; individuals, including scholarships (other than those awarded as part of the company-sponsored college scholarship program); travel support; fund-raising activities related to individual sponsorship; and fund-raising dinners other than those for health care or medical research organizations aligned with company research and product interests.
Amount $5000-$30,000 average, education and community; $15,000-$75,000 health and medicine
Contact Community Relations, fax: (510) 601-6952; email: Chiron_foundation@chiron.com
Internet http://www.chiron.com/foundation/index.html
Sponsor Chiron Foundation
4560 Horton St
Emeryville, CA 94608

Christensen Fund Regional Grants **1320**
The fund (TCF) focuses its grantmaking on maintaining the rich diversity of the world--biological and cultural--over the long run, by focusing on four geographic regions: the greater South West (Southwest United States and Northwest Mexico); Central Asia, Turkey, and Iran; the African Rift Valley (Ethiopia); and Northern Australia and Melanesia. Grants within the regional programs are generally directed to organizations based within those regions or, where appropriate, to internationally based organizations working in support of people and institutions on the ground. In general, grants are of one year or less duration; currently grants up to two years are by invitation only.
Requirements 501(c)3 nonprofit organizations and non-USA institutions with nonprofit or equivalent status in their country of origin are eligible. Partnerships or associations with USA-based nonprofit organizations are preferred.
Restrictions The fund does not make grants directly to individuals but rather assists individuals through institutions qualified to receive nonprofit support with which such individuals are affiliated.
Amount $200,000 maximum; $5000-$100,000 first-time grants
Date(s) Application Is Due Jan 15; Mar 31; Jun 30; Sep 30.
Contact Grants Administrator, (650) 462-8600 ext 106; email: info@christensenfund.org
Internet http://www.christensenfund.org/index.html

Sponsor Christensen Fund
145 Addison Ave
Palo Alto, CA 94301

Christian Gauss Award **1321**
This award is offered for books published in the field of literary scholarship or criticism. An edition of a literary work is not eligible unless it contains an introduction amounting to a substantial critical or historical estimate that might have been published independently. Entries must be submitted by the publisher who will have obtained a copy of the conditions of eligibility prior to submission.
Requirements Entries must be published in the United States during the 12-month period between May 1 (of the past year) and the April 30 (of the current year) deadline date. Entries will ordinarily be the work of a single author. Exceptions may be made for books written by small teams of scholars working in close collaboration. Authors must be US citizens or residents.
Restrictions Works of fiction and unpublished manuscripts are not eligible.
Amount $2500 maximum
Date(s) Application Is Due Apr 30.
Contact Sandra Beasley, Awards Coordinator, (202) 265-3808; fax: (202) 986-1601; email: SBeasley@pbk.org
Internet http://www.pbk.org/scholarships/books.htm
Sponsor Phi Beta Kappa Society
1606 New Hampshire Ave NW
Washington, DC 20009

Christine Mirzayan Science and Technology Policy Internship Program **1322**
The program is designed to engage graduate and postdoctoral science, engineering, medical, veterinary, business, and law students in science and technology policy and to familiarize them with the interactions between science, technology, and government. Students develop essential skills different from those attained in academia and make the transition from a graduate student to a professional. Internships are tenable for 12 weeks in January, 10 weeks in June and 12 weeks in September. Candidates should submit the on-line application and reference letter forms, both available on the Web site.
Requirements Graduate and postdoctoral science, engineering, medical, veterinary, business, and law students are eligible.
Amount $5700 stipend for the 12 week program; $4800 stipend for the 10 week program; $500 travel allowance
Date(s) Application Is Due Mar 1; Jun 1; Nov 1.
Contact Christine Mirzayan Internship Program, (202) 334-2455; fax: (202) 334-1667; email: internship@nas.edu
Internet http://www.nationalacademies.org/internship
Sponsor National Academies
500 5th St, NW, Rm 508
Washington, DC 20001

Christine O. Gregoire Youth/Young Adult Award for Outstanding Use of Tobacco Industry Documents **1323**
The award recognizes a person 24 years of age or younger who has made a contribution to the health of the public in the recent past through use of tobacco documents. The award also honors innovation in the use and application of tobacco industry documents to improve the public's health and, where applicable, to further the goals of tobacco prevention and control in order to help build a world where young people reject tobacco and anyone can quit. Those nominated should be individuals who have made a notable impact through innovative use of tobacco industry documents as applied to research, policy, or advocacy.
Requirements At least one of the following two criteria must be met by the nominated individual: Nominees must have made a remarkable research, policy, or advocacy contribution with the use of tobacco industry documents, and/or; Nominees must have employed innovative, creative approaches to the employment of tobacco industry documents that result in an improvement in the health or public awareness of a community or nation. Nominations may be made by individuals such as colleagues, peers, coworkers, instructors/professors, governments, or CBOs that are qualified to make such a nomination because of their familiarity with the nominee's work and contribution. The preferred method of submission is through the Legacy Awards website.
Restrictions Nominees must not have any affiliation with the tobacco industry. Members of the awards committee may not nominate potential recipients, although they may provide written support as part of a nomination package. Employees and directors of the American Legacy Foundation and their relatives are not eligible.
Amount $7,500
Date(s) Application Is Due Jul 11.
Contact Jennifer Bramble, (202) 454-5555; fax: (202) 454-5599; email: awards@americanlegacy.org
Internet http://www.americanlegacy.org/49.htm
Sponsor American Legacy Foundation
Legacy Awards, 2030 M Street, NW, 6th Floor
Washington, DC 20036

Christopher Columbus Fellowship Foundation Frank Annunzio Award **1324**
This program presents one $25,000 award in the Science/Technology field for a cutting edge innovation and one $25,000 award in the Alternative Energy Sources (AES) field. The awards recognize individual Americans who are improving the world through ingenuity and innovation, and provide incentive for continuing research and/or a specific project.
Requirements U.S. citizens may apply.
Amount $25,000
Date(s) Application Is Due May 13.
Contact Judith M. Shellenberger, Executive Director, (315) 258-0090; fax: (315) 258-0093; email: judithmscolumbus@cs.com
Internet http://www.columbusfdn.org/otherprograms/frankannunzio/
Sponsor Christopher Columbus Fellowship Foundation
110 Genesee Street, Suite 390
Auburn, NY 13021

Christopher Columbus Fellowship Foundation Homeland Security Awards **1325**
The Foundation bestows this award upon United States individual citizens or companies that are making a measurable and constructive contribution related to basic and/or advanced research in the area of homeland security which will result in a significant and positive benefit to society. Nominations are categorized in five fields: Biological, Radiological, Nuclear, Chemical and Explosive Attacks; Border and Transportation Security; Cyber Security and Information Sharing; Emergency Response to Natural and Man-Made Disasters; and Other. The winner may be chosen from any of the fields.
Requirements Nominees must be United States citizens or companies. Nomination materials must consist of an official Nomination form available only online.
Amount $25,000
Date(s) Application Is Due May 25.
Contact Judith M. Shellenberger, Executive Director, (315) 258-0090; fax: (315) 258-0093; email: judithmscolumbus@cs.com
Internet http://www.columbusfdn.org/homelandsecurity/
Sponsor Christopher Columbus Fellowship Foundation
110 Genesee Street, Suite 390
Auburn, NY 13021

Christopher D. Smithers Foundation Research Grants **1326**
Activities of the foundation are concentrated in the field of alcoholism. The foundation supports research on treatment, prevention, and public education to create a public awareness of alcoholism as a treatable disease. Small groups, such as treatment groups, shelters, and halfway houses, may apply for one-year seed grants to help them get started. There are no deadlines; applications are accepted year-round. The foundation requests that organizations first write, call, or fax for an annual report and guidelines before applying.
Restrictions Grants are not awarded to individuals.
Contact Grants Administrator, (516) 676-0067; fax: (516) 676-0323; email: info@smithersfoundation.org
Internet http://www.smithersfoundation.org
Sponsor Christopher D. Smithers Foundation
P.O. Box 67, Oyster Bay Rd
Mill Neck, NY 11765

Christopher Reeve Paralysis Foundation Individual Research Grants **1327**
The mission of the foundation is to support cutting-edge research to develop effective treatments and cures for paralysis caused by spinal cord injury and other central nervous system disorders. International individual grants support research that seeks to promote neuronal growth and survival, encourage the formation of synapses, enhance the production of myelin, and restore conduction capabilities in the acutely and chronically injured spinal cord; evaluate drugs or other interventions that protect against secondary neuronal injury or provide insight into the mechanisms causing such damage; elucidate the biological mechanisms underlying approaches to improve concomitant function; and understand anatomical characteristics of injury in both animals and human spinal cord, documenting neuronal systems that are most vulnerable to injury and resultant losses in function. The program is designed to encourage promising new investigators to undertake research on spinal cord regeneration and recovery; encourage researchers who are well-established in other areas to transfer their efforts to spinal cord research; and enable researchers with novel ideas to test their ideas and develop pilot data for seeking larger awards from NIH and other funding sources.
Requirements Senior scientists, young investigators, and postdoctoral fellows are eligible to serve as principal investigators.
Amount $75,000 maximum per year, senior scientists and young investigators; $60,000 maximum per year postdoctoral fellowships
Date(s) Application Is Due Jun 15; Dec 15.
Contact Dr. Douglas Landsman, (800) 225-0292; email: dlandsman@crpf.org
Internet http://www.christopherreeve.org/research/researchmain.cfm
Sponsor Christopher Reeve Paralysis Foundation
500 Morris Ave
Springfield, NJ 07081

Christopher Reeve Paralysis Foundation Quality of Life and Health Promotions Grants **1328**
The foundation awards grants to organizations nationwide that help improve opportunities, access, and day-to-day quality of life for individuals living with disabilities--primarily paralysis--and their families. This program recognizes the unique and numerous needs

of these individuals and the importance of providing services and programs that enable them to participate in all areas of life. Quality of Life grants are given to programs or projects that improve the daily lives of people living with disabilities, particularly spinal cord injuries. Funding is awarded twice yearly to programs that provide assistance through access, advocacy, education, recreation, and technology, among others. Health Promotion Grants seek to remove societal and environmental barriers that limit the abilities of individuals with paralysis to participate in life activities. Participation in these activities improves physical and emotional health and prevents secondary conditions for persons living with paralysis. Priority funding goes to programs that focus on paralysis generally and are not specific to one condition or disease that results in paralysis. Complete guidelines are available online.
Requirements 501(c)3 tax-exempt organizations are eligible.
Restrictions No grants will be made to individuals, for benefit tickets, or for courtesy advertising.
Amount $5000-$25,000 quality of life grants; $25,000 program awards (health promotion); $5000-$10,000 direct impact awards (health promotion)
Date(s) Application Is Due Mar 1; Sep 1.
Contact Donna Valente, Quality of Life Grants Coordinator, (800) 539-7309 or (973) 467-8270 ext 211; email: qol@crpf.org
Internet http://www.christopherreeve.org/qlgrants/qlgrantsmain.cfm
Sponsor Christopher Reeve Paralysis Foundation
500 Morris Ave
Springfield, NJ 07081

Chrysalis Scholarships **1329**
The association offers scholarships each year to aid women in finishing their theses and completing MS or PhD degree programs in geoscience fields. The support can be used for anything necessary to assist the candidate in completing her thesis, such as typing, drafting expenses, field work, or child care. The applicant should write a letter stating her background, career goals and objectives, involvement in both the geosciences and her community, how she will use the money, and explaining the length and nature of the interruption to her education. The applicant should also submit two letters of reference.
Requirements Applicants must be women whose educations have been interrupted for at least one year, candidates for advanced degrees in geoscience field, and who need the money to complete their theses during the current academic year.
Amount $2000
Date(s) Application Is Due Mar 15.
Contact Program Contact; email: chrysalis@awg.org
Internet http://www.awg.org/AWGFoundation/chrysalis.html
Sponsor Association for Women Geoscientists
P.O. Box 30645
Lincoln, NE 68503-0645

Churchill Fellowships--Australia **1330**
The fellowships are awarded each year to Australians to undertake overseas study or to conduct an investigative project needing facilities not available in Australia. The value of an applicant's work to the community and the extent to which it will be enhanced by the applicant's overseas study project are considered, as well as the applicant's merit based on past achievements or on demonstrated ability for future achievements in any field.
Requirements Australian citizens over the age of 18 are eligible. Applicants must be able to complete a minimum of four weeks overseas travel to complete their research.
Amount $20,000 average
Date(s) Application Is Due Feb 28.
Contact Norman Owens (02) 9683 9900 or 0418 667 208; email: norman.owens@abw.org.au
Internet http://e-bility.com/churchill/trust.htm
Sponsor Winston Churchill Memorial Trust
218 Northbourne Ave
Braddon 2612 Australia

CIA Postdoctoral Research Fellowship **1331**
The Center for the Study of Intelligence invites applications for a two-year fellowship that focuses on problems or issues of intelligence. Priority will be given to research proposals that enhance the understanding of the application of technology to intelligence issues. The fellowship provides a stipend for two years. The fellow is required to submit one article per year for publication. The applicant selected will not be required to have any security clearances but will be asked to provide periodic research updates to the CIA chief historian. Applicants should submit proposals and include a cover sheet with name, mailing address, telephone and fax numbers, email address, present rank and institution, title of project, and the names of two recommenders; a curriculum vita; a two- to three-page research proposal that explains the research topic, the main sources to be examined, and how the research paper will enhance the understanding of US intelligence; and two letters of recommendation.
Requirements US citizens with the PhD degree are eligible.
Amount $100,000 per year
Date(s) Application Is Due Jul 1.
Contact Chief Historian, (703) 482-0623; fax: (703) 482-1739
Internet http://web.missouri.edu/~gradschl/financial/extramural/bulletin/Fellowships/CentralIntelligenceAgencyPostdoctoralResearchFellowship.htm
Sponsor Central Intelligence Agency
Center for the Study of Intelligence
Washington, DC 20505

CICU James C. Ross Research Fellowship **1332**
The nine-month research fellowship focuses on higher education and its relationship to state and national priorities. Preference is given to candidates who have a doctorate or have completed all but their dissertation and have a proven track record of communicating research findings to a general audience. The fellow will work in CICU's Albany office, and is expected to produce a final paper by the first Monday in October of next year. Housing is the responsibility of the fellow. To apply, submit a cover letter, 500-1000 word outline of a proposed course of research, resume, recent publication or unpublished manuscript, and two confidential letters of reference. Annual deadlines may vary; contact program staff for exact dates.
Restrictions Class work is prohibited during the full-time fellowship, though credit arrangements for fellowship participation are permissible.
Amount $20,000 stipend
Date(s) Application Is Due Dec 1.
Contact Sheila Seery, (518) 436-4781; fax: (518) 436-0417; email: sheila@cicu.org
Internet http://www.cicu.org/CMT/frontpage/04RossApplication.pdf
Sponsor Commission on Independent Colleges and Universities
P.O. Box 7289, 17 Elk St
Albany, NY 12224

CIES African Regional Special Program and Country Grants **1333**
The program makes up to 12 awards in all academic fields for research in sub-Saharan Africa. Fellows will conduct research in one country for three to nine months or in two or three countries for five to nine months. Grantees are expected to give occasional lectures and seminars in consultation with host universities and US embassies. Lecturing/research awards in specified fields also are available in some countries: contact program staff for a current listing.
Requirements Applicants must be US citizens with the PhD or equivalent professional/terminal degree at the time of application. Foreign language proficiency in the field of the advertised assignment or proposed lecturing/research activity is required.
Contact Debra Egan, Program Contact, (202) 686-6230; email: degan@cies.iie.org
Internet http://www.iie.org/cies/download/2006_07AWARDS_CATALOG.pdf
Sponsor Council for International Exchange of Scholars
3007 Tilden St NW, Ste 5L
Washington, DC 20008-3009

CIIT Postdoctoral Fellowships **1334**
Ten to 15 fellowships are offered annually to support persons holding recently earned PhD, MD, or DVM degrees during further training in genetic toxicology, immunotoxicology, biochemical toxicology, pathology, reproductive toxicology, epidemiology, teratology, and carcinogenesis. Fellowships are tenable at the institute for two to three years. The institute holds 501(c)6 status. Applications are available on the Web site.
Requirements Applicants who recently were awarded PhD degrees in a discipline related to toxicology are eligible to apply; those holding recently awarded DVM or MD degrees are expected to have substantial research experience.
Restrictions Traineeships and fellowships are awarded only for research conducted at the CIIT. Awardees may not use their stipends to supplement funds from other awards.
Amount $27,000 first year; $28,500 second year
Contact Rusty Bramlage, Human Resources Manager, (919) 558-1331; fax: (919) 558-1300; email: bramlage@ciit.org
Internet http://www.ciit.org/careers/openings_postdoc.asp
Sponsor Chemical Industry Institute of Toxicology
P.O. Box 12137
Research Triangle Park, NC 27709

Cinnabar Foundation Grants **1335**
The foundation awards grants to nonprofits to promote environmental and wildlife conservation and protection. Types of support include general operating support, conferences and seminars, research, and scholarships to individuals. There are no application forms.
Requirements Idaho, Montana, and Wyoming nonprofit organizations may apply.
Amount $1000-$15,000 range
Date(s) Application Is Due Mar 15.
Contact James Posewitz, c/o Holmes and Turner, (406) 449-2795; fax: (406) 449-9985; email: cinnabar@mt.net
Sponsor Cinnabar Foundation
P.O. Box 5088
Helena, MT 59604

CINOA Prize **1336**
This art history prize is given by the International Confederation of Art Dealers (Confederation Internationale des Negociants en Oeuvres d'Art) to encourage the study of the history of art in the 19 countries where the confederation is represented--Australia, Austria, Belgium, Czech Republic, Denmark, England, France, Germany, Ireland, Italy, the Netherlands, New Zealand, Portugal, San Marino, South Africa, Spain, Sweden, Switzerland, and the United States. An author wishing to be considered

in the competition should forward a copy of his/her bound manuscript, a curriculum vita, a brief summary, and a support letter from a professor or other qualified scholar in the field to which the work relates, as well as a letter from an editor/publisher willing to publish the work if it is granted the CINOA Prize. Contact the organization via email for more information.
Requirements To be eligible, a candidate must be a resident of one of the member nations, and his/her work should preferably be concerned with an aspect of the art or art history of one of the CINOA countries.
Amount $10,000 to the publisher and an all-expense paid trip to the next annual CINOA meeting
Date(s) Application Is Due Nov 15.
Contact CINOA Prize, (212) 940-8925; fax: (212) 940-6484; email: secretary@cinoa.org
Internet http://www.cinoa.org
Sponsor Art Dealers Association of America
575 Madison Ave
New York, NY 10022

CIRCLE Civic Education at the High School Level Research Grants **1337**
The program seeks research that will help educators and policymakers to improve civic outcomes for US students of high-school age (roughly 14 to 18). Civic outcomes include, but are not limited to knowledge of politics, democracy and civil society; knowledge of social issues; values such as tolerance, trust, patriotism, concern for others' rights and well-being, and efficacy (the belief that one can make a difference); skills and habits of deliberating about public issues and participating in politics and community affairs; volunteering and membership in voluntary and/or nonprofit groups; and intentions to vote or to consider careers in public service (in the government or nonprofit sectors). CIRCLE is interested in research on interventions and reforms that may enhance civic outcomes. These interventions and reforms include, but are not limited to programs of civic education and classes on history, democracy, or law; approaches to the teaching of other disciplines that may have civic benefits; co-curricular activities, including student government and student media; service-learning; games and simulations that involve political or civic issues; student voice or participation in the governance of their schools; the basic structure of high schools (including their size, focus, requirements, climate, admissions criteria, or composition); professional development for teachers, so long as the effects on students can be assessed; and after-school or community-based programs, insofar as these have the potential to reach large numbers of adolescents or to change mainstream education. In most CIRCLE-funded research projects, the outcomes will be civic knowledge, values, skills, or behaviors. However, research that explores whether being civically engaged helps academic outcomes or positive adolescent development also will be considered. The listed application deadline is for letters of inquiry; full proposals are by invitation.
Requirements CIRCLE welcomes proposals from academics, students (especially PhD candidates at the dissertation stage), independent scholars, practitioners, and research nonprofits and firms. CIRCLE also welcomes proposals from youth of high school age, perhaps working in partnership with adults. Such youth-led research proposals will be evaluated separately and not compared directly to proposals from adults.
Restrictions CIRCLE funds rigorous research, not advocacy, education, or other forms of practice.
Amount $500,000 total; $100,000 maximum
Date(s) Application Is Due Dec 15.
Contact Carrie Donovan, (301) 405-2790; email: cdonovan@umd.edu
Internet http://www.civicyouth.org/grants/index.htm
Sponsor University of Maryland
School of Public Policy
College Park, MD 20742

CIUS Darcovich Memorial Doctoral Fellowship **1338**
The institute invites applications for one doctoral thesis fellowship, nonrenewable. The award is intended to aid a student in completing a thesis on a Ukrainian or Ukrainian Canadian topic in education, history, law, humanities, arts, social sciences, women's studies, and library sciences. The fellowship will be awarded only in the thesis year of an academic program and only for thesis work. Only in exceptional circumstances may an award be held concurrently with other awards.
Requirements A Canadian citizen or permanent resident may hold the fellowship at any institution of higher learning in Canada or elsewhere. For non-Canadian applicants, preference will be given to students enrolled at the University of Alberta.
Amount $C12,000 maximum
Date(s) Application Is Due Mar 1.
Contact Helen Darcovich Memorial Endowment Fund, (780) 492-2973; fax: (780) 492-4967; email: cius@ualberta.ca
Internet http://www.ualberta.ca/CIUS/cius-grants.htm
Sponsor Canadian Institute of Ukrainian Studies
University of Alberta, 450 Athabasca Hall
Edmonton, AB T6G 2E8 Canada

CIUS Master's Fellowship **1339**
The institute invites applications for one master's thesis fellowship, nonrenewable. The award is intended to aid a student to complete a thesis on a Ukrainian or Ukrainian Canadian topic in education, history, law, humanities, arts, social sciences, women's studies, and library sciences. The fellowship will be awarded only in the thesis year of an academic program and only for thesis work. Only in exceptional circumstances may an award be held concurrently with other awards.
Requirements A Canadian citizen or permanent resident may hold the fellowship at any institution of higher learning in Canada or elsewhere. For non-Canadian applicants, preference will be given to students enrolled at the University of Alberta.
Amount $C10,000 maximum
Date(s) Application Is Due Mar 1.
Contact Marusia and Michael Dorosh Endowment Fund, (780) 492-2973; fax: (780) 492-4967; email: cius@ualberta.ca
Internet http://www.ualberta.ca/CIUS/cius-grants.htm
Sponsor Canadian Institute of Ukrainian Studies
University of Alberta, 450 Athabasca Hall
Edmonton, AB T6G 2E8 Canada

CIUS Neporany Research and Teaching Fellowship **1340**
A research and training fellowship in Ukrainian studies will be awarded by the Osyp and Josaphat Neporany Educational Fund. The fellowship will be tenable at any university with research facilities at which the fellow's academic Ukrainian studies specialty may be pursued and the fellow enabled to teach a course related to the specialty. The duration of the fellowship will normally be one term, i.e., half of the academic year. This may be extended where the applicant has been successful in receiving supplemental funding from other sources. Institutions and departments who wish to explore the possibility of hosting a fellow also are encouraged to request information.
Requirements Applicants must hold doctorates, or have equivalent professional achievement, in Ukrainian studies.
Amount $C20,000 maximum
Date(s) Application Is Due Mar 1.
Contact Fellowships Coordinator, (780) 492-2973; fax: (780) 492-4967; email: cius@ualberta.ca
Internet http://www.ualberta.ca/CIUS/cius-grants.htm
Sponsor Canadian Institute of Ukrainian Studies
University of Alberta, 450 Athabasca Hall
Edmonton, AB T6G 2E8 Canada

CIUS Research Grants **1341**
The Michael and Daria Kowalsky Endowment Fund invites applications for research grants in Ukrainian and Ukrainian Canadian studies in history, literature, language, education, social sciences, and library sciences. Application forms and the guide to research applications are available from the office.
Date(s) Application Is Due Mar 1.
Contact Program Officer, (780) 492-2973; fax: (780) 492-4967; email: cius@ualberta.ca
Internet http://www.ualberta.ca/CIUS/cius-grants.htm
Sponsor Canadian Institute of Ukrainian Studies
University of Alberta, 450 Athabasca Hall
Edmonton, AB T6G 2E8 Canada

Civic Education Project Grants **1342**
The Special Project Grants Program will provide support for projects designed to strengthen community, secondary and higher education by introducing innovative content, methods and materials of teaching and research, strengthening academic and scholarly exchange and fostering school and university linkages to the community. The Program will award Special Project Grants to the graduates of Muskie/FSA Graduate Fellowship Program currently residing in the NIS and Baltic States.
Requirements Applicants must be fluent in English. Teaching experience is preferred. Applicants must have successfully completed a Muskie/FSA Graduate Fellowship Program and reside in one of the following countries: Armenia, Azerbaijan, Belarus, Estonia, Georgia, Kazakhstan, Kyrgyzstan, Latvia, Lithuania, Moldova, Russia, Tajikistan, Turkmenistan, Ukraine, Uzbekistan. Applications from groups led by Muskie/FSA alumni will be accepted.
Restrictions Members of staff of CEP, OSI, American Councils, other organizations directly involved in the SCOUT or any other Muskie/FSA alumni support program supervision or administration, and individuals holding similar grants or fellowships supporting their academic activity, which overlap in time with the proposed SCOUT grant activity, are not eligible to receive any SCOUT program grants.
Amount $1000-$5000
Date(s) Application Is Due Apr 1.
Contact Sara Werth, Program Director, (202) 663-7793; fax: (202) 663-7799; email: swerth2@jhu.edu
Internet http://www.cep.org.hu/programs/spannouncement.html
Sponsor Civic Education Project
2360 N Vermont St
Arlington, VA 22207

CLA Nurses Respiratory Society Fellowships **1343**
The objective of the fellowships is to permit nurses to pursue graduate study so that they may be better able to contribute to the Canadian field of respiratory illness and health care. Applicants may register in any master's or doctoral program where knowledge, skill, and expertise may develop toward this objective. The program should show evidence of a

plan to foster theory, research, and either a clinical or functional area of specialization. Application forms may be obtained from the association.
Requirements Applicant must be a Canadian citizen or permanent Canadian resident, be a registered nurse, be enrolled full-time in a graduate program at the master's or doctoral level, and be a member of CNRS.
Amount $C3750-$C7500
Date(s) Application Is Due Feb 1.
Contact Grants Administrator, (416) 864-9911; fax: (416) 864-9916; email: orcs@on.lung.ca
Internet http://www.on.lung.ca/orcs/fellowships.html
Sponsor Canadian Lung Association
1900 City Park Dr, Ste 508
Gloucester, ON K1J 1A3 Canada

CLA Nurses Respiratory Society Nursing Research Grants **1344**
Research grants are offered to those studying respiratory nursing, chronic or acute lung disease, which will result in improved quality of patient care. Research may include clinical investigation of any nursing-related phenomenon; be pertinent to illness assessment, management, or responses; or be aimed at health promotion and prevention issues. Studies may use either quantitative or qualitative methodologies.
Requirements Applicant must be a Canadian citizen or permanent Canadian resident; a registered nurse; hold an appointment in, or have an affiliation with, a health care agency, educational institution, or other organization in Canada that can administer the funds in an approved manner; and be a member of CNRS.
Amount $C3000-$C30,000
Date(s) Application Is Due Nov 1.
Contact Grant Administrator, (613) 747-6776; fax: (613) 747-7430; email: dhogg@cha.ab.ca
Internet http://www.lung.ca/resp/Fellowships/Fellow_Grants.htm
Sponsor Canadian Lung Association
1900 City Park Dr, Ste 508
Gloucester, ON K1J 1A3 Canada

CLA Physiotherapy Cardio-Respiratory Society Fellowships **1345**
The purpose of the research program is to pursue increased scientific knowledge in the area of cardio-respiratory physiotherapy practice. Fellowships are offered to physiotherapists pursuing postgraduate training, with respiratory research as the major component. The award period is one year.
Requirements Applicants must be Canadian citizens or permanent Canadian residents, be registered physiotherapists, be enrolled or accepted for full-time study in a graduate program at the master's or doctoral level, and be a member of the Canadian Physiotherapy Cardio-Respiratory Society.
Amount $C6000-$C12,000
Date(s) Application Is Due Nov 1.
Contact Administrator, Societies & Special Projects, (613) 569-6411; email: nprt@lung.ca
Internet http://www.lung.ca/crhp/index.html
Sponsor Canadian Lung Association
1900 City Park Dr, Ste 508
Gloucester, ON K1J 1A3 Canada

CLA Scholarship for Minority Students in Memory of Edna Yelland **1346**
Awards encourage and support ethnic minority group students in the attainment of a graduate library degree in library or information science. Award announcement will be made June 15. Application forms will be sent upon written request.
Requirements California residents and US citizens and permanent US residents may apply. To be eligible, applicants must be either enrolled or accepted for enrollment in a master's program in an accredited California graduate library school. The applicant must be an ethnic minority of one of the following groups: Native American, African American, Mexican American, Latin/Hispanic origin, Asian American or Pacific Islander, or Filipino. Applicants must also provide evidence of financial need.
Amount $2500
Date(s) Application Is Due May 31.
Contact Scholarship Committee Chair, (916) 447-8541; fax: (916) 447-8394; email: info@cla-net.org
Internet http://cla-net.org/awards/ednayelland.php
Sponsor California Library Association
717 20th St, Ste 200
Sacramento, CA 95814

Claneil Foundation Grants **1347**
The foundation awards grants to nonprofit organizations in its areas of interest, including community development, education, arts and culture, environment, health, women, domestic abuse, and social services. Types of support include capital campaigns, equipment acquisition, continuing support, building construction/renovation, exchange programs, and research. Deadlines listed are for letters of intent. Application forms are required.
Requirements Nonprofit organizations are eligible. Preference is given to organizations serving Pennsylvania counties including Bucks, Montgomery, Chester, Delaware, and Philadelphia.
Restrictions Grants are not awarded to governmental organizations, individuals, or religious organizations.
Amount $3000-$50,000 range
Date(s) Application Is Due Jun 30; Dec 15.
Contact Cathy Weiss, Executive Director, (610) 941-1131; email: cweiss@claneil.com
Internet http://www.claneil.org
Sponsor Claneil Foundation Inc
630 W Germantown Pike, Ste 400
Plymouth Meeting, PA 19462

Clapham Prize for Historical Research **1348**
The prize is awarded under the auspices of the William Wilberforce Papers Project and will be awarded biannually to the scholar judged to have completed the most outstanding scholarly work related to Wilberforce during the preceding two-year period. All nominees will be contacted for further information.
Amount $5000
Date(s) Application Is Due Feb 1.
Contact Debbie Drost, Program Manager, (978) 867-4365; fax: (978) 867-4673; email: drost@gordon.edu
Internet http://www.gordon.edu/ccs
Sponsor Gordon College
255 Grapevine Rd
Wenham, MA 01984

Clarence E. Heller Charitable Foundation Grants **1349**
The charitable foundation supports nonprofit organizations, with priority given to proposals from California, in its areas of interest, including environment and health--to prevent serious risk to human health from toxic substances and other environmental hazards by supporting programs in research, education, and policy development; management of resources--to protect and preserve the earth's limited resources by assisting programs that demonstrate how natural resources can be managed on a sustainable and an ecologically sound basis, and supporting initiatives for sustainable agriculture, and for promoting the long-term viability of communities and regions; music--to encourage the playing, enjoyment, and accessibility of symphonic and chamber music by providing scholarship and program assistance at selected community music organizations and schools, and by helping community-based ensembles of demonstrated quality implement artistic initiatives, diversify and increase audiences, and improve fund-raising capacity; and education--to focus on support for programs that improve the teaching skills of educators and artists in environmental and arts education. Types of support include continuing support, general operating expenses, publications, research, seed money, and special projects. The foundation's board meets typically in March, June, and October. Letters of inquiry are accepted at any time.
Requirements 501(c)3 tax-exempt organizations are eligible.
Restrictions Grants are not made to individuals.
Amount $5000-$600,000; $10,000-$50,000 average
Contact Bruce Hirsch, Executive Director, (415) 989-9839; fax: (415) 989-1909; email: info@cehcf.org
Internet http://cehcf.org/app_info.html
Sponsor Clarence E. Heller Charitable Foundation
1 Lombard St, Ste 305
San Francisco, CA 94111-1130

Clark Foundation Grants **1350**
The foundation awards grants in New York, NY, and upstate New York for charitable and educational purposes and in support of health care, youth, cultural, environmental, and community organizations. Types of support include general operating support, continuing support, annual campaigns, capital campaigns, building construction/renovation, equipment acquisition, program development, seed money, and scholarships to Cooperstown County residents.
Requirements Nonprofit organizations in upstate New York and New York, NY, are eligible.
Amount $20,000-$200,000 average range
Date(s) Application Is Due Jan 1; Apr 1; Jul 15; Oct 1.
Contact Charles Hamilton, Executive Director, (212) 977-6900
Sponsor Clark Foundation
1 Rockefeller Plz, 31st Fl
New York, NY 10020

Clark Library Short-Term Resident Fellowships **1351**
These short-term fellowships facilitate access to the Department of Special Collections for researchers and scholars residing outside of the Los Angeles area. Fellowships are held April through December for periods of one to three months. The department collects primary resources in the humanities and social sciences. Application requirements include a cover letter, a curriculum vita, a brief outline of the research and specific collections to be used (two-page maximum), dates to be spent in residence, and three letters of recommendation. Information on the library's holdings, application, and guidelines are available on the Web site.
Requirements Scholars holding PhD or equivalent degrees involved in a project suitable to the collection are eligible to apply.
Amount $2000 per month

Date(s) Application Is Due Feb 1.
Contact Fellowship Coordinator, (323) 731-8529; fax: (323) 731-8617; email: clarklib@humnet.ucla.edu
Internet http://www.humnet.ucla.edu/humnet/c1718cs/Postd.htm
Sponsor William Andrews Clark Memorial Library
2520 Cimarron St
Los Angeles, CA 90018

Clark-Huntington Joint Bibliographical Fellowship **1352**
Sponsored jointly by the Clark and the Huntington Libraries, this two-month fellowship provides support for bibliographical research in early modern British literature and history as well as other areas where the two libraries have common strengths.
Requirements Applicants should hold a PhD degree or have appropriate research experience.
Date(s) Application Is Due Feb 1.
Contact Fellowship Administrator, fax: (310) 206-8577; email: clarklib@humnet.ucla.edu
Internet http://www.humnet.ucla.edu/humnet/c1718cs/applic4.htm
Sponsor UCLA Center for 17th- and 18th-Century Studies
405 Hilgard Ave, 310 Royce Hall
Los Angeles, CA 90095-1404

Claude Pepper Foundation Grants **1353**
The foundation makes grants primarily to support the work of the Claude Pepper Center and the Pepper Institute on Aging and Public Policy, both located at Florida State University, Tallahassee, FL. The foundation makes limited grants to other organizations to continue the work and vision of Claude and Mildred Pepper. The foundation also supports a visiting scholars program and an oratory competition for Florida students. Grants are usually made for a period of one year and except in rare instances no grant will be made for longer than a three-year period of time. Deadlines are April 15 and October 15 for the visiting scholars program. Guidelines are available online.
Requirements 501(c)3 tax-exempt organizations are eligible.
Date(s) Application Is Due Apr 15; Oct 15.
Contact Lisa Maynard, Associate Director for Programs, (850) 644-9309; fax: (850) 644-9301; email: llmaynar@mailer.fsu.edu
Internet http://www.claudepepper.org/foundation/programs/grant.htm
Sponsor Claude Pepper Foundation
636 W Call St
Tallahassee, FL 32306-1122

Claude S. Hudson Award in Carbohydrate Chemistry **1354**
This award, sponsored by the National Starch and Chemical Co and administered by ACS, is given biennially in odd-numbered years to recognize outstanding contributions to carbohydrate chemistry, whether in education, research, or application. The award is granted without regard to age or nationality. Applications are accepted in even-numbered years.
Requirements Any individual, except a member of the award committee, may submit one nomination or seconding letter for the award in any given year. Nominating documents consist of a letter of not more than 1000 words containing an evaluation of the nominee's accomplishments and a specific identification of the work to be recognized, a biographical sketch including date of birth, and a list of publications and patents authored by the nominee. Six copies of all items to be included in the nomination must be submitted.
Restrictions Self-nominations are not accepted.
Amount $3000 and up to $1000 for travel expenses to award meeting
Date(s) Application Is Due Feb 1.
Contact Awards Administrator, (202) 452-2109; fax: (202) 776-8211; email: awards@acs.org
Internet http://www.chemistry.org/portal/a/c/s/1/acsdisplay.html?DOC=awards%5Chudson.html
Sponsor American Chemical Society
1155 16th St NW
Washington, DC 20036

Claude Worthington Benedum Foundation Grants **1355**
Grants are made in the areas of education, health and human services, community and economic development, environment, and the arts. Grants have been awarded to support education reform, teacher education, higher education, workforce development, rural health, professional developing in healthcare, human services, affordable housing, and economic development. Grants are awarded to organizations in West Virginia and southwestern Pennsylvania. Funds are provided for general operations for projects, sometimes including building and equipment, in West Virginia, and for projects in Pittsburgh that address regional problems and needs, that establish demonstration projects with strong potential for replication in West Virginia, or make outstanding contributions to the area. Additional types of support include matching funds, consulting services, technical assistance, capital campaigns, conferences and seminars, research, and seed grants. Organizations wishing to apply should request a copy of the annual report, which includes application guidelines. Applications may be submitted at any time; the board meets for review in March, June, September, and December.
Requirements Southwestern Pennsylvania and West Virginia nonprofit organizations may apply.
Restrictions Support is not given for national health and welfare campaigns, medical research, religious activities, fellowships, scholarships, annual campaigns, or travel.
Amount $14.4 million total
Contact William P. Getty, President, (800) 223-5948 or (412) 288-0360 ext 224; fax: (412) 288-0366; email: info@benedum.org
Internet http://www.benedum.org
Sponsor Claude Worthington Benedum Foundation
1400 Benedum-Trees Bldg, 223 Fourth Ave
Pittsburgh, PA 15222

Clay Foundation Grants **1356**
The primary mission of the foundation is to promote and enhance the quality of life of the citizens of West Virginia. Initially, grants will be confined to organizations or projects within the greater Kanawha Valley that significantly affect its residents. The foundation considers a broad range of organizations, though special interest is given to programs in the field of aging; health care, research, and education; vocational education; and services to disadvantaged youth and their families. Applicants are asked to submit a preliminary letter. If foundation priorities and resources permit consideration of the request, a detailed formal proposal may be requested. There are no deadline dates for the submission of preliminary letters. The board meets four times annually, generally in January, April, July, and October, at which times applications are considered and grants made.
Requirements IRS 501(c)3 tax-exempt organizations in West Virginia are eligible.
Restrictions Grants are not made for ongoing normal operations, debt retirement or operational deficits, contributions to endowment or scholarship funds, annual appeals or other fund-raising events, national fund-raising campaigns, religious organizations for religious purposes, or grants to conduit organizations.
Amount $5000-$75,000 average
Contact Charles Avampato, President, (304) 344-8656; fax: (304) 344-3805
Sponsor Clay Foundation
1426 Kanawha Blvd E
Charleston, WV 25301

Clements Center for Southwest Studies Research Fellowships **1357**
The fellowship is open to individuals in any field in the humanities or social sciences doing research on Southwestern America. The fellowships are designed to provide time for senior or junior scholars to bring book-length manuscripts to completion. Fellows are expected to spend the academic year at SMU, teach one course during the two-semester duration of the fellowship, and participate in center activities. Applicants should send two copies of their vita, a description of their research project, and a sample chapter or extract, and arrange to have letters of reference sent from three persons who can assess the significance of the work and the ability of the scholar to carry it out.
Amount $37,000 stipend
Date(s) Application Is Due Jan 16.
Contact David Weber, Director, (214) 768-3684; email: swcenter@smu.edu
Internet http://www.smu.edu/swcenter/announce.htm
Sponsor William P. Clements Center for Southwest Studies
P.O. Box 750176, Dallas Hall, Rm 356
Dallas, TX 75275-0176

Clements-DeGolyer Library Fellowships **1358**
The center and the DeGolyer Library offer fellowships to encourage broader and more intensive research on its holdings, which focus largely on the history of the trans-Mississippi west and railroad history.
Requirements Any serious researcher in any field is invited to apply. In general, the library awards fellowships to those individuals who have demonstrated strong qualifications in scholarship, publication, or teaching.
Restrictions Fellowships are not awarded to individuals living within the Dallas/Fort Worth metropolitan area.
Amount $500 per week
Contact Russell Martin, Director, (214) 768-1233 or (214) 768-3234; email: swcenter@smu.edu or rlmartin@smu.edu
Internet http://www.smu.edu/swcenter/clemdeg.htm
Sponsor William P. Clements Center for Southwest Studies
P.O. Box 750176
Dallas, TX 75275-0176

Cleveland-Cliffs Foundation Grants **1359**
Contributions are made to nonprofit organizations to enhance the quality of life of Cleveland-Cliffs Inc employees and in recognition of a corporate responsibility toward educational, health, welfare, civic, and cultural matters within the communities where the company operates. The foundation was formed for the purpose of making contributions to groups organized and operated exclusively for religious, charitable, scientific, literary, or educational purposes and for the prevention of cruelty to children or animals. Types of support include general operating support, annual campaigns, capital campaigns, building/renovation, professorships, scholarship funds, research, and employee matching gifts. The foundation's major emphasis is on supporting education through a matching gift program and direct contributions to educational institutions. Requests for support must be in writing.

Requirements Nonprofit organizations in the mining communities in which Cleveland-Cliffs Inc operates, including Michigan, Minnesota, and the greater Cleveland area, are eligible.
Amount $250-$50,000
Contact Dana Byrne, Vice President, (216) 694-5700; fax: (216) 694-4880; email: publicrelations@cleveland-cliffs.com
Internet http://www.cleveland-cliffs.com/general/community/foundation.asp
Sponsor Cleveland-Cliffs Foundation
1100 Superior Ave
Cleveland, OH 44114-2589

CLF Fellowships **1360**
The fellowships provide support for specialized clinical or experimental training in hepatic function or disease to individuals who have already completed the basic graduate program. The value of the fellowship is based on the qualifications and seniority of the applicant and will include, if applicable, a travel grant equivalent to return economy airfare for the grantee and spouse between the university of origin and the place of training. Guidelines and application forms are available from the office and in medical schools through the office of the Dean of the Faculty of Medicine.
Requirements Candidates must hold an MD or PhD degree or equivalent. Canadian citizens and landed immigrants who are resident in Canada at the time of application or Canadian citizens who are normally resident in Canada are eligible. Applications must be sponsored by a Canadian Faculty of Medicine or Health Sciences and accompanied by a letter of support from the Dean (or designee).
Amount $C30,000 maximum per year
Date(s) Application Is Due Mar 31.
Contact Research Awards Administrator, (800) 563-5483 or (416) 491-3353; fax: (416) 491-4952; email: clf@liver.ca
Internet http://www.liver.ca/Research/Grant_Program
Sponsor Canadian Liver Foundation
2235 Sheppard Ave E, Ste 1500
Toronto, ON M2J 5B5 Canada

CLF Graduate Studentships **1361**
Studentships enable academically superior students to undertake full-time studies in Canadian universities in disciplines relevant to liver function, structure, and disease. Awards are for one academic year and may be renewed three times for a total of four years of support. Registrants in an MS program are restricted to a maximum of three years of support. Guidelines are available from the office or at medical schools through the office of the Dean of the Faculty of Medicine.
Requirements The candidate must be accepted into a full-time university graduate science program in a medically related discipline related to a master's or doctoral degree; hold a record of superior academic performance; and be sponsored by a faculty supervisor with a record of productive medical research and sufficient, competitively acquired research funding to ensure the satisfactory conduct of the student's research during the term of the award.
Amount $C16,500 per year
Date(s) Application Is Due Mar 31.
Contact Billie Potkonjak, (800) 563-5483; fax: (416) 491-4952; email: bpotkonjak@liver.ca
Internet http://www.liver.ca/Research/Grant_Program
Sponsor Canadian Liver Foundation
2235 Sheppard Ave E, Ste 1500
Toronto, ON M2J 5B5 Canada

CLF Operating Grants **1362**
The grants provide funding to help fully qualified and trained hepatologists and basic scientists begin liver research projects in their own laboratories at Canadian universities. Candidates must be prepared to spend 80 percent of their time in research and to commit the remaining time to active participation in teaching and/or patient care.
Requirements Candidates must hold an MD or PhD or equivalent and have a proven interest in liver structure, function, or disease. The applicant must have completed a minimum of two and preferably three years of formal research training (post medical specialty training in the case of MDs) and have obtained additional research experience as a clinical investigator or postdoctoral fellow under the supervision of a well-established, competitively funded, senior basic or clinical scientific faculty colleague who holds a faculty level position.
Amount $C60,000 maximum per year for two years
Date(s) Application Is Due Mar 31.
Contact Research Awards Administrator, (416) 964-1953; fax: (416) 964-0024; email: bpotkonjak@liver.ca
Internet http://www.liver.ca/Research/Grant_Program
Sponsor Canadian Liver Foundation
2235 Sheppard Ave E, Ste 1500
Toronto, ON M2J 5B5 Canada

CMA Foundation Grants **1363**
The foundation seeks to improve the quality of life for central Ohio residents through the promotion of wellness, prevention of disease, and delivery of services and research. The foundation will review funding requests for matching or challenge grants, multiyear commitments, and capital expenditures on a project-by-project basis. The foundation is the leading local source of funding for health care projects benefiting the local community. Application may be made online.
Requirements Nonprofit organizations in central Ohio, including Franklin, Delaware, Fairfield, Licking, Madison, Pickaway, and Union Counties, are eligible.
Contact Program Contact, (614) 240-7410; email: yourthoughts@goodhealthcolumbus.org
Internet http://www.cmaf-ohio.org/cmaf/grants.html
Sponsor Columbus Medical Association Foundation
431 E Broad St
Columbus, OH 43215

CMAP Physician Advocacy Fellowship **1364**
This program supports doctors to develop or enhance their advocacy skills by implementing a project in partnership with an advocacy organization. The fellowship seeks to make advocacy a core professional value for physicians by developing a cadre of advocates with expertise in achieving system or policy-level social change at the local, state, and national level. Projects must be focused within the United States and should identify system or policy level changes as the outcomes of the fellowship work. Application guidelines are available online. Deadline listed is for short proposals; full proposals are by invitation.
Requirements US physicians at all stages of their careers are eligible; however, the most competitive applicants are practicing physicians. Prospective applicants must secure the commitment of an advocacy organization that is prepared to house, mentor, and support them throughout the fellowship period. A list of advocacy organizations that are interested in participating in the fellowship is available online. Applicants also may apply with organizations other than those listed online.
Amount $40,000-$80,000 salary support; $2000 travel funds to MAP-sponsored meetings; $5000 maximum overhead support to organizations
Date(s) Application Is Due Oct 7.
Contact Claudia Calhoon, Program Manager, (212) 342-4769; email: cmc100@columbia.edu
Internet http://www.cmap.columbia.edu/research_fellowship.shtml
Sponsor Columbia University
630 W 168th St, P&S Box 11
New York, NY 10032

CMHC External Research Program Grants for Housing Research **1365**
The objective of this program is to encourage and enable individuals in the private and nonprofit sectors to carry out independent housing research of high quality. Current housing research priority areas include sustainable development, housing in the national/international economy, housing affordability, people with differing needs, rental markets, housing renovation, and building performance and technical innovation. Competitions are held annually following distribution of application brochures. Successful applicants enter into grant agreements with CMHC, the end products of which are research reports, disseminated free of charge to the public by CMHC.
Requirements Financial assistance is provided to Canadian citizens or those having permanent resident status in Canada who are independent housing researchers, as well as to those employed in Canadian universities, institutions, private consulting firms, the professions, and the housing industry.
Restrictions Full-time students at the graduate or undergraduate level are not eligible to apply but may be used as research assistants on the project.
Amount $C25,000 maximum
Date(s) Application Is Due Oct 31.
Contact Administrator, CMHC External Research Program, (613) 748-2300 ext. 3061; fax: (613) 748-2402; email: erp@cmhc-schl.gc.ca
Internet http://www.cmhc-schl.gc.ca/en/prfias/gr/exrepr/index.cfm
Sponsor Canada Mortgage and Housing Corporation
700 Montreal Rd
Ottawa, ON K1A 0P7 Canada

CMS Historically Black Colleges and Universities Health Services Research Grants **1366**
The purpose of the grant program is to support researchers in implementing health services research activities to meet the needs of diverse CMS beneficiary populations. The goals of the grant program are to: 1) encourage HBCU health services researchers to pursue research issues which impact the Medicare, Medicaid, and SCHIP (State Children's Health Insurance Program) programs, 2) assist CMS in implementing its mission focusing on health care quality and improvement for its beneficiaries, 3) assist HBCU researchers by supporting extramural research in health care capacity development activities for the African American communities, 4) increase the pool of HBCU researchers capable of implementing the research, demonstration, and evaluation activities of CMS, and 5) assist in fostering interuniversity communication and collaboration regarding African American health disparity issues. Funding is available for grants to implement research related to health care delivery and health financing issues affecting African American communities, including issues of access to health care, utilization of health care services, health outcomes, quality of services, cost of care, health and racial disparities, socio-economic differences, cultural barriers, managed care systems, and activities related to health screening, prevention, outreach, and education.

Requirements To be eligible for grants under this program, an organization must be an HBCU (Historically Black College or University) and meet one of the following three *Requirements* 1) offer a Ph.D. or Master's Degree Program in one or more of the following disciplines - Allied Health, Gerontology, Health Care Administration, Health Education, Health Management, Nursing, Nutrition, Pharmacology, Public Health, Public Policy, Social Work; or 2) have a School of Medicine; or 3) a member of the National HBCU Network for Health Services and Health Disparities. All proposals should describe research to be conducted with relevance to the CMS Medicare, Medicaid, and SCHIP programs and which area of Healthy People 2010 is served by this project. Applications must be submitted electronically (via grants.gov).
Restrictions Grant funds may not be used for any of the following: to provide direct services to individuals except as explicitly permitted under the grant solicitation; to match any other Federal funds; to provide services, equipment, or supports that are already the legal responsibility of another party under Federal law.
Amount $200,000 - $250,000
Date(s) Application Is Due Jul 2.
Contact Joi Grymes, (410) 786-7251; email: Joi.Grymes@cms.hhs.gov
Internet http://www.cms.hhs.gov/ResearchDemoGrantsOpt/02_Historically_Black_Colleges_and_Universities.asp#TopOfPage
Sponsor Centers for Medicare & Medicaid Services
Office of Acquisition and Grants Management, 7500 Security Boulevard, C2-21-15
Baltimore, MD 21244-1850

CMS Research and Demonstration Grants **1367**
The general purpose of the Centers for Medicare & Medicaid Services' (CMS) research and demonstration program is to conduct and support projects to develop, test, and implement new health care financing and payment policies and to evaluate the impact of the agency's programs on its beneficiaries, providers, States, and other customers and partners. The scope of the agency's activities embraces all areas of health care: costs, access, quality, service delivery models, and financing and payment approaches.
Requirements The following themes represent the agency's current priorities in research. Note that all projects must fall into the agency's statutory authorities to operate and improve Medicare, Medicaid, and other CMS programs and activities: (1) Monitoring and Evaluating CMS Programs; (2) Strengthening Medicaid, State Children's Health Insurance Program (SCHIP), and State Programs; (3) Expanding Beneficiaries' Choices and Availability of Managed Care Options; (4) Developing FFS Payment and Service Delivery Systems; (5) Improving Quality of Care and Performance Under CMS Programs; (6) Improving the Health of Our Beneficiary Population; (7) Prescription Drugs; (8) Building Research Capacity. Application packet is available online.
Restrictions Applicants are expected to contribute towards the project costs. Generally 5 percent of the total project costs is considered acceptable. CMS rarely approves grants or cooperative agreements for research or demonstration projects in which the Federal Government covers 100 percent of the project's costs. The budget may not include costs for construction or remodeling or for project activities that take place before the applicant has received official notification of our approval of the project.
Amount $25,000 - $1,000,000; avg. $235,000
Date(s) Application Is Due none.
Contact Grant Officer, Office of Acquisition and Grants Management; (410) 786-5130; email: Jnorrisl@cms.hhs.gov
Internet http://www.cms.hhs.gov/ResearchDemoGrantsOpt/04_Other_CMS-Grant_Opportunities.asp
Sponsor Centers for Medicare & Medicaid Services
Office of Acquisition and Grants Management, 7500 Security Boulevard, C2-21-15
Baltimore, MD 21244-1850

CMU Arts in Society Fellowship **1368**
The program awards postdoctoral fellowships to scholars and artists in any field of humanistic inquiry or artistic endeavor. Two fellows will be appointed to the Center for the Arts in Society and will be awarded a stipend plus a small research grant. Fellows will teach one undergraduate course each semester that contributes to the center's arts-histories curriculum. Fellows also participate in the work of the center, which sponsors conferences, lectures, and colloquia on various topics, and give one public lecture. Candidates should submit a statement of current research interests as they relate to the current year's fellowship theme; a one-page proposal for a one-semester undergraduate course related to at least two disciplines--one in the arts and one in the humanities; a full curriculum vita; and at least three letters of recommendation. Applications should be submitted by postal mail.
Requirements Scholars and artists who have received their terminal degree within the last four years in any field of humanistic inquiry or artistic endeavor are eligible.
Amount $35,000 stipend plus $5000 research grant
Date(s) Application Is Due Feb 3.
Contact Judith Schachter, Director, (412) 268-3239; email: jm1e@andrew.cmu.edu
Internet http://www.hss.cmu.edu/cas/Content/visiting_fellows.htm
Sponsor Carnegie Mellon University
Dean's Office, BH 154
Pittsburgh, PA 15213

Coastal Bend Community Foundation Grants **1369**
The community foundation awards grants to nonprofit organizations in the Aransas, Bee, Jim Wells, Kleberg, Nueces, Refugio and San Patricio counties of Texas. Grants are usually made to provide seed money for innovative and start-up programs that will generate additional future funding or revenues. Capital projects will also receive favorable consideration. The board of directors approves grant recipients in early November after considering recommendations presented by the Grants Committee. Areas of interest include alcohol and drug abuse, libraries and literacy, arts and culture, higher and other education, adult basic education, child welfare, hospitals, community development, animal welfare, human services, and general charitable giving. Grants are awarded for general operating support, program and project development, equipment, seed money, scholarship funds, and fellowships. Application forms are not required.
Requirements Nonprofit organizations in Texas in Aransas, Bee, Jim Wells, Kleberg, Nueces, Refugio, and San Patricio counties, may submit grant proposals.
Amount $3.4 million total; $250-$50,000
Date(s) Application Is Due Sep 1.
Contact Jim Moloney, Executive Vice President, (361) 882-9745; fax: (361) 882-2865; email: jmoloney@cbcfoundation.org
Internet http://www.cbcfoundation.org/grant.html
Sponsor Coastal Bend Community Foundation
600 Building, Ste 1716
Corpus Christi, TX 78473

Coca-Cola Foundation Grants **1370**
The foundation has established education as its philanthropic focus and set aside most of its funds to support educational initiatives that address pressing needs. To help prepare youth for life, the foundation gives in three areas: higher education--pipeline programs that connect various levels of education and help students stay in school, scholarships, and minority advancement; classroom teaching and learning--innovative K-12 projects, teacher development, and small projects that deal with classroom activities; and global education--projects that encourage international studies, global understanding, and student exchange. Grants are awarded to both public and private institutions at all levels of education: universities, colleges, and secondary and elementary schools. International educational institutions and health care organizations also receive consideration. Types of support include annual campaigns, donated equipment, employee matching gifts, operating budgets, special projects, capital campaigns, continuing support, fellowships, internships, endowment funds, matching funds, and scholarship funds. Proposals may be submitted at any time.
Requirements IRS 501(c)3 nonprofits are eligible.
Restrictions The foundation does not make grants to individuals, religious endeavors, political or fraternal organizations, or organizations without 501(c)3 status.
Amount $25,000-$200,000 average
Date(s) Application Is Due Mar 1; Jun 1; Sep 1; Dec 1.
Contact Executive Director, (404) 676-2568; fax: (404) 676-8804
Internet http://www2.coca-cola.com/citizenship/foundation_guidelines.html
Sponsor Coca-Cola Foundation
P.O. Box 1734
Atlanta, GA 30301

Cockrell Foundation Grants **1371**
The foundation awards grants to Texas nonprofit organizations in its areas of interest, including higher education, cultural programs, social services, youth agencies, religious education and religious welfare, and hospitals. Types of support include annual campaigns, capital campaigns, building construction/renovation, endowment funds, general operating support, program development, fellowships, professorships, scholarship funds, research, and matching grants. There are no application forms or deadline dates. The board meets in the spring and fall each year.
Requirements Texas 501(c)3 nonprofit organizations in Houston are eligible.
Amount Median award in 2005, $12,000
Contact M. Nancy Williams, Executive Vice President, (713) 209-7500; email: foundation@cockrell.com
Internet http://www.cockrell.com/foundation/grant_guidelines.asp
Sponsor Cockrell Foundation
1000 Main St, Ste 3250
Houston, TX 77002

Coeta and Donald Barker Foundation Grants **1372**
The foundation awards grants to California and Oregon nonprofit organizations in its areas of interest, including arts, children and youth, community development, disabled, environmental conservation, family services, federated giving, health care and health organizations, heart and circulatory research, higher education, hospitals, mental health, and secondary school education. Types of support include building construction/renovation, equipment acquisition, general operating support, program development, and scholarship funds.
Requirements California and Oregon nonprofit organizations are eligible.
Restrictions Grants do not support sectarian religious purposes, federal and tax-dependent organizations, individuals, or endowment funds.
Amount $100-$20,450 range
Date(s) Application Is Due Mar 1; Aug 1.
Contact Nancy Harris, Executive Administrator, (760) 324-2656; fax: (760) 321-8662
Sponsor Coeta and Donald Barker Foundation
P.O. Box 936
Rancho Mirage, CA 92270

Coleman Foundation Grants 1373

The foundation awards grants in the Chicago area and the Midwest in the areas of entrepreneurship awareness education; cancer research, care, and treatment in the Midwest; housing and education for the disabled; religion (Christian, interdenominational, Lutheran, Methodist, Presbyterian, and Roman Catholic); and a wide range of other educational programs. Types of support include general operating expenses, projects, research, conferences and seminars, building funds, equipment, land acquisition, professorships, internships, scholarship funds, fellowships, capital campaigns, renovation projects, endowment funds, emergency funds, continuing support, matching funds, and program-related investments. Letters of interest are accepted. Full proposals will be invited at the request of the foundation.
Requirements Nonprofits across the Midwest are eligible. Preference is given to requests from Illinois and Chicago.
Restrictions The program does not fund for-profit businesses, individuals, individual scholarships, ad books, tickets, equipment purchases (including computer hardware or software), or advertising.
Contact Michael Hennessy, President, (312) 902-7120; fax: (312) 902-7124; email: coleman@colemanfoundation.org
Internet http://www.colemanfoundation.org/index1.html
Sponsor Coleman Foundation, Inc
651 W. Washington Blvd, Ste 306
Chicago, IL 60661

College Art Association Professional Development Fellowships 1374

The fellowship provides two years of funding: a grant in the first, and in the second, CAA provides assistance in securing employment or an internship at a museum, university, or art center and subsidizes the position. Contact the office to request an application form. Applications will also be available in most art and art history graduate departments.
Requirements Artists and art historians from culturally diverse backgrounds who have been underrepresented in the field due to their race, religion, gender, age, national origin, sexual orientation, disability, or history of economic disadvantage who demonstrate distinction in approach, technique, or perspective in their contribution to the discipline of art or art history and will receive the MFA, terminal MA, or PhD degree in the current funding year, who can demonstrate financial need, and who are citizens or permanent residents of the United States are eligible to apply.
Amount $5000 for the first year
Date(s) Application Is Due Jan 31.
Contact Stacy Miller, (212) 619-1051 ext 242; fax: (212) 627-2381; email: smiller@collegeart.org or fellowship@collegeart.org
Internet http://www.collegeart.org/caa/career/fellowship.html
Sponsor College Art Association
275 Seventh Ave
New York, NY 10001

College of Human Sciences Scholarships 1375

Human sciences undergraduate and graduate scholarships are available in the College of Human Sciences at Texas Tech University. Programs include human development and family studies, marriage and family therapy, interior design, merchandising, family financial planning, clothing and textiles, restaurant/hotel management, food and nutrition, early childhood, family and consumer sciences education, consumer economics, environmental design, and fashion design. Application deadline is February 1 unless specifically stated otherwise. Check Web site for current details and criteria of available scholarships.
Requirements Scholarships are awarded only to students who have officially applied to Texas Tech University. Unless the scholarship award is for multiple years, students are required to resubmit scholarship applications during the spring semester to be eligible for renewal of their scholarship.
Amount $200-$2000 generally
Date(s) Application Is Due Feb 1.
Contact Beverly Pinson, Coordinator, Human Sciences Scholarship Committee, (806) 742-3031; email: beverly.pinson@ttu.edu
Internet http://www.hs.ttu.edu/aas/scholarships/default.php
Sponsor Texas Tech University, College of Human Sciences
Box 41162
Lubbock, TX 79409-1162

College of Saint Rose Dissertation Fellowships 1376

The college supports two minority scholars in the completion of dissertations leading to a doctoral degree. In addition to completing the dissertation by the end of the year, fellows will teach one course, usually in their discipline. They will discuss their research and work with Saint Rose faculty and students at selected events throughout the year. After successful completion of the fellowship year, fellows will be invited to apply for full-time faculty positions. To apply, submit a letter of application, curriculum vita, and contact information of three references.
Requirements Eligibility requirements include: record of outstanding academic achievement; member of historically underrepresented racial or ethnic group, including, but not limited to: African Americans, Alaskan Natives, American Indians or Native Americans, Asian Americans, Latino/as, Chicano/as, and Pacific Islanders; enrollment in a full-time academic program leading to the doctoral degree at the time of application; admission to degree candidacy before the dissertation fellowship is awarded; approval of dissertation proposal by the applicant's committee prior to application; and US citizenship.
Amount $20,000 stipend; $5000 research expenses
Date(s) Application Is Due Nov 15.
Contact Dr. Davide Szcerbacki, Provost, email: szcerbd@strose.edu
Internet http://www.strose.edu
Sponsor College of Saint Rose
432 Western Ave
Albany, NY 12203

Colonel Stanley R. McNeil Foundation Grants 1377

The foundation awards grants to eligible Illinois nonprofit organizations in its areas of interest, including child welfare, education, health care, and youth. Types of support include building construction/renovation, equipment acquisition, general operating support, matching grants, research, and special projects. There are no application deadlines or forms.
Requirements Illinois nonprofit organizations serving the Chicago metropolitan area are eligible.
Restrictions Grants are not made to individuals.
Amount $7000-$250,000 range
Contact Charles Slamar, Jr., Vice President, Bank of America, (312) 828-8028
Sponsor Colonel Stanley R. McNeil Foundation
231 S LaSalle St
Chicago, IL 60697-0246

Columbia Earth Institute Postdoctoral Fellowships 1378

The institute seeks applications from innovative postdoctoral candidates interested in pathbreaking disciplinary research as well as multidisciplinary initiatives on sustainable development issues. The program provides young scholars with the opportunity to enhance their foundation in one of the institute's core disciplines--earth sciences, biological sciences, engineering sciences, social sciences, and health sciences--while at the same time acquiring the cross-disciplinary expertise and breadth needed to address critical issues related to reducing poverty, hunger, disease, and environmental degradation, placing special emphasis on the needs of the world's poor. Application and guidelines are available online. The institute prefers applicants to apply online.
Requirements Candidates are asked to submit a proposal for research, based in one of the core disciplines, that will contribute to the goal of global sustainable development. Applicants also are requested to indicate the general direction of multidisciplinary training and research opportunities that they would like to pursue at the Earth Institute.
Date(s) Application Is Due Dec 1.
Contact Program Coordinator, (212) 854-3893; fax: (212) 854-6309; email: hd6@columbia.edu
Internet http://www.earthinstitute.columbia.edu/postdoc
Sponsor Columbia University
2910 Broadway, B-16 Hogan Hall, MC 3277
New York, NY 10025

Columbia Foundation Grants Program 1379

The foundation currently has three program areas: arts and culture, human rights, and sustainable communities and economies. Types of support include general operating support, program development, publication, seed money, and research. Multiyear grants are made on occasion. A complete application includes application, one-page proposal summary, proposal not to exceed five pages, budgets, funding sources, board of directors, certificate of tax-exempt status, and other descriptive materials. The board of directors generally meets twice a year to consider grant applications. Applicants should submit a one- to two-page inquiry letter with cover sheet. Proposals are invited from the foundation. The deadline is May 1 for arts and culture grants; August 1 for human rights grants; and December 1 for sustainable communities and economies grants. Annual deadlines may vary; contact program staff for exact dates.
Requirements The foundation considers proposals only from organizations certified by the IRS as public charities. Priority will be given to applications from the San Francisco Bay, CA, area. International grants support the arts in London.
Restrictions The foundation does not customarily provide support for operating budgets of established agencies, recurring expenses for direct services or ongoing administrative costs, individual fellowships or scholarships, or agencies wholly supported by federated campaigns or heavily subsidized by government funds.
Amount $25,000-$100,000
Date(s) Application Is Due May 1; Aug 1; Dec 1.
Contact Susan Clark, Executive Director, (415) 561-6880; fax: (415) 561-6883; email: info@columbia.org
Internet http://www.columbia.org
Sponsor Columbia Foundation
P.O. Box 29470
San Francisco, CA 94129

Columbia University Center for Comparative Literature and Society Postdoctoral Fellowship 1380

The main purpose of the center is to rethink comparative literary and cultural studies in their relation to area studies and the historically oriented social sciences. The fellow will be given time and resources to develop his or her scholarship in a broadening and

experimental cross-disciplinary and cross-regional context. The fellow will join an intellectually vibrant community of scholars from the humanities, the social sciences, architecture, and law affiliated with the center.
Requirements Applicants must have received the PhD between January 1, 1999, and July 1, 2005, to be eligible.
Amount $41,000 stipend, $1000 travel
Date(s) Application Is Due Oct 15.
Contact Director, Center for Comparative Literature and Society, (212) 854-4541; fax: (212) 662-7289; email: ccls@columbia.edu
Internet http://www.columbia.edu/cu/ccls/academics/postdocs/intro/index.html
Sponsor Columbia University
2960 Broadway, MC 5700
New York, NY 10027

Columbia University Society of Fellows in the Humanities 1381
The Columbia Society of Fellows, with support from the Andrew W. Mellon Foundation and the Kenan Trust, will appoint a number of postdoctoral fellows in the humanities. The society seeks to enhance the role of the humanities in the university by exploring and clarifying the interrelationship within the humanities, as well as their relationship to the natural and social sciences. The appointment as fellow, considered as equivalent to the rank of lecturer, is for one year with the expectation of renewal for a second year. The award covers costs of independent research and for teaching in the undergraduate program in general education. Normal fringe benefits will be added. Additional funds are available to support research.
Requirements Applicants must have received their PhD between January 1 and July 1.
Amount $50,000 stipend
Date(s) Application Is Due Oct 1.
Contact Judy Huyck, (212) 854-4631; fax: (212) 854-4069; email: sof-fellows@columbia.edu
Internet http://ci.columbia.edu/w0250/fellowship.html
Sponsor Columbia University
2960 Broadway, Mail Code 5700
New York, NY 10027

Columbus Foundation Ann Ellis Fund Grants 1382
The Fund is used for eye research, with primary emphasis on sponsoring scientific research on the diagnosis, prevention, and treatment of glaucoma. Once this is accomplished, the fund will assist in the research of other hidden eye problems. For more information, please contact the Community Research and Grant Management Department at the Foundation
Restrictions Individuals are ineligible. Requests for religious purposes, budget deficits, endowments, conferences, or projects that are normally the responsibility of a public agency are generally not funded.
Contact Grant Management Department, (614) 251-4000; fax: (614) 251-4009; email: tcfinfo@columbusfoundation.org
Internet http://www.columbusfoundation.org/GD/Templates/Pages/TCF/TCFSecondary.aspx?page=73
Sponsor Columbus Foundation
1234 East Broad Street
Columbus, OH 43205

Commonfund Endowment Management Prize 1383
Commonfund, which manages the world's largest pool of endowment and cash assets for universities, colleges, independent schools, and health care facilities, sponsors this competition for research and scholarship in the advancement of endowment management. The prize is awarded in two installments--upon announcement of the winner and upon acceptance of the final paper. This paper will be published and distributed by Commonfund. The winner is announced in March.
Requirements Applicants must submit a sample completed paper or working paper written for an academic or other audience, a proposal of 1000 words or less outlining how the applicant would develop a derivative paper written for the endowment management audience, and a curriculum vita.
Amount $50,000
Date(s) Application Is Due Dec 31.
Contact John Griswold Jr., Senior Vice President, (203) 563-5185; email: jgriswol@cfund.org
Internet http://www.commonfund.org/Commonfund/About+Us/pillars_educational_programs_2004.htm
Sponsor Commonfund
P.O. Box 812, 15 Old Danbury Rd
Wilton, CT 06897-7717

Commonweal Foundation Community Assistance Grants 1384
The foundation supports educational programs and projects assisting disadvantaged, at-risk youth. The foundation focuses on secondary and, to a lesser extent, elementary education. The foundation also considers grants for educational research and, to a limited extent, health care. Guidelines are available online.
Requirements 501(c)3 tax-exempt organizations located in the District of Columbia, Maryland, or Northern Virginia are eligible. Applicant organizations should have an annual budget not exceeding $1 million.
Amount $25,000 maximum
Date(s) Application Is Due Mar 1; Aug 1.
Contact Gloria Dairsow, (240) 450-0000; fax: (240) 450-4115; email: gdairsow@cweal.org
Internet http://www.cweal.org/cag.htm
Sponsor Commonweal Foundation
10770 Columbia Pike, Ste 150
Silver Spring, MD 20901

Commonweal Foundation Grants 1385
The foundation awards grants to eligible nonprofit organizations serving disadvantaged youth in the area comprising the corridor between Baltimore, MD, and Washington, DC. It also offers some assistance to elementary education, educational research, and some health care causes. Programs include Partners in Learning (address low literacy skills of economically disadvantaged children), community assistance grants (i.e., after-school tutoring, parenting classes, and shelters for the homeless or abused women), and learning disabilities support program (special education services to economically disadvantaged children). Contact the office for application procedures.
Requirements 501(c)3 tax-exempt organizations serving disadvantaged youth in the corridor between Baltimore, MD, and Washington, DC, are eligible.
Amount $10,000-$25,000
Date(s) Application Is Due Feb 1; May 1; Aug 1; Nov 1.
Contact Renee Cottman-Reyes, (240) 450-0000; fax: (240) 450-4115; email: gdairsow@cweal.org
Internet http://www.commonweal-foundation.org/index.html
Sponsor Commonweal Foundation
10770 Columbia Pke, Ste 150
Silver Spring, MD 20901

Commonwealth Fund Grants 1386
The fund awards grants for projects in its three major program areas: international health care policy and practice; improving the quality of health care services; and improving insurance coverage and access to care. Types of support include employee-matching gifts, program development, program evaluation, and research. Preference is given to projects that seek to solve problems, especially those affecting vulnerable groups; that analyze the effects of policies and trends on well-defined health issues; and that develop and test practical solutions. Prospective grantees should submit a letter of inquiry via regular or electronic mail. Program staff will contact applicants if more detailed information is required. Proposals recommended by fund staff are reviewed and voted upon by the board of directors, which meets in July, April, and November. Letters of inquiry should be brief, no more than two pages.
Requirements The fund makes grants only to tax-exempt organizations and public agencies.
Restrictions The fund does not support general planning and ongoing activities or existing deficits; endowment or capital costs, including construction, renovation, or equipment; basic biomedical research; conferences, symposia, major media projects or documentaries, unless they are an outgrowth of one of the fund's programs; individuals; scholarships; churches or other religious organizations, unless the project is entirely secular in nature; or work for which achievements cannot be measured.
Contact Andrea Landes, Director of Grants Management, (212) 606-3800; fax: (212) 606-3508; email: acl@cmwf.org
Internet http://www.cmwf.org/grantseekers/index.asp?link=4
Sponsor Commonwealth Fund
1 E 75th St
New York, NY 10021-2608

Commonwealth Fund/Harvard University Fellowship in Minority Health Policy 1387
The program is designed to prepare physicians, particularly minority physicians, for leadership roles in formulating and implementing public health policy and practice on a national, state, or local level. Under the auspices of the Minority Faculty Development Program at Harvard Medical School, five one-year fellowships will be awarded per year. Fellows will complete academic work leading to a master's level degree and, through additional program activities, gain exposure to and understanding of the major health issues facing minority and disadvantaged populations. It is expected that the fellowship will support the development of a cadre of leaders in minority health, well-trained academically and professionally in public health, health policy, health management, and clinical medicine, as well as committed to pursuing careers in public service.
Requirements Applicants are required to complete applications to both the Commonwealth Fund/Harvard University Fellowship in Minority Health Policy and the Harvard School of Public Health. Applicants must have finished residency and be US citizens.
Amount $50,000 stipend
Date(s) Application Is Due Jan 3.
Contact CFHUF Program Coordinator, c/o Minority Faculty Development Program, email: mfdp_cfhuf@hms.harvard.edu
Internet http://www.cmwf.org/fellowships/fellowships.htm
Sponsor Commonwealth Fund
164 Longwood Ave, 2nd Fl
Boston, MA 02115-5818

Communities Foundation of Texas Grants **1388**

The unrestricted funds of the foundation support programs and projects intended to improve the quality of life for the citizens of the Dallas, TX, area. The funds support education, health and hospitals, social services, youth, and cultural programs. The foundation encourages projects developed in consultation with other agencies and planning groups and that promote coordination, cooperation, and sharing among organizations. Types of support include seed grants, emergency funds, building funds, equipment acquisition, matching funds, technical assistance, research, capital campaigns, and operating budgets. Requests for operating funds generally are not granted.
Requirements 501(c)3 organizations in the Dallas, TX, area may apply.
Restrictions Grants are not made to or for individuals, endowments, sectarian religious purposes, political or lobbying efforts, deficit financing, media projects, or for operational expenses of established organizations.
Date(s) Application Is Due Jan 15; Sep 14.
Contact Leslie Parks, (214) 750-4222; fax: (214) 750-4210; email: Rdear@cftexas.org
Internet http://www.cftexas.org
Sponsor Communities Foundation of Texas
5500 Caruth Haven Ln
Dallas, TX 75225-8146

Community Campus Partnerships for Health Fellowships **1389**

Community-based professionals, academic administrators, and faculty with significant knowledge and expertise in building and sustaining service-learning, community-based participatory research, and community-campus partnerships are encouraged to apply for a fellowship with CCPH. The expected outcome of the program is to advance and support these concepts in the context of health professions education and practice. Fellows will receive a stipend for a one-year fellowship period, with the potential for a second year of funding. Funding provides support for time spent participating in fellow-related activities. Fellows also receive a certificate of recognition upon completing the fellowship. Application procedures and additional information are available online.
Requirements CCPH members and nonmembers are eligible.
Amount $5000
Contact Sarena Seifer, Executive Director, (206) 616-4305; fax: (206) 685-6747; email: sarena@u.washington.edu or ccphuw@u.washington.edu
Internet http://depts.washington.edu/ccph
Sponsor Community Campus Partnerships for Health
UW Box 354809
Seattle, WA 98195-4809

Community Foundation AIDS Endowment Awards **1390**

The foundation administers an annual special grants program called the AIDS Endowment Awards. Grants of $1,000 will be awarded to one or two organizations that demonstrate a commitment to working towards the prevention, education and treatment of AIDS so that they may continue their efforts. Services provided could include education programs for the prevention of HIV/AIDS, medical and social services for those living with HIV/AIDS, housing services for those living with HIV/AIDS and medical research for the treatment and prevention of HIV/AIDS.
Requirements Selected organizations in the metropolitan Richmond area interested in the field of AIDS education, research or community service and care are encouraged to apply. Organizations interested in applying should submit a brief proposal to foundation which should be no more than two single-spaced pages and include: [1] a description of the organization's mission; and [2] a description of the agency's work in the field of AIDS. Include a list of Board of Governors, a copy of the most recent IRS Form 990, an audited financial statement if available, and an IRS Tax Exempt Letter designating your organization a 501(c)(3) non-profit.
Amount $1,000
Date(s) Application Is Due Feb 15.
Contact Susan Hallett, Program Officer, (804) 330-7400; fax: (804) 330-5992; email: shallett@tcfrichmond.org
Internet http://www.tcfrichmond.org/Page2954.cfm
Sponsor Community Foundation Serving Richmond and Central Virginia
7501 Boulders View Drive, Suite 110
Richmond, VA 23225

Community Foundation for Greater Buffalo Grants **1391**

Grants are made to organizations in and for the benefit of Erie County, NY, residents. The foundation supports charitable, educational, and civic purposes and awards grants for educational institutions, scholarships, family and child health and welfare, and community development. Highest priority is given to projects that support creative and innovative responses to existing or emerging community problems.
Requirements IRS 509(a) organizations in or benefiting residents of Allegany, Cattaraugus, Chautauqua, Erie, Genesee, Niagara, Orleans, and Wyoming Counties, NY, are eligible.
Restrictions Grant requests are not considered for endowment funds, religious purposes, projects outside the western New York region, or schools not registered with the state education department.
Amount $1000-$25,000 typically
Date(s) Application Is Due Feb 1; Aug 1.
Contact Jean McKeown, Program Officer, (716) 852-2857, ext. 204; fax: (716) 852-2861; email: jeanm@cfgb.org
Internet http://www.cfgb.org/page17000.cfm
Sponsor Community Foundation for Greater Buffalo
712 Main St
Buffalo, NY 14202

Community Foundation for Muskegon County Grants **1392**

The community foundation was established to serve the needs of the people of Muskegon County and nearby western Michigan. The foundation's strategic plan for grant making focuses on the prevention of problems rather than the cure; encourages programs that are collaborative, comprehensive, and have the potential to be continuous; encourages leveraging and matching grant opportunities from multiple funders; and supports seed money opportunities for innovative projects. Major grant interest areas include the arts, community development and urban revitalization, education, environment, health/ human services, and needs of young children (ages 0-3). Types of support include seed money grants, special projects, matching funds, equipment, scholarship funds, loans, research, publications, conferences and seminars, endowment funds, consulting services, continuing support, emergency funds, internships, professorships, and renovation projects. Although the foundation generally makes one-year grant commitments, it will consider making longer term commitments for new efforts that show strong promise for positive impact.
Requirements IRS 501(c)3 organizations and institutions in Muskegon County and nearby western Michigan are eligible.
Restrictions Support will not be provided for routine operating expenses; capital equipment, computer hardware and software, and motor vehicles; conferences, publications, videos, films, television, or radio programs; endowment campaigns; special fund-raising events; religious programs that serve specific denominations; existing obligations or debts; individual schools or districts; or individuals.
Amount $250-$50,000 average
Contact Gina Van Bruggen or Arn Boezaart, Program Officers, (231) 722-4538; fax: (231) 722-4616; email: gvanbruggen@cffmc.org or aboezaart@cffmc.org
Internet http://www.cffmc.org/grantapply.php
Sponsor Community Foundation for Muskegon County
425 W Western Ave, Ste 200
Muskegon, MI 49440

Community Foundation for Southern Arizona Grants **1393**

The foundation awards grants in southern Arizona for a broad array of charitable purposes in the areas of arts and humanities, education, the environment, health, social services. Types of support include challenge/matching grants, conferences and seminars, scholarships, equipment acquisition, fellowships, general support, multiyear support, project development, publications, research, seed funding, and technical assistance. Priority is given to proposals that promote collaboration and build on the strengths of individuals and communities. Deadlines are determined on a yearly basis.
Requirements Nonprofit and grassroots organizations in southern Arizona communities are eligible. Southern Arizona communities include all of Cochise, Santa Cruz, and Pima Counties; and the areas of Yuma, Mariposa, Pinal, Graham, and Greenlee Counties that lie south of the Gila River.
Restrictions Funds are generally not available for ongoing operating or capital campaigns, debt retirement, endowments, individuals, individual schools, sectarian activities, or underwriting of fund-raising events.
Amount $1000-$10,000 average range
Contact Barbara Brown, Executive Vice President, (520) 770-0800 ext 107; fax: (520) 770-1500; email: bbrown@CFSoAZ.org
Internet http://www.cfsoaz.org/page17480.cfm
Sponsor Community Foundation for Southern Arizona
2250 E Broadway Blvd
Tucson, AZ 85719

Community Foundation of Broward Grants **1394**

Through its competitive grantmaking process, the foundation supports programs that strengthen families within low socioeconomic communities in Florida's Broward County. Grantmaking priorities include the arts, foster care, out-of-school time, and technology. Proposals also are accepted in specific areas of interest, including animal welfare--protect and educate; cancer and arthritis research--finding a cure; patient care--relief and assistance to individuals with cancer or other terminal diseases; literacy--opening worlds through language, an AIDS/HIV--through issued RFP. Proposals are accepted anytime throughout the year. Application and guidelines are available online.
Requirements 501(c)3 organizations, public charities as defined by the IRS code, and governmental agencies located in Broward County or directly benefiting the residents of Broward County are eligible.
Restrictions Grants are not awarded in the following areas: annual fundraising, capital campaign/improvements, deficit financing, endowment efforts, grants to individuals, religious purposes, or routine operating needs.
Amount $10,000 average
Contact Sheri Brown, Vice President of Strategic Community Initiatives, (954) 761-9503 ext 103; fax: (954) 761-7102; email: jbull@cfbroward.org
Internet http://www.cfbroward.org/new/grant.html
Sponsor Community Foundation of Broward
1401 E Broward Blvd, Ste 100
Fort Lauderdale, FL 33301

Community Foundation of Champaign County Grants 1395

The community foundation awards grants from its unrestricted funds to Champaign County, IL, nonprofit organizations to use for charitable purposes. Representative categories include arts and humanities, environmental concerns, education, health, human services, research, urban affairs, church, and youth programs. Types of support include continuing support, annual campaigns, building/renovation, equipment, publication, consulting services, and scholarships.

Requirements Champaign County, IL, nonprofit organizations are eligible.
Amount $1000-$2000 typically
Date(s) Application Is Due Aug 31.
Contact Joan Dixon, Executive Director, (217) 359-0125; fax: (217) 352-6494; email: cfcc@soltec.net
Sponsor Community Foundation of Champaign County
404 W Church St
Champaign, IL 61820

Community Foundation of Greater Tampa Grants 1396

Program interests of the foundation include arts and culture, community enablement, education, environment and animals, health and human services, history, neighborhoods, senior citizens, and youth and families.

Requirements Florida 501(c)3 organizations in Hillsborough, Pasco and Pinellas counties are eligible.
Restrictions Political causes/organizations will not be supported. Grants also will not be made to purchase tickets or advertising space in programs or other publications. The foundation generally is not interested in capital campaigns, funding of operating costs, experimental medical research, religious or sectarian purposes, loans, or multiple year funding.
Date(s) Application Is Due Mar 1; Sep 1.
Contact Paula Fraher, Grants Director, (813) 282-1975; fax; (813) 282-3119; email: pfraher@cftampabay.org
Internet http://www.cftampabay.org/Grants/grants_process.htm
Sponsor Community Foundation of Greater Tampa
4950 W Kennedy Blvd, Ste 250
Tampa, FL 33609

Community Foundation of the Fox River Valley 1397

The foundation awards full-time scholarships to graduating high school seniors, undergraduate college students, and graduate school students within its service area, comprising the City of Aurora, Kendall County, and southern Kane County in the State of Illinois. The residency requirement does not apply to graduating high school students whose parent(s) are employed by Nicor Gas; graduating high school students residing within Community High School District 94, West Chicago; and graduating community/junior college students whose parent(s) are employed by a company that maintains membership with the Valley Industrial Association. The majority of scholarships are based on academic ability and financial need. Some awards are renewable. Students who attend the following high schools must obtain applications from their high school guidance office (deadline date for applications determined by the school): Aurora Central Catholic, Aurora Christian, East Aurora, Hinckley-Big Rock, IMSA Kaneland, Marmion, Oswego, Plano, Rosary Waubonsie Valley, West Aurora, and Yorkville High School. All other students may obtain an application by calling the office. The deadline date for receipt of applications is generally mid-February.

Requirements Eligibility is restricted to students who will be attending school on a full-time basis and whose permanent residence is within the foundation's service area. The foundation's service area includes the City of Aurora, Kendall County, and southern Kane County in the state of Illinois.
Amount $1000-$3000
Contact Rhonda Soos, (630) 896-7800; email: rsoos@communityfoundationFRV.org
Internet http://www.CommunityFoundationFRV.org
Sponsor Community Foundation of the Fox River Valley
111 W Downer Pl, Ste 312
Aurora, IL 60506-6106

Community Foundation of the Napa Valley Grants 1398

The foundation awards one-year grants to preserve the assets of the community and to fill gaps in funding to Napa Valley nonprofit agencies and organizations. Grants may be renewed. Applicants should send a letter of inquiry outlining the organization, the program, and amount requested. Letters of inquiry should be submitted three months in advance of the project start date.

Requirements California 501(c)3 organizations serving the Napa Valley are eligible.
Contact Patricia Struntz, Executive Director, (707) 254-9565; fax: (707) 254-7955; email: info@cfnv.org
Internet http://www.cfnv.org/grant/grantguide.html
Sponsor Community Foundation of the Napa Valley
433 Soscol Ave, Ste B-151
Napa, CA 94559

Community Health Scholars Program Fellowships 1399

The Community Health Scholars Program (CHSP) is a postdoctoral fellowship program designed to meet the growing needs of schools of public health and other health professions for faculty with community competency. The 12-month fellowship enables scholars to develop and enhance skills in working with communities and engaging in participatory community-based research at institutions where these skills are present. Applications are welcome from junior faculty as well as those recently completing doctoral-level training so long as the above eligibility requirements are met. Women and other underrepresented groups are encouraged to apply.

Requirements Applicants must be US citizens located at one of three training sites (Johns Hopkins, University of Michigan, or University of North Carolina) and have completed all formal requirements for professional and postprofessional training (e.g., internships or residencies) at the doctoral level (e.g., PhD, MD, JD, or DrPH) by the date of entry into the program.
Restrictions Scholars may not hold other training fellowships or be enrolled full time in another degree program during their tenure in this program.
Amount $50,000 fellowship award plus $10,000 research fund
Contact Saundra Bailey, Program Administrator, (734) 647-3065; fax: (734) 936-0927; email: chsp@umich.edu
Internet http://www.sph.umich.edu/chsp
Sponsor University of Michigan
109 Observatory St, M4142
Ann Arbor, MI 48109-2029

Comprehensive Health Education Foundation Grants 1400

The foundation awards grants to support programs that address health inequities. The initial grantmaking effort will focus on Clark, Pierce, and Spokane Counties in Washington State. One-year grants of up to $20,000 each will be awarded to culturally appropriate, community-led collaborations to test their best idea on how to make it easier for people who suffer from health inequities to move more and eat healthier. Health inequities are defined as differences in the incidence, prevalence, mortality, and burden of diseases that exist for specific populations in the United States. Low-income individuals and people of color within the United States generally have higher rates of poor health and injury than those who are in higher-income groups and are Caucasian.

Requirements 501(c)3 tax-exempt organizations located in Clark, Pierce, and Spokane Counties in Washington State and units of government that are nondiscriminatory in policy and practice regarding disabilities, age, sex, sexual orientation, race, ethnic origin, or creed are eligible.
Restrictions Support will not be provided for building or land acquisitions; equipment or furniture purchases; endowment funds; emergency funds; grants to individuals; fellowships/scholarships; research; debt retirement; fundraising activities; general fund drives; indirect overhead; or CHEF programs or products.
Amount $500-$20,000 typically
Date(s) Application Is Due Jun 15.
Contact Kari L. Lewis, (206) 824-2907 or (800) 323-2433; fax: (206) 824-3072; email: KariL@chef.org
Internet http://www.chef.org/about/grants.php
Sponsor Comprehensive Health Education Foundation
22419 Pacific Hwy S
Seattle, WA 98198-5106

Compton Foundation Grants Program 1401

The foundation was founded to address community, national, and international concerns in the fields of peace and world order, population, and the environment. Other concerns of the foundation include equal educational opportunity, community welfare and social justice, and culture and the arts. The foundation makes three kinds of grants. Project grants generally are made to national organizations for projects that fall within the primary areas of peace and world order, population, and the environment. The grants may be for regional (Pacific Coastal states), national, or international activities and are usually for projects of limited duration. Project grants are considered by the board two times a year. Discretionary grants are made at the discretion, and usually at the initiation, of individual board members. Most grants in this area are made for community welfare and social justice, and culture and the arts. Renewal grants provide general support to organizations whose activities have been funded by the foundation for many years and whose work continues to be considered particularly effective by the board. Many of the foundation's grants in the area of equal educational opportunity, and some grants in peace and world order and population, are renewal grants.

Requirements The foundation makes grants only to tax-exempt organizations and institutions.
Restrictions Grants will not be made to individuals.
Amount $5000-$50,000 average
Date(s) Application Is Due Mar 15; Sep 7.
Contact Edith Eddy, Executive Director, (650) 508-1181; fax: (650) 508-1191; email: info@comptonfoundation.org
Internet http://www.comptonfoundation.org/application.html
Sponsor Compton Foundation
255 Shoreline Dr, Ste 540
Redwood City, CA 94065

Compton Foundation Mentor Fellowships 1402

The fellowship program focuses on graduating college students from the United States. This program is designed to promote creativity and support the commitment of graduating seniors as they move beyond academic preparation to real-world application and contribution. Each year five fellows are selected from participating universities and

awarded a one-year, fellowship. The stipend is to implement a self-directed project, contributing their talents and energy to real-world situations. At the core of the fellowship is the partnership between a fellow and a mentor, who provides guidance, encouragement, and impetus for continued learning and service.
Amount $35,000
Contact Edith Eddy, Executive Director, (650) 328-0101; fax: (650) 328-0171; email: info@comptonfoundation.org
Internet http://www.comptonfoundation.org/mentor_fellowship.html
Sponsor Compton Foundation
535 Middlefield Rd, Ste 160
Menlo Park, CA 94025

Computing in Chemical Engineering Award **1403**
The award, which is sponsored by Mitsubishi Chemical Company and the Dow Chemical Company, recognizes outstanding contributions in the application of computing and systems technology to chemical engineering. All members as well as other interested persons are urged to nominate deserving candidates. All information and supporting documentation are to be included with completed forms. Nominations will remain active for three years. The awardee is invited to deliver an address at a CAST Division luncheon or dinner at the AIChE annual meeting.
Amount $3000
Date(s) Application Is Due Apr 15.
Contact AIChE Awards Programs, (212) 591-7107; fax: (212) 591-8882; email: awards@aiche.org
Internet http://www.aiche.org/awards/awarddtl.asp?AwardID=28
Sponsor American Institute of Chemical Engineers
3 Park Ave
New York, NY 10016-5901

Conference on Latin American History Prize **1404**
The prize is awarded annually for a distinguished English-language article on any significant aspect of Latin American history published in the year preceding the award and appearing in journals edited or published in the United States, including Puerto Rico (exclusive of the Hispanic American Historical Review), the Journal of Latin American Studies (Cambridge), or in volumes of collected articles.
Amount $500
Contact CLAH, University of California at Davis, (530) 752-3046; fax: (530) 752-8964; email: clah@ucdavis.edu
Internet http://www.h-net.msu.edu/~clah/about/index.html
Sponsor Conference on Latin American History
One Shields Ave
Davis, CA 95616

Congressional Fellowships for African Americans **1405**
This program is a comprehensive, nine-month paid fellowship designed to prepare minority graduate students and professionals for senior-level careers in the public policy arena. The goal of the program is twofold: to offer talented people the opportunity to learn all aspects of policy development by working on congressional committees and to produce scholarly research on critical issues before the US Congress. The program includes an in-depth orientation to Capitol Hill; a nationally recognized lecture series with policy experts including members of Congress; an educational enrichment component that complements practical work experiences; and a professional development component under the guidance of a mentor. Application forms are available on the Web site.
Requirements To be considered, an applicant must be a full-time graduate student; an individual with five years of professional work experience presently pursuing part-time graduate studies; or a college faculty member with a demonstrated interest in the legislative or public policy process. All applicants must be US citizens who have demonstrated commitment to black political empowerment.
Amount $25,000
Date(s) Application Is Due Apr 2.
Contact Program Contact, (800) 784-2577 or (202) 263-2800; fax: (202) 775-0773; email: info@cbcfinc.org
Internet http://cbcfinc.org/Leadership%20Education/Fellowships/congressional.html
Sponsor Congressional Black Caucus Foundation
1720 Massachusetts Ave NW
Washington, DC 20036

Congressional Hispanic Caucus Institute Fellowships **1406**
Every year, the fellowship program offers up to 21 promising Latinos from across the country the opportunity to gain hands-on experience at the national level in the public policy area of their choice. Fellows have the opportunity to work in such areas as international affairs, economic development, education policy, housing, or local government. CHCI also aims to develop leaders in the areas of public health administration (Edward Roybal Public Health Fellowship), telecommunications policy (Telecommunications Fellowship), financial services (Financial Services Fellowship), and corporate-public interest (Corporate Fellowship). Fellowships include domestic round-trip transportation to Washington, DC; health insurance; and a monthly stipend to help cover housing and local expenses. Annual deadline dates may vary; contact program staff for exact dates.
Requirements Applicants must have a BA/BS or graduate degree within one year of the application deadline or be currently enrolled as graduate students. US citizenship is required.
Restrictions Relatives of CHCI staff or of its board of directors are not eligible.
Amount $2061 monthly stipend; $2500 monthly fee to fellows with a graduate degree
Date(s) Application Is Due Mar 1.
Contact Fellowships Administrator, (800) 392-3532 or (202) 543-1771; fax: (202) 546-2143; email: chci@chci.org
Internet http://www.chci.org/chciyouth/fellowship/fellowshipprogram.htm
Sponsor Congressional Hispanic Caucus Institute
911 Second St NE
Washington, DC 20002

Congressional Research Awards Program **1407**
The center's primary interest is to fund the study of the leadership in the Congress, both House and Senate. Topics could include external factors shaping the exercise of congressional leadership, institutional conditions affecting it, resources and techniques used by leaders, and the prospects for change or continuity in the patterns of leadership. The program was developed to support work intended for publication in some form or for application in a teaching or policy-making setting. Types of support include seed grants, travel grants, and dissertation/thesis research support. Grants will normally extend for one year.
Requirements The competition is open to individuals with a serious interest in studying Congress. Political scientists, historians, biographers, scholars of public administration or American studies, and journalists are among those eligible. The center encourages graduate students to apply.
Restrictions Grants will not be awarded for purchase of equipment or for subsidizing publication costs. Organizations are not eligible, and the award does not fund undergraduate or pre-PhD study.
Amount $200-$3500
Date(s) Application Is Due Feb 1.
Contact Executive Director, Congressional Research Grants Program, (309) 347-7113; fax: (309) 347-6432; email: fmackaman@dirksencenter.org
Internet http://www.dirksencenter.org/print_grants_CRAs.htm
Sponsor Dirksen Congressional Center
2815 Broadway
Pekin, IL 61554-4219

Connecticut Community Foundation Grants **1408**
The foundation supports nonprofits in the Waterbury, CT, area to enrich the quality of life of residents. Categories of support include teenage growth and development--education, employment, culture, delinquency prevention, family support, and emotional and physical health; and arts and humanities--increasing access to the arts, new art forms, performances, and education for youth and adult audiences. A broad range of program types will be funded, including seed money, emergency funds, building/renovation, equipment, land acquisition, matching grants, research, projects/programs, publications, conferences and seminars, capital campaigns, consulting services, scholarship funds, student aid, and technical assistance. Applicants must discuss their application with the program officer before submission.
Requirements Nonprofit organizations in Beacon Falls, Bethlehem, Bridgewater, Cheshire, Goshen, Litchfield, Middlebury, Morris, Naugatuck, New Milford, Oxford, Prospect, Roxbury, Southbury, Thomaston, Warren, Watertown, Washington, Wolcott, and Woodbury, CT, may submit applications.
Restrictions Grants are not awarded for religious purposes, political activities, deficit financing, continuing support, fund-raising events, annual campaigns, newly established arts organizations, commissioning of new works of art, general operating support, or endowments.
Amount $8000-$10,000 average
Date(s) Application Is Due Jan 10; Apr 4; Sep 5.
Contact Carol O'Donnell, Director of Grants and Community Services, (203) 753-1315; fax: (203) 756-3054; email: info@waterburyfoundation.org
Internet http://www.conncf.org/grants/grants.htm
Sponsor Connecticut Community Foundation
43 Field St
Waterbury, CT 06702

Connecticut Health Foundation Health Initiative Grants **1409**
The foundation awards grants to organizations and institutions that directly respond to its current priority areas and result in improving the health status of Connecticut's underserved and unserved populations. Program priorities include children's mental health--projects related to children's mental health, including research, community grants, creating resources for clinical effective practices, and parent advocacy groups; oral health--improving oral health care access, quality, and utilization; and racial and ethnic health disparities--improving the diversity of the health care workforce, and increasing cultural competency in the existing workforce. The foundation awards two major types of grants: strategic and responsive. Application and guidelines are available online.
Requirements Connecticut state and local units of government, community health centers, health advocacy organizations, community-based organizations, community and cultural groups, schools, and faith-based organizations are eligible. Applicants must

have IRS 501(c)3 tax-exempt status or be public entities. Unincorporated organizations may apply through 501(c)3 fiscal agents.
Restrictions Foundation grants do not support awards to individuals; construction of buildings; capital projects, endowments, or chairs associated with universities, and medical schools; conferences (unless part of a greater project or program); projects that do not benefit Connecticut residents; lobbying or influencing the outcomes of a proposed piece of legislation or election; and indirect cost for discretionary grants.
Amount $50,000-$200,000 typically
Date(s) Application Is Due Mar 15; Jun 15; Sep 15; Dec 15.
Contact Onell Jesus Calderas, Grants Administrator, (860) 224-2200; fax: (860) 224-2230; email: onell@cthealth.org
Internet http://www.cthealth.org/matriarch
Sponsor Connecticut Health Foundation
74B Vine St
New Britain, CT 06052

ConocoPhillips Grants Program **1410**
ConocoPhillips maintains a philanthropic contributions budget for nonprofit, charitable programs closely tied to its corporate goals and focused primarily in locations of strong business interests. Submit an executive summary outlining the purpose of the program or project, how it will be accomplished, expected results, a budget (noting administrative expenses such as: salaries and fees, program expenses and total income), other sources of financial support and a copy of the IRS tax determination letter that confirms 501(c)3 status. The grant must be used in the United States. Requests for grants in non-US locations should be made directly to the ConocoPhillips international office doing business in that part of the world. Education and youth, civic and arts, employee volunteerism, safety and social services, and the environment are focus areas.
Requirements Applications are accepted from areas where ConocoPhillips has a strong business presence, e.g., Texas and Oklahoma. All contributions are to be used within the United States.
Restrictions ConocoPhillips does not award funds to individuals, sectarian or religious organization, promotional sponsorship and advertising (marketing related) or an endowment.
Contact Program Contact, (281) 293-2685
Internet http://www.conocophillips.com/about/Contribution+Guidelines/index.htm
Sponsor ConocoPhillips Corporation
600 N Dairy Ashford, MA 3144
Houston, TX 77079

Conservation, Food, and Health Foundation Grants for Developing Countries **1411**
The geographic focus of the foundation is the developing world. Through grants to support research and through targeted grants to help solve specific problems, the foundation helps build capacity within developing countries in three areas of interest: conservation, food, and health. The foundation concentrates its grantmaking on research, technical assistance, and training projects of benefit to the Third World; favors grants for pilot projects and special programs that have a potential for replication; prefers to support projects that employ and/or train personnel from the developing world; and favors research concerning problems of importance to the developing world. Concept papers may be submitted at any time, but must be received in the office by the listed application deadlines for consideration at board meetings; full proposals are by invitation.
Requirements 501(c)3 tax-exempt organizations and foreign organizations with the equivalent of 501(c)3 status may apply.
Restrictions The foundation does not normally provide support for buildings or for land purchase; quantity purchases of durable medical equipment; endowments or fundraising activities; famine or emergency relief; films, videos, or web-site production; re-granting through intermediaries; general operating support; or individuals (however, the foundation may support an individual engaged in research on a problem of significance to the developing world where the research is sponsored by an established, nonprofit organization such as an educational institution and conducted in close partnership with a local nongovernmental organization).
Amount $11,000 average; $25,000 maximum
Date(s) Application Is Due Feb 1; Aug 1.
Contact Prentice Zinn, c/o Grants Management Associates, (617) 426-7172; fax: (617) 426-7087; email: cfh@grantsmanagement.com
Internet http://www.grantsmanagement.com/cfhguide.html
Sponsor Conservation, Food, and Health Foundation
77 Summer St, Ste 800
Boston, MA 02110

Consortium for Graduate Study in Management Minority Fellowships **1412**
An 11-university consortium, designed to hasten the entry of minorities into managerial positions in business, is offering fellowships to capable young men and women to allow them the opportunity to pursue a high-quality educational program leading to the MBA. Fellowships are made possible through the support and contributions of American business. Summer opportunities are also provided to each student accepted for the program. The 11 participating universities are University of California-Berkley, Indiana University-Bloomington, New York University, University of Michigan-Ann Arbor, University of North Carolina at Chapel Hill, University of Rochester, University of Southern California, University of Texas at Austin, University of Virginia, Washington University-Saint Louis, and University of Wisconsin-Madison. Application forms may be downloaded from the Web site. Applications are accepted between December 1 and January 15.
Requirements Young African Americans, Puerto Ricans, Cubans, Dominicans, Mexican Americans, or Native Americans who are US citizens or nationals who aspire to managerial careers in business are invited to apply. Applications will be received from college seniors and those holding bachelor's degrees from accredited colleges and universities. Degrees may be in the humanities, life, social and physical sciences, and engineering, as well as business or economics. Those already embarked on other careers but wishing to change careers are also encouraged to apply.
Amount $2500 per year plus tuition and fees
Date(s) Application Is Due Jan 15; Dec 1.
Contact Jackie Olden, (888) 658-6814 or (314) 877-5540; email: frontdesk@cgsm.org or oldenj@cgsm.org
Internet http://www.cgsm.org
Sponsor Consortium for Graduate Study in Management
5585 Pershing, Ste 240
Saint Louis, MO 63112-4621

Consortium of College and University Media Centers Annual Research Grants **1413**
Grants support research related to production, selection, distribution, and/or utilization of film/video to better meet the needs of the educational community. The research should be in progress or expected to be completed within 18 months of the submission of the proposal. Selection of an award recipient will be made on the basis of how well the proposed study focuses on needs or opportunities related to the production, selection, cataloging, distribution, and/or utilization of educational media. Grants are made for one year and are not usually renewable. The application must include a one- to two-page description of the study, a proposed budget, and a resume of the investigator. Mail or fax the required materials to Research Awards Committee, CCUMC, 1200 Communications Building, ITC, Iowa State University, Ames, IA 50011-3243.
Requirements Eligible to apply are undergraduate or graduate student faculty or staff persons or any constituent member of the consortium. Greater consideration will be given to studies with general application to the field.
Amount $2000 maximum
Date(s) Application Is Due May 1.
Contact Research Awards Committee, (515) 294-1811; fax: (515) 294-8089; email: ccumc@ccumc.org
Internet http://www.indiana.edu/~ccumc
Sponsor Consortium of College and University Media Centers
Iowa State University, 1200 Communications Bldg
Ames, IA 50011-3243

Consumers Energy Foundation **1414**
The corporate foundation provides financial support to Michigan nonprofits whose social welfare programs provide solutions to problems faced by individuals and families who are unable to address their own needs without help; Michigan growth and environmental enhancement efforts that protect and enhance Michigan's physical environment; education initiatives that coordinate and develop partnerships for systemic reform in grades K-12 and programs that support schools of higher learning, with special interest in curricula and capital improvements in the study of business, political science, economics, engineering and natural/physical sciences; community and civic endeavors that support programs focusing on Michigan's economic development at the community, regional, and statewide levels, with preference given to volunteer-driven efforts, public/private partnerships and short- or long-term projects with significant evaluation components; culture and the arts programs that increase awareness of the values of artistic and cultural achievements and encourage their growth. The foundation considers requests from qualified organizations to support operating budgets and capital fund programs for construction, refurbishment or purchase of buildings, structures, equipment, or other physical enhancements, and matching grants. The initial application should be in narrative format, not exceeding two pages, and must include confirmation of the applicant organization's 501(c)3 status. The foundation provides support for minority scholarship programs administered by the United Negro College Fund (UNCF) and the Michigan Colleges Foundation (MCF). For each of these programs, scholarships are awarded to women and minority students enrolled in business or science-related curriculums, including math, engineering and computers.
Requirements Michigan 501(c)3 organizations are eligible. The principal focus includes communities in Michigan's Lower Peninsula where Consumers Energy has a business presence. Projects that benefit the state of Michigan and the communities served by Consumers Energy will be considered from organizations based elsewhere.
Restrictions Contributions are not made to individuals, including individual scholarships; organizations to which contributions are not tax deductible; organizations that practice discrimination on the basis of sex, age, height, weight, etc.; those whose operating activities are already supported by the United Way; political organizations and campaigns; religious organizations for religious purposes; or labor or veterans organizations, fraternal orders, or social clubs.
Amount $500-$10,000 average
Contact Carolyn Bloodworth, Secretary/Treasurer, (517) 788-0432; fax: (517) 788-2281; email: foundation@consumersenergy.com
Internet http://www.consumersenergy.com/ocompany/index.asp?SSID=34&pop=true

Sponsor Consumers Energy
1 Energy Plz, Rm EP8-210
Jackson, MI 49201

Cooley's Anemia Research Fellowships 1415
The grants-in-aid program supports research that will add to current knowledge about Cooley's anemia and related disorders. The ultimate goal is to find the cause and cure or effective treatment of these diseases. This involves a great deal of basic research in hematology, pathology, physiology, biochemistry, physical chemistry, and related sciences. Fellowships are also available and are awarded for one year, with possible renewal for a second year upon reapplication. The deadline for both fellowships and grants in aid of research is mid-March each year; awards are announced by June 1.
Requirements Grants are made to institutions and researchers of any country. Individual applicant must have a doctoral degree and no more than five years postdoctoral training.
Amount $40,000 maximum stipend per year
Date(s) Application Is Due Mar 1.
Contact Chairperson, Medical Advisory Board, (718) 321-2873 or (800) 522-7222; fax: (718) 321-3340; email: info@cooleysanemia.org
Internet http://www.cooleysanemia.org/sections.php?sec=58
Sponsor Cooley's Anemia Foundation
129-09 26th Ave, Ste 203
Flushing, NY 11354

Cooperative Institute for Research in Environmental Sciences Visiting Fellows Program 1416
With support from the Environmental Research Laboratories of the National Oceanic and Atmospheric Administration, the Cooperative Institute for Research in Environmental Sciences (CIRES) at the University of Colorado at Boulder offers up to six one-year visiting fellowships to scientists with research interests in the areas of advanced observing and modeling systems, climate system variability, geodynamics, planetary metabolism, regional processes, and integrating activities. The program provides opportunities for interactions between CIRES scientists and visiting fellows to pursue common research interests. Selections for this program are based in part on the likelihood of interactions between the visiting fellow and the scientists at CIRES and the degree to which both parties will benefit from the exchange of new ideas. To further this goal, priority is given to candidates with research experience at institutions outside the Boulder scientific community. Salary, benefits, and a research budget are provided.
Requirements Awards may be made to PhD scientists at all levels; faculty planning sabbatical leave and recent PhD recipients are especially encouraged to apply. The program is open to scientists of all countries.
Date(s) Application Is Due Dec 31.
Contact Karen Dempsey, Program Contact, (303) 492-1168; fax: (303) 492-1149; email: dempsey@cires.colorado.edu
Internet http://cires.colorado.edu/visfell
Sponsor Cooperative Institute for Research in Environmental Sciences
Human Resources Dept, 216 UCB
Boulder, CO 80309-0216

Cooperstown Graduate Fellowships 1417
The program, cosponsored by the State University of New York and the association, awards assistantships, fellowships, and scholarships to individuals in the museum field to enhance their professional training. Candidates should apply for admission to the program and for a fellowship at the same time. Write to the program at Cooperstown for a catalog and application.
Requirements Applicants must be US citizens who are graduates of accredited four-year colleges with a 3.0 average or above in their major field of study for the last two years. In addition, they must have obtained satisfactory scores on the Graduate Record Exam.
Amount $2000-$10,000 over four semesters
Date(s) Application Is Due Jan 10.
Contact Director of Admissions, Cooperstown Graduate Program, (607) 547-2586; fax: (607) 547-8926; email: wrightlg@oneonta.edu
Internet http://cgp.oneonta.edu
Sponsor New York State Historical Association
P.O. Box 800
Cooperstown, NY 13326

Coors Brewing Corporate Contributions Grants 1418
The company has a firm commitment to giving back to its home-market communities--including Denver, CO; Memphis, TN; and Elkton, VA--and supports grassroots, nonprofit organizations that address community, civic and industry issues. The primary focus is on programs that enhance the quality of life. Vehicles of support include cash grants, Coors products for events, Coors logo items for fund-raisers, volunteer hours by Coors employees or retirees, or used equipment or in-kind services. Preference will be given to groups that focus on issues of national scope. Corporate Contributions usually reviews requests the first Wednesday of every month. A minimum of two months lead time is required before the event or funding need.
Requirements IRS 501(c)3 nonprofit organizations located in Denver, CO; Memphis, TN; and Elkton, VA; are eligible.
Restrictions Requests will not be considered for individuals in personal programs; individual scholarships; teams, groups, or races; travel expenses; third-party fund-raisers or sales promotions; political activities; or requests by telephone.
Contact Buck Boze, Corporate Contributions, (800) 642-6116 or (303) 277-5953; fax: (303) 277-6132
Internet http://www.coors.com/part_community_funding.asp
Sponsor Coors Brewing Company
P.O. Box 4030, Dept NH420
Golden, CO 80401

Cord Foundation Grants 1419
The foundation makes grants to a variety of groups in three broad areas: education, social services, and the arts. Grant recipients have included higher education institutions, research groups, youth organizations, community service agencies, religious organizations, and performing and visual arts centers. Types of support include general operating support, building construction/renovation, equipment acquisition, emergency funds, program development, scholarship funds, research, and matching funds. Grants are awarded nationwide, with preference given to requests from northern Nevada. Application forms are not required.
Requirements Nonprofit organizations are eligible but giving is primarily in the northern NV area.
Restrictions The foundation does not support general fund-raising events, memorial campaigns, deficit fundings, conferences, dinners, or mass mailings.
Amount $10,000-$100,000 average
Date(s) Application Is Due May 15.
Contact William Bradley, Trustee, (775) 323-0373
Sponsor Cord Foundation
418 Flint St
Reno, NV 89501

Corning Foundation Community Service Grants 1420
The foundation supports a variety of organizations that serve a broad base of constituents. Included in this category are hospitals and hospices, community foundations, youth and women's centers, YMCAs, local chapters of Girl Scouts and Boy Scouts of America, and selected United Ways.
Requirements All requests to the foundation for support must be made in writing. Grant seekers are advised to submit a two- to three-page letter of inquiry, signed by the senior administrative officer of the organization.
Restrictions Grants do not support individuals; political parties, campaigns, or causes; labor or veterans' organizations; religious or fraternal groups; volunteer emergency squads; athletic activities; courtesy advertising; or fundraising events.
Contact Karen Martin, Associate Director, (607) 974-8746; fax: (607) 974-4756
Internet http://www.corning.com/inside_corning/foundation.asp
Sponsor Corning Foundation
MP-BH-07
Corning, NY 14831

Corning Incorporated Foundation Educational Grants 1421
The grants improve education by supporting selected K-12 school districts, community colleges and four-year institutions of higher learning primarily in communities where the sponsor company has operations. Areas of involvement have included community service programs for students, curriculum enrichment, student scholarships, facility improvement, and instructional technology projects for the classroom.
Requirements Support goes to institutions that are tax-exempt under Section 501 (c)(3) of the Internal Revenue Code and which are public charities as defined in Section 509(a) of the Code. All requests to the foundation for support must be made in writing. Grant seekers are advised to submit a two- to three-page letter of inquiry, signed by the senior administrative officer of the organization.
Restrictions Grants do not support individuals; political parties, campaigns, or causes; labor or veterans' organizations; religious or fraternal groups; volunteer emergency squads; athletic activities; courtesy advertising; or fundraising events.
Amount $1000-$25,000 average
Contact Karen Martin, Associate Director, (607) 974-8722; fax: (607) 974-4756; email: martinkc@corning.com
Internet http://www.corning.com/inside_corning/foundation.asp
Sponsor Corning Incorporated Foundation
MP-LB-02
Corning, NY 14831

Corpus Christi College Research Scholarships 1422
Successful candidates will pursue, as members of college, a course of study in any field leading to a research-based higher degree in the University of Cambridge. Awards are usually made to those studying for the PhD degree. Subject to satisfactory progress, awards may be extended to a maximum of three years.
Requirements The awards are open to both men and women who have graduated before October 1 of the year of application. Applicants must first apply for university admission to the Board of Graduate Studies at 4 Mill Ln, Cambridge, CB2 1RZ and must have acceptance as a condition of receiving a scholarship.
Restrictions Those eligible for United Kingdom State Awards may not apply.
Amount @L500 maximum

Contact Tutor for Advanced Students, 44 01223-338038; fax: 44 01223-338057; email: graduate-tutor@corpus.cam.ac.uk
Internet http://www.admin.cam.ac.uk/univ/gsprospectus/colleges/corpuschristi.html
Sponsor Corpus Christi College
Trumpington St
Cambridge, England CB2 1RH United Kingdom

Coughlin-Saunders Foundation Grants Program **1423**
The foundation awards grants to nonprofit organizations in its areas of interest, including arts and arts education, higher education, religion, social services, and youth organizations. Types of support include general operating support, capital campaigns, building construction/renovation, equipment acquisition, emergency funds, program development, professorships, and scholarship funds. Proposals are preferred in January or February. Grants are made primarily for projects which benefit Alexandria, Louisiana, and the surrounding area. New Orleans and the surrounding area will be considered.
Requirements 501(c)3 tax-exempt organizations in central Louisiana may apply.
Restrictions Grants are not made to individuals or for fund raisers. Endowments will not be funded.
Amount $100-$40,000 range
Contact Ed Crump Jr., Grants Administrator, (318) 561-4070; fax: (318) 487-7339; email: csfoundation@kricket.net
Sponsor Coughlin-Saunders Foundation
2010 Gus Kaplan Dr
Alexandria, LA 71301

Council of Logistics Management Doctoral Dissertation Fellowships **1424**
Each year a number of grants are awarded to support doctoral dissertation research leading to the advancement of theory and practice in logistics management, inventory management, transportation management, materials management, and related fields. The dissertation should emphasize the research problem, major aspects of the research design and analysis, and the findings, including their implications and significance for logistics theory and practice.
Requirements This program is open to individuals who will have completed their doctoral work in logistics or a related field during the period January 1 to March 1 of the year of application.
Amount $5000
Contact Doctoral Dissertation Fellowships, (630) 574-0985; fax: (630) 574-0989; email: clmAdmin@clm1.org
Internet http://clm1.org/Default.asp?XX=1
Sponsor Council of Logistics Management
2805 Butterfield Rd, Ste 200
Oak Brook, IL 60523

Council on Foundations Emerging Philanthropic Leaders Fellowships **1425**
The program is designed to help future foundation leaders become more effective within their communities and the larger field of organized philanthropy. Each year, two two-year fellowships are awarded. Each fellow is matched with a mentor who is a recognized leader in philanthropy. The fellows are asked to identify their professional growth goals and organizational development needs that they would like to address as part of their fellowship. The mentors, drawn from the council's membership, are asked to help develop two-year plans for providing information, advice, and referrals. Applications may be sent by mail, fax, or email.
Requirements The nominee or applicant must have at least two years experience in the philanthropic area, with at least one year in a leadership position. The nominee or applicant's organization must have a focus on increasing and expanding philanthropic programs within communities that are historically underrepresented in institutional philanthropy. All applicants must submit a simple application letter. The chief executive of the organization also must write a brief letter of support or co-sign the applicant's submission. Nominees or applicants must be associated with a Council on Foundations member or member-eligible organization.
Date(s) Application Is Due Dec 31.
Contact Grants Administrator, (202) 466-6512; fax: (202) 785-3926; email: inclusive@cof.org
Internet http://www.cof.org/files/Documents/Diversity/diversitybrochure.pdf
Sponsor Council on Foundations
1828 L Street NW, Suite 300
Washington, DC 20036-5168

Council on Legal Education Opportunity Program **1426**
The program provides economically and educationally disadvantaged students, many with less than traditional admissions credentials, an opportunity to attend accredited law schools. Students accepted into the program are assigned to a summer institute where immediately prior to commencing law school they are exposed to and prepared for the ensuing law school regimen. Stipend is available for three years while recipient is attending an American Bar Association-approved law school.
Requirements Applicants must have completed an undergraduate degree program and have taken the LSAT examination.
Restrictions Persons who are currently enrolled in law school and did not enter through the CLEO program, as well as those individuals who have previously attended law school, are ineligible to apply.
Amount $7000 for the first year and approximately $5000 for each of the second and third years
Date(s) Application Is Due Feb 1.
Contact CLEO Admissions Analyst, (202) 662-8630; email: williatm@staff.abanet.org
Internet http://cleoscholars.com/all_about_cleo/index.htm
Sponsor Council on Legal Education Opportunity
740 15th St NW
Washington, DC 20005

Cowles Charitable Trust Grants **1427**
The foundation awards grants, primarily in New York, Florida, and on the East Coast, for the arts and culture, including museums and the performing arts; environment; education, including early childhood education, secondary and higher education, medical school education, adult basic education and literacy, and adult continuing education; hospitals and AIDS programs, including research; social services, including family planning, human services, and federated giving; and community funds, including leadership development, civil rights, and race relations. Types of support include general operating support, capital campaigns, annual campaigns, equipment acquisition, endowment funds, continuing support, seed money, building construction/renovation, matching funds, professorships, and program development. Application forms are required; initial approach should be by letter. The board meets in January, April, July, and October.
Requirements Nonprofit organizations may apply for grant support. Grants are awarded primarily along the Eastern Seaboard.
Amount $1000-$40,000 range
Date(s) Application Is Due Mar 1; Jun 1; Sep 1; Dec 1.
Contact Gardner Cowles III, President, (732) 936-9826
Sponsor Cowles Charitable Trust
P.O. Box 219
Rumson, NJ 07760

CPB American History and Civics Initiative **1428**
The program is a major commitment by the CPB to use its educational mandate, reach, and creative capacity to address critical shortfalls in middle and high school students' knowledge of American history, our political system, and their roles as citizens. This initiative will award grants to forge unique and sustainable partnerships between public television producers and broadcast outlets, the educational community, curriculum developers, the high-tech industry and other appropriate partners, to design, test and create integrated interactive multimedia platforms that improve learning. Grants will be awarded in three phases: research and development, prototype creation, and production and implementation. The current round is for research and development grants. Only research and development grantees may apply for phase 2 and phase 3 grants. Guidelines are available online.
Requirements Public broadcasting stations are eligible. Any public or private, nonprofit, educational, or commercial entity is eligible to apply for a research and development grant as a managing partner. Any public or private, nonprofit, educational, or commercial entity is eligible to serve as a subordinate key partner in a proposal.
Amount $50,000-$250,000
Date(s) Application Is Due Nov 1.
Contact Grants Administrator, (202) 879-9600; email: History.Civics@cpb.org
Internet http://www.cpb.org/grants/historyandcivics
Sponsor Corporation for Public Broadcasting
401 Ninth St NW
Washington, DC 20004-2129

CPC Catherine H. Beattie Fellowship **1429**
The fellowship was created to promote the conservation of rare and endangered flora in the United States through the programs of the CPC. The research grant enables a student in either biology or horticulture to conduct field research on rare plants. Preference is given to students whose projects focus on the endangered flora of the Carolinas and the southeastern United States. Additional information and applications may be obtained by contacting the office.
Requirements Graduate students in biology, horticulture, or a related field are eligible to apply.
Amount $1000-$4000
Date(s) Application Is Due Dec 31.
Contact Conservation Programs Manager, (314) 577-9450; fax: (314) 577-9465; email: cpc@mobot.org
Internet http://www.centerforplantconservation.org/beattie.html
Sponsor Center for Plant Conservation
P.O. Box 299, Missouri Botanical Garden
St. Louis, MO 63166

Cranbrook Academy of Art Guest Artist/Scholar Grants **1430**
Applications for the position of guest artist/scholar are invited from scholars in the humanities or from writers, poets, musicians, filmmakers, visual artists, etc. who are active in their field, who have manifested a significant body of work, and who can frame their interests in an interdisciplinary manner. The format of each program is flexible. Possible models include a set of five or six public lectures, weekly or biweekly, with follow-up seminars or studio critiques; or a four- to six-week residency on campus with informal performances, readings, and studio visits. A letter of interest; curriculum

vita; publications, slides, or other representation of recent work; title, abstract, outline, and format of proposed program; and indication of scheduling requirements comprise application materials.
Contact Ruth Ann Clark, Assistant Director for Annual Programs, (248) 645-3065; fax: (248) 646-0046; email: RClark@cranbrook.edu
Internet http://www.cranbrookart.edu
Sponsor Cranbrook Academy of Art
Box 801, 39221 Woodward Ave
Bloomfield Hills, MI 48303-0801

Credit Union Foundation of British Columbia Grants 1431
The purpose of the foundation is to administer funds for the encouragement, promotion, and advancement of postsecondary education by means of grants-in-aid assistance to British Columbia resident students in need of financial assistance in pursuing vocational, technical, or academic training within British Columbia. Areas of interest include adult and continuing education, education institutions, universities, community colleges, and vocational training. Types of support through the program include scholarships, grants, awards, and bursaries. The majority of student grants are considered in the fall. Contact the office for application forms.
Amount $300-$2000 range
Contact email: cufoundation@shaw.ca
Internet http://www.cufoundation.org
Sponsor Credit Union Foundation of British Columbia
1441 Creekside Dr
Vancouver, BC V6J 4S7 Canada

CRF Graduate Research Grants 1432
Proposals are welcome from students enrolled in graduate programs in any accredited colleges or universities. Grants will support fully or partially funded projects. Travel expenses may be included if justified by the research. Guidelines are available online.
Amount $15,000 maximum
Date(s) Application Is Due Nov 28.
Contact Craft Research Fund, email: info@craftcreativitydesign.org
Internet http://www.craftcreativitydesign.org/research/grants.php
Sponsor Center for Craft, Creativity, and Design
P.O. Box 1127
Hendersonville, NC 28793

CRF Project Research Grants 1433
Support is provided for research on American studio craft. Research involving international craft must be in relationship to craft in America. The fund seeks proposals that address the goals of the fund through monographs on individual craft artists or themes, historical research, and cross-disciplinary research involving craft. Applicants requesting support for monographs on individual craft artists should refer to www.aaa.si.edu on how the research will compliment or expand the Smithsonian Laitman Documentation Project for Craft and Decorative Arts in America.
Requirements Proposals are welcome from academic researchers, independent scholars, doctoral students, and museum curators.
Restrictions General overhead (indirect administrative expenses) is not eligible for university-based projects. No capital equipment purchases are eligible for support.
Amount $10,000 maximum graduate research grants; $15,000 maximum research grants
Date(s) Application Is Due Nov 28.
Contact Craft Research Fund, email: info@craftcreativitydesign.org
Internet http://www.craftcreativitydesign.org/research/grants.php
Sponsor Center for Craft, Creativity, and Design
P.O. Box 1127
Hendersonville, NC 28793

CRI Clinical Investigator Award in Cancer Immunology 1434
Investigator awards are available to six qualified scientists at the assistant professor level who are working in the field of clinical cancer immunology. The four-year award may be used at the recipient's discretion for salary, technical assistance, supplies, or capital equipment. CRI has no citizenship restrictions, and research supported by the award may be conducted anywhere in the United States or abroad, excluding for-profit institutions. Applications may be downloaded from the Web site.
Requirements Candidate must hold a doctoral degree and be a tenure-track assistant professor or equivalent rank at the time of the award.
Amount $50,000 a year for four years for each investigator
Date(s) Application Is Due Mar 1.
Contact Lynne Harmer, Grants Administrator, (212) 688-7515; fax: (212) 832-9376; email: grants@cancerresearch.org
Internet http://www.cancerresearch.org/clinical.html
Sponsor Cancer Research Institute
681 Fifth Ave
New York, NY 10022-4209

CRI Postdoctoral Fellowships 1435
Each year the institute awards postdoctoral fellowships to qualified individuals in the formative stages of their career who wish to receive training in cancer immunology with special emphasis on tumor immunology. Work may be carried out in the United States or abroad. The fellowships are awarded for a period of two years, with the possibility of renewal for one additional year. CRI requires all fellowship applicants to complete an electronic application as well as a paper application.
Requirements Applicant of any nationality must have a doctoral degree and must conduct research under a sponsor who holds a formal appointment at the sponsoring institution.
Amount $40,000 first year, $42,000 second year, $44,000 third year; plus $1500 institutional allowance per year
Date(s) Application Is Due Apr 1; Oct 1.
Contact Brian Brewer, Grants Administrator, (212) 688-7515 ext 242 or (800) 992-2623; fax: (212) 832-9376; email: grants@cancerresearch.org
Internet http://www.cancerresearch.org/postdoc.html
Sponsor Cancer Research Institute
681 Fifth Ave
New York, NY 10022-4209

CRI Prostate Cancer Initiative Grants 1436
The program supports Phase I and Phase I/II clinical trials that test novel therapies for advanced prostate cancer, with particular emphasis on hormonal therapy and immunotherapy. CRI does not provide funds for indirect costs. The completed application consists of 15 sets of the following items collated in the order specified: application form; biographical sketches for all key personnel; abstract of proposed project explaining the importance of the proposed research and ramifications; five-page description of research program, including summary of past work and future plans; and IRB-approved protocol. Applications must be typed or printed (using both sides of the paper, if possible). In addition, a self-addressed, stamped postcard is required if applicant would like to receive notification of receipt of application. Annual deadline dates may vary; contact the program office for exact dates.
Amount $150,000 over two years
Date(s) Application Is Due Apr 15.
Contact Grants Administrator, (212) 688-7515 or (800) 992-2623; fax: (212) 832-9376; email: info@cancerresearch.org
Internet http://www.cancerresearch.org/pciinit.html
Sponsor Cancer Research Institute
681 Fifth Ave
New York, NY 10022-4209

Crohn's Disease and Colitis Research Fellowships 1437
Three-year fellowships are awarded to encourage the development of individuals with research potential to help them prepare for careers of independent research in the areas of Crohn's disease and ulcerative colitis. Yearly renewal is dependent on the receipt of satisfactory progress reports. Application forms must be obtained from the foundation. Letters of intent are due May 1 and November 1. Submission deadlines for full applications are January 14 and July 1 of each year. Annual deadline dates may vary; contact program staff for exact dates.
Requirements The applicant must hold an MD, PhD, or equivalent degree and be currently employed by an institution engaged in health care and/or health-related research within the United States. Candidates who have obtained MD degrees must have at least two years of postdoctoral experience, one year of which must be documented research experience relevant to inflammatory bowel disease. Candidates holding PhD degrees must have one year of postdoctoral experience and at least one year of documented research experience relevant to IBD.
Amount $58,250 maximum salary per year
Date(s) Application Is Due Jan 14; May 1; Jul 1; Nov 1.
Contact Carol Cox, Director of Research and Scientific Programs, (212) 685-3440 or (800) 932-2423; fax: (212) 779-4098; email: ccox@ccfa.org
Internet http://www.ccfa.org/research/?LMI=4
Sponsor Crohn's & Colitis Foundation of America Inc
386 Park Ave S, 17th Fl
New York, NY 10016-8804

Crohn's Disease and Ulcerative Colitis Senior Research Grants 1438
Grants are awarded to individuals for up to two years for research in the basic biomedical and clinical sciences that will increase the understanding of the cause, mechanisms of symptoms, and treatment of inflammatory bowel disease including Crohn's disease and ulcerative colitis. Support for additional one-year periods will be by competitive renewal. Application forms must be secured from the foundation. Submission deadlines for letters of intent are November 1 and May 1. Submission deadlines for full applications are January 14 and July 1 of each year, unless noted otherwise.
Requirements Applicants must be established researchers in the field of inflammatory bowel disease.
Amount $115,000 maximum
Date(s) Application Is Due Jan 14; May 1; Jul 1; Nov 1.
Contact Carol Cox, Research and Scientific Programs, (212) 685-3440 or (800) 932-2423; fax: (212) 779-4098; email: ccox@ccfa.org
Internet http://www.ccfa.org/research/?LMI=4
Sponsor Crohn's & Colitis Foundation of America Inc
386 Park Ave S, 17th Fl
New York, NY 10016-8804

Croucher Foundation Grants **1439**
The foundation promotes education, learning, and research in the areas of natural science, technology, and medicine. Each year, 20 to 25 scholarships and fellowships, tenable in the United Kingdom, Hong Kong, Canada, Australia, or New Zealand, are awarded.
Requirements The competition is open to permanent residents of Hong Kong.
Contact Administrator, (852) 2736 6337; fax: (852) 2730 0742; email: cfadmin@croucher.org.hk
Internet http://www.croucher.org.hk
Sponsor Croucher Foundation
9 Queen's Rd Central, Ste 501
Hong Kong

Cruise Industry Charitable Foundation Grants **1440**
The foundation awards grants to improve the quality of life in US cities and towns where the cruise industry maintains vessel operations, employs a significant number of individuals, and purchases products and services. Areas of interest include civic and community development, educational assistance and training programs, public health programs, and environmental initiatives. Funding has supported job creation and training programs; efforts to improve access to community services and youth and adult education, particularly for minority and disadvantaged students; literacy and basic life skills education; and mentoring services. Proposals are encouraged for programs serving the needs of at-risk populations. There are no application deadlines. Letters of inquiry are accepted at any time; full proposals are by invitation.
Requirements US 501(c)3 organizations and state and local government units, such as public schools and child welfare agencies, are eligible.
Restrictions Requests will not be considered from individuals, fraternal organizations, religious organizations, political organizations, or organizations that conduct lobbying activity.
Contact Cynthia Colenda, Executive Director, (703) 522-3160; fax: (703) 522-3161; email: cicf@iccl.org
Internet http://www.iccl.org/foundation/guidelines.cfm
Sponsor Cruise Industry Charitable Foundation
2111 Wilson Blvd, 8th Fl
Arlington, VA 22201

CSRPC Dissertation Fellowships **1441**
The goal of the fellowship is to enable an outstanding doctoral student interested in the study of race and ethnicity to devote his or her full energies to the completion of the dissertation. The fellowship carries a stipend; a travel and research budget; and will cover advanced residence tuition, fees, and basic university student health insurance, if needed. The successful applicant will be provided with an office and use of a computer at the center. The fellow will be expected to be in residence during the award year, present his or her work at one of the Reproduction of Race and Racial Ideologies Workshop meetings and to actively participate in the workshop and other activities sponsored by the center.
Requirements University of Chicago doctoral students who have completed all requirements for the PhD but the dissertation, including formal admission to candidacy, and expect to complete all field work by September 26 are eligible to apply. Any dissertation that has as its central focus issues related to race or racialized groups will be considered. Special consideration will be given to projects that attend to the intersection of race or ethnicity with other identities such as gender, class, sexuality, and nationality.
Restrictions The fellow may not engage in any remunerative activity, including teaching either on or off campus, while holding the award, and will be ineligible for further internal University funding from any source, including teaching appointments, if the degree is not completed within six months of the end of the CSRPC fellowship tenure.
Amount $18,000 stipend; $1000 travel and research budget
Date(s) Application Is Due Mar 4.
Contact Center for the Study of Race, Politics, and Culture, (773) 702-8063; fax: (773) 834-2200; email: csrpc@uchicago.edu
Internet http://csrpc.uchicago.edu/resources_funding.shtml
Sponsor University of Chicago
5733 S University Ave
Chicago, IL 60637

CSRPC Postdoctoral Fellowship for Advanced Scholars **1442**
The goal of the fellowship is to support the work of an outstanding advanced scholar whose research focuses on the study of race or ethnicity by allowing the fellow to devote his or her energies to the further development of their research agenda. The fellowship carries a stipend, a travel and research budget, and an allowance for moving expenses. The fellow will be provided with office space, a computer at the center, and full access to University libraries and other facilities. Awardees will be expected to be in full-time residence during the academic year; teach a 10-week course related to race and/or ethnicity (one quarter); give a public lecture; present his or her work at one of the Reproduction of Race and Racial Ideologies Workshop meetings; and actively participate in the workshop and other activities sponsored by the center. Guidelines are available online.
Requirements Applicants are required to have a PhD; must have been awarded tenure at the time of application; and must be US citizens or permanent residents at the time of application.
Amount $55,000 stipend; $5000 travel and research budget; $2500 for moving expenses
Date(s) Application Is Due Feb 11.
Contact Center for the Study of Race, Politics, and Culture, (773) 702-8063; fax: (773) 834-2200; email: csrpc@uchicago.edu
Internet http://csrpc.uchicago.edu/resources_funding.shtml
Sponsor University of Chicago
5733 S University Ave
Chicago, IL 60637

CSRPC Postdoctoral Fellowship for Junior Scholars **1443**
The goal of the fellowship is to support the work of an outstanding junior scholar whose research focuses on the study of race or ethnicity by allowing the fellow to devote his or her energies to the further development of their research agenda. The fellowship carries a stipend, a travel and research budget, and an allowance for moving expenses. The fellow will be provided with office space, a computer at the center, and full access to university libraries and other facilities. Awardees will be expected to be in full-time residence during the academic year; teach a 10-week undergraduate course related to race and/or ethnicity (one quarter); present his or her work at one of the Reproduction of Race and Racial Ideologies Workshop meetings; and actively participate in the workshop and other activities sponsored by the center. Guidelines are available online.
Requirements Applicants are required to have a PhD; must be non-tenure track scholars or tenure track faculty who do not expect to receive tenure prior to the start of the fellowship year; and must be US citizens or permanent residents at the time of application.
Amount $45,000 stipend; $5000 travel and research budget; $2500 maximum for moving expenses
Date(s) Application Is Due Feb 11.
Contact Center for the Study of Race, Politics, and Culture, (773) 702-8063; fax: (773) 834-2200; email: csrpc@uchicago.edu
Internet http://csrpc.uchicago.edu/resources_funding.shtml
Sponsor University of Chicago
5733 S University Ave
Chicago, IL 60637

CTCRI Idea Grants **1444**
Idea Grants are designed to encourage unique or original research that has the potential to advance knowledge in tobacco control. Grants will allow investigators with innovative ideas and observations to conduct pilot studies, to perform secondary analysis of data sets or to gather new evidence necessary to determine the viability of research directions or hypotheses. Innovative projects are a priority for the Idea Grant program. Preference will be given to proposals that address research priorities identified by the Canadian Tobacco Control Research Summit. Research employing new or unconventional methodologies is encouraged. Proposed methods must be appropriate to the research question(s). Each successful proposal may receive a one-time grant of up to $50,000. Work is expected to be completed in one year's time.
Requirements Research proposals must meet the following eligibility criteria: The Principal Applicant (PA) is a Canadian citizen or legal resident (Co-applicants may be citizens or residents of other countries); The research proposal demonstrates basic relevance to tobacco abuse / nicotine addiction / tobacco control and addresses research priorities identified by the Canadian Tobacco Control Research Summit; Applicant(s) has disclosed other sources of funding; Commercial interests have been disclosed or applicant(s) has indicated no commercial interests; Applicant(s) has affirmed lack of support from the tobacco industry; Applicant(s) can demonstrate that he/she works in an environment that adequately supports research through ethical review, administration of funds, provision of space and equipment, etc.; Research plans include gender analysis, or it has been demonstrated that this is not appropriate; Proposal avoids duplication of previous research, unless it can be demonstrated that replication is of value; Research proposal involves pilot testing of research methods, tools, or hypotheses by a research team in order to strengthen proposals prepared for submission to traditional funding sources; Proposal articulates preliminary plans for development of a full research proposal -OR- Research proposal constitutes a novel idea which falls outside the normal scope of traditional research, either in topic or methodology; Proposal demonstrates that adequate funding is not available from other sources for this purpose.
Restrictions Members of the staff or Board of Directors of the CTCRI, or a staff member of any CTCRI funding partner organization are not eligible to apply.
Amount up to $50,000
Date(s) Application Is Due Apr 1; Oct 1.
Contact Research Grant Programs; (416) 934-5666; fax: (416) 961-4189; email: info@ctcri.ca
Internet http://ctcri.ca/~ctcri/en/index.php?option=content&task=view&id=207&Itemid=68
Sponsor Canadian Tobacco Control Research Initiative
10 Alcorn Ave., Suite 200
Toronto, ON M4V 3B1 Canada

CTCRI Knowledge Synthesis Grants **1445**
The goal of the Knowledge Synthesis program is to support interdisciplinary teams of researchers and practitioners / decision-makers to conduct collaborative reviews of evidence for particular tobacco control interventions. The maximum amount awarded for a single grant is $120,000. It is anticipated that at least two applications will be

supported in the present competition, contingent upon the availability of funds and the quality of proposals received.
Requirements Teams are requested to develop proposals to carry out reviews addressing ONE of the following topics: (1) Anti-contraband measures – An issue that undermines the effectiveness of a high tobacco tax strategy is contraband activity that includes the smuggling of tobacco products from lower tax jurisdictions, illicit manufacturing and counterfeiting. Though large price increases may provide incentive for some smokers to quit, it will impel others to seek out lower cost sources. A number of smokers are turning to contraband. (2) The effect of tax and price on prevalence and consumption in subpopulations (defined as tobacco users including 15 to 24 year olds, aboriginal people, persons diagnosed with mental health or substance abuse disorders, and lowest categories of income and formal education). (3) Discount cigarettes (defined as lower-priced brands by small manufacturers and cheaper brands by big tobacco companies) – With the price increase of tobacco products, a number of smokers are turning to price discounted cigarettes. Price discounted cigarettes now comprise more than 40% of market share in cigarette sales. Research proposals must meet the following eligibility criteria: The Principal Applicant (PA) is a Canadian citizen or legal resident (Co-applicants may be citizens or residents of other countries); The research proposal demonstrates basic relevance to tobacco abuse / nicotine addiction / tobacco control and addresses research priorities identified by the Canadian Tobacco Control Research Summit; Applicant(s) has disclosed other sources of funding; Commercial interests have been disclosed or applicant(s) has indicated no commercial interests; Applicant(s) has affirmed lack of support from the tobacco industry; Applicant(s) can demonstrate that he/she works in an environment that adequately supports research through ethical review, administration of funds, provision of space and equipment, etc.; Research plans include gender analysis, or it has been demonstrated that this is not appropriate; Proposal avoids duplication of previous research, unless it can be demonstrated that replication is of value; Proposal demonstrates the inclusion of and consultation with end-users (practitioners, policy and decision-makers) throughout the research process; Applicant demonstrates understanding and application of the Better Practices methodology, including definition of the scope of the review.
Restrictions Members of the staff or Board of Directors of the CTCRI, or a staff member of any CTCRI funding partner organization are not eligible to apply.
Amount up to $120,000
Date(s) Application Is Due Apr 1.
Contact Research Grant Programs; (416) 934-5666; fax: (416) 961-4189; email: info@ctcri.ca
Internet http://ctcri.ca/en/index.php?option=com_content&task=view&id=212&Itemid=72
Sponsor Canadian Tobacco Control Research Initiative
10 Alcorn Ave., Suite 200
Toronto, ON M4V 3B1 Canada

CTCRI Policy Research Grants **1446**
Policy Research grants are intended to stimulate research that will influence, guide or have a direct impact on policy decisions in tobacco control. Suggested research areas and methodologies include: The full policy process from agenda setting and decision making through to development and implementation, enforcement, evaluation and refinement; All areas in which policy might be used to influence tobacco use including fiscal, legislative, regulatory and educational policies; Public and private policy at all levels of government/locale; Preference will be given to projects that address research priorities identified by the Canadian Tobacco Control Research Summit (2002). Research employing new or unconventional methodologies is encouraged, but proposed methods must be appropriate to the research question(s). Each successful proposal may receive a one-time grant of up to $80,000. The project may be completed over the course of two years.
Requirements Research proposals must meet the following eligibility criteria: The Principal Applicant (PA) is a Canadian citizen or legal resident (Co-applicants may be citizens or residents of other countries); The research proposal demonstrates basic relevance to tobacco abuse / nicotine addiction / tobacco control and addresses research priorities identified by the Canadian Tobacco Control Research Summit; Applicant(s) has disclosed other sources of funding; Commercial interests have been disclosed or applicant(s) has indicated no commercial interests; Applicant(s) has affirmed lack of support from the tobacco industry; Applicant(s) can demonstrate that he/she works in an environment that adequately supports research through ethical review, administration of funds, provision of space and equipment, etc.; Research plans include gender analysis, or it has been demonstrated that this is not appropriate; Proposal avoids duplication of previous research, unless it can be demonstrated that replication is of value; Research proposal is relevant to public policy issues surrounding tobacco control in Canada. FastTrack proposals only: Applicants must demonstrate that their proposal is dependent upon policy or legislation which is timely and that the project cannot be delayed until the April 1 or October 1 deadlines.
Restrictions Members of the staff or Board of Directors of the CTCRI, or a staff member of any CTCRI funding partner organization are not eligible to apply.
Amount up to $80,000
Date(s) Application Is Due Apr 1; Oct 1.
Contact Research Grant Programs; (416) 934-5666; fax: (416) 961-4189; email: info@ctcri.ca
Internet http://ctcri.ca/~ctcri/en/index.php?option=content&task=view&id=206&Itemid=87
Sponsor Canadian Tobacco Control Research Initiative
10 Alcorn Ave., Suite 200
Toronto, ON M4V 3B1 Canada

CTCRI Research Planning Grants **1447**
Research Planning Grants are offered for the purpose of bringing together new, multi-sectoral and interdisciplinary research teams to construct research proposals for submission to traditional open funding competitions. The specific objectives of the program are: To facilitate the development of excellent research proposals which are relevant to the priorities of the CTCRI's research agenda; To support the formation of strong, interdisciplinary teams that can compete for research funding through traditional sources. Each successful proposal may receive a one-time grant of up to $15,000. Work is expected to be completed in one year's time. The number of applications supported each year is contingent upon the availability of funds and the quality of proposals.
Requirements Preference will be given to proposals that address research priorities identified by the Canadian Tobacco Control Research Summit. Suggested methodologies include: Physically gathering members of a team to develop a research plan; Conducting a literature review or other background work to develop a research project; Hiring a research assistant to help write a well grounded proposal (if applicable). Research proposals must meet the following eligibility criteria: The Principal Applicant (PA) is a Canadian citizen or legal resident (Co-applicants may be citizens or residents of other countries); The research proposal demonstrates basic relevance to tobacco abuse / nicotine addiction / tobacco control and addresses research priorities identified by the Canadian Tobacco Control Research Summit; Applicant(s) has disclosed other sources of funding; Commercial interests have been disclosed or applicant(s) has indicated no commercial interests; Applicant(s) has affirmed lack of support from the tobacco industry; Applicant(s) can demonstrate that he/she works in an environment that adequately supports research through ethical review, administration of funds, provision of space and equipment, etc.; Research plans include gender analysis, or it has been demonstrated that this is not appropriate; Proposal avoids duplication of previous research, unless it can be demonstrated that replication is of value.
Restrictions Conducting work to pilot surveys or methods does not qualify for support through this program. Members of the staff or Board of Directors of the CTCRI, or a staff member of any CTCRI funding partner organization are not eligible to apply.
Amount up to $15,000
Date(s) Application Is Due Feb 28; May 30; Aug 31; Nov 30.
Contact Research Grant Programs; (416) 934-5666; fax: (416) 961-4189; email: info@ctcri.ca
Internet http://ctcri.ca/~ctcri/en/index.php?option=content&task=view&id=209&Itemid=88
Sponsor Canadian Tobacco Control Research Initiative
10 Alcorn Ave., Suite 200
Toronto, ON M4V 3B1 Canada

CTCRI Researcher Travel Grants **1448**
Researcher Travel Grants are offered to provide opportunities for graduate and post-doctoral students and individuals affiliated with non-governmental organizations/community groups to attend conferences/meetings related to tobacco abuse and nicotine addiction. Any poster or presentation of research related to tobacco abuse and nicotine addiction is eligible for support. Preference will be given to proposals that address research priorities identified by the Canadian Tobacco Control Research Summit. Research employing new or unconventional methodologies is encouraged, but proposed methods must be appropriate to the research question(s). Grants of up to $3,000 are available to support travel and accommodations. In some cases, the value of the grant may exceed $,3000 (for example, for conferences involving international travel). The number of applications supported annually is contingent upon the availability of funds and the quality of proposals.
Requirements Research proposals must meet the following eligibility criteria: The Principal Applicant (PA) is a Canadian citizen or legal resident (Co-applicants may be citizens or residents of other countries); The research proposal demonstrates basic relevance to tobacco abuse / nicotine addiction / tobacco control and addresses research priorities identified by the Canadian Tobacco Control Research Summit; Applicant(s) has disclosed other sources of funding; Commercial interests have been disclosed or applicant(s) has indicated no commercial interests; Applicant(s) has affirmed lack of support from the tobacco industry; Applicant(s) can demonstrate that he/she works in an environment that adequately supports research through ethical review, administration of funds, provision of space and equipment, etc.; Research plans include gender analysis, or it has been demonstrated that this is not appropriate; Proposal avoids duplication of previous research, unless it can be demonstrated that replication is of value; The Principal Applicant must be conducting graduate or post-doctoral work and must be affiliated with an accredited academic program. OR The Principal Applicant must be affiliated with a non-governmental organization or community group conducting tobacco control research or evaluation; The Principal Applicant's abstract has been accepted for the upcoming conference for which the funding is requested (funding cannot be applied for retroactively); The proposal demonstrates that any current funding will not adequately support the stated objectives of the proposal; The Principal Applicant has not been awarded another CTCRI travel grant to present at a conference or event in the same calendar year as the current application. This does not include attendance at the special tobacco control conferences such as the World Conference on Tobacco or Health (WCOTH) or the Society for Research on Nicotine and Tobacco (SRNT) conference.

Restrictions Members of the staff or Board of Directors of the CTCRI, or a staff member of any CTCRI funding partner organization are not eligible to apply.
Amount up to $3,000
Date(s) Application Is Due none.
Contact Research Grant Programs; (416) 934-5666; fax: (416) 961-4189; email: info@ctcri.ca
Internet http://ctcri.ca/~ctcri/en/index.php?option=content&task=view&id=208&Itemid=89
Sponsor Canadian Tobacco Control Research Initiative
10 Alcorn Ave., Suite 200
Toronto, ON M4V 3B1 Canada

CTCRI Student Research Grants **1449**
The objectives of the program are to support learning opportunities through a one-time grant for students wishing to conduct research projects related to tobacco abuse and nicotine addiction; and to provide opportunities for graduate and post-doctoral students to improve skills in tobacco abuse and nicotine addiction research. The grant program is intended to support a broad range of research topics and areas as long as the proposed research is led by the applicant under professional research supervision. The program is not intended to support the applicant's regular course of study or background work required to prepare a research project, nor is it intended to support the research supervisor's existing project(s). Preference will be given to proposals that address research priorities identified by the Canadian Tobacco Control Research Summit. Each successful proposal may receive a one-time grant of up to $10,000. Work is expected to be completed in one year's time. The number of applications supported each year is contingent upon the availability of funds and the quality of proposals.
Requirements Graduate and post-doctoral students are eligible for Student Research grant. Research proposals must meet the following eligibility criteria: The Principal Applicant (PA) is a Canadian citizen or legal resident (Co-applicants may be citizens or residents of other countries); The research proposal demonstrates basic relevance to tobacco abuse / nicotine addiction / tobacco control and addresses research priorities identified by the Canadian Tobacco Control Research Summit; Applicant(s) has disclosed other sources of funding; Commercial interests have been disclosed or applicant(s) has indicated no commercial interests; Applicant(s) has affirmed lack of support from the tobacco industry; Applicant(s) can demonstrate that he/she works in an environment that adequately supports research through ethical review, administration of funds, provision of space and equipment, etc.; Research plans include gender analysis, or it has been demonstrated that this is not appropriate; Proposal avoids duplication of previous research, unless it can be demonstrated that replication is of value.; Proposal demonstrates that any current funding will not adequately support the stated objectives of the proposal; The Research Supervisor has provided a letter of support for the applicant's proposal.
Restrictions Members of the staff or Board of Directors of the CTCRI, or a staff member of any CTCRI funding partner organization are not eligible to apply.
Amount up to $10,000
Date(s) Application Is Due Mar 31; Jun 30; Sep 30; Dec 30.
Contact Research Grant Programs; (416) 934-5666; fax: (416) 961-4189; email: info@ctcri.ca
Internet http://ctcri.ca/~ctcri/en/index.php?option=content&task=view&id=211&Itemid=90
Sponsor Canadian Tobacco Control Research Initiative
10 Alcorn Ave., Suite 200
Toronto, ON M4V 3B1 Canada

CTCRI Workshop and Learning Opportunities Grants **1450**
Workshop and Learning Opportunity grants are offered to support workshops, meetings and other events to build research capacity and promote collaboration between researchers and end-users. Priority is given to first-time applicants, to regions or populations where development of research is more acutely needed and to events that address research priorities identified by the CTCRI Research Summit: Building capacity for tobacco-related research in the region or population; Providing unique opportunities to bring together individuals from different disciplines and sectors; Supporting the sharing of knowledge, initiation of collaborations or the planning of relevant research activities. Workshops, courses and other educational methods or tools are appropriate for this grant program. Each successful proposal may receive a one-time grant of up to $15,000. Work is expected to be completed in four (4) months time. The number of applications supported annually is contingent upon the availability of funds and the quality of proposals.
Requirements Proposals to this program must meet the following eligibility criteria: Topic is related to both research and tobacco abuse and/or addiction and intervention; Research could involve identifying research priorities, discussing and/or developing research frameworks and/or disseminating research results; Method involves multiple participants and could be in the form of a workshop or another educational opportunity; Approach is innovative and deals with engaging new topics and methods or involves new populations (e.g., researchers or practitioners new to tobacco control, historically under-represented regions or populations); Proposal demonstrates that any current funding will not adequately support the stated objectives of the proposal. Additionally, the following criteria apply: Research proposals must meet the following eligibility criteria: The Principal Applicant (PA) is a Canadian citizen or legal resident (Co-applicants may be citizens or residents of other countries); The research proposal demonstrates basic relevance to tobacco abuse / nicotine addiction / tobacco control and addresses research priorities identified by the Canadian Tobacco Control Research Summit; Applicant(s) has disclosed other sources of funding; Commercial interests have been disclosed or applicant(s) has indicated no commercial interests; Applicant(s) has affirmed lack of support from the tobacco industry; Applicant(s) can demonstrate that he/she works in an environment that adequately supports research through ethical review, administration of funds, provision of space and equipment, etc.; Research plans include gender analysis, or it has been demonstrated that this is not appropriate; Proposal avoids duplication of previous research, unless it can be demonstrated that replication is of value.
Restrictions Members of the staff or Board of Directors of the CTCRI, or a staff member of any CTCRI funding partner organization are not eligible to apply.
Amount up to $15,000
Date(s) Application Is Due none.
Contact Research Grant Programs; (416) 934-5666; fax: (416) 961-4189; email: info@ctcri.ca
Internet http://ctcri.ca/~ctcri/en/index.php?option=content&task=view&id=210&Itemid=91
Sponsor Canadian Tobacco Control Research Initiative
10 Alcorn Ave., Suite 200
Toronto, ON M4V 3B1 Canada

Cudd Foundation Grants **1451**
The foundation awards grants to eligible nonprofit organizations in its areas of interest, including arts, culture, performing arts, children and youth, education, environment, health care, historic preservation, and social services. Types of support include annual campaigns, building construction/renovation, capital campaigns, continuing support, curriculum development, emergency grants, endowments, program development, research, and scholarship funds. The listed application deadline is for letters of intent; full proposals are by invitation.
Requirements Louisiana and New Mexico nonprofit organizations are eligible.
Amount $250-$222,088 range
Contact Amanda Stuermer, (505) 986-8416; fax: (505) 986-8427; email: cuddfdn@aol.com
Sponsor Cudd Foundation
P.O. Box 2322
Santa Fe, NM 87504

Cushwa Center Research Travel Grants **1452**
This program is designed to foster research in the archives and library of the University of Notre Dame. The library collection is particularly rich in the following areas: Catholic newspapers, history of midwestern Catholicism, Catholic literature, and history of Catholicism in the United States. The archives have manuscripts of historical personages, records of 20th-century Catholic organizations, reports of European missionary societies, and other material related to the American Catholic community. Grants to help defray travel and lodging costs are made to scholars of any academic discipline who are engaged in projects which require substantial use of the collections of the library and archives. Submit one copy of the completed application form, current curriculum vita, a 1,000-word description of the project to be undertaken at the center, and a budget estimating travel, lodging, and research expenses. Two letters of recommendation from two people who know your work should be sent directly to the Cushwa Center.
Requirements The research project must be related to the study of the American Catholicism. Applicants should describe the relevance of the project for American Catholic studies, indicate the specific resources of interest at Notre Dame, and specify any plans for publication of the project.
Amount $2000 maximum
Date(s) Application Is Due Dec 31.
Contact Director, Cushwa Center for the Study of American Catholicism, (219) 631-5441; fax: (219) 631-8471; email: cushwa.1@nd.edu
Internet http://www.nd.edu/~cushwa/grants/
Sponsor University of Notre Dame
1135 Flanner Hall
Notre Dame, IN 46556-5611

Cystic Fibrosis Research Grants **1453**
The trust was founded to find a complete solution for cystic fibrosis and to improve upon current methods of treatment. Research grants are awarded in the United Kingdom and internationally in the fields of science and medicine.
Requirements Only researchers from recognized academic institutions are eligible to apply.
Contact Research Administrator, Research Administrator, 020 8290 7906; email: researchgrants@cftrust.org.uk
Internet http://www.cftrust.org.uk/scope/page/view.go?layout=cftrust&pageid=54
Sponsor Cystic Fibrosis Trust
11 London Rd
Bromley BR1 1BY United Kingdom

D.F. Halton Foundation Grants **1454**
The foundation awards grants to nonprofit organizations in Charlotte, NC, and San Miguel County, CO, primarily in the areas of youth, education, social services, and the performing arts. Additional areas of interest include historical preservation, education, vocational education, business school education, substance abuse, cancer research,

heart/circulatory diseases and research, human and family services, and community development. Grants are awarded for general operating support, annual campaigns, capital campaigns, and scholarship funds. There are no application deadlines or forms.
Requirements Nonprofit organizations in North Carolina counties, including Mecklenburg, Union, Cleveland, Cabarrus, Stanly, Lincoln, and Gaston, may submit proposals. Nonprofit organizations in San Miguel county, CO. may also submit proposals.
Restrictions No grants will be awarded to individuals.
Contact Dale Halton, President
Sponsor D.F. Halton Foundation
P.O. Box 834
Ophir, CO 81426

DAAD Bilateral Programs for Co-Operative Research Grants **1455**
These programs aim to intensify academic collaborative research projects by promoting the project-related exchange of academics. These are bilateral programs agreed between the DAAD in Germany and partner organizations in a number of countries. Support is given to persons participating in specific academic collaborative research projects. Particular importance is attached to the continuing education and training and specialization of young academics working within the framework of research collaboration projects. Financial support is only offered to fund specifically person-related additional costs in as far as these arise through the exchange of participating scientists, scholars, graduates and, for some countries, advanced students. Diploma-level candidates can only be included in the support framework if their final dissertation forms part of the project. The German or respectively the foreign side will pay the travel costs and the stay at the partner institute for the participants of their country on the basis of the generally applicable conditions. Payments by the host institute (for example, for accommodation) will be taken into account. Project-related additional costs (for example, computer time, material purchases, documentation, photocopying, printing) cannot be reimbursed by the DAAD, nor is there any element in the grant to cover bench fees or equipment. To date, programs have been implemented with Argentina, Brazil, Bulgaria, Canada, Chile, China, Croatia, Czech Republic, Finland, France, Greece, Hong Kong, Hungary, India, Italy, Mexico, Norway, Poland, Portugal, Slovakia, Spain, Taiwan, Thailand, the United Kingdom and the United States. Country-specific information, dates and deadlines, and application addresses differ from one country to the next.
Requirements Applications must be accompanied by a specific academic or scientific research project proposal. Academics from Germany and from the respective partner country must be collaborating in this project. Primary financing for the collaborative research project (personnel and running costs on both sides) must be provided by other sources.
Restrictions Proposals based purely on study and training are not funded.
Contact Scholarship Administrator, (212) 758-3223; fax: (212) 755-5780; email: kim@daad.org or daadny@daad.org
Internet http://www.daad.de/deutschland/foerderung/stipendiendatenbank/00462.en.html?detailid=10&fachrichtung=15&land=44&status=4&seite=1&daad=1
Sponsor German Academic Exchange Service (DAAD)
871 United Nations Plaza
New York, NY 10017

DAAD Emigre Memorial German Internship Program- Bundestag **1456**
The Program offers internship opportunities for US and Canadian students in the German parliament, the Bundestag. The internships are two months long in positions matching the student's interest and experience. Interns will be placed with their preferred Fraktion, Ausschuss, with individual members of the Bundestag and their offices. In addition to contributing to the respective offices, interns have the opportunity to study legislative and administrative procedures in the German parliament. The successful applicant will receive compensation of approximately 1,100 Euros per month from the German Bundestag. Subsidized health insurance is available for a monthly fee of about 23 Euros. DAAD can help the interns to obtain housing in Berlin (the average rent for a room is 250 Euros/month) and make contacts with fellow international interns and German students.
Requirements Applicants for EMGIP – Bundestag should possess outstanding academic records and personal integrity as well as some knowledge of the German legislative process. Participants should be advanced undergraduates or graduate students in fields such as political science, international relations, law, history, economics or German. Students must be able to fully communicate in German. US and Canadian citizens and permanent residents are eligible to apply. International students who are enrolled in a full time course of study in the US or Canada may also apply. Applicants must be younger than 32 at the start of the internship. Applicants who are graduating seniors should be prepared to show acceptance to a graduate school or further affiliation with their college to ensure student status in Germany. Travel expenses are the intern's responsibility.
Restrictions German nationals are not eligible.
Amount Euro 1100 per month
Date(s) Application Is Due Nov 17.
Contact Program Administrator, (212) 758-3223; fax: (212) 755-5780; email: schenkl@daad.org or daadny@daad.org
Internet http://www.daad.org/page/53287/
Sponsor German Academic Exchange Service (DAAD)
871 United Nations Plaza
New York, NY 10017

DAAD Faculty Research Visit Grants **1457**
This program offers grants for one to three months in all academic disciplines to scholars at US and Canadian institutions of higher education to pursue research at universities, libraries, archives, institutes or laboratories in Germany. Grants are awarded for specific research projects. Stipends consist of a monthly maintenance allowance.
Requirements Candidate must hold a PhD, have been engaged in teaching or research for at least two years after receipt of the doctorate, be a US citizen or permanent resident affiliated with an American institution for at least five years, and have a previous research record in the proposed field. The period for which the grant is awarded must fall entirely within one calendar year.
Restrictions Grants cannot be used for travel, attendance at conferences or conventions, editorial meetings, lecture tours, or extended guest-professorships. No extra allowance is given for dependents who might accompany the grantee. Three years must elapse before another application by a former study visit grantee will be considered; applicant may not hold a DAAD grant or a grant from another German or American organization consecutively or concurrently.
Amount 1,840 - 2,240 Euro per month
Date(s) Application Is Due Feb 1; Aug 1.
Contact Grants Administrator; (212) 758-3223; fax: (212) 755-5780; email: daadny@daad.org or schenkl@daad.org
Internet http://www.daad.org/page/68573/
Sponsor German Academic Exchange Service (DAAD)
871 United Nations Plaza
New York, NY 10017

DAAD German Studies Research Grants **1458**
This specialized program offers up to five German Studies Research Grants to highly qualified undergraduate and graduate students who are nominated by their department/program chairs. The grant may be used for short-term research (one to two months) in either North America or Germany. The program is designed to encourage research and promote the study of cultural, political, historical, economic and social aspects of modern and contemporary German affairs from an inter- and multidisciplinary perspective. Research support ranging in value from $1,500 to $2,500 is available to individual recipients and is intended to offset living and travel costs during the research phase.
Requirements Undergraduates with at least junior standing pursuing a German Studies track or minor may be nominated for the grant by their department and/or program chair. Applicants are expected to have completed two years of college German and a minimum of three courses in German Studies (literature, history, politics or other fields) at the time of nomination. Grants are restricted to citizens of the US who are enrolled full time at the university that nominates them. Applicants must be younger than 32 at the start of the grant period.
Restrictions Support cannot be provided for stays in Germany in the context of study abroad programs.
Amount $1,500 to $2,500
Date(s) Application Is Due Nov 1; May 1.
Contact Program Administrator, (212) 758-3223; fax: (212) 755-5780; email: graaff@daad.org or daadny@daad.org
Internet http://www.daad.org/page/51532/
Sponsor German Academic Exchange Service (DAAD)
871 United Nations Plaza
New York, NY 10017

DAAD Intensive Language Courses Grants **1459**
DAAD offers grants to graduate students at North American universities to attend 8-week intensive language courses at leading institutes in Germany. Extensive descriptions of the institutes, their teaching philosophies, course content, as well as course dates are available on the website of each institute. Scholarships are awarded to students currently enrolled full-time in a graduate or PhD program in all fields of study except English, German, or any other modern language or literature. Applicants will be assessed on academic record and statements of projected academic and professional future.
Requirements As a rule, applicants must be citizens of the US or Canada. Foreign nationals may be eligible if they have been full-time graduate students at a US or Canadian University for at least one academic year at the time of application. Applicants must have completed three semesters of college German or have achieved an equivalent level of language proficiency. Applicants must be younger than 32 at the start of the grant period.
Restrictions Applicants who have received a DAAD summer language grant in the past three years are not eligible to apply.
Amount 2,650 Euro
Date(s) Application Is Due Jan 31.
Contact Program Administrator, (212) 758-3223; fax: (212) 755-5780; email: graaff@daad.org or daadny@daad.org
Internet http://www.daad.org/page/54773/
Sponsor German Academic Exchange Service (DAAD)
871 United Nations Plaza
New York, NY 10017

DAAD Learn German in Germany Grants **1460**
The Goethe-Institut, through DAAD, offers one to two grants to faculty members in all academic fields except modern languages and literatures to attend intensive language

courses at Goethe-Instituts in Germany. Four and eight-week courses are offered year-round. Preference will be given to applicants in the social sciences, the natural sciences, engineering and professional schools, who are in mid-career and are under 46 years of age.
Requirements Scholars who hold a PhD (or equivalent) and have been working in research or teaching full-time at a United States university or research institution for at least two years after receipt of the doctorate are eligible. Applicants must have a basic knowledge of German and be able to demonstrate a need for acquiring a better proficiency in the German language for their future studies or research.
Restrictions Applicants must be citizens or permanent residents of the United States. Faculty members who teach in the fields of English, German or any modern languages or literatures are not eligible.
Amount 1,700 Euro
Date(s) Application Is Due Jan 31.
Contact Program Administrator, (212) 758-3223; fax: (212) 755-5780; email: graaff@daad.org or daadny@daad.org
Internet http://www.daad.org/page/47845/
Sponsor German Academic Exchange Service (DAAD)
871 United Nations Plaza
New York, NY 10017

DAAD Re-invitation Program for Former Scholarship Holders **1461**
The Program helps the DAAD maintain contacts with its former one-year scholarship holders and with former scholarship holders who had studied in East Germany (GDR) for at least one year. Former scholarship holders meeting these requirements can apply for re-invitation to Germany to complete a research or work project at a state (public) or state-recognized higher education institution or non-university research institute. Depending on the applicant's work schedule, the research stay can last between one and three months. Depending on the applicant's academic status, the monthly award will amount to 1,840 Euros for assistant lecturers, assistant professors and young lecturers, and 1,990 Euros for professors. In some rare exceptions, 2,240 Euros may be available. In addition to these payments, the DAAD generally will pay an appropriate flat-rate travel allowance, unless these costs are covered by the home country or by another funding source.
Requirements Applications for the re-invitation program can only be submitted by former one-year scholarship holders who have been back in their home country for at least three years. The most important selection criterion is a convincing and well-planned research or work project to be completed during the stay in Germany.
Amount Euro 1,840 - Euro 2,240 per month
Date(s) Application Is Due Jan 15; Aug 1.
Contact Scholarship Administrator, (212) 758-3223; fax: (212) 755-5780; email: kim@daad.org or daadny@daad.org
Internet http://www.daad.de/deutschland/foerderung/stipendiendatenbank/00462.en.html?detailid=38&fachrichtung=15&land=44&status=4&seite=1&daad=1
Sponsor German Academic Exchange Service (DAAD)
871 United Nations Plaza
New York, NY 10017

DAAD Research Grants **1462**
Research grants are awarded to highly qualified undergraduate and graduate students who are nominated by their department/program chairs. The grant may be used for short-term research (one to two months) in either North America or Germany. The program is designed to encourage research and promote the study of cultural, political, historical, economic and social aspects of modern and contemporary German affairs from an inter- and multidisciplinary perspective.
Requirements Master's level graduate students in the humanities and social services earning a certificate or working on a project in German Studies may be nominated for the grant by their department and/or program chair. Applicants are expected to have completed a minimum of three courses in German Studies (literature, history, politics, or other fields) at the time of nomination. Doctoral degree students in the humanities and social science disciplines in the process of preparing their dissertation proposals on modern German topics may be nominated. Students whose dissertation proposals have already been formally accepted are not eligible for nomination. The intent of the program is to provide an opportunity for short-term exploratory research to determine the viability or to delimit the scope of their proposed dissertations. The program is not intended to supplement or substitute for regular dissertation field work abroad which should lag the short-term research stay by at least one semester. All applicants are expected to have completed two years of college level German language studies. Applicants must be younger than 32 at the start of the grant period.
Restrictions Grants are restricted to citizens of the US who are enrolled full time at the university that nominates them. Support cannot be provided for stays in Germany in the context of study abroad programs.
Amount $1,500-$2,500
Date(s) Application Is Due May 1; Nov 1.
Contact Grants Administrator, (212) 758-3223; fax: (212) 755-5780; email: kim@daad.org or daadny@daad.org
Internet http://www.daad.org/?p=gradresearch
Sponsor German Academic Exchange Service (DAAD)
871 United Nations Plaza
New York, NY 10017

DAAD Research Grants for Doctoral Candidates and Young Academics and Scientists **1463**
The Program provides young foreign academics and scientists with an opportunity to carry out a research project or a course of continuing education and training at a German state (public) or state-recognized higher education institution or non-university research institute. Research grants can be used to carry out; research projects at a German higher education institution for the purpose of gaining a doctorate in the home country; research projects at a German university for the purpose of gaining a doctorate in Germany; or research projects or continuing education and training, but without aiming at a formal degree/qualification. Depending on the project in question and on the applicant's work schedule, grants can be paid generally for between one and ten months, in the case of full doctoral programs in Germany for up to three years, and in exceptions for up to a maximum of four years. Applications for research grants to run for more than six months are decided once a year, and must be submitted by November 15. Applications by musicians, architects and visual artists must be submitted by November 1. Applications for research grants to run for up to six months are decided twice a year, and must be submitted by August 1 or November 15. At the earliest, the grant can begin 6 months after the date of application. Support can only be provided for the completion of a full doctoral program in Germany when special support policy reasons exist. Depending on the award holder's academic level, the program will pay a monthly award of 715 Euros (graduates holding a first degree) or 975 Euros (doctoral candidates). As a rule, the scholarship additionally includes certain payments towards health insurance coverage in Germany. Furthermore, the program generally will pay an appropriate flat-rate travel allowance, unless these costs are covered by the home country or by another funding source.
Requirements Applications for DAAD research grants are open to excellently-qualified university graduates who hold a Diplom or Master's degree at the time they commence the grant-supported research and, in exceptional cases, graduates holding a Bachelor's degree or already holding a doctorate/PhD (post-docs). It is required that doctoral candidates wishing to take a doctorate/PhD in their home country will already have been admitted to an appropriate course at their home university. Besides previous study achievements, the most important selection criterion is a convincing and well-planned research or continuing education and training project to be completed during the stay in Germany and which has been coordinated and agreed with an academic supervisor at the chosen German host institute. German language skills are generally required, although the required level also depends on the applicant's project and topic, as well as on the available opportunities for learning German in the applicant's home country.
Restrictions The award of grants is subject to an age limit of 32 years at the time of starting the grant.
Amount Euro 715 - Euro 975 per month
Date(s) Application Is Due Aug 1; Nov 1; Nov 15.
Contact Scholarship Administrator, (212) 758-3223; fax: (212) 755-5780; email: kim@daad.org or daadny@daad.org
Internet http://www.daad.de/deutschland/foerderung/stipendiendatenbank/00462.en.html?detailid=7&fachrichtung=4&land=44&status=3&seite=1&daad=1
Sponsor German Academic Exchange Service (DAAD)
871 United Nations Plaza
New York, NY 10017

DAAD Research Internships in Science and Engineering (RISE) **1464**
DAAD, in cooperation with science organizations in North America and Germany, offers summer internships in Germany for US and Canadian undergraduate students in the fields of biology, chemistry, physics, earth sciences and engineering. RISE fellows work directly with doctoral students in research groups at top German universities and institutions and can expect to gain serious hands-on research experience. RISE placements provide students the opportunity to live and work in an international context, to gain confidence in their practical and theoretical skills, and to improve their (or begin learning!) German. Last but not least, the research internship should be a source of mutual cultural enrichment for both the interns and their hosts. Every RISE intern receives a pro-rated monthly scholarship of approximately 615 Euros for any period of six weeks to three months between June and August. The program also provides health and accident insurance.
Requirements To apply for a placement an applicant must: be currently enrolled at an United States or Canadian university/college as a full-time student in the field of Biology, Chemistry, Physics, Earth Sciences or Engineering (or a closely related field); be an undergraduate who will have completed at least 2 years of a degree program by the time of the placement; and prove that he/she will be registered as an undergraduate at a university/college for the academic year.
Amount Euro 615
Date(s) Application Is Due Feb 1.
Contact Michaela Gottschling; +49 (0)228-882-567; fax: +49 (0)228-882-551; email: knieps@daad.de or rise@daad.de
Internet http://www.daad.de/rise/en/index.html
Sponsor German Academic Exchange Service (DAAD)
Referat 315, Kennedyallee 50
Bonn 53175 Germany

DAAD Research Stays for University Academics and Scientists **1465**
These grants and scholarships aim to provide foreign academics and scientists working in higher education or at research institutes with an opportunity to carry out a research project at a state (public) or state-recognized higher education institution or non-

university research institute in Germany. Depending on the applicant's work schedule, the research stay will last between one and three months. Depending on the applicant's academic status, the monthly award will amount to 1,840 Euros for assistant lecturers, assistant professors and young lecturers, and 1,990 Euros for professors. In some rare exceptions, 2,240 Euros may be available. In addition to these payments, the DAAD generally will pay an appropriate flat-rate travel allowance, unless these costs are covered by the home country or by another funding source. Applications for research grants are decided twice a year. Applications must have been submitted by 1 August or 15 January. At the earliest, grants can begin 4 months after the date of application.
Requirements Applications for DAAD research stays are open to excellently-qualified academics and scientists who should generally hold a doctorate/PhD. All applicants must be working in higher education or at a research institute in their home country. Besides their previous academic achievements (for example, recent publications), the most important selection criterion is a convincing and well-planned research project to be completed during the stay in Germany. The application must provide proof of a workplace being provided at the host institute.
Restrictions DAAD support for a research stay can only be awarded once in any three-year period. No travel expenses can be paid from the grant.
Amount Euro 1,840 - Euro 2,240 per month
Date(s) Application Is Due Jan 15; Aug 1.
Contact Scholarship Administrator, (212) 758-3223; fax: (212) 755-5780; email: kim@daad.org or daadny@daad.org
Internet http://www.daad.de/deutschland/foerderung/stipendiendatenbank/00462.en.html?detailid=39&fachrichtung=15&land=44&status=4&seite=1&daad=1
Sponsor German Academic Exchange Service (DAAD)
871 United Nations Plaza
New York, NY 10017

DAAD RISE Professional Internships 1466
The Program offers practical, career-building experience in the fields of Biology, Chemistry, Physics, Earth Sciences and Engineering (or closely related subjects). Aimed at Bachelor, Master or PhD students from the US or Canada, the RISE professional internship placements provide students the opportunity to live and work in an international context, to gain confidence in their practical and professional skills, and to improve their German. Further, the internship will be a source of mutual cultural and professional enrichment for both the interns and their host companies. Every intern receives a pro-rated monthly scholarship of about 615 Euros for any period of six weeks to three months between June and August. DAAD also provides health and accident insurance.
Requirements To apply for a placement an applicant must: be currently enrolled at an United States or Canadian university/college as a full-time student in the field of Biology, Chemistry, Physics, Earth Sciences or Engineering (or a closely related field); be an undergraduate who will have completed at least 2 years of a degree program by the time of the placement; and prove that he/she will be registered as an undergraduate at a university/college for the academic year.
Amount Euro 615
Date(s) Application Is Due Jan 25.
Contact Martina Ludwig; +49 (0)228) 882-104; fax: +49 (0)228) 882-551; email: rise-pro@daad.de
Internet http://www.daad.de/rise-pro/en/index.html
Sponsor German Academic Exchange Service (DAAD)
Referat 315, Kennedyallee 50
Bonn 53175 Germany

DAAD Scholarships for Artists: Study Visits for Academics 1467
The study visits for academics program aims to enable lecturers from the fields of Fine Art, Design, Film, Music and Architecture as well as Drama, Direction, Dance and Choreography to apply for a supported study visit for the purpose of artistic cooperation with a German host institution. Depending on the applicant's work schedule, the study visit will last between one and three months. Depending on the applicant's academic status, the monthly award will amount to 1,840 euros for assistant lecturers, assistant professors and young lecturers, and 1,990 euros for professors, in exceptions, 2,240 euros. In addition to these payments, the DAAD generally will pay an appropriate flat-rate travel allowance, unless these costs are covered by the home country or by another funding source.
Requirements To qualify for support under the study visits for artists program, the applicant must be lecturing at a higher education institution in the home country. A well-planned and convincing project is an important selection criterion. The application papers must be accompanied by written confirmation of academic supervision or confirmation of agreement having been reached with a German institution of higher education.
Restrictions DAAD support for study visits by artists can only be awarded once in any three-year period.
Amount Euro 1,840 - Euro 2,240 per month
Date(s) Application Is Due Jan 15; Aug 1.
Contact Scholarship Administrator, (212) 758-3223; fax: (212) 755-5780; email: kim@daad.org or daadny@daad.org
Internet http://www.daad.de/deutschland/foerderung/stipendiendatenbank/00462.en.html?detailid=41&fachrichtung=8&land=44&status=4&seite=1&daad=1
Sponsor German Academic Exchange Service (DAAD)
871 United Nations Plaza
New York, NY 10017

DAAD Study & Internship Program (SIP) in Germany 1468
This program offers students a full academic semester of study abroad at one of the UAS7 universities in Germany followed by a one-semester professional internship experience in a company or research institute in Germany. Scholarships are granted for one semester (6 months). Recipients will be awarded a monthly stipend of about 675 Euro to cover living expenses, including a monthly contribution to cover health and accident liability insurance. In addition, they receive 850 Euro as a contribution to travel expenses. During the internship the company will pay a minimum of 500 Euro/month to help cover the monthly living expenses.
Requirements Students must: be full-time, in good academic standing, and currently enrolled in an undergraduate degree-granting program at an accredited US or Canadian college or university; be currently enrolled as Sophomores or Juniors in engineering, science, life sciences, business, management, economics, architecture, art, design, journalism, or social work; possess an outstanding academic record and personal integrity, as proven by academic achievement and letters of recommendation; hold US or Canadian citizenship or be a permanent resident thereof (foreign nationals are eligible if they have been full-time students at an accredited US or Canadian university for more than one year at the time of application and intend to return to the US or to Canada after the scholarship period to complete their Bachelor's degree); and meet the age limit of 32 at the start of the grant period.
Amount 675 Euro per month, plus 850 Euro travel expense
Contact Program Administrator, (212) 758-3223; fax: (212) 755-5780; email: daadny@daad.org
Internet http://www.uas7.org/content/programs__projects/study__internship_program/index_en.html
Sponsor German Academic Exchange Service (DAAD)
871 United Nations Plaza
New York, NY 10017

DAAD Study Visits / Study Seminars and Practicals in Germany by Foreign Students 1469
The program aims to provide students with subject-related knowledge by arranging appropriate visits, tours and information meetings (Study Visits) or by organizing subject-related seminars and practical courses (e.g. specialist courses, block seminars, workshops) at the invitation of a German university. This university is also responsible for organizing practical courses with universities, companies and, possibly, public institutions (Study Seminars and Practicals). The program goals also include: facilitating meetings with German students, academics and researchers to establish and maintain contacts between German and foreign universities; and giving students a greater understanding of and insight (regional and area studies) into economic, political and cultural life in Germany. Cultural events (e.g. concert tours) can be funded when the focus is on meeting students and university teachers from a relevant academic field and this academic relevance is appropriately documented. Study visits, study seminars or practicals should last no less than 7 days. Funding is available for a maximum of 12 days (including travel days), although the visits themselves may last longer. The DAAD takes out health, accident and public/private liability insurance for each funded group.
Restrictions Funding cannot be provided for annual repeat visits (by applicants, faculties or departments); each applicant, faculty or department can only be considered for a maximum of one application per year. Funding cannot be provided for required/obligatory excursions or for measures that have already been completed. The Program regrets that it is unable to pay any international travel costs.
Contact Katharina Klein; +49 (0)228/882-370; fax: +49 (0)228/882-447; email: k.klein@daad.de
Internet http://www.daad.de/deutschland/foerderung/stipendiendatenbank/00462.en.html?detailid=15&fachrichtung=15&land=44&status=4&seite=1&daad=1
Sponsor German Academic Exchange Service (DAAD)
Referat 224, Kennedyallee 50
Bonn D-53175 Germany

DAAD Undergraduate Scholarships 1470
Highly qualified undergraduate students are invited to apply for scholarships funding study, senior thesis research, and/or internships in Germany. The goal of this program is to support study abroad in Germany and at German universities. Preference will be given to students whose projects or programs are based at and organized by a German university. Scholarships are available either as part of an organized study abroad program or as part of an individual, student-designed study abroad semester or year. The scholarship periods must take place during the German academic year. (short term: October 1 through January 31; long term: October 1 through July 31). Recipients receive a monthly stipend and funds to help defray travel and research expenses, as well as health insurance. Guidelines are available online.
Requirements Eligible students are current sophomores or juniors of all academic fields; are seeking DAAD support for a four- to ten-month period in Germany during the German academic year; possess outstanding academic records and personal integrity, as evidenced by both their grades and letters of recommendation; are able to receive academic credit at their home institutions or ECTS credits for their activity in Germany; are US or Canadian citizens or permanent residents thereof (Foreign nationals are eligible if they have been full-time students at an accredited US or Canadian university for more than one year at the time of application and will return to the US or Canada after the scholarship period to complete their bachelor's degree.); have well-defined study, research, or internship plans for their stay in Germany; submit the DAAD language

evaluation form with their application, although German language competency is not mandatory; demonstrate an interest in contemporary German and European affairs and who explain the significance of their project in Germany to their future studies, research, or professional goals; are enrolled, full-time students in an undergraduate degree-granting program at an accredited North American college or university; and are younger than 32 at the start of the grant period.
Amount Euro 615 per month
Date(s) Application Is Due Jan 31.
Contact Scholarship Administrator, (212) 758-3223; fax: (212) 755-5780; email: daadny@daad.org
Internet http://www.daad.org/?p=47220
Sponsor German Academic Exchange Service (DAAD)
871 United Nations Plaza
New York, NY 10017

DAAD Visiting Professorship Grants **1471**
This program serves to strengthen the internationalization of the educational experience for scholars, host institutions and students by welcoming educators from abroad to university campuses in Germany for guest teaching assignments. The recent development of international degree programs and traditional curricula looking to infuse an international aspect provide opportunities for professors from other countries to contribute their expertise in particular subjects and teaching methods. Courses need not be taught in German. As the applicant, the German host institution receives the DAAD funding. Visiting Professors are paid by the host institution according to the salary schemes for German university faculty. Funding is available for one semester to two years. Additional allowances can be made for travel, luggage and health insurance.
Requirements Highly qualified scholars in all academic disciplines, preferably those who hold a doctoral or other terminal degree and have an affiliation with an institution of higher education, are eligible. Candidates must secure an invitation from a German host institution and teach courses integrated into the regular curriculum.
Restrictions Funds cannot be made available to replace faculty on sabbatical.
Date(s) Application Is Due Jul 15; Jan 15.
Contact Grants Administrator; (212) 758-3223; fax: (212) 755-5780; email: daadny@daad.org or gastdozentur@daad.org
Internet http://www.daad.org/page/50132/
Sponsor German Academic Exchange Service (DAAD)
871 United Nations Plaza
New York, NY 10017

DAAD-AICGS Research Fellowships **1472**
The program is designed to bring scholars and specialists working on Germany, Europe, and/or transatlantic relations to AICGS for research stays of two months each. Project proposals should address a topic closely related to one or more of the Institute's five research and programming areas: Globalization and the German and American Economies; Germany in Europe; Security and Foreign Policy--Changing Agendas and New Challenges; Culture and Politics; or Transnational Issues and German-American Cooperation. Fellowships include a monthly stipend of up to $4,600, depending on the seniority of the applicant, economy class round-trip airfare and transportation to and from Washington (for a maximum of $770), and office space at the Institute.
Requirements Applicants must be German or American citizens.
Amount $4,600 per month, plus $770 round-trip airfare
Date(s) Application Is Due Apr 30; May 31; Sep 30.
Contact Program Contact, (202) 332-9312; fax: (202) 265-9531; email: kverclas@aicgs.org or info@aicgs.org
Internet http://www.daad.org/page/98696/
Sponsor German Academic Exchange Service (DAAD)
871 United Nations Plaza
New York, NY 10017

DAAD-Leo Baeck Institute Fellowships **1473**
Fellowships are awarded for research in New York or Germany on the social, communal, and intellectual history of German-speaking Jewry. Financial assistance is provided to doctoral students for dissertation research and to young academics for the preparation of a scholarly essay or book. The New York fellowship consists of a stipend of $2,000 paid in two installments of $1,000 each. The fellowship for Germany follows the terms of award for the DAAD Research Grant.
Requirements Applicants must be US citizens and PhD candidates or recent PhDs (degree awarded within the last two years).
Amount $2,000
Date(s) Application Is Due Nov 15.
Contact Program Contact, Leo Baeck Institute; (212) 744-6400; fax: (212) 988-1305; email: lbaeck@lbi.cjh.org
Internet http://www.daad.org/page/48513/
Sponsor German Academic Exchange Service (DAAD)
15 West 16th Street
New York, NY 10011

Dade Community Foundation Grants **1474**
The funding for this program is made available through the Foundation's unrestricted and field of interest funds. This program is designed to honor both the donors interests and address significant community issues such as: education; health; human services; arts and culture; environment; economic development; at-risk youth; abused and neglected children; living with HIV/AIDS; homelessness; social justice; care of animals; heart disease and more.
Requirements Eligible applicants include nonprofit tax-exempt organizations, as defined by the Internal Revenue Code, which are serving the residents of Miami-Dade County. Preference will be given to organizations based in Miami-Dade County or if located outside the county, are working in partnership with an organization based in Miami-Dade.
Restrictions The Foundation does not provide grants to individuals, for memberships, fundraising events or memorials. Grants to government agencies are made on a very restricted basis.
Amount $7,500
Date(s) Application Is Due Nov 15.
Contact Gianne Ewing-Chow, Program Officer, (305) 371-2711; fax: (305) 371-5342; email: gianne.ewingchow@dadecommunityfoundation.org
Internet http://www.dadecommunityfoundation.org/Site/programs/overview.jsp
Sponsor Dade Community Foundation
200 South Biscayne Boulevard, Suite 505
Miami, FL 33131-5330

DaimlerChrysler Corporation Fund Grants **1475**
The fund contributes to organizations grouped under the general categories of education, health and human services, civic and community, religion, and culture and the arts. Within these categories, grants are made available for public welfare or for charitable, scientific, educational, environmental, safety, building, and affirmative action purposes. Higher education grants largely support science and engineering education and business management. A major interest of the corporation is the establishment of national certification standards for elementary and secondary teachers. Another area of concern is the encouragement of early reading skills, and a pilot project has been funded for research in this area. The fund earmarks funds for its future workforce initiatives, which support business and engineering departments, community-based job-skill training, and entry-level work preparation. Types of support include matching gifts, program grants, scholarships, annual campaigns, building construction/renovation, general support, and employee matching gifts. In considering requests, the fund evaluates each applicant organization on its own merits; considered are the programs in which it is engaged, constituencies served, operation procedures, services offered, quality of management, its accountability, finances, and fund-raising practices. Applications are accepted at any time.
Requirements Eligible for support are nonprofit, tax-exempt educational, health, civic, and cultural organizations primarily in locations where the greatest number of employees of Chrysler and its US-based subsidiaries live and work (Alabama, Delaware, Illinois, Indiana, Michigan, Missouri, New York, Ohio, and Wisconsin). Some support is targeted for national organizations as well.
Restrictions Grants are not awarded to support endowments, conferences, trips, direct health care delivery, multiyear pledges, capital campaigns, fund-raising activities related to sponsorships, advertising, or debt retirement.
Contact Brian Glowiak, Vice President, (248) 512-2502; fax: (248) 512-2503; email: mek@dcx.com
Internet http://www.fund.daimlerchrysler.com
Sponsor DaimlerChrysler Corporation Fund
1000 Chrysler Dr
Auburn Hills, MI 48326-2766

Damon Runyon Cancer Foundation Fellowships **1476**
The foundation encourages all theoretical and experimental research relevant to the study of cancer and the search for cancer causes, mechanisms, therapies, and prevention. Candidates must apply for the fellowships under the guidance of a sponsor--a senior member of the scientific research community. The sponsor should be actively engaged in the planning, execution, and supervision of the proposed research and should encourage the fellow to report the results of the research in scientific journals and meetings. Awards are made to institutions for the support of the fellow under direct supervision of the sponsor.
Requirements Applicants must have completed one or more of the following degrees or its equivalent: MD, PhD, DDS, and DVM.
Amount $41,000 and $55,000 year one (level I and level II); $43,000 and $56,000 year two; $44,000 and $57,000 year three; $2000 in expenses each year
Date(s) Application Is Due Mar 15; Aug 15.
Contact Fellowship Administrator, (212) 455-0520; email: awards@drcrf.org
Internet http://www.drcrf.org/apFellowship.html
Sponsor Damon Runyon Cancer Research Foundation
675 Third Ave, 25th Fl
New York, NY 10017

Dana Clinical Hypotheses Program in Brain and Immuno-Imaging Research Grants **1477**
The program focuses on improving human brain and immune system functioning in health and disease. The program consists of two tracks. Track A is for conventional systems imaging of brain tissues (imaging white or gray matter in the brain). Track B is for the evolving field of cellular and molecular imaging of brain cells, or immune cells, or

their interactions (imaging at the level of cells rather than tissues). Applicants undertaking cellular and molecular imaging also can employ systems imaging in their proposals to view the actions of cells within their system. Institutions may submit only one application per track. Both tracks are designed to support pilot-testing of promising but high-risk innovative ideas that have direct clinical application and that, when successful, could be supported on a larger scale by other funders. Although one goal of the program is to make support available to researchers early in their careers, any researcher with a promising new hypothesis is eligible. Guidelines are available online.
Requirements Each US medical school dean, and the presidents of the few selected biomedical research institutions that have been invited by letter, may nominate a total of two applicants, one for Track A, conventional brain systems imaging research, and one application for Track B, using cellular and molecular imaging techniques alone or in combination with brain tissue (systems) imaging techniques. Each application must be countersigned by the medical school dean or invited biomedical institution's president.
Amount $100,000 maximum per year
Date(s) Application Is Due May 27.
Contact Rebecca Husman, email: danainfo@dana.org
Internet http://www.dana.org/grants/health/proposals/brainimaging.cfm
Sponsor Charles A. Dana Foundation
745 Fifth Ave, Ste 900
New York, NY 10151

Dana Foundation Science and Health Grants **1478**
The Foundation supports research in neuroscience, immunology, and the effects of arts training on cognition. Areas of focus are: Brain and Immuno-imaging; Human Immunology; Neuroimmunology; Clinical Neuroscience Research; and Arts and Cognition. All other Science and Health Grants are made solely by invitation.
Requirements The Foundation requires institutions, in many cases, to share the cost of a project or raise matching funds.
Restrictions The foundation makes no grants directly to individuals; does not support annual operating budgets of organizations, deficit reduction, capital campaigns, or individual sabbaticals; and does not schedule meetings with applicants, other than by specific invitation initiated by the foundation.
Contact Grants Administrator, (212) 223-4040; fax: (212) 317-8721; email: danainfo@dana.org
Internet http://www.dana.org/grants
Sponsor Charles A. Dana Foundation
745 Fifth Avenue, Suite 900
New York, NY 10151-0002

Dana Science and Health Research Grants **1479**
Science and health grants support brain research in neuroscience and immunology and their interrelationship in human health and disease. Areas of interest include brain and immuno-imaging--anatomical, physiological, or cellular and molecular imaging techniques to pilot-test novel clinical hypotheses of the brain, immune cells, or their interactions; and human immunology--clinical studies that measure human immune system functioning in health and disease, including the measurement of immune system responses to experimental therapeutic trials supported by other sources. Guidelines are available online.
Requirements RFPs for the brain and immuno-imaging category are sent twice yearly to deans of US medical schools and other invited biomedical research institutions. Individual investigators as well as collaborating investigators are eligible to apply in the human immunology category.
Amount $300,000 maximum over three years
Contact Grants Administrator, (212) 223-4040; fax: (212) 317-8721; email: danainfo@dana.org
Internet http://www.dana.org/grants/health
Sponsor Dana Foundation
745 Fifth Ave, Ste 900
New York, NY 10151-0002

Dance Advance Grants **1480**
The program, which supports dance projects in Pennsylvania's five-county region surrounding and including Philadelphia, is designed to cultivate artistic excellence, strengthen creative capacity, and promote professional standards in the area. One-year grants are awarded to individual choreographers and dance artists and dance organizations. Grants are awarded on a project basis (research and development, rehearsal and creation, production and presentation, and capacity-building projects) and not for unrestricted or general operating support. Complete guidelines and application are available online. Letters of intent are due September 21; full applications are due November 9.
Requirements Grants are awarded to Philadelphia individual dance artists and 501(c)3 dance organizations in Bucks, Chester, Delaware, Montgomery, and Philadelphia counties. Individual applicants who are full-time employees of a university, college, or institution of higher learning may be considered.
Amount $10,000 maximum, individual choreographers and dance artists; $20,000 maximum, organizations with annual budgets up to $200,000
Date(s) Application Is Due Sep 21; Nov 9.
Contact Grants Administrator, (215) 732-9060; fax: (215) 732-9057; email: info@danceadvance.org
Internet http://www.danceadvance.org/02guidelines/index.html
Sponsor Dance Advance
1500 Walnut St, Ste 305
Philadelphia, PA 19102

Daniel Mendelsohn New Investigator Award **1481**
The Daniel P. Mendelsohn award is intended to encourage new investigators whose work is compatible with this mission. New investigators in the field of research or education whose work relates to health and well being are eligible for the award. Candidates, who may or may not be members of the FRI organization, must have demonstrated scholarly research potential compatible with the mission of FRI. They must show future promise, evidenced by energy and enthusiasm in research that addresses prevention, treatment or education activities. Candidates for the biennial award are reviewed by the Awards Review Committee of FRI that presents their recommendation to the Board of Directors at their October Annual Meeting. Deadline for recommending candidates is May 1 of even numbered years. The Award is $5000 payable to the recipient for her or his personal or professional use, and will be presented in the fall of the awarding year.
Amount $5,000
Date(s) Application Is Due May 1.
Contact Janet Klein Brown, Chair, (410) 823-5116; fax: (410) 823-5131; email: fri@friendsresearch.org
Internet http://www.friendsresearch.org/awards_summary.htm
Sponsor Friends Research Institute
505 Baltimore Avenue, P.O. Box 10676
Baltimore, MD 21285

Danone Institute Belgium Doctoral Scholarship in Nutrition **1482**
The scholarship, given every four years, is allocated to a candidate who has decided on a career in research on nutrition, and to this end, is enrolled in a doctoral program in a Belgian university in either the French-speaking community or in the Flemish-speaking community. All degrees must be obtained with a minimum grade of distinction.
Requirements Applicants should be either: holders of a degree of doctor of medicine, pharmacologist, chemical and agricultural engineering, or bioengineering; a graduate in nutrition, physical education and physiotherapy, psychology; or be holders of an equivalent recognized degree obtained in a country of the European Union.
Amount 30,000 Euro annually
Contact Fabienne Trinon; + 32 2 770 63 54; fax: + 32 2 771 98 97; email: institute@danone.com
Internet http://www.danoneinstitute.be/
Sponsor Danone Institute Belgium
Rue du Duc - 100 - Hertogstraat
Brussels 1000
Belgium

Danone Institute Belgium Research in Human Nutrition Grants **1483**
The grants for human nutrition are designed to help promote research in human nutrition, including applied research on an animal model, in Belgium university-level institutions. Candidates should be members of, or an employee with, a research service, research department, research institute or research body within the institution to which he belongs or is affiliated. Three grant awards are given each year.
Requirements Candidates must be: less than 40 years of age. He/she must also be a member of the permanent academic or scientific staff at a Belgian university-level institution, a permanent researcher at the Fund for Scientific Research, or a research fellow specifically recommended by an university authority.
Amount 12,000 Euro / $16,500 approximately
Contact Fabienne Trinon; + 32 2 770 63 54; fax: + 32 2 771 98 97; email: institute@danone.com
Internet http://www.danoneinstitute.be/
Sponsor Danone Institute Belgium
Rue du Duc - 100 - Hertogstraat
Brussels 1000
Belgium

DAR American Indian Scholarship **1484**
The American Indians Committee of the DAR awards this scholarship to Native Americans. This award is intended to help Native American students of any age, any tribe, in any state striving to get an education. All awards are judged based on financial need and academic achievement. This scholarship is applicable to programs of vocational training or college/university at the undergraduate or graduate level. Graduate students are eligible; however, undergraduate students are given preference.
Requirements Applicants must be Native Americans(proof of American Indian blood is required by letter or proof papers)in financial need, and have a grade point average of 2.75 or higher. There will be no exceptions.
Amount $500
Date(s) Application Is Due Apr 1; Oct 1.
Contact Scholarship Administrator, (202) 628-1776
Internet http://www.dar.org/natsociety/edout_scholar.cfm#amInd
Sponsor Daughters of the American Revolution
1776 D St NW
Washington, DC 20006

DARPA Military Research and Technology Development Grants 1485

The program objective is to support and stimulate basic research, applied research, and technology development at educational institutions, nonprofit organizations, and commercial firms, of interest to DOD and the military services. This support may take the form of grants, cooperative agreements, or other transactions. Funds may support symposia and conferences, programs to encourage careers in science and technology, programs assisting laboratory research instrumentation at universities, and programs intended to produce fundamentally different approaches to relevant technologies. The assistance is generally for a three- to five-year period.

Requirements For grants, eligibility is limited to public and private educational institutions and nonprofit organizations operated for purposes of special interest. For cooperative agreements, eligibility is limited to educational institutions, nonprofit organizations, and commercial firms.

Restrictions Individuals are ineligible.

Amount $100,000-$100 million; average $1.15 million

Contact Director, Contract Management Office, Defense Advanced Research Projects Agency, (703) 696-2399

Internet http://www.darpa.mil/index.html

Sponsor Department of Defense
3701 N Fairfax Dr
Arlington, VA 22203

Dart Center Ochberg Fellowship 1486

The Dart Center provides six or more expense-paid fellowships to midcareer journalists who want to apply knowledge of emotional trauma to improving coverage of violent events. Fellows will attend a two-day seminar on the role emotional trauma plays in coverage of violent events, then will have access to all events and speakers in the annual conference of the International Society for Traumatic Stress Studies (istss.org). Guidelines are available online.

Requirements Fellowships are open to print and broadcast reporters, photographers, editors, and producers with at least five years of journalism experience.

Date(s) Application Is Due Jul 22.

Contact Fellowship Administrator, (800) 332-0565; fax: (206) 543-9285; email: info@dartcenter.org

Internet http://www.dartcenter.org/awards_fellowships/index.html

Sponsor Dart Center for Journalism and Trauma
Box 353740, 102 Communications Bldg
Seattle, WA 98195-3740

Dartmouth College Andrew W. Mellon Postdoctoral Fellowship 1487

The program offers one two-year postdoctoral teaching/research fellowship in the humanities and related social sciences. Though there are no citizenship requirements, preference will be given to individuals likely to make their careers in the United States.

Requirements Applicants should have received the PhD during the past three years.

Amount $46,250 plus benefits; $1500 research allowance; $3500 computer allowance (first year only)

Date(s) Application Is Due Jan 31.

Contact Administrator, Leslie Humanities Center, (603) 646-0896; fax: (603) 646-0998; email: lhc@dartmouth.edu

Internet http://www.dartmouth.edu/~lhc/mellon.html

Sponsor Dartmouth College
6240 Gerry Hall, Rm 205
Hanover, NH 03755-3526

Datatel Scholars Foundation Scholarship Program 1488

The tax-exempt foundation awards undergraduate and graduate scholarships to eligible students to attend a higher learning institution selected from Datatel's more than 600 college, university, and nonprofit client sites. The program reflects the foundation's long-standing commitment to higher education and to give back to the company's client base by focusing Datatel's corporate charitable giving on scholarship. Applicants apply through the institution, which may nominate up to two students. The scholarships are awarded annually on May 1, in conjunction with Datatel's corporate anniversary.

Requirements To be eligible to apply for a Datatel scholarship, a student must be planning to attend a Datatel client college or university for the year of the award. Students who transfer to another college or university during the award year only maintain their eligibility if the institution to which they transfer is a Datatel client site. Applicants must also be employed at a Datatel non-education client site and attending a college or university of the applicant's choice for the year of the award.

Amount $1000-$2400

Contact Scholarship Program Administrator, (703) 968-9000 ext 4549; fax: (703) 968-4573; email: scholars@datatel.com

Internet http://www.datatel.com/objectViewerBlank.cfm?objectID=EA7DA3E2-F913-11D4-AE900002A5070708

Sponsor Datatel Scholars Foundation
4375 Fair Lakes Ct
Fairfax, VA 22033

Dave Thomas Foundation for Adoption Grants 1489

The foundation supports advocacy and social service organizations working in the field of adoption. The primary goal of the foundation is to raise public awareness about children in the public welfare system awaiting adoption and to form public and private partnerships to make the adoption process easier and more affordable. Types of support include challenge/matching grants, conferences and seminars, demonstration grants, professorships, program development grants, research grants, seed money grants, and technical assistance. National, regional, or statewide projects will be considered. Priority will be given to projects that request seed money; include matching or other material support from other organizations, government agencies, or funders; coordinate service providers; include a measurement component to evaluate the project's success; and are easily replicable. Proposals are accepted throughout the year. Funding decisions are made four times per year. In order to receive serious consideration, proposals must be received by the submission deadline date for each quarter. Guidelines are available online.

Requirements Eligible applicants are nonprofit 501(c)3 organizations.

Restrictions The foundation will not consider funding individual adoption expenses; operating budgets or budget deficits; endowments or capital campaigns; adoption searches or reunions; scholarships; special events; institutions that discriminate on the basis of race, creed, gender, national origin, age, disability, or sexual orientation; or organizations engaged in sectarian religious activities. Unless solicited by the foundation, the following will not be considered: research, educational or promotional videos, publications, television productions, conferences, or public service announcements.

Amount $35,000-$50,000

Date(s) Application Is Due Jan 5; Apr 6; Jul 6; Sep 7.

Contact Rita Soronen, Executive Director, (800) 275-3832 ; fax: (614) 766-3871; email: adoption@wendys.com

Internet http://www.davethomasfoundationforadoption.org

Sponsor Dave Thomas Foundation for Adoption
4150 Tuller Rd, Ste 204
Dublin, OH 43017

David & Lucile Packard Foundation - Preschool for California's Children Grants 1490

The goal of this program is to secure high-quality preschool opportunities for all three and four-year-olds in the state by funding leadership and constituency-building, technical assistance and systems building, research, and public preschool programs in selected California communities. The Foundation seeks to: expand and strengthen statewide advocacy efforts and engage a diverse cross-section of groups in support of preschool; support further research on topics related to ensuring preschool for California's children; provide ongoing support to local flagship preschool efforts that demonstrate the promise of high-quality preschool when implemented on a large scale.

Requirements The Foundation accepts grant proposals only for charitable, educational, or scientific purposes, primarily from tax-exempt, charitable organizations. We do not provide funding for projects that benefit specific individuals or that serve religious purposes.

Restrictions The Foundation does not fund attempts to influence specific legislation or ballot measures. We also do not fund direct service programs (i.e., individual child care centers, preschools, or schools), individual facility construction or renovation, isolated curriculum or professional development efforts, or local programs that do not have a central goal of helping to achieve preschool for every child on a district-, city-, county-, or statewide level.

Contact Children, Famlies, and Communities Program, (650) 917-7238; fax: 9650) 948-1361; email: cfc@packard.org

Internet http://www.packard.org/searchGrants.aspx?RootCatID=3&CategoryID=226

Sponsor David and Lucile Packard Foundation
300 Second Street, Suite 200
Los Altos, CA 94022

David and Lucile Packard Foundation Fellowships 1491

The goal of the program is to provide support for unusually creative researchers early in their careers; faculty members who are well established and well funded are less likely to receive the award. The foundation emphasizes support for innovative individual research that involves the fellows, their students, and junior colleagues, rather than extensions or components of large-scale, ongoing research programs. Guidelines are available online.

Requirements Every year, the foundation invites the presidents of 50 universities to nominate two professors each from their institutions. Nominations are reviewed by an advisory panel of distinguished scientists and engineers.

Amount $125,000 per year for five years

Date(s) Application Is Due Mar 15.

Contact Fellowships for Science and Engineering, (650) 917-7275; fax: (650) 948-2957; email: fellows@packard.org

Internet http://www.packard.org/index.cgi?page=consci-fellow

Sponsor David and Lucile Packard Foundation
300 Second St, Ste 200
Los Altos, CA 94022

David Berry Essay on Scottish History Prize 1492

This competition is held every year for a prize to be awarded to the writer of the best essay on a subject, to be selected by the candidate, dealing with Scottish history. The society may require evidence that the person submitting the essay is the author thereof and shall not be liable if any essay is lost or mislaid nor be called upon to return any essay. The essay submitted must be a genuine work of research based on original (manuscript

or printed) materials. The essay should be between 6000 and 10,000 words in length, excluding footnotes and appendices, and must be submitted in typescript. The author's name should not appear on the typescript and should be submitted separately.
Restrictions Previous winners of the prize may not enter.
Amount @L250
Contact Administrative Assistant, 0171-387 7532; fax: 0170-387 7532; email: royalhistsoc@ucl.ac.uk
Internet http://www.rhs.ac.uk/rhspri.html#david
Sponsor Royal Historical Society
Gower St, University College London
London WC1E 6BT United Kingdom

David Bohnett Foundation Grants **1493**
The foundation's mission is to improve society through social activism. Focus areas include the promotion of the positive portrayal of lesbians and gay men in the media; voter registration activities; animal language research, animal companions, and eliminating rare animal trade; environmental conservation; the reduction and elimination of the manufacture and sale of handguns in the United States; community-based social services that benefit gays and lesbians; and the development of mass transit and non-fossil fuel transportation. Types of support include general operating support, program specific grants, seed money, and multiyear grants. Applicants should email a letter of inquiry to the program officer.
Requirements Nonprofit organizations are eligible.
Restrictions Grants do not support individuals, videos or other film productions, or organizations outside the United States.
Amount $2 million total; $5000-$50,000 typically
Date(s) Application Is Due Jan 27; Jul 28.
Contact Michael Fleming, Executive Director, (310) 277-4611; fax: (310) 203-8111; email: mfpfleming@yahoo.com
Internet http://www.bohnettfoundation.org/grants/grantapplication.htm
Sponsor David Bohnett Foundation
2049 Century Park E, Ste 2151
Los Angeles, CA 90067-3123

David E. Finley Predoctoral Fellowship **1494**
The fellowship is intended to fund a 36 month period for travel and research in Europe on a well-advanced dissertation in western art and an additional year in residence at the National Gallery of Art. Half the year in residence will be devoted to gallery research projects designed to complement the subject of the dissertation. A primary requirement for the awarding of this fellowship is that the candidate have a real interest in museum work. However, there is no requirement as to the candidate's subsequent choice of a career. The fellowship begins on September 1 and is not renewable. Application must be made through the chair of the graduate department of art history or other appropriate department. Departments should limit nominations to one candidate.
Requirements Applicants must have completed their residence requirements and coursework for a PhD and general or preliminary examinations before the date of application and know two foreign languages related to the topic of the dissertation. Applicants must be either US citizens or enrolled in a university in the United States.
Amount $24,000 annually for three years
Date(s) Application Is Due Nov 15.
Contact Fellowships Program, Center for Advanced Study in the Visual Arts, (202) 842-6482; fax: (202) 789-3026; email: advstudy@nga.gov
Internet http://www.nga.gov/resources/casvapre.htm
Sponsor National Gallery of Art
Fourth St and Constitution Ave NW
Washington, DC 20565

David H. Smith Conservation Research Fellowship **1495**
The fellowship program identifies and supports innovative young scientists who are beginning their careers in applied conservation biology. The program will provide two years of postdoctoral support in applied conservation biology. Awards will be made to the individual fellows, who select the academic institution best suited for carrying out the proposed scientific research. Research will focus on one or more of the conservancy's priority conservation sites, or questions germane to these sites.
Requirements Applicants must either hold a PhD or be awarded a PhD during the academic year in which the application is made.
Amount $36,000 annual salary, plus benefits; $30,000 research fund; $8000 travel budget
Date(s) Application Is Due Oct 28.
Contact Smith Conservation Research Fellowship Program, (800) 628-6860; email: info@smithfellows.org
Internet http://smithfellows.org/proposalguidelines.cfm
Sponsor The Nature Conservancy
4245 N Fairfax Dr
Arlington, VA 22203

Davis Family Foundation Grants **1496**
The foundation provides grants primarily to Maine-based educational, medical, and cultural/arts charitable organizations in support of a wide variety of worthwhile projects. Application and guidelines are available online.
Requirements Eligible educational organizations include colleges, universities, and other educational institutions (grants are not made to public elementary and secondary schools, nor to schools whose financial support is derived primarily from a church or other religious organization. Trustees will consider grant requests from other educational organizations whose purpose is to promote systemic change in education or to provide innovative programs whose objectives are to improve education). Medical organizations eligible for support include hospitals, clinics, and medical research organizations. Grant requests will also be considered from other similar health organizations for programs designed to increase the effectiveness or decrease the cost of medical care. Eligible cultural/arts organizations include organizations whose customary and primary activity is to promote music, theater, drama, history, literature, the arts, or other similar cultural activities.
Restrictions The Foundation does not make grants to individuals, religious programs, fellowships, or in the form of loans. The Foundation does not normally provide support for annual giving campaigns or general operating needs. Grants to endowment campaigns have a low priority.
Date(s) Application Is Due Feb 10; May 10; Aug 10; Nov 10.
Contact Grants Administrator, (207) 781-5504; email: info@davisfoundations.org
Internet http://www.davisfoundations.org/site/family.asp
Sponsor Davis Family Foundation
4 Fundy Road
Falmouth, ME 04105

Deafness Research Foundation Research Grants **1497**
The grants are intended for research directed to any aspect of the ear, e.g., investigation of function, physiology, biochemistry, genetics, anatomy, or pathology. Grants cover a range of subjects from basic neuroscience research to studies on corrective hearing/speech testing and training. Grants may be renewed for one to two years.
Requirements Current policy favors awarding grants in support of projects directed by new investigators, so-called seed money support for studies in generally unexplored areas of research. It does not exclude grant support for new research by established researchers. Application should state whether the same project is receiving support from another source and whether an application has been submitted to another source of funding. The principal investigator and grantee institution must notify the DRF when and if this same project receives support from another granting agency.
Amount $20,000
Date(s) Application Is Due Dec 1.
Contact Grants Administrator, (800) 829-5934 or (703) 610-9025; email: grants@drf.org
Internet http://www.drf.org/grants/grants.htm
Sponsor Deafness Research Foundation
8201 Greensboro Dr, Ste 300
McLean, VA 22102

Dean Witter Foundation Grants **1498**
The Foundation supports graduate schools of business and organizations to promote research and higher education in finance. The Foundation makes additional grants, often on a matching basis, to support specific wildlife research and conservation projects in Northern California and seminal opportunities to improve and extend environmental education and to stimulate learning. The Foundation will consider requests for multi-year funding for two or three years into the future to facilitate effective program planning by the institutions supported. Applicants are encouraged to telephone or write the Consultant to determine whether their proposed program falls within the Foundation's areas of interest and grantmaking priorities.
Requirements The Foundation accepts grant proposals from tax-exempt charitable institutions as defined under Section 501(c)(3) of the Internal Revenue Code on a continuing basis. The Foundation does not have a standard application form. Applicants should send one complete proposal to the Consultant with the following elements: cover letter; specific request; personnel information; organizational information; financial information; and addenda.
Restrictions The Foundation does not: accept funding requests from individuals or award loans, scholarships and grants to specific individuals; assume any obligation to provide continuing support to grantee programs; make grants for annual fundraising events, operating deficits, and capital campaigns; or support sectarian religious activities or sectarian religious facilities.
Contact Kenneth Blum, Consultant, (415) 981-2966; fax: (415) 981-5218; admin@deanwitterfoundation.org
Internet http://www.deanwitterfoundation.org/FundingGuidelines.html
Sponsor Dean Witter Foundation
57 Post Street, Suite 510
San Francisco, CA 94104

DeBakey Medical Foundation Fellowships and Scholarships **1499**
The foundation fosters and encourages medical education and graduate training and promotes medical research in any field of medicine, but it is especially interested in investigations that have direct clinical application, particularly those concerned with cardiovascular disease. Financial aid may be extended to persons in the form of scholarships or fellowships and to institutions in the form of grants or funds for hospital care. Applications are accepted at any time.

Contact Program Director, (713) 798-8600; fax: (713) 793-1192; email: pa@bcm.tmc.edu
Sponsor DeBakey Medical Foundation
1 Baylor Plz, Baylor College of Medicine
Houston, TX 77030

DEED Grants **1500**
APPA's Demonstration of Energy-Efficient Developments (DEED) program sponsors grants intended for demonstration or early commercialization projects at DEED member utilities that promise either to improve efficiencies or lower costs in the provision of energy services to the consumers of publicly owned electric utilities. DEED grants also are open to all organizations for applied research to early demonstration projects with long-term potential either to improve efficiencies or lower costs in the provision of energy services to the consumers of publicly owned electric utilities; these outside organizations, however, must apply through a DEED member utility. Maximum funding is limited to 25 percent of available DEED funds; amounts greater than $50,000 must be approved by the APPA board after review by the DEED directors. The DEED board of directors meets each year in March and September; therefore, deadlines for receipt of applications are usually in February and August. Call for exact dates and application forms or visit the Web site.
Requirements Proposals for DEED grants may be submitted only by DEED member utilities that have been DEED members for at least six months prior to grant submission. All proposals shall include a project plan showing tasks, schedule, costs, and decision criteria for termination versus further research.
Amount $75,000 maximum; $25,000-$50,000 typically
Date(s) Application Is Due Feb 15; Aug 15.
Contact Michele Ghosh, DEED Program Manager, (202) 467-2960; fax: (202) 467-2992; email: DEED@appanet.org
Internet http://www.appanet.org/research/index.cfm?ItemNumber=2671&sn.ItemNumber=2415
Sponsor American Public Power Association
2301 M St NW
Washington, DC 20037-1484

DEED Student Research Grants and Internships **1501**
DEED (Demonstration of Energy-Efficient Developments) student research grants/internships are intended to promote the involvement of students studying in energy-related disciplines in the public power industry, and to provide host utilities with technical assistance. Successful applicants are expected to conduct research on a project approved by the sponsoring utility and submit a final report on the project, describing activities, cost, bibliography, achievements, problems, results, and recommendations. Additional information is available online.
Requirements Only graduate or undergraduate students in energy-related disciplines from accredited colleges or universities are eligible. Students must be attending school in a country with at least one DEED member. Applications must be sent from a DEED member utility. Applicants will not be discriminated against on the basis of sex, race, religion, national origin, or citizenship.
Amount $4,000
Date(s) Application Is Due Feb 15; Oct 1.
Contact DEED Administrator, (202) 467-2960; email: DEED@APPAnet.org
Internet http://www.appanet.org/research/index.cfm?ItemNumber=2671&sn.ItemNumber=2415
Sponsor American Public Power Association
2301 M. Street NW
Washington, DC 200371484

Del E. Webb Foundation Grants **1502**
The Foundation applies its resources only for the benefit of the residents of Arizona, California and Nevada for improved and expanded medical services, medical research and education. Within these broad areas of interest, the Foundation draws upon the talent and experience of leaders from many walks of life to select organizations of demonstrated competence which have sound programs that will be able to reach and sustain high levels of performance. In choosing particular projects for support, the Foundation's Board acts on the basis of how the public welfare most effectively may be served. Application information is available online.
Requirements Grants are confined to the support of nonpartisan, non-profit organizations that are operated in the public interest and have tax-exempt status as charitable organizations granted by the Internal Revenue Service and the states in which the respective organizations are incorporated and/or engage in activities.
Restrictions Grants are not made to the following: governmental agencies or subdivisions; sectarian or religious organizations whose principle activity is exclusively for the benefit of their own members; organizations soliciting funds in support of projects or programs operated by organizations other than the applicant; expenditures before the recipient incurs and makes such expenditures, and, in the absence of compelling circumstances, the Foundation does not make grants to recipients to liquidate or reduce previously incurred obligations or operating deficits. No grants or loans are awarded or made to individuals for any purpose. Grants are not made for scholarships, student aid or medical assistance. Grants may be made to organizations that provide scholarships, student aid or medical assistance when the organization selects recipients in conformity with accepted standards. The Foundation does not participate in the administration of program(s) that the Foundation funds through the award of the application. The Foundation does not fund or underwrite: galas or gala-like events, testimonial or fund-raising luncheons or dinners, advertising in programs or similar fund-raising activities; organizations that in turn make grants to others; purchase of uniforms, equipment, or trips for school related organizations or amateur sports teams; honoraria for guest speakers or panelists; charities operated by service clubs; or educational seminars.
Amount $5000-$100,000 average
Date(s) Application Is Due Nov 30; Feb 28; May 31; Aug 31.
Contact Program Contact, (928) 684-7223; fax: (928) 684-5665
Internet http://www.dewf.com/DEFAULT.shtml
Sponsor Del E. Webb Foundation
300 E. Willis, Suite C
Prescott, AZ 86301-3110

Deland Fellowships in Health Care and Society **1503**
This one-year fellowship provides a training opportunity for graduates interested in pursuing careers in health care management. Appointees will explore the most challenging issues of health care delivery today, including problems of access to quality health care for the poor, uninsured, and underinsured; the changing roles of physicians, nurses, social workers, administrators, and allied health professionals; ethical, legal, and human considerations arising from new biomedical technologies; the impact of for-profit ventures on the work of teaching and community hospitals; and development of integrated delivery systems in the health care marketplace. Stipends are commensurate with the seniority, prior educational experience, and living requirements of the appointees. Fellowship tenure begins in July. For current deadline information, please email Kevin Gahagan at kgahagan@partners.org.
Requirements It is anticipated that candidates will come from a variety of careers and educational backgrounds including business, law, economics, public policy, and medicine. Candidates are required to have an advanced degree.
Contact Kevin Gahagan, (617) 732-5500; TTY/TTD: (617) 732-6458; email: kgahagan@partners.org
Internet http://www.brighamandwomens.org/general/Deland_Fellowship.asp
Sponsor Brigham and Women's Hospital
75 Francis St
Boston, MA 02115

Dell Foundation Open Grants **1504**
The foundation, the giving arm of Dell Computer, seeks to fund collaborative and innovative solutions to community and children's issues addressing youth (ages newborn to high-school seniors) in Texas, Tennessee, Idaho, and Oregon. Through these efforts, Dell strives to effect change in its local community, while providing lessons and best practices for communities everywhere. Funded areas include arts, education, social services, and health. The foundation supports specific, preventative, and measurable programs with cash, in-kind, and volunteer contributions. Grants are awarded quarterly. An online application form is available on the Web site.
Requirements Eligibility is open to 501(c)3 nonprofit organizations in Texas--Travis, Williamson County, and McLennan County; Tennessee--Wilson, Davidson County; Idaho--Twin Falls County; and Oregon--Roseburg, Douglas County.
Restrictions Grants do not support individuals; academic or research projects; civic, religious, or political institutions; school fundraisers; marketing opportunities; or sports events and organizations.
Amount $5000 maximum
Date(s) Application Is Due Jan 15; Apr 15; Jul 15; Oct 15.
Contact Grants Administrator, (512) 338-4400; email: the_dell_foundation@dell.com
Internet http://www1.us.dell.com/content/topics/global.aspx/corp/foundation/en/open_grants?c=us&l=en&s=corp
Sponsor Dell Foundation
1 Dell Wy
Round Rock, TX 78682

Della Martin Foundation Grants **1505**
The foundation awards grants to organizations located in southern California for research seeking to find the causes of and cures for mental illness. Types of support include challenge/matching grants, endowments, fellowships, professorships, and research grants. There is no application deadline, but the foundation usually makes grants for mental health research at the year's end.
Requirements Grants are made only to California 501(c)3 organizations.
Amount $263,000
Contact Laurence Gould Jr., Director, (213) 617-4143; fax: (213) 620-1398
Sponsor Della Martin Foundation
333 S Hope St, 48th Fl
Los Angeles, CA 90071

Deloitte Foundation Grants **1506**
The foundation, funded by Deloitte and Touche USA LLP, supports accounting, business, and related fields of study within the United States. Its national programs benefit university students and faculty and promote excellence in teaching and research, curriculum innovation, and cooperation among practitioners and the academic community. It funds the Deloitte Doctoral Fellowship Program, Trueblood Seminars for Professors, matching gifts program, and many other higher education initiatives. Applications for the doctoral

fellowship program must meet the listed deadline; there are no deadlines or application forms for other requests.
Requirements Doctoral fellowship applicants must be doctoral candidates pursuing their PhD in accounting.
Restrictions Grants are not awarded to support general purposes, capital campaigns, special programs, publications, or loans.
Amount $5000-$50,000 average
Contact Janet Butchko, Manager, Academic Development, (203) 761-3474
Internet http://www.deloitte.com/dtt/section_node/0,2332,sid%253D2257,00.html
Sponsor Deloitte Foundation
P.O. Box 820, 10 Westport Rd
Wilton, CT 06897-0820

Delta Air Lines Foundation Grants 1507
The foundation awards grants to nonprofits in the areas of: community enrichment - focusing on involvement and participation in volunteer, civic, and social activities; health and wellness - with support to organizations that dedicate their efforts to the health and well-being of communities with a focus on broad-reaching research for cures and education around diseases that affect all walks of life; youth development - offering support to organizations focusing on keeping young people interested in math and science and helping them develop leadership skills and positive self esteem; and arts and culture to include fine art, theatre, music, or other creative endeavors which enhance a community's quality of life.
Requirements For proposals which meet the Foundation's area of focus, priority will be given to: programs meeting compelling needs in communities where Delta has a presence; proposals that exhibit clean, reasonable goals, and measurable outcomes; distinctive projects where the Foundation's involvement will leave a legacy; projects that include collaboration or cooperation with other nonprofit organizations; projects that offer opportunities for Delta employee involvement.
Restrictions The Foundation will generally not consider: individual applicant's request for support of personal needs; religious activities; political organizations or campaigns; specialized single-issue health organizations; annual or automatic renewal grants; general operating expenses; endowment campaigns; capital campaigns; multi-year commitments; fraternal organizations, professional associations, or membership groups; fundraising events such as benefits; charitable dinners, or sporting events.
Date(s) Application Is Due Mar 1; Jun 1; Sep 1; Nov 1.
Contact Administrator, (404) 715-5487; fax: (404) 715-3267
Internet http://www.delta.com/about_delta/community_involvement/delta_foundation/index.jsp
Sponsor Delta Air Lines
P.O. Box 20706, Dept 979
Atlanta, GA 30320-6001

Delta Dental Master's Thesis Award 1508
The fund invites Master of Science students at the dental schools in Michigan, Ohio, and Indiana to submit proposals for the thesis award program. This program is intended to encourage thesis research that is of direct relevance to the costs or outcomes of dental care. The award provides a stipend to cover costs associated with the conduct of master's thesis research, including materials, supplies, and rental of necessary equipment. A detailed budget with justification for expenditures is required. Partial funding may be approved, dependent on reasonableness of the budget and availability of funds. A copy of the final thesis must be provided to Delta Dental Fund upon its completion. Applications may be submitted at any time. Application and guidelines are available online.
Requirements Master of Science students at the dental schools in Michigan, Ohio, and Indiana are eligible.
Restrictions Salaries, wages, indirect costs, and the purchase of equipment will not be covered.
Amount $3000 maximum
Contact Dental Master's Thesis Award Program, (517) 347-5333; fax: (517) 347-5320; email: ddfund@ddpmi.com
Internet http://www.ddpmi.com/ddf/masterThesis.htm
Sponsor Delta Dental Plan of Michigan
P.O. Box 293
Okemos, MI 48805-0293

Delta Gamma Foundation Fellowships for Graduate Study 1509
Fellowships are offered annually for graduate study in any chosen field. Selection is based on scholarship, potential for achievement, and financial need. Annual deadline dates may vary. Contact the committee for application form.
Requirements Applicants must be Delta Gammas who will have completed their undergraduate study by June 30 of the year in which the fellowship is granted. Application consists of completed application form, official transcripts, two passport-style photos, statement of graduate school acceptance, autobiographical sketch, self-addressed stamped envelope, and sealed letters of recommendation from two persons familiar with applicant's academic work, one alumna of Delta Gamma, and employer.
Amount $2500
Date(s) Application Is Due Apr 1.
Contact Jacquelyn Geving Everson, Scholarship and Fellowship Director, (614) 481-8169; fax: (614) 481-0133; email: ScholarFellowandLoans@deltagamma.org
Internet http://www.deltagamma.org/scholarships_fellowships_and_loans_2.shtml
Sponsor Delta Gamma Foundation
P.O. Box Box 21397, 3250 Riverside Dr
Columbus, OH 43221-0397

Delyte and Dorothy Morris Doctoral Fellowships 1510
Graduate students of the highest caliber are invited to compete for fellowships to support doctoral study in any field at SIU at Carbondale. Fellowships will be awarded for up to three years of full-time study. Application materials and more information are available from the graduate school.
Requirements Applicant must have an undergraduate grade point average of at least 3.25 overall, or a grade point average for the last two years of bachelor's degree work of 3.5 (A=4.0); if prior graduate study has been undertaken, the applicant must have an overall graduate grade point average of at least 3.7; must have a score in the 75th percentile or higher on a standard test such as the GRE, MAT, GMAT, or ATGSB; and may not already be enrolled in a doctoral program. Preference will be given to citizens or permanent residents of the United States, or immigrants to the United States, and to those who have not previously been enrolled in a graduate program or at SIU.
Amount $18,000 stipend plus waiver of tuition for up to three years of full-time doctoral study
Date(s) Application Is Due Jan 23.
Contact Assistantship/Fellowship Office, (618) 453-4555; fax: (618) 453-4562; email: gaoffice@siu.edu
Internet http://www.siu.edu/gradschl/grad_fellowship.htm
Sponsor Southern Illinois University at Carbondale
Graduate School, Woody Hall B130
Carbondale, IL 62901-4716

DeMatteis Family Foundation Grants 1511
The foundation makes grants in the New York metropolitan area to eligible institutions whose mission involves education, health and human services, medical research, social services, and the arts. Types of support include facilities construction, expansion, renovation; acquisition of capital equipment; scientific/medical research; projects and programs that enable the applicant to expand its mission through new or expanded programs to reach a greater segment of the community served; project-oriented capital campaigns. In general, most grants are made to cover projects that can be accomplished within one year. For construction and longer duration projects, grants may be structured to conform to identified milestones. For major projects, the payment of the grant may be over a number of years.
Requirements Metropolitan New York 501(c)3 tax-exempt agencies, institutions, and organizations are eligible.
Restrictions In general, the foundation does not support grants for operating deficits; general operating support; endowments; loans, or financing of any kind; annual appeals, dinner functions, and other special fund raising events; or unrestricted funds.
Contact Grants Administrator, (516) 705-4974
Internet http://fdncenter.org/grantmaker/dematteis/about.html
Sponsor DeMatteis Family Foundation
P.O. Box 25
Glen Head, NY 11545

Democracy Fellows Program 1512
The program, coordinated by World Learning Inc and funded primarily by the US Agency for International Development (USAID), seeks applicants for one-year fellowships that promote professional development of the fellow and the advancement of democratic institutions worldwide. Fellows will be placed with USAID missions in transitional or newly emerging democracies or with USAID offices in Washington, DC. Applications are accepted on a rolling basis.
Requirements US citizens with the JD or master's degree who have expertise in political science, government, law, public administration, human rights, election administration, justice systems, conflict resolution, or other social sciences relevant to the advancement of democratic institutions abroad may apply. Applicants also must have professional-level foreign language proficiency as appropriate. The program is targeted to junior- and mid-level individuals with one to 10 years of experience and interests in international democracy and governance.
Amount $79,000 maximum mid-level; $54,000 junior level; $87,000 senior level
Contact Democracy Fellows Program, (202) 408-5420; fax: (202) 408-5397; email: dfp.info@worldlearning.org
Internet http://www.worldlearning.org/wlid/cssc/dfp/available.html
Sponsor World Learning Inc
1015 15th St, NW, Ste 750
Washington, DC 20005

Dennis Leslie Mahony Prize in Legal Theory 1513
The prize will go to the author or authors of an outstanding published work in the field of jurisprudence that best reflects an approach combining legal theory with sociological inquiry, in the tradition of the jurisprudence of the late Professor Julius Stone. A published work need not necessarily be in the form of a traditional book or journal publication. Other types of publication, including reports or papers, are eligible. The recipient of the prize will receive a cash prize, with the offer of an invitation to participate in the activities of the Faculty of Law at the University of Sydney for a period of up to one semester. He or she may also receive an invitation to deliver the prestigious Julius Stone Address in

the year following the award of the prize. Entrants are required to submit an application form and five copies of the work, plus five copies of their curriculum vita. Four copies will be returned following judging, and one will be kept in the archive of the Julius Stone Institute. Guidelines are available online.
Requirements Entries may be directly submitted by the author(s), or on the nomination of a third party.
Amount AU$50,000
Contact Helen Irving, 61-2-9351- 0232; fax: 61-2-9351-0200; email: heleni@law.usyd.edu.au
Internet http://www.law.usyd.edu.au/~jurisprudence
Sponsor University of Sydney
Julius Stone Institute of Jurisprudence Director, Level 12, 173-175 Phillip Street
Sydney 2000 NSW Australia

DENSO North America Foundation Grants **1514**
The Foundation is committed to supporting higher education in engineering and business programs. Priority is given to programs that advance automotive engineering and supply-side business practices. Capital funding is available for equipment, lab development, technological advancements and/or installations, building campaigns and expansion projects. Student projects are supported for university-sanctioned student projects and training competitions. Funding is available for tooling and equipment offering a major, sustaining investment.
Requirements 501(c)3 nonprofit organizations, educational institutions, and universities located throughout North America are eligible. Proposals should contain: details on how funding will advance student development and training; demonstrate principle(s) of innovation and/or training for efficiency gains in the workplace; contain a clearly articulated desired result.
Restrictions Grants are not awarded for administrative costs, stipends or trips, conferences and travel expenses.
Amount $2000 minimum
Contact Grants Administrator, (248) 372-8233; fax: (248) 213-2550; email: DENSOfoundation@denso-diam.com
Internet http://www.densofoundation.org/foundation/foundation.html
Sponsor DENSO North America Foundation
24777 Denso Drive, MC 4610
Southfield, MI 48086-5047

Dental Teaching and Research Fellowships **1515**
Fellowships are awarded to individuals who plan to become dental teachers and/or researchers in dental schools in Canada and who must guarantee to pursue careers in teaching and research at a university for a minimum of two years following fellowship tenure. A formal application form must be filed with official transcripts and letters of support. The award is given for one year with possible renewal for a second year based on satisfactory progress.
Requirements Candidates must be Canadian citizens or permanent residents who have completed an undergraduate course in dentistry, a dental hygiene program, or a program in science and who are also eligible for admission to a graduate or other advanced education program.
Amount $C1800-$C8000
Date(s) Application Is Due Feb 1.
Contact Richard Munro, Executive Director, (613) 236-4763; fax: (613) 236-3935; email: Information@dcf-fdc.ca
Internet http://www.dcf-fdc.ca/grants.html
Sponsor Dentistry Canada Fund
427 Gilmour St
Ottawa, ON K2P OR5 Canada

Denton A. Cooley Foundation Grants **1516**
The foundation awards grants in Texas in support of health care, health education, hospitals, and medical research. Types of support include endowments, general operating grants, program grants, and research grants. There are no application forms or deadlines. The board meets quarterly to consider requests.
Restrictions Grants do not support conferences, loans, individuals, scholarships, fellowships, or publication.
Amount $100-$250,000
Contact Grants Administrator, (713) 799-2700
Sponsor Denton A. Cooley Foundation
6624 Fannin, Suite 1640
Houston, TX 77030

Department of Black Studies Dissertation Fellowships **1517**
One or two dissertation fellowships are available to assist scholars whose research focuses on areas significant to African, Caribbean, and/or African-American studies. Recipients are required to be in residence at UC Santa Barbara during the academic year, to teach one undergraduate course, and to present one public lecture. It is expected that the dissertation will be completed during residence. Applicants should submit curriculum vita, a brief description of the dissertation project, a writing sample (approximately 25 pages), and three letters of reference.
Requirements Individuals advanced to candidacy at an accredited university are eligible. Candidates from the humanities, social sciences, and interdisciplinary fields are encouraged to apply.
Amount $20,000 stipend
Date(s) Application Is Due Mar 1.
Contact Gwenner Miller, Black Studies Department, (805) 893-7624; fax: (805) 893-3597; email: gmiller@blackstudies.ucsb.edu
Internet http://www.blackstudies.ucsb.edu/student_info/fellowship.html
Sponsor University of California, Santa Barbara
3631 South Hall, Dept of Black Studies
Santa Barbara, CA 93106-3150

Dept of Ed Adult Education--National Leadership Activities Grants **1518**
This program supports research, evaluation, information dissemination, and other activities to help states improve adult education and literacy programs. Types of projects include: professional development; national evaluations and surveys; curriculum development; distance learning; data analysis; professional papers; seminars and colloquia.
Requirements Eligible applicants: Institutions of Higher Education, Local Education Agencies, Nonprofit Organizations, Other Organizations and/or Agencies, State Education Agencies, Postsecondary education institutions, public or private agencies, or consortia of these institutions, agencies, or organizations are eligible for grants, cooperative agreements, and contracts.
Contact Dennis Berry, Division of Adult Education and Literacy, (202) 245-7814; fax: (202) 245-7837; email: dennis.berry@ed.gov
Internet http://www.ed.gov/programs/aenla/index.html
Sponsor Department of Education
400 Maryland Avenue, S.W., 11131, PCP
Washington, DC 20202-7240

Dept of Ed American Overseas Research Centers **1519**
Grants are available to consortia of institutions of higher education (IHEs) that plan to establish overseas centers that promote postgraduate research, exchanges, and area studies. Funds are to be used for activities such as stipends, salaries, travel, facility operation and maintenance, materials, research, and visitor exchanges.
Requirements Eligible applicants are consortia of US-based, nonprofit IHEs that have a permanent presence in the host country; 501(c)3 organizations; and organizations that receive more than 50 percent of their funding from public or private US sources.
Amount $83,333 average per year
Date(s) Application Is Due Nov 15.
Contact Cheryl Gibbs, (202) 502-7634; fax: (202) 502-7859; email: cheryl.gibbs@ed.gov
Internet http://www.ed.gov/programs/iegpsaorc/index.html
Sponsor Department of Education
1990 K St, NW, 6th Fl
Washington, DC 20006-8521

Dept of Ed Disability and Rehabilitation Research Project and Centers Program Grants **1520**
The purpose of this program is to improve the effectiveness of services authorized under the Rehabilitation Act of 1973. The priority is intended to improve rehabilitation services and outcomes for individuals with disabilities. Applications are invited for an information technology technical assistance and training center to conduct research, development, demonstration, training, dissemination, utilization, and technical assistance activities to expand access to computer technology and resources for individuals with disabilities.
Requirements Parties eligible to apply for grants are states; public or private agencies, including for-profit agencies; public or private organizations, including for-profit organizations; institutions of higher education; and Indian tribes and tribal organizations.
Amount $300,000-$750,000 range; $300,000 average
Date(s) Application Is Due Sep 13.
Contact Donna Nangle, (202) 245-7462; fax: (202) 245-7323; email: donna_nangle@ed.gov
Internet http://www.ed.gov/programs/drrp/index.html
Sponsor Department of Education
400 Maryland Ave SW, Rm 6030, PCP
Washington, DC 20202-2500

Dept of Ed Fund for the Improvement of Education - Programs of National Significance **1521**
FIE provides authority for the secretary of education to support nationally significant programs to improve the quality of elementary and secondary education at the state and local levels and help all students meet challenging state academic content standards and student achievement standards. The types of programs that may be supported include: activities to promote systemic education reform at the state and local levels; programs at the state and local levels that are designed to yield significant results, including programs to explore approaches to public school choice and school-based decision making; recognition programs; and scientifically based studies and evaluations of education reform strategies and innovations. All funded programs must be designed so that their

effectiveness is readily ascertainable and is assessed using rigorous, scientifically based research and evaluations.
Requirements State educational agencies, local educational agencies, institutions of higher education, public and private organizations, and institutions may apply.
Contact Linda Jones, (202) 205-4352; fax: (202) 205-5631; email: linda.jones@ed.gov
Internet http://www.ed.gov/programs/fie/index.html
Sponsor Department of Education
400 Maryland Avenue S.W., Room 4W203, FB-6
Washington, DC 20202

Dept of Ed Fund for the Improvement of Postsecondary Education Grants 1522
The objective of this program is to provide assistance for innovative programs that improve the access to and the quality of postsecondary education. Project grants are provided for activities sponsored by institutions and agencies that develop and demonstrate more effective approaches to the provision of postsecondary education. Priority is given to activities that relate to improving access, retention, and graduation rates; improving college-school cooperation; using and developing new educational technologies; supporting curriculum reform; making campus culture more conducive to academic progress; developing faculty as professionals; experimenting with new ways to maintain quality and accessibility of education despite shrinking resources; and disseminating properly researched and documented solutions to national problems in higher education. The fund will support multiyear projects on a declining fund basis; grants are awarded for one to three years. Annual deadline dates may be obtained by contacting the office. Application materials are available on the Web site.
Requirements Eligible to apply are providers of postsecondary educational services including, but not limited to, two- and four-year colleges and universities, community organizations, libraries, museums, consortiums, student groups, and local government agencies.
Restrictions Grant award amounts are seed money and may not be used for construction. Requests for equipment and stipends are given low priority.
Contact Fund for the Improvement of Postsecondary Education, Office of the Assistant Secretary for Postsecondary Education, (202) 502-7500; fax: (202) 502-7877; email: fipse@ed.gov
Internet http://www.ed.gov/programs/fipsecomp/index.html
Sponsor Department of Education
1990 K St, NW
Washington, DC 20006-8544

Dept of Ed Graduate Assistance in Areas of National Need Project Grants 1523
The objective of this program is to provide federal support to graduate academic departments, programs, and units of institutions of higher education for the purpose of sustaining and enhancing the capacity for teaching and research in academic areas of national need, as designated by the Department of Education Secretary, through the provision of fellowships to assist graduate students of superior ability who demonstrate financial need. Awards made to institutions under this program are used exclusively to provide direct fellowship aid that will include need-based stipends. A project funded under this priority must propose to provide fellowships in one or more of the following areas of national need: Biology, Chemistry, Computer and Information Sciences, Engineering, Geological and Related Sciences, Mathematics, and Physics. Contact the program office for application deadlines.
Requirements Accredited institutions of higher education may apply. Institutions receiving the awards will provide direct fellowship aid to graduate students accepted and approved by the institution. A grantee must match the award by 25 percent. Funds must be used for stipends, tuition fees, and other educational costs of students.
Restrictions Students are ineligible to apply for funding.
Amount $30,000 maximum
Date(s) Application Is Due Dec 1.
Contact Rebecca Green, (202) 502-7779; fax: (202) 502-7859; email: ope_gaann_program@ed.gov
Internet http://www.ed.gov/programs/gaann/index.html
Sponsor Department of Education
1990 K St NW, 6th Fl
Washington, DC 20006-8524

Dept of Ed International Business Education Centers Grants 1524
This program provides a comprehensive university approach to improve the teaching of international business by bringing together faculty from numerous disciplines to engage in research to promote the international competitiveness of US business. Institutions of higher education eligible for grant funding must establish a center advisory council to conduct extensive planning regarding the scope of the center's activities and the design of its programs prior to establishing the center; ensure ongoing collaboration in the center's establishment and operation by appropriate faculty from business, management, foreign language, international studies, and other professional schools/departments; ensure that the center's programs are open to students concentrating in these areas; and ensure that the recipient institution will use the aid provided to supplement and not to supplant their activities. Grants are awarded for up to a 36-month period.
Requirements Accredited public and nonprofit private institutions of higher education, or combinations of such institutions, that establish a center advisory council before the date federal assistance is received may apply. This advisory council will conduct extensive planning concerning the scope of the center's activities and the design of its program prior to establishing the center.
Amount $370,000 average
Contact Susanna Easton, International Studies Branch, Center for International Education, Department of Education, (202) 502-7628; fax: (202) 502-7859; email: Susanna.easton@ed.gov
Internet http://www.ed.gov/programs/iegpscibe/index.html
Sponsor Department of Education
400 Maryland Ave SW
Washington, DC 20202

Dept of Ed International Research and Studies Project Grants 1525
This program supports surveys, studies, and development of instructional materials to improve and strengthen instruction in modern foreign languages, area studies, and other international fields. In addition to surveys and studies, the program provides funds for the development of foreign language materials designed to improve and strengthen foreign language and area and related studies in the U.S. education system.
Requirements Public and private agencies, organizations, institutions, and individuals may apply.
Restrictions Funds awarded may not be used for the training of students and teachers.
Contact Ed McDermott, International Education Programs Service, (202) 502-7636; fax: (202) 502-7860; email: ed.mcdermott@ed.gov
Internet http://www.ed.gov/programs/iegpsirs/index.html
Sponsor Department of Education
1990 K Street, N.W., 6th Floor
Washington, DC 20006-8521

Dept of Ed Jacob K. Javits Fellowships 1526
The program provides fellowships to individuals of superior ability to undertake studies leading to a doctoral degree or master of fine arts in selected fields of arts, humanities, or social sciences. The recipient is entitled to use the fellowship in a doctoral or master of fine arts program at any accredited institution of higher education in which the recipient may decide to enroll. Individuals will receive payments only during the periods that they are maintaining satisfactory proficiency and devoting essentially full-time status to study or research in the field in which the fellowships were awarded. Stipends are determined in accordance with the fellows' demonstrated level of need. The grant is awarded for a period of one year. Annual deadline dates may vary.
Requirements An eligible applicant must be a national of, or reside in, the United States for other than a temporary purpose and must intend to become a permanent resident. Eligibility is limited to students who are eligible to receive any other federal grant, loan, or work study assignment.
Restrictions No institutional payment will be made to a school or department of divinity for an individual studying for a religious vocation.
Amount $41,822 maximum
Date(s) Application Is Due Oct 3.
Contact Teacher and Student Development Programs Service , (202) 502-7542; TTY: (800) 437-0833; fax: (202) 502-7859; email: ope_javits_program@ed.gov
Internet http://www.ed.gov/programs/iegpsjavits/index.html?exp=0
Sponsor Department of Education
1990 K St NW, 6th Fl
Washington, DC 20006

Dept of Ed Jacob K. Javits Gifted and Talented Students Education Program-National Research and Development Center 1527
This program conducts research for the purpose of carrying out activities described in Sec. 5464(b) of the statute including research on methods and techniques for identifying and teaching gifted and talented students and for using gifted and talented programs and methods to serve all students. It also conducts program evaluations and surveys. As part of its work, the center collects, analyzes, and develops information about gifted and talented education. Emphasis is given to the identification of and services for students traditionally not included in gifted and talented education, including individuals with limited English proficiency (LEP), individuals with disabilities, and individuals living under economically disadvantaged conditions.
Requirements Institutions of Higher Education, State Education Agencies and a consortium of IHEs and SEAs may apply.
Contact Anne Sweet, U.S. Department of Education, IES (202) 219-2043; fax: (202) 219-2030; email: anne.sweet@ed.gov
Internet http://www.ed.gov/programs/nrdcjavits/index.html
Sponsor Department of Education
555 New Jersey Avenue, N.W., Suite 615B
Washington, DC 20208-5573

Dept of Ed National Resource Centers for Languages, Area Studies, and International Studies Grants 1528
Centers grants promote instruction in those modern foreign languages and area and international studies critical to national needs by supporting the development, establishment, strengthening, and operation of such programs at colleges and universities. Centers may focus on undergraduate training only or may be comprehensive, including undergraduate, graduate, and professional training components. Funds may be used for instructional costs of language, area, and international studies programs; administration;

lectures and conferences; library resources and staff; and staff travel. Grants are awarded for 12-month periods subject to renewals of one to two years. Application forms are available from the program. Higher education institutions currently receiving funds for three-year phased program support may submit annual proposals for the continuation of such support. Deadlines for applications are announced in the Federal Register.
Requirements Accredited US colleges and universities may apply. Applying institutions must provide evidence of existing resources and institutional commitment to language and area and international studies through a curriculum that provides instruction dealing with a particular world area and its languages, with comparative world area studies, or with the international aspects of professional or other fields of study.
Contact Cheryl Gibbs, U.S. Department of Education, (202) 502-7634; fax: (202) 502-7680; email: cheryl.gibbs@ed. gov
Internet http://web99.ed.gov/GTEP/Program2.nsf/a5b8d6c38fdd4ca08525644400514f2c/126194fff55a27c68525659b00582060?OpenDocument
Sponsor Department of Education
600 Independence Ave SW
Washington, DC 20202

Dept of Ed Native Hawaiian Higher Education Grants **1529**
Direct grants are made to Native Hawaiian education organizations or education entities with experience in developing or operating Native Hawaiian programs or programs of instruction conducted in the Native Hawaiian language to enable them to provide a program of baccalaureate and graduate fellowship assistance to Native Hawaiian students. Grants must be used to provide full or partial fellowship support for Native Hawaiian students enrolled at two- or four-year degree-granting institutions of higher education. Priority is given to providing fellowship support for professions that are underrepresented in the Native Hawaiian community.
Requirements Native Hawaiian education organizations or entities with experience in developing or operating Native Hawaiian programs may apply.
Amount $1.5 million average
Contact Susanna Easton, International Education Programs Service, (202) 502-7628; fax: (202) 502-7859 or (202) 502-7860; email: susanna.easton@ed.gov
Internet http://www.ed.gov/programs/iegpshawaiian/index.html
Sponsor Department of Education
1990 K St NW
Washington, DC 20006-8500

Dept of Ed Rehabilitation Engineering Research Centers **1530**
This program is intended to support long-term projects aimed at improving the lives of individuals with disabilities. The Rehabilitation Engineering Research Center (RERC) awards will be made in four areas: prosthetics and orthotics, wheeled mobility, technology transfer, and telerehabilitation centers. These centers will conduct research, demonstration, and training activities regarding assistive technologies, rehabilitation engineering, and similar technology-based rehabilitation services and products.
Requirements Applications will be accepted from states, institutions of higher education, tribal organizations, and other public and private agencies.
Amount $950,000 average
Contact Donna Nangle, (202) 245-7462; fax: (202) 245-7323; email: Donna_Nangle@ed.gov
Internet http://web99.ed.gov/GTEP/Program2.nsf/a5b8d6c38fdd4ca08525644400514f2c/8199bc8504044b10852563bc005404ea?OpenDocument
Sponsor Department of Education
600 Independence Ave SW
Washington, DC 20202

Dept of Ed Rehabilitation Fellowships **1531**
The purpose of this program is to build research capacity by providing support to highly qualified individuals, including those who are individuals with disabilities, to perform research on the rehabilitation of individuals with disabilities. Fellows may conduct original research in any area relating to rehabilitation services and may address any problem faced by persons with disabilities. Two types of fellowships are available. Merit Fellowships are awarded to individuals who have advanced training or experience in independent study. Distinguished Fellowships are available to individuals who have seven or more years of research experience in related fields.
Requirements Only individuals are eligible to be recipients of fellowships.
Restrictions Institutions are not eligible to be recipients of fellowships.
Amount $45,000 for Merit fellows; $55,000 for Distinguished fellows
Date(s) Application Is Due Jun 24.
Contact Donna Nangle, (202) 245-7462; email: donna.nangle@ed.gov
Internet http://www.ed.gov/legislation/FedRegister/announcements/2005-2/042505c.html
Sponsor Department of Education
600 Independence Ave SW
Washington, DC 20202

Dept of Ed Ronald E. McNair Postbaccalaureate Achievement Program **1532**
The program provides grants for higher education institutions to prepare low-income, first-generation college students and students underrepresented in graduate education for doctoral study. Funds may be used to provide eligible participants enrolled at undergraduate or graduate levels with services such as opportunities for research and other scholarly activities; summer internships; seminars; tutoring; academic counseling; and securing admission and financial assistance for graduate study. At least two-thirds of the project participants must be low-income individuals who are first-generation college students. The remaining participants must be from a group that is underrepresented in graduate education. Deadlines are published each year in the Federal Register.
Requirements Institutions of higher education or combinations of institutions of higher education may apply.
Amount $240,000 average
Contact Federal TRIO Programs, U.S. Department of Education, OPE, (202) 502-7600; fax: (202) 502-7857 or (202) 219-7074; email: OPE_TRIO@ed.gov
Internet http://www.ed.gov/programs/triomcnair/applicant.html
Sponsor Department of Education
1990 K St NW, Ste 7000
Washington, DC 20006-8510

Dept of Ed Safe and Drug-Free Schools and Communities State Grants **1533**
This program provides support to SEAs for a variety of drug and violence prevention activities focused primarily on school-age youths. Activities may include: developing instructional materials; providing counseling services and professional development programs for school personnel; implementing community service projects and conflict resolution, peer mediation, mentoring and character education programs; establishing safe zones of passage for students to and from school; acquiring and installing metal detectors; and hiring security personnel.
Requirements State Education Agencies may apply. Local Education Agencies or intermediate education agencies or consortia must apply to the State Education Agency.
Contact Paul Kesner, Office of Safe and Drug-Free Schools, (202) 205-8134; fax: (202) 260-7767; email: paul.kesner@ed.gov
Internet http://www.ed.gov/programs/dvpformula/index.html
Sponsor Department of Education
400 Maryland Avenue, S.W., Room 3E230, FB-6
Washington, DC 20202-6450

Dept of Ed Star Schools Program Grants **1534**
The purpose of this program is to support distance education projects that: encourage improved instruction in mathematics, science, foreign languages, and other subjects; and serve underserved populations, including disadvantaged, nonreading, and limited English proficient (LEP) populations and individuals with disabilities. Star Schools grants are made to eligible telecommunications partnerships, to enable such partnerships to: develop, construct, acquire, maintain, and operate telecommunications audio and visual facilities and equipment; develop and acquire educational and instructional programming; and obtain technical assistance for the use of such facilities and instructional programming. Annual deadline dates may vary; contact the program office for exact dates.
Requirements Eligible applicants include either one of the following that is organized on a statewide or multistate basis: a public agency or corporation established for the purpose of developing and operating telecommunications networks to enhance education opportunities provided by education institutions, teacher training centers, and other entities, except that any such agency or corporation shall represent the interests of elementary schools and secondary schools that are eligible to participate in the program under Title I, Part A, of the Elementary and Secondary Education Act of 1965; or a partnership that will provide telecommunications services and that include three or more of the following entities (a-g), at least one of which must be an agency as described in (a) or (b): (a) a local education agency that serves a significant number of elementary and secondary schools that are eligible for assistance under Title I, Part A, of the ESEA, or elementary and secondary schools operated or funded for Indian children by the Department of the Interior; (b) a state education agency; (c) an adult and family education program; (d) an institution of higher education or a state higher education agency; (e) a teacher-training center or academy that provides teacher preservice and in-service training, and receives federal financial assistance or has been approved by a state agency; (f) a public or private entity with experience and expertise in the planning and operation of a telecommunications network, including entities involved in telecommunications through satellite, cable, telephone, or computer; or a public broadcasting entity with such experience; and (g) a public or private elementary or secondary school.
Contact Brian Lekander, Office of Innovation and Improvement, (202) 205-5633; fax: (202) 205-5720; email: brian.lekander@ed.gov
Internet http://www.ed.gov/programs/starschools/index.html
Sponsor Department of Education
400 Maryland Avenue, S.W., Room 4W226, FB-6
Washington, DC 20202

Dept of Ed Vocational Education National Programs **1535**
This program supports research, evaluation, information dissemination, and other activities aimed at improving the quality and effectiveness of vocational and technical education. Projects include: research, development, demonstration, dissemination, identification of best methods, capacity building, technical assistance, evaluation, and assessment activities.

Requirements Institutions of Higher Education, Nonprofit Organizations, Other Organizations and/or Agencies may apply.
Contact Ricardo Hernandez, U.S. Department of Education, OVAE, (202) 245-7818; fax: (202) 245-7837; email: ricardo.hernandez@ed.gov
Internet http://www.ed.gov/programs/venp/index.html
Sponsor Department of Education
400 Maryland Avenue, S.W., 11137, PCP
Washington, DC 20202-7242

Dept of Ed Vocational Rehabilitation Services Demonstration and Training Programs **1536**
This program provides competitive grants to eligible entities to expand and improve the provision of rehabilitation and other services authorized under the Rehabilitation Act of 1973 , as amended. Funding also is provided to further the purposes and policies of the act. More specifically, the program supports activities that increase the provision, extent, availability, scope, and quality of rehabilitation services under the act. Sec. 303 authorizes support of activities serving individuals with disabilities in an array of project types. These diverse projects may include the effective practices that demonstrate methods of service delivery to individuals with disabilities, as well as activities such as technical assistance, systems change, model demonstration, special studies and evaluations, and dissemination and utilization of findings from successful, previously funded projects. The expansion and improvement of rehabilitation and other services will lead to more employment outcomes for individuals with disabilities.
Requirements State vocational rehabilitation (VR) agencies, community rehabilitation programs, Indian tribes or tribal organizations, or other public or nonprofit agencies or organizations or, as the Rehabilitation Services Administration (RSA) commissioner determines appropriate, for-profit organizations, may apply.
Contact Timothy Muzzio, Rehabilitation Services Administration, (202) 245-7458; fax: (202) 245-7591; email: Timothy.Muzzio@ed.gov
Internet http://www.ed.gov/programs/demotrain/index.html
Sponsor Department of Education
400 Maryland Avenue, S.W., Room 5052, PCP
Washington, DC 20202-2800

Dept of Ed Women's Educational Equity Program Grants **1537**
This program promotes education equity for women and girls through competitive grants. The program designates most of its funding for local implementation of gender-equity policies and practices. Research, development, and dissemination activities also may be funded. Projects may be funded for up to four years. Examples of allowable activities include: training for teachers and other school personnel to encourage gender equity in the classroom; evaluating exemplary model programs to advance gender equity; school-to-work programs; guidance and counseling activities to increase opportunities for women in technologically demanding workplaces; and, developing strategies to assist LEAs in evaluating, disseminating, and replicating gender-equity programs.
Requirements Public agencies; private nonprofit agencies; organizations, including community and faith-based organizations; institutions; student groups; community groups; and individuals developing programs that promote gender equity may apply.
Contact Beverly Farrar, Women's Educational Equity Program, (202) 205-3145; fax: (202) 205-5630; email: beverly.a.farrar@ed.gov
Internet http://www.ed.gov/programs/equity/index.html
Sponsor Department of Education
400 Maryland Avenue, S.W., Room 4W242, FB-6
Washington, DC 20202-5950

Dermatology Clinical Career Development Awards **1538**
The purpose of this award is to enhance the academic careers of clinician-scientists in the early stages of their career development. The program is aimed at junior investigators with significant creativity in clinically relevant research. Research must be conducted in the United States. Such studies could include research on diagnostic and/or prognostic indicators, as well as outcome and/or epidemiologic studies. Creativity in developing new treatment modalities, including novel pharmacologic approaches and clinical trials, is encouraged. Studies need not involve direct laboratory investigation. The primary criteria for selection of a successful awardee are the quality of the research proposal, the environment of the candidate, and ability of the proposal to clarify the place of dermatologic practice in a changing health care environment. Award recipients are expected to spend at least 75 percent of their time in clinical research. Awardees are encouraged to seek simultaneous grant support from other agencies to provide for the nonsalary components of research being performed under the auspices of this award.
Requirements Applications are accepted from faculty members in a department or division of dermatology who have completed clinical training in a US dermatology residency program. Applicants must demonstrate a strong commitment to skin research and have already had appropriate initial training (a two- to three-year research fellowship or postdoctoral training) in relevant research.
Restrictions The foundation does not fund awards to be performed as part of the US government research program (with the exception of the Veterans Administration) or awards to private foundations without an academic affiliation to dermatology.
Amount $55,000
Date(s) Application Is Due Oct 17.
Contact Sandra Rahn Benz, Executive Director, (847) 328-2256; fax: (847) 328-0509; email: dfgen@dermatologyfoundation.org
Internet http://www.dermfnd.org
Sponsor Dermatology Foundation
1560 Sherman Ave, Ste 870
Evanston, IL 60201

Dermatology Foundation Grants **1539**
Limited funds are available for investigators at the early stages of their career development to initiate research projects in dermatology and cutaneous biology. Applications are reviewed by the Medical and Scientific Committee and awarded on a competitive basis for projects not funded from other sources. The research has to be performed under the sponsorship of a division or department of dermatology. The maximum period of funding is for one year. Only one grant application will be considered from a single academic center.
Restrictions Awards cannot be used for payment of indirect costs.
Amount $10,000 average
Date(s) Application Is Due Oct 17.
Contact Sandra Rahn Benz, Executive Director, (847) 328-2256; fax: (847) 328-0509; email: dfgen@dermatologyfoundation.org
Internet http://dermatologyfoundation.org
Sponsor Dermatology Foundation
1560 Sherman Ave, Ste 870
Evanston, IL 60201

Dermatology Postdoctoral Research Fellowships **1540**
Financial support is available to postdoctoral fellows with commitments to careers in academic dermatology who desire research training. Applications will be accepted in two categories. Dermatologist Investigator Research Fellowships are designed to support dermatologists who desire research training and have commitments to careers in academic dermatology. Research Fellowships support training in research skills relevant to dermatology and cutaneous biology. Highest priority will be given to new applicants. A limited number of second-year awards may be given. Although it is recognized that fellowships will encompass specific research projects, they are intended primarily for the support of research training. Fellowship recipients must spend at least 75 percent of their total effort in cutaneous research.
Requirements Applications for Dermatologist Investigator Research Fellowships are accepted from individuals holding the MD, MD-PhD, or DO degree who have completed their clinical training in US dermatology residency programs. Research Fellowship applications are accepted from individuals holding the MD or PhD or equivalent.
Restrictions In general, investigators at more than four years past their terminal degrees or two years beyond their residencies at the time of the initial application are not eligible. (Consideration will be given to individuals with substantial training in other areas and who are entering into skin research.) Individuals with academic appointments at the level of assistant professor or above are not ordinarily eligible.
Amount $25,000 maximum for one year
Date(s) Application Is Due Oct 17.
Contact Sandra Rahn Benz, Executive Director, (847) 328-2256; fax: (847) 328-0509; email: dfgen@dermatologyfoundation.org
Internet http://dermatologyfoundation.org/rap
Sponsor Dermatology Foundation
1560 Sherman Ave, Ste 870
Evanston, IL 60201

Dermatology Research Career Development Awards **1541**
Awards are available to assist in the transition from fellowship to established investigator in cancer and other diseases of the skin, hair, and nails. The intent of the program is to advance the research careers of young individuals in dermatology and cutaneous biology, with the emphasis on research benefiting the dermatology community at large. Award recipients are expected to spend at least 75 percent of their time in cutaneous research. Awardees are encouraged to seek simultaneous grant support from other agencies to provide for the nonsalary components of research being performed.
Requirements Applicants must be faculty members in a department or division of dermatology who demonstrate a strong commitment to skin research and have already had appropriate initial training (a two- to three-year research fellowship or postdoctoral training) in biomedical research.
Restrictions The foundation does not fund awards to be performed as part of the US government research program (with the exception of the Veterans Administration) or awards to private foundations without an academic affiliation to dermatology.
Amount $55,000
Date(s) Application Is Due Oct 17.
Contact Sandra Rahn Benz, Executive Director, (847) 328-2256; fax: (847) 328-0509; email: dfgen@dermatologyfoundation.org
Internet http://dermatologyfoundation.org/rap
Sponsor Dermatology Foundation
1560 Sherman Ave, Ste 870
Evanston, IL 60201

Detroit Lions Charities Grants **1542**
The organization supports charitable and community causes in Michigan. Funding interests include child abuse and domestic violence prevention, youth recreation, and spinal cord injury research. Grants have been awarded to support the Never, Never

Shake a Baby billboard campaign; Pigskin Geography, a learning initiative for youth; Big Brothers/Big Sisters; Grand Rapids Metropolitan YMCA--for swimming lessons for inner-city youth; and Saint Joseph Mercy Hospital--for a domestic violence education program. Requests are accepted between October 1 and December 31.
Date(s) Application Is Due Dec 31.
Contact Detroit Lions Community Affairs Information Hotline, (313) 216-4056
Internet http://detroitlions.com/community/index.cfm?cont_id=49715
Sponsor Detroit Lions Charities
222 Republic Dr
Allen Park, MI 48101

DHHS AIDS and HIV Epidemiologic Research Studies Grants 1543
The purpose of this program is to encourage studies using the new rapid HIV tests in different settings (Operational Research), specifically focused on African American, Latino, and other racial and ethnic minorities that are underserved and/or disproportionally affected by the HIV epidemic, and conducted by researchers who have experience working with these populations; to learn more about the effects of rapid HIV testing on motivators and barriers to HIV testing at the individual, provider, and system levels; and to foster collaborations between organizations serving minority communities and their respective state and local health departments in the design and implementation of innovative practical strategies using rapid HIV tests to increase knowledge of HIV serostatus and facilitate entry into prevention and care systems. The research should contribute to the health services knowledge base from which empirically based information can be derived by policy makers, both immediately and over the coming decades. Assistance is available for a 12-month budget period within project periods ranging from one to five years. Contact the office for deadline dates.
Requirements Applications may be submitted by public and private nonprofit organizations; community-based, national, and regional organizations; state and local governments or their bona fide agents or instrumentalities; federally recognized Indian tribal governments; and Indian tribes or organizations.
Amount $5000-$270,000; $200,265 average
Contact JAllyn Nakashima, Epidemiology Branch, Division of HIV/AIDS Prevention/ Surveillance and Epidemiology, (404) 639-0900; Cheryl Maddux, Grants Management, (770) 498-1911
Internet http://www.dhhs.gov
Sponsor Department of Health and Human Services
1600 Clifton Rd NE, MS-E-45
Atlanta, GA 30333

DHHS AIDS Education and Training Centers Grants 1544
Grants are awarded for the establishment of AIDS education and training centers. The purpose is to provide education and training to primary care providers and others on the treatment and prevention of AIDS, in collaboration with health professions schools, local hospitals, and health departments; to provide updates of new and timely information about HIV infection to primary and secondary health care providers; and to serve as the support system for area health professionals through the AIDS hotline, clearinghouse, and referral activities. Awards will also support community-based organizations and community health clinics affiliated with accredited public and private nonprofit entities. Preference will be given to qualified projects that will train or result in the training of health professionals who will provide treatment for minority individuals with HIV, other individuals who are at high risk of contracting HIV, or to minority health professionals and allied health professionals who will provide treatment for persons with HIV. Awards will be made for a three-year project period. Annual deadline dates vary.
Requirements Public and nonprofit entities, schools, and academic health science centers are eligible to apply.
Amount $450,000-$5.1 million range; $2.3 million average
Contact Deborah Willis-Fillinger, HIV Education Branch, (301) 443-6364; fax: (301) 443-9887
Internet http://hab.hrsa.gov
Sponsor Department of Health and Human Services
5600 Fishers Ln, Parklawn Bldg
Rockville, MD 20857

DHHS AIDS Project Grants 1545
The grants are intended to fund programs that develop and implement surveillance, epidemiological research, health education, school health, and risk reduction activities of AIDS in states and major cities. The program also gives support for cooperative agreements for AIDS activities. The funding period will be from one to five years, renewable. Applicants should contact the CDC for deadline information.
Requirements Public and private organizations, both nonprofit and for profit, state and local governments, US territories and possessions, small and minority businesses, and businesses owned by women are encouraged to apply.
Amount $45,000-$2 million; $390,174 average
Contact Allyn Nakashima , Division of HIV/AIDS Prevention, Centers for Disease Control and Prevention, (404) 639-0900; Cheryl Maddux, Grants Management Branch, (770) 498-1911
Internet http://www.dhhs.gov
Sponsor Department of Health and Human Services
2920 Brandywine Rd
Atlanta, GA 30341

DHHS Chiropractic Demonstration Project Grants 1546
The objective of the program is to make grants and enter into contracts with schools, colleges, and universities of chiropractic for the purposes of carrying out demonstration projects in which chiropractors and physicians collaborate to identify and provide effective treatment for spinal and lower back conditions. Grant funds may be used for personnel, equipment, supplies, domestic travel, consultants and guest lecturers, rental of space, renovations, and other costs directly related to the project as described in the approved application. Application materials are available on the World Wide Web at address: http://www.hrsa.gov/bhpr/grants.html.
Requirements Public or private nonprofit schools, colleges, and universities of chiropractic medicine are eligible to apply.
Restrictions Grant funds may not be used for construction of facilities, acquisition of land, foreign travel, or support of students, including fellowships, stipends, tuition, fees, or travel allowances.
Amount $381,048 -$389,214; $386,456 average
Contact Jennifer Hannah, Health Resources and Services Administration, (301) 443-0908
Internet http://bhpr.hrsa.gov/interdisciplinary/chiro.html
Sponsor Department of Health and Human Services
5600 Fishers Ln, Parklawn Bldg
Rockville, MD 20857

DHHS Comprehensive Community Mental Health Services Grants for Children with Serious Emotional Disturbances 1547
This program provides community-based systems of care for children and adolescents with serious emotional disturbances and their families. The program will ensure that services are provided collaboratively across child-serving systems; that each child or adolescent served through the program receives an individualized service plan developed with the participation of the family; that each individualized plan designates a case manager to assist the child and family; and that funding is provided for mental health services required to meet the needs of youngsters in these systems.
Requirements States; political subdivisions of a state, such as county or local governments; and federally recognized Native American tribal governments are eligible to apply.
Amount $200,064-$3.5 million; $1.85 million average
Contact Gary Blau, Chief, Child Adolescent and Family Branch, (301) 443-1333
Internet http://mentalhealth.samhsa.gov/publications/allpubs/CA-0013/default.asp
Sponsor Department of Health and Human Services
5600 Fishers Ln, Parklawn Bldg
Rockville, MD 20857

DHHS Developmental Disabilities University Affiliated Programs Grants 1548
Grants assist with the cost of administration and operation of facilities for providing interdisciplinary training for personnel concerned with developmental disabilities, demonstrations of the provision of exemplary services related to the developmentally disabled, demonstration of technical assistance for generic and specialized agencies, dissemination of findings related to the provision of services to researchers and government agencies, and generation of information on the need for further service-related research. Grants may cover salaries for administrators, coordinators, and others needed to operate a training facility, such as clerical and financial personnel, and maintenance and housekeeping personnel; overhead expenses and expenses required to start up new programs; and faculty for training programs that will meet critical personnel shortages and are not eligible for support from other sources. Deadline dates are available from the office.
Requirements Public and private nonprofit organizations and agencies are eligible to apply.
Amount $480,000
Date(s) Application Is Due Sep 1.
Contact Jennifer Johnson, Administration on Developmental Disabilities, Administration for Children and Families, (202) 690-5982
Internet http://www.dhhs.gov
Sponsor Department of Health and Human Services
370 L'Enfant Promenade, SW
Washington, DC 20447

DHHS Emergency Medical Services for Children (EMSC) Program 1549
The purpose of this program is to support demonstration projects for the expansion and improvement of emergency medical services for children who need treatment for trauma or critical care. It is expected that maximum distribution of projects among the states will be made and that priority will be given to projects targeted toward populations with special needs, including Native Americans, minorities, and the disabled. Annual deadline dates may vary; contact program staff for exact dates.
Requirements States and accredited schools of medicine are eligible to apply.
Amount $200,000 average
Contact Dan Kavanaugh, (301) 443-1321; email: dkavanaugh@hrsa.gov
Internet http://mchb.hrsa.gov/programs/emsc
Sponsor Department of Health and Human Services
5600 Fishers Lane
Rockville, MD 20857

DHHS Geriatric Training for Physicians and Dentists Grants 1550

These grants are intended to assist in the operation of postdoctoral training preparing current and future faculty for leadership roles in geriatric medicine and dentistry and to provide support, including traineeships and fellowships, for geriatric medicine training projects to train physicians and dentists who plan to teach geriatric medicine or geriatric dentistry. Geriatric training is to be provided through one or both of the following projects: one grant is offered for a one-year retraining program in geriatrics for physicians who are faculty members in departments of internal medicine, family medicine, gynecology, geriatrics, and psychiatry at schools of medicine and osteopathy; and dentists who are faculty members at schools of dentistry or at hospital departments of dentistry. A grant is offered for a two-year internal medicine or family medicine fellowship program with emphasis in geriatric research for physicians who have completed graduate medical education programs in internal medicine, family medicine, psychiatry, neurology, gynecology, geriatrics, or rehabilitation medicine; and dentists who have completed postdoctoral dental education programs. Each project for which a grant is made must be staffed by full-time teaching physicians who have experience or training in geriatric medicine, be staffed by full-time or part-time teaching dentists who have experience or training in geriatric dentistry, and be based in a graduate medical education program in a department of internal medicine or family medicine or a department of geriatrics that has been in existence over a year. Each project must provide participants with exposure to a diversified population of elderly individuals and provide training in geriatrics and exposure to the physical and mental disabilities of elderly individuals through a variety of service rotations, such as geriatric consultation services, acute care services, dental services, geriatric psychiatry units, day and home care programs, rehabilitation services, extended care facilities, geriatric ambulatory care and comprehensive evaluation units, and community care programs for elderly mentally retarded individuals. Applications and deadline dates can be obtained on the Web site or by contacting the office.

Requirements Grants will be made to accredited public or private nonprofit schools of medicine, schools of osteopathic medicine, teaching hospitals, and graduate medical education programs.

Amount $178,721-$632,825; $374,575 average

Contact Kathleen Bond, Department of Health and Human Services, (301) 443-8681

Internet http://www.dhhs.gov

Sponsor Department of Health and Human Services

5600 Fishers Ln, Parklawn Bldg

Rockville, MD 20857

DHHS Great Lakes Human Health Effects Research Program Grants 1551

The objectives of this program are to build upon and amplify the results from past and ongoing research; develop information, databases, and/or research methodology that will provide long-term benefit to the Great Lakes human health research effort; develop directions and methodology for future human health effects research; provide health information to the subjects of the research and their medical professions; and increase the public awareness of the health implications of the toxic pollution problem in the Great Lakes. Grant funds may be used to conduct research on the impact on human health of fish consumption in this region and to extend the knowledge of the effects of contaminants on human reproductive/developmental, behavioral, neurological, and endocrinological adverse health. Contact the office for deadline dates.

Requirements Eligible applicants are the official public health agencies or their bona fide agents or instrumentalities and political subdivisions thereof, which may include state universities, state colleges, state research institutions, state and local health departments, and federally recognized Native American tribal governments located in the Great Lakes states (Illinois, Indiana, Michigan, Minnesota, Ohio, Pennsylvania, New York, and Wisconsin).

Amount $200,000 average

Contact Heraline Hicks, Division of Toxicology, Agency for Toxic Substances and Disease Registry, (404) 489-0717; fax: (404) 498-0094; email: HEH2@cdc.gov; Edna Green, Grants Management Contact, (770) 488-2743; email: ecg4@cdc.gov

Internet http://www.atsdr.cdc.gov/grtlakes.html

Sponsor Department of Health and Human Services

1600 Clifton Rd NE

Atlanta, GA 30333

DHHS Health Care Systems Cost and Access Research and Development Grants 1552

Grants are made to support health services research to create new knowledge and better understanding of the process by which health services are made available and how they may be provided more efficiently and effectively. The AHCPR has a broad legislative mandate to support general health services research on problems related to health care cost, quality, and access to health services. Major categories of research issues include consumer decision making, managed care and the health care marketplace, primary care, rural health services, and AIDS. Annual deadline dates may vary; contact program staff for exact dates.

Requirements Government agencies (federal, state, and local), federally recognized tribal governments, US territories, sponsored organizations, nongovernment organizations, minority groups, specialized groups, public or private institutions of higher education, and other public or nonprofit private agencies, institutions, or organizations are eligible. Research project grants may also be awarded to individuals.

Restrictions Profit-making organizations are not eligible for grants.

Amount $5000-$2.8 million; $310,000 average

Date(s) Application Is Due Feb 1; Jun 1; Oct 1.

Contact Mable Lam, Grants Management Officer, (301) 427-1447

Internet http://www.dhhs.gov

Sponsor Department of Health and Human Services

2101 E Jefferson St, Executive Office Ctr

Rockville, MD 20852

DHHS Health Conference Support Program for Toxic Substances and Disease Registry 1553

Funds are available through this program for partial support for nonfederal conferences on disease prevention, health promotion, and projects related to hazardous substances. The purpose of this program is to work closely with state, local, and other federal agencies to reduce or eliminate illness, disability, and death resulting from exposure of the public and workers to toxic substances at spill and waste disposal sites.

Amount $130,000-$300,000; $200,000 average

Contact Caroline McDonald, Agency for Toxic Substances and Disease Registry, (404) 498-0270; fax: (404) 498-0059; email: COS4@cdc.gov; Mildred Garner, Grants Management Branch, (770) 488-2745, fax: (770) 488-2777

Internet http://www.dhhs.gov

Sponsor Department of Health and Human Services

1600 Clifton Rd NE

Atlanta, GA 30333

DHHS Health Professions Preparatory Scholarship Program for Indians 1554

The program makes scholarship grants for a maximum of two years to individuals of Native American or Alaskan Native descent for the purpose of completing compensatory preprofessional education to enable the recipient to qualify for enrollment or re-enrollment in a health professions school. Grants for stipends and books are made directly to the individual applicant; tuition payments are made to the college or university. New applications are usually available in February with an annual submission deadline in April. Annual deadline dates may vary; contact program staff for exact dates.

Requirements Scholarship awards are made to individuals of Native American or Alaskan Native descent who have successfully completed high school education or high school equivalency and who have been accepted for enrollment in a compensatory, preprofessional general education course or curriculum.

Amount $17,500-$26,019; $17,366 average

Date(s) Application Is Due Apr 1.

Contact Harold Jess Brier, Chief, Scholarship Branch, (301) 443-6197; Lois Hodge, Grants Management Officer, (301) 443-0243

Internet http://www.ihs.gov

Sponsor Department of Health and Human Services

12300 Twinbrook Pkwy, Twinbrook Metro Plz

Rockville, MD 20852

DHHS Health Professions Scholarship Program 1555

The program makes scholarship grants to Native Americans and other students for the purposes of completing health professional education--nursing; medicine including allopathic, osteopathic, and veterinary medicine; dentistry; x-ray technology; optometry; pharmacy; public health nutrition (graduate); medical social work (graduate); speech pathology/audiology (graduate); podiatry; health care administration; and other allied health professions--to obtain health professionals to serve Native Americans. Not all disciplines participate each year. Upon completion, grantees are required to fulfill an obligated service payback. Maximum length of funding is four years. Grants for stipends and books are made directly to the individual applicant; tuition payments are made to the college or university. New applications are available in February with a submission deadline in April. Annual deadline dates may vary; contact program staff for exact dates.

Requirements Priority consideration for scholarship awards is granted to persons of Native American or Alaskan Native descent. Applicants for new awards must be accepted by an accredited US educational institution for a full-time course of study leading to a degree in medicine, osteopathy, dentistry, or other participating health profession that is deemed necessary by the Indian Health Service; be eligible for or hold an appointment as a commissioned officer in the regular or reserve corps of the Public Health Service; or be eligible for civilian service in the Indian Health Service.

Amount $24,128-$38,222; $24,694 average

Date(s) Application Is Due Apr 1.

Contact Harold Jess Brier, Chief, Scholarship Branch, (301) 443-6197; Lois Hodge, Grants Management Officer, (301) 443-0243

Internet http://www.dhhs.gov

Sponsor Department of Health and Human Services

12300 Twinbrook Pkwy, Twinbrook Metro Plz

Rockville, MD 20852

DHHS Health Promotion and Disease Prevention Research and Demonstration Centers Grants 1556

Grants are awarded to qualified schools to establish, maintain, and operate academic-based centers for high-quality research and demonstration with respect to health promotion and disease prevention; to establish linkages between ongoing basic research in a wide array of fields and applied research in disease prevention and health promotion; to bring the knowledge and expertise of academic health centers to bear on practical

public health problems; to field test and rigorously evaluate more cost-effective methods and strategies for preventing unnecessary illness and promoting good health; and to shorten the time lag between the development of new and proven effective disease prevention and health promotion techniques and their widespread application. The length of assistance will be from one to five years, renewable based on competitive applications and availability of funds. Deadlines will be announced in the Federal Register.
Requirements Eligible applicants are schools of medicine, schools of osteopathy, and schools of public health.
Restrictions Grantees may not award subgrants but may enter into consortia agreements or contracts as necessary to achieve the aims of the program.
Amount $740,000-$770,000; $755,000 average
Contact Dr. Eduardo Simoes, Program Director, National Center for Chronic Disease Prevention and Health Promotion, (770) 488-5919; Carlos Smiley, Grants Management Officer, (770) 488-2754
Internet http://www.cdc.gov/prc
Sponsor Department of Health and Human Services
4770 Buford Hwy, K-45
Atlanta, GA 30333

DHHS HIV Demonstration Program for Children, Adolescents, and Women 1557
Grants are awarded to support, improve, and expand the system of comprehensive care services for children, youth, women, and families who are infected with or affected by HIV and AIDS and to link comprehensive care systems with clinical research. Projects should promote collaboration between research institutions and primary care medical and social service programs. Funding priority will be given to projects that demonstrate established models of care that are comprehensive and coordinated, sensitive to differing cultural needs, and family and community based. Grants may be made for up to three-year project periods, renewable competitively after the first year. Contact the office for deadline dates.
Requirements All public and private nonprofit organizations that provide or arrange for primary health care are eligible for grants. This includes state or local health departments, hospitals, community health centers, drug abuse treatment agencies, school-based clinics, tribal health programs, colleges, and hemophilia treatment centers.
Amount $230,384-$2.5 million; $766,222 average
Contact Dr. Jose Rafael Morales, Division of Community Based Programs/Title IV, HIV/AIDS Bureau, (301) 443-9051
Internet http://www.dhhs.gov
Sponsor Department of Health and Human Services
5600 Fishers Ln, Parklawn Bldg
Rockville, MD 20857

DHHS Independence Demonstration Program 1558
The objective of the program is to provide for the establishment of demonstration projects designed to determine the social, civic, psychological, and economic effects of providing to individuals and families with limited means an incentive to accumulate assets by saving a portion of their earned income; the extent to which an asset-based policy that promotes saving for postsecondary education, homeownership, and microenterprise development may be used to enable individuals and families with limited means to increase their economic self-sufficiency; and the extent to which an asset-based policy stabilizes and improves families and the community in which the families live. Deadlines are announced in the Federal Register.
Requirements Nonprofit 501(c)3 tax-exempt organizations and state or local government agencies or tribal governments submitting an application jointly with such a nonprofit organization are eligible to apply.
Amount $360,000 average
Contact James Gatz, Office of Community Services, (202) 401-4626; email: AFIProgram@acf.hhs.gov
Internet http://www.acf.hhs.gov/grants/open/HHS-2004-ACF-OCS-EI-0027.html
Sponsor Department of Health and Human Services
370 L'Enfant Promenade SW, Ste 500 W
Washington, DC 20447

DHHS Maternal and Child Health Research and Training Program Grants 1559
Grants fund special projects that develop new data and improve the professional development of health practitioners who serve women and children. Research grants will fund projects that address minority and disadvantaged populations, health-promoting behaviors, quality outcome measures, and systems integration and reform. Long-term training grants will be awarded to train health professionals at the graduate and postgraduate levels. Training should focus on family-centered, community-based care. Continuing education grants support continuing education for workers in the maternal and child health field. Priority will be given to projects focusing on emergency medical services for children, violence prevention in schools, and core public health. Application kits may be obtained by calling toll-free (877) 477-2123.
Requirements Training grants may be made to public or nonprofit private institutions of higher learning. Research grants may be made to public or nonprofit institutions of higher learning and public or nonprofit private agencies and organizations engaged in research, maternal and child health, or programs for children with special health care needs.
Amount $14,000-$1.5 million; $179,248 average
Contact Program Contact, Maternal and Child Health Bureau, (301) 443-2170; Lawrence Poole, Director, Division of Grants Management Operations, (301) 443-2385
Internet http://www.dhhs.gov
Sponsor Department of Health and Human Services
5600 Fishers Ln, Parklawn Bldg
Rockville, MD 20857

DHHS National Health Service Corps Loan Repayment Awards 1560
To help ensure an adequate supply of trained health professionals for the National Health Service Corps, this program provides for the repayment of educational loans for participants who agree by written contract to serve an applicable period of time in a health-related workforce shortage area or in an Indian health program or facility. Awards provide payments toward participants' qualified government and commercial health professions education loans during each year of practice at a selected NHSC loan repayment service site with a two-year service minimum. Health professions given priority for selection are those determined by the workforce needs of the NHSC and the Indian Health Service. Beneficiaries include primary care physicians; dentists; certified nurse midwives; certified nurse practitioners; physicians assistants; clinical psychologists; clinical social workers; psychiatric nurse specialists; marriage and family therapists; licensed professional counselors; and dental hygienists. Deadline dates are published in the Federal Register.
Requirements US citizens who are enrolled as full-time students in the final year of study in an accredited health profession education institution or possess a health professions degree and are either enrolled in postgraduate health professions training or are in professional practice are eligible to apply. They must hold an unrestricted health professions license in a state and be eligible for or hold an appointment as a commissioned officer in the regular or reserve corps of the Public Health Service or be eligible for selection for a federal civil service appointment.
Amount $25,000 maximum per year plus a tax assistance payment of 39 percent
Date(s) Application Is Due Mar 26.
Contact Chief, Loan Repayment Programs Branch, Division of Health Services Scholarships, (301) 594-4400; Public Information Phone, (800) 435-6464
Internet http://www.hrsa.gov
Sponsor Department of Health and Human Services
4350 East-West Hwy
Rockville, MD 20857

DHHS National Health Service Corps Scholarships Program 1561
To obtain adequate numbers of trained physicians, dentists, and other health-related specialists for the National Health Service Corps, scholarships are given in exchange for service in health personnel shortage areas within the United States. Disciplines have included allopathic and osteopathic medicine, dentistry, nursing (baccalaureate and graduate), public health nutrition (graduate), medical social work (graduate), speech pathology/audiology (graduate), veterinary medicine, optometry, podiatry, and pharmacy. Not all disciplines participate each year. Deadlines for receipt of applications for each academic year are the last Friday in March. A student may not receive more than a total of four years of support. Each award covers one academic year of support (including monthly living stipend, tuition, and fees), as specified by signed contracts, with annual continuation awards if funds are available.
Requirements Applicants for new awards must be accepted by accredited US educational institutions for full-time courses of study leading to degrees in medicine, osteopathy, or dentistry; be former recipients of the federal scholarship program for first-year students of exceptional financial need; be eligible for or hold appointments as commissioned officers in the regular or reserve corps of PHS or be eligible for civilian service in the NHSC; and submit applications and signed contracts to accept payment of scholarships and to serve for the applicable period of obligated service in health workforce shortage areas.
Restrictions Each year of scholarship support incurs a year of federal service obligation with the minimum obligation being two years. Failure to fulfill the service obligation incurs financial damages, payable in one year, calculated at three times the scholarship benefits plus interest.
Amount $1128 plus tuition, fees and other reasonable costs
Contact Division of National Health Service Corps, (301) 594-4400 or (800) 221-9393
Internet http://www.dhhs.gov
Sponsor Department of Health and Human Services
4350 East-West Hwy
Bethesda, MD 20814

DHHS Native American Health Service Loan Repayment Awards 1562
To help ensure an adequate supply of trained health professionals for IHS facilities, the program provides for the repayment of educational loans for participants who agree by written contract to serve an applicable period of time at a facility IHS has designated as a retention/recruitment priority site or in a designated specialty at a site with an appropriate position. Recipients must agree to serve an applicable period of time in such a site with a minimum period of participation of two years. Contact the program office for deadline dates.
Requirements Eligible applicants must be individuals who are enrolled as full-time students in the final year of a course of study or program leading to a degree in allopathic or osteopathic medicine, dentistry, or other health profession in a state; are enrolled in an approved graduate training program in allopathic or osteopathic medicine, dentistry, or other health profession; or have a degree in allopathic or osteopathic medicine, dentistry, or other health profession and have completed an approved graduate training program and

have a current and valid license to practice such health profession in a state. In addition, applicants must be eligible for appointment as commissioned officers in the regular or reserve corps of Public Health Service (PHS) or be eligible for selection for civilian service in IHS, submit an application to participate in the loan repayment program, and sign and submit it to DHHS at the time of agreeing to accept repayment of educational loans, and serve for the applicable period of service in a retention/recruitment site as determined by DHHS.
Amount $3000-$48,000 for a 2-year obligation
Contact Jackie Sanitago, Chief, Loan Repayment Program, IHS, (301) 443-3396
Internet http://www.dhhs.gov
Sponsor Department of Health and Human Services
12300 Twinbrook Pkwy
Rockville, MD 20852

DHHS Native American Programs **1563**
To provide financial assistance, training and technical assistance, and research, demonstration and evaluation activities to public and private nonprofit organizations including Indian Tribes, urban Indian centers, Alaska Native villages, Native Hawaiian organizations, rural off-reservation groups, and Native American Pacific Island groups for the development and implementation of social and economic development strategies that promote self-sufficiency. These projects are expected to result in improved social and economic conditions of Native Americans within their communities and to increase the effectiveness of Indian Tribes and Native American organizations in meeting their economic and social goals. Additional competitive areas include (1) Environmental Regulatory Enhancement, designed to assist Tribal and Alaska Village governments in developing environmental programs responsive to tribal needs; and (2) Native Languages Preservation and Enhancement, a program to assist Native American tribes and communities in ensuring the survival and continued vitality of their languages.
Requirements Public and private nonprofit agencies, including but not limited to, governing bodies of Indian tribes on Federal and State reservations, Alaska Native villages and regional corporations established by the Alaska Native Claims Settlement Act, such public and nonprofit private agencies serving Native Hawaiians, Indian and Alaska Native organizations in urban or rural nonreservation areas, and Native American Pacific Islanders (American Samoan Natives, and indigenous peoples of Guam, the Commonwealth of the Northern Mariana and the Republic of Palau) are eligible to apply.
Amount $125,000 average tribal grant; $100,000 average urban grant
Contact Sheila Cooper, Director of Program Operations, (202) 690-5787
Internet http://www.acf.hhs.gov/programs/ana/programs/index.html
Sponsor Department of Health and Human Services
370 L'Enfant Promenade SW, MS HHH 326-F
Washington, DC 20447

DHHS Neurodevelopmental Test Methods Research Grants **1564**
The purpose of the program is to determine and validate a battery of neurodevelopmental tests for use in assessing the effects of prenatal or postnatal exposure to developmental toxicants. The battery of tests should be applicable to a wide range of potential neurodevelopmental toxicants found at waste sites and in the environment including metals and solvents; be applicable to a wide range of exposure levels found in the environment; and cover a broad range of developmental domains including cognitive function, sensory function, motor function, and complex multi-tasking performance. These research methods will address an agency goal to develop methods and tools for evaluating human health consequences from exposure to toxic substances in the environment.
Requirements Applications may be submitted by official public health agencies of the states, or their bona fide agents. This includes the District of Columbia, American Samoa, the Commonwealth of Puerto Rico, the Virgin Islands, the Federated States of Micronesia, Guam, the Northern Mariana Islands, the Republic of the Marshall Island, the Republic of Palau, federally recognized Indian tribal governments, public and private nonprofit and for-profit universities, colleges, and research institutions.
Amount $130,000-$300,000; $200,000 average
Date(s) Application Is Due Jul 15.
Contact Mildred Garner, Grants Management Officer, (770) 488-2745; fax: (770) 488-2777; email: info@cdc.gov
Internet http://www.cdc.gov
Sponsor Department of Health and Human Services
2920 Brandywine Rd
Atlanta, GA 30341-4146

DHHS Oral Health Promotion Research Across the Lifespan **1565**
The National Institute of Dental and Craniofacial Research has invited proposals for improving the oral health of people of all ages. The research team must include someone with extensive experience in health promotion, behavioral and/or social science research. The health promotion intervention proposed for funding must be based on a previously conducted assessment of the epidemiology, social, behavioral and/or environmental factors related to the disease or condition under study. Research could focus on maternal and child health, adolescent and young adult health, or health of adults with complex diseases. For example, an applicant might propose to study approaches to involving families, social networks, communities, or neighborhoods in behaviors that promote and improve oral health; improving patient-provider communication related to oral preventive measures; or effective ways to train oral health professional students to communicate with diverse patient populations.
Requirements Any person with the skills, knowledge, and resources necessary to carry out the proposed research as the project director/principal investigator (PD/PI) is invited to work with his/her organization to develop an application for support. Applications must be submitted electronically through Grants.gov (http://www.grants.gov) using the SF424 research and related forms and the SF424 application guide.
Date(s) Application Is Due Mar 5; Jul 5; Nov 5.
Contact Maria Teresa Canto, (301) 594-5497; fax: (301) 480-8322; email: maria.canto@nih.gov
Internet http://grants.nih.gov/grants/guide/pa-files/PA-07-225.html
Sponsor National Institute of Dental and Craniofacial Research (NIDCR)
Building 45, Room 4AS43D, 45 Center Drive MSC 6401
Bethesda, MD 20892

DHHS Podiatric Primary Care Residency Training Grants **1566**
This program intends to promote the postgraduate education of podiatrists in primary care podiatric practice. Grants are to assist in meeting the costs of the program that cannot be met from other sources. Grants may include support for the program only, residents only, or support for both the program and residents but are not intended to absorb costs of existing or new positions that can be supported from other available funds. Project period is a maximum of 36 months; a noncompeting continuation application is required at the end of each budget period. Contact the office for deadline dates.
Requirements Public or nonprofit private accredited schools of podiatric medicine and teaching hospitals may apply.
Amount $205,291-$286,362; $245,826 average
Contact Chris McLaughlin, Division of Medicine, (301) 443-1568; email: cmclaughlin@hrsa.gov
Internet http://www.dhhs.gov
Sponsor Department of Health and Human Services
5600 Fishers Ln, Parklawn Bldg
Rockville, MD 20857

DHHS Preventive Medicine **1567**
The grants promote the postgraduate education of physicians in preventive medicine. Grants are intended to assist in meeting the costs of planning and developing new preventive medicine programs; maintaining or improving existing residency training programs in preventive medicine; and providing financial assistance to trainees enrolled in such programs. Contact the office for deadlines and application materials.
Requirements Any accredited public or private school of medicine, osteopathy, or public health may apply. To be eligible for a grant, the applicant must demonstrate that it has or will have available, full-time faculty members with training and experience in the fields of preventive medicine.
Restrictions Grants may not be used for construction or patient services.
Amount $101,897-$430,188; $206,768 average
Contact Dr. Douglas Lloyd, Public Health and Dental Education Branch, (301) 443-0157
Internet http://www.dhhs.gov
Sponsor Department of Health and Human Services
5600 Fishers Ln, Parklawn Bldg
Rockville, MD 20857

DHHS Primary Medical Care National Research Service Awards (NRSA) **1568**
This program is intended to promote postdoctoral research training programs in primary medical care. NRSAs are made directly to individuals for research training in primary medical care; in addition, grants may be made to institutions to enable them to award NRSAs to individuals selected by them. Each individual who receives an NRSA is obligated, upon termination of the award, to comply with certain service and payback provisions. Recipients agree to engage in primary medical care research and/or teaching for a period equal to the period of the NRSA support in excess of 12 months. Contact the office for deadline dates.
Requirements Domestic public or private nonprofit organizations may apply for training grants. States or local governments and US territories are eligible. Individual applicants for fellowships must have received doctoral degrees. All persons supported as fellows or trainees must be citizens or noncitizen nationals of the United States or have been lawfully admitted for permanent residence. Eligibility is limited to individuals affiliated with entities having received grants or contracts under Sections 780, 784, or 786 of the Public Health Service Act.
Amount $258,100-$538,167; $389,688 average
Contact Christopher McLaughlin and Anne Patterson, Division of Medicine, (301) 443-6785
Internet http://www.dhhs.gov
Sponsor Department of Health and Human Services
5600 Fishers Ln, Parklawn Bldg
Rockville, MD 20857

DHHS Priority Health Conditions Studies Initiative **1569**
The primary purpose of this program is to solicit scientific proposals designed to study the occurrence of and risk factors for priority adverse health conditions. The priority health conditions are birth defects and reproductive disorders, cancers, immune function

disorders, kidney dysfunction, liver dysfunction, lung and respiratory diseases, and neurotoxic disorders. Each fiscal year, one of the seven priority health conditions will be emphasized; however, applications may address any of the seven. This will improve recipients' ability to address potential public health problems related to exposure to hazardous substances. Contact the office for deadline dates.
Requirements Eligible applicants are state health departments and the District of Columbia; the Commonwealth of Puerto Rico; the Virgin Islands; Guam; the Federated States of Micronesia; the Republic of the Marshall Islands; the Republic of Palau; the Northern Mariana Islands; American Samoa; the political subdivisions thereof, which may include state universities, state colleges, and state research institutions; and federally recognized Native American tribal governments.
Amount $50,000-$500,000; $100,000 average
Contact Caroline McDonald, Division of Health Studies, Agency for Toxic Substances and Disease Registry, (404) 498-0270; fax: (404) 498-0059; email: COS4@cdc.gov
Internet http://www.dhhs.gov
Sponsor Department of Health and Human Services
1600 Clifton Rd NE
Atlanta, GA 30333

DHHS Professional Nurse Traineeships Program **1570**
Grants are awarded to eligible institutions to provide financial support through traineeships for registered nurses enrolled in advanced education nursing programs to prepare nurse practitioners, clinical nurse specialists, nurse midwives, nurse anesthetists, nurse administrators, nurse educators, public health nurses and nurses in other specialties determined by the Secretary to require advanced education.
Requirements Schools of nursing and public health, public or nonprofit private hospitals, and other public or nonprofit entities are eligible for funds. Trainees are selected by participating institutions. A candidate must be a US citizen or have been lawfully admitted to the United States for permanent residence; a graduate of a state-approved school of nursing; licensed as a professional nurse in a state or territory; and able to enroll full-time in a course of study.
Amount $1000-$235,000; $45,000 average
Contact Karen Breeden, Division of Nursing, (301) 443-6333
Internet http://www.dhhs.gov
Sponsor Department of Health and Human Services
5600 Fishers Ln, Parklawn Bldg
Rockville, MD 20857

DHHS Promoting Safe and Stable Families Grants **1571**
The National Center on Child Abuse and Neglect is interested in research on the impact of community-based family support and family preservation programs on child abuse and neglect. Research should focus on expanding the current knowledge base, build on previous research, and provide insights into new approaches to preventing child maltreatment and preserving families through support and preservation services. The center is particularly interested in projects that address specific populations and outcomes. The populations are families who receive family support services but have had no previous contact with child protective services; families who have been referred to child protective services whose cases were unsubstantiated but were found to need services and were referred to family support programs; families who have been in the system whose child abuse or neglect cases were substantiated, who received family preservation or support services, and whose cases are now closed; and families who have open cases whose children have not been removed and who are receiving family preservation services. Outcomes of interest are case finding, which involves families who were not referred to child protective services, and the impact of family support and/or preservation services on prevention, recidivism, and removal of children. Applicants should plan and design the proposed research in collaboration with state and local CPS and Title IV-B agencies as well as community-based entities providing family support services, such as family resource centers. Contact the office for deadline dates.
Requirements Agencies of state and local governments, public and private nonprofit agencies, and institutions engaged in child and family welfare activities and research are eligible for these grants.
Amount $194,000-$48 million range
Contact Joseph Bock, Deputy Associate Commissioner, Children's Bureau, (202) 205-8618
Internet http://www.acf.hhs.gov/programs/cb/programs/fpfs.htm
Sponsor Department of Health and Human Services
330 C St, SW
Washington, DC 20447

DHHS Public Health Students Traineeships and Other Graduate Public Health Programs **1572**
The programs support traineeships for students in graduate educational programs in schools of public health or other public or nonprofit educational entities that offer graduate programs for training in biostatistics or epidemiology; health administration, health planning, or health policy analysis and planning; environmental or occupational health; dietetics or nutrition; maternal and child health; or approved residency training in preventive medicine or dentistry. Deadlines and application kits are forwarded to all eligible applicants. Annual deadline dates may vary.
Requirements Accredited schools of public health and other public or nonprofit educational entities providing graduate or specialized training in public health may apply. Trainees must be US citizens or noncitizen nationals possessing visas permitting permanent residence in the United States and must be pursuing a graduate degree in an eligible school of public health or be enrolled in an eligible program.
Amount $8109-$148,850; $50,150 average
Contact Cecelia Maryland, Public Health Branch, Division of State, Community and Public Health, (301) 443-1973
Internet http://www.dhhs.gov
Sponsor Department of Health and Human Services
5600 Fishers Ln, Parklawn Bldg
Rockville, MD 20857

DHHS Residency Training in Family Practice, General Internal Medicine, or General Pediatrics Grants **1573**
Grants are awarded to assist graduate training programs in family medicine, general internal medicine and/or general pediatrics to expand and improve the quality of residency training programs that prepare graduates to enter primary care practice. Residency training programs should emphasize national innovations aimed at primary care residency education across disciplines.
Requirements An accredited public or private nonprofit school of medicine, a school of osteopathic medicine, and a public or private nonprofit hospital or other entity located in a state is eligible to apply. Each allopathic program must be fully or provisionally approved by the Accreditation Council for Graduate Medical Education. Each osteopathic program must be approved by the American Osteopathic Association.
Restrictions Grants may not be used for construction, patient services, or student assistance.
Amount $27,000-$657,344; $178,803 average
Contact Dr. P. Preston Reynolds, Division of Medicine and Dentistry of the Bureau of Health Professions, (301) 443-1467
Internet http://www.dhhs.gov
Sponsor Department of Health and Human Services
5600 Fishers Ln, Parklawn Bldg
Rockville, MD 20857

DHHS Rural Telemedicine Grants **1574**
The objective of this program is to demonstrate and collect information on the feasibility, costs, appropriateness, and acceptability of telemedicine for improving access to health services for rural residents and reducing the isolation of rural practitioners, and to demonstrate how telemedicine can be used as an effective tool for the development of integrated systems of health care for rural areas. Application kits may be obtained by calling toll-free (888)300-4772. Annual deadline dates may vary; contact program staff for exact dates.
Requirements Eligible applicants are nonprofit public (nonfederal) or private health care providers or a consortium of providers, nonprofit or for profit, that are members of an existing or proposed telemedicine network.
Restrictions Not more than 40 percent of grant funds may be expended for equipment. Not more than 20 percent of grant funds may be expended for direct costs. Grant funds may not be used for purchasing and installing telecommunications transmission equipment.
Amount $250,000 maximum
Contact Monica Cowan, Administrative Assistant, Office for the Advancement of Telehealth, (301) 443-1730
Internet http://www.telehealth.hrsa.gov
Sponsor Department of Health and Human Services
4350 East-West Hwy
Rockville, MD 20814

DHHS Special Programs for the Aging Training, Research, and Discretionary Projects and Programs Grants **1575**
Funds are given to provide adequately trained personnel in the field of aging, improve knowledge of the problems and needs of the elderly, and to demonstrate better ways of improving the quality of life for the elderly. Funds may be used to train persons to work in the field of aging, to increase the availability and accessibility of training and education programs in the field of aging, and to conduct activities for the development of knowledge to improve the circumstances of older people. Deadlines are posted in the Federal Register.
Requirements Grants may be made to any public or nonprofit private agency, organization, or institution.
Restrictions Grants are not available to individuals.
Amount $250,000 average
Contact Center for Planning and Policy Development, Administration on Aging, (202) 619-0724
Internet http://aspe.hhs.gov/SelfGovernance/inventory/Aoa/048.htm
Sponsor Department of Health and Human Services
330 Independence Ave SW
Washington, DC 20201

DHHS Tuberculosis Demonstration, Research, Public, and Professional Education Cooperative Agreements **1576**
The purpose of the program is to assist states, political subdivisions of states, and other public and nonprofit private entities to conduct research into the prevention and control of tuberculosis, especially research concerning strains of tuberculosis resistant

to drugs and research concerning cases of tuberculosis that affect certain populations; conduct demonstration projects for the prevention and control of tuberculosis; provide public information and provide education programs for prevention and control of tuberculosis; and develop education, training, and clinical skills improvement activities in the prevention and control of tuberculosis for health professionals, including allied health personnel. Project periods are for one to five years with 12-month budget periods. Applications will be evaluated on the extent of the tuberculosis problem; the establishment of specific and measurable objectives; and the development of a sound operational plan that will ensure the implementation of each program element. Contact the office for deadline dates.
Requirements States, political subdivisions of states, and other public and nonprofit private entities are eligible.
Amount $150,000-$200,000; $165,000 average
Contact Dr. Kenneth Castro, National Center for HIV, STD, and TB Prevention, (404) 639-8120; William Ryan, Grants Management Officer, (770) 488-2717
Internet http://www.dhhs.gov
Sponsor Department of Health and Human Services
1600 Clifton Rd NE
Atlanta, GA 30333

DHHS Universal Newborn Hearing Screening and Intervention 1577
This program supports the implementation of universal physiologic newborn hearing screening prior to hospital discharge with linkages to medical home, ongoing family-to-family support, diagnostic evaluation by three months of age, and enrollment in a program of early intervention by six months of age for those infants identified with hearing loss. Applicants are expected to notify the Maternal and Child Health Bureau's Division of Services for Children with Special Health Care Needs by November 10; the deadline for receipt of applications is December 8.
Requirements This program is open to state agencies with the capacity to implement a statewide universal newborn hearing screening and intervention program for all newborn infants in the state.
Amount $43,650-$515,382; $161,017. average
Contact Irene Forsman, Integrated Services Branch, Division of Services for Children with Special Health Needs, (301) 443-2370; email: iforsman@hrsa.gov; Lawrence Poole, Director, Division of Grants Management Operations, (301) 443-0354
Internet http://www.dhhs.gov
Sponsor Department of Health and Human Services
5600 Fishers Ln, Parklawn Bldg
Rockville, MD 20857

DHHS Welfare Reform Research, Evaluations, and National Studies Grants 1578s
The objectives of the funding are to support research on the benefits, effects, and costs of different welfare reform interventions; and studies such as on the effects of different programs on welfare dependency, illegitimacy, teen pregnancy, employment rates, child well-being, and related areas; and to assist in the development and evaluation of innovative approaches for reducing welfare dependency and increasing the well-being of minority children in welfare families. Grants, cooperative agreements, and contracts are awarded for innovative research, demonstrations, and evaluations that are responsive to the Administration for Children and Families program priorities. Deadlines for grants are announced in the Federal Register.
Requirements Grants and cooperative agreements may be made to or with governmental entities, colleges, universities, nonprofit, and for-profit organizations (if fee is waived). Contracts may be awarded to nonprofit or for-profit organizations. Grants or cooperative agreements cannot be made directly to individuals.
Amount $10,000-$6 million range; $500,000 average
Contact Karl Koerper, Office of Planning, Research, and Evaluation, Administration for Children and Families, (202) 401-4535; fax: (202) 205-3598; email: KKoerper@acf.dhhf.gov
Internet http://www.acf.hhs.gov/programs/opre
Sponsor Department of Health and Human Services
370 L'Enfant Promenade, SW
Washington, DC 20447

DHHS/ASPE Welfare Outcomes Short-Term Policy Research Grants 1579
The purpose of these grants is to support policy relevant research to complement ongoing research and evaluations on the outcomes of welfare reform, and to broaden our understanding of the outcomes of welfare reform. These grants are meant to supplement other leavers grants that ASPE has previously funded and support short-term research and data analysis efforts that are designed to be completed within 12 months. ASPE hopes to support efforts to analyze a variety of information about individuals (adults and children) and their families, including their economic and non-economic well-being and their participation in government programs. ASPE seeks to gain some understanding of the broader issues of the labor market and individual behaviors, such as the differential effects of the business cycle on subgroups of the eligible population. The identification of important subgroups such as rural residents and individuals with significant barriers to success (e.g., mental illness, domestic violence, substance abuse, illiteracy, people with disabilities) and analyses of outcomes for these groups is also encouraged. Analyses that focus on differential outcomes by race/ethnicity are also encouraged. In addition, while average effects or outcomes are important, it is also important in the context of welfare reform to look at the distribution of the outcomes, to identify and understand the winners and losers, and to understand the reasons why some individuals are winners and others are losers. Thus researchers are encouraged to look beyond averages.
Requirements Public or private nonprofit organizations may apply.
Amount $300,000-$1.2 million; $575,000 average
Contact Program Contact, Office of the Assistant Secretary for Planning and Evaluation, (202) 690-8794
Internet http://aspe.os.dhhs.gov
Sponsor Department of Health and Human Services
200 Independence Ave SW
Washington, DC 20201

Diaz-Ayala Cuban and Latin American Popular Music Collection Travel Grants 1580
The Diaz-Ayala Cuban and Latin American Popular Music Collection is the most extensive publicly available collection of Cuban music in the United States. The grants will provide graduate students and scholars the opportunity to visit the Diaz-Ayala Music Collection at the FIU Green Library, thereby enhancing its value as a national resource. The program provides a research stipend to offset the costs of a minimum of one-week stay to use the collection. Application and guidelines are available online.
Requirements Scholars in the humanities and the social sciences whose work will be enhanced by using the resources of the collection are encouraged to apply.
Amount $1,500
Date(s) Application Is Due Feb 15.
Contact Alma DeRojas, Coordinator, (305) 348-1991; email: derojasa@fiu.edu
Internet http://lacc.fiu.edu/centers_institutes/?body=centers_cri_whatsnew&rightbody=centers_cri
Sponsor Florida International University
Cuban Research Institute, DM 363
Miami, FL 33119

Dibner Institute Postdoctoral Fellows Program 1581
Postdoctoral fellowships are available for advanced research in the history of science and technology. Fellowships run for one year, from September 1 through August 15, and may be extended for a second and final year at the discretion of the institute. Fellows are expected to reside in the Boston area during the fellowship term, to participate in institute activities, and to present their work at appropriate occasions. The institute provides office space, support facilities, full privileges at the libraries of consortium universities as well as Burndy Library, and access to programs, events, and many resources at consortium member institutions, and to the entire spectrum of activities that will take place at the institute.
Requirements Fellowships are awarded to outstanding young scholars of diverse countries of origin who have obtained the PhD or equivalent within the previous five years.
Date(s) Application Is Due Dec 31.
Contact Trudy Kontoff, Program Coordinator, (617) 253-6989; fax: (617) 253-9858; email: dibner@mit.edu
Internet http://dibinst.mit.edu/DIBNER/Fellows/FellowsProgram.htm
Sponsor Dibner Institute for the History of Science and Technology
MIT E56-100, 38 Memorial Dr
Cambridge, MA 02139

Dibner Institute Science Writing Fellowships 1582
This is an opportunity for a senior science writer with a proven track record of writing and/or reporting for a general audience to pursue a substantial project of his or own choosing that bears on history of science or technology. The fellow will pursue his or her project and have the opportunity to interact with the other Dibner fellows and the community of scholars in history of science and technology in the Boston/Cambridge area. He or she will also be able to participate with faculty, students, and fellows in the Graduate Program in Science Writing and the Knight Science Journalism Fellowship program, both at MIT. Fellowships provide a stipend with added expenses negotiable, office space, support facilities, and full privileges at the Burndy Library and at the libraries of the consortium universities. In judging applications, the primary criterion will be the significance of the project. Guidelines are available online.
Requirements Science writers with a proven track record of writing and/or reporting for a general audience are eligible.
Amount $35,000 stipend
Date(s) Application Is Due Dec 31.
Contact Trudy Kontoff, Program Coordinator, (617) 253-6989; fax. (617) 253-9858; email: dibner@mit.edu
Internet http://dibinst.mit.edu/DIBNER/Fellows/Application/SciWriterFellowship.htm
Sponsor Dibner Institute for the History of Science and Technology
MIT E56-100, 38 Memorial Dr
Cambridge, MA 02139

Dibner Institute Senior Fellows Program 1583
The institute is an international center for advanced research in the history of science and technology. Scholars may apply to the program for the fall (beginning September 1), the spring term (beginning January 1), or both. At the time of application, Term 1 candidates may request an arrival date in August; Term 2 candidates may request an extension into June/July. The institute prefers that senior fellows apply for a two-term, full-year residency if possible. Fellows are expected to reside in the Cambridge/Boston area during

the award period, participate in the activities of the Dibner Institute community, and present their current work once during their fellowship appointments.
Requirements Candidates should have advanced degrees in disciplines relevant to their research and show evidence of substantial scholarly accomplishment and experience.
Date(s) Application Is Due Dec 31.
Contact Trudy Kontoff, Program Coordinator, (617) 253-6989; fax: (617) 253-9858; email: dibner@mit.edu
Internet http://dibinst.mit.edu/DIBNER/Fellows/Application/Introduction.htm
Sponsor Dibner Institute for the History of Science and Technology
MIT E56-100, 38 Memorial Dr
Cambridge, MA 02139

Dietetic Outcomes Research Study Grants **1584**
The program seeks proposals for a prospective, controlled trial study on the effectiveness of nutrition services. The objective is to investigate the cost and clinical effectiveness of nutrition services provided by registered dietitians compared to other health practitioners or health care teams with and without dietitians in an ambulatory setting. The study must focus on one of four disease states: diabetes, hyperlipidemia, congestive heart failure, or obesity with metabolic complications. Key personnel requirements include an experienced research dietitian and ADA members as a principal or co-principal investigator. Specifications are contained in the RFP posted on the Web site.
Amount $225,000 maximum
Contact Elisabeth Puga, (800) 877-1600 ext 4803; email: epuga@eatright.org
Internet http://www.eatright.org/Public/7713_7808.cfm
Sponsor American Dietetic Association Foundation
120 S Riverside Plz, Ste 2000
Chicago, IL 60606

Diversifying Higher Education Faculty in Illinois Program (DFI) **1585**
The program aims to increase access of underrepresented students to graduate degree programs in Illinois public and private universities and, ultimately, to increase the number of underrepresented faculty and staff in Illinois colleges and universities. Each recipient is awarded an annual stipend and an institutional scholarship that covers tuition and fees. Doctoral recipients may receive awards for up to four years. Those in master's or professional degree programs may receive awards for up to two years.
Requirements To be considered for an award, an applicant must be an Illinois resident and a United States citizen or permanent resident; a member of an underrepresented group in higher education such as African American, Hispanic, Asian American, or Native American; the recipient of an earned baccalaureate degree; of above-average academic ability as evidenced by admission to a graduate or professional degree program at a participating ICEOP institution; and unable to pursue a graduate or professional degree in the absence of an ICEOP award.
Amount $12,500-$16,000 for full time enrollment
Date(s) Application Is Due Feb 15.
Contact Program Contact, Graduate School, (618) 453-4558; fax: (618) 453-5313; email: fellows@siu.edu
Internet http://www.dfi.siu.edu
Sponsor Southern Illinois University at Carbondale
Woody Hall C-224, MC 4723
Carbondale, IL 62901

DOA Agricultural Competitive Research Grants **1586**
The grants promote basic research in food, agriculture, and related areas to further the programs of USDA. Funds may be used for costs necessary to conduct research (salaries and wages, scientific equipment, materials and supplies, travel, publication costs, and other allowable direct and indirect costs). Primary responsibility for general supervision of all grant activities rests with the grantee organization; the principal investigator is responsible for the scientific work. Deadlines are announced annually in the Federal Register.
Requirements State agricultural experiment stations, US colleges/universities, other US research institutions and organizations, federal agencies, private organizations or corporations, and individuals are eligible to submit proposals.
Restrictions Funds may not be used for purposes other than those specified in the grant.
Amount $4000-$5 million; $183,607 average
Contact Chief Scientist, National Research Initiative Competitive Grants Program, Cooperative State Research, Education, and Extension Service, (202) 401-5022
Internet http://www.usda.gov
Sponsor Department of Agriculture
1400 Independence Ave SW
Washington, DC 20250

DOA Agricultural Special Research Grants **1587**
The program supports research to facilitate or expand promising breakthroughs in areas of the food and agricultural sciences of importance to the nation and to facilitate or expand ongoing state-federal food and agricultural research programs. Areas of basic and applied research are generally limited to high-priority problems of a regional or national scope. Areas currently considered are water quality, integrated pest management, and rangeland research. Application deadlines are announced each fiscal year in the Federal Register and may also be obtained by calling the Office of Extramural Programs below.
Requirements State agricultural experiment stations, all colleges and universities, other research institutions and organizations, federal agencies, private organizations or corporations, and individuals having a demonstrable capacity to conduct research to facilitate or expand promising breakthroughs in areas of the food and agricultural sciences of importance to the United States are eligible to apply.
Amount $56,664-$9.5 million; $46,183 average
Contact Competitive Programs, (202) 401-5048
Internet http://www.usda.gov
Sponsor Department of Agriculture
1400 Independence Ave SW
Washington, DC 20250

DOA Animal Health and Disease Research Grants **1588**
The grants support animal health and disease research to improve the health and productivity of food animals and horses through effective prevention, control, or treatment of disease; to reduce losses from transportation and other hazards; and to protect human health through control of animal diseases transmissible to people. Research can be conducted under the following categories: infectious diseases; internal and external parasites; noninfectious diseases, toxins, poisons, transportation losses, predators, and other hazards; diseases and parasites of wildlife transmissible to food animals and horses; and diseases and parasites of animals transmissible to people. Applications are accepted at any time.
Requirements Eligibility is restricted to schools and colleges of veterinary medicine and state agricultural experiment stations.
Amount $1,586-$408,854; $65,515 average
Contact Grants Administrator, Cooperative State Research, Education, and Extension Service, (202) 401-4329
Internet http://www.usda.gov
Sponsor Department of Agriculture
1400 Independence Ave SW
Washington, DC 20250

DOA Biological Nitrogen Fixation Research Grants **1589**
The grants help build a foundation of basic information concerning nitrogen fixation as it relates to enhancing the process in currently known systems and in providing a base for developing new nitrogen-fixing associations by genetic transfer or other means for crop species not now possessing such capability. Program priorities will be on innovative approaches that may contribute to a thorough understanding of nitrogen cycling encompassing biochemistry, cellular and developmental biology, genetics and genetic manipulation, and other relevant life science disciplines. An understanding of these processes is essential to the development of strategies that maximize nitrogen fixation, minimize inputs of nitrogenous fertilizers, and optimize their utilization in agriculture. Deadlines are announced in the Federal Register, usually November through March.
Requirements State agricultural experiment stations, US colleges/universities, other US research institutions and organizations, federal agencies, private organizations or corporations, and individuals may submit proposals.
Amount $4000-$5 million; $183,607 average
Contact Chief Scientist, National Research Initiative Competitive Grants Program, (202) 401-5022
Internet http://www.usda.gov
Sponsor Department of Agriculture
1400 Independence Ave SW
Washington, DC 20250

DOA Biological Stress on Plants Research Grants **1590**
The grants support research on stresses on plants arising from their interactions with other plants or with other biological agents such as weeds, insects, nematodes, fungi, bacteria, viruses, and mycoplasma-like organisms. The goal is to reduce losses in plant productivity from damage caused by biologically generated stresses. The program seeks to develop an understanding of how stressful interactions are established between plants and other biological agents, how such interactions are influenced by environmental and other factors inherent to the interacting organisms, how the interactions reduce plant productivity and usefulness to man, how plants react to stresses generated by such interactions, and how damage from such interactions may be reduced or eliminated. Deadlines are announced in the Federal Register between December and April.
Requirements State agricultural experiment stations, US colleges/universities and other research institutions and organizations, federal agencies, private organizations or corporations, and individuals may apply.
Amount $4000-$5 million; $183,607 average
Contact Chief Scientist, National Research Initiative Competitive Grants Program, (202) 401-5022
Internet http://www.usda.gov
Sponsor Department of Agriculture
1400 Independence Ave SW
Washington, DC 20250

DOA Biotechnology Risk Assessment Research Grants **1591**
The purpose of this program is to assist agencies in making science-based decisions about genetically modified organisms. Research funded through this program will be

relevant to risk assessment and the regulatory process. Although investigators are not required to perform actual risk assessments in the research they propose, they should design studies that will provide information useful to regulators for making science-based decisions in their assessments of genetically-modified organisms. Deadlines are published in the Federal Register.
Requirements Eligible applicants include any public or private research or educational institution or organization.
Restrictions Funds may not be used for purposes other than those approved in the grant award documents.
Amount $50,220-$223,269; average award $147,583
Contact Deputy Administrator, Competitive Programs, (202) 401-1761
Internet http://www.reeusda.gov
Sponsor Department of Agriculture
1400 Independence Ave SW
Washington, DC 20250

DOA Cooperative Forestry Research Grants **1592**
The grants encourage and assist states in carrying on programs of forestry research at forestry schools and in developing a trained pool of forest scientists capable of conducting needed forestry research. Categories of forestry research supported include reforestation and management of land for the production of crops of timber and other related products of the forest; management of forest and related watershed lands to improve conditions of waterflow and to protect resources against flood and erosion; management of forest and related rangeland for production of forage for domestic livestock and game and improvement of food and habitat for wildlife; management of forest lands for outdoor recreation; protection of forest resources against fire, insects, diseases, and other destructive agents; utilization of wood and other forest products; development of sound policies for the management of forest lands and the harvesting and marketing of forest products; and other studies necessary to obtain the fullest and most effective use of forest resources. Applications are accepted at any time.
Requirements Applicants must be state or territorial institutions certified as eligible by a state representative designated by the governor.
Amount $30,281-$694,074; $322,889 average
Contact Deputy Administrator, Cooperative State Research Service, (202) 720-4318
Internet http://www.usda.gov
Sponsor Department of Agriculture
1400 Independence Ave SW
Washington, DC 20250

DOA Emerging Markets Program Grants **1593**
The purpose of the program is to assist US organizations, public and private, to improve the market access and to develop and promote US agricultural products and/or processes in low- to middle-income countries that offer promise of emerging market opportunities in the near to medium term. This is to be accomplished by providing US technical assistance through projects and activities in those emerging markets consistent with US foreign policy interests. The program funds technical assistance activities to leverage the export and marketing of US agricultural products to emerging markets. The emphasis is on marketing opportunities where there are risks that the private sector would not normally undertake alone, with funding provided on a project-by-project basis. The program is intended to support primarily small- to medium-sized US firms that may need federal assistance in realizing or maintaining access in overseas markets. Application deadline is announced in the Federal Register.
Requirements Any US agricultural and/or agribusiness organization, university, or state department of agriculture is eligible to participate in the program. Priority will be given to those proposals that include significant support and involvement by private industry. Proposals from research and consulting organizations will be considered if they provide evidence of substantial participation by US industry. US market development cooperators may seek funding to address priority, market-specific issues and to undertake activities not already serviced by or unsuitable for funding under other FAS marketing programs.
Restrictions No proposal will be considered without the element of cost-sharing.
Amount $500,000 maximum
Contact Emerging Markets Office, Foreign Agricultural Service; (202) 720-4327; fax: (202) 690-4369; email: emo@fas.usda.gov
Internet http://www.cfda.gov/public/viewprog.asp?progid=1575
Sponsor Department of Agriculture
6506 S Bldg
Washington, DC 20250

DOA Federal-State Marketing Improvement Program (FSMIP) **1594**
The program is a matching fund program designed to assist state departments of agriculture or other appropriate state agencies in conducting studies or developing innovative approaches related to the marketing of agricultural products. Funds can be requested for a wide range of marketing research and marketing service activities, including projects aimed at developing and testing new or more efficient methods of processing, packaging, handling, storing, transporting, and distributing food and other agricultural products; assessing customer response to new or alternative agricultural products or marketing services and evaluating potential opportunities for US producers, processors, and other agribusinesses, in both domestic and international markets; and identifying problems and impediments in existing channels of trade between producers and consumers of agricultural products and devising improved marketing practices, facilities, or systems to address such problems.
Requirements Only state departments of agriculture or other appropriate state agencies are eligible to apply for funds.
Amount $12,000-$74,000; $49,556 average
Contact Janise Zygmont, Agricultural Marketing Service, (202) 720-2704
Internet http://www.ams.usda.gov/tmd/fsmip.htm
Sponsor Department of Agriculture
Dept of Agriculture
Washington, DC 20250

DOA Food and Agricultural Sciences National Needs Graduate Fellowships **1595**
This program awards grants to colleges and universities that have superior teaching and research competencies in the food and agricultural sciences to encourage outstanding students to pursue and complete graduate degrees at such institutions in areas of the food and agricultural sciences for which there is a national need for the development of scientific expertise. Therefore, institutions that currently have excellent programs of graduate study and research in these areas dealing with targeted national needs are particularly encouraged to apply. The Cooperative State Research, Education, and Extension Service (CSREES) will provide support on a biennial basis and combine appropriations from two fiscal years into one competition to be held during odd-numbered years. Deadline dates may vary; contact the program office for exact dates.
Requirements Proposals may be submitted by all US colleges and universities that confer a master's or doctoral degree in at least one area of the food and agricultural sciences targeted for national needs fellowships. Eligibility also applies to research foundations maintained by eligible colleges or universities.
Restrictions Individuals selected by the institutions may not have been enrolled previously in the program at the same degree level.
Contact National Program Leader, Higher Education Programs, (202)720-7854
Internet http://www.reeusda.gov
Sponsor Department of Agriculture
1400 Independence Ave SW
Washington, DC 20250

DOA Food and Agricultural Sciences Small Business Innovation Research (SBIR) Grants **1596**
Grants are made to stimulate technological innovation in the private sector, strengthen the role of small businesses in meeting federal research and development needs, increase private-sector commercialization of innovations derived from USDA-supported research and development efforts, and foster and encourage minority and disadvantaged participation in technological innovation. Selected areas for research are forests and related resources; plant production and protection; animal production and protection; air, water, and soils; food science and nutrition; rural and community development; aquaculture; and industrial applications. Phase I awards will be made for periods normally not to exceed six months to determine, if possible, the scientific or technical feasibility of ideas in the selected research areas. Phase II awards will be made to firms with approaches that appear sufficiently promising as a result of Phase I studies for a period not to exceed 24 months. Phase III will be nonfederally funded through the exercising of funding commitment to stimulate technological innovation and the national return on investment from research through the pursuit of commercial objectives resulting from the USDA-supported work carried out in Phases I and II. Deadlines are announced in the Federal Register and SBIR program solicitation for each fiscal year.
Requirements Small businesses that meet the SBIR program specifications may apply.
Amount $80,000-$300,000
Contact Dr. Charles Cleland, National Program Leader, (202) 401-4002; fax: (202) 401-6070; email: ccleland@csrees.usda.gov
Internet http://www.csrees.usda.gov/fo/fundview.cfm?fonum=1220
Sponsor Department of Agriculture
1400 Independence Ave SW
Washington, DC 20250

DOA Forestry Research Grants **1597**
The program extends the fundamental research activities of the Forest Service by awarding grants to nonprofit organizations, institutions of higher education, and organizations engaged in renewable resources research. Grants will be used for research in the fields of timber management, watershed management, forest range management, wildlife habitat management, forest recreation, forest fire protection, forest insect and disease protection and control, forest products utilization, forest engineering, forest production economics, forest products marketing, and forest survey. Grants are awarded for one to five years. Contact the regional experiment stations for deadlines.
Requirements Eligible to apply are state agricultural experiment stations, universities and colleges, state and local governments, US territories, for-profit and nonprofit research institutions and organizations, and international organizations.
Amount $2000-$300,000; $35,000 average
Contact Deputy Chief for Research, Forest Service, (202) 205-1075
Internet http://www.usda.gov
Sponsor Department of Agriculture
P.O. Box 96090
Washington, DC 20090

DOA Higher Education Challenge Grants **1598**

The objective of the program is to increase institutional capacities to respond to state, regional, national, or international educational needs by strengthening college and university teaching programs in the food and agricultural sciences. Funds may be used only in targeted areas, e.g., curricula design and materials development, faculty preparation and enhancement for teaching, instruction delivery systems, scientific instrumentation for teaching, student experiential learning, and student recruitment and retention. A dollar-for-dollar match is required from nonfederal sources. Grants are awarded for a one- to three-year period. Deadlines are published in the Federal Register. USDA-GRANTS-092605-004

Requirements Any US college or university having a demonstrable capacity to teach the food and agricultural sciences is eligible.

Amount $150,000-$400,000

Date(s) Application Is Due Feb 2.

Contact Gregory Smith, National Program Leader, (202) 720 - 2067; fax: (202) 720 - 2030; email: gsmith@csrees.usda.gov

Internet http://www.csrees.usda.gov/fo/fundview.cfm?fonum=1082

Sponsor Department of Agriculture
1400 Independence Ave SW, Stop 2201
Washington, DC 20250-2201

DOA International Agricultural Training Grants **1599**

Grants are to assist US colleges and universities in strengthening their capabilities for food, agricultural, and related research training and extension relevant to agricultural development activities in other countries. Projects funded are most often in course development and/or evaluation. In general, cooperative agreements are established for a 12-month period but may be extended with justification. Applications are accepted at any time.

Requirements US institutions of higher education or nonprofit organizations involved with agricultural development and educational activities are eligible to apply.

Amount $10,000-$40,000; average $18,900

Contact Dr. Frank Fender, FAS/International Cooperation and Development, Food Industries Division, (202) 690-1339

Internet http://www.fas.usda.gov

Sponsor Department of Agriculture
2121 K St NW, 2nd Fl
Washington, DC 20250

DOA International Collaborative Agricultural Research Program Grants **1600**

Grant support is provided to US scientists working in cooperation with foreign researchers to implement collaborative research and to maximize the utilization of US agricultural commodities and products in domestic and export markets; to respond quickly to pressing high-priority plant and animal disease or pest problems that have their roots in international origins and may also have trade implications; and to conduct targeted cooperative research with friendly countries having resources or expertise needed to solve urgent US agricultural problems. Projects funded are to be conducted by the United States and cooperating foreign scientists. Collaborating scientists should be identified in the proposal. Generally, cooperative agreements are funded for a 12- to 36-month period. Funding will be provided only to US researchers. Applications are accepted at any time.

Requirements US institutions of higher education and public/private nonprofit organizations whose primary purpose is scientific research are eligible to apply, including those located in US territories.

Restrictions The program does not fund the foreign collaborator because foreign institutions are expected to have sufficient interest in collaborating with US scientists to provide for their portion of the research.

Amount $10,000-$40,000; $18,900 average

Contact Dr. Frank Fender, FASInternational Cooperation and Development, Food Industries Division, (202) 690-1339

Internet http://www.fas.usda.gov

Sponsor Department of Agriculture
2121 K St NW, 2nd Fl
Washington, DC 20250

DOA National Integrated Food Safety Initiative **1601**

The purpose of this program is to support competitive projects that address selected priority issues in food safety that are best solved using an integrated approach. Special emphasis is given to research describing multi-functional activities (i.e., research that contains research, education, and extension components). The research component of the National Integrated Food Safety Initiative focuses on applied food safety research. The education component focuses on education and training in a formal classroom setting, which may include elementary, secondary, undergraduate, or graduate education. The extension component addresses education and training outside of the classroom. Where there is no extension program, outreach activities that deliver science-based and informational education to people in a variety of non-formal settings are appropriate. The RFP is usually announced in the Federal Register in February or March of each year, and proposals are due eight weeks following the release of the RFP. Funding opportunity number: USDA-GRANTS-090304-001

Requirements Faculty at all four year accredited colleges and universities are eligible to apply.

Amount $500,000 maximum

Contact Chris Wozniak , Food Science and Food Safety, (202) 401-6020; fax: (202) 401-6156; email: cwozniak@csrees.usda.gov

Internet http://www.csrees.usda.gov/fo/fundview.cfm?fonum=1087

Sponsor Department of Agriculture
1400 Independence Ave SW
Washington, DC 20250

DOA Photosynthesis Research Grants **1602**

The grants support research in aspects of photosynthetic energy conversion including such areas as early events in photon capture by photosynthetic systems and the mechanisms of charge separation, the structure and function of photosynthetic membranes and constituents and associated reactions; photosynthetic carbon assimilation including CO2 fixation, biochemistry of photosynthetic pathways, photorespiration and aspects of cellular metabolism control of photosynthate partitioning and translocation by hormones and other metabolic factors; factors controlling development and senescence of photosynthetic competence; genetic and cellular manipulation to improve photosynthetic efficiency in plants; and the photosynthetic process in leaves and whole plants including involvement of the stomatal aperture, and water and temperature extremes. Deadlines are announced each fiscal year in the Federal Register, usually falling between November and March.

Requirements State agricultural experiment stations, US colleges/universities and other research institutions and organizations, federal agencies, private organizations or corporations, and individuals may apply.

Amount $4000-$5 million; $183,607 average

Contact Chief Scientist, National Research Initiative Competitive Grants Program, (202) 401-5022

Internet http://www.usda.gov

Sponsor Department of Agriculture
1400 Independence Ave SW, Ag Box 2241
Washington, DC 20250

DOA Plant and Animal Disease, Pest Control, and Animal Care Grants **1603**

The objectives of this program are to protect US agriculture from economically injurious plant and animal diseases and pests, ensure the safety and potency of veterinary biologics, and ensure the humane treatment of animals. Project and training grants are awarded to eligible organizations to carry out these objectives. Initial contact should be a letter outlining the project proposed.

Requirements Eligible to apply are foreign, state, local, and US territorial government agencies; nonprofit institutions of higher education; and nonprofit associations or organizations requiring federal support to eradicate, control, or assess the status of injurious plant and animal diseases and pests that are a threat to regional or national agriculture and to conduct related demonstration projects.

Contact Anita Ridley, Budget and Accounting Division, Animal and Plant Health Inspection Service, (301) 734-8792

Internet http://www.aphis.usda.gov

Sponsor Department of Agriculture
4700 River Rd, Unit 55, Sta 4B80
Riverdale, MD 20737

DOA Rangeland Research Grants **1604**

Applications are solicited for projects covering research on rangeland, both open and contained. Project areas may include multiple forage factors; soil and water erosion; climate, wind, and rain; and growth replenishment. Also supported are innovative projects of interest to all those involved in rangeland use. Deadline dates vary; contact the Office of Extramural Programs for exact dates.

Requirements Land-grant colleges and universities; state agricultural experimental stations; and college, university, and federal laboratories having a demonstrable capacity in rangeland research are eligible to apply.

Amount $56,664-$9.5 million; $46,183 average

Contact Competitive Programs, (202) 401-5048

Internet http://www.reeusda.gov

Sponsor Department of Agriculture
1400 Independence Ave SW, Stop 2245
Washington, DC 20250

DOA Resource Conservation and Development Grants **1605**

The grants are intended to encourage and improve the capability of state and local units of government and local nonprofit organizations in rural areas to plan, develop, and carry out programs for resource conservation and development. Assistance is available for the planning and installation of approved measures in RC&D areas for land conservation, water management, community development, and environmental enhancement. Applications are accepted at any time.

Requirements State and local governments and nonprofit organizations with authority to plan or carry out activities relating to resource use and development in multijurisdictional areas are eligible to apply. The program is also available in Puerto Rico, the Virgin Islands, Guam, and the Mariana Islands.

Contact Terry D'Addio, National RC&D Program Manager, (202) 720-0557; email: terry.d'addio@usda.gov

Internet http://www.nrcs.usda.gov/programs/rcd

Sponsor Department of Agriculture
1400 Independence Ave SW
Washington, DC 20250

DOA Rural Business Enterprise Grants **1606**
Grants are made to finance and facilitate development of small and emerging private business enterprises located in areas outside the boundary of a city or unincorporated areas of 50,000 or more and its immediately adjacent urbanized or urbanizing area. Costs that may be paid from grant funds include the acquisition and development of land and the construction of buildings, plants, equipment, access streets and roads, parking areas, and utility and service extensions; refinancing; fees for professional services; technical assistance and related training for adults; startup operating costs and working capital, providing financial assistance to a third party; and production of television programs to provide information to rural residents and to create, expand, and operate rural distance learning networks. Grants may also be made to establish or fund revolving loan programs.
Requirements Eligibility is limited to public bodies, private nonprofit corporations, and federally recognized Indian tribal groups. Small and emerging businesses with less than 50 new employees and less than $1 million in gross annual revenues are eligible.
Amount $2000-$500,000; $83,309 average
Contact Program Contact, Rural Development Specialist, (202) 720-1400
Internet http://www.rurdev.usda.gov/rbs/busp/rbeg.htm
Sponsor Department of Agriculture
1400 Independence Ave SW
Washington, DC 20250

DOA Small Business Innovation Research (SBIR) Grants **1607**
Firms with strong scientific research capabilities in the topic areas listed below are encouraged to participate. Objectives of the three-phase program include stimulating technological innovation in the private sector, strengthening the role of small businesses in meeting federal research and development needs, increasing private sector commercialization of innovations derived from USDA-supported research and development efforts, and fostering and encouraging participation of women-owned and socially and economically disadvantaged small business concerns in technological innovation. Research areas include forests and related resources; plant production and protection; animal production and protection; air, water, and soils; food science and nutrition; rural and community development; aquaculture; industrial applications; and marketing and trade. The deadline for Phase I is August 31; for Phase II is February 5.
Amount $80,000 maximum for Phase I; $300,000 maximum for Phase II
Date(s) Application Is Due Feb 2; Sep 1.
Contact Dr. Charles Cleland, Director, SBIR Program, Cooperative State Research, Education, and Extension Service, (202) 401-4002; fax: (202) 401-6070; email: ccleland@reeusda.gov
Internet http://www.csrees.usda.gov/fo/fundview.cfm?fonum=1220
Sponsor Department of Agriculture
1400 Independence Ave SW
Washington, DC 20250

DOA Sustainable Agriculture Research and Education Grants **1608**
The intent of these grants is to facilitate and increase scientific investigation and education to reduce the use of chemical pesticides, fertilizers, and toxic materials in agricultural production; improve management of on-farm resources to enhance productivity, profitability, and competitiveness; promote crop, livestock, and enterprise diversification and facilitate the conduct of research projects to study agricultural production systems that are located in areas that possess various soil, climatic, and physical characteristics; study farms that have been and continue to be managed using farm production practices that optimize the use of on-farm resources and conservation practices; take advantage of the experience of farmers and ranchers through their direct participation and leadership in projects; transfer practical, reliable, and timely information to farmers and ranchers concerning low-input sustainable practices and systems; and promote a partnership between farmers, nonprofit organizations, agribusiness, and public and private research and extension institutions. Funds may be used for transportation, per diem, salaries, office supplies, printing, and other direct costs for activities approved in cooperative agreements or interagency reimbursable transfers. Contact the office for deadlines.
Requirements Land-grant colleges or universities, other universities, state agricultural experiment stations, nonprofit organizations, or federal or state governmental entities that have demonstrated appropriate expertise in agricultural research and technology transfer may apply.
Restrictions Funds may not be used to pay indirect costs or tuition.
Amount $8000-$1.7 million; $855,540 average
Contact Administrator, Cooperative State Research, Education, and Extension Service, (202) 720-7948
Internet http://www.reeusda.gov
Sponsor Department of Agriculture
1400 Independence Ave SW
Washington, DC 20250

DOA Technical Agricultural Assistance Research Grants **1609**
The objective of the program is to identify and apply the most appropriate solutions to international agricultural problems and to increase the capabilities of US educational institutions and nonprofit agencies in agricultural research and technical assistance. Generally, cooperative agreements are funded for a 12- to 24-month period. Applications are accepted at any time.
Requirements US institutions of higher learning and public/private nonprofit organizations whose primary purpose is scientific research are eligible to apply, including those in US territories.
Amount $30,000-$600,000; $160,000 average
Contact Dr. Howard Anderson, FAS/International Cooperation and Development Office, Development Resources Division, (202) 690-1924
Internet http://www.fas.usda.gov
Sponsor Department of Agriculture
2121 K St NW, 2nd Fl
Washington, DC 20250

DOA Wildlife Services Grants **1610**
Grants are given to reduce damage caused by mammals and birds and those mammal and bird species that are reservoirs for zoonotic diseases, except for urban rodent control. Wherever feasible, humane methods will be employed. Recipients are to work closely with state departments of fish and game, agriculture, health, and counties in joining efforts to alleviate wild animal damage. Recipients are expected to conduct surveys and campaigns to reduce wild animal damage, including bird problems at airports; develop methods to control wild animal damage; and provide technical advice and assistance. For direct technical assistance, state fish and game departments should be contacted.
Requirements State and local governments, federally recognized Indian tribal governments, public/private nonprofit organizations, nonprofit institutions of higher education, and individuals are eligible to apply.
Contact Anita Ridley, Budget and Accounting Division, Animal and Plant Health Inspection Service, (301) 734-8792
Internet http://www.aphis.usda.gov/ws
Sponsor Department of Agriculture
4700 River Rd, Unit 55, Sta 4B80
Riverdale, MD 20737

DOC National Technical Assistance: Training, Research, and Evaluation Grants **1611**
The purpose of the program is to provide grants and cooperative agreements for technical assistance projects that are useful in creating or retaining jobs and promoting economic growth. Awards are made for national technical assistance projects, local technical assistance projects, and university center projects. Supported activities include feasibility studies; management and operational assistance; demonstration projects; administrative support for local, regional, and national nonprofit economic development organizations; and other forms of technical assistance and support.
Requirements Eligible applicants are private individuals, firms, colleges, universities, and other institutions; profit and nonprofit organizations are also eligible.
Amount $12,000-$209,000 average range
Contact John McNamee, Director, Research and National Technical Assistance Division, (202) 482-4085
Internet http://www.commerce.gov/grants.html
Sponsor Department of Commerce
14th St and Constitution Ave NW, Herbert C. Hoover Bldg
Washington, DC 20230

DOC NERRS Graduate Research Fellowships **1612**
The National Estuarine Research Reserve System (NERRS) supports research and training opportunities for graduate students in estuarine ecology. The program is intended to fund high-quality research focused on improving coastal zone management while providing students with hands-on training in conducting ecological monitoring. Fellowships are offered for up to three years and require development of training programs with on-site staff at the NERRS sites. Research projects must focus on one of the following issues: non-point source pollution, biodiversity and the effects of invasive species, estuarine ecosystem restoration, and mechanisms for sustaining estuarine resources. Annual deadline dates may vary; contact the program office or visit the Web site for specific dates and application materials.
Requirements Students admitted to or enrolled in full-time master's or doctoral programs at US-accredited universities are eligible to apply. Students should have completed a majority of their course work at the beginning of their fellowships and have approved thesis research programs. Fellowships must be matched by the applicant by at least 30 percent of the total project cost.
Amount $20,000 per year for up to three years
Date(s) Application Is Due Nov 1.
Contact Susan White, Research Coordinator, (301) 713-3155 ext 224; email: susan.white@noaa.gov
Internet http://nerrs.noaa.gov/Fellowship
Sponsor Department of Commerce
1305 East-West Hwy, N/ORM5, SSMC4, Sta 10500
Silver Spring, MD 20910

DOC Special American Business Internship Training Program Grants **1613**
The SABIT program awards funding to qualified US companies for training business executives and scientists from the New Independent States of the former Soviet Union.

SABIT exposes NIS business managers and scientists to a completely new way of thinking in which demand, consumer satisfaction, and profits drive production. Mid- to senior-level interns visiting the US for internship programs with public or private sector companies will be exposed to an environment that will provide them with practical knowledge for restructuring their enterprises. The program provides firsthand, eye-opening experience to managers and scientists that cannot be duplicated by American managers traveling to their countries. Annual deadline dates may vary; contact the program office for exact dates.
Requirements Any profit or nonprofit US corporation, association, organization or other public or private entity is eligible.
Restrictions Agencies or divisions of the federal government are not eligible.
Amount $8400-$40,400 range; $18,000 average
Contact Program Contact, SABIT Program, (202) 482-0073; fax: (202) 482-2443
Internet http://www.mac.doc.gov/sabit
Sponsor Department of Commerce
14th St and Constitution Ave NW, Herbert C. Hoover Bldg
Washington, DC 20230

DOC Special American Business Internship Training (SABIT): Sakhalin-Oil and Gas Internship Program 1614
The SABIT program awards funding to qualified US companies for training business executives and scientists from the New Independent States (NIS) of the former Soviet Union. SABIT exposes NIS business managers and scientists to a completely new way of thinking in which demand, consumer satisfaction, and profits drive production. Mid-to senior-level interns visiting the United States for internship programs with public or private sector companies will be exposed to an environment which will provide them with practical knowledge for restructuring their enterprises. The program provides first-hand, eye-opening experience to managers and scientists which cannot be duplicated by American managers traveling to their territories.
Requirements All for-profit or nonprofit US corporations, associations, organizations, or other public or private entities are eligible to apply. Interns must be from the Sakhalin region in Russia. At the end of the training program, interns must return to Sakhalin, Russia.
Restrictions Agencies or divisions of the federal government are not eligible.
Amount $8400-$40,400; $18,000 average
Contact Tracy Rollins, Director, (202) 482-0073; fax: (202) 482-2443
Internet http://www.mac.doc.gov/sabit
Sponsor Department of Commerce
1401 Constitution Ave NW, 4th Fl, 4100W
Washington, DC 20230

DOC Technology Administration Fellows Program Grants 1615
The purpose of the ComSci program is to provide a hands-on learning experience for participants and to increase their understanding of: technological innovation as a source of national and international economic growth; the relationship of science and technology to government policies on economics, trade, education, and fiscal matters; the organization of scientific and technological activities in the federal government; and the technical activities and problems that exist in other executive, legislative, and judicial agencies of the government. Two program options are offered: ComSci program with a work assignment-- a 10-month intensive and challenging work assignment in an executive or legislative branch office (preferably different from one's home agency) in the Washington metropolitan area; and ComSci program without a work assignment--a nine-month program offering all of the benefits of the program, without the full-time work assignment. This option allows individuals in the Washington metropolitan area to participate on a part-time basis. Participants continue to work at their home agencies throughout the duration of the program while attending ComSci events. For participants in both program options, the program combines intensive education and orientation activities. Fellows receive a broadening of knowledge and understanding not achievable through traditional fellowship programs.
Requirements The program provides federal government employees in a professional or management series with an opportunity to study national and international issues relating to the development, application, and management of science and technology. Candidates are selected through recommendation procedures developed by participating agencies. In general, recommendations are based on candidates' qualifications, accomplishments, and potential for career growth. All agencies of the federal government may participate.
Amount $3800 for option with a work assignment, and $3400 for option without a work assignment), and expenses associated with the one-week field trip (estimated to be about $1900)
Date(s) Application Is Due Nov 21.
Contact Cynthia Lynn, (202) 482-6103; fax: (202) 482-4306; email: cynthia.lynn@technology.gov
Internet http://www.technology.gov/comsci/Intro.htm
Sponsor Department of Commerce
14th St and Constitution Ave NW, Rm 4823
Washington, DC 20230

DOC/ITA Market Development Cooperator Program (MDCP) 1616
The goal of the MDCP is to develop, maintain, and expand foreign markets for nonagricultural goods and services produced in the United States. The intended beneficiaries of the program are US producers of nonagricultural goods or services that seek to export such goods or services. ITA encourages applicants to propose activities that would be most appropriate to the market development needs of their US industry or industries. Examples of activities might include: opening an overseas office or offices to perform a variety of market development services for companies joining a consortium to avail themselves of such services; detailing a private-sector representative to a US&FCS post in accordance with 15 USC 4723(c); commissioning overseas market research, participating in overseas trade exhibitions, and trade missions to promote US exports, and/or hosting reverse trade missions; conducting US product demonstrations abroad; and other eligible activities. The applicant must contribute at least two dollars for each federal dollar provided. Full guidelines are available on the Web site or may be obtained by contacting the office listed.
Requirements US trade associations; nonprofit industry organizations; state trade departments and their regional associations, including centers for international trade development; and private industry firms or groups of firms in cases where no entity described above represents that industry are eligible.
Amount $400,000 maximum; $298,000 average
Date(s) Application Is Due Jul 1.
Contact Brad Hess, Manager, Trade Development, International Trade Administration, (202) 482-2969; fax: (202) 482-5828; email: Brad_Hess@ita.doc.gov
Internet http://www.ita.doc.gov/mdcp
Sponsor Department of Commerce
14th St and Constitution Ave NW, Herbert C Hoover Bldg
Washington, DC 20230

DOD Breast Cancer Center of Excellence Award 1617
The award mechanism supports multidisciplinary, multi-institutional teams of gifted scientists, clinicians, and consumer advocates in making groundbreaking advances toward the eradication of breast cancer. The Breast Cancer Research Program (BCRP) encourages highly accomplished scientists renowned for their contributions to the proposed areas of research and promising young investigators who can provide fresh insight to work together to accelerate the solution of a central, overarching research problem in a way that could not be accomplished by a single investigator or group. In addition, the BCRP strongly endorses the integration of scientists from nontraditional disciplines such as computer science, mathematics, economics, physics, and other quantitative disciplines. The BCRP also encourages centers of excellence to incorporate study components addressing ethical issues in breast cancer research. Breast cancer consumer/survivor groups must be active participants in all aspects of these awards. The listed application deadline is for preproposals; full proposals are by invitation. Preproposals must be submitted through the CDMRP eReceipt system. Guidelines are available online.
Requirements All individuals, regardless of ethnicity, nationality, or citizenship status, may apply as long as they are employed by, or affiliated with, an eligible institution. Eligible institutions include for-profit, nonprofit, public, and private organizations. Agencies of local, state, and federal governments are eligible to the extent that proposals do not overlap with their fully funded intramural programs. Federal agencies will be expected to explain how their proposals do not overlap with their intramural programs.
Amount $20 million maximum
Date(s) Application Is Due Apr 5.
Contact Commander, US Army Medical Research and Materiel Command, (301) 619-7079; fax: (301) 619-7792; email: cdmrp.pa@det.amedd.army.mil
Internet http://cdmrp.army.mil/funding/bcrp.htm
Sponsor Department of Defense
1077 Patchel St (Bldg 1077), MCMR-ZB-C (BC05-COE)
Fort Detrick, MD 21702-5024

DOD Clinical Translational Research Grants 1618
The award is designed to sponsor innovative research that will result in substantial improvements over current approaches to breast cancer chemoprevention and therapy by accelerating the progression of recent, highly promising findings in preclinical breast cancer research from the laboratory to the clinic. These awards are intended to support both new and established scientists across a broad spectrum of disciplines. Partnerships between academic institutions and biotechnology companies are encouraged. Proposals are being sought only in the areas of chemoprevention and therapeutics. Successful applicants must initiate a prospective clinical trial and accrue participants for a minimum of one year during the award period. They must also include preliminary data to support the feasibility of their hypotheses and approaches. Funding for these awards may be requested for up to five years. The listed application deadline is for preproposals; full proposals are by invitation. Preproposals must be submitted through the CDMRP eReceipt system. Guidelines are available online.
Requirements All individuals, regardless of ethnicity, nationality, or citizenship status, may apply as long as they are employed by, or affiliated with, an eligible institution. Eligible institutions include for-profit, nonprofit, public, and private organizations. Agencies of local, state, and federal governments are eligible to the extent that proposals do not overlap with their fully funded intramural programs. Federal agencies will be expected to explain how their proposals do not overlap with their intramural programs.
Restrictions This award is not intended to support early drug discovery or development, correlative studies, or the study of new combinations of standard breast cancer therapies.
Amount $20 million total
Date(s) Application Is Due Apr 5.

Contact Commander, US Army Medical Research and Materiel Command, (301) 619-7079; fax: (301) 619-7792; email: cdmrp.pa@det.amedd.army.mil
Internet http://cdmrp.army.mil/funding/bcrp.htm
Sponsor Department of Defense
1077 Patchel St (Bldg 1077), MCMR-ZB-C (BC05-CTR)
Fort Detrick, MD 21702-5024

DOD Era of Hope Scholar Award **1619**
The Breast Cancer Research Program sponsors this grant to identify individuals with high potential for innovation in breast cancer research early in their careers. Candidates should be exceptionally talented, early-career scientists who have demonstrated that they are the best and brightest in their field(s) through extraordinary creativity, vision, and productivity. They should also exhibit strong potential for leadership in the breast cancer research community that supports a vision for the eradication of breast cancer. These individuals should challenge current dogma and demonstrate an ability to look beyond tradition and convention. Award recipients will be expected to successfully challenge the status quo through creative, high-risk research that may lead ultimately to the eradication of breast cancer. Proposals must focus on the candidate's emerging record of creative and original accomplishments and potential for leadership in the field. Experience in breast cancer is not a requirement; however, the proposal must focus on breast cancer, and the applicant must commit a minimum of 50 percent effort during the award period to breast cancer research. All nominations must be converted into an electronic PDF file for electronic submission. Nominations guidelines are available online.
Requirements Applicants must be nominated to be considered for this award. Applicants must be independent, nonmentored investigators within six years of their last training position. All individuals, regardless of ethnicity, nationality, or citizenship status, may apply as long as they are employed by, or affiliated with, an eligible institution. Eligible institutions include for-profit, nonprofit, public, and private organizations. Agencies of local, state, and federal governments are eligible to the extent that proposals do not overlap with their fully funded intramural programs.
Restrictions Self-nominations will not be accepted. Postdoctoral fellows, clinical fellows (including residents and interns), and other mentored researchers are not eligible.
Amount $2.5 million for up to five years
Date(s) Application Is Due Apr 5.
Contact Commander, US Army Medical Research and Materiel Command, (301) 619-7079; fax: (301) 619-7792; email: cdmrp.pa@det.amedd.army.mil
Internet http://cdmrp.army.mil/bcrp/era/default.htm
Sponsor Department of Defense
1077 Patchel St (Bldg 1077), MCMR-ZB-C (BC05-EHSA)
Fort Detrick, MD 21702-5024

DOD HBCU/MI Partnership Training Award **1620**
This program's goal challenges the scientific community to design innovative research that will foster new directions for, address neglected issues in, and bring new investigators to the field of breast cancer research. The program focuses its funding on innovative projects, particularly those involving multidisciplinary and/or multi-institutional collaborations and alliances that have the potential to make a significant impact on breast cancer. Proposals that address the needs of minority, low-income, rural, and other underrepresented and/or medically underserved populations are strongly encouraged. The listed application deadline is for preproposals. Preproposals must be submitted through the CDMRP eReceipt system. Guidelines are available online.
Requirements Applicants must be HBCU/MI doctoral-level faculty members. All individuals, regardless of ethnicity, nationality, or citizenship status, may apply as long as they are employed by, or affiliated with, an eligible HBCU/MI institution. Eligible institutions are those approved as HBCU/MIs by the Department of Education.
Contact Commander, US Army Medical Research and Materiel Command, (301) 619-7079; fax: (301) 619-7792; email: cdmrp.pa@det.amedd.army.mil
Internet http://cdmrp.army.mil/bcrp/default.htm
Sponsor Department of Defense
1077 Patchel Street (Building 1077), MCMR-ZB-C (BC05-HPT)
Fort Detrick, MD 21702-5024

DOD Idea Award for Breast Cancer Research **1621**
The award supports innovative, high-risk/high-reward breast cancer research. Proposals should describe new paradigms and challenge existing dogma in the study of breast cancer. The award also supports efforts to examine existing problems from a new perspective; however, these proposals will face a greater burden to demonstrate innovation. Special consideration will be given to proposals that focus on biological signal integration, and/or systems implications. Proposals must be submitted electronically at https://cdmrp.org/. This website will contain all the information, forms, documents, and links needed to apply.
Requirements All individuals, regardless of ethnicity, nationality, or citizenship status, may apply as long as they are employed by, or affiliated with, an eligible institution. Eligible institutions include for-profit, nonprofit, public, and private organizations. Agencies of local, state, and federal governments are eligible to the extent that proposals do not overlap with their fully funded intramural programs.
Amount $300,000 maximum for up to three years; $625,000 maximum for population-based studies
Date(s) Application Is Due May 24.
Contact Commander, US Army Medical Research and Materiel Command, (301) 619-7079; fax: (301) 619-7792; email: cdmrp.pa@det.amedd.army.mil
Internet http://cdmrp.army.mil/bcrp/default.htm
Sponsor Department of Defense
1077 Patchel St (Bldg 1077), MCMR-ZB-C (BC05-IDEA)
Fort Detrick, MD 21702-5024

DOD Multidisciplinary Postdoctoral Award for Breast Cancer Research **1622**
The award is designed to identify and fund exceptionally talented recent doctoral graduates committed to broadening the scope of their research by adding significant, mentored training in more than one major discipline. Mentors should be identified for each discipline represented in the proposed project. Major disciplines for this award include, but are not limited to, laboratory, clinical, social/behavioral science, and public health research. The Breast Cancer Research Program is especially interested in proposals that integrate training in disciplines currently underrepresented in breast cancer, such as engineering, physics, and mathematics; however, innovative proposals that incorporate any combination of the major disciplines listed above will be considered. Proposals must be submitted electronically at https://cdmrp.org. Guidelines are available online.
Requirements Eligible applicants should have been in the laboratory or research setting in which the proposed research is to be performed for no longer than two years at the time of submission and should have a total of less than five years of postdoctoral research experience (excluding clinical residency or fellowship training). All individuals, regardless of ethnicity, nationality, or citizenship status, may apply as long as they are employed by, or affiliated with, an eligible institution as defined below. Eligible institutions include for-profit, nonprofit, public, and private organizations. Agencies of local, state, and federal governments are eligible to the extent that proposals do not overlap with their fully funded intramural programs.
Amount $375,000 maximum
Date(s) Application Is Due May 24.
Contact Commander, US Army Medical Research and Materiel Command, (301) 619-7079; fax: (301) 619-7792; email: cdmrp.pa@det.amedd.army.mil
Internet http://cdmrp.army.mil/funding/bcrp.htm
Sponsor Department of Defense
1077 Patchel St (Bldg 1077), MCMR-ZB-C (BC05-MPA)
Fort Detrick, MD 21702-5024

DOD National Defense Science and Engineering Graduate Fellowships **1623**
The NDSEG program is a DOD fellowship program sponsored by AFOSR, the Army Research Office, the Office of Naval Research, and the Advanced Research Projects Agency. The DOD selects about 90 fellows per year; the Air Force sponsors about 25 of those fellows. AFOSR has a goal of awarding 10 percent of these fellowships to applicants who are members of an ethnic minority group underrepresented in the advanced levels of the US science and engineering personnel pool (i.e., Native American, African American, Hispanic, Native Alaskan, or Native Pacific Islander). These fellowships are for study and research in areas of interest to the Air Force. Stipends are prorated for fellowship periods of less than 12 months; however, the duration of the fellowship will not be less than nine months. In addition to the stipend, the Air Force pays the student's tuition and fees. Those fellows selected and sponsored by the Air Force will be offered the opportunity to become associated with an Air Force laboratory, but they are not required to spend a summer at an Air Force laboratory. Contact the office listed or the AFOSR/NR 4040 Fairfax Dr, Arlington, VA 22203, (703) 696-7310, DSN: 426-7310, or fax: (703) 696-7320. Applications are available on the Web site.
Requirements Applicants must be US citizens who have received their baccalaureate degrees. Air Force graduate fellowships are tenable at any US institution of higher education offering a PhD in science or engineering. Fellowships are awarded for study and research in mathematical, physical, biological, ocean, and engineering sciences. Preference is given to applicants in aeronautical and astronautical engineering; biosciences (including toxicology); chemical engineering; chemistry; cognitive, neural, and behavioral sciences; computer science; electrical engineering; mathematics; mechanical engineering; naval architecture and ocean engineering; oceanography; and physics (including optics).
Amount $18,000 first year; $19,000 second year; $20,000 third and fourth years
Date(s) Application Is Due Jan 20.
Contact Dr. George Outterson, NDSEG Fellowship Program, (919) 549-8505; fax: (919) 549-8205; email: ndseg@aro-emh1.army.mil
Internet http://www.acq.osd.mil/ddre/researchtest/opportunities.html
Sponsor Department of Defense
P.O. Box 13444, 200 Park Dr, Ste 211
Research Triangle Park, NC 27709-3444

DOD National Security Education Program (NSEP) Scholarships **1624**
The purpose of this undergraduate scholarship program is to equip Americans with an understanding of less commonly taught languages and cultures; to build a critical base of future leaders both in the marketplace and in government service; to develop a cadre of professionals with more than the traditional knowledge of language and culture; and to enhance institutional capacity and increase the number of faculty who can educate US citizens toward achieving these goals.
Requirements Any US citizen enrolled in an accredited two or four year public or private US institution of higher education is eligible to apply.
Restrictions Students enrolled in federal government schools are not eligible.

Amount $8000 maximum per term, not to exceed two terms per year
Contact Dr. Edmond Collier, Department of Defense, Office of the Secretary of Defense, (703) 696-1991; email: collier@nsep.policy.osd.mil
Internet http://www.defenselink.mil
Sponsor Department of Defense
1101 Wilson Blvd
Arlington, VA 22209

DOD Predoctoral Traineeship in Breast Cancer Research 1625
The award prepares promising graduate students with a strong commitment to breast cancer research for successful and competitive careers. This award promotes creative approaches to training breast cancer investigators. Successful trainees will be selected for their talent, potential, and commitment to breast cancer research; the mentor's qualifications and experience in breast cancer research; the strong breast cancer research training program at the trainee's institution; the innovative research environment; and the institution's commitment to training future leaders in breast cancer research. The proposed training must focus on breast cancer research. Historically Black Colleges and Universities/Minority Institutions are highly encouraged to apply. Proposals must be submitted electronically at https://cdmrp.org. Guidelines are available online.
Requirements Applicants must be graduate students under the guidance of a designated mentor. Individuals enrolled in a PhD or MD/PhD program are encouraged to apply. All individuals, regardless of ethnicity, nationality, or citizenship status, may apply as long as they are employed by, or affiliated with, an eligible institution. Eligible institutions include for-profit, nonprofit, public, and private organizations. Examples include universities, colleges, hospitals, laboratories, and companies. Agencies of local, state, and federal governments are eligible to the extent that proposals do not overlap with their fully funded intramural programs.
Amount $30,000 per year for a maximum of three years
Date(s) Application Is Due May 24.
Contact Commander, US Army Medical Research and Materiel Command, (301) 619-7079; fax: (301) 619-7792; email: cdmrp.pa@det.amedd.army.mil
Internet http://cdmrp.army.mil/funding/archive/05bcrppredoc_pa.pdf
Sponsor Department of Defense
1077 Patchel St (Bldg 1077), MCMR-ZB-C (BC05-PREDOC)
Fort Detrick, MD 21702-5024

DOE Academies Creating Teacher Scientists (ACTS) Grants 1626
This program is based upon research and best practices in teacher professional development and is aligned with the National Standards for Science Education, the National Teaching Standards, and National Board for Professional Teaching Standards. Instruction is offered to middle and high school teachers in four content areas: biotechnology-genetic engineering; fusion-astrophysics; and energy technologies. Each of these programs teaches knowledge and skills derived from science research and provides a context that when shared with students can help them understand how classroom science is linked to the big science. Teachers will have access to a wealth of mentoring talent that will guide and enrich their understanding of the scientific and technological world. Participants and mentors will create supportive relationships that can follow them into their classrooms. The Teacher Researchers (TR) model provides the teacher with four-weeks of hands-on instruction in a content discipline of their choosing in their initial year followed by two, eight-week summer research internships. Teachers in K-12 classrooms and community college faculty of science, technology, engineering, or mathematics are encouraged to apply. Housing allowances, transportation, and stipends are offered to participants at all the laboratories.
Requirements All applicants must: be teaching full time in a public or private elementary or secondary school and continue to be full time employees of a school system throughout the duration of the program; have a current teaching assignment with at least 3/4 of classroom contact hours in science, mathematics, and/or technology (applies to secondary school teachers and community college instructors only); be at least 21 years old at the time the appointment starts; be U.S. citizens at the time of application; have current health insurance coverage; and commit to a minimum of 3 years involvement in the program.
Amount $800 per week
Date(s) Application Is Due Apr 1.
Contact Todd Clark; (202) 586-7174; fax: (202) 586-0019; email: todd.clark@science.doe.gov; ; Cindy Musick; (202) 586-0987; fax: (202) 586-0019; email: cindy.musick@science.doe.gov
Internet http://www.scied.science.doe.gov/SciEd/LSTPD/about.htm
Sponsor U.S. Department of Energy, Office of Science
1000 Independence Avenue SW
Washington, DC 20585

DOE Advanced Detector Research Grants 1627
The purpose of this program is to support the development of the new detector technologies needed to perform future high-energy physics experiments. Such experiments will require higher performance detectors to exploit the higher beam energies and intensities of new or upgraded accelerators. Higher performance detectors are also needed to probe for new physical processes in both accelerator- and nonaccelerator-based-experiments. Proposed detector research should be driven by the anticipated needs of experiments to be built within the foreseeable future, as well as upgrades to current experiments. Interesting technologies would include but not be limited to charged particle track detectors, calorimeters, or particle identification detectors that are less sensitive to radiation, have higher resolution, are lower in cost, or can be read out faster than currently available detectors. Applicants are requested to submit a Letter of Intent (LOI) by November 15 which includes the title of the proposal, the name of the principal investigator(s), the requested funding, and a one-page abstract. Failure to submit a letter of intent will not negatively prejudice a responsive formal application submitted in a timely manner. Full applications are due by December 12.
Requirements Investigators who are currently involved in experimental high-energy physics are eligible to apply and should do so through a US academic institution.
Amount $10,000-$600,000
Date(s) Application Is Due Nov 15; Dec 12.
Contact Dr. Saul Gonzalez, Program Manager; (301) 903-2359; fax: (301) 903-2597; email: Saul.Gonzalez@science.doe.gov
Internet http://www.science.doe.gov/grants/FAPN07-33.html
Sponsor U.S. Department of Energy
19901 Germantown Road
Germantown, MD 20874-1290

DOE Advanced Energy Projects/Laboratory Technology Research Grants 1628
The Advanced Energy Projects program funds research to establish the feasibility of novel, energy-related concepts. These concepts are usually derived from recent advances in basic research, but require additional research to establish their feasibility. A common theme for each concept is the initial linkage of new, or previously neglected, research results to a practical energy payoff. The Laboratory Technology Research program conducts high-risk, energy-related research that advances fundamental science and technology toward innovative applications that could significantly impact the United States' energy economy. Scientists at the Office of Science laboratories enter into cost-shared research partnerships with industry to explore energy applications of research advances in areas of mission relevance to both parties. The partners jointly bring technology research to a point where industry or the department's technology development programs can pursue final development or commercialization. Applications are available on the Web site and may be submitted at any time.
Amount $10,000-$2 million; $200,000 average
Date(s) Application Is Due May 31.
Contact Martin Rubinstein, Grants and Contracts Division, Office of Science, (301) 903- 5212
Internet http://www.er.doe.gov/production/grants/guide.html
Sponsor Department of Energy
19901 Germantown Rd
Germantown, MD 20874

DOE Advanced Nuclear Energy Systems Basic Research Grants 1629
Areas of focus in this program include: understanding of nanoscale interactions under extreme conditions; mastering the behavior of actinides and of fission products; solution behavior under extreme conditions of radiation and temperature; and interfacial behavior under extreme environmental conditions. Research funded under this initiative will pursue breakthroughs in scientific understanding that will advance materials design, will improve characterization of materials and processes, will enhance chemical processes under the extreme conditions present in nuclear energy systems, and will extend interdisciplinary theory-modeling-simulation-experimentation methodology to surmount the existing scientific and technical barriers for nuclear energy systems of the future. Pre-applications are required, and are due no later than November 22. A response to the pre-applications encouraging or discouraging formal applications will be communicated to the applicants by January 4, and formal applications are due March 14.
Requirements Eligible to apply are institutions of higher education, industry (particularly small and disadvantaged businesses), and nonprofit institutions. Unsolicited research proposals are screened by program officials and, if appropriate, are evaluated by peer review. Successful proposers are awarded one-year or multi-year special research contracts or grants with renewals or incremental funding available, provided performance has been satisfactory. A one- to two-year phase-out period is normally granted to those finishing research projects. Equipment items may be purchased from contract funds with the agreement of DOE.
Amount $10,000-$2 million; $200,000 average
Date(s) Application Is Due Nov 22; Mar 14.
Contact Dr. Lester Morss; (301) 903-9311; email: lester.morss@science.doe.gov; ; Dr. Tim Fitzsimmons; (301) 903-9830; email: tim.fitzsimmons@science.doe.gov
Internet http://www.science.doe.gov/grants/FAPN07-04.html
Sponsor U.S. Department of Energy, Office of Basic Energy Sciences (BES)
19901 Germantown Road
Germantown, MD 20874-1290

DOE Albert Einstein Distinguished Educator Fellowship Program 1630
The Albert Einstein Distinguished Educator Fellowship Act was signed into law in November 1994. The law gives the Department of Energy responsibility for administering the program of distinguished educator fellowships for elementary and secondary school mathematics and science teachers. Selected teachers spend up to one year in a Congressional Office or a federal agency. Agencies that have participated include: the Department of Energy (DOE), the National Science Foundation (NSF), the National Aeronautics and Space Administration (NASA), the National Institutes of Health (NIH),

the Department of Education (ED), National Institute of Standards and Technology (NIST), the White House Office of Science and Technology Policy (OSTP) and the National Oceanic and Atmospheric Administration (NOAA). The Fellows provide their educational expertise, years of experience and personal insights to these offices. Costs for relocation will be reimbursed based on the distance of current location to Washington DC. During the Fellowship, awardees receive funds for travel to conferences, workshops, and other professional development opportunities.
Requirements To be eligible, applicants must be US citizens at the time of selection; have a minimum of five years full-time classroom teaching experience; be teaching full-time in a public or private elementary or secondary school; have a current teaching assignment with at least 3/4 of classroom contact hours in science, mathematics, and/or technology (applies to secondary school teachers only); and provide a recommendation from a current school administrator and two additional recommendations.
Amount $5,000 per month stipend
Date(s) Application Is Due Jan 13.
Contact Todd Clark; (202) 586-7174; fax: (202) 586-0019; email: todd.clark@science.doe.gov; ; Cindy Musick; (202) 586-0987; fax: (202) 586-0019; email: cindy.musick@science.doe.gov
Internet http://www.scied.science.doe.gov/scied/Einstein/about.htm
Sponsor U.S. Department of Energy, Office of Science
1000 Independence Avenue SW
Washington, DC 20585

DOE Atomic, Molecular, and Optical Sciences Research Grants **1631**
The AMOS Program supports a balanced portfolio of experiment and theory to study the fundamental properties of atoms, ions and small molecules and the interactions between electrons, photons and ions in collisions with atoms, molecules and surfaces. Research is focused on the most complete quantum mechanical description of these properties and interactions and is intended to provide a basic understanding of physical processes. The AMOS program plays an underpinning role in relation to other programs within BES in Chemical and Materials Sciences, in relation to current and future BES facilities in which matter is probed with photons, electrons or heavy ions, and in relation to applied efforts in plasma science. AMOS also contributes at the most fundamental level to the science-based optimization of current energy sources and the development of new ones. Some topics of current interest: studies of the interactions of intense electromagnetic fields, induced by highly charged ions or lasers, with atoms and molecules; coherent control of quantum mechanical processes; development and application of ultrafast x-ray light sources, both laser-based and at BES synchrotron facilities; and theory and experiment on ultracold collisions and quantum condensates.
Requirements Eligible to apply are institutions of higher education, industry (particularly small and disadvantaged businesses), and nonprofit institutions. Unsolicited research proposals are screened by program officials and, if appropriate, are evaluated by peer review. Successful proposers are awarded one-year or multi-year special research contracts or grants with renewals or incremental funding available, provided performance has been satisfactory. A one- to two-year phase-out period is normally granted to those finishing research projects. Equipment items may be purchased from contract funds with the agreement of DOE.
Amount $10,000-$2 million; $200,000 average
Contact Dr. Eric A. Rohlfing, Director; (301) 903-8165; fax: (301) 903-4110; email: Eric.Rohlfing@science.doe.gov
Internet http://www.science.doe.gov/bes/chm/Programs/programs.html
Sponsor U.S. Department of Energy, Office of Science
1000 Independence Avenue, SW
Washington, DC 20585-1290

DOE Basic Energy Sciences (BES) Grants **1632**
The mission of the program is to foster and support fundamental research to expand the scientific foundations for new and improved energy technologies and for understanding and mitigating the environmental impacts of energy use. Research is sponsored in a variety of disciplines to broaden the energy supply and technological base knowledge. The disciplines represented are biosciences, chemical sciences, geosciences, engineering, and materials sciences. The program also supports exploratory research on advanced energy projects. Research projects are selected for funding on the basis of scientific merit, the possible relevance to meeting BES long-range research goals, and the contribution toward a balanced, responsive research program. The detailed substance of the program is determined by the selection from among many unsolicited proposals of ideas from the university/scientific community. Applications are accepted at any time.
Requirements Eligible to apply are institutions of higher education, industry (particularly small and disadvantaged businesses), and nonprofit institutions. Unsolicited research proposals are screened by program officials and, if appropriate, are evaluated by peer review. Successful proposers are awarded one-year or multiyear special research contracts or grants with renewals or incremental funding available, provided performance has been satisfactory. A one- to two-year phase-out period is normally granted to those finishing research projects. Equipment items may be purchased from contract funds with the agreement of DOE.
Amount $10,000-$2 million; $200,000 average
Contact Martin R. Rubinstein, Supervisor of Grants and Contracts; (301) 903-4946; fax: (301) 903-4194; email: Martin.Rubinstein@science.doe.gov
Internet http://www.science.doe.gov/grants/FAPN08-01.html
Sponsor U.S. Department of Energy, Office of Basic Energy Sciences
19901 Germantown Road
Germantown, MD 20874-1290

DOE Catalysis and Chemical Transformations Research Grants **1633**
This Program supports basic research to understand the chemical aspects of catalysis, both heterogeneous and homogeneous; the chemistry of fossil resources; and the chemistry the molecules used to create advanced materials. Catalysts are crucial to energy conservation in creating new, less-energy- demanding routes for the production of basic chemical feedstocks and value-added chemicals. Catalysts are also indispensable for processing and manufacturing fuels that are a primary means of energy storage. Results from a fundamental, molecular-level understanding of the syntheses of advanced catalytic materials have the potential of providing new chemicals or materials that can be fabricated with greater energy efficiency or function as energy-saving media themselves. This activity is the Nation's major supporter of catalysis research, and it is the only activity that treats catalysis as a discipline integrating all aspects of homogeneous and heterogeneous catalysis research.
Requirements Eligible to apply are institutions of higher education, industry (particularly small and disadvantaged businesses), and nonprofit institutions. Unsolicited research proposals are screened by program officials and, if appropriate, are evaluated by peer review. Successful proposers are awarded one-year or multi-year special research contracts or grants with renewals or incremental funding available, provided performance has been satisfactory. A one- to two-year phase-out period is normally granted to those finishing research projects. Equipment items may be purchased from contract funds with the agreement of DOE.
Amount $10,000-$2 million; $200,000 average
Contact Dr. Eric A. Rohlfing, Director; (301) 903-8165; fax: (301) 903-4110; email: Eric.Rohlfing@science.doe.gov
Internet http://www.science.doe.gov/bes/chm/Programs/programs.html
Sponsor U.S. Department of Energy, Office of Science
1000 Independence Avenue, SW
Washington, DC 20585-1290

DOE Chemical Energy and Chemical Engineering Research Grants **1634**
This activity supports research on electrochemistry, thermophysical and thermochemical properties, and physical and chemical rate processes. Emphasis is given to improving and/or developing the scientific base for engineering generalizations and their unifying theories. Also included is fundamental research in areas critical to understanding the underlying limitations in the performance of electrochemical energy storage and conversion systems including anode, cathode, and electrolyte systems and their interactions with emphasis on improvements in performance and lifetime. The program covers a broad spectrum of research including fundamental studies of composite electrode structures; failure and degradation of active electrode materials; thin film electrodes, electrolytes, and interfaces; and experimental and theoretical aspects of phase equilibria, especially of mixtures, including supercritical phenomena.
Requirements Eligible to apply are institutions of higher education, industry (particularly small and disadvantaged businesses), and nonprofit institutions. Unsolicited research proposals are screened by program officials and, if appropriate, are evaluated by peer review. Successful proposers are awarded one-year or multi-year special research contracts or grants with renewals or incremental funding available, provided performance has been satisfactory. A one- to two-year phase-out period is normally granted to those finishing research projects. Equipment items may be purchased from contract funds with the agreement of DOE.
Amount $10,000-$2 million; $200,000 average
Contact Dr. Eric A. Rohlfing, Director; (301) 903-8165; fax: (301) 903-4110; email: Eric.Rohlfing@science.doe.gov
Internet http://www.science.doe.gov/bes/chm/Programs/programs.html
Sponsor U.S. Department of Energy, Office of Science
1000 Independence Avenue, SW
Washington, DC 20585-1290

DOE Chemical Physics Research Grants **1635**
The program supports basic research on fundamental molecular processes related to the mission of the Department in such areas as combustion, catalysis, and environmental restoration. It is the Nation's principal supporter of high temperature chemical kinetics and gas phase chemical physics. Specific areas of research emphasis include, but are not limited to: gas phase chemical reaction theory, computational chemistry, experimental dynamics and spectroscopy, thermodynamics of reaction intermediates, chemical kinetics and reaction mechanisms at high temperatures in the gas phase and at surfaces, combustion diagnostics, and chemical dynamics and kinetics at surfaces and with metal and semiconductor clusters.
Requirements Eligible to apply are institutions of higher education, industry (particularly small and disadvantaged businesses), and nonprofit institutions. Unsolicited research proposals are screened by program officials and, if appropriate, are evaluated by peer review. Successful proposers are awarded one-year or multi-year special research contracts or grants with renewals or incremental funding available, provided performance has been satisfactory. A one- to two-year phase-out period is normally granted to those finishing research projects. Equipment items may be purchased from contract funds with the agreement of DOE.
Amount $10,000-$2 million; $200,000 average

Contact Dr. Eric A. Rohlfing, Director; (301) 903-8165; fax: (301) 903-4110; email: Eric.Rohlfing@science.doe.gov
Internet http://www.science.doe.gov/bes/chm/Programs/programs.html
Sponsor U.S. Department of Energy, Office of Science
1000 Independence Avenue, SW
Washington, DC 20585-1290

DOE Chemical Sciences Research Grants **1636**
The Chemical Sciences program supports a major portion of the nation's fundamental research in the chemical sciences. The research covers those areas of the chemical sciences that impact the Department's energy and environmental missions. Research supported covers atomic, molecular and optical (AMO) sciences; chemical physics; photo- and radiation chemistry; surface chemistry and heterogeneous catalysis; organometallic chemistry and homogeneous catalysis; analytical and separation science; heavy element chemistry; and aspects of chemical engineering sciences. This research provides a foundation for fundamental understanding of the interactions of atoms, molecules, and ions with photons and electrons; the making and breaking of chemical bonds in gas phase, in solutions, at interfaces, and on surfaces; and understanding the energy transfer processes within and between molecules. Applications are accepted at any time.
Requirements Eligible to apply are institutions of higher education, industry (particularly small and disadvantaged businesses), and nonprofit institutions. Unsolicited research proposals are screened by program officials and, if appropriate, are evaluated by peer review. Successful proposers are awarded one-year or multi-year special research contracts or grants with renewals or incremental funding available, provided performance has been satisfactory. A one- to two-year phase-out period is normally granted to those finishing research projects. Equipment items may be purchased from contract funds with the agreement of DOE.
Amount $10,000-$2 million; $200,000 average
Contact Dr. Eric A. Rohlfing, Director; (301) 903-8165; fax: (301) 903-4110; email: Eric.Rohlfing@science.doe.gov
Internet http://www.science.doe.gov/bes/chm/chmhome.html
Sponsor U.S. Department of Energy, Office of Science
1000 Independence Avenue, SW
Washington, DC 20585-1290

DOE Coal Liquefaction Research Grants **1637**
The objectives of the program are to develop advanced technology and an engineering and operations database sufficient for the production of marketable liquid fuels from coal by the year 2015 at a cost competitive with crude oil, between $25 and $30 per barrel. The implementation strategy is based on catalytic staged direct liquefaction, coprocessing of coal/waste and petroleum resid, slurry-phase indirect liquefaction technology, and advanced processes based on exploratory research. Areas covered by the program include direct/indirect coal liquefaction processes, coprocessing of coal-petroleum mixture/coal-waste mixture, refining and chemicals, and supporting research. Proposals are accepted at any time.
Requirements States, local governments, universities, governmental entities, consortia, nonprofit institutions, commercial corporations, joint federal/industry corporations, US territories, and individuals are eligible to apply.
Amount $50,000-$400,000 range; $154,000 average
Contact Fred Glaser, Office of Advanced Research, Assistant Secretary of Fossil Energy, (301) 903-2786
Internet http://www.fe.doe.gov
Sponsor Department of Energy
19901 Germantown Rd, MS FE-3
Germantown, MD 20874

DOE Combustion Systems Research Grants **1638**
The program emphasizes the development of technologies which would allow more cost-effective and efficient coal use. The objectives of this program include developing the technology necessary for electric power applications with lower cost, increased efficiency, and emission significantly lower than current NSPS. Applications are accepted at any time.
Requirements States, local governments, universities, governmental entities, consortia, nonprofit institutions, commercial corporations, joint federal/industry corporations, US territories, and individuals are eligible to apply.
Amount $10,000-$25 million range
Contact Mary Roland, Department of Energy, Fossil Energy Program, (301) 903-3514
Internet http://www.fe.doe.gov
Sponsor Department of Energy
19901 Germantown Rd, MS FE-3
Germantown, MD 20874

DOE Competitive Financial Assistance for Renewable Energy and Energy Efficiency Programs **1639**
DOE announces a competitive solicitation for information dissemination, public outreach, training, and related technical analysis and technical assistance activities involving renewable energy and energy efficiency. Areas of interest involving renewable energy include wind, photovoltaic, hydrogen, and bioenergy technologies. Energy efficiency areas of interest include energy efficiency in the transportation, buildings, and industrial sectors.
Requirements Profit organizations, nonprofit institutions and organizations, state and local governments, universities, individuals, Native American organizations, and Alaskan Native corporations are eligible to apply.
Amount $6 million total
Contact James Damm, Contract Specialist, fax: (303) 275-4788; email: gostate@nrel.gov
Internet http://www.tgci.com/fedrgtxt/01-10503.txt
Sponsor Department of Energy
1000 Independence Ave SW
Washington, DC 20585

DOE Computational Science Graduate Fellowships **1640**
Sponsored by the DOE Office of Science and Office Defense Programs and administered by the institute, the program supports highly capable students pursuing graduate study at US universities in scientific or engineering disciplines with applications in high-performance computing. Fellows also participate in off-campus research at DOE laboratories. The program offers an annual stipend and payment of tuition and fees for graduate study in scientific and technical disciplines using computational science methods. Appointments are reviewed annually and may be renewed up to a limit of four years.
Requirements The program is open to US citizens and permanent residents who are in their first or second year of graduate school and working toward a PhD at the time of application. Exceptional senior undergraduates who can meet all of the requirements listed in the application booklet also may apply.
Amount $28,000 annual stipend
Date(s) Application Is Due Jan 11.
Contact Graduate Fellowships, (515) 956-3696; email: csgf@krellinst.org
Internet http://www.krellinst.org/csgf
Sponsor Krell Institute
1609 Golden Aspen Dr, Ste 101
Ames, IA 50010

DOE Conservation Research and Development Grants **1641**
Grants are awarded to programs to conduct a balanced, long-term research effort in the areas of buildings, industry, and transportation. Grants are offered to develop and transfer various energy conservation technologies to the nonfederal sector. The program is willing to suggest potential areas for new research initiatives. Applications are accepted at any time.
Requirements Profit organizations, private nonprofit organizations, and state and local governments are eligible to apply.
Amount $50,000-$500,000 average
Contact Polly Perando, Office of Building Technology, State, and Community Programs, (202) 586-2300; email: polly.perando@ee.doe.gov
Internet http://energy.gov/engine/content.do?BT_CODE=ST_SS11
Sponsor Department of Energy
1000 Independence Ave SW, Forrestal Bldg
Washington, DC 20585

DOE Control Technology and Coal Preparation Research Grants **1642**
The activities of the program emphasize the development of technologies which will allow greater use of coal in an environmentally acceptable manner. These technologies include coal characterization and cleaning, combined flue gas cleanup, processes for cleanup of hot coal combustion and gasification streams, and management of wastes generated in coal conversion and utilization. Applications are accepted at any time.
Requirements States, local governments, universities, governmental entities, consortia, nonprofit institutions, commercial corporations, joint federal/industry corporations, US territories, and individuals are eligible to apply.
Amount $10,000-$25 million
Contact Mary Roland, Department of Energy, Fossil Energy Program, (301) 903-3514
Internet http://www.fe.doe.gov
Sponsor Department of Energy
19901 Germantown Rd, MS FE-3
Germantown, MD 20874

DOE Electric Energy Systems Research Grants **1643**
The program assists the private sector in the development of advanced technology options for the nation's electric energy networks; methodologies for integrating new technologies into electric utility systems; and analytical procedures to assess and enhance the stability and efficiency of the country's increasingly complex interconnected electric energy system. Supported are innovative research in such areas as high-voltage systems, new materials, and sophisticated control methods. Basic research is supported on increasing the efficiency of electric energy supply and distribution, thus reducing primary energy use per unit of real GNP. Subprograms include reliable electric power delivery, electric field effects, and systems technologies. Proposals are accepted at any time.
Amount $50,000-$500,000
Contact Office of Utility Technologies, (202) 586-4142
Internet http://www.eere.energy.gov
Sponsor Department of Energy
1000 Independence Ave SW, Forrestal Bldg
Washington, DC 20585

DOE Energy Biosciences Research Grants **1644**
To provide financial support for fundamental research in the basic sciences and advanced technology concepts, and assessments in fields related to energy. Financial support, in whole or in part, may be provided for such purposes as the salaries, materials and supplies, equipment, travel, publication costs, and services required for conducting research, related activities, and advanced technology projects or assessments. Restrictions on use of funds depend on grant provisions. Applications may be submitted at any time. Specific grant solicitation notices, issued from time to time, usually contain due dates. Applicants are encouraged to contact the office regarding specific grant due dates and other requirements.
Requirements Colleges and universities, non-profit organizations, for-profit commercial organizations, State and local governments, and unaffiliated individuals.
Amount $10,000-$2 million; $200,000 average
Contact Martin Rubinstein, Grants and Contracts Division, Department of Energy, (301) 903-5212
Internet http://www.cfda.gov/public/viewprog.asp?progid=875
Sponsor Department of Energy
19901 Germantown Rd
Germantown, MD 20874

DOE Energy Conservation Research and Development Grants **1645**
This program supports scientific and technical research in fields where new knowledge can expand the generic technology base underlying energy conservation. This will allow the private sector to develop ways to make more efficient use of available energy and to facilitate use of nonpetroleum energy sources. Programs include basic and applied research in fields of scientific inquiry that can provide a general technology base that the private sector will be able to use in developing advanced conservation applications and actually getting these technology applications into the marketplace. Applications are accepted at any time.
Requirements Eligible applicants include profit organizations, private nonprofit institutions/organizations, and state and local governments.
Amount $50,000-$500,000
Contact Office of Transportation Technologies, (202) 586-6715; Office of Building Technology, State, and Community Programs, (202) 586-2300; Office of Industrial Technologies, (202) 586-0098
Internet http://www.eere.energy.gov
Sponsor Department of Energy
1000 Independence Ave SW, Forrestal Bldg
Washington, DC 20585

DOE Energy Conversion Technology Research Grants **1646**
Under the Energy Conversion and Utilization Technologies Program, the energy conversion technology subprogram's problem areas that require additional research include thermodynamics and fluid mechanics of closed system energy conversion, combustion processes of internal combustion engines, and physical and chemical aspects of alternative fuels for furnaces and boilers. Potential areas for new research include development of a complete understanding of velocities and turbulence levels at various points during engine operation and how they can be controlled to appropriately tailor combustion processes of advanced engine concepts; complete incorporation of technology base information and development of validated multidimensional large-scale computer models of complete engines for use in solving specific design problems; assemblage of an adequate database of physical and chemical properties for select alternative fuels and experimental evaluation of several combustion parameters of interest to designers of furnaces and boilers; and experimental and analytical investigation of thermodynamic and fluid dynamic aspects of advanced closed-cycle systems and components. Proposals are accepted at any time.
Amount $50,000-$500,000
Contact Office of Transportation Technologies, (202) 586-6715; Office of Building Technology, State, and Community Programs, (202) 586-2300; Office of Industrial Technologies, (202) 586-0098
Internet http://www.eere.energy.gov
Sponsor Department of Energy
1000 Independence Ave SW, Forrestal Bldg
Washington, DC 20585

DOE Energy from Municipal Waste Projects Grants **1647**
Grants support research to provide a database on liquids and gas production and to provide a basis for environmental and feedstock preparation. Potential areas for new research initiatives include thermochemical studies to provide a generic technology base for systems producing liquid and gaseous fuels; combustion tasks concerned with kinetics, efficiency, and products formation for corrosion and pollution control; pyrolysis tasks concerned with base data development on effects of various feedstock components and of time, temperature, pressure, and so forth; biochemical studies to provide data on biochemistry and life support systems of anaerobes; water and wastewater studies to provide information to improve energy efficiency in treatment systems; mechanical studies to provide generic data on systems design; and improved densification techniques and binders. Proposals are accepted at any time.
Amount $50,000-$500,000
Contact Office of Utility Technologies, (202) 586-4142
Internet http://www.eere.energy.gov
Sponsor Department of Energy
1000 Independence Ave SW, Forrestal Bldg
Washington, DC 20585

DOE Energy Research Analyses Grants **1648**
This program supports energy research analyses of the department's basic and applied research activities. Specific objectives include assessments to identify any duplication or gaps in scientific research activities, and impartial and independent evaluations of scientific and technical research efforts. Applications are accepted at any time and are available on the Web site.
Requirements Profit organizations, nonprofit institutions, intrastate, interstate, local agencies, and universities are eligible for funding. Preapplication coordination is recommended for unsolicited proposals.
Amount $10,000-$2 million; $200,000 average
Contact Martin Rubinstein, Grants and Contracts Division, Office of Science, (301) 903- 5212
Internet http://www.er.doe.gov/production/grants/guide.html
Sponsor Department of Energy
1000 Independence Ave SW, Forrestal Bldg
Washington, DC 20585

DOE Energy-Related Inventions Grants **1649**
Grants encourage innovation in developing nonnuclear energy technology by providing assistance in the development of promising energy-related inventions. Assistance provided includes evaluation of energy-related inventions, limited funding assistance where appropriate, advice concerning engineering, marketing, and business planning.
Requirements There are no restrictions on eligibility. Small businesses, individual inventors, and entrepreneurs are especially invited to participate.
Amount $50,000-$500,000
Contact Lisa Barnett, Department of Energy, (202) 586-2212
Internet http://www.eere.energy.gov/inventions
Sponsor Department of Energy
1000 Independence Ave SW, Forrestal Bldg
Washington, DC 20585

DOE Engineering Research Grants **1650**
The objectives of the engineering research program are to extend the body of knowledge underlying current engineering practice in order to open new ways for enhancing energy savings and production, prolonging useful equipment life, and reducing costs while maintaining output and performance quality; and to broaden the technical and conceptual base for solving future engineering problems in the energy technologies. Long-term research topics of current interest include foundations of bioprocessing fuels and energy related wastes; fracture mechanisms; experimental and theoretical studies of multiphase flows; intelligent machines; and diagnostics and control for plasma processing of materials.
Amount $10,000-$2 million; $200,000 average
Date(s) Application Is Due May 31.
Contact Martin Rubinstein, Grants and Contracts Division, Office of Science, (301) 903- 5212
Internet http://www.er.doe.gov/production/grants/guide.html
Sponsor Department of Energy
19901 Germantown Rd
Germantown, MD 20874-1290

DOE Environmental Processes Research Grants **1651**
This program addresses global environmental change from increases in atmospheric carbon dioxide and other greenhouse gases. The scope of the global change program encompasses the carbon cycle, climate modeling and diagnostics, atmospheric sciences and meteorology, ecosystem responses, and impacts on resources. The role of clouds and radiation in climate prediction is a particular emphasis. Applications are available on the Web site and are accepted at any time.
Amount $10,000-$2 million; $200,000 average
Contact Martin Rubinstein, Grants and Contracts Division, Office of Science, (301) 903- 5212
Internet http://www.er.doe.gov/production/grants/guide.html
Sponsor Department of Energy
19901 Germantown Rd
Germantown, MD 20874

DOE Environmental Remediation Grants **1652**
The objectives of the program relate to environmental processes affected by energy production and use. The program develops information on the physical, chemical, and biological processes that cycle and transport energy-related material, particularly contaminates that arose during nuclear weapons production, through the earth's surface and subsurface. Emphasis is put on the development of a strong basis for understanding and implementing the appropriate and efficient use of bioremediation, particularly at the department's sites. Applications are accepted at any time and are available on the Web site.
Amount $10,000-$2 million range; $200,000 average

Contact Martin Rubinstein, Grants and Contracts Division, Office of Science, (301) 903- 5212
Internet http://www.science.doe.gov/production/grants/grants.html
Sponsor Department of Energy
19901 Germantown Rd
Germantown, MD 20874

DOE Experimental Program to Stimulate Competitive Research (EPSCoR) 1653
The objective of the EPSCoR program is to enhance the capabilities of EPSCoR states to conduct nationally competitive energy-related research and to develop science and engineering manpower to meet current and future needs in energy-related fields. This program addressees research needs across all of the Department of Energy research interests. Research supported by the EPSCoR program is concerned with the same broad research areas addressed by the Office of Science programs that are described above. States eligible for DOE/EPSCoR support include: Alabama, Alaska, Arkansas, Delaware, Hawaii, Idaho, Kansas, Kentucky, Louisiana, Maine, Mississippi, Montana, Nebraska, Nevada, New Mexico, North Dakota, Oklahoma, South Carolina, South Dakota, Tennessee, Vermont, West Virginia, Wyoming, Commonwealth of Puerto Rico, and the Virgin Islands. Applicants are encouraged, but not required, to submit a preliminary proposal to DOE by April.
Amount $750,000 maximum
Date(s) Application Is Due Sep 21.
Contact Dr. Matesh Varma, Office of Science, (301) 903-3209; fax: 301-903-9513; email: matesh.varma@science.doe.gov
Internet http://www.science.doe.gov/bes/EPSCoR/OVER1.HTM
Sponsor Department of Energy
19901 Germantown Rd
Germantown, MD 20874-1290

DOE Faculty and Student Teams (FaST) Program Grants 1654
The program provides hands-on research opportunities in DOE national laboratories during the summer, and will support a team comprised of one faculty member and 2 - 3 undergraduate students. The faculty member identifies a mutually beneficial research area amenable to collaboration by the faculty member and the laboratory scientist. Potential areas of collaboration are based upon the Project Descriptions described at the specific DOE Office of Science laboratory. Faculty from colleges and universities with limited research facilities and those institutions serving populations, women, and minorities underrepresented in the fields of science, engineering, and technology are encouraged to apply. The amounts targeted for the student stipends are $4,500 for each student (allocated as ten weekly stipends of $400, and up to $500 for travel), and faculty stipends up to 2/9 academic year salary (up to $12,000) for faculty team members. Both faculty and student team members will receive funding assistance with travel. Student team members will receive funding assistance with housing.
Requirements Faculty applicants must be United States Citizens or Permanent Resident Aliens. Student team members must: be currently enrolled as an undergraduate student and completed at least one semester of college course work; be 18 years or older at the start of the program; have earned a high school diploma or GED; be United States Citizens or Permanent Resident Aliens; participate in a maximum of two FaST internships; and have coverage under a health insurance plan.
Amount $4,500 maximum per student; $12,000 maximum per faculty member
Date(s) Application Is Due Feb 1.
Contact Todd Clark; (202) 586-7174; fax: (202) 586-0019; email: todd.clark@science.doe.gov; ; Cindy Musick; (202) 586-0987; fax: (202) 586-0019; email: cindy.musick@science.doe.gov
Internet http://www.scied.science.doe.gov/scied/PST/about.htm
Sponsor U.S. Department of Energy, Office of Science
1000 Independence Avenue SW
Washington, DC 20585

DOE Fossil Advanced Research and Technology Development Grants 1655
The Advanced Research and Technology Development (AR&TD) Program is directed toward the scientific and technical areas that underlie the development of all fossil energy coal technologies. The AR&TD coal science program conducts fundamental research into coal combustion and conversion and addresses scientific and engineering problems that are barriers to fossil energy technological goals. Areas covered by current projects include materials research; fluids and solids handling; instrumentation and diagnostics; bioprocessing of coal; component development; structure and reactions of coal; multiphase flow and thermodynamics; fundamental problems in combustion of pulverized coal, synfuels, and coal-liquid mixtures; environmental aspects of coal use and conversion; control technology and coal preparation; coal gasification; and coal liquefaction. Applications are accepted at any time.
Requirements States, local governments, universities, governmental entities, consortia, nonprofit institutions, commercial corporations, joint federal/industry corporations, US territories, and individuals are eligible to apply.
Amount $10,000-$25 million average
Contact Mary Roland, Department of Energy, Fossil Energy Program, (301) 903-3514
Internet http://www.fe.doe.gov
Sponsor Department of Energy
19901 Germantown Rd, MS FE-3
Germantown, MD 20874

DOE Fossil Energy Research and Development Grants 1656
The fossil energy program's role is to support long-term research toward providing an improved capability to convert coal and oil shale to liquid and gaseous fuels; increase domestic production of coal, oil, and gas; ensure that current and new facilities that burn coal can do so in an economically feasible and environmentally acceptable manner; and allow more efficient and more economically attractive utilization of fossil energy resources. Applications are accepted at any time.
Requirements States, local governments, universities, recognizant industrial governments, US territories, and individuals are eligible to apply.
Amount $10,000-$25 million
Contact Mary Roland, Department of Energy, Fossil Energy Program, (301) 903-3514
Internet http://www.fe.doe.gov
Sponsor Department of Energy
19901 Germantown Rd
Germantown, MD 20874

DOE Fusion Energy Science Division Grants 1657
Basic and applied research is carried out in the following areas: (1) basic plasma science research directed at furthering the understanding of fundamental processes in plasmas; (2) improving the theoretical understanding of fusion plasmas necessary for interpreting results from present experiments and the planning and design of future confinement devices; (3) obtaining the critical data on plasma properties, atomic physics, and new diagnostic techniques for support of confinement experiments; (4) supporting exploratory research into concepts that are alternatives to the tokamak; and (5) carrying out research on issues that support the development of inertial fusion energy, for which target development is carried out by the Department of Energy's defense programs. Application forms are available on the Web site. Applications may be submitted at any time.
Requirements Unsolicited research proposals should be preceded by an informal preproposal of no more than two or three pages that briefly describes the research project and the proposed level of funding.
Amount $10,000-$2 million; $200,000 average
Date(s) Application Is Due May 31.
Contact Martin Rubinstein, Grants and Contracts Division, Office of Science, (301) 903- 5212
Internet http://www.er.doe.gov/production/grants/guide.html
Sponsor Department of Energy
19901 Germantown Rd
Germantown, MD 20874

DOE Fusion Energy Science Technology Division Grants 1658
The technology division's science-oriented goal is to provide the technologies that are required to successfully design, build, and operate near-term experiments aimed at producing, understanding, and optimizing the fusion energy process. The division's energy-oriented goal is to develop the technologies that will be needed in the long term for an economically and environmentally attractive fusion energy source. These goals are pursued through multi-institutional domestic programs and international collaboration partnerships. Applications are accepted at any time and are available on the Web site.
Requirements Unsolicited research proposals should be preceded by an informal preproposal of no more than two or three pages that briefly describes the research project and the proposed level of funding.
Amount $10,000-$2 million; $200, 000 average
Date(s) Application Is Due May 31.
Contact Martin Rubinstein, Grants and Contracts Division, Office of Science, (301) 903- 5212
Internet http://www.science.doe.gov/production/grants/grants.html
Sponsor Department of Energy
19901 Germantown Rd
Germantown, MD 20874-1290

DOE Geosciences Research Grants 1659
The Program supports research aimed at developing an understanding of fundamental Earth processes that can be used as a foundation for efficient, effective, and environmentally sound use of energy resources, and provide an improved scientific basis for advanced energy and environmental technologies. The program funds projects that develop a quantitative and predictive understanding of the energy-related aspects of processes within the earth. Emphasis is on the upper levels of the earth's crust and the focus is on geophysics and geochemistry of rock-fluid systems and interactions. Specific topical areas receiving high emphasis include high-resolution geophysical imaging; rock physics; fundamental properties of rocks, minerals, and fluids; scientific drilling; and sedimentary basin systems. The resulting improved understanding and knowledge base are needed to assist efforts in the utilization of the nation's energy resources in an environmentally acceptable fashion. Applications are accepted at any time and are available on the Web site.
Requirements Eligible to apply are institutions of higher education, industry (particularly small and disadvantaged businesses), and nonprofit institutions. Unsolicited research proposals are screened by program officials and, if appropriate, are evaluated by peer review. Successful proposers are awarded one-year or multi-year special research contracts or grants with renewals or incremental funding available, provided performance has been satisfactory. A one- to two-year phase-out period is normally granted to those

finishing research projects. Equipment items may be purchased from contract funds with the agreement of DOE.
Amount $10,000-$2 million; $200,000 average
Contact Dr. Eric A. Rohlfing, Director; (301) 903-8165; fax: (301) 903-4110; email: Eric.Rohlfing@science.doe.gov
Internet http://www.science.doe.gov/bes/geo/geohome.html
Sponsor U.S. Department of Energy, Office of Science
19901 Germantown Road
Germantown, MD 20874-1290

DOE Health Effects and Life Sciences Research Grants 1660
The objectives of this program of basic and biological research are to create and apply new technologies and resources in mapping, sequencing, and information management for characterizing the molecular nature of the human genome; to develop and support DOE national user facilities for use in fundamental structural biology; to use model organisms to understand human genome organization, human gene function and control, and the functional relationships between human genes and proteins; to characterize and exploit the genomes and diversity of microbes with potential relevance for energy, bioremediation, or global climate; to understand and characterize the risks to human health from exposures to low levels of radiation and chemicals; to develop novel technologies for high throughput determination of protein structure; and to anticipate and address ethical, legal, and social implications arising from genome research. Applications are accepted at any time and are available on the Web site.
Requirements Unsolicited research proposals should be preceded by an information preproposal of no more than two or three pages that briefly describes the research project and the proposed level of funding.
Amount $10,000-$2 million range; $200,000 average
Contact Martin Rubinstein, Grants and Contracts Division, Office of Science, (301) 903- 5212
Internet http://www.science.doe.gov/production/grants/grants.html
Sponsor Department of Energy
19901 Germantown Rd
Germantown, MD 20874

DOE Heavy Element Chemistry Research Grants 1661
This Program supports research in actinide and fission product chemistry. Areas of interest include aqueous and non-aqueous coordination chemistry; solution and solid-state speciation and reactivity; measurement of chemical and physical properties; synthesis of actinide-containing materials; chemical properties of the heaviest actinide and transactinide elements; theoretical methods for the prediction of heavy element electronic and molecular structure and reactivity; and the relationship between the actinides, lanthanides, and transition metals. This activity represents the Nation's only funding for basic research in the chemical and physical principles of actinide and fission product materials. The program is primarily based at the national laboratories because of the special licenses and facilities needed to obtain and safely handle radioactive materials. However, research in heavy element chemistry is supported at universities, and collaborations between university and laboratory programs are encouraged. The training of graduate students and postdoctoral research associates is viewed as an important responsibility of this activity.
Requirements Eligible to apply are institutions of higher education, industry (particularly small and disadvantaged businesses), and nonprofit institutions. Unsolicited research proposals are screened by program officials and, if appropriate, are evaluated by peer review. Successful proposers are awarded one-year or multi-year special research contracts or grants with renewals or incremental funding available, provided performance has been satisfactory. A one- to two-year phase-out period is normally granted to those finishing research projects. Equipment items may be purchased from contract funds with the agreement of DOE.
Amount $10,000-$2 million; $200,000 average
Contact Dr. Eric A. Rohlfing, Director; (301) 903-8165; fax: (301) 903-4110; email: Eric.Rohlfing@science.doe.gov
Internet http://www.science.doe.gov/bes/chm/Programs/programs.html
Sponsor U.S. Department of Energy, Office of Science
1000 Independence Avenue, SW
Washington, DC 20585-1290

DOE High-Energy Physics Research Grants 1662
The primary objectives of this program are to understand the nature of and relationships among fundamental forces of nature and to understand the ultimate structure of matter in terms of the properties and interrelations of its basic constituents. The research falls into three broad categories: experimental research, theoretical research, and technology R&D in support of the high-energy physics program.
Requirements Unsolicited proposals from universities for research support are analyzed by the program staff and undergo external peer review on an individual basis. Independently, experimental research proposals are submitted to national accelerator laboratories for review. The final decision to make accelerator facilities available for a particular experiment rests with the laboratory management. Successful research proposals usually receive one-year contracts (project grants) with provisions for review and renewal on an annual basis.
Amount $10,000-$2 million; $200,000 average
Date(s) Application Is Due May 31.
Contact Martin Rubinstein, Grants and Contracts Division, Office of Science, (301) 903- 5212
Internet http://www.science.doe.gov/production/grants/grants.html
Sponsor Department of Energy
19901 Germantown Rd
Germantown, MD 20874-1290

DOE Human Genome Program--Ethical, Legal, and Social Implications 1663
DOE announces its interest in receiving applications in support of the Ethical, Legal, and Social Implications (ELSI) subprogram of the Human Genome Program (HGP). Applications should focus on issues of genetics and the workplace, storage of genetic information and tissue samples, education, or complex or multigenic traits. The HGP is a coordinated, multidisciplinary, directed research effort aimed at obtaining a detailed understanding of the human genome at the molecular level.
Amount $10,000-$2 million range; $200,000 average
Contact Martin Rubinstein, Grants and Contracts Division, Office of Science, (301) 903-5212
Internet http://www.sc.doe.gov/production/grants/grants.html
Sponsor Department of Energy
19901 Germantown Rd
Germantown, MD 20874

DOE Hydrogen Program 1664
In a supplemental announcement to a broad-based solicitation, DOE is seeking research and development (R&D) proposals that can advance hydrogen production, storage, and utilization technologies. The solicitation contains information that must be used in conjunction with this supplemental announcement when applying for an award. Thus, in order to prepare a complete application, it is mandatory to comply with the requirements of the overall broad-based solicitation document, DE-PS36-00GO10482, which can be found on the Web site.
Date(s) Application Is Due Dec 15.
Contact Steven Chalk, Program Manager, (202) 586-3388; email: steven.chalk@ee.doe.gov
Internet http://www.eere.energy.gov/hydrogenandfuelcells/financial.html
Sponsor Department of Energy
1617 Cole Blvd
Golden, CO 80401

DOE Industrial Materials for the Future Program 1665
This program is a national effort to research, design, develop, engineer, and test new and improved materials to achieve improvements in energy efficiency, emissions and waste reduction, productivity, product quality, and global competitiveness.
Requirements Proposals are solicited from universities, and nonprofit research institutes for research and development leading to new materials and processing methods for eventual use in the Industries of the Future. Universities, and nonrofits are required to form partnerships for technology development and to work with industry to ensure that core activities will ultimately lead to successful applications in industry.
Amount $50,000-$500,000
Date(s) Application Is Due May 31.
Contact Polly Perando, Contract Specialist; email: polly.perando@ee.doe.gov
Internet http://www.tgci.com/fedrgtxt/01-11274.txt
Sponsor Department of Energy
850 Energy Dr, MS 1221
Idaho Falls, ID 83401-1563

DOE Inventions and Innovation Grant Program (I&I) 1666
The goal of the program is to improve energy efficiency through the promotion of innovative ideas and inventions that have a significant potential energy impact and a potential future commercial market. Additionally, DOE provides awardees with nonfinancial support by assisting them with business development and commercialization planning through a network of national and regional resource providers. This assistance is provided at three levels: Up to $50,000 for technologies in early-stage development, up to $250,000 for technologies approaching the point of prototype, and up to $500,000 for technology demonstrations. Cost-share is strongly encouraged to receive a Category 1 or 2 award, and cost-share is required to receive a Category 3 award. Funding Opportunity Number: DE-PS36-06GO96001
Requirements US individual inventors, small businesses (profit or nonprofit with less than 500 employees) may apply for category 1 or 2 applications. Universities and nonprofit research institutes may apply for category 1 applications.
Amount $50,000-$500,000
Date(s) Application Is Due Oct 11.
Contact Michael Schledorn, Grant Specialist, (303) 275-4993; email: goii@go.doe.gov
Internet http://www.eere.energy.gov/inventions
Sponsor Department of Energy--Golden Field Office
1617 Cole Blvd
Golden, CO 80401

DOE Low Dose Radiation Research Program 1667
Research is specifically sought for pilot projects that involve innovative collaborations between experimentalists and modelers to model the mechanisms of key radiation-induced

biological responses and to describe or identify strategies for developing biologically-based risk models that incorporate information on mechanisms of radiation-induced biological responses. Potential applicants should submit a one-page preapplication referencing Program Notice 01-17 by February 1; formal applications are due May 1. Annual deadline dates may change; contact program staff for exact dates.
Amount $10,000-$2 million range; $200,000 average
Date(s) Application Is Due Feb 1; May 1.
Contact Martin Rubinstein, Grants and Contracts Division, Office of Science, (301) 903-5212
Internet http://www.science.doe.gov/grants
Sponsor Department of Energy
19901 Germantown Rd
Germantown, MD 20874

DOE Materials Sciences and Engineering Research Grants **1668**
Research support is directed toward understanding materials properties and phenomena of importance to all energy systems. Emphasis is placed on areas where problems are known to exist or are anticipated. Research is supported in metallurgy, ceramics, solid state physics, materials chemistry, and related disciplines where the emphasis is on the science of materials. Applications are accepted at any time and are available on the Web site.
Requirements Eligible to apply are institutions of higher education, industry (particularly small and disadvantaged businesses), and nonprofit institutions. Unsolicited research proposals are screened by program officials and, if appropriate, are evaluated by peer review. Successful proposers are awarded one-year or multi-year special research contracts or grants with renewals or incremental funding available, provided performance has been satisfactory. A one- to two-year phase-out period is normally granted to those finishing research projects. Equipment items may be purchased from contract funds with the agreement of DOE.
Amount $10,000-$2 million; $200,000 average
Contact Martin R. Rubinstein, Supervisor of Grants and Contracts; (301) 903-4946; fax: (301) 903-4194; email: Martin.Rubinstein@science.doe.gov
Internet http://www.science.doe.gov/grants/FAPN08-01.html
Sponsor U.S. Department of Energy, Office of Basic Energy Sciences
19901 Germantown Road
Germantown, MD 20874-1290

DOE Mathematical, Information, and Computational Sciences Grants **1669**
This program supports a spectrum of fundamental research in applied mathematical sciences, computer science, and networking from basic through prototype development. Results of these efforts are used to form partnerships with users in scientific disciplines to validate the usefulness of the ideas and to develop them into tools. Testbeds on important applications for DOE are supported by this subprogram. Applications are accepted at any time, and application forms can be found on the Web site.
Amount $10,000-$2 million; $200,000 average
Date(s) Application Is Due May 31.
Contact Martin Rubinstein, Grants and Contracts Division, Office of Science, (301) 903- 5212
Internet http://www.er.doe.gov/production/grants/guide.html
Sponsor Department of Energy
19901 Germantown Rd
Germantown, MD 20874-1290

DOE Medical Applications and Measurement Science Grants **1670**
The objectives of this program are to develop technologies for the beneficial applications of radiation and in-vivo radiotracer detection in the study, diagnosis, and treatment of human diseases and disorders; to develop new instrumentation for biological and medical research; and to develop new concepts and techniques for detecting and measuring the hazardous agents of biochemical, physical, and environmental consequences related to energy production. Applications are accepted at any time; application forms are available on the Web site.
Amount $10,000-$2 million range; $200,000 average
Contact Martin R. Rubinstein, Grants and Contracts Division, Office of Science, (301) 903- 5212
Internet http://www.er.doe.gov/production/grants/guide.html
Sponsor Department of Energy
19901 Germantown Rd
Germantown, MD 20874

DOE Million Solar Roofs (MSR) Program **1671**
The purpose of this initiative is to install solar energy systems on one million US buildings. The department hopes to achieve this goal by establishing state and local MSR partnerships involving states and local governments, businesses, and community-based organizations to promote the use of solar roofs. Matching grants are not required, but will be considered in the application process.
Requirements Existing and new MSR state and local partnerships are eligible to apply.
Restrictions Partnerships that received funding under this program or the State Energy Program Special Projects Solicitation in the last fiscal year are ineligible.
Amount $10,000-$50,000
Contact Sandra Burton, (215) 656-6983; fax: (215) 656-6981; email: sandra.burton@ee.doe.gov
Internet http://www.millionsolarroofs.com
Sponsor Department of Energy
19901 Germantown Rd
Germantown, MD 20874

DOE Natural and Accelerated Bioremediation Research Program **1672**
DOE announces its interest in receiving applications for research grants in the Natural and Accelerated Bioremediation Research (NABIR) Program. Applications should describe research projects in one of the following categories: research projects that address the scientific aims of individual NABIR elements including biogeochemistry, biotransformation, community dynamics, biomolecular science and engineering, and assessment; or research projects to be performed at a field research center addressing field scale biostimulation of microbiological processes that immobilize metals and/or radionuclides. Interdisciplinary teams should include, at a minimum, experts in the fields of microbiology, geochemistry, and hydrology. Refer to program notice 02-12.
Amount $10,000-$2 million range; $200,000 average
Contact Dr. Anna Palmisano, Environmental Sciences Division, (301) 903-9963; fax: (301) 903-8519; email: anna.palmisano@science.doe.gov
Internet http://www.sc.doe.gov/production/grants/Fr02-12.html
Sponsor Department of Energy
19901 Germantown Rd
Germantown, MD 20874

DOE Nonproliferation and National Security Research **1673**
The purpose of the program is to conduct basic and applied research and development on verification technologies needed for effective treaty negotiations and for international agreements on the control of special nuclear materials, nuclear weapons, and weapons of mass destruction. Financial support, in whole or in part, may be provided for salaries, materials, supplies, equipment, travel, publication costs, services required for conducting research, and for developing advanced detection technologies. Contact DOE for deadlines.
Requirements Eligible to apply are public and private universities and institutions of higher education with postdoctoral programs.
Amount $100,000-$250,000 per year
Contact Paul Morrison, Office of Nonproliferation Research and Engineering (NA-22), (202) 586-5751
Internet http://www.nnsa.doe.gov/na-20
Sponsor Department of Energy
19901 Germantown Rd
Germantown, MD 20874

DOE Nuclear Energy Research Initiative (NERI) **1674**
NERI is designed to support innovative research, primarily to address the principal technical and scientific obstacles to future use of nuclear power in the United States. NERI is also intended to reinvigorate the vital nuclear scientific and engineering infrastructure within US universities, industry, and DOE national laboratories.
Requirements US universities or other institutions of higher learning, industry, nonprofit and R&D organizations are eligible for grant or cooperative agreement awards under this program. DOE national laboratories are eligible to participate, but not as the lead organization in the application. All segments of the US private sector (nonfederal) are eligible to apply. Non-citizens employed by US institutions also are eligible.
Amount $100,000-$500,000 range; $350,000 average
Contact Denise Berry, Contract Specialist, (510) 637-1873; fax: (510) 637-2025
Internet http://neri.ne.doe.gov
Sponsor Department of Energy
1301 Clay St, 700N
Oakland, CA 94612

DOE Nuclear Physics Research Grants **1675**
The primary objectives of this program are an understanding of the interactions and structures of atomic nuclei and nuclear matter, and an understanding of the fundamental forces of nature as manifested in nuclear matter. Applications are accepted at any time and are available on the Web site.
Requirements The DOE Nuclear Physics Program supports university-based user groups that plan experiments at the home institution, execute and partially analyze experiments at the national facility, and complete the analyses and publication of results at the home institution. Support of work under Nuclear Theory is almost equally divided between national laboratory-based theorists and university-based theorists. Written proposals for direct funding should be sent to the DOE. Written proposals for access to the accelerator installations should be sent to the director of the facility.
Amount $10,000-$2 million; $200,000 average
Date(s) Application Is Due May 31.
Contact Martin Rubinstein, Grants and Contracts Division, Office of Science, (301) 903- 5212
Internet http://www.science.doe.gov/production/grants/grants.html
Sponsor Department of Energy
19901 Germantown Rd
Germantown, MD 20874-1290

DOE On-Line Temperature Measurement Instrumentation for Gasification Process Control Development Grants **1676**

DOE seeks applications for innovative technical approaches to develop an accurate, reliable, robust, and cost-effective real-time temperature-monitoring system capable of measuring temperatures in the high temperature (typically ranging from 2000-2600F) section of pressurized, coal-fired slagging gasifiers. A variety of approaches, including the use of thermocouple or optically based techniques, are acceptable as long as they offer the clear potential to meet the aforementioned objectives. Furthermore, all proposed temperature measurement instrumentation must be suitable for use on large-scale slagging gasification systems and applications must address issues such as laboratory scale-up, potential placement, and method of mounting on actual operating systems. Solicitation DE-PS26-99FT40565.
Amount $10,000-$25 million range
Contact John Augustine, Program Director, (412) 386-4524
Internet http://www.netl.doe.gov
Sponsor Department of Energy
19901 Germantown Rd
Germantown, MD 20874

DOE Photochemistry and Radiation Research Grants **1677**

The program supports fundamental molecular-level research on interactions of radiation with matter in the condensed phase. The photochemistry research effort emphasizes fundamental processes aimed at the capture and chemical conversion of solar energy. The radiation sciences research effort supports fundamental studies on chemical effects produced by absorption of energy from ionizing radiation.
Requirements Eligible to apply are institutions of higher education, industry (particularly small and disadvantaged businesses), and nonprofit institutions. Unsolicited research proposals are screened by program officials and, if appropriate, are evaluated by peer review. Successful proposers are awarded one-year or multi-year special research contracts or grants with renewals or incremental funding available, provided performance has been satisfactory. A one- to two-year phase-out period is normally granted to those finishing research projects. Equipment items may be purchased from contract funds with the agreement of DOE.
Amount $10,000-$2 million; $200,000 average
Contact Dr. Eric A. Rohlfing, Director; (301) 903-8165; fax: (301) 903-4110; email: Eric.Rohlfing@science.doe.gov
Internet http://www.science.doe.gov/bes/chm/Programs/programs.html
Sponsor U.S. Department of Energy, Office of Science
1000 Independence Avenue, SW
Washington, DC 20585-1290

DOE Program for Ecosystem Research **1678**

The mission of this program is to improve the scientific basis for predicting or detecting effects of simultaneous changes in climate and atmospheric composition on terrestrial ecosystems and their component organisms and processes. Ecosystem processes and components of importance to humanity are of special concern. Climatic and atmospheric changes of key interest include (but need not be limited to): warming (and changes in diurnal, seasonal, and interannual temperature cycles), changes in precipitation and evapotranspiration (e.g., intensification of the hydrologic cycle), changes in frequency and/or magnitude of extreme weather events and patterns, and rising atmospheric carbon dioxide and ozone concentrations. Potential applicants are strongly encouraged (but not required) to submit a preapplication for programmatic review. The deadline for preapplications is July 2; deadline for receipt of formal applications is August 13. Annual deadline dates may vary; contact program staff for exact dates.
Amount $10,000-$2 million; $200,000 average
Date(s) Application Is Due Jul 2; Aug 13.
Contact Martin Rubinstein, Grants and Contracts Division, Office of Science, (301) 903- 5212
Internet http://www.tgci.com/fedrgtxt/01-12539.txt
Sponsor Department of Energy
19901 Germantown Rd
Germantown, MD 20874-1290

DOE Programs in Fusion Energy Sciences **1679**

DOE announces its interest in receiving grant applications for new research in fusion energy sciences. The specific areas of interest are Magnetic Fusion Concept Exploration Experiments; Inertial Fusion Energy Concept Exploration Research; Inertial Fusion Energy Chamber and Target Research; Magnetic Fusion Liquid Wall Experiments; and Fusion Materials Modeling. Annual deadlines may vary; contact program staff for exact dates. Refer to program notice 00-07.
Requirements Colleges and universities, nonprofit organizations, for-profit commercial organizations, State and local governments, and unaffiliated individuals.
Amount $10,000-$2 million; $200,000 average
Contact Martin Rubinstein, Grants and Contracts Division, Office of Science, (301) 903-5212
Internet http://www.science.doe.gov/production/grants/grants.html
Sponsor Department of Energy
19901 Germantown Rd
Germantown, MD 20874

DOE Rebuild America Energy-Efficiency Grants **1680**

The Rebuild America program aims to increase the energy efficiency of commercial buildings and multifamily housing in the United States. Partnerships must include at least one state or local government member, as well as businesses, educational institutions, and nonprofits. Projects must apply retrofit improvements to a substantial portion of the floor space of targeted buildings, such as schools, offices, libraries, churches, stores, hospitals, and correctional facilities, within five years of the grant award.
Contact John Meeker, Procurement, (303) 275-4748; fax: (303) 275-4754
Internet http://www.rebuild.org/index.asp
Sponsor Department of Energy
1617 Cole Blvd
Golden, CO 80401

DOE Reliable Electric Power Delivery Research Grants **1681**

Under this program of the Electric Energy Systems Division, recent breakthroughs in new materials and control concepts show the potential for significantly improving our ability to maintain electric power continuity during periods of severe emergencies. New research is needed in such areas as electromagnetic pulse protection, basic mechanisms of insulation failure, emergency detection and control, new systems analysis and equipment research, and system dynamic performance. Proposals are accepted at any time.
Amount $50,000-$500,000; $200,000 average
Contact Office of Utility Technologies, (202) 586-4142
Internet http://www.eere.energy.gov
Sponsor Department of Energy
1000 Independence Ave SW, Forrestal Bldg
Washington, DC 20585

DOE Separations and Analysis Research Grants **1682**

This Program supports fundamental research covering a broad spectrum of separation concepts, including membrane processes, extraction under both standard and supercritical conditions, adsorption, chromatography, photo-dissociation, and complexation. Also supported is work to improve the sensitivity, reliability, and productivity of analytical determinations and to develop entirely new approaches to analysis. This activity is the Nation's most significant long-term investment in many aspects of separations and analysis, including solvent extraction, ion exchange, and mass spectrometry.
Requirements Eligible to apply are institutions of higher education, industry (particularly small and disadvantaged businesses), and nonprofit institutions. Unsolicited research proposals are screened by program officials and, if appropriate, are evaluated by peer review. Successful proposers are awarded one-year or multi-year special research contracts or grants with renewals or incremental funding available, provided performance has been satisfactory. A one- to two-year phase-out period is normally granted to those finishing research projects. Equipment items may be purchased from contract funds with the agreement of DOE.
Amount $10,000-$2 million; $200,000 average
Contact Dr. Eric A. Rohlfing, Director; (301) 903-8165; fax: (301) 903-4110; email: Eric.Rohlfing@science.doe.gov
Internet http://www.science.doe.gov/bes/chm/Programs/programs.html
Sponsor U.S. Department of Energy, Office of Science
1000 Independence Avenue, SW
Washington, DC 20585-1290

DOE Small Business Innovation Research (SBIR) Commercialization Assistance Program **1683**

The purpose of this program is to accelerate the development, demonstration, and commercialization of products, services, or technology resulting from the research of SBIR Phase II financial assistance award recipients. The major objective of the program is to provide individualized assistance to SBIR Phase II financial assistance recipients that will lead to the successful commercialization of products, services, or technology developed in the SBIR program.
Requirements Small businesses are eligible to apply.
Amount $750,000 maximum
Date(s) Application Is Due Dec 2.
Contact Grants Administrator, (301) 903-1414; email: sbir-sttr@science.doe.gov
Internet http://www.science.doe.gov/sbir
Sponsor Department of Energy
9800 S Cass Ave
Argonne, IL 60439-4899

DOE State Energy Program Special Projects **1684**

The goal of this project is to assist states in deploying energy-efficient and renewable energy technologies; to facilitate the acceptance of emerging and underutilized technologies; and to increase the responsiveness of federally funded technology development efforts to private sector energy needs. DOE is providing funding in the areas of Clean Cities/Alternative Fuels, Industrial Technologies, Codes and Standards, Rebuild America, Federal Energy Management Program, Hydrogen Reformer Field Verification, Building America, Wind Energy Case Studies, Biomass Power Projects, and Photovoltaic Projects.
Requirements All 50 states plus the District of Columbia, the US Virgin Islands, Puerto Rico, Guam, Samoa, and the Commonwealth of the Northern Mariana Islands may apply.

Amount $20,000-$1 million range; $17 million total
Contact John Millhone, Weatherization and Intergovernmental Program, Department of Energy, (202) 586-1510
Internet http://12.46.245.173/pls/portal30/CATALOG.PROGRAM_TEXT_RPT.show
Sponsor Department of Energy
1000 Independence Ave SW
Washington, DC 20585

DOE University Coal Research Grants **1685**
The grants are awarded to improve scientific and technical understanding of the chemistry and physics involved in the conversion and utilization of coal, furnish technical support for the ongoing and developing coal conversion process, produce clear fuels in an environmentally acceptable manner, and develop new approaches to the design of future coal conversion and utilization technologies. Proposals should be submitted to the National Energy Technology Laboratory, Attn: MS921-107, Department of Energy, P.O. Box 10940, 626 Cochrans Mill Road, Pittsburgh, PA.
Requirements US institutions of higher education may apply for these grants.
Amount $50,000-$400,000; $154,000 average
Contact Fred Glaser, Office of Advanced Research, (301) 903-2786
Internet http://www.netl.doe.gov/coal/Advanced%20Research
Sponsor Department of Energy
1000 Independence Ave SW, Forrestal Bldg
Washington, DC 20585

DOE University Nuclear Science and Reactor Support **1686**
The purpose of this program is to provide financial support for research design, analysis, and assessments in science and technology in fields related to nuclear energy. Project grant funds may be used in support of nuclear energy-related research and development financial support, in whole or in part, may be provided for salaries, materials, supplies, equipment, travel, publication costs, supporting costs required for technical activities, market analyses, financing plans, and other activities necessary to achieve the objective.
Requirements Any individual, partnership, corporation, association, joint venture, institution of higher education, or nonprofit organization may apply.
Amount $50,000-$300,000 range
Contact Nancy Hebron-Isreal , Office of Nuclear Energy, Science and Technology, (301) 903-1536
Internet http://nuclear.gov
Sponsor Department of Energy
19901 Germantown Rd
Germantown, MD 20874

DOE University Reactor Instrumentation (URI) Program **1687**
The purpose of this program is to upgrade and improve the US university nuclear research and training reactors and to contribute to strengthening the academic community's nuclear engineering infrastructure.
Requirements US colleges and universities having a duly licensed, operating nuclear research or training reactor are eligible to apply.
Contact Suzette Olson, DOE Idaho Operations Office, (208) 526-7385; fax: (208) 526-5548; email: Suzette.Olson@nuclear.energy.gov
Internet http://www.id.doe.gov/doeid/psd/proc-div.html
Sponsor Department of Energy, Idaho Operations Office
P.O. Box 1625, MS 3860
Idaho Falls, ID 83415-3860

DOE Vehicle and Engine Research and Development Grants **1688**
The grants support research to reduce the transportation sector's vulnerability to petroleum shortages by developing more energy-efficient vehicle propulsion system options and by developing the ability to switch from petroleum to electricity and alternative fuels. Emphasis is placed on advancing heat engine technology through the development of component and materials technologies; supporting long-term, high-risk technology research and development for petroleum savings in the heavy-duty transport sector; advancing electric and hybrid vehicle technology; and developing means of using alternative fuels in vehicles. Identified potential areas for new research initiatives may be requested from one of the program information contacts. Proposals are accepted at any time. For further information on specific programs and prior to submitting formal proposals, contact Advanced Heat Engines, (202) 252-8012; Heavy Duty Transport, (202) 252-8055; Alternative Fuels, (202) 252-8055; and Electric and Hybrid Vehicles, (202) 252-8044.
Amount $50,000-$500,000
Contact Polly Perando, Energy Efficiency and Renewable Energy Program, email: polly.perando@ee.doe.gov
Internet http://www.eere.energy.gov
Sponsor Department of Energy
1000 Independence Ave SW, Forrestal Bldg
Washington, DC 20585

DOI African Elephant Conservation Grants **1689**
The program objectives are to provide financial assistance to any organization or individual responsible for African elephant conservation and to any organization or individual with experience in African elephant conservation, for approved projects to support research, conservation, management, and protection of African elephants. Funds may be used for approved conservation projects. Funds are matched by nonfederal funds or in-kind support, which must be equal to or exceed the amount of federal funds provided.
Requirements Individuals and public or private organizations with experience in African elephant conservation may apply. All private sector project proposals must contain evidence of support by governmental entities of countries where the project is to be conducted.
Amount $50,000 average
Contact Division of International Conservation, (703) 358-1754
Internet http://international.fws.gov/grants/grants.html
Sponsor Department of the Interior
4401 N Fairfax Dr, Rm 730
Arlington, VA 22203

DOI Biological Resource Division Brucellosis Program **1690**
Applications are invited for a research project on the improvements in ballistic delivery systems for brucellosis vaccination of free-ranging elk and bison of the Greater Yellowstone area. The purpose of this project is to develop methods of ballistic delivery that improve the distance, reliability, ease, and/or rapidity of brucella vaccine parenteral delivery.
Requirements Applications may be submitted by educational institutions, private firms, private foundations, individuals, and agencies of state and local governments.
Amount $1000-$582,000; $50,000 average
Contact Branch of Acquisition and Federal Assistance; (703) 648-7478 or (703) 648-7361
Internet http://www.usgs.gov/contracts
Sponsor Department of the Interior
P.O. Box 25046, MS 204B
Denver, CO 80225

DOI Earthquake Hazards Reduction Research Grants **1691**
Applications are being sought for grants for research projects under the National Earthquake Hazards Reduction Program to mitigate earthquake losses that can occur in many parts of the nation by providing earth science data and assessments essential for warning of imminent damaging earthquakes, land-use planning, engineering design, and emergency preparedness decisions. Specific objectives are identified in the annual program announcement.
Requirements Colleges, universities, for-profit and nonprofit organizations, and state and local governments may submit applications for support by a named principal investigator.
Amount $5887-$1.1 million; $76,474 average
Date(s) Application Is Due May 10.
Contact Michael Blanpied, Earthquake Hazards Program Office, US Geological Survey, National Center, (703) 648-6696; fax: (703) 648-6642; email: gd-erp-coordinator@usgs.gov
Internet http://aspe.os.dhhs.gov/cfda/p15807.htm
Sponsor Department of the Interior
12201 Sunrise Valley Dr
Reston, VA 22092

DOI Geological Research and Data Acquisition Grants **1692**
Project grants are awarded to support research in any field of study that helps fulfill the Geological Survey's mission, which is to collect, organize, interpret, and publish information about the nation's energy, minerals, water, and land resources; to determine the geologic structure of the United States; and to develop an understanding of earth processes and hydrologic principles. Applications must be for scientific research projects that are within the survey's area of responsibility. Conferences and symposia will be supported only if it is clear that equivalent results cannot be obtained at regular meetings of professional societies. Cost sharing is encouraged. Applications may be presented at any time.
Requirements Colleges, universities, profit-making and nonprofit organizations, and state and local governments may make application for support by a named principal investigator.
Restrictions Office furniture, office equipment, and foreign travel are not normally considered for support.
Amount $1000-$582,000; $50,000 average
Contact Assistant Director for Research, US Geological Survey, National Center, (703) 648-4460
Internet http://www.usgs.gov/contracts
Sponsor Department of the Interior
12201 Sunrise Valley Dr
Reston, VA 22092

DOI National Center for Preservation Technology and Training Grants **1693**
The objectives of the program are to develop and distribute preservation and conservation skills and technologies for the identification, evaluation, conservation, and interpretation of prehistoric and historic resources; to develop and facilitate training for federal, state, and local resource preservation professionals, cultural resource managers, maintenance

personnel, and others working in the preservation field; to apply preservation technology benefits from ongoing research by other agencies and institutions; to facilitate the transfer of preservation technology among federal agencies, state and local governments, universities, international organizations, and the private sector; and to cooperate with related international organizations including, but not limited to, the International Council on Monuments and Sites, the International Center for the Study of Preservation and Restoration of Cultural Property, and the International Council of Museums.
Requirements Eligible applicants are universities and colleges; nonprofit organizations, including museums, research laboratories, professional societies, and similar organizations that are directly associated with educational or research activities; federal and nonfederal laboratories; offices, units, and Cooperative Park Study Units of the National Park System; federal, state, local, and tribal preservation offices; and Native Hawaiian organizations. For-profit organizations and individuals are eligible provided their proposal partners with an eligible entity to be the recipient.
Amount $7856-$50,000; $36,000 average
Contact Kirk Cordell, Executive Director, (318) 356-7444 ext 222; fax: (318) 356-9119; email: kirk_cordell@nps.gov
Internet http://www.ncptt.nps.gov/default.aspx?m=36
Sponsor Department of the Interior
1849 C St NW
Washington, DC 20240

DOI National Spatial Data Infrastructure Cooperative Agreements Program Grants **1694**
The objectives of the program are to help the Federal Geographic Data Committee form partnerships with the nonfederal sector that will further the development and implementation of the National Spatial Data Infrastructure. NSDI means the technology, policies, standards, and human resources necessary to acquire, process, store, distribute, and improve utilization of geospatial data. Partnership activities must be directed towards the creation of the National Geospatial Data Clearinghouse for finding and accessing geospatial data; the development and promulgation of the use of standards in data collection, documentation, transfer, and search and query; the development and creation of a National Digital Geospatial Data Framework; and/or the development and implementation of educational outreach programs to increase awareness and understanding of the major NSDI initiatives.
Requirements Proposals from federal, state and local government agencies, educational institutions, private firms, private foundations, nonprofit organizations and federally acknowledged or state-recognized Native American tribes or groups are invited. Proposals must demonstrate that more than one organization or agency is involved in the project.
Amount $20,000-$75,000 range; $29,000 average
Date(s) Application Is Due May 15.
Contact David Painter, FGDC CAP Coordinator, (703) 648-5513; fax: (703) 648-5755; email: dpainter@fgdc.gov
Internet http://www.fgdc.gov/funding/cap2002.html
Sponsor Department of the Interior
Mail Stop 590, 12201 Sunrise Valley Dr
Reston, VA 20192

DOI Rhinoceros and Tiger Conservation Grants **1695**
The objectives of the program are to increase conservation of rhinoceros and tigers through strengthening habitat/ecosystem management; surveys and monitoring; conservation education; wildlife inspection, law enforcement, and forensic skills; protected area/reserve management; sustainable development in buffer zones surrounding tiger/rhinoceros habitat; management of human behavior and livestock to decrease conflicts with tigers/rhinoceros; and the use of substitute for tiger/rhinoceros products in oriental medicine. Projects which provide training to strengthen capabilities in these areas will receive priority. Funds may be used for approved conservation projects. Projects proposed should have the support of the local government(s) and have matching funds (cash) or in-kind support (salaries, equipment, etc.) provided by the organization receiving the grant or other partners. Project duration must be one year or less. Proposals may be submitted at any time.
Requirements US public and private nonprofit institutions and organizations are eligible.
Amount $50,000 maximum
Contact Division of International Conservation, (703) 358-1754; fax: (703) 358-2849
Internet http://www.fws.gov/international/grants/grants.html
Sponsor Department of the Interior
4401 N Fairfax Dr
Arlington, VA 22203

DOI State Partnership Program Grants **1696**
The purpose of the SPP is to provide support through grants and cooperative agreements to states and tribal agencies whose primary focus is on gathering, analyzing, and distributing biological science information needed for natural resource management decision making. This program requires complementary study participation and interaction between state/tribal institutions and science centers or cooperative research units of the USGS, Eastern Region. Eligible institutions may request a preproposal solicitation package. Preproposals must be submitted to USGS by state/tribe institutions only, but must include information on participating USGS Science Center or Cooperative Research Unit. Full proposals will be requested in writing by the USGS from institutions that have submitted preproposals of high merit and who have met all of the preproposal requirements. Guidelines are available online.
Requirements State, tribal, and/or US territories and possessions that conduct natural resources studies and associated information management are eligible to apply.
Restrictions No federal or private agencies may apply.
Amount $4000-$300,000 range; $50,000 average
Contact Gary Brewer, State Partnership Program Coordinator, (304) 724-4507; fax: (304) 724-4505; email: gary_brewer@usgs.gov
Internet http://www.doi.gov
Sponsor Department of the Interior
1849 C St NW
Washington, DC 20240

DOI Upper Mississippi River System Long-Term Resource Monitoring Program Grants **1697**
The mission of this program is to provide decision makers with information needed to maintain the Upper Mississippi River System (UMRS) as a sustainable large river ecosystem given its multiple-use character. The long-term goals of this program are to: understand the UMRS ecosystem, monitor trends and effects with respect to selected resources, develop resource management alternatives, manage information, and develop useful products. This is a 15-year program. There are no deadlines.
Requirements Eligible to apply are states, local governments, intrastate/interstate agencies, sponsored organizations, private nonprofit institutions/organizations.
Amount $392,426 average
Contact Dr. Leslie Holland-Bartels, Center Director, Upper Midwest Environmental Sciences Center, (608) 781-6221; fax: (608) 783-6066; fax: (608) 783-6066; email: Leslie_Holland-Bartels@usga.gov
Internet http://www.umesc.usgs.gov/ltrmp.html
Sponsor Department of the Interior
2630 Fanta Reed Rd
La Crosse, WI 54603

DOJ Corrections Technical Assistance Grants **1698**
This program provides assistance for upgrading the operation of correctional facilities, programs, and services at State and local levels. Services are available to the entire range of correctional agencies, including probation, parole, institutions, jails, and community programs. The purpose is to encourage and assist federal, state, and local government programs and services, and programs and services of other public and private agencies, institutions, and organizations in their efforts to develop and implement improved corrections programs. It also seeks to assist and serve in a consulting capacity to federal, state, and local courts, departments, and agencies in the development, maintenance, and coordination of programs, facilities, services, training, treatment, and rehabilitation with respect to criminal and juvenile offenders.
Requirements States, general units of local government, public and private agencies, educational institutions, organizations, and individuals involved in the development, implementation or operation of correctional programs and services are eligible.
Amount $1500-$50,000; $7500 average
Date(s) Application Is Due Jul 30.
Contact Grants Administrator, (202) 307- 3106 or (800) 995-6423; fax: (202) 307-3361; TDD: (202) 307- 3156
Internet http://www.usdoj.gov
Sponsor Department of Justice
320 First St NW
Washington, DC 20534

DOJ Grants to Reduce Violent Crimes Against Women on Campus **1699**
The purpose of this program is to encourage institutions of higher education to adopt comprehensive, coordinated responses to violence against women, including sexual assault, stalking, dating and domestic violence. Funds are authorized to enhance the apprehension, investigation, and adjudication of persons committing violent crimes against women on campuses; train campus administrators, security personnel, and disciplinary or judicial boards to effectively identify and respond to violent crimes against women on campuses; implement and operate education programs for the prevention of violent crimes against women on campuses; develop, enlarge or strengthen support services for victims; create, disseminate, or otherwise provide assistance and information about victims' options on and off campus to bring disciplinary or other legal action; develop and implement more effective campus policies, protocols, orders, and services specifically devoted to prevent, identify, and respond to violent crimes against women on campuses; develop, install, or expand data collection and communication systems, including computerized systems, linking campus security to the local law enforcement for the purpose of identifying and tracking arrests, protection orders, violations of protection orders, prosecutions, and convictions; develop, enlarge or strengthen victim service programs for the campus and to improve the delivery of victim services on campus; provide capital improvements (including improved lighting and communication facilities but excluding construction of buildings) on campuses to address violent crimes against women; and to support improved coordination among campus administrators, campus security personnel, and local law enforcement to reduce violent crimes against women on campuses.

Requirements Eligible applicants for this program are institutions of higher education as defined under the Higher Education Amendments of 1998. A consortium of higher education institutions also may apply for these grants provided that each individual consortium member is also eligible to apply.
Amount $143,000-$550,000; $360,000 average
Contact Violence Against Women Office, (202) 307-6026; fax (202) 307-3911; TTY: (202) 307-2277
Internet http://www.ojp.usdoj.gov/vawo/campus_desc.htm
Sponsor Department of Justice
810 Seventh St NW
Washington, DC 20531

DOJ Juvenile Justice and Delinquency Prevention Special Emphasis Grants 1700
Grants support investigative research into and the development and implementation of programs that design, test, and demonstrate effective approaches, techniques, and methods for preventing and controlling juvenile delinquency, such as community-based alternatives to institutional confinement; developing and implementing effective means of diverting juveniles from the traditional juvenile justice and correctional system; developing and supporting programs stressing advocacy activities aimed at improving services to youth impacted by the juvenile justice system; developing model programs to strengthen and maintain the family unit, including self-help programs; developing and implementing special emphasis prevention and treatment programs relating to juveniles who commit serious crimes; developing programs to prevent hate crimes; and developing and implementing further a coordinated, national law-related education program of delinquency prevention. Deadlines are published in program announcements.
Requirements Public and private nonprofit agencies, organizations, individuals, state and local units of government, and combinations of state and local units are eligible to apply.
Contact Office of Juvenile Justice and Delinquency Prevention, (202) 307-5914; email: AskDOJ@usdoj.gov
Internet http://www.usdoj.gov
Sponsor Department of Justice
950 Pennsylvania Ave NW
Washington, DC 20530-0001

DOJ National Incident-Based Reporting System 1701
The purpose of this program is to provide funding for states and units of local government to help create a uniform national standard for reporting crime trends that go beyond simple tallies of crimes and arrests, including as much detailed information about the individual crimes as possible. Funds may be used to develop or enhance NIBRS data collection programs; develop or provide NIBRS training programs, including attending conferences; and develop, implement, or license software that supports NIBRS data collection. A 10 percent matching grant is required from applicants.
Requirements Eligible applicants are states applying at the state level or on behalf of one or more cities or counties. States may apply on behalf of more than one jurisdiction.
Restrictions Funds may not be used to purchase equipment or to pay salaries or overtime for persons attending NIBRS training sessions.
Contact Dr. Charles Kindermann, Senior Statistician, (202) 616-3489; Carol Kaplan, Chief, Criminal History Improvement Programs, (202) 307-0759
Internet http://www.ojp.usdoj.gov/bjs/ibrs.htm
Sponsor Department of Justice
Bureau of Justice Statistics, Rm 2406, 810 7th St
Washington, DC 20531

DOJ National Institute for Juvenile Justice and Delinquency Prevention Grants 1702
The objective of the grants is to encourage, coordinate, and conduct research and evaluation of juvenile justice and delinquency prevention activities; to provide for public and private agencies, institutions, justice system agencies, a clearinghouse and information center for collecting, disseminating, publishing, and distributing information on juvenile delinquency; to conduct national training programs of juvenile-related issues and provide technical assistance and training to federal, state, and local governments, courts, corrections, law enforcement, probation, public and private agencies, institutions, and individuals in the planning, establishment, funding, operation, or evaluation of juvenile delinquency programs. Deadlines are published in program announcements.
Requirements Public or private agencies, organizations, and individuals are eligible to apply.
Contact Office of Juvenile Justice and Delinquency Prevention, (202) 307-5940; email: AskDOJ@usdoj.gov
Internet http://www.usdoj.gov/10grants/index.html
Sponsor Department of Justice
950 Pennsylvania Ave NW
Washington, DC 20530-0001

DOJ National Institute of Corrections Training and Staff Development Grants 1703
The grants provide assistance to devise and conduct in various geographical locations seminars, workshops, and training programs for law enforcement officers, judges and judicial personnel, probation and parole personnel, correctional personnel, welfare workers, and other personnel, including lay ex-offenders and paraprofessionals, connected with the treatment and rehabilitation of criminal and juvenile offenders. In addition, the grants develop technical training teams to aid in the development of seminars, workshops, and training programs within the several states and with the state and local agencies that work with prisoners, parolees, probationers, and other offenders.
Requirements States, general units of local government, as well as public and private agencies, educational institutions, organizations, and individuals involved in the development, implementation, or operation of correctional programs and services are eligible to apply.
Amount $1500-$300,000; $100,000 average
Contact Staff Development Branch, National Institute of Corrections, (202) 307-3106 or (800) 995-6423; fax: (202) 307-3361; email: AskDOJ@usdoj.gov
Internet http://www.usdoj.gov/10grants/index.html
Sponsor Department of Justice
950 Pennsylvania Ave NW
Washington, DC 20530-0001

DOJ National Institute of Justice Graduate Research Fellowships 1704
The fellowships are intended to improve the quality and quantity of knowledge about crime and the criminal justice system, while helping to increase the number of persons who are qualified to teach in collegiate criminal justice programs; to conduct research related to criminal justice issues; and help such persons perform more effectively within the criminal justice system. A fellowship is funded for up to two years. Applications may be submitted at any time throughout the year. Proposals will be due and subsequently reviewed three times a year, in February, June, and October, with funding decisions made within 60-90 days of the review date.
Requirements Applicants must be accredited institutions of higher education offering doctoral degree programs. Eligible students are doctoral candidates engaged in dissertation research and writing on a problem relating to law enforcement, crime, or criminal justice. This competitive program provides fellowship stipends, major project costs, and certain university fees.
Amount $20,000 stipend
Contact Sarah Hart, Director, National Institute of Justice, (202) 307-2942; fax: (202) 307-6394
Internet http://www.ojp.usdoj.gov/nij/funding.htm
Sponsor Department of Justice
810 Seventh St, NW
Washington, DC 20531

DOJ National Institute of Justice Research, Development, and Evaluation Project Grants 1705
The grants encourage and support research and development for further understanding of the causes and control of crime and improvement of the criminal justice system. The funds may be used to conduct research and development pertaining to these objectives, including the development of new or improved approaches, techniques, and systems; carry out programs of research on the causes of crime and means of preventing crime; and evaluate criminal justice programs and procedures. In addition to larger grant requests, the institute invites proposals for smaller funding amounts, including grants of less than $50,000 across all goals and subject areas in criminal justice. Each year, NIJ announces its program plan of research opportunities with specific deadline dates and contacts for each program. Contact the program office for guidelines.
Requirements Grants and contracts may be made to and with state and local governments, profit and nonprofit organizations, institutions of higher education, and qualified individuals. Territories of the United States are also eligible to participate in this program.
Contact National Institute of Justice, (202) 307-2942; fax: (202) 307-6394
Internet http://www.ojp.usdoj.gov/fundopps.htm
Sponsor Department of Justice
810 Seventh St NW
Washington, DC 20531

DOJ National Institute of Justice Visiting Fellowships 1706
Fellowships provide opportunities for experienced criminal justice practitioners and researchers to pursue projects aimed at improved understanding of crime, delinquency, and criminal justice administration by sponsoring research projects of their own creation and design. Funds may be used to conduct research on crime causation, crime measurements, crime prevention, law enforcement, criminal justice administration, and the effectiveness and efficiency of anti-crime programs. Juvenile delinquency research projects also are eligible for support under this program. Fellows conduct their studies while based at NIJ. Concept papers may be submitted at any time. Applicants should anticipate a decision time frame of six to nine months from concept paper to award. Fellowship guidelines are available at no charge by sending a self-addressed mailing label to Announcement-Visiting Fellowship Program, NCJRS, Box 6000, Rockville, MD 20849-6000, or by phone (800) 851-3420.
Requirements Fellowships are awarded to individuals or to their parent agencies or organizations. Generally, professionals working in the criminal justice field, including university- or college-based academic researchers and upper-level managers in criminal justice agencies are eligible.
Contact National Institute of Justice, Department of Justice, (202) 307-2942
Internet http://www.usdoj.gov/nij

Sponsor Department of Justice
810 Seventh St NW
Washington, DC 20531

DOJ/NIJ Violence Against Women Research Grants **1707**
NIJ's Violence Against Women and Family Violence program provides funds for research and evaluation, including research fellowships. The program's objectives are to estimate the scope of violence against women and family violence, identify their causes and consequences, evaluate promising prevention and intervention programs, disseminate research results to the field, and build partnerships among a wide variety of disciplines to accomplish these objectives. Visit the Web site for current solicitations for these programs.
Amount $1.25 million total
Contact Leora Rosen, Program Manager, (202) 616-2452; email: Leora.Rosen@usdoj.gov
Internet http://www.ojp.usdoj.gov/nij/vawprog/funding.html
Sponsor Department of Justice
810 Seventh St NW
Washington, DC 20531

Dolores Zohrab Liebmann Fellowships **1708**
The fellowships are awarded to graduate degree candidates who have outstanding undergraduate records, have demonstrated a need for financial assistance, are enrolled in selected US college and universities, are US citizens, and have received baccalaureate degrees. Applications are mailed to selected schools in late fall.
Requirements The dean of the school must nominate qualified candidates.
Date(s) Application Is Due Jan 31.
Contact Fellowships Administrator, c/o JPMorgan Private Bank, Philanthropic Services, (212) 789-5682; email: jones_ed_l@jpmorgan.com
Internet http://fdncenter.org/grantmaker/liebmann
Sponsor Dolores Zohrab Liebmann Fund
345 Park Ave, 4th Fl
New York, NY 10154

Donaghue Investigator Program Grants **1709**
The program supports particularly promising medical researchers holding faculty appointments at Connecticut institutions. The funding emphasis is on the investigator and his or her program of research rather than on a specific study. Approximately four to six awards will be made each year.
Requirements A prototypical recipient will be committed to pursuing his or her career in Connecticut for the foreseeable future; show potential for an outstanding independent research career, and for leadership in his or her field(s) of research; be accepting of the importance of earning support for research by actively explaining to the public his or her field of work and specific results and their value; be enthusiastic about and committed to disciplinary and interinstitutional collaboration in integrative research; be strongly supported by his or her institution; and possess evidence of external recognition of his or her work.
Amount $100,000 maximum for five years
Contact Lynne Garner, (860) 521-9011 ext 11; fax: (860) 521-9018; email: garner@donaghue.org
Internet http://www.donaghue.org/granttype.htm
Sponsor Patrick and Catherine Weldon Donaghue Medical Research Foundation
18 N Main St
West Hartford, CT 06107

Donaghue Practical Benefit Initiatives Grants **1710**
The foundation initiates research projects showing particular promise for producing practical benefit to human health and works in an interactive process with prospective investigators to develop projects for funding. Organizations with project ideas aimed at productive ways to deliver practical benefit to the public through health research should submit a short summary letter. There is no specific timeline for application or designated grant award amount.
Contact Director of Operations, (860) 521-9011; fax: (860) 521-9018; email: office@donaghue.org
Internet http://www.donaghue.org
Sponsor Patrick and Catherine Weldon Donaghue Medical Research Foundation
18 N Main St
West Hartford, CT 06107-1919

Donald and Sylvia Robinson Family Foundation Grants **1711**
The foundation awards grants to US nonprofit organizations in its areas of interest, including animal and wildlife protection, arms control, arts (general, performing arts, and visual arts), environmental conservation and protection, eye diseases and eye research, family planning and human reproductive health, food distribution, international affairs, Israel, Jewish social services, and social service delivery programs. Types of support include annual campaigns, building construction/renovation, capital campaigns, and general operating support. There are no application deadlines or forms.
Requirements National nonprofit organizations are eligible to apply.
Restrictions Individuals are ineligible.
Contact Donald Robinson, (412) 661-1200; fax: (412) 661-4645
Sponsor Donald and Sylvia Robinson Family Foundation
6507 Wilkins Ave
Pittsburgh, PA 15217

Donald P. Eckman Award **1712**
This award is given for outstanding accomplishments by a young engineer in the field of automatic control. Nominees must be younger than 35 years on January 1 of the year of the award and have made contributions to the field while residing in the United States. Contributions may be technical or scientific publications, theses, patents, inventions, or combinations or the above in the field of automatic control. The award consists of a certificate and honorarium, which are presented at the annual conference. Nomination forms as well as additional information may be obtained from the AACC secretary.
Requirements Nomination packages should consist of letter of nomination, three to five letters of reference, current resume, current list of publications and patents, any other supporting material, and nomination form. The nomination letter should clearly identify the primary reason that the nominee should receive the award, as well as up to four ancillary reasons. All materials should be submitted in a single package.
Date(s) Application Is Due Dec 1.
Contact AACC Secretariat, c/o Department of Electrical Engineering, Wright State University, (937) 775-5062; fax: (937) 775-3936; email: pmisra@cs.wright.edu
Internet http://www.a2c2.org/awards/index.php
Sponsor American Automatic Control Council
3640 Col Glenn Hwy
Dayton, OH 45435

Donald Q. Kern Award in Heat Transfer or Energy Conversion **1713**
This award is given annually by the Heat Transfer and Energy Conversion Division of AIChE for expertise in a given field of heat transfer or energy conversion. Special emphasis is given to recognition of contributions that have had significant practical applications. A plaque accompanies the award. The recipient will be required to prepare a written review covering an area selected by the recipient.
Requirements Three to five supporting letters are required that discuss specific contributions by the nominee and the reasons for their value.
Amount $1500
Date(s) Application Is Due Jun 1.
Contact AIChE Awards Programs, (212) 591-7107; fax: (212) 591-8882; email: awards@aiche.org
Internet http://www.aiche.org/awards/awarddtl.asp?AwardID=40
Sponsor American Institute of Chemical Engineers
3 Park Ave
New York, NY 10016-5901

Dora Brahms Historic Preservation and Restoration Award **1714**
One award is made on a biennial basis to educational institutions on behalf of their students in historic preservation and/or restoration studies, to encourage and support the advancement of professional activities in historic preservation and/or restoration. Institutions must illustrate how the award will best assist the student and the historic preservation and design education community.
Amount $3000
Date(s) Application Is Due Mar 26.
Contact Grants Administrator, (202) 546-3480; fax: (202) 546-3240; email: asid@asid.org
Internet http://www.asid.org/learning/asid_ed_foundation/awards_ed.asp
Sponsor American Society of Interior Designers Educational Foundation Inc
608 Massachusetts Ave NE
Washington, DC 20002-6006

Doreen Kronick Scholarship **1715**
This scholarship is awarded annually to a graduate student in a program that will lead to the recipient's being able to assist persons with learning disabilities. Application forms are available from the association or the faculty of graduate studies at Canadian universities.
Requirements Any student, 18 or older, enrolled in any graduate program of any university in Canada is eligible.
Restrictions Scholarship recipients will not be eligible to reapply for three years.
Amount $C500
Date(s) Application Is Due May 15.
Contact Kronick Scholarships, (613) 238-5721; fax: (613) 235-5391; email: information@ldac-taac.ca
Internet http://www.ldac-taac.ca/Scholarships/scholarships-e.asp
Sponsor Learning Disabilities Association of Canada
323 Chapel St, Ste 200
Ottawa, ON K1N 7Z2 Canada

Doris Duke Charitable Foundation Clinical Interfaces Award Program **1716**
The program seeks to catalyze activity at the interface of clinical and other research disciplines by: supporting the formation of new collaborations and strengthening existing collaborations of outstanding scientists across disciplines; demonstrating successful models for clinical research at the interface of multiple disciplines; and supporting interdisciplinary and interinstitutional endeavors that go beyond the program project

mindset. Full grants, awarded over five years, are made to established teams with key investigators from at least three disciplines. Planning grants are awarded to new teams for the development of full proposals over 18 months. The listed application deadline is for preproposals; full proposals are by invitation. Though new grants are not being offered continually, potential applicants can sign up to be notified of future competitions.
Requirements Teams of at least three key investigators whose primary expertise lie in different disciplines are eligible to apply. Key investigators must have advanced degrees (MD, PhD, MD/PhD, or the equivalent), and one of the key investigators must be a clinical researcher. The team leader must work in a U.S. nonprofit institution, such as an academic medical center. The team may include investigators at other institutions in the United States and overseas.
Restrictions Planning grants will not be awarded in the current competition.
Amount $2.25 million maximum over 5 years
Date(s) Application Is Due Nov 2.
Contact Elaine K. Gallin, Program Director, (212) 974-7104; fax: (212) 974-7590; email: egallin@ddcf.org
Internet http://www.ddcf.org/page.asp?pageId=299
Sponsor Doris Duke Charitable Foundation
650 Fifth Avenue, 19th Floor
New York, NY 10019

Doris Duke Charitable Foundation Clinical Research Fellowships for Medical Students **1717**

The fellowship program is designed to encourage medical students to pursue careers in clinical research by giving exceptional students the opportunity to take a year to experience clinical research first hand. The CRF program is available at the following medical schools: Columbia University College of Physicians and Surgeons; Harvard Medical School; Mount Sinai School of Medicine; University of California at San Francisco School of Medicine; University of Iowa Roy J. and Lucille A. Carver College of Medicine; University of North Carolina at Chapel Hill School of Medicine; University of Pennsylvania School of Medicine; University of Texas Southwestern Medical Center at Dallas; Washington University Medical School; and Yale University School of Medicine. An additional 11-12 fellowships will be available to medical students interested in conducting clinical research in Africa. Each participating medical school provides medical students with a one-year fellowship experience in clinical research that includes both didactic and research components; matches students to outstanding clinical research mentors; and offers fellowships to at least five students per year.
Requirements Medical students matriculated at any US medical school who have completed two or more years of medical school prior to the start of the fellowship and who have completed some clinical experience are eligible to apply to any of the participating schools.
Amount $27,000 plus health insurance
Date(s) Application Is Due Jan 18.
Contact Elaine K. Gallin, Program Director, (212) 974-7104; fax: (212) 974-7590; email: egallin@ddcf.org
Internet http://www.ddcf.org/page.asp?pageId=292
Sponsor Doris Duke Charitable Foundation
650 Fifth Avenue, 19th Floor
New York, NY 10019

Doris Duke Charitable Foundation Clinical Research Systems Grants **1718**

The Program is founded on the premise that clinical research requires not only human and research capital, facilities, and equipment, but it also requires robust support systems, including appropriate regulatory organizations and processes, common language, analytical tools, databases and information systems, as well as mechanisms to distribute findings and interface with the public. The Program is interested in supporting activities that seek to identify ways to strengthen the regulatory processes and systems for clinical research, such as the protection of human subjects. The foundation is willing to consider any exceptional opportunities that may arise.
Contact Elaine Gallin, Program Director for Medical Research, (212) 974-7104; fax: (212) 974-7590; email: egallin@ddcf.org
Internet http://www.ddcf.org/page.asp?pageId=302
Sponsor Doris Duke Charitable Foundation
650 Fifth Avenue, 19th Floor
New York, NY 10019

Doris Duke Charitable Foundation Clinical Scientist Development Award **1719**

Grants are awarded to junior physician-scientists to facilitate their transition to independent clinical research careers. The program is designed to help prepare and support new investigators with an MD or MD/PhD as they begin their careers as independent clinical researchers. The program is aimed at conducting clinical research in any disease area. The listed application deadline is for preproposals, which must be submitted electronically.
Requirements Applicants must: be a physician-scientist conducting clinical research in any disease area; have received an M.D. or a foreign equivalent from an accredited institution; be working in a U.S. degree-granting institution, but do not have to be a U.S. citizen; have a full-time faculty level position not higher than the Assistant Professor level; and have been appointed to their first full-time faculty level position between January 31, 2002 and January 31 of the grant year. (All full-time post-fellowship Instructor level positions will be considered full-time faculty level appointments).
Restrictions Funds cannot be used on experiments that utilize animals or primary tissues derived from animals. An award will not be made if, prior to the commencement of the award, the applicant becomes the principal investigator on a federal government, peer-reviewed, research or career development award or any nongovernment award averaging more than $126,000 per year in direct costs and of a duration of three or more years.
Amount $125,000 (direct costs) per year and $10,000 (indirect costs) per year for three years
Date(s) Application Is Due Jan 23.
Contact Elaine K. Gallin, Program Director, (212) 974-7104; fax: (212) 974-7590; email: egallin@ddcf.org
Internet http://www.ddcf.org/page.asp?pageId=291
Sponsor Doris Duke Charitable Foundation
650 Fifth Avenue, 19th Floor
New York, NY 10019

Doris Duke Charitable Foundation Distinguished Clinical Scientist Award Program **1720**

The purpose of the program is to recognize outstanding physician-scientists who are engaged in applying the latest basic science advances to the prevention, diagnosis, treatment, and cure of disease, and to enable the physician-scientist to support and mentor the next generation of physician-scientists conducting translational clinical research. Awards will be granted to physician-scientists conducting translational clinical research in any disease area; this award cycle is not limited to specific disease areas.
Requirements Grantees must hold an M.D. degree from an accredited institution in the United States (holders of M.D./Ph.D. degrees are also eligible, as are holders of M.D.-equivalent degrees from non-U.S. institutions); hold a full-time university faculty appointment at the level of Associate Professor or above as of the date of nomination; have been appointed to their first full-time, faculty-level position for no more than 15 years; and have an established translational clinical research program.
Restrictions Experiments that utilize animals or primary tissues derived from animals are not eligible for support through this award program. An award will not be made if, prior to the commencement of the foundation's award, the applicant becomes the principal investigator of a federal government, peer-reviewed, research or career development award or of any nongovernment award averaging $100,000 or more per year and of three years or more duration.
Amount $1.5 million maximum
Date(s) Application Is Due Feb 14.
Contact Elaine Gallin, Program Director for Medical Research, (212) 974-7104; fax: (212) 974-7590; email: egallin@ddcf.org
Internet http://www.ddcf.org/page.asp?pageId=297
Sponsor Doris Duke Charitable Foundation
650 Fifth Avenue, 19th Floor
New York, NY 10019

Doris Duke Charitable Foundation International AIDS Research in Africa Grants **1721**

The Program seeks to improve the care and treatment of AIDS patients in Africa by supporting clinical research and related capacity-building projects that fill critical gaps. Each year, the foundation awards a few individual, one-time grants to support clinical research, training and infrastructure. In addition, the Program has funded or co-funded competitive grant programs focused on the following three areas: operations research related to antiretroviral therapy to inform policy and practice and improve outcomes; development of low-cost clinical diagnostics to improve the medical management of antiretroviral therapy; and support for young African investigators through the AIDS Care Research in Africa small grants program. Detailed descriptions are available at the web site.
Contact Elaine Gallin, Program Director for Medical Research, (212) 974-7104; fax: (212) 974-7590; email: egallin@ddcf.org
Internet http://www.ddcf.org/page.asp?pageId=301
Sponsor Doris Duke Charitable Foundation
650 Fifth Avenue, 19th Floor
New York, NY 10019

Dorothea Haus Ross Foundation Grants **1722**

The foundation awards grants to eligible nonprofit organizations that work to relieve suffering among children who are sick, handicapped, injured, disfigured, orphaned, or otherwise vulnerable. Types of support include direct services, medical research, equipment and supplies, and small renovation projects. There are no application deadlines. Grants have supported projects for children in Native American schools and schools that serve populations of children who are disadvantaged or underserved.
Requirements U.S. Charities may apply if: they have 501(c)(3) status; they are listed in the current edition of the Cumulative List of Charities published by the U.S. Department of the Treasury; they are a Catholic organization listed in the current edition of the Catholic Director; or they are listed in the Free Methodist Yearbook, or other Protestant Denomination Directory that has a group ruling for tax exemption from the IRS. Although grants are made internationally, Foundation by-laws prohibit sending money directly to foreign charities.
Restrictions The Foundation does not fund day-to-day operations, individuals, conferences, day care, or public education. Although the Foundation makes international grants, there are restrictions in some countries for the following reasons: war, widespread

violence, or breakdown of law and order; or countries where grants are restricted by the U.S. Government due to a boycott or other reason.
Contact Wayne Cook, Executive Director, (716) 473-6006; fax: (716) 473-6007; email: rossfoundation@frontiernet.net
Internet http://www.dhrossfoundation.org/index.html
Sponsor Dorothea Haus Ross Foundation
1036 Monroe Avenue
Rochester, NY 14620

Dorothea Klumpke-Roberts Award **1723**
An award and plaque are given annually for outstanding contributions to public understanding and appreciation of astronomy. The contributions may be in the form of popular books and articles; lectures; radio, TV, or movie productions; or service to public education in astronomy of any other nature. Nominations are welcome from all members of the Society and the public at large. Nominations are made by a special committee of the Astronomical Society of the Pacific; suggestions from the public are welcome.
Amount $500
Date(s) Application Is Due Dec 31.
Contact Marilyn Delgado, Awards Committee, (415) 337-1100; fax: (415) 337-5205; email: mdelgado@astrosociety.org
Internet http://www.astrosociety.org/membership/awards/klumpke.html
Sponsor Astronomical Society of the Pacific
390 Ashton Ave
San Francisco, CA 94112

Dorothy Leet Grants **1724**
This competition is held in even-numbered years to award grants that assist women graduates from countries with low per capita income, or they may be given to other women graduates who wish to work as experts in these countries or whose research is of value to such countries. Grant is to be used preferably in a country other than that in which the applicant received her education or habitually resides. Grants may be used for obtaining special training essential to research and survey work; training in new techniques in group research and further study; or carrying out independent research or surveys, including completion of projects well advanced at the time of application. Members of the IFUW should apply through their national IFUW unit (in the United States, the American Association of University Women, 1111 16th St NW, Washington, DC 20036; info@aauw.org). Deadline for applications is determined by each affiliate, but normally falls between early September and mid-October of the year preceding the competition. Contact national headquarters for the exact deadline date.
Amount Sf3000-Sf6000 average
Date(s) Application Is Due Oct 1.
Contact Fellowships Officer, 41-22-731-23-80; fax: 41-22-738-04-40; email: info@ifuw.org
Internet http://www.ifuw.org/fellowships/international.htm
Sponsor International Federation of University Women
8 rue de l'Ancien Port
Geneva CH 1201
Switzerland

Dorothy Rider Pool Health Care Grants **1725**
The Foundation's intent is to serve as a means to improve the quality of life in the Lehigh Valley community, to build on community strengths and add to its vitality, and to increase the capacity of the community to serve the needs of all its citizens. Within this objective the Foundation's funding program is focused on education, health and welfare, culture and art and community development. Interested applicants should submit a letter of intent of five pages or less.
Requirements Allentown, PA, nonprofit organizations are eligible.
Restrictions The Foundation is restricted from providing funds to individuals, legislative or lobbying efforts, political or fraternal organizations or organizations outside the United States and its territories. The Foundation as a policy does not provide operating or capital funds to Sectarian institutions, organizations or programs in which funds will be used primarily for the propagation of religion, hospitals or United Way member agencies. Further, the Foundation does not underwrite charitable or testimonial dinners, fund-raising events or related advertising or the subsidization of books, mailings or articles in professional journals.
Amount $100,000
Date(s) Application Is Due Apr 1; Aug 15.
Contact Ronald Dendas, Program Manager, (610) 770-9346; fax: (610) 770-9361; email: drpool@ptd.net
Internet http://www.pooltrust.com
Sponsor Dorothy Rider Pool Health Care Trust
1050 S. Cedar Crest Boulevard, Suite 202
Allentown, PA 18103

Dorr Foundation Grants **1726**
Grants are made primarily for programs designed to develop new science curricula from sixth-12th grade. Support is also given to special education projects for youth relating to conservation and the environment if such projects involve the school's curriculum. In addition, some grants are made available to promote research and disseminate information on chemical, metallurgical, and sanitation engineering. Grants are awarded on a national basis, with emphasis in the Northeast. Types of support include equipment, emergency funds, program development, seed money, curriculum development, scholarship funds, and research. Initial contact should be a phone call. There is no deadline. No response can be expected unless there is interest on the part of the trustees. Applications are accepted at any time.
Requirements 501(c)3 tax-exempt organizations are eligible.
Restrictions Grants are not made to individuals or for operation budgets, continuing support, annual campaigns, deficit financing, endowment funds, or conferences and seminars.
Amount $1000-$40,000 range
Contact Barbara McMillan, Chairperson, (212) 433-6438
Sponsor Dorr Foundation
P.O. Box 328
Eastchester, NY 10709

Dorrance Family Foundation Grants **1727**
The foundation awards general support grants in grant-making priority areas, including arts and culture, civic affairs, education, health, religion, science, and social services. Specific interests include arts associations, museums, galleries, music, and theater; botanical gardens and zoos; higher education, precollege private education, and special education; AIDS/HIV, arthritis, kidney diseases, hospices, and hospitals; religious organizations; science museums; and United Way organizations. Capital campaigns also are supported. Priority is given to requests from Arizona. There are no application deadlines. Contact Program Officer before application.
Contact Carolyn O'Malley, Program Officer, (480) 367-7000
Sponsor Dorrance Family Foundation
7600 East Doubletree Ranch Road, Suite 300
Scottsdale, AZ 85258

DOS Freedom Support Educational Partnerships with Eurasia **1728**
The Office of Global Educational Programs of the Bureau of Educational and Cultural Affairs announces an open competition for the Freedom Support Educational Partnerships Program with Eurasia. The objectives of the program are to support democratic systems and market economies in Armenia, Azerbaijan, Belarus, Georgia, Kazakhstan, Kyrgyzstan, Moldova, Russia, Tajikistan, Ukraine, and Uzbekistan, and to strengthen mutual understanding and cooperation between these countries and the United States. The means of achieving these objectives may include faculty exchange, curriculum development, and outreach to professionals and other members of the communities served by the participating institutions. The purpose of the program is to support the development or revision of courses, curricula, outreach programs and programs of study at participating institutions in ways that strengthen democracy and free markets in Eurasia as well as mutual understanding between the people of the United States and those of Eurasia. Applicants are strongly encouraged to discuss their project ideas during the proposal development process with the relevant program officer, who may be able to provide additional insight into priorities by country as well as background information on what types of projects are most competitive for funding.
Requirements Accredited, postsecondary educational institutions meeting the provisions described in Internal Revenue Code section 26 USC 501(c)(3) may submit proposals to pursue institutional or departmental objectives in partnership with foreign counterpart institutions.
Amount $250,000 maximum
Contact Office of Global Educational Programs, (202) 647-4000
Internet http://exchanges.state.gov/education/partnership
Sponsor Department of State
2201 C St NW
Washington, DC 20520

DOS Partners in Education Program **1729**
Partners in Education (PiE), a project of the Office of Global Educational Programs, brings secondary level social science teachers, teacher trainers and administrators from targeted regions in Russia, Ukraine, Kyrgyzstan, Uzbekistan, Armenia, Azerbaijan and Georgia for a six-week, school-based internship program focusing on citizenship education. Host institutions, often university level schools of education, also provide professional development seminars, cultural activities and homestays. US teachers from host communities return the visit to their NIS counterparts. Both participants and US host institutions are selected through an open merit-based competition. Since 1998, the program has brought to the U.S. more than 500 educators from the Eurasia to learn about different approaches to civic education, curriculum development, and teaching methodologies. The program is administered by the American Councils for International Education.
Requirements Public and private nonprofit organizations meeting the provisions described in IRS regulation 26 CFR 1.501(c) are eligible to apply.
Restrictions Proposals relating to the teaching of English or English as a foreign language (EFL) are not eligible.
Amount $150,000
Contact Office of Global Educational Programs, (202) 619-5289; fax: (202) 401-1433
Internet http://exchanges.state.gov/education/partnership/fulbright.htm
Sponsor Department of State
301 Fourth St SW
Washington, DC 20547

DOS Study of the United States Institutes 1730

The program seeks grant proposals from US colleges and universities to develop and implement summer institutes. Each institute is a six-week US-based seminar, including up to two weeks of travel, designed for multinational groups of 18 foreign university teaching faculty or 30 secondary school educators. Institute include Study of the United States for Foreign Secondary School Educators; Religious Pluralism in the United States; US Foreign Policy; American Politics and Political Thought; and Contemporary American Literature. The application of the Study of the United States for Foreign Secondary Educators institute is December 13; the January 10 deadline applies to the other institutes. Guidelines are available at the website.
Requirements US colleges and universities are eligible.
Date(s) Application Is Due Jan 10; Dec 13.
Contact Jennifer Phillips, (202) 453-8537; fax: (202) 453-8533
Internet http://exchanges.state.gov/education/rfgps/menu.htm
Sponsor Department of State
301 4th St, SW, Rm 314
Washington, DC 20547

DOS Women's Political, Educational, and Economic Development for Afghanistan Grants 1731

The program supports a series of exchanges and training programs promoting women's political, educational, and economic development in Afghanistan. Eligible US applicants may submit proposals to develop and implement exchanges and training programs involving participants from Afghanistan, including training conducted in Afghanistan. These US organizations should have a current presence in Afghanistan, or experience working in Afghanistan, and work in conjunction with Afghan NGO partners. The program solicits proposals for exchange projects that involve the following priority themes: women's leadership, educational development and literacy for women and girls, women-led small business development, job skills training, and NGO management. Up to five grants may be awarded.
Requirements US public and private nonprofit organizations meeting the provisions described in IRS Code section 26 USC 501(c)3 may submit proposals.
Amount $150,000 maximum
Date(s) Application Is Due Feb 6.
Contact Office of Citizen Exchanges, (202) 619-5320; fax: (202) 619-4350
Internet http://exchanges.state.gov/education/rfgps
Sponsor Department of State
301 4th St SW, ECA/PE/C/NEA-AF, Rm 216
Washington, DC 20547

DOT Dwight David Eisenhower Transportation Fellowship Program 1732

The program's goals are to attract people to the field of transportation, to enhance the careers of transportation professionals by encouraging them to seek advanced degrees, and to retain top talent in the transportation community. The fellowship awards are: the Eisenhower Graduate Fellowships to allow students to pursue master's degrees or doctorates in transportation-related fields; the Eisenhower Historically Black Colleges and Universities Fellowships to provide HBCU students with additional opportunities to enter careers in transportation; the Eisenhower Hispanic Serving Institutions Fellowships to provide HSI students with opportunities to enter transportation careers; the Eisenhower Tribal Colleges Initiatives, which provide fellowships for Native American students and faculty at tribal colleges; and the Eisenhower Faculty Fellowships to provide faculty in transportation fields with opportunities to improve their transportation knowledge by attending conferences, courses, seminars, or workshops.
Date(s) Application Is Due Apr 15; Oct 15.
Contact Gwen Sutton, Program Manager, (703) 235-0535; fax: (703) 235-0593; email: transportationedu@fhwa.dot.gov
Internet http://www.nhi.fhwa.dot.gov/uandg.asp
Sponsor Federal Highway Administration
4600 N Fairfax Dr, Ste 800
Arlington, VA 22203

DOT Recreational Boating Safety Grants 1733

These grants are used to fund projects on various subjects promoting boating safety on the national level. It targets specific boat market segments and recreational boating safety topics.
Requirements National nongovernmental, nonprofit, public service organizations are eligible to apply.
Amount $3 million total
Contact Capt. Scott Evans, Office of Boating Safety, US Coast Guard, (202) 267-0950; Vickie Hartberger, Office of Boating Safety, US Coast Guard, (202) 267-0974
Internet http://www.uscgboating.org/grants/state/rbs.htm
Sponsor Department of Transportation
2100 Second St SW
Washington, DC 20593

DOT Transit Planning and Research Grants 1734

The objectives of the program are to foster innovation in public transit systems, through local demonstrations of promising, but risky, new technologies and service or operational concepts to provide information that can be used nationally; to address economic and social issues resulting from human impacts on the environment, and develop risk assessment methodologies, integrated assessments, and other analytical tools for effective policy formulation; to develop practical know-how for solving fundamental industry-wide problems, such as how to accommodate the travel needs of persons with disabilities, how to finance transit infrastructure construction and maintenance, and how to meet requirements of the Clean Air Act; and to support development of information and technical assistance to convey results of research, technology development, and innovative demonstrations for adaptation and local implementation.
Requirements Eligible applicants include public bodies, nonprofit institutions, state and local agencies, universities, and legally constituted public agencies and operators of public transportation services.
Contact Associate Administrator for Research, Demonstration, and Innovation, Federal Transit Administration, (202) 366-4052
Internet http://www.fta.dot.gov
Sponsor Department of Transportation
400 Seventh St SW
Washington, DC 20590

DOT Transportation Statistics Research Grants 1735

The purpose of this grant program is to provide financial assistance to eligible organizations to help advance the discipline of transportation statistics. The Bureau of Transportation Statistics (BTS) is an operating administration within the DOT. Its mission is to lead in developing transportation data and information of high quality, and to advance their effective use in public and private transportation decisionmaking. The ultimate goal is to make transportation better--to enhance safety, mobility, economic growth, the human and natural environment, and national security.
Requirements Public and private nonprofit institutions of higher education are eligible to apply.
Amount $25,000-$200,000; $75,000 average
Contact Mary Hutzler, Acting Director, Bureau of Transportation Statistics, (202) 366-9913; fax: (202) 366-3640; email: answers@bts.gov
Internet http://www.bts.gov
Sponsor Department of Transportation
400 Seventh St SW
Washington, DC 20590

Douglass Institute Fellowships 1736

The Frederick Douglass Institute for African and African American Studies supports a program of predoctoral and postdoctoral fellowships on the prospects for cultural, social, and economic development in Africa and its diaspora. Annual themes vary; contact the associate director of the institute for details of the program.
Requirements Scholars holding a PhD degree in a field related to the African and African-American experience are eligible for the postdoctoral fellowship. Graduate students of any university who are studying aspects of the African and African-American experience are eligible for the predoctoral fellowship. Students who want to begin their graduate work in African and African-American studies at the university are eligible for the graduate fellowship.
Amount $35,000 postdoctoral fellowship stipend, $18,000 predoctoral fellowship stipend
Date(s) Application Is Due Jan 31.
Contact Associate Director for Research Fellowships, Frederick Douglass Institute, (585) 275-7235; fax: (585) 256-2594; email: fdi@troi.cc.rochester.edu
Internet http://www.rochester.edu/College/AAS/fellowships.php
Sponsor University of Rochester
RC Box 270440, 302 Morey Hall
Rochester, NY 14627-0440

Dover Foundation Grants 1737

The primary purpose of the foundation is to serve the interests of Cleveland County and other areas of North Carolina. Foundation grants seek to strengthen the spiritual, mental, and moral fiber of the community; give priority to those initiatives and programs that will elevate the life and educational opportunities of deserving recipients; and discover ways to encourage others to come together to address needs for the common welfare of the community. Types of support include general operating support, annual campaigns, capital campaigns, building/renovation, emergency funds, scholarship funds, and research. A formal grant request must be submitted by letter. The board of directors meets four times a year to consider grant awards--January, April, July, and October.
Requirements Applicants must reside in North Carolina.
Restrictions The foundation ordinarily does not make grants to organizations whose principal activities are outside the United States; political activities or entities; individuals or their projects; advertising; newsletters, magazines, or books; or trips or tours.
Amount $500-$25,000 average
Contact Hoyt Bailey, President, (704) 487-8888; fax: (704) 482-6818; email: doverfnd@shelby.net
Sponsor Dover Foundation
P.O. Box 208
Shelby, NC 28151

Dr. Arthur E. Bisson Prize for Naval Technology Achievement 1738

This award is presented to recognize and reward an individual's successes in technology achievement. It is granted annually to a current or former navy scientist, engineer, or S&T

program manager that has a significant, direct transitional impact from S&T to naval operations or systems. Such impact shall be so outstanding as to be widely recognized in the navy and the relevant technical community nationally. While the impact must have been realized in the year prior to nomination, it is recognized that the efforts leading to transition may have been ongoing for many years. The award consists of an individual plaque, a certificate, and a cash award. Additionally, the recipients name is placed on the master plaque located on the Honorary Wall of Fame at ONR Headquarters.
Requirements High-quality science and/or technology accomplishment, well-conducted transition of that accomplishment from S&T to naval acquisition or operations, and a significant impact upon the warfighting and/or peacekeeping capabilities of naval forces are criteria for the award. At the time of the achievement cited as the basis for the prize, nominees must have been military or civilian employees of the navy in positions managing or performing S&T.
Amount $3000
Date(s) Application Is Due Feb 15.
Contact Awards Administrator, (703) 696-5031; fax: (703) 696-5940; email: onrpao@onr.navy.mil
Internet http://www.onr.navy.mil/sci%5Ftech/personnel/342/training/transitions/bisson.htm
Sponsor Office of Naval Research
875 N Randolph St, Ste 1425
Arlington, VA 22203-1995

Dr. Bob and Jean Smith Foundation Grants **1739**
The foundation awards grants to Texas nonprofit organizations in its areas of interest, including arts and culture, higher education, medical education, medical research, and health care. Types of support include annual campaigns, building construction/renovation, capital campaigns, general operating support, matching/challenge grants, and scholarship funds. There are no application deadlines; the board meets quarterly.
Requirements Texas nonprofit organizations are eligible. Preference is given to Dallas-based organizations.
Restrictions Individuals are ineligible.
Amount $100-$500,000 range
Contact Sally Smith, Grants Administrator, (214) 521-3461
Sponsor Dr. Bob and Jean Smith Foundation
3811 Turtle Creek Ctr, No 2150 LB 53
Dallas, TX 75219

Dr. Courtney W. Shropshire Scholarship Grant **1740**
All qualified applicants will be considered without regard to race, creed, sex, or national origin. The grant is to be used only for tuition and approved purposes that are invoiced from the school. Necessary forms are available annually after September 1 from the Civitan International Foundation; please include a self-addressed business envelope with postage to cover two-ounce US mailing.
Requirements Candidates must be a Civitan member (or a Civitan's immediate family member) and must have been a Civitan for at least two years and/or must be or have been a junior Civitan for no less than two years. Candidates must be enrolled in a degree or certificate program at an accredited community college, vocational school, four-year college, or graduate school.
Amount $1000 maximum
Date(s) Application Is Due Jan 31.
Contact Shropshire Scholarship Grant, (205) 591-8910; fax: (205) 592-6307; email: civitan@civitan.org
Internet http://www.civitaninternational.com/templates/cuscivitan/details.asp?id=23844&PID=155457
Sponsor Civitan International Foundation
P.O. Box 130744
Birmingham, AL 35213-0744

Dr. J. Roberto Villavicencio Foundation Grants **1741**
The foundation operates in Rosario and its surrounding area in the fields of education, medicine and health, and science and technology. Types of support include research grants to institutions and individuals, scholarships and fellowships, prizes, conferences, training courses, and publications.
Contact Dra. Ana Maria Uriarte, Director, fax: 54-341-449 0152; email: info@villavicencio.org.ar
Internet http://www.villavicencio.org.ar
Sponsor Dr. J. Roberto Villavicencio Foundation
Alvear 854
Rosario, Santa Fe 2000
Argentina

Dr. Robert H. Goddard Historical Essay Award **1742**
A competition is held annually for essays dealing with any significant aspect of the historical development of rocketry and astronautics. The essay may, through research, bring new information to light or may cast a new and different light upon events or individuals influencing rocketry and astronautics in the United States. Essays should not exceed 5000 words and should be fully documented. Complete contest rules are available; send a self-addressed envelope with inquiries.
Requirements Applicant must be a US citizen.
Restrictions Previous winners are not eligible.
Amount $1000
Date(s) Application Is Due Dec 1.
Contact Goddard Historical Essay Award, (202) 973-8661
Internet http://www.nscfl.com/awards.html
Sponsor National Space Club
2025 M St NW, Ste 800
Washington, DC 20036-4907

Dr. Robert H. Goddard Research Fellowships **1743**
These one-year, nonrenewable fellowships are awarded for full-time graduate study at the institute. In addition to the fellowship stipend, the award includes up to 20 credits of tuition, $1,591/month for 12 months, one year fellowship. Interested persons should contact the graduate admissions office for details on enrolling for graduate study and eligibility for the fellowships. Preference given to doctoral applicants.
Requirements Applicants must be US citizens with acceptance to a WPI graduate-degree program. GRE or GMAT test scores are required.
Amount $1,591 annual stipend
Date(s) Application Is Due Feb 15.
Contact Graduate Admissions, (508) 831-5301; fax: (508) 831-5717; email: gse@wpi.edu
Internet http://www.grad.wpi.edu/Financial/fellowships.html
Sponsor Worcester Polytechnic Institute
100 Institute Rd
Worcester, MA 01609-2280

Dr. Robert H. Goddard Scholarship **1744**
The club awards a scholarship for the academic year to stimulate the interest of talented students in the opportunity to advance scientific knowledge through space research and exploration. The award is given at the Goddard Memorial Dinner in the latter part of March. The National Space Club will pay travel and lodging costs so that the winner may attend the dinner. Applicants should apply by letter and provide the data requested. Funds awarded are paid to the winner through his/her university before the next academic year begins. The winner is eligible to compete for a second year if the circumstances and his/her accomplishments warrant it. Deadline usually is the first Friday in January.
Requirements Applicant must be a US citizen in at least the junior year of an accredited university and have the intention of pursuing undergraduate or graduate studies in science or engineering during the interval of the scholarship. Selection is based on official transcripts, letters of recommendation from faculty, accomplishments demonstrating personal qualities of creativity and leadership, scholastic plans that would lead to future participation in some phase of the aerospace sciences and technology, and proven past research and participation in space-related science and engineering. Personal need is considered but is not controlling.
Amount $10,000
Date(s) Application Is Due Jan 8.
Contact Goddard Scholarship, (202) 973-8661
Internet http://www.wpi.edu/Academics/FS/entrydetail.php?award_id=139
Sponsor National Space Club
2000 L St NW, Ste 710
Washington, DC 20036-4907

Dr. Sydney Segal Research Grants **1745**
Research grants are awarded to enable students to pursue full-time higher degree studies at a Canadian institution researching the possible causes, effects, and/or prevention of sudden infant death syndrome. The research grants are awarded for one year in any discipline--medical, psychological, biological, sociological, nursing, or other. Contact the foundation for applications.
Requirements Applications are invited from suitably qualified graduate students who are undertaking full-time training in research in the health sciences leading to an MSC, PhD, or equivalent degree.
Amount $C35,000 maximum
Date(s) Application Is Due Jun 1.
Contact Executive Director, (800) 363-7437 or (416) 488-3260; fax: (416) 488-3864; email: sidsinfo@sidscanada.org
Internet http://www.sidscanada.org/segal_research_grants.htm
Sponsor Canadian Foundation for the Study of Infant Deaths
586 Eglinton Ave E, Ste 308
Toronto, ON M4P 1P2 Canada

Draper Richards Foundation Fellowships **1746**
The foundation awards three-year grants to selected social entrepreneurs to start new nonprofit organizations that are national or global in scope and that have broad social impact. Selected projects will demonstrate innovative ways to solve existing social problems. Proposals are accepted for a variety of public service areas, including, but not limited to, education, youth and families, the environment, arts, health, and community and economic development. The foundation offers financial support as well as strategic and organizational assistance. Proposals are accepted at any time; full proposals are by request.
Requirements Experienced, dedicated social entrepreneurs with a developed idea for a US nonprofit organization are invited to apply.

Restrictions The fund does not support research, scholarships, or local community-based organizations.
Amount $100,000 annually
Contact Jenny Shilling Stein, Executive Director, (415) 616-4050; fax: (415) 616-4060; email: proposals@draperrichards.org
Internet http://www.draperrichards.org/process/index.html
Sponsor Draper Richards Foundation
50 California St, Ste 2925
San Francisco, CA 94111

Dreyfus Faculty Start-Up Grants for Undergraduate Institutions 1747
The program aims to provide funding for new faculty members at non-PhD-granting institutions at the start of their research and teaching activities. While most talented young faculty apply for external funding to support their research, in most cases such support does not ordinarily become available before the end of the first year of appointment. The key feature of the award is an unrestricted research grant that is awarded in September of the year the new faculty member formally begins the first-year appointment. Normally, 10 awards are made each year based on institutional nominations. Nominating materials, including supporting letters, must be received at the foundation by the listed deadline date.
Requirements Institutions that grant a BA or MA degree, but not a PhD, in chemistry, chemical engineering, or biochemistry may submit nominations. Nominees are normally expected to have no more than three years of postdoctoral experience and to begin the first year of their first full-time tenure-track academic appointment at the time of the award.
Restrictions Faculty members who already hold full-time tenure-track appointments at eligible institutions may not be nominated for the program.
Amount $30,000
Date(s) Application Is Due May 11.
Contact Mark Cardillo, Executive Director, (212) 753-1760; email: admin@dreyfus.org or mcardillo@dreyfus.org
Internet http://www.dreyfus.org/su.shtml
Sponsor Camille and Henry Dreyfus Foundation
555 Madison Ave, 20th Fl
New York, NY 10022-1301

Dreyfus New Faculty Awards Program 1748
This program was established to recognize and encourage the teaching and research careers of talented young faculty in the chemical sciences. The program is designed to provide discretionary funding to faculty at early stages in their careers. These faculty must have demonstrated a commitment to education and have produced an independent body of scholarship that signals the promise of continuing outstanding contributions to research and teaching. Nomination and all letters of recommendation must be received in the foundation office by the listed application deadline date. Nominations must be made online. Electronic nomination forms are available on the Web site.
Requirements Institutions that grant doctorates in chemistry, chemical engineering, or biochemistry may submit nominations. Nominee must hold a full-time tenure-track academic appointment.
Amount $50,000
Date(s) Application Is Due May 11.
Contact Mark Cardillo, Executive Director, (212) 753-1760; fax: (212) 593-2256; email: admin@dreyfus.org or mcardillo@dreyfus.org
Internet http://www.dreyfus.org/nf.shtml
Sponsor Camille and Henry Dreyfus Foundation
555 Madison Ave, 20th Fl
New York, NY 10022-1301

Dreyfus Postdoctoral Program in Environmental Chemistry 1749
The Foundation seeks to further the development of scientific leadership in the field of environmental chemistry with a postdoctoral fellowship program. The award is given to a principal investigator who submits a proposal judged to be exceptional, both in its potential for leading edge contributions to environmental science, and in the arrangements for the education of the Fellow. Successful applicants are expected to recruit excellent young Ph.D. graduates from the fields of physical, organic, inorganic, biological chemistry or associated fields in chemical engineering, and provide them with the highest caliber of research experience and broad education in environmental science. Instructions for application submission are available online.
Requirements The program is open to all academic and other not-for-profit organizations that have well-established research efforts in environmental science or engineering in the States, Districts, and Territories of the US. These research activities need not be located in traditional departments in the chemical sciences, and collaboration across departments and institutions is encouraged.
Restrictions No part of the award may be used for institutional administrative purposes.
Amount $120,000 over two years
Date(s) Application Is Due May 24.
Contact Executive Director, (212) 753-1760; email: admin@dreyfus.org or mcardillo@dreyfus.org
Internet http://www.dreyfus.org/ep.shtml
Sponsor Camille and Henry Dreyfus Foundation
555 Madison Avenue, 20th Floor
New York, NY 10022-1301

Dreyfus Senior Scientist Mentor Program Grants 1750
The program enables undergraduates to conduct research in the chemical sciences in a close working relationship with emeritus faculty members. Only one faculty member may apply per application, although more than one application per department or institution is permitted. A letter of support must be sent directly to the Foundation from a colleague, preferably from outside the institution, who is familiar with the applicant's research and teaching and who can speak to the applicant's experience in mentoring and advising undergraduates. Letters of support cannot be accepted via electronic mail or facsimile.
Requirements Faculty with emeritus status on or before January of the current year, and who maintain active research programs in the chemical sciences may apply for one of a limited number of awards that will allow undergraduates to do research under their guidance. Successful applicants, who are expected to be closely engaged in a mentoring relationship with the students will receive grants annually for two years for undergraduate stipends and modest research support.
Amount $10,000 annually for up to two years
Date(s) Application Is Due Nov 15.
Contact Senior Scientist Mentor Program, (212) 753-1760; email: admin@dreyfus.org
Internet http://www.dreyfus.org/si.shtml
Sponsor Camille and Henry Dreyfus Foundation
555 Madison Avenue, 20th Floor
New York, NY 10022-3301

Dreyfus Special Grants Program in the Chemical Sciences 1751
This program offers support to eligible institutions for projects that propose to advance the science of chemistry in innovative ways. Proposals are invited in any area consistent with the Foundation's broad objective of advancing the chemical sciences. For projects that require sustaining support, note that this program is intended to seed the initial phases, with the expectation that grant recipients will find continuing funding from other sources.
Requirements Institutions in the States, Districts, and Territories of the US that have a focus in the chemical sciences are eligible and may submit a preliminary inquiry to the Special Grant Program in the Chemical Sciences. Institutions include schools, colleges and universities, as well as other not-for-profit organizations, such as museums and libraries.
Restrictions Awards are not made directly to individuals, nor, in general, to private foundations.
Date(s) Application Is Due Jun 7.
Contact Grants Administrator, (212) 753-1760; email: admin@dreyfus.org or mcardillo@dreyfus.org
Internet http://www.dreyfus.org/sg.shtml
Sponsor Camille and Henry Dreyfus Foundation
555 Madison Avenue, 20th Floor
New York, NY 10022-3301

Drs. Bruce and Lee Foundation Grants 1752
The Foundation's goal is to advance the general welfare and the quality of all life in the Florence, S.C. area by providing economic support to qualified programs and non-profit organizations. The Foundation will support a broad range of charitable purposes including, but not limited to: medical; health; human services; education; arts; religion; civic affairs; and the conservation, preservation and promotion of cultural, historical and environmental resources. There are no application deadlines. Contact the office for application materials and guidelines.
Requirements Florence, SC, nonprofit organizations are eligible.
Restrictions The Foundation does not purchase tickets for fundraising events. Grants to individuals will not be considered.
Contact L. Bradley Callicott, Executive Director, (843) 664-2870; email: blfound@bellsouth.net
Sponsor Drs. Bruce and Lee Foundation
181 East Evans Street, BTC Box 022
Florence, SC 29506

DSO Cognitive Technology Threat Warning System Grants 1753
The objective of the CT2WS program is to drive a breakthrough in soldier-portable visual threat warning devices. Recent developments and discoveries in the disparate technology areas of flat-field, wide-angle optics, large pixel-count digital imagers, cognitive visual processing algorithms, neurally-based target detection signatures and ultra-low power analog-digital hybrid signal processing electronics have led DARPA to believe that focused technology development, system design, and system integration efforts may produce revolutionary capabilities for the warfighter. The final objective of the DARPA CT2WS program is the development of prototype soldier-portable digital imaging threat queuing systems capable of effective detection ranges of 1-10 km against dismounts and vehicles while simultaneously surveying a 120-degree or greater field of view (FOV). DARPA requests proposals for the full scope of development (e.g., an end-to-end system designed by a team of multidisciplinary research organizations, plus an integrator for coordination and implementation support). Proposals addressing only individual component-level technologies may be considered non-compliant to this BAA. This BAA affords proposers the choice of submitting proposals for the award

of a Grant, Cooperative Agreement, Procurement Contract, Technology Investment Agreement, Other Transaction for Prototype Agreement, or other such appropriate award instrument.
Requirements The Government anticipates proposals submitted under this BAA will be Unclassified.
Date(s) Application Is Due Apr 11.
Contact Amy Kruse, Program Manager; (571) 218-4338; fax: (703) 248-1908; email: amy.kruse@darpa.mil or BAA07-25@darpa.mil
Internet http://www.darpa.mil/baa/BAA07-25.html
Sponsor Defense Sciences Office within the Defense Advanced Research Projects Agency (DARPA)
3701 North Fairfax Drive
Arlington, VA 22203-1714

DSO Computer Science Study Group (CSSG) Grants **1754**
This Research Announcement (RA) initiates Phase 1 of the 2008 Computer Science Study Group (CSSG). The objective of the CSSG is to rapidly identify ideas in the field of computer science that will provide revolutionary advances, rather than incremental benefit, to the Department of Defense. Phase 1 (12 months) consists of participation on the CS Study Panel. The CS Study Panel anticipates meeting at least four times throughout the 2008 calendar year, totaling approximately twenty days. Two of the meetings will occur during the academic year and will take place in the Washington, D.C. metropolitan area. Two extended meetings, lasting approximately one week each, will take place during the summer, and will involve travel throughout the United States. For successful proposers, host institutions will receive grants or other assistance instruments for up to $100,000. The funding to the host institution will support participant travel expenses for Panel meetings; it will also support participant salary, to include time spent while participating in the CS Study Panel and time to connect the participants' computer science research to critical DoD needs identified during their Panel trips. The funding may also support research assistants' summer salary and costs for administrative support.
Requirements All responsible sources may submit a proposal that shall be considered by DARPA. Historically Black Colleges and Universities (HBCUs) and Minority Institutions (MIs) are encouraged to submit proposals.
Restrictions Only U.S. institutions of higher learning are eligible for awards under this RA, and participants must be junior faculty members who are able to receive a U.S. Department of Defense SECRET security clearance.
Date(s) Application Is Due Aug 10.
Contact Dr. Benjamin Mann, Program Manager; (571) 218-4246; fax: (571) 218-4553; email: benjamin.mann@darpa.mil or RA07-43@darpa.mil
Internet http://www.darpa.mil/baa/RA07-43.html
Sponsor Defense Sciences Office within the Defense Advanced Research Projects Agency (DARPA)
3701 North Fairfax Drive
Arlington, VA 22203-1714

DSO Controlling Pathogen Evolution Workshop Grants **1755**
The goal of the workshop is to explore: the potential of computational methods to precisely predict pathogen evolution; and vaccination and/or therapeutic strategies to control direction of pathogen evolution. The workshop will investigate tools for predicting protective epitopes, pathogen evolution and protein structure, and then review strategies to force pathogens into an evolutionary trap that prevents escape through mutation. From there, vaccines and therapies can be developed against the particular pathogen strain. Workshop participants are strongly encouraged to prepare posters describing previous or potential research in the area in order to facilitate discussions and/or formation of well-rounded teams.
Requirements Attendees should have specific expertise in infectious disease, epitope prediction (computational and/or immunomic), vaccinology, mathematical modeling, protein structure, pathogen evolution, drug design, and/or animal modeling.
Date(s) Application Is Due Mar 16.
Contact Dr. Michael V. Callahan, Program Manager; (571) 218-4596; fax: (571) 218-4553; email: michael.callahan@darpa.mil
Internet http://www.darpa.mil/baa/SN07-21.html
Sponsor Defense Sciences Office within the Defense Advanced Research Projects Agency (DARPA)
3701 North Fairfax Drive
Arlington, VA 22203-1714

DSO Defense Sciences Research and Technology Grants **1756**
TThe mission of the DSO is to identify and pursue high-risk/high-payoff research initiatives throughout a broad spectrum of the science and engineering disciplines, and to transform these initiatives into important, radically new military capabilities. To carry out this mission, DSO seeks research ideas and areas that might lead to innovations in science and engineering. Therefore, the office is soliciting proposals for advanced research and development in a variety of enabling technical areas. Proposals may be either basic or applied research. However, in all cases, proposers should demonstrate that their proposed effort is aimed at high-risk/high-payoff technologies that have the potential for making, in the 5-10 year time frame, revolutionary rather than incremental improvements to national security, including emerging threats and operational challenges. Multiple awards are anticipated. The amount of resources made available to this BAA will depend on the quality of the proposals received and the availability of funds. While there is no specific requirement for cost and duration of the proposed effort, it is recommended that proposers include a Phase I of 12 to 18 months in length that addresses the most critical issues on the path to success.
Requirements All responsible sources may submit a proposal.
Date(s) Application Is Due Feb 14.
Contact Barbara K. McQuiston, Deputy Director; (703) 526-4759; fax: (703) 248-1916; email: barbara.mcquiston@darpa.mil or BAA07-21@darpa.mil
Internet http://www.darpa.mil/baa/baa07-21mod1.html
Sponsor Defense Sciences Office within the Defense Advanced Research Projects Agency (DARPA)
3701 North Fairfax Drive
Arlington, VA 22203-1714

DSO Radiation Biodosimetry (RaBiD) Grants **1757**
The DSO is seeking proposals for new technologies for rapid, high-throughput, portable and low-cost biodosimeters to determine radiation dose to individuals after acute radiation exposure. This technology would provide rapid identification of individuals who have been exposed to high-dose radiation in order to accurately assess radiation exposure levels. The Program is a single phase, 15-month program with a goal of revolutionizing radiation exposure detection. The first 12 months consist of scientific research and development during which the proposer will develop a non- or minimally-invasive radiological biodosimeter and demonstrate accurate radiological detection from biological samples into quartiles of doses for humans with a detection time less than 10 minutes. This will include radiological dose/detection curves, as well as multipoint data regarding decay of biological signal as a function of time after radiation exposure. A successful proposal will demonstrate a clear path to these deliverables, including a timeline for technology development, experimentation, and delivery of results.
Requirements All proposers must provide evidence of a competent team capable of developing a new radiation biodosimetry technology meeting all program objectives and milestones. The Program requires that each proposal include a team with demonstrated (or established) capability. At a minimum, proposers are expected to possess expertise or demonstrate collaboration with professionals in the following areas: radiation biologist/radiation oncologist--with expertise in radiation exposure to animal models; and engineering--with developmental expertise needed to translate biological sampling to radiation readout.
Restrictions Only unclassified proposals will be accepted in response.
Date(s) Application Is Due Jul 9.
Contact Dr. Mildred Donlon, Program Manager; (703) 696-2289 or (703) 248-1527; fax: (571) 218-4553; email: mildred.donlon@darpa.mil or BAA07-29@darpa.mil
Internet http://www.darpa.mil/baa/BAA07-29.html
Sponsor Defense Sciences Office within the Defense Advanced Research Projects Agency (DARPA)
3701 North Fairfax Drive
Arlington, VA 22203-1714

DuBois-Mandela-Rodney Fellowship Program **1758**
The center invites applications for the fellowship program from scholars working on Africa or the African diaspora. Consideration will be given to all disciplines including - but not limited to - the humanities, social sciences, physical sciences and professional schools. Scholars from or who study the Gullah speaking Sea islands, Cape Verde islands, the Anglophone Caribbean, the Canary Islands, and Madagascar and/or other less studied areas are especially encouraged to apply. Successful candidates can expect to maintain affiliations with CAAS as well as with departments and research institutes that relate to their projects. Each fellow will also be expected to conduct a CAAS work-in-progress seminar during one semester in residence.
Requirements Candidates must have the PhD in hand and be no more than 5 years beyond the completion of the degree.
Amount $45,000 total
Date(s) Application Is Due Nov 30.
Contact V. Robin Grice, Center for African American and African Studies, (734) 647-5361; email: gricer@umich.edu
Internet http://www.umich.edu/~iinet/caas/fellow&grants/dubois-mandela-intro.htm
Sponsor University of Michigan
106 W Hall Bldg
Ann Arbor, MI 48109-1092

Duchossois Family Foundation Grants **1759**
The foundation focuses its efforts in the Chicago metropolitan area and gives primary consideration to nonprofit organizations that contribute to the community in the area of health. Contributions to health programs are pledged to organizations and agencies whose services include research and education in the primary area of cancer and cancer research. A one-page summary-request letter should include a description of the organization and its specific needs and purposes, the amount requested, and a list of members of the board of directors and their business/professional affiliations.
Requirements 501(c)3 tax-exempt public charities serving the Chicago metropolitan area are eligible.
Contact Iris Krieg, Executive Director, (312) 641-5765
Sponsor Duchossois Family Foundation
203 N. Wabash, Suite 1800
Chicago, IL 60601

Duke Foundation Fellowships **1760**
Beginning in the fall semester of 2009, a limited number of graduate fellowships will be available for students in the Ph. D. Program in Public Policy Analysis in the Terry Sanford Institute of Public Policy who intend to focus their dissertation on the theory of foundations, foundation strategy, the measurement of foundation impact, and foundation accountability.
Contact Bruce Kuniholm, Director, (919) 613-7309; email: bruce.kuniholm@duke.edu
Internet http://www.pubpol.duke.edu/centers/dfrp/fellowship.php
Sponsor Duke Foundation, Sanford Institute of Public Policy
Box 90239
Durham NC 27708-0239

Dumbarton Oaks Fellowships **1761**
Dumbarton Oaks offers fellowships in the three areas of Byzantine studies (including related aspects of late Roman, early Christian, western medieval, Slavic, and Near Eastern studies); Pre-Columbian studies of Mexico, Central America, and Andean South America; and studies in landscape architecture. Fellowships are for scholars who hold or expect to have, at the beginning of the fellowship, a doctorate or who have done comparable advanced work and wish to pursue research on projects of their own. Fellowships are not renewable, but initial application may be made for two successive years (two annual fellowships and one intervening summer fellowship, part of which may be spent away from Dumbarton Oaks). Applications not postmarked by due date will be returned.
Requirements Fellowships are open to scholars of any nationality holding a PhD or relevant advanced degree and pursuing research on a project of their own or one sponsored by the center.
Restrictions Applications from former fellows are accepted if five years have elapsed since tenure of previous fellowship.
Amount $25,990 plus housing, lunch on weekdays; $2000 (if needed) to assist with the cost of bringing and maintaining dependents; $975 maximum for research expenses; $1300 maximum travel reimbursement
Date(s) Application Is Due Nov 1.
Contact Carol Sellery, Director's Office, (202) 339-6410; fax: (202) 339-6419; email: DumbartonOaks@doaks.org
Internet http://www.doaks.org/fellowships.html
Sponsor Dumbarton Oaks
1703 32nd St NW
Washington, DC 20007

Dumbarton Oaks Junior Fellowships **1762**
Junior fellowships are awarded to students who at the time of application have fulfilled all preliminary requirements for a higher degree and plan to work at Dumbarton Oaks on a dissertation or a final project under the direction of a faculty member at their own university. In exceptional cases, applications will be accepted from students before fulfilling preliminary requirements. Junior fellowships are awarded in the three areas of Byzantine studies (including related aspects of late Roman, early Christian, western medieval, Slavic, and Near Eastern studies); Pre-Columbian studies of Mexico, Central America, and Andean South America; and studies in landscape architecture. Applications not postmarked by due date will be returned.
Requirements Fellowships are open to individuals of any nationality who have passed all preliminary examinations for a higher degree and are writing a dissertation or equivalent. Fellows are expected to have a working knowledge of the languages necessary for their research and be sufficiently advanced to pursue research on their own.
Amount $14,635 plus housing, lunch on weekdays, contribution to health insurance; $975 research allowance; $2000 (if needed) to assist with the cost of bringing and maintaining dependents; $1300 maximum travel expense
Date(s) Application Is Due Nov 1.
Contact Carol Sellery, Director's Office, (202) 339-6410; fax: (202) 339-6419; email: DumbartonOaks@doaks.org
Internet http://www.doaks.org/fellowships.html
Sponsor Dumbarton Oaks
1703 32nd St NW
Washington, DC 20007

Dumbarton Oaks Project Grants **1763**
Dumbarton Oaks makes grants to assist with scholarly projects in the three areas of Byzantine studies (including related aspects of late Roman, early Christian, western medieval, Slavic, and Near Eastern studies); Pre-Columbian studies of Mexico, Central America, and Andean South America; and studies in landscape architecture. Support is generally for archaeological research or for the recovery, recording, and analysis of materials that would otherwise be lost. Grants may cover modest expenses such as photography, supplies, special services, and sometimes travel, although Dumbarton Oaks does not make travel grants as such. Applicants must contact Dumbarton Oaks by October 1 to determine whether the project is within the institution's purview; applications must be received by November 1.
Restrictions Project awards are not offered purely for the purpose of travel, nor for work associated with a degree, for library or archive research, for catalogues, or for conservation and restoration per se.
Amount $3000-$10,000 typically
Date(s) Application Is Due Oct 1; Nov 1.
Contact Carol Sellery, Director's Office, (202) 339-6410; fax: (202) 339-6419; email: DumbartonOaks@doaks.org
Internet http://www.doaks.org/project.html
Sponsor Dumbarton Oaks
1703 32nd St NW
Washington, DC 20007

Dumbarton Oaks Summer Fellowships **1764**
Dumbarton Oaks offers summer fellowships for periods of six to nine weeks in the three areas of Byzantine studies (including related aspects of late Roman, early Christian, western medieval, Slavic, and Near Eastern studies); Pre-Columbian studies of Mexico, Central America, and Andean South America; and studies in landscape architecture. Awards are for scholars (on any level of advancement) who are not incumbent fellows. Applications not postmarked by due date will be returned.
Amount $230 per week plus housing and lunch on weekdays; $1300 maximum travel expenses
Date(s) Application Is Due Nov 1.
Contact Carol Sellery, Director's Office, (202) 339-6410; fax: (202) 339-6419; email: DumbartonOaks@doaks.org
Internet http://www.doaks.org/fellowshipsann.html
Sponsor Dumbarton Oaks
1703 32nd St NW
Washington, DC 20007

Duncan L. Gordon Fellowships **1765**
Fellowships are available for research in pediatric medicine including nutrition, infectious diseases, mental retardation, environmental health, and clinical pharmacology, tenable in any agreed institution within Canada for one or two years. Candidates should be nominated by the head of the department in which they are employed or in which they will be employed upon completion of the fellowship. Nominating institutions must affirm their intention to employ the fellow upon completion of studies and to continue or establish a program in the field concerned. Award includes a full-time stipend, paid on a quarterly basis, plus a modest transportation allowance to take up the fellowship if required.
Requirements Fellowships are available to Canadian citizens or landed immigrants at a post-doctoral level and who are of outstanding academic achievement in a pediatric related health care field and who can provide evidence of aptitude for pediatric patient care, teaching, and research.
Amount $C47,500 maximum
Date(s) Application Is Due Oct 1.
Contact Pam Gilliland, Coordinator, National Grants Program, (416) 813-6166 ext 2354; fax: (416) 813-7311; email: national.grants@sickkids.ca
Internet http://www.sickkidsfoundation.com
Sponsor Sick Kids Foundation
555 University Ave
Toronto, ON M5G 1X8 Canada

Dysautonomia Research Grants **1766**
Grants are awarded to promote research into control and/or cure for familial dysautonomia with particular emphasis on genetic screening; prenatal and/or carrier tests are necessary. Funds awarded are variable and depend on research proposed.
Requirements Postdoctoral candidates must be connected with a recognized medical and/or teaching institution. There are no geographic limitations.
Amount $100,000
Date(s) Application Is Due Nov 30.
Contact Grants Administrator, (212) 949-6644; fax: (212) 682-7625; email: info@familialdysautonomia.org
Internet http://www.familialdysautonomia.org/researchgrantprogram.htm
Sponsor Dysautonomia Foundation
633 Third Ave, 12th Fl
New York, NY 10017

Dystonia Medical Research Grants and Fellowships **1767**
The research grants provide assistance in supporting investigations in specified areas of biomedical research pertinent to dystonia and related disorders. Research grants are being sought to develop important tools for DYT1 dystonia research; these include cell culture models, proteomics, genetic animal models of DYT1 dystonia, including transgenic and knock-in/ knock-out mice, Drosophila, C. elegans, and Zebrafish models. Grants are also being sought to develop new assays suitable for high throughput drug screening. Funding is available up to $40,000 for one-year pilot studies. A limited number of two-year grants are also available for larger studies with funding up to $75,000 per year. Fellowships assist post-doctoral students in establishing careers in dystonia research.
Requirements Eligible for research grants are all nonprofit organizations or institutions. Eligible for research fellowships are investigators with MD or PhD degrees. For all investigations involving humans, approval by the institution's human subject protection committee is necessary. The regulations pertaining to recombinant DNA research and animal welfare as established by PHS have been adopted by DMRF.
Restrictions Grant support will not be given for medical care of dystonia patients or for constructions and alterations.

Amount $50,000 per year for two years for fellowships; $75,000 per year for two years for research grants and contracts
Date(s) Application Is Due Dec 30.
Contact Dr. Robert McAlister, Executive Director, (312) 755-0198; fax: (312) 803-0138; email: dystonia@dystonia-foundation.org
Internet http://www.dystonia-foundation.org/research/other.asp?id=1
Sponsor Dystonia Medical Research Foundation
One E Wacker Dr, Ste 2430
Chicago, IL 60601-2001

E. Bright Wilson Award in Spectroscopy **1768**
Sponsored by Rohm and Haas Company and administered by ACS, this award recognizes outstanding accomplishments in fundamental or applied spectroscopy in chemistry. The award shall be granted to an individual without regard to age or nationality. The scope of the award is to cover all fields of spectroscopy in chemistry, both fundamental and applied. The recipient will deliver a lecture at the spring awards symposium of the ACS Division of Physical Chemistry.
Amount $5000 and up to $1500 travel expenses
Date(s) Application Is Due Feb 1.
Contact Awards Administrator, (202) 872-4408; fax: (202) 872-6317; email: awards@acs.org
Internet http://www.chemistry.org/portal/a/c/s/1/acsdisplay.html?DOC=awards%5Cwilson.html
Sponsor American Chemical Society
1155 16th St NW
Washington, DC 20036

E.A. Baker Foundation for the Prevention of Blindness Grants **1769**
The foundation awards grants to Canadian hospitals and universities conducting research in ophthalmology and eye diseases and awards fellowships for advanced training for Canadian ophthalmologists. The advanced training may be undertaken outside of Canada, but the ophthalmologist must return to Canada to teach or practice, particularly in remote areas.
Amount $C40,000 average
Date(s) Application Is Due Dec 1.
Contact Barbara Marjeram, Canadian National Institute for the Blind, (416) 486-2500 ext 7586; email: barbara.marjeram@cnib.ca
Internet http://www.cnib.ca/eng/eabaker/eabf
Sponsor E.A. Baker Foundation for the Prevention of Blindness
1929 Bayview Ave
Toronto, ON M4G 3E8 Canada

E.B. Hershberg Award for Important Discoveries in Medicinally Active Substances **1770**
This award, sponsored by Schering-Plough Corporation and administered by the American Chemical Society, is given biennially in odd-numbered years to recognize and encourage outstanding discoveries in the chemistry of medicinally active substances. The discovery for which the award is given should have been made during the last two decades. The award is given without regard to age or nationality of the recipient. Nominations are accepted in even-numbered years.
Requirements Any individual, except a member of the award committee, may submit one nomination or seconding letter for the award in any given year. The nominating documents consist of a letter of not more than 1000 words containing an evaluation of the nominee's accomplishments and a specific identification of the work to be recognized, a biographical sketch including date of birth, and a list of publications and patents authored by the nominee. Six copies of all items to be included in the nomination must be submitted.
Restrictions Self-nominations are not accepted.
Amount $3000 and reimbursement of up to $1000 for travel expenses to award meeting
Date(s) Application Is Due Feb 1.
Contact Awards Administrator, (202) 227-5558; fax: (202) 872-4615; email: awards@acs.org
Internet http://www.acs.org/portal/Chemistry?PID=acsdisplay.html&DOC=awards\hershberg.html
Sponsor American Chemical Society
1155 16th St NW
Washington, DC 20036

E.D.Thomas Fellowship **1771**
The foundation supports research into the diagnosis, prevention, and cure of leukemia and related hematological malignancies. The fellowship is awarded for one year, renewable yearly for two additional years upon satisfactory performance. The award supports costs not to exceed 8% and salary not to exceed $35,000 including fringe benefits, with the remainder for supplies and/or equipment. Applications must be requested by October 15.
Requirements Candidates must hold an MD or PhD degree and have completed at least three years postdoctoral training but must be less than 10 years post their first doctoral degree when the award begins. There are no restrictions based on nationality, but only one application will be considered from each sponsoring institution. Candidates must be committed to the research goals of the foundation, must be able to devote at least 80% of their time to the project and must have a sponsoring institution with the academic environment to provide adequate support for the proposed project.
Amount $50,000
Date(s) Application Is Due Nov 2.
Contact Grants Administrator, 34 93 414 55 66; fax: 34 93 201 0588; email: fundacio@fcarreras.es
Internet https://www.fcarreras.org/eng/seccio.php?opcion=5
Sponsor Jose Carreras International Leukemia Foundation
Muntaner, 383 2n
Barcelona 08021
Spain

E.J. Sierleja Memorial Fellowship **1772**
The fellowship is available annually to a graduate student pursuing advanced studies in the area of transportation, with priority consideration given to, but not limited to, students focusing on rail transportation. The institute supports the advancement of engineering education and research. The program is open to individuals in the United States, Canada, and Mexico.
Requirements Candidates for these awards must be active institute members, as reflected on the October chapter roster or before. New member applications must be completely processed prior to the end of September in order for students to be eligible. Students must be enrolled full-time in graduate or undergraduate industrial engineering programs for the upcoming year and must have an overall point-hour average of 3.40 on a scale of 4.00; graduate students must have had a 3.40 average as undergraduates to qualify. Students may not apply directly for this scholarship, they must be nominated.
Amount $600 for academic year
Date(s) Application Is Due Nov 15.
Contact Bonnie Cameron, Headquarters Operations Administrator, (770) 449-0461 ext 105; email: bcameron@iienet.org
Internet http://www.iienet.org/public/articles/index.cfm?cat=525
Sponsor Institute of Industrial Engineers
3577 Parkway Ln, Ste 200
Norcross, GA 30092

E.L. Wiegand Foundation Grants **1773**
The foundation provides grants to develop and strengthen programs and projects at Arizona, California, the District of Columbia, Idaho, Nevada, New York, Oregon, Utah, and Washington educational institutions in the academic areas of science, business, fine arts, and law; and medicine and health organizations in the areas of heart, eye, and cancer surgery, treatment, and research. The foundation also considers requests for projects that enrich children, communities, public policy, and art. Grants for education, including funds for computers and scientific equipment, are awarded. The board of trustees meets in February, June, and October to choose recipients, but applications may be submitted at any time. Application guidelines are available upon request.
Requirements Nonprofit organizations in Arizona, California, District of Columbia, Idaho, Nevada, New York, Oregon, Utah, and Washington State are eligible.
Amount $10,000-$200,000 average
Contact Kristen Avansino, Executive Director, (775) 333-0310; fax: (775) 333-0314
Sponsor E.L. Wiegand Foundation
165 W Liberty St, Ste 200
Reno, NV 89501

E.V. Murphree Award in Industrial and Engineering Chemistry **1774**
This award, sponsored by the ExxonMobile Research and Engineering Company and the ExxonMobile Chemical Company, is given annually to stimulate fundamental research in industrial and engineering chemistry, the development of chemical engineering principles, and their application to industrial processes. A nominee must have accomplished outstanding research of a theoretical or experimental nature in the fields of industrial chemistry or chemical engineering. The award is granted without regard to age or nationality.
Requirements Any individual, except a member of the award committee, may submit one nomination or seconding letter for the award in any given year. Nominating documents consist of a letter of not more than 1000 words containing an evaluation of the nominee's accomplishments and a specific identification of the work to be recognized, a biographical sketch including date of birth, and a list of publications and patents authored by the nominee.
Restrictions Self-nominations are not accepted.
Amount $5000 and $1000 maximum for travel to award meeting
Date(s) Application Is Due Feb 1.
Contact Awards Administrator, (202) 872-4408; fax: (202) 872-6317; email: awards@acs.org
Internet http://www.chemistry.org/portal/a/c/s/1/acsdisplay.html?DOC=awards%5Cmurphree.html
Sponsor American Chemical Society
1155 16th St NW
Washington, DC 20036

Earhart Foundation Institutional Grants **1775**
The foundation supports research fellowships for individual projects in economics, history, philosophy, international affairs, and political science. Fellowships are awarded

upon direct application to faculty members. Grants for research in these areas also are awarded to educational and research organizations. H.B. Earhart Fellowships are awarded for graduate study (recipients must be nominated). Fields of interest include history and archaeology, philosophy/ethics, economics, political science, and international studies. Types of support include professorships, publication, fellowships, research, grants to individuals, and scholarships to individuals. Application forms are not required.
Restrictions Grants are not awarded for capital, building, endowment funds, operating budgets, continuing support, annual campaigns, seed money, ermegency funds, deficit financing, matching gifts, or loans.
Amount $1000-$25,000 average
Contact Ingrid Gregg, President, (734) 761-8592
Sponsor Earhart Foundation
2200 Green Road, Suite H
Ann Arbor, MI 48105

Earle B. Barnes Award for Leadership in Chemical Research Management 1776
This award, sponsored by the Dow Chemical Company and administered by the American Chemical Society, is awarded yearly to recognize outstanding achievements in chemical research management. The award is intended to recognize those individuals who have demonstrated outstanding leadership and creativity in promoting the sciences of chemistry and chemical engineering in research management. Nominees should have demonstrated success in research management by exhibiting the proven ability to manage research projects and people. This leadership and creativity must have been demonstrated by a record of successful research projects and by a strong motivation of the researchers on those projects. Recognition of these accomplishments by peers is essential.
Requirements Any individual, except a member of the award committee, may submit one nomination or seconding letter for the award in any given year. The nominating documents consist of a letter of not more than 1000 words containing an evaluation of the nominee's accomplishments and a specific identification of the work to be recognized, a biographical sketch including date of birth, and a list of publications and patents authored by the nominee. A nominee must be a citizen of the United States. Six copies of all items to be included in the nomination must be submitted.
Restrictions Self-nominations are not accepted.
Amount $5000
Date(s) Application Is Due Feb 1.
Contact Awards Administrator, (202) 872-4408; fax: (202) 776-8211; email: awards@acs.org
Internet http://chemistry.org/portal/Chemistry?PID=acsdisplay.html&DOC=awards\barnes.html
Sponsor American Chemical Society
1155 16th St NW
Washington, DC 20036

Early American Industries Research Grants 1777
Awards are made to support research conducted by serious students and scholars for the study and better understanding of early American industries in homes, shops, farms, and on the sea; as well as the discovery, identification, classification, and preservation of obsolete tools, implements, and mechanical devices. Three to five grants will be awarded. Application must be made on forms supplied by the Grants in Aid Committee.
Requirements Grants in aid are available to all qualified applicants in general, but those who have completed the graduate level of their education will be given preference. Successful applicant is required to file a project report on a form supplied by the association that must include a statement of finances as well as a half-page abstract of the grantee's research.
Restrictions Grants may not be used to pay for salaries in whole or in part.
Amount $2000 maximum
Date(s) Application Is Due Mar 15.
Contact Grants in Aid Committee, (302) 652-7297
Internet http://www.eaiainfo.org/Grants.htm
Sponsor Early American Industries Association
1324 Shallcross Ave
Wilmington, DE 19806

Early Southern History and Decorative Arts Summer Institute 1778
The summer institute offers a four-week curriculum in a museum setting with lectures, object and room studies, research projects, field trips, and workshops, all dealing with early (pre-1821) southeastern US material culture. The program is sponsored by the museum and the University of North Carolina at Greensboro. Six hours of graduate credit in history can be earned. The program is designed for persons interested in American art, art history, American history, American studies, and museum studies.
Requirements Applicant must have graduate student status or be presently employed in a museum-related profession.
Amount $150-$350 for partial tuition
Date(s) Application Is Due Apr 20.
Contact Sally Gant, Director of Education, (336) 721-7360; fax: (336) 721-7367; email: sgant@oldsalem.org
Internet http://www.oldsalem.org/about/mesda.htm
Sponsor Museum of Early Southern Decorative Arts
P.O. Box 10310, Salem Sta
Winston-Salem, NC 27108

Earthwatch Institute Student Fellowships 1779
Earthwatch Student Fellowships offer students with limited exposure to science the opportunity to experience research first hand. Award recipients will: work and learn alongside inspiring professional scientists; discover how science and technology can advance our understanding of the world; interact with talented and committed peers and mentors.
Requirements High school teachers and counselors are encouraged to nominate one to two students with limited opportunities for enrichment and resources, and no prior experience helping a scientist conduct research. Current juniors are preferred, but sophomores and seniors are welcome to apply. Students with disabilities may be eligible for this program.
Contact Fellowship Program Officer, (800) 776-0188 ext 118; fax: (978) 461-2332; email: EducationAwards@earthwatch.org
Internet http://www.earthwatch.org/site/pp.asp?c=dsJSK6PFJnH&b=2221765
Sponsor Earthwatch Institute
3 Clock Tower Place, P.O. Box 75
Maynard, MA 01754-0075

East Stroudsburg University Graduate Assistantships 1780
Graduate assistantships are available in a variety of academic disciplines including pedagogy, sciences (biology, computer science, and general), social sciences (history and political science), and health sciences and human performance (public health, community health, movement studies, athletic training, cardiac rehabilitation, and exercise sciences). Stipends are based on 10-hour and 20-hour assignments with tuition waiver for the academic year. Minorities and women are strongly encouraged to apply.
Requirements A minimum 2.5 overall GPA and 3.0 GPA in applicant's major field are required.
Amount $2500-$5000
Date(s) Application Is Due Jun 15.
Contact Graduate Assistantships, Office of the Graduate School, (866) 837-6130 or (570) 422-3536; fax: (570) 422-3506; email: grad@po-box.esu.edu
Internet http://www.esu.edu/grants/gradcat/newasst.shtml
Sponsor East Stroudsburg University
200 Prospect St
East Stroudsburg, PA 18301-2999

East-West Center Graduate Fellowships 1781
The fellowship program is designed to give students the opportunity to undertake graduate studies at the University of Hawaii and interact with staff of the East-West Center on research subjects of interest to the center. Awards to master's candidates are for up to 24 months, to doctoral candidates up to 48 months.
Requirements Applicant must be a citizen or permanent resident of the United States or an Asian/Pacific Islander on the Exchange Visitor Program and must meet center guidelines and academic requirements for completing his or her degree. Recipients of the fellowship who are single or married with no accompanying dependents below 18 years of age are required to reside in Center dormitories.
Amount $17,000 approximately
Date(s) Application Is Due Nov 1.
Contact Awards Services Officer, EWC-UHM Scholarship Office, (808) 944-7111; fax: (808) 944-7730; email: EWCUHM@EastWestCenter.org
Internet http://www.eastwestcenter.org/semedu-program.asp?program_ID=1&Topic=Student&Area=Education
Sponsor East-West Center
1601 East-West Rd
Honolulu, HI 96848

East-West Center Jefferson Fellowships 1782
Each spring the center invites 12 to 14 midcareer American and Asian journalists in print and broadcasting to apply for the fellowships. The journalists spend four weeks at the center in an intensive program of seminars that examine Asian and American political, economic, energy, environmental, population, cultural, and security issues. The American fellows then embark on a four-week trip through Asia while the Asian fellows travel to the US mainland. All return to Honolulu for a final session of discussion and review. The selection committee gives priority to gatekeepers such as news editors, editorial editors and writers, broadcast producers, and assignment editors and producers. A stipend in Honolulu for five weeks at the center plus travel and a modest per diem for the travel portion of the program are provided; employers are expected to share costs where feasible.
Requirements The program is open to qualified journalists from the United States and from the Asian/Pacific area, ranging from Japan to Pakistan, to Australia and New Zealand, including the Pacific Island nations.
Date(s) Application Is Due Oct 26.
Contact Ann Hartman, Coordinator, (808) 944-7384; fax: (808) 944-7600; email: seminars@EastWestCenter.org
Internet http://www.eastwestcenter.org//semedu-program.asp?program_ID=10&Topic=Media%20Program&Area=Seminars
Sponsor East-West Center
1601 East-West Rd
Honolulu, HI 96848

Eastern Europe and the Independent States of the Former Soviet Union Research and Training Grants 1783

Grants are awarded to organizations to support national programs of advanced research; graduate training; language training; public dissemination of research data, methods, and findings; contact and collaboration among government and private specialists; and/or firsthand experience of the area by US specialists. Organizations that receive the grants act as intermediaries for the federal funds by conducting their own national, open competitions to make awards at the graduate level and above to individual students, scholars, or other institutions. Grant recipients have up to three years to spend their awards. Application deadline will be published in the Federal Register.
Requirements Applicants must be nonprofit organizations or institutions of higher education with an established track record in conducting research and training programs on the independent states of the former Soviet Union and countries of Eastern Europe. These organizations must run national programs of advanced research; graduate training; language training; public dissemination of research data, methods, and findings; contact and collaboration among Government and private specialists; and/or firsthand experience of the area by U.S. specialists.
Amount $129,000-$1.2 million range
Contact Kenneth Roberts, Executive Director, (202) 736-4572; fax: (202) 736-4851
Internet http://www.state.gov
Sponsor Department of State
2201 C St NW, Rm 2251
Washington, DC 20520

Eastman School of Music Graduate Awards Program 1784

The program offers financial support through the work opportunities that come with the awards. The award includes variable stipends plus approximately one-third to full tuition. The deadline of January 1 is for support of study beginning the following September.
Requirements Eligibility is restricted to persons who have been accepted for graduate study at the Eastman School of Music of the University of Rochester.
Contact Director, (585) 274-1560; email: cmccamman@esm.rochester.edu
Internet http://www.rochester.edu/Eastman/apply/finaid_grad.php
Sponsor University of Rochester, Eastman School of Music
26 Gibbs St
Rochester, NY 14604

Eaton Charitable Fund Grants 1785

The Fund is dedicated to supporting programs that improve the quality of life in communities where the company operates. The Fund gives primary consideration to requests for programs located in an Eaton community, recommended by an Eaton manager and where employees demonstrate leadership involvement. Programs selected for funding will have clearly defined objectives, measurable end results, and provide a positive return on the Funds investment. The Fund's primary interests are in support of community improvement, education, and arts and cultural programs. Program, project and capital grants are awarded. Capital grants are made for special purposes that meet specific community needs within the company's funding focus. On occasion, operating grants are awarded. Proposals should be sent to the manager of the Eaton facility located in an Eaton community.
Requirements Applicant organizations must be 501(c)3 tax exempt charities and be located in communities where the company has operations.
Restrictions Eaton does not make contributions to: annual operating budgets of United Way agencies or hospitals; medical research; endowment funds; debt retirement; religious organizations unless they are engaged in a significant program benefiting the entire community; fraternal or labor organizations; individuals or individual endeavors; fund raising benefits, sponsorships or other events.
Contact (216) 523-4944; fax: (216) 479-7013
Internet http://www.eaton.com/EatonCom/OurCompany/AboutUs/CorporateResponsibility/SocialCommitment/CorporateGiving/index.htm
Sponsor Eaton Charitable Fund
1111 Superior Avenue
Cleveland, OH 44114-2584

EBSCO Community College Learning Resources/Library Achievement Awards 1786

Two annual awards are given to recognize significant achievement in the areas of program development and leadership. Nominees for the program award should demonstrate significant achievement in development of an innovative learning resources/library program. Nominees for the leadership award should demonstrate significant achievement in advocacy of learning resources/library programs or services or leadership in professional organizations that are associated with the mission of community, junior, or technical colleges.
Requirements Individuals or groups from two-year institutions, as well as the two-year institutions themselves, are eligible to receive the awards.
Amount $500 each
Date(s) Application Is Due Dec 1.
Contact Matthew Burrell, Librarian, (850) 769-1551; email: mburrell@gulfcoast.edu
Internet http://www.ala.org/ala/acrl/acrlawards/ebscoawards.htm
Sponsor Association of College and Research Libraries
50 E. Huron Street
Chicago, IL 60611

Echoing Green Fellowships 1787

The program awards full-time fellowships to emerging entrepreneurs to create innovative domestic or international public service projects that seek to catalyze positive social change. The proposed project may be in any public service area, including but not limited to, the environment, arts, education, health, youth service and development, civil and human rights, and community and economic development. The fellowship provides a two-year stipend, healthcare benefits, online connectivity; access to Echoing Green's network of social entrepreneurs, training, and technical assistance. Application and guidelines are available online.
Requirements Applicants must be at least 18 years old and commit to leading the project for at least two years. Partnerships of up to two individuals also are eligible.
Restrictions Faith-based and research projects and lobbying activities are not eligible.
Amount $30,000 per year for two years, individual fellowships; $45,000 per year (per project, not per individual) for two years, partnership fellowships
Date(s) Application Is Due Dec 1.
Contact Fellowship Administrator, (212) 689-1165 ext 80; fax: (212) 689-9010; email: info@echoinggreen.org
Internet http://www.echoinggreen.org/index.cfm?useaction=Page.viewPage&pageID=41
Sponsor Echoing Green Foundation
60 E 42nd St, Ste 2901
New York, NY 10165

Edilia and Francois-Auguste De Montequin Fellowship in Iberian and Latin American Architecture 1788

The fellowship is awarded each year in support of travel costs for research on Spanish, Portuguese, or Ibero-American architecture. The fellowship is intended for graduate students and junior scholars, but senior scholars may also apply.
Amount $2000
Date(s) Application Is Due Oct 15.
Contact Pauline Saliga, Executive Director, (312) 573-1365; fax: (312) 573-1141; email: psaliga@sah.org or info@sah.org
Internet http://www.sah.org/index.php?module=ContentExpress&func=display&btitle=CE&mid=&ceid=59
Sponsor Society of Architectural Historians
1365 N Astor St
Chicago, IL 60610-2144

Edmund Niles Huyck Preserve Graduate and Postgraduate Research Grants 1789

Graduate and postgraduate investigators may apply for grants for the support of research utilizing the natural resources of the Biological Station of the Huyck Preserve. Included within the preserve are 2000 acres of natural and reforested woodlands, old fields, Lake Myosotis (100 acres), Lincoln Pond (10 acres), and approximately three miles of permanent and intermittent streams. Housing and laboratory space are provided. Write for instructions on application and additional information.
Requirements Applicants must be predoctoral and postdoctoral scientists whose research utilizes the natural resources of the Edmund Niles Huyck Preserve.
Amount $2500 maximum
Date(s) Application Is Due Feb 1.
Contact Richard Wyman, Executive Director, (518) 797-3440; fax: (518) 797-3440; email: rlwyman@capital.net
Internet http://www.huyckpreserve.org
Sponsor Edmund Niles Huyck Preserve
P.O. Box 189
Rensselaerville, NY 12147

Education Through Astronomy and Space Science Initiative 1790

This program was developed to establish a comprehensive approach to providing education and public outreach to enhance the publics understanding of space science. The spirit of the program is to provide start-up funding to explore innovative, creative ways to integrate astronomy and space science into US education and public outreach venues through partnerships between the astronomers/space scientists and education professionals.
Requirements Professionals in astronomy or space science with an affiliation to an institution within the United States are eligible to apply. The proposal must incorporate a partnership with at least one professional educator as coinvestigator.
Amount $20,000 maximum for small projects; $50,000 maximum for large projects
Contact Grant Administrator, Office of Public Outreach, (410) 338-4798; email: ideas@stsci.edu
Internet http://oposite.stsci.edu/pubinfo/edugroup/grants.html#top
Sponsor Space Telescope Science Institute
3700 San Martin Drive
Baltimore, MD 21218

Educational Communications and Technology Awards 1791

The awards given through the ECT Foundation promote scholarship and leadership in the field of educational communications and technology. Awards are made to defray doctoral dissertation research expenses, for the papers reporting studies addressing a question related to educational technology, and for the papers describing research findings that could be used to improve the process of instructional design, development,

and evaluation. Contact the awards program office for official guidelines for presenting a nomination or application.
Contact K.J. Saville, AECT Awards Chair, (906) 227-2413; email: ksaville@nmu.edu or aect@aect.org
Internet http://www.aect.org/Foundation/Awards/Awards.htm
Sponsor Association for Educational Communications and Technology
1800 N Stonelake Dr, Ste 2
Bloomington, IN 47408

Educational Ventures International Foundation Grants **1792**
The foundation funds nonprofits addressing important educational issues in areas where adequate funding from other sources is unavailable. The foundation's areas of interest include grants for educational technology, which provide grants for hardware, software, and peripherals for K-12 and underserved areas; grants for educational resources, which provide funding for resources to enhance teaching and learning environments in underserved areas; grants to encourage the development of new and innovative uses of technology to enhance teaching and learning; and grants for research, which provide funds to support research in math and technology education. Submit a three- to four-page proposal stating the program's goals and budget needs. Full proposals by invitation.
Requirements Nonprofit organizations are eligible.
Contact Grants Administrator, fax: (801) 659-2233
Sponsor Educational Ventures International Foundation
P.O. Box 5887
Carefree, AZ 85377-5887

Educause Jane N. Ryland Fellowships **1793**
This fellowship expands opportunities for information technology professionals to attend Educause events, thus helping to build future leaders. Fellowships recognize a combination of past achievement, personal and institutional commitment, potential benefit, and financial need. Awards are made on an annual basis, depending on an applicant's educational goals and the needs of his or her institution.
Requirements Recipients are selected annually on a competitive basis. Applicants may serve their institutions in any information technology management area: central IT organizations, academic units, or administrative departments.
Amount $500-$3000
Date(s) Application Is Due Nov 1.
Contact Fellowships Administrator, (303) 449-4430; fax: (303) 440-0461; email: ryland-fellowships@educause.edu
Internet http://www.educause.edu/awards/fellow
Sponsor Educause
4772 Walnut St, Ste 206
Boulder, CO 80301

Edward Bangs Kelley and Elza Kelley Foundation Grants **1794**
The Foundation's interest is primarily in Barnstable County, Massachusetts. The Foundation has been the leader in improving the health and welfare of the community. Grants are made to a great variety of health, social and human service agencies, as well as to cultural and environmental organizations. Town libraries, theatre and art groups, and musical organizations have been supported. Grants are sometimes utilized as seed money by young organizations.
Requirements Grant applicants must be tax-exempt organizations which are not private foundations and must be located in Barnstable County. The proposed project/program must have a direct benefit to the inhabitants of Barnstable County. If the tax-exempt organization is located outside of Barnstable, but the proposed project/program will have a direct and substantial benefit to the inhabitants of Barnstable, the grant application may be eligible for funding.
Restrictions Applicants must be residents of Barnstable County, Massachusetts, or must demonstrate very significant ties to Barnstable County.
Contact Henry Murphy Jr., Administrative Manager, (508) 775-3117; email: contact@kelleyfoundation.org
Internet http://www.kelleyfoundation.org
Sponsor Edward Bangs Kelley and Elza Kelley Foundation
243 South Street, P.O. Drawer M
Hyannis, MA 02601

Edward C. and Ann T. Roberts Foundation Grants **1795**
The foundation awards grants to support arts (visual arts and performing arts) and culture, including education and programs that benefit the disadvantaged and children in Hartford, CT. Types of support include capital campaigns, building construction/renovation, and program development. The board meets in March, June, September, and December. There are no application forms.
Requirements 501(c)3 nonprofit organizations in Hartford, CT, may apply.
Restrictions Grants are not made to individuals or for scholarship aid.
Date(s) Application Is Due Feb 1; May 1; Aug 1; Nov 1.
Contact Elizabeth Normen, Executive Director, (860) 233-0228; fax: (860) 236-8098; email: EJNormen@aol.com
Internet http://www.fdncenter.org/grantmaker/e&aroberts
Sponsor Edward C. and Ann T. Roberts Foundation
P.O. Box 271588
West Hartford, CT 06127-1588

Edward F. Kook-USITT Endowment Fund Grants **1796**
The goal of this program is to further the objectives of the institute. Only new projects and research with the purpose of advancement of the industry will be considered for annual grants. The program must benefit the industry of theatrical design and technology and clearly seek new knowledge through experimentation, research, or collection of resources; serve a cross-section of the institute; and provide results that are made available to institute members. Projects may involve theoretical research, applied research, statistical survey, or historical research. A formal application form must be obtained from the Web site or directly from the institute.
Requirements An applicant must be a current member of USITT to apply; membership is open to anyone.
Amount $10,000 for project support grants; $15,000 maximum for fellowships
Date(s) Application Is Due Jan 10.
Contact Grants Administrator, Marketing and Development, (800) 938-7488; fax: (866) 398-7488; email: info@office.usitt.org
Internet http://www.usitt.org/activities/GrantsFellowshipsIntro.html
Sponsor United States Institute for Theater Technology Inc
6443 Ridings Rd
Syracuse, NY 13206-1111

Edward G. McDowell Traveling Scholarships **1797**
The scholarships are awarded annually for a one-year period of travel, research, and study in Paris and Europe; and are open to unmarried members of the league of either sex, who must have pursued a course of study at the league for at least 16 months in a full-time class of which a minimum six months must have been during the current school year. Applications are available in mid-March, and recipients are announced in early May.
Requirements Candidates must be league members for at least 16 months.
Restrictions Winners are not eligible for subsequent McDowell competitions.
Amount $10,000 approximately
Contact Gaetano Scognamillo, Scholarship Coordinator, (212) 247-4510; fax: (212) 541-7024
Internet http://www.theartstudentsleague.org/Navigation/Home/HP-FRAME.html
Sponsor Art Students League of New York
215 W 57th St
New York, NY 10019

Edward S. Moore Foundation Grants **1798**
The foundation awards grants to nonprofits in Connecticut and New York in its areas of interest, including youth, hospitals, education, cultural programs, museums, and Christian religion. Types of support include operating budgets, continuing support, annual campaigns, seed money, emergency funds, building funds, equipment, land acquisition, endowment funds, matching funds, internships, scholarship funds, special projects, and research. There are no application deadlines. The board meets in January, April, July, and October to consider proposals.
Requirements Nonprofits in Connecticut and New York may submit proposals.
Restrictions Grants are not awarded to individuals or for deficit financing, publications, or conferences.
Amount $10,000-$50,000 average
Contact John W. Cross III, President, (203) 629-4591
Sponsor Edward S. Moore Foundation
30 Lismore Ln
Greenwich, CT 06831

Edwin F. Church Medal Award **1799**
This award is given annually to an individual who has rendered eminent service in increasing the value, importance, and attractiveness of mechanical engineering education. Mechanical engineering is used here in its broadest sense of preparation for any aspect or level of mechanical engineering through any appropriate mechanism including universities, technical institutes, professional societies and private groups, in-house professional development programs of industrial concerns and governmental agencies, or programmed learning and self-instruction systems. The qualifications for this medal are detailed and rigorous and a prospective nominator may secure the nomination form and details from the ASME. The award is not intended to recognize professional educators on that merit alone.
Requirements The award may be made to one recipient of any age who need not be a member of ASME.
Amount $2500
Date(s) Application Is Due Feb 15.
Contact Gilda DiTullio, Manager, (212) 591-7736; fax: (212) 705-7739; email: ditulliog@asme.org
Internet http://www.asme.org/honors/ms71/gaa/church.html
Sponsor American Society of Mechanical Engineers
3 Park Ave
New York, NY 10016

Edwin O. Reischauer Institute of Japanese Studies Postdoctoral Fellowships **1800**
The program awards postdoctoral fellowships to give recipients the opportunity to turn dissertations into publishable manuscripts. Fellowships are for 10 to 12 months, beginning July 1 or September 1, and include a stipend and health insurance coverage

for grantee. Fellows receive office space and access to libraries and resources of Harvard University.
Requirements Applicants should have received the PhD in Japanese studies in any area of the humanities or social sciences since 1999. Those without the degree must complete all requirements by July 1 of the current year.
Amount $20,000 stipend
Date(s) Application Is Due Mar 1.
Contact Ruiko Connor, Staff Assistant Administrative Officer, (617) 495-3220; email: rconnor@fas.harvard.edu
Internet http://www.gsas.harvard.edu/pdfs/reischauer_dcapp.pdf
Sponsor Harvard University
1737 Cambridge St
Cambridge, MA 02138

Edwin S. Webster Foundation Grants **1801**
The policy of the foundation is to support charitable organizations that are well known to the trustees, with emphasis on special projects and capital programs, or operating income for hospitals, medical research, education, youth agencies, cultural activities, and programs addressing the needs of minorities. Types of support include operating budgets, continuing support, annual campaigns, building funds, equipment, land acquisition, endowment funds, matching funds, scholarship funds, professorships, internships, fellowships, special projects, and research. Deadlines are in April and September; the board meets in June and December. A recipient is notified usually within 15 days from meeting date.
Requirements Grantees must provide evidence of their tax-exempt status. Requests for grants must be submitted in letter form. Funding is confined primarily to the New England area.
Restrictions Grants are not made to organizations outside the United States or to individuals.
Amount $10,000-$50,000 average
Date(s) Application Is Due Apr 15; Sep 30.
Contact Michelle Jenney, (617) 426-7080; fax: (617) 426-7087; email: mjenney@grants.management.com
Sponsor Edwin S. Webster Foundation
c/o Grants Management Assocs, 77 Summer St, 8th Fl
Boston, MA 02110

EF Behavioral Sciences Student Fellowships **1802**
This fellowship stimulates individuals to pursue careers in epilepsy in either research or practice settings. Appropriate fields include sociology, social work, psychology, anthropology, nursing, economics, vocational rehabilitation, counseling, political science, and others relevant to epilepsy research or practice. Annual deadline dates may vary; contact program staff for exact dates.
Requirements Applicant must be actively enrolled in a degree program at the time the fellowship is to be undertaken. The fellowship must be undertaken during a free period in the student's year, e.g., during the summer. Both graduate and undergraduate students are eligible provided all other eligibility criteria are met. The project must be carried out at an approved facility.
Amount $3000 stipend
Date(s) Application Is Due Mar 1.
Contact Fellowship Programs, Research and Professional Education, (301) 459-3700; fax: (301) 577-2684; email: grants@efa.org
Internet http://www.epilepsyfoundation.org/research/grants.cfm
Sponsor Epilepsy Foundation
4351 Garden City Dr, Ste 406
Landover, MD 20785-7223

EF Health Sciences Student Fellowships **1803**
Three-month fellowships are awarded to medical and health science students for work on epilepsy study projects. The project may be carried out at the US institution of the student's choice where there are ongoing programs of research, training, or service in epilepsy. Application forms and guidelines are available upon request. Annual deadline dates may vary; contact program staff for exact dates.
Requirements Predoctoral training students in the Health Sciences may be accepted at any point in their schooling-following acceptance but before beginning the first year, or in the period immediately following their final year. A supervisor or preceptor must accept responsibility for the supervision of the student program and for the submission of a full report to the institute upon completion of the program.
Amount $3000 stipend
Date(s) Application Is Due Mar 1.
Contact Fellowship Programs, Research and Professional Education, (301) 459-3700; fax: (301) 577-2684; email: grants@efa.org
Internet http://www.epilepsyfoundation.org/research/grants.cfm
Sponsor Epilepsy Foundation
4351 Garden City Dr, Ste 406
Landover, MD 20785

EF Postdoctoral Research Training Fellowships **1804**
The foundation awards grants and fellowships for cutting-edge research into the causes of epilepsy. Program goals include understanding basic mechanisms, developing new therapeutic approaches, understanding the behavioral and psychosocial aspects of having epilepsy, and encouraging the professional development of scientists and healthcare professionals. The purpose of the fellowship is to support predoctoral students with dissertation research related to epilepsy. Applications from all fields of research pertinent to epilepsy will be considered.
Requirements Physicians or PhD neuroscientists who desire postdoctoral research experience are eligible for these fellowships, which must be carried out at an approvable facility where there is an ongoing epilepsy research program. Applicants must be licensed to practice medicine in the United States or Canada.
Restrictions Individuals holding faculty appointments at the level of assistant professor or higher are ineligible.
Amount $40,000 maximum
Date(s) Application Is Due Sep 1.
Contact Research and Professional Education, (301) 459-3700; fax: (301) 577-2684
Internet http://www.epilepsyfoundation.org/research/grants.html
Sponsor Epilepsy Foundation
4351 Garden City Dr, Ste 406
Landover, MD 20785

EF Predoctoral Research Training Fellowship **1805**
The predoctoral research training fellowship supports predoctoral students with dissertation research related to epilepsy, thus strengthening their interest in establishing epilepsy research as a career direction. Annual deadline dates may vary; contact program staff for exact dates.
Requirements Graduate students pursuing a PhD degree in neuroscience, physiology, pharmacology, psychology, biochemistry, genetics, nursing, or pharmacy may apply.
Amount $20,000 ($19,000 stipend plus $1000 travel allowance)
Date(s) Application Is Due Sep 1.
Contact Research and Professional Education, (301) 459-3700; fax: (301) 577-2684; email: grants@efa.org
Internet http://www.epilepsyfoundation.org/research/grants.cfm
Sponsor Epilepsy Foundation
4351 Garden City Dr, Ste 406
Landover, MD 20785

EF Research and Training Fellowships for Clinicians **1806**
These fellowships offer qualified individuals the opportunity to develop expertise in epilepsy research through a one-year training experience and involvement in an epilepsy research project. The purpose of the fellowships is to develop academic clinicians to teach patient care of persons with epilepsy and advance knowledge about epilepsy through clinical investigation. Applications from individuals interested in acquiring experience in the conduct of human clinical studies and who plan to study epilepsy as a human disorder are encouraged. Emphasis is placed on individuals who will be trained in clinical research in epilepsy rather than use epilepsy as a tool in their research in other fields. Applications from women, members of minority groups, and people with disabilities are especially encouraged.
Requirements Individuals with the MD or DO degree who will have completed residency training in neurology, neurosurgery, pediatrics, internal medicine, or psychiatry by the time the fellowship commences and desire additional postdoctoral clinical research experience are eligible. Applicants planning to work in the United States receive preference.
Restrictions These are training fellowships and will not be granted to individuals who have received faculty appointments at the level of assistant professor or higher. Individuals may not receive concurrent support for more than one EFA or AES grant or fellowship.
Amount $50,000
Date(s) Application Is Due Oct 14.
Contact Research and Professional Education, (301) 459-3700; fax: (301) 577-2684
Internet http://www.epilepsyfoundation.org/research/grants.cfm
Sponsor Epilepsy Foundation
4351 Garden City Dr, Ste 406
Landover, MD 20785

EFWA Accounting Research Grants **1807**
The foundation funds issues papers by faculty, individuals, or business to research technical accounting issues or other issues furthering women in the accounting profession. The foundation also provides research grants for women faculty members to contribute to the field of accounting and assist faculty in their careers.
Amount $3000
Date(s) Application Is Due May 1.
Contact Cynthia Hires, (610) 407-9229; fax: (610) 644-3713; email: info@efwa.org
Internet http://www.efwa.org/research.htm
Sponsor Educational Foundation for Women in Accounting
P.O. Box 1925
Southeastern, PA 19399-1925

EFWA Accounting Scholarships **1808**
The program provides a one-year academic scholarship for women who are pursuing a PhD in accounting. Applications are posted online in January.
Amount $1000-$5000

Date(s) Application Is Due Mar 15.
Contact Cynthia Hires, (610) 407-9229; fax: (610) 644-3713; email: info@efwa.org
Internet http://www.efwa.org/scholarships.htm
Sponsor Educational Foundation for Women in Accounting
P.O. Box 1925
Southeastern, PA 19399-1925

Eileen J. Garrett Scholarship **1809**
The foundation awards an annual scholarship for research and study in parapsychology. Any student attending an accredited college or university who has already demonstrated an academic interest in parapsychology and plans to pursue the subject as a career may apply. Applications and collateral material may be submitted via post, fax, or as MS Word or Adobe Acrobat attachments. Guidelines are available online.
Amount $3000
Date(s) Application Is Due Jul 15.
Contact Garrett Scholarship, (212) 628-1550; fax: (212) 628-1559; email: office@parapsychology.org
Internet http://www.parapsychology.org/dynamic/040200.html
Sponsor Parapsychology Foundation
P.O. Box 1562
New York, NY 10021

Eisenhower Exchange International Fellowships **1810**
These competitive fellowships are for US citizens to go abroad for a professional exchange program. The program includes travel throughout the selected country/region for research/inquiry purposes. Countries participating have included Argentina, Germany, Hungary, Ireland, Malaysia, Peru, and Taiwan. Fellowships include travel and living expenses and program arrangements/appointment scheduling for a one- to three-month program. Spouse participation is encouraged. Fellowships are awarded in the year preceding departure. Contact the office or visit the Web site for the most current information on participating countries and deadline dates.
Requirements Midcareer professionals who are US citizens with demonstrated leadership ability and significant contributions to their fields are eligible to apply.
Contact USA Fellowships, (215) 546-1738; fax: (215) 546-4567; email: ike@eisenhowerfellowships.org
Internet http://eisenhowerfellowships.org
Sponsor Eisenhower Exchange Fellowships
256 S 16th St
Philadelphia, PA 19102

Ekhagastiftelsen Foundation Grants **1811**
The foundation operates in Sweden and supports research into agricultural production without the use of poisons and artificial means; and research into the production of natural foods and medical methods based on the capacity of human beings to cure themselves. Types of support include grants to organizations and scholarships and fellowships to individuals.
Contact Grants Administrator, 46 70 240 81 81; fax: 46-08-21-83-76; email: info@ekhagastiftelsen.se
Internet http://www.ekhagastiftelsen.se/eng/stiftelsen.html
Sponsor Ekhagastiftelsen Foundation
Box 34012
Stockholm SE-100 26 Sweden

El Pomar Leadership Development and Community Engagement Postgraduate Fellowship **1812**
The program educates young leaders about the role of nonprofit organizations and the foundation within the communities of Colorado. The two-year postgraduate program also focuses on professional development and prepares fellows for positions of leadership in Colorado and the nation. Fellows serve the foundation's operating programs, such as EPYCS, a high school philanthropy initiative. In addition, fellows will be thoroughly educated in the nature of the nonprofit sector and the role of foundations. At a minimum, fellows participate in monthly courses in public speaking, financial and investment management, nonprofit management, fundraising and strategic planning, and an annual Outward Bound course in the central mountain ranges of Colorado.
Requirements Applicant must be a graduate of a four-year university or college, have a Colorado affiliation (e.g., be a state resident, have attended an in-state university or college, or have immediate family who are residents or past residents), and demonstrate a strong leadership capability and potential.
Amount $27,000 starting salary
Contact Grants Administrator, (800) 554-7711 or (719) 633-7733; email: fellowship@elpomar.org
Internet http://www.elpomar.org/page.asp?pageid=0|6|30&id=0|fellowship
Sponsor El Pomar Foundation
10 Lake Cir
Colorado Springs, CO 80906

Eleanor Naylor Dana Charitable Trust Grants **1813**
The trust supports biomedical research and the performing arts. In the biomedical program, grants are awarded to support clinical investigation by established scientists to pursue innovative projects designed to improve medical practice or prevent disease. Grants do not support large-scale field studies of a therapeutic or epidemiological nature. Grants for the performing arts support US programs benefiting the public with long-range potential. Giving primarily is in areas east of the Mississippi River. The foundation is interested in the organization's history and its public service.
Requirements Established scientists working under a qualified US institution's approval and US arts organizations are eligible to apply.
Restrictions The biomedical program does not make grants for instrumentation alone or solely for conference or individual travel. The arts program will not fund deficits; exhibits, publications, or conclaves; or individuals.
Amount $5000-$50,000 average
Date(s) Application Is Due Feb 1; May 1; Sep 1; Nov 1.
Contact Trust Administrator, (212) 754-2890; fax: (212) 754-2892
Sponsor Eleanor Naylor Dana Charitable Trust
c/o The Trustees, P.O. Box. 1803, Murray Hill Sta
New York, NY 10156

Eli Lilly & Company Foundation Grants Program **1814**
Discretionary grants are awarded in two categories: nonprofit groups aligned with company interests, and grants in Indianapolis and several other communities with significant employee populations. Company-aligned giving focuses on public policy research, health and human services aligned with major therapeutic interests, and academic relations. Community-aligned giving focuses on culture, K-12 education and youth development, locally aligned healthcare organizations, fencerow neighborhood groups, and diversity. The foundation supports organizations within these categories that have a well-defined sense of purpose, a demonstrated commitment to maximizing available resources, and a reputation for meeting objectives and delivery quality programs and services.
Restrictions Grants do not support individuals; endowments; debt reduction; religious or sectarian programs for religious purposes; bands or fraternal, labor, athletic, or veterans organizations; political contributions; beauty or talent contests; fundraising activities related to individual sponsorship; conferences or media productions; nonaccredited education groups; or memorials.
Date(s) Application Is Due Jun 30; Dec 31.
Contact Thomas King, President, (317) 276-3177; fax: (317) 277-2025
Internet http://www.lilly.com
Sponsor Eli Lilly & Company Foundation
Lilly Corporate Ctr
Indianapolis, IN 46285

Eli Lilly & Company Reintegration Scholarships **1815**
The goal of the scholarship is to help people with schizophrenia and related schizophrenia-spectrum disorders to acquire the educational and vocational skills necessary to reintegrate into society, secure jobs, and regain their lives. The program is designed to offer financial assistance for a wide range of educational opportunities in which students work to attain a certificate or degree, including high school equivalency programs; trade or vocational school programs; and associate, bachelor, and graduate degrees. Guidelines and application are available online.
Requirements Applicants must be diagnosed with schizophrenia, schizophreniform, or schizoaffective disorder; be currently receiving medical treatment for the disease, including medications and psychiatric follow-up; be actively involved in rehabilitative or reintegrative efforts, such as clubhouse membership, part-time work, volunteer efforts, or school enrollment; and complete an application package that includes an application form, essay, transcripts (if applicable), recommendation forms from three references, and school financial requirements.
Contact Lilly Secretariat, (800) 809-8202; email: lillyscholarships@reintegration.com
Internet http://www.reintegration.com/resources/scholarships
Sponsor Eli Lilly & Company
310 Busse Hwy, PMB 327
Park Ridge, IL 60068-3251

Elisabeth Severance Prentiss Foundation Grants Program **1816**
The foundation awards the majority of its support in the field of health and medicine. Scientific and medical research, hospitals, health projects, medical education, and care and support of the elderly are funded. Types of support include building programs, equipment needs, research, operating budgets, continuing support, seed grants, endowment funds, and projects/programs. Decision makers favor specific projects over general operating support. The maximum term of a commitment is five years, with preference for proposals for three years or less. Special consideration will be given to requests from applicants in the Cuyahoga County area. The board meets in June and December.
Requirements Grants are awarded to promote and improve medical services in the greater Cleveland, OH, area.
Restrictions Grants are not awarded to individuals for scholarships, fellowships, or grants in aid; or to organizations for fund-raising campaigns, surveys, assessments, studies, or planning activities.
Amount $10,000-$100,000 average
Date(s) Application Is Due May 15; Nov 15.
Contact Michael Galland, c/o National City Bank, (216) 222-2736
Sponsor Elisabeth Severance Prentiss Foundation
P.O. Box 94651
Cleveland, OH 44104

Elizabeth Glaser Pediatric AIDS Foundation International Leadership Awards 1817

The Award program is designed to invest in trained individuals in resource-poor countries who have the potential to develop programs which will have a direct impact on the pediatric HIV epidemic in their country, but that lack the resources to do so. This program will complement existing training programs by providing support after training is completed. The Award specifically seeks to identify individuals who are likely to have an enduring impact on control of the epidemic. Applicants may apply for support to create and or scale-up effective pediatric HIV/AIDS research and/or implementation programs including those addressing epidemiology, prevention of mother-to-child transmission, treatment of infected mothers and infants, continuum of care and scale up of prevention services to include care and treatment, development of national policies or strategies to combat pediatric HIV, assessment of the economic impact of disease and its prevention, or to help train additional in-country and regional scientists and program leaders. Award recipients will be asked to mentor a minimum of three additional people who would benefit from the experience and could help them achieve their goals. These are individuals who would be hired and trained to work on the project proposed by the applicant. The Award provides up to $100,000 in total costs per year for three years for a total of $300,000. Funding in years 2 and 3 is dependant on progress in year one and is not guaranteed. Letters of Intent are due by August 24th, with full applications solicited by August 31st and full applications due on September 28th. Awards are made to institutions on behalf of individuals.
Requirements Applicants must be from either Africa or India, and performing work in either Africa or India in order to apply. Special interested will be given to applications from the African nations of South Africa and Tanzania, but the foundation will consider applicants from other African countries as well. Applicants must demonstrate commitment to continuing to work in a developing country on HIV/AIDS when the award is complete, which is a requirement of the award. Applicants are expected to be in the process of establishing successful careers and programs. Most applicants will have completed training within the past 5 years. Senior investigators such as Full Professors will usually not be eligible for the award. Applicants must hold a position at a public or private non-profit institution that will allow him or her adequate time and provide appropriate facilities to perform the work proposed.
Restrictions U.S. citizens or European citizens living in these countries are not eligible to apply. Previous International Leadership Award recipients will not be eligible for this round of funding. Grants can not be made directly to individuals.
Amount $100,000 in total costs per year for three years
Date(s) Application Is Due Sep 28.
Contact Chris Hudnall; (310) 314-1459, ext. 154; fax: (310) 314-1469; email: Chris@pedaids.org or research@pedaids.org
Internet http://www.pedaids.org/GrantsandAwards/Awards/International%20Leadership%20Award.aspx
Sponsor Elizabeth Glaser Pediatric AIDS Foundation
2950 31st Street, Suite 125
Santa Monica, CA 90405

Elizabeth Glaser Pediatric AIDS Foundation Research Grants 1818

The goal of this program is to provide initial funding to pediatric AIDS investigators, which will enable them to gather preliminary data to answer questions quickly and/or obtain sufficient results to apply to other granting agencies. One- and two-year grants are available. The grant-making process begins when the Foundation issues a formal Request for Applications (RFA), which is distributed to thousands of researchers worldwide. General RFAs allow the Foundation to identify promising new ideas on the cutting edge of HIV/AIDS research; targeted RFAs are designed to elicit applications from scientists working in areas that have been deemed critically important by Foundation think tanks and scientific advisors. Investigators are required to submit a pre-application letter of intent (LOI). LOIs are reviewed and pre-screened by internal Foundation staff and members of the advisory board assigned to a particular program committee, and full grant applications are solicited from those investigators whose LOIs are most highly recommended.
Requirements Applicant must have a full-time academic and/or institutional appointment. Investigators outside the United States may apply.
Restrictions Only one application per investigator will be accepted.
Amount $80,000 per year
Contact Chris Hudnall; (310) 314-1459, ext. 154; fax: (310) 314-1469; email: Chris@pedaids.org or research@pedaids.org
Internet http://www.pedaids.org/GrantsandAwards/Grant%20Application%20and%20Review%20P.aspx
Sponsor Elizabeth Glaser Pediatric AIDS Foundation
2950 31st Street, Suite 125
Santa Monica, CA 90405

Elizabeth Glaser Pediatric AIDS Foundation Two-Year International Scholar Award 1819

The Foundation is offering a postdoctoral fellowship for clinicians/scientists from developing countries. The program is aimed at health care professionals who have specific training or experience with HIV/AIDS and hold an M.D. or Ph.D. Applicants must demonstrate commitment to continuing to work in a developing country on HIV/AIDS when the award is complete, as the emphasis of this program is on building long-term scientific capacity in developing countries. The subjects for these projects could include, but are not limited to, the following: epidemiology; issues related to implementation of either prevention or therapy programs; transmission of the HIV virus from mother to infant, including breast-milk transmission and prevention; pediatric HIV vaccine development; antiretroviral drug treatment including pharmacology, complications, and resistance; and microbicide research.
Requirements Applicants must be from a developing country, and performing work in a developing country. The Foundation encourages those who are determined to improve care in the international setting, as well as those interested in basic science, to apply.
Restrictions United States or European citizens living in developing countries are not eligible to apply.
Amount $57,225
Contact Chris Hudnall; (310) 314-1459, ext. 154; fax: (310) 314-1469; email: Chris@pedaids.org or research@pedaids.org
Internet http://www.pedaids.org/GrantsandAwards/Awards/Two-Year%20International%20Award.aspx
Sponsor Elizabeth Glaser Pediatric AIDS Foundation
2950 31st Street, Suite 125
Santa Monica, CA 90405

Elizabeth Glaser Pediatric AIDS Foundation Two-Year Scholar Awards 1820

The Awards are postdoctoral fellowships that provide two years of salary support, plus supplies and/or travel costs toward medical research on pediatric HIV/AIDS. Annual salaries—based on years of postdoctoral experience—range from $30,000 to $46,000. These awards provide a powerful incentive for a new generation of scientists to take an early professional interest in studying pediatric HIV/AIDS. Scientists are supported by a mentor experienced in HIV/AIDS research. Through this mentoring relationship, a growing number of talented investigators are focusing their efforts on helping to bring an end to HIV/AIDS in children.
Requirements Scholars must select an experienced sponsor with appropriate qualifications to oversee the proposed research. The sponsor should be a faculty member with an advanced degree (M.D. or Ph.D.) who will oversee the research, provide guidance to the applicant, and can provide evidence of the institution's commitment to the career development of the applicant.
Amount $60,000 maximum
Contact Chris Hudnall; (310) 314-1459, ext. 154; fax: (310) 314-1469; email: Chris@pedaids.org or research@pedaids.org
Internet http://www.pedaids.org/GrantsandAwards/Awards/Two-YearScholar.aspx
Sponsor Elizabeth Glaser Pediatric AIDS Foundation
2950 31st Street, Suite 125
Santa Monica, CA 90405

Elizabeth M. Irby Foundation Grants 1821

The foundation awards grants to Mississippi nonprofits in its areas of interest, including arts and culture, elementary education, secondary education, higher education, social services, and Christian churches and religious organizations. Types of support include general operating support, continuing support, annual campaigns, capital campaigns, building construction/renovation, endowment funds, emergency funds, program development, research, scholarship funds, and matching funds. There are no application forms or deadlines.
Requirements Mississippi nonprofit organizations may apply.
Restrictions Individuals are ineligible.
Amount $250-$500,000 range
Contact Stuart Irby, President, (601) 989-1811
Sponsor Elizabeth M. Irby Foundation
P.O. Box 1819
Jackson, MS 39215

Elizabeth McGraw Foundation Grants 1822

The foundation awards grants nationally, with a focus on the US Northeast, in its areas of interest, including cancer research, elementary and secondary education, art museums, performing arts (opera and theater), and culture. There are no application deadlines or specific guidelines.
Contact Charles B. Fischer, Jr., Managing Director, (561) 659-8844; fax: (561) 659-8829; email: charles.b.fischer@bd.com
Sponsor Elizabeth McGraw Foundation
c/o Deutsche Bank, 350 Royal Palm Way
Palm Beach, FL 33480

Elizabeth Ordway Dunn Foundation Grants 1823

The foundation's grants program awards funds for special projects in conservation and environmental concerns that benefit Florida. Some support is also given for historic preservation. Special interests in the environmental field include preservation of biological diversity, protection of coastal and fresh water ecosystems, conservation of land and wildlife resources, comprehensive planning and growth management, environmental education, environmental health, energy conservation and the development of renewable resources, marine conservation, and pollution prevention and toxics use reduction. Special interests in the field of historic preservation include education and appropriate use of architecturally and historically significant properties, particularly those that are located in fragile and threatened natural areas. Types of support include programs/

projects and seed grants. Applicants are urged to submit concept papers; full proposals will be invited. Grants are often awarded in partial support of a project.
Requirements 501(c)3 organizations that are not 509(a) private charities are eligible.
Restrictions The foundation does not award grants to support individuals or sectarian religious activities or for capital purposes, operating budgets, endowments, or deficit financing.
Amount $5000-$30,000 range
Date(s) Application Is Due Mar 15; Sep 15.
Contact Robert Jensen, Managing Director, (305) 667-5521; email: eodf@worldnet.att.net
Sponsor Elizabeth Ordway Dunn Foundation
P.O. Box 016309
Miami, FL 33101-6309

Ellison Medical Foundation Senior Scholar Awards **1824**
The awards enable established investigators working at US institutions to conduct up to four years of research in the basic biological and clinical sciences relevant to understanding aging processes and age-related diseases and disabilities. The award is intended to provide significant support to established investigators in order to allow the development of new, creative research programs by investigators who may not currently be conducting aging research or who may wish to develop new research programs in aging. Acceptable uses for award funds include salary, other personnel, equipment, supplies, resource acquisition, and travel. (Carry-overs in excess of $25,000 must be approved by the Ellison Medical Foundation Scholars Program Office.) Full indirect costs at the NIH negotiated rate will be provided. Ten awards are made annually. Application deadline is for letters of intent.
Requirements Established investigators working at US institutions are eligible.
Amount $150,000 maximum per year
Date(s) Application Is Due Mar 9.
Contact Dr. Richard Sprott, Executive Director, (301) 657-1830; fax: (301) 657-1828; email: rsprott@ellison-med-fn.org
Internet http://www.ellison-med-fn.org/emf_applications.jsp
Sponsor Ellison Medical Foundation
4710 Bethesda Ave, Ste 204
Bethesda, MD 20814

Ellison Medical Foundation Senior Scholar Awards in Global Infectious Diseases **1825**
The program funds up to four years of basic research on molecular and cellular mechanisms of parasitology and infectious diseases that result from microbial, protozoan, or viral pathogenesis--with special focus on tuberculosis, malaria, and parasitoses. Awards are intended to inspire new directions that may entail substantial risk. Ten awards are made annually. The listed application deadline is for letters of intent; full applications are by invitation.
Requirements Investigators at least four years beyond their postdoctoral fellowship, employed by US 501(c)3 institutions, or US colleges or universities, are eligible to apply. Whereas the foundation only makes awards to US nonprofit institutions, the program encourages formation of research consortia between US institutions and those in other disease-endemic countries, as through a subcontract mechanism, when such collaborations will benefit the proposed research.
Restrictions The awards are not intended to supplement ongoing, already funded programs.
Amount $150,000 maximum per year
Date(s) Application Is Due Mar 9.
Contact Dr. Richard Sprott, Executive Director, (301) 657-1830; fax: (301) 657-1828
Internet http://www.ellison-med-fn.org/emf_applications.jsp
Sponsor Ellison Medical Foundation
4710 Bethesda Ave, Ste 204
Bethesda, MD 20814

Ellison Medical Foundation/AFAR Senior Postdoctoral Fellowships **1826**
The program seeks to encourage and further the careers of senior postdoctoral fellows with outstanding promise in the basic biological and biomedical sciences relevant to understanding aging processes and age-related diseases and disabilities. The award is intended to provide significant support to permit these postdoctoral fellows to become established in the field of aging. Projects concerned with understanding the basic mechanisms of aging will be considered. Projects investigating age-related diseases are also supported, if approached from the point of view of how basic aging processes may lead to these outcomes. Projects concerning mechanisms underlying common geriatric functional disorders are also considered. It is anticipated that three two-year grants will be awarded each year.
Requirements Postdoctoral fellows, both MDs and PhDs, are eligible. Fellows with at least three and not more than five years of prior postdoctoral training are eligible.
Amount $100,000
Date(s) Application Is Due Dec 15.
Contact Grants Manager, (212) 703-9977; fax: (212) 997-0330; email: grants@afar.org
Internet http://www.afar.org/ellison.html
Sponsor American Federation for Aging Research
70 W 40th St, 11th Fl
New York, NY 10018

Elmer O. and Ida Preston Educational Trust Scholarships **1827**
The trust awards scholarships to Iowa male college students of the Protestant faith who currently are at the sophomore through graduate level of study. The applicant must be a current student or plan on attending a college and/or university in Iowa.
Requirements Applications are accepted from male college students (currently at the freshman through graduate level) who are residents of Iowa, for study at a college/university in Iowa.
Amount $500-$700
Contact Trust Administrator, (515) 243-4191
Sponsor Elmer O. and Ida Preston Educational Trust
801 Grand Ave, Ste 3700
Des Moines, IA 50309

ELP Fellowships **1828**
The fellowship is an innovative national program designed to build the leadership capacity of the environmental field's most promising emerging professionals from the United States and US territories. Each year, a new group of fellows is chosen to join the ELP community of US environmental professionals from diverse backgrounds, sectors, and areas of expertise. The three-year fellowship offers unique networking opportunities, intensive leadership and skills training, project seed money, support, and time for personal and professional reflection. Fellows join a community of diverse emerging leaders, and have the opportunity to meet established environmental practitioners and experts in the field. Fellows receive a stipend; travel and accommodations for four fellowship retreats; access to funding for leadership-building projects; and national recognition through the program. Application materials are available online.
Requirements Applicants must be residents of the United States or US territories. Individuals should be relatively new to the environmental field, with approximately three to 10 years of experience.
Amount $10,000 maximum
Date(s) Application Is Due Oct 1.
Contact Fellowship Administrator, (413) 268-0035; fax: (413) 268-0036; email: info@elpnet.org
Internet http://www.elpnet.org/fellowship_application.html
Sponsor Environmental Leadership Program
P.O. Box 446
Haydenville, MA 01039

Elsa U. Pardee Foundation Grants **1829**
The foundation has three main grantmaking focuses: ongoing research grants to established institutions for cancer research, the funding of worthwhile new cancer research projects, and grants to committees providing financial assistance to cancer victims in specified areas. The foundation particularly welcomes innovative, small-scale, short-term projects that may be difficult to fund elsewhere until some interesting results are obtained. Application forms are available on written request and must accompany all project proposals. Applications are accepted at any time.
Requirements Application must include completed form, description of project, itemized budget, approval from the institution where the project will be done, amount requested, duration of project, and any other supportive material deemed helpful.
Restrictions Grants are limited to research toward the cure and control of cancer and in general do not provide for building funds, equipment (except that used in a specific project), fellowships, or fund-raising campaigns.
Amount $50,000-$200,000 average
Contact James Kendall, Secretary, (989) 832-3691; email: info@pardeefoundation.org
Internet http://www.pardeefoundation.org
Sponsor Elsa U. Pardee Foundation
P.O. Box 2767
Midland, MI 48641-2767

Emerson Charitable Trust Grants **1830**
Grants are given to support higher education, especially for engineering and related fields; youth programs; cancer research; and, to a lesser degree, welfare, cultural, and community programs. Types of support include general operating support, employee matching gifts, and employee-related scholarships. Giving is targeted to the communities where Emerson Electric has a plant or facilities. Organizations seeking support should send a formal proposal. Proposals are accepted at any time.
Amount $5000-$300,000 average
Contact Jo Ann Harmon, Senior Vice President, (314) 553-3722; fax: (314) 553-1605
Sponsor Emerson Charitable Trust
P.O. Box 4100, 8000 W Florissant Ave
Saint Louis, MO 63136

EMIERT Coretta Scott King Awards **1831**
Two awards are given annually to recognize outstanding inspirational and educational contributions toward the goals of peace and brotherhood. The category for the awards is creative writing and illustration. Books must have been published one year preceding the year of the award. Nominations should be sent to the office.
Requirements African American authors and illustrators are eligible to apply.
Amount $1000 to author; $1000 to illustrator
Date(s) Application Is Due Dec 1.

Contact ALA Awards Staff Liaison, (800) 545-2433; fax: (312) 280-3257; email: olos@ala.org
Internet http://www.ala.org/ala/emiert/corettascottkingbookawards/corettascott.htm
Sponsor American Library Association
50 E Huron Street
Chicago, IL 60611

Emil Buehler Perpetual Trust Grants **1832**
The Trust accepts inquiries from organizations with requests that promote the field of aviation science and technology. Grants are made in support of specific programs or projects. Grants are occasionally made for specific capital purchases if a clear need is demonstrated. Priority is given to cost-effective programs that offer the broadest benefit to the community. The Board of Trustees meets monthly to make grant decisions. Proposals must be received by the 10th day of the month for consideration.
Requirements Grants are only made to organizations qualifying for tax exemption under Section 501(c)(3) of the Internal Revenue Code.
Restrictions The Trust does not provide grants for general operating support; endowments; individuals; political activities; loans; or fund-raising events including dinners, benefits and athletic events.
Contact Deborah Janof, Grants Administrator, (201) 967-8040
Sponsor Emil Buehler Perpetual Trust
305 Route 17 South
Paramus, NJ 07652

Emma B. Howe Memorial Foundation Grants **1833**
The Emma B. Howe Memorial Foundation makes grants through the Minneapolis Foundation. The focus of all grants is to improve: the health and well-being of children, youth and families; opportunities for educational achievement; access to quality affordable housing; and economic vitality throughout the region. Information on the application process is available online.
Requirements Eligible organizations include 501(c)(3) nonprofits, public institutions; and emerging groups organized for nonprofit purposes.
Restrictions Funds are not available for: individuals; organizations/activities outside of Minnesota; conference registration fees; memberships; direct religious activities; political organizations or candidates; direct fundraising efforts; telephone solicitations; courtesy advertising; financial deficits.
Contact Community Philanthropy, (612) 672-3836; email: grants@mplsfoundation.org
Internet http://www.mplsfoundation.org/partners/emma.htm
Sponsor Emma B. Howe Memorial Foundation
80 South Eighth Street
Minneapolis, MN 55402

Endangered Language Fund Grants **1834**
The Fund provides grants for language maintenance and linguistic field work. The work most likely to be funded is that which serves both the native community and the field of linguistics. Work which has immediate applicability to one group and more distant application to the other will also be considered. Publishing subventions are a low priority, although they will be considered. Proposals can originate in any country. The language involved must be in danger of disappearing within a generation or two. Endangerment is a continuum, and the location on the continuum is one factor in our funding decisions. Eligible expenses include consultant fees, tapes, films, travel, etc. Grants are normally for a one year period, though extensions may be applied for. The Fund expects grants to be less than $4,000 in size, and to average about $2,000.
Restrictions Overhead expenses are not allowed.
Amount $4,000 maximum
Date(s) Application Is Due Apr 20.
Contact Grants Coordinator, (203) 865-6163, ext. 265; fax: (203) 865-8963; email: elf@endangeredlanguagefund.org
Internet http://www.endangeredlanguagefund.org/request.html
Sponsor Endangered Language Fund
300 George Street, Suite 900
New Haven, CT 06511

Energy Foundation Grants **1835**
The foundation's mission is to assist in the nation's transition to a sustainable energy future by promoting energy efficiency and renewable energy. To this end, grants are awarded in five areas: utility--competitive structures for the electric industry, energy efficiency, clean energy, and fair competition; buildings--energy-efficient structures, better codes and equipment standards; transportation--alternatives to single-occupancy vehicle use, new highways, and increased vehicle efficiency; renewable energy--accelerate the commercialization of renewable energy; and integrated issues--deepen understanding of energy and its relationship to the health of the economy. The foundation's board meets in March (first week), June (last week), and November (first week) to review proposals, which are accepted at any time. Guidelines and forms are available online.
Requirements Applicants must be nonprofit 501(c)3 charitable organizations.
Restrictions The foundation does not support individuals; for-profit organizations; local projects, unless they have been designed for replication or have broad-based regional or national implications; candidates for political office; legislation; sectarian or religious purposes; research and development of technology; demonstration projects; endowments; the planning, renovation, maintenance, or purchase of buildings; or the purchase of equipment or the acquisition of land, even if the intent is to save energy.
Amount $2000-$850,000 typically; $11.2 million total approximately
Contact Program Office, (415) 561-6700; fax: (415) 561-6709; email: energyfund@ef.org
Internet http://www.ef.org/applications.cfm
Sponsor Energy Foundation
1012 Torney Ave, #1
San Francisco, CA 94129

Energy Foundation State and Regional Climate Program Grants **1836**
The foundation's funding area focuses on state and regional climate policy initiatives. The efforts supported will have reducing greenhouse gas emissions as their main objective. Potential areas of work include state and regional carbon cap-and-trade programs; state and regional greenhouse gas plans and targets; greenhouse gas reporting and reduction initiatives; and financial mechanisms like incentives or carbon taxes. The foundation's geographic focus is the United States, with special emphasis on regional initiatives. There is no fixed format for proposals. The foundation's Board of Directors meets three times a year (the first week of March, the last week of June, and the first week of November). Proposals are accepted on an ongoing basis. There are no specific deadlines; however, proposals should be received 12 weeks in advance of the next board meeting.
Requirements 501(c)3 nonprofit, charitable organizations are eligible.
Restrictions The foundation does not support individuals or for-profit organizations; local projects, unless they have been consciously designed for further replication or have broad regional or national implications; candidates for political office, to influence legislation, or to support sectarian or religious purposes; research and development of technology (e.g., funds to develop hybrid automobiles or commercialization of an invention); demonstration projects (e.g., model solar homes); community energy projects; endowments or debt reduction; general-support grants; annual fundraising campaigns or capital construction; planning, renovation, maintenance, retrofit, or purchase of buildings; the purchase of equipment; or the acquisition of land, even if the intent is to save energy.
Contact Grants Administrator, (415) 561-6700; fax: (415) 561-6709; email: energyfund@ef.org
Internet http://www.ef.org/programs.cfm
Sponsor Energy Foundation
1012 Torney Ave, No 1
San Francisco, CA 94129

Engineering Awards of Excellence **1837**
The purpose of this program is to give national recognition to structural engineering excellence and innovation in steel-framed building projects.
Requirements Projects must be located in the United States, Canada, or Mexico. A significant part of the framing system must be steel wide-flange structural shapes or hollow structural sections. Both new buildings and renovation projects are eligible. Building construction must have been completed between January 1, 2001, and December 31, 2003.
Date(s) Application Is Due Mar 1.
Contact Becky LeDonne, Excellence Awards, (312) 670-5433; fax: (312) 670-5403; email: ledonne@aisc.org
Internet http://www.aisc.org/Content/NavigationMenu/About_AISC/Competition_and_Awards/Project_Awards/Engineering_Awards_of_Excellence/Engineering_Awards_of_Excellence.htm
Sponsor American Institute of Steel Construction
One E Wacker Dr, Ste 3100
Chicago, IL 60601-2001

Engineering Information Foundation Grants **1838**
The Foundation supports developmental projects, instructional projects, and training programs in engineering education and research that fit their fields of interest. These currently include the availability and use of published information, women in engineering, and information access in developing countries. The Foundation has a specific interest in innovative projects with measurable results, projects that promote significant and lasting change, projects that can be successfully replicated elsewhere and methodologies that are specific, well-defined and cost-effective.
Requirements US 501(c)3 tax-exempt organizations are eligible.
Restrictions Funds are not available for: operating expenses; requests solely for equipment; general overhead; campaigns; conferences; scholarships, fellowships, assistantships; support for doctoral candidates; loans.
Amount $5000-$25,000
Contact Program Contact, (212) 579-7596; fax: (212) 579-7517; email: info@eifgrants.org
Internet http://www.eifgrants.org
Sponsor Engineering Information Foundation
180 West 80th Street, Suite 207
New York, NY 10024-6301

Ensign-Bickford Foundation Grants **1839**
The corporate foundation gives primarily in areas of company operations, with emphasis on the Simsbury and Avon, CT, areas. Grants are awarded to nonprofit organizations for

welfare, education, cultural programs, employee-related scholarships, and community development activities. Types of support include continuing support, annual campaigns, building/renovation, equipment acquisition, land acquisition, programs and projects, conferences and seminars, publication, seed money, internships, scholarships, research, and employee matching gifts. Applications are accepted throughout the year.
Requirements Nonprofit organizations in company operating areas of Connecticut are eligible to apply.
Restrictions Grants are not awarded to individuals (except for employee-related scholarships) or for operating budgets, endowment funds, emergency funds, deficit financing, or loans.
Amount $50-$50,000 for organizations; $500-$2500 for individuals
Contact Jan Delissio, (860) 843-2388
Internet http://www.ensign-bickfordind.com/community.html
Sponsor Ensign-Bickford Foundation
P.O. Box 7, 100 Grist Mill Rd
Simsbury, CT 06070-0007

Entente Cordiale Scholarships **1840**
Scholarships are awarded to 28 outstanding British or French postgraduates to study or undertake research in France. Applicants may study any discipline at any French institution of higher education or research. The scholarship is for one academic year. Expenses covered are tuition and registration fees, books, and arrival and departure costs. A stipend is also included. Deadline is February 10th for French application and March 31 for British application. An application form is available on the Web site.
Requirements Applicants must be British or French nationals in their final year of undergraduate study, so that when the scholarship is awarded they will go on to postgraduate doctoral or postdoctoral studies or research on the other side of the Channel. Candidates should contact their chosen institutions before applying.
Amount @L8000 maximum, paid in three monthly installments
Contact French Cultural Department, 020 7073 1312; fax: 020 7073 1326; email: entente.cordiale@mail.ambafrance.org.uk
Internet http://www.francealacarte.org.uk/entente
Sponsor Entente Cordiale
French Embassy, 23 Cromwell Rd
London SW7 2EL United Kingdom

Enterprise Foundation Frederick P. Rose Architectural Fellowship **1841**
The fellowship creates partnerships between new architects and community-based organizations to direct the skills and passions of the architects in the service of low- and moderate-income communities and to encourage architects to become life-long leaders in public service and community development. The proposal should identify specific, tangible bricks-and-mortar projects that can be achieved or be well underway by the time the fellowship is completed. Fellows are expected to make a commitment of three years and are expected to offer their time and energy to work as part of the partner organization's staff. Fellows will contribute to the strengthening of the partner organization and the communities within which they work. The partnering organization is expected to provide space and general overhead costs, as necessary. Applicants who are interested in developing a partnership but have not found a partner organization should contact the program director.
Requirements The partner organization must be a community development corporation (CDC) or other community-based organization (CBO) with 501(c)(3) status or a tribally designated housing entity (TDHE). It must also be a member of The Enterprise Foundation Network. Prior to application, both the architect and the CDC, CBO, or TDHE must develop a partnership based on their shared vision and goals. As part of the application process, they must develop a proposal that highlights a three-year work plan with tangible, measurable objectives. The partnership and proposal should be developed in conjunction with local or regional foundation staff.
Amount $40,000 stipend per year
Date(s) Application Is Due Mar 27.
Contact Stephen Goldsmith, Director, (801) 364-6593; fax: (801) 532-0709; email: sgoldsmith@enterprisefoundation.org
Internet http://www.enterprisefoundation.org/RoseFellowship
Sponsor Enterprise Foundation
1283 E South Temple, No 203
Park City, UT 84102

Environmental Excellence Awards **1842**
The awards recognize the outstanding efforts of students across the country who are working at the grassroots level to protect and preserve the environment. Eight projects will be selected. Each winning school will receive: all-expenses-paid trip for three students and one chaperon/teacher to one of the SeaWorld or Busch Gardens parks for a special awards event; 100 t-shirts to share with school and community partners; and award trophy for the school and certificates for every student/teacher participant. From the eight projects, one outstanding environmental educator will be recognized. That educator will receive: all-expenses-paid trip for him/herself and one guest to one of the SeaWorld or Busch Gardens parks for a special awards event in April; all-expenses-paid trip to the National Science Teachers Association (NSTA) national conference; and award trophy and certificate. Previous award-winning projects have been in the areas of habitat restoration, school yard beautification, energy and waste reduction, environmental education and community outreach, wildlife protection, and natural resource conservation.
Requirements Public and private elementary, secondary, and home schools in the United States and Canada are eligible to apply. Community-based projects, such as those managed and operated by community service organizations, public recreation centers, 4-H clubs and other public, nonprofit groups working to protect the environment at the grassroots level, also are eligible.
Restrictions Individual students and previous award-winning schools are ineligible.
Amount $10,000; $5000 to educator
Date(s) Application Is Due Nov 30.
Contact Program Officer, (877) 792-4332 or (407) 363-2389; (877) 792-4332 (toll free)
Internet http://www.seaworld.org/conservation-matters/eea
Sponsor Anheuser-Busch Adventure Parks
7007 Sea World Dr
Orlando, FL 32821

Environmental Protection Agency Summer Faculty Fellowships **1843**
EPA Summer Faculty Fellowships are awarded to faculty with research experience and will include assistant, associate, and full professors. Each award is for one summer. The participant may reapply for and possibly receive awards for up to two additional summers (three total). Participants receive a stipend based on the level of the award and may receive a daily expense allowance, where applicable. Holders of summer fellowships must devote their full-time effort to the research program proposed in their applications and must be in residence at the sponsoring laboratory during the entire period of the summer fellowship. Holders of summer fellowships must devote their full-time effort to the research program proposed in their applications and must be in residence at the sponsoring laboratory during the entire period of the summer fellowship. Guidelines are available online.
Requirements US citizens and permanent residents with the PhD in science or engineering who are full-time faculty at accredited baccalaureate-granting US institutions are eligible.
Amount $1250 assistant professor; $1450 associate professor; $1650 full professor
Date(s) Application Is Due Nov 1.
Contact National Academies Summer Faculty Fellowships, (202) 334-2760; fax: (202) 334-2759c; email: rap@nas.edu
Internet http://www4.nationalacademies.org/pga/rap.nsf/vwLabInformation/FDF66DEFC1427CD385256B11006A213E?OpenDocument#8
Sponsor National Research Council
500 Fifth St NW
Washington, DC 20001

EPA Baseline Assessment of Risks of Exposure to Lead Poisoning of Native American Children **1844**
This program supports efforts to identify the risks of lead poisoning among children by conducting a baseline assessment of potential lead exposures. Tribes may use this data to determine whether there is a need to implement an authorized lead-reduction program.
Requirements Federally recognized Indian tribes, tribal consortia, and tribal organizations are eligible to apply.
Restrictions Funds may not be used to purchase property, provide lead hazard reduction activities, conduct renovation or construction activities, or cover case management costs.
Amount $75,000 maximum
Contact Darlene Watford, (202) 566-0516; fax: (202) 566-0469; email: Watford.Darlene@epa.gov
Internet http://www.epa.gov/lead
Sponsor Environmental Protection Agency
1200 Pennsylvania Ave, NW
Washington, DC 20460

EPA Children's Health Protection Grants **1845**
The objectives of this program are to catalyze community-based and regional projects and other actions that enhance public outreach and communication; assist families in evaluating risks to children and in making informed consumer choices; build partnerships that increase a community's long-term capacity to advance the protection of children's environmental health and safety; leverage private and public investments to enhance environmental quality by enabling community efforts to continue past EPA's ability to provide assistance to communities; and promote protection of children from environmental threats through lessons learned. There are no deadline dates.
Requirements Eligible applicants include community groups, public nonprofit institutions/organizations, tribal governments, specialized groups, profit organizations, private nonprofit institutions/organizations, and municipal and local governments. Potential applicants are strongly encouraged to discuss proposed projects with or submit preapplications to program staff prior to the completion of a full proposal.
Amount $5000-$250,000 average
Contact Bettina Fletcher, Office of Children's Health Protection, (202) 564-2188; fax: (202) 564-2733; email: fletcher.bettina@epa.gov
Internet http://yosemite.epa.gov/ochp/ochpweb.nsf/content/grants.htm
Sponsor Environmental Protection Agency
1200 Pennsylvania Ave NW, Mail Code 1107A, Rm 2512 Ariel Rios N
Washington, DC 20004

EPA Five-Star Restoration Challenge Grant Program 1846
Projects must include a strong on-the-ground wetland or riparian restoration component, and should also include education, outreach, and community stewardship. Projects involving only education, research, outreach, monitoring, or planning are not eligible for funding. Projects must demonstrate measurable ecological, educational, social, and/or economic benefits resulting from the completion of the project. Projects may be a discrete part of a larger restoration effort but must be ready to complete within a one-year time frame upon receipt of funding. Preference will be given to projects that are part of a larger watershed or community stewardship effort, include specific provisions for long-term management and protection, and demonstrate the value of innovative, collaborative approaches to restoring the nation's waters. The stars in Five-Star are the partners, funders, and/or participants necessary to complete the project, including schools or youth organizations (e.g. state or local youth conservation corps or county job training programs); local or tribal governments (e.g. boards of county commissioners, departments of planning, environment, or parks and recreation); local businesses or corporations; conservation organizations or local citizen groups; state and federal resource management agencies; and foundations or other funders. Projects must therefore involve diverse partnerships of ideally five organizations that contribute funding, land, technical assistance, workforce support, and/or other in-kind services. Annual deadline dates may vary; contact program staff for exact dates.
Requirements Any public or private entity in a community with wetlands, riverbanks, or shoreline areas in need of help are eligible to apply.
Restrictions Projects that are part of a mitigation requirement are not eligible for funding.
Amount $5000-$20,000; $10,000 average
Date(s) Application Is Due Mar 1.
Contact Tom Kelsch, Wetlands Division, (202) 857-0166; fax: (202) 857-0162; email: kelsch@nfwf.org
Internet http://www.nfwf.org/programs/5star-rfp.htm
Sponsor Environmental Protection Agency
1120 Connecticut Ave NW, Ste 900
Washington, DC 20036

EPA Grants for Research 1847
The EPA research programs focus on reducing uncertainty associated with risk assessment and risks to human health and ecosystems. Areas where risk assessors are most in need of new concepts, methods, and data will be given highest priority. Projects are invited in the following areas: ecological assessment; exposure of children to pesticides; air quality; analytical and monitoring methods; drinking water; environmental fate and treatment of toxic and hazardous wastes; environmental statistics; high-performance computing; and exploratory research. In all areas, EPA is interested in research that recognizes issues relating to environmental justice, the agency's effort to achieve equal protection from environmental and health hazards for all people without regard to race, economic status, or culture. For specific program deadlines and information, contact the program office or visit the Web site.
Requirements Academic and nonprofit institutions and state and local governments are eligible for EPA research grants in all areas. For-profit firms are eligible only under certain programs and then under restrictive conditions, including the absence of any profit from the project.
Restrictions Federal agencies and federal employees are not eligible to participate.
Contact Office of Research and Development, National Center for Environmental Research and Quality Assurance, (202) 260-3837 or (800) 490-9194; fax: (202) 260-2039; email: ord.grants@epamail.epa.gov
Internet http://www.epa.gov/epahome/program2.htm
Sponsor Environmental Protection Agency
1200 Pennsylvania Ave NW, Ariel Rios Bldg
Washington, DC 20460

EPA Interagency Project to Clean Up Open Dumps on Tribal Lands 1848
This project is intended to demonstrate the federal government's ability to work closely with tribal governments to provide comprehensive solid waste management funding and technical support for the closure or upgrade of high-priority waste disposal sites and the development and strengthening of tribal or multitribal solid waste management programs. In determining whether a site is high priority, the Workgroup will generally rely on the Indian Health Service's Report to Congress on open dumps on American Indian lands. For further information contact the regional solid waste Indian coordinator in your area (see web site for details).
Requirements Federally recognized tribes and multitribe 501(c)3 organizations whose membership consists of federally recognized tribes are eligible to apply.
Contact Carol Jorgensen, Director, American Indian Environmental Office, (202) 564-0303; email: jorgensen.carol@epa.gov
Internet http://www.epa.gov/epaoswer/non-hw/tribal/finance.htm#dumps
Sponsor Environmental Protection Agency
401 M St SW
Washington, DC 20460

EPA Lead Awareness Outreach for Native American Tribes 1849
This program provides financial assistance to tribes to launch outreach efforts that would educate Native American families about the dangers of exposure to lead-based paint hazards among children, distribute educational information and encourage families to have their children screened and homes tested for lead hazards. Activities may include providing medical training, developing culturally specific lead outreach materials, distributing pamphlets and establishing an in-home education program.
Requirements Federally recognized Indian tribes, tribal consortia, and tribal organizations are eligible to apply.
Restrictions Funds may not be used to purchase property, provide lead hazard reduction, conduct renovation or construction activities, or cover case management costs.
Amount $50,000 maximum per outreach project
Contact Darlene Watford, Office of Pollution Prevention and Toxics, (202) 566-0516; fax: (202) 566-0469; email: Watford.Darlene@epa.gov
Internet http://www.epa.gov/lead
Sponsor Environmental Protection Agency
1200 Pennsylvania Ave, NW
Washington, DC 20460

EPA National Environmental Education Grant Program 1850
The purpose of this program is to provide training and related support services to education professionals who are or can become leaders in ensuring the quality and long-term sustainability of coordinated and comprehensive environmental education efforts across a state or states.
Requirements US institutions of higher education or nonprofit institutions or a consortia of such institutions are eligible to apply.
Amount $2 million-$3 million range; $15,000 average
Date(s) Application Is Due Nov 15.
Contact Diane Berger or Sheri Jojokian, (202) 260-8619; email: berger.diane@epa.gov or jojokian.sheri@epa.gov
Internet http://www.epa.gov/enviroed/grants.html
Sponsor Environmental Protection Agency
401 M St SW
Washington, DC 20460

EPA Pollution Prevention Information Network 1851
The Pollution Prevention Act provides funds to states to strengthen the efficiency and effectiveness of state technical assistance programs in providing source reduction information to businesses. These funds will be targeted for applicants that are willing to work as part of a collective service providing pollution prevention information to state and local governments' technical assistance providers. The purpose of this request for proposals is to coordinate work among new and existing grantees to minimize duplication of effort in information collection and synthesis, training for the promotion of pollution prevention technologies, and establish information standards that will facilitate information exchange among centers. Grants for this program are competed through a Federal Register notice or through a more limited announcement usually sent to state technical assistance providers every three years. These grants are intended for state entities as described under the Pollution Prevention Act of 1990. Since this program has operated for seven years, there are eight existing P2 information centers. New applicants would need to work with established centers and be willing to collaborate on some cooperative projects the group has in progress. New proposals should address work with the existing "P2Rx centers" (see www.p2rx.org) as well as any new tasks or projects that would fit into this program.
Requirements Eligible applicants for purposes of funding under this grant program include the 50 states, the District of Columbia, the US Virgin Islands, the Commonwealth of Puerto Rico, any territory or possession of the United States, any agency or instrumentality of a state including state universities, and all federally recognized American Indian tribes.
Restrictions Local governments, private universities, private nonprofit entities, private businesses, and individuals are not eligible to apply.
Amount $120,000 maximum
Date(s) Application Is Due Jul 6.
Contact Jean Waters, Pollution Prevention Resource Exchange, (402) 595-2381; fax: (402) 554-6260; email: jwaters@mail.unomaha.edu
Internet http://www.epa.gov/p2/grants/ppin/ppin.htm
Sponsor Environmental Protection Agency
1200 Pennsylvania Ave NW, Ariel Rios Bldg
Washington, DC 20460

EPA Senior Environmental Employment Program Project Grants 1852
The objective of the program is to use the talents of Americans 55 years of age or older to provide technical assistance to federal, state, and local environmental agencies for projects of pollution research, prevention, abatement, and control. Applications are accepted at any time. Prediscussion with the office is advisable.
Requirements Private, nonprofit organizations designated by the Secretary of Labor under Title V of the Older Americans Act are eligible to apply.
Amount $184,900 average
Contact Susan Street, Director, SEE Program, (202) 564-0410; fax: (202) 564-0735; email: street.susan@epa.gov
Internet http://www.epa.gov
Sponsor Environmental Protection Agency
401 M St SW
Washington, DC 20460

EPA Solid Waste Management Assistance Grants **1853**
The objective of this program is to promote use of integrated solid waste management systems to solve municipal solid waste generation and management problems at the local, regional, and national levels. Funds are available for the allowable direct cost expenditures incident to program performance plus allocatable portions of allowable indirect costs of the institution. Projects can include training, surveys, public education programs, studies, and demonstrations. Grants will normally be funded on a 12-month basis; total approved project period may not exceed three years. Applications are accepted at any time.
Requirements Eligible to apply are nonprofit entities including public authorities (federal, state, interstate, and local); public agencies and institutions; private agencies, institutions, and individuals; and Indian tribes.
Restrictions For-profit organizations are not eligible to apply.
Amount $100,000 average
Contact Nick Vizzone, (703) 308-8460; email: vizzone.nick@epa.gov
Internet http://www.epa.gov/epaoswer/osw
Sponsor Environmental Protection Agency
401 M St SW
Washington, DC 20460

Epilepsy Postdoctoral and Clinical Research Fellowships **1854**
A few fellowships will be awarded to scientists (PhD or MD) wishing to carry out full-time research projects in the field of epilepsy. The period of support may begin at any time between May and October. The grant will be for one year but will be renewable once and exceptionally twice, upon request.
Requirements Fellowships are available to Canadian citizens or for projects conducted in Canada.
Amount $C30,000
Date(s) Application Is Due Jan 15.
Contact Caroline Savoy, (450) 358-9779; fax: (450) 346-1045; email: epilepsy@savoy-foundation.ca
Internet http://www.savoy-foundation.ca/eng/mission/defaut.htm
Sponsor Savoy Foundation
230 Foch St
St Jean Sur Richelieu, PQ J3B 2B2 Canada

Epilepsy Research Award for Outstanding Contributions to the Pharmacology of Antiepileptic Drugs **1855**
This award, donated by Warner-Lambert/Parke-Davis and administered by ASPET, is given biennially (odd-numbered years) to recognize outstanding research leading to better clinical control of epileptic seizures. This may include basic screening and testing of new therapeutic agents, mechanism of action studies, metabolic disposition, pharmacokinetics, and clinical pharmacology studies.
Requirements Candidates may be nominated by members of any recognized scientific association, domestic or foreign.
Amount $2000
Date(s) Application Is Due Sep 15.
Contact Dr. Christine Carrico, Executive Officer, (301) 530-7060; fax: (301) 530-7061; email: ccarrico@aspet.faseb.org
Internet http://www.aspet.org/public/awards/epilepsy_award.html
Sponsor American Society for Pharmacology and Experimental Therapeutics
9650 Rockville Pike
Bethesda, MD 20814-3995

Epilepsy Research Foundation New Therapy Grants **1856**
The foundation supports innovative research leading to new insights into a cure for epilepsy. The primary focus of this program is to bring new approaches and therapies to patients through translational research. Other areas of consideration include but are not limited to: meaningful grants to senior-level scientific and clinical investigators on the brink of new discoveries, working at the nation's leading academic and research institutions, and in private industry; seed funding for preliminary work necessary to explore novel approaches; building innovative platform technologies; research to bring new approaches and therapy to children; innovative cutting edge projects that could lead to breakthrough discoveries; support for applying work in other areas with potential for promise in epilepsy; research programs that might not otherwise be funded through traditional sources; projects that encourage collaboration among scientists and industry; and proposals dealing with commercializing academic research projects. Grant funds may be used to support the direct costs of research such as salary support for personnel directly engaged in the project, consumable supplies and services, and travel essential to the conduct of the research. Multi-year awards will be considered.
Requirements Investigators must hold a relevant advanced degree (MD and/or PhD) and have completed all research training. The program is open to investigators at corporations as well as the academic/university arena. All applications will be judged on a competitive basis, without regard to the academic rank or title of the investigator. Applicants whose research involves patient care or direct involvement with patients must be licensed to practice their profession and must obtain Institutional Review Board (IRB) approval of their research. IRB approval must be included with the original application.
Restrictions Grant funds may not be used for indirect costs or institutional overhead, and the purchase of permanent equipment that exceeds 10 percent of the budget without prior approval.
Amount $100,000-$200,000
Date(s) Application Is Due Apr 1; Oct 1.
Contact Research Department, (800) 332-1000 or (301) 459-3700; email: grants@efa.org or EpilepsyCure@aol.com
Internet http://www.epilepsytdp.org/sec/support_translational
Sponsor Epilepsy Research Foundation
4351 Garden City Dr
Landover, MD 20785-7223

Episcopal Church Foundation Graduate Fellowships **1857**
Fellowships are awarded to encourage doctoral study by recent seminary graduates to qualify themselves for the teaching ministry in seminaries of the Episcopal Church. Fellowships may be held at accredited institutions and are renewable for a second and third year. Applications should be obtained from the dean's office at any of the 11 accredited Episcopal seminaries, Harvard Divinity, or Union Theological Seminary.
Requirements Applicants should be seniors or graduates from an accredited Episcopal seminary or an Episcopal candidate from Harvard Divinity School or Union Theological Seminary. Applicants must be recommended by the deans of their theological seminaries in order to apply. If the applicant is a graduate of a non-Episcopal seminary, nomination for a fellowship must be approved by the dean of an accredited Episcopal seminary.
Amount $10,000 per year
Date(s) Application Is Due Dec 1.
Contact Elizabeth Rauen Sciaino, Fellows Program Manager, (800) 697-2858 or (212) 716-6246; fax: (212) 297-0142; email: beth@episcopalfoundation.org
Internet http://www.episcopalfoundation.org/education/doctoral.html
Sponsor Episcopal Church Foundation
815 Second Ave, Rm 400
New York, NY 10017

Eppendorf & Science Prize for Neurobiology **1858**
The Eppendorf & Science Prize for Neurobiology acknowledges the increasingly active and important role of neurobiology in advancing our understanding of the functioning of the brain and the nervous system -- a quest that seems destined for dramatic expansion in the coming decades. This international prize, established in 2002, encourages the work of promising young neurobiologists by providing support in the early stages of their careers. It is awarded annually for the most outstanding neurobiological research by a young scientist, as described in a 1,000-word essay based on research performed during the past three years. The winner is awarded money and publication of his or her essay in 'Science'. The essay and those of up to three finalists are also published on 'Science Online'. The award is announced and presented at a ceremony at the annual meeting of the Society for Neuroscience. Eppendorf provides financial support to help enable the grand prize winner to attend the meeting.
Requirements Entrants must be a neurobiologist with an advanced degree and not older than 35 years. The research described in the entrant's essay must be based on the methods of molecular and cell biology. The entrant must have performed or directed the work described in the essay. The research must have been performed during the previous three years.
Restrictions Employees of Eppendorf AG, its subsidiaries, Science and AAAS, and their relatives are not eligible for the prize.
Amount $25,000 and publication of his or her essay in 'Science'.
Date(s) Application Is Due Jun 15.
Contact Maryrose Police, email: mpolice@aaas.org
Internet http://www.sciencemag.org/feature/data/prizes/eppendorf/eppenprize.dtl
Sponsor American Association for the Advancement of Science
1200 New York Ave., NW, Room 1049B
Washington, DC 20005

Eppley Foundation Postdoctoral Grants **1859**
The foundation supports research in advanced scientific subjects, both in the biological and physical sciences, and is interested in supporting research where federal support is not available or to provide seed money toward larger undertakings. Work must be original and independent. Approximately 12 grants are awarded each year.
Requirements Individuals who have several years of postdoctoral research experience in the biological and physical sciences are eligible. Grant proposals from foreign countries are considered only when a US institution will administer the grant on their behalf.
Restrictions Grants are not made to individuals and rarely for support of newly awarded PhDs or MDs. Social sciences, computer sciences, and education programs will not be supported. Under most circumstances, the foundation will not support heart, HIV, cancer, or DNA research.
Amount $15,000 average
Contact Huyler Held, Secretary-Treasurer, (212) 448-1100 or (212) 371-1660; fax: (212) 448-6260; email: bblauner@Mclaughlinstern.com
Sponsor Eppley Foundation for Research
260 Madison Ave
New York, NY 10016

Equal Sweetener Foundation Grants **1860**
The foundation invests in programs that improve the health and well being of people throughout the world, and supports programs in which Merisant employees are actively involved as contributors or volunteers. The foundation prefers to support projects that

fit within its focus area--diabetes research and education. Collaborative projects that achieve stated, measurable objectives receive preference. There are no deadlines for preliminary requests; full proposals are by invitation.
Requirements 501(c)3 tax-exempt organizations are eligible. The grantseeking organization must be reputable, experienced, and show capable, responsible financial management.
Restrictions Grants do not support individual aid or personal support; religious activities, politically partisan groups or activities, or fraternal orders; veterans or labor organizations; athletic teams; capital campaigns; endowments; scholarship programs; or projects from start-up organizations. The foundation will not contribute to any organization that discriminates on the basis of race, color, creed, sex, marital status, or physical ability.
Contact Jo-Ann Digman, President
Internet http://www.merisant.com/pages/about_merisant/career_center/community_involve.asp
Sponsor Equal Sweetener Foundation
#1 N Brentwood Blvd, Ste 510
Clayton, MO 63105

Equipment Leasing and Finance Foundation Research Grants **1861**
Grants are available to encourage academics in all fields of scholarship to study topics of interest to the equipment leasing and finance industry. Research topics of interest include: transitioning the business model and avoiding the commoditization of a finance product through the bundling of services; best practice case studies; analysis of publicly held lease financing companies--does the current model work?; changes in accounting rules--how does this affect the lessee and lessor in the financial decision making process?; what will finance companies of the future look like?; study of successful industry consolidates; corporate size--when does efficiency of size become inefficient?; limited purpose bank charters--are they the vehicle of the future in leasing?; FASB-and changes to synthetic leases; specialty finance in banking--what is the future?; and maintaining residual values--the challenges and solutions. General topics of research interest are: strategic management/planning, accounting/financial reporting, and finance; tax and legislative/regulatory; credit/collections; economics; portfolio management; contracts/documentation; technology benchmarking; strategic importance of captives; operations; and best practices. Grants may be used for research studies; booklets, pamphlets and video production; surveys and statistical gathering; and other initiatives that are considered on a case-by-case basis.
Requirements For-profit and nonprofit organizations and applicants--which may include individuals, universities, foundations, associations, and corporations--are eligible.
Amount $5000-$50,000 range; $12,000 average
Date(s) Application Is Due Jan 15; May 15; Sep 1.
Contact Lisa Levine, Executive Director, (703) 516-8363; email: llevine@elamail.com
Internet http://www.leasefoundation.org/grant
Sponsor Equipment Leasing and Finance Foundation Grants
4301 N Fairfax Dr, Ste 550
Arlington, VA 22203

Erasmus Institute Fellowships **1862**
The institute will admit six postdoctoral fellows to its center on the campus of the University of Notre Dame. The institute invites applications from academics who by their scholarship and/or faith seek to cultivate Catholic intellectual and cultural traditions. Fellows devote their time in residence to concentrated research and writing on individual projects related to the institute's goals. The fellows will also be expected to teach one course during the academic year, likely in the spring term of next year.
Requirements Postdoctoral applicants must have received the PhD after May 1, 2001; ABD applicants must fulfill the PhD requirements by June 1 in order to be eligible.
Restrictions Dissertation and salaried senior and junior faculty fellowships are no longer offered.
Amount $35,000
Date(s) Application Is Due Jan 27.
Contact Residential Fellowships, (574) 631-9346; fax: (574) 631-3585; email: erasmus@nd.edu
Internet http://www.nd.edu/~erasmus
Sponsor University of Notre Dame
1124 Flanner Hall
Notre Dame, IN 46556-5611

Erasmus Prize **1863**
This prize is awarded annually to a person or institution that has made an exceptionally important contribution to European culture in the fields of humanities and the arts or social and social-scientific sphere.
Requirements There are no restrictions as to age, sex, or citizenship of the recipient.
Amount NLG150,000
Contact Program Contact, 31-0-20-6752753; fax: 31-0-20-6752231; email: spe@erasmusprijs.org
Internet http://www.erasmusprijs.org/eng/index.htm
Sponsor Erasmus Prize Foundation (Stichting Praemium Erasmianum)
Jan van Goyenkade 5
Amsterdam 1075 HN The Netherlands

EREF Grants **1864**
The Foundation awards several grants each year for research or education in topics pertaining to any aspect of solid waste management. Applications are accepted three times each year. There is no formal application. Your submission, in English, should include a description of proposed activity, project timeline, budget, and resumes of principal investigators.
Restrictions Grants will not be provided for capital campaigns; political contributions; religious causes; operating funds; loans; or support of lobbying activities. The Foundation will not pay overhead in excess of 25%.
Amount $10,000-$500,000
Contact Michael Cagney, President, (703) 299-5139; fax: (703) 299-5145; email: mjcagney@erefdn.org
Internet http://www.erefdn.org/guide.html
Sponsor Environmental Research and Education Foundation
901 N. Pitt Street, Suite 270
Alexandria, VA 22314

EREF Scholarships **1865**
Scholarships are awarded in memory of Francois Fiessinger, PhD, to support the work of outstanding students interested in excellence in environmental research. Awards are based on academic or professional performance; relevance of one's work to the advancement of environmental science; and potential for success. Applicants should request an application packet or download the online pdf application.
Requirements Applications will be considered from full-time PhD students who have a clearly demonstrated interest in environmental research. Awards are made without regard to race, religion, national or ethnic origin, citizenship, or disability. Applications will be considered from students outside the United States or studying abroad.
Amount $12,000 maximum per year paid monthly, renewable for two additional years for a total of $36,000
Date(s) Application Is Due Aug 1.
Contact Michael Cagney, President, (703) 299-5139; fax: (703) 299-5145; email: mcagney@erefdn.org
Internet http://www.erefdn.org/scholar.html
Sponsor Environmental Research and Education Foundation
120 S Fayette St
Alexandria, VA 22314

Eric Berne Fund for the Future Grants **1866**
Grants support research or projects that demonstrate an interest in the evaluation of the effectiveness of various applications of transactional analysis (TA) theory. Preference is given to projects that are expected to generate particular benefits within a region or community, that extend TA to new areas of the world, support development of measurable professional standards of competency, and/or build bridges between TA and other disciplines. The deadline for making nominations for the EBMA is December 1 of the year preceding the award.
Requirements Grants are open to individuals or nonprofit organizations. If profit-making organizations wish to submit proposals, special royalty or profit-sharing agreements may be required.
Contact Eric Berne Fund Distribution Committee, (925) 600-8110; fax: (925) 600-8112
Internet http://www.itaa-net.org/itaa/grants.htm
Sponsor International Transactional Analysis Association
2186 Rheem Dr #B-1
Pleasanton, CA 94588

Erikson Institute Child Development Doctoral Fellowships **1867**
The PhD program, offered jointly with the Department of Psychology at Loyola University Chicago, prepares students for careers in college teaching and research, administration, program design and evaluation, and child advocacy. Named fellowships include the Fellowship in Applied Research in Child Development and the Irving B. Harris Leadership Fellowship in Child Development. The fellowships include tuition plus a research/teaching assistantship or living stipend and are awarded on the basis of academic promise, experience, and research interest.
Date(s) Application Is Due Apr 1.
Contact Dr. Robert Halpern, (312) 893-7142; email: rhalpern@erikson.edu
Internet http://www.erikson.edu/students.asp?file=applyfinaid&highlight=fellowships
Sponsor Erikson Institute
420 N Wabash Ave
Chicago, IL 60611

Ernest Guenther Award in the Chemistry of Natural Products **1868**
This award, sponsored by Givaudan and administered by the American Chemical Society, is given annually to recognize and encourage outstanding achievements in analysis, structure elucidation, and chemical synthesis of natural products. Special consideration will be given to the independence of thought and originality shown. This award is granted without regard to age or nationality.
Requirements Any individual, except a member of the award committee, may submit one nomination or seconding letter for each award in any given year. Nominating documents consist of a letter of not more than 1000 words containing an evaluation of the nominee's accomplishments and a specific identification of the work to be recognized, a biographical

sketch including date of birth, and a list of publications and patents authored by the nominee. Six copies of all items to be included in the nomination must be submitted.
Restrictions Self-nominations are not accepted.
Amount $5000 and an allowance of $2500 toward traveling expenses to award meeting
Date(s) Application Is Due Feb 1.
Contact Awards Administrator, (202) 872-4408; fax: (202) 872-6317; email: awards@acs.org
Internet http://chemistry.org/portal/Chemistry?PID=acsdisplay.html&DOC=awards\guenther.html
Sponsor American Chemical Society
1155 16th St NW
Washington, DC 20036

Ernest M. Eller Prize in Naval History 1869
The Naval Historical Center, in cooperation with the Naval Historical Foundation, offers this prize to encourage excellence in research and writing on the history of the US Navy. The annual prize goes to the author of the best article on US naval history published in a scholarly journal. Entry deadline is June 1 of the year following publication.
Amount $1000
Date(s) Application Is Due Jun 1.
Contact Senior Historian, Washington Naval Yard
Internet http://www.history.navy.mil/prizes/grants.htm
Sponsor Naval Historical Center
805 Kidder Breese SE, Washington Navy Yard
Washington, DC 20374-5060

Erskine A. Peters Dissertation-Year Fellowship 1870
This initiative has two overall goals: to enable two outstanding African-American doctoral candidates (at the ABD level) to devote their full energies to the completion of the dissertation; and to provide an opportunity for African-American scholars at the beginning of their academic careers to experience life at a major Catholic research university. The fellowship is tenable for a full academic year beginning in August and concluding in May. Each fellow is provided with office space, use of a personal computer, an official academic home in the department of the fellow's specialization, access to a faculty mentor in the fellow's discipline, and access to all university facilities. The candidate is expected to be in residence at the university and to devote most of her/his time to the completion of dissertation research. In addition, she/he will be expected to present a public lecture dealing with her or his current research at the end of the spring term, to give one lecture in the university's introductory course in African and African-American Studies, and to sponsor a short-term mutual learning event for faculty and students (e.g., brown bag series, roundtable discussion, etc.). Application is available online.
Requirements The program invites applications from African-American doctoral candidates in the humanities, social sciences, and theological disciplines who have completed all degree requirements with the exception of the dissertation.
Amount $25,000 stipend; $2000 research budget
Date(s) Application Is Due Dec 3.
Contact African and African-American Studies Program, (574) 631-5628 or (219) 631-5666; email: astudies@nd.edu
Internet http://www.nd.edu/~astudies/erskinepeters.htm
Sponsor University of Notre Dame
O'Shaughnessy Hall
Notre Dame, IN 46556

ESF Latsis Prize 1871
The foundation invites nominations for the European Latsis Prize. Presented each year at the ESF's Annual Assembly, the European Latsis Prize is awarded to an individual scholar or research group in recognition of outstanding and innovative contributions in a selected field of European research.
Requirements Nominations may be received from institutions and individuals for an individual scholar, or from institutions generally for research groups.
Restrictions Self-nominations are not accepted.
Amount Sf100,000 (EU62,000)
Contact Secretary General, 33-0-3-88-76-71-00; fax: 33-0-3-88-37-05-32; email: prize@esf.org
Internet http://www.esf.org/prize
Sponsor European Science Foundation
1 quai Lezay Marnesia, BP 90015
Strasbourg Cedex F-67080 France

ESRI Conservation Program Grants 1872
The conservation grants program provides donations and discounts of GIS software, data, books, and training. There are no application deadlines. The program does not grant hardware or cash, but partners with many other groups who do (list available online). General grants and basic grants are available. Grants are awarded to organizations that can demonstrate a strong commitment to conservation; compelling reasons to use GIS in obtaining their objectives; and the organizational capacity to use GIS effectively over a long period of time. All applicants must present a credible case for how GIS and the support from ESRI will advance their cause of conservation and environmental protection, broadly defined. Successful applicants will effectively make their case about how they propose to integrate and analyze disparate spatial data to accomplish their goals. To request application materials, send a blank email message (no subject, no content) to ecpgrant@esri.com, or visit the Web site.
Requirements Eligible applicants are US-based 501c(3) nonprofit organizations that actively engage the public in resource conservation and environmental protection. This includes, but is not limited to, grassroots conservation and environmental organizations, community action groups, economic development organizations, sustainable development groups, community-based conservation groups, growth management organizations, environmental justice groups, and tribal conservation organizations. International groups must have a US-based tax-exempt organization as their sponsor.
Restrictions The following types of organizations are not eligible to apply: colleges and universities; public schools or school districts; local, state, and federal government agencies or natural resource conservation districts; association and coalitions organized to fund-raise for or to benefit local, state, and federal government agencies; natural resource conservation districts; and CTSP's nonprofit sponsors and their associated members.
Contact Charles Convis, (909) 793-2853 ext 2488; fax: (909) 307-3025; email: ecp@esri.com
Internet http://www.conservationgis.org/aaesrigrants.html
Sponsor Environmental Systems Research Institute
380 New York St
Redlands, CA 92373

Ethical Research Grants and Fellowships 1873
Graduate fellowships are available for investigations into the discovery, development, validation, and implementation of alternatives to the use of live animals in research, testing, and teaching. Areas of interest include tissue cultures, bacteria cultures, protozoan studies, gas chromatography, mass spectrometry, radioimmunoassay, mathematical and computer models, quantum pharmacology, mechanical models, and clinical and epidemiological surveys. Awards include stipend plus supplies. Students from all over the world are eligible to apply.
Requirements Nonprofit educational and research institutions are eligible for grants. Students who are enrolled in master's and PhD programs in the sciences, humanities, psychology, and journalism are eligible for graudate fellowships.
Amount $15,000 maximum
Date(s) Application Is Due Mar 15.
Contact Peter O'Donovan, Executive Director, (312) 427-6025; fax: (312) 427-6524; email: ifer@navs.org
Internet http://www.ifer.org
Sponsor International Foundation for Ethical Research
53 W Jackson Blvd, Ste 1552
Chicago, IL 60604

Ethics and Excellence in Journalism Foundation Grants 1874
This Foundation was founded for charitable, scientific and educational purposes, including the improvement of the quality of the practice of journalism among various media. Support includes funding for creative projects and research that promotes excellence in journalism and instills and encourages high ethical standards in journalism. Funding is available to organizations via an application and review process.
Requirements US nonprofit organizations, including universities and colleges, are eligible.
Restrictions Individuals are not eligible.
Date(s) Application Is Due Apr 15; Oct 15.
Contact Nancy Hodgkinson, Senior Program Officer, (405) 604-5388; fax: (405) 604-0297; email: nancy.hodgkinson@journalismfoundation.org
Internet http://www.journalismfoundation.org
Sponsor Ethics and Excellence in Journalism Foundation
210 Park Avenue, Suite 3150
Oklahoma City, OK 73102

ETS Postdoctoral Fellowships 1875
Up to three fellows are selected annually to conduct independent research in Princeton, NJ, in one of the following areas: psychology; education; teaching; learning; literacy; statistics; computer science; educational technology; minority issues; and testing issues, including new forms of assessment and alternate forms of assessment for special populations. The program goals are to provide research opportunities to individuals who hold a doctorate in the fields indicated and to increase the number of women and underrepresented minority professionals conducting research in educational measurement and related fields. Prior to applying, candidates need to send a one-page abstract of their research via email. Guidelines are available online.
Requirements The program is open to any individual who holds a doctorate in a relevant discipline and provides evidence of prior research.
Amount $50,000 stipend
Date(s) Application Is Due Feb 1.
Contact Linda DeLauro, (609) 734-1806 or 734-5949; fax: (609) 497-6032; email: fellowships@ets.org
Internet http://www.ets.org/research/fellowships.html
Sponsor Educational Testing Service
MS 09R, Rosedale Rd
Princeton, NJ 08541-0001

ETS Predoctoral Summer Program 1876

Students chosen for the eight-week program will participate in ongoing independent research with access to a mentor in one of the following areas: education; educational technology; learning; linguistics; literacy; minority issues; new constructs; policy research; psychology; psychometrics; statistics; teaching; and testing issues (including alternate forms of assessment for special populations and new forms of assessment). An explicit goal of the program is to increase the number of women and minority professionals in educational measurement and related fields. Applicants must submit their application materials electronically. Guidelines are available online.
Requirements Graduate students who are currently enrolled in a doctoral program and have completed a minimum of two years of full-time graduate study in a program emphasizing one of the areas specified are eligible. A letter of recommendation from the major advisor or committee chair and transcripts, undergraduate and graduate, must be included with completed application form.
Amount $5000 stipend
Date(s) Application Is Due Feb 1.
Contact Grants Administrator, (609) 734-5543; email: internfellowships@ets.org
Internet http://www.ets.org/research/fellowships.html
Sponsor Educational Testing Service
MS 07R, Rosedale Rd
Princeton, NJ 08541-0001

ETS Sylvia Taylor Johnson Minority Fellowship in Educational Measurement 1877

The two-year fellowship, renewable after the first year by mutual agreement, is designed to provide talented minority scholars an opportunity to carry out independent research under the mentorship of ETS senior researchers. The stipend will be set in relation to the successful applicant's compensation at the home institution. Applicants may obtain the center's brochure before they apply.
Requirements Applicants must have received their doctoral degree within the past ten years and must be US citizens or permanent residents.
Date(s) Application Is Due Feb 1.
Contact Linda DeLauro, (609) 734-1806; fax: (609) 734-5410; email: internfellowships@ets.org
Internet http://www.ets.org/portal/site/ets/menuitem.c988ba0e5dd572bada20bc47c3921509/?vgnextoid=1dadaf5e44df4010VgnVCM10000022f95190RCRD&vgnextchannel=49f5be3a864f4010VgnVCM10000022f95190RCRD
Sponsor Educational Testing Service
MS-09R, Rosedale Rd
Princeton, NJ 08541-0001

EU Center for Humanistic Inquiry Junior and Postdoctoral Fellowships 1878

The purpose of the program is to stimulate and support humanistic research by providing scholars in early stages of their careers with the necessary time, space, and other resources. Research projects must be humanistic, but fellows may hold the PhD in any discipline. Fellows are expected to offer an upper-level undergraduate course on a subject of their choice during the spring of their fellowship year. The program provides stipends, research budgets, office space, and access to the university libraries. Application forms and further information are available from the office and online.
Requirements Junior fellows are scholars who, at the beginning of the fellowship year, will be at least three years beyond receipt of the PhD, and normally no more than 10. Postdoctoral fellows, who must have the PhD before the submission of their applications, are awarded to those who have held the PhD for no more than three years before receiving the fellowship.
Amount $38,500 stipend
Date(s) Application Is Due Feb 23.
Contact Center for Humanistic Inquiry, (404) 727-6424; fax: 404-727-1669; email: chi@emory.edu
Internet http://www.chi.emory.edu/Fellowships/index.html
Sponsor Emory University
1715 N Decatur Rd
Atlanta, GA 30307

EU Robert W. Woodruff Library Research Fellowships 1879

Short-term fellowships support scholarly use of the library's research collections in the areas of modern literature and African American studies. The Special Collections Department has extensive holdings related to the Irish literary renaissance and the finest collection outside of Ireland for the study of contemporary Irish poetry. The library also holds the literary archive of the late poet laureate of England, Ted Hughes, and related British literary collections. The department also houses extensive collections focusing on black print culture, the civil rights and post-civil rights movements, communism and the Left, and African American religion and culture. Fellowships help defray expenses in traveling to and residing in Atlanta during the fellowship tenure, usually one month.
Amount $2000 maximum
Date(s) Application Is Due May 31.
Contact Fellowship Program, fax: (404) 727-0360; email: speccollref@emory.edu
Internet http://web.library.emory.edu/services/hr/fellows.html
Sponsor Emory University
Robert W. Woodruff Library, 540 Asbury Cir, Emory University
Atlanta, GA 30322-2870

Eugene and Agnes E. Meyer Foundation Grants 1880

The Foundation awards grants to nonprofit organizations that serve the people and communities in the Washington, D.C. region. Grants are awarded in ten program areas: arts; heritage, and culture; children, youth and families; civic engagement; education; employment and skills training; health and mental health; homelessness and hunger; housing and community development; immigrant communities; and law and justice. Candidates are required to first submit a letter of inquiry. Instructions for completion of LOI are available online.
Requirements Eligible applicants must be a nonprofit organization with tax-exempt status and be located within and primarily serve the Washington, D.C. region which is defined as: the District of Columbia; the Maryland counties of Montgomery, Prince George's, Calvert, Charles, and St. Mary's; and the Virginia counties of Arlington, Fairfax, Loudoun, Prince William, and Stafford and cities of Alexandria, Falls Church, Manassas, and Manassas Park in Virginia.
Restrictions The Foundation generally will not consider requests to fund: individuals, either through scholarships or other forms of financial assistance; scientific or medical research; sectarian purposes (programs that promote religious doctrine); special events or conferences; endowments.
Date(s) Application Is Due Feb 9; Jun 8; Oct 1.
Contact Julie Rogers, President, (202) 483-8294; fax: (202) 328-6850; email: jrogers@meyerfdn.org
Internet http://www.meyerfoundation.org
Sponsor Eugene and Agnes E. Meyer Foundation
1400 16th Street, N.W., Suite 360
Washington, DC 20036

Eugene M. Lang Foundation Grants 1881

The foundation awards grants in New York and Pennsylvania in its areas of interest, including education (early childhood education and higher education), medical and health programs, arts, health organizations, medical research, minorities, and performing arts. Types of support include annual campaigns, conferences and seminars, continuing support, fellowships, general operating support, internship funds, professorships, program development, scholarship funds, and seed money. The foundation favors social services such as those helping homeless or single mothers. Locally based groups wanting support must involve a Lang family member. There are no application deadlines; initial approach should be by letter.
Requirements Organizations in New York and Pennsylvania are eligible to apply.
Restrictions Grants are not made to individuals, or for building funds, equipment and materials, capital or endowment funds, deficit financing, publications, or matching gifts.
Amount $500-$50,000 average
Contact Program Contact, (212) 949-4100
Sponsor Eugene M. Lang Foundation
535 5th Avenue, Suite 906
New York, NY 10017

Eugene McDermott Foundation Grants 1882

The foundation awards grants to Texas nonprofit organizations in its areas of interest, including children and youth, community development, education (early childhood through higher education), health care/organizations, international human rights, medical research, minorities, and social service delivery programs. Types of support include annual campaigns, building construction/renovation, capital campaigns, equipment/land acquisition, general operating grants, matching/challenge grants, professorships, programs/project support, research grants, scholarship funds, and seed grants. There are no application deadlines or forms. The board meets quarterly to consider requests.
Requirements Texas nonprofit organizations are eligible.
Amount $1000-$25,000 average
Contact Grants Administrator, (214) 521-2924
Sponsor Eugene McDermott Foundation
3808 Euclid Ave
Dallas, TX 75205

Eugene S. Pulliam Fellowship for Editorial Writing 1883

The fellowship is awarded to an outstanding editorial writer to help broaden his or her journalistic horizons and knowledge of the world. The annual award can be used to cover the cost of study, research, and/or travel in any field. In some cases, the fellowship results in editorials and other writings, including books. All entries must be in English.
Requirements A candidate must hold a position as a full-time editorial writer at a news publication located in the United States; have at least three years experience as an editorial writer; demonstrate outstanding writing and analytical abilities; and secure assurances by the editor or publisher that the applicant will be allowed sufficient time to pursue the fellowship without jeopardizing employment.
Amount $75,000
Date(s) Application Is Due Jul 1.
Contact Bobby Deckard, Awards Coordinator, (317) 927-8000 ext 215; email: bdeckard@spj.org
Internet http://www.spj.org/fellowships_pulliam.asp
Sponsor Sigma Delta Chi Foundation
3909 N Meridian St
Indianapolis, IN 46208-4045

Eurasia Foundation Grantmaking Program 1884

The grantmaking program supports innovative projects in the foundation's three program areas: private enterprise development, public administration and policy, and civil society. The foundation supports projects aimed at strengthening human capital, developing locally sustainable forms of financing, and promoting a favorable legal and regulatory environment. Projects that cross over programmatic areas and geographic boundaries are particularly encouraged. The Washington office supports partnership projects that are developed and implemented jointly between US or other foreign institutions and New Independent States (NIS) organizations. Proposals are accepted at any time. The foundation occasionally sponsors targeted initiatives. Grant seekers should contact the nearest field office (listed on the Web site) for more information. The foundation strongly encourages applicants to submit a two- to three-page letter of inquiry describing the objectives of the program before making a formal application.
Requirements Grants are made to 501(c)3 nonprofit organizations as well as universities and government agencies. Organizations must be involved in a US-NIS partnership project.
Restrictions Grants are not made to individuals, nor does the foundation provide scholarships.
Amount $20,000 field grants
Contact Grantmaking Program, (202) 234-7370; fax: (202) 234-7377; email: eurasia@eurasia.org
Internet http://www.eurasia.org/grant.html
Sponsor Eurasia Foundation
1350 Connecticut Ave NW, Ste 1000
Washington, DC 20036

Eureka-Boston Fellowships 1885

The program awards two-year fellowships to CEOs of Massachusetts-based nonprofit organizations serving children, youth, and families in Boston, Cambridge, Chelsea, and Somerville.
Requirements CEOs of Massachusetts nonprofit organizations serving Boston, Cambridge, Chelsea, and Somerville are eligible.
Contact Grants Administrator, (617) 859-8218; fax: (617) 507-7738; email: info@eureka-boston.org
Sponsor Eureka-Boston
32 Rutland St
Boston, MA 02118

Evan Frankel Foundation Grants 1886

The foundation awards grants in its areas of interest, including higher education in the humanities and the environment. Giving is primarily in Manhattan and Suffolk County, NY and Los Angeles, CA. Submit a letter to request guidelines and deadline dates.
Restrictions Individuals are not eligible.
Amount $500-$100,000 average
Contact Nancy Wendell, (631) 329-2833; fax: (631) 329-7102; email: frankelfound@hamptons.com
Sponsor Evan Frankel Foundation
P.O. Box 5072
East Hampton, NY 11937

Evanston Community Foundation Grants 1887

Grants awarded by the Foundation: encourage and support new initiatives and innovative approaches to addressing community needs; build the capacity of local nonprofit organizations to fulfill their missions more effectively; encourage collaborative ventures that will strengthen the community; provide initial support of projects that will have impact beyond the scope and timeline of the proposed project; build community partnerships and resources; and strengthen the area's nonprofit community. Grants typically provide initial seed money to launch new projects, capstone dollars for a larger project that will grow over a longer period, and support a one-time activity or initial phase of a new program. The Foundation's area of interests include: arts and culture; basic human needs; community development; education; environment; health; women and girls and youth and families. The Foundation's RFP and application instructions are available online.
Requirements IRS 501(c)3 organizations serving the Evanston, IL, community are eligible.
Date(s) Application Is Due Feb 26.
Contact Sara Schastok, Executive Director, (847) 492-0990; fax: (847) 492-0904; email: schastok@evcommfdn.org or info@evcommfdn.org
Internet http://www.evcommfdn.org/grant_making.htm
Sponsor Evanston Community Foundation
1007 Church Street, Suite 108
Evanston, IL 60201

Evjue Foundation Grants 1888

The Foundation contributes each year to worthy educational, cultural and charitable organizations that contribute to the quality of life in Madison and Dane County. The Foundation's interests include: theater, hunger, troubled youth, and universities. The Foundation looks favorably upon projects responding to overall community needs and priorities that do not duplicate existing services. Application and guidelines are available online.
Requirements Grants are only made to nonprofit organizations.
Restrictions Grants are not made to individuals. All grants for scholarships are given to educational institutions, which have full responsibility for selecting the individual recipients. Grants are not usually made to establish or add to endowment funds. Grants are not ordinarily made to fund specific medical or scientific research inquiries, nor to support operating expenses and general administrative expenses of organizations.
Date(s) Application Is Due Mar 12.
Contact Arlene Hornung, Executive Director, (608) 252-6401; email: ahornung@madison.com
Internet http://www.madison.com/tct/evjue/policy/index.php
Sponsor Evjue Foundation
1901 Fish Hatchery Road
Madison, WI 53713

Ewing Halsell Foundation Grants 1889

The foundation awards grants to eligible Texas nonprofit organizations in its areas of interest, including education, environment, health care and health organizations, medical research, social services, and youth services. Types of support include annual campaigns, building construction/renovation, equipment acquisition, land acquisition, publication, research, seed grants, and technical assistance. There are no application deadlines or forms.
Requirements Texas nonprofit organizations are eligible. Preference is given to requests from southwestern Texas, particularly San Antonio.
Restrictions The foundation's grants do not support individuals or requests for deficit financing, emergency funds, general endowments, matching gifts, scholarships, fellowships, demonstration projects, general purposes, conferences, or loans.
Contact Grants Administrator, (210) 223-2640
Sponsor Ewing Halsell Foundation
711 Navarro Street, Suite 537
San Antonio, TX 78205

Ewing Marion Kauffman Entrepreneurial Leadership Emerging Scholars Grants 1890

The foundation's Kauffman Center for Entrepreneurial Leadership will award approximately 10 grants to PhD students for the support of scholarly entrepreneurship research. Proposals submitted must address research issues of theoretical and practical importance to the domain of entrepreneurship. Special consideration is given to submissions that also provide insight on the topic of entrepreneurship and women, minorities, education, finance, or the environment. The primary purpose of this initiative is to help launch a cohort of world-class scholars into the field. In addition, it is hoped that the findings generated will be translated into knowledge with immediate application for policymakers, educators, service providers, and entrepreneurs.
Requirements PhD students from accredited US institutions of higher education are eligible.
Contact Program Contact, (816) 932-1000; fax: (816) 932-1100; email: info@emkf.org
Internet http://www.kauffman.org/pages/150.cfm
Sponsor Ewing Marion Kauffman Foundation
4801 Rockhill Rd
Kansas City, MO 64110-2046

ExxonMobil Education Foundation Grants 1891

The program addresses the use of mathematics specialists in grades K-3, the status of mathematics instruction at the college level, and the analysis of policy issues in mathematics education. Types of support include general operating grants, matching gifts, scholarship funds, and program grants. The foundation also funds the Elementary and Secondary School Improvement program, which is intended to help the educational community gain a better understanding of the changing demographics of the school-age population and the implications for changes in the schools; to help educators learn how to restructure schools to make them instructionally more effective with more students, particularly with educationally at-risk and minority students; and to improve teacher education to help teachers take better advantage of changing school structures. The foundation also sponsors a program addressing the reform of undergraduate science, technology, engineering, and mathematics education.
Requirements The foundation makes grants only to tax-exempt organizations. A two-page letter of inquiry is required.
Restrictions The foundation rarely contributes to endowments or make grants for construction or remodeling of facilities. Funds are not provided for equipment acquisition. Scholarships and grants to individuals are not awarded.
Contact Program Contact, (972) 444-1106; fax: (972) 444-1405; email: contributions@exxonmobil.com
Internet http://www.exxonmobileurope.com/corporate/Citizenship/Corp_Cit_EducationInter.asp
Sponsor ExxonMobil Education Foundation
5959 Las Colinas Blvd
Irving, TX 75039-2298

ExxonMobil Grants 1892

The corporation favors grants that relate to the conduct of US business in general and the conduct of the petroleum and chemical industries in particular. The company is also concerned about social and economic conditions in corporate areas. Philanthropic

giving is concentrated in the areas of the environment, public policy and public research; health; united appeals and civic and community-service organizations; minority- and women-oriented service organizations; arts, museums, and historical associations; and education. There are no application forms; submit a letter of inquiry that includes a brief history of the organization, the operating budget, a list of the board of directors and contributors, and a copy of the tax-exemption letter.
Requirements Grants are made to tax-exempt organizations within principal company-operating areas.
Restrictions Grants are not made to individuals for scholarships, fellowships, research, or travel. Organizations that are primarily religious in nature are ineligible.
Amount $126 million total
Contact Public Affairs, Contributions, Exxon Mobil Corporation, (972) 444-1103; fax: (972) 444-1405; email: contributions@exxonmobil.com
Internet http://www.exxon.mobil.com
Sponsor ExxonMobil
5959 Las Colinas Blvd
Irving, TX 75039-2298

Ezra Jack Keats/Kerlan Collection Memorial Fellowship 1893
This fellowship provides a talented writer and/or illustrator of children's books with funds from the Children's Literature Research Collections at the University of Minnesota-Twin Cities Campus to use the Kerlan Collection for artistic development. Special consideration will be given to someone who would find it difficult to finance the visit to the Kerlan Collection. The fellow will receive transportation and a per diem allotment.
Requirements Grants are awarded to individuals based on need. Candidates may be of any nationality.
Amount $1,500
Date(s) Application Is Due Jun 1.
Contact Ezra Jack Keats/Kerlan Collection Memorial Fellowship Committee, (612) 624-4576; fax: (612) 625-5525; email: clrc@tc.umn.edu
Internet http://special.lib.umn.edu/clrc/awards.php
Sponsor University of Minnesota Children's Literature Research Collections
222 21st Avenue South, 113 Andersen Library
Minneapolis, MN 55455

F.J. O'Neill Charitable Corporation Grants 1894
The corporation awards general operating grants to eligible Ohio nonprofit organizations in its areas of interest, including higher and secondary education, medical research, and Roman Catholic groups and churches. There are no application deadlines or forms.
Requirements Ohio nonprofit organizations serving the Cleveland area are eligible.
Amount $25,000-$100,000 average
Contact Grants Administrator, (216) 464-2121
Sponsor F.J. O'Neill Charitable Corporation
3550 Lander Rd
Cleveland, OH 44124

F.W. Olin Foundation Construction Grant 1895
Each year, the foundation accepts applications for a grant to pay the entire cost of constructing and equipping a new academic building or library on a US independent college or university campus with a full-time undergraduate enrollment of 500 or more; the cost will not be shared with any other donor. Submit the original application to the New York office and one copy to the Minneapolis office c/o William Horn, 1500 Forshay Tower, Minneapolis, MN 55402; (612) 341-2581; fax: (612) 341-3801.
Contact Dr. Richard Miller, President, (212) 832-0508; email: richard.miller@olin.edu
Internet http://www.olin.edu/about_olin/olin_foundation.asp
Sponsor F.W. Olin Foundation
780 Third Ave, Ste 3403
New York, NY 10017-7090

FACHE Albert W. Dent Scholarships 1896
These scholarships have been established to provide financial aid and to increase the enrollment of minority students in health care management graduate programs and to encourage students, through structured, formalized study, to obtain positions in middle and upper levels of health care management. Applications are accepted between January 1 and March 31, and scholarship awards are announced in July. Interested persons should request application forms from the director of their graduate program in health care administration or from the foundation.
Requirements To be eligible, an applicant must be a US or Canadian student associate in good standing in the ACHE, a minority student who has been enrolled for full-time study for the upcoming fall term, which is his/her final year in a health care management graduate program. Financial need also must be demonstrated.
Restrictions Previous recipients are ineligible.
Amount $3500
Date(s) Application Is Due Mar 31.
Contact Membership, (312) 424-2800; fax: (312) 424-0023; email: membership1@ache.org
Internet http://www.ache.org/Faculty_Students/dent_scholarship.cfm
Sponsor Foundation of the American College of Healthcare Executives
1 N Franklin St, Ste 1700
Chicago, IL 60606-3491

Fairbank Center An Wang Postdoctoral Fellowships in Chinese Studies 1897
The fellowships support well-designed research projects in Chinese studies. The award includes a stipend and research fund for 12 months. Priority will be given to candidates working in late imperial and 20th-century fields and candidates who have had no previous postdoctoral fellowships. The center supports projects at any stage from initial research to revision for publication. Application guidelines are available on the Web site.
Requirements Candidate must have a PhD at the time of application and may not have held the PhD for more than five years.
Amount $40,000 stipend
Date(s) Application Is Due Feb 1.
Contact Postdoctoral Fellowship Coordinator, (617) 495-4046; fax: (617)495-9976; email: fairbank@fas.harvard.edu
Internet http://www.fas.harvard.edu/~fairbank/An_Wang.html
Sponsor Harvard University
625 Massachusetts Ave, 2nd Fl
Cambridge, MA 02139

Families USA Wellstone Fellowship for Social Justice 1898
The annual, one-year fellowship is designed to foster the advancement of social justice through participation in health care advocacy work that focuses on the unique challenges facing many communities of color. The fellowship, from August through July, will be based in the Families USA office in Washington, DC, and will afford the fellow the opportunity to learn about Medicare, Medicaid, efforts to achieve universal coverage, and other important health policy issues. At the same time, the fellow will learn about conducting health care campaigns through communication and collaboration with a network of state grassroots advocates and organizations. The goals of the program are to address disparities in access to health care; inspire fellows to continue to work for social justice throughout their lives; and increase the number and racial and ethnic diversity of up-and-coming social justice advocates and leaders. Guidelines are available online.
Requirements Candidates must demonstrate an interest in both health care and grassroots organizing and a commitment to contributing to social justice work following their year of hands-on experience as a fellow. Preference will be given to applicants who have experience with, or demonstrate a keen interest in, working with communities of color. While there is no bias in favor of any specific academic discipline, a college degree is preferred.
Amount $35,000 stipend plus health benefits
Date(s) Application Is Due Jan 7.
Contact Melissa Rosenblatt, (202) 628-3030; fax: (202) 347-2417; email: wellstonefellowship@familiesusa.org
Internet http://www.familiesusa.org/site/PageServer?pagename=Wellstone_Fellowship_About
Sponsor Families USA
1334 G St NW
Washington, DC 20005

Fan Fox and Leslie R. Samuels Foundation Grants Program 1899
The foundation's areas of funding are the performing arts and healthcare. Healthcare funding supports patient-based and social service activities that directly help the elderly of New York City. The foundation supports performing arts organizations in the City of New York, principally, but not exclusively, in the borough of Manhattan. The foundation's primary mission is to support major performing arts institutions of national or international eminence. In addition to providing direct support, the foundation also assists presenting entities that have the requisite expertise, knowledge, and artistic judgment to present groups or individuals, new works, varied repertoire, and arts-in-education projects that will be contributions to the aesthetic and intellectual life of New York. Application guidelines are available on the Web site or upon request.
Requirements The foundation funds organizations in the New York City area only. Only 501(c)3 tax-exempt organizations are invited to apply.
Restrictions The foundation does not give grants to individuals or for scholarships, and does not support research, film, or video, nor does it fund education or social services. The foundation no longer actively solicits applications for support of arts-in-education programs at the primary and secondary level.
Amount $25,000-$250,000 average
Date(s) Application Is Due Mar 1; Jun 1: Sep 1; Dec 1.
Contact Joseph Mitchell, President , (212) 239-3030; fax: (212) 239-3039; email: info@samuels.org
Internet http://www.samuels.org
Sponsor Fan Fox and Leslie R. Samuels Foundation
350 Fifth Ave, Ste 4301
New York, NY 10118

Fannie and John Hertz Foundation Graduate Fellowship Program 1900
The foundation supports graduate students working towards the PhD degree in the applied physical sciences. Fellows must have proposed fields of graduate study in engineering, applied physics, computer science, math, chemistry, or other area in the applied physical sciences; have excellent previous scholastic performance, typically including at least an A- grade average during the last two years of undergraduate work; be a US citizen or a permanent resident of the United States; and be ready to make themselves, their skills, and abilities available for the common defense in the event of national emergency.

Requirements Applicant must be a US citizen and have a bachelor's degree and propose to complete a program of graduate study leading to an advanced degree, but not in a professional degree program or a joint PhD/professional degree program.
Restrictions Joint-professional degree programs are not funded.
Amount $28,000-$33,000
Date(s) Application Is Due Oct 28.
Contact Graduate Fellowship Program, (510) 373-1642; fax: (510) 373-6329; email: askhertz@aol.com
Internet http://www.hertzfndn.org/awards.shtml
Sponsor Fannie and John Hertz Foundation
2456 Research Dr
Livermore, CA 94550-3850

Fannie E. Rippel Foundation Grants **1901**
The foundation aids, assists, funds, equips, and provides maintenance for corporations, institutions, associations, organizations, or societies maintained for the relief and care of aged women; provides funds for the building, equipping, and maintenance of hospitals; and provides funds for corporations, institutions, and other organizations existing for treatment of and/or research on heart disease or cancer. The foundation gives emphasis to the equipment and programmatic needs of major teaching medical centers and local rural hospitals, particularly where opportunities exist for leveraging the expertise or capabilities of the medical centers/rural hospitals. Programs should reach underserved rural and urban groups, advocate preventive care, present strategies to change behaviors of the people served, and promote humanistic medicine and mind-body-spirit connections in the healing process. Preference also is given to proposed projects where the benefits can be leveraged through challenge grants.
Requirements Organizations, associations, institutions, and hospitals in the Northeast are eligible.
Restrictions Grants are not awarded to individuals.
Amount $50,000-$300,000 average
Contact Barbara Vanderkolk Gardner, Trustee, (908) 766-0404; fax: (908) 766- 0527; email: rippel@attglobal.net
Internet http://fdncenter.org/grantmaker/rippel/index.html
Sponsor Fannie E. Rippel Foundation
180 Mount Airy Rd, Ste 200
Basking Ridge, NJ 07920

Fannie Mae Foundation Grants for Research **1902**
The foundation's Innovation, Research, and Community Technology (IRCT) division focuses on housing finance topics, such as affordable mortgage products and services and alternative mortgage finance structures and systems; ways to expand homeownership opportunities for low- and moderate-income and minority households and communities; the production and ongoing maintenance and management of affordable housing; fair housing and fair lending practices; community development; housing demography; and urban and regional policy. IRCT makes research grants and a limited number of grants to support research conferences. Research grants are awarded to individuals and organizations with the ability to make a significant contribution to the state of knowledge in housing economics and finance, housing and urban policy, housing demography, or community development issues related to the foundation's areas of focus. Grants to organizations also support research conferences disseminating new information in the areas of the foundation's research interests. Guidelines are available online.
Requirements US 501(c)3 nonprofit organizations are eligible.
Restrictions Grants are not awarded to fund individuals; private foundations; organizations/projects/programs that do not fit within the foundation's funding priorities; organizations that channel grant funds to third parties; organizations whose dominant purpose is to influence legislation or participate/intervene in political campaigns on behalf of or against any candidate for public office; organizations/projects/programs for which the foundation is asked to serve as the sole funder; organizations that already have an active Fannie Mae Foundation grant; sectarian purposes (i.e., programs that promote religious doctrine or exclude participants on the basis of religion); endowment or capital campaigns; existing program or organizational deficits; or local affiliates of national organizations with which the foundation has a relationship.
Contact Program Contact, (202) 274-8057; email: grants@fanniemaefoundation.org
Internet http://www.fanniemaefoundation.org/grants/grants_research.shtml
Sponsor Fannie Mae Foundation
4000 Wisconsin Ave NW
Washington, DC 20016

Fannie Mae Foundation Kennedy School of Government Fellowships **1903**
The foundation offers up to 35 fellowships annually as part of its partnership with the John F. Kennedy School of Government at Harvard University. The program enhances the management and decision-making skills of senior public and nonprofit officials committed to improving affordable housing opportunities in the United States. The program engages accomplished leaders experienced in managing housing and related community development programs. The curriculum focuses on organizational strategy, political management, policy development, management control and operations, and management of human resources. Fellowship funds cover the cost of the admission deposit, program tuition, and room and board for the session. Applicants must be able to attend the entire three-week session and are responsible for their own transportation and other incidental costs.
Requirements Admissions decisions are made solely by the Kennedy School of Government. Applicants must satisfy the requirements for admission to be accepted by the Kennedy School to attend one of the state and local program sessions.
Date(s) Application Is Due Apr 1.
Contact Fellowship Administrator, (202) 274-8000; fax: (202) 274-8100
Internet http://www.fanniemaefoundation.org/grants/kennedy_school.shtml
Sponsor Fannie Mae Foundation
4000 Wisconsin Ave NW, N Tower, Ste 1
Washington, DC 20016-2804

Fannie Mae James A. Johnson Fellowships **1904**
Each year, the program selects up to six fellows. These fellows design and pursue development plans that can include research, travel, study, self-designed internships, and other activities that enhance their skills and knowledge. The program's chief goals are to recognize and reward individual dedication and contribution to the affordable housing and community development fields; increase leadership and professional development of the fellows; foster opportunities for new solutions to affordable housing and community development challenges; and inform the affordable housing and community development knowledge base and influence long-term strategies in the field. The fellowship provides each fellow with a grant and a stipend for travel and education-related expenses. The nonprofit organization with which each fellow is associated (through paid or volunteer employment) may receive a grant of up to $25,000 for transitional costs related to the temporary absence of the employee or volunteer. Fellows are selected through a two-step nomination process. Each January, the foundation requests nominations from national housing and community development organizations and and national neighborhood funders. Regional review committees then select a number of individuals as finalists.
Requirements Nominees must meet the following criteria: a minimum of eight years in the affordable housing and community development field; current full-time (paid or volunteer) duties in the field; employment and affiliation with a neighborhood-based nonprofit or community-based nonprofit organization focused on affordable housing and community development; demonstrated leadership abilities; demonstrated ability to think creatively and design and implement innovative solutions to community development and affordable housing issues on a local, regional, or national level and in rural or urban settings; a continuing commitment to the field upon completion of the fellowship; a significant impact from the fellowship on the neighborhood/communities in which the nominee serves; no other venues or resources to pursue the opportunities that the fellowship will provide; and validation that timing is optimal for the nominee to utilize this experience, professionally and personally.
Amount $70,000 grant; $20,000 maximum for travel and education-related expenses
Date(s) Application Is Due Dec 31.
Contact Josie Gross, (202) 274-8031; fax: (202) 274-8100; email: jgross@fanniemaefoundation.org
Internet http://www.fanniemaefoundation.org/grants/johnson.shtml
Sponsor Fannie Mae Foundation
4000 Wisconsin Ave NW, N Tower, Ste 1
Washington, DC 20016-2804

FAR Fund **1905**
The Fund focuses its resources in three domains: improving and expanding services and systems for people on the autistic spectrum; preventing violence against youth; and preventing homelessness. The Fund encourages the creation of projects that operate across domains. The Fund also encourages projects that increase the participation and influence of consumers in shaping the service system that affect their lives. Particular interest is in projects that incorporate psychodynamic thinking in their program philosophy and service delivery. Proposal information is available on the website.
Requirements The application proposal should be brief and describe the following: the organization where the project will be located; the problem; the project, including the project title; the expected impact; a plan for project evaluation, including outcome indicators; plans for the project beyond the grant period; project staff; project expense budget and income budget, and an organization expense and income budget; the percentage of the project budget that would be supported by the Fund; a monitorable work plan; and the name of the tax-exempt organization that would receive the grant.
Amount $25,000
Date(s) Application Is Due Feb 1; Jun 1; Oct 1.
Contact Kaajal Shah, Program Officer
Internet http://www.farfund.org/
Sponsor Fund for Social Change
135 East 15th Street
New York, NY 10003

Farm Foundation Extension Graduate Training Fellowships **1906**
The foundation provides a number of extension fellowships for graduate training in extension administration and the social sciences, with emphasis on agricultural economics, rural sociology, psychology, political science, and agricultural geography, to improve the capability of active extension workers to function in managerial and supervisory roles in the extension service. The period of study may be one quarter, one semester, or nine months. The amount of each award will be determined individually on the basis of each applicant's qualifications and needs, ranging from tuition only to tuition and additional expenses including family subsistence. Extension fellowships are granted effective June 1 for the ensuing year.

Requirements Active federal-state agricultural extension workers in the United States are eligible to apply. Priority is given to administrators and supervisory personnel.
Amount $5500 maximum for nine months
Date(s) Application Is Due Mar 1.
Contact Walter Armbruster, President, (630) 571-9393; fax: (630) 571-9580; email: walt@farmfoundation.org
Internet http://www.farmfoundation.org
Sponsor Farm Foundation
1211 W 22nd St, Ste 216
Oak Brook, IL 60523

Farmers Insurance Group of Companies Grants **1907**
The corporate community relations program awards grants in the areas of education, public safety, arts and culture, civic improvement, and health and human services. Education giving focuses on literacy programs, mentoring programs, adopt-a-school programs, employee matching grants, and aid-to-education undergraduate scholarships. Public safety awards support tougher laws against drunk driving, drug/alcohol-free graduation night parties, neighborhood crime prevention, highway safety, and earthquake relief. Arts and culture funding supports children's programs and public television. Civic improvement focuses on recognizing exemplary youth, voter registration drives, adopt-a-highway programs, and community paint-a-thons. Health and human services giving supports March of Dimes, United Way, aid for families with cancer, aid to migrant farmworkers, and feeding the hungry. There are no application deadlines. Requests for contributions should be in the form of a letter outlining the purpose of the organization or program. The letter also should include the amount requested, its intended use, and a description of how Farmers' support will be recognized. Additional information should include a budget, annual report, proof of tax-exempt status, and a roster of the board.
Requirements 501(c)3 tax-exempt organizations are eligible.
Restrictions Farmers does not make charitable contributions to individuals, political candidates, or religious groups or for sports events, advertising or raffle tickets, construction projects, or international programs.
Amount $4.3 million total
Contact Angela Easton, Director of Community Affairs and Sponsorship, (213) 932-3518
Internet http://www.farmers.com/FarmComm/content/CC010153.jsp
Sponsor Farmers Insurance Group of Companies
4680 Wilshire Blvd
Los Angeles, CA 90010

FASSE Demonstration Project Grant **1908**
This research award is to engage and support educators in strengthening and advocating social studies, defined as the integrated study of the social sciences and humanities to promote civic competence. This annual award includes a commemorative gift, annual conference session for research presentation and publicity.
Requirements Nomination *Requirements* no self nominations; cover page; letter of nomination supporting, rationalizing the nomination; vitae or professional resume prepared by nominee; nominated study.
Date(s) Application Is Due May 1.
Contact Prema Parmar, Programs Assistant, (301) 588-1800; email: excellence@ncss.org
Internet http://www.socialstudies.org/awards/research/exemplary/
Sponsor Exemplary Research in Social Studies Award
8555 Sixteenth Street, Suite 500
Silver Spring, MD 20910

Father James B. Macelwane Annual Awards **1909**
To stimulate interest in meteorology among college students through the encouragement of original student papers concerned with some phase of the atmospheric sciences, these awards, supported by Weather Corporation of America and administered by the American Meteorological Society, are given for three papers submitted that are judged to be the best in the previous 12-month period; also considered may be papers from the previous 12-month period if they did not receive any award during the previous competition. To be considered, the paper must be accompanied by a letter of application from the author and a letter from the department head or other faculty member of the major department confirming that the author was an undergraduate student at the time the paper was written and indicating the elements of the paper that represent original contributions by the student.
Requirements All registered undergraduates in a college or university in the Americas are eligible to participate.
Restrictions Participating students must be enrolled as undergraduates at the time the paper is written, and no more than two students from any one institution may enter papers in any one contest.
Amount $300 first place, $200 second place, $100 third place
Contact Donna Fernandez, Fellowship and Scholarship Coordinator (617) 227-2426 ext 246; fax: (617) 742-8718; email: dfernand@ametsoc.org; or Stephanie Armstrong, Director of Development, (617) 227-2426 ext 235; email: dfernand@ametsoc.org
Internet http://www.ametsoc.org/amsstudentinfo/scholfeldocs
Sponsor American Meteorological Society
45 Beacon Street
Boston, MA 02108-3693

Faye McBeath Foundation Grants **1910**
Grants are made within the state of Wisconsin and principally to support projects or programs having primary focus on the welfare of the residents of the greater Milwaukee community including Milwaukee, Waukesha, Ozaukee and Washington counties. Generally, the Foundation supports programs for children, aging and elders, health, health education, and civic and governmental affairs. Capital grants are limited to projects with community-wide impact that reflect the program interests of the Foundation. There are no published deadlines for proposals. The common application form is available online.
Requirements 501(c)3 nonprofit organizations in the metropolitan Milwaukee area are eligible. The Foundation requires its grant applicants to use the Milwaukee-area common application form when submitting a full proposal.
Restrictions The Foundation does not consider or acknowledge general solicitation letters. Basic health sciences research is not funded. The Foundation does not award grants for annual fund drives, scholarships, support of individuals, or provide funds on an emergency basis.
Amount $12.5 million total; $10,000-$50,000 average
Contact Sarah Dean, Executive Director, (414) 272-2626; fax: (414) 272-6235; email: info@fayemcbeath.org
Internet http://www.fayemcbeath.org
Sponsor Faye McBeath Foundation
1020 N Broadway
Milwaukee, WI 53202

FCAR General Scholarships **1911**
Scholarships and fellowships are for master's and doctoral studies and for postdoctorate research or improvement in the arts, to encourage the most gifted students residing in the province of Quebec, and to emphasize special fields of study where a need is felt in the province. Salary for postdoctoral fellowships depends on area and quality of research. Visit the Web site for details on special requirements and restrictions. Annual deadline dates may vary; contact FCAR for exact dates.
Requirements Applicants must be Canadian citizens or permanent residents who have been residents of Quebec for at least one year at the time of application. Candidates must have obtained a bachelor's or master's degree in the past five years for master's and doctoral fellowships, and have a cumulative B+ or equivalent grade. Grantees must reside in Quebec for the duration of the grant period.
Restrictions Applicants for postdoctoral fellowships must not have been involved in research they intend to continue during the training period. The following will not be funded: supplies, publication, development, offices/laboratories, or elaborate projects.
Amount $C15,000 maximum per year for master's scholarships; $C20,000 maximum per year for doctoral scholarships
Date(s) Application Is Due Oct 13.
Contact Philippe-Edwin Belanger, Program Administer, (418) 643-8560 ext 3447 or 3446 or (888) 653 6512; fax: (418) 643-1451; email: boursesm@fqrnt.gouv.qc.ca or bourses@fqrnt.gouv.qc.ca
Internet http://www.fcar.qc.ca/nateq/bourses/regles/boGenerauxAng.htm
Sponsor Formation de Chercheurs et L'Aide a la Recherche
140 Grande-Allee Est, Bureau 450
PQ G1R 5M8 Canada

FCAR Quebec-France Fellowships **1912**
Fellowships are for master's and doctoral studies and for postdoctorate research or improvement in the arts, to encourage the most gifted students residing in the province of Quebec, and to emphasize special fields of study where a need is felt in the province. Salary for postdoctoral fellowships depends on area and quality of research. Visit the Web site for details on special requirements and restrictions. Five grants are awarded to masters students, and five are awarded to doctoral students to encourage advanced study in France. Annual deadline dates may vary; contact the program office for exact dates.
Requirements Applicants must be Canadian citizens or permanent residents who have been residents of Quebec for at least one year at the time of application. Candidates must have obtained a bachelor's or master's degree in the past five years for master's and doctoral fellowships, and have a cumulative B+ or equivalent grade. Grantees must reside in Quebec for the duration of the grant period.
Restrictions Applicants for postdoctoral fellowships must not have been involved in research they intend to continue during the training period. The following will not be funded: supplies, publication, development, offices/laboratories, or elaborate projects.
Date(s) Application Is Due Oct 15.
Contact Philippe-Edwin Belanger, Program Administrator, (418) 643-8560 ext 3447 or 3446 or (888) 653 6512; fax: (418) 643-1451; email: boursesm@fqrnt.gouv.qc.ca or bourses@fqrnt.gouv.qc.ca
Internet http://www.fcar.qc.ca/nateq/bourses/index.htm
Sponsor Formation de Chercheurs et L'Aide a la Recherche
140 Grande-Allee Est, Bureau 450
PQ G1R 5M8 Canada

FCD Changing Faces of America's Fellowships **1913**
The program focuses on understanding the changing faces of America's children and seeks to support a new generation of scholars conducting research on the development of young immigrant children from birth to age 10. The goals of the program are to stimulate both fundamental and policy-relevant research in this area, and to support young investigators from a variety of behavioral or social sciences or in an allied professional

field. Fellowship recipients are expected to produce a book or article(s)suitable for publication and to articulate how their research may potentially inform policies regarding young newcomer children. Approximately three or four fellowships are available for support of individual scholarship by junior faculty. The funds, to be used over a one to three years, cover each fellow's research expenses and salary and are paid directly to the recipient's academic institution. Complete guidelines are available online.
Requirements Fellowships are available to scholars who have earned their PhD within the last 15 years. Applicants must hold a PhD or its equivalent in one of the behavior or social sciences or in an allied professional field (i.e., public policy, public health, education, social work, nursing). Applicants must hold a position as a full-time, tenure-track faculty member of a US college or university.
Restrictions The foundation does not consider requests for: capital campaigns, the purchase, construction or renovation of buildings, grants for projects outside the United States, the direct provision of preschool education or child care, or health care; or under the foundation's health focus, research, policy, or direct-service projects concerned with specific illnesses.
Amount $150,000 maximum
Date(s) Application Is Due Nov 1.
Contact Changing Faces of America's Children, (212) 213-8337 ext 203; fax: (212) 213-5897; email: inforequest@ffcd.org
Internet http://www.fcd-us.org/ourwork/y-index.html
Sponsor Foundation for Child Development
145 E 32nd St, 14th Fl
New York, NY 10016

FCD Child Development Grants **1914**
The foundation awards grants to support programs for children, particularly the disadvantaged, and promote their well-being through basic and policy-relevant research about the factors that promote optimal development of children and adolescents; policy analysis, advocacy, services, and public education to enhance the discussion and adoption of social policies that support families in their important child-raising responsibilities; and leadership development activities linked to the programmatic focus of the foundation. Grants focus on the integration of research, policy, and advocacy in two areas: the availability of and access to early childhood education programs and health care for children. Most grants support research, but a small number of direct service grants are made for New York City-based projects that advance the foundation's research and policy analysis efforts. There are no application deadlines; submit a brief letter of inquiry. Full proposals are by invitation.
Requirements Nonprofit organizations are eligible.
Restrictions The foundation does not consider requests for scholarships or support for individuals, capital campaigns, building purchase or renovation, or equipment purchase. The foundation does not make grants outside the United States.
Contact Grants Administrator, (212) 213-8337; fax: (212) 213-5897; email: info@fcd-us.org
Internet http://www.ffcd.org/ourwork/g-how.html
Sponsor Foundation for Child Development
145 E 32nd St, 14th Fl
New York, NY 10016

FCER Chiropractic Research Grants **1915**
The grants support basic and clinical research and research program development related to chiropractic. Types of support include awards/prizes, challenge/matching grants, conferences and seminars, demonstration grants, fellowships, research grants, residencies, and research contracts. Fellowships are for a maximum of five years.
Amount $10,000-$130,000 per year
Date(s) Application Is Due Mar 1; Oct 1.
Contact Dr. Anthony Rosner, Director of Research, (617) 734-3397; fax: (617) 734-0989; email: rosnerfcer@aol.com
Internet http://www.fcer.org/html/Research/Grants/guidelines.htm#Instructions%20for%20Application
Sponsor Foundation for Chiropractic Education and Research
1330 Beacon St, Ste 315
Brookline, MA 02446-3202

FCER Research Grants and Fellowships **1916**
The fellowships support research training primarily for graduate chiropractors enrolled in academic programs in basic sciences and clinical health-related areas. Grants are for basic research and related expenses.
Requirements Priority for funding will be based on merit and the relevance/importance of the proposed research of chiropractic theory and practice, as well as the ability of the investigator and sponsoring institutions to bring the project to successful completion.
Amount $10,000-$120,000 range
Contact Dr. Anthony Rosner, Director of Research & Education, (617) 734-3397; fax: (617) 734-0989; email: rosnerfcer@aol.com
Internet http://www.fcer.org/research.htm
Sponsor Foundation for Chiropractic Education and Research
1330 Beacon St, Ste 315
Brookline, MA 02446-3202

FDA Orphan Products Clinical Studies Grants **1917**
The objective of the grants is to support clinical trials on the safety and effectiveness of products to treat a rare disease or condition. These include conditions for which no current therapy exists or the therapy that does exist is in need of improvement. The FDA provides grants to conduct clinical studies intended to provide data that will either result in or substantially contribute to approval of these medical products. All studies of new drugs and biological products must be conducted under the FDA's investigational new drug procedure. Studies of medical devices must be conducted under the investigational device exemption procedures.
Requirements Public or private for-profit or nonprofit organizations may apply. Profit organizations must commit to excluding fees or profit in their request for support.
Amount $100,000 maximum for new awards; $200,000 maximum for continuation awards
Contact Rosemary Springer, Chief Grants Management Officer, (301) 827-7182; fax: (301) 827-7101; email: rspringe@oc.fda.gov
Internet http://www.fda.gov
Sponsor Food and Drug Administration
5630 Fishers Ln, HFA-520, Rm 2129
Rockville, MD 20857

FDA Scientific Conferences Grants **1918**
The FDA accepts applications for grants for scientific conferences held in the United States and Canada on topics relating directly to the agency's mission and funding priorities. This initiative is intended to support and encourage state food regulatory agencies to establish (or provide support of existing) regularly scheduled Food Safety Task Force meetings. These meetings should foster communication and cooperation within the state among state and local food safety regulatory agencies and is part of the President's Food Safety Initiative (FSI).
Requirements Awards can be made to any public or private nonprofit university, college, hospital, laboratory, or other institution, including state and local units of government. Commercial and nonprofit organizations are also eligible.
Amount $5000-$3 million; $225,970 average
Contact Rosemary Springer, Chief, Grants and Agreements Management Branch, Division of Contracts and Assistance Management, (301) 827-7182; fax: (301) 827-7101; email: rspringe@oc.fda.gov
Internet http://www.fda.gov
Sponsor Food and Drug Administration
5600 Fishers Ln, HFA-520, Rm 2129
Rockville, MD 20857

FDHN Bridging Grants **1919**
Awards of $50,000 each are available to assist investigators were not awarded their first R01 or the first renewal of their R01 to continue their gastroenterology related research. Two awards will be made following each of the three annual NIH review cycles and availability of Summary Statements. The primary objective of the award is to provide interim support to AGA Members who have submitted grants to NIH that were approved on the basis of scientific merit, but received priority scores out of the funding range.
Requirements Applicants must: be AGA members who are applying for their first R01 or their second R01 either as a competitive renewal or a new R01 (this includes investigators going from a K award to their first R01); hold an MD, PhD, or equivalent degree (e.g., MB, ChB, MBBS, DO); hold full-time faculty positions at North American universities or professional institutes at the time of application; and have submitted a proposal to NIH that has undergone the peer review process and was either approved and not funded or received high commendation but not funded.
Restrictions Applicants cannot receive more than $75,000 of any additional extramural research support. Up to 25% of total amount the award may be used for salary support of the Principal Investigator. Indirect costs, including travel are not allowed.
Amount $50,000
Date(s) Application Is Due Feb 14; Jun 14; Oct 14.
Contact Research Awards Manager, (301) 222-4012; fax: (301) 652-3890; email: awards@fdhn.org
Internet http://www.fdhn.org/wmspage.cfm?parm1=119
Sponsor Foundation for Digestive Health and Nutrition
4930 Del Ray Avenue
Bethesda, MD 20814

FDHN Centocor International Research Fellowship in Gastrointestinal Inflammation & Immunology **1920**
This award provides $50,000 to enable promising young investigators from outside the United States to spend a year at a U.S. institution engaged full-time in research related to the fundamental processes in gastrointestinal inflammation and immunology. The primary objectives of the award are: to provide the opportunity for young investigators from outside the U.S. to participate in basic research on inflammatory disease processes at prominent institutions in the U.S. (the award provides salary support for fulltime research); to initiate future international collaborative research efforts in inflammatory digestive diseases; and to address an important question in such a way as to provide a meaningful answer.
Requirements Candidates must hold an MD or equivalent degree (eg, MB. ChB, MBBS). Applicants should currently be on the faculty of an academic institution outside the

U.S. Applicants must be AGA members or be eligible for and submit an application for membership.
Restrictions At the time of application, candidates are not allowed to hold any other similar research grant. These awards may not be renewed. No more than one application will be accepted from any institution in a given year.
Amount $50,000
Date(s) Application Is Due Jan 14.
Contact Research Awards Manager, (301) 222-4012; fax: (301) 652-3890; email: awards@fdhn.org
Internet http://www.fdhn.org/wmspage.cfm?parm1=105
Sponsor Foundation for Digestive Health and Nutrition
4930 Del Ray Avenue
Bethesda, MD 20814

FDHN Designated Outcomes Award in Geriatric Gastroenterology 1921
Two awards in the amount of $35,000 for one year are available to support investigator-initiated outcomes research in geriatric gastroenterology. In general, outcomes studies examine clinical outcomes, patient satisfaction, quality of life, economic evaluation, quality of care, functional status, appropriateness of care, conformance of recommended/desirable standards of performance, or change in practice patterns. The objective of this award is to promote research by young investigators in the area of outcomes, broadly defined above, as it relates to geriatric gastroenterology. Please review the AGA Future Trends Committee Report: Effects of Aging of the Population on Gastroenterology Practice, Education and Research to learn more about research topics encouraged for study. Funds may be used for salary support of personnel and technicians only, supplies and/or equipment/services. Women and minorities are strongly encouraged to apply.
Requirements Investigators must possess an MD, PhD or equivalent and must hold faculty positions at accredited North American academic institutions by the time of the start date of the award. MD applicants: No more than five years should elapse following the completion of your clinical training (GI fellowship or equivalent) and the start date of this award. Applicants must be AGA Members.
Restrictions The award is intended for junior faculty; therefore, established investigators are not eligible. Candidates may not hold awards on a similar topic from other agencies. Indirect costs are not allowed.
Amount $35,000
Date(s) Application Is Due Sep 5.
Contact Research Awards Manager, (301) 222-4012; fax: (301) 652-3890; email: awards@fdhn.org
Internet http://www.fdhn.org/wmspage.cfm?parm1=234
Sponsor Foundation for Digestive Health and Nutrition
4930 Del Ray Avenue
Bethesda, MD 20814

FDHN Designated Research Award in Geriatric Gastroenterology 1922
This award provides $75,000 per year for three years (total $225,000) for young investigators working toward independent careers in academic research related to geriatric gastroenterology. The overall objective is to enable young investigators to develop independent and productive research careers, with a focus on research related to geriatric gastroenterology, by ensuring that a major proportion of their time is protected for research. Non-recipient applicants for this award will be considered for the Research Scholar Awards. Applicants should review the AGA Future Trends Committee Report: Effects of Aging of the Population on Gastroenterology Practice, Education and Research to learn more about research topics encouraged for study. The award is not intended for fellows, but for young faculty who have demonstrated unusual promise and have some record of accomplishment in research.
Requirements Candidates must hold an MD, PhD, or equivalent degree (e.g., MB, ChB, MBBS, DO). Applicants must hold full-time faculty positions at North American universities or professional institutes at the time award begins. Applicants must be Members of the AGA. # MD applicants: no more than five years shall have elapsed following the completion of your clinical training (GI fellowship or its equivalent) and the start date of this award. PhD applicants: no more than five years shall have elapsed from the completion of your postdoctoral training and the start date of this award. Candidates must devote at least 70 percent of their efforts to research related to geriatric gastroenterology.
Restrictions Candidates should be in the beginning years of their careers; therefore, established investigators are not appropriate candidates.
Amount $75,000 per year for three years
Date(s) Application Is Due Sep 15.
Contact Research Awards Manager, (301) 222-4012; fax: (301) 652-3890; email: awards@fdhn.org
Internet http://www.fdhn.org/wmspage.cfm?parm1=224
Sponsor Foundation for Digestive Health and Nutrition
4930 Del Ray Avenue
Bethesda, MD 20814

FDHN Designated Research Award in Research Related to Pancreatitis 1923
The overall objective of this Award is to enable young investigators to develop independent and productive research careers, with a focus on pancreatic disease, by ensuring that a major proportion of their time is protected for research. The Award provides $75,000 per year for three years (total $225,000) for young investigators working toward independent careers in academic research related to understanding, improving treatments or curing Pancreatitis.
Requirements Candidates must hold an MD, PhD, or equivalent degree (e.g., MB, ChB, MBBS, DO). Applicants must hold full-time faculty positions at North American universities or professional institutes at the time award begins. Applicants must also be members of the AGA. The award is not intended for fellows, but for young faculty who have demonstrated unusual promise and have some record of accomplishment in research. Candidates should be in the beginning years of their careers; therefore, established investigators are not appropriate candidates. MD applicants: No more than five years shall have elapsed following the completion of your clinical training (GI fellowship or its equivalent) and the start date of this award. PhD applicants: No more than five years shall have elapsed from the completion of your postdoctoral training and the start date of this award.
Amount $75,000 per year for three years
Date(s) Application Is Due Apr 17.
Contact Research Awards Manager, (301) 222-4012; fax: (301) 652-3890; email: awards@fdhn.org
Internet http://www.fdhn.org/wmspage.cfm?parm1=100
Sponsor Foundation for Digestive Health and Nutrition
4930 Del Ray Avenue
Bethesda, MD 20814

FDHN Fellow Abstract Prizes 1924
Two awards of $1000 each will be given to fellows who have submitted abstracts chosen to be presented during Digestive Disease Week®. Awards will be presented at a ceremony during DDW. The primary objective of this award is to stimulate interest in GI research careers through competition and recognition
Requirements Qualified candidates are MD or PhD postdoctoral fellows who are trainee members the AGA. Women and minority investigators are strongly encouraged to apply. Applicants must: be sponsored by an AGA member; and be the first author of an abstract accepted for presentation at DDW and provide evidence of abstract acceptance. Individuals with faculty appointments are not eligible. Applicants may only submit one abstract for consideration.
Restrictions Fellows who have been awarded must present the abstract. No substitute presenters are allowed. Abstracts must have been selected for presentation at DDW. A letter of recommendation from the sponsor is required.
Amount $1,000
Date(s) Application Is Due Mar 21.
Contact Research Awards Manager, (301) 222-4012; fax: (301) 652-3890; email: awards@fdhn.org
Internet http://www.fdhn.org/wmspage.cfm?parm1=124
Sponsor Foundation for Digestive Health and Nutrition
4930 Del Ray Avenue
Bethesda, MD 20814

FDHN Fellowship to Faculty Transition Awards 1925
This award provides $40,000 per year for two years for current trainees in gastroenterology related fields so they may gain additional research training in gastrointestinal, liver function or related diseases. The objective is to prepare physicians for independent research careers in digestive diseases. The award provides salary support for additional full-time research training in basic science to acquire modern laboratory skills. The additional two years of research training provided by this award should broaden and expand the scope of investigative tools available to the recipient, generally in basic disciplines such as cell or molecular biology or immunology.
Requirements Applicants must be MDs or MD/PhDs currently in a gastroenterology-related fellowship at an accredited North American institution, committed to academic careers. They will have completed two years of research training at the start of this award. Applicants must be AGA Trainee Members and be sponsored by an AGA Member.
Restrictions Individuals who hold a PhD are ineligible. Although the institution may supplement the award, the applicant may not concurrently hold a similar training award or grant from another organization, such as the NIH, ALF, CCFA, or the Glaxo Institute of Digestive Health.
Amount $40,000 per year for two years
Date(s) Application Is Due Sep 5.
Contact Research Awards Manager, (301) 222-4012; fax: (301) 652-3890; email: awards@fdhn.org
Internet http://www.fdhn.org/wmspage.cfm?parm1=102
Sponsor Foundation for Digestive Health and Nutrition
4930 Del Ray Avenue
Bethesda, MD 20814

FDHN Funderburg Research Scholar Award in Gastric Biology Related to Cancer 1926
This grant of $25,000 per year for two years (total $50,000) is awarded to an established investigator working on novel approaches in gastric cancer, including the fields of gastric mucosal regeneration and regulation of cell growth (not as they relate to peptic ulcer disease inflammation (including Helicobacter pylori) as precancerous lesions; genetics of gastric oncogenes in gastric epithelial malignancies; epidemiology of gastric cancer; etiology of malignancies; or clinical research in the diagnosis or treatment of gastric carcinoma. The primary objective of the award is to support an active, established

investigator in the field of gastric biology who enhances the fundamental understanding of gastric cancer pathobiology in order to ultimately develop a cure for the disease.
Requirements Applicants must hold faculty positions at accredited North American institutions and must have established themselves as independent investigators in the field of gastric biology. Women and minority investigators are strongly encouraged to apply. Applicants must be Members of the AGA.
Amount $25,000 per year for two years
Date(s) Application Is Due Sep 5.
Contact Research Awards Manager, (301) 222-4012; fax: (301) 652-3890; email: awards@fdhn.org
Internet http://www.fdhn.org/wmspage.cfm?parm1=90
Sponsor Foundation for Digestive Health and Nutrition
4930 Del Ray Avenue
Bethesda, MD 20814

FDHN Graduate Student Awards **1927**
Two awards of $20,000 a year for two years are offered to fund graduate students undertaking research in the biology and epidemiology of diseases of the gastrointestinal tract, liver or pancreas. The award includes $18,000 for stipend and $2,000 to be used towards fringe benefits such as medical insurance and travel to a national meeting. The primary objective of the award is to provide a salary stipend for graduate students performing doctoral research related to the gastrointestinal tract, liver or pancreas.
Requirements Applicants should have completed at least one year and no more than three years of training towards the doctoral degree and have selected and confirmed the laboratory or department in which they will conduct doctoral research. Research is to be conducted at an accredited academic institution within North America and the research advisor must be a Member of the AGA. Applicants should be US citizens, permanent residents or overseas students who have a current visa to pursue education within North America.
Restrictions Indirect costs, excluding travel, are not allowed. Tuition costs are expected to be covered by the institution or host department and laboratory.
Amount $20,000 per year for two years
Date(s) Application Is Due Mar 14.
Contact Research Awards Manager, (301) 222-4012; fax: (301) 652-3890; email: awards@fdhn.org
Internet http://www.fdhn.org/wmspage.cfm?parm1=154
Sponsor Foundation for Digestive Health and Nutrition
4930 Del Ray Avenue
Bethesda, MD 20814

FDHN Jon I. Isenberg International Research Scholar Award **1928**
This award provides a total of $50,000 for one year of study, $25,000 from the AGA and $25,000 in matching funds from the applicant's national GI society. The award provides for non-US citizen young investigators to spend one year performing GI-related research at an American institution under the tutelage of an AGA member. Four awards will be given annually. The primary objective of this award is to promote international scholarship, increase AGA's involvement within the international GI community and foster international collaboration in training GI investigators.
Requirements An eligible candidate must be nominated by his or her national GI Society. The national GI society must match the $25,000 contribution from the AGA. Before submitting an application, a candidate must identify a sponsoring American institution and a research preceptor who agrees in writing to supervise his or her training and research. Qualified candidates must possess a doctoral degree, either an MD, or equivalent degree, and/or a PhD degree. In keeping with the intent to support the career development of young investigators, the candidate must be within five (5) years of completing GI training or, if a PhD, within five (5) years of the receipt of the degree, at the time of initiation of the award. A documented parental leave of absence will not be counted towards the five (5) years of eligibility.
Amount $50,000
Date(s) Application Is Due Mar 1.
Contact Research Awards Manager, (301) 222-4012; fax: (301) 652-3890; email: awards@fdhn.org
Internet http://www.fdhn.org/wmspage.cfm?parm1=101
Sponsor Foundation for Digestive Health and Nutrition
4930 Del Ray Avenue
Bethesda, MD 20814

FDHN June & Donald O. Castell MD, Esophageal Clinical Research Award **1929**
One award of $35,000 is made annually to provide research and/or salary support for junior faculty involved in clinical research in esophageal diseases. This award is funded by the June and Donald O. Castell, MD, Gastroenterology Research and Education Trust. The primary objective of the award is to support investigators who have demonstrated high potential to develop independent, productive research careers.
Requirements Candidates must hold a MD or PhD or equivalent. Applicants must hold a full-time faculty position at a North American universities or professional institute. Applicants must be members of the AGA. The recipient must be at or below the level of assistant professor, and his/her initial appointment to the faculty position must have been within seven (7) years of the time of application. This award is not intended for fellows, but for junior faculty who have demonstrated unusual promise; have some record of accomplishment in research; and have established independent research programs at the time of the award. Candidates must devote at least 50 percent of their efforts to research related to esophageal function or diseases.
Restrictions If an award recipient receives notification of another award with overlapping scientific objectives, prior to the start date of an AGA or FDHN award, the applicant must choose between the two awards.
Amount $35,000
Date(s) Application Is Due Jan 14.
Contact Research Awards Manager, (301) 222-4012; fax: (301) 652-3890; email: awards@fdhn.org
Internet http://www.fdhn.org/wmspage.cfm?parm1=104
Sponsor Foundation for Digestive Health and Nutrition
4930 Del Ray Avenue
Bethesda, MD 20814

FDHN Moti L. & Kamla Rustgi International Travel Awards **1930**
This program awards grants to young basic, translational and clinical investigators to support their travel and related expenses to attend Digestive Disease Week®. Two awards of $500 each will be given to selected individuals residing outside North America. The primary objective of the award is to enable young investigators outside of North American (U.S. or Canada) institutions to attend Digestive Disease Week and encourage international trainees to become more involved in digestive tract, pancreatic and liver disease research.
Requirements Candidates must: be MD or PhD or MD PhD postdoctoral fellows who are international trainee members of the AGA; be sponsored by an International member of AGA; be 35 years of age or younger at the time of the meeting; be fluent in English; and have a sufficient number of scientific papers (impact factor) published and/or poster presentations.
Amount $500
Date(s) Application Is Due Mar 21.
Contact Research Awards Manager, (301) 222-4012; fax: (301) 652-3890; email: awards@fdhn.org
Internet http://www.fdhn.org/wmspage.cfm?parm1=126
Sponsor Foundation for Digestive Health and Nutrition
4930 Del Ray Avenue
Bethesda, MD 20814

FDHN Non-Career Research Awards **1931**
This award provides approximately $10,000 (per symposia) for travel support for young investigators and selected established investigators to participate in symposia on gastrointestinalrelated topics. The primary objective of the award is to foster interactions and enhance the exchange of information between clinical and basic science investigators, and established and junior investigators working in gastrointestinal research. Eligibility women and minority organizers are strongly encouraged to apply. Travel support may be provided for: junior investigators who are within 5 years of completing their clinical training in GI or from completion of their PhD doctoral thesis and are at or below the rank of assistant professor; and up to two established investigators who are invited speakers. Biosketches of these individuals and a letter addressing their contribution to the scientific content and atmosphere of the meeting should be submitted with the application.
Requirements Within 60 days of the conclusion of the meeting, a one-page summary of the highlights of the meeting and an accounting of the use of funds must be submitted. The names of participants and speakers in the symposium, addresses, dates of birth and academic ranks of the attending scientists and their itemized expenses, must be sent to the Foundation. Any unexpended funds must be returned.
Restrictions Indirect costs are not allowed.
Amount $10,000 average
Date(s) Application Is Due Feb 1; May 1; Oct 1.
Contact Research Awards Manager, (301) 222-4012; fax: (301) 652-3890; email: awards@fdhn.org
Internet http://www.fdhn.org/wmspage.cfm?parm1=123
Sponsor Foundation for Digestive Health and Nutrition
4930 Del Ray Avenue
Bethesda, MD 20814

FDHN Non-Career Research Grants **1932**
A research initiative grant of $25,000 for one year is offered to investigators to support pilot research projects in gastroenterology- or hepatology-related areas. The primary objective of the award is to provide non-salary funds for new investigators to help them establish their research careers or to support pilot projects that represent new research directions for established investigators. The intent is to stimulate research in gastroenterology- or hepatology-related areas by permitting investigators to obtain new data that can ultimately provide the basis for subsequent grant applications of more substantial funding and duration. Women and minorities are strongly encouraged to apply.
Requirements Investigators must possess an MD or PhD degree or equivalent and must hold faculty positions at accredited North American institutions. Candidates may not hold awards on a similar topic from other agencies. Applicants must be AGA Members. Applicants for this award may not simultaneously apply for the AGA/Miles and Shirley Fiterman Foundation Basic Research Award or the AGA June and Donald O. Castell, MD, Esophageal Clinical Research Award.

Restrictions If an award recipient receives notification of another award with overlapping scientfic objectives, prior to the start date of an AGA or FDHN award, the applicant must choose between the two awards.
Amount $25,000
Date(s) Application Is Due Jan 14.
Contact Research Awards Manager, (301) 222-4012; fax: (301) 652-3890; email: awards@fdhn.org
Internet http://www.fdhn.org/wmspage.cfm?parm1=121
Sponsor Foundation for Digestive Health and Nutrition
4930 Del Ray Avenue
Bethesda, MD 20814

FDHN Research Scholar Awards 1933
These awards provide salary support for young investigators working in any area of gastrointestinal, liver function, or related diseases. The primary intent of the program is to support physician-investigators who have a high potential to develop independent, productive research careers in gastroenterology and hepatology. Candidates must devote at least 70 percent of their effort to research related to the gastrointestinal tract or liver. There must be a strong commitment from the candidate's division and department to support the candidate by protecting time for research and providing adequate laboratory space and facilities.
Requirements Applicants must hold full-time faculty positions at North American universities or professional institutes. Nonphysician candidates with a PhD will also be considered. Candidates should be early in their research careers and commonly will have recently completed their fellowship training.
Restrictions Indirect costs are not allowed. Candidates who have been at the assistant professor level or equivalent for more than five years are not eligible. Nor can applicants hold, or have held, an RO1, R29, K11, K08, or VA research award or any award with similar objectives from nonfederal sources (such as ALF, CCFA, or Glaxo Institute of Digestive Health). However, awards or grants obtained after receipt of this award need not be surrendered.
Amount $75,000 per year for three years
Date(s) Application Is Due Sep 5.
Contact Research Awards Manager, (301) 222-4012; fax: (301) 652-3890; email: awards@fdhn.org
Internet http://www.fdhn.org/wmspage.cfm?parm1=103
Sponsor Foundation for Digestive Health and Nutrition
4930 Del Ray Avenue
Bethesda, MD 20814

FDHN Student Research Fellowships 1934
This program offers financial support for students to spend a minimum of 10 weeks performing research in digestive diseases or nutrition and is intended to stimulate interest in research careers in these areas. The work may take place at any time during the year. Up to 20 fellowships will be available for full-time research with a preceptor, who must be a faculty member who directs a research project in a gastroenterology-related area at an accredited North American institution. A complete financial statement and scientific progress report are required upon completion of the program. The AGA has recognized the need to attract and encourage minority individuals to enter and pursue gastroenterology research careers. In response to this concern, seven of the student research fellowship awards will be reserved for underrepresented minority students. For the purpose of this award, minorities have been defined as African American, Hispanic, Native American/Alaskan Native, and Pacific Islander.
Requirements Candidates may be high school, undergraduate, medical, or graduate students (not yet engaged in thesis research) in accredited North American institutions. Women and minority students are strongly encouraged to apply. The preceptor must be a faculty member who directs a research project in a gastroenterology-related area at an accredited North American institution.
Restrictions Candidates may not hold similar salary support from other agencies: e.g., American Liver Foundation, Crohn's and Colitis Foundation.
Amount $2,000-$3,000
Date(s) Application Is Due Mar 5.
Contact Research Awards Manager, (301) 222-4012; fax: (301) 652-3890; email: awards@fdhn.org
Internet http://www.fdhn.org/wmspage.cfm?parm1=115
Sponsor Foundation for Digestive Health and Nutrition
4930 Del Ray Avenue
Bethesda, MD 20814

FDHN TAP Endowed Designated Research Award in Acid-Related Diseases 1935
This award provides $75,000 per year for three years (total $225,000) for young investigators working toward independent careers in acid-related diseases. The overall objective is to enable young investigators to develop independent and productive careers in acid-related research by ensuring that a major proportion of their time is protected for research.
Requirements Candidates must hold an MD, PhD, or equivalent degree (e.g., MB, ChB, MBBS, DO). Applicants must hold full-time faculty positions at North American universities or professional institutes at the time award begins. Applicants must be Members of the AGA. The award is not intended for fellows, but for young faculty who have demonstrated unusual promise and have some record of accomplishment in research. Candidates should be in the beginning years of their careers; therefore, established investigators are not appropriate candidates. Candidates must devote at least 70 percent of their efforts to research related to geriatric gastroenterolgy.
Restrictions MD applicants: no more than five years shall have elapsed following the completion of your clinical training (GI fellowship or its equivalent) and the start date of this award. PhD applicants: no more than five years shall have elapsed from the completion of your postdoctoral training and the start date of this award.
Amount $75,000 per year for three years
Date(s) Application Is Due Sep 5.
Contact Research Awards Manager, (301) 222-4012; fax: (301) 652-3890; email: awards@fdhn.org
Internet http://www.fdhn.org/wmspage.cfm?parm1=132
Sponsor Foundation for Digestive Health and Nutrition
4930 Del Ray Avenue
Bethesda, MD 20814

FDHN Translational Research Awards 1936
One award of $100,000 per year for two years will be made annually to support translational research in gastroenterology and/or hepatology. Translational research will be defined as the process of applying ideas, insights and discovery generated through basic science research to the diagnosis, treatment or prevention of human disease. The primary objective of the award is to enhance interaction between researchers with basic science and clinical backgrounds with the goal of accelerating the pace of discovery that is directly applicable to patient care. The creation of teams including both a Ph.D. and an M.D. researcher is particularly encouraged.
Requirements This award must be applied for jointly by a team of researchers (typically consisting of two members), including at least one researcher with significant training and experience in a basic science discipline (including areas outside the traditional biomedical sciences, such as physical sciences and engineering) and at least one researcher who is qualified to provide direct clinical care to patients. Junior investigators in either or both categories are particularly encouraged to apply. Applicants must be members of the AGA. Research must be conducted at an accredited North American institution.
Restrictions Candidates may not hold support for the same project from another agency. If a proposed award recipient receives notification of another award with overlapping scientific objectives prior to the start date of an AGA or FDHN award, the applicant must choose only one of the awards to accept.
Amount $100,000 per year for two years
Date(s) Application Is Due Mar 14.
Contact Research Awards Manager, (301) 222-4012; fax: (301) 652-3890; email: awards@fdhn.org
Internet http://www.fdhn.org/wmspage.cfm?parm1=148
Sponsor Foundation for Digestive Health and Nutrition
4930 Del Ray Avenue
Bethesda, MD 20814

Fellowships at American Schools of Oriental Research--Amman 1937
ASOR offers seven different award opportunities for study in humanistic disciplines of the Middle East from prehistoric times through the 19th century. Islamic studies are especially encouraged. (1) The Kress Fellowship in the Art and Archaeology of Jordan: One or more three- to six-month fellowships for predoctoral students completing dissertation research in an art historical topic are awarded. (History of art is defined to include art history, archaeology, architectural history, and in some cases classical studies.) (2) CAORC Fellowship: Six or more two- to six-month fellowships for predoctoral students and postdoctoral scholars are awarded. Fields of study include all areas of the humanities and the natural and social sciences. Topics should contribute to scholarship in Near Eastern studies. (3) CAORC Post-Graduate Fellowship: Two or more two- to six-month fellowships for postdoctoral scholars pursuing research or publication projects in the natural and social sciences, humanities, and associated disciplines relating to the Near East are awarded. (4) National Endowment for the Humanities (NEH) Fellowship: One four-month fellowship is awarded for scholars who have a PhD or have completed their professional training. Fields of research include modern and classical languages, linguistics, literature, history, jurisprudence, philosophy, archaeology, comparative religion, ethics, and the history, criticism, and theory of the arts. Social and political scientists are encouraged to apply. (5) Jennifer C. Groot Fellowship: Three awards to help support beginners in archaeological fieldwork, who have been accepted as staff members on archaeological projects with ASOR/CAP affiliation in Jordan, are given. (6) Harrell Family Fellowship: One award to help support a graduate student for participation in an ACOR-approved archaeological research project, which has passed an academic review process, is given. Senior project staff whose expenses are being borne largely by the project are ineligible. (7) Pierre and Patricia Bikai Fellowship: One or more awards for one or two months of residency at ACOR during the period of June 1 through May 31 are given. Visit the Web site for further details.
Requirements Requirements corresponding to the seven awards listed in the description are as follows: (1) Kress applicants must be PhD candidates and US citizens or foreign nationals who have matriculated at US institutions. (2 & 3) CAORC applicants must be US citizens. (4) NEH applicants must be US citizens or foreign nationals living in the United States three years immediately preceding the application deadline. (5) Groot Fellowships applicants must be undergraduate or graduate students who are US or Canadian citizens. (6) Harrell Fellowship applicants must be enrolled graduate students

of any nationality. (7) Bikai Fellowship applicants must be graduate students of any nationality participating in an archaeological project or a research project in Jordan.
Amount $1500-$25,000
Date(s) Application Is Due Feb 1.
Contact Dr. Britt Hartenberger, (617) 353-6571; fax: (617) 353-6575; email: acor@bu.edu
Internet http://www.bu.edu/acor/fellowsh.htm
Sponsor American Schools of Oriental Research
656 Beacon St, 5th Fl
Boston, MA 02215

Fellowships for Research in Egypt **1938**
Fellowships support graduate and postgraduate research in Egypt for single continuous periods. Areas of research include archaeology, architecture, art, economics, egyptology, history, humanistic social sciences, humanities, Islamic studies, literature, political science, and religious studies. Research can cover all periods from ancient times to the present. Fellowships are granted for not less than three months nor more than 12 months. Award recipients must be physically present in Egypt to receive stipends; dependents' allowances will be granted for up to two dependents who are physically present in Egypt. Up to 15 fellowships are awarded annually. Also available from ARCE is the Kress Predoctoral Fellowship in Egyptian Art and Architecture that awards funding for up to eight months of research in Egypt, and special fellowships for Egyptian graduate students enrolled in American universities at the ABD stage who seek maintenance support for research in Egypt on topics relating to Egyptian development. Each fellow receives one round-trip ticket.
Requirements Applicants must be doctoral candidates or postdoctoral scholars. Candidates must complete application forms (available from ARCE) and submit three letters of recommendation. Predoctoral students must also submit transcripts.
Restrictions Awards are generally limited to the fields of humanities, fine arts, and social sciences; admission to candidacy is a prerequisite for student fellowships; fellows must devote full time to their research and may not accept outside teaching assignments or employment without written consent of program officers. Doctoral candidates must be either US or Egyptian citizens. Postdoctoral scholars must be either US citizens or have been teaching at an American or Canadian university for a minimum of three years.
Amount $1530 per month for students; $3019 per month for full professors
Date(s) Application Is Due Jan 7.
Contact Center for Arabic Study Abroad, (404) 727-2575; fax: (404) 727-6187; email: casa@emory.edu
Internet http://www.casa.emory.edu/programs
Sponsor American Research Center in Egypt
1385 Oxford Rd
Atlanta, GA 30322

Fellowships in Infectious Diseases **1939**
The program encourages and assists young qualified physicians to become specialists and investigators in the field of infectious diseases. The fellowship will be awarded to individuals who do not or will not have training or research grant support during the period of this grant and who are seeking support for one to three years of postdoctoral fellowship experience. Preference will be given to those applying for the third year of such support. The applicant must be sponsored by a university affiliated medical center. A letter from the chair of the infectious diseases department expressing a willingness to assume responsibility for training the applicant must accompany the application. In addition, each application must be accompanied by a letter from the host laboratory and signed by the laboratory director or appropriate department chair attesting willingness to accept the applicant and provide guidance, research space, and necessary research equipment. One thousand dollars of the award amount may be used for travel and supplies.
Requirements Applicants must be US physicians who have satisfactorily completed three or more years of postgraduate medical training (internal medicine, surgery, pediatrics, epidemiology, etc.).
Restrictions The fellowship will not be awarded if the applicant has received or will receive a major fellowship, research grant, or traineeship in excess of the amount of this award from the federal government or another foundation.
Amount $25,000 stipend
Date(s) Application Is Due Feb 15.
Contact Senior Executive Director, (301) 656-0003; fax: (301) 907-0878; email: info@nfid.org
Internet http://www.nfid.org/fellow
Sponsor National Foundation for Infectious Diseases
4733 Bethesda Ave, Ste 750
Bethesda, MD 20814-5278

Fermilab Postdoctoral Fellowship Programs **1940**
Fermilab, a Department of Energy laboratory, offers postdoctoral fellowships for work in experimental physics. The objective of the programs is to broaden or intensify the research experience of recent PhDs through involvement in experimental or theoretical research. Recent PhDs receive research associate appointments generally for two or more years.
Contact Dr. Michael Albrow, Head-Experimental Physics Projects Department, Particle Physics Division, (630) 840-3922; email: albrow@fnal.gov
Internet http://www.fnal.gov
Sponsor Fermi National Accelerator Laboratory
P.O. Box 500, MS 116
Batavia, IL 60510-0500

Fetzer Institute Research Grants **1941**
The Foundation uses the bulk of its income to actively run its own programs or services. The Institute's mission is to foster awareness of the power of love and forgiveness through research, education, and service programs. Current focus includes scientific research on altruistic love, compassionate love, and forgiveness. Individuals and organizations invited by the Institute to participate in the creation and implementation of its programs can receive funding. Requests are posted on the Foundation's website. The Foundation does not accept unsolicited proposals.
Contact Heidi Ihrig, (269) 375-2000; email: educationrfp@fetzer.org
Internet http://www.fetzer.org/Programs.aspx?PageID=Programs&NavID=1
Sponsor Fetzer Institute
9292 W. KL Avenue
Kalamazoo, MI 49009-9398

FIC International Cooperative Biodiversity Groups Grants **1942**
Funding for this program has been provided by six components of the National Institutes of Health (NIH), the Biological Sciences Directorate of the National Science Foundation (NSF) and the Foreign Agriculture Service of the USDA. The cooperating NIH components are the Fogarty International Center (FIC), National Cancer Institute (NCI), National Institute of Allergy and Infectious Diseases (NIAID), National Institute of Mental Health (NIMH), National Institute on Drug Abuse (NIDA) and the National Heart, Lung, and Blood Institute (NHLBI). The purpose of these groups will be to address the interdependent issues of biodiversity conservation, sustained economic growth, and human health in terms of drug discovery for cancer, infectious diseases including AIDS, cardiovascular diseases, mental disorders, and diseases of primary concern to developing countries. A group, under a single group leader (principal investigator), is expected to be a consortium of associate programs working together to form a multidisciplinary and/or multi-institutional team from academic, nonprofit, and/or commercial organizations. At least one of the group's associate programs must be located in a developing country. It is strongly advised that applicants contact program staff early in the planning process to discuss prospective applications and to obtain supplemental clarifying information and instructions. RFA-TW-04-004
Requirements Public and private nonprofit institutions, governments and their agencies, and foreign institutions are eligible. Applicant institutions must be in the United States or in a participating developing country. For-profit institutions may participate as members of the group.
Amount $500,000-$600,000 per year
Contact Dr. Joshua Rosenthal, Director, (301)496-1653; fax: (301) 402-2056; email: Joshua_Rosenthal@nih.gov
Internet http://www.fic.nih.gov/programs/grants.html#research
Sponsor Fogarty International Center
31 Center Dr MSC 2220, Bldg 31, B2C39
Bethesda, MD 20892-2220

FIC International Malaria Research Training Program Award **1943**
FIC invites applications to train or expand the capabilities of scientists and health professionals from malaria endemic developing countries to engage in malaria research. Proposals are requested that would create innovative, collaborative malaria research training programs and that would contribute to the long-term goal of harnessing scientific knowledge and skills to enhance efforts to prevent malaria-related morbidity and mortality and to control malaria transmission in endemic developing countries. To develop sustainable research capacity in endemic developing countries, FIC will support malaria research training efforts as part of ongoing, productive malaria research projects in collaboration with internationally recognized research institutions in Africa and other highly endemic regions of the world.Annual deadlines may vary; contact program staff for exact dates. RFA: TW-00-006
Requirements Applications may be submitted by US nonprofit public and private institutions, such as universities, colleges, hospitals, laboratories, and eligible agencies of the federal government capable of meeting the objectives of the RFA.
Restrictions Principal Investigators currently supported by other FIC malaria focused research training awards (D43) are not eligible to apply.
Amount $45,000 maximum stipend per year
Contact Grants Administrator, (301) 496-2075; fax: (301) 594-1211; email: ficinfo@nih.gov
Internet http://www.fic.nih.gov/programs/malaria.html
Sponsor Fogarty International Center
31 Center Dr, Bldg 31
Bethesda, MD 20892

FIC International Research and Training in Population and Health Grants **1944**
FIC, NICHD, and NIA have developed this program to support international research and training in population-related sciences and to enable NIH grant recipients to extend the geographic base of research and training efforts to developing nations, in support of international population priorities. Types of training for foreign scientists or health professionals may include predoctoral training in research related to population;

postdoctoral training in laboratory procedures and research projects and techniques conducted at the host US institutions or in the trainee's home country; and participation in advanced research training conducted by US faculty in the host country and also short-term in-country training for foreign scientists and health professionals in the host country. A letter of intent is requested by December 13; full application is due January 13. Annual deadline dates may vary; contact program staff for exact dates. RFA-TW-05-002)
Requirements Applicants must be US principal investigators on at least one NIH-sponsored research grant, cooperative agreement, or contract. The grantee institution must be a US nonprofit private or public institution.
Amount $139,000-$185,000
Date(s) Application Is Due Jan 13; Dec 13.
Contact Dr. Jeanne McDermott , Division of International Training and Research, (301) 496-1492; fax: (301) 402-0779; email: mcdermoj@mail.nih.gov
Internet http://grants.nih.gov/grants/guide/rfa-files/RFA-TW-05-002.html
Sponsor Fogarty International Center
31 Center Dr MSC 2220, Bldg 31, Rm B2C39
Bethesda, MD 20892-2220

FIC International Research Fellowship Program **1945**
The program provides opportunities for non-US postdoctoral biomedical or behavioral scientists in the formative stages of their research careers to gain further research experience by working in the laboratories of distinguished US scientists on problems of mutual interest. Nominations are made by the national nominating committee in each participating country. These committees submit applications to the Fogarty International Center. More than 50 countries or regions in the Americas, Africa, Asia, the Far East, Australia, Europe, and New Zealand participate in the program. Fellowships are awarded for a minimum of 12 months and provide stipend, travel, and institutional allowance. Fellowships provide round-trip travel for the fellow only. In addition, the host institution receives a modest allowance to cover such costs as the fellow's health insurance, supplies, equipment, and travel to scientific meetings or laboratories in the US or Canada.
Requirements Candidate must hold a doctoral degree or equivalent in a health science field at the time of submission of application to a nominating committee, have demonstrated the ability to engage in independent basic or clinical research, have a sponsor in the United States at a nonprofit institution who has accepted the applicant for research on his/her proposed project, and have assurance from a nonprofit institution in the home country that there is a position for him/her upon return. Applicant must be proficient in spoken and written English.
Contact Program Officer, (301) 496-1653; fax: (301) 402-0779/2056; email: nugentr@mail.nih.gov
Internet http://www.fic.nih.gov/programs/grants.html#fellowships
Sponsor Fogarty International Center
31 Center Dr, Bldg 31
Bethesda, MD 20892

FIC International Research Scientist Development Award **1946**
The award supports basic research for behavioral and clinical scientists who are committed to a career in international health research and would benefit from an additional period of mentored research as part of a strong, established collaboration between a US sponsor and leading scientists at a developing country center of scientific excellence. The specific research training may be new to the candidate or in an area that would demonstrably enhance the candidate's pursuit of a career focusing on international research pertinent to health in developing countries. Applications are encouraged to address one of the global health research priorities defined by the World Health Organization (http://www.who.ch), which include both infectious and chronic/degenerative conditions and mental health disorders. It is expected that following this experience, the candidate will be able to pursue an independent and productive international research career involving ongoing collaboration with developing country scientists to more effectively pursue research relevant to stemming a major global health problem. Annual deadlines may vary; contact program staff for exact dates. PAR-04-058
Requirements An applicant must be a US citizen or non-citizen national; hold doctoral or medical degree or the equivalent in a health science field; have earned the relevant degree within seven years of the application receipt date (not including clinical training); have demonstrated a commitment and competence in international health research as well as the potential to engage in independent and productive basic biomedical, behavioral, or epidemiological/clinical research in the period following the award; and have a sponsor in an internationally recognized developing country research institution addressing one or more of that country's major health problems. Eligible countries are in regions that include Africa, Asia (except Japan, Singapore, South Korea, and Taiwan), Central and Eastern Europe, Latin America and the Caribbean, the Middle East (except Israel) and the Pacific Ocean Islands (except Australia and New Zealand). Contact the program office or visit the Web site for full eligibility requirements.
Amount $70,000 maximum direct costs per year
Date(s) Application Is Due Feb 16.
Contact Dr. Rachel Nugent, Division of International Training and Research, (301) 496-8733; fax: (301) 402-0779; email: nugentra@mail.nih.gov
Internet http://www.fic.nih.gov/programs/irsda.html
Sponsor Fogarty International Center
31 Center Dr, Bldg 31
Bethesda, MD 20892

FIC International Training and Research in Emerging Infectious Diseases Grants **1947**
The Fogarty Center and NIAID have developed this program to train laboratory scientists and public health workers in developing countries and the United States in emerging and re-emerging infectious diseases research, control, and prevention strategies and their implementation and evaluation; facilitate international collaboration on emerging infectious diseases research, including the conduct of research in developing countries; enhance domestic infectious diseases research programs and improve the protection of the US population from infectious diseases by early detection and response to epidemics internationally and nationally; and develop international leaders in science and public health. Training will include predoctoral and postdoctoral programs, participation in advanced and/or short-term in-country training conducted by US faculty in the host country; and participation in training of health workers in the diagnosis, patient management, control, and prevention of disease. RFA: TW-96-001
Requirements Applicant must be a US principal investigator of at least one NIH-sponsored research grant related to infectious diseases.
Contact Dr. Joel Breman, International Training and Research, (301) 496-0815; email: Joel_Breman@.nih.gov
Internet http://www.fic.nih.gov/programs/erid.html
Sponsor Fogarty International Center
31 Center Dr, Bldg 31
Bethesda, MD 20892

FIC International Training and Research in Environmental and Occupational Health **1948**
This program, sponsored by the Fogarty International Center, NIEHS, NIOSH, and CDC, was developed to train foreign health scientists, clinicians, epidemiologists, toxicologists, engineers, industrial hygienists, chemists, and allied health workers from developing countries and emerging democracies in both general environmental health and occupational health. Types of training may include training in epidemiology concepts and methods, environmental monitoring, industrial hygiene, field studies, and other research related to environmental and occupational health that will lead to the MS or PhD degree for individuals with previous field research experience; short-term comprehensive courses in epidemiology, toxicology, chemistry, industrial hygiene, and environmental and safety engineering, with an emphasis on control of occupational injuries and illnesses, for health and safety professionals to be given in the United States; training in laboratory procedures and research techniques related to environmental and occupational health for individuals with the MS or PhD degree to be given in the United States; and postdoctoral research training for foreign scientists who want to expand their abilities in the epidemiology, diagnosis, prevention, and treatment of environmental and occupational disease and injury. Postdoctoral training can take place both in the United States and in foreign countries. RFA: TW-01-002.
Requirements The grantee institution must be a US, nonprofit private or public institution. Although most applications will be from academic institutions, a nonacademic, nonprofit institution may apply.
Contact Dr. Christopher Schonwalder, Senior Environmental Health Advisor to the Director, (919) 541-4794 ; fax: (919) 541-2583; email: cs64c@nih.gov
Internet http://www.fic.nih.gov/programs/environ.html
Sponsor Fogarty International Center
31 Center Dr, Bldg 31
Bethesda, MD 20892

FIC Israeli Ministry of Health Postdoctoral Research Fellowships **1949**
The program provides postdoctoral fellowships to US health scientists to conduct biomedical research in Israel. The purpose is to enhance the exchange of research experience and information in the biomedical and behavioral sciences with emphasis on heart diseases, aging, cancer, human reproduction, and child development. Short- and long-term fellowships are available for appointments at Hebrew University, Hadassah Medical School; Sackler Faculty of Medicine, Tel Aviv University; Weizmann Institute of Science; Technion-Israel Institute of Technology; and Ben Gurion University of the Negev. Information and applications are available from NIH Fogarty International Center; funding is from the Israeli Ministry of Health.
Requirements Applicants must be citizens or permanent residents of the United States; have doctorates in one of the clinical, biomedical, or behavioral sciences; and have professional experience in the proposed area.
Restrictions Support is not provided for brief observational visits, attendance at scientific meetings, or independent study.
Contact Bruce Butrum, Grants Management Officer, (301) 496-1653
Internet http://www.fic.nih.gov
Sponsor Fogarty International Center
31 Center Dr, Bldg 31
Bethesda, MD 20892

FIC Research Collaboration Award **1950**
Project grants facilitate collaborative research efforts between US and foreign scientists that will expand and enhance the NIH-supported research program of the US principal investigator, while at the same time benefiting the scientific interests of the collaborating foreign scientist. These small grants will provide funds for up to three years to purchase supplies, materials, and small equipment items necessary to conduct the collaborative research in the foreign scientist's laboratory. Travel support for both the US principal

investigator and the foreign collaborator also is provided. Applications will be reviewed on the basis of scientific and technical merit of the research proposal. Collaborative potential, significance of the proposed research, and the competence of the foreign collaborator are also prime factors. All biomedical and behavioral research topics supported by the NIH are eligible for inclusion under this program. Contact the office for deadline dates. PAR: PA-02-057
Requirements The grant applicant is the US institution where the US principal investigator is employed. The foreign collaborator must hold a position at a public or nonprofit private institution.
Amount $32,000 per year in direct costs for up to three years
Date(s) Application Is Due Jan 21; May 21; Sep 21.
Contact Dr. Kathleen Michels, Program Director, (301) 496-1653; fax: (301) 402-0779; email: FIRCA@nih.gov
Internet http://www.fic.nih.gov/programs/firca.html
Sponsor Fogarty International Center
31 Center Dr, Bldg 31
Bethesda, MD 20892

FIC Swedish Medical Research Council Fellowships **1951**
The Swedish Medical Research Council (SMRC) provides a limited number of research fellowships to US health scientists to conduct research in Sweden and to enhance the exchange of research experience and information in the biomedical and behavioral sciences. Activities supported include collaboration in basic or clinical research and the familiarization with or utilization of special techniques and equipment not otherwise available to the applicant. The program is administered by the Fogarty International Center and funded by the SMRC; applications may be obtained from the center.
Requirements Candidate must be a citizen or permanent resident of the United States; have a doctorate in clinical, behavioral, or biomedical science; have 10 years or less of postdoctoral experience; and have professional experience in the health sciences for at least two of the last four years. A letter of invitation from the host sponsor is required.
Restrictions Support is not provided for brief observational visits, attendance at scientific meetings, or independent study.
Amount $30,000-$45,000 per year; $41,000 average
Contact Bruce Butrum, Grants Management Officer, (301) 496-1653
Internet http://www.fic.nih.gov/programs/grants.html#fellowships
Sponsor Fogarty International Center
31 Center Dr, Bldg 31
Bethesda, MD 20892

FIC/NIH AIDS International Training and Research Program **1952**
The primary goal of this program is to build research capacity. This program is intended to complement ongoing HIV/AIDS and TB research efforts of the NIH and to the extent possible, of other government, nongovernment, and international organizations. Programs are encouraged to develop human resources in those developing and other participating countries that currently are or are likely to be sites of HIV/AIDS-related research on HIV and/or TB vaccines, anti-HIV and TB drugs, and other HIV and TB interventions. A letter of intent is requested by November 21; full application is due December 21. Annual deadline dates may change; contact program staff for exact dates. PAR-05-140)
Requirements Countries in Central and Eastern Europe and the New Independent States are eligible to participate, as are countries in Africa, the Americas, Asia, and the Pacific Region. The grantee institution must be a US nonprofit private or public institution capable of meeting the objectives in this RFA.
Restrictions Institutions that currently hold an award are not eligible to submit a second application.
Date(s) Application Is Due Nov 21; Dec 21.
Contact Dr. Jeanne McDermott, Program Officer, (301) 496-1653; fax: (301) 402-0779; email: mcdermoj@mail.nih.gov
Internet http://www.fic.nih.gov/programs/aitrp/aitrp.html
Sponsor Fogarty International Center
31 Center Dr, Bldg 31
Bethesda, MD 20892

FIC/ORMH Minority International Research Training Grants **1953**
FIC and ORMH jointly support scientific training programs that offer international research training opportunities to qualified minority undergraduates and graduate/medical students underrepresented in biomedical and behavioral research careers. Applications are invited from innovative programs that provide international research and training to encourage underrepresented minority students to pursue biomedical research careers, broaden minority research efforts and scientific training to encompass international health problems, stimulate novel approaches to studying health problems that disproportionately affect underserved groups in the United States or in developing countries, and assist minority scientists to participate in international collaborative relationships and work effectively in the rapidly evolving global scientific environment. A letter of intent is requested by December 10; full application is due January 14. Annual deadline dates may vary; contact program staff for exact dates. RFA: TW-00-001
Requirements Applicant institution and its associated consortia institutions must be colleges or universities that offer baccalaureate degrees in fields relevant to biomedical science. Only one application per institution will be accepted. Priority is given to consortia which include historically black colleges and universities, hispanic serving institutions, or tribal colleges and universities. Participant students and faculty must be US citizens or permanent residents.
Amount $1.8 million total
Date(s) Application Is Due Jan 14; Dec 10.
Contact Dr. Barbara Sina, Division of International Training and Research, (301) 496-1653; fax: (301) 402-0779; email: barbara_sina@nih.gov
Internet http://www.fic.nih.gov/programs/mirt.html
Sponsor Fogarty International Center
31 Center Dr, Bldg 31
Bethesda, MD 20892

Field Museum Graduate Student Fellowships **1954**
A limited number of Field Museum fellowships are available for graduate students engaged in dissertation research associated with the museum. These fellowships provide stipend support.
Requirements Candidates will be expected to have formal involvement with the museum; a curator should serve on the student's academic committee, and the research should rely heavily upon the collections and facilities of the museum. Students must be in residence in the Chicago area and are expected to spend a significant portion of their research time at the museum. The period of appointment is one year and starts on September 1st. Applicants must contact the sponsoring curator well in advance of the application deadline.
Restrictions Only electronic applications using the museum's web site will be accepted.
Date(s) Application Is Due Feb 1.
Contact Scholarship Coordinator; (312) 922-9410
Internet http://www.fieldmuseum.org/research_collections/scholarships/default.htm#grad_fellow
Sponsor Field Museum
1400 S. Lake Shore Dr.
Chicago, IL 60605-2496

Field Museum High School Internships **1955**
A few salaried internships per year are available for high school students or recent graduates to work directly with collections and research staff at the Museum. Internships are 10 weeks long and are usually taken in the summer. Other internships, including those in administrative areas, are also available.
Requirements Applicants for these internships must contact the museum curator who seems most appropriate, since the internship project and work schedule will be arranged with her/him (see website for list of curators and contact information). The museum curators travel frequently and should be contacted well in advance of the application deadline.
Date(s) Application Is Due Feb 1.
Contact Sam Burns, Human Resources; (312) 665-7279; email: sburns@fieldmuseum.org
Internet http://www.fieldmuseum.org/research_collections/scholarships/default.htm#ungrad_intern
Sponsor Field Museum
1400 S. Lake Shore Dr.
Chicago, IL 60605-2496

Field Museum Undergraduate Internships **1956**
A limited number of internships per year are available for undergraduate students or recent graduates to work directly with collections and research staff at the Museum. Internships are 10 weeks long and are usually taken in the summer. Other internships, including those in administrative areas, are also available.
Requirements Applicants for these internships must contact the museum curator who seems most appropriate, since the internship project and work schedule will be arranged with her/him (see website for list of curators and contact information). The museum curators travel frequently and should be contacted well in advance of the application deadline.
Date(s) Application Is Due Feb 1.
Contact Sam Burns, Human Resources; (312) 665-7279; email: sburns@fieldmuseum.org
Internet http://www.fieldmuseum.org/research_collections/scholarships/default.htm#ungrad_intern
Sponsor Field Museum
1400 S. Lake Shore Dr.
Chicago, IL 60605-2496

Field Museum Visiting Scholarships **1957**
Providing opportunities for scientists who wish to use the Field Museum's collections, funds are earmarked for travel and for subsistence while visitors are conducting their research. Young professionals and graduate students can be funded for periods of a few days to several weeks. Owing to the limited availability of these funds, awards are typically less than $1,500 per scholar. Short or extended-term visits by distinguished national and international scientists can be funded for periods of several weeks up to one year. These stipends are negotiable.
Requirements Applications must be endorsed by a Field Museum curator (see website for list of curators responsible for the collection you wish to study). Contact the appropriate

curator beforehand to communicate your background, goals and objectives. Applications require statements regarding: (a) purpose and significance of the proposed research, (b) relevance of the Field Museum's collections to the project, (c) collaboration(s) with Field Museum curators, if any, (d) procedures and methods used in the project.
Restrictions Only electronic applications using the museum's web site will be accepted.
Date(s) Application Is Due May 1; Nov 1.
Contact Scholarship Coordinator; (312) 922-9410
Internet http://www.fieldmuseum.org/research_collections/scholarships/default.htm#visiting_scholar
Sponsor Field Museum
1400 S. Lake Shore Dr.
Chicago, IL 60605-2496

Field Psychology Research Grants **1958**
Grants support promising graduate students exploring the history, contributions, and further development of perceptual (field) psychology in relationship to the research and writings of Arthur W. Combs, PhD. Applications of Dr. Combs's theoretical position to the improvement of educational, community, conflict-resolution, therapeutic efforts, etc. are also encouraged.
Amount $500-$1500
Date(s) Application Is Due Jan 31; Oct 5.
Contact Anne Richards, Trustee, (770) 834-8143; email: arichard@westga.edu
Internet http://www.fieldpsychtrust.org/application.asp
Sponsor Field Psychology Trust
301 Dixie St
Carrollton, GA 30117

Fight for Sight Research Grants **1959**
Grants support basic or clinical research of high scientific merit into diseases of the eye. The award may cover salaries, equipment, necessary travel, and/or research expenses. Awards are tenable at the Institute of Ophthalmology or other institutes or universities in the United Kingdom for up to three years.
Requirements Awards are open to all medical and scientific researchers.
Contact Janice Benson, Grants Manager, (212) 679-6060; fax: (212) 679-4466; email: janice@fightforsight.com
Internet http://www.fightforsight.com
Sponsor Fight for Sight
381 Park Ave S, Ste 809
New York, NY 10016

Fight for Sight Research Grants and Fellowships **1960**
The primary purpose of the program is to encourage and finance research in ophthalmology, vision, and related sciences. The goal is to restore and preserve sight through research in detection, prevention, treatment, and curing of visual disorders, as well as diseases leading to impaired sight and partial or total blindness. Funding priority is given to pilot projects for research relating to clinically important eye diseases. Fight for Sight will continue to support younger investigators, promoting the development of scientific skills that will lead to more substantial funding from other sources. Preference will be given to clinical and disease-oriented grants and training fellowships in the areas of age-related macular degeneration, diabetic retinopathy, retinitis pigmentosa, glaucoma, amblyopia, strabismus, AIDS-related eye disorders, cataract, and uveal and corneal inflammation. Award mechanisms include grants in aid, postdoctoral fellowships, and student fellowships.
Requirements Applicant must have a doctoral degree in medicine, optometry, or basic science and have less than one year of postdoctoral training. Fellowships are available to US and Canadian residents and are not offered for study abroad. Undergraduate, graduate, and medical students may apply for student fellowships.
Restrictions An applicant may not currently be financed by other research funds.
Amount $25,000-$50,000
Date(s) Application Is Due Mar 1.
Contact Program Coordinator, Fight for Sight Research Division, (847) 843-2020; fax: (847) 843-8458; email: info@preventblindness.org
Internet http://www.preventblindness.org/research
Sponsor Prevent Blindness America
500 E Remington Rd
Schaumburg, IL 60173

Finnish Cultural Foundation Grants **1961**
The foundation awards grants to scientists and artists in Finland. Internationally, the foundation awards travel and research grants. Long-term projects, especially relating to Finnish cultural history, are also supported. The Mirjam Helin International Singing Competition is offered every five years (e.g., 2000, 2005, etc.).
Contact Grants Administrator, 358 9 612 810; fax: 358-9-640474; email: info@skr.fi; Mirjam Helin International Singing Competition, 358 9 612 810; fax: 358 9 640 474; email: info@skr.fi
Internet http://www.skr.fi/english/welcome.html
Sponsor Finnish Cultural Foundation
P.O. Box 203, Bulevardi 5A
Helsinki 00121 Finland

Finnish Literature Translation Grants **1962**
Each year, FILI awards translation grants for the translation of Finnish, Finland-Swedish, and Saami language literature into other languages; the translation of both fiction and non-fiction from abroad into Finnish; the translation of academic publications and nonfiction into Swedish and the translation of fiction and nonfiction written in Finnish into Swedish. In addition, FILI also awards travel grants to translators from abroad. Application and guidelines are available online.
Date(s) Application Is Due Apr 1; Nov 1.
Contact Tiina Lehtoranta, +358 (0)9 1312 3344; email: tiina.lehtoranta@finlit.fi
Internet http://dbgw.finlit.fi/fili/eng/apurahat/apurahat-1.html
Sponsor Finnish Literature Information Center
Mariankatu 7A2
Helsinki 17 00170 Finland

Fischelis Grants for Research in the History of American Pharmacy **1963**
The institute supports a wide range of scholarly activities as long as they promise to contribute significantly to historical understanding and are clearly related to the modern practice of pharmacy in the United States. Projects must be connected directly to American pharmacy practice. Preference will be given to 20th-century topics, although studies of earlier periods will be considered. Historical discussions of current practice issues are also eligible. An application received after the deadline date will be evaluated individually if any funds remain unawarded; otherwise it will be considered in the next year's program.
Requirements Each application is referred for evaluation to a committee of the institute. Principal criteria used in evaluating an application are a candidate's qualifications and record relevant to the intended purpose, relevance to the history of modern American pharmacy, and the adequacy of resources to fulfill the stated purpose.
Amount $5000 maximum
Date(s) Application Is Due Mar 1.
Contact Gregory Higby, Director, (608) 262-5378; email: grants@aihp.org
Internet http://www.pharmacy.wisc.edu/aihp/fischelis.htm
Sponsor American Institute of the History of Pharmacy
777 Highland Ave
Madison, WI 53705-2222

FishAmerica Foundation Marine and Anadromous Fish habitat Restoration Grants **1964**
The program requests proposals for local efforts to accomplish meaningful on-the-ground restoration of marine, estuarine and riparian habitats, including salt marshes, seagrass beds, mangrove forests, and freshwater habitats important to anadromous fish species (fish like salmon and striped bass that spawn in freshwater and migrate to the sea). Emphasis is on using a hands-on, grassroots approach to restore fisheries habitat across coastal America and the Great Lakes.
Requirements Nonprofit organizations such as sporting clubs, civic organizations, conservation groups, and to a lesser extent state agencies, in the United States and Canada are eligible. Projects must result in on-the-ground habitat restoration, clearly demonstrate significant benefits to marine, estuarine or anadromous fisheries resources, particularly sportfish, and must involve community participation through an educational or volunteer component tied to the restoration activities.
Amount $5,000 - $50,000
Date(s) Application Is Due Feb 5.
Contact Erica George, Grants Manager; (703) 519-9691, ext. 247; fax: (703) 519-1872; email: egeorge@asafishing.org or fishamerica@asafishing.org
Internet http://www.fishamerica.org/grants/index.html
Sponsor FishAmerica Foundation
225 Reinekers Lane, Suite 420
Alexandria, VA 22314

FishAmerica Foundation Research Grants **1965**
Overall, the Foundation will fund research projects that further the National Fish Habitat Plan. Specifically, the program funds research projects that have regional or national implication, not local. Grants support research in the following areas: fisheries management, water quality, habitat studies, stock enhancement, economic impact studies related to sport fishing, and tagging.
Requirements Nonprofits such as sporting clubs, civic organizations, conservation groups, and to a lesser extent state agencies, in the US and Canada are eligible.
Restrictions Grants do not support the following projects or purposes: donations of fishing tackle; salaries, administration, overhead, or travel for conservation projects; individuals; local stream monitoring programs; political activities that attempt to influence political campaigns or legislation; access projects such as road construction, boat ramps, or fishing piers; loans, endowments, trips, tours, tickets, advertising, or publications; or permitting and related costs.
Amount $15,000 average
Date(s) Application Is Due Jul 31.
Contact Erica George, Grants Manager; (703) 519-9691, ext. 247; fax: (703) 519-1872; email: egeorge@asafishing.org or fishamerica@asafishing.org
Internet http://www.fishamerica.org/grants/index.html
Sponsor FishAmerica Foundation
225 Reinekers Lane, Suite 420
Alexandria, VA 22314

Fishman Family Foundation Grants **1966**

The Foundation considers grants for: research, education, and cultural development of and for the community; scholarships related to Jewish services, education, social, and community activities; medical and scientific research; providing resources to meet critical needs in Israel; and educational grants and scholarships. Proposals are reviewed in April and October. Application information is available online.
Requirements 501(c)3 nonprofits are eligible.
Date(s) Application Is Due Mar 31; Sep 30.
Contact Betty Fishman, President, email: info@fishman.org
Internet http://www.fishman.org/apply.html
Sponsor Fishman Family Foundation
730 E. Cypress Avenue
Monrovia, CA 91016

FIU Wolfsonian Fellowships **1967**

The program supports research on the material culture of the modern world. All proposals addressing humanities themes that can be supported by materials in the Wolfsonian's collection are welcome. The Wolfsonian also encourages research projects in areas related to its curatorial program. Fellowships are intended to support full-time research, generally for a period of three to five weeks. All fellows are expected to reside in the greater Miami area duing the fellowship period and are encouraged to participate in the activities of the Wolfsonian and other divisions of Florida International University. The fellowship includes a stipend for living expanses, round-trip travel, and an allowance for making reproductions. The application deadline is for projects beginning no earlier than July 1 of the next year. Candidates are asked to indicate preferred dates in residence on their application. Guidelines and application are available online.
Requirements Fellowships are granted on the basis of outstanding professional or academic accomplishment and are limited to those with at least a master's degree. Doctoral students may apply for dissertation research related to the Wolfsonian collections.
Date(s) Application Is Due Dec 31.
Contact Fellowship Coordinator, (305) 535-2613; fax: (305) 531-2133; email: research@thewolf.fiu.edu
Internet http://www.wolfsonian.fiu.edu/education/research/index.html
Sponsor Wolfson-Florida International University
1001 Washington Ave
Miami Beach, FL 33139

Five College Women's Research Center Ford Associateships **1968**

The center invites applications from international applicants for two one-semester Ford Associateships (fall and spring), which offer a stipend plus a housing/travel allowance in return for teaching (in English) one undergraduate course in the women's studies program at the University of Massachusetts or the Women and Gender Studies Department at Amherst College. UMass and Amherst seek a total of two experienced researchers and teachers to strengthen their undergraduate curriculum and, in the case of the university, to complement their graduate program. For the fall, the University of Massachusetts seeks a researcher with expertise in the Middle East or Latin America with an emphasis on globalization, transnational studies, or postcolonial studies. Research should focus on gender, race, ethnicity, class, and sexuality within the context of globalization. For fall or spring 2006, Amherst College seeks a researcher who is also an experienced teacher and who works on the Middle East, Latin America, Asia, or Africa with expertise in the field of gender in the media especially in the context of war and civil unrest. Ford Associates need not be studying their own region of origin. Ford Associates are expected to be in residence in the Five College area, working full-time at the center on the project outlined in their application, during the period of appointment. Each Ford Associate is expected to give a public presentation on her work, lead a faculty seminar, and participate actively in the daily life of the center. Application and guidelines are available online.
Requirements Applications are welcomed worldwide from writers, visual artists, film and video makers, as well as academic scholars. Ford applicants may work on any and all regions of the world and need not be studying their own region of origin.
Amount $12,000 stipend plus $3000 housing/travel allowance
Date(s) Application Is Due Feb 13.
Contact Ford Associateships Administrator, Mount Holyoke College, (413) 538-2275; fax: (413) 538-3121; email: fcwsrc@wscenter.hampshire.edu
Internet http://www.fivecolleges.edu/sites/fcwsrc/about
Sponsor Five Colleges Inc
50 College St
South Hadley, MA 01075-6406

Five College Women's Studies Ford Associateships **1969**

Open to international researchers in women's studies, this special program is supported by the Ford Foundation. Ford Associates spend a semester in residence at the center pursuing their own research, participating in faculty seminars with women's studies and area studies colleagues from the Five Colleges, and forging connections with the feminist community in Western Massachusetts. Each associate also teaches or co-teaches (in English) an undergraduate women's studies course at one of the Five Colleges (Amherst, Hampshire, Mount Holyoke, and Smith Colleges, and the University of Massachusetts, Amherst) during her semester at the center. International applicants may apply for one of the two special one-semester Ford Associateships for fall or spring, which offer a stipend and a housing/travel allowance in return for teaching (in English) one undergraduate women's studies course at Smith College. Ford applicants' research should focus on how the economics of globalization regulate gender, race, ethnicity, nationality, class, and sexuality in Latin America, the Caribbean, Africa, the Middle East, the former Soviet bloc, or Asia. Two Ford Associate positions are available. For one position preference will be given to those whose work focuses on sexuality in a global context, including sex work, global sex trafficking, health issues, international gay and lesbian activism, and advocacy for sexual minorities. For the second position, preference will be given to those whose work focuses on cultural production and resistance, including political performance, the transformation and use of international media, and new technologies. Application and guidelines are available online.
Requirements Applications are welcomed from writers, visual artists, film and video makers, as well as academic scholars. Ford applicants may work on any and all regions of the world and need not be studying their own region of origin.
Amount $12,000 stipend plus $3000 housing/travel allowance
Date(s) Application Is Due Feb 28.
Contact Five College Women's Studies Research Center, (413) 538-2275; fax: (413) 538-3121; email: fcwsrc@fivecolleges.edu
Internet http://www.fivecolleges.edu/sites/fcwsrc/about
Sponsor Mount Holyoke College
50 College St
South Hadley, MA 01075-6406

Five Colleges Fellowship Program for Minority Scholars **1970**

The program provides a year in residence for minority graduate students in the final phase of the doctoral degree. Each fellow will be hosted within a particular department or program at one of the five colleges in the consortium--Amherst, Hampshire, Mount Holyoke, Smith College, and the University of Massachusetts. (At Smith, recipients hold a Mendenhall Fellowship.) The purposes of the program are to enable fellows to complete their dissertations; to encourage their interest in college teaching; and to acquaint them with the schools. Although the primary goal is completion of the dissertation, each fellow is expected to do some formal teaching or its equivalent (no more than a single, one-semester course).
Requirements Eligible to apply are minority graduate students who have completed all of the requirements for the PhD except the dissertation.
Amount $30,000 stipend, housing assistance, office space, library privileges, departmental affiliation
Date(s) Application Is Due Dec 1.
Contact Five College Fellowship Program Committee, (413) 256-8316
Internet http://www.fivecolleges.edu/academic_programs/academprog_fellowship.html
Sponsor Five Colleges Inc
97 Spring St
Amherst, MA 01002

Fletcher Jones Foundation Grants **1971**

The foundation considers grants for charitable, scientific, literary, and educational support, with primary emphasis given to private colleges and universities, particularly in California. Prior to any written submission, it is advisable to call or to meet with the executive director in order to discuss a tentative proposal and to determine the suitability of the intended request. The board of trustees meets on a quarterly basis to review and act upon grant proposals. There are no deadlines; proposals are accepted throughout the year. Guidelines are available online.
Requirements Applicants must be private, accredited colleges or universities, primarily in California.
Restrictions Grants are not made to individuals, K-12 educational institutions, for operating funds, deficit financing, conferences, traveling exhibits, or for projects supported by government agencies.
Amount $9.4 million total
Contact Christine Sisley, Executive Director, (213) 943-4646; fax: (213) 943-4648
Internet http://www.fletcherjonesfdn.org/Fletcher_Jones_Application.htm
Sponsor Fletcher Jones Foundation
523 W Sixth St, Ste 301
Los Angeles, CA 90014

Flinn Foundation Grants **1972**

The foundation's grantmaking programs, limited to Arizona, include enhancing community-based solutions to local health care needs, especially those for children and youth; strengthening medical education and biomedical research programs in Arizona; strengthening Arizona's universities through an undergraduate scholarship program for outstanding Arizona high school students; and enhancing the visibility and long-term artistic mission of Arizona's principal visual and performing arts organizations. Types of support include program development, seed money, scholarship funds, and research grants.
Requirements Arizona-based institutions or organizations whose programs are operated for the benefit of Arizona institutions and individuals are eligible to apply. Applications are accepted at any time. There is no application form, but a preliminary letter of inquiry or phone call is requested to determine the appropriateness of a full submission.
Restrictions The foundation rarely provides grants to individuals, building projects (capital campaigns), purchase of equipment, endowment projects, annual fund-raising campaigns, ongoing operating expenses, or deficit needs. Requests to support conferences

and workshops, publications, or the production of films and video are considered only when these activities are an integral component of a larger foundation initiative.
Amount $2500-$150,000 average
Contact JoAnn Fazio, Grants Coordinator, (602) 744-6800; fax: (602) 744-6815; email: info@flinn.org
Internet http://www.flinn.org/about/grants.cms
Sponsor Flinn Foundation
1802 N Central Ave
Phoenix, AZ 85004-1506

Florida Sea Turtle Grants Program 1973
Funded by a portion of revenues from Florida's Sea Turtle Specialty License Plate, the grants program distributes funds each year to support sea turtle research, conservation, and education programs throughout Florida. Types of grants include competitive grants, funding for ongoing activities, and emergency grants. Application and guidelines are available online.
Requirements Florida coastal local governments, Florida-based nonprofit organizations, and education and research institutions that actively participate in marine turtle research, conservation, and educational activities within the state of Florida are eligible to apply.
Contact Grants Administrator, (352) 373-6441; fax: (352) 375-2449; email: stgp@helpingseaturtles.org
Internet http://www.helpingseaturtles.org/stgp.htm
Sponsor Caribbean Conservation Corporation
4424 N.W. 13th Street, Suite B11
Gainesville, FL 32609

Florida Vocational Rehabilitation Grants 1974
The foundation provides grants to Florida nonprofit organizations and to Florida citizens with documented disabilities. Types of support include services, education, training, research, demonstration, and other activities leading to the employment of persons with disabilities. The planning, research, and policy development of issues related to the employment and training of disabled citizens and the publication and dissemination of such information also is of interest. There also is a grants program specifically for individual Floridians with disabilities to assist them in obtaining competitive employment or advancing in current employment. There are no application forms. The grant-information booklet that includes the proposal format is available online.
Requirements Citizens of Florida with documented disabilities and Florida-based nonprofit 501(c)3 organizations are eligible to apply.
Contact Ryan Burhnell, Manager of Grants Administration, (888) 838-2253 or (850) 224-4493; fax: (850) 224-4496; email: info@abletrust.org
Internet http://www.abletrust.org/grant
Sponsor Able Trust
106 E College Ave, Ste 820
Tallahassee, FL 32301

Fluor Foundation Grants 1975
The Fluor Corporation achieves its contribution objectives through the Fluor Foundation and corporate giving. The Foundation's areas of interest are: education; human services; cultural outreach; and public/civic affairs. The Foundation considers requests for operating, program, capital or endowment support. Priority is given to funding organizations with employee volunteer participation. Interested applicants should submit a letter of inquiry. Application information is available online.
Requirements Funding is considered for community organizations located where Fluor has a permanent office or project site presence.
Restrictions Funding is not available for: film production/publishing activities; individuals; sports organizations/programs; veterans, fraternal, labor or religious organizations; or lobbying/political organizations or campaigns.
Contact Margarita Miranda, Senior Community Relations Coordinator, (949) 349-6797; fax: (949) 349-7175; email: community.relations@fluor.com
Internet http://www.fluor.com/communities/default.asp
Sponsor Fluor Foundation
One Enterprise Drive
Aliso Viejo, CA 92656-2606

FMC Foundation Grants 1976
The foundation supports education, community improvement, urban affairs, health and human services, and public issues/economic education. Higher education is supported through scholarships and employee matching gifts. Education support tends to be in business, engineering, chemistry, and some minority education programs. Eligible applicants need to contact the FMC in their geograhic area. Each individual FMC location determines how their contributions will be given.
Requirements Grants are awarded to 501(c)3 organizations in FMC-plant communities. US-based organizations with an international focus are also eligible.
Restrictions Grants are not made to individuals.
Contact Program Contact, (215) 299-6000; fax: (215) 299-6140
Internet http://www.fmc.com
Sponsor FMC Foundation
1735 Market Street
Philadelphia, PA 19103

FNN Alice P. Kenney Award 1977
This annual prize is awarded to an individual or group that has made a significant contribution to colonial Dutch studies and/or has encouraged understanding of the significance of the Dutch colonial experience in North America by research, teaching, writing, speaking, or in other ways. Reasonable travel expenses will be reimbursed. The winner will be selected by a four-person committee consisting of the director of the New Netherland Project, two members of the Friends of New Netherland, and a representative of the Alice P. Kenney Memorial Trust Fund. The award will be presented each year at an event in connection with the New Netherland Project. Nominating guidelines are available online.
Requirements Persons or groups to be considered for this award can be involved in any pursuit of any aspect of Dutch colonial life in North America. Candidates can be nominated by members of the Friends of New Netherland, by historical organizations, or by the general public.
Amount $500
Date(s) Application Is Due Apr 1.
Contact Award Selection Committee, (518) 474-6067; fax: (518) 473-0472; email: nyslfnn@mail.nysed.gov
Internet http://www.nnp.org/fnn/kenny.html
Sponsor Friends of New Netherland
P.O. Box 2536, Empire State Plaza Sta
Albany, NY 12220-0536

Fogarty International Center/Ellison Medical Foundation Overseas Fellowships in Global Health and Clinical Research 1978
The fellowship is a one-year mentored clinical research training experience for graduate-level US students in the health professions. The program enables individuals to experience mentored research training at top-ranked NIH-funded research centers in developing countries. Fellowship sites include Bangladesh; Botswana; Brazil; Haiti; Chennai, India; China; Vellore, India; Kenya; Mali, West Africa; Lima, Peru; Durban, South Africa; Pretoria, South Africa; Russia; Tanzania; Thailand; Uganda; and Zambia. Each fellowship is for a one-year period. The term will begin with an intensive orientation program on the NIH campus in Bethesda, MD, in July. This will be followed by approximately 10-plus months of intense research training at the foreign site. Application and guidelines are available online.
Requirements This program is designed for students meeting all of the following qualifications: a strong interest in, and potential for, a career in international health activities and/or clinical research; advanced standing in a US medical (M3) or osteopathic school, or enrollment in a doctoral-level program at a US school of public health, nursing, or dentistry; and support of their home academic institution, including a committed mentor. Applicants must have strong academic records and must be US citizens or permanent US residents. Medical and osteopathic students must have completed their basic science courses and one year of clinical clerkship; public health doctoral students must have completed their coursework and passed their qualifying exams prior to the beginning of the fellowship.
Amount $18,000-$20,000 per year (adjusted to cost of living expenses at the foreign site) plus $6000 per year for travel, insurance, and educational materials
Date(s) Application Is Due Dec 28.
Contact Yolanda Thomas, email: fic-fellowship@aamc.org
Internet http://www.aamc.org/students/medstudents/overseasfellowship/2006fogartyapp.doc
Sponsor Association of American Medical Colleges
2450 N St NW
Washington, DC 20037-1127

Folger Institute Consortium Grants 1979
The grants are available to faculty members and graduate students from affiliated universities and are offered to reimburse travel and some lodging expenses in support of participation in institute programs. Awards for released-time may also be made to consortium faculty members.
Date(s) Application Is Due Jan 3; Jun 1; Sep 1.
Contact Virginia Millington, Program Assistant, (202) 675-0333; fax: (202) 544-4623; email: institute@folger.edu
Internet http://www.folger.edu/template.cfm?cid=1346
Sponsor Folger Institute
201 E Capitol St SE
Washington, DC 20003

Folger Institute Grants in Aid 1980
The institute offers an interdisciplinary program of seminars, workshops, symposia, colloquia, and lectures. Faculty and graduate students from affiliated universities may apply for reimbursement of travel and lodging expenses in support of their attendance at any Folger Institute program. Some awards for released time are also made to consortium faculty members. Full-time faculty from any US college or university who attend Folger programs funded by the NEH may apply for NEH at-large grants. A limited number of registration fee waivers are available by application to independent scholars.
Requirements Grants in aid are awarded for participation in institute programs for advanced graduate students and faculty from institute-affiliated universities.
Amount $2000
Date(s) Application Is Due Jan 3; Jun 1; Sep 1.

Contact Virginia Millington, Program Assistant, (202) 675-0333; fax: (202) 544-4623; email: institute@folger.edu
Internet http://www.folger.edu/template.cfm?cid=1346
Sponsor Folger Institute
201 E Capitol St SE
Washington, DC 20003-1094

Folger Long-Term Postdoctoral Research Fellowships **1981**
The Folger holds the largest collection outside Britain of books and manuscripts on early English history from the 15th through 18th centuries. The library offers a limited number of residential fellowships for periods of six to nine months. Three National Endowment for the Humanities and two Andrew W. Mellon Foundation fellowships are offered. Fellowships are open to scholars from any country. Applicants should submit seven copies of each of the following: an application form, a 1000-word description of the research project, a curriculum vita, and three letters of reference (under separate cover).
Requirements Successful candidates will be advanced scholars who have made substantial contributions in their fields and whose research projects are appropriate to the library's collections.
Amount $40,000 NEH fellowships; $50,000 and $35,000 Mellon fellowships
Date(s) Application Is Due Nov 1.
Contact Carol Brobeck, Fellowships Coordinator, (202) 675-0348; email: cbrobeck@folger.edu
Internet http://www.folger.edu/academic/fellows.asp
Sponsor Folger Shakespeare Library
201 E Capitol St SE
Washington, DC 20003

Folger Postdoctoral Short-Term Research Fellowships **1982**
Applications are welcome in all areas covered by the Folger collection for work on projects that draw significantly from the Folger holdings from the 16th through 18th centuries: English, American, and European literature and drama; English, American, and Continental history; political, economic, and legal history; and history of philosophy, art, music, religion, science and medicine, and exploration. Short-term postdoctoral fellowships are offered for independent research for a term of one to three months during the period of July to June of the next year. Application consists of a completed Folger's application form, four copies of the applicant's curriculum vita, four copies of a 1000-word description of the research project, and three letters of recommendation submitted directly to the fellowship committee.
Requirements Applicants for NEH fellowships must be US citizens who have completed the PhD or equivalent and have a research project appropriate to the collections at the Folger Library. Applications for the Folger long-term or short-term fellowships are open to scholars from any country. A fellow is expected to be in residence in Washington, DC, during the term of the fellowship and to conduct his/her research at the Folger Library.
Amount $2000 per month
Date(s) Application Is Due Mar 1.
Contact Carol Brobeck, Fellowships Coordinator, (202) 675-0348; email: cbrobeck@folger.edu
Internet http://www.folger.edu/academic/fellows.asp
Sponsor Folger Shakespeare Library
201 E Capitol St SE
Washington, DC 20003

Food, Pharmaceutical, and Bioengineering Division Award in Chemical Engineering **1983**
This award is given to recognize outstanding chemical engineering contributions and achievements by an individual in those industries involved in food, pharmaceutical, and bioengineering activities. The recipient need not be a member of AIChE, and there is no age limit. The individual's contributions may have been made in industrial, governmental, or academic areas, or with other organizations.
Requirements All members, as well as other interested persons, are urged to nominate deserving candidates.
Amount $4000
Date(s) Application Is Due Mar 25.
Contact AIChE Awards Programs, (212) 591-7107; fax: (212) 591-8890; email: awards@aiche.org
Internet http://www.aiche.org/awards/awarddtl.asp?AwardID=36
Sponsor American Institute of Chemical Engineers
3 Park Ave
New York, NY 10016-5910

Ford Foundation International Fellowships **1984**
The program supports advanced study by exceptional individuals who will use this education to become leaders in their respective fields, furthering development in their own countries and greater economic and social justice worldwide. Eligible fields of study are any academic discipline or field of study related to the foundation's three grant-making areas: asset building and community development--children, youth and families, sexuality and reproductive health, work-force development, development finance and economic security, environment and development, community development; education, media, and arts and culture--education reform; higher education and scholarship; religion, society and culture; media; and arts and culture; peace and social justice--human rights; international cooperation; governance; and civil society. The international fellowships provide support for up to three years of formal graduate-level study leading to a masters or doctoral degree. Fellows are selected from countries where the foundation maintains active overseas programs. Once selected, fellows may enroll in an appropriate university program anywhere in the world, including their country of residence. The program also enables fellows to undertake short-term language study and training in research and computer skills prior to graduate school enrollment.
Requirements Applicants must be resident nationals or residents of Asia, Africa, the Middle East, Latin America, and Russia. Successful candidates will demonstrate superior achievement in their undergraduate studies and hold a baccalaureate degree or its equivalent; have substantial experience in community service or development-related activities; possess leadership potential evidenced by their employment and academic experience; propose to pursue a post-baccalaureate degree that will directly enhance their leadership capacity in a practical, policy, academic, or artistic discipline or field corresponding to one or more of the foundation's areas of endeavor; present a plan specifying how they will apply their studies to social problems or issues in their own countries; and commit themselves to working on these issues following the fellowship period.
Restrictions US nationals are not eligible, although fellows may study in the United States.
Contact Grant Administrator, (212) 573-5000; fax: (212) 351-3677; email: office-secretary@fordfound.org
Internet http://www.fordfound.org/news/more/11272000ifp/index.cfm
Sponsor Ford Foundation
320 E 43rd St
New York, NY 10017

Ford Foundation Peace and Social Justice Grants **1985**
This program area supports two categories: human rights and international cooperation, and governance and civil society. Grants under human rights and international cooperation support projects involving women's rights and civil rights in the United States, international human rights, international law, multilateral conflict prevention, and US foreign policy. Governance and civil society grants support projects concerning civic participation, electoral reform, and innovations in state and local government. Most grants are given to organizations. The foundation also makes grants to individuals, though they are few in number relative to demand and are limited to research, training, and other activities related to the foundation's program interests. Support for graduate fellowships is generally provided through grants to universities and other organizations, which select recipients. Applications are considered throughout the year; a letter of inquiry is the first step of the application process.
Requirements The letter of inquiry should include the purpose of the project, problems and issues addressed, information about the applicant organization, estimated overall budget, time period for which funds are requested, and qualifications of those engaged in the project.
Restrictions Support is not normally given for routine operating costs of institutions or for religious activities. Except in rare cases, funding is not available for the construction or maintenance of buildings. The foundation does not award undergraduate scholarships or make grants for purely personal or local needs.
Amount $75,000-$250,000 average
Contact Office of Communications, (212) 573-5000; fax: (212) 599-4584; email: office-secretary@fordfound.org
Internet http://www.fordfound.org
Sponsor Ford Foundation
320 E 43rd St
New York, NY 10017

Ford Motor Company Fund Grants Program **1986**
The fund supports not-for-profit organizations in three major areas: innovation and education; community development and American legacy, and auto-related safety education. The fund seeks to build partnerships with organizations that have a well-defined sense of purpose, a demonstrated commitment to maximizing available resources, and a reputation for meeting objectives and delivering quality programs and services. Priority is placed on the support and development of organizations that promote diversity and inclusion. Requests for support are accepted and reviewed throughout the year. The fund now implements an online application system. Details are available online.
Restrictions Ford does not fund: advocacy-directed programs; animal-rights organizations; beauty or talent contests; day-to-day business operations; debt reduction; donation of vehicles; efforts to influence legislation, or the outcome of any elections or any specific election of candidates to public office or to carry on any voter registration drive; endowments; fraternal organizations; general operating support to hospitals and health care institutions; individual sponsorship related to fundraising activities; individuals; labor groups; loans for small businesses; loans to program-related investments; organizations that do not have 501(c)(3) status; organizations that unlawfully discriminate in their provision of goods and services based on race, color, religion, gender, gender identity or expression, ethnicity, sexual orientation, national origin, physical challenge, age, or status as a protected veteran; political contributions; private K-12 schools; profit-making enterprises; religious programs or sectarian programs for religious purposes; species-specific organizations; sports teams.
Contact Ford Fund Coordinator, (888) 313-0102; email: Fordfund@ford.com

Internet http://www.ford.com/en/goodWorks/fundingAndGrants/fordMotorCompanyFund/default.htm
Sponsor Ford Motor Company Fund
P.O. Box 1899
Dearborn, MI 48121-1899

Fordham Prizes **1987**
The foundation awards two prizes annually. The Thomas B. Fordham Prize for Distinguished Scholarship is awarded to a scholar who has made major contributions to education reform via research, analysis, and successful engagement in the war of ideas. The Thomas B. Fordham Prize for Valor is awarded to a leader who has made major contributions to education reform via noteworthy accomplishments at the national, state, local, and/or school levels. Nominations from individuals or organizations familiar with the work of outstanding education reformers and scholars are welcome. Self-nominations will not be considered. Nomination guidelines are available online.
Requirements Anyone can be nominated whose work has had a profound impact on education in the United States. Candidates may be nominated either for cumulative lifetime achievement or for extraordinary one-time accomplishments.
Restrictions Employees and trustees of the foundation are not eligible, nor are members of the prize committee.
Contact Jennifer Leischer, Prize Coordinator, (202) 223-5452; fax: (202) 223-9226; email: jleischer@edexcellence.net
Internet http://www.edexcellence.net/foundation/global/page.cfm?id=305
Sponsor Thomas B. Fordham Foundation
1701 K Street, N.W., Suite 1000
Washington, DC 20006

Foreign Language and Russian and East European Area Studies Fellowships **1988**
Fellowships are awarded in the fall to advance students' knowledge of the Russian or an East European language and culture. Selection of fellows is based on academic record, letters of recommendation, intent of study plan, and priorities of the Department of Education, which gives final approval to awardees.
Requirements Applicants must be US citizens or permanent residents of the United States and full-time students in an advanced degree program at the University of Pittsburgh as well as in the graduate certificate program of the Center for Russian and East European studies. Students with Russian background must have completed Russian through the second-year level of college to be eligible. Application must be submitted by the dean/chairperson of the school/department in which the student will study.
Amount $11,000 stipend plus tuition and fees for two terms
Date(s) Application Is Due Feb 1.
Contact Center for Russian and East European Studies, (412) 648-7407; fax: (412) 648-2199
Internet http://sli.slavic.pitt.edu/administrative.html#financial
Sponsor University of Pittsburgh
4G15 Forbes Quadrangle
Pittsburgh, PA 15260

Forest Products Society Wood Award **1989**
The Forest Products Society (FPS), Borden Inc, and Dynea USA Inc, sponsor the annual wood awards. Two awards are made for the best 2000- to 4000-word paper on the forestry industry. Topics may cover any of a wide range of problems from harvesting trees, to development and manufacture of products, to distribution and marketing of such products. Judges will rate the essays on the basis of subject, skill of treatment, conclusions, applicability, and conformance to competition rules. Winners will make a presentation at the annual meeting of the FPS. Tentative titles are due by the deadline.
Requirements The competition is open to all graduate students who are registered for a full quarter or full semester at any university or college the year previous to application.
Amount $1000 first place; $500 second place
Date(s) Application Is Due Feb 6.
Contact Vickie Bruce, (608) 231-1361 ext 210; fax: (608) 231-2152; email: vbruce@forestprod.org or info@forestprod.org
Internet http://www.forestprod.org/awa-wood.html
Sponsor Forest Products Society
2801 Marshall Ct
Madison, WI 53705-2295

Forrest C. Lattner Foundation Grants **1990**
The Foundation's primary objectives are in six areas of interest: arts and humanities; education; environment; health and social services; historic preservation; and medical research. The Foundation encourages the development of innovative model programs.
Restrictions The foundation is unable to fulfill grant requests to individuals, or to support programs that are the primary responsibility of the public sector.
Date(s) Application Is Due Mar 1; Sep 1.
Contact Susan Lattner Lloyd, President, (561) 278-3781; fax: (561) 278-3167; email: lattner@bellsouth.net
Internet http://www.lattnerfoundation.org
Sponsor Forrest C. Lattner Foundation Inc
777 E. Atlantic Avenue, Suite 317
Delray Beach, FL 33483

Foundation for Enhancing Communities Grants **1991**
The foundation awards grants to Pennsylvania nonprofit organizations in the greater Harrisburg area. Areas of interest include art/cultural programs, education, health care and health organizations, human services, and community development. Types of support include program development, publication, seed money, and scholarships.
Requirements 501(c)3 tax-exempt organizations in Pennsylvania's Dauphin, Cumberland, Franklin, and Perry Counties are eligible.
Restrictions Grants do not support individuals, operating budgets, or capital expenses.
Amount $10,000 maximum; $2500-$5000 average
Contact Rosemary Moore, Program Officer, (717) 236-5040; fax (717) 231-4463; email: rosemary@ghf.org
Internet http://www.ghf.org
Sponsor Foundation for Enhancing Communities
P.O. Box 678, 200 N 3rd St
Harrisburg, PA 17108-0678

Foundation for Medical Research Grants **1992**
The foundation promotes all forms of scientific medical research, in particular clinical research and that connected with the basic biological sciences directly or indirectly related to medicine. Grants are awarded to individuals and institutions in France and on an international basis. Types of support include subsidies for travel and study abroad and equipment acquisition. Major annual awards include the Rosen Prize for Cancer Research and the Delahautemaison Prize, which is awarded every two years, alternately for research in nephrology and cancer; the annual Grand Prix; and five prizes for molecular biology, endocrinology, immunology, clinical investigation, and neurobiology.
Amount $10 million total annually
Contact Program Contact, 33-1-44-39-75-75; fax: 33-1-44-39-75-99; email: frm@frm.org
Internet http://www.frm.org
Sponsor Foundation for Medical Research
54 rue de Varenne
Paris 75007 France

Foundation for Physical Therapy Mary McMillan Dotoral Scholarships **1993**
The purpose of this program is to assist physical therapists with outstanding potential for doctoral studies in the first year of graduate studies towards a doctorate.
Requirements Applicants must be entering post professional full-time or part-time doctoral study during the current academic year. Applicants must possess a license to practice physical therapy in a U.S. jurisdiction or have met all the requirements for licensure in a U.S. jurisdiction, including having received a passing score on the licensure exam.
Amount $5000
Date(s) Application Is Due Aug 15.
Contact Lucy Dickson, Program Contact, (800) 999-2782 ext 8505; email: foundation@apta.org
Internet http://www.apta.org/AM/Template.cfm?Section=Awards_and_Scholarships&TEMPLATE=/CM/ContentDisplay.cfm&CONTENTID=23362
Sponsor Foundation for Physical Therapy
1055 N Fairfax St, Ste 350
Alexandria, VA 22314

Foundation for Physical Therapy Research Grants **1994**
The foundation provides sole support or matching funds to individuals and groups of researchers to pursue scientifically based and clinically related physical therapy research, focused on studies initiated by emerging investigators. Emerging investigators are individuals who have had some previous research experience, may or may not have completed graduate or postgraduate work, or are beginning a new field of research or making strategic changes in research direction within an existing line of research. Proposed studies should add to or refine the body of theoretical, scientific, and clinical knowledge on which physical therapy practice is based, using any of a variety of recognized investigative methods such as experimental, descriptive, or correlational.
Requirements Proposals may be submitted by individuals or groups of investigators independently or through a sponsoring institution or organization with which they are affiliated. Groups must designate one member as the principal investigator responsible for directing the project. This person must be eligible for licensure as a physical therapist. Other members of the group may be physical therapists, physical therapist assistants, or persons from other fields that are relevant to the proposed study.
Amount $40,000 maximum per year for up to two years
Date(s) Application Is Due Aug 15.
Contact Lucy Dickson, Scientific Program Administrator, (800) 999-2782 ext 8505; email: foundation@apta.org
Internet http://www.apta.org/AM/Template.cfm?Section=Awards_and_Scholarships&TEMPLATE=/CM/ContentDisplay.cfm&CONTENTID=23363
Sponsor Foundation for Physical Therapy
1111 N Fairfax St
Alexandria, VA 22314-1488

Foundation for Psychocultural Research Doctoral Fellowships **1995**
The foundation will competitively award limited dissertation research fellowships aimed at advancing interdisciplinary research projects and scholarship at the intersection of

psychology, culture, neuroscience, and psychiatry, with emphasis on psycho-cultural factors as central, not peripheral. The dissertation topic will involve substantial engagement in Trauma and the Interaction of Early Relational Experiences, Social Context, and Developmental Trajectories. The interdisciplinary approach will emphasize the cultural and neuroscientific approaches to the study of PTSD. Grants will be awarded on a one-time basis. An institutional allowance is allotted to the host institution on a monthly basis for one year, to be used at the sponsor's discretion to help pay for the fellow's research supplies, travel to scientific meetings, or health insurance. If a deadline falls on a weekend, applications will be accepted on the following Monday. Application guidelines are available online.
Requirements Candidates must be enrolled at an accredited US university or institution. Applicant must be a doctoral candidate in anthropology, psychology, neuroscience, or health sciences, and should have interest in completing a dissertation involving interdisciplinary research in culture, neuroscience, and psychiatry.
Amount $25,000; $1250 institutional allowance
Date(s) Application Is Due Feb 15.
Contact Director, fax: (310) 454-1417; email: info@thefpr.org
Internet http://www.thefpr.org/programs_funding/applications/doctoral_app.html
Sponsor Foundation for Psychocultural Research
P.O. Box 826
Pacific Palisades, CA 90272

Foundation for Psychocultural Research Postdoctoral Fellowships **1996**
The foundation funds research aimed at advancing interdisciplinary research projects and scholarship at the intersection of psychology, culture, neuroscience, and psychiatry, with emphasis on psychocultural factors as central, not peripheral. The current topical focus is Interdisciplinary Approach to Post Traumatic Stress and Resilience. The research will integrate cultural and neuroscientific approaches to the study of PTSD, in its design and/or clinical application. Candidates must conduct their proposed research under a sponsor who holds an academic appointment at an accredited US university or institution. The fellowship may be extended up to the maximum of three years, based on the evaluation of the previous year's performance. An institutional allowance is allotted monthly to the host institution, to be used at the sponsor's discretion to help pay for the fellow's research supplies, travel to scientific meetings, or health insurance. If a deadline falls on a weekend, applications will be accepted on Monday. Guidelines are available online.
Requirements Applicants must have a doctoral or MD degree and should have interest in pursuing a career involving interdisciplinary research in neuroscience, culture, and psychiatry.
Amount $40,000 stipend; $1500 per-year for supplies, travel or health insurance
Date(s) Application Is Due Feb 15.
Contact Director, email: foundationpsycul@aol.com
Internet http://www.thefpr.org/programs_funding/applications/post_doctoral_app.html
Sponsor Foundation for Psychocultural Research
P.O. Box 826
Pacific Palisades, CA 90272

Foundation for Science and Disability Grant Program for Physically Disabled Students in the Sciences **1997**
A grant may be awarded annually to a disabled student who is interested in obtaining a graduate degree in science, mathematics, medicine, engineering, or computer science. Selection is based on financial need, sincerity of purpose, and scholarship and/or research ability. Funds may be used for an assistive device or instrument, or as financial support to work with a professor on an individual research project, or for some other special need. The number of grants awarded each year varies depending on funds available. Application must include a 250-word essay on professional goals and objectives, as well as the specific purpose for which the grant monies will be used, and two letters of recommendation from faculty members, one of whom must be the student's academic research advisor.
Requirements College seniors who have some physical or sensory disability and who have been accepted to graduate or professional school, as well as students already in graduate or professional schools, are eligible to apply.
Restrictions Undergraduate students are not eligible.
Amount $1000
Date(s) Application Is Due Dec 1.
Contact Dr. Richard Mankin, Co-Chair, Science Student Grant Committee, (352) 374-5774; fax: (352) 374-5804; email: rmankin@nervm.nerdc.ufl.edu
Internet http://www.as.wvu.edu/~scidis/organize/fsdinfo.html
Sponsor Foundation for Science and Disability
503 NW 89th St
Gainesville, FL 32607

Foundation for Seacoast Health Grants **1998**
The mission of the foundation is to invest its resources to improve the health and well being of Seacoast residents. The foundation considers a very limited number of new grant initiatives which address one or more of the following prioritized health needs; access to affordable mental health services; access to preventative and restorative dental services; access to affordable child care and after school care; access to affordable primary medical care; and coordination and dissemination of health information related to identified priority needs. The deadline for the submission of the letter of intent is March 1 for Infants, Children and Adolescence and June 1 for Promoting Health and Preventing Disease. Annual deadline dates may vary; contact program staff for exact dates.
Requirements Nonprofit organizations in cities and towns in the New Hampshire/Maine Seacoast area, including Greenland, New Castle, Newington, North Hampton, Portsmouth, and Rye, NH; and Eliot, Kittery, and York, ME, may submit applications.
Restrictions Grants do not support ongoing general operating expenses, deficit elimination, political activities, travel, conferences, or lodging.
Date(s) Application Is Due Mar 1; Jun 1.
Contact Susan Bunting, President, (603) 422-8200; email: ffsh@communitycampus.org
Internet http://www.ffsh.org/grants.cfm
Sponsor Foundation for Seacoast Health
100 Campus Drive, Suite 1
Portsmouth, NH 03801

Foundation for the Advancement of Mesoamerican Studies Grants **1999**
The foundation awards grants to support scholarly contributions to the understanding of ancient Mesoamerican cultures (M'xico, Belize, Guatemala, Honduras, and El Salvador). The foundation supports projects in the disciplines of archaeology, art history, epigraphy, linguistics, ethnohistory, ethnography, and sociology. Interdisciplinary projects are encouraged, especially those that combine disciplines in novel and potentially productive ways. The program provides research grants and contingency grants. Contingency grants provide emergency funds for unforeseen situations encountered during initial research, secondary analysis, and/or the final dissemination of findings. Application guidelines are available online.
Restrictions FAMSI does not provide funds for equipment purchases, salaries, stipends, or honoraria.
Amount $500-$10,000 research grants
Date(s) Application Is Due Sep 15.
Contact Sandra Noble, Director, (352) 795-5990; fax: (352) 795-1970; email: sandra@famsi.org
Internet http://www.famsi.org/grants
Sponsor Foundation for the Advancement of Mesoamerican Studies
268 S Suncoast Blvd
Crystal River, FL 34429-5498

Foundation for the Carolinas Grants **2000**
The foundation supports nonprofit organizations in North and South Carolina, especially in the greater Charlotte, NC, area. The foundation awards grants in the following program areas: education, religion, human services, the environment, historic preservation, public and civic affairs, health, the arts, youths, and senior citizens. Building Youth grants help school-age children make the transition from youth to adulthood.
Requirements The foundation awards grants to nonprofit organizations serving the following areas in North Carolina: Cebarrus, Cleveland, Iredell, Lincoln, Mecklenburg, Richmond, Stanley, and Union Counties and the cities of Lexiington and Salisbury; and Cherokee, Lancaster, and York Counties in South Carolina.
Restrictions Grants are not awarded for capital campaigns, operating budgets, endowments, publications, equipment, videos, or conferences, nor to individuals.
Contact Dr. Don Jonas, Senior Vice President of Community Philanthropy, (704) 973-4500 or (800) 973-7244; fax: (704) 973-4599; email: djonas@fftc.org
Internet http://www.fftc.org/grants
Sponsor Foundation for the Carolinas
P.O. Box 34769
Charlotte, NC 28234-4769

Foundation for the Future Grants **2001**
The program awards grants to support scholars undertaking research that is directly related to a better understanding of the factors affecting the quality of life of the long-term future of humanity. Preliminary Grant Applications must be submitted between January 1 and April 30 of the year in which grant funding is sought. An application form is available on the Web site.
Requirements Individuals and organizations worldwide may apply.
Amount $5000-$25,000
Date(s) Application Is Due Apr 30.
Contact Sesh Velamoor, Deputy Director, Programs, (425) 451-1333; fax: (425) 451-1238; email: seshvelamoor@futurefoundation.org
Internet http://www.futurefoundation.org/grants/index.html
Sponsor Foundation for the Future
123-105th Ave SE
Bellevue, WA 98004-6265

Foundation Global Ethic Grants **2002**
The foundation is based on the Declaration toward a Global Ethic endorsed by the Parliament of the World's Religions, which declares a commitment to a culture of nonviolence and respect for life, solidarity and a just economic order, tolerance and a life of truthfulness, and equal rights and partnership between men and women. Fields of interest include arts and humanities, education, international affairs, law and human rights, and social welfare. Types of support include grants to individuals and institutions, scholarships, fellowships, and prizes.

Contact Stephan Schlensog, Managing Director, 49-7071-640334; fax: 49-7071-610140; email: office@stiftung-weltethos.uni-tuebingen.de
Internet http://www.weltethos.org/dat_eng/index_e.htm
Sponsor Foundation Global Ethic
Waldhauser Strasse 23
Tubingen 72076 Germany

Fragile X Syndrome Postdoctoral Research Fellowships Program **2003**
The purpose of this program is to promote research aimed at finding a specific treatment for fragile X syndrome, the primary inherited cause of mental retardation. The foundation is particularly interested in preclinical studies of potential pharmacological and genetic treatments for fragile X and studies aimed at understanding the function of the FMR1 gene. The goal is to bring practical treatment into current medical practice as quickly as possible; therefore, preference will be given to research projects that have a clear practical application and the results of which will be shared with other qualified researchers in a timely fashion. Fellowships are awarded for one year and may be renewed for a second year.
Requirements Tax-exempt 501(c)3 institutions are eligible for funding. Individuals are nominated by applicant institutions for the fellowships and should have training and experience at least equal to the PhD or MD level.
Amount $40,000 maximum
Date(s) Application Is Due May 1; Dec 1.
Contact Katie Clapp, (978) 462-1866; fax: (978) 463-9985; email: kclappFRAXA@comcast.net
Internet http://www.fraxa.org/research_howtoapply.aspx
Sponsor FRAXA Research Foundation
45 Pleasant St, 2nd Fl
Newburyport, MA 01950

Frances C. and William P. Smallwood Foundation Grants **2004**
The foundation awards grants in support of education, higher education, and social services. Applications will be received from the following organizations; educational institutions, both public and private, primarily at the college or university level, as well as other non-profit organizations involved in American education and is confined to the area within a 100 mile radius of the Dallas/Fort Worth Metroplex, the area within a 100 mile radius of the city of Gainesville, FL, and the area within a 100 mile radius of Minden, Nevada. Potential applicants should request guidelines prior to applying.
Requirements Contributions are limited to non-profit, tax-exempt organizations which have obtained IRS status under Section 501(c)(3) of the IRS code, and, where appropriate, under Section 170(c).
Restrictions Funding will not be considered for: general endowment funds of an organization; fund-raising events, i.e. tickets, dinner, telethons; corporate memberships or contributions to Chambers of Commerce, taxpayer associations, and other similar bodies; and contributions to political organizations, campaigns and candidates.
Date(s) Application Is Due Feb 28.
Contact Rick Piersall, Foundation Contact; Suzanne Stockdale, (775) 782-3678 or Sally Muller, (352) 378-9646
Sponsor Frances C. and William P. Smallwood Foundation
P.O. Box 2050
Fort Worth, TX 76113

Frances L. and Edwin L. Cummings Memorial Fund Grants **2005**
The foundation supports nonprofits in New York City and northern New Jersey in the areas of education, especially programs that serve public school children from disadvantaged backgrounds; social welfare concerns; and campaigns to build endowments through establishment of challenge grants. Other areas of interest include elementary education, secondary education, vocational education, adult basic education and literacy, and higher education; hospitals, medical care, AIDS, and cancer; children, youth, and human services; and community development. Support is provided for endowment funds, seed money, consulting services, matching funds, technical assistance, professorships, and program development. Application forms are not required.
Requirements Grants are awarded to nonprofit organizations in the metropolitan New York, NY, area, with emphasis on New York City, southern Westchester County, and northern New Jersey.
Restrictions Grants are not awarded to individuals or for capital building campaigns, general operating support, moving expenses, conferences, surveys, annual fund-raising campaigns, or research conducted by individuals or private institutions.
Amount $10,000
Contact Elizabeth Costas, Administrative Director, (212) 286-1778; fax: (212) 682-9458
Sponsor Frances L. and Edwin L. Cummings Memorial Fund
501 Fifth Avenue, Suite 708
New York, NY 10017-6103

Francis Bacon Award in the History and Philosophy of Science and Technology **2006**
The institute and the Francis Bacon Foundation support this biennial prize in the history of science, the history of technology, or historically engaged philosophy of science. The prize will be awarded biennially to an outstanding scholar whose work continues to have a substantial impact on any of the three fields. Submit a one-page letter of nomination that addresses the candidate's qualifications and potential; and a copy of the nominee's curriculum vita and contact information.
Amount $20,000
Date(s) Application Is Due Dec 1.
Contact Sanja Ilic, Secretary to the Bacon Committee, (626) 395-4065; fax: (626) 405-9841; email: sanja@hss.caltech.edu
Internet http://www.hss.caltech.edu/humanities/fbaward
Sponsor California Institute of Technology
1200 E California Blvd, Baxter 228-77
Pasadena, CA 91125

Francis Butler Simpkins Award **2007**
The award is given in odd-numbered years for the best first book by an author or authors in the field of US southern history published during the preceding two years. The application due date is March 1 of the year in which the prize is to be awarded. Books should be forwarded to the committee members listed on the Web site.
Date(s) Application Is Due Mar 1.
Contact Francis Butler Simpkins Award, (706) 542-8848; fax: (706) 542-2455
Internet http://www.uga.edu/~sha/franci~1.htm
Sponsor Southern Historical Association
University of Georgia, Department of History
Athens, GA 30602

Francis C. Wood History of Medicine Fellowships **2008**
The institute offers fellowships to scholars engaged in projects requiring personal use of the historical collections of the library of the College of Physicians of Philadelphia and/or the collections of the Mutter Museum. The historical collections constitute one of the largest medical history repositories in the United States, documenting the evolution of medicine from the medieval period to the present. Its resources include rare medical books and journals; manuscript case records, papers, and lecture notes of many physicians; and prints, engravings, and photographs of medical subjects. The Mutter Museum is renowned for its collections of medical artifacts, instruments, and pathological and anatomical specimens. Recipients may be requested to present a seminar at the institute and will be required to submit a report on their research. Awards will be announced in March.
Requirements Letters of application outlining the proposed project (proposal should not exceed five pages); length of residence; historical materials to be used; and a budget with specific information on travel, lodging, and research expenses should be submitted, along with a curriculum vita and two letters of recommendation.
Amount $1000 maximum
Date(s) Application Is Due Apr 1.
Contact Margaret Patton, Program Contact, (215) 563-3737 ext 305; email: mpatton@collphyphil.org
Internet http://www.collphyphil.org/woodfell.htm
Sponsor College of Physicians of Philadelphia
19 S 22nd St
Philadelphia, PA 19103

Francis C. Wood Scholar in Residence Program **2009**
Short-term grants will be awarded to scholars engaged in projects requiring personal use of the historical collections of the library and/or Mutter Museum. Letters of application outlining the proposed project (proposal should not exceed five pages), necessary length of residence, historical materials to be used and a budget with specific information on travel, lodging, and research expenses should be submitted, along with a curriculum vitae and two letters of recommendation by January 31.
Requirements The program is restricted to individuals pursuing advanced research. Candidates must have a PhD or an equivalent record of professional experience and scholarly publication.
Restrictions The award will not be made to degree candidates or to persons seeking support for work leading to a degree.
Amount $30,000, office, and research and computer facilities
Contact Ed Morman, Committee on Awards, (215) 563-3737 ext 265; fax: (215) 561-6477; email: emorman@collphyphil.org
Internet http://www.collphyphil.org/woodpg1.shtml
Sponsor College of Physicians of Philadelphia
19 S 22nd St
Philadelphia, PA 19103

Francis P. Garvan-John M. Olin Medal **2010**
This award, sponsored by the the Francis P. Garvan-John M. Olin Medal Endowment and administered by the American Chemical Society, is given annually to recognize distinguished service to chemistry by women chemists who are US citizens.
Requirements Any individual, except a member of the awards committee, may submit one nomination or seconding letter for the award in any given year. The nominating documents consist of a letter of not more than 1000 words containing an evaluation of the nominee's accomplishments and a specific identification of the work to be recognized, a biographical sketch including date of birth, and a list of publications and patents authored by the nominee. Nominee must be a US citizen. Six copies of all items to be included in the nomination must be submitted.
Restrictions Self-nominations are not accepted.

Amount $5000 and an allowance of $1000 toward traveling expenses to award meeting
Date(s) Application Is Due Feb 1.
Contact Awards Administrator, (800) 227-5558 or (202) 872-4408; fax: (202) 776-8258; email: awards@acs.org
Internet http://www.chemistry.org/portal/a/c/s/1/acsdisplay.html?DOC=awards%5Cgarvin-oiln.html
Sponsor American Chemical Society
1155 16th St NW
Washington, DC 20036

Frank B. Sessa Scholarship for Continuing Education **2011**
The scholarship is available to society members who are intending to enroll in programs for continuing education. Application form must be obtained from the society and returned with a resume and explanation of the proposed study or research. Applications for all scholarships and fellowships are accepted beginning November 15.
Amount $1250
Date(s) Application Is Due Mar 15.
Contact Dr. Jane Robbins, Executive Director, School of Information Studies, (850) 644-3907; fax: (850) 644-9763; email: Beta_Phi_Mu@lis.fsu.edu
Internet http://www.beta-phi-mu.org/scholarships.html
Sponsor Beta Phi Mu International Library and Information Science Honor Society
Beta Phi Mu, School of Information Studies, 101 Louis Shores Bldg, Florida State University
Tallahassee, FL 32306-2048

Frank H. Field and Joe L. Franklin Award for Outstanding Acievements in Mass Spectrometry **2012**
This award, sponsored by Bruker Daltonics, Inc. and administered by ACS, is given annually to recognize outstanding achievement in the development or application of mass spectrometry. The award shall be granted without regard to age, nationality, or the date of the achievement recognized by the award. In odd-numbered years the award will be presented for advances in techniques or fundamental processes in mass spectrometry. Recognition will be given in even-numbered years to development of the applications of mass spectrometry.
Requirements Any individual, except a member of the award committee, may submit one nomination or seconding letter for each award in any given year. The nominating documents consist of a letter of not more than 1000 words containing an evaluation of the nominee's accomplishments and a specific identification of the work to be recognized, a biographical sketch including date of birth, and a list of publications and patents authored by the nominee.
Restrictions Self-nominations are not accepted.
Amount $5000, certificate, and an allowance of up to $1000 for travel expenses to award meeting
Date(s) Application Is Due Feb 1.
Contact Awards Administrator, (800) 227-5558; fax: (202) 872-6317; email: awards@acs.org
Internet http://www.chemistry.org/portal/a/c/s/1/acsdisplay.html?DOC=awards\field-franklin.html
Sponsor American Chemical Society
1155 16th St NW
Washington, DC 20036

Frank J. McDevitt, DO, Excellence in Research Awards for Health Service, Policy, and Clinical Care **2013**
The program recognizes research that contributes to improving health and medical care in Michigan Grants of unrestricted research support are made to physician and doctoral-level researchers for research on health policy, health services, and clinical care. Submissions to the health policy or health services research categories should focus on public health, the financing and organization of health services, population health, reimbursement, or resource allocation. Submissions to the clinical care category should focus on outcomes, clinical effectiveness, or clinical protocol research. Submissions of basic biomedical research are not encouraged. The award will be made to the recipient's 501(c)3 nonprofit or educational organization. Guidelines are available online.
Requirements Self-nominations and nominations made by an individual researcher or by any interested party will be accepted. Nominations must include two copies of the nominated article and the name, degree, title, address, organizational affiliation, and contact information of the nominee.
Amount $10,000
Date(s) Application Is Due Jan 1.
Contact Grants Administrator, (313) 225-8706; fax: (313) 225-7730; email: foundation@bcbsm.com
Internet http://www.bcbsm.com/foundation/pdf/fmcdevitt.pdf
Sponsor Blue Cross Blue Shield of Michigan Foundation
600 Lafayette E, X520
Detroit, MI 48226

Frank Knox Memorial Fellowships **2014**
The program enables graduates from Canada to spend one year studying at one of the faculties of Harvard University. Fellowships are available only to citizens of Canada. All applications and supporting documents must be submitted in English only.
Requirements Applicants must be Canadian citizens or permanent residents who have graduated no earlier than the spring of 2003 or who will graduate before September 2005 from an institution which is a member, or affiliated with a member of AUCC.
Restrictions Applications from students currently studying in the United States will not be considered.
Amount $18,500
Date(s) Application Is Due Dec 31.
Contact Canadian Awards Program, (613) 563-1236; fax: (613) 563-9745; email: awards@aucc.ca
Internet http://www.aucc.ca/programs/scholarships/knox_e.html
Sponsor Frank Knox Fellowships
350 Albert St, Ste 600
Ottawa, ON K1R 1B1 Canada

Frank Stanley Beveridge Foundation Grants **2015**
The foundation welcomes proposals in the areas of: animal care; arts, culture and humanities; civil rights, social action, advocacy; education; employment/jobs; environmental quality, protection and beautification; food, nutrition and agriculture; health; housing; human services; medical research; mental health; philanthropy; safety; recreation; religion; science; social services; and youth development. The board meets in October and April to consider requests. Multiyear grants are rare. Contact the foundation via the Web site only. No phone or written inquiries will be accepted.
Requirements Applicants must be 501(c)3 nonprofit organizations or foundations in Massachusetts's Hampden and Hampshire Counties.
Restrictions The Foundation prefers not to support: awards or prizes; commissioning of new artistic work; conferences/seminars; curriculum development; debt reduction; employee matching gifts; employee-related scholarships; endowment funds; exhibitions; faculty/staff development; fellowship funds; fellowships to individuals; film/video/radio production; foundation administered programs; general operating support; grants to individuals; income development; internship funds; management development; performance/production costs; professorships; program-related investment/loans; publications; scholarships to individuals; student aid; technical assistance.
Amount $50,000
Date(s) Application Is Due Feb 1; Aug 1.
Contact Philip Caswell, President, email: administrator@beveridge.org or caswell@beveridge.org
Internet http://www.beveridge.org/
Sponsor Frank Stanley Beveridge Foundation
1340 US Highway 1, Suite 102
Jupiter, FL 33469

Franklin Mosher Baldwin Fellowships **2016**
The Baldwin fellowship is intended for scholars with citizenship in an African country who seek to obtain an advanced degree or specialized training in an area of study related to human origins research. This award is for a program of approved special training and/or advanced training towards an MA, PhD, or equivalent and is limited to two years of support.
Requirements Scholars with citizenship in an African country are eligible to apply.
Amount $12,000 maximum per year
Date(s) Application Is Due Feb 15.
Contact Grants Officer, (415) 561-4646; fax: (415) 561-4647; email: grants@leakeyfoundation.org
Internet http://www.leakeyfoundation.org/grants/g3.jsp
Sponsor L.S.B. Leakey Foundation
P.O. Box 29346, 1002A O'Reilly Ave
San Francisco, CA 94129-0346

Fraser-Parker Foundation Grants **2017**
The foundation awards general operating grants in its areas of interest, including Christian religion organizations, education and higher education, and hospitals. There are no application forms.
Amount $5000-$50,000 average
Date(s) Application Is Due Apr 15; Oct 15.
Contact John Stephenson, Executive Director, (404) 658-9066
Sponsor Fraser-Parker Foundation
50 Hurt Plz, Ste 850
Atlanta, GA 30303

Frederic Stanley Kipping Award in Silicon Chemistry **2018**
This award, sponsored by Dow Corning Corporation and administered by the American Chemical Society, is given biennially in even-numbered years to recognize distinguished achievement in research in silicon chemistry and to stimulate the creativity of others toward further advancement of this field of chemistry. A nominee must have accomplished distinguished achievement in research in silicon chemistry during the preceding 10 years. The measure of this achievement should focus primarily on the nominee's significant publications in the field of silicon chemistry but may include consideration of contributions to the related field of organometallic chemistry, particularly embracing the elements of Group IV. There are no limits on age or nationality. Applications are accepted in odd-numbered years. Annual deadline dates may vary; contact program staff for exact dates.

Requirements Any individual, except a member of the award committee, may submit one nomination or seconding letter for the award in any given year. Nominating documents consist of a letter of not more than 1000 words containing an evaluation of the nominee's accomplishments and a specific identification of the work to be recognized, a biographical sketch including date of birth, and a list of publications and patents authored by the nominee.
Amount $5000 and allowance for travel expenses to award meeting
Date(s) Application Is Due Feb 1.
Contact Awards Administrator, (202) 872-4408; fax: (202) 776-8211; email: awards@acs.org
Internet http://www.chemistry.org/portal/a/c/s/1/acsdisplay.html?DOC=awards%5Ckipping.html
Sponsor American Chemical Society
1155 16th St NW
Washington, DC 20036

Frederick Douglass Summer Fellowships **2019**
The summer fellowships offer teaching oppotunities to minority graduate students who are pursuing careers in college teaching and are in their final year of a terminal degree program. The fellowships are intended to attract graduate studnts primarily from historically black colleges and universities. Fellows will teach and/or team teach one course during a five-week summer session.
Requirements Applicants must be US citizens, and must have completed all doctoral work, except the dissertation, by the end of the next academic year.
Amount $2381
Date(s) Application Is Due Jan 31.
Contact Fellowships Administrator, (814) 393-2109; email: info@clarion.edu
Internet http://www.clarion.edu/admin/socequ/fd.shtml
Sponsor Clarion University
The Frederick Douglass Teaching Scholars, c/o Clarion University, Office of Social Equity, 207 Carrier
Clarion, PA 16214

Frederick Douglass Teaching Scholars Program **2020**
The Pan African Studies program of the university offers teaching opportunities to graduate students entering the final year of terminal degree programs and preparing to be college teachers, and for the purpose of attracting graduate students from historically underrepresented and underserved populations. Application information and form are available on the Web site.
Requirements Minimum requirements are: master's degree completed or equivalent and currently enrolled in a terminal degree program; academic background in one of the fields taught at the university; and at least three favorable letters of recommendation from faculty or professionals in the student's field.
Date(s) Application Is Due Feb 9.
Contact Dr. Veronica Watson, Coordinator, The Frederick Douglass Institute, (724) 357-2280; email: maat@grove.iup.edu
Internet http://www.chss.iup.edu/fdi/teach_scholars.htm
Sponsor Indiana University of Pennsylvania
421 North Walk, 110 Leonard Hall
Indiana, PA 15705

Frederick Gardner Cottrell Foundation Grants **2021**
The foundation awards grants to educational and scientific organizations to advance research and chair teaching positions. The foundation's areas of interest include eye research, higher education, marine science, and science. There are no application deadline. Submit a written request for application.
Amount $100,000-$300,000 average
Contact Gary Munsinger, President
Sponsor Frederick Gardner Cottrell Foundation
101 N Wilmot Rd, Ste 600
Tucson, AZ 85711-3365

Freedom of Information Internships/Kilgore **2022**
The foundation accepts applications each year for two freedom of information internships with the Society of Professional Journalists. The 10-week internships enable two students to research and write about freedom of information issues while assisting in the preparation of the annual SPJ Freedom of Information Report. Each intern will work during a mutually agreeable 10-week period in the late spring or summer. A candidate must submit a completed application form, a resume, a two- to three-page essay detailing expectations from experience, up to five samples of writing, a listing of past FOI-related activities, names and phone numbers of three references, and a black-and-white photograph suitable for publication. Applicants' overall GPA and GPA for journalism courses will be considered.
Requirements Candidates must be senior or graduate journalism students, or law students with journalism backgrounds.
Amount $400 per week
Date(s) Application Is Due Mar 1.
Contact Grants Administrator, (317) 927-8000; fax: (317) 920-4789; email: quill@spj.org
Internet http://www.spj.org/internships_pk.asp
Sponsor Sigma Delta Chi Foundation
3909 N Meridian St
Indianapolis, IN 46208-4045

Freedom of the Press Fellowships and Internships **2023**
The Reporters Committee hires a journalism fellow each year. The journalism fellow plans, supervises, and edits articles for the website, newsletter, and magazine and works with staff attorneys to ensure that all work is appealing to and useful for journalists, not just lawyers. The Reporters Committee hires two or three legal fellows each year. Fellows will monitor significant developments in media law, assist with responding to legal defense requests from reporters, prepare legal memoranda, and handle other special projects. In addition, fellows will write for the Committee's publications, the quarterly magazine The News Media & The Law, and the bi-weekly newsletter, News Media Update.
Requirements A journalism fellowship candidate must have at least three years experience as a reporter or editor, and should have a background in free press issues.
Contact Rebecca Daugherty, Internship Coordinator, (703) 807-2100; fax: (703) 807-2109; email: rfcp@rfcp.org
Internet http://www.rcfp.org/interns.html
Sponsor Reporters Committee for Freedom of the Press
1101 Wilson Blvd, Ste 1100
Arlington, VA 22209

Freeman Fellowships **2024**
Grants to aid and encourage young engineers, especially in research work, are made to fund expenses for experiments, observations, and compilations to discover new and accurate data that will be useful in engineering. The fellowships also recognize underwriting fully or in part some of the loss that may be sustained in the publication of meritorious books, papers, or translations pertaining to hydraulic science and art that might, except for some such assistance, remain mostly inaccessible. Traveling scholarships are available to members younger than 45 years of age in recognition of achievement or promise for the purpose of aiding the candidate to visit engineering works in the United States or any other part of the world where there are good prospects of obtaining information useful to engineers. The grant may be used for assisting in the translation or publication in English of papers or books in foreign languages pertaining to hydraulics. The grant is available annually. In a given year there may be more than one recipient, or no recipient if no meritorious applications are received. Stipend is based on funds available annually from the endowment. An application form is available upon request.
Requirements Application consists of a completed form and a statement in general terms of the purposes for which the funds are expected to be used. Any member of ASCE is eligible to apply.
Amount $2000-$5000
Date(s) Application Is Due Feb 9.
Contact Grants Coordinator, (800) 548-2723; fax: (703) 295-6132; email: student@asce.org
Internet http://www.asce.org/inside/stud_freeman.cfm
Sponsor American Society of Civil Engineers
1801 Alexander Bell Dr
Reston, VA 20191-4400

Freeman Scholar Award **2025**
This program is conducted biennially in even-numbered years; a person of wide experience in fluids engineering is selected as the Freeman scholar. He/she is expected to review a coherent topic in his/her specialty, including a comprehensive statement of the state of the art, and to suggest key future research needs. The results will be presented at the winter meeting and published in the ASME Journal of Fluids Engineering. Deadline date for applications and nominations is February 1 of odd-numbered years.
Requirements The recipient may be from industry, government, education, or private professional practice, and need not be an ASME member.
Amount $7500 and expense supplement
Date(s) Application Is Due Aug 1.
Contact Gulda DiTullio, Manager, (212) 591-7736; fax: (212) 705-7739; email: ditulliog@asme.org
Internet http://www.asme.org/honors/ms71/sla/freeman.html
Sponsor American Society of Mechanical Engineers
3 Park Ave
New York, NY 10016

French-American Studies Fellowships **2026**
The Institut Francais de Washington offers two Gilbert Chinard fellowships and an Edouard Morot-Sir fellowship in literature for maintenance (excluding travel) during research in France for a period of at least two months. The applicable fields of French study are art, economics, history, history of science, linguistics, literature, and social sciences. There is no application form; applicants must write two pages maximum describing their research projects and planned trips, and include curriculum vita. A letter from the dissertation director is also required for PhD candidates. Upon return, the awardee will send a brief report to the institute.
Requirements Applications are invited from US citizens or permanent residents of the US who are PhD candidates at the final stage of their dissertations or who have held the

PhD for no more than six years prior to January 15 of the award year. Candidates should be studying, teaching, or doing postdoctoral research at an American university.
Amount $1500
Date(s) Application Is Due Jan 15.
Contact Catherine Maley, Department of Romance Languages, (919) 962-0154; fax: (919) 962-5457; email: cmaley@email.unc.edu
Internet http://www.unc.edu/depts/institut/institutapp.htm
Sponsor Institut Francais de Washington
The University of North Carolina, Department of Romance Languages & Literatures, CB# 3170
Chapel Hill, NC 27599-3170

Frese Senior Research Fellowship **2027**
The fellowship is awarded for study in the history, theory, and criticism of sculpture, prints and drawings, and the decorative arts of any geographical area and of any period. Applications are also solicited from scholars in other disciplines whose work examines visual material in these media. The fellowship is for full-time research. Fellows are expected to reside in Washington, DC, throughout the academic year and participate in the activities of the center. Lectures, colloquia, and informal discussions complement the fellowship program. The award is limited to one-half of the applicant's salary. Senior Fellows who relocate to Washington are eligible for a housing allowance (up to $12,000.
Requirements The fellowship is intended for those who have held the PhD for five years or more or who possess an equivalent record of professional accomplishment at the time of application.
Amount $50,000 maximum
Date(s) Application Is Due Oct 1.
Contact Fellowships Program, Center for Advanced Study in the Visual Arts, (202) 842-6482; fax: (202) 789-3026; email: advstudy@nga.gov
Internet http://www.nga.gov/resources/casvasen.htm
Sponsor National Gallery of Art
Fourth St and Constitution Ave NW
Washington, DC 20565

Friedman-Klarreich Family Foundation Grants **2028**
The foundation supports innovative projects, programs, and research in educational, social, and cultural areas. Grants fund efforts to improve educational and economic equality for girls and women and to enhance the stability of families.
Requirements Organizations must have 501(c)3 tax-exempt status to be eligible.
Amount $5000 maximum
Date(s) Application Is Due Jun 1.
Contact Susan Klarreich, Grants Administrator, fax: (650) 948-3148; email: klarff@worldnet.att.net
Sponsor Friedman-Klarreich Family Foundation
551 Tyndall St
Los Altos, CA 94022

Friedrich Ebert Foundation Doctoral Research Fellowships **2029**
These fellowships are intended to provide doctoral candidates in the fields of sociology, political science, economics, and history an opportunity to conduct research necessary for their dissertations in Germany. A German university professor competent in the subject of study will assist fellowship holders and provide academic advice during their stay. This assistance also applies in the case of doctoral candidates who intend to spend most of their time engaged in archival, library, or other types of research outside the university. Sociohistorical studies, studies in contemporary history, and studies on current political problems (including comparative studies) will be given special consideration. These fellowships will be granted for stays of between five and 12 months. Guidelines are available from the foundation's US offices in New York City or from the foundation headquarters at Godesberger Allee 149, D-53715 Bonn, Germany; (49) 228 883-0.
Requirements The applicant must be a qualified PhD candidate at an American university and must have completed all of the prerequisites for a doctorate except for the dissertation, have an approved dissertation proposal and submit a recommendation from his/her academic advisor, indicate a German counterpart who would be available for cooperation and assistance during his/her stay in the Federal Republic, be a US citizen, and provide evidence that his/her knowledge of German is adequate for research purposes.
Amount DM1390 monthly maintenance allowance plus airfare between the United States and Berlin; domestic travel expenses; an allowance for luggage costs, health insurance, and books; tuition and fees if applicable; and family allowance
Date(s) Application Is Due Feb 28.
Contact Doctoral Research Fellowships, (212) 687-0208; fax: (212) 687-0261; email: info@fesny.org
Internet http://www.fesny.org
Sponsor Friedrich Ebert Foundation
823 United Nations Plz, Ste 711
New York, NY 10017

Friedrich Ebert Foundation Postdoctoral-Young Scholar Fellowships **2030**
These fellowships are intended to provide young scholars who have already accumulated a certain amount of experience in teaching and/or research an opportunity to conduct independent research in Germany in the disciplines of political science, sociology, history, and economics. Priority consideration will be given to applicants who wish to carry out studies on politically relevant subjects, particularly those involving a comparative approach. Considerable importance is attached to the establishment of contacts and cooperative relationships with competent German counterparts in the same field. The fellowships will be granted for stays of between five and 12 months. Guidelines are available from the foundation's US offices in New York City or from the foundation headquarters, at Godesberger Allee 149, D-53170 Bonn, Germany; (49) 228 883-0.
Requirements Applicant must have a PhD or equivalent university degree and at least two years of subsequent experience in research and/or teaching at a university or in a related research institution; be a US citizen; submit copies of relevant academic publications; indicate a German counterpart who would be available for cooperation and assistance during his/her stay in Germany; and have an appropriate knowledge of German.
Amount DM1700 monthly maintenance allowance plus airfare between the United States and Germany; domestic travel expenses; an allowance for luggage costs, health insurance, and books; tuition and fees if applicable; and a family allowance
Date(s) Application Is Due Feb 28.
Contact Postdoctoral-Young Scholars Fellowships, (202) 331-1819; fax: (202) 331-1837; email: fesdc@fesdc.org
Internet http://www.fesdc.org
Sponsor Friedrich Ebert Foundation
1155 15th St, NW, Ste 1100
Washington, DC 20005

Friedrich Ebert Foundation Predissertation-Advanced Grad Fellowships **2031**
These fellowships are intended to provide advanced graduates an opportunity for study and research in Germany in the disciplines of political science, sociology, history, and economics; an opportunity to familiarize themselves with the current state of research in their fields in Germany; and to conduct independent research. Applicants should have special interest in contemporary or past German or European affairs and/or German-American relations, particularly comparative studies. These fellowships are designed to enable the holders to engage in advanced studies at a university in Germany under the guidance of a German university professor. The expected outcome is the development of a dissertation proposal or the accomplishment of a specific research issue. The fellowship will be granted for a stay of between five to 12 months. Additional information and application guidelines may be obtained from the foundation's US offices in New York City or from the foundation headquarters at Godesberger Allee 149, D-53170 Bonn, Germany, (49) 228 883-0. Applications must be filed at foundation headquarters.
Requirements The applicant must be a qualified graduate student intending to pursue a doctoral degree and/or participating in a specific research project, must have successfully completed at least two years of graduate studies at an American university before initiating the intended period of study in Germany, be a US citizen, indicate a German counterpart who would be available for cooperation and assistance during his/her stay in the Federal Republic, and provide proof that he/she has sufficient knowledge of German.
Amount DM1250 monthly maintenance allowance plus airfare between the United States and Berlin; domestic travel expenses; an allowance for luggage costs, health insurance, and books; tuition and fees if applicable; and a family allowance should fellowship hol
Date(s) Application Is Due Feb 28.
Contact Predissertation-Advanced Graduate Fellowships, (212) 687-0208; fax: (212) 687-0261; email: fesny@fesny.org
Internet http://www.fesny.org
Sponsor Friedrich Ebert Foundation
823 United Nations Plaza, Ste 711
New York, NY 10017

Fritz B. Burns Foundation Grants **2032**
The foundation supports nonprofit organizations in southern California by awarding grants for education, with an emphasis on buildings, equipment, endowments (except for ordinary operating expenses), student scholarship and loan funds, and faculty fellowships; to/for hospitals, hospital equipment, and medical research; and religious organizations (Christian, Jewish, Latter-day Saints, nondenominational, Presbyterian, Protestant, Roman Catholic, and Salvation Army). Proposals should be concise, containing a brief description of what is planned, with a clear statement of the objective sought; IRS letter certifying tax exemption; financial statements; and a list of officers and directors. No formalized application or proposal format is required. Proposals are considered on a quarterly basis.
Requirements Nonprofit, tax-exempt organizations in southern California may apply.
Restrictions Grant requests are not considered from individuals nor from tax-supported entities.
Amount $10,000-$250,000 average
Contact Joseph Rawlinson, President, (818) 840-8802
Sponsor Fritz B. Burns Foundation
4001 W Alameda Ave, Ste 203
Burbank, CA 91505-4338

From The Heart Productions Grants **2033**
The program's goal is to make films that might otherwise never be made. Grants are made in a variety of categories, including Writers Grant (August 30 deadline); Editing Grant (September 30 deadline); New York Grant (April 30 deadline); LA Film Grant

(May 30 deadline); and LA Video Grant (June 30 deadline). The program seeks film and video projects that are unique and benefit society; new projects; and works-in-progress. Length is not a consideration. New York City and Los Angeles grants are not restricted geographically; anyone may apply for either or both grants. Information (including application fees), guidelines, and applications are available online.
Requirements This grant is available for shorts and low-budget independents as well as documentary filmmakers. Student filmmakers, independent producers, or independent production companies are all welcome to apply. There is a $38 application fee ($28 for students).
Restrictions Employee of From the Heart Productions, an employee of any of the sponsors, or a family member of any employee of From the Heart Productions or any of the sponsors are ineligible.
Date(s) Application Is Due Apr 30; May 30; Jun 30; Aug 30; Sep 30.
Contact Carole Dean, email: Caroleedean@att.net
Internet http://www.fromtheheartproductions.com/index.shtml
Sponsor From The Heart Productions
1455 Mandalay Beach Rd
Oxnard, CA 93035-2845

FTE Dissertation Fellowships **2034**
The fellowships support African American PhD or ThD students in their final year of dissertation work in religious or theological studies. The objectives of the program are to increase completion rates of African American students in the field of theological studies; collaborate with graduate programs in identifying and supporting students at this juncture of their studies; and offer doctoral students special opportunities for scholarly exchange and peer contacts, as well as assistance in the enhancement of writing and research skills. The fellowship includes a stipend for living expenses and other educational costs; full tuition grants; and attendance at a summer conference of workshops to assist in the development of research, writing, and teaching skills. Applicants must be able to write full time during the fellowship year. Application materials are available on the Web site.
Requirements US African American PhD or ThD students at the final writing stage of their graduate work in religious or theological studies are eligible. The applicant's dissertation research proposal and writing plan must have been approved by the dissertation committee.
Amount $15,000 stipend
Date(s) Application Is Due Feb 1.
Contact Sharon Watson Fluker, Director, (404) 727-1450; email: sfluker@thefund.org
Internet http://www.thefund.org/programs/fellowships/dissertation/index.html
Sponsor Fund for Theological Education
825 Houston Mill Rd, Ste 250
Atlanta, GA 30329-4211

FTE Doctoral Fellowships **2035**
The fellowships support African American students entering a PhD or ThD program in religious or theological studies. The objectives of the program are to increase the number of qualified African American students in the field of theological studies; establish partnerships with graduate programs and theological schools to strengthen their efforts toward the recruitment and support of these students; provide opportunities for intellectual stimulation and encouragement through conferences, mentoring, and peer relationships; and undertake assessment of how racial/ethnic minority doctoral candidates are best supported in their work and the factors that contribute to successful completion of their programs. The fellowship includes a stipend for living expenses and other educational costs; full tuition grants; and attendance at a summer conference of workshops to assist in the development of research, writing, and teaching skills. Application materials are available on the Web site.
Requirements African American students entering their first year of an accredited graduate program leading to a PhD or ThD degree in religious or theological studies are eligible. Applicants must be committed to providing leadership within theological education and strongly considering a career in seminary teaching and research.
Amount $15,000 maximum
Date(s) Application Is Due Mar 1.
Contact The Rev. Ellen Echols Purdum, Director, (404) 727-1450; email: epurdum@thefund.org
Internet http://www.thefund.org/programs/fellowships/doctoral/index.html
Sponsor Fund for Theological Education
825 Houston Mill Rd, Ste 250
Atlanta, GA 30329-4211

FTE Expanding Horizons Partnership Grants **2036**
The program supports African American students in PhD and ThD programs in religious and theological studies. It links educators, academic institutions, and those pursuing doctoral work for the purpose of promoting quality in the preparation for and practice of scholarly research and teaching in theological seminaries. The program supports doctoral fellows entering their first year of a PhD or ThD program in religious or theological studies; and dissertation support to fellows at the final stage of their doctoral work in religious or theological studies. Dissertation fellowship applications are due February 1; doctoral fellowship applications are due March 1.
Requirements African American students in PhD and ThD programs in religious and theological studies are eligible.
Amount $15,000
Date(s) Application Is Due Feb 1; Mar 1.
Contact The Rev. Ellen Echols Purdum, (404) 727-1450; fax: (404) 727-1490; email: sfluker@thefund.org or fte@thefund.org
Internet http://www.thefund.org/programs/horizons/index.html
Sponsor Fund for Theological Education
825 Houston Mill Rd, Ste 250
Atlanta, GA 30329-4211

FTE North American Doctoral Fellowships **2037**
The fellowships support talented racial or ethnic minority students currently enrolled in a PhD or ThD program in religious or theological studies. Candidates must pursue full-time study with high academic performance; be committed to teaching and scholarship; and demonstrate capacity for leadership in theological education. Preference is given to students nearing the end of their studies. Application materials are available online.
Requirements US or Canadian PhD or ThD students who are members of racial or ethnic groups traditionally underrepresented in graduate education are eligible.
Restrictions DMin students are ineligible.
Amount $5000 maximum
Date(s) Application Is Due Mar 1.
Contact Sharon Watson Fluker, Director, (404) 727-1450; email: sfluker@thefund.org
Internet http://www.thefund.org/programs/fellowships/doctoral/northamerican.html
Sponsor Fund for Theological Education
825 Houston Mill Rd, Ste 250
Atlanta, GA 30329-4211

Fulbright Alumni Initiatives Awards Program Grants **2038**
The objective of the AIA program is to help translate the individual Fulbright experience into long-term institutional impact. To this end, the program provides small institutional grants to Fulbright alumni to develop innovative projects that will foster institutionally supported linkages and sustainable, mutually beneficial relationships between the Fulbright scholar's home and host institutions. Just about any activity resulting in the creation or fostering of a sustainable institutional relationship that will have an impact on both the Fulbright alum's home institution and the Fulbright host institution abroad and which both institutions are prepared to support in both the long and short terms will be considered. The program has been temporarily suspended for the foreseeable future. Please check back for updates.
Requirements Applicants must be US citizens. The program is open to eligible alumni whose grants occurred at any time from the 1998/1999 academic year through the present academic year.
Restrictions This program is limited to application by a Fulbright alum (whether U.S. or Visiting Scholar) in partnership with his/her host institution colleague. However, other faculty members from both applicants' institutions may be part of the proposal and participate in the project.
Contact Stacey Bustillos, Program Officer, (202) 686-6252; email: sbustillos@cies.iie.org; Hajra Zahid, Senior Program Associate, (202) 686-6250; email: hzahid@cies.iie.org
Internet http://www.cies.org/aia/
Sponsor Institute of International Education, Council for International Exchange of Scholars
3007 Tilden Street, NW, Suite 5L
Washington, DC 20008-3009

Fulbright Business Grants in Mexico **2039**
This program is designed to enhance the knowledge, expertise, and understanding of business in Mexico for U.S. students in business, law, or engineering. It combines graduate courses (a minimum of 3 and a maximum of 6) in the pertinent academic area (e.g., business, finance, international trade, or comparative law among others) with an internship with a Mexico-based company, firm, or NGO dedicated to international business. Candidates with a BA degree and recent M.B.A., J.D. or master's degree in business administration, finance, economics, international relations, engineering, or accounting, and some work experience are preferred. A Master's degree is recommended but not required. Significant work experience in a business environment is strongly recommended for these candidates and for candidates who do not have a business-related degree.
Requirements Applicants must: be U.S. citizens at the time of application (permanent residents are not eligible); be in good health (grantees will be required to submit a satisfactory Medical Certificate of Health from a physician); and hold a B.A. degree or the equivalent before the start of the grant (applicants who have not earned a B.A. degree or the equivalent, but who have extensive professional study and/or experience in business, may be considered). Excellent spoken and written Spanish is required at the time of application.
Contact Jody Dudderar, Program Manager, (212) 984-5565; fax: (212) 984-5325; email: jdudderar@iie.org; Joseph Livingston, Program Manager in Central America and the Caribbean, (212) 984-5366; email: jlivingston@iie.org
Internet http://us.fulbrightonline.org/program_country.html?id=70#binational
Sponsor Institute of International Education
809 United Nations Plaza
New York, NY 10017-3580

Fulbright Business Grants in Spain **2040**

These awards are co-sponsored by the Instituto de Empresa Foundation in Madrid. Instituto de Empresa is one of Europe's leading business schools and has hosted nearly 28,000 students, representing 71 different nationalities. Awards are for full-time study in the bilingual English/Spanish International MBA program which offers the basic MBA core, two components of elective courses, and a Global Affairs Seminar in which students analyze business problems focusing on five different geographic areas.

Requirements Applicants must: be U.S. citizens at the time of application (permanent residents are not eligible); be in good health (grantees will be required to submit a satisfactory Medical Certificate of Health from a physician); and hold a B.A. degree or the equivalent before the start of the grant (applicants who have not earned a B.A. degree or the equivalent, but who have extensive professional study and/or experience in business, may be considered). Excellent spoken and written Spanish is required at the time of application.

Contact Valerie Hymas, Program Manager, (212) 984-5326; email: vhymas@iie.org
Internet http://us.fulbrightonline.org/program_country.html?id=98#MBA
Sponsor Institute of International Education
809 United Nations Plaza
New York, NY 10017-3580

Fulbright Critical Language Enhancement Awards **2041**

The Award, a component of the National Security Language Initiative, is available to students who have been awarded a Fulbright U.S. Student full grant and who intend to use the eligible languages in their Fulbright project. Students must also demonstrate the equivalent of an academic year of study in that language by the grant start date. Application for an Award is made in conjunction with the Fulbright Program application. Awards will be granted based on recommendations made by the selection committees, and final selections by Fulbright Commissions or U.S. Embassies in the corresponding countries. The purpose of the Award is to cultivate higher levels of language proficiency prior to and during the Fulbright grant period and beyond. Ultimately, awardees will achieve a high level of proficiency in a targeted language and will go on to careers or further study which will incorporate the use of this and/or related languages. The languages available for the Award are: all dialects of Arabic, Azeri, Bengali, Chinese (Mandarin only), Farsi, Gujarati, Hindi, Korean, Marathi, Pashto, Punjabi, Russian, Tajik, Turkish, Urdu, and Uzbek. It is preferred that language training take place in the same country as that of the award.

Requirements The grant include pre- and post-testing in the relevant language, a minimum of 20 hours of formal study per week in-country, and a commitment to study beyond the Critical Language Enhancement Award training period. Applicants must: be U.S. citizens at the time of application (permanent residents are not eligible); be in good health (grantees will be required to submit a satisfactory Medical Certificate of Health from a physician); and hold a B.A. degree or the equivalent before the start of the grant (applicants who have not earned a B.A. degree or the equivalent, but who have extensive professional study and/or experience in fields in which they wish to pursue a project, may be considered). In the creative and performing arts area, four years of professional study and/or experience meets the basic eligibility requirement.

Restrictions Due to scheduling constraints, Fulbright English Teaching Assistants (ETAs) are ineligible for this award. The following persons are ineligible: anyone who has already held a U.S. Department of State-funded Fulbright student grant of any type; anyone who has previously received a Department of Education-funded Doctoral Dissertation Research Abroad (Fulbright Hays grant); employees of the U.S. Department of State, and their immediate families, for a period ending one year following termination of such employment; employees of private and public agencies (excluding educational institutions) under contract to the U.S. Department of State to perform administrative or screening services on behalf of the U.S. Department of State's exchange program, for a period ending one year following the termination of their services for the U.S. Department of State provided such employees have been directly engaged in performing services related to the exchange programs; applicants holding a doctoral degree at the time of application; applicants seeking enrollment in a medical degree program abroad; or applicants currently residing in the countries of Australia, Belgium/Luxembourg, Canada, Chile, Finland, Hungary, Mexico, Netherlands, New Zealand, Sweden, or Switzerland.

Contact Jermaine Jones, Program Manager, (212) 984-5341; email: jjones@iie.org
Internet http://us.fulbrightonline.org/thinking_type.html#businessgrants
Sponsor Institute of International Education
809 United Nations Plaza
New York, NY 10017-3580

Fulbright Distinguished Chairs Program Grants **2042**

Awards in the Fulbright Distinguished Chairs Program are viewed as among the most prestigious appointments in the Fulbright Scholar Program. Candidates should be senior scholars and have a significant publication and teaching record. Applicants should submit hard copies of the Distinguished Chairs Application Form (one page), a letter of interest (about three pages), a curriculum vitae (maximum eight pages) and, if required, a sample syllabus (maximum four pages). Chairs are available in Australia, Austria, Brazil, Canada, Denmark, Finland, France, Germany, Hungary, Ireland, Israel, Italy, Netherlands, Poland, Portugal, Russia, and Sweden. Because an objective of the Fulbright Program is to provide an educational exchange experience for those not previously afforded such an opportunity, preference will usually be given to candidates who have not had substantial recent experience in the country to which they are applying.

Requirements Applicants must meet all of the following eligibility *Requirements* U.S. citizenship at the time of application (permanent resident status is not sufficient); possess a Ph.D. or equivalent professional terminal degree at the time of application (for professionals and artists outside academe, recognized professional standing and substantial professional accomplishments); have college or university teaching experience at the level and in the field of the proposed lecturing activity as specified in the award description (for Distinguished Chairs awards, candidates should be senior scholars with a significant publication and teaching record); have foreign language proficiency only if specified in the award description or required for the completion of the proposed project; be of sound physical and mental health; and disclose prior conviction or current indictment for commission of a felony.

Restrictions Previous Fulbright scholar grantees are eligible to apply only if five years will have elapsed between the ending date of one scholar award and the beginning date of the new scholar award. This rule does not apply if the previous grant was for less than two months. Employees, spouses or dependent children of the United States Department of State or public and private organizations under contract to the United States Department of State are ineligible to apply for a Fulbright grant until one year after the employee's termination.

Date(s) Application Is Due May 1.
Contact Maria Bettua, (202) 686-6245; email: mbettua@cies.iie.org; Tozer Hammond, (202) 686-6232; email: thammond@cies.iie.org
Internet http://www.cies.org/ab_dc/
Sponsor Institute of International Education, Council for International Exchange of Scholars
3007 Tilden Street, NW, Suite 5L
Washington, DC 20008-3009

Fulbright English Teaching Assistantships (ETAs) **2043**

The Fulbright program has offered opportunities for U.S. students to serve as English teachers and teaching assistants at schools, colleges and universities abroad for many years. Since an applicant may only apply to one country and one program, it is vital to select carefully, based on educational and career goals, academic background and preparation, language proficiency, and geographic interests. ETAs in Asia are placed primarily in elementary and secondary schools and knowledge of the host country language at the time of application is not required; however, ETAs in South America will be working with university and adult students and must have proficiency in the host country language. In most cases, ETAs: are placed in schools or universities outside of capital cities; are assigned various activities designed to improve their students' language abilities and knowledge of the United States; are fully integrated into the host community, increasing their own language skills and knowledge of the host country; may pursue individual study/research plans in addition to ETA responsibilities; and have some background or training in education and/or teaching English. Check the guidelines on line for the ever-changing list of host countries.

Requirements Applicants must: be U.S. citizens at the time of application (permanent residents are not eligible); be in good health (grantees will be required to submit a satisfactory Medical Certificate of Health from a physician); and have sufficient proficiency in the written and spoken language of the host country (where required) to communicate with the people and to carry out the proposed ETA.

Restrictions The following persons are ineligible: anyone who has already held a U.S. Department of State-funded Fulbright student grant of any type; anyone who has previously received a Department of Education-funded Doctoral Dissertation Research Abroad (Fulbright Hays grant); employees of the U.S. Department of State, and their immediate families, for a period ending one year following termination of such employment; employees of private and public agencies (excluding educational institutions) under contract to the U.S. Department of State to perform administrative or screening services on behalf of the U.S. Department of State's exchange program, for a period ending one year following the termination of their services for the U.S. Department of State provided such employees have been directly engaged in performing services related to the exchange programs; or applicants holding a doctoral degree at the time of application.

Amount Varies
Date(s) Application Is Due Oct 21.
Contact Walter Jackson, Program Manager, (212) 984-5327; email: wjackson@iie.org
Internet http://www.us.fulbrightonline.org/thinking_teaching.html
Sponsor Institute of International Education
809 United Nations Plaza
New York, NY 10017-5330

Fulbright European Union Scholar-in-Residence Program Grants **2044**

The primary objective of the European Union Scholar-in-Residence (EUSIR) program is to strengthen expertise in European Union affairs. Through an arrangement with the EU, grants will be available to bring European scholars specializing in EU affairs to U.S. campuses as resident scholars for one term of the academic year. The scholars will give guest lectures and conduct seminars as appropriate, consult with faculty and students on research, engage in collaborative study and provide outreach to neighboring institutions and the local community. The resident scholars are not expected to teach regular course offerings. Detailed program guidelines, proposal forms, and further information are available upon request; materials are available in May prior to deadline date.

Date(s) Application Is Due Oct 15.

Contact Karen Watts, Senior Program Officer, (202) 686-4004; fax: (202) 362-3442; email: kwatts@cies.iie.org
Internet http://www.cies.org/sir/eusir/
Sponsor Institute of International Education, Council for International Exchange of Scholars
3007 Tilden Street NW, Suite 5L
Washington, DC 20008-3009

Fulbright German Studies Seminar Program Grants **2045**
The program allows participation in a group seminar on current German society and culture. The program will begin in Berlin and include visits to other cities in Germany. The program will focus on the formation of policies in current issues at the core of modern society such as climate change, food technology, gene technology, stem cell research and the broad scope of education. The seminar will explore how Germany and its European neighbors view the role of science in their societies, examining the factors that result in differing approaches to these issues and the challenges of harmonizing different standards under a uniform EU-policy umbrella. With an eye to the global marketplace and worldwide competition in science, the seminar will further examine the multiple interests which structure relations between national governments, economic corporations, political and supranational bodies as well as research and development institutions. Scholars from U.S. universities, colleges, and community colleges who hold full-time teaching appointments and meet other academic requirements (Ph.D., Ph.D. candidacy or other equivalent degree or qualifications) are eligible. The seminar lasts two weeks, typically during the month of June.
Requirements Applicants must be US citizens with permanent residence in the United States at the time of application.
Date(s) Application Is Due Nov 1.
Contact Tara Campbell, Senior Program Officer, (202) 686-6240; email: tcampbell@cies.iie.org; Alisha Scott, (202) 686-6244; email: ascott@cies.iie.org
Internet http://www.cies.org/award_book/award2008/award/Ful8257.htm
Sponsor Institute of International Education, Council for International Exchange of Scholars
3007 Tilden Street, NW, Suite 5L
Washington, DC 20008-3009

Fulbright International Education Administrators (IEA) Seminars Program Grants **2046**
The IEA seminars are designed to introduce participants to the society, culture and higher education systems of these countries through campus visits, meetings with foreign colleagues and government officials, attendance at cultural events and briefings on education. Participants in the International Education Administrators Program gain a firsthand look into the host country's academic infrastructure and culture. They gain new perspective on the need to internationalize U.S. campuses and insight into how it can be done. The deadline for the German program is February 1, while the deadline for both Japan and Korea is November 1.
Requirements To be eligible, applicants must: be U.S. citizens; be international education professionals and senior university administrators (e.g., deans, provosts, vice presidents) with significant responsibility for international programs and activities; have an affiliation with an accredited college or university or nonprofit international exchange organization administering postsecondary student or faculty exchange; and have a minimum of three years of work experience in international education. Applicants for the Japan program must be affiliated with a four-year college or university, while Germany and Korea will consider applicants from both two- and four-year institutions.
Restrictions Employees, spouses or dependent children of the United States Department of State or public and private organizations under contract to the United States Department of State are ineligible to apply for a Fulbright grant until one year after the employee's termination. TEFL administrators are ineligible for these seminar programs, but they are encouraged to view a listing of other Fulbright opportunities.
Date(s) Application Is Due Feb 1; Nov 1.
Contact Tara Campbell, Senior Program Officer for Germany, (202) 686-6240; email: tcampbell@cies.iie.org; David B.J. Adams, Senior Program Officer for Japan and Korea, (202) 686-4021; email: dadams@cies.iie.org
Internet http://www.cies.org/IEA/
Sponsor Institute of International Education, Council for International Exchange of Scholars
3007 Tilden Street, NW, Suite 5L
Washington, DC 20008-3009

Fulbright mtvU Awards **2047**
Up to four awards will be available to pursue projects around an aspect of international contemporary or popular music as a cultural force for expression. Preference will be given to creative projects that are conveyed in a dynamic fashion and are accompanied by a feasible plan. In addition to presenting unique projects on music as a global force for mutual understanding, applicants must submit a documentation and outreach plan describing how they intend to share their activities with their peers during their Fulbright year abroad through mtvU print, broadcast and/or online mediums.
Requirements Applicants must: be U.S. citizens at the time of application (permanent residents are not eligible); be in good health (grantees will be required to submit a satisfactory Medical Certificate of Health from a physician); have sufficient proficiency in the written and spoken language of the host country (where required) to communicate with the people; and hold a B.A. degree or the equivalent before the start of the grant (applicants who have not earned a B.A. degree or the equivalent, but who have extensive professional study and/or experience in fields in which they wish to pursue a project, may be considered). In the creative and performing arts area, four years of professional study and/or experience meets the basic eligibility requirement. All candidates for the Europe and Eurasia region are required to obtain their own affiliations, generally established with an educational and/or research institution in the host country or countries. Candidates are responsible for securing their own research clearance as required by the host country.
Restrictions The following persons are ineligible: anyone who has already held a U.S. Department of State-funded Fulbright student grant of any type; anyone who has previously received a Department of Education-funded Doctoral Dissertation Research Abroad (Fulbright Hays grant); employees of the U.S. Department of State, and their immediate families, for a period ending one year following termination of such employment; employees of private and public agencies (excluding educational institutions) under contract to the U.S. Department of State to perform administrative or screening services on behalf of the U.S. Department of State's exchange program, for a period ending one year following the termination of their services for the U.S. Department of State provided such employees have been directly engaged in performing services related to the exchange programs; or applicants currently residing in the countries of Australia, Belgium/Luxembourg, Canada, Chile, Finland, Hungary, Mexico, Netherlands, New Zealand, Sweden, or Switzerland.
Date(s) Application Is Due Aug 1.
Contact Valerie Hymas, Program Manager, (212) 984-5326; email: vhymas@iie.org
Internet https://us.fulbrightonline.org/thinking_mtv.html
Sponsor Institute of International Education
809 United Nations Plaza
New York, NY 10017-5330

Fulbright New Century Scholars (NCS) Program Grants **2048**
The NCS Program brings 30 top academics and professionals from around the world together each year to collaborate on an issue of global importance. Of the thirty, approximately one-third will be U.S. citizens while the remaining two thirds will be visiting scholars from countries with an operational Fulbright Scholar Program. NCS will provide a platform for scholars from the US and around the world to engage in debate and dialogue based on multidisciplinary research and to develop new global models for understanding the social context within which nations and communities shape their responses to the many challenges of the 21st century. This particular aspect of the New Century Scholars program is a unique feature that distinguishes it from the core Fulbright Scholar Program.
Requirements Applicants must be conducting current research relevant to the program's theme and objectives, be open to exploring and incorporating comparative, interdisciplinary approaches in their investigations, and interested in developing collaborative activities with other NCS Scholars. U.S. applicants must have U.S. citizenship and be residing permanently in the United States. For academic applicants, a Ph.D. or equivalent terminal degree in a relevant field is required. For applicants in the professional fields, the appropriate terminal degree in a relevant field is required. Non-U.S. applicants must be citizens or permanent residents of and residing in the country from which they are applying at the time of application. All applicants must have fluency in English.
Restrictions Non-U.S. applicants holding permanent residency green cards, whether or not they reside in the U.S., are not eligible.
Date(s) Application Is Due June 16.
Contact Stacey Bustillos, Program Officer, (202) 686-6252; email: sbustillos@cies.iie.org; Hajra Zahid, Senior Program Associate, (202) 686-6250; email: hzahid@cies.iie.org
Internet http://www.cies.org/NCS/
Sponsor Institute of International Education, Council for International Exchange of Scholars
3007 Tilden Street, NW, Suite 5L
Washington, DC 20008-3009

Fulbright Occasional Lecturer Program (OLP) Grants **2049**
The Council for International Exchange of Scholars provides travel awards through the Occasional Lecturer Program (OLP), that enable Fulbright Visiting Scholars to accept guest lecturing invitations at colleges and universities throughout the United States. OLP Travel Awards are granted at three different levels ranging from $250 to $750, which CIES determines based on distances involved.
Amount $250; $500; $750
Contact Karen Watts, Senior Program Officer, (202) 686-4004; fax: (202) 362-3442; email: kwatts@cies.iie.org
Internet http://www.cies.org/sir/olp/
Sponsor Institute of International Education, Council for International Exchange of Scholars
3007 Tilden Street NW, Suite 5L
Washington, DC 20008-3009

Fulbright Scholar-in-Residence (SIR) Program Grants **2050**
Grants strengthen the institutional commitment of US higher education to international education and scholarship by enabling colleges and universities to invite visiting scholars from abroad in the humanities and social sciences or in professional specializations with

strong international focus. A Fulbright Scholar in Residence may teach regular courses from a foreign area perspective, serve as a resource person in interdisciplinary courses, assist in developing new courses, or participate in special seminars. Host institutions are expected to share the scholar's expertise with a wide range of departments and with neighboring institutions, involve him/her in community activities and professional organizations, and provide opportunities for the visitor to pursue personal research interests. Detailed program guidelines, proposal forms, and further information are available upon request; materials are available in May prior to deadline date.
Date(s) Application Is Due Oct 15.
Contact Karen Watts, Senior Program Officer, (202) 686-4004; fax: (202) 362-3442; email: kwatts@cies.iie.org
Internet http://www.cies.org/sir/
Sponsor Institute of International Education, Council for International Exchange of Scholars
3007 Tilden Street NW, Suite 5L
Washington, DC 20008-3009

Fulbright Senior Specialists Program Grants **2051**
The Program is designed to provide short-term academic opportunities (two to six weeks) for U.S. faculty and professionals. Shorter grant lengths give specialists greater flexibility to pursue a grant that works best with their current academic or professional commitments. Applications for the Program are accepted on a rolling basis, and peer review of applications is conducted eight times per year. Program goals include: to increase the participation of leading U.S. scholars and professionals in Fulbright academic exchanges; to encourage new activities that go beyond the traditional Fulbright activities of lecturing and research; and to promote increased connections between U.S. and non-U.S. post-secondary academic institutions.
Requirements Applicants must: be U.S. citizen at the time of application (permanent resident status is not sufficient; if a naturalized citizen, applicant must provide actual date of naturalization); possess a Ph.D. or equivalent professional/terminal degree at the time of application; have a minimum of five years of post-doctoral teaching or professional experience in the field in which you are applying (for professionals and artists outside academe, recognized professional standing and substantial professional accomplishments plus a minimum of five years of professional experience in the field in which you are applying); disclose prior conviction or current indictment for commission of a felony; and be residing in the United States at the time they are approved for a grant and intend to return to their U.S. institution after the grant's completion.
Restrictions Employees, spouses or dependent children of the United States Department of State or public and private organizations under contract to the United States Department of State exchange programs are ineligible to apply for a Fulbright grant until one year after the employee's termination.
Date(s) Application Is Due Feb 1; Mar 26; May 9; Jun 20; Aug 1; Sep 12; Oct 22; Dec 19.
Contact Ryan Hathaway, Senior Program Coordinator, (202) 686-4026; email: rhathaway@cies.iie.org
Internet http://www.cies.org/specialists/#program
Sponsor Institute of International Education, Council for International Exchange of Scholars
3007 Tilden Street, NW, Suite 5L
Washington, DC 20008-3009

Fulbright Traditional Scholar Program in Europe and Eurasia **2052**
The traditional Fulbright Scholar Program sends 800 U.S. faculty and professionals abroad each year. Grantees lecture and conduct research in a wide variety of academic and professional fields. Distribution of awards to countries in the region will vary annually according to the caliber of the applicants. Grants are available to: Albania, Andorra, Armenia, Austria, Azerbaijan, Belarus, Belgium, Bosnia and Herzegovina, Bulgaria, Croatia, Cyprus, Czech Republic, Denmark, Estonia, European Union, Finland, France, Georgia, Germany, Greece, Hungary, Iceland, Ireland, Italy, Latvia, Lithuania, Luxembourg, Macedonia, Moldova, Netherlands, Norway, Poland, Portugal, Romania, Russia, Slovakia (Slovak Republic), Slovenia, Spain, Sweden, Switzerland, Turkey, Ukraine, and United Kingdom. Only countries Considered to be in the Eastern Europe or Eurasia regions may be part of a multi-country application (2 to 3 countries). Multi-country proposals are not permitted for Western Europe. Language requirements vary by country, and prior knowledge of the local language may not be required, particularly where language is not commonly taught in the U.S.
Requirements Applicants must: be U.S. citizens at the time of application (permanent residents are not eligible); be in good health (grantees will be required to submit a satisfactory Medical Certificate of Health from a physician); have sufficient proficiency in the written and spoken language of the host country (where required) to communicate with the people and to carry out the proposed study; and hold a B.A. degree or the equivalent before the start of the grant (applicants who have not earned a B.A. degree or the equivalent, but who have extensive professional study and/or experience in fields in which they wish to pursue a project, may be considered). In the creative and performing arts area, four years of professional study and/or experience meets the basic eligibility requirement. All candidates for the Europe and Eurasia region are required to obtain their own affiliations, generally established with an educational and/or research institution in the host country or countries. Candidates are responsible for securing their own research clearance as required by the host country.
Restrictions The following persons are ineligible: anyone who has already held a U.S. Department of State-funded Fulbright student grant of any type; anyone who has previously received a Department of Education-funded Doctoral Dissertation Research Abroad (Fulbright Hays grant); employees of the U.S. Department of State, and their immediate families, for a period ending one year following termination of such employment; employees of private and public agencies (excluding educational institutions) under contract to the U.S. Department of State to perform administrative or screening services on behalf of the U.S. Department of State's exchange program, for a period ending one year following the termination of their services for the U.S. Department of State provided such employees have been directly engaged in performing services related to the exchange programs; applicants holding a doctoral degree at the time of application; applicants seeking enrollment in a medical degree program abroad; or applicants currently residing in the countries of Australia, Belgium/Luxembourg, Canada, Chile, Finland, Hungary, Mexico, Netherlands, New Zealand, Sweden, or Switzerland.
Date(s) Application Is Due Aug 1.
Contact Valerie Hymas, Program Manager, (212) 984-5326; email: vhymas@iie.org
Internet http://us.fulbrightonline.org/program_regions_countries.php?id=3
Sponsor Institute of International Education
809 United Nations Plaza
New York, NY 10017-5330

Fulbright Traditional Scholar Program in Sub-Saharan Africa **2053**
The traditional Fulbright Scholar Program sends 800 U.S. faculty and professionals abroad each year. Grantees lecture and conduct research in a wide variety of academic and professional fields. Selection for countries in sub-Saharan Africa, with the exception of South Africa, will be made based on the quality of the applications, rather than per-country quotas. Distribution of awards to countries in the region will vary annually according to the caliber of the applicants. Grants are available to: Benin, Botswana, Burkina Faso, Cameroon, Chad, Eritrea, Ethiopia, Ghana, Guinea, Ivory Coast, Kenya, Madagascar, Malawi, Mali, Mauritius, Mozambique, Namibia, Niger, Nigeria, Senegal, South Africa, Swaziland, Tanzania, Togo, Uganda, Zambia, and Zimbabwe. All countries within the sub-Saharan Africa Region, with the exception of South Africa, may be part of a multi-country application (2 to 3 countries). For unlisted countries, applications may be considered on a case-by-case basis, but for dissertation research only.
Requirements Applicants must: be U.S. citizens at the time of application (permanent residents are not eligible); be in good health (grantees will be required to submit a satisfactory Medical Certificate of Health from a physician); have sufficient proficiency in the written and spoken language of the host country to communicate with the people and to carry out the proposed study; and hold a B.A. degree or the equivalent before the start of the grant (applicants who have not earned a B.A. degree or the equivalent, but who have extensive professional study and/or experience in fields in which they wish to pursue a project, may be considered). In the creative and performing arts area, four years of professional study and/or experience meets the basic eligibility requirement. All candidates for Africa are required to obtain their own affiliations, generally established with an educational and/or research institution in the host country or countries.
Restrictions Grants are not available to: Burundi, Central African Republic, Guinea-Bissau, Liberia, Somalia, or Sudan. The following persons are ineligible: anyone who has already held a U.S. Department of State-funded Fulbright student grant of any type; anyone who has previously received a Department of Education-funded Doctoral Dissertation Research Abroad (Fulbright Hays grant); employees of the U.S. Department of State, and their immediate families, for a period ending one year following termination of such employment; employees of private and public agencies (excluding educational institutions) under contract to the U.S. Department of State to perform administrative or screening services on behalf of the U.S. Department of State's exchange program, for a period ending one year following the termination of their services for the U.S. Department of State provided such employees have been directly engaged in performing services related to the exchange programs; applicants holding a doctoral degree at the time of application; applicants seeking enrollment in a medical degree program abroad; or applicants currently residing in the countries of Australia, Belgium/Luxembourg, Canada, Chile, Finland, Hungary, Mexico, Netherlands, New Zealand, Sweden, or Switzerland.
Date(s) Application Is Due Aug 1.
Contact Jermaine Jones, Program Manager, (212) 984-5341; email: jjones@iie.org
Internet http://us.fulbrightonline.org/program_regions_countries.php?id=1
Sponsor Institute of International Education
809 United Nations Plaza
New York, NY 10017-3580

Fulbright Traditional Scholar Program in the East Asia Pacific Region **2054**
The traditional Fulbright Scholar Program sends 800 U.S. faculty and professionals abroad each year. Grantees lecture and conduct research in a wide variety of academic and professional fields. Distribution of awards to countries in the region will vary annually according to the caliber of the applicants. Grants are available to: Australia, Cambodia, China, Hong Kong, Indonesia, Japan, Korea, Laos, Macau, Malaysia, Mongolia, New Zealand, Philippines, Singapore, Taiwan, Thailand, and Vietnam. All countries within the East Asia/Pacific region, with the exception of China, may be part of a multi-country application (2 to 3 countries). For unlisted countries, applications may be considered on a case-by-case basis, but for dissertation research only. Language requirements vary by

country, and prior knowledge of the local language may not be required, particularly where language is not commonly taught in the U.S.
Requirements Applicants must: be U.S. citizens at the time of application (permanent residents are not eligible); be in good health (grantees will be required to submit a satisfactory Medical Certificate of Health from a physician); have sufficient proficiency in the written and spoken language of the host country to communicate with the people and to carry out the proposed study; and hold a B.A. degree or the equivalent before the start of the grant (applicants who have not earned a B.A. degree or the equivalent, but who have extensive professional study and/or experience in fields in which they wish to pursue a project, may be considered). In the creative and performing arts area, four years of professional study and/or experience meets the basic eligibility requirement. All candidates for the East Asia/Pacific region are required to obtain their own affiliations, generally established with an educational and/or research institution in the host country or countries. Candidates are responsible for securing their own research clearance as required by the host country.
Restrictions Grants are not available to: Brunei, the Cook Islands, East Timor, Fiji, Myanmar, the Pacific Island Nations, Papua New Guinea, or Western Samoa. The following persons are ineligible: anyone who has already held a U.S. Department of State-funded Fulbright student grant of any type; anyone who has previously received a Department of Education-funded Doctoral Dissertation Research Abroad (Fulbright Hays grant); employees of the U.S. Department of State, and their immediate families, for a period ending one year following termination of such employment; employees of private and public agencies (excluding educational institutions) under contract to the U.S. Department of State to perform administrative or screening services on behalf of the U.S. Department of State's exchange program, for a period ending one year following the termination of their services for the U.S. Department of State provided such employees have been directly engaged in performing services related to the exchange programs; applicants holding a doctoral degree at the time of application; applicants seeking enrollment in a medical degree program abroad; or applicants currently residing in the countries of Australia, Belgium/Luxembourg, Canada, Chile, Finland, Hungary, Mexico, Netherlands, New Zealand, Sweden, or Switzerland.
Date(s) Application Is Due Aug 1.
Contact Jonathan Akeley, Program Manager, (212) 984-5487; email: jakeley@iie.org
Internet http://us.fulbrightonline.org/program_regions_countries.php?id=2
Sponsor Institute of International Education
809 United Nations Plaza
New York, NY 10017-3580

Fulbright Traditional Scholar Program in the Near East and North Africa 2055
The traditional Fulbright Scholar Program sends 800 U.S. faculty and professionals abroad each year. Grantees lecture and conduct research in a wide variety of academic and professional fields. Selection for countries in the Near East and North Africa region will be made based on the quality of the applications, rather than per-country quotas. Distribution of awards to countries in the region will vary annually according to the caliber of the applicants. Grants are available to: Bahrain, Egypt, India, Jordan, Kuwait, Morocco, Oman, Qatar, Syria, Tunisia, United Arab Emirates, and Yemen. Multi-country applications (2 to 3 countries) are available, except in Egypt, India, Jordan, and Morocco. For unlisted countries, applications may be considered on a case-by-case basis.
Requirements Applicants must: be U.S. citizens at the time of application (permanent residents are not eligible); be in good health (grantees will be required to submit a satisfactory Medical Certificate of Health from a physician); have sufficient proficiency in the written and spoken language of the host country to communicate with the people and to carry out the proposed study; and hold a B.A. degree or the equivalent before the start of the grant (applicants who have not earned a B.A. degree or the equivalent, but who have extensive professional study and/or experience in fields in which they wish to pursue a project, may be considered). In the creative and performing arts area, four years of professional study and/or experience meets the basic eligibility requirement. Candidates are responsible for securing research clearance, as required. In countries with Fulbright Commissions, assistance may be provided.
Restrictions Grants are not available to: Algeria, Iran, Iraq, Lebanon, Saudi Arabia, the West Bank, or Gaza. The following persons are ineligible: anyone who has already held a U.S. Department of State-funded Fulbright student grant of any type; anyone who has previously received a Department of Education-funded Doctoral Dissertation Research Abroad (Fulbright Hays grant); employees of the U.S. Department of State, and their immediate families, for a period ending one year following termination of such employment; employees of private and public agencies (excluding educational institutions) under contract to the U.S. Department of State to perform administrative or screening services on behalf of the U.S. Department of State's exchange program, for a period ending one year following the termination of their services for the U.S. Department of State provided such employees have been directly engaged in performing services related to the exchange programs; applicants holding a doctoral degree at the time of application; applicants seeking enrollment in a medical degree program abroad; or applicants currently residing in Australia, Belgium/Luxembourg, Canada, Chile, Finland, Hungary, Mexico, Netherlands, New Zealand, Sweden, or Switzerland.
Date(s) Application Is Due Aug 1.
Contact Jermaine Jones, Program Manager, (212) 984-5341; email: jjones@iie.org
Internet http://us.fulbrightonline.org/program_regions_countries.php?id=4
Sponsor Institute of International Education
809 United Nations Plaza
New York, NY 10017-3580

Fulbright Traditional Scholar Program in the South and Central Asia 2056
The traditional Fulbright Scholar Program sends 800 U.S. faculty and professionals abroad each year. Grantees lecture and conduct research in a wide variety of academic and professional fields. Selection for countries in the South and Central Asia region will be made based on the quality of the applications, rather than per-country quotas. Distribution of awards to countries in the region will vary annually according to the caliber of the applicants. Grants are available to: Bangladesh, India, Kazakhstan, Kyrgyz Republic, Nepal, Sri Lanka, Tajikistan, and Uzbekistan. Multi-country applications (2 to 3 countries) are not available. Language requirements vary by country. Applicants to India who are recommended for final review will need to submit research visa applications in January or February.
Requirements Applicants must: be U.S. citizens at the time of application (permanent residents are not eligible); be in good health (grantees will be required to submit a satisfactory Medical Certificate of Health from a physician); have sufficient proficiency in the written and spoken language of the host country to communicate with the people and to carry out the proposed study; and hold a B.A. degree or the equivalent before the start of the grant (applicants who have not earned a B.A. degree or the equivalent, but who have extensive professional study and/or experience in fields in which they wish to pursue a project, may be considered). In the creative and performing arts area, four years of professional study and/or experience meets the basic eligibility requirement. Candidates are responsible for securing research clearance, as required. In countries with Fulbright Commissions, assistance may be provided.
Restrictions Grants are not available to: Afghanistan, Bhutan, Pakistan, Republic of Maldives, or Turkmenistan. The following persons are ineligible: anyone who has already held a U.S. Department of State-funded Fulbright student grant of any type; anyone who has previously received a Department of Education-funded Doctoral Dissertation Research Abroad (Fulbright Hays grant); employees of the U.S. Department of State, and their immediate families, for a period ending one year following termination of such employment; employees of private and public agencies (excluding educational institutions) under contract to the U.S. Department of State to perform administrative or screening services on behalf of the U.S. Department of State's exchange program, for a period ending one year following the termination of their services for the U.S. Department of State provided such employees have been directly engaged in performing services related to the exchange programs; applicants holding a doctoral degree at the time of application; applicants seeking enrollment in a medical degree program abroad; or applicants currently residing in Australia, Belgium/Luxembourg, Canada, Chile, Finland, Hungary, Mexico, Netherlands, New Zealand, Sweden, or Switzerland.
Date(s) Application Is Due Aug 1.
Contact Jonathan Akeley, South Asia Program Manager, (212) 984-5487; email: jakeley@iie.org; Valerie Hymas, Central Asia Program Manager, (212) 984-5326; email: vhymas@iie.org
Internet http://www.iie.org/Template.cfm?Section=Students&template=/ContentManagement/ContentDisplay.cfm&ContentID=3589
Sponsor Institute of International Education
809 United Nations Plaza
New York, NY 10017-3580

Fulbright Traditional Scholar Program in the Western Hemisphere 2057
The traditional Fulbright Scholar Program sends 800 U.S. faculty and professionals abroad each year. Grantees lecture and conduct research in a wide variety of academic and professional fields. Selection for countries in Central America and the Caribbean will be made based on the quality of the applications, rather than per-country quotas. Distribution of awards to countries in the region will vary annually according to the caliber of the applicants. Grants are available to: Argentina, Barbados and the Eastern Caribbean, Bolivia, Brazil, Canada, Chile, Colombia, Costa Rica, Dominican Republic, Ecuador, El Salvador, Guatemala, Honduras, Jamaica, Mexico, Nicaragua, Panama, Paraguay, Peru, Trinidad and Tobago, Uruguay, and Venezuela. English Teaching Assistantship are available in Argentina, Brazil, Chile, Uruguay and Venezuela. Language proficiency may be preferred or required. Applicants for English Teaching Assistantships can apply to only one country. Multi-country applications (2 to 3 countries) are available in all other disciplines throughout the Western Hemisphere. For unlisted countries, applications may be considered on a case-by-case basis, but for dissertation research only.
Requirements Applicants must: be U.S. citizens at the time of application (permanent residents are not eligible); be in good health (grantees will be required to submit a satisfactory Medical Certificate of Health from a physician); have sufficient proficiency in the written and spoken language of the host country to communicate with the people and to carry out the proposed study; and hold a B.A. degree or the equivalent before the start of the grant (applicants who have not earned a B.A. degree or the equivalent, but who have extensive professional study and/or experience in fields in which they wish to pursue a project, may be considered). In the creative and performing arts area, four years of professional study and/or experience meets the basic eligibility requirement. Candidates are responsible for securing research clearance, as required. In countries with Fulbright Commissions, assistance may be provided.
Restrictions Grants are not available to: Bahamas, Belize, Cuba, French Guiana, Guyana, Haiti, Martinique, or Suriname. The following persons are ineligible: anyone who has already held a U.S. Department of State-funded Fulbright student grant of any type; anyone who has previously received a Department of Education-funded Doctoral Dissertation Research Abroad (Fulbright Hays grant); employees of the U.S. Department of State, and their immediate families, for a period ending one year following termination of such employment; employees of private and public agencies (excluding educational

institutions) under contract to the U.S. Department of State to perform administrative or screening services on behalf of the U.S. Department of State's exchange program, for a period ending one year following the termination of their services for the U.S. Department of State provided such employees have been directly engaged in performing services related to the exchange programs; applicants holding a doctoral degree at the time of application; applicants seeking enrollment in a medical degree program abroad; or applicants currently residing in the countries of Australia, Belgium/Luxembourg, Canada, Chile, Finland, Hungary, Mexico, Netherlands, New Zealand, Sweden, or Switzerland.
Date(s) Application Is Due Aug 1.
Contact Jody Dudderar, Program Manager in South America, Mexico and Canada, (212) 984-5565; fax: (212) 984-5325; email: jdudderar@iie.org; Joseph Livingston, Program Manager in Central America and the Caribbean, (212) 984-5366; email: jlivingston@iie.org
Internet http://us.fulbrightonline.org/program_regions_countries.php?id=5
Sponsor Institute of International Education
809 United Nations Plaza
New York, NY 10017-3580

Fulbright Travel Grants **2058**
Travel grants are available only to Germany, Hungary, or Italy. They are available to supplement an award from a non-IIE source that does not provide funds for travel or to supplement a student's own funds for study. Travel grants provide round-trip transportation to the country where the student will pursue studies for an academic year, supplemental health and accident insurance, and the cost of all orientation courses abroad, if applicable.
Requirements Applicants must be US citizens with at least the bachelor's degree and capable of meeting the eligibility criteria for Fulbright grants.
Contact Valerie Hymas, Program Manager, (212) 984-5326; email: vhymas@iie.org
Internet http://us.fulbrightonline.org/thinking_type.html#travelgrants
Sponsor Institute of International Education
809 United Nations Plaza
New York, NY 10017-3580

Fulbright Visiting Specialists Program: Direct Access to the Muslim World **2059**
The program aims to promote Americans' understanding of Islamic civilization and the history, politics, and culture of today's Muslim world. The program further aims to strengthen resources for enriching understanding of relevant global issues. The program offers a unique opportunity for U.S. colleges and universities to host specialists from countries with significant Muslim populations for short-term programs of intensive lecturing, public outreach, and consultation. The Fulbright Visiting Specialists will lecture on and off campus in a variety of humanities and social science disciplines, including the arts, with a focus on Islamic society or civilization. The Program encourages inter-religious dialog through on-campus and off-campus activities. The Visiting Specialists will also work together with the U.S. host institutions on projects with lasting benefits such as curriculum consultation, faculty development, and institutional linkage-building.
Requirements Institutions with few or no programs/courses related to Islam or the Muslim world are encouraged to apply. Institutions that have well-established Islam-related or area studies programs should clearly indicate that their proposed program for the Fulbright Visiting Specialists Program is in a field/subject that is not currently supported at the institution. Community colleges and minority-serving institutions, such as Historically Black Colleges and Universities, Hispanic Serving Institutions, and Tribal Colleges and Universities, are encouraged to apply and will receive preference for an award. At the time of program participation, the Fulbright Visiting Specialist should be a resident of his/her home country.
Restrictions The program does not support the teaching of languages or research projects. Institutions that have already hosted a Fulbright Visiting Specialist are no longer eligible. While more than one application may be submitted by the same institution, only one award to the same institution will be offered. Persons holding U.S. citizenship or permanent residency in the U.S. are not eligible.
Date(s) Application Is Due May 1.
Contact Mamiko Hada, (202) 686-7873; fax: (202) 362-3442; email: vstngspec@cies.iie.org
Internet http://www.cies.org/Visiting_Specialists/
Sponsor Institute of International Education, Council for International Exchange of Scholars
3007 Tilden Street NW, Suite 5L
Washington, DC 20008-3009

Fulbright-Hays Seminars Abroad Bilateral Projects Grants **2060**
The program provides short-term study and travel seminars abroad for U.S. educators in the social sciences and humanities for the purpose of improving their understanding and knowledge of the peoples and cultures of other countries. Support is generally made available through inter-agency agreements. There are approximately seven to ten seminars with fourteen to sixteen participants in each seminar annually. Seminars are four to six weeks in duration. All seminars are held in countries outside of Western Europe. Terms of the award include a round-trip economy airfare, room and board, tuition and fees, and program-related travel within the host country.
Requirements Applicants must: be a citizen of the US or a permanent resident; hold at least a bachelor's degree from an accredited college or university; have at least three years of full-time experience by the time of departure for the seminar; be currently employed full-time in a US school system, institution of higher education, local education agency (LEA), state education agency (SEA), library, or museum; meet the general language requirement; and be physically and psychologically able to participate in all phases of the seminar.
Contact Gail Holdren, International Education Graduate Programs Service, (202) 502-7691; fax: (202) 502-7859; email: gale.holdren@ed.gov
Internet http://www.ed.gov/programs/iegpssap/index.html
Sponsor U.S. Department of Education
1990 K Street N.W., 6th Floor
Washington, DC 20006-8521

Fund for French-American Academic Partnerships **2061**
The program enables French and American researchers, professors, and administrators from all academic disciplines to enter long-term agreements that jointly develop new curricula to be integrated into the programs of their respective graduate schools. In addition to fostering the creation of innovative joint curricula, the fund seeks to give French and American graduate students the opportunity to explore cross-cultural, interdisciplinary approaches in their courses and/or research, thereby training globally minded professionals. The program's long-term goal is to strengthen ties between France and the United States through these structured partnerships. Partnership grants are awarded each year. Guidelines are available online.
Requirements Only nonprofit institutions may submit applications. US institutions must demonstrate 501(c)3; French organizations must provide proof of equivalent status for eligibility. Projects must be submitted and co-signed jointly by one or several American universities with a matching commitment from one or several French institutions of higher learning, or by one or several French institutions with a matching commitment from one or several American matching institutions.
Restrictions Grants are not allocated to individuals.
Date(s) Application Is Due Feb 25.
Contact Christian Tual, (202) 944 6414; fax: (202) 944 6268; email: Christian.TUAL@diplomatie.gouv.fr
Internet http://www.facecouncil.org/word/UniversityFund.doc
Sponsor French Embassy, Cultural Services
4101 Reservoir Rd
Washington, DC 20007

Fund for Investigative Journalism Grants **2062**
The fund makes grants to reporters--often unknown and financially struggling--to probe abuses of authority or the malfunctioning of institutions and systems that harm the public. Their reports are published in newspapers, magazines, and books or are broadcast. Applications are accepted at any time.
Requirements To apply, send a letter to the executive director describing the subject of the proposed investigation, its significance, the proof in hand, further evidence needed, and how the project will be completed. The letter should include an itemized budget, resume, and samples of the applicant's published work. A statement of intent from an editor or producer or a contract from a book publisher is also required to ensure that the report will be published if the finished product meets expectations. Grants from the fund ordinarily cover expenses only. The board meets several times a year to review proposals.
Amount $500-$10,000 average
Date(s) Application Is Due Feb 1; Jun 1; Oct 1.
Contact John Hyde, Executive Director, (202) 362-0260; fax: (301) 576-0804; email: johnchyde@yahoo.com
Internet http://www.fij.org/grants
Sponsor Fund for Investigative Journalism
P.O. Box 60184
Washington, DC 20039-0184

Fund for New Jersey Grants **2063**
Grants support nonprofit organizations in New Jersey or organizations that benefit the state, with particular attention given to projects seeking to affect public policy. Although a few grants are provided for local activities, direct services, and general operating support, such proposals are considered usually at the fund's invitation. Grant applicants are asked to submit a single-page proposal cover sheet containing the following information: organization and contact person, summary of request, amount requested, and problem or need addressed by proposed activity. All proposals must be accompanied by a copy of the IRS tax-exemption letter, names and affiliations of the board of directors, and a budget. The board normally meets in March, June, September, and December to consider proposals.
Requirements 501(c)3 organizations are eligible. Proposals are not accepted via email.
Restrictions The fund does not accept proposals for support of individuals nor for capital projects such as acquisition, renovation, or equipment. The fund is unable to support day care centers, drug treatment programs, arts programs, health care delivery, or scholarships.
Amount $3.3 million total
Contact Mark Murphy, Executive Director, (732) 220-8656; fax: (732) 220-8654; email: info@fundfornj.org
Internet http://www.fundfornj.org/app_guide.html

Sponsor Fund for New Jersey
94 Church St, Ste 303
New Brunswick, NJ 08901

Fund for Santa Barbara Grants **2064**
The fund gives preference to projects working to address the root causes of social, economic, and environmental problems. Types of support include seed grants to new grassroots projects, general support, or project grants to small organizations, and grants to larger, more established organizations only for specific targeted purposes. Affirmative action considerations are among the criteria used in all funding decisions.
Requirements Applications are invited from organizations that are working against discrimination based on race, sex/gender, age, religion, economic status, sexual orientation, physical/mental ability, ethnicity, language, or immigration status; struggling for the rights of workers; promoting self-determination in low-income and disenfranchised communities; promoting international peace and organizing locally for a just foreign policy; working on improving the environment, especially organizing a constituency usually without access or input to environmental concerns; and operating in a democratic manner, responsive to and directed by the constituency being served.
Restrictions Grants do not support projects involved in electoral campaigns on behalf of candidates or parties; private (vs. public) interests; direct labor organizing; projects located outside of Santa Barbara County; projects providing direct services without a social change component; or direct support to individuals, capital ventures, or building improvements.
Amount $10,000 maximum; $4000 average
Date(s) Application Is Due Mar 12; Sep 9.
Contact Fund Administrator, (805) 962-9164; fax: (805) 965-0217; email: email@fundforsantabarbara.org
Internet http://www.fundforsantabarbara.org/apply/apply.htm
Sponsor Fund for Santa Barbara
924 Anacapa St, Ste 4H
Santa Barbara, CA 93101-2192

Fund for Scientific Research--Flanders Grants **2065**
The foundation awards pre- and postdoctoral fellowships and grants for research in Flemish universities and research institutions in all fields of science, including medicine, technology, environmental studies, social science, law, and the humanities. National and international research is supported.
Contact Secretary General, 32 (2) 512-91-10; fax: 32 (2) 512-58-90; email: post@fwo.be
Internet http://sun.fwo.be/page1en.php?lang=en
Sponsor Fund for Scientific Research--Flanders
Egmontstraat 5
Brussels 1000 Belgium

Fund for the Advancement of the Discipline **2066**
The American Sociological Association invites submissions for the Fund for the Advancement of the Discipline (FAD) awards. Supported by the American Sociological Association through a matching grant from the National Science Foundation, the goal of this award is to nurture the development of scientific knowledge by funding small, ground breaking research initiatives and other important scientific research activities. FAD awards provide scholars with venture capital for innovative research that has the potential for challenging the discipline, stimulating new lines of research, and creating new networks of scientific collaboration. The award is intended to provide opportunities for substantive and methodological breakthroughs, broaden the dissemination of scientific knowledge, and provide leverage for acquisition of additional research funds.
Requirements Proposals are reviewed for scientific merit and the importance of the proposed research project. Within this context, specific evaluation criteria include the following elements: innovativeness and promise of the research idea; originality and significance of research goals; the potential of the study as a building block in the development of future research; appropriateness and significance of the research hypothesis; feasibility and adequacy of project design; plans for analysis and evaluation of data; plans for dissemination of results; appropriateness of requested budget. The awards are limited to individuals with PhD degrees or the equivalent. Preference is given to applicants who have not previously received a FAD award.
Amount $7000 maximum
Date(s) Application Is Due Jun 15; Dec 15.
Contact Roberta Spalter-Roth, FAD Awards, (202) 383-9005 ext. 317; email: spalter-roth@asanet.org
Internet http://asanet.org/page.ww?section=Funding&name=Fund+for+the+Advancement+of+the+Discipline
Sponsor American Sociological Association
1307 New York Ave NW, Ste 700
Washington, DC 20005-4107

Furthermore Grants in Publishing **2067**
The program is concerned with nonfiction book publishing about the city; natural and historic resources; art, architecture, and design; cultural history; and civil liberties and other public issues of the day. Grants apply to writing, research, editing, design, indexing, photography, illustration, and printing and binding. Work is sought that appeals to an informed general audience; gives evidence of high standards in editing, design, and production; promises a reasonable shelf life; might not otherwise achieve top quality or even come into being; and represents a contribution without which we would be the poorer. Book proposals to which a university press or trade publisher is already committed and for which there is a feasible distribution plan are usually preferred. In geographical reach, the program is drawn, but in no way limited, to New York City and to New York State and its Hudson Valley. Guidelines and application are available online.
Requirements 501(c)3 tax-exempt organizations are eligible. Trade publishers and public agencies may apply for Furthermore grants in partnership with an eligible nonprofit project sponsor.
Amount $500-$15,000
Date(s) Application Is Due Mar 15; Sep 15.
Contact Grants Administrator, (518) 828-8900; fax: (518) 828-8901; email: info@furthermore.org
Internet http://www.furthermore.org
Sponsor J.M. Kaplan Fund
P.O. Box 667
Hudson, NY 12534

Fyssen Foundation Postdoctoral Study Grants **2068**
The foundation awards postdoctoral research grants for research on cognitive mechanisms, including thought and reasoning, that underlie animal and human behavior; their biological and cultural bases; and phylogenetic and ontogenetic development. Research should be in ethology and psychology, neurobiology, anthropology/ethnology, and human paleontology. Grants support French scientists for research abroad and foreign researchers conducting research in France. Annual deadline dates may vary; contact program staff for exact dates.
Date(s) Application Is Due Mar 31.
Contact Postdoctoral Study Grants, 331 42975316; fax: 331 42601795; email: secretariat@fondation-fyssen.org
Internet http://www.fondation-fyssen.org
Sponsor Fyssen Foundation
194 rue de Rivoli
Paris 75001 France

G. Harold and Leila Y. Mathers Charitable Foundation Grants **2069**
The foundation awards grants to support research in the basic life sciences. Requests for general operating support also will be considered. There are no application forms or deadlines. The board meets two or three times each year.
Requirements US research organizations are eligible.
Amount $10,000-$200,000 average per year
Contact James Handelman, Executive Director, (914) 242-0465; email: bcheikin@mathersfoundation.org
Internet http://www.mathersfoundation.org
Sponsor G. Harold and Leila Y. Mathers Charitable Foundation
118 N Bedford Rd, Ste 203
Mount Kisco, NY 10549-2555

G. Unger Vetlesen Foundation Grants **2070**
The foundation's mission is to aid and contribute to religious, charitable, scientific, literary, and educational purposes throughout the world. Grants have been concentrated in the fields of oceanography, climate studies, earth sciences, cultural programs emphasizing Norwegian-American relations, environmental programs, libraries, international affairs, and public policy. A letter of inquiry, 3 pages or less, should be submitted at any time during the year. Proposals are to be submitted only upon invitation. Unsolicited proposals will not be reviewed.
Requirements 501(c)3 nonprofit organizations are eligible.
Restrictions The Foundation does not make grants to individuals.
Date(s) Application Is Due Apr 30; Oct 31.
Contact George Rowe Jr, President, (212) 586-0700; fax: (212) 245-1863; email: info@monellvetlesen.org
Internet http://www.monellvetlesen.org/vetlesen/appguide.htm
Sponsor G. Unger Vetlesen Foundation
c/o Fulton, Rowe & Hart, One Rockefeller Plaza, Suite 301
New York, NY 10020-2002

G.D. Searle Charitable Trust Grants **2071**
Searle awards grants through its charitable trust to tax-exempt organizations for education at all levels, health, social services, arts and humanities, and civic affairs. A major part of the funding is to United Way/Crusade of Mercy and employee matching gift programs, preventive medicine, and medical research. Most projects funded have a duration of two years or less. Applications outlining the project for which funds are needed should be submitted in the first quarter of each year. Address applications to Searle Charitable Trust, 5200 Old Orchard Rd, Skokie, IL 60077.
Requirements Grants are not made to individuals for personal education or to organizations funded by United Way.
Amount $500-$30,000 average
Contact Judith Van der Vort, Administrator, (708) 982-7000
Sponsor G.D. Searle Charitable Trust
50 S LaSalle St
Chicago, IL 60675

Gaius Charles Bolin Fellowships for Minority Graduate Students **2072**
This fellowship enables a minority graduate student who is working toward the PhD in the humanities or in the natural, social, or behavioral sciences, and who plans to pursue a career in college teaching, to devote the bulk of his or her time during the academic year to the completion of dissertation work. During the year of residence at Williams, the Bolin fellow will be assigned a faculty advisor in the appropriate department and will be expected to teach a one-semester course. Two minority graduate students are awarded fellowships each year. The fellowship includes a stipend and research allowance; housing assistance; and academic support including office space and computer and library privileges.
Requirements Applicants must be US citizens who have completed all doctoral work except the dissertation by the end of the current academic year.
Amount $31,000 for academic year plus $4000 maximum research expense allowance
Date(s) Application Is Due Dec 1.
Contact Thomas Kohut, Dean of Faculty, (413) 597-4351
Internet http://www.williams.edu
Sponsor Williams College
P.O. Box 141
Williamstown, MA 01267

Gallaudet University Alumni Association Graduate Fellowship Fund **2073**
These fellowships are offered to deaf and hard-of-hearing college graduates who wish to pursue doctoral study at a university for people who hear normally. Recipients must carry a full-time semester load. The amount awarded varies, depending on the needs of the recipient and the availability of funds. The fellowship is awarded for one year and may be renewed.
Requirements Applicants must be deaf or hard-of-hearing graduates of accredited colleges and universities who have been accepted for graduate study at colleges or universities for people who hear normally. Preference is given to US applicants who possess a master's degree or equivalent and who are seeking the doctorate.
Date(s) Application Is Due Apr 20.
Contact Peikoff Alumni House; fax: (202) 651-5062; TTY: (202) 651-5081; email: alumni.relations@gallaudet.edu
Internet http://alumni.gallaudet.edu/article.asp?ID=2646
Sponsor Gallaudet University Alumni Association
800 Florida Ave NE
Washington, DC 20002-3695

Galveston Shriners Hospital Postdoctoral Fellowships **2074**
The program awards postdoctoral clinical and research fellowships to individuals interested in trauma, critical care, and burn-related practice or research. Fellowships are for a minimum of one year (clinical) and two years (research). The UTMB Trauma and Burn Services have NIH- supported active investigators with comprehensive laboratories working in the fields of wound healing, metabolism, cardiopulmonary pathophysiology, molecular biology, and immunology. Graduate programs, including master's and PhD degrees, are also available.
Requirements Applicants who have attained an MD, DO, PhD, or DVM degree are eligible. Applicants for clinical fellowships should be board eligible or board certified in general surgery; however, senior residents from academically oriented university programs will be considered or those who have completed USMLE part III.
Amount $30,000-$45,000
Contact Dr. David Herndon, Shriners Burns Hospital, (409) 770-6731; fax: (409) 770-6919; email: dherndon@utmb.edu
Internet http://www.shrinershq.org/shc/galveston/postdoc.html
Sponsor University of Texas Medical Branch-Galveston
815 Market St
Galveston, TX 77550

Gas Technology Institute Basic Research Program **2075**
The institute supports a broad program of basic research relevant to the US natural gas industry. Research topics include solid oxide fuel cell stacks and new drilling concepts. Contracts may run as long as three years. Research topics may change in content or timing during the year; changes will be posted on the Internet. Only written, fax, and Internet requests for individual proposal requests (RFPs) will be accepted.
Requirements Potential applicants must contact the office for specific individual requests for proposals.
Contact GTI Managers, (847) 768-0500; fax: (847) 768-0501; email: vp_rd@gastechnology.org
Internet http://www.gastechnology.org/webroot/app/xn/xd.aspx?it=enweb&xd=gtihome.xml
Sponsor Gas Technology Institute
1700 S Mt Prospect Rd
Des Plaines, IL 60018-1804

Gates Global HIV/AIDS Vaccine Grants **2076**
The program seeks research proposals to apply new technologies, concepts, and approaches to the design of safe and effective preventive vaccines against HIV/AIDS, in the context of the Scientific Strategic Plan of the Global HIV/AIDS Vaccine Enterprise. The foundation will fund a number of consortia or centers targeting three different priority areas identified in the Scientific Strategic Plan of the Global HIV/AIDS Vaccine Enterprise: Design of Immunogens that Induce Broadly Reactive Neutralizing Antibodies (RFP: GH-HTR-05-01); Design of Immunogens that Induce Persistent High Levels of Cell-mediated Immunity (RFP: GH-HTR-05-02); and Standardization and Development of Laboratory Assays to Comparatively Measure the Immunogenicity of HIV Vaccine Candidates in Pre-clinical and Clinical Trials (RFP: GH-HTR-05-03). The complete RFPs are available online. The listed application deadline is for letters of intent; full proposals are by invitation.
Requirements Governmental entities and 501(c)3 tax-exempt organizations are eligible. Foreign governmental agencies and equivalent organization also are eligible.
Restrictions Grants are not awarded to support individuals or projects that serve an exclusively religious purpose.
Date(s) Application Is Due Apr 1.
Contact Grants Administrator, (206) 709-3140; email: info@gatesfoundation.org
Internet http://www.gatesfoundation.org/GlobalHealth/Grantseekers/GrantmakingAreas/default.htm
Sponsor Bill and Melinda Gates Foundation
P.O. Box 23350
Seattle, WA 98102

Gates Millennium Scholars Program **2077**
The foundation funds college scholarships for low-income minority students. Students receiving scholarships may major in any field. Graduate scholarships support postgraduate study up to and including doctoral degrees for work in mathematics, science, engineering, education, and library science.
Requirements Applicants must be a citizen of the United States; have a minimum GPA of 3.3 on a 4.0 scale; be a high school senior applying to an accredited college or university for the academic year; or a college student planning to continue undergraduate study; or a college senior or college graduate enrolled or about to enroll in graduate school. Graduate students must be enrolled in a degree program in engineering, mathematics, science, education, or library science; and demonstrate significant financial need.
Contact Gates Millennium Scholars, (877) 690-4677
Internet http://www.gmsp.org
Sponsor Bill and Melinda Gates Foundation
P.O. Box 10500
Fairfax, VA 22031-80214

GCA Interchange Fellowship **2078**
The program provides a reciprocal exchange of British and American students in horticulture, landscape architecture, and related fields. The intent of the program is to foster cultural understanding, as well as to promote horticultural studies and the exchange of information in this field. GCA offers an academic year of graduate work for a British student in America. The Martin McLaren Scholarship provides a noncredit work/study program for an American recipient at universities such as Reading, Wye College of University of London, Gloucester College, and the Royal Botanic Gardens, Kew; Royal Horticultural Society Gardens, Wisley; and Royal Botanic Garden, Edinburgh. The program is jointly sponsored with the Institute of Horticulture in the British Isles.
Requirements Recent college graduates who have earned the bachelor's degree in related fields are eligible. Because of a 26-year-old age limit on student travel vouchers in Great Britain and Europe, it is strongly advised that the applicant be 26 or younger.
Date(s) Application Is Due Nov 15.
Contact Connie Sutton, Scholarship Committee, (212) 753-8287; fax: (212) 753-0134; email: csutton@gcamerica.org
Internet http://www.gcamerica.org/scholarship/gcainterchange.html
Sponsor Garden Club of America
14 East 60th St
New York, NY 10022-1002

GCA Katharine M. Grosscup Scholarships **2079**
Scholarships provide assistance to college juniors, seniors, and graduate students pursuing the study of horticulture, agriculture, and related subjects. Preference is given to students from Ohio, Pennsylvania, West Virginia, Michigan, Kentucky, and Indiana.
Amount $3000 maximum per scholarship
Date(s) Application Is Due Feb 1.
Contact Nancy Stevenson, Grosscup Scholarship Committee, (no phone calls); fax: (216) 721-2056
Internet http://www.gcamerica.org/scholarship/grosscup.html
Sponsor Garden Club of America
11030 East Boulevard
Cleveland, OH 44106

GCA Summer Environmental Studies Scholarships **2080**
Each year the GCA Awards for Summer Environmental Studies provide financial aid toward summer studies doing field work or research in the environmental field. The awards offer students who have demonstrated a keen interest in the betterment of the environment an opportunity for further study in the field of ecology. With these scholarships, young men and women can pursue summer programs beyond the regular course of study to gain additional knowledge and experience. Work may award academic credit but should be in addition to required courses. College students may apply for these awards to pursue study following their freshman, sophomore, or junior year. Guidelines and application are available online.

Amount $1500
Date(s) Application Is Due Feb 10.
Contact Connie Sutton, GCA Scholarship Committee, (212) 753-8287; fax: (212) 753-0134; email: csutton@gcamerica.org
Internet http://www.gcamerica.org/scholarship/summeraward_org.html
Sponsor Garden Club of America
14 East 60th St
New York, NY 10022-1002

GCA Tropical Botany Research Awards **2081**
The program was established to promote the preservation of tropical forests by enlarging the body of botanists with field experience. The awards enable recipients to pursue independent field research in the tropics. Two awards will be offered annually.
Requirements PhD candidates are eligible to apply.
Amount $5500
Date(s) Application Is Due Dec 31.
Contact Judith Mashinya, GCA Awards in Tropical Botany, World Wildlife Fund, (202) 861-8316; fax: (202) 887-5293; email: judith.mashinya@wwfus.org
Internet http://www.gcamerica.org/scholarship/tropical.html
Sponsor Garden Club of America
1250 24th St NW
Washington, DC 20037

GCSAA Essay Contest **2082**
The contest is open to undergraduate and graduate students pursuing degrees in turfgrass science, agronomy, or any field related to golf course management. Essays should be seven to 12 pages and should focus on the relationship between golf courses and the environment.
Requirements Undergraduate and graduate students pursuing degrees in turfgrass science, agronomy, or any field related to golf course management are eligible to apply. Applicants must be a member of GCSAA.
Amount $2000 for first place; $1500 for second place; $1000 for third plac
Date(s) Application Is Due Mar 31.
Contact Scholarship Coordinator, (800) 472-7878 ext 4424; email: ahoward@gcsaa.org
Internet http://www.gcsaa.org/Students/scholarships/essay/default.asp
Sponsor Golf Course Superintendents Association of America Foundation
1421 Research Park Dr
Lawrence, KS 66049

GCSAA Watson Fellowships **2083**
These awards are available to candidates for master's and doctoral degrees in fields related to golf course management. The goal of this program is to identify tomorrow's leading teachers and researchers.
Requirements To be eligible applicants must be in the second year of a recognized graduate program in turfgrass science or a related field. Typically, this includes candidates for masters degrees or doctorates in appropriate fields of study. Applicants must also be planning to pursue a career in research, instruction, or extension in a university setting.
Amount $5000 minimum
Date(s) Application Is Due Oct 1.
Contact Amanda Howard, Scholarship Coordinator, (800) 472-7878 ext 4424 or (785) 832-3678; email: ahoward@gcsaa.org
Internet http://www.gcsaa.org/students/scholarships/default.asp
Sponsor Golf Course Superintendents Association of America Foundation
1421 Research Park Dr
Lawrence, KS 66049

GE & Science Prize for Young Life Scientists **2084**
The GE & Science Prize for Young Life Scientists has been established to provide support to scientists at the beginning of their careers, because Science/AAAS and GE Healthcare believe that such support is critical for continued scientific progress. The prize will recognize outstanding graduate students in molecular biology from all regions of the world. This international prize will be awarded for the outstanding thesis in the general area of molecular biology as described in a 1000-word essay. The winning essay will be published in Science; essays of the regional award winners will appear in the online version of Science. For judging purposes, the essays will be grouped according to the geographic location of the degree-granting institution: North America, Europe, Japan, and all other countries. Initial screening of the submissions will be done by regional judges. Essays will be judged on the quality of the research and the entrant's ability to articulate the contribution of the research to the field of molecular biology. The top five essays from each geographic region will be forwarded to a panel of judges. All regional winners will compete for the grand prize of US$25,000. The regional winners who do not receive the grand prize will be awarded US$5,000. Winners will be announced in Science and the prize will be awarded in a location to be announced. The grand prize essay will be published in 'Science', and essays of the regional winners will be published on the online version of 'Science'.
Requirements Entrants must have been awarded their Ph.D. between 1 January and 31 December 2006. Candidates for M.D./Ph.D. degrees are eligible to compete for the prize in either the year the Ph.D. is awarded or the year the final degree is awarded. The research described in the entrant's thesis must be in the field of molecular biology as described above. The prize will recognize only work that was performed while the entrant was a graduate student. The prize will be awarded without regard to sex, race, or nationality.
Restrictions Employees of GE, Science and AAAS, and their relatives are not eligible for the prize.
Amount $25,000
Date(s) Application Is Due Jul 15.
Contact Sylvia Kihara, Prize Coordinator, (202) 326-6507; fax: (202) 289-7562; email: skihara@aaas.org
Internet http://www.sciencemag.org/feature/data/prizes/ge/index.dtl
Sponsor American Association for the Advancement of Science
1200 New York Ave., NW, Room 1049B
Washington, DC 20005

GEM MS Engineering Fellowships **2085**
The objective of the master's program is to increase the pool of minority MS engineering graduates. Each participant is provided with a summer internship experience for a GEM corporate member and a portable academic fellowship of tuition, fees, and stipend that must be used at a GEM university member. Fellows are supported for three semesters or four quarters.
Requirements Eligibility includes US citizenship; ethnic identification of Native American, African American, Mexican American, or Puerto Rican; academic classification of junior, senior, or baccalaureate degree recipient in an accredited engineering discipline; and an undergraduate record that indicates the ability to successfully pursue graduate studies in engineering.
Amount $10,000 stipend per academic year
Date(s) Application Is Due Nov 1.
Contact Fellowships Program, (219) 631-7771; fax: (219) 287-1486; email: gem@nd.edu
Internet http://was.nd.edu/gem/gemwebapp/public/gem_01_100.htm
Sponsor National GEM Center
P.O. Box 537
Notre Dame, IN 46556

GEM PhD Engineering Fellowships **2086**
The objective of this program is to offer doctoral fellowships to underrepresented minority students. Fellowships may be used at any participating GEM member university. Tuition, fees, and a yearly stipend are provided. Fellows may be required to accept a research or teaching assistantship. A paid summer internship may be required.
Requirements Eligibility includes US citizenship and ethnic identification of Native American, African American, Mexican American, or Puerto Rican. Applicants must have or be in the process of attaining a master's degree in engineering and have an academic record that indicates the ability to successfully pursue doctoral studies in engineering.
Amount $14,400 per calendar year plus $5500 cost of instruction grant for first year
Date(s) Application Is Due Nov 1.
Contact Fellowships Program, (219) 631-7771; fax: (219) 287-1486; email: gem@nd.edu
Internet https://ws4.nd.edu/gem/gemwebapp/public/gem_01_100.htm
Sponsor National GEM Center
P.O. Box 537
Notre Dame, IN 46556

GEM PhD Science Fellowships **2087**
The goal of this program is to increase the number of minority students pursuing doctoral degrees in the natural, physical, and life sciences (chemistry, physics, mathematics, and computer science, as well as the earth, biological, and pharmaceutical sciences). Fellowships are portable to any participating GEM member university, and include a stipend, tuition, and fees. The award is renewable through the university for up to four additional years. Fellows may be required to accept a research or teaching assistantship. A paid summer internship is required prior to entering a doctoral program.
Requirements Eligibility includes US citizenship; ethnic identification of Native American, African American, Hispanic, or Puerto Rican; academic classification of junior, senior, or baccalaureate degree recipient in an accredited science discipline; and an undergraduate record that indicates the ability to successfully pursue doctoral studies in the natural sciences.
Amount $14,400 per calendar year plus $5500 cost of instruction grant for first year
Date(s) Application Is Due Nov 1.
Contact Fellowships Program, (219) 631-7771; fax: (219) 287-1486; email: gem@nd.edu
Internet http://was.nd.edu/gem/gemwebapp/public/gem_01_100.htm#03
Sponsor National GEM Center
P.O. Box 537
Notre Dame, IN 46556

General L. Kemper Williams Prize in Louisiana History **2088**
The Historic New Orleans Collection, in cooperation with the Louisiana Historical Association, awards one prize for the best published work (book or article) dealing with Louisiana history. The award contains an engraved plaque. The nomination form is available on the Web site.

Requirements Works about all aspects of Louisiana history and culture are eligible, as are works that treat the history of Louisiana in a regional, national, or international context.
Amount $1500
Date(s) Application Is Due Jan 15.
Contact Chair, Williams Prize Committee, (504) 523-4662; fax: (504) 598-7108; email: WRC@hnoc.org
Internet http://www.hnoc.org/index.html
Sponsor Historic New Orleans Collection
533 Royal St
New Orleans, LA 70130

General Motors Foundation Grants Support Program **2089**
With a strong commitment to diversity in all areas, the targeted areas of focus for the Foundation are: education; health and human services; civic and community; public policy; arts and culture; and environment and energy. Primary consideration is given to requests that meet the following criteria: exhibit a clear purpose and defined need in one of the foundation's areas of focus; recognize innovative approaches in addressing the defined need; demonstrate an efficient organization and detail the organization's ability to follow through on the proposal; and, explain clearly the benefits to the foundation and the plant city communities. Paper applications are no longer accepted. Completion of an online eligibility quiz is the first step in the application process.
Requirements Nonprofit, tax-exempt organizations and institutions are eligible to apply. Applications must be made online.
Restrictions The Foundation not not support organizations that discriminate on the basis of race, religion, creed, gender, age, veteran status, physical challenge or national origin. Contributions are generally not provided for: individuals; religious organizations; political parties or candidates; U.S. hospitals and health care institutions (general operating support); capital campaigns; endowment funds; conferences, workshops or seminars not directly related to GM's business interests.
Contact Grant Coordinator, (313) 556-5000
Internet http://www.gm.com/company/gmability/community/guidelines/index.html
Sponsor General Motors Foundation
P.O. Box 300, 300 Renaissance Center
Detroit, MI 48265-3000

General Service Foundation International Peace Grants **2090**
The foundation awards grants in three program areas: international peace, reproductive health and rights, and resources. International peace grants address the root causes of conflict in Mexico, Central America, and the Caribbean. Reproductive health and rights grants address the issues of rapid population growth and unintended pregnancies in the United States and Latin America. Resources grants support improvement of the use, quality, and management of water in regions west of the Mississippi River. It is recommended that applicants carefully review the foundation's annual report before sending letters of inquiry. Apply online.
Requirements Grants are made to organizations that are tax-exempt under US laws. The foundation prefers projects and/or programs that give promise of significant contribution and that are new, innovative, demonstrational, and/or research in nature.
Restrictions In general, contributions are not made to operating budgets, nor to annual campaigns of established organizations. The foundation ordinarily does not contribute to capital expenses (physical plant, equipment, endowment), to individuals, nor for relief.
Amount $3.1 million total; $2500-$35,000 average
Date(s) Application Is Due Jan 14; Sep 1.
Contact Program Officer, International Peace, (970) 920-6834; fax: (970) 920-4578; email: peace@generalservice.org
Internet http://www.generalservice.org
Sponsor General Service Foundation
557 N Mill St, Ste 201
Aspen, CO 81611

General Service Foundation Reproductive Health and Rights Grants **2091**
The foundation is concerned with the related issues of rapid population growth and unintended pregnancies, particularly the availability of high-quality reproductive health care and access to that care. The foundation funds research for policy analysis, litigation, public education, and advocacy. Grants are made for programs in the United States and Latin America that address the needs of low-income women, women of color, adolescents, and the issue of access. Apply online.
Requirements Grants are made to organizations that are tax-exempt under US laws. The foundation prefers projects and/or programs that give promise of significant contribution and that are new, innovative, demonstrational, and/or research in nature.
Restrictions Generally, grants are not made for service delivery, contraceptive development, or university-based research. In addition, contributions are not made to operating budgets or to annual campaigns of established organizations. The foundation ordinarily does not contribute to capital (physical plant, equipment, endowment), to individuals, nor for relief.
Amount $3.1 million total; $2500-$35,000 average
Date(s) Application Is Due Feb 1.
Contact Holly Bartling, Program Contact, (202) 232-1005 or (970) 920-6834; fax: (970) 920-4578; email: holly@generalservice.org or rhr@generalservice.org
Internet http://www.generalservice.org/Reproductive%20Health.htm
Sponsor General Service Foundation
557 N Mill St, Ste 201
Aspen, CO 81611

General Service Foundation Western Water Grants **2092**
The goal of the program is to preserve, secure, and protect water flows for aquatic and riparian ecosystems in the rivers of the interior West. Within the target states of Idaho, Montana, Wyoming, Colorado, New Mexico, Utah and Arizona, the foundation will support projects with significant promise of basin-wide, state-wide, or regional (multi-state) impact. The foundation will also continue to consider projects addressing water policies and laws affecting the West as a region. While the foundation supports a broad range of activities, including advocacy, litigation, public education and outreach, research, and media, priority will be given to organizations attempting to affect legal and/or policy changes. Apply online.
Requirements Grants are made to organizations that are tax-exempt under US laws. The foundation prefers projects and/or programs that give promise of significant contribution and that are new, innovative, demonstrational, and/or research in nature.
Restrictions In general, contributions are not made to operating budgets or to annual campaigns of established organizations, nor does the foundation ordinarily contribute to capital expenses (physical plant, equipment, endowment), to individuals, or for relief.
Amount $3.1 million total; $2500-$35, 000 average
Date(s) Application Is Due Jan 14; Sep 1.
Contact Lani Shaw, Executive Director, (970) 920-6834; fax: (970) 920-4578; email: info@generalservice.org
Internet http://www.generalservice.org
Sponsor General Service Foundation
557 N Mill St, Ste 201
Aspen, CO 81611

Genuardi Family Foundation Grants **2093**
The Foundation supports direct providers of services in the areas of education, health, human services, and culture. The Foundation gives preference to projects which receive broad-based community support and provides for reasonable costs associated with conducting the proposed project or program. Grant proposals may include the allocation of a reasonable percentage of grant monies towards general support of the recipient organization. On a limited basis, the Foundation will also consider grants in support of capital campaigns for facilities or equipment, and organizational capacity building.
Requirements The Foundation only considers grant requests from organizations designated as tax exempt under Section 501(c)(3) of the Internal Revenue Code. Preference will be given to non-profit organizations based in the Greater Philadelphia Area.
Restrictions The Foundation's funding will not process grant requests from: individuals; fraternal and/or civic organizations; political candidates or to influence legislation; other foundations; general fund raising and endowment drives; debt reduction; environmental issues or initiatives; annual appeals or letters of solicitation; or public, private or parochial schools that serve the general public.
Amount $5,000-$50,000
Date(s) Application Is Due Oct 31.
Contact Robert C. Fernandez, Executive Director, email: info@genuardifamilyfoundation.org
Internet http://www.genuardifamilyfoundation.org/pages/home.html
Sponsor Genuardi Family Foundation
Blue Bell Executive Campus, 470 Norristown Road, Suite 300
Auburn, NY 13021

Geographic Education Dissertation Award **2094**
Awards are made for outstanding doctoral research to encourage research in geography teaching and learning. Applications for the award must be made through a 15-page paper based on the applicant's doctoral dissertation.
Requirements Scholars eligible for the award must have received the doctoral degree within the previous two years. All applicants are expected to present their research at the annual meeting.
Amount $300 first prize, $100 second prize
Date(s) Application Is Due Mar 15.
Contact Executive Director, (256) 782-5293; fax: (256) 782-5336; email: ncge@ncge.org
Internet http://www.ncge.org/resources/awards/dissertation.cfm
Sponsor National Council for Geographic Education
Jacksonville State University, 206A Martin Hall
Jacksonville, AL 36265-1602

George A. and Eliza Gardner Howard Humanities Fellowships **2095**
These fellowships assist individuals in the middle stages of their professional humanities or social sciences careers. Support is intended to augment paid sabbatical leaves. Preference will be given to individuals who are professionally based in the United States through institutional affiliation or by residence. Awards are granted in a sequence: arts in odd-numbered years and social sciences in even-numbered years; contact the foundation for current subcategories. Nominations must be received by October 17. Details of the nomination procedure are available from the foundation upon request.

Requirements Candidates must be nominated by a representative of an affiliated college or university, a professional critic, or editor, or the director of a professional society. Grants are available to men and women of any nationality, generally between the ages of 25 and 45, who are below the rank of full professor.
Restrictions Fellowships are not available for work leading to an academic degree of for private study.
Amount $25,000 stipend
Date(s) Application Is Due Oct 17.
Contact Henry Majewski, Director, (401) 863-2640; fax: (401) 863-7341; email: howard_foundation@brown.edu
Internet http://www.stg.brown.edu/projects/gradschool/howard
Sponsor George A. and Eliza Gardner Howard Foundation
42 Charlesfield St
Providence, RI 02912

George A. Olah Award in Hydrocarbon or Petroleum Chemistry **2096**
The award is conferred to recognize, encourage, and stimulate outstanding research achievements in hydrocarbon or petroleum chemistry. The award consists of a stipend, certificate, and travel expenses to the meeting at which the award will be presented.
Requirements Any individual, except a member of the award committee, may submit one nomination or seconding letter for the award in any given year. The nominating documents consist of a letter of not more than 1000 words, containing an evaluation of the nominee's accomplishments and a specific identification of the work to be recognized, a biographical sketch including date of birth, and a list of publications and patents authored by the nominee. Six copies of all items to be included in the nomination must be submitted. Nominee must be a US or Canadian citizen.
Amount $5000 award and $1500 travel expenses to meeting
Date(s) Application Is Due Feb 1.
Contact Awards Administrator, (800) 227-5558; (202) 872-4408; fax: (202) 872-6317; email: awards@acs.org
Internet http://www.chemistry.org/portal/a/c/s/1/acsdisplay.html?DOC=awards%5Colah.html
Sponsor American Chemical Society
1155 16th St NW
Washington, DC 20036

George B. Storer Foundation Grants **2097**
The foundation awards grants, primarily in Florida, in its areas of interest, including higher education, social services--particularly for the blind, youth organizations, conservation, hospitals, and cultural programs. Types of support include building construction/renovation, capital campaigns, general operating support, matching/challenge grants, and research grants. There are no application forms. Applications should be submitted between October 15 and the listed deadline.
Date(s) Application Is Due Nov 15.
Contact Grants Administrator, c/o Thomas McDonald, CPA
Sponsor George B. Storer Foundation
P.O. Box 1040
Tavernier, FL 33070

George C. Pimentel Award in Chemical Education **2098**
This award, sponsored by the Dow Chemical Company and administered by the American Chemical Society, is given annually to recognize outstanding contributions to chemical education. A nominee must have made outstanding contributions to chemical education considered in its broadest meaning, including the training of professional chemists; the dissemination of reliable information about chemistry to prospective chemists, to members of the profession, to students in other fields, and to the general public; and the integration of chemistry into our educational system. The activities recognized by the award may lie in the fields of teaching (at any level), organization and administration, influential writing, educational research, the methodology of instruction, establishment of standards of instruction, and public enlightenment. Preference shall be given to US citizens. Award includes certificate and travel expenses to award meeting.
Requirements Any individual, except a member of the award committee, may submit one nomination or seconding letter for the award in any given year. The nominating documents consist of a letter of not more than 1000 words containing an evaluation of the nominee's accomplishments and a specific identification of the work to be recognized, a biographical sketch including date of birth, and a list of publications and patents authored by the nominee. Six copies of all items to be included in the nomination must be submitted.
Restrictions Self-nominations are not accepted.
Amount $5000
Date(s) Application Is Due Feb 1.
Contact Awards Administrator, (800) 227-5558; (202) 872-4408; fax: (202) 776-8211; email: awards@acs.org
Internet http://www.chemistry.org/portal/a/c/s/1/acsdisplay.html?DOC=awards%5Cpimentel.html
Sponsor American Chemical Society
1155 16th St NW
Washington, DC 20036

George Foundation Grants **2099**
The Foundation prioritizes its funding opportunities across the following areas: basic needs; health and wellness; education; early childhood - 3rd grade; economic success; scholarship programs; security and safety; community enhancement; and preservation of regional heritage. To support family stability by creating an environment in which families can support one another and children can be nurtured, the Foundation strongly favors programs that: target service delivery to populations with less access to resources, with priority given to programming for children; recognize that providing basic human needs is the first step to assisting the most impoverished; seek to understand the needs of children and promote their well-being; understand today's families are complex and may include kin-ship guardians, non-custodial fathers, foster families, and adoptive families; support preventative rather than intervening efforts by identifying the root cause of community issues preventing the growth of self-reliant and productive families; and understand the cultural diversity and values of the families residing in Fort Bend County. Application information is available online.
Requirements Nonprofit groups in Fort Bend County, TX, may submit proposals.
Restrictions The Foundation does not fund: grants to organizations that do not have a current 501(c)(3) determination letter; churches or other organized religious bodies; grants to another organization that distributes money to recipients of its own selection, i.e., a regranting organization; regional, national or international programs; grants for research or studies; grants for travel, conferences, conventions, group meetings, or seminars; the purchase of event tickets, tables, ads or sponsorships; support to fairs and festivals; religious or private schools; request for funds to develop films, videos, books or other media projects; direct mail campaigns; loans of any kind; grants to individuals; grants to fraternal organizations; political interests of any kind; and institutions that discriminate on the basis of race, creed, gender, national origin, age, disability or sexual orientation in policy or in practice.
Date(s) Application Is Due Jan 15; Apr 15; Jul 15; Oct 15.
Contact Dee Koch, Grant Officer, (281) 342-6109; fax: (281) 341-7635; email: dkoch@thegeorgefoundation.org
Internet http://www.thegeorgefoundation.org
Sponsor George Foundation
310 Morton Street, PMB Suite C
Richmond, TX 77469

George Frederick Jewett Foundation Grants Program **2100**
The foundation is concerned primarily with people and values. The grants program focuses on the future and on stimulating and supporting activities and projects of established, voluntary, nonprofit organizations that are of importance to human welfare. Grants are made in the fields of arts and humanities, conservation and preservation, education, health care and medical services, population, religion, and social welfare. The foundation may support research on and studies of important problems of public concern solely for the purpose of aiding in the gathering and presenting of facts that may assist the public to better understand such problems and to arrive at realistic and effective solutions to them. From time to time, support may be given to the scholarship, fellowship, and research programs of established institutions when sufficient evidence is available to establish clearly that the applicant organization is awarding such grants in accordance with the regulations established by the IRS. Grants are awarded to support activities in progress, research into potential projects, building and equipment, general operations, program development, seed funding, research, technical assistance, and matching funds. Inquiries for clarification of the foundation's policy and program emphasis are encouraged.
Requirements Preference is given to public charities or nonprivate foundations. The foundation confines its grants largely to requests from eastern Washington and the San Francisco Bay area.
Restrictions Grants do not support advertising; advocacy, athletic, international, religious, political, or veterans organizations; or individuals.
Amount $5000-$50,000
Contact Ann Gralnek, (415) 421-1351; fax: (415) 421-0721; email: ADGjewettf@aol.com or tfbjewettf@aol.com
Sponsor George Frederick Jewett Foundation
235 Montgomery St, Ste 612
San Francisco, CA 94104

George Gund Foundation Grants **2101**
The Foundation's guidelines reflect their long-standing interests in: arts; economic development and community revitalization; education; the environment; and human services. The Foundation supports opportunities that cross program boundaries and that integrate elements of the Foundation's interests. Although the Foundation's focus is centered in Greater Cleveland, a portion of their grantmaking will continue to support state and national policy making that bolsters their work. Application information is available online.
Requirements The foundation makes grants only to nonprofit, tax-exempt organizations or to qualified governmental units or agencies. The Foundation currently does not accept faxed proposals or proposals submitted electronically.
Date(s) Application Is Due Mar 30; Jun 30; Sep 30; Dec 30.
Contact David Abbott, Executive Director, (216) 241-3114; fax: (216) 241-6560; email: info@gundfdn.org
Internet http://www.gundfdn.org
Sponsor George Gund Foundation

45 Prospect Avenue West, 1845 Guildhall Building
Cleveland, OH 44115

George H. Hitchings New Investigator Award in Health Research **2102**
Provides awards to provide flexible support for young researchers in their second year of graduate school. Students planning to follow a career path in academic teaching and research that is closely tied to the health of North Carolinians and the strength of North Carolina Science are particularly encouraged to apply.
Requirements Applications/nominations must be submitted by the institution on behalf of the student(s). Nomination applications are accepted from Duke, NCCU, NCSU, and UNC-Chapel Hill.
Restrictions Only one nomination/application per graduate program/department within the university will be accepted.
Amount $4,000
Date(s) Application Is Due Mar 15.
Contact Robyn Fehrman, Community Program Officer; (919) 474-8370; fax: (919) 941-9208
Internet http://www.trianglecf.org/page33713.cfm
Sponsor Triangle Community Foundation
324 Blackwell Street, Suite 1220
Durham, NC 27701

George Kress Foundation Grants **2103**
The foundation awards grants to eligible Wisconsin nonprofit organizations in its areas of interest, including arts and culture, children and families, Christian churches and organizations, health care/health organizations/hospitals, historical preservation, human and social services, and sports and recreation. Types of support include building construction and renovation, capital campaigns, emergency services, professorships, program development, research grants, and scholarship funds. There are no application deadlines or forms.
Requirements Wisconsin nonprofit organizations are eligible. Preference is given to requests benefiting Green Bay and Madison
Contact John Kress, Secretary, (920) 433-3109
Sponsor George Kress Foundation
P.O. Box 408
Neenah, WI 54957-0408

George M. Brooker Collegiate Scholarship for Minorities **2104**
The scholarship supports graduate and undergraduate minority students entering careers in real estate, and specifically real estate management, upon graduation. Applicants for the one-time award must have declared a major in real estate or a related field; must have completed two courses in real estate or indicate intent to complete them; must have at least a 3.0 grade point average within the major; and must submit recommendation letters, themed essay, and official transcript.
Requirements To be eligible, the applicant must be a member of a minority group and a US citizen.
Amount $2500 for graduates; $1000 for undergraduates
Date(s) Application Is Due Mar 31.
Contact Kimberly Holmes, Foundation Administrator, (312) 329-6008; fax: (312) 410-7908; email: kholmes@irem.org or foundatn@irem.org
Internet http://www.irem.org/sec1ins.cfm?sec=iremfoundation&con=scholarships.cfm&par=#4
Sponsor Institute of Real Estate Management Foundation
430 N Michigan Ave
Chicago, IL 60611-8775

George S. and Dolores Dore Eccles Foundation Grants **2105**
The foundation awards grants to eligible Utah organizations in its areas of interest, including arts, children and youth, economics, higher education, hospitals, medical research, performing arts, visual arts, and social services. Types of support include building construction/renovation, capital campaigns, equipment acquisition, general operating grants, matching/challenge grants, professorships, program development, research grants, and scholarship funds. A request for application is available online.
Requirements Giving primarily in Utah.
Restrictions Funding requests will not be considered from the following types of organizations: those that have not received a tax exemption letter establishing 501(c)(3) status from the Internal Revenue Service, unless they are a unit of government, in which case such a letter is not required; other private foundations; those of a political nature that attempt to influence legislation and/or candidacy of persons for elected public office; conduit organizations, unified funds, or those that use funds to make grants to support other organizations; those that do not have fiscal responsibility for the proposed project. Funds will also not be considered for: contingencies, deficits, or debt reduction; general endowment funds; direct aid to individuals; conferences, seminars, or medical research; requests which do not fall within the Foundation's specified areas of interest.
Contact Director, (801) 246-5340; fax: (801) 350-3510; email: gseg@gseccles.org
Internet http://www.gsecclesfoundation.org
Sponsor George S. and Dolores Dore Eccles Foundation
79 South Main Street, 12th Floor
Salt Lake City, UT 84111

George W. Codrington Charitable Foundation Grants **2106**
The foundation's support is limited to public charitable or educational projects within Cuyahoga County, OH, and immediately adjacent areas. Areas of interest include museums, performing arts, arts and cultural programs, higher education, other education, hospitals (general), and children and youth services. Types of support include continuing support, general operating support, annual campaigns, capital campaigns, equipment, program development, and research. The application should state fully but briefly the amount requested, need for the grant, area served by the applicant, brief history of the applicant organization, description of applicant's contribution to the area, listing of the applicant's officers and trustees, and evidence of 501(c)3 status. Grants generally are made on an annual basis. Meetings of the supervisory board are usually held in March, June, September, November and December, at which time pending applications are considered.
Requirements IRS 501(c)3 organizations serving residents of Cuyahoga County, OH, and immediately adjacent areas are eligible.
Restrictions Grants are not made to individuals.
Amount $500-$25,000 average
Contact Raymond Sawyer, Chair, Supervisory Board, (216) 566-5837; fax: (216) 566-5800
Sponsor George W. Codrington Charitable Foundation
127 Public Sq, 39th Fl
Cleveland, OH 44114-1216

George Westinghouse Medals **2107**
Medals are bestowed annually for eminent achievement or distinguished service in the power field of mechanical engineering. Considering power in the broad sense, the basis of the awards shall include contributions of utilization, application, design, development, research, and the organization of such activities in the power field. Any individual member, group of members, or committee may nominate candidates for the awards. A certificate accompanies the award.
Requirements Candidates are not restricted by profession nor by membership in any engineering society or organization. Silver medals are awarded to candidates under 45 years of age.
Amount $1500 and vermeil medal; $1000 and silver medal
Date(s) Application Is Due Sep 1.
Contact Gilda DiTullio, Manager, (212) 591-7736; fax: (212) 705-7739; email: ditulliog@asme.org
Internet http://www.asme.org/honors/ms71/saa/westinghouse.html
Sponsor American Society of Mechanical Engineers
3 Park Ave
New York, NY 10016-5990

Georgetown University Chemistry Department Grad Research Fellowships **2108**
Fellowships enable qualified students to pursue graduate work leading to PhD degrees while gaining valuable experience assisting in undergraduate courses during at least one of the years of graduate study. The graduate program provides a firm foundation in all areas of chemistry as well as opportunities for research under 17 faculty members on a considerable variety of topics.
Requirements Applicant must have a BS degree in chemistry or its equivalent.
Amount $21,400
Contact Chairperson, (202) 687-6073; fax: (202) 687-6209; email: chemad@georgetown.edu
Internet http://www.georgetown.edu/departments/chemistry/graduate.htm
Sponsor Georgetown University
Department of Chemistry, Box 571227
Washington, DC 20057-2222

Georgia Institute of Technology Postdoctoral Fellowship **2109**
The 12-month postdoctoral fellowship starts in mid-August. Duties include individual/group counseling, outreach, crisis intervention, consultation, and testing/evaluation. The fellowship provides a stipend plus benefits. Applicants should send resumes to the office.
Requirements Individuals with the PhD in psychology and experience in counseling/clinical psychology are eligible.
Amount $22,000
Date(s) Application Is Due Mar 9.
Contact Dr. Irene Dalton, (404) 894-2575; fax: (404) 894-1804
Internet http://www.ohr.gatech.edu
Sponsor Georgia Institute of Technology
500 Tech Pkwy
Atlanta, GA 30332-0286

Georgia Power Foundation Grants **2110**
Giving is focused on issues that directly affect customers, employees, business and shareholders. These include: improving the quality of education by partnering with organizations to assist students with personal development, mentoring and career exploration; protecting the environment by promoting programs to improve air and water quality, preserve natural resources and protect endangered species; preventing cancer; and promoting diversity. The Foundation gives strong preference to Georgia-

based organizations and programs that seek to improve the quality of life for the state's residents. Applicants may apply online or with a written proposal.
Requirements The foundation makes grants to tax-exempt organizations that seek to improve the quality of life for Georgia's residents.
Restrictions The Foundation does not provide grants to individuals, private elementary or secondary schools, and religious organizations, nor political campaigns or causes. The Foundation does not provide multi-year funding commitments.
Amount $10,000
Date(s) Application Is Due Feb 15; May 15; Aug 15; Nov 15.
Contact Grants Administrator, (404) 506-6784; email: gpfoundation@southernco.com
Internet http://www.georgiapower.com/community/apply.asp
Sponsor Georgia Power Foundation
241 Ralph McGill Boulevard, N.E., Bin 10131
Atlanta, GA 30308-3374

Gerald R. Ford Foundation Research Travel Grants **2111**
Grants are available for research that makes significant use of the Gerald R. Ford Library's archival collections, which focus on US domestic affairs, foreign relations, economic policies, and politics in the 1970s. The library can provide free database searches and other information to help scholars determine whether the collections are useful to their research. The grants defray travel, living, and photocopy expenses incurred while conducting research at the library. Applications are available on the Web site.
Amount $20,000 total; $2000 each
Date(s) Application Is Due Mar 15; Sep 15.
Contact Grants Coordinator, (734) 205-0555; fax: (734) 205-0571; email: ford.library@nara.gov
Internet http://www.ford.utexas.edu/library/hpgrants.htm
Sponsor Gerald R. Ford Foundation
1000 Beal Ave, Gerald R. Ford Library
Ann Arbor, MI 48109

Geraldine R. Dodge Foundation Frontiers for Veterinary Medicine Fellowships **2112**
Fellowships enable motivated and creative veterinary students to pursue either summer projects or research undertakings of their own design centered on endeavors they are passionate about and that hold promise for advancing the humane treatment of animals. The program gives veterinary students the opportunity to step outside the traditional bounds of veterinary education to explore and bring new, creative problem-solving perspectives to pressing, animal-related issues. Proposals may be for work that is project-based (such as developing a humane education program) or research-based. Projects or research must be completed by September of the upcoming year. A wide range of fellowship topics and issues are open for consideration. They include companion animals, wildlife, livestock, laboratory animals, zoo animals, pet overpopulation, the human-animal bond, animal-assisted therapies, conservation medicine, shelter medicine, animal ethics, and humane and/or veterinary education. Preference will be given to projects that occur in the United States. International work, however, will be considered if the proposal is exceptionally compelling. To be considered, an applicant must submit a fellowship proposal, including an abstract and budget, and have the support of a sponsoring mentor. Applications and mentor letters via standard mail must be postmarked no later than the listed application deadline. Applications via email must be received by the listed deadline.
Requirements The applicant must be currently enrolled as a full-time veterinary student at a US or Canadian school or college of veterinary medicine accredited by the American Veterinary Medical Association.
Amount $7000 maximum
Date(s) Application Is Due Dec 16.
Contact Lisa Bregman, (973) 540-8443 ext 131; fax: (973) 540-1211; email: lbregman@grdodge.org
Internet http://www.grdodge.org/frontiers_guidelines.htm
Sponsor Geraldine R. Dodge Foundation
P.O. Box 1239, 163 Madison Ave
Morristown, NJ 07962-1239

Geraldine R. Dodge Foundation Teacher Fellowships **2113**
The program awards fellowships to full-time New Jersey teachers in public and public charter schools in Camden County, NJ. The program seeks to support life-expanding, rejuvenating projects that may even fulfill a lifetime dream in addition to proposals that will expand intellectual capacity and appreciation of diversity and culture. Consideration will be given to teams of one or more teachers with one common proposal. The deadline is January 17, and submissions should be made online.
Requirements K-12 New Jersey teachers in Camden County are eligible.
Restrictions The Fellowship program does not fund: training that your school district would normally be expected to fund such as block scheduling or differentiated instruction; projects whose funds are directly used for classroom supplies, classroom activities, or classroom field trips; funds for equipment purchase or rental (such as a video camera, computer, etc.); funds used for college or graduate level classes leading to dissertation work or degree credit; individual project proposals from administrators; or retroactive financial support for projects, workshops, or travel that has already taken place.
Amount $2,000-$7,500 for individuals; $5,000-$10,000 for teams
Date(s) Application Is Due Jan 17.
Contact Shannon Joerchel, Teacher Fellowship Coordinator; (973) 540-8442, ext. 106; fax: (973) 540-1211; email: tfellows@grdodge.org
Internet http://www.grdodge.org/initiatives/teacherfellowship/index.htm
Sponsor Geraldine R. Dodge Foundation
163 Madison Avenue, P.O. Box 1239
Morristown, NJ 07962-1239

Gerber Foundation Grants **2114**
The foundation awards grants to support national programs that have a significant impact on issues facing infants and young children. Areas of interest include pediatric health--promoting health and preventing disease, including projects geared toward research or interventions that will reduce the incidence of serious chronic illnesses (e.g., diabetes, heart disease, obesity, or cancer) or improve cognitive, social, and emotional aspects of development; pediatric nutrition--assuring adequate nutrition for infants and young children through projects of research or interventions; and the effects of environmental hazards. The listed deadlines are for letters of inquiry. Guidelines and application are available online.
Requirements 501(c)3 nonprofit organizations are eligible. Priority is given to projects that improve infant and young children nutrition, care, and development from the first year before birth to three years of age.
Restrictions The foundation does not make grants or loans to individuals. Outside the West Michigan area, the foundation does not support capital campaigns, operating support, national child welfare programs, international based programs, or food/baby products giveaway programs.
Amount $1 million maximum; $20,000-$500,000 typically
Date(s) Application Is Due Jun 1; Dec 1.
Contact Program Contact, (231) 924-3175; fax: (231) 924-7906; email: cobits@ncresa.org
Internet http://www.gerberfoundation.org
Sponsor Gerber Foundation
4747 W 48th St, Ste 153
Fremont, MI 49412-8119

Gerd Muehsam Award **2115**
Papers should be submitted by graduate students for consideration for the Gerd Muehsam Award for the most outstanding research paper on art or visual resources librarianship. Contact the society for complete guidelines.
Amount $500
Date(s) Application Is Due Nov 21.
Contact Paul Gabbard, Award Committee Chair, (212) 854-6745; fax: (212) 854-8904; email: gabbard@columbia.edu
Internet http://www.arlisna.org/about/awards/muehsam_info.html
Sponsor Art Libraries Society of North America
1172 Amsterdam Ave, MC 0301
New York, NY 10027

Gerda Henkel Foundation Grants **2116**
The Foundation funds activities concentrating on German and foreign academia in the fields of historical humanities. In particular, research projects in the following fields are supported: history, prehistory and early history; archaeology; art history; history of Islam; and legal history. Funds are provided for: specific temporary research projects through grants for personnel, travel and material expenses; research and doctoral scholarships for German and foreign scholars; innovative academic conferences; publications of particularly successful projects supported by the Foundation. Application information is available online.
Restrictions Support is not provided for: permanent positions; academic institutions through endowments; festschrifts or dictionaries; annual meetings and academic anniversaries; publications which are not related to projects already being supported by the Foundation; excursions; exhibition projects which are not related to projects already being supported by the Foundation.
Date(s) Application Is Due Jun 29.
Contact Grants Adminstrator, 49-(0)211-359853; fax: 49-(0)211-357137; email: info@gerda-henkel-stiftung.de
Internet http://www.gerda-henkel-stiftung.de/02_foerderung/en_foerderung.htm
Sponsor Gerda Henkel Foundation
Malkastenstrasse 15
Dusseldorf 40211 Germany

German National Scholarship Foundation Program **2117**
The foundation awards grants, scholarships, and fellowships to German university students in the fields of education, science and medicine, arts and humanities, and law and other professions. Scholars may participate in summer schools arranged by the foundation, be offered special research grants, and receive tuition at German and many foreign universities.
Requirements Students must be recommended by professors, academic advisers for doctoral students, headmasters, or school principals. Only the most academically well-qualified students will be considered.
Restrictions Students cannot directly apply for a scholarship.
Amount DM960.00 maximum to cover living expenses; DM100.00 monthly book allowance

Contact Dr. Gerhard Teufel, 49-228-820960; fax: 49-228-82096103; email: info@studienstiftung.de
Internet http://www.studienstiftung.org
Sponsor German National Scholarship Foundation
MirbachstraBe 7
Bonn 53173 Germany

Germanistic Society of America Fellowships 2118
Usually up to six fellowships are awarded annually to enable prospective specialists to study for an academic year in Germany, primarily in art history; economics and banking; German language and literature; history; international law; philosophy; political science; and public affairs. Candidates selected for these awards, administered in the United States by the IIE, will be considered for Fulbright travel grants.
Requirements A master's degree is desirable, but candidates must have a bachelor's degree and be US citizens by November 1 of the year preceding the award.
Amount $12,000
Contact US Student Programs Division, (212) 984-5330; fax: (212) 984-5325; email: info@iie.org
Internet http://www.iie.org/Content/NavigationMenu/Fulbright_Demo_Site/U_S__Student_Program/Fulbright_Grant_Opportunities/Germany.htm
Sponsor Institute of International Education
809 United Nations Plz
New York, NY 10017

Gerrish/FTE Technology Education Graduate Fellowship 2119
The fellowship is available to technology teachers at the K-12 grade level. Candidates must be accepted into a graduate degree program in technology education and beginning or continuing full-time graduate work. All applicants must be members of the International Technology Education Association. Additional information is available upon request.
Amount $5000
Date(s) Application Is Due Dec 1.
Contact Kendall Starkweather, Executive Director, (703) 860-2100; fax: (703) 860-0353; email: iteaordr@iris.org
Internet http://www.doe.mass.edu/tgfa/tech.html#2
Sponsor Foundation for Technology Education
1914 Association Dr, Ste 201
Reston, VA 22091

Gertrude B. Elion Mentored Medical Student Research Awards 2120
An annual award granted to support women medical students interested in pursuing health-related research projects.
Requirements Students must have the support of a faculty mentor and must conduct their research at one of the four medical schools in North Carolina. Applications are accepted from Duke University Medical Center, East Carolina University School of Medicine, UNC-Chapel Hill School of Medicine or Wake Forest University Baptist Medical Center only.
Restrictions Candidates must be women, enrolled as full-time students, and will have completed at least one year of medical school prior to the start of the award. They must conduct their research at the applying institution. Candidates must be citizens or permanent residents of the United States or Canada at the time of application. Documentation of permanent residency status must be provided with the application. Persons who have applied for permanent residency but have not received their government documentation by the time of application are not eligible.
Amount $10,000
Date(s) Application Is Due Apr 20.
Contact Libby Long; (919) 474-8370, ext. 134; email: libby@trianglecf.org
Internet http://www.trianglecf.org/page10000237.cfm
Sponsor Triangle Community Foundation
4813 Emperor Boulevard, Cambridge Hall, Suite 130
Durham, NC 27703

Getty Graduate Internships 2121
Full-time internships are available to graduate students who intend to pursue careers in art museums and related fields of the visual arts, humanities, and sciences. Internships are offered by several programs of the Getty Trust, including curatorial--prepare exhibitions, as well as engage in research and writing projects; conservation--inspection, care, and treatment of objects; education and research--museum education, professional education of conservators, provenance research, or public programs; information management--museum registration, Web services, institutional archives, or library special collections; and grantmaking--select and award grants in the areas of research, conservation, and education. Each internship is full time (five day, 38-hour week. Most internships are for eight months; conservation internships last 12. The grant includes health benefits and an educational travel allowance. Housing is not provided. Applications are available online.
Requirements Graduate internships at the Getty are open to applicants of all nationalities. Students must either be currently enrolled in a graduate program leading to an advanced degree in a field relevant to the internship(s) for which they are applying or have completed a relevant graduate degree in 2002 or later.
Amount $17,300 for eight months, $25,000 for 12 months; plus health benefits and $1200 educational travel allowance
Date(s) Application Is Due Dec 15.
Contact Internships Administrator, (310) 440-7320; fax: (310) 440-7703; email: gradinterns@getty.edu
Internet http://www.getty.edu/grants/education/grad_interns.html
Sponsor J. Paul Getty Museum
1200 Getty Center Dr, Ste 800
Los Angeles, CA 90049-1685

Getty Research Grants for Institutions - Archival Grants 2122
These grants support the basic arrangement and description of important archival collections of art-historical material in order to make them more accessible to scholars. Most projects result in the creation of an electronic finding aid. These grants do not support digitization of already catalogued archival materials, nor do they support archival research or transcription projects. Applicants should submit a preliminary letter of inquiry.
Requirements Nonprofit institutions that own significant archival collections (including both documentary and photographic archives) relevant to the study of art history are eligible to apply for support. The collections must be open for use by interested scholars.
Restrictions Requests for support to preserve archival collections are not eligible; however, certain preservation costs may be considered as a part of a larger arrangement and description project.
Contact Research Grants for Institutions, (310) 440-7320; fax: (310) 440-7703
Internet http://www.getty.edu/grants/research/institutions/archival.html
Sponsor J. Paul Getty Trust
1200 Getty Center Drive, Suite 800
Los Angeles, CA 90049-1685

Getty Research Grants for Institutions - Art History Research Grants 2123
Grants in this category support projects that advance the scholarly mission of Art History Research Centers. Projects that enhance scholarly access to library and archival resources are particularly encouraged. Applicants should submit a preliminary letter of inquiry to determine eligibility.
Requirements Grants are reserved for independent advanced research centers for the history of art that have significant library holdings and residential fellowship programs, and are open to scholars worldwide.
Contact Art History Research Center, (310) 440-7320; fax: (310) 440-7703
Internet http://www.getty.edu/grants/research/institutions/art_historical.html
Sponsor J. Paul Getty Trust
1200 Getty Center Drive, Suite 800
Los Angeles, CA 90049-1685

Getty Research Grants for Institutions - Cataloguing of Museum Collections Grants 2124
These grants support full scholarly research and documentation of one or more distinct groups of objects in a museum's permanent collection by experienced scholars. Support is also available for the publication costs of catalogues. Applicants should submit a preliminary letter of inquiry to determine eligibility.
Requirements Museums and other nonprofit organizations that own and house art collections and are open to the public on a regular basis are eligible to apply.
Restrictions These grants do not support electronic collection catalogues, special exhibition catalogues, registrars' inventories, checklists, or summary catalogues.
Contact Research Grants for Institutions, (310) 440-7320; fax: (310) 440-7703
Internet http://www.getty.edu/grants/research/institutions/cataloguing.html
Sponsor J. Paul Getty Trust
1200 Getty Center Drive, Suite 800
Los Angeles, CA 90049-1685

Getty Research Grants for Institutions - Critical Reference Resource Grants 2125
These grants support the preparation and publication of scholarly databases, reference works, innovative electronic resources, and other research tools that provide critical resource materials for art-historical scholarship. Priority is given to projects of international importance for which resources are otherwise limited. Applicants should submit a preliminary letter of inquiry to determine eligibility.
Requirements Nonprofit institutions are eligible to apply. Grants are intended to support a crucial phase or portion of a larger project, not to provide long-term, ongoing support.
Contact Research Grants for Institutions, (310) 440-7320; fax: (310) 440-7703
Internet http://www.getty.edu/grants/research/institutions/critical_reference.html
Sponsor J. Paul Getty Trust
1200 Getty Center Drive, Suite 800
Los Angeles, CA 90049-1685

Getty Research Institute Library Research Grants 2126
These grants provide short-term support to scholars at all levels to pursue independent projects that will benefit from research in the collections housed in the Getty library. Projects need not relate to the theme of the scholar year. Grantees receive partial support for costs related to research, travel, and living expenses for periods ranging rom several days to a maximum of three months. Applications are available on the Web site.

Requirements Scholars at any level who demonstrate a compelling need to use materials housed in the research library and whose place of residence is more than 80 miles from the center are eligible to apply.
Amount $500-$2500
Date(s) Application Is Due Nov 1.
Contact Library Research Grants, (310) 440-7374; fax: (310) 440-7703; email: researchgrants@getty.edu
Internet http://www.getty.edu/grants/research/scholars/library_research.html
Sponsor J. Paul Getty Trust
1200 Getty Center Dr, Ste 800
Los Angeles, CA 90049-1685

Getty Research Institute Nonresidential Grants - Collaborative Research 2127
These grants provide opportunities for teams of scholars to pursue interpretive research projects that offer new explanations of art and its history. Collaborations that foster a cross-fertilization of ideas and methodologies are particularly encouraged. Grants also fund the research in preparation for scholarly exhibitions. Grants provide support for projects during a determined time frame. Grant periods vary according to the needs of the individual projects, but are generally available for research periods of one to two years. Although team members may alternate their period of leave to work on the project, the proposed plan for the project's completion must include a portion of time dedicated to joint study; such periods of joint study may include travel. Applications are welcome from scholars of all nationalities. Potential applicants are strongly encouraged to send a brief letter of inquiry. Grant amounts may vary. Application information is available online.
Requirements These grants are intended to support established scholars who have attained distinction in their fields. Teams may consist of two or more art historians, or of one or more art historians together with one or more scholars from other disciplines. Teams for exhibition projects should include scholars from both museums and universities.
Restrictions Individual scholars may not apply as a member of more than one team. Applications for the development of basic research tools, such as computer databases or art-historical reference works, are not eligible in this grant category.
Date(s) Application Is Due Nov 1.
Contact Collaborative Research Grants, (310) 440-7374; fax: (310) 440-7703; email: researchgrants@getty.edu
Internet http://www.getty.edu/grants/research/scholars/research_collaborative.html
Sponsor J. Paul Getty Trust
1200 Getty Center Drive, Suite 800
Los Angeles, CA 90049-1685

Getty Research Institute Nonresidential Grants - Curatorial Research 2128
This fellowship supports the professional scholarly development of curators by providing them with time off from regular museum duties to undertake short-term research or study projects that advance the understanding of art and its history. Applicants may apply for a research period of one to three consecutive months. Fellowships provide stipends toward salary replacement and travel expenses. Eligible projects may include research for an exhibition or publication, travel to visit sites or collections, revision of a dissertation for publication, an intensive period of reading or writing, or other projects that support professional scholarly development. Application information is available online.
Requirements Fellowships are reserved for full-time curators of all nationalities who have a minimum of three years' professional experience and are employed at museums with art collections. Applicants must obtain authorization from their museums for the proposed fellowship term.
Restrictions Funding is not available to cover institutional overhead costs or for carrying out the planning requirements of an exhibition apart from research. Fellowships are not intended to fund research for the completion of an academic degree.
Amount $3,500-$5,000
Date(s) Application Is Due Nov 1.
Contact Curatorial Research Fellowships, (310) 440-7374; fax: (310) 440-7703; email: researchgrants@getty.edu
Internet http://www.getty.edu/grants/research/scholars/research_curatorial.html
Sponsor J. Paul Getty Trust
1200 Getty Center Drive, Suite 800
Los Angeles, CA 90049-1685

Getty Research Institute Nonresidential Grants - Postdoctoral Fellowships 2129
These fellowships provide support for outstanding scholars in the early stages of their careers, allowing them the flexibility to travel and study wherever necessary to undertake their work. Grants support interpretive research projects that make a substantial and original contribution to the understanding of art and its history. Fellowships provide a stipend for a twelve-month period. Application information is available online.
Requirements Scholars of all nationalities whose doctoral degrees in art history (or the equivalent in countries outside the United States) have been or will be officially conferred between 1/1/01 and 1/1/07 are eligible to apply. Candidates who hold doctoral degrees in fields outside art history are eligible to apply if they can demonstrate that their work promises to make a substantial and original contribution to the understanding of art and its history.
Restrictions During the tenure of the fellowship, fellows may not accept other awards or grants, nor may they undertake any form of employment. These awards may not be deferred, and they are not renewable.
Amount $40,000
Date(s) Application Is Due Nov 1.
Contact Postdoctoral Fellowships, (310) 440-7374; fax: (310) 440-7703; email: researchgrants@getty.edu
Internet http://www.getty.edu/grants/research/scholars/research_postdoc.html
Sponsor J. Paul Getty Trust
1200 Getty Center Drive, Suite 800
Los Angeles, CA 90049-1685

Getty Research Institute Predoctoral and Postdoctoral Residential Fellowships 2130
Pre- and postdoctoral fellowships provide support for emerging scholars to complete work on projects related to the Getty Research Institute's annual theme. The theme for the current program is Duration. Recipients are in residence at the institute, where they pursue research to complete their dissertations or to expand them for publication. Fellows make use of the Getty collections, join in a weekly meeting devoted to the annual theme, and participate in the intellectual life of the Getty Center. Pre- and postdoctoral fellows are in residence for the entire academic year. Both fellowships provide an office at the institute, airfare to Los Angeles, an apartment in the Getty scholar housing complex, and health benefits.
Requirements Applications are welcome from scholars of all nationalities who are working in the arts, humanities, or social sciences. Predoctoral fellowship applicants must have advanced to candidacy and expect to complete their dissertations during the fellowship period. Postdoctoral fellowship applicants must have received their degree no earlier than 1998.
Amount $18,000 predoctoral fellowships; $22,000 postdoctoral fellowships
Date(s) Application Is Due Nov 1.
Contact Pre- and Postdoctoral Fellowships, (310) 310) 440-7374; fax: (310) 440-7703; email: researchgrants@getty.edu
Internet http://www.getty.edu/grants/research/scholars/pre_post_fellows.html
Sponsor J. Paul Getty Trust
1200 Getty Center, Ste 800
Los Angeles, CA 90049-1688

Getty Scholars and Visiting Scholars Grants 2131
These grants provide a unique research experience. Recipients are in residence at the Getty Research Institute or the Getty Villa in Malibu where they are able to pursue their own projects free from academic obligations, make use of Getty collections, and participate in the intellectual life of the Getty. Scholars are in residence for the entire academic year. A salary replacement stipend is awarded. The grant also includes an office, research assistance, airfare to and from Los Angeles, an apartment and health benefits. Application information is available online.
Requirements These grants are for established scholars, artists, or writers who have attained distinction in their fields. Applications are welcome from researchers of all nationalities who are working in the arts, humanities, or social sciences.
Date(s) Application Is Due Nov 1.
Contact Getty Residential Scholar and Visiting Scholar Grants, (310) 440-7374; fax: (310) 440-7703; email: researchgrants@getty.edu
Internet http://www.getty.edu/grants/research/scholars/research_grischolars.html
Sponsor J. Paul Getty Trust
1200 Getty Center Drive, Suite 800
Los Angeles, CA 90049-1685

Giant Food Corporation Scholarships 2132
The corporation awards scholarships for pharmacy education leading to a bachelor of science or doctorate degree. Scholarships include the Izzy Cohen Memorial Scholarship and the Esther Peterson Memorial Education Scholarship. Information regarding these programs is posted online in February.
Amount $1000 Esther Peterson Memorial Education Scholarship; $4000 Izzy Cohen Memorial Scholarship
Contact Barry Scher, Vice President of Public Affairs, (301) 341-4710; fax: (301) 618-4972
Internet http://www.giantfood.com/corporate/company_charitable.htm
Sponsor Giant Food Corporation
6300 Sheriff Rd, Dept. 599
Landover, MD 20785

Gilbert F. White Postdoctoral Fellowships 2133
The fellowships support professionals who wish to devote a year to scholarly work on social science or policy problems in the areas of natural resources, energy, or the environment. Two fellowships per year are awarded for a minimum of nine and a maximum of 12 months. The amount of the stipend is commensurate with experience. Fellows will reside in one of three RFF units: the energy and natural resources division, the quality of the environment division, or the center for risk management. Applications via fax are not accepted.
Requirements The award is open to individuals in any discipline who will have completed their doctoral requirements by the beginning of the academic year for which the fellowship is requested. Faculty members who will be on sabbatical leave during the fellowship are also encouraged to apply.

Restrictions Individuals holding positions in government as well as at academic institutions are eligible.
Amount $1000 for moving and living expenses plus stipend based on current salary
Date(s) Application Is Due Feb 28.
Contact Fellowship Program, (202) 328-5155; fax: (202) 939-3460; email: white-award@rff.org
Internet http://www.rff.org/rff/About/Fellowships_and_Internships/White/Gilbert-F-White-Postdoctoral-Fellowship-Program.cfm
Sponsor Resources for the Future
1616 P St NW
Washington, DC 20036

Gilbreth Memorial Fellowships **2134**
These fellowships are awarded to recognize graduate students pursuing advanced degrees in industrial engineering in accredited industrial engineering programs at colleges and universities in the United States, Canada, or Mexico. Consideration is given to proven scholastic ability, character, leadership qualities, potential service to industrial engineering, and the need for financial assistance. Nominations are solicited from department heads at the end of August for candidates for the following academic year. Nomination packets are then sent to the nominees.
Requirements Institute members who are enrolled full time in graduate industrial engineering programs and have had a 3.4 to 4.0 GPA as undergraduates are eligible. Nominations are accepted only from department heads of accredited industrial engineering programs.
Amount $4000 maximum
Date(s) Application Is Due Nov 15.
Contact Fellowship Coordinator, (800) 494-0460 or (770) 449-0460; fax: (770) 441-3295; email: info@iienet.org
Internet http://www.iienet.org/public/articles/index.cfm?cat=525
Sponsor Institute of Industrial Engineers
3577 Parkway Ln Ste 200
Norcross, GA 30092

Gilder Lehrman Institute of American History Scholarly Fellowships **2135**
The fellowships support work in one of five archives: the Gilder Lehrman Collection, on deposit at the New-York Historical Society; the Library of the New-York Historical Society; the Columbia University Rare Book and Manuscript Library; the New York Public Library - Humanities and Social Sciences Library; and the Schomburg Center for Research in Black Culture (NYPL). To apply, candidates must submit a cover sheet with name, mailing address, email address, telephone and fax numbers; current rank, department, and institution; title of project; duration and amount of proposed fellowship; and names of recommenders. They must also submit a curriculum vitae, a 2-3-page project proposal that lists the specific holdings in the collection they intend to use (please specify only one archive in the application), two letters of recommendation, and a schedule and proposed budget of expenses during the tenure of the fellowship.
Requirements Fellowships range in duration from a week to two months and research must be completed within a year of notification of the award.
Restrictions Fellowships are not available for scholars who live within commuting distance of New York City.
Amount $1500-$4000 per month
Date(s) Application Is Due May 6; Dec 1.
Contact Fellowship Program, (646) 366-9666; fax: (646) 366-9669
Internet http://www.gilderlehrman.org/historians/scholar4.html
Sponsor Gilder Lehrman Institute of American History
19 W 44th St, Ste 500
New York, NY 10036

Gilroy and Lillian P. Roberts Charitable Foundation Grants **2136**
The foundation awards grants to eligible nonprofit organizations in its areas of interest, including arts and fine arts, health care and health organizations, higher education, Jewish temples and organizations, and social services. Types of support include annual campaigns, capital campaigns, continuing support, fellowships, general operating grants, professorships, program development, and scholarships. Most grants are awarded in Montgomery and Delaware Counties, PA. There are no application deadlines or forms.
Restrictions Individuals are not eligible.
Amount $408,750 total
Contact Stanley Merves, Treasurer, (610) 668-1998
Sponsor Gilroy and Lillian P. Roberts Charitable Foundation
101 W Elm St, Ste 500
Conshohocken, PA 19428

Gina Finzi Memorial Student Summer Fellowship **2137**
Fellowships are awarded to encourage clinical, basic or psychosocial research related to the causes, treatments, prevention, or cure of lupus. Awards are made in May to the top 10 applicants for support during the summer months. Application materials are available in December of each year. There are no renewals; applicant must submit a new proposal.
Requirements Junior investigators, defined as assistant professor and below rank if in academic medicine, are eligible to apply.
Amount $2000
Date(s) Application Is Due Mar 15.
Contact Grants Coordinator, (202) 349-1155; fax: (202) 349-1156; email: Finzifellowship@lupus.org
Internet http://www.lupus.org/research/studentannounc.html
Sponsor Lupus Foundation of America
2000 L St NW, Ste 710
Washington, DC 20036-4916

Girl's Best Friend Foundation Grants **2138**
The foundation supports and promotes programs by and for girls and young women in Illinois (ages eight through 21). The foundation is dedicated to effecting change at the grassroots level by funding community-based organizations statewide. Types of grants made include general operating support, project specific support, planning or start-up support, technical assistance, and collaborative action research (research that lays the groundwork for policy changes conducted by a partnership between two nonprofits or a nonprofit contracting with a researcher or academic institution). When multiyear funding is requested, the foundation will consider making two-year grants if the requesting organization has received at least two previous grants from GBF, is seeking two years of funding for the same purpose, and has clearly demonstrated the need for a two-year grant. Applications are due the first Monday in August.
Requirements Letters of intent will be accepted from 501(c)3 nonprofits for projects that serve or have a direct impact on girls living in the Chicago metropolitan area including Cook, DuPage, Kane, Lake, McHenry, and Will counties.
Restrictions Organizations with budgets that exceed $650,000 may apply only for technical assistance and/or collaborative action research grants. The foundation generally does not fund individuals, capital campaigns, debt reduction, scholarships, or government or religious organizations.
Amount $5000-$20,000 typically
Contact Robin Dixon, Senior Program Officer, (312) 266-2842; fax: (312) 266-2972; email: robin@girlsbestfriend.org or contact@girlsbestfriend.org
Internet http://www.girlsbestfriend.org/apply/index.html
Sponsor Girl's Best Friend Foundation
900 N Franklin, Ste 210
Chicago, IL 60610

Gladys Krieble Delmas Foundation Grants for Venetian Research **2139**
Predoctoral and postdoctoral grants will be awarded for travel to and residence in Venice and Veneto for research on Venice and the former Venetian empire and for study of contemporary Venetian society and culture. Disciplines of the humanities and social sciences are eligible areas of study, including, but not limited to, archaeology, architecture, art, bibliography, economics, history, history of science, law, literature, music, political science, religion, and theater. Prospective applicants should write to the foundation for application forms.
Requirements Applicants must be US citizens or permanent residents, have some experience in advanced research, and, if graduate students, have completed all doctoral requirements except for the dissertation at the time of application.
Amount $19,900 maximum for academic year
Date(s) Application Is Due Dec 15.
Contact Program Contact, (212) 687-0011; fax: (212) 687-8877; email: info@delmas.org
Internet http://www.delmas.org/guidelines/v_ir_a.html
Sponsor Gladys Krieble Delmas Foundation
521 Fifth Ave, Ste 1612
New York, NY 10175-1699

Glaucoma Foundation Grants in Aid **2140**
The foundation funds research initiatives to determine the causes of glaucoma, to improve methods of treatment, and to develop cures for the various kinds of glaucoma. Two areas of particular focus are: optic nerve rescue and restoration--research into new approaches designed to protect the optic nerve against glaucomatous damage, to restore vision lost to glaucoma and eventually reverse blindness by restoring or regenerating the function of the optic nerve cells, and to explore the feasibility of achieving transplantation of optic nerve cells; and molecular genetics--research into the genetic causes of the various forms of glaucoma, particularly the identification of the responsible genes, with the long-term goal of finding ways to reverse these genetic defects. Grants are awarded for a one-year period and are renewable. Guidelines and application are available online.
Requirements Applicants must have a full time faculty position or the equivalent.
Restrictions The foundation does not provide funds for investigator salaries, travel, overhead, or other indirect costs.
Amount $35,000 maximum initial grant; $50,000 maximum renewal grant
Date(s) Application Is Due Mar 1; Sep 1.
Contact Grants Administrator, (212) 285-0080; fax: (212) 651-1888; email: info@glaucomafoundation.org
Internet http://www.glaucomafoundation.org/info.php?i=5
Sponsor Glaucoma Foundation Grants
80 Maiden Ln, Ste 1206
New York, NY 10038

Glaucoma Research Pilot Project Grants **2141**
These grants provide funds to encourage innovative and pilot research, as well as to aid ongoing studies that seek to protect and restore the optic nerve, accurately monitor

glaucoma's progression, find the genes responsible for the glaucoma, understand the intraocular pressure system and develop better treatments, and determine the risk factors for glaucoma damage. Grants are awarded for one year with the possibility of renewal. Preliminary proposals are due December 1.
Requirements Applicants must have a graduate degree.
Restrictions Funding is not granted for equipment purchases, overhead commercial applications, or indirect costs.
Amount $15,000-$50,000
Date(s) Application Is Due Feb 1.
Contact Grants Administrator, (800) 826-6693 or (415) 986-3162; fax: (415) 986-3763; email: info@glaucoma.org
Internet http://www.glaucoma.org/research
Sponsor Glaucoma Research Foundation
490 Post St, Ste 1427
San Francisco, CA 94102

Glenn/AFAR Breakthroughs in Gerontology Awards **2142**
The goal of the program is to provide timely support to a small number of pilot research programs that may be of high risk but offer significant promise of yielding transforming discoveries in the fundamental biology of aging. The hope is that one or more of the funded research projects will lead to major new insights into the molecular factors that coordinate aging in multiple cells and tissues, and the ways in which the aging process is differentially timed in long-lived species. Projects that focus on genetic controls of aging and longevity, on delay of aging by pharmacological agents or dietary means, or that elucidate the mechanisms by which alterations in hormones, anti-oxidant defenses, or repair processes promote longevity are all well within the intended scope of this competition. Projects that focus instead on specific diseases or on assessment of health care strategies will receive much lower priority, unless the research plan makes clear and direct connections to fundamental issues in the biology of aging. Studies of invertebrates, mice, human clinical materials, or cell lines are all potentially eligible for funding. Although preliminary data are always helpful for evaluating the feasibility of the experiments proposed, the emphasis in review will be on creativity and the likelihood that the findings will open new vistas and approaches to aging research that might merit intensive follow-up studies. Applications from individuals not previously engaged in aging research are particularly encouraged, as long as the research proposals show high promise for leading to important new discoveries in biological gerontology. The proposed research must be conducted at any type of nonprofit setting in the United States. Guidelines are available online.
Requirements Applicants must at the time they submit their proposal be full-time faculty members at the rank of assistant professor or higher. A strong record of independent publication beyond the postdoctoral level is a requirement.
Restrictions Applicants who are employees in the NIH Intramural program are not eligible.
Amount $125,000 maximum
Date(s) Application Is Due May 2.
Contact Grants Manager, (212) 703-9977; fax: (212) 997-0330; email: grants@afar.org
Internet http://www.afar.org/GlennBIG.html
Sponsor American Federation for Aging Research
70 W 40th St, 11th Fl
New York, NY 10018

Glenn/AFAR Research Grants for Postdoctoral Fellows **2143**
AFAR funds research projects concerned with understanding the basic mechanisms of aging. Projects investigating age-related diseases are also supported, especially if approached from the point of view of how basic aging processes may lead to these outcomes. Projects concerning mechanisms underlying common geriatric functional disorders are also encouraged. Examples of promising areas of research include aging and immune function; genetic control of longevity; neurobiology and neuropathology of aging; invertebrate or vertebrate animal models; cardiovascular aging; aging and cellular stress resistance; metabolic and endocrine changes; age-related changes in cell proliferation; caloric restriction and aging; DNA repair and control of gene expression; biology of the menopause; aging and apoptosis; and biodemographic analysis of aging. Funding begins July 1. Guidelines and application are available online.
Requirements Postdoctoral fellows (MDs and PhDs) who will have had at least two and not more than five years of prior postdoctoral training at the time of the award are eligible.
Restrictions Funds may not be requested for overhead or indirect costs. Fellows may not hold any concurrent foundation or not-for-profit funding.
Amount $60,000
Date(s) Application Is Due Dec 15.
Contact Grants Manager, (212) 703-9977; fax: (212) 997-0330; email: amfedaging@aol.com
Internet http://www.afar.org/grants.html
Sponsor American Federation for Aging Research
70 W 40th St
New York, NY 10018

Global Center for Dispute Resolution Research Grants **2144**
The center is dedicated to research that provides insight, information, and guidance on the growth and practice of alternative dispute resolution (ADR) methods throughout the world, particularly in the area of cross-border commerce. The grants program funds research papers. Areas of interest include pattern and trend analysis of the collected data, such as global trends in ADR by industry, by country, by process type, and by forces in the marketplace that lead to caseload fluctuations in different sectors; and designed experiment research that will examine specific aspects of dispute resolution processes, such as process effectiveness, cost savings, time savings, quality of result, party satisfaction, and optimization of results. Research findings and their application will inform policy development in the field and increase process knowledge of practitioners.
Contact Grants Administrator, (212) 716-3900; fax: (212) 716-5913; email: woodw@adr.org
Internet http://www.globalcenteradr.org/english/research.jsp
Sponsor Global Center for Dispute Resolution Research
335 Madison Ave, 10th Fl
New York, NY 10017

Global Change Education Program **2145**
This program provides research opportunities in areas related to global change such as atmospheric sciences, ecology, global carbon cycles, climatology, and terrestrial processes. Types of support include graduate research environmental fellowships (GREF) and summer undergraduate research experiences (SURE).
Requirements College juniors, seniors, and graduate students are eligible to apply.
Amount $475 weekly, plus travel for undergratuages; $1500 monthly stipend, plus tuition and fees for graduates
Contact Dr. Milton Constantin, Program Manager, (865) 576-7009; email: constanm@orau.gov; Dr. Jeffrey Gaffney, Argonne National Laboratory, (630) 252-5178; email: constanm@orau.gov
Internet http://see.orau.org/ProgramDescription.aspx?Program=10125
Sponsor Oak Ridge Institution for Science and Education
P.O. Box 117, 120 Badger Ave, MS 36
Oak Ridge, TN 37831-0117

GMFUS Grants **2146**
The fund's grantmaking promotes the study of international and domestic policies, supports comparative research and debate on key issues, and assists policy and opinion leaders' understanding of these issues. Grants are allocated in the areas of economics, environment, foreign policy, and immigration and integration. On occasion, grants are awarded to fund projects or institutions that are worthy of support but that do not fall within one of the fund's established program areas. Initial inquiries should be submitted in a letter or brief proposal, written in English, and should outline the project's: purpose and importance; relation to the fund's program areas; budget; other potential funding sources; qualifications of the applicant; and plans for dissemination and follow-up.
Restrictions The fund generally does not offer support for projects chiefly concerned with countries outside Europe and the United States; building and operating funds; education below the doctoral level; scientific research; or the arts.
Contact Grants Administrator, (202) 745-3950; fax: (202) 265-1662; email: info@gmfus.org
Internet http://www.gmfus.org/grants/index.cfm
Sponsor German Marshall Fund of the 1744 R St NW
Washington, DC 20009

GMFUS Transatlantic Environmental Fellowship Program **2147**
The fund aims to promote collaboration between Americans and Europeans on efforts that increase understanding of policy differences between the United States and Europe on transportation, agriculture, and air quality issues. Projects should involve people on both sides of the Atlantic, develop leadership, and transfer experience and innovations between practitioners and policymakers.
Requirements Nonprofits in the United States and Western Europe are eligible.
Restrictions The fund generally does not offer support for building and operating funds, graduate or undergraduate education, research, or the arts.
Amount $9000-$40,000
Contact Lea Rosenbohm, Director of Programs, (202) 745-6663; email: lrosenbohm@gmfus.org
Internet http://www.gmfus.org/fellowships/index.cfm
Sponsor German Marshall Fund of the 1744 R St, NW
Washington, DC 20009

GMFUS Transatlantic Policy Research Fellowships **2148**
The aim of this program is to support research-driven conferences of scholars and policymakers working on transatlantic policy issues that will be selected and change on a yearly basis. GMF will award six grants for transatlantic policy conferences in the academic year. Conference proposals should include scholars from the United States and Europe, and preference will be given to those proposals with a comparative and interdisciplinary approach. Proposals will be evaluated on their intellectual merits, transatlantic cooperation, engagement with the policy community, and potential policy impact through publications or other means. This year, GMF will consider proposals in three areas: democracy promotion, immigration, and economic competitiveness policy.
Requirements American and European university-based scholars from any discipline may apply.

Amount $25,000 maximum
Date(s) Application Is Due Mar 1.
Contact Program Officer, (202) 745-3950; fax: (202) 265-1662; email: epope@gmfus.org or info@gmfus.org
Internet http://www.gmfus.org/fellowships/research.cfm
Sponsor German Marshall Fund of the 1744 R St NW
Washington, DC 20009

Goddess Scholars Grants **2149**
The purpose of these grants is to develop young researchers at the entry faculty level (Instructor or Assistant Professor) who will focus a research career on studying the unique aspects of stroke in women. Such research may be basic or clinical in orientation, including areas such as mechanisms of ischemic brain injury, neuroprotective treatments, primary or secondary stroke prevention, epidemiological studies, educational programs for patients or health care providers, rehabilitation, and outcome research. The grant provides funding for two years, with potential non-competitive renewal for a third year should satisfactory progress be demonstrated. These grants are intended to provide bridging funds for individuals who are finishing or have completed residency or postdoctoral training and require additional support before their subsequent establishment as independent investigators.
Requirements Goddess Scholar grants are targeted at individuals who: hold an M.D., Ph.D., or equivalent degree; are at the fellow, instructor, or assistant professor rank; and are within 5 years of completion of residency or post-doctoral fellowship at the time of grant activation. Individuals who are currently enrolled in a fellowship program may apply if there is assurance of a faculty position at the time of the grant's activation.
Amount $65,000 direct salary plus research costs (e.g. research or laboratory assistant, materials, small equipment)
Contact Willow Heske, Program/Operations Assistant, (212) 713-6789; fax: (212) 288-2160; email: willow@thegoddessfund.org
Internet http://www.thegoddessfund.org/grantprograms.html
Sponsor Hazel K. Goddess Fund for Stroke Research in Women
785 Park Avenue
New York, NY 10021-3552

Goethe-Institut Grants **2150**
The institute was founded to promote the German language abroad and for the fostering of international cultural relations. It operates internationally in the fields of science and medicine, arts and humanities, and international relations. Types of support include grants to institutions and individuals and scholarships. The institute is particularly concerned with the teaching and promotion of the German language abroad and provides professional assistance to foreign teachers of German and students of German philology, and for the development and improvement of teaching methods and materials.
Contact Dr. Hilmar Hoffman, President, 49-89-159210; fax: 49-89-15921450; email: zentralverwaltlung@goethe.de
Internet http://www.goethe.de
Sponsor Goethe-Institut
Helene-Wever-Allee 1
Munich 80637 Germany

Goldhirsh Foundation Brain Tumor Research Grants **2151**
The foundation is interested in providing strategic investment in both pediatric and adult brain tumor research to accelerate progress toward more effective treatment for malignant diffuse glioma tumors. Responses are sought from investigators working in the continuum between basic research and clinical application, integrating and translating knowledge in various disciplines into meaningful progress for patients. Examples of funding areas include but are not limited to oncogenomics and proteomics, genetically engineered models, the discovery and testing of small molecule therapies, unusual drug delivery systems, or improved brain imaging techniques. The foundation also encourages submission of research projects at the interface of developmental biology and cancer along the stem cell to glial axis. Eligibility is not limited to those investigators currently working in brain tumor research. Investigators from other fields are encouraged to apply with proposals relevant to malignant diffuse glioma tumors. Projects must be relevant to malignant diffuse gliomas, i.e., diffuse astrocytomas, oligodendrogliomas and oligoastrocytomas, including glioblastoma. The sponsoring institution accepts responsibility for the scientific, administrative, and financial management of the overall project including subcontracts. The candidate may collaborate with investigators from other institutions and these institutions may include for-profit companies. Letters of intent must be submitted online by the listed application deadline; full proposals are by invitation. Guidelines are available online.
Requirements Applications are accepted from candidates working in the United States or Canada who meet the following eligibility *Requirements* have an MD and/or PhD degree(s) or equivalent degree; hold at least the position of Assistant Professor or equivalent at a US-based 501(c)3 or equivalent nonprofit Canadian institution.
Restrictions Projects in benign/WHO grade I gliomas, nonglial nonepithelial tumors, meningeal tumors, nerve sheath tumors, CNS lymphomas, germ-cell tumors, and tumors of the sella region are beyond the scope of the grant program focus. Projects that characterize genes and gene products of normal cellular development are not eligible, nor are epidemiological studies.
Amount $600,000 three-year and $100,000 one-year pilot studies
Date(s) Application Is Due Jan 10.
Contact Dr. Sally E. McNagny, (617) 279-2254; fax: (617) 423-4619; email: smcnagny@goldhirshfoundation.org
Internet http://www.goldhirshfoundation.org/application_information.htm
Sponsor Goldhirsh Foundation
95 Berkeley Street, Suite 201
Boston, MA 02116

Goldman Philanthropic Partnerships Program **2152**
Since its founding, the Program has solicited, validated and helped donors co-fund innovative research with the potential to quickly find cures for life-altering diseases, and supported these donors using for-profit business tools to insure that the research and philanthropic goals are met through proper project and resource management. The Program provides funding research for cures for a range of catastrophic diseases by exploring groundbreaking research in all disciplines of medicine, including those areas of research outside of conventional medicine such as alternative medicine. The Program usually co-funds a venture with at least one organizational, institutional, or corporate partner. The Partnerships maintains a strong interest in diseases of children and young adults, although it will fund research into any patient population where it believes there is a high likelihood of return on disease prevention, treatment or cure.
Contact Dr. Bruce E. Bloom, (312) 601-8856 or (312) 780-3440; fax: (312) 780-3459; email: bruce@goldmanpartnerships.org
Internet http://www.goldmanpartnerships.org/aboutus.html
Sponsor Goldman Philanthropic Partnerships
70 West Madison Street, Suite 1500
Chicago, IL 60602

Goldsmith Awards Program **2153**
The program, funded by the Goldsmith-Greenfield Foundation, is sponsored by the Joan Shorenstein Center on the Press, Politics, and Public Policy at Harvard University's John F. Kennedy School of Government. The program annually awards both the Goldsmith Prize for Investigative Reporting and the Goldsmith Book Prize. The Goldsmith Prize is given annually to the journalist(s) whose investigative reporting in a story or series of related stories best promotes more effective and ethical conduct of government, the making of public policy, or the practice of politics. The Goldsmith Book Prize is given annually to the author(s) of the best book that aims at improving the quality of government or politics through an examination of the press and government or the intersection of press and politics in the formation of public policy. Both prizes have a submission deadline of December 31. The program also grants Goldsmith Research Awards on an ongoing basis to scholars, graduate students, and journalists in the field of press/politics. Applications are available on the Web site.
Requirements Publication must have occurred within 12 months (January 1 through December 31) preceding the submission deadline, and all submissions must be in English.
Restrictions Edited volumes will not be accepted for the book prize. Books will not be accepted as submissions for the investigative reporting prize.
Amount $25,000 for investigative reporting prize, $2000 to finalists; $2500 for book prize
Date(s) Application Is Due Jan 5.
Contact Administrator, Goldsmith Awards Program, Joan Shorenstein Center, (617) 495-1329; fax: (617) 495-8696; email: alison_kommer@harvard.edu
Internet http://www.ksg.harvard.edu/presspol/goldsmith.shtml
Sponsor Harvard University
John F. Kennedy School of Government, 79 John F. Kennedy St
Cambridge, MA 02138

Goodman and Gilman Award in Drug Receptor Pharmacology **2154**
This award is given biennially (even-numbered years) to recognize and stimulate outstanding research in the pharmacology of biological receptors. It is the hope that such research might provide a better understanding of the mechanism of biological processes and potentially provide the basis for the discovery of drugs useful in the treatment of diseases. The award includes a monetary prize and travel support for winner and spouse to attend the award ceremony. Nominations must be received September 15 of the year prior to the year in which the award will be made.
Requirements Nominations must be made by ASPET members; however, there are no restrictions as to age, sex, nationality, or institutional affiliation. Nominee need not be a member of ASPET.
Amount $2500
Date(s) Application Is Due Sep 15.
Contact Dr. Christine Carrico, Executive Officer, (301) 530-7060; fax: (301) 530-7061; email: ccarrico@aspet.faseb.org or info@aspet.org
Internet http://www.aspet.org/public/awards/g&g_award.html
Sponsor American Society for Pharmacology and Experimental Therapeutics
9650 Rockville Pike
Bethesda, MD 20814-3995

Gordon Allport Intergroup Relations Prize **2155**
This prize is awarded annually to the best paper or article submitted on intergroup relations concerning race, sex, age, and socioeconomic status. The manuscript need not have been published. Entries should be submitted in quadruplicate and will not be returned.

Requirements Papers submitted for consideration must have been written during the current year on intergroup relations. Competitors need not be society members. Graduate students are particularly urged to compete.
Amount $1000
Date(s) Application Is Due Nov 1.
Contact Intergroup Relations Prize, email: awards@spssi.org
Internet http://www.spssi.org/Allport_flyer.html
Sponsor Society for the Psychological Study of Social Issues
1901 Pennsylvania Ave NW, Ste 901
Washington, DC 20006-3405

Gottlieb Daimler and Karl Benz Foundation Grants **2156**
Grants are awarded to individuals for doctoral research, to German nationals wishing to conduct research abroad, and to foreign young scientists carrying out research at German institutions. In addition, several grants support the scientific cooperation with the Kaliningrad State University (open for applications), with young economists from East Europe, with Peking University, with Vietnam, and with South Africa. Types of support include awards, general operating support, basic research, dissertation research support, fellowships, international exchange programs and grants, seed grants, and conferences and workshops.
Date(s) Application Is Due Mar 1; Oct 1.
Contact Dr. Jorg Klein, Managing Director, 49-6203-1092-0; fax: 49-6203-1092-5; email: klein@daimler-benz-stiftung.de
Internet http://www.daimler-benz-stiftung.de/home/fellowship/en/start.html
Sponsor Gottlieb Daimler and Karl Benz Foundation
Dr Larl-Benz-Platz 2
Ladenburg 68526 Germany

GPP Charles E. Culpeper Foundation Biomedical Pilot Projects Initiative Grants **2157**
The initiative is designed to encourage the investigation of novel ideas in cures for disease, particularly in the areas of molecular genetics, bio-engineering, and molecular pharmacology. Research into complimentary and alternative medicine will also be considered. Grants will be made on a one-time basis with the possibility for renewal for a second year upon reapplication. No more than 8 percent of the grant may be allocated to cover indirect costs. The purpose of these grants is to explore new and even untested hypotheses, thus substantial preliminary information is not required. Proposals are accepted throughout the year and each successful
Requirements Nonprofit health care organizations, accredited medical schools, and universities in the United States are eligible.
Amount $25,000 maximum
Date(s) Application Is Due Nov 16.
Contact Grants Administrator, (847) 948-5512; fax: (847) 948-5516
Internet http://www.goldmanpartnerships.org/Culpeper/CulpeperBiomedicalPilotInitiativegrants.htm
Sponsor Goldman Philanthropic Partnerships
155 N Pfingsten Rd, Ste 109
Deerfield, IL 60015

Graduate Institute of International Studies Scholarships **2158**
A number of scholarships are awarded each year by the institute for doctoral instruction in international law and politics, international economics, political science, international institutions, and international development. Limited financial assistance is obtained and maintained on the basis of both the academic performance and the financial status of the applicants. The Gallatin Fellowship is awarded competitively to an advanced American student to permit him/her to engage in research work at the institute for one year, and to an advanced doctoral student from the institute to enable him/her to study and do research for 10 months at an American university of his/her choosing. In addition, the Paul Guggenheim Foundation awards a prize every two years to a work in international law that is distinguished by its exceptional quality and that is the first outstanding work of its author. Obtain instructions for scholarships and this award from the secretariat. The Swiss Confederation also grants scholarships to foreign graduates; candidates for such scholarships should apply to the Swiss diplomatic representatives in their countries. For US citizens, information on other scholarships and fellowships is available from the Institute of International Education, 809 United Nations Plaza, New York, NY 10017.
Requirements Generally, these scholarships are reserved for advanced students, especially those working toward doctorates, who have been enrolled at least one year.
Amount Sf10,000 per year
Date(s) Application Is Due Jan 10; Mar 1.
Contact Jean-Claude Frachebourg, Secretaire General, 41 22 908 59 59; fax: 41 22 733 30 49; email: info@hei.unige.ch
Internet http://heiwww.unige.ch/sections/ec/admissions/tuition.html
Sponsor Graduate Institute of International Studies
Avenue de la Paix 11A
Geneva 1202
Switzerland

Graduate Writing Fellowships **2159**
Fellowships are given to talented writers of fiction or poetry intending to make writing their vocation. Five departmental fellowships are awarded annually for the master's program in creative writing: the Raymond Carver, Hayden Carruth, Loring Williams (Academy of American Poets), Delmore Schwartz, and the Jeremy Lake Memorial prizes in poetry and in fiction, the Raymond Carver, the Peter Neagoe, and the Stephen Crane prizes in fiction. These fellowships include an academic-year award stipend and a full-tuition scholarship for 24 credits for the academic year (12 credit hours per semester). Normally, these are awarded to new students and are not renewable.
Requirements Applicant must have a bachelor's degree, preferably in English.
Amount $9800-$12,300 plus remitted tuition for all fellowships
Date(s) Application Is Due Jan 10.
Contact Christopher Kennedy, Director of Creative Writing Program, (315) 443-3755; fax: (315) 443-5390; email: ckennedy@syr.edu
Internet http://www-hl.syr.edu/depts/english/cwp/cwsupport.htm#10
Sponsor Syracuse University
English Department, 401 Hall of Languages
Syracuse, NY 13244-1170

Graham Foundation Carter Manny Award **2160**
The foundation supports advanced-level architectural projects and other areas of the arts. This award is made for doctoral dissertation research at international schools of architecture.
Requirements Candidates must be nominated by their departments.
Amount $15,000 maximum
Date(s) Application Is Due Mar 15.
Contact Richard Solomon, Director, (312) 787-4071; email: rsolomon@grahamfoundation.org
Internet http://www.grahamfoundation.org/grants/carter-desc.asp
Sponsor Graham Foundation
4 W Burton Pl
Chicago, IL 60610

Graham Foundation Grants **2161**
Grants are offered to individuals and institutions in support of activities focused on architecture and the built environment; and generally for activities that lead to the public dissemination of ideas through publication, exhibition, or educational programming. The Foundation has supported a variety of endeavors, including research by scholars; grants to architectural schools for special projects, enrichment programs, or new curricula; grants to museums, schools, and libraries for exhibitions, catalogues, and, in rare cases, for acquisitions; and support for publications, usually to help make an important publication better or more affordable. When large sums are necessary, the foundation is willing to consider a seed grant to explore possibilities, or a challenge grant when feasibility already seems clear and help is needed to corroborate worthiness of purpose and stimulate broad support. Occasionally multiyear grants are offered, though they normally will not extend beyond three consecutive years.
Requirements Both individuals and organizations may apply. For individuals, consideration is given to those demonstrating mature creative talents who have specific project objectives.
Restrictions There is no direct scholarship aid. The foundation does not award grants to cover costs of endowments, annual operating expenses, construction, or architectural fees in support of construction or renovation projects.
Amount $10,000 average
Date(s) Application Is Due Jan 15; Jul 15.
Contact Richard Solomon, Director, (312) 787-4071; email: rsolomon@grahamfoundation.org or info@grahamfoundation.org
Internet http://www.grahamfoundation.org/grants/gen-desc.asp
Sponsor Graham Foundation
4 W Burton Pl
Chicago, IL 60610

Grammy Foundation Grants **2162**
The foundation awards grants in two program areas. Research Projects grants are made to organizations and individuals to support efforts that advance the research and/or broad- reaching implementations of original research projects related to the impact of music study on early childhood development, the human development, and the medical and occupational well-being of music professionals. Archiving and Preservation Projects grants are made to organizations and individuals to support efforts that advance the archiving and preservation of the music and recorded sound heritage of the Americas. The foundation funds preservation of original, preexisting media and source material; preservation projects that follow the recommended methodology; projects of historical, artistic, cultural, and or/national significance; and archiving projects including the rescue, organization of, and access to preexisting media and materials. Application and guidelines are available online.
Restrictions The foundation does not fund Recording Academy chapters, trustees, governors, officers, or staff; organizations that discriminate on the basis of race, sex, religion, national origin, disability, or age; projects promoting advocacy issues; a single organization or individual for more than three consecutive years; organizations or individuals not based in the Americas; purchase of collections; recording projects, demo tapes, or performance events; proposals for commercial purposes (i.e., CD reissue or textbook/ A/V package); purchase of repairs of equipment; purchase or repairs of musical instruments; maintenance or upgrading of computer systems; competitions or any expense associated with competitions; work toward academic degrees; music

education or in-residence programs; documentaries; endowments and fundraising; buildings and facilities; marketing, publicity, design costs; or projects where copyright status is unknown.
Amount $10,000-$40,000
Date(s) Application Is Due Oct 1.
Contact Kristin Murphy, (310) 392-3777 ext 8662; fax: (310) 392-2188; email: grant@grammy.com
Internet http://www.grammy.com/GRAMMY_Foundation/Grants/
Sponsor Grammy Foundation
3402 Pico Blvd
Santa Monica, CA 90405

Grass Foundation Marine Biological Laboratory Fellowships **2163**
The foundation awards fellowships to encourage independent research for scientific discovery by investigators early in their careers and to increase research opportunities for persons trained for careers in neurobiological investigation. Neurobiological approaches supported include neurophysiology, membrane biophysics, integrative neurobiology and neuroethology, neuroanatomy, neuropharmacology, systems neuroscience, cellular and developmental neurobiology, and computational approaches to neural systems. Fellowships provide funds to support an investigator, his/her spouse or domestic partner, and dependent children for one summer at the Marine Biological Laboratory in Woods Hole, MA. Laboratory research space, equipment, housing and board, and travel expenses to and from the MBL are covered. Guidelines and application are available online.
Requirements Applicants may be researchers in the late stages of predoctoral training or postdoctoral researchers. Priority is given to applicants who have demonstrated a commitment to a research career, who have no more than five years of postdoctoral research and who have no prior research experience at the Marine Biological Laboratory. All US citizens, permanent residents, and foreign applicants with or able to obtain J-1 Visas for the duration of the fellowship are eligible to participate in this program. The foundation must have a copy of the J-1 Visa prior to participation in the program.
Restrictions Applicants should not attempt to combine a fellowship at the Marine Biological Laboratory with writing a dissertation (PhD thesis).
Date(s) Application Is Due Dec 15.
Contact Fellowship Administrator, (781) 843-0219; fax: (781) 843-0474; email: grassfdn@aol.com
Internet http://www.grassfoundation.org/fellowships/grass_fellowship/index.html
Sponsor Grass Foundation
400 Franklin St, Ste 302
Braintree, MA 02184

Grawemeyer Education Awards **2164**
This award is given to the author(s) of the theory, policy proposal, technological advance, program initiative, or research study published in the recent past that is judged to have the most potential for educational improvement. The program intent is to stimulate worldwide the dissemination, public scrutiny, and implementation of ideas that have potential to contribute to improvement in educational practice and attainment. The award is intended not only to recognize the individual(s) responsible, but also to draw critical attention to the award-winning ideas, proposals, or achievements. Annual deadline dates may vary; contact program staff for exact dates.
Requirements The university invites nominations from professional educators, educational institutions and organizations, and editors and publishers of journals and books worldwide.
Restrictions Self-nominations will not be considered.
Amount $200,000 payable in five annual installments of $40,000
Date(s) Application Is Due Feb 1.
Contact Dr. Allan E. Dittmer, Executive Director, (502) 852-0791; fax: (502) 852-1497; email: allan@louisville.edu
Internet http://www.louisville.edu/ur/onpi/grawemeyer/education/index.html
Sponsor University of Louisville
School of Education, University of Louisville
Louisville, KY 40292

Great Lakes Fishery Trust Grants **2165**
The mission of the trust is to provide funding to nonprofit organizations, educational institutions, and government agencies to enhance, protect, and rehabilitate Great Lakes fishery resources. Preproposals are sought in the following themes: research and related management activities consistent with the goals in the Lake Michigan Fish-Community Objectives; innovative research intended to lead to effective means to prevent the introduction of invasive species in the Great Lakes and limit the range and/or abundance of invasive species already present; research that models critical ecosystem components essential to sustainable fish population management; and research and analysis that documents the contribution (economic, environmental, and/or social) of various elements of the fishery. The trust will accept preproposals only submitted thought eh e-Grant application system.
Requirements Preproposals are encouraged from educational, governmental, tribal, and 501(c)3 tax-exempt organizations.
Date(s) Application Is Due Jan 25.
Contact Trust Administrator, (517) 371-7468; fax: (517) 484-6549; email: glft@glft.org
Internet http://www.glft.org/geninfo.htm
Sponsor Great Lakes Fishery Trust
600 W Saint Joseph, Ste 10
Lansing, MI 48933-2265

Great Lakes Protection Fund Grants **2166**
The Great Lakes Protection Fund welcomes preproposals for projects that enhance the health of the Great Lakes ecosystem. Applicants should propose projects that will return the greatest ecosystem benefits. Current funding interests include preventing biological pollution, restoring natural flow regimes; and using market mechanisms for environmental improvement. Additional projects are sought to add to, and expand fund-supported work in these areas. The fund also welcomes projects that are designed to identify and explore other master variables that if acted upon, will result in tangible improvements to the health of the Great Lakes ecosystem. Proposals may be submitted at any time. The board makes grant decisions at its March, June, September, and December meetings.
Requirements Nonprofit organizations (including environmental organizations, trade associations, and universities), for-profit businesses, government agencies, and individuals are eligible for fund support.
Restrictions The fund does not give to general operating funds, environmental education, and groups from Indiana.
Amount $25,000-$420,000 typically
Contact Program Contact, (847) 425-8150; fax: (847) 424-9832; email: preproposals@glpf.org
Internet http://www.glpf.org/interest/index.html
Sponsor Great Lakes Protection Fund
1560 Sherman Ave, Ste 880
Evanston, IL 60201

Green Foundation Grants **2167**
The Foundation's resources are focused on the four specific areas of arts, education, medical/scientific research and special projects. Preferential attention will be given to institutions exhibiting the following positive factors: a history of achievement, good management, and a stable financial condition; significant programs with the promise of making a measurable impact; programs that are self-sustaining and will not necessitate continued dependence on the Foundation. Interested applicants must complete the Foundation's online eligibility questionnaire. Information is available online.
Requirements 501(c)3 nonprofits (as per the IRS Service Code of 1986) are eligible. Most grantmaking is limited to institutions that serve the Los Angeles community; however the Foundation will consider requests beyond this geographic boundary for those institutions with the potential to impact communities statewide or nationally.
Restrictions The Foundation does not provide funds for: those with net assets or fund balances of less than $100,000; multi-year commitments; annual meetings, conferences, and/or seminars; religious programs; capital campaigns; direct mail campaigns; conduit institutions, unified funds, fiscal agents, or institutions using grant funds from donors to support other institutions or individuals; private foundations; individuals.
Contact Kylie Schwerdtfeger, (626) 584-1285; fax: (626) 577-9400; email: kylies@ligf.org
Internet http://ligf.org/index.html
Sponsor Green Foundation
201 South Lake Avenue, Suite 605
Pasadena, CA 91101

Greenburg-May Foundation Grants **2168**
Grants are almost entirely awarded for medical research, primarily in the fields of cancer, heart, and neurological research. In addition, some support is given to hospitals, Jewish welfare funds, temple support, and the aging. Types of support include general operating support, continuing support, annual campaigns, endowment funds, emergency funds, program development, internships, scholarship funds, research, and consulting services. Organizations in Florida and New York City receive the largest part of the funds. Applications may be submitted at any time.
Requirements Nonprofit organizations in southern Florida and New York are eligible.
Restrictions Grants are not given to individuals or for endowment funds, special projects, publications, or conferences, and generally not for scholarships and fellowships.
Amount $295,282 total
Contact Isabel May, President, (305) 864-8639
Sponsor Greenburg-May Foundation
P.O. Box 54-5816
Miami Beach, FL 33154

Greenspun Family Foundation Grants **2169**
The foundation awards grants to eligible Nevada organizations in its areas of interest, including cancer research, children's services, higher education, the physically and mentally disabled, and religious welfare programs that provide for the homeless. There are no application forms or deadlines. Submit a letter of request.
Requirements Nevada nonprofit organizations are eligible. Preference is given to requests from the Las Vegas area.
Contact Grants Administrator
Sponsor Greenspun Family Foundation
901 N Green Valley Pkwy, Ste 210
Henderson, NV 89074

Greenwall Foundation Bioethics Grants 2170
The Foundation provides funding for physicians, lawyers, philosophers, theologians and other professionals to address micro and macro issues in bioethics, providing guidance for those engaged in decision-making at the bedside as well as those responsible for shaping institutional and public policy. The Foundation is especially interested in the work of junior investigators and pilot projects that may lead to NIH support, and it is prepared to address issues regarded by some as sensitive or potentially controversial.
Restrictions The Foundation is not normally interested in proposals to support equipment purchase, facility construction or renovation, or general operating expenses, and will not normally consider grants to private foundations, endowment funds, or individual applicants.
Amount $5000-$50,000 average
Date(s) Application Is Due Feb 1; Aug 1.
Contact Sam Teigen, Grants Administrator; (212) 679-7266; fax: (212) 679-7269; email: steigen@greenwall.org
Internet http://www.greenwall.org/guidebio.htm
Sponsor Greenwall Foundation
420 Lexington Avenue, Suite 2500
New York, NY 10170

Greenwall Foundation Faculty Scholars Program in Bioethics 2171
The Program is a career development program that enables junior faculty members to carry out original research on policy and moral dilemmas at the intersection of ethics and the life sciences. To maximize scholarly development, three years of support are provided, requiring a 50% time commitment (carefully monitored) in each of the three years. Each year the Scholars participate in a learner-centered educational program that includes required attendance at two workshops (spring and fall). Continued involvement in this activity, after each Scholar's support period is over, provides Scholar-alumni/ae with ongoing professional development and engages them in the training of successor cohorts. Preliminary applications are due on December 3. Approximately 15 to 20 applicants will be invited to submit full proposals due in February.
Requirements Applicants must be junior faculty members holding at least a 60% appointment at a university or non-profit research institute in the U.S. Priority will be given to applicants who are below the rank of Associate Professor, who have not received a comparable career development award, and whose work will have an impact on public policy or clinical practice. Within this group, priority will be given to applicants whose research addresses innovative and emerging topics.
Date(s) Application Is Due Dec 3.
Contact Sam Teigen, Grants Administrator; (415) 476-6241 or (212) 679-7266; fax: (212) 679-7269; email: steigen@greenwall.org or greenwall@medicine.ucsf.edu
Internet http://www.greenwallfsp.org/
Sponsor Greenwall Foundation
420 Lexington Avenue, Suite 2500
New York, NY 10170

Greenwall Foundation Fellowship Program in Bioethics and Health Policy 2172
The Fellowship program and its faculty cover much of the waterfront of issues and methodologies in bioethics, from ethics and advances in biomedical science, to ethics and public health and health policy, to ethics and clinical care. The defining focus of the Program, however, is bioethics and public policy. The Program is intended for people who are early in their careers. Greenwall applicants are subdivided by discipline (medicine, philosophy and law) and reviewed by a selection committee composed of program faculty with relevant disciplinary backgrounds. Typically, only one Fellow per year is accepted from each discipline.
Amount $111,650 over two years
Date(s) Application Is Due Dec 1.
Contact Gail Geller; (410) 955-7894; email: ggeller@jhmi.edu; ; Maria Merritt; (410) 614-6335; email: mmerritt@jhsph.edu
Internet http://www.greenwall.org/guideaffil.htm
Sponsor Greenwall Foundation
420 Lexington Avenue, Suite 2500
New York, NY 10170

GSA Research Grants 2173
The society offers research grants to provide partial support of master's and doctoral thesis research in earth science for graduate students at universities in the United States, Canada, Mexico, and Central America. Application forms are available on the Web site. faxed or email applications will not be accepted.
Requirements Eligibility is restricted to GSA members. Applicant must be enrolled in a graduate program in the United States, Canada, Mexico, or Central America and must outline the proposed research. Application must be on current GSA forms, which are available from the geology departments of most colleges and universities in the United States or upon request from the Research Grants Administrator of the society. Completed forms must be accompanied by two faculty evaluations of the applicant. Applicants must use forms for the current grant year.
Restrictions The program does not offer scholarships to be used for tuition, housing, etc., nor are students in seeking acceptance into graduate school given assistance.
Amount $1533 average
Date(s) Application Is Due Feb 1.
Contact Program Officer, (303) 357-1028; email: awards@geosociety.org
Internet http://www.geosociety.org/profdev/grants/index.htm
Sponsor Geological Society of America
P.O. Box 9140
Boulder, CO 80301-9140

Guggenheim Foundation Charitable Contribution Grants 2174
The Foundation concentrates its efforts in the criminal justice field. Accordingly, requests for grants should only be presented if there is criminal justice content. Grants are awarded as seed money for organizations to use to develop successful programs that continue beyond the life of the grant. Application information is available online.
Requirements Connecticut, New Jersey, and New York organizations are eligible.
Restrictions Grants are not awarded to individuals or for scholarships.
Date(s) Application Is Due Apr 15.
Contact President, (212) 755-3199
Internet http://www.dfguggenheimfoundation.org/apply.html
Sponsor Daniel and Florence Guggenheim Foundation
950 Third Avenue, 30th Floor
New York, NY 10022

GUITS Post-Doctoral Summer Travel-Research Grants 2175
The Institute of Turkish Studies is a non-profit, private educational institution devoted solely to the advancement of training, research, and teaching in the field of Ottoman and modern Turkish Studies. The grant is intended to provide partial support for travel and research to Turkey for those who hold a Ph.D. in social sciences or humanities discipline. The time period for the grant varies with each individual application. Normally, the recipients of the grants are expected to spend a minimum of four weeks in Turkey. Maximum award is round-trip airfare to Turkey.
Requirements Eligible recipients must be U.S. citizens or U.S. permanent residents and currently live/work in the U.S.
Date(s) Application Is Due Mar 9.
Contact David Cuthell, Intercultural Center, (202) 687-0295; fax: (202) 687-3780; email: dcc@turkishstudies.org
Internet http://www.turkishstudies.org/grant.html
Sponsor Georgetown University Institute of Turkish Studies
Intercultural Center--Box 571033-Room 305R
Washington, DC 20057-1033

GUITS Research and Writing Grant: Turkey's Bid for EU Membership 2176
The Institute of Turkish Studies is a non-profit, private educational institution devoted solely to the advancement of training, research, and teaching in the field of Ottoman and modern Turkish Studies. This is a single award to support research and/or writing for the academic year with a particular weight assigned to work directed towards scholarly publication.
Requirements This grant is open to scholars in the field of contemporary Turkish Studies who hold American citizenship or permanent resident status.
Amount $10,000
Date(s) Application Is Due Mar 11.
Contact David Cuthell, Intercultural Center, (202) 687-0295; fax: (202) 687-3780; email: dcc@turkishstudies.org
Internet http://www.turkishstudies.org/grant.html
Sponsor Georgetown University Institute of Turkish Studies
Intercultural Center--Box 571033-Room 305R
Washington, DC 20057-1033

GUITS Research Grants in Comparative Studies of Modern Turkey 2177
The Institute of Turkish Studies is a non-profit, private educational institution devoted solely to the advancement of training, research, and teaching in the field of Ottoman and modern Turkish Studies. A significant portion of the project should be devoted comparatively to one or more states or political entities in Europe, Latin America, the Middle East, and Asia in addition to the Turkish Republic. The grants are primarily, but not exclusively, in the field of Political Science. The grant is for the academic year, and permission to postpone the tenure of the grant beyond this period will normally not be given.
Requirements Grants are awarded to graduate students at the dissertation research stage and for post-doctoral scholars in the U.S. who study aspects of the Republic of Turkey (post 1922) in a comparative context. Applicants must be U.S. citizens or permanent residents in the U.S. and affiliated with a university at the U.S. at the time of the application.
Amount $10,000
Date(s) Application Is Due Mar 9.
Contact David Cuthell, Intercultural Center, (202) 687-0295; fax: (202) 687-3780; email: dcc@turkishstudies.org
Internet http://www.turkishstudies.org/grant.html
Sponsor Georgetown University Institute of Turkish Studies
Intercultural Center--Box 571033-Room 305R
Washington, DC 20057-1033

GUITS Sabbatical Research Grant 2178
The Institute of Turkish Studies is a non-profit, private educational institution devoted solely to the advancement of training, research, and teaching in the field of Ottoman and

modern Turkish Studies. The grants are for the academic year and permission to postpone the tenure of the grant beyond this period will normally not be given.
Requirements To be eligible for a grant, applicants should be: faculty in any field of the social sciences and/or humanities; and US citizens or permanent residents at the time of the application. The grants will be awarded only to applicants who certify that they are taking sabbatical leave and will be conducting research in the field of Turkish Studies.
Amount $25,000
Date(s) Application Is Due Mar 9.
Contact David Cuthell, Intercultural Center, (202) 687-0295; fax: (202) 687-3780; email: dcc@turkishstudies.org
Internet http://www.turkishstudies.org/grant.html
Sponsor Georgetown University Institute of Turkish Studies
Intercultural Center--Box 571033-Room 305R
Washington, DC 20057-1033

GUITS Summer Research Grants in Turkey for Graduate Students **2179**
The Institute of Turkish Studies is a non-profit, private educational institution devoted solely to the advancement of training, research, and teaching in the field of Ottoman and modern Turkish Studies. Grants are awarded for summer travel to Turkey to carry out projects. The time period for grants varies with each individual application. Normally, the recipients of the Summer Research Grants are expected to spend a minimum of two months in Turkey. Application information is available online.
Requirements Eligible recipients must be: graduate students in any field of the social sciences and/or humanities in the United States; U.S. citizens or permanent residents at the time of the application; and currently not engaged in dissertation writing.
Amount $1,000-$2,000
Date(s) Application Is Due Mar 9.
Contact David Cuthell, Intercultural Center, (202) 687-0295; fax: (202) 687-3780; email: dcc@turkishstudies.org
Internet http://www.turkishstudies.org/grant.html
Sponsor Georgetown University Institute of Turkish Studies
Intercultural Center--Box 571033-Room 305R
Washington, DC 20057-1033

Gustavus and Louise Pfeiffer Research Foundation Grants **2180**
The Foundation makes grants to US tax-exempt institutions for projects or programs for the advancement of medicine and pharmacy, including scientific research; postgraduate scholarship and fellowship assistance; and studies in nutrition, blindness, deafness and other physical disabilities. The letter of inquiry should not exceed two pages and should state the nature and purpose of the project, the field of interest of the foundation to which it relates, the amount requested, and a general description of the items to be funded; full proposals are by invitation. Applications are considered by the foundation's directors at two meetings a year, one in spring and one in fall. The listed application deadlines are for letters of inquiry; full applications are by invitation.
Requirements US tax-exempt organizations are eligible.
Restrictions Grants will not be made for delivery of health care services; that benefit a limited geographical area; for endowment, general institutional support, building programs, chairs, or the like; where a major part of the funds are for equipment, exhibits, conferences, seminars, lectures, workshops, sabbatical leave, or the like; for indirect costs; for general programs of research rather than specific research projects of limited duration; to other foundations or fund raising organizations for the purpose of their making grants to others; that are more appropriate for support by other sources, such as pharmaceutical companies for commercial applications of existing products; that involve animal experimentation (other than insects); or to institutions for projects not in the United States.
Amount $75,000 maximum
Date(s) Application Is Due Jan 8; Jul 25.
Contact Matt Herold Jr., Secretary, (973) 983-0480; fax: (973) 586-3456
Internet http://fdncenter.org/grantmaker/pfeiffer
Sponsor Gustavus and Louise Pfeiffer Research Foundation
89 Diamond Spring Rd, CN 3050
Danville, NJ 07834

Gustus L. Larson Memorial Award **2181**
This award, sponsored jointly by the Pi Tau Sigma Honorary Mechanical Engineering Fraternity and ASME, is given annually to the engineering graduate who has demonstrated outstanding achievement in mechanical engineering within 10 to 20 years after graduating from a regular engineering course of a recognized college or university. Achievement shall be all or in part in any field including industrial, educational, political, research, civic, and artistic. The candidate's achievements will be examined for an application of basic engineering methods or principles. A special nominating form must be obtained from ASME.
Amount $1000
Date(s) Application Is Due Feb 1.
Contact Gilda DiTullio, Manager, (212) 591-7736; fax: (212) 705-7739; email: ditulliog@asme.org
Internet http://www.asme.org/honors/ms71/gaa/larson.html
Sponsor American Society of Mechanical Engineers
3 Park Ave
New York, NY 10016

H.A. and Mary K. Chapman Charitable Trust Grants **2182**
Grants are provided to support nonprofit organizations involved in a wide variety of charitable purposes, including education, medical research, health and human services, arts and culture, civic and community, and nature and wildlife. Priority is given to: funding projects or programs that will serve a documented need and have a significant impact on the community; financial support of the organization management and board of directors, individuals of the general community affected by the program or project, and other private foundations; sound financial planning for maintenance and continuation of the project or program after the initial funding is complete; projects or programs that potentially benefit a significant segment of people; applicants with committed volunteers and staff leadership. Application information is available online.
Requirements 501(c)3 nonprofits in Oklahoma, are eligible. Priority will normally be given to Tulsa and surrounding counties and eastern Oklahoma. Depending on the availability of funds, Arkansas and Texas may also be eligible for funding for Colleges and Universities.
Restrictions Grants are not made for the following purposes: to be passed-through to another organization that is not a 501(c)(3) public charity or a governmental entity; to attempt to influence legislation or the outcome of any election, or to political campaigns. Grant requests for the following purposes are not favored: endowments; deficit financing and debt retirement; projects or programs for which the Chapman Trusts would be the sole source of financial support; travel, conferences, conventions, group meetings, or seminars, camp programs and other seasonal activities; religious programs of religious organizations; project or program planning; start-up ventures are not excluded, but organizations with a proven strategy and results are preferred; purposes normally funded by taxation or governmental agencies; requests made less than nine months from the declination of a previous request by an applicant, or within nine months of the last payment made on a grant made to an applicant; requests for more than one project.
Contact Jerry Dickman or Donne Pitman, (918) 496-7882; fax (918) 496-7887; jerry@chapmantrusts.com
Internet http://www.chapmantrusts.org/grants_programs.html
Sponsor H.A. and Mary K. Chapman Charitable Trust
6100 South Yale, Suite 1816
Tulsa, OK 74136

H.B. Earhart Fellowships **2183**
These fellowships are awarded to move talented individuals through graduate study in the fields of international studies, economics, political science, and history in optimum time to embark upon careers in college or university teaching or in research. Awards are made to graduate students nominated by faculty sponsors whose participation is invited annually. Sponsors also monitor performance. Direct applications from candidates or from noninvited sponsors are not accepted.
Amount $1000-$25,000 average
Contact Ingrid Ann Gregg, President, (734) 761-8592
Sponsor Earhart Foundation
2200 Green Rd, Ste H
Ann Arbor, MI 48105

H.R. Lissner Award **2184**
This award has been established in honor of H.R. Lissner for his pioneering contributions in biomechanical research. The award is bestowed annually for outstanding accomplishments in the area of bioengineering in the form of: significant research contributions; development of new methods of measuring; design of new equipment and instrumentation; educational impact in the training of bioengineers; or service to the bioengineering community and/or the ASME Bioengineering Division.
Amount $1000 honorarium and expense supplement
Date(s) Application Is Due Jan 1.
Contact Honors and Awards Department, (212) 705-7735; fax: (212) 705-7739
Internet http://www.asme.org/honors/ms71/list.html
Sponsor American Society of Mechanical Engineers
345 E 47th St
New York, NY 10017-2392

H.W. Wilson Foundation Grants **2185**
The foundation awards grants nationwide in its areas of interest, including libraries, library schools, and library science; higher education; and cultural outreach. Types of support include program grants, scholarships, and research grants. There are no application forms or deadlines. The board meets in January, March, May, August, and October.
Restrictions Grants do not support building construction/renovation, endowment funds, or operating expenses.
Contact William Stanton, President, (718) 588-8400
Sponsor H.W. Wilson Foundation
950 University Avenue
Bronx, NY 10452

Hadassah Foundation Grants **2186**
The foundation's mission is to improve the status, health, and well-being of women and girls; bring their contributions, issues, and needs from the margins to the center of Jewish concern; and encourage and facilitate their active participation in decision-making and leadership in all spheres of life. The foundation funds projects that empower

Israeli women by providing them with the tools they need to become economically self-sufficient. The foundation also supports training for girls so that they will develop into self-confident adults and leaders. Letters of intent must meet the listed deadline.
Requirements 501(c)3 nonprofit organizations and organizations who have amutah or mossad tziburi status in Israel are eligible.
Amount $100,000 maximum; $30,000-$40,000 typically
Date(s) Application Is Due Jul 6.
Contact Grants Administrator, (212) 451-6245; fax: (212) 303-8282; email: Hadassahfoundation@hadassah.org
Internet http://www.hadassahfoundation.org
Sponsor Hadassah Foundation
50 W 58th St
New York, NY 10019-2505

Hagley Museum and Library Grants in Aid **2187**
These grants support short-term (two to eight weeks) research in the imprint, manuscript, pictorial, and artifact collections of the Hagley Museum and Library, which contain materials on significant businesses and individuals of the Middle Atlantic region and the nation as well as published material with strong research value in the areas of business, economic, technological, and social history.
Requirements Degree candidates, advanced scholars, and independent scholars may apply.
Amount $1400 maximum per month
Date(s) Application Is Due Mar 31; Jun 30; Oct 31.
Contact Carol Lockman, Center for the History of Business, Technology, and Society, (302) 658-2400 ext 243; fax: (302) 655-3188; email: clockman@hagley.org
Internet http://www.hagley.lib.de.us/grants.html
Sponsor Hagley Museum and Library
P.O. Box 3630
Wilmington, DE 19807-0630

Hagley Museum and Library Henry Belin DuPont Fellowships **2188**
Fellowships enable individual out-of-state scholars to pursue advanced research and study in the library, archival, and artifact collections of the Hagley Museum and Library. Preference will be given to those whose travel costs to Hagley will be higher. Fellows must devote full time to their studies and may not accept teaching assignments or undertake any other major activities during the tenure of their fellowships. Tenure must be continuous and last from two to six months. At the end of their tenure, fellows must submit final reports on their activities and accomplishments. Fellows are expected to participate in seminars, as well as attend noontime colloquia, lectures, concerts, exhibits, and other public programs offered during their tenure.
Requirements The following information must be submitted for consideration: fellowship application cover sheet; cover letter, noting applicant's social security number and notice of any sabbatical or other funding to be received during tenure at Hagley; copy of current resume or vita, not to exceed five pages in length; description of the proposed project, not more than 15 pages in length, providing methodology, plan of work, Hagley collections to be used, the relevance of Hagley's fields of interest to the project, and the intended product; and two letters of recommendation from persons familiar with the project.
Restrictions Degree candidates are ineligible.
Amount $1400 maximum
Date(s) Application Is Due Mar 31; Jun 30; Oct 31.
Contact Dr. Philip Scranton, Center for the History of Business, Technology, and Society, (302) 658-2400 ext 208; fax: (302) 658-3188; email: pscranton@hagley.org
Internet http://www.hagley.lib.de.us/grants.html
Sponsor Hagley Museum and Library
P.O. Box 3630
Wilmington, DE 19807

Hagley/Winterthur Research Fellowships in Arts and Industries **2189**
This is a cooperative program of short-term research fellowships for scholars interested in the historical and cultural relationships between economic life and the arts including design, architecture, crafts, and the fine arts. Fellowships are awarded for periods of from one to six months. Fellows receive stipends; make use of the rich research collections of the Winterthur Museum, Garden, and Library and the Hagley Museum and Library; and participate in seminars that meet at both sponsoring institutions. Applicants doing dissertation research are welcome to apply. Guidelines are available upon request from the Research Fellowship Program, Winterthur Museum, Garden, and Library, Winterthur, DE 19735; (302) 888-4649; or from the Hagley Museum.
Amount $1400 stipend per month
Date(s) Application Is Due Dec 1.
Contact Dr. Philip Scranton, Center for the History of Business, Technology, and Society, (302) 658-2400 ext 208; fax: (302) 655-3188; email: pscranton@hagley.org
Internet http://www.hagley.lib.de.us/grants.html
Sponsor Hagley Museum and Library
P.O. Box 3630
Wilmington, DE 19807

Hague Academy of International Law Doctoral Scholarships **2190**
The academy offers a limited number of residential scholarships for doctoral candidates whose theses in areas of international law are in advanced stages of preparation. Scholarships are given for periods of two months beginning July 1. Time is to be spent at the academy to facilitate the completion of the thesis.
Requirements The doctoral scholarships are intended for candidates from developing countries who reside in their home countries and who do not have access to scientific sources. The upper age limit of applicants is 45. Application must be accompanied by a recommendation from the professor under whose direction the thesis is being written, giving the title of the thesis. Each candidate must show proof that she/he is at postgraduate level and that his/her thesis is necessary to obtain the doctoral degree. The thesis may be concerned with either private or public international law.
Amount 2250 Euros; 910 Euros maximum travel
Date(s) Application Is Due Mar 1.
Contact M. Croese, Head of the Secretariat, (070) 302 42 42
Internet http://www.hagueacademy.nl/eng-home.html
Sponsor Hague Academy of International Law
Peace Palace, Carnegieplein 2
The Hague 2517 KJ The Netherlands

Hague Academy of International Law Summer Scholarships **2191**
The Hague Academy of International Law awards scholarships for one of two summer sessions of study in public and private international law taught by selected authorities. Sessions are for three weeks of intensive study in French or in English; diplomas are available if arrangements for taking the tests are made prior to acceptance of the application deadline of March 1 of each year. Forms may be obtained by writing directly to the academy or to the heads of diplomatic missions and other authorities and scientific institutions connected with international law.
Requirements Application must be submitted by the applicant and must be accompanied by a recommendation from a professor of international law, a curriculum vita, and a statement of evidence that the applicant considers to be of value in support of his/her candidacy. Applicants must be under 40 years of age.
Restrictions No more than two scholarships will be awarded to applicants from any one country during the same year; an applicant may obtain only one scholarship.
Amount Dfl900
Date(s) Application Is Due Mar 1.
Contact Secretariat, 070-302-42-42
Internet http://www.hagueacademy.nl/eng-home.html
Sponsor Hague Academy of International Law
Peace Palace, Carnegieplein 2
The Hague 2517 KJ The Netherlands

Halliburton Foundation Grants **2192**
The foundation supports education at all levels and charitable organizations in the following ways: matching US- based employee donations on a two-for-one basis up to $20,000 annually per employee for accredited junior colleges, colleges, and universities; matching US-based employee donations to accredited elementary and secondary schools on a two-for-one basis up to $500 annually per employee; making direct donations to US-based elementary and secondary schools and colleges and universities; and recognizing and supporting active US-based employee volunteerism with direct donations through the Halliburton Volunteer Incentive Program. The corporate giving program makes donations to tax-exempt nonprofit organizations dedicated to education, health/welfare, civic issues, and arts and culture. The board meets quarterly. There are no application deadlines or forms.
Amount $250-$20,000 average
Contact Margaret Carriere, (713) 676-3717; email: fhoufoundation@halliburton.com
Internet http://www.halliburton.com/about/community.jsp
Sponsor Halliburton Foundation
4100 Clinton Dr, Bldg 1, 7th Fl
Houston, TX 77020

Harold Alfond Foundation Grants **2193**
The foundation awards grants to eligible organizations in its areas of interest, including secondary education, higher education, medical research, health care, and general charities. Grants support: education--public and private colleges and universities, as well as private secondary schools, to fund athletically oriented capital projects and scholarship endowments; medical research--individual research projects are considered when sponsored by a recognized medical research center; health--community support for capital campaigns and endowment funds; and general charities--community organizations that support youth, the arts, persons with disabilities, underprivileged, substance abuse rehabilitation, and annual fund drives of national organizations focusing on the above areas. There are no application deadlines or forms.
Restrictions Grants are not made to individuals.
Amount $250-$15,000 range
Contact Gregory Powell, c/o Dexter Enterprises
Sponsor Harold Alfond Foundation
Two Monument Square
Portland, ME 04101

Harold Amos Medical Faculty Development Program **2194**
This program offers four-year, postdoctoral research fellowships to minority physicians who have demonstrated superior academic and clinical skills and who are committed to careers in academic medicine. The program seeks to increase the number of minority

faculty physician scientists who can achieve senior rank in academic medicine and who will encourage and foster the development of succeeding classes of minority physicians. Applications are accepted from African American, Mexican American, Native American, and mainland Puerto Rican physicians. (Mainland Puerto Ricans are those who have completed at least their postsecondary education on the mainland.) Fellows will pursue biomedical research, clinical investigation, or health services research. Participants will conduct research in association with senior faculty members at academic centers.
Requirements Eligible to apply are minority physicians who are US citizens at the time of application, have excelled in their postsecondary education within the United States, are now completing or will have completed formal clinical training, and are committed to academic careers.
Amount $65,000 stipend per year plus $26,350 for research support
Date(s) Application Is Due Mar 23.
Contact National Program Office, (301) 565-4080; email: amfdp@starpower.net
Internet http://www.amfdp.org/applicat.htm
Sponsor Robert Wood Johnson Foundation
P.O. Box 2316, Rt 1 and College Rd E
Princeton, NJ 08543-2316

Harold Howe II Youth Policy Fellowship **2195**
The annual fellowship is awarded to a promising young scholar or practitioner to support a self-designed project on significant issues in youth policy, practice, research, or program evaluation, focusing particularly on disadvantaged youth. It may support dissertation research in any of the fields related to youth policy. It is expected that in the 12-month period of the fellowship, a report of high quality will be produced. The resulting paper may be the basis for an article in a peer-reviewed journal and may be the basis for one or more AYPF forums to be held on Capitol Hill. The fellow will join the AYPF staff, accruing leave and working a regular 40-hour week. Proposal guidelines are available online.
Requirements Candidates must have received a MA degree or higher within the five years preceding commencement of the fellowship or completed coursework toward a PhD within the five years preceding commencement of the fellowship. Candidates must possess excellent writing skills and sufficient computer competency to carry out research and writing related to the project.
Amount $25,000
Contact Samuel Halperin, Fellowship Administrator, (202) 775-9731; fax: (202) 775-9733; email: aypf@aypf.org
Internet http://www.aypf.org/publications/harold_howe.htm
Sponsor American Youth Policy Forum
1836 Jefferson Pl NW
Washington, DC 20036

Harold Lancour Scholarship for Foreign Study **2196**
This scholarship is awarded to a librarian or graduate library science student for foreign study and research in the library sciences. Application form must be obtained from the society and returned with resume and brief letter describing relevance of the proposed foreign study to work or schooling.
Amount $1500
Date(s) Application Is Due Mar 15.
Contact Dr. Jane Robbins, Executive Director, (850) 644-3907; fax: (850) 644-9763; email: Beta_Phi_Mu@lis.fsu.edu
Internet http://www.beta-phi-mu.org/scholarships.html#lancour
Sponsor Beta Phi Mu International Library and Information Science Honor Society
101 Louis Shores Bldg, Florida State University
Tallahassee, FL 32306-2048

Harold Simmons Foundation Grants **2197**
The foundation awards grants to Texas nonprofit organizations, with emphasis on social services, religion, health, the arts, and youth. Grants also support community programs and projects, child development, and adult basic education/literacy programs. The foundation also supports international development and relief efforts in Third World countries. Grants are awarded for general operating support, annual campaigns, capital campaigns, building construction/renovation, continuing support, seed money, and program development. Application forms are not required, and there are no deadline dates.
Requirements Dallas, TX, nonprofits are eligible.
Restrictions Grants are not awarded to support individuals or for endowment funds or loans.
Contact Lisa Simmons Epstein, President, (972) 233-2134
Sponsor Harold Simmons Foundation
5430 LBJ Freeway, Suite 1700
Dallas, TX 75240-2697

Harold Whitworth Pierce Charitable Trust Grants **2198**
The trust awards grants to Boston-area nonprofit organizations in its areas of interest, including green and public spaces--projects that support community gardens, parks, and other natural areas, and projects that enhance space for recreation; capital projects--projects that reduce the operating costs for an institution and projects that improve and/or restore the physical heritage of Boston; and research--environmental research and/or for making the results of such research available for public policy. Occasionally other areas are supported. Types of support include program development, seed money, capital projects, and operating grants on occasion. The first step in the application process is a phone call to determine whether the project is eligible. The listed application deadlines are for concept letters (two-page maximum). Full proposals are by invitation.
Requirements 501(c)3 tax-exempt organizations in the Boston, MA, area are eligible.
Restrictions Grants do not support scholarships, individuals, fund-raising events or training, films, videos, travel, or advocacy.
Amount $1000-$100,000
Date(s) Application Is Due Mar 1; Sep 15.
Contact Elizabeth Nichols, c/o Nichols and Pratt, (617) 523-8368; fax: (617) 523-8949; email: piercetrust@nichols-pratt.com
Sponsor Harold Whitworth Pierce Charitable Trust
50 Congress St, Ste 832
Boston, MA 02109

Harriet and Leon Pomerance Fellowship **2199**
One fellowship will be awarded annually for the following academic year to enable an individual to work on a scholarly project relating to Aegean Bronze Age archaeology. Preference will be given to a candidate whose project requires travel to the Mediterranean. Official application materials are available upon request from the institute in the spring of each year.
Requirements Applicants must be residents of the United States or Canada.
Restrictions Previous Harriet Pomerance fellows are ineligible.
Amount $4000
Date(s) Application Is Due Nov 1.
Contact Elizabeth Gilgan, AIA Program Administrator, (617) 353-8705; fax: (617) 353-6550; email: aia@aia.bu.edu or egilgan@aia.bu.edu
Internet http://www.archaeological.org/webinfo.php?page=10008
Sponsor Archaeological Institute of America
656 Beacon Street
Boston, MA 02215-2006

Harriet Hale Woolley Scholarships **2200**
The Fondation des Etats-Unis annually offers four or five Woolley Scholarships for graduate study in art and music in Paris; specifically, grants are for persons studying painting, printmaking and sculpture and for instrumentalists. Grantees live at the Fondation des Etats-Unis and are expected to participate in the cultural and social activities. They should have a keen interest not only in furthering their own careers, but in contributing to international friendship by showing an active interest in meeting persons of other nationalities. A flyer documenting all materials needed to support an application is available upon request. Preference is given to mature students who have already done graduate study.
Requirements Candidates must be single American citizens; have proficiency in the French language; must be between 21 and 29 years of age; and have a bachelor's degree in arts, fine arts, or music or show evidence of equivalent training. Applicants' projects must include enrollment at recognized schools or instruction with private teachers. Letters of acceptance must accompany application. Although recipients must remain in Paris for the full academic year, they are free to travel during the Christmas and Easter vacation periods.
Restrictions Grants do not cover transportation costs to and from Europe. Grants are not given for research in art history, or musicology, nor for students of dance or the theater.
Amount $8500 stipend paid in five installments in francs from October 1 through June 29 for room, board, transportation in Paris, and miscellaneous expenses
Date(s) Application Is Due Mar 1.
Contact Director, (+33) 1 53 80 68 87; fax: (+33) 1 53 80 68 99; email: elizabeth.askren-brie@feusa.org
Internet http://www.feusa.org/index.php?page=harriet
Sponsor Fondation des Etats-Unis
15 blvd Jourdan
Paris, Cedex 14 75690 France

Harriman Institute Postdoctoral Fellowships **2201**
The goals of the institute are the preparation of graduate students for scholarly and professional careers in Russian, Soviet, and post-Soviet studies; the promotion of advanced research on Russia, the CIS, and the post-Soviet reality; and the dissemination of information, analyses, and opinions derived from institute-sponsored research and activities. Postdoctoral fellowships allow scholars to spend a period of time at the institute without any obligations other than to revise their dissertations for publication as a book. Fellows are welcome to participate in the intellectual life of the institute. All fellows will have access to the university's libraries, the institute's reading room, archives, lectures, and discussions.
Requirements Applicants must have completed dissertations within the preceding five years. To apply, a scholar must write the assistant director a letter outlining how she or he will spend time revising a dissertation for publication. Besides forwarding a curriculum vita and substantial portions of the dissertation, applicants should ask three scholars who are familiar with their work to forward letters of evaluation and recommendation.
Amount $10,000 maximum per semester
Date(s) Application Is Due Jan 2.

Contact Barbara Singleton, Administrative Aide, Postdoctoral Fellowships, Harriman Institute, (212) 854-6219 or (212) 854-4623; email: harriman@columbia.edu
Internet http://sipa.columbia.edu/REGIONAL/HI/post-doc.html
Sponsor Columbia University
420 W 118th St
New York, NY 10027

Harris and Eliza Kempner Fund Grants **2202**
The foundation provides grants primarily in the Galveston, TX, area to qualifying organizations in the broad areas of the arts, historic preservation, community development, education, health, and human services. The foundation gives preference to requests for seed money, operating funds, small capital needs, and special projects partnering with other funding sources. Application information is available online.
Requirements Grants are made primarily to Texas residents.
Restrictions Funding is not available for: fund-raising benefits; direct mail solicitations; grants to individuals; and grants to non-USA based organizations.
Date(s) Application Is Due Mar 15; Oct 15.
Contact Grants Manager, (409) 762-1603; fax: (409) 762-5435; email: information@kempnerfund.org
Internet http://www.kempnerfund.org/app/programs.html
Sponsor Harris and Eliza Kempner Fund
2201 Market Street, Suite 601
Galveston, TX 77550-1529

Harris Graduate School of Public Policy Studies Research Development Grants **2203**
The Harris School supports this program for social science scholars interested in food assistance research. Awards will be made to scholars who propose research including, but not limited to interactions between food assistance programs and other welfare programs with respect to participation, administration, budget exposure, and the role of food assistance as a personal and fiscal stabilizer; the effects of the macroeconomic environment on the need for food assistance, level of participation, and food assistance program costs; and the well-being of current and former food assistance recipients. Other topics related to welfare reform and macroeconomic interactions with food assistance will be considered. This program is designed to encourage experienced researchers in other areas to start projects in the area of food assistance; research on food assistance using innovative approaches and research methods; smaller, start-up projects with the potential to make a significant contribution to food assistance research; and younger and junior scholars to develop research agendas in the area of food assistance. Funding may include compensation for the principal investigator's time; research assistance; travel; and purchase of data, computers, or other research related items. Application guidelines are available online.
Requirements Applicants must hold a PhD degree.
Amount $40,000 maximum; $20,000-$25,000 typically
Date(s) Application Is Due May 1.
Contact USDA Research Development Grants Program, (773) 702-2028; email: spopa@uchicago.edu.
Internet http://harrisschool.uchicago.edu/Research/funding.asp
Sponsor University of Chicago
1155 E 60th St
Chicago, IL 60637

Harry A. and Margaret D. Towsley Foundation Grants **2204**
The foundation awards grants to Michigan organizations in its areas of interest, including environment, medical and preschool education, social services, continuing education, and research in the health sciences. Types of support include annual campaigns, building construction and renovation, capital campaigns, continuing support, employee matching gifts, endowments, general operating support, matching/challenge support, professorships, program development, research, and seed grants. There are no application forms; submit a letter of inquiry between January and the listed application deadline.
Restrictions Grants are not awarded to individuals or for travel, scholarships, fellowships, conferences, books, publications, films, tapes, audio-visual or communication media, or loans.
Date(s) Application Is Due Mar 31.
Contact Lynn White, President, (989) 837-1100; fax: (989) 837-3240
Sponsor Harry A. and Margaret D. Towsley Foundation
P.O. Box 349, 140 Ashman St
Midland, MI 48640

Harry and Laura Jacques Scholarship **2205**
This endowed award is given annually to a Canadian graduate student in a field of study related to the petroleum industry. Period of time covered by the award is four months. Both academic standing and financial need will be considered in making the selection of a recipient.
Requirements The award is open to qualified graduates of any recognized university who are registered in or admissible to a program leading to a master's or doctoral degree at the University of Calgary.
Amount $C3500
Date(s) Application Is Due Feb 1.
Contact Connie Busch, Faculty of Graduate Studies, (403) 220-5690; email: cbusch@ucalgary.ca
Internet http://www.ucalgary.ca/pubs/calendar/current/what/Awards/03GradAwards.htm#66
Sponsor University of Calgary
2500 University Dr NW, Earth Sciences Bldg, Rm 720
Calgary, AB T2N 1N4 Canada

Harry Frank Guggenheim Foundation Dissertation Fellowships **2206**
Ten or more dissertation fellowships are awarded each year to individuals who will complete their dissertations within the award year. These fellowships are designed to help doctoral candidates finish writing their dissertations rather than to support dissertation research. Awards are made only for projects clearly relevant to human dominance, aggression, and violence, but are not necessarily restricted to studies of humans. The foundation will consider proposals from any discipline that will further the foundation's intellectual and practical objectives including, but not limited to, anthropology, biology, history, psychology, sociology, and political science.
Requirements Applicants may be citizens of any country and studying at colleges or universities in any country.
Amount $15,000
Date(s) Application Is Due Feb 1.
Contact Dissertation Fellowships, (212) 644-4907; fax: (212) 644-5110
Internet http://www.hfg.org/df/guidelines.htm
Sponsor Harry Frank Guggenheim Foundation
527 Madison Ave
New York, NY 10022-4304

Harry Frank Guggenheim Foundation Research Grants **2207**
The foundation invites proposals for natural and social science research that may increase understanding of the causes, manifestations, and control of human violence and aggression. Grants are awarded for one-year support of postdoctoral research. Issues of particular interest are violence and aggression in children, the relationship between drugs and violence, violence in families, techniques for controlling aggression and violence, and political and religious violence. Types of support include salaries, employee benefits, research assistants, supplies, equipment, fieldwork, and technical assistance. Funded programs average two years in duration.
Requirements The grants are intended to fund individual investigators, not institutional programs.
Restrictions Funds are not for studies directed toward requirements for the doctoral degree, institutional overhead, nor for conference support.
Amount $15,000-$30,000 for one or two years
Date(s) Application Is Due Aug 1.
Contact Program Officer, (646) 428-0971; fax: (646) 428-0981; email: hfgacf@aol.com
Internet http://www.hfg.org/rg/guidelines.htm
Sponsor Harry Frank Guggenheim Foundation
25 W 53rd St
New York, NY 10019-5401

Harry Ransom Humanities Research Center Research Fellowships **2208**
The center offers a number of fellowships on an international basis to scholars for the purpose of conducting research based on the center's collections. The center is the principal rare book and manuscript library of the University of Texas at Austin and noted for its collections of British, American, and French literary materials, with major strengths in photography, music, film, and theater arts. Most fellowships are for one month, but a limited number of fellowships may be awarded for periods of residency up to four months to scholars with longer-term projects. Recipients are expected to be in continuous residence for the duration of their awards. The program also awards domestic and foreign travel stipends to scholars with research projects that require less than one month's research at the center (stipends may not be combined with other Ransom Center fellowships); and dissertation fellowships, which are designated for graduate students who are working on doctoral dissertations. Guidelines are available online.
Requirements Applicants must have received the PhD and be engaged in postdoctoral or equivalent research based on the center's collections. A two-page proposal, one-page curriculum vita, and two letters of recommendation are required for application.
Restrictions Individuals who have received the HRHRC Research Fellowship are ineligible to reapply for one year. Fellowships do not support work on the dissertation.
Amount $3000 per month; $1000 domestic and $1500 foreign travel stipends; $1200 dissertation fellowships
Date(s) Application Is Due Feb 1.
Contact Grants and Research, (512) 471-8944; fax: (512) 471-9646; email: fellows@hrc.utexas.edu
Internet http://www.hrc.utexas.edu/about/fellowships/application
Sponsor University of Texas at Austin
P.O. Box 7219
Austin, TX 78713-7219

Harry S. Truman Fellowship in National Security Science and Engineering **2209**
The fellowship enables recipients to pursue independent research of their own choosing that supports the national security mission of Sandia National Laboratories. The appointee is expected to foster creativity and to stimulate exploration of forefront

science and technology and high-risk, potentially high-value research and development. candidates are expected to have solved a major scientific or engineering problem in their thesis work or will have provided a new approach or insight to a major problem, as evidenced by a recognized impact in their field. The fellowship carries a stipend and a competitive benefits package that includes health, vision, and dental insurance; savings and income plan (401K); and paid holidays and vacation. Fellows may work at either of the laboratories' principal locations, in Albuquerque, NM, and Livermore, CA. The fellowship is a three-year appointment normally commencing on October 1, although exceptions may be made to accommodate special circumstances.
Requirements Eligibility criteria include: US citizenship, the ability to obtain a DOE Q clearance; research in areas of interest to national security; the candidate must have been awarded a PhD within the past three years at the time of application or will have completed all PhD requirements by commencement of appointment; and, candidates seeking their first national laboratory appointment.
Amount $94,200
Date(s) Application Is Due Dec 5.
Contact Yolanda Moreno, (505) 284-2106
Internet http://www.sandia.gov/employment/special-prog/truman/index.html
Sponsor Sandia National Laboratories
P.O. Box 5800, MS-1351
Albuquerque, NM 87185-1351

Harry S. Truman Library Institute Book Awards **2210**
One prize is awarded biennially in even-numbered years for the best book written during the previous two years, dealing primarily and substantially with some aspect of US history between April 12, 1945, and January 20, 1953, or with the public career of Harry S. Truman. The institute will accept applications after October 1 for funding after January 1. Information concerning the current status of the program may be obtained by writing to the secretary at the address shown.
Requirements Three copies of each book entered must be submitted to the secretary of the institute.
Amount $1000
Contact Grants Administrator, (816) 833-0425; fax: (816) 833-2715; email: lisa.sullivan@nara.gov
Internet http://www.trumanlibrary.org/grants.htm
Sponsor Harry S. Truman Library Institute
500 W US Hwy 24
Independence, MO 64050-1798

Harry S. Truman Library Institute Dissertation-Year Fellowships **2211**
To support the writing of doctoral dissertations on the public career of Harry S. Truman and on the history of the Truman administration, the institute is offering two one-year fellowships to individuals who have completed their dissertation research and are ready to begin writing. Persons receiving dissertation-year fellowships will not be required to come to the Truman Library but will be expected to furnish the library with a copy of their dissertation (or any publications resulting therefrom). Persons interested in applying may obtain application forms from the committee on research and education.
Requirements Applicants should have substantially completed their research and be prepared to devote full time to writing their dissertation. Preference will be given to projects based on extensive research at the Truman Library.
Amount $16,000
Date(s) Application Is Due Feb 1.
Contact Grants Administrator, (816) 833-0425; fax: (816) 833-2715; email: lisa.sullivan@nara.gov
Internet http://www.trumanlibrary.org/grants.htm#diss
Sponsor Harry S. Truman Library Institute
500 W US Hwy 24
Independence, MO 64050-1798

Harry S. Truman Library Institute Research Grants **2212**
The institute offers research grants to graduate students and postdoctoral scholars to enable them to spend one to three weeks conducting research at the library. Applicants must be working on a project pertaining to the public career of Harry S. Truman or to some facet of the history of the Truman administration. Awards are meant to cover round-trip air transportation between the applicant's home and Independence, MO, and a modest sum to cover living expenses while working at the library. Major factors in the awards decision will be the amount of pertinent material available at the Truman Library and the extent to which the particular topic has already been worked on by other scholars. Applications must be submitted on forms available from the office.
Restrictions Individuals may receive no more than two grants in this category in any one five-year period.
Amount $2500 maximum
Date(s) Application Is Due Apr 1; Oct 1.
Contact Grants Administrator, (816) 833-0425; fax: (816) 833-2715; email: lisa.sullivan@nara.gov
Internet http://www.trumanlibrary.org/grants.htm#ress
Sponsor Harry S. Truman Library Institute
500 W US Hwy 24
Independence, MO 64050-1798

Harry S. Truman Library Institute Scholar's Awards **2213**
In even-numbered years, the institute will make one award, either to an established scholar or to a scholar about to embark on his or her career, who is engaged in a study of either the public career of Harry S. Truman or some aspect of the history of the Truman administration or of the United States during that administration. The scholar's work must be based on major utilization of the resources of the Truman Library and must be designed to result in the publication of a book-length manuscript. One copy of such book (and/or any other publications resulting from work done under this award) shall be deposited by the author with the Harry S. Truman Library. Proposals should be submitted by December 15 of the odd-numbered year preceding the year of the award. The amount of the award shall be based on a proposed budget submitted by the applicant but will not exceed one-half of the applicant's academic year salary (or a comparable figure in the case of persons not affiliated with an institution of higher learning).
Requirements The application process is in two stages. Applicants should submit an informal proposal, indicating what work has already been done toward completion of the project, what remains to be done, and the specific resources in the Truman Library that will be utilized. Applicants will be advised of the outcome of this preliminary screening no later than February 1. Candidates selected to continue in the second phase of the process will receive forms (including a budget form) to be submitted by February 15. Applicants in this second stage will be notified of the committee's decision no later than April 15.
Amount $30,000 maximum
Date(s) Application Is Due Dec 15.
Contact Grants Administrator, (816) 833-0425; fax: (816) 833-2715; email: lisa.sullivan@nara.gov
Internet http://www.trumanlibrary.org/grants.htm#scholars
Sponsor Harry S. Truman Library Institute
500 W US Hwy 24
Independence, MO 64050-1798

Harry Shwachman Clinical Investigator Award **2214**
This three-year award provides the opportunity for clinically trained physicians to develop into independent biomedical research investigators who have active involvement in cystic fibrosis-related areas. It is also intended to facilitate the transition from postdoctoral training to a career in academic medicine. Applications are due the first Wednesday in September.
Requirements US citizenship or permanent resident status is required.
Amount $70,000 maximum per year plus $15,000 for supplies
Date(s) Application Is Due Sep 1.
Contact Office of Grants Management, (301) 951-4422; fax: (301) 951-6378; email: grants@cff.org
Internet http://www.cff.org/research/cystic_fibrosis_foundation_grants/research_grants
Sponsor Cystic Fibrosis Foundation
6931 Arlington Rd, 2nd Fl
Bethesda, MD 20814

Hartford Aging and Health Program Awards **2215**
The foundation's two principal programs are Health Care Cost and Quality and Aging and Health. The Health Care Cost and Quality program supports the community health management initiative, health care quality measures, and reducing inappropriate health care services. The Aging and Health program supports strengthening physicians' knowledge of geriatrics, reducing medication problems of the elderly, and demonstrating integrated financing and service delivery for comprehensive geriatric services. Types of support include operating budgets, continuing support, projects/programs, research, publications, and conferences and seminars. The foundation also welcomes inquiries regarding projects that may not fit these specific interests but would further its broad goal of improving health care in America. Types of support include general operations, continuing support, projects/programs, research, publications, and conferences and seminars. Applications are accepted at any time and are reviewed four times each year when the board meets.
Requirements US health, education, and social service organizations may apply.
Restrictions Requests will be denied for general research or for projects lasting more than three years.
Contact Corinne Rieder, Executive Director, (212) 832-7788; fax: (212) 593-4913; email: mail@jhartfound.com
Internet http://www.jhartfound.org
Sponsor John A. Hartford Foundation
55 E 59th St, 16th Fl
New York, NY 10022-1178

Hartford Geriatrics Health Outcomes Research Scholars Program **2216**
This program supports physician-scientists committed to improving the health care of older adults during the critical transition from junior faculty to independent researcher. Outcomes research is defined as the study of functional status, impairments, perceptions, social opportunities, and health services utilization that are influenced by disease, injury, treatment, or health policy, including etiology, diagnosis, and intervention. Research must be focused on older adults and may address clinical strategies and effectiveness, innovative outcomes measures, and quality of life. Scholars must have a research sponsor who should have a strong background in training and outcomes research, as well as

expertise and interest in the outcomes research that is being proposed. Guidelines and an application request form are available online.
Requirements The applicant must be a US citizen or permanent resident; be sponsored at a US allopathic or osteopathic institution by a full-time faculty member; have an MD or DO degree; hold a full-time faculty appointment at the level of assistant professor for no longer than two years at the time the grant becomes effective; demonstrate the motivation and ability to devote at least 75 percent of his or her time to conduct outcomes research related to improving the care of older adults with the goal of devoting his/her research career to this area; be a geriatrician or geriatric psychiatrist who has completed all of the requirements to be eligible to sit for a Certificate of Added Qualifications by the time the award commences (July 1), or a general internist (or family physician, neurologist, or subspecialist of internal medicine) who is pursuing a career devoted to aging research and who has completed all the requirements to be eligible to sit for board certification in his/her discipline; and have at least two years of training with one year of clinical experience at an accredited US institution, and one year of research training at a US academic institution.
Amount $75,000 per year for two years
Date(s) Application Is Due Jan 15.
Contact Funding Administrator, (800) 247-8779 or (212) 308-1414; fax: (212) 832-8646; email: sreinthaler@americangeriatrics.org
Internet http://www.healthinaging.org/research
Sponsor American Geriatrics Society Foundation for Health in Aging
350 Fifth Ave, Ste 801
New York, NY 10118

Harvard Postdoctoral Fellowships on Education **2217**
The graduate school invites applications from scholars for a two-year residential postdoctoral fellowship. Applications are encouraged from a broad range of scholarly traditions and backgrounds whose research links theory, practice, and policy in education. Special consideration will be given to applicants committed to careers in university research and teaching related to the improvement of education, particularly K-12 education. Fellows will teach one course during each of the two academic years and will give an annual lecture to the graduate school community about their research. Fellows receive an annual stipend plus a small housing supplement, are eligible for a travel supplement for participation in professional conferences, and receive additional support for course development or research. Applicants should send a letter of application, including a proposal for a two-year plan of research and teaching that identifies a member of the HGSE faculty who might serve as a mentor and provides a rationale for the selection of the mentor. Contact the office for additional information.
Requirements Applicants must be within two years of receiving the PhD or EdD. Their degree must be completed by July and cannot have been awarded prior to May 2003.
Amount $40,000 annual stipend; $1000 possible travel supplement; $3000 maximum for course development or research support
Date(s) Application Is Due Feb 11.
Contact Kenje Ogata, (617) 496-2805; email: kenje_ogata@gse.harvard.edu
Internet http://www.gse.harvard.edu/~finaid/fellowship.html
Sponsor Harvard University
122 Longfellow Hall
Cambridge, MA 02138

Harvard Study of New Scholars Postdoctoral Fellowship **2218**
The program will evaluate the satisfaction of junior faculty at the colleges and universities where they are currently employed. Researchers will survey all full-time tenure-track faculty members at 12 pilot sites to learn how they view specific institutional policies, structural and cultural barriers, work climate, ability to balance professional and personal lives, current job satisfaction, and estimated likelihood of success in achieving tenure or contract renewal. The purposes of the program are to enable the academy to attract the best and brightest scholars and teachers; and to increase the recruitment, retention, success, and satisfaction of all new scholars, with special attention to women and faculty of color. Applications are invited for one- or two-year postdoctoral fellowships. Candidates should send a letter of application including: evidence of a scholarly interest in higher education; two examples of academic writing; three references; and a three- to five-page statement that describes the fellow's intended research.
Requirements Applicants must have a doctoral degree awarded between May 2001 and June 2003 and a demonstrable, research-based interest in faculty work life or American higher education.
Amount $40,000 annual stipend plus $500 maximum travel supplement
Date(s) Application Is Due Mar 15.
Contact Graduate School of Education, email: newscholars@gse.harvard.edu
Internet http://www.gse.harvard.edu/~newscholars
Sponsor Harvard University
6 Appian Wy, Gutman Library
Cambridge, MA 02138

Harvard University Administrative Fellowships **2219**
The program seeks to attract candidates, especially those from underrepresented ethnic minority groups and those committed to addressing the underrepresentation of ethnic minorities in university administration, to administrative careers in higher education. The fellowship offers a 12-month management experience complemented by a professional development program. Fellows from business, government, education, and the professions will be selected. Each participant receives a salary from Harvard University and is placed in a full-time work assignment in Harvard schools or central administration departments for the duration of the program. All costs for the required educational seminar will be covered by Harvard University. Participants must secure and cover the cost of their housing. Guidelines and application are available online.
Requirements Applicants must have a bachelors degree and at least five years of work experience. The program seeks applicants with degree and backgrounds in the fields of athletics/sports management, information technology, alumni affairs and development, finance, human resources, and library science and management.
Date(s) Application Is Due Feb 10.
Contact Teresa Malonzo, Program Coordinator, (617) 495-8919; email: teresa_malonzo@harvard.edu
Internet http://www.oap.harvard.edu/afp
Sponsor Harvard University
1350 Massachusetts Ave
Cambridge, MA 02138

Harvard University Faculty Fellowships in Ethics **2220**
The Center for Ethics and the Professions encourages teaching and research about ethical issues in public life and the professions. Applications are welcomed from scholars and teachers who wish to develop their ability to address questions of moral choice in such areas as business, education, government, law, and medicine. Application forms are information are available online.
Requirements Applicants should hold a doctorate in philosophy, political theory, theology, or related disciplines; or a professional degree in business, education, public policy, law, or medicine. Preference will be given to applicants at an early stage of their careers, normally no more than 10 years from their terminal degree.
Amount $40,000 maximum stipend
Date(s) Application Is Due Nov 1.
Contact Center for Ethics and the Professions, (617) 495-1336; fax: (617) 496-6104; email: ethics@harvard.edu
Internet http://ethics.harvard.edu/fellowships.php
Sponsor Harvard University
79 John F. Kennedy St
Cambridge, MA 02138

Harvard University Graduate School of Education Fellowships and Awards **2221**
Harvard's graduate school of education (HGSE) offers several merit-based fellowships and awards. Presidential Fellowships, awarded to entering doctoral students, provide full tuition and fees for four years of study and an annual stipend for the first three years of study. Recipients must be full-time and are determined by the admissions committee based on the strength of the individual's application for admission. Entering Awards are awarded to first-year doctoral students who are either highly promising future professors or school leaders. These awards are for one year only and provide full tuition and fees plus a stipend. Roy E. Larsen Awards are awarded to first-year doctoral students who exhibit superior achievement and outstanding research potential. These awards are for one year only and provide full tuition and fees plus a stipend. Conant Fellowships support the professional growth of outstanding teachers and administrators in the Boston and Cambridge public schools. To be eligible, applicants must be teachers or administrators with professional status, under contract with either the Boston or the Cambridge public schools, and admitted to a degree program at HGSE. These fellowships cover the cost of full tuition are pro-rated for part-time study. Awards for doctoral Conant Fellowships carry the possibility of a one-year renewal. Guidelines for these programs are available online.
Amount $7000 entering award; $7000 stipend Roy E. Larsen Award
Date(s) Application Is Due Feb 4.
Contact Fellowship Office, (617) 496-2805; fax: (617) 496-0840; email: kenje_ogata@harvard.edu
Internet http://www.gse.harvard.edu/~finaid/fellowship.html#merit
Sponsor Harvard University
108 Longfellow Hall, 13 Appian Wy
Cambridge, MA 02138

Harvard Women and Public Policy Postdoctoral Fellowship **2222**
The program will award a postdoctoral residential fellowship to an outstanding scholar in security affairs from the United States and elsewhere working to promote basic research in the broad area of international security with a particular focus on gender, prevention, peace building, and sustainable security. The fellow will hold his/her fellowship jointly with the International Security Program of the Belfer Center for Science and International Affairs. The fellow will be expected to participate actively in the weekly ISP seminar and in the intellectual life of the Women and Public Policy Program; take an active organizational role in the monthly Boston Consortium meetings on Gender Security and Human Rights and devote some portion of his/her time to collaborative endeavors; and complete a book, monograph, scholarly article, or other significant publication during the period of residence. Residential fellowships also provide for individual health insurance, institutional support, and some research-related travel stipends.
Requirements The fellow must hold a PhD by September.
Amount $30,000 stipend
Date(s) Application Is Due Jan 31.

Contact Theresa Lund, John F. Kennedy School of Government , (617) 496-6609; fax: (617) 496-6154; email: theresa_lund@harvard.edu
Internet http://www.ksg.harvard.edu/wappp/research/fellowship.html
Sponsor Harvard University
79 John F. Kennedy St
Cambridge, MA 02138

Harvey Prizes **2223**
Two prizes are awarded annually to outstanding personalities whose achievements in one of the following fields have served as a source of inspiration to many others: science and technology, human health, and outstanding contribution to peace in the Mideast. Recipients are invited to Israel as guests of the Technion and to spend time at the institute teaching their subjects. Those interested in nominating candidates should contact the society for deadline date and guidelines. Inquiries may also be directed to Ruth Eckstein in Israel at 011-972-4-8292863, email: andree@tx.technionac.il.
Requirements Nominations may be made by members of the board of governors of Technion and by request from the prize committee. Persons making nominations are requested not to inform the proposed candidates of the nomination.
Restrictions Candidates may not nominate themselves.
Amount $35,000 each
Date(s) Application Is Due Oct 1.
Contact Miriam Golzman, Coordinator, Office of Vice President for Development and Harvey Prize, Haifa 32000, Israel; New York office: (212) 407-6300; fax: (212) 753-2925; email: info@ats.org
Internet http://www.admin.technion.ac.il/harvey/Philosophy.html
Sponsor American Technion Society--Israel Institute of Technology
55 E 59th St
New York, NY 10022

Hastings Center International Biomedical Ethics Research Program for International Scholars **2224**
This program was inaugurated in response to the growing interest in comparative bioethics and to the number of foreign scholars and medical professionals interested in the work of the center. The center carries out an active research program on timely and crucial subjects, working in a variety of fields--law, medicine, science, philosophy, and religion, among others. The center is presently studying ethical issues related to abortion, neonatal care, surrogate motherhood, organ transplantation, occupational health, health professional-patient relationships, allocation of resources, animal welfare, aging, AIDS, care of the dying and termination of treatment, chronic illness, artificial reproduction, genetic screening, rehabilitation medicine, and justice in health care delivery. International scholars stay at the center for four to six weeks, dividing their time between their own research and the ongoing activities at the center. There is a modest stipend for foreign citizens who require financial assistance. Applications should be submitted four to six months in advance of proposed stay. Applications are accepted at any time.
Requirements The program is designed for advanced scholars and practitioners who have made or will make a significant contribution to bioethics in their own countries.
Amount $500-$2000
Contact Director of Education, (845) 424-4040 ext 203; fax: (845) 424-4545; email: visitors@thehastingscenter.org
Internet http://www.thehastingscenter.org/visitors/visitorsint.asp
Sponsor Hastings Center
21 Malcolm Gordon Rd
Garrison, NY 10524-5555

Hastings Center International Visiting Scholars Program **2225**
This program responds to the growing interest in comparative bioethics and to the number of foreign scholars and medical professionals interested in the center's work--examining critical ethical issues in medicine, the life sciences, and the professions. The program is designed for advanced scholars and practitioners who have made or will make significant contributions to bioethics in their own countries. International scholars usually stay two weeks to six weeks, dividing their time between their own research and ongoing activities at the center. There is a modest stipend for foreign citizens who require financial assistance. Applications are due four to six months in advance of proposed stay.
Amount $500-$1500
Contact Daniel Callahan, Director, International Programs, (845) 424-4040 ext 222; fax: (845) 424-4545; email: callahand@thehastingscenter.org
Internet http://www.thehastingscenter.org/visitors/visitorsint.asp
Sponsor Hastings Center
Rte 9D, 21 Malcolm Gordon Rd
Garrison, NY 10524-5555

Hawaii Community Foundation Medical Research Grants **2226**
Funding will be provided for medical research in the fields of: cancer; heart disease; lung disease; blindness prevention, with particular emphasis on macular degeneration; juvenile diabetes; Alzheimer's disease and other mental and physical diseases of old age; pharmaceutical development; immunology; and genetic research. Priority is given to projects that: demonstrate a foreseeable benefit to the people of Hawai'i; support new investigators in Hawai'i; and support collaborative efforts. Proposal submission information is available online.
Requirements To be eligible for consideration an organization must be a 501(c)(3) organization or a unit of government. The Principal Investigator must be based in Hawaii and conducting the research in Hawaii.
Amount $25,000-$50,000
Date(s) Application Is Due Mar 1; Aug 15.
Contact Amy Luersen, (808) 566-5550 or (888) 731-3863; email: aluersen@hcf-hawaii.org
Internet http://www.hawaiicommunityfoundation.org/index.php?id=71&categoryID=23
Sponsor Hawaii Community Foundation
1164 Bishop Street, Suite 800
Honolulu, HI 96813

Haystack Mountain School of Crafts Summer Scholarships **2227**
Scholarships are awarded for research and study at the school in blacksmithing (as related to craftwork), graphics, ceramics, weaving, jewelry, glass, or wood. Candidates must be at least 18 years of age, of any nationality, and capable of doing professional work. Six sessions are held each summer lasting for two to three weeks each. Obtain guidelines before applying. Tuition plus partial room and board are provided.
Date(s) Application Is Due Mar 25.
Contact Director, Scholarship Program, (207) 348-2306; fax: (207) 348-2307; email: haystack@haystack-mtn.org
Internet http://www.haystack-mtn.org/workshops_summer_financial_assistance.php
Sponsor Haystack Mountain School of Crafts
P.O. Box 518
Deer Isle, ME 04627-0518

Hazel Hatcher International Home Economics Award **2228**
The international award will be granted biennially (even-numbered years) to assist the applicant in returning to the United States for the purpose of updating professional information through attending a conference, seminar, or national professional meeting.
Requirements Applicant must hold a degree in home economics or one of its specialized areas from a US college/university and have had at least five years of professional service outside of the United States since receiving the degree.
Amount $1500
Date(s) Application Is Due Feb 1.
Contact Fellowships Administrator, National Office, (304) 368-0612; email: rickards@mountain.net
Internet http://www.ianr.unl.edu/phiu/webdoc3.htm
Sponsor Phi Upsilon Omicron
P.O. Box 329
Fairmont, WV 26555

HCR Manor Care Foundation Grants **2229**
Grants are awarded to communities nationwide where Manor Care Health Services has operations. The foundation has two grantmaking interests: organizations involved in research of diseases and disorders affecting the elderly and community programs that offer support and outreach services to seniors. The foundation concentrates on research organizations that treat and look for cures for illnesses such as Alzheimer's disease and stroke. Grants also are made to community organizations that offer support and information services to seniors. Initial contact should be made through a letter of inquiry (five pages or less). Letters are reviewed on an ongoing basis. If the foundation is interested, a formal grant proposal will be invited, with application deadlines as indicated.
Requirements Nonprofits must have 501(c)3 status, be located in a state where Manor Care Health Services operates (AZ, CA, CO, CT, DE, FL, GA, IL, IN, IA, KS, KY, MD, MI, MN, MO, NV, NJ, NM, NC, ND, OH, OK, PA, SC, SD, TN, TX, UT, VA, WA, WV, and WI), and have at least one other source of support for the project.
Restrictions The foundation does not support fundraising events, advertising, individuals, for-profit organizations, building or capital campaigns, political purposes or campaigns, endowment funds, multiple year grants, overhead fees, or general purpose/operating grants.
Amount $8300-$35,000 average
Date(s) Application Is Due Apr 1; Oct 1.
Contact Executive Director, (419) 252-5989; fax: (419) 252-5521; email: foundation@hcr-manorcare.com
Internet http://www.hcr-manorcare.org
Sponsor HCR Manor Care Foundation
P.O. Box 10086, 333 N Summit St
Toledo, OH 43699-0086

Health Care Financing Research, Demonstrations, and Evaluations Grants **2230**
Project grants (including cooperative agreements) are awarded to support analyses, experiments, demonstrations, and pilot projects in efforts to resolve major health care financing issues or to develop innovative methods for the administration of Medicare and Medicaid. HCFA has identified priority areas for the current fiscal year, including access and quality of care, coordinated care systems, provider payment, health care systems reform and financing, program evaluation and analysis, service delivery systems, and

subacute and long-term care. Awardees are required to share in the cost of projects; normally, the minimum cost-sharing requirement is 5 percent of total project costs. Projects are generally funded on a 12-month basis, with support beyond the first year contingent upon acceptable evidence of satisfactory progress, continuing program relevance, and availability of funds. Applications may be submitted at any time.
Requirements Grants or cooperative agreements may be made to private or public and nonprofit or for-profit agencies/organizations.
Amount $25,000-$1 million; $235,000 average
Contact Judy Norris, (410)786-5130; email: jnorrisl@cms.hhs.gov
Internet http://www.cms.hhs.gov/contracts
Sponsor Health Care Financing Administration
7500 Security Blvd
Baltimore, MD 21244-1850

Health Care Research Awards **2231**
The awards recognize research that advances healthcare delivery and management and include a monetary prize in each of two categories: general healthcare, and children's healthcare. The research submitted must have been published between December 31 and September 1 of the previous year. Authors can be from any field, and may come from higher education settings, research firms, or policy organizations.
Requirements Healthcare researchers are eligible.
Amount $5000 prize
Date(s) Application Is Due Mar 31; Sep 22.
Contact Grants Administrator, (202) 296-4426; fax: (202) 296-4319; email: nihcm@nihcm.org
Internet http://www.nihcm.org/awardframe.html
Sponsor National Institute for Health Care Management Foundation
1225 19th St NW, Ste 710
Washington, DC 20036

Health Foundation of Southern Florida Grants **2232**
The foundation supports projects and organizations that improve healthcare in southern Texas. Areas of interest include healthcare services, preventive health services, health education, medical research, and organizational and system capacity building. The foundation is interested in supporting start-up projects; expansion projects; projects whose governmental funding has recently been discontinued; project models with a clear explanation of how improved outcomes will be achieved; education measuring project performance and outcome; integration of services from multiple organizations; development or replication of evidence-based, best practice models; recognition and development of skills and competencies of individuals, organizations, and communities; projects that improve the system(s) of healthcare delivery; and sustainability and replicability of project models. Proposal guidelines are available online.
Requirements Southern Florida nonprofit organizations in Broward, Miami-Dade, and Monroe Counties are eligible.
Restrictions The foundation does not make grants as the sole revenue source; fund projects outside of Broward, Miami-Dade, and Monroe Counties; or provide grant support to projects focused outside the following content areas: healthcare services, preventive health services, health education, medical research, or capacity building for healthcare organizations and systems.
Amount $300,000 maximum
Date(s) Application Is Due Mar 11; Oct 21.
Contact Peter Wood, Chief Program Officer, (305) 374-7200; fax: (305) 374-7003; email: pwood@hfsf.org
Internet http://www.hfsf.org/index.cfm?fa=grantmaking
Sponsor Health Foundation of Southern Florida
601 Brickell Key Dr, Ste 901
Miami, FL 33133

Health Management Scholarships and Grants for Minorities **2233**
This financial assistance program provides scholarships and grants to ethnic minority students for graduate study in health care administration/management. Annual tuition scholarships and grants are made to outstanding students in health services management and related programs. Grants are provided to cover the costs of books, tutorial assistance, and other nontuition educational aids. Students are eligible to receive a combination of awards during the same time period.
Requirements To be eligible, applicants must be members of an ethnic minority group; must be US citizens or have permanent resident status (birth certificate, green card, or current passport); they must be college juniors, seniors or graduate students; they must be health care administration/management majors; they must have a strong academic background (2.5 GPA on a 4.0 scale); and they must have strong extracurricular and community service activities.
Amount $2500 scholarship, $500 grant
Contact Program Contact, (800) 233-0996 or (312) 422-2680; fax: (312) 422-4566
Internet http://www.diversityconnection.org/asp/programs_conferences/leadership_conference.asp
Sponsor Institute for Diversity in Health Management
1 N Franklin, 30th Fl
Chicago, IL 60606

Health Research Board Clinical Research Fellowships in Nursing and Midwifery **2234**
Fellowships provide experienced nurses and midwives with an opportunity to carry out research in Ireland in clinical nursing and midwifery, leading to a postgraduate qualification at master's and doctoral level. Awards are available for one to three years, depending on the project and the postgraduate qualification sought. Postgraduate fees will be paid where applicable. Fellowships will be held on a full-time basis. Fellowships are tenable by nurses or midwives employed in a recognized health service or an Irish academic department of nursing and registered with an academic department of nursing or other relevant academic department for a postgraduate degree. One of the academic sponsors must be a nurse or midwife. Applications are available on the Web site.
Requirements Applicants must be registered as a nurse or midwife; have practiced professional nursing or midwifery for at least five years; hold a post in nursing or midwifery practice or a post related to nursing or midwifery; have been employed in the Irish health services, or an Irish academic department of nursing, within two years prior to the closing date for application to the fellowship; have a research proposal involving a field of nursing or midwifery in either Ireland as a whole or the Republic of Ireland; have obtained the prior approval of the head of an academic department of nursing for the research study being carried out; secure ethical approval for the research, if such approval is required; be an EU citizen or be entitled to permanent resident status in Ireland.
Amount IR@L41,902; IR@L43,319; IR@L44,727
Date(s) Application Is Due Jan 13.
Contact Dr. Mairead O'Driscoll, (01) 6761176 ext 114 or 6766076; fax: (01) 6611856; email: modriscoll@hrb.ie or hrb@hrb.ie
Internet http://www.hrb.ie/display_content.php?page_id=98
Sponsor Health Research Board
73 Lower Baggot St
Dublin 2
Ireland

Health Research Board Project Grants **2235**
The aim of the board's research grant schemes is to support high-quality, internationally competitive health research in Ireland and to promote the development of a world-class research community in biomedical sciences, clinical research, and health and health services research. Grants currently support research in all areas of health and health services, including basic biomedical sciences (cell biology, endocrinology, genetics, immunology, microbiology, molecular biology, neurosciences, pathology, physiology, and virology); clinical research; health services; nursing; mental health; public health; general practice; and epidemiology. Assistance may be in the form of a postgraduate scholarship or funding toward other relevant personnel, whichever is most applicable. Applications for project grants are normally advertised in January each year. Application forms are available on the Web site at time of advertisement.
Requirements The principal applicant must hold a full-time academic post in an Irish academic institution and his/her specialty should be within the range of disciplines stated above. Applicants must reside in the Republic of Ireland and grants are tenable in that country.
Amount IR@L44,000
Contact Dr. Mairead O'Driscoll, (01) 6761176 or 6766076; fax: (01) 6611856; email: grants@hrb.ie
Internet http://www.hrb.ie/display_content.php?page_id=92
Sponsor Health Research Board
73 Lower Baggot St
Dublin 2
Ireland

Health Services Research Impact Awards **2236**
The program requests nominations of health services research that has made a positive impact on health policy and/or practice. The winning impacts will be disseminated widely as part of AcademyHealth's ongoing efforts to promote the field of health services research and communicate its value for health care decision-making. Nominated research may be published or unpublished, a single study or a body of work, the work of an individual or a team. The time frame for when the research was conducted is open, but the impact should have occurred recently. Nominators and nominees are not required to be AcademyHealth members. Self-nominations are accepted. Award winners are announced at the National Health Policy Conference, February 6 and 7, and the winners receive complimentary registration, travel, and lodging to the conference.
Requirements Each nomination must include a summary describing the research used, the method of translation, and the impact on policy and/or practice (no more than 500 words); a letter of recommendation from the user of this research discussing the impact the research has had; contact information for the lead researcher; and contact information for the nominator (may be the lead researcher).
Amount $2000
Date(s) Application Is Due Jul 29.
Contact Jennifer Muldoon, (202) 292-6700; fax: (202) 292-6800; email: jennifer.muldoon@academyhealth.org
Internet http://www.academyhealth.org/awards/hsrimpacts.htm
Sponsor AcademyHealth
1801 K St NW, No 701-L
Washington, DC 20006

Healthcare Foundation of New Jersey Grants 2237
The Foundation's funding priorities are the vulnerable populations of the greater Newark New Jersey community; the emergent health needs of serving at-risk individuals and families in the MetroWest Jewish community; and clinical research/medical education initiatives that significantly and directly impact these populations. The Foundation seeks grant proposals that promise innovation and change or a significant enhancement of services. Proposals are accepted on a rolling basis throughout the calendar year. Proposal submission instructions are available online.
Requirements Nonprofit organizations in the Greater Newark area are eligible to apply. The Foundation strongly suggests that applications be submitted electronically.
Restrictions Grants are made only to private nonprofit organizations that have tax-exempt status under Section 501(c)(3) of the Internal Revenue Code and that are not private foundations. The Foundation does not make grants to individuals or government agencies. The Foundation does not typically fund the following: organizations outside of Essex, Morris or Union County, New Jersey; programs not related to health care; direct support of an individual's healthcare needs; fundraising events or endowment campaigns; advertising campaigns; lobbying; or scholarships.
Contact Program Contact, (973) 921-1210; fax: (973) 921-1274; email: info@hfnj.org
Internet http://www.hfnj.org
Sponsor Healthcare Foundation of New Jersey
60 East Willow Street, 2nd Floor
Millburn, NJ 07041

Heart Rhythm Society Fellowships 2238
Fellowships and research grants are available for projects pertaining to cardiac pacing and/or cardiac electrophysiology. All awards are made for one year, renewable in competition. Also available are traveling fellowships, for a one- to three-month duration, to enable a researcher to observe research at other institutions or attend seminars and conferences. One traveling Canadian fellowship is offered; the applicant must be a Canadian citizen or must train at a site in Canada. Annual deadline dates may vary; contact program staff for exact dates.
Requirements Fellowships are open to applicants who have a doctor of medicine, philosophy, osteopathy, science, or equivalent training or experience in the field of biomedical engineering. Applicants must be citizens or permanent residents of a North American country and include cardiac pacing or cardiac electrophysiology as a central part of his/her long-range career goals.
Amount $40,000 for fellowships, $6000 for traveling fellowships, $6000 for traveling Canadian fellowship
Date(s) Application Is Due Sep 15.
Contact Stephanie Mascetta, (508) 647-0100 ext 3046; fax: (508) 647-0124; email: fellowship@HRSonline.org
Internet http://www.hrsonline.org/society_in_action/fellowships/default.asp
Sponsor Heart Rhythm Society
Six Strathmore Rd
Natick, MA 01760-2499

Hebrew University Lady Davis Trust Fellowships 2239
The trust offers fellowships to visiting professors, postdoctoral researchers, and doctoral students at the Hebrew University of Jerusalem and at the Technion, Israel Institute of Technology in Haifa. Distinguished scholars spend from three months to one year at one of these institutions developing research networks, teaching and enjoying the world-class academic environment.
Requirements Scholars of any age, in any field, and from any region may apply.
Contact Coordinator of Graduate Programs, Office of Academic Affairs, (800) 404-8622 or(212) 472-2288; fax: (212) 517-4548; email: admission@roth.mscc.huji.ac.il
Internet http://www.huji.ac.il/unew/main.html
Sponsor Hebrew University of Jerusalem
Givat Ram, Jerusalem 91904
Israel

Hedco Foundation Grants 2240
The foundation awards grants domestically and internationally to nonprofit organizations in its areas of interest, including education at all levels; health care, including hospitals and health organizations; and organizations serving children and youth. Types of support include building construction/renovation and equipment acquisition. Past grants have supported biomedical research, but research grants generally are not awarded. There are no application deadlines or forms. An audited financial statement and IRS tax-exemption letter must accompany all proposals.
Requirements 501(c)3 nonprofit organizations are eligible.
Restrictions Grants do not support individuals or requests for general operating support, publications, special projects, or loans.
Amount $5000-$75,000 average
Contact Grants Administrator, (925) 242-0257
Sponsor Hedco Foundation
P.O. Box 1980
San Ramon, CA 94583

HEI Grants 2241
The institute awards research grants for scientific information about the health effects of motor vehicle emissions on the environment and on human health.
Amount $70,000-$300,000
Contact Daniel Greenbaum, President, (617) 886-9330 ext 311; fax: (617) 886-9335; email: dgreenbaum@healtheffects.org
Internet http://www.healtheffects.org/funding.htm
Sponsor Health Effects Institute
120 Second Ave
Boston, MA 02129-4533

Heinz Latin American Social and Public Policy Fellowships 2242
The Center for Latin American Studies awards the fellowships, made possible from the Howard Heinz Endowment, Alcoa Foundation, and the Mine Safety Appliances Company Charitable Foundation, to assist scholars interested in various dimensions of social and public policy to pursue advanced graduate studies in a department or professional school of the University of Pittsburgh. Fellowship support is for a maximum of two years. Applicants must be accepted into one of the following departments or schools to be eligible: anthropology, economics, history, linguistics, political science, religious studies, sociology, business, education, law, public health, public and international affairs, and social work. Recipients are appointed for fall and spring terms and in addition to pursuing their studies as full-time students, work on collaborative projects with Latin American social and public policy specialists. Applications are due in late January.
Requirements Individuals of all nationalities who are enrolled as full-time graduate students at the University of Pittsburgh and are pursuing master's or PhD degrees in some aspect of social and/or public policy are eligible.
Amount $1325 per month stipend, full tuition for fall and spring terms, medical insurance, and $400 book allowance per year
Contact Luis Van Fossen Bravo, Center for Latin American Studies, (412) 648-7393; fax: (412) 648-2199; email: bravo@ucis.pitt.edu
Internet http://www.ucis.pitt.edu/clas/students/fellowships_scholarships.html
Sponsor University of Pittsburgh
University of Pittsburgh, 4E Wesley W Posvar Hall
Pittsburgh, PA 15260

Heiser Leprosy and Tuberculosis Research Postdoctoral Fellowships 2243
The program fosters research on leprosy and tuberculosis by supporting the research training of a limited number of young biomedical scientists interested in the field. The program is designed to encourage national and international cooperation and research interchange in the study of the diseases. A maximum of two years of support will be provided to successful applicants at stipend levels adjusted according to US government guidelines for geographical location at which the training is to take place. There are no application forms. Application may be made either by the individual seeking training or by the head of a laboratory engaged in research related to leprosy. In the latter case, the head of the laboratory must name the prospective fellow in the application.
Requirements Biomedical scientists with either the PhD or MD degree are eligible for these fellowships. Applicants should be at the beginning or in an early phase of their postdoctoral training and interested in obtaining research training in a basic science field directly related to the study of leprosy. There are no citizenship requirements.
Amount $35,000 maximum stipend per year; $2000 training allowance; $1500 maximum for health insurance
Date(s) Application Is Due Mar 1.
Contact Len McNally, Program Director, (212) 686-0010 ext 556; email: lm@nyct-cfi.org
Sponsor Heiser Program for Research in Leprosy and Tuberculosis
c/o The New York Community Trust , 909 Third Ave
New York, NY 10022

Heiser Leprosy Research Grants 2244
The grants provide support to laboratories involved in leprosy research training. Proposals of high scientific caliber related to leprosy will be considered. Seed grants may be requested for new projects or facilities that show promise of support from other sources within one year. Leprosy postdoctoral research fellowships and tuberculosis postdoctoral research fellowships also are awarded. There are no application forms. Applicants should submit proposals and budgets along with curriculum vita and relevant bibliographies of participating scientists.
Requirements Senior investigators who are experienced in leprosy and tuberculosis research and associated with laboratories providing training opportunities in these areas are eligible.
Restrictions Grants do not support clinical trials, salaries of personnel, or more than 10 percent of institutional overhead.
Amount $35,000 maximum
Date(s) Application Is Due Mar 1.
Contact Len McNally, Program Director, (212) 686-0010 ext 556; email: lm@nyct-cfi.org
Sponsor Heiser Program for Research in Leprosy and Tuberculosis
c/o The New York Community Trust, 909 Third Ave
New York, NY 10022

Helen Bader Foundation Grants 2245
The foundation supports innovative pilot projects and programs that are research based, have strong evaluation components, and involve community collaboration. The foundation's primary focus areas are Alzheimer's disease and dementia, early childhood

development in Israel, education, economic development, and Jewish life and learning. Modest grants are awarded to support neighborhood renewal and youth development in Milwaukee's Sankofa area. Grants will be awarded primarily in the Delaware River Valley and in particular Milwaukee, WI, with the exception of the Alzheimer's disease and dementia program, which accepts applications from organizations nationwide. International grants are made for projects conducted in Israel. The foundation often funds multiple-year projects but rarely for a period of more than three years. Preliminary proposals must be received by the listed application deadline dates. If the foundation is interested in exploring the grant request further, a member of the program staff will contact the applicant to arrange a meeting or site visit. Applications are available on the Web site.
Requirements Grants are awarded for projects consistent with one or more of the Helen Bader Foundation's program areas. Grants are given only to U.S. organizations which are tax exempt under Section 501(c)(3) of the Internal Revenue Code or to government entities. Grants will only be approved for foreign entities which meet specific charitable status requirements.
Restrictions The Foundation does not provide direct support for individuals, such as individual scholarships.
Amount $10,000-$100,000 average
Date(s) Application Is Due Jun 25; Feb 25.
Contact Program Contact, (414) 224-6464; fax: (414) 224-1441
Internet http://www.hbf.org
Sponsor Helen Bader Foundation
233 North Water Street, 4th Floor
Milwaukee, WI 53202

Helen Carr Minority Fellowships **2246**
These fellowships provide support to African American engineering students or faculty at Hampton University, Morgan State University, Howard University, North Carolina A&T State University, Prairie View A&M University, Tennessee State University, Tuskegee University, and Southern University who have not yet completed their doctorates and wish to do so. The fellowships are awarded for one year and may be renewed. The amount awarded is dependent on the educational requirements and financial needs of the recipients.
Requirements Eligible to apply are African American students or engineering faculty who are interested in earning doctoral degrees and returning to one of the historically black engineering colleges to teach.
Amount $10,000 maximum per year
Date(s) Application Is Due May 1.
Contact Historically Black Engineering Colleges Committee, (202) 331-3525 or 331-3500; fax: (202) 265-8504; email: projects@asee.org
Internet http://www.asee.org/fellowships/hbecc.cfm
Sponsor American Society for Engineering Education
1818 N St NW, Ste 600
Washington, DC 20036

Helen Hay Whitney Foundation Postdoctoral Research Fellowships **2247**
The program provides three-year fellowships for beginning postdoctoral training in basic biomedical research. The program is intended for individuals planning careers in biological or medical research to receive financial support of sufficient duration to help further their professional careers. It is expected that fellowship training will be obtained in an academic setting. The foundation will not consider applicants who plan tenure of the fellowship in the laboratory in which they have already received extensive predoctoral or postdoctoral training; the aim of the fellowship is to broaden postdoctoral training and experience. Applications are available online.
Requirements Residents of the United States, Canada, and Mexico who are in the final stages of obtaining the MD, PhD, or equivalent degree and are seeking beginning postdoctocral training in basic biomedical research are eligible.
Restrictions Applications from established scientists or advanced fellows will not be considered. Applicants who have already had one year of postdoctoral laboratory training by the listed deadline date will not be considered.
Amount $41,000 for first year, $42,500 for second year, and $44,000 for the third year, plus $2500 to the fellow's laboratory to help defray research expenses
Date(s) Application Is Due Jul 15.
Contact Grants Administrator, (845) 639-6799; fax: (845) 639-6798 or (646) 304-7133; email: hhwf@earthlink.net
Internet http://www.hhwf.org/HTMLSrc/ResearchFellowships.html
Sponsor Helen Hay Whitney Foundation
20 Squadron Blvd, Ste 630
New York, NY 10956

Helen Kellogg Institute for International Studies Residential Fellowships **2248**
The institute seeks fellows of high scholarly accomplishment and promise, at both senior and junior levels, whose work and presence will contribute creatively to its major research themes. The institute's research reflects commitments to democracy, development, and social justice, and focuses on five major themes: Democratization and the Quality of Democracy, Paths to Development, Religion and the Catholic Church, Social Movements and Organized Civil Society, and Public Policies for Social Justice. Stipends vary according to seniority; fellows from abroad may receive one direct round-trip economy airfare from the institute. Applications and further information are available on the Web site.
Requirements Applications are welcome from candidates from any country holding the PhD or equivalent degree in any discipline of the social sciences or history. Candidates will be evaluated individually but joint projects will be considered. All fellows from abroad are requested to apply for travel grants to aid with transportation expenses in the United States.
Date(s) Application Is Due Nov 1.
Contact Sharon Schierling, Program Coordinator, (219) 631-6580; fax: (219) 631-6717; email: Sharon.K.Schierling.1@nd.edu
Internet http://www.nd.edu/~kellogg/guest.html
Sponsor University of Notre Dame
216 Hesburgh Ctr
Notre Dame, IN 46556-5677

Helen M. Robinson Dissertation Research Award **2249**
This award may be made annually to support doctoral students who are IRA members at the early stages of their dissertation research. The award will be made only in those years when the committee concludes that there are applications of very high quality.
Requirements Doctoral student applicant should submit an abstract, not to exceed 1000 words, of an approved dissertation proposal; a brief statement, not to exceed 500 words, indicating how the grant will be used to support the research; a copy of the full proposal with a cover sheet, including signatures of approval by a supervisory committee; and a letter from the student's major advisor that includes a brief rationale as to why the grant should be awarded to this applicant.
Amount $1500
Date(s) Application Is Due Jan 15.
Contact Program Contact, (302) 731-1600 ext 423; fax: (302) 731-1057; email: research@reading.org
Internet http://www.reading.org/association/awards/research_robinson.html
Sponsor International Reading Association
P.O. Box 8139, 800 Barksdale Rd
Newark, DE 19714-8139

Helen M. Woodruff AIA and American Academy in Rome Archaeology Fellowship **2250**
A pre- or postdoctoral fellowship for study of archaeology and classical studies has been established by the institute at the American Academy in Rome. This fellowship, combined with other funds from the American Academy in Rome, will support a Rome Prize Fellowship, which will be open to citizens or permanent residents of the United States. For application forms, write to the American Academy in Rome, 7 E 60th St, New York, NY 10022; (212) 751-7200; or visit the Web site (http://www.aarome.org).
Restrictions Current officers and governing board members of the Institute at the American Academy in Rome are not eligible.
Contact Program Contact, (617) 353-9361; fax: (617) 353-6550; email: aia@aia.bu.edu
Internet http://www.archaeological.org/webinfo.php?page=10008
Sponsor Archaeological Institute of America
656 Beacon St
Boston, MA 02215-2010

Helen McWilliam Memorial Scholarship **2251**
This scholarship is open to full-time graduate students at the University of Calgary interested in pursuing careers in school psychology. Recipients will be selected on the basis of academic excellence, skill in the handling of children referred for testing or guidance, and evidence of interest and ability in the area of school psychology. The award will be based on grades and observations by faculty members of academic and practical work. Annual deadline dates may vary; contact program staff for exact dates.
Requirements Applicants must be full-time graduate students enrolled in the school psychology program of the Department of Educational Psychology at the master's or doctoral level. Applications should be made at the end of the first academic year.
Amount $C2000
Contact Program Contact, Faculty of Graduate Studies, (403) 220-5690; email: cbusch@acs.ucalgary.ca or ucawards@ucalgary.ca
Internet http://www.grad.ucalgary.ca/funding/internal_scholarships/lev_4/mcwilliam.htm
Sponsor University of Calgary
2500 University Dr NW, Earth Sciences Bldg
Calgary, AB T2N 1N4 Canada

Helen V. Brach Foundation Grants **2252**
The foundation operates to prevent cruelty to animals or to children; for religious, charitable, scientific, literary, and education purposes; and for public safety testing through support of Midwest 501(c)3 tax-exempt organizations carrying out programs and activities in these areas. Brach provides grants nationally and has wide-ranging interests. For instance, it supports homeless and women's emergency shelters, teen pregnancy prevention programs, parenting education, summer school for disadvantaged children, job training for welfare mothers, orphanages, and scholarships for economically disadvantaged students. Types of support include annual campaigns, building construction/renovation, equipment, general operating support, publications, research, and special projects. The foundation ordinarily does not make multiyear grants

or commitments. Applicants are required to complete in full a brief application form, which may be obtained from the office. The board of directors gives final consideration to all applications received in a given year at the board's meeting, which is usually held in March.
Requirements Although 501(c)3 nonprofits from across the nation are eligible, giving is primarily made in the Midwest and California, Massachusetts, Ohio, Pennsylvania, and South Carolina.
Restrictions Grants are not made to individuals or to organizations outside the United States. Typically grants are not made in excess of 10 percent of a group's operating budget, which automatically excludes start-up grants.
Amount $10,000-$25,000 average
Date(s) Application Is Due Dec 31.
Contact Raymond Simon, President, (312) 372-4417; fax: (312) 372-0290
Sponsor Helen V. Brach Foundation
55 W Wacker Dr, Ste 701
Chicago, IL 60601

Henry Dreyfus Teacher-Scholar Awards Program **2253**
The program is intended to support and encourage young scholars who demonstrate excellence in both research and teaching. The award is based on accomplishments in scholarly research with undergraduates, as well as a compelling commitment to teaching with respect to primarily undergraduate institutions. Institutions may make only one nomination annually. Application information is available online.
Requirements Institutions in US states, districts, and territories that grant a bachelor's or higher degree in chemistry, chemical engineering, or biochemistry may submit nominations. Nominees must hold a full-time tenure-track academic appointment, be between the fourth and twelfth years of their independent academic careers, and engage in research and teaching primarily with undergraduates.
Restrictions Awards are not made directly to individuals.
Amount $60,000
Date(s) Application Is Due Jun 28.
Contact Program Contact, (212) 753-1760; email: admin@dreyfus.org
Internet http://www.dreyfus.org/th.shtml
Sponsor Camille and Henry Dreyfus Foundation
555 Madison Avenue, 20th Floor
New York, NY 10022-1301

Henry Hess Award **2254**
The award is given annually for an original technical paper submitted to ASME for presentation and publication during the calendar year prior to the year of award by a student or associate member who was not yet 31 years of age at the time the paper was submitted to ASME. Joint authorship is permissible provided all authors meet the requirements. The paper shall be specifically recommended for the award by a review committee or a qualified individual.
Requirements Author must not be older than 31 at the time of submission and must be an ASME student member or associate member to be eligible to apply.
Amount $1000 and expense supplement
Date(s) Application Is Due Mar 1.
Contact Gilda DiTullio, Manager, (212) 591-7736; fax: (212) 705-7739; email: ditulliog@asme.org
Internet http://www.asme.org/honors/ms71/gla/hess.html
Sponsor American Society of Mechanical Engineers
3 Park Ave
New York, NY 10016

Henry J. Kaiser Family Foundation Grants **2255**
The foundation concentrates giving in the following areas: US government's role in health, health of low-income and minority groups with major emphasis on HIV/AIDS policy, reproductive health policy, and health system innovation and reform in California. The foundation also operates a major program to improve health and health care and promote social justice in South Africa. Grants are awarded for one to three years and support a range of activities, including policy analysis, applied research to define and measure public health problems, demonstration and pilot projects, and communications activities that help sharpen health care debates and improve quality of health information. Prospective applicants should submit a preliminary letter (two to three pages in length) that briefly describes the proposed project, along with an estimate of the total budget and the amount requested from the foundation. There are no deadlines and no application forms. Inquiries for projects in South Africa may be addressed to Dr. Michael Sinclair, Senior Vice President, The Henry J. Kaiser Family Foundation, 1450 G St NW, Ste 250, Washington, DC 20005, (202) 347-5270, fax: (202) 347-5274.
Requirements Grants in response to unsolicited proposals are made only to governmental agencies and to private organizations with IRS 501(c)3 tax-exempt status.
Restrictions The foundation does not award grants to individuals. Support is not given to ongoing general operating expenses, indirect costs, capital campaigns, annual appeals or other fundraising events, construction, purchase or renovation of facilities, or equipment purchases.
Amount $1000-$500,000 typically
Contact Renee Wells, Grants Manager, (415) 854-9400; fax: (415) 854-4800; email: rwells@kff.org
Internet http://www.kff.org
Sponsor Henry J. Kaiser Family Foundation
2400 Sand Hill Rd
Menlo Park, CA 94025

Henry J. Kaiser Family Foundation Media Fellowships **2256**
The purpose of the fellowship is to help journalists and commentators do the best possible job of keeping the public informed about health issues at this critical time in the evolution of the health care system. The goal of the fellowship is to provide a highly flexible range of opportunities tailored to each fellow's interests; help journalists improve the quality of the work they do; provide time to research specific topics; and deepen participants' commitment to becoming specialists in health reporting. Fellows may want to participate in the fellowship program on a part-time basis and continue writing or reporting during their fellowship. Fellows are encouraged to do reporting based on their fellowship research and to experiment with different media or forms of writing. Most fellows work from home, or base themselves at a local academic or research institution. There is no obligation to pursue academic coursework, although that is an option open to all fellows. There is no application form. Guidelines are available online.
Requirements Fellowships will be awarded to US journalists interested in US health policy issues.
Amount $50,000 maximum for nine-month fellowship
Date(s) Application Is Due Mar 16.
Contact Penny Duckham, Executive Director, (650) 234-9220; fax: (650) 854-4800; email: pduckham@kff.org
Internet http://www.kff.org/about/mediafellowships.cfm
Sponsor Henry J. Kaiser Family Foundation
2400 Sand Hill Rd
Menlo Park, CA 94025

Henry L. Guenther Foundation Grants **2257**
The foundation awards grants to California nonprofit organizations in its areas of interest, including medical services, creating opportunities for youth, and community services. Grants support hospitals, medical research, and social services. The board meets in January and July. Contact the office for application procedures.
Requirements California nonprofit organizations are eligible. Grants are awarded primarily in Lost Angeles.
Restrictions Grants do not support government agencies, religious organizations for religious purposes, individuals, or debt-reduction requests.
Amount $10,000-$100,000 average
Date(s) Application Is Due May 31; Nov 30.
Contact W.D. Milliken, Secretary, (310) 785-0658
Sponsor Henry L. Guenther Foundation
2029 Century Park D, Ste 4392
Los Angeles, CA 90067

Henry Luce Foundation Special Projects in Higher Education Grants **2258**
This award is a responsive grant made to colleges and universities for special projects which fall outside the context of the Foundation's funding categories. Higher education is an underlying theme for most of the Foundation's programs, through support for research, training, and the creation of new resources. The current primary focus of the program has reflected the Foundation's commitment to strengthen America's capacity for international understanding. No special forms are required for the application process. An initial letter of inquiry should be addressed to the appropriate program contact. Requests are accepted at any time. Awards are determined by the board of directors, which meets three times a year.
Restrictions The Foundation does not support health care or medical projects and does not fund development assistance work overseas. It does not normally assist journalism, media and film projects or the performing arts.
Contact Special Projects in Higher Education, (212) 489-7700; fax: (212) 581-9541; email: hlf1@hluce.org
Internet http://www.hluce.org/4heddefm.html
Sponsor Henry Luce Foundation
111 West 50th Street, Room 4601
New York, NY 10020

Henry Luce Foundation Theology Program Grants **2259**
The foundation's theology program emphasizes theological education and reflects a commitment to support the role of religion in daily life. Six areas of funding illustrate the breadth of the program: seminary education, leadership, publications, religion and the arts, ecumenical programs, and special initiatives. The program supports innovative research and publication by full-time seminary faculty. Requests may be submitted at any time. The board meets three times each year to consider requests.
Restrictions The foundation does not support health care or medical projects and does not fund development assistance work overseas. It does not normally assist journalism, media and film projects, or the performing arts.
Contact Theology Program, (212) 489-7700; fax: (212) 581-9541; email: hlf@hluce.org
Internet http://www.hluce.org/3theofm.html
Sponsor Henry Luce Foundation
111 W 50th St, Ste 4601
New York, NY 10020

Henry Luce Foundation/ACLS American Art Dissertation Fellowships **2260**
The fellowships, which are made possible by funding from the Henry Luce Foundation, support graduate students in any stage of PhD dissertation research or writing. To be eligible, a student must be a PhD candidate in a department of art history, and the candidate's dissertation must be focused on a topic in the history of the visual arts of the United States. Students whose degrees will be granted by another department may be eligible if their principal dissertation advisor is in a department of art history and their dissertation topic is object-oriented. The fellowships are for a one-year nonrenewable term beginning in the summer. Fellowship funds may not be used to defray tuition costs.
Requirements Applicants must have completed all requirements for the PhD except the dissertation before beginning the one-year tenure.
Restrictions Students who received grants of $5000 or more from the Henry Luce Program previously administered through university art departments are not eligible, nor are students preparing theses for the master of fine arts degree.
Amount $22,500
Date(s) Application Is Due Nov 14.
Contact Saul Fisher, Director of Fellowship Programs, (212) 697-1505 ext 124; fax: (212) 949-8058; email: sfisher@acls.org
Internet http://www.acls.org/luceguid.htm
Sponsor American Council of Learned Societies
228 E 45th St
New York, NY 10017-3398

Henry Luce Foundation/ACLS Grants to Individuals in East Asian Archaeology and Early History **2261**
Research fellowships and training grants will be awarded for study of the peoples and cultures of early East Asia. For the purposes of this program, East Asia refers to northeast Asia (China, Hong Kong, Japan, Korea, Macau, Mongolia, and Taiwan) and southeast Asia (Brunei, Burma/Myanmar, Cambodia, Indonesia, Laos, Malaysia, Philippines, Singapore, Thailand, and Vietnam). Proposals may cover prehistoric or historical periods, but must focus on research or training that involves excavations and/or excavated materials. Comparative projects and those that build scholarly networks are especially encouraged. Application information is available online.
Requirements Applicants must be residents of the United States or Canada and have their primary professional affiliation at an institution in this region. Applicants must hold an advanced degree in a relevant discipline such as archaeology, anthropology, art history, literature, or history, must be nearing completion of such a degree, or must possess commensurate experience in scholarship, archives, museums, or field sites. Linguistic ability sufficient to conduct the work proposed is required.
Restrictions Applications will not be accepted by fax or email.
Contact Grants Administrator, (212) 697-1505; fax: (212) 949-8058; email: grants@acls.org
Internet http://www.acls.org/eaaeh.htm
Sponsor American Council of Learned Societies
633 Third Avenue
New York, NY 10017-6795

Henry Luce Fund in American Art Grants **2262**
The program consists of three areas: the Luce Fund in American Art, which places emphasis on scholarly exhibitions and publications; responsive grants, generally for institutional enhancement; and dissertation fellowships, aimed at the next generation of art historians specializing in this field. Grants are made three times a year. Letters of request may be submitted at any time but should be received by March 1 for the annual summer review of approximately 20 proposals. It is helpful if applicant speaks with appropriate staff members in advance of sending a letter or proposal.
Requirements American museums may apply by invitation only.
Date(s) Application Is Due Mar 1; Jun 15.
Contact Helene Redell, Program Director, (212) 489-7700; fax: (212) 581-9541; email: hlf@hluce.org
Internet http://www.hluce.org/4lfaafm.html
Sponsor Henry Luce Foundation
111 W 50th St, Rm 4601
New York, NY 10020

Henry Luce Scholars Program **2263**
This program is one aspect of the foundation's continuing efforts to improve American understanding of Asia. Each year, 15 young Americans of outstanding promise are selected by the foundation and sent to East and Southeast Asia to undertake internships in their chosen fields under the guidance of leading Asian professionals. A distinguishing feature of the program is that it is directed toward those who are not, and do not plan to become, specialists in Asian affairs. The object is to develop among a broad cross-section of future American leaders an understanding of the nature of Asian societies and cultures. At the program's core are individual internships and job placements arranged for the scholars on the basis of their individual career interests, experience, and training. Though it is hoped that the work of the scholars will be useful to their Asian hosts, a scholar's most significant contribution may simply be an honest attempt to assimilate the wealth of Asian experience and in the process to develop a much broader world perspective. The program relies on a network of 65 colleges and universities for its nominations; individual applications submitted directly to the foundation cannot be considered. Applications must reach the foundation from the nominating institutions by the first Monday of December. A guidelines brochure is available upon request.
Requirements Candidates must be American citizens who have received at least a bachelors degree and are no more than 29 years old on September 1 of the year they enter the program. Institutions may submit two nominations.
Restrictions Individual applications submitted directly to the foundation cannot be considered. Those who already have significant experience in Asia or Asian studies are not eligible to apply.
Contact Luce Scholars Program, (212) 489-7700; fax: (212) 581-9541; email: hlf@hluce.org
Internet http://www.hluce.org/3scholfm.html
Sponsor Henry Luce Foundation
111 W 50th St, Rm 3710
New York, NY 10020

Henry P. Kendall Foundation Grants **2264**
The foundation focuses almost entirely on the environment and securing its physical, biological, and aesthetic wealth for future generations. Geographic priorities for grants are New England and the Maritime Provinces of Eastern Canada and the Pacific Northwest, including Western Canada and Alaska. Current program themes include Gulf of Maine ecosystem, Northeastern landscape, Northeast climate change initiative, North country institution capacity-building, Yellowstone to Yukon conservation, watershed innovations in North America, public lands management, and special project initiatives. The foundation provides funding for general operating needs and for specific programs and initiatives. Activities funded include advocacy, public education, policy research and analysis, on-the-ground resource management experiments, and institutional development. Grants are normally made for one or two years. Unsolicited proposals and inquiries will not be reviewed.
Restrictions Grants do not support endowments or capital fund campaigns, land acquisition, television and film projects, fellowships, basic scientific research, building construction or maintenance, equipment, debt reduction, or conferences unrelated to current foundation institutional grants. Nor does the foundation normally fund waste clean-ups, toxics or air/water pollution prevention or pollution monitoring initiatives, individual land trusts, or species-specific preservation efforts.
Amount $20,000-$50,000 typically
Date(s) Application Is Due Feb 1; May 1; Oct 1.
Contact Jennifer Patrick, Associate Program Officer, (617) 951-2525; fax: (617) 443-1977
Internet http://www.kendall.org/grants/types.html
Sponsor Henry P. Kendall Foundation
176 Federal St
Boston, MA 02110

Henry R. Worthington Medal **2265**
This award is given annually for eminent achievement in the field of pumping machinery. Such achievement may be, for example, in the areas of research, development, design, innovation, management, education, or literature. Any individual member, group of members, or committee may nominate candidates for this award.
Amount $5000; $1000
Date(s) Application Is Due Feb 1.
Contact Gilda DiTullio, Manager, (212) 591-7736; fax: (212) 705-7739; email: ditulliog@asme.org
Internet http://www.asme.org/honors/ms71/saa/worthington.html
Sponsor American Society of Mechanical Engineers
3 Park Ave
New York, NY 10016

Henry W. Bull Foundation Grants **2266**
The foundation awards grants nationwide in its areas of interest, including higher education, the disabled, healthcare, Christian religion, music, and the arts. Types of support include annual campaigns, building construction/renovation, equipment acquisition, general operating support, continuing support, and research. There is no formal grant application form. Submit a simple, concise statement of needs and objectives with pertinent supportive data.
Requirements 501(c)3 nonprofits are eligible.
Restrictions Foreign grants are not considered.
Amount $500-$20,000 range
Date(s) Application Is Due Apr 1; Sep 1.
Contact Janice Gibson, Vice-President, Santa Barbara Bank & Trust, (805) 899-8405; fax: (805) 884-1404
Sponsor Henry W. Bull Foundation
P.O. Box 2340
Santa Barbara, CA 93120-2340

HERA Foundation Ovarian Cancer OSB1 Seed Grant **2267**
The Foundation is a non-profit organization whose mission is to prevent ovarian cancer and improve prognosis through innovative scientific research and education. The HERA Foundation will fund two basic, translational and/or clinical research projects: one grant of $25,000 is for projects that include, but are not limited to, those that study high grade ovarian carcinoma etiology and pathogenesis, and those that explore novel approaches

to early ovarian cancer detection and targeted therapy; a second grant of $20,000 is earmarked for low grade/micropapillary serous carcinoma/low malignant potential ovarian tumor research for research leading to a better understanding and/or more effective treatment. The goal is to encourage outside the box thinking and solutions and provide seed money for such projects. Chemotherapy has been in use for many years and to date we have not improved overall survival by 1%. New approaches to understanding and treating this disease are needed and are what is of interest to the Foundation.
Requirements Applicants must hold either a Ph.D. and/or an M.D. degree, and be either a post-doctoral research fellow or clinical fellow. A previous research background in ovarian cancer is not essential, as the HERA Foundation seeks to encourage new young investigators to enter the field. However, candidates should demonstrate the relevance of their previous research background to the proposed work, and indicate a strong long-term commitment to research in the field of ovarian cancer.
Restrictions Dr. Brant Wang, Johns Hopkins University (2006); Dr. Hiroyuki Yoshida, Anderson Cancer Center (2006); Dr. Martina Bazzaro, Johns Hopkins University.
Amount $20,000-$25,000
Date(s) Application Is Due Jan 15.
Contact Sheridia Daniels, (970) 948-7360; email: sdaniel6@jhmi.edu
Internet http://www.herafoundation.org/research.cfm
Sponsor HERA Foundation
P.O. Box 664
Carbondale, CO 81623

Herb Society of America Research and Education Grants **2268**
Grants are meant to further the knowledge and use of herbs and contribute the results of the study and research to the records of horticulture, science, literature, history, art, or economics. The research could involve such varied topics as history, medicinal research and usage from a historical perspective, fragrance, flavor, horticulture, landscaping, economic importance, chemurgy, taxonomy, and political and social influence. Grants are made for periods up to one year.
Requirements Applicants should be graduate students with proposed programs of scientific or academic investigation of herbal plants, or persons capable of demonstrating in-depth knowledge of herbs.
Restrictions The grant is not given for financial aid to individuals, rather for specific research on herbal projects. The grant does not provide for indirect costs or personal travel for the benefit of any individual.
Amount $5000 maximum per year
Date(s) Application Is Due Jan 31.
Contact Grants Administrator, (440) 256-0514; fax: (440) 256-0541; email: herbs@herbsociety.org
Internet http://www.herbsociety.org/research.php
Sponsor Herb Society of America
9019 Kirtland Chardon Rd
Kirtland, OH 44094

Herbert C. Brown Award for Creative Research in Synthetic Methods **2269**
This award, sponsored by Purdue Borane Research Fund and the Herbert C. Brown Award Endowment, is to recognize and encourage outstanding and creative contributions to research in synthetic methods. A nominee must have accomplished outstanding and creative research that involved the discovery and development of novel and useful methods for chemical synthesis. The synthetic method that is the basis for the award may be related to any area of chemistry.
Requirements Any individual, except a member of the award committee, may submit one nomination or seconding letter for the award in any given year. The nominating documents consist of a letter of not more than 1000 words containing an evaluation of the nominee's accomplishments and a specific identification of the work to be recognized, a biographical sketch including date of birth, and a list of publications and patents authored by the nominee. Six copies of all items to be included in the nomination must be submitted.
Restrictions Self-nominations are not accepted.
Amount $5000 and travel to award meeting
Date(s) Application Is Due Feb 1.
Contact Awards Administrator, (800) 227-5558 or (202) 872-4408; fax: (202) 872-6317; email: awards@acs.org
Internet http://www.chemistry.org/portal/a/c/s/1/acsdisplay.html?DOC=awards%5Cbrown.html
Sponsor American Chemical Society
1155 16th St NW
Washington, DC 20036

Herbert Eugene Bolton Memorial Prize **2270**
The prize is awarded for the best book in English on any significant aspect of Latin American history that is published during the imprint year previous to the year of the award. Sound scholarship, grace of style, and importance of the scholarly contribution are among the criteria for the award. Translations, anthologies of selections by several authors, reprints or reeditions of works published previously, and works not primarily historiographical in aim or content are not normally considered for an award. An honorable mention award may be made for an additional distinguished work.
Requirements To be considered for the prize, a book must bear the imprint of the year prior to the year for which the award is made.
Amount $1000
Contact CLAH, (530) 752-3046; fax: (530) 752-8964; email: clah@ucdavis.edu
Internet http://www.h-net.org/~clah/about/index.html
Sponsor Conference on Latin American History
University of California at Davis, One Shields Ave
Davis, CA 95616

Herbert H. and Grace A. Dow Foundation Grants **2271**
The Foundation has charter goals to improve the educational, religious, economic and cultural lives of Michigan's people. Priority is given to organizations that: have clearly stated objectives, strong and purposeful management and are publicly accountable; have needs which are in areas not normally funded by governmental or public financing; are not hesitant to explore, initiate, volunteer, or execute original ideas or concepts; are willing to collaborate with other persons or organizations to give synergy to a common objective or goal; have purposes which tend to advance private enterprise and the preservation of a free, open and self-resourceful society. Application information is available online.
Requirements Only organizations in Michigan are eligible to apply.
Restrictions The Foundation does not make grants directly to individuals. It cannot legally support: organizations to which contributions are not tax deductible, according to Internal Revenue Service regulations; organizations that practice discrimination by race, sex, creed, age or national origin; political organizations or organizations whose purposes are to influence legislation.
Contact Margaret Ann Riecker, President, (989) 631-3699; fax: (989) 631-0675; email: info@hhdowfoundation.org
Internet http://www.hhdowfdn.org
Sponsor Herbert H. and Grace A. Dow Foundation
1018 West Main Street
Midland, MI 48640-4292

Herbert Hoover Travel Grant Competition **2272**
Travel grants are awarded to encourage scholarly use of the Herbert Hoover Presidential Library in West Branch, IA. The program is intended to promote the study of subjects of interest and concern to Herbert Hoover, Lou Henry Hoover, their associates, and other public figures as reflected in the library's collections. It is strongly suggested that the applicant contact the archival staff at (319) 643-5301 to determine whether library holdings are pertinent to the applicant's research. Three separately mailed references must be submitted.
Requirements The program is open to graduate and postdoctoral scholars and to qualified nonacademic researchers on a competitive basis.
Amount $500-$1500
Date(s) Application Is Due Mar 1.
Contact Patricia Hand, Manager of Academic Programs, (800) 828-0475 or (319) 643-5327; fax: (319) 643-2391; email: pathand@hooverassociation.org or info@hooverassoc.org
Internet http://www.hooverassociation.org/grants.html
Sponsor Herbert Hoover Presidential Library Association
P.O. Box 696
West Branch, IA 52358

Herman Kahn Fellowship **2273**
One fellowship is given annually in the area of national security studies, domestic or international economics, education policy, or the study of political institutions to support PhD candidates who have completed their coursework and have only their dissertations remaining. Studies will be carried out in Indianapolis, IN, for one academic year. The fellow's time will be equally divided between dissertation work and policy research assigned by the institute. Application requirements are available upon request. Selected candidates will be interviewed in Indianapolis.
Requirements Eligible to apply are graduate students who have completed all PhD coursework within the last five years and who can provide evidence that they have been formally admitted to candidacy for the PhD. Consideration will be given only to applicants with outstanding academic records who are strongly recommended by faculty members and have demonstrated interest in and capability for policy-oriented research.
Amount $18,000 plus some travel expenses
Date(s) Application Is Due Apr 1.
Contact Director of Research and Programs, (202) 974-2400; fax: (202) 974-2410 ; email: rsvp@hudson.org
Internet http://www.hudson.org/learn/index.cfm?fuseaction=mission_statement
Sponsor Hudson Institute
1015 15th St NW, 6th Fl
Washington, DC 20005

Heublein Foundation Inc Grants **2274**
The foundation offers grant support in the areas of preschool through higher education, including a scholarship program for dependents of employees, health and social care, culture and art, problems of the inner cities, and education to combat alcohol abuse. A large percentage of grants within all categories is targeted at disadvantaged populations. Heublein also contributes directly to the alcoholism prevention programs of several

organizations and to research by noted universities. Application deadline for scholarships is December 1.
Restrictions Grants may not be made to individuals, religious groups, political organizations, or for endowments. The foundation principally supports programs in communities where the company has major facilities: greater Hartford, CT, area; Allen Park, MI; and Madera, Menlo Park, and Napa Valley, CA.
Date(s) Application Is Due Dec 1.
Contact Treasurer, (860) 231-5000
Sponsor Heublein Foundation Inc
P.O. Box 778
Farmington, CT 06142-0778

HHMI Gilliam Fellowships for Advanced Study **2275**
The Fellowships provide full support for up to five years of study toward a Ph.D. for outstanding students who are from groups underrepresented in the sciences or from disadvantaged backgrounds. Gilliam fellows attend the university of their choice and work alongside distinguished scientists. Chosen for their academic excellence and scientific potential, they will become the leaders of a new generation of biomedical researchers. The Fellowship is available up to 5 years at $44,000 per year.
Requirements Must be: past participants in the HHMI Exceptional Research Opportunities Program (EXROP); graduating seniors or recent baccalaureate recipients (within two years) who have completed no more than one year of Ph.D. training. Former EXROP students pursuing an M.D./Ph.D. degree may apply, but the fellowship supports only the Ph.D. portion of the studies. There is no citizenship requirement.
Amount $44,000
Date(s) Application Is Due Oct 18.
Contact Office of Grants and Special Programs; (800) 424-9924 or (301) 215-8873; fax: (301) 215-8888; email: gilliam@hhmi.org
Internet http://www.hhmi.org/grants/individuals/gilliam.html
Sponsor Howard Hughes Medical Institute
4000 Jones Bridge Road
Chevy Chase, MD 20815-6789

HHMI Grants and Fellowships Programs **2276**
The institute administers a grants program that focuses on improving science education from preschool through postdoctoral training, enhancing the science literacy of the general public, and supporting the research of biomedical scientists in selected foreign countries. Grants are administered through five programs: an international program that supports biomedical scientists outside the United States and provides funding for selected courses and workshops; a precollege science-education program that offers grants for educational activities to science museums, botanical and zoological gardens, etc.; a biomedical-research program that supports medical schools and research organizations; a graduate science-education program that provides fellowships for graduate students, medical students, and physicians, and supports special courses; and a biological-sciences education program that awards grants to selected undergraduate institutions.
Amount $50 million total annually
Contact Office of Grants and Special Programs, Department AD98, (301) 215-8889; fax: (301) 215-8888; email: grantswww@hhmi.org
Internet http://www.hhmi.org/grants
Sponsor Howard Hughes Medical Institute
4000 Jones Bridge Rd
Chevy Chase, MD 20815-6789

HHMI Initiative for Colleges Grants **2277**
HHMI awards four-year grants to colleges (baccalaureate and master's institutions) to support science education at the undergraduate, K-12, and community college levels. Grants support a range of activities that engage students in research and broaden their access to science; create courses that convey the excitement of contemporary science; develop new, current, and future faculty members; and establish or expand outreach programs that extend to elementary, high school, and community college faculty and students. The registration deadline is May 16, with final proposals due by October 17.
Requirements Only invited institutions are eligible to apply. Invitations are based on an institution's classification by the Carnegie Foundation for the Advancement of Teaching as a baccalaureate and master's institution and on the institution's record of postbaccalaureate student achievement in the sciences.
Amount $800,000-$1.6 million
Date(s) Application Is Due May 16; Oct 17.
Contact Grants Program Officer; (301) 215-8870 or (301) 215-8500; fax: (301) 215-8888; email: grantugr@hhmi.org
Internet http://www.hhmi.org/grants/institutions/colleges.html
Sponsor Howard Hughes Medical Institute
4000 Jones Bridge Road
Chevy Chase, MD 20815-6789

HHMI Initiative for Universities Grants **2278**
HHMI awards four-year grants to research and doctoral universities to support science education at the undergraduate and K-12 levels. The program supports initiatives that strengthen education in the biological sciences and other scientific disciplines as they relate to biology. Program objectives include: to strengthen research and teaching in undergraduate education and to support student involvement in faculty research; to prepare undergraduates for graduate studies and careers in biomedical research, medicine, and science education; to bring fresh perspectives to established scientific disciplines, and develop novel programs and courses in emerging areas; to foster linkages between universities and elementary and secondary schools; and to develop approaches that encourage teamwork among faculty, postdoctoral fellows, graduate students, and undergraduates. The registration deadline is May 12, with proposals due October 18.
Requirements Only invited institutions are eligible to apply. Invitations are based on an institution's classification by the Carnegie Foundation for the Advancement of Teaching as a baccalaureate and master's institution and on the institution's record of postbaccalaureate student achievement in the sciences.
Amount $1.2-$2.2 million
Date(s) Application Is Due May 12; Oct 18.
Contact Grants Program Officer; (301) 215-8870 or (301) 215-8500; fax: (301) 215-8888; email: 2006ugcomp@hhmi.org
Internet http://www.hhmi.org/grants/institutions/universities.html
Sponsor Howard Hughes Medical Institute
4000 Jones Bridge Road
Chevy Chase, MD 20815-6789

HHMI International Research Scholars Program **2279**
This five year grant program supports non-U.S. biomedical scientists, scientific meetings for grant-supported scientists, and other international educational activities. Grants are awarded to promising biomedical scientists who have made significant contributions to fundamental research. Application information is available online.
Requirements To be considered, individuals must hold a full-time academic or research appointment at a university, medical school, or other nonprofit scientific institution. They are not permitted to have major administrative responsibilities.
Contact Jill G. Conley, Ph.D., Program Director; (301) 215-8873; fax: (301) 215-8888
Internet http://www.hhmi.org/grants/for_grantees/
Sponsor Howard Hughes Medical Institute
4000 Jones Bridge Road
Chevy Chase, MD 20815/6789

HHMI K-12 Science Education Improvement Grants **2280**
HHMI awards four-year grants to biomedical research institutions to improve K-12 science education. The primary program objectives are to address national concerns about the level of general scientific knowledge and interest in both school-aged and adult populations, to provide teachers with research opportunities and access to new teaching tools, and to encourage students to pursue science careers. Projects should encourage interaction between scientists and students through a variety of channels, such as mentoring programs; stimulate students' interest in science through hands-on activities; and push students toward meeting state and local education standards that already are in place.
Requirements Eligible entities are medical schools, academic health centers, independent biomedical research institutions, and nonprofits with active biomedical research programs and personnel to help implement the education activities. Applicants will need schools' participation to demonstrate the fulfillment of their proposals.
Amount $200,000-$500,000 typically
Contact Patricia Soochan, Program Officer, (301) 215-8872; fax: (301) 215-8888; email: 2004ugcomp@hhmi.org
Internet http://www.hhmi.org/grants/institutions
Sponsor Howard Hughes Medical Institute
4000 Jones Bridge Rd
Chevy Chase, MD 20815-6789

HHMI Med into Grad Initiative Grants **2281**
HHMI will award grants to institutions to improve the understanding of medicine and pathobiology by scientists conducting biomedical research. Grants will be used to modify existing graduate training or initiate new programs to develop a cadre of Ph.D. researchers who understand pathophysiology and are committed to working at the interface of the basic sciences and clinical medicine. Applications will be accepted from any university in the United States that offers Ph.D.-level training in an appropriate science or engineering discipline. It is expected that as much as $10 million will be awarded in this competition. Awards will range from $400,000 to $1 million, and the grant funds will be allocated over four consecutive years. Registration for intent to apply is due by April 20, with the proposal submission deadline September 8.
Requirements US institutions that grant PhD degrees in the appropriate science and engineering disciplines are eligible to apply.
Amount $400,000-$1 million
Date(s) Application Is Due Apr 20; Sep 8.
Contact Maryrose Franko, Senior Program Officer; (800) 448-4882, ext. 8880; fax: (301) 215-8888; email: medintograd@hhmi.org
Internet http://www.hhmi.org/grants/institutions/medintograd.html
Sponsor Howard Hughes Medical Institute
4000 Jones Bridge Road
Chevy Chase, MD 20815-6789

HHMI Physician-Scientist Early Career Award **2282**
Through this competitive grant initiative, HHMI awards five-year grants to selected alumni of the HHMI-NIH Research Scholars Program and the HHMI Research Training

Fellowships for Medical Students Program to support these individuals as they begin careers as independent physician-scientists. The award provides $375,000 over a five-year period for direct research costs.
Requirements Only alumni of the HHMI-NIH Research Scholars Program and the HHMI Research Training Fellowship for Medical Students Program who have received an M.D., M.D./Ph.D., D.D.S, or equivalent degree are eligible to apply.
Restrictions The funds may not be used for the salary of the awardee or institutional indirect costs.
Amount $375,000 over a five-year period
Contact Office of Grants and Special Programs; (800) 448-4882, ext. 8889 or (800) 424-9924; fax: (301) 215-8888; email: earlycareer@hhmi.org
Internet http://www.hhmi.org/grants/individuals/earlycareer.html
Sponsor Howard Hughes Medical Institute
4000 Jones Bridge Road
Chevy Chase, MD 20815-6789

HHMI Precollege Outreach Initiative for Biomedical Research Institutions Grants 2283
HHMI will award five-year grants to support pre-K to 12th-grade science education. Funding will be provided to medical schools, dental schools, veterinary schools, public health schools, hospitals, academic health centers, and independent research institutions to enable these science-rich organizations to work with school systems, museums, and other partners skilled in delivering science content to students. Letters of Intent to submit a proposal are due by June 13, and proposal submissions are due by September 12.
Requirements HHMI does not make grants directly to individuals, school systems, or to pre-K to 12th-grade schools under this initiative.
Amount $200,000-$500,000
Date(s) Application Is Due Jun 13; Sep 12.
Contact Grants Program Officer; (301) 215-8870 or (301) 215-8500; fax: (301) 215-8888; email: grantprc@hhmi.org
Internet http://www.hhmi.org/grants/institutions/biomedical.html
Sponsor Howard Hughes Medical Institute
4000 Jones Bridge Road
Chevy Chase, MD 20815-6789

HHMI Research Training Fellowships 2284
Medical fellowships are intended to strengthen and expand the nation's pool of medically trained researchers. These fellowships provide funds to help meet fellows' research-related expenses and education costs during the research training period. Fellowships are awarded annually to provide support for one year of full-time training in fundamental biomedical, clinical, translational, or applied research. The fellowship includes a stipend, a research allowance to meet research-related expenses, and a fellow's allowance to be used on behalf of the fellow for health care, tuition and fees, and other research-related expenses. Application information is available online.
Requirements Fellowships are awarded to students enrolled in medical and dental programs in the U.S.
Contact Anh-CHI Le, Ph.D., Program Officer, (301) 215-8879 or (800) 448-4882 ext. 8879; fax: (301) 215-8888; email: grantmed@hhmi.org
Internet http://www.hhmi.org/grants/individuals/medfellows.html
Sponsor Howard Hughes Medical Institute
4000 Jones Bridge Road
Chevy Chase, MD 20815-6789

HHMI Undergraduate Science Education Grants for Professors 2285
The Program awards four-year grants to research-active undergraduate faculty. The grants are intended to empower leading scientists at doctoral and research universities to work more closely with undergraduates at their home institutions and provide other institutions with innovative models for transmitting the excitement and values of scientific research to undergraduate education.
Requirements Institutions must be invited by HHMI to nominate faculty members to compete for the HHMI professors awards. Invitations are based on the institutions' classifications by the Carnegie Foundation for the Advancement of Teaching as doctoral and research universities and the institutions' records of postbaccalaureate student achievement in the sciences. Invitees are listed in the program announcement.
Contact Office of Grants and Special Programs; (800) 424-9924 or (301) 215-8873; fax: (301) 215-8888; email: grantugr@hhmi.org
Internet http://www.hhmi.org/grants/individuals/professors.html
Sponsor Howard Hughes Medical Institute
4000 Jones Bridge Road
Chevy Chase, MD 20815-6789

HHMI-NIBB Interfaces Initiative Grants 2286
HHMI and the National Institute of Biomedical Imaging and Bioengineering have formed a partnership to support biomedical research institutions in developing graduate-level research training programs in emerging interdisciplinary fields. The primary goal of this initiative is to train a cadre of PhD scientists who possess the knowledge and skills to conduct interdisciplinary research at the interface between the biomedical sciences and the physical science, computational, engineering, or mathematical disciplines. These fields may include, but are not limited to, chemistry, imaging, science, materials science, nanotechnology, and physics. Another goal is to reduce barriers to interdisciplinary graduate science education. Proposals should reflect the unique educational and scientific capabilities and strengths of the applicant institution(s) as well as address the specific goals of the initiative. The initiative consists of two phases: Phase I supports the establishment of new interdisciplinary training programs; Phase II will sustain the training programs through their critical years. Registration letters of intent to apply are due by January 20, with the proposal submission deadline June 15.
Requirements All US institutions that grant PhD degrees in appropriate science or engineering disciplines are eligible to apply. Collaborative programs between two or more institutions are acceptable.
Amount $1 million maximum for three years
Date(s) Application Is Due Jan 20; Jun 15.
Contact Maryrose Franko, Senior Program Officer; (800) 448-4882, ext. 8880; fax: (301) 215-8888; email: interdisc@hhmi.org
Internet http://www.hhmi.org/grants/institutions/nibib.html
Sponsor Howard Hughes Medical Institute
4000 Jones Bridge Road
Chevy Chase, MD 20815-6789

HHMI-NIH Cloister Research Scholars Program 2287
The goal of this program, a joint venture of HHMI and NIH, is to expand the pool of medically trained researchers by encouraging medical students to pursue research careers. The program provides support for an intensive nine months to one year of full-time research, with a possible one-year extension, at NIH in Bethesda, MD. Most students enter after their second year of medical school. The Cloister, a residential facility for scholars, is available on the NIH campus. The research project is selected upon arrival at NIH, after a round of laboratory visits. Application forms may be downloaded from the Web site or requested from the program officer.
Requirements Applicant must be in good standing at a medical or dental school in the US or Puerto Rico and must receive permission from the school to participate in the program. The school does not have to be a major academic medical center or research-oriented school.
Restrictions Enrollees in an M.D./Ph.D. or D.D.S./Ph.D. program are not eligible.
Amount $17,800 annual salary
Date(s) Application Is Due Jan 10.
Contact Office of Grants and Special Programs; (800) 424-9924 or (301) 215-8873; fax: (301) 215-8888; email: research_scholars@hhmi.org
Internet http://www.hhmi.org/research/cloister/program.html
Sponsor Howard Hughes Medical Institute
4000 Jones Bridge Road
Chevy Chase, MD 20815-6789

HHMI/EMBO Start-up Grants for Central Europe 2288
The program encourages young scientists to obtain independent faculty positions in select countries that have ongoing HHMI and EMBO science programs. Applications are encouraged from scientists to set up their first independent laboratories in a Central European EMBC member state (Croatia, Czech Republic, Estonia, Hungary, Poland, and Slovenia). Application forms should be completed by the individual scientist and the receiving institute. It is expected that the institute make the applicant an offer that goes beyond that of a position and laboratory space. HHMI will contribute $50,000, while the participating member state must provide the remaining $25,000. Application and guidelines are available online.
Requirements Eligible scientists should have an excellent publication record; have a maximum of 10 years postdoctoral experience; be negotiating a position at an institute/university in Central Europe by the date of the application; and be located outside Central Europe at the time of application.
Amount $75,000 per year for three years
Date(s) Application Is Due Aug 1.
Contact Grants Administrator, (301) 215-8500
Internet http://www.embo.org/projects/yip/embo_hhmi_startup_grants.html
Sponsor Howard Hughes Medical Institute
4000 Jones Bridge Rd
Chevy Chase, MD 20815-6789

HHS Children's Hospitals Graduate Medical Education Payment Program 2289
The program provides funds to freestanding children's hospitals to support the training of pediatric and other residents in graduate medical education (GME) programs. This program compensates for the disparity in the level of federal funding for teaching hospitals for pediatrics versus other types of hospitals.
Requirements To be eligible, a children's hospital must meet all of the following criteria: participates in an approved graduate medical education (GME) program; has a Medicare provider agreement; is excluded from the Medicare inpatient prospective payment system (PPS) under section 1886(d)(1)(B)(iii) of the Social Security Act, and its accompanying regulations; and ss a freestanding hospital.
Amount $40 million total
Date(s) Application Is Due May 1; Aug 1.
Contact Kara Castellow, (301) 443-1058; email: kcastellow@hrsa.gov
Internet http://bhpr.hrsa.gov/childrenshospitalgme/default.htm
Sponsor Department of Health and Human Services
5600 Fishers Ln, Parklawn Bldg, Rm 9A-05
Rockville, MD 20857

HIAS Scholarship Awards 2290
The annual competition offers scholarships to deserving students in the United States and Israel. The awarding of scholarships is based on academic excellence, financial need, and involvement within the Jewish community. Guidelines and application are available online.
Amount $1500 average award
Date(s) Application Is Due Mar 15; Jun 30.
Contact Scholarship Committee, (212) 613-1358; email: scholarship@hias.org
Internet http://www.hias.org/Scholarships/apply.html
Sponsor HIAS Scholarship Program
333 Seventh Ave, 16th Fl
New York, NY 10001-5004

Higher Education Graduate Scholarships, Fellowships, and Grants 2291
The program in higher education at New York University offers graduate assistantships and fellowships to graduate students. Degree programs in higher education include the MA, EdD (community college leadership focus), and PhD. Information and applications are available on the Web site.
Requirements These opportunities are open specifically to students enrolled in the master's and doctoral degree programs in higher education at New York University.
Amount $1000-$15,000
Contact Office of Graduate Admissions, School of Education, (212) 998-5030; email: ed.gradadmissions@nyu.edu
Internet http://www.nyu.edu/financial.aid
Sponsor New York University
82 Washington Sq E, 2nd Fl
New York, NY 10003-6680

Hilda and Preston Davis Foundation Grants 2292
The Foundation provides funds to charitable organizations whose programs advance the development of all areas of the lives of children and young adults. The Foundation places special emphasis on, and channels most of its financial resources toward, those organizations whose attention is concentrated on eating disorders and education for the underprivileged. Applicants are encouraged to use the on-line grant application form.
Requirements 501(c)3 tax-exempt organizations are eligible.
Restrictions The foundation generally will not provide grants to: non-501(c)3 tax-exempt organizations; individuals; general fundraising drives; endowments; government agencies; or organizations that subsist mainly on third-party funding and have demonstrated no ability or expended little effort to attract private funding.
Amount $10,000-$100,000
Contact Grants Administrator, (203) 629-8552; fax: (203) 547-6112; email: info@fsllc.net
Internet http://www.hpdavis.org/application.htm
Sponsor Hilda and Preston Davis Foundation
640 West Putnam Avenue, 3rd Floor
Greenwich, CT 06830

Hill Crest Foundation Grants 2293
The foundation awards grants to Alabama nonprofits in its areas of interest, including health, the elderly, arts and culture, community development, higher education, and youth. Types of support include general operating support, capital campaigns, building construction/renovation, equipment acquisition, endowment funds, program development, professorships, publication, seed money, scholarship funds, research, technical assistance, and matching funds. There are no application forms or deadlines.
Requirements Alabama nonprofit organizations may apply.
Amount $5000-$50,000 average
Contact Charles Terry, Senior Chair, (205) 425-5800
Sponsor Hill Crest Foundation
P.O. Box 530507
Mountain Brook, AL 35253

Hirtzel Memorial Foundation Grants 2294
The foundation awards grants to eligible organizations in New York and Pennsylvania in its areas of interest, including medical research and health care; community and neighborhood improvement; higher education; and social and human services. Types of support include building construction and renovation, capital campaigns, scholarships, equipment acquisition, general operating support, research, and scholarships. There are no application deadlines; contact the office for appropriate forms.
Requirements New York nonprofit organizations in Ripley, Chautauqua County, and Pennsylvania nonprofit organizations in North East, Erie County, are eligible.
Amount $750-$250,000 range
Contact Laurie Moritz, Grants Administrator, c/o Mellon Financial Corporation, (412) 234-0023
Sponsor Orris C. Hirtzel and Beatrice Dewey Hirtzel Memorial Foundation
P.O. Box 185
Pittsburgh, PA 15230

Hispanic Scholarships 2295
Scholarships are intended for undergraduate and graduate students of Hispanic American background. Successful candidates are chosen on the basis of academic achievement, personal strengths, leadership, and financial need. For more information and application requirements, write to the selection committee at the Hispanic Scholarship Fund. Applications can be downloaded from Web site.
Requirements Applicants must be US citizens or legal permanent residents who come from Mexican American, Puerto Rican, Cuban, Caribbean, Central American, or South American parentage and who attend college in one of the 50 states or Puerto Rico on a full-time basis, must have completed a minimum of 12 units of college work prior to submission of an application, and must have a GPA of 2.7 on a 4.0 scale. Community college applicants must be enrolled in majors transferable to a four-year institution offering a baccalaureate degree.
Restrictions HSF is unable to make awards to fully employed persons or practicing professionals.
Amount $2000-$10,000
Contact Sara Martinez Tucker, President, (877) 473-4636 or (415) 445-9930; fax: (415) 808-2302; email: info@hsf.net
Internet http://www.hsf.net/scholarship/Special.htm#nhfa
Sponsor Hispanic Scholarship Fund
55 Second St., Ste 1500
San Francisco, CA 94105

Historical Analysis Senior and Postdoctoral Research Fellowships 2296
The center provides a setting to discuss issues of broad contemporary relevance in historical perspective. Organizing its annual activities around major themes of inquiry or research projects, the center each year welcomes two to three visiting senior and two postdoctoral fellows chosen through an open, international competition, along with a dozen faculty and graduate fellows from within Rutgers University. Senior fellowship applicants are urged to combine the fellowship with their home university's leave programs or other external grants to be in residence at the center for the full academic year. Formal teaching responsibilities are not expected, but past fellows have welcomed opportunities to work with students on projects of mutual interest. Postdoctoral fellows receive 10-month stipend and benefits. They teach one undergraduate seminar each semester. Both senior and postdoctoral fellows are provided with a modest research fund. The center also awards about a dozen fellowships to Rutgers faculty and graduate students from various disciplines who receive modest research grants and office space if available.
Requirements Applications are welcome from all disciplines and regional specializations. Senior fellows are defined as persons of any academic rank, including independent scholars. Postdoctoral fellows must hold PhDs no more than four years old.
Amount $27,500 senior fellowships; $35,000 teaching salary postdoctoral fellowships
Date(s) Application Is Due Dec 15.
Contact Program Administrator, (732) 932-8701; fax: (732) 932-8708; email: rcha@rci.rutgers.edu
Internet http://rcha.rutgers.edu/fellowshipinfo.php
Sponsor Rutgers Center for Historical Analysis
88 College Ave
New Brunswick, NJ 08901

Historical Studies Research Fellowships 2297
Research fellowships are offered for one or two semesters, from September to January and from February to June, to enable scholars in historical studies to pursue postdoctoral research projects at the center and to contribute actively to the seminar on Friday mornings during the term. Proposals that deal with the material, ethical, and symbolic dimensions of the role of animals in human culture are welcomed. Fellows are expected to live in Princeton to take an active part in intellectual interchange with other members of the seminar. Funds are limited; candidates are strongly urged to apply to other grant-giving institutions as well as the center, if they wish to remain in residence for a full year. Travel funds for fellow, spouse, and children are provided.
Requirements Fellowships are designed for highly recommended younger scholars, as well as senior scholars with established reputations, either from the United States or abroad; candidates must have finished dissertations and have full-time paid positions to which they can return.
Amount $72,000 maximum per academic year or $36,000 per semester plus maximum of $900 per semester research expenses
Date(s) Application Is Due Dec 1.
Contact Gyan Prakash, Director, (609) 258-4997; fax: (609) 258-5326
Internet http://dav.princeton.edu
Sponsor Shelby Cullom Davis Center for Historical Studies
Princeton University, 129 Dickinson Hall
Princeton, NJ 08544

History of Art Graduate Fellowships at the University of Michigan 2298
The Department of the History of Art and the Museum of Art at the University of Michigan offer a variety of financial aid to students who have completed the first year of graduate work. The sources of aid include departmental, graduate school, and museum funds, and grants in aid from external agencies. For first-year students, Regents fellowships provide support for three years, and CIC and University Merit fellowships provide support for four years for those students who intend to continue through the doctorate. Other graduate fellowships and financial assistance include Rackham Graduate School fellowships; Charles L. Freer and Area Center fellowships in non-Western Art (China, South and Southeast Asia, Near East, Japan); Rackham Nontraditional fellowships;

teaching, research, and grading assistantships; as well as assistance with photographic and library collections. Some travel stipends are available for seminar and individual research projects, including a fund for students of medieval art. Applications can be obtained from the departmental graduate secretary. In the case of both new applications and renewal applications, the student must see that letters of recommendation are sent directly to the chairperson of the department. Applicants are urged to be thorough and candid in their appraisal of their resources and needs.
Requirements Those who qualify for national and international grants must exhaust this possibility before applying for departmental funds.
Amount $1000-$1500 monthly
Date(s) Application Is Due Jan 1.
Contact Student Services Assistant, Art History Department, (734) 764-5400; fax: (313) 647-4121; email: histartadmiss@umich.edu
Internet http://www.lsa.umich.edu/histart/graduate/financial
Sponsor University of Michigan
519 S State St
Ann Arbor, MI 48109-1357

History of Pharmacy Thesis Research Grants in Aid **2299**
Grants in aid are awarded yearly for thesis research (master's or PhD). Thesis projects should be devoted to history of pharmacy, history of drugs, or other humanistic study with a strong historical pharmacy component. The grants cover direct thesis expenses.
Requirements Graduate students in US colleges and universities are eligible to apply.
Amount $5000 maximum
Date(s) Application Is Due Feb 1.
Contact Dr. Gregory Higby, Director, (608) 262-5378
Internet http://www.pharmacy.wisc.edu/aihp/grant.htm
Sponsor American Institute of the History of Pharmacy
777 Highland Ave
Madison, WI 53705-2222

HKU Foundation Postgraduate Studentships **2300**
The purpose of the studentships is to provide selected students with financial assistance in the form of a scholarship to study full-time for the degrees of MPhil or PhD during the prescribed periods of study. A postgraduate studentship holder may be required to undertake, under supervision, duties such as assistance with research; assistance with scheduled laboratory, studio, and fieldwork classes and with tutorials; assistance with the preparation of materials for scheduled classes; assistance with marking practical notebooks and answers from exercise classes; and assistance with invigilation of university degree examinations. Guidelines are available online.
Amount HK$13,000-HK$15,100 per month
Date(s) Application Is Due Jan 31.
Contact Graduate School, (852) 2857-3470; fax: (852) 2857-3543; email: gradsch@hkucc.hku.hk
Internet http://www.hku.hk/rss/index4.htm
Sponsor University of Hong Kong
Graduate House, Rm P403
Pokfulam Rd, Hong Kong
Hong Kong

Hoffmann-La Roche Foundation Grants **2301**
The corporate contributions program supports nonprofits in company operating areas. Funds may be requested in two categories: health programs that focus on health promotion and health education and educational projects that encourage math and science literacy and promote secondary school teacher enrichment. Seed grants are awarded for new activities for which Hoffman-La Roche may spark other funders to pitch-in operating support.
Requirements Nonprofits in company-operating communities are eligible to apply, with some preference given to groups near the New Jersey headquarters.
Restrictions Funds will not be awarded in support of endowments; scholarships; facility expansion or construction; purchase of equipment; capital expenditures; good will advertising; and political, veterans, or labor organizations. Telephone, facsimile, and email requests will not be honored.
Amount $2500-$50,000
Contact Vivian Beetle, Administrative Director, (973) 562-2055; fax: (973) 562-2999
Internet http://www.rocheusa.com/about/responsibility.html
Sponsor Hoffmann-La Roche Foundation
340 Kingsland St
Nutley, NJ 07110-1199

Holley Medal **2302**
The medal is bestowed on an individual who by some great and unique act(s) of an engineering nature has accomplished a great and timely public benefit. In judging the merits of any candidate for this award, no limitations shall arise out of the nominee's formal degree of education, membership in any society or organizations, or the circumstances of employment or official position. Attention shall be concentrated on the brilliance of the art--not the individual. The achievement should be of such public importance as to be worthy of the gratitude of the nation and to call forth admiration of engineers. More than one individual may be recognized for a single achievement provided that each individual made equal or comparable contribution.
Requirements Any individual member, group of members, or committee may nominate candidates for this award.
Amount $1000
Date(s) Application Is Due Mar 1.
Contact Gilda DiTullio, Manager, (212) 591-7736; fax: (212) 705-7739; email: ditullio@asme.org
Internet http://www.asme.org/honors/ms71/gaa/holley.html
Sponsor American Society of Mechanical Engineers
3 Park Ave
New York, NY 10016

Home Depot Foundation Grants **2303**
The foundation's funding initiatives include affordable housing--organizations that work to create and rehabilitate affordable housing, such as Habitat for Humanity affiliates, Rebuilding Together affiliates, community development corporations, and neighborhood housing initiatives; and environment--organizations that direct efforts toward protecting the environment, with a focus on forestry, sustainability and green design, cleanup and recycling, and lead poisoning prevention, such as The Nature Conservancy, Institute for Sustainable Development, Keep America Beautiful, and World Wildlife Fund. The foundation gives first priority to organizations that have been invited to apply for a grant. Unsolicited requests that match foundation eligibility requirements also receive consideration.
Requirements 501(c)3 tax-exempt public charities in the United States and charitable organizations in Canada are eligible. The foundation only funds programs that meet its eligibility test, which is available online.
Restrictions The foundation does not support organizations that are not 501(c)3 or Revenue Canada designated charities; scholarships or other direct support to individuals; religious, fraternal, political, labor, athletic, or social groups; capital campaigns, endowments, or endowed chairs; institutional overhead/indirect costs; capital investments; equipment purchases not part of a larger program request; projects for political or religious purposes; special events, such as conferences, sports competitions, or art exhibits; courtesy or journal advertising campaigns; film, music, television, video, or media production projects or broadcast underwriting; activities of organizations serving primarily their own membership; or United Way chapters (the company provides support to United Way).
Amount $10,000-$50,000
Date(s) Application Is Due Jan 15; Apr 15; Jul 15; Oct 15.
Contact Community Affairs, (866) 593-7019 or (770) 384-3889; fax: (866) 593-7027; email: hd_foundation@homedepot.com
Internet http://www.homedepotfoundation.org
Sponsor Home Depot Foundation
2455 Paces Ferry Rd
Atlanta, GA 30339-4024

HomeBanc Foundation Grants **2304**
The Foundation has three main goals: provide support to cancer related causes through funding education, advocacy, and research; support the American dream of homeownership for those who might not reach it on their own; and provide college funding to students who strive to achieve their goals through education beyond high school. Scholarship forms are available online. Contact the Foundation to obtain application information for grants.
Requirements Nonprofit organizations providing services in Georgia and Florida are eligible.
Contact Amanda Albertelli, (404) 459-7618; email: AAlbertelli@HomeBanc.com
Internet http://www.homebancfoundation.org/grant_information.aspx
Sponsor HomeBanc Foundation
2002 Summit Boulevard, Suite 100
Atlanta, GA 30319-1497

Horace Mann ALPLM Fellowships **2305**
Horace Mann and the Abraham Lincoln Presidential Library and Museum (ALPLM) offer 50 teachers a fellowship to study the life and legacy of the country's 16th president. Winning fellows will attend a five-day institute in June and July, at the presidential library and museum in Springfield, IL. Teachers submit their resumes and answer two essay questions (250 word max). Within the first essay, teachers briefly describe the subject area(s) and grade level(s) they teach, and how they anticipate this experience will benefit them and their students. In the second essay, teachers show why it is essential to understand Abraham Lincoln today. Teachers must submit their application online. Guidelines are available online.
Requirements The fellowship is open to any full-time teacher, teaching kindergarten through 12th grade, in the United States.
Restrictions
Amount $1000
Date(s) Application Is Due Mar 4.
Contact Fellowships Administrator, (800) 999-1030
Internet http://www.horacemann.com/educator-resources/abraham-lincoln-fellowship.html
Sponsor Horace Mann Insurance Company
1 Horace Mann Plaza
Springfield, IL 62715-0001

Horowitz Foundation for Social Policy Grants 2306

The foundation supports and advances research and understanding in the major fields of the social sciences, specifically in the fields of psychology, anthropology, sociology, economics, urban affairs, area studies, political science, and other disciplines. Grants provide direct assistance to individual scholars worldwide who require small grants to further their research with emphasis on policy-oriented studies. Preference will be given to projects that deal with contemporary issues in the social sciences or issues of policy relevance, as well as to scholars in the initial stages of work. Five to 10 grants are awarded each year. Guidelines and application are available online.
Amount $3000-$5000 range
Date(s) Application Is Due Dec 31.
Contact Mary Curtis, Vice Chairman and Secretary; email: applications@horowitz-foundation.org
Internet http://www.horowitz-foundation.org
Sponsor Horowitz Foundation for Social Policy
P.O. Box 7
Rocky Hill, NJ 08553-0007

Horton Research Grants 2307

One or more grants are awarded annually in support of a research project in hydrology and water resources, with the objective of fostering graduate student research leading to the completion of doctoral dissertations. Appropriate topics may be in hydrology including its physical, chemical, or biological aspects, or in water resources policy sciences including economic systems analysis, sociology, and law. A proposal must be signed by the student and by the faculty supervisor; a formal application form must accompany the proposal.
Requirements Applicant must be a PhD candidate.
Amount $10,000 plus travel allowance to attend the awards luncheon
Date(s) Application Is Due Apr 15.
Contact Horton Research Grants, (800) 966-2481 or (202) 462-6900; email: service@agu.org
Internet http://www.agu.org/inside/honors.html#SH
Sponsor American Geophysical Union
2000 Florida Ave NW
Washington, DC 20009

Hospital for Sick Children Foundation External Grants 2308

Grants are awarded for research in child health (up to age 18). Application forms should be obtained from the foundation. Listed application deadlines are for receipt of letters of intent. Annual deadline dates may vary; contact program staff for exact dates.
Requirements Individuals affiliated with Canadian registered charities (including hospitals and universities) are eligible to apply.
Restrictions The foundation does not support projects related to support of children outside Canada; established, ongoing research projects; computer hardware; building construction; operating expenses; or general endowments.
Amount $C65,000 maximum per year for two years
Date(s) Application Is Due Mar 1; Sep 1.
Contact Grants Officer, (416) 813-6166 ext 2354; fax: (416) 813-5024; email: national.grants@sickkids.ca
Internet www.sickkids.ca/foundation/grants.asp
Sponsor Hospital for Sick Children Foundation
555 University Ave
Toronto, ON M5G 1X8 Canada

Houghton Library Visiting Fellowships 2309

Short-term fellowships are available to scholars pursuing research in literature, history, philosophy, religion, history of science, theater, dance, and printing and graphic arts. Fellows also have access to collections in Widener as well as throughout the world's largest university library.
Amount $2750 stipend
Date(s) Application Is Due Jan 13.
Contact Dennis Marnon, Administrative Officer, (617) 495-2441; email: dmarnon@fas.harvard.edu
Internet http://hcl.harvard.edu/libraries/houghton/public_programs.html#fellowships
Sponsor Harvard University
Houghton Library
Cambridge, MA 02138

Household International Corporate Giving Program Grants 2310

Grants made in support of Household's corporate social responsibility fall into three main focus areas: education, housing, and community enrichment. Special attention is given to requests from nonprofits that address issues related to financial and credit education, economic development, housing, youth development, and education, particularly for low-income and minority populations. Types of support include annual campaigns, capital campaigns, challenge/matching grants, employee-related scholarships, scholarship funds, equipment, fellowships, general operating support, continuing support, research grants, and technical assistance. Grants are made at three levels: companywide grants, local-facility grants, and the Help for Communities program administered through local branch offices. Each level has its own deadline. Obtain guidelines, which contain a list of contacts for the company's US and foreign subsidiaries.
Requirements Nonprofit organizations in corporate operating areas are eligible.
Restrictions The corporation generally does not support the following: nonprofit organizations that do not have 501(c)3 tax deductible status; fraternal, veteran, labor, athletic, or religious organizations serving a limited constituency; for-profit student aid or scholarship programs, aside from those already established by Household or its business groups; political, lobbying, or voter registration programs, or those supporting the candidacy of a particular individual; funds to support travel for groups or individuals; organizations that might in any way pose a conflict with corporate values, products, customers, or employees; unsolicited requests from secondary, elementary, and post-secondary schools; single disease research initiatives outside of corporate sponsored programs; unsolicited proposals from colleges and universities; advertising; or individuals.
Amount $8 million total
Date(s) Application Is Due Dec 15.
Contact Contributions Administrator, (847) 564-6010; fax: (847) 564-7094; email: communityrelations@household.com
Internet http://www.hsbcusa.com/corporateresponsibility/contributions_grants
Sponsor Household International Corporate Giving Program
2700 Sanders Rd
Prospect Heights, IL 60070

Houston Young Lawyers Foundation Grants 2311

Grants are awarded to support, promote, and encourage charitable organizations and activities in Harris County, TX, including activities for the furtherance of justice and legal education through the sponsorship and encouragement of legal research, publications, and institutes and forums; the institution and maintenance of legal-aid facilities for the indigent or working poor and the acceptance of aid grants from the governmental and private sources; the support of youths through athletic and educational forums; and any other activity that will promote and aid an improved system for the administration of justice and the improvement of the Bench and Bar in Harris County, TX, and elsewhere. Priority is given to organizations and programs serving the people of the Houston metropolitan area.
Requirements Charitable organizations and projects that primarily benefit the greater Houston metropolitan community are eligible.
Amount $500-$2500
Date(s) Application Is Due Jan 7.
Contact Vivica Simmons, Grants Administrator, (713) 546-5637; email: vsimmons@shb.com
Internet http://www.hyla.org/hyla/Grant_Guidelines_EN.asp?SnID=381093844
Sponsor Houston Young Lawyers Foundation
P.O. Box 61208
Houston, TX 77208-1208

Howard Francis Cline Memorial Prize 2312

The prize is awarded biennially to the book or article in English, German, or a Romance language judged to make the most significant contribution to the history of Indians in Latin America, referring to any time before the immediate present. Items appearing in the two calendar years just preceding may be considered for a given year's award.
Amount $500
Contact CLAH, (530) 752-3046; fax: (530) 752-8964; email: clah@ucdavis.edu
Internet http://www.h-net.org/~clah/about/index.html
Sponsor Conference on Latin American History
University of California at Davis, One Shields Ave
Davis, CA 95616

Howard Gilman Foundation Grants 2313

The foundation is dedicated to the preservation of natural and cultural resources, with a focus on environmental, especially animal, conservation; the preservation and advancement of artistic and cultural endeavors; and medical research, especially in the fields of HIV/AIDS, cardiology, and sports medicine. The arts and culture component of the program is focused primarily in the New York metropolitan area. Types of support include general operating grants, program grants, research grants, and seed money grants. Staff prefer to respond to a brief letter of inquiry outlining the project's aim and general budgetary requirements before asking potential grantees to prepare full proposals.
Requirements 501(c)3 nonprofit organizations are eligible.
Restrictions Religious and political agencies are ineligible.
Amount $1000-$100,000 average
Contact Harry Brown, Program Associate, (212) 307-1073; fax: (212) 262-4108; email: hbrown@gilman.com
Sponsor Howard Gilman Foundation
111 W 50th St, 40th Fl
New York, NY 10020

Howe Foundation Grants 2314

The foundation supports youth organizations, social services, medical research, hospitals, religion, child welfare, drug abuse, education, and family services. Types of support include continuing support, general operating funds, and research. Requests from qualified organizations must be received prior to the second Tuesday of March for the grant year. There is only one consideration meeting a year.

Requirements Only nonprofit organizations to the Pasadena area of the San Gabriel Valley of California are eligible. A brief letter and a copy of the organizations 501(c)3 form are the requirements for application.
Restrictions No restricted grants will be funded by the foundation.
Amount $1000 minimum
Contact Mitchell Howe, President, (626) 792-0514; email: mbromouse@earthlink.net
Sponsor Howe Foundation
180 South Lake Avenue
Pasadena, CA 91101-2619

HRB Clinical Research Training Fellowships 2315
These fellowships are designed to enable medical and dental graduates at any stage in their career to gain specialized clinical research training in a biomedical field in Ireland. Awards are available for up to two years. Fellowships are tenable only in institutions approved of by the board, such as teaching hospitals, universities and research institutes in Ireland. Applications are available on the Web site.
Requirements Applicants should be graduates in medicine or dentistry from post-registration up to and including senior registrar or equivalent academic level. Applicants should be EU citizens or be graduates from outside the EU with permanent Irish resident status.
Amount IR@L46,909-IR@L56,066
Date(s) Application Is Due Sep 16.
Contact Patricia Cranley, Research Grants Officer, (353) 1 6761176 ext 120; fax: (353) 1 6611856; email: pcranley@hrb.ie
Internet http://www.hrb.ie/display_content.php?page_id=95
Sponsor Health Research Board
73 Lower Baggot St
Dublin 2
Ireland

HRB Health Services Research Fellowships 2316
Fellowships provide an opportunity to graduates with appropriate experience to undertake health services research in Ireland. Research may be interdisciplinary in nature and may involve clinical, epidemiological, public health, statistics, health economics, social science, operational, and management disciplines. Awards are available for up to three years. Application forms are available on the Web site.
Requirements To be eligible, candidates must hold a primary degree in a discipline relevant to health services research; have acquired appropriate postgraduate experience in the field of health services research; have support from an approved academic department or center; have obtained the prior approval of a head of department for the research study being proposed; be European Union citizens or be graduates from outside the European Union with permanent Irish resident status.
Amount IR@L41,902; IR@L43,319; IR@L44,727
Date(s) Application Is Due Oct 14.
Contact Patricia Cranley, Research Grants Officer, (353) 1 6761176 ext 120; fax: (353) 1 6611856; email: pcranley@hrb.ie
Internet http://www.hrb.ie/display_content.php?page_id=96
Sponsor Health Research Board
73 Lower Baggot St
Dublin 2
Ireland

HRB Postdoctoral Research Fellowships 2317
Fellowships enable researchers with a PhD, MD, or equivalent research experience to develop research careers at an advanced level in medicine, dentistry, health-related biological sciences, or epidemiology in Ireland. Awards are available for up to three years. Applications are available on the Web site.
Requirements Applicants must have a PhD or MD in a related biomedical science field or have submitted a thesis for such at the time of application, or have equivalent research experience. Applicants should not have more than five years postdoctoral experience at the time of application and be European Union citizens or be graduates from outside the European Union with permanent Irish resident status. Applications should be made by the prospective fellow with the support of the head of an appropriate sponsoring laboratory in the Republic of Ireland.
Amount IR@L41,902; IR@L43,319; IR@L44,727
Date(s) Application Is Due Oct 7.
Contact Patricia Cranley, Research Grants Officer, (353) 1 6761176 ext 120; fax: (01) 6611856; email: pcranley@hrb.ie
Internet http://www.hrb.ie/display_content.php?page_id=97
Sponsor Health Research Board
73 Lower Baggot St
Dublin 2
Ireland

HRDC Employability and Social Partnerships Grants 2318
The program supports initiatives that develop and promote nationally significant research and identify and develop models of best practices or of new service delivery initiatives designed to meet the social development and employability needs of populations who are or may be at risk. Eligible activities include applied research--identification of new and critical social/employment issues that affect the participation of targeted groups and individuals in the community and in the labor market, and the quality of child care; development--testing and evaluation of models or best practices that will enhance the quality of child care and the social development and employability of populations who are most at risk; capacity building--support national nongovernmental organizations whose mandates reflect those of HRDC in serving their target populations and enhancing civic participation through partnerships among nongovernmental organizations and the public and private sectors; and data development and dissemination--of information on social development, employability of populations most at risk, and child care.
Amount $C12.5 million total budget
Contact Employability and Social Partnerships, (819) 997-1452; fax: (819) 997-1359; email: epb-dgpe@hrdc-drhc.gc.ca
Internet http://www.hrsdc.gc.ca/en/gateways/nav/top_nav/program/gc.shtml
Sponsor Human Resources Development Canada
140 Promenade du Portage, Phase IV
Hull, PQ K1A OJ9 Canada

HRSA Basic Nurse Education and Practice Grants 2319
This program is intended to help schools of nursing and other institutions improve the quality and availability of nursing education through projects for specified purposes such as expanding enrollment in professional nursing programs, improving access to primary health care in noninstitutional settings, providing continuing education for nurses in medically underserved communities, and providing long-term care fellowships for certain paraprofessionals. Grant funds may be used for salaries of personnel specifically employed for the project, consultant fees, supplies and equipment necessary to conduct the project, and essential travel expenses and other expenses related to the project. Indirect administrative costs incurred as a result of the project are allowed but limited to 8 percent of direct costs. Applications are reviewed two times a year by the Advisory Council on Nurses Education. Assistance is available up to five years. Contact the office or visit the Web site for deadline dates.
Requirements Public and nonprofit private schools of nursing and other public or nonprofit private entities may apply.
Amount $250,000 average
Contact Grants Administrator, Division of Nursing, Bureau of Health Professions, (301) 443-5688; fax: (301) 443-8586
Internet http://bhpr.hrsa.gov/nursing
Sponsor Health Resources and Services Administration
5600 Fishers Lane, Rm 9-35
Rockville, MD 20857

HRSA Eliminating Disparities in Perinatal Health Grants 2320
The purpose of this program is to enhance a community's capacity to address significant disparities in several perinatal health indicators, with an emphasis on infant mortality rates.
Requirements Public and private nonprofit community-based organizations are eligible to apply.
Restrictions Entities that are currently receiving a Healthy Start implementation grant are not eligible to apply.
Amount $100,000-$2.3 million; $782,971 average
Contact Director, Division of Perinatal Systems and Women's Health, (301) 443-0543
Internet http://www.hrsa.gov
Sponsor Health Resources and Services Administration
5600 Fishers Ln, Parklawn Bldg
Rockville, MD 20857

HRSA Geriatric Education Centers 2321
The purpose of this program is to develop geriatric education centers to support development of collaborative arrangements involving several health professions schools and healthcare facilities. Geriatric centers facilitate the training of health professional faculty, students, and practitioners in the diagnosis, treatment, and prevention of disease, disability, and other health problems of the aged. Projects must improve training of health professionals; develop and disseminate curricula relating to treatment; support training and retraining of faculty and continuing education of health professionals who provide geriatric care; and provide students with clinical training in geriatrics in nursing homes, hospitals, ambulatory care centers, and senior centers. HRSA-05-077
Requirements Accredited health professions schools, physicians assistants training programs, allied health schools, and nursing schools are eligible to apply.
Amount $200,000 average
Date(s) Application Is Due Mar 1.
Contact Donna Nash, Grants Managment Specialist, (301) 443-6960; fax: (301) 443-6343; email: dnash@hrsa.gov
Internet http://www.hrsa.gov/grants/preview/guidanceprofessions/hrsa05077.htm
Sponsor Health Resources and Services Administration
5600 Fishers Ln, Rm 11A-05
Rockville, MD 20857

HRSA Health Professions Scholarships for Disadvantaged Students 2322
The program makes funds available for grants to schools of medicine; osteopathic medicine; dentistry; optometry; pharmacy; podiatric medicine; veterinary medicine; nursing (associate, diploma, baccalaureate, and graduate degree); public health; chiropractic; allied health (baccalaureate or graduate degree programs of dental hygiene,

medical laboratory technology, occupational therapy, physical therapy, radiologic technology, speech pathology, audiology, and registered dietitians); graduate programs in behavioral and mental health practice (includes clinical psychology, clinical social work, professional counseling, or marriage and family therapy); and programs providing training of physician assistants for the purpose of assisting such schools in providing scholarships to individuals from disadvantaged backgrounds who are enrolled (or accepted for enrollment) as full-time students in the schools. Notice of awards is issued to the schools, which, in turn, select and issue the awards to the eligible students. Consultation and technical assistance is provided to institutions wishing to apply. Annual deadline dates may vary; contact the office to confirm exact dates.
Requirements Accredited public or private nonprofit schools of medicine, nursing, osteopathic medicine, dentistry, pharmacy, podiatric medicine, optometry, veterinary medicine, public or allied health, or schools offering graduate programs in clinical psychology are eligible.
Amount $727-$650,000; $102,468 average
Contact Andrea Stampone, Bureau of Health Professions, (301) 443-4776
Internet http://bhpr.hrsa.gov/dsa/sds.htm
Sponsor Health Resources and Services Administration
5600 Fishers Ln, Parklawn Bldg
Rockville, MD 20857

HRSA Nurse Anesthetist Traineeships Program **2323**
Grants are awarded to eligible institutions to provide financial support through traineeships for licensed registered nurses enrolled as full-time students beyond the twelfth month of study in a master's nurse anesthesia program. HRSA-05-062
Requirements Eligible applicants are schools of nursing, academic health centers, and other public or private nonprofit entities which provide registered nurses with full-time anesthetist master's education and have evidence of earned accreditation status from the American Association of Nurse Anesthetists (AANA) Council on Accreditation of Nurse Anesthesia Education Programs.
Amount $7100 average
Date(s) Application Is Due Nov 18.
Contact Karen Breeden, Division of Nursing, Bureau of Health Professions, (301) 443-6333; fax: (301) 443-8586; email: kbreeden@hrsa.gov
Internet http://www.hrsa.gov/grants/preview/professions.htm#hrsa05062
Sponsor Health Resources and Services Administration
5600 Fishers Ln, Parklawn Bldg
Rockville, MD 20857

HRSA Nursing Education Opportunities for the Disadvantaged Project Grants **2324**
This program is intended to provide financial assistance to eligible schools of nursing and other applicants to meet the costs of special projects to increase nursing education opportunities for individuals from disadvantaged backgrounds. Funds may be used for salaries of personnel specifically employed for the project; consultant fees; supplies and equipment necessary to conduct the project; essential travel expenses; and other expenses related to the project. Indirect administrative costs are allowed, limited to 8 percent of direct costs. Grants may be made for up to three-year project periods and may be renewed competitively for an additional two years.
Requirements Public and nonprofit private schools of nursing and other public or nonprofit private entities are eligible.
Amount $58,800-$518,600; $255,100 average
Contact Dr. Janice Young, Division of Nursing, Bureau of Health Professions, (301) 443-6193
Internet http://bhpr.hrsa.gov/dsa/sds.htm
Sponsor Health Resources and Services Administration
5600 Fishers Ln, Parklawn Bldg
Rockville, MD 20857

HRSA Physician Assistant Training **2325**
Grants are awarded for projects for the training of physician assistants and for the training of individuals who will teach in programs to provide such training. A project supported must meet the following definition of a training program for physician assistants as defined under Section 799B of the Public Health Service Act: has as its objective the education of individuals who will, upon completion of their studies in the program, be qualified to provide primary care under the supervision of a physician; extends for at least one academic year and consists of supervised clinical practice and at least four months (in the aggregate) of classroom instruction directed toward preparing students to deliver health care; has an enrollment of not less than eight students; and trains students in primary care, disease prevention, health promotion, geriatric medicine, and home health care. The program assists schools to meet the costs of projects to plan, develop, and operate or maintain programs for the training of physician assistants and for the training of individuals who will teach in programs to provide such training. Programs must develop and use methods designed to encourage graduates of the program to work in health professional shortage areas. Programs also must develop and use methods for placing graduates in positions for which they have been trained.
Requirements Public or nonprofit private hospitals, schools of medicine or osteopathic medicine, or public or private nonprofit entities are eligible to apply. Eligible physician assistant programs are those that are either accredited by the American Medical Association's Committee on Allied Health Education and Accreditation (AMA-CAHEA) or its successor organization, the Commission on Accreditation of Allied Health Education Programs (CAAHEP).
Amount $13,487-$257,297; $120,076 average
Contact Ellie Grant, (301) 443-5404; email: egrant@hrsa.gov
Internet http://www.hrsa.gov
Sponsor Health Resources and Services Administration
5600 Fishers Ln, Parklawn Bldg
Rockville, MD 20857

HSBC in the Community (USA) Grants **2326**
The foundation awards grants in its areas of interest, including education and the environment. Education grants focus on K-12 public schools and postsecondary institutions as well as adult education, such as public library programs and welfare-to-work programs. K-12 education may target students, teachers, and/or parents. Higher education grants support scholarship programs, primarily for disadvantaged students. Grants will be awarded to schools, colleges, and universities as well as to other institutions. In the area of environment, the foundation will award grants to nonprofit organizations that have programs targeting conservation, sustainable development, or environmental education. Programs that promote good environmental practices, and programs that increase environmental public awareness will be considered. Proposals also are welcome for programs that strive to prevent potential environmental degradation, those that focus on scientific research on environmental issues, and activities promoting energy conservation, recycling, preservation of green spaces, waste reduction, and ecological concerns. Proposals may be submitted throughout the calendar year.
Requirements 501(c)3 public charities, public schools and school districts, or other government agencies are eligible.
Restrictions The foundation will not make grants to non-education or non-environment organizations; individuals, except for scholarships through a third party; or political organizations or for political purposes.
Contact Group Public Affairs, (212) 525-8239; TTY/TTD: (800) 898-5999
Internet http://www.us.hsbc.com/inside/community/foundation/print.html
Sponsor HSBC in the Community (USA)
452 Fifth Ave
New York, NY 10018

Hubbard Scholarship **2327**
One scholarship is awarded each year for study at an American Library Association-accredited school for up to two years. The purpose of this scholarship is to recruit excellent librarians for Georgia and provide financial assistance toward completing a degree in library science. The scholar is required to work in a library or in a library-related capacity in Georgia for one year following completion of the program or refund the amount awarded plus interest within two years. Applicants should submit the following materials: official application form, proof of acceptance in an accredited library school, three letters of reference sent directly from the reference, and official transcripts of all academic work sent directly from each institution of higher education. Other considerations being equal, residents of Georgia will be given preference.
Requirements US citizens accepted for admission to a master's program who intend to complete their study within two years at an ALA-accredited library school are eligible.
Amount $3000
Date(s) Application Is Due May 1.
Contact Elizabeth Bagley, Scholarship Committee Chair, (404) 651-2172; fax: (404) 651-2476; email: ebagley@gsu.edu
Internet http://www.library.gsu.edu/gla/committees/scholarship
Sponsor Georgia Library Association
P.O. Box 3967, 100 Decatur St SE
Atlanta, GA 30303-3967

HUD Community Outreach Partnership Centers Grants **2328**
The program provides funds to Institutes of Higher Learning (IHLs) to establish and operate Community Outreach Partnership Centers. These centers carry out research and administer outreach programs in the surrounding communities that focus on addressing the problems of urban areas. Centers should conduct not only outreach but technical assistance, applied research, and empowerment activities for the local neighborhood and community-based organizations. Centers will be required to address at least three urban problems in their outreach programs; these can include issues relating to housing, economic development, neighborhood revitalization, infrastructure, health care, job training, education, crime prevention, planning, and community organization. Outreach activities may include technical assistance, counseling, workshops, and assistance to community and neighborhood organizations.
Requirements Institutions of higher education with demonstrated ability to carry out eligible activities are eligible. A 50 percent match of the total cost of research activities is required, as well as a 25 percent match of the total cost of establishing and operating outreach activities.
Amount $200,000-$400,000 range
Contact Kinnard Wright, Office of University Partnerships, Policy Development and Research, (202) 708-3061 ext 7495; email: Kinnard_D._Wright@hud.gov
Internet http://www.hud.gov/grants
Sponsor Department of Housing and Urban Development
451 Seventh St SW
Washington, DC 20410

HUD Doctoral Dissertation Research Grants 2329

The program awards grants to doctoral candidates completing their dissertations on housing and urban development issues. HUD encourages research based on relationships among universities, communities, distressed public housing developments, public schools, municipal agencies, and community-based organizations. Applications are encouraged from students of any discipline that can provide policy-relevant insight on HUD's mission and program commitments to reduce homelessness, revitalize severely distressed public housing, increase housing production, reduce racial barriers to residential mobility, and reinvigorate economically distressed communities. Support from the university such as tuition waivers, office space, or computer time is required. HUD sends program announcements to relevant PhD- granting departments of accredited universities and posts the announcements on the Internet.
Requirements Any currently enrolled student accepted into candidacy in an accredited doctoral program who has a fully developed and approved dissertation proposal that addresses the program's purpose may apply. Applicants must provide proof that they will have satisfactorily completed all written and oral PhD requirements except the dissertation by September 1 of the current year and that the dissertation can be completed within two years.
Amount $15,000 maximum
Contact University Partnerships Clearinghouse, (800) 245-2691
Internet http://www.hud.gov/progdesc/ddrg.cfm
Sponsor Department of Housing and Urban Development
451 Seventh St SW
Washington, DC 20410

HUD General Research and Technology Activity Grants 2330

Grants are awarded to organizations to carry out research and demonstration projects of high priority and preselected by HUD to improve the operations of their programs. Research relating to low-income housing and housing assistance; public finance and urban economic development; national housing needs; evaluation of existing housing and community development programs; and improving the management and planning of state and local governments are areas eligible for award of grants or cooperative agreements. Specific deadline dates are shown in requests for proposals.
Requirements State and local governments, academic institutions, and public and/or private profit and nonprofit organizations that have the authority and capacity to carry out projects are eligible to compete for these grants.
Amount $13,000-$1.4 million range
Contact Assistant Secretary for Policy Development and Research, (202) 708-1796
Internet http://www.hud.gov
Sponsor Department of Housing and Urban Development
451 Seventh St SW
Washington, DC 20410

HUD Urban Scholars Postdoctoral Fellowships 2331

The program is intended to expand urban research and ensure a continued pipeline of new researchers who will be vitally important to both research and public policy. The fellowships enable recent doctoral recipients to make a positive impact on the scholarship relating to housing and urban development. Applicants must have an academic appointment that will extend beyond the 15-month duration of the fellowship. The institution of higher education where the fellow is employed must designate a faculty adviser with relevant technical and subject expertise to monitor progress on the research project; provide office space and computer access; and waive indirect costs above the 8 percent allowed by the fellowship. Applicants must identify a mentor at their institution or elsewhere who is a respected scholar in the area of the research topic. (The mentor and faculty adviser can be, but do not need to be, the same person.) Fellows will also have a mentor at HUD who conducts research on a related topic and who will keep the fellow advised of policy developments.
Requirements Applicants must have earned a PhD degree no earlier than January 1, 1997, in a field that relates to the research topic eligible for support.
Restrictions A fellow may not hold another comparable major fellowship concurrently.
Amount $55,000 maximum
Contact Fellowship Program-HUD, (202) 334-2872; fax: (202) 334-3419; email: infofell@nas.edu
Internet http://www7.nationalacademies.org/fellowships
Sponsor Department of Housing and Urban Development
2101 Constitution Ave
Washington, DC 20418

Hudson River Graduate Fellowships 2332

The foundation will award up to six full-time research graduate fellowships to doctoral- and master's-level students conducting research on the Hudson River system. The student's home university will be expected to be the primary source of support for materials and expenses required to do the thesis research. In special cases, applicants can apply for a 15-month fellowship to extend the proposed project through an additional summer. (Applications will not be accepted for extensions of existing fellowships.) The award is conditional on a full tuition waiver or reimbursement by the university.
Requirements Applicants must be enrolled in an accredited doctoral or master's program, must have a thesis advisor and advisory committee, and must have a thesis research plan approved by the student's institution or department.
Amount $15,000 plus $1000 for supplies for doctoral fellowships; $11,000 plus $1000 for supplies for master's fellowships
Date(s) Application Is Due Apr 11.
Contact Grants Administrator, (212) 483-7667; fax: (212) 924-8325; email: info@hudsonriver.org
Internet http://www.hudsonriver.org/graduate_fellow.htm
Sponsor Hudson River Foundation
17 Battery Pl, Ste 915
New York, NY 10004

Hudson River Research Grants 2333

The foundation supports basic and applied research in the natural and social sciences and educational programs concerning all aspects of the Hudson River ecosystem, with an emphasis on studies that bear on potential human uses of the system. The geographical area of primary interest is the estuarine portion of the river. General areas of interest for scientific research include resource species, dynamics of Hudson River trophic webs, toxic substances, and hydrodynamics and sediment transport. The program also awards travel grants and expedited grants for the study of emergency situations affecting the Hudson River. Proposals must be preceded by a preproposal consisting of a maximum three-page, single-spaced project description including an abstract and an estimated budget. Preproposals must be received by the listed application deadline date.
Requirements Proposals are welcomed from individual researchers, researchers at colleges and universities, nonprofit/academic institutions, profit-making institutions, and governmental agencies. The foundation prefers that individual researchers seek some institutional affiliation for the purpose of carrying out the proposed research.
Amount $50,000-$90,000 generally
Contact Dr. Dennis Suszkowski, Science Director, (212) 483-7667; fax: (212) 924-8325; email: info@hudsonriver.org
Internet http://www.hudsonriver.org/toc.htm
Sponsor Hudson River Foundation
17 Battery Pl, Ste 915
New York, NY 10004

Huebner Foundation Fellowships 2334

The purpose of the fellowships is to increase the number of qualified professors specializing in insurance and risk management by providing financial assistance to graduate students aspiring to academic careers at the college or university level. Postdoctoral fellowships also are available. A successful candidate for a Foundation grant must certify that it is his or her intention to (1) follow a career as a full-time college or university faculty member with a teaching or research specialization in insurance economics and risk management; (2) specialize in insurance economics and risk management, and in a related discipline such as finance, for a graduate degree; and (3) not engage in any outside work for pay or profit without the consent of the Executive Director of the Foundation during the period of the fellowship.
Requirements Applicant must be a citizen of the United States or Canada and have a bachelor degree from an accredited college or university. Candidates for Foundation grants must apply on a special form available from the Foundation. Candidates for Foundation grants must apply separately and directly for admission to the Wharton Doctoral Program. They must take the Graduate Management Examination Test (GMAT) or the Graduate Record Examination (GRE) administered by the Educational Testing Service in Princeton, New Jersey. A copy of the GMAT or GRE results must be sent by ETS to the Wharton Doctoral Program office, located at 1150 Steinberg Hall- Dietrich Hall at the University of Pennsylvania.
Amount $15,000 annually for four years
Contact Executive Director, (215) 898-9631; fax: (215) 573-2218
Internet http://www.huebnergeneva.org
Sponsor S.S. Huebner Foundation
3733 Spruce St, Wharton School, 430 Vance Hall
Philadelphia, PA 19104-6301

Hugh Atkinson Memorial Award 2335

This award recognizes outstanding achievement, including risk taking, by academic librarians that have contributed significantly to improvements in the area of library automation, library management, and/or library development or research. Nominations include a letter that indicates: the name, address, and phone number of both the nominator and the nominee; a narrative supporting the nomination; and a current vita.
Requirements The nominee must be a librarian employed in a university, college, or community college library in the year prior to application for the award and must have a minimum of five years of professional experience in an academic library. Individuals may nominate themselves or be nominated by others.
Amount $2000
Date(s) Application Is Due Dec 1.
Contact Carlen Ruschoff, Chair (301) 314-0409, email: ruschoff@umd.edu; Megan Bielefeld (800) 545-2433 ext.2514, email mbielefeld@ala.org
Internet http://www.ala.org/ala/alcts/divisiongroups/alctsdivawards/atkinsonaward/hughcatkinson.htm
Sponsor Association of College and Research Libraries
50 E Huron St
Chicago, IL 60611-2795

Huie-Dellmon Trust Grants 2336

The trust awards grants to Louisiana nonprofits in its areas of interest, including hospitals, higher and secondary education, libraries, and Protestant churches and organizations. Types of support include general operating support, capital campaigns, building construction/renovation, equipment acquisition, program development, scholarship funds, research, and matching funds. There are no application forms or deadlines.
Requirements Central Louisiana nonprofit organizations are eligible.
Amount $250-$100,000 range
Contact Richard Crowell Jr., Trustee, (318) 748-8141
Sponsor Huie-Dellmon Trust
P.O. Box 330
Alexandria, LA 71309-0330

Huisking Foundation Grants 2337

The foundation awards grants in its areas of interest, including Catholic higher and secondary education, church support and social services, hospitals, and religion associations. Types of support include general operating support, building construction/renovation, research grants, endowment funds, scholarship funds, special projects, and continuing support. The board meets in April and November; letters of intent are due in February and August.
Amount $200-$60,000 range
Contact Frank Huisking, Treasurer, (203) 426-8618
Sponsor Huisking Foundation
291 Peddlers Rd
Guilford, CT 06437

Human Growth Foundation Small Grants 2338

The foundation awards grants for investigation of human growth and its disorders, with special consideration given for the chondrodystrophies. Special consideration will be given to new investigators and ideas new to the field. Postdoctoral research dealing with all aspects of normal and abnormal human growth and development including, but not limited to, the areas of biological, psychological, educational, and diet and nutrition will be considered. Up to three grants will be awarded. A synopsis of the research results is required to be submitted the following year. An NIH-type biographical sketch and two-page letter of intent should be sent by May 15; full applications are due by September 1.
Restrictions No portion of the grant can be used for administrative overhead.
Amount $7500-$10,000
Date(s) Application Is Due May 15; Sep 1.
Contact Program Contact, (800) 451-6434 or (516) 671-4041; fax: (516) 671-4055; email: hgf1@hgfound.org
Internet http://www.hgfound.org/smallgrants.html
Sponsor Human Growth Foundation
997 Glen Cove Ave
Glen Head, NY 11545

Human Rights Fellows Program 2339

The aim of this two-year program is to support the further development of a civil liberties network of lawyers in the countries of Eastern Europe and the former Soviet Union. Three lawyers from Central and Eastern Europe and the former Soviet Union will be selected to participate in the program. Fellows reside in the United States for one year and audit courses related to human rights at the American University Washington College of Law during the fall semester and spend the spring and summer semesters in internships with civil liberties organizations or legal services agencies in the United States. Fellows return to their home countries after the first year, where they spend at least one year working with NGOs on human rights advocacy on a nonprofit basis--providing legal services, litigating test cases, training and educating in human rights, etc. Criteria for selection includes the applicant's experience, the potential of the applicant to contribute to the protection and promotion of human rights in Eastern Europe and the former Soviet Union, and the suitability of the applicant's proposed role in the nominating NGO. Preference will be given to applicants under 35 years of age.
Requirements Applicants from Central and Eastern Europe and the former Soviet Union with a law degree, a strong commitment to human rights, eligibility for legal practice in home country, and English proficiency may apply.
Amount $1500 monthly stipend for up to 12 months, round-trip airfare to the United States, $500 textbook allowance, and medical insurance for one year while in the *Contact* Eszter Filippinyi, Program Coordinator or Zaza Namoradze, Director, 36 1 327-3102; fax: 36 1 327-3103; email: justiceinitiative@sorosny.org
Internet http://www.justiceinitiative.org/activities/lcd/fellows/index
Sponsor Open Society Justice Initiative
Oktober 6 u 12
Budapest 1051
Hungary

Humanities Institute Visiting Scholars Fellowships 2340

The institute offers residential fellowships each academic year to one or two visiting scholars to pursue advanced work in the humanities. Projects may contribute to scholarly knowledge or to the general public's understanding of the humanities. Recipients might eventually produce scholarly articles, a monograph on a specialized subject, a book on a broad topic, an archaeological site report, a translation, an edition, or other scholarly tools. Fellowships support projects that can be completed during the tenure of an award or those that are part of a long-term endeavor. Applicants may be faculty or staff members of colleges or universities, or scholars and independent writers.
Requirements Applicants should have held the PhD for five years or more or possess a record of professional accomplishment.
Restrictions Fellowships do not support projects to study teaching methods or theories. Neither do they support surveys of courses and programs or the preparation of institutional curricula.
Amount $40,000 stipend
Date(s) Application Is Due Jan 15.
Contact UCHI, (860) 486-9057 or 486-9058; fax: (860) 486-9136; email: UCHI@uconn.edu
Internet http://www.humanities.uconn.edu
Sponsor University of Connecticut
215 Glenrook Rd, U-4234
Storrs, CT 06269-4234

Humanities Summer Research Fellowships at the University of Oregon 2341

The University of Oregon Humanities Center invites applications for summer research fellowships. This is a residential research program supporting high-quality research in the humanities; arts; and interpretive fields of the social sciences, natural sciences, and professional studies. Research fellows are provided offices with computers and support services, use of the Knight Library at the university, and a small stipend for temporary relocation expenses. Fellowships are available for six to eight weeks from mid-June to mid-September. Fellows must pursue research projects full time during the fellowship period and may simultaneously have other support. Write for application form.
Restrictions Fellowships are not awarded for dissertation research or writing.
Amount $1400 maximum
Date(s) Application Is Due Dec 1.
Contact Julia Heydon, Associate Director, Oregon Humanities Center, (541) 346-1001; email: jheydon@uoregon.edu
Internet http://darkwing.uoregon.edu/~humanctr/fellowship/index.html
Sponsor University of Oregon Humanities Center
5211 Oregon Humanities Ctr
Eugene, OR 97403-5211

Hunter's Hope Foundation Grants 2342

Hunter's Hope funds projects directly related to Krabbe disease or other leukodystrophies. Eligible studies may investigate new treatment approaches, or study basic mechanisms related to these diseases. Areas of relevant research include, among others, gene therapy, myelin development, neurodegeneration and transplantation, developmental neurobiology, and molecular biology. Applications are accepted in three project categories: postdoctoral fellowships provide stipend support for individuals who are within five years of receiving their terminal degree (MD, DVM, PhD, or equivalent degree). Fellows will be working with senior investigators within their sponsoring institution. Fellowships are awarded for two years. Pilot studies are one-year projects designed to test new concepts or ideas and can serve as a source of preliminary data for future studies. Major research grants provide support to senior investigators conducting major research studies. Projects may be funded for one to three years. Applications are reviewed twice annually.
Amount $100,000 maximum major research grants; $40,000-$60,000 postdoctoral fellowships; $30,000 maximum pilot studies
Date(s) Application Is Due Apr 15; Sep 15.
Contact Executive Director, (877) 984-4673 or (716) 667-1200; fax: (716) 667-1212; email: info@huntershope.org
Internet http://www.huntershope.org/research/default.asp
Sponsor Hunter's Hope Foundation
P.O. Box 643
Orchard Park, NY 14127

Huntington Library Fellowships 2343

The Huntington Library welcomes applications from scholars for awards to help them carry on significant research in the collections. The library offers many short- and long-term awards. In selecting persons to receive awards, attention is paid to the value of the project, the ability of the scholar, and the degree to which special strengths of the library will be utilized. Holders of the awards are expected to be in residence through the tenure. One month is the minimum period for which awards are made. The stipends are to assist in balancing budgets of persons who are on leave at reduced pay and in meeting the additional expenses of living away from home and travel to and from San Marino. Applications are accepted from October 1 to December 15 each year for awards within the 12-month period beginning the following June 1; selection announcements will be made no later than April 1.
Requirements Applicant scholars must have the PhD or equivalent degree or be doctoral candidates at the dissertation stage. Non-tenured faculty are available for one of the fellowships.
Amount $2000-$40,000
Date(s) Application Is Due Dec 15.
Contact Robert Ritchie, Director of Research, (626) 405-2194; fax: (626) 449-5703; email: cpowell@huntington.org
Internet http://www.huntington.org/ResearchDiv/Fellowships.html

Sponsor Huntington Library and Art Gallery
1151 Oxford Rd
San Marino, CA 91108

Huntington's Disease Research Grants **2344**
Support will be for research projects that contribute to identifying and understanding the basic defect in Huntington's disease. Grants are usually for one year, with the possibility of renewal for up to three years. Areas of interest include trinucleotide expansions, animal models, gene therapy, neurobiology and development of the basal ganglia, cell survival and death, and intercellular signaling in striatal neurons. In addition to its regular grants, the foundation also offers the Lieberman Award for innovative proposals accelerating the discovery of a treatment and cure of Huntington's disease. Grants that receive funding are considered seed money. If the project shows promise, it is hoped that other institutions will fund it thereafter. To obtain an application, submit a one-page letter of intent. Letter of intent forms may be submitted electronically via the Web site.
Amount $50,000 maximum
Date(s) Application Is Due Feb 15; Jun 15; Oct 15.
Contact Dr. Carl Johnson, (212) 928-2121; fax: (212) 928-2172; email: carljohnson@hdfoundation.org
Internet http://www.hdfoundation.org/fundinga.htm
Sponsor Hereditary Disease Foundation
3960 Broadway, 6th Fl
New York, NY 10032

Huntington's Disease Society of America Research Fellowships **2345**
The fellowships are designed to assist promising young postdoctoral investigators in the early stages of their careers who are engaged in research at the basic and clinical levels relating to the cause and treatment of Huntington's disease. The amount of the award will depend on the policy of the sponsoring accredited medical school or university and the training and experience of the applicant. Fellowships are awarded for one year with the possibility of renewal. Application forms and requested information on curriculum vita, publications, research proposal, sponsorship, and other sources of funding are provided by the society.
Requirements Applicants must have an MD or PhD degree or the equivalent and work must be related to Huntington's disease. There is no citizenship requirement.
Amount $80,000 maximum over two years
Date(s) Application Is Due Dec 15.
Contact Grants Administrator, (800) 345-4372 ext 27; email: rgraze@hdsa.org
Internet http://www.hdsa.org/site/PageServer?pagename=HDSA_Research_Grants_and_Fellowships_Programs
Sponsor Huntington's Disease Society of America
158 W 29th St, 7th Fl
New York, NY 10001-5300

Huntington's Disease Society of America Research Grants **2346**
The society awards research grants for one year for support of basic or clinical research related to Huntington's disease. Grant awards are provided as seed monies for new or innovative research projects in the hope that they will develop sufficiently to attract funding from other sources. Application forms are provided by the society and generally follow the format of NIH grant applications.
Requirements Applicants may be doctorate or graduate students or equivalent professionals. There is no citizenship requirement.
Amount $100,000 maximum over two years
Date(s) Application Is Due Dec 15.
Contact Grants Administrator, (800) 345-4372 ext 27 or (212) 242-1968 ext 13; fax: (212) 239-3430; email: rgraze@hdsa.org
Internet http://www.hdsa.org/site/PageServer?pagename=HDSA_Research_Grants_and_Fellowships_Programs
Sponsor Huntington's Disease Society of America
158 W 29th St, 7th Fl
New York, NY 10001

Hutchinson Community Foundation Grants **2347**
While the Foundation provides support for a broad range of causes, particular interest is in the following program areas: projects that focus on early childhood development, youth development, and school to work; projects that promote developmental assets and thriving behavior in children and youth; men and fathers; and family economic success. Grant proposal applications must be requested by email.
Requirements Nonprofit organizations in Kansas are eligible to apply. Special purpose units of government can apply for support of innovative projects located in Reno County.
Restrictions Grant proposals from individuals or non-qualifying organizations will not be considered.
Date(s) Application Is Due Aug 13.
Contact Audrey Abbott Patterson, President, (620) 663-5293; fax: (620) 663-9277; email: aubrey@hutchcf.org
Internet http://www.hutchcf.org
Sponsor Hutchinson Community Foundation
First National Bank Building, One North Main, Suite 501
Hutchinson, KS 67504

Hyde and Watson Foundation Grants Program **2348**
The foundation's primary concern is supporting capital projects that increase the quality, capacity, or efficiency of a grantee's programs or services, such as purchase or relocation of facilities, facilities improvements, capital equipment, instructive materials development, or certain medical research areas. Broad fields include health, education, religion, social services, arts, and humanities.
Requirements Primary geographic areas served include the New York City metropolitan region and primarily Essex, Union, and Morris Counties in New Jersey.
Restrictions Requests for endowment or operating support or from fiscal agents generally will be denied. Grants are not made to individuals.
Amount $5000-$25,000 average
Date(s) Application Is Due Feb 15; Sep 15.
Contact Hunter Corbin, President, (973) 966-6024; fax: (973) 966-6404; email: Hcorbin@HydeandWatson.org
Internet http://fdncenter.org/grantmaker/hydeandwatson
Sponsor Hyde and Watson Foundation
437 Southern Blvd
Chatham Township, NJ 07928

i2 Foundation Grants **2349**
The foundation promotes advancements in education, technology, environmental practices, medicine, and economic opportunity through programs improving the quality of life and creating a better society. Although the foundation's main priority is the development and education of youth, proposals related to a wide array of issues are accepted, including illiteracy, youth violence, early childhood development, poverty, improved healthcare, and scientific research. All future grant cycles are currently postponed and new proposals are not being accepted.
Requirements Nonprofit organizations closely aligned with the foundation's goals are eligible.
Restrictions Individuals, religious institutions, political organizations, and government entities are ineligible.
Amount $5000-$50,000
Contact Grants Administrator, (469) 357-4200; fax: (469) 357-7777; email: Melis_Jones@i2.com
Internet http://www.i2.com/company/i2foundation/index.cfm
Sponsor i2 Foundation
One i2 Pl, 11701 Luna Rd
Dallas, TX 75234

Ian Axford Public Policy Fellowships in New Zealand **2350**
The fellowships give outstanding midcareer American professionals an opportunity to study, travel, and gain practical experience in public policy in New Zealand, including first-hand knowledge of economic, social and political reforms, and management of the government sector. Two to three fellowships per year are awarded for six months of study in New Zealand. Fellowships are offered in any area of public policy.
Requirements Applicants must be US citizens with at least five years experience in their professions. There are no formal age limits, but the focus of the fellowships is on midcareer development, and successful candidates are likely to be in their early 30s to early 50s. Applications are welcome equally from men and women, from members of any ethnic group, and regardless of physical abilities.
Restrictions Fellowships are not awarded to support basic research or to enable study for an academic degree.
Amount NZ$500- NZ$4,000 per month living expenses (on top of salary); NZ$1,500 per month for a partner to accompany a fellow; NZ$250 per month per child for a maximum of two children up to 18 years
Date(s) Application Is Due Mar 1.
Contact Diana Davenport, (212) 606-3800; fax: (212) 606-3500; email: dd@cmwf.org
Internet http://www.cmwf.org/fellowships/fellowships_list.htm?attrib_id=9159
Sponsor Commonwealth Fund
1 E 75th St
New York, NY 10021

Ian N. McKinnon Memorial Fellowship **2351**
This four-month fellowship is open to qualified graduates of any recognized university who are registered in or admissible to a full-time program leading to a master's or doctoral degree at the University of Calgary. Fields of study supported are all areas relevant to the effective development and utilization of energy resources with special emphasis on economics, engineering, and geology.
Requirements Candidates must be Canadian citizens or landed immigrants at the time of taking up the award.
Amount $C3500
Date(s) Application Is Due Apr 15.
Contact Faculty of Graduate Studies, (403) 220-5417; email: graduate@ucalgary.ca
Internet http://www.grad.ucalgary.ca/funding/internal_scholarships/lev_4/mckinnon.htm
Sponsor University of Calgary
2500 University Dr NW, Earth Sciences Bldg
Calgary, AB T2N 1N4 Canada

IARC Cancer Research Training Fellowships PhD Program 2352
A limited number of Ph.D. Fellowships are available for junior scientists from low- or medium-resource countries who are committed to pursuing a career in cancer research and have a Master's degree in an appropriate subject area (medicine, epidemiology, biostatistics, genetics, laboratory research) and wish to study for a Ph.D. degree in the field of epidemiology or biostatistics in a research Group at IARC in Lyon. The cost of tuition will be covered by IARC. The annual stipend will cover living expenses and cost of travel for the Fellow as well as health insurance cover.
Requirements Candidates must be proficient in English, both oral and written and those for whom English is not their first language must supply evidence of competency. Candidates should be under the age of 40 at the application deadline and are expected to return to their home country upon completion of their training and to keep working in cancer research.
Date(s) Application Is Due Sep 15.
Contact Dr. Paolo Boffetta, +33-(0)472-73-84-48; fax: +33-(0)472-73-80-80; email: vsa@iarc.fr
Internet http://www.iarc.fr/ENG/Fellowships/phd.php
Sponsor International Agency for Research on Cancer
150 cours Albert-Thomas
Lyon Cedex 08 69372 France

IARC Expertise Transfer Fellowship 2353
The Fellowship is intended to enable an established investigator to spend normally from six to twelve months in an appropriate host institute in a low- to medium-resource country in order to transfer knowledge and expertise in a research area relevant for the host country and related to epidemiology, biostatistics, environmental chemical carcinogenesis, cancer etiology and prevention, infection and cancer, molecular cell biology, molecular genetics, molecular pathology and mechanisms of carcinogenesis. Applications should include a proposed collaborative research project, specifying the link to IARC's on-going activities and a letter of support from the host lab giving details of feasibility and anticipated benefit to the receiving institute. Priority will be given to projects directly linked to IARC's on-going research program, involving at least one contact at IARC. There will be an annual remuneration of up to $70,000, which will take into account the on-going salary of the Fellow. This amount may include limited support for the project. The cost of travel will also be met.
Requirements Applicants should be established cancer researchers actively engaged in the field with appropriate scientific or medical qualifications and an excellent publications' record. They must also belong to the staff of a university or a research institution.
Amount $70,000 maximum
Date(s) Application Is Due Nov 30.
Contact Dr. Paolo Boffetta, +33-(0)472-73-84-48; fax: +33-(0)472-73-80-80; email: vsa@iarc.fr
Internet http://www.iarc.fr/ENG/Fellowships/expertisetransfer.php
Sponsor International Agency for Research on Cancer
150 cours Albert-Thomas
Lyon Cedex 08 69372 France

IARC Postdoctoral Fellowships for Training in Cancer Research 2354
Applications for training fellowships are invited from junior scientists from low- or medium-resource countries wishing to complete their training in those aspects of cancer research related to coordinate and conduct both epidemiological and laboratory research into the causes of cancer. Disciplines covered include: epidemiology, biostatistics, environmental chemical carcinogenesis, cancer etiology and prevention, infection and cancer, molecular cell biology, molecular genetics, molecular pathology and mechanisms of carcinogenesis, with emphasis on interdisciplinary projects. The fellowship is for a period of one year, with the possibility of an extension for a second year subject to satisfactory appraisal.
Requirements Candidates should have spent less than five years abroad (including doctoral studies) and have finished their doctoral degree within five years of the closing date for application or be in the final phase of completing their doctoral degree (M.D. or Ph.D.). They must provide evidence of their ability to return to their home country and keep working in cancer research. The working languages at IARC are English and French. Candidates must be proficient in English at a level sufficient for scientific communication.
Restrictions Candidates already working as a postdoctoral fellow at the Agency at the time of application or who have had any contractual relationship with IARC during the 6 months preceding the application deadline or who have already spent more than one year at IARC cannot be considered.
Amount 25,000 Euros
Date(s) Application Is Due Nov 30.
Contact Dr. Paolo Boffetta, +33-(0)472-73-84-48; fax: +33-(0)472-73-80-80; email: vsa@iarc.fr
Internet http://www.iarc.fr/ENG/Fellowships/postdoc.php
Sponsor International Agency for Research on Cancer
150 cours Albert-Thomas
Lyon Cedex 08 69372 France

IARC Visiting Scientist Award for Senior Scientists 2355
The IARC is offering this Award for a qualified and experienced investigator with recent publications in international peer-reviewed scientific journals who wishes to spend from six to twelve months at the IARC working on a collaborative project in a research area related to the Agency's programs: epidemiology, biostatistics, environmental chemical carcinogenesis, cancer etiology and prevention, infection and cancer, molecular cell biology, molecular genetics, molecular pathology and mechanisms of carcinogenesis. There will be an annual remuneration of up to $80,000, which will take into account the on-going salary of the visiting scientist plus the cost of travel.
Requirements Applicants must belong to the staff of a university or a research institution and should provide written assurance of a post to return to at the end of the period of award.
Amount $80,000 maximum
Date(s) Application Is Due Nov 30.
Contact Dr. Paolo Boffetta, +33-(0)472-73-84-48; fax: +33-(0)472-73-80-80; email: vsa@iarc.fr
Internet http://www.iarc.fr/ENG/Fellowships/vsa.php
Sponsor International Agency for Research on Cancer
150 cours Albert-Thomas
Lyon Cedex 08 69372 France

IAS Mellon Fellowships for Assistant Professors 2356
The School of Historical Studies at the institute, with the support of the Andrew Mellon Foundation, has established a program of one-year memberships for assistant professors at universities and colleges in the United States and Canada to support promising young scholars who have embarked on professional careers. While at the institute they will be expected to engage exclusively in scholarly research and writing. Appointments will be for one full year (July 1 through June 30 with the option of staying through the second summer until August 15) and will carry all the privileges of membership at the Institute for Advanced Study. The stipend will match the combined salary and benefits at the member's home institution at the time of application.
Requirements Assistant professors in areas represented in the School of Historical Studies (Greek and Roman civilization, the history of Europe, the Islamic world, East Asian studies, the history of art, and modern international relations) may apply, provided at the time of their arrival they will have served at least two and not more than four years as assistant professors in institutions of higher learning in the United States or Canada and provided they can return to their institution.
Date(s) Application Is Due Nov 15.
Contact Administrative Officer, email: mzelazny@ias.edu
Internet http://www.hs.ias.edu/mellon.htm
Sponsor Institute for Advanced Study
Einstein Dr
Princeton, NJ 08540

IBM Center for the Business of Government Grants 2357
Through grants for research and forums, the organization stimulates research and facilitates discussion on new approaches to improving the effectiveness of government at the federal, state, local, and international levels. Individuals may apply for grants to produce a 30-40 page research report in one of four areas. Categories vary by year; contact program staff for current topics. Interested individuals should submit a three-page description of the proposed research and a resume, including a list of publications. Application and guidelines are available online.
Requirements Individuals working in universities, nonprofit organizations, and journalism are eligible.
Amount $15,000 for each research paper
Date(s) Application Is Due Mar 1; Nov 1.
Contact Mark Abramson, (202) 515-4504; fax: (202) 515-4375; email: mark.abramson@us.ibm.com
Internet http://www.endowment.pwcglobal.com/about.asp
Sponsor IBM Center for the Business of Government
1301 K St NW, 4th Fl, West Tower
Washington, DC 20005

ICCP Outstanding Young Investigator Award 2358
The annual award recognizes the recent contributions of a promising young investigator and, in so doing, encourages and facilitates his/her lifelong commitment to the field of spinal cord repair. The award is intended to encourage young scientists to devote their careers to spinal cord research; promote and enrich the international research field in repair of the damaged spinal cord; and stimulate collaborative research in the field. The award supports inter-laboratory travel and expenses to complete a collaborative new study or a clearly defined project to learn a specific technique. The goal of the award is to benefit the grantee and the field for a spinal cord study or learning experience.
Requirements To be eligible, a candidate must be a postdoctoral fellow who possesses a doctoral degree at the time of proposal submission and who is in his/her first to seventh year of postdoctoral work. The winning nominee must be a postdoctoral fellow during the 12-month award period, and the study must be completed within one year of the award.
Amount $10,000
Date(s) Application Is Due Sep 1.
Contact Dr. John Steeves, fax: (604) 822-2924; email: steeves@icord.or
Internet http://www.campaignforcure.org/Young%20Investigator%20Award.htm
Sponsor International Campaign for the Cure for Spinal Cord Paralysis
ICORD at UBC, 2469-6270 University Blvd
Vancouver, BC V6T 1Z4 Canada

ICCS Graduate Students Scholarships 2359

The scholarships enable successful candidates to spend four to six weeks at a Canadian university or research site other than their own doing research related to their thesis or dissertation in the field of Canadian studies. Scholarships are not intended to initiate a thesis or dissertation, but rather to provide access to crucial scholarly information and resources in Canada in support of a thesis/dissertation that is close to or at the point of being written.

Requirements Each applicant must be nominated by his/her national Canadian studies association The student must obtain in writing the support of a faculty member at a Canadian university who has agreed to act as the student's academic sponsor during the tenure of his/her award.

Amount $C5000 maximum

Date(s) Application Is Due Dec 31.

Contact Grants Administrator, (613) 789-7834 ext 242; fax: (613) 789-7830; email: csppec@iccs-ciec.ca

Internet http://www.iccs-ciec.ca/pages/4_ICCSprogs/a_gradstu.html

Sponsor International Council for Canadian Studies
75 Albert, Ste 908
Ottawa, ON K1P 5E7 Canada

ICCS Publishing Fund 2360

The fund assists with the publication and distribution in Canada of scholarly monographs on Canada written by foreign Canadianists who are members of a Canadian Studies Association or associate member belonging to the International Council for Canadian Studies. This fund assists foreign Canadianists by granting financial aid to a recognized scholarly press once the work is published. The fund may also grant financial assistance for the translation from English or French into a third language and from a third language into French or English. The funds allocated will apply to the printing or translating costs of a manuscript/book and not to the costs of research, typing, reproduction or any other stage in the manuscript preparation process. Applications must be presented to the ICCS in either of Canada's official languages. Guidelines are available online.

Requirements Only scholarly manuscripts on Canada written by foreign Canadianists are eligible. Manuscripts must be previously unpublished. Manuscripts consisting of previously published texts, such as excerpts of books or articles, are eligible if a third of the texts have not previously been published. The author must be a member in good standing of an ICCS member association or associate member. A letter of support from a Canadian Studies Association or associate member belonging to the ICCS must accompany the application.

Restrictions Collections of poetry, novels, plays, magazine articles or conference proceedings are not eligible.

Date(s) Application Is Due Oct 31.

Contact Guy LeClair, (613) 789-7834 ext 228; fax: (613) 789-7830; email: gleclair@cs-ciec.ca

Internet http://www.iccs-ciec.ca/pages/4_ICCSprogs/f_publishfund.html

Sponsor International Council for Canadian Studies
75 Albert St., Ste 908
Ottawa, Ontario K1P 5E7 Canada

ICF Korean Literature Translation Fellowship 2361

The program was established to provide prospective translators with financial assistance for studying at Korean universities or at their home institutions to develop their skills as translators of Korean Literature. The important function is to cultivate translators of Korean literature, with the long-term goal of introducing Korean literature abroad. Fellowship term is one year, renewable. Each applicant should submit a recommendation letter from a professor of Korean literature, English literature, or Creative writing in any university department.

Requirements Applications are invited from candidates whose English is native and who want to specialize in translating Korean literature into English.

Amount $5000 quarterly

Date(s) Application Is Due Sep 30.

Contact Foundation Administrator, 82+2 2280-7233; fax: 82+2 2269-4310; email: yds@icfkorea.net

Internet http://exam.ybmsisa.com/icf/icfe02_1.asp

Sponsor International Communication Foundation
#56-15 Jongno 2 ga
Jongno-Gu Seoul 110-122
Korea

ICJ World Affairs Journalism Fellowships 2362

The fellowship is aimed at news managers, editors, commentary writers, and other gatekeepers of news--basically those who decide which stories appear in the paper--from US community-based dailies. Twelve experienced media professionals will be selected to travel overseas for one to three weeks on assignment. While overseas, fellows will explore issues of local importance and submit articles to their home newspapers for publication. Up to 12 fellows will be selected each year. The program covers all domestic and international travel costs and provides support in setting up contacts while overseas. Guidelines and application are available online.

Date(s) Application Is Due Mar 1.

Contact World Affairs Journalism Fellowships, (202) 737-3700; fax: (202) 737-0530; email: wajf@icfj.org

Internet http://www.icfj.org/worldaffairs.html

Sponsor International Center for Journalists
1616 H St NW, 3rd Fl
Washington, DC 20006

Ida Smedley MacLean International Fellowship 2363

The fellowship shall be awarded to encourage advanced scholarship by enabling university women to undertake original research in some country other than that in which the holder has received her education or habitually resides. Fellowships are intended to cover at least eight months of work and should be taken up within a reasonable period from the date of the award. Members of the IFUW should apply through their national affiliates (in the United States, the American Association of University Women, 1111 16th St NW, Washington, DC 20036). The competition is held in even-numbered years. The deadline for receipt of applications is determined by each affiliate but normally falls between early September and mid-October of the year preceding the competition. Contact the national headquarters for the exact deadline date.

Requirements An applicant must be a woman graduate who is a member of IFUW and must be well started on the research program to which the application relates.

Restrictions A fellowship will not be awarded for the first year of a PhD program.

Amount Sf8000

Date(s) Application Is Due Oct 1.

Contact Fellowships Officer, 41-22-731-23-80; fax: 41-22-738-04-40; email: info@ifuw.org

Internet http://www.ifuw.org/fellowships/international.htm

Sponsor International Federation of University Women
8 rue de l'Ancien Port
Geneva CH 1201
Switzerland

Idaho Humanities Council Fellowships 2364

The goals of this program are to stimulate scholarship in the humanities, to provide support for individuals who need to devote time and money to specific research projects, and to share the results of research with academic and public communities. The council invites research fellowship proposals from Idaho scholars or out-of-state scholars undertaking work on a subject of special relevance to Idaho. Scholar should have a minimum of a master's degree in the humanities, though individuals will be considered by their previous record of research. Up to four fellowships are awarded each year.

Requirements Eligible applicants include Idaho scholars who are residents working in any area of the humanities and nonstate scholars undertaking work on a subject of special relevance to Idaho. Also, any scholar pursuing work on a special initiative put forth by the council in that year is eligible.

Amount $3500

Date(s) Application Is Due Sep 15.

Contact Program Contact, (208) 345-5346; fax: (208) 345-5347; email: jennifer@idahohumanities.org or rick@idahohumanities.org

Internet http://www2.state.id.us/ihc/grantfrm.htm

Sponsor Idaho Humanities Council
217 W State St
Boise, ID 83702

IDEM Section 319(h) Nonpoint Source Program Grants 2365

This program funds projects that will work on a watershed level to reduce nonpoint source pollution in Indiana's lakes, rivers, and streams. Nonpoint source pollution does not come from a pipe. It results when water (rain or snowmelt) moves across land, such as city streets, agricultural fields and residential backyards, and picks up dirt, fertilizers, pesticides, animal wastes, road salt, motor oil and other pollutants. Nonpoint source pollution is also caused by wind, which like rain, can pick up soil particles and deposit them in lakes and streams. These pollutants have harmful effects on drinking water supplies, recreation, fisheries and wildlife. Nonpoint source pollution is the leading cause of water quality problems in Indiana and is responsible for many of the impairments identified on the 303(d) List of Impaired Waterbodies. Funding for selected projects will be provided by Clean Water Act Section 319 grant funds and match is provided by grant recipients and partners.

Requirements To be considered for funding, the project sponsor (the entity responsible for the project and its overall success), must be one of the following: 1) Municipality; 2) County Government; 3) State Government; 4) Federal Government; 5) College/University; 6) Nonprofit 501(c)(3). The program provides funding and technical assistance to groups that work on the watershed level with citizens to develop locally-based solutions to nonpoint source pollution. Specific ways to address nonpoint source water pollution include education/outreach on watershed management, information gathering activities such as conducting watershed inventories and water quality assessments for the purpose of developing comprehensive watershed management plans and implementing those plans, including implementation of best management practices that directly reduce sources of nonpoint source pollution. IDEM provides sixty percent (60%) of an approved project's total cost with Section 319 funds. A grant recipient must provide the remaining forty percent (40%) of the total project cost as match. Match may be in-kind services or cash. Match cannot come from any federal funding sources. Guidelines and application forms are available for download at the website. Do not use forms from previous years – they will not be accepted by IDEM.

Restrictions The following is a list of activities that cannot be funded with Section 319 funds and cannot be counted as matching funds for a Section 319 grant: Permit fees; Food for meetings or other events; Purchase of agricultural equipment, or other large pieces of equipment (equipment modifications and leasing are allowable); Purchase of land or land easements (these activities can be counted as matching funds in some cases); Any project which is directed at water quantity rather than water quality, such as dredging, drainage, or flood control; Any practices, equipment, or supplies used to fulfill the requirements of any federal permit (NPDES permit, Section 401 Water Quality Certification, permits from the U.S. Army Corps of Engineers, as examples) or to comply with IDEM's Confined Feeding Operation rule or permit requirements, or to meet enforcement requirements; Wetland mitigation sites; Incentive payments or yield losses; Nonpoint source best management practices not sanctioned by IDEM or not sanctioned by a partner agency of IDEM; Practices not installed in accordance with standards and specifications developed by NRCS, IDNR or other recognized standards; Office furniture; Sales tax. Additionally, the following will not be funded by this grant program: Septic system pump outs, repairs, rehabilitations, or demonstrations of alternative septic systems; Projects whose sole purpose is data collection, research, demonstration of best management practices, or education/outreach. However, these activities may be incorporated as elements into a proposal that meets one of the three priorities.
Date(s) Application Is Due Sep 1.
Contact Andrew Pelloso, Section Chief, (317) 233-2481; Doug Campbell, Solicitation Coordinator, (317) 233-8491; Laura Bieberich, Team Leader, 317-233-1863
Internet http://www.in.gov/idem/resources/grants_loans/319h/index.html
Sponsor Indiana Department of Environmental Management (IDEM)
Indiana Government Center North, 100 N. Senate Ave.
Indianapolis, IN 46204

IDNR C2000 Ecosystem Project Grants **2366**
The purpose of the Program is to integrate the interests and participation of local communities and private, public and corporate landowners to enhance and protect watersheds through ecosystem-based management. The program is made up of partnerships, which are coalitions of local stakeholders (private landowners, businesses, scientists, environmental organizations, recreational enthusiasts, and policy makers). Application deadlines are February 28 for online applications and January 31 for hard-copy applications. Applicants are encouraged to pre-submit project applications to the appropriate Local Partnership Councils (LPCs) for their review and comments before completing their formal submissions to IDNR. Guidelines are available online
Date(s) Application Is Due Jan 31; Feb 28.
Contact Grants Administrator, (217) 782-6232; email: dnr.grants@illinois.gov
Internet http://www.dnr.state.il.us/orep/c2000/ecosystem/fy06/index.htm
Sponsor Illinois Department of Natural Resources
One Natural Resources Way
Springfield, IL 62702-1271

IEEE Electrical History Fellowship **2367**
This fellowship supports one year of full-time graduate study in the history of electrical engineering and technology at an engineering school of recognized standing in the United States or Canada.
Requirements Individuals doing graduate or postgraduate work in the history of electrical technology are eligible.
Amount $15,000
Date(s) Application Is Due Feb 1.
Contact Director, Center for the History of Electrical Engineering, (732) 932-1066; fax: (732) 932-1193; email: history@ieee.org
Internet http://www.ieee.org/portal/index.jsp?pageID=corp_level1&path=membership/students/awards&file=sc_ehistory.xml&xsl=generic.xsl
Sponsor Institute of Electrical and Electronics Engineers
39 Union St
New Brunswick, NJ 08901-8538

IERF Sepmeyer Research Grant Program **2368**
The Foundation's mission is to conduct research and disseminate information on world educational systems and to facilitate the integration of individuals educated outside the United States into the U.S. educational environment and work force. The Foundation conducts and supports comprehensive, quality research on world education systems, shares research findings with the international community, and provides research-based credentials, evaluations, and related services. The purpose of the research grant is to aid the Foundation in carrying out its mission. There is no application form. Applicants should submit a research project summary. Application information is available online.
Requirements Research grants are available to all persons, irrespective of citizenship and country of residence.
Amount $5000 maximum
Date(s) Application Is Due Feb 1.
Contact Susan Bedil, Executive Director, (310) 258-9451; fax: (310) 342-7086; email: grants@ierf.org
Internet http://www.ierf.org/grants.asp
Sponsor International Education Research Foundation
P.O. Box 3665
Culver City, CA 90231-3665

IES Scholarships **2369**
The institute offers financial aid to students studying for a semester or full year at one of its centers abroad. IES centers are located in Durham, London, Freiburg, Berlin, Dijon, Dublin, Madrid, Milan, Nantes, Paris, Salamanca, and Vienna. Asian programs are located in Adelaide, Beijing, Nagoya, and Tokyo. South American programs are located in La Plata, Argentina. Most financial aid is awarded on the basis of need and scholarship and is applied to the comprehensive fee for the appropriate program. Competitive merit awards are also made to students for all programs. Scholarships are available in the areas of international business, urban issues, science, foreign languages, fine and performing arts, international relations, cross-cultural and comparative studies, leadership, and community involvement; special scholarships are available for study in Beijing, Dijon, Nantes, and Tokyo. Go to Web site or write for application materials and deadlines for various scholarships.
Requirements Candidates must be accepted to an IES/IAS study abroad program.
Amount $1 million total per year
Contact Scholarships, (800) 995-2300 or (312) 944-1750; fax: (312) 944-1448; email: info@IESabroad.org
Internet http://www.iesabroad.org/info/finaid.html
Sponsor Institute for the International Education of Students (IES)
33 N LaSalle St, 15th Fl
Chicago, IL 60602

IFP/MSP McKnight Artist Fellowships for Filmmakers **2370**
IFP Minnesota in partnership with the McKnight Foundation awards fellowships to two Minnesota filmmakers annually. These fellowships recognize Minnesota artists for talent in working with film/video as demonstrated by two examples of completed, original works in any of the genres and formats of narrative, documentary, experimental, or animation in feature or short lengths. The program is intended to support mid-career artists by providing financial assistance, professional encouragement, and industry recognition. Work examples and application material are judged by a panel of industry professionals from outside the state of Minnesota. Judges look for consistent artistic excellence and merit, clarity and uniqueness of vision, professional quality in the technical aspects of production, and demonstrable, sustained growth in the artist's career. Additionally, judges assess the ability of the artist to present their application in an articulate and professional manner. Guidelines are available online.
Amount $25,000
Date(s) Application Is Due Feb 3.
Contact McKnight Filmmakers Fellowships, email: cmick@ifpmsp.org or word@ifpmsp.org
Internet http://www.ifp.org/common/page.php?ref=grants
Sponsor IFP Minneapolis/Saint Paul
2446 University Ave W, Ste 100
St Paul, MN 55114

IFP/MSP McKnight Artist Fellowships for Screenwriters **2371**
IFP Minnesota in partnership with the McKnight Foundation awards fellowships to two Minnesota screenwriters annually. These fellowships recognize Minnesota artists for talent in writing for the screen as demonstrated by one completed feature-length screenplay. The program is intended to support mid-career writers by providing financial assistance, professional encouragement, and industry recognition. Screenplays and application material are judged by two panels of industry professionals from outside the state of Minnesota. In addition to the monetary award, the winners receive entrance into the IFP Market in New York, as well as a live reading on stage at the Jungle Theater in Minneapolis with professional actors. Screenplays and applicants are judged on originality of ideas and uniqueness of writer's voice, skillful story structure, talent with creating dialog, and talent with character development. Guidelines are available online.
Restrictions The following are ineligible: organizations and companies; full-time and part-time students in any film-, video- or screenwriting-related degree program; screenplays associated with a degree-granting program; and employees of IFP/MSP or the McKnight Foundation. Fellows cannot attend school full time during the fellowship year. The screenplay may not be an adaptation of any previously written performed or filmed work by another artist; or have been submitted to the fellowship more than three times previously, under any title.
Amount $25,000
Date(s) Application Is Due Feb 3.
Contact Christopher Mick, McKnight Screenwriters Fellowships, email: cmick@ifpmsp.org or word@ifpmsp.org
Internet http://www.ifp.org/common/page.php?ref=grants
Sponsor IFP Minneapolis/Saint Paul
2446 University Ave W, Ste 100
St Paul, MN 55114

IFP/New York Anthony Radziwill Documentary Fund **2372**
The fund provides grants to emerging and established documentary filmmakers in the form of development funds (seed money) for specific new projects. Administered by IFP/New York, the fund seeks to provide funding for independent nonfiction filmmakers at the earliest stage of new work, traditionally a difficult point at which to secure funding. Grants will be awarded to documentary projects that are seeking funds needed for research, treatment and script development, initial interviews and shooting,

the production of trailers/clips for further funding needs, etc. Typically a grant will be seed money, though in some cases it could be a supplement to another initial small grant. Application and guidelines are available online.
Requirements Grants are given to individuals with creative and financial control on the project. The grantee must be a US legal resident 18 years of age or older. Grants are for nonfiction projects intended to be: feature length (over 50 minutes); for general audiences; and primarily for wide distribution via theatrical, television, and festival markets.
Restrictions The following are not eligible: international projects for which neither the producer nor director is a legal US resident; projects by students in undergraduate or graduate degree programs, or for fulfillment of any course requirement by nonmatriculated students; projects intended primarily for the educational or industrial markets or for promotional purposes; projects for which film or video is not the primary artistic component (work designed to accompany a larger theater piece or multimedia installation); individuals and immediate family members who are employees of any IFP chapter, or currently serving as evaluators, panelists, or on the fund advisory committee; and grantees who have received funding from the fund for any grant cycle within the previous two-year period.
Date(s) Application Is Due Mar 1; Sep 1.
Contact Fund Administrator, (212) 465-8200 ext 830
Internet http://market.ifp.org/newyork/docfund
Sponsor IFP/New York
104 E 29th St, 12th Fl
New York, NY 10001

IFT Foundation Grants 2373
The foundation awards funding in science communications and career guidance. Science communications delivers the scientific perspective on food issues to media, policy makers, allied societies, and members. Priority topics include food safety, biotechnology, diet and health, food labeling, food and the environment, and support for research in food science and technology. Career guidance includes educational videos on food science and food science careers. Funds available for distribution by the foundation vary yearly. It is recommended that applicants contact the foundation prior to preparing a proposal. The intent of the foundation is to serve as a catalyst to establish programs rather than a permanent funding source for programs.
Contact Tekla Syers, Director of Foundation Development, (312) 782-8424; email: tasyers@ift.org
Internet http://www.ift.org/cms/?pid=1000260
Sponsor Institute of Food Technologists Foundation
525 W Van Buren St, Ste 1000
Chicago, IL 60601

Ignacio Martin-Baro Fund for Mental Health and Human Rights Grants 2374
The organization supports children's programs in health and mental health and is a resource for advocacy, education, prevention, service, and action research. The fund has a strong preference for projects that are developing innovative and progressive ways to deal with the mental health consequences of violence and political repression. Applicants should understand that the foundation does not view mental health and human rights as issues that can be addressed separately, but are seeking to fund activities that explore the links between them. Groups with budgets under $25,000 receive priority consideration. The listed application deadline applies to letters of interest; full proposals are by invitation.
Amount $7000 maximum
Date(s) Application Is Due Sep 1.
Contact Grants Administrator, (617) 469-7454; fax: (617) 469-3379; email: apply@martinbarofund.org
Internet http://www.martinbarofund.org/contact/applying.htm
Sponsor Ignacio Mart'n-Bar' Fund for Mental Health and Human Rights
P.O. Box 2122
Jamaica Plain, MA 02130

IHS Filmmaking and Writing Scholarships 2375
Scholarships up to $10,000 in tuition and stipend will be awarded to support students who: are pursuing a Master of Fine Arts (MFA) degree in filmmaking, fiction writing, or playwriting; have a demonstrated interest in classical liberal ideas and their application in contemporary society; and demonstrate the desire, motivation, and creative ability to succeed in their chosen profession. In recognition of the important role that films and novels play in the world of ideas, IHS provides support to promising young filmmakers and writers who share an appreciation for the potential and promise of a free society.
Amount $10,000 maximum
Date(s) Application Is Due Jan 14.
Contact Scholarship Administrator, (800) 697-8799 or (703) 993-4880; fax: (703) 993-4890
Internet http://www.theihs.org/subcategory.php/15.html
Sponsor Institute for Humane Studies
3301 N Fairfax Dr, Ste 440
Arlington, VA 22201

IHS Humane Studies Fellowships 2376
The institute awards fellowships to support the studies of excellent students who have demonstrated an interest in the classical liberal tradition of individual liberties and free markets. The program is open to graduate students and advanced undergraduates pursuing degrees in the social sciences, humanities, jurisprudence, journalism, and related fields. The disciplines of law and business also are eligible if students intend intellectual careers. Application forms are available on the Web site. Annual deadline dates may vary; contact the institute for exact dates.
Requirements Graduate and advanced undergraduate students enrolled at accredited colleges or universities in the United States or abroad who are intending academic or other intellectual careers, including public policy and journalism, are eligible.
Amount $12,000 maximum
Contact Humane Studies Fellowships, (703) 993-4880 or (800) 697-8799; fax: (703) 993-4890; email: ihs@gmu.edu
Internet http://www.theihs.org/subcategory.php/2.html
Sponsor Institute for Humane Studies
3301 N Fairfax Dr, Ste 440
Arlington, VA 22201-4432

IHS Native American and Alaskan Native Health Research Centers 2377
The purpose of this program is to establish centers that would encourage research on diseases that affect Native American populations and other health issues of importance to tribes and tribal organizations. Funds may be used to reduce health disparities that affect Native Americans and Alaskan Natives, train scientists and health professionals, help encouraging partnerships among health organizations, and for health research. A letter of intent is requested by October 1; full application is due by December 12. Annual deadline dates may vary; contact program staff for exact dates. RFA: GM-00-007
Requirements Federally recognized tribes, tribal consortia, and nonprofit Indian health organizations are eligible to apply.
Amount $27,000-$300,000; $115,000 average
Date(s) Application Is Due Oct 1; Dec 12.
Contact Lois Hodge, Grants Management Officer, (301) 443-5204
Internet http://www.ihs.gov
Sponsor Indian Health Service
12300 Twinbrook Plz
Rockville, MD 29852

IIE Cintas Fellowships 2378
Administered for Cintas Foundation by IIE, these fellowships are intended to acknowledge demonstrated creative accomplishments and to encourage the professional development of talented creative artists in the fields of visual arts, including film installation, art, painting, photography, sculpture, and other plastic arts. Each year fellowships are offered in different artistic disciplines. Fellows are free to pursue their arts activities either in the United States or in other countries approved by Cintas Foundation.
Requirements Eligibility is limited to professionals in the arts who are of Cuban citizenship or lineage (at least one parent a Cuban) living outside of Cuba and who have completed their academic and technical training.
Restrictions Individuals wishing to pursue academic programs are not eligible for awards nor are performing artists as opposed to creative artists. The fellowships, under ordinary circumstances, are not awarded more than twice to the same person.
Amount $10,000
Date(s) Application Is Due Mar 10.
Contact US Student Programs Division, (212) 984-5330; fax: (212) 984-5325; email: cintas@iie.org
Internet http://www.iie.org/Template.cfm?&Template=/programs/fulbright/cintas/default.htm
Sponsor Institute of International Education
809 United Nations Plz
New York, NY 10017

IIE Professional Development Fellowships 2379
Support is provided for young American researchers in professional, policy, and public administration-related fields who want to develop specialized knowledge of East Central Europe, the Baltic States, and the New Independent States (NIS). Candidates may apply for grants to Albania, Armenia, Azerbaijan, Belarus, Bulgaria, Croatia, Estonia, Georgia, Kazakhstan, Kyrgyzstan, Latvia, Lithuania, Macedonia, Moldova, Romania, Russia, Slovak Republic,Tajikistan, Turkmenistan, Ukraine, or Uzbekistan. The program is intended to support young specialists in the fields of business and economics, law, journalism, public administration, and international relations. Grants are available for periods of three to seven months. No provisions will be made for fellows' dependents. Round-trip international airfare, monthly living stipend, insurance, and book and travel allowance are provided. Annual deadline dates may vary; contact program staff for exact dates.
Requirements Applicants must be US citizens and be at least in the second (or terminal) year of a graduate or professional degree program, have graduated within five years from a graduate or professional degree program, or have language ability sufficient to carry out the proposed project by the time of departure from the United States.
Restrictions Fellows may not receive any other Title VIII support during the fellowship tenure.
Date(s) Application Is Due Mar 15.
Contact US Student Programs Division, (212) 984-5326; fax: (212) 984-5325; email: pdfnis@iie.org
Internet http://www.iie.org/pgms/pdfnis

Sponsor Institute of International Education
809 United Nations Plaza
New York, NY 10017

IIPP Graduate Fellowship **2380**
The program supports graduate education toward a masters degree in international affairs or a related field. Fellows apply to and enroll in the nation's leading graduate programs, most members of the Association of Professional Schools of International Affairs (APSIA). Participating graduate schools provide monetary support over the course of a two-year program. IIPP, in turn, provides each of its fellows with a matching grant to be applied in accordance with an agreement between IIPP and the institution the fellow attends.
Requirements To date, IIPP fellows have enrolled at the following institutions: American University, Columbia University, Georgetown University, George Washington University, Harvard University, Johns Hopkins University, Princeton University, Syracuse University, Tufts University, University of Denver, University of Maryland, University of Michigan, University of Washington, and Yale University. Non-APSIA schools include Cornell University, Pepperdine University, New York University, and the Bush School at Texas A&M.
Amount $15,000 matching grants ($30,000 total)
Date(s) Application Is Due Mar 15.
Contact Fellowship Administrator, (800) 530-6232 or (703) 205-7623; fax: (703) 205-7645
Internet http://161.58.87.106/content/program.cfm#grad
Sponsor Institute for International Public Policy
2750 Prosperity Ave, Ste 600
Fairfax, VA 22031

Ildaura Murillo-Rohde Scholarships **2381**
The association awards these scholarships for tuition to outstanding Hispanic associate, diploma, baccalaureate, or graduate students. Recipients will be selected on the basis of potential to graduate, current academic standing in an accredited school of nursing (minimum 3.0 GPA), potential for contribution to the profession, and financial need. The amount awarded each year depends on the availability of funds.
Requirements An applicant must be currently enrolled in an accredited school of nursing and be a US citizen or legal resident of the United States, Puerto Rico, or the US territories. Applicant must be a member of the association.
Date(s) Application Is Due Apr 30.
Contact Scholarships, (202) 387-2477; fax: (202) 483-7183; email: info@thehispanicnurses.org
Internet http://www.thehispanicnurses.org
Sponsor National Association of Hispanic Nurses
1501 16th St NW
Washington, DC 20036

Illinois Arts Council Arts-in-Education Residency Artists Roster Program **2382**
The IAC AIE Residency Program provides support to primary and secondary educational institutions, community colleges, and not-for-profit local arts and community organizations to work with an individual artist from one month to six months. Residencies involving performing artist companies range from two weeks to six months.
Requirements Artists who conduct these residencies must be listed in the current IAC AIE Residency Program Artists Roster. Applicant must be a professional artist in the disciplines of creative writing, dance, interdisciplinary arts, media, music, theater, or visual arts or a performing arts company in the disciplines of dance, music, theater, or interdisciplinary arts.
Restrictions Applicant may not be enrolled in a degree or certification granting program of any kind between October 1, 2008 – August 31, 2010.
Date(s) Application Is Due Jan 16.
Contact Arts-in-Education Program staff, (312) 814-6780; email: iac.aie@illinois.gov
Internet http://www.state.il.us/agency/iac/Guidelines/guidelines.htm#aieroster
Sponsor Illinois Arts Council
James R. Thompson Center; 100 W. Randolph Street, Suite 10-500
Chicago, IL 60601-3298

Illinois Schoolyard Habitat Action Grants **2383**
The program is a means of funding for teachers and students who are interested in creating or enhancing schoolyard habitat areas. Examples include: trail development; vegetation planting; designing, establishing and maintaining a schoolyard prairie plot; butterfly garden; watering station; designing and building a bird feeder or feeding station. Guidelines are available online.
Requirements Schools, nature centers, and youth groups may apply. Although not required, it is preferred that an educator trained in either Project WILD, Learning Tree or WET be involved with the project (contact the Illinois Department of Natural Resources, Educational Services Section at (217) 524-4126) or visit http://dnr.state.il.us.
Restrictions Funding cannot be used for consultant fees, bird seed, fuel, equipment (shovels, rakes, trowels), labor, books, web site development, or land acquisition.
Amount $300 average; $600 maximum
Date(s) Application Is Due Oct 15.
Contact Grants Administrator, (217) 782-6232; email: dnr.grants@illinois.gov
Internet http://dnr.state.il.us/lands/education/CLASSRM/Grants/Brochure.htm
Sponsor Illinois Department of Natural Resources
One Natural Resources Way
Springfield, IL 62702-1271

Illinois Space Grant Consortium (ISGC) Graduate Fellowships **2384**
These graduate fellowships support outstanding graduate students pursuing aerospace, space science, Earth system science and other interdisciplinary space-related science, engineering or mathematics fields. A total of up to $80,000 is available for fellowship awards each academic year. Individual awards will range from $5,000 to $10,000. Deadline for submission is February 2, with awards being announced by February 22.
Requirements Applicants must have: U.S. citizenship; full-time current enrollment at an ISGC institution; a minimum 3.0 to 4.0 GPA; a good academic record; and research or design experience in a field related to space or aerospace.
Amount $5,000 - $10,000
Date(s) Application Is Due Feb 2.
Contact Diane Jeffers, Associate Director; (217) 244-8048; fax: (217) 244-0720; email: dejeffer@uiuc.edu
Internet http://www.ae.uiuc.edu/ISGC/funding/grad-fellowship.html
Sponsor Illinois Space Grant Consortium (ISGC)
306 Talbot Laboratory, 104 South Wright Street
Urbana, IL 61801-2935

Illinois Space Grant Consortium (ISGC) Individual Undergraduate Research Project Grants **2385**
These grants are designed to facilitate undergraduate participation in research in aerospace engineering, space or Earth system science at ISGC institutions. Awards of up to $4,000 will be allocated. The objective of this grant is to encourage undergraduate participation in research. The majority of requested funds must be used for undergraduate student stipends. A small amount may be used for salary, supplies, and travel support. Proposals will be reviewed by a ISGC Review Panel and selected based on adherence to the described criteria, scientific merit, and equitable distribution of resources across the Consortium. Deadline for submission is February 2, with awards being announced by February 22.
Requirements The undergraduate student must be a US citizen or permanent resident, and be identified in the proposal. The grants are available to faculty members or research scientists at all ISGC institutions. Grants must be matched (at least one-to-one) with funds from non-federal sources. The source of matching funds must be identified and confirmed by a letter from the appropriate authority. Waived indirect costs and faculty effort can qualify as matching funds. Women, under-represented minorities and persons with disabilities are encouraged to apply.
Restrictions Funds cannot be used for the purchase of equipment.
Amount $4,000 maximum
Date(s) Application Is Due Feb 2.
Contact Diane Jeffers, Associate Director; (217) 244-8048; fax: (217) 244-0720; email: dejeffer@uiuc.edu
Internet http://www.ae.uiuc.edu/ISGC/funding/ind-ug.html
Sponsor Illinois Space Grant Consortium (ISGC)
306 Talbot Laboratory, 104 South Wright Street
Urbana, IL 61801-2935

Illinois Space Grant Consortium (ISGC) Multiple Undergraduate Research Program Grants **2386**
These grants are designed to fund programs of undergraduate research in aerospace engineering, space or Earth system science at ISGC institutions. The objective of this grant is to encourage undergraduate participation in research. Proposals can include requests for salary, supplies, and travel support. The program should involve multiple students working with multiple research advisors. The grants are available to faculty members or research scientists at all ISGC institutions. A total of $140,000 has been allocated to these grants.
Requirements The undergraduate students must be US citizens or permanent residents. Grants must be matched (at least one-to-one) with funds from non-federal sources. The source of matching funds must be identified and confirmed by a letter from the appropriate authority. Waived indirect costs and faculty effort can qualify as matching funds. Women, under-represented minorities and persons with disabilities are encouraged to apply. Participation in this program is limited to faculty (research and professorial) at ISGC affiliate and lead institutions.
Restrictions ISGC funds cannot be used for the purchase of equipment.
Date(s) Application Is Due Feb 2.
Contact Diane Jeffers, Associate Director; (217) 244-8048; fax: (217) 244-0720; email: dejeffer@uiuc.edu
Internet http://www.ae.uiuc.edu/ISGC/funding/multi-undergrad.html
Sponsor Illinois Space Grant Consortium (ISGC)
306 Talbot Laboratory, 104 South Wright Street
Urbana, IL 61801-2935

Illinois Space Grant Consortium (ISGC) Research Seed Grants **2387**
These seed grants are designed to facilitate the development of research expertise in aerospace engineering/space science at ISGC institutions and allow the award recipients to obtain the preliminary results needed to support larger proposals to other federal or non-federal funding agencies. The objective of this grant is to support new areas

of research. Selected proposals may reapply for a second year of funding. Proposals can include requests for salary, supplies, and travel support. Waived indirect costs and faculty effort can qualify as matching funds. The grants are available to faculty members or research scientists at all ISGC institutions. A total of $40,000 has been allocated to these grants for the period March 1 to February 29. The funding level of each seed grant is up to $10,000. Proposals will be reviewed by a ISGC Review Panel and selected based on adherence to the described criteria, scientific merit, and equitable distribution of resources across the Consortium. Deadline for submission is February 2, with awards being announced by February 22.
Requirements Seed grant must support research in an area of interest to NASA (aerospace engineering, space or Earth system science). Grants must be matched (at least one-to-one) with funds from non-federal sources. The source of matching funds must be identified and confirmed by a letter from the appropriate authority. Women, under-represented minorities and persons with disabilities are encouraged to apply. Participation in this program is limited to faculty (research and professorial) at ISGC affiliate and lead institutions.
Restrictions Funds cannot be used for the purchase of equipment.
Amount $10,000 maximum
Date(s) Application Is Due Feb 2.
Contact Diane Jeffers, Associate Director; (217) 244-8048; fax: (217) 244-0720; email: dejeffer@uiuc.edu
Internet http://www.ae.uiuc.edu/ISGC/funding/seedgrant.html
Sponsor Illinois Space Grant Consortium (ISGC)
306 Talbot Laboratory, 104 South Wright Street
Urbana, IL 61801-2935

Illinois Space Grant Consortium (ISGC) Undergraduate Scholarships **2388**
Scholarships support outstanding undergraduate students pursuing aerospace, space science, Earth system science and other interdisciplinary space-related science, engineering or mathematics fields. A total of up to $70,000 is available for scholarship awards each academic year. Individual awards of approximately $2,500 per scholarship will be made. Award winners will be chosen based on student qualifications, scientific and educational relevance of the proposed activity, faculty member's expressed commitment to the project, and the application. Deadline for submission is February 2, with awards being announced by February 22.
Requirements Applicants must have: U.S. citizenship; full-time current enrollment at an ISGC institution; a minimum 2.5 to 4.0 GPA; a good academic standing; and participation in an extra-curricular activity (i.e. Design/Build/Fly project, outreach, research, etc.). Women, under-represented minorities, and persons with disabilities are strongly encouraged to apply.
Amount $2,500
Date(s) Application Is Due Feb 2.
Contact Diane Jeffers, Associate Director; (217) 244-8048; fax: (217) 244-0720; email: dejeffer@uiuc.edu
Internet http://www.ae.uiuc.edu/ISGC/funding/undergrad-scholarship.html
Sponsor Illinois Space Grant Consortium (ISGC)
306 Talbot Laboratory, 104 South Wright Street
Urbana, IL 61801-2935

IMLS 21st Century Museum Professionals Grants **2389**
The 21st Century Museum Professionals program supports a range of activities, including professional training in all areas of museum operations and leadership development. This program provides the museum community with support for a variety of training and personnel development activities for museum staff members across all types of museums, as well as the collection and dissemination of information to museum professionals and the public. Project design could include direct dissemination of information through workshops, seminars, and courses, or indirect communication through publications and Web sites. Projects should benefit multiple institutions or diverse constituencies.
Requirements Museums that fulfill the Eligibility Criteria for Museums may apply. Private not-for-profit museum services organizations or associations that engage in activities designed to advance the well-being of museums and the museum profession also may apply. In addition, institutions of higher education, including public and not-for-profit universities, are eligible. Please see Program Guidelines for specific eligibility criteria.
Amount $15,000 - $500,000
Date(s) Application Is Due Mar 15.
Contact Christopher J. Reich, Senior Program Officer, 202-653-4685; email: creich@imls.gov
Internet http://www.imls.gov/applicants/grants/21centuryMuseums.shtm
Sponsor Institute of Museum and Library Services
1800 M Street NW, 9th Floor
Washington, DC 20036-5802

IMLS Conservation Project Support Grants **2390**
The grants provide matching funds to help museums identify conservation needs and priorities and perform activities to ensure the safekeeping of their collections. Projects may assess four types of collections: nonliving, systematics/natural history, living plants, and living animals. Grants are available for different types of conservation projects, such as environmental improvements, research, surveys and long-range plans, training, and treatment. Projects may not exceed two years. IMLS will pay up to one-half the cost of the project. A museum's matching funds must come from cash contributions, earned income, in-kind contributions, or nonfederal funds. This program also funds Exceptional Projects. These are projects with broad-reaching effects that benefit multiple institutions. The November 1 deadline apples to programs for museums in counties of Alabama, Florida, Louisiana, and Mississippi that have been declared disaster areas by the federal government. Application and guidelines are available online.
Requirements Museums located in one of the 50 states, the Commonwealth of Puerto Rico, American Samoa, the Virgin Islands, the Northern Mariana Islands, the Trust Territory of the Pacific Islands, Guam, or the District of Columbia may apply. Applicant organizations must have provided museum services, including exhibiting objects to the general public, on a regular basis for at least two years prior to application. A public or private nonprofit organization such as a municipality, college, or university that is responsible for the operation of a museum may, if necessary, apply on behalf of the museum.
Restrictions A museum operated by a department or agency of the federal government is not eligible to apply. Funds may not be used for the acquisition of objects, contributions to endowment funds, costs of social activities, major renovations, new construction, or preaward costs.
Amount $250,000 maximum
Date(s) Application Is Due Oct 1.
Contact Steven Shwartzman, Senior Program Officer, (202) 653-4641; fax: (202) 606-8591; email: sshwartzman@imls.gov
Internet http://www.imls.gov/applicants/grants/conservProject.shtm
Sponsor Institute of Museum and Library Services
1800 M Street NW, 9th Floor
Washington, DC 20036

IMLS Grants to State Library Administrative Agencies **2391**
Through the program, the Institute of Museum and Library Services provides funds to State Library Administrative Agencies (SLAAs) using a population-based formula. State libraries may use the appropriation to support statewide initiatives and services. They also may distribute the funds through subgrant competitions or cooperative agreements to public, academic, research, school, and special libraries in their state.
Amount Based on state population
Date(s) Application Is Due Apr 1.
Contact George V. Smith, Associate Deputy Director, (202) 653-4650; email: stateprograms@imls.gov
Internet http://www.imls.gov/programs/programs.shtm
Sponsor Institute of Museum and Library Services
1800 M Street NW, 9th Floor
Washington, DC 20036-5802

IMLS Laura Bush 21st Century Librarian Program Grants **2392**
The program supports efforts to recruit and educate the next generation of librarians and the faculty who will prepare them for careers in library science. It also supports grants for research related to library education and library staffing needs, curriculum development, and continuing education and training. Program priorities are masters-level programs, doctoral programs, preprofessional programs, research, programs to build institutional capacity, and continuing education and training. The grant period is up to three years, except doctoral programs, which may be up to four years. Applications, guidelines, and examples of successful proposals are available online.
Requirements Beginning with the FY 2007 grant cycle, all applicants for the Laura Bush 21st Century Librarian program are required to file their applications, including all attachments, online through Grants.gov. All types of libraries, except federal and for-profit libraries, may apply. Eligible libraries include public, school, academic, special, private (not-for-profit), archives, library agencies, library consortia, and library associations. In addition, research libraries that give the public access to services and materials suitable for scholarly research not otherwise available to the public and that are not part of a university or college are eligible. Institutions of higher education, including public and not-for-profit universities and colleges, also are eligible. Graduate schools of library and information science may apply as part of an institution of higher education.
Amount $50,000-$1 million
Date(s) Application Is Due Dec 15.
Contact Stephanie Clark, Senior Program Officer, (202) 653-4662; email: sclark@imls.gov; Karmen Bisher, Program Specialist, (202) 653-4664; email: kbisher@imls.gov
Internet http://www.imls.gov/applicants/grants/21centuryLibrarian.shtm
Sponsor Institute of Museum and Library Services
1800 M Street NW, 9th Floor
Washington, DC 20036-5802

IMLS National Leadership Grants (NLG) **2393**
National Leadership Grants enable libraries and museums to help people gain the knowledge, skills, attitudes, behaviors, and resources that enhance their engagement in community, work, family, and society. Projects should enable libraries and museums to address current problems in creative ways, develop and test innovative solutions, and expand the boundaries within which cultural heritage institutions operate. The results of these projects will help equip tomorrow's libraries and museums to better meet the needs of a Nation of Learners. Successful proposals will show evidence that they will have national impact and generate results—new tools, research, models, services, practices, or alliances—that can be widely adapted or replicated to extend the benefit of federal

support. Proposals will reflect an understanding of current issues and needs, showing the potential for far-reaching impact throughout the museum and/or library community. Projects will provide creative solutions to issues of national importance and provide leadership for other organizations.
Requirements All types of libraries, except federal and for-profit libraries, may apply. Eligible libraries include public, school, academic, special, private (notfor- profit), archives, library agencies, library consortia, and library associations. Research libraries and archives that give the public access to services and materials suitable for scholarly research not otherwise available and that are not part of a university or college also are eligible. Digital libraries that make library materials publicly available and provide services including selection, organization, description, reference, and preservation under the supervision of at least one permanent professional staff librarian are eligible to apply. Institutions of higher education, including public and not-for-profit universities and colleges, also are eligible. An academic unit, such as a graduate school of library and information science, may apply as part of an institution of higher education. Library applicants may apply individually or as partners. Additionally, all types of museums, large and small, are eligible for funding. Eligible museums include aquariums, arboreta and botanical gardens, art museums, youth museums, general museums, historic houses and sites, history museums, nature centers, natural history and anthropology museums, planetariums, science and technology centers, specialized museums, and zoological parks. Private nonprofit museum services organizations or associations that engage in activities designed to advance the well-being of museums and the museum profession also may apply. In addition, institutions of higher education, including public and nonprofit universities, are eligible.
Amount $25,000-$1 million
Date(s) Application Is Due Mar 1.
Contact Martha Crawley, Senior Program Officer (libraries), (202) 653-4667; email: mcrawley@imls.gov; Dan Lukash, Senior Program Officer (museums), (202) 606-4644; fax: (202) 606-8591; email: dlukash@imls.gov
Internet http://www.imls.gov/applicants/grants/nationalLeadership.shtm
Sponsor Institute of Museum and Library Services
1800 M Street NW, 9th Floor
Washington, DC 20036-5802

Implant Dentistry Research and Education Foundation Grants **2394**
The objective of the grant is to encourage new investigators by providing seed or start-up funding for promising research projects. Grants support basic research and education relating to dental implants. Areas include, but are not limited to, biology, biochemistry, biomechanics, biomaterials, and molecular biology. Grants are awarded after thorough review by an independent scientific advisory board. Grant applications are available upon request.
Requirements The principal investigator or coprincipal investigator must hold an appropriate terminal degree. A dental resident or PhD candidate may apply if the appropriate department or division chair provides a letter confirming he/she is coming on staff the year a project is funded.
Amount $20,000-$25,000
Date(s) Application Is Due Jan 1.
Contact Craig Johnson, Executive Director, IDREF, (800) 442-0525 or (973) 783-6300; fax: (973) 783-1175; email: icoi@dentalimplants.com
Internet http://www.dentalimplants.com
Sponsor Implant Dentistry Research and Education Foundation
248 Lorraine Ave, #3
Upper Montclair, NJ 07043-1454

Inamori Foundation Kyoto Prize **2395**
The Kyoto Prize is awarded annually to persons who have made significant contributions in the three categories of Advanced Technology, Basic Sciences, and Arts and Philosophy. Through this Prize, the and groups worldwide Foundation seeks not only to recognize outstanding achievements but also to promote academic and cultural development and to contribute to mutual international understanding.
Amount 50 million yen
Contact Program Director, (075) 353-7272; fax: (075) 353-7270
Internet http://www.inamori-f.or.jp/e_fd_out_out.html
Sponsor Inamori Foundation
620 Suiginya-cho
Shimogyo-ku, Koyoto 600-8411
Japan

Inamori Foundation Research Grants **2396**
Through the Inamori Grants and other research funding, the Foundation supports a wide variety of activities by young researchers in Japan in the fields of natural sciences, humanities, and social sciences. It aims to cultivate and nurture human resourses who will contribute to the future of our global society, to promote academic and cultural development, and to contribute to international understanding. In the founder's own words, "It is my sincere hope that the activities of the Foundation contribute to the progress and development of humankind and thereby allow me to repay, in some way, my indebtedness to all those in my local community, in my country, and throughout the world who have helped make me and my company what they are today."
Requirements Must be a resident researcher living in Japan.
Contact Research Program Director, (075) 353-7272; fax: (075) 353-7270
Internet http://www.inamori-f.or.jp/e_fd_out_out.html
Sponsor Inamori Foundation
620 Suiginya-cho
Shimogyo-ku, Koyoto 600-8411
Japan

Independent Institute Olive W. Garvey Fellowship **2397**
The program awards fellowships to outstanding college students around the world through a competitive essay contest on the meaning and significance of economic and personal liberty. The program aims to encourage critical thinking and educational excellence by college students in examining the nature and relevance of human liberty. Fellowships are awarded in two categories: students up to age 35, and junior faculty members not yet tenured. The institute publishes the winning essays on its Web site and seeks to have them published elsewhere in major magazines and journals. Complete guidelines, an entry form, and additional information are available online.
Requirements College or university students who are part-time, full-time, undergraduate, graduate, and from all nations and academic disciplines are eligible. (Student must be enrolled on date of essay submission.) Students must be no older than 35 years. Junior faculty members must hold a position of assistant professor or higher, not yet tenured, and may not be older than 35 years.
Restrictions Previous fellowship recipients, judges, and current or past institute employees are ineligible.
Amount $2500 first prize, $1500 second prize, $1000 third prize to students; $10,000 first prize, $5000 second prize, $1500 third prize to junior faculty
Date(s) Application Is Due May 1.
Contact Carl Close, (510) 632-1366; fax: (510) 568-6040; email: CClose@independent.org
Internet http://www.independent.org/students/garvey
Sponsor Independent Institute
100 Swan Way
Oakland, CA 94621-1428

India Studies Language Training Fellowships **2398**
The institute, with funding from the Canadian International Development Agency, will award a number of language training fellowships for the summer term to students in Canadian universities. The fellowships are tenable at North American institutions in cities other than the one in which the student studied in the previous term and that offer training in the Indian language of choice.
Requirements Applicants must be Canadian citizens or permanent residents enrolled as full-time students in a Canadian university working toward a degree in the social sciences or the humanities (including management and law) with a substantial India studies or development studies component.
Amount $C2500
Date(s) Application Is Due Jun 30.
Contact Program Officer, (403) 220-7467; fax: (403) 289-0100; email: sici@ucalgary.ca
Internet http://www.ucalgary.ca/~sici/2004shastri/english/indiastudies.htm
Sponsor Shastri Indo-Canadian Institute
2500 University Dr NW
Calgary, AB T2N 1N4 Canada

Indian Council of Social Science Research Grants **2399**
The council funds research projects of scientists in the social sciences and sponsors projects on its own initiatives (e.g., research on the northeastern region of India, women's studies, and entrepreneurship). Types of support include research fellowships, contingency grants, grants for study and publications, and conferences and seminars. The council collaborates in research and exchange programs with a number of countries and evaluates research proposals submitted by foreign nationals intending to undertake research in India.
Contact Professor Andre Beteille, Chair, (0) 26179679; email: chairman@icssr.org
Internet http://www.icssr.org/rp_main.htm
Sponsor Indian Council of Social Science Research
35 Ferozeshah Rd
New Delhi 110 001
India

Indiana 21st Century Research and Technology Fund Awards **2400**
The Indiana 21st Century Research and Technology Fund of the Indiana Economic Development Corporation (IEDC) is open to proposals from all public and private entities for technology-based commercialization activities encompassing science/technology creation, innovation, and transfer intended to have commercial impacts. The fund intends to increase the numbers, and rates of development, of new and expanding technology-based companies by funding promising opportunities that, in some cases, the financial markets might find too risky. The Fund makes awards in two broad categories: Science and Technology Commercialization and Centers of Excellence. In addition, the Fund provides cost-share on behalf of Federal proposals submitted by Indiana-based entities. Generally awards are made in multiples of $50,000 up to $2,000,000. Support for awards in excess of $2,000,000 will be rare.
Requirements The IEDC defines a technology-based company as one that is involved in transferring advanced technology into products, developing technologies with the near-term intention of creating products, or using new or advanced technologies in its design,

development, and/or manufacturing of products. The Fund emphasizes the creation of academic-sector - commercial-sector partnerships. In making awards, the Fund expects significant leverage from the partners involved in the projects. Important: before applying, contact Fund staff (email preferred) to discuss your interest in submitting a proposal and to discuss your technology and commercialization goals. While not a review criterion, the fund encourages the inclusion of interns from any academic institution, or participating commercial sector partner, in order to increase project-related involvement of students at all levels.
Restrictions Only direct costs will be supported. Institutions will not be provided indirect (overhead) cost support. Entities with previous Fund awards that are not current with regard to financial or technical reporting requirements will be disqualified from making new submissions to the Fund. Resubmissions of previously declined proposals will be considered only if substantive changes have been made to the proposal. Fund staff will determine whether to review resubmissions.
Amount $500,000 - $2,000,000
Contact Linda Peterson-Roe; (317) 234-4652; email: lpeterson-roe@iedc.in.gov
Internet http://www.21fund.org/
Sponsor Indiana Economic Development Corporation
One North Capitol Avenue, Suite 900
Indianapolis, IN 46204

Indiana Library Federation Graduate Scholarships **2401**
The purpose of the program is to give financial assistance upon availability of funding, in the form of scholarship grants, for library science education to candidates who give sufficient evidence of possessing exceptional talent for librarianship and who show economic need. Scholarship may be used at any ALA-accredited graduate library education program for the master's degree in library science (MLS).
Requirements A recipient must be a legal resident of Indiana; must accept employment in an Indiana library within three months after completing library education; and must continue to work in an Indiana school or a public or university/college library for at least one year.
Amount $1000 maximum
Date(s) Application Is Due Jan 2.
Contact Jason Gilbert, Program Manager, (317) 257-2040; fax: (317) 257-1389; email: jgilbert@ilfonline.org
Internet http://www.ilfonline.org/Scholarship.htm
Sponsor Indiana Library Federation
941 E 86th St, Ste 260
Indianapolis, IN 46220

Indiana SBIR/STTR Commercialization Enhancement Program **2402**
ISCEP provides funds to enhance commercialization activities of Indiana-based SBIR/STTR (Small Business Innovation Research/Small Business Technology Transfer) awardees. Specific ISCEP goals include: Support of thoughtfully structured commercialization plans of SBIR/STTR Phase II awardees; Accelerate and enhance commercial impacts of SBIR/STTR technologies, and; Establish and enhance successful technology-based businesses in Indiana. Proposals will be accepted from a small business that has received a federal Phase II SBIR or STTR and at least 50% of the federal program dollars must be expended prior to submission of a proposal in response to the RFP. Review considers both the technology development stage and the related business plan. The final stage of review involves a presentation to the IEDC. Between two and four awards of up to $350,000 may be made per funding cycle. The awards will be made with performance periods of up to 2 years and are contingent on the availability of funds.
Requirements Eligible applicants must have a principal place of business in Indiana and the benefits from commercialization must accrue to an Indiana small business. Applicants must be a small business that has received a federal Phase II SBIR or STTR and at least 50% of the federal program dollars must be expended prior to submission of a proposal in response to the RFP, because an essential metric used in judging suitability for an award will involve assessing current progress toward achievement of Phase II objectives. The technology being commercialized must be directly related to the technology funded under the SBIR or STTR Phase II award. There is no limit as to the number of proposals that a single company can submit. However, only one award per company will be made per RFP cycle. The RFP, proposal tips and application are available at the website.
Restrictions Awardees must maintain a principal place of business in Indiana for a term of 10 years beginning on the effective date of the agreement. Successful applicants must adhere to specific reporting requirements, including: quarterly progress reports, annual reports, annual site visits and a final report.
Amount $350,000 maximum
Date(s) Application Is Due Jul 20.
Contact Brooke Pyne, Director, SBIR/STTR Program; office: (812) 384-3078; mobile: (812) 381-0350; fax: (812) 384-3487; email: bpyne@iedc.in.gov
Internet http://www.in.gov/iedc/sbir/index.html
Sponsor Indiana Economic Development Corporation
SBIR/STTR Program Office, 32 E. Main St.
Bloomfield, IN 47424

Indiana Waste Tire Fund (WTF) Program Grants **2403**
The Indiana Waste Tire Fund (WTF) Program was created to help Indiana businesses undertake research, development, and/or commercial manufacturing projects that develop markets for use of scrap tires. Funds are made available through grants of up to $100,000 with a 50% match requirement are available for innovative research and development projects. Key elements include project partnerships and technology transfer. Provisions will be made for confidentiality of proprietary information.
Requirements Eligible applicants are limited to Indiana businesses and not-for-profits. Interested applicants must contact OPPTA (Office of Pollution Prevention and Technical Assistance) to receive a grant application. Activities that may be funded through the program include the following: Civil engineering applications using shredded tires; Asphalt-rubber applications using ground rubber; Development of advanced technology and processes for production of products from scrap tires and; Tire-derived-fuel.
Restrictions Projects must take place within the state of Indiana.
Amount $100,000 maximum
Contact Call 800-988-7901 to find the Regional Grant Representative in your area.; email: recycling@idem.in.gov
Internet http://www.in.gov/recycle/funding/wtf.html
Sponsor Indiana Department of Environmental Management (IDEM)
Office of Pollution Prevention and Technical Assistance, 100 North Senate Avenue, MC 64-01
Indianapolis, IN 46204-2251

Infinity Foundation Grants **2404**
The foundation awards grants in a broad array of areas including charitable, scientific, religious, educational, and holistic healing activities by organizations and public agencies that work to better the lives of people. Grants also support individuals' research and development of educational materials to improve the authenticity of the portrayal of Indic traditions in the educational system. Proposed projects could result in one or more of the following: books, curriculum development, articles, conferences, CD-Roms, digital slide shows, Internet presentations, and audio/video materials. Topics covered may include philosophy, history, religion, science, art, and sociology, as they pertain to the educational curricula on Indic traditions. Proposals should be submitted by email.
Requirements Grantee may be a scholar, teacher, visionary, or spiritual leader whose work in the designated topics would be enhanced by a foundation grant.
Contact Rajiv Malhotra, (609) 683-0548; fax: (609) 683-0478; email: rm.infinity@gmail.com
Internet http://www.infinityfoundation.com/callforgrantproposals.htm
Sponsor Infinity Foundation
66 Witherspoon Street, Suite 400
Princeton, NJ 08542

Informix for Innovation Software Grants **2405**
The program objective is to provide education institutions around the world and nonprofit institutions in the United States free access to the world's leading database technology. The Informix for Innovation Educational Grant Program offers educators the opportunity to use the latest technology as a teaching tool in the classroom and as an engine for academic research. Software is provided to encourage breakthroughs in technology and the development of next-generation data management applications. The Informix for Innovation Philanthropic Grant Program awards grants to US nonprofits to help the organizations deliver their messages and information to further their cause. Projects should directly contribute to the nonprofit organization's vision and be visible to the public. Most software grants are for the development and enhancement of Web sites. The grant includes software, support, and training.
Requirements The project or organization must be located in a community where Informix has a business presence. The project must be highly visible in the organization and the community and must have a projected time span, specific goals, and measurable results. Nonprofit organizations must be located in the United States.
Amount $30,000 average
Contact Amy Fenstermaker, Grant Programs Manager, (510) 628-3932; fax: (510) 628-3951; email: grants@informix.com
Internet http://www-306.ibm.com/software/data/informix
Sponsor Informix Software Inc
300 Lakeside Dr, Ste 2700
Oakland, CA 94612

Innovations Deserving Exploratory Analysis (IDEA) Program Grants **2406**
The Transportation Research Board of the National Research Council funds projects testing innovative highway and intelligent transportation technologies and products. IDEA projects should examine the feasibility of innovative concepts or review new applications of advanced technologies or products from other industries that could be converted to transportation use. Requests for support may be submitted at any time. Applications are reviewed after March 31 and September 30 each year. Program announcements are posted on the Web site as are contacts for each area.
Requirements US and international investigators, businesses, universities, and research institutions may apply.
Amount $25,000-$250,000
Date(s) Application Is Due Mar 1; Sep 1.
Contact Debbie Irvin, IDEA Administrative Assistant, (202) 334-3310; email: dirvin@nas.edu or ideaprogram@nas.edu
Internet http://www4.trb.org/trb/dive.nsf/web/idea_programs
Sponsor National Research Council
500 Fifth St NW, Keck Ctr, WS 401
Washington, DC 20001

Innovative Technology Development Award Program 2407

The center annually funds biotechnology research projects that promise development of commercializable technologies. In this way, the center aims to further establish and strengthen ties between academic scientists and industry. Grants are for one year, with a continuation seed grant offered for the second and third year if necessary. Proposals are evaluated based on the quality of the science, the commercial potential, and how the project might impact New York state economy. Applications are posted on the Web site or are available by fax or mail.

Requirements Faculty at any New York state research institution may apply for an ITD award.

Amount $40,000-$80,000

Contact Dr. Anil Dhundale, Director of Scientific Affairs, (516) 632-8521; fax: (516) 632-8577; email: anil.dhundale@sunysb.edu

Internet http://www.biotech.sunysb.edu/techDev/ITD/index.html

Sponsor Center for Biotechnology
Psychology A Bldg, 3rd Fl, SUNY Stony Brook
Stony Brook, NY 11794-5208

Institute Award for Excellence in Industrial Gases Technology 2408

Sponsored by Praxair Inc and administered by AIChE, the award is given to recognize sustained excellence in the contribution to the advancement of technology for the production, distribution, and application of industrial gases. The recipient of the award shall have a record of sustained contribution recognized for its impact on advancing the frontier of industrial gases technology. The contribution can be characterized by a sustained record of important fundamental research, innovation, technological development, or the novel application of technology, either fostering or leading to important commercial results. Recipients need not be members of the institute.

Requirements All members of AIChE as well as other interested persons are urged to nominate deserving candidates. All information and supporting documents are to be included with the completed form; nomination forms and instructions may be obtained from the institute.

Amount $3000 plus $500 travel allowance

Date(s) Application Is Due Feb 15.

Contact AIChE Awards Programs, (212) 591-7107; fax: (212) 591-8890; email: awards@aiche.org

Internet http://www.aiche.org/awards/awarddtl.asp?AwardID=59

Sponsor American Institute of Chemical Engineers
3 Park Ave
New York, NY 10016-5901

Institute for Advanced Studies in Culture Postdoctoral Fellowships 2409

The Institute supports research addressing the complex and dynamic relationship between religion and democratic ideals, institutions, and practices. Residential and nonresidential fellowships are available. Application materials and information are available online.

Requirements Applicants may be from any discipline, but must be working on a project concerned with religion and public life, and must have defended their dissertation by May 1.

Amount $35,000

Date(s) Application Is Due Jan 15.

Contact James Davison Hunter, Executive Director, (434) 924-7705; email: iasc@virginia.edu

Internet http://www.virginia.edu/iasc/programs.html

Sponsor University of Virginia
Institute for Advanced Studies in Culture, P.O. Box 400816
Charlottesville, VA 22904-4816

Institute for Ecumenical and Cultural Research Resident Scholars Program 2410

The institute is a postdoctoral residential research center for study, reflection, and writing, located on the campus of Saint John's Abbey and University. The institute encourages constructive and creative thought in theology and religious studies and, more generally, in the humanities, natural sciences, and social sciences as they relate to Christian tradition, including the interplay of Christianity and culture. Applicants may apply for a semester (September-December or January-May) or an entire academic year (September-May). Furnished apartments are provided for resident scholars and their families. Application materials are available upon request.

Requirements The resident scholars program is normally for persons who already have academic doctoral degrees. The Admissions Committee occasionally considers persons with other qualifications. Applicants without a doctoral degree should seek advice from the institute's executive director prior to applying.

Amount $3500 per year

Contact Program Contact, (320) 363-3366; fax: (320) 363-3313; email: iecr@iecr.org

Internet http://www.iecr.org/resident.htm

Sponsor Institute for Ecumenical and Cultural Research
P.O. Box 2000
Collegeville, MN 56321-2000

Institute for European History Research Fellowships 2411

The institute annually awards 20 fellowships to young historians from Europe and abroad for research on the history of occidental religion and the history of Europe from the 16th to 20th centuries. Fellows live and work at the institute; their rooms serve both as work and living quarters. An open-stack library provides fellows with over 195,000 volumes pertaining to their specialized fields. A separate reading room for periodical literature offers a recent selection of more than 550 journals and newspapers.

Requirements All fellows must have completed their undergraduate education. Candidates must have a thorough command of German and be either at the advanced stages of their dissertations or already in possession of their doctorates.

Contact Dr. Heinz Duchhardt, European History Awards, +49 6131 39 93 60; fax: +49 6131 23 79 88; email: ieg2@inst-euro-history.uni-mainz.de

Internet http://www.ieg-mainz.de/02-Zielsetzung/Index.htm

Sponsor Institute for European History (Institut fur Europaische Geschichte)
Alte Universitatstrasse 19
Mainz 55116 Germany

Institute for Palestine Studies, Publishing, and Research Organization Grants 2412

The institute operates in the United States, Lebanon, France, and Jerusalem and awards research grants on all aspects of the Palestine problem, including the history and development of Palestine, the Palestinian problem and the Arab-Israeli conflict, and possible ways of arriving at a peaceful resolution.

Contact Linda Butler, Acting Director, (202) 342-3990; fax: (202) 342-3927; email: ipsdc@palestine-studies.org

Internet http://www.palestine-studies.org/final/en/intro/research.php

Sponsor Institute for Palestine Studies, Publishing, and Research Organization
3501 M St NW
Washington, DC 20007

Institute for Research in the Humanities Postdoctoral Fellowships 2413

The institute invites applications for postdoctoral Friedrich Solmsen Fellowships, tenable at the institute in the upcoming academic year in literary and historical studies with a European focus, antiquity through the 17th century.

Requirements Candidates must have doctoral degrees by the time of application; expectation of the degree by the beginning of the fellowship is insufficient.

Amount $30,000

Date(s) Application Is Due Oct 15.

Contact Loretta Freiling, Executive Secretary, Institute for Research in the Humanities, (608) 262-3855; fax: (608) 265-4173; email: freiling@facstaff.wisc.edu

Internet http://www.wisc.edu/irh/research.html

Sponsor University of Wisconsin--Madison
1401 Observatory Dr
Madison, WI 53706

Institute of American Cultures Graduate and Predoctoral Fellowships 2414

The UCLA Center for Asian American Studies, American Indian Studies Center, Center for African American Studies, and the Chicano Studies Research Center, in conjunction with the Institute of American Cultures, offer a limited number of predoctoral fellowships to support scholarly work in relevant ethnic studies. The awards are for one year. Reapplication for a second year of support is permitted. The deadline for African American and Chicana/o studies is January 13 and the deadline for American Indian and Asian American studies is March 30. On occasion, centers have chosen to divide the graduate fellowship between two or among three students. Application and guidelines are available online.

Requirements The fellow must be a full-time UCLA graduate student and make a contribution to the ongoing activities of the center. Application for the fellowship in African American Studies is open only to doctoral students who will have advanced to candidacy by the beginning of the fellowship year.

Amount $17,000 per year stipend plus registration fees

Date(s) Application Is Due Jan 13; Mar 30.

Contact Program Contact, (310) 825-1233; email: IACcoordinator@gdnet.ucla.edu

Internet http://www.gdnet.ucla.edu/iacweb/preweber.htm

Sponsor UCLA Institute of American Cultures
1237 Murphy Hall, Box 951419
Los Angeles, CA 90095-1419

Institute of American Cultures Postdoctoral and Visiting Scholar Fellowships 2415

The UCLA Center for Asian American Studies, American Indian Studies Center, Center for African American Studies, and the Chicano Studies Research Center, in conjunction with the Institute of American Cultures, offers a limited number of postdoctoral fellowships. Currently, the IAC, in cooperation with UCLA's four Ethnic Studies Research Centers and the UCLA Library's Center for Oral History Research offers four postdoctoral fellowships (one per Center) that focus on conducting and theorizing oral history research in African American, American Indian, Asian American, and Chicano communities. Awards will depend on experience for those who have recently received a PhD. Senior scholars will receive a supplement to their sabbatical salaries to support work in ethnic studies. Application and guidelines are available online.

Requirements Applicants must be citizens or permanent residents of the United States and hold a PhD from an accredited college/university (or, in the case of the arts, a terminal degree) in the appropriate field at the time of appointment. Fellows must teach or do research in the programs of the center.

Restrictions UCLA faculty, staff, and currently enrolled students are not eligible to apply.
Amount $32,000-$34,000 per year plus health benefits and up to $4000 in research support
Date(s) Application Is Due Jan 13.
Contact IAC Coordinator, (310) 825-1233; email: iaccoordinator@gdnet.ucla.edu
Internet http://www.gdnet.ucla.edu/iacweb/pstweber.htm
Sponsor UCLA Institute of American Cultures
Box 951419, 1237 Murphy Hall
Los Angeles, CA 90095-1419

Institute of Current World Affairs Fellowships 2416
The purpose of the Institute of Current World Affairs, also known as the Crane-Rogers Foundation, is to identify promising young (under 36) internationalists with the drive, self-discipline, and ability to spend a minimum of two years studying and writing about areas and issues outside the United States. Full support is provided for the fellows and their immediate families, requiring that they write monthly reports or newsletters to the executive director. Applications are accepted at any time. It is suggested that applicant write for a brochure explaining the fellowship program, application procedure, and current areas of particular interest. Listed deadlines are for letters of interest; full application is by invitation. Annual deadlines vary; contact program staff for exact dates.
Date(s) Application Is Due Feb 28; Aug 1.
Contact Peter Martin, Executive Director, (603) 643-5548; fax: (603) 643-9599; email: icwa@valley.net
Internet http://www.icwa.org/#anchor110081
Sponsor Institute of Current World Affairs
4 W Wheelock St
Hanover, NH 03755

Institute of Food Technologists Graduate Fellowships and Undergraduate Scholarship Program 2417
The IFT-administered scholarships/fellowships program is available each year to outstanding undergraduate and graduate students. These awards are given by food industry companies, organizations, divisions, and sections of the IFT, and the IFT to assist young scientists in obtaining the education and training necessary to fill positions in industry, government, and education. Graduate and junior/senior applications are due to department heads February 1; freshman applications, February 15; and sophomore applications, March 1. Instructions and applications are available on the Web site, or from the fax-on-demand system: (800) 234-0270.
Requirements Applicants for undergraduate scholarships must be enrolled or planning to enroll in an IFT-approved food science/technology program. Graduate fellowship applicants can be enrolled in any college or university that is conducting fundamental studies to further food science/technology.
Restrictions Research in such disciplines as genetics, horticulture, nutrition, microbiology, biochemistry, engineering, chemistry, etc., is not eligible unless it is directly related to food science/technology.
Amount $1000-$5000 graduate fellowships; $1000-$2250 undergraduate scholarships
Date(s) Application Is Due Feb 1; Feb 15; Mar 1.
Contact Patti Pagliuco, Fellowships Administrator, (312) 782-8424; email: pgpagliuco@ift.org
Internet http://www.ift.org/cms/?pid=1000438
Sponsor Institute of Food Technologists
221 N LaSalle St
Chicago, IL 60601

Institute of Global Conflict and Cooperation Research, Conference, and Teaching Grants 2418
Institute of Global Conflict and Cooperation (IGCC) research and teaching grants are awarded to University of California (UC) faculty to stimulate independent research and education projects on international issues of contemporary importance. Grants support research and teaching on the nine UC campuses on the causes of international conflict and opportunities to promote international cooperation. IGCC research, research conference, and teaching grants are designed to stimulate independent research and education projects on international issues of contemporary importance. Topics of interest are posted on the Web site, as are application procedures.
Requirements Applications are accepted from UC faculty in all disciplines. Collaborative work is encouraged; however, the principal investigator must have an integral role in the project. Collaborative projects between UC faculty and the scientific and the technical staff of the national laboratories are eligible. Research projects may be either theoretical or policy analytical.
Amount $35,000 maximum
Date(s) Application Is Due Mar 7.
Contact Kim Newin, IGCC Campus Programs Representative, (858) 534-8602; email: ktnewin@ucsd.edu
Internet http://www-igcc.ucsd.edu/cprograms/fac_grant_menu.php
Sponsor University of California, San Diego
9500 Gilman Dr, Dept 0518
La Jolla, CA 92093-0518

Institute of Human Values in Health Care Interdisciplinary Fellowships 2419
The program is designed to provide non-clinical professionals who work in health related fields (e.g., law, government, economics, sociology, philosophy, journalism, religion, and history) with first-hand exposure to and involvement with intensive inpatient and ambulatory care of the critically ill within a major academic medical center. The fellowship runs from January through May.
Requirements Professionals who are active and established in their fields and can devote full time to the program for five months may submit fellowship applications. Postdoctoral candidates also will be considered.
Amount $7500
Date(s) Application Is Due Sep 15.
Contact Dr. Robert Sade, Director, (843) 792-5278; fax: (843) 792-8286; email: sader@musc.edu
Internet http://www.values.musc.edu/news/if_announcement.htm
Sponsor Medical University of South Carolina
P.O. Box 250612, 96 Jonathan Lucas St, Ste 409
Charleston, SC 29425

Institute of Mental Hygiene Grants 2420
The program invests in children through its grantmaking programs, active involvement with grantees, and leadership in improving mental health programs and policies. Grants support organizations that are tax-exempt and provide services in New Orleans. The foundation supports the following programs: early childhood mental health grants, children's mental health grants, early childhood mini-grants, and technical assistance grants. Applications and guidelines, including deadline dates, are available online.
Requirements Louisiana nonprofit organizations are eligible.
Restrictions Capital projects, general fund drives, or grants to individuals will not be considered.
Contact Nancy Freeman, Executive Director, (504) 566-1852; fax: (504) 566-1853; email: nfreeman@imhno.org or imh@imhno.org
Internet http://www.imhno.org/imh_guidelines.html
Sponsor Institute of Mental Hygiene
1055 St Charles Ave, Ste 350
New Orleans, LA 70130

Institute of Paper Science and Technology Fellowships 2421
Fellowships are awarded in the interdisciplinary program in chemistry, chemical engineering, mechanical engineering, physics, biology, and mathematics leading to the MS and PhD degrees. Alumni have obtained responsible positions in research, development, production, and management in the pulp and paper industry and in the chemical and related industries, with a small but increasing number in advanced education.
Requirements Applicants generally have BA or BS degrees in chemistry, paper science, chemical engineering, or mechanical engineering, but well-qualified individuals with degrees in other physical sciences and engineering areas will be considered. Citizens or permanent legal residents of the United States, Canada, or Mexico enrolled at the institute are eligible.
Amount $16,000 per year plus tuition waiver, master's level; $18,000 per year plus tuition waiver, doctoral level
Contact Project Manager, (800) 558-6611; email: energy.challenge@ipst.gatech.edu
Internet http://www.ipst.gatech.edu/energy_challenge/website/challenger/ipst.html
Sponsor Institute of Paper Science and Technology
500 10th St NW
Atlanta, GA 30318

Institute of Russian and East European Studies Postgraduate Studentships 2422
The studentships, open to applicants worldwide, will pay university fees for a one-year course of full-time study for the postgraduate degree of M.Phil in Russian and East European Studies. The M.Phil consists of three courses and a dissertation, plus a language exam. Language tuition is provided. Program may be temporarily suspended; contact the institute for current availability.
Requirements Applicants should have an undergraduate degree or an equivalent qualification in a social science subject. Candidates must commence their study at the institute in Glasgow.
Contact Richard Berry, Director ICEES, Postgraduate Studentships, 44 141 330 5585; fax: 44 141 330 5594; email: R.R.Berry@socsci.gla.ac.uk
Internet http://www.gla.ac.uk/departments/dcees
Sponsor University of Glasgow
Hetherington Bldg, Bute Gardens
Glasgow, Scotland G12 8RS United Kingdom

Institute of Textile Technology Graduate Fellowships 2423
Up to 10 students will each be awarded a tuition scholarship and a nonservice fellowship. Each ITT fellowship provides the student with a stipend for the nine months of the academic year. The Academic Committee will decide which students receive these financial awards. Students also may apply for Federal aid in the form of student loans. Fellowships require no service, such as assistance with laboratory work or teaching, and are continued for the second year, provided the student's performance during the first year is satisfactory. All students are expected to maintain a minimum average of B in the course work.

Requirements Fellowships are intended for US citizens holding bachelor's degrees and interested in careers in the textile industry.
Restrictions If at the end of the first year the required average is not attained, the fellowship cannot be renewed for the second year.
Amount $12,000 stipend plus tuition and fees per academic year
Date(s) Application Is Due Mar 15.
Contact Program Officer, (919) 513-7583; fax: (919) 882-9410
Internet http://www.itt.edu/Education/FinancialAid.asp
Sponsor Institute of Textile Technology
2401 Research Dr, Box 8301
Raleigh, NC 27695-8301

Institute of Turkish Studies Dissertation Writing Grants 2424
The institute is devoted solely to the advancement of training, research, and teaching in the field of Ottoman and modern Turkish studies. These grants are intended for advanced students who have finished the research stage of their dissertation, and they may not be used for dissertation research. The dissertation writing grants will be awarded only to applicants who certify that they will not be involved in teaching beyond the half-time level. Application and guidelines are available online.
Requirements Graduate students in any field of the social sciences and/or humanities, who are US citizens or permanent residents at the time of application; currently enrolled in a PhD degree program in the United States; and expecting to complete all PhD requirements except their dissertation by March are eligible.
Amount $5000-$10,000 stipend
Contact David Cuthell, (202) 687-0295; fax: (202) 687-3780; email: dcc@turkishstudies.org
Internet http://www.turkishstudies.org/grand_app.html
Sponsor Institute of Turkish Studies
Intercultural Center, Box 571033-Room 305R
Washington, DC 20057-1033

Institute of Turkish Studies Research Grants in Comparative Studies of Modern Turkey 2425
The program supports and encourages the development of research, scholarship, and learning in the field of Turkish Studies in the United States. This grant is for graduate students at the dissertation research stage and for post-doctoral scholars in the U.S. who study aspects of the Republic of Turkey (post-1922) in a comparative context. A significant portion of the project should be devoted comparatively to one or more states or political entities in Europe, Latin America, the Middle East, and Asia in addition to the Turkish Republic. These grants are primarily, but not exclusively, in the field of Political Science. Applications and further information are available online.
Requirements Applicants must be U.S. citizens or permanent residents in the U.S. and affiliated with a university in the U.S at the time of the application.
Amount $10,000
Contact David Cuthell, (202) 687-0295; fax: (202) 687-3780; email: dcc@turkishstudies.org
Internet http://www.turkishstudies.org/grand_app.html
Sponsor Institute of Turkish Studies
Intercultural Center, Box 571033-Room 305R
Washington, DC 20057-1033

Institute of Turkish Studies Summer Language Study Grants in Turkey 2426
These grants are for summer travel to Turkey for language study in preparation for graduate research. The time period for these grants varies with each individual application. Normally, recipients are expected to spend a minimum of two months in Turkey at an established Ottoman or Turkish language training facility. Application guidelines are available online.
Requirements Applicants must be graduate students in any field of the social sciences and/or humanities; US citizens or permanent residents at the time of the application; and currently enrolled in a university in the United States.
Amount $1000-$2000
Date(s) Application Is Due Mar 11.
Contact David Cuthell, (202) 687-0295; fax: (202) 687-3780; email: dcc@turkishstudies.org
Internet http://www.turkishstudies.org/grantsprogram.html
Sponsor Institute of Turkish Studies
Box 571033, Intercultural Ctr
Washington, DC 20057-1033

Institute of Turkish Studies Summer Research Grants in Turkey 2427
These grants are for summer travel to Turkey to carry out projects. The time period for these grants varies with each individual application. Normally, grant recipients are expected to spend a minimum of two months in Turkey. Application and guidelines are available online.
Requirements Applicants must be graduate students in any field of the social sciences and/or humanities in the United States; US citizens or permanent residents at the time of the application; and currently not engaged in dissertation writing.
Amount $1000-$2000
Contact David Cuthell, (202) 687-0295; fax: (202) 687-3780; email: dcc@turkishstudies.org
Internet http://www.turkishstudies.org/grand_app.html
Sponsor Institute of Turkish Studies
Intercultural Center, Box 571033-Room 305R
Washington, DC 20057-1033

Inter-University Board for Chinese Language Studies 2428
This year-long program provides graduate and undergraduate students with intensive oral-aural language instruction and furthers reading ability in general materials and in disciplinary or professional fields. Acceptance is granted to students of all countries affiliated with recognized academic institutions and to unaffiliated students who provide evidence of serious intention to pursue advanced work after attending the program or use Chinese in their profession. Full tuition may be provided, and fellowships are available.
Requirements Admission is open to all qualified students from the United States. Applicants from other English-speaking countries are also eligible for admission, as are others who speak and read English fluently. Applicants must demonstrate proficiency in Chinese.
Contact Karen Cheong, Program Administrator, (510) 642-3873; fax: (510) 643-7062; email: iub@socrates.berkeley.edu
Internet http://ieas.berkeley.edu/iup
Sponsor Inter-University Board for Chinese Language Studies
2223 Fulton St, Ste 2318
Berkeley, CA 94720-2318

International Affairs Fellowship Program 2429
The program is designed to bridge the gap between theory and practice in international relations and to encourage the better use of scholarly or reflective wisdom in decisions on international problems. The fellowships also provide career experiences for young foreign policy professionals. Interested qualified individuals should write to the council in the spring of the year and briefly describe the proposed project and methods to carry it out. Nominations, including self-nominations, must meet the listed deadline. Annual deadline dates may vary; contact program staff for exact dates.
Requirements The council awards a number of fellowships to US citizens between the ages of 27 and 35 with demonstrated intellectual ability and promise who come from academic, government, business, and/or professional communities. While a PhD or its equivalent is not a firm requirement, successful candidates generally hold advanced degrees and possess a solid record of work experience.
Restrictions The program does not support research toward a postgraduate degree. The program will not support research as traditionally understood, or the gathering of new information and the development of generalizations concerning it, if the results will be of primary interest only to scholars or theoreticians.
Amount $40,000 maximum per year
Date(s) Application Is Due Oct 24.
Contact Aysha Ghadiali, (212) 434-9489; fax (212) 434-9801; email: Fellowships@cfr.org
Internet http://www.cfr.org/about/fellowships/iaf.html
Sponsor Council on Foreign Relations
58 E 68th St
New York, NY 10021

International Cancer Technology Transfer Fellowships 2430
The fellowships are funded by a group of cancer institutes, leagues, societies, associations, foundations, and governmental agencies in North America, Europe, and Australia. The aims of the awards are threefold: to facilitate rapid international transfer of cancer research and clinical technology; exchange knowledge and enhance skills in basic, clinical, behavioral, and epidemiological areas of cancer research and in cancer control and prevention; and acquire up-to-date clinical management, diagnostic, and therapeutic expertise. Applications are particularly encouraged for projects in the fields of cancer control and prevention, epidemiology and cancer registration, public education, and behavioral sciences. The short-term fellowships permit successful candidates to spend up to three months at a suitable host institute abroad. They are particularly aimed at investigators and clinicians working in places where such teaching is not yet available and where the necessary facilities exist to apply and disseminate the new skills upon return. Applications may be submitted at any time, and funding decisions are generally communicated to candidates within 60 days of receipt of a complete application.
Requirements Qualified cancer investigators should be at the early stages in their careers; clinicians should be well established in their oncology practice. Experts from any country who have been invited to teach specialized skills abroad also may apply.
Amount $3000 average
Contact International Cancer Research Program, (4122) 809 18 40; fax: (41-22) 809 18 10; email: fellows@uicc.org
Internet http://fellows.uicc.org/fell4icr.shtml
Sponsor International Union against Cancer
3, rue de Conseil-General
Geneva 1205
Switzerland

International Center for Tolerance Education Scholars in Residence Awards 2431
The International Center for Tolerance Education (ICTE) announces an initiative to support junior and senior research fellows in keeping with its mission to understand

the origins of tolerance and intolerance in children and to develop educational and clinical interventions that encourage respect for diversity. The center seeks applicants who will pursue complementary scholarly projects in early childhood and elementary education and human rights. ICTE is especially interested in distinctive new approaches to the prevention of intolerance and the promotion of tolerance, and the possibility for translational research that will have an impact on practices and policies. Scholars from the social sciences are especially encouraged to apply, and interdisciplinary efforts will be of particular interest. ICTE will reimburse the research fellows' home institutions for their salaries and benefits. In addition, for fellows not living in New York there will be a modest housing stipend to be determined as the fellowship is negotiated.
Contact Connie Kendig, (212) 421-5244; fax: (212) 421-5243; email: tmf.usa@verizon.net
Internet http://www.seedsoftolerance.org/initiative_scholars.html
Sponsor Third Millennium Foundation
340 West 12th Street
New York, NY 10014

International College of Surgeons Grants and Scholarships **2432**
The ICS makes grants and scholarships available to surgeons who wish to enhance their surgical skills through postgraduate training. Applicants are responsible for making their own arrangements for the program of study; must clearly indicate the place of study, with whom they will be studying, and acceptance by the institution and surgeon for the course of study as defined; and must indicate what it is they expect to achieve upon completion of the study program (e.g. learn a particular procedure, etc.). Guidelines are available online. No formal application form is required.
Requirements Applicants must have graduated from an accredited medical school, completed their residency, and be licensed to practice surgery in their home country (documentation of licensure must be provided). Applicants need not be ICS fellows.
Contact Max Downham, Executive Director, (312) 787-6274; fax: (312) 787-9289; email: max@icsglobal.org
Internet http://www.icsglobal.org/RandS/index.asp
Sponsor International College of Surgeons
1516 N Lake Shore Dr
Chicago, IL 60610-1694

International Crane Foundation Internships **2433**
This is a formal stipend program with internships being offered in the fields of aviculture and restoration. In the aviculture program, interns will receive intensive hands-on training in the care and management of endangered cranes, including husbandry, handling techniques, behavior, stimulating reproduction, incubation, chick rearing, artificial insemination, health care, and genetic management. The associate also manages the volunteer chick parent program. Each intern is responsible for developing and completing a research project with assistance from the staff. Internships usually run from March through May, June through August, September through November, and December through February. Application deadlines are for spring, summer, fall, and winter internships. Under the restoration program, interns will be involved in the ecosystems restoration program, which directs the restoration of prairie, savanna, and wetland communities on the ICF property. Interns will develop important ecological, hydrological, botanical, and horticultural skills. Depending on the season, interns may be involved in prescribed burns, field studies of wild sandhill care populations; seed collecting, planting, and site preparation for community restorations; and interaction with foreign scientists. The associate also will manage the seed collection program. Internships usually run for six months from March through August and from June through November. Application deadlines are January 1 and April 1 for the spring-summer and summer-fall internships, respectively. The program runs for nine months from March through November.
Requirements Applications may be made by recent college sophomores through college graduates in biology, zoology, or botany who have a willingness to work at manual tasks and can work in a self-directed manner. Individuals seeking graduate training are especially encouraged.
Amount $350 per month plus housing for interns
Date(s) Application Is Due Jan 1; Apr 1; Jul 1; Oct 1.
Contact Korie Klink, (608) 356-9462 ext 127; fax: (608) 356-9465; email: korie@savingcranes.org
Internet http://www.savingcranes.org/about/get_involved/intern.cfm
Sponsor International Crane Foundation
P.O. Box 447
Baraboo, WI 53913-0447

International Doctoral Scholarships in Jewish Studies **2434**
Scholarships assist in training future Jewish scholars for careers in Jewish scholarship and research and help religious, educational, and other Jewish communal workers obtain advanced training for leadership positions in the Jewish community. Scholarships are awarded for one academic year, renewable up to a maximum of four years. References are required on the background and scholastic ability of the applicant. Final action is taken by the foundation in July with applicants being advised in August. Applicant must submit a written request for an application form.
Requirements Any graduate student specializing in a Jewish field who is officially enrolled or registered in a doctoral program at a recognized university is eligible to apply. Preference is given to students at the dissertation level.
Amount $2000-$7500
Date(s) Application Is Due Oct 31.
Contact Dr. Jerry Hochbaum, Executive Vice President, (212) 425-6606; fax: (212) 425-6602; email: office@mfjc.org
Internet http://www.mfjc.org
Sponsor Memorial Foundation for Jewish Culture
50 Broadway, 34th Fl
New York, NY 10004

International ePhilanthropy Awards **2435**
These awards honor those individuals, organizations, and companies working in the ePhilanthropy field. Nominees will have demonstrated extraordinary talent, creativity, and insight in drawing the public's attention to the important use of the Internet for philanthropic purposes and have created services or strategies that support this effort. Award categories include: Best ePhilanthropy Research Project; Best Online Donations/ Fundraising (revenue generating) Campaign; Best Event Registration and/or Membership Campaign; and Best Community Building/ Volunteerism and/or Activism (non-revenue) Campaign. It is acceptable to nominate individuals, companies, and organizations in multiple categories. Nomination form and guidelines are available online.
Requirements Individuals, organizations, and companies working in the ePhilanthropy field who have demonstrated extraordinary talent, creativity and insight in drawing the public's attention to the important use of the Internet for philanthropic purposes and/or have created services or strategies that support this effort are encouraged to apply.
Restrictions Employees of the ePhilanthropy Foundation, members of the International ePhilanthropy Awards Judging panel, and their immediate family (spouse, siblings, parents, and children) are not eligible for consideration.
Amount $500 to charities of awardees' choice
Date(s) Application Is Due Aug 1.
Contact Awards Administrator, (877) 536-1245 ext 1; fax: (202) 478-0910; email: Awards@ephilanthropy.org
Internet http://www.ephilanthropy.org/awards
Sponsor ePhilanthropy Foundation
1101 15th St NW, Ste 200
Washington, DC 20005

International Essential Tremor Foundation Grants **2436**
The foundation awards grants for clinical or basic research specific to essential tremor. Data to be derived should lead to grant proposals to governmental or other sources of funds. Two grants are available in the current year. Under exceptional circumstances, funding may be allowed for a second year as a competing renewal. No more than one award can be given to an individual investigator per year. Funding begins in June or July.
Requirements Grants are awarded to MDs and/or PhDs.
Amount $20,000 per year
Contact Catherine Rice, (888) 387-3667 or (913) 341-3880; fax: (913) 341-1296; email: crice@essentialtremor.org
Internet http://www.essentialtremor.org/research/index.php
Sponsor International Essential Tremor Foundation
P.O. Box 14005
Lenexa, KS 66285-4005

International Federation of University Women Research Fellowships **2437**
This competition is open to women graduates for research for a period of at least eight months, preferably in a country other than the one in which the candidate has received her education or habitually resides. In addition, the Study and Action Program Fellowship is awarded for research related to the IFUW Study and Action Program--Woman's Role in Changing Society. Members of the IFUW should apply through their national affiliates (in the United States, the American Association of University Women, 1111 16th St NW, Washington, DC 20036). Competitions are held in even-numbered years. The deadline for receipt of applications is determined by each affiliate but normally falls between early September and November of the year preceding the competition.
Requirements An applicant must be a woman graduate who is an IFUW member and must be started on the research program to which the application relates.
Restrictions A fellowship will not be awarded for the first year of a PhD program.
Amount Sf3000-Sf6000 approximately
Date(s) Application Is Due Nov 1.
Contact Fellowships Officer, (022) 731 23 80; fax: (022) 738 04 40; email: info@ifuw.org
Internet http://www.ifuw.org/fellowships/index.htm
Sponsor International Federation of University Women
8 rue de l'Ancien Port
Geneva CH 1201
Switzerland

International Fellowships in Jewish Studies **2438**
Fellowships assist qualified individuals to carry out independent scholarly, literary, or art projects in a field of Jewish specialization that will make a significant contribution to the understanding, preservation, enhancement, or transmission of Jewish culture. Fellowships are awarded for one academic year, renewable for one more year.

Requirements Any recognized and/or qualified scholar, researcher, writer, or artist who possesses knowledge and experience to formulate and implement a project in a field of Jewish specialization may apply.
Amount $7500 maximum per year
Date(s) Application Is Due Oct 31.
Contact Dr. Jerry Hochbaum, Executive Vice President, (212) 425-6606; fax: (212) 425-6602; email: office@mfjc.org
Internet http://www.mfjc.org/index.htm
Sponsor Memorial Foundation for Jewish Culture
50 Broadway, 34th Fl
New York, NY 10004

International Fellowships in Medical Education 2439
The program provides opportunities for faculty from schools of medicine outside the United States to study aspects of medical education in the United States that have the potential to improve medical education in their home country institutions. Mentoring will be provided by preceptors in US basic and clinical science departments, medical education departments, and health system institutions. Eligible study areas include educational methodology, curriculum design, evaluation systems, medical school governance, development of basic and clinical science departments, and the design and operation of health care and public health system programs linked to medical education. Fellows may concurrently pursue collaborative research interests with US basic science faculty or observe some clinical activity with clinical faculty. Fellowship allowance generally includes a monthly stipend, round-trip economy-class air fare for the fellow, and travel to one scientific meeting in the United States. Programs may range from six months to one year. The interactive, web-based application is now available online; paper applications are no longer accepted.
Requirements Candidates must reside and work in their home countries at the time of application; have a graduate or professional degree in medicine or in a basic medical science; have not less than three years of work experience in their chosen field in the home country; hold an academic appointment as a faculty member in a school of medicine; have the ability to communicate effectively in English; have the endorsement of a home country medical school or organization; and have a position to return to in the home country medical school or organization.
Restrictions Fellowships are not provided for programs in basic or clinical research; degree-granting educational programs that require acceptance to an institution and tuition payments; tuition grants for short-term courses; specialty training in residency programs, or solely for training in clinical procedures.
Amount $2400 monthly stipend
Contact Grants Administrator, (215) 386-5900; fax: (215) 386-9196; email: info@ecfmg.org
Internet http://www.ecfmg.org/about.html
Sponsor Educational Commission for Foreign Medical Graduates
3624 Market St
Philadelphia, PA 19104-2685

International Human Rights Funders Grants 2440
Human rights grantmaking supports a wide range of efforts to ensure that all people have the opportunity to enjoy a genuinely human existence. Grants varying in type and amount support a broad range of approaches, including: public education to inform people about their human rights and how to exercise them; documentation, reporting, and fact-finding to expose human rights violations; litigation to uphold human rights and hold abusers accountable; policy advocacy to ensure that states and non-state actors conform to human rights standards; research and scholarship to define the content of rights; networking and coalition building to further the effectiveness of a global human rights movement; and capacity building for organizations engaged in the above work, locally and internationally. Humanitarian funding contributes essential support for direct services that meet vital needs of communities the world over; and supports efforts to ensure that states and non-state actors comply with laws promulgated for the protection of people throughout the world.
Requirements The applicant must be an organization that works to defend or promote human rights; and is based in India, Bangladesh, Pakistan, and be working, in whole or in part, on human rights issues in the country in which the organization is based, or is based in Algeria, Tunisia, or Morocco, and be working, in whole or in part, on human rights issues in the country in which the organization is based.
Restrictions The fund does not support stand-alone conferences, individuals, businesses, scholarships, fundraising events, university-based research, government agencies, or activities directly or indirectly intended to support candidates for political office.
Amount $5000-$30,000
Date(s) Application Is Due Jul 1.
Contact Grants Administrator, (202) 347-7488; fax: (202) 783-8499; email: info@globalhumanrights.org
Internet http://www.hrfunders.org/fghr/apply.html
Sponsor International Human Rights Funders Group
1634 I St NW, Ste 1001
Washington, DC 20006

International League of Antiquarian Booksellers Bibliographical Prize 2441
Every four years (next in 2006) the ILAB awards a prize to the author of the best work, published or unpublished, of learned bibliography or of research into the history of books or of typography, and books of general interest on the subject. Two copies of each work to be considered must be deposited at the office of the secretary at the very latest 16 months before date of award. The award period covers the four years prior to the year of deadline date.
Requirements Entries must be submitted in a language that is universally used. A work already published is eligible only if publication occurred within the four years immediately preceding the closing date for submission or if it has an imprint bearing a date within those four years.
Restrictions Entries in the form of a specialized catalog of one or more books destined for sale are not eligible, nor are periodicals or public library catalogs.
Amount $10,000
Date(s) Application Is Due Dec 31.
Contact Raymond Kilgarriff, Prize Secretary, +44 (0)1424 426146; email: rmkilgarriff@btinternet.com
Internet http://www.ilab-lila.com/english/prize.htm
Sponsor International League of Antiquarian Booksellers
Hauptstrasse 19 A
Bad Honnef D-53604 Germany

International Lelio Basso Foundation for the Rights and Liberation of Peoples Grants 2442
The foundation awards research grants internationally to individuals in the fields of environment, development studies, and human rights issues in developing countries. The work of the foundation concentrates on the environment and development, industrial hazards and human rights, refugee rights, and the rights of children and young people.
Contact Elmar Altvater, President, 39-6-68801468; fax: 39-6-6877774; email: filb@iol.it
Internet http://www.grisnet.it/filb/filbeng.html
Sponsor International Lelio Basso Foundation for the Rights and Liberation of Peoples
Via della Dogana Vecchia 5
Rome 00186
Italy

International Oncology Nursing Fellowships 2443
The fellowships are funded by the Oncology Nursing Society and provide an opportunity for qualified nurses to augment their professional knowledge and experience through short-term observerships at a renowned comprehensive cancer center in Australia, North America, or the United Kingdom. A project description must provide full details of the particular cancer nursing skills that the candidate wishes to observe. It should elaborate on the treatment and nursing facilities at the home institute and how the newly acquired knowledge and techniques would be used and disseminated to other nursing staff upon return. Projects need the approval of the candidate's home and host supervisors. The maximum fellowship duration is three months; stipend support is for one month only. The program also contributes to the least expensive international two-way airfare or other appropriate form of transport. Financial support is not provided for dependents.
Requirements English-speaking registered nurses who are actively engaged in the management of cancer patients in their home institutes and who come from developing or Eastern European countries are eligible, as are established oncology nurses from any country who wish to disseminate their skills in these regions.
Amount $2800 average
Date(s) Application Is Due Nov 1.
Contact International Cancer Research Program, (41-22) 809 18 40; fax: (41-22) 809 18 10; email: fellows@uicc.org
Internet http://fellows.uicc.org/fell5ion.shtml
Sponsor International Union against Cancer
3, rue de Conseil-General
Geneva 1205
Switzerland

International Peace Research Institute, Oslo Grants 2444
PRIO offers scholarships for graduate students, mainly at Norwegian universities. In addition to a student stipend, the scholarship includes supervision by PRIO's researchers and office space at the institute's building in Oslo. Residence in Oslo during the scholarship period is essential. Guidelines are available online. The scholarship lasts for an agreed period of time, up to one year. If the thesis is finalized within the agreed period, PRIO may offer an extension of the stipend period to secure academic publishing of the results, e.g. by writing an article for an international journal.
Amount NOK 3500 per month
Date(s) Application Is Due Oct 1.
Contact Stein Tonnesson, Director, 47-22-54-77-31; fax: 47-22-54-77-01; email: stein@prio.no or info@prio.no
Internet http://www.prio.no/page/preview/preview/9346/21744.html
Sponsor International Peace Research Institute, Oslo
Fuglehauggta 11
Oslo 0260 Norway

International Spinal Research Trust Grants 2445
The trust awards grants worldwide for research into the treatment of paralysis caused by spinal cord injury. Grants also are available for the purchase of relevant equipment.

Contact John Cavanagh, Head of Research, 01483 898786; fax: 01483 898763; email: research@spinal-research.org or john@spinal-research.org
Internet http://www.spinal-research.org/display_section.asp?section=researchers
Sponsor International Spinal Research Trust
Station Rd, Bramley
Guildford GU5 0AZ
United Kingdgom

International Studies Graduate Fellowships **2446**
The Graduate Programs in International Studies department at the university offers MA and PhD fellowships to train graduate students and promote scholarship on transnational issues. The program focuses on traditional problems of foreign and security policy, international business and economics, as well as post-Cold-War priorities such as gender, human rights, and migration.
Contact Graduate Programs in International Studies, (757) 683-5700: fax: (757) 683-5701; email: isgpd@odu.edu
Internet http://al.odu.edu/gpis
Sponsor Old Dominion University
Batten Arts and Letters Bldg, Rm 620
Norfolk, VA 23529-0086

InterUniversity Fellowship Program in Jewish Studies **2447**
The program awards fellowships to graduate students in Jewish Studies who wish to spend a year working in the Department of Jewish Studies at one of Israel's universities. Fellows can take courses, do research in Israel's Judaic libraries, and have personal contact with Israeli scholars in the field. In addition, fellows attend an ongoing seminar program coordinated by an on-site mentor. Fellows are expected to spend the full academic year in Israel. Fellowships are renewable upon consideration.
Requirements Applicants can be earning their degrees in any discipline, but a primary focus must be placed on some aspect of Jewish life. Fellows must normally have enough fluency in Hebrew to enable them to participate in graduate courses and seminars taught in Hebrew. All nationalities accepted.
Amount $4500 for doctoral students; $2500 for master's students
Contact Fellowship Administrator, (718) 951-5146; fax: (718) 951-4639
Internet http://www.nyu.edu/pages/gsas/files/interuni
Sponsor Brooklyn College
Rm 3612, James Hall
Brooklyn, NY 11210

IPA George Washington Williams Fellowship **2448**
The fellowship funds stories written by journalists of color about issues such as the environment, global trade policy, healthcare, race, and education. Fellows receive access to some research support, consultants, advanced professional training, and a large network of journalists working in the public interest sector. In addition, program staff work closely with fellows to publish their stories in major publications. Individuals may apply for financial and institutional support to write a single story, or they may seek an investigative or depth reporting fellowship of between three and 12 months to research a specific social issue. The fellowship will pay national commercial rates for individual stories or $1500 per month plus expenses for depth reporting fellowships.
Requirements Any journalist of color with at least three years of solid professional reporting and writing experience may apply. Individuals with backgrounds in investigative or enterprise reporting are preferred. Previous reporting or other experience in the chosen subject area is desirable. The fellowship is open only to US citizens or to foreign journalists who have established relationships with US publications.
Restrictions College journalism or internship experience do not qualify as professional experience.
Date(s) Application Is Due May 30; Nov 15.
Contact Fellowship Administrator, (415) 643-4401 ext 116 or ext 117; email: gww@indypress.org
Internet http://www.indypress.org/programs/gwwfellow.html
Sponsor Independent Press Association
2729 Mission St, Ste 201
San Francisco, CA 94110-3131

Ipatieff Prize **2449**
This award is given every three years (2004, 2007, etc.) to recognize outstanding chemical experimental work in the field of catalysis or high pressure, carried out by individuals of any nationality and not over 40 years of age (by date of presentation). If experimental investigations in these fields shall have been abandoned to such a degree that no outstanding results have been achieved, then the award may be given for highly meritorious work in a closely allied field of chemistry. Special weight shall be given to the independence of thought and the originality shown. The award may be made for investigations carried out in any country and without consideration of the nationality of the recipient; however, preference will be given to American chemists.
Requirements Any individual, except a member of the award committee, may submit one nomination or seconding letter for the award in the award year. Nominating documents consist of a letter of not more than 1000 words containing an evaluation of the nominee's accomplishments and a specific identification of the work to be recognized, a biographical sketch including date of birth, and a list of publications and patents authored by the nominee. Six copies of all items to be included in the nomination must be submitted.
Restrictions Self-nominations are not accepted.
Amount $5000, depending on income from the trust fund, and travel to award meeting
Date(s) Application Is Due Feb 1.
Contact Awards Administrator, (202) 872-4408; fax: (202) 872-6317; email: awards@acs.org
Internet http://chemistry.org/portal/Chemistry?PID=acsdisplay.html&DOC=awards\ipatieff.html
Sponsor American Chemical Society
1155 16th St NW
Washington, DC 20036

IRA Jeanne S. Chall Research Fellowship **2450**
The fellowship was established to encourage and support reading research by promising scholars. The special emphasis of the fellowship is to support research efforts in the following areas: beginning reading (theory, research, and practice that improves the effectiveness of learning to read); readability (methods of predicting the difficulty of texts); reading difficulty (diagnosis, treatment, and prevention); stages of reading development; the relation of vocabulary to reading; and diagnosing and teaching adults with limited reading ability.
Requirements The fellowship is open to IRA members.
Amount $6000
Date(s) Application Is Due Jan 15.
Contact Program Contact, (301) 731-1600 ext 423; fax: (301) 731-1057; email: research@reading.org
Internet http://www.reading.org/association/awards/research_chall.html
Sponsor International Reading Association
P.O. Box 8139, 800 Barksdale Rd
Newark, DE 19714-8139

IRA Nila Banton Smith Research Dissemination Support Grants **2451**
The grant is intended to assist any IRA member to spend from two to 10 months working on a research dissemination activity. The grant is funded from the Nila Banton Smith Endowment.
Amount $5000 maximum
Date(s) Application Is Due Jan 15.
Contact Program Contact, Division of Research, (302) 731-1600 ext 423; fax: (302) 731-1057; email: research@reading.org
Internet http://www.reading.org/association/awards/research_smith_grant.html
Sponsor International Reading Association
P.O. Box 8139, 800 Barksdale Rd
Newark, DE 19714-8139

IRA Outstanding Dissertation of the Year Award **2452**
The competition is intended for those doctoral students who have focused their research in the reading field or who have conducted related research having implications for reading. Studies using any research approach (ethnographic, experimental, historical, survey, etc.) are encouraged. Each study will be assessed in the light of this approach, the scholarly qualification of its report, and its significant contributions to knowledge within the reading field. Application forms and guidelines are available from the association.
Requirements Dissertations must have been completed between May 15 and May 14 of the following year.
Amount $1000
Date(s) Application Is Due Oct 1.
Contact Division of Research, (302) 731-1600 ext 423; fax: (302) 731-1057; email: research@reading.org
Internet http://www.reading.org/association/awards/research_outstanding.html
Sponsor International Reading Association
P.O. Box 8139, 800 Barksdale Rd
Newark, DE 19714-8139

IRA Outstanding Teacher Educator in Reading Award **2453**
This award honors an outstanding college or university teacher of reading methods or reading-related courses. Nominee must be an IRA member, affiliated with a college or a university, and engaged in teacher preparation in reading at the undergraduate and/or graduate level. Entry forms and current guidelines are available from the Executive Office, International Reading Association, P.O. Box 8139, Newark, DE 19714-8139.
Amount $1000
Date(s) Application Is Due Oct 15.
Contact Program Contact, (302) 731-1600 ext 221; fax: (302) 731-1057; email: exec@reading.org
Internet http://www.reading.org/association/awards/teachers_outstanding.html
Sponsor International Reading Association
P.O. Box 8139, 800 Barksdale Rd
Newark, DE 19714-8139

IRA Print Media Award **2454**
The award recognizes outstanding reporting in newspapers, magazines, and wire services. Entries may include in-depth studies of reading instruction, discussion of research, or ongoing coverage of reading programs in the community and must have appeared during the previous calendar year.

Requirements The competition for the award is limited to professional journalists.
Date(s) Application Is Due Jan 7.
Contact Program Contact, (302) 731-1600 ext 293; fax: (302) 731-1057; email: pubinfo@reading.org
Internet http://www.reading.org/association/awards/media_print.html
Sponsor International Reading Association
P.O. Box 8139, 800 Barksdale Rd
Newark, DE 19714-8139

IRA-Elva Knight Research Grants **2455**
The grant supports reading and literacy research. Research is defined as that which addresses significant questions for the disciplines of literacy research and practice. Projects should be completed within two years. Studies may be carried out using any research method or approach so long as the focus of the project is on research in reading or literacy. Activities such as developing new programs or instructional materials are not eligible for funding except to the extent that these activities are necessary procedures for the conduct of the research. Each year it is expected that at least one grant will be awarded to a researcher outside the United States and Canada as well as one grant being awarded to a teacher-initiated research project.
Requirements All applicants must be members of the International Reading Association.
Amount $10,000 maximum
Date(s) Application Is Due Jan 15.
Contact Program Contact, Division of Research, (302) 731-1600 ext 423; fax: (302) 731-1057; email: research@reading.org
Internet http://www.reading.org/association/awards/research_knight.html
Sponsor International Reading Association
P.O. Box 8139, 800 Barksdale Rd
Newark, DE 19714-8139

Irene and Daisy MacGregor Memorial Scholarship **2456**
The scholarship is awarded to a student who has been accepted into an accredited school of medicine to pursue an MD degree. This scholarship is also available to students who have been accepted into or who are pursuing an approved course of study in the field of psychiatric nursing, graduate level, at accredited medical schools, colleges, or universities. There is a preference to females, if equally qualified.
Requirements Applicants must be US citizens and must attend an accredited US college or university. All applicants must obtain letters of sponsorship from local DAR chapters.
Amount $20,000 maximum; $5000 per year
Date(s) Application Is Due Apr 15.
Contact Office of the Committees/Scholarships, (202) 628-1776; fax: (202) 879-3252
Internet http://www.dar.org/natsociety/edout_scholar.cfm
Sponsor National Society of the Daughters of the American Revolution
1776 D St NW
Washington, DC 20006-5303

IREX ECA Alumni Small Grants Program **2457**
The Program is a professional and community development program open to alumni of the Eurasian Undergraduate Program (UGRAD) formerly known as FSAU and Edmund S. Muskie Graduate Fellowship Program. Alumni must complete their small grant activities within Eurasia. Currently, Eurasia is defined as Armenia, Azerbaijan, Belarus, Georgia, Kazakhstan, Kyrgyz Republic, Moldova, Russia, Tajikistan, Turkmenistan, Ukraine and Uzbekistan. Possible project ideas include: initiating a public or community service program; launching a pilot program at an NGO or academic institution; organizing training programs or conferences for professional colleagues and/or other alumni; funding travel of U.S. colleagues to eligible Eurasian countries for conferences, training programs and professional collaboration; development and publication of curricula, textbooks, or related reference or educational materials; publication of public information pamphlets or brochures; and conducting any other projects judged by the selection committee and/or ECA to be in the interest of program goals.
Amount $3,000 maximum
Date(s) Application Is Due Jun 1.
Contact Program Contact, (202) 628-8188; fax: (202) 628-8189; email: asgp@irex.org
Internet http://www.irex.org/programs/asgp/index.asp
Sponsor International Research & Exchanges Board
2121 K Street, NW, Suite 700
Washington, DC 20037

IREX Edmund S. Muskie Graduate Fellowship Program (Muskie) **2458**
The program provides opportunities for graduate students and professionals from Armenia, Azerbaijan, Belarus, Georgia, Kazakhstan, Kyrgyzstan, Moldova, Russia, Tajikistan, Turkmenistan, Ukraine and Uzbekistan for one-year non-degree, one-year degree or two-year degree study in the United States. Eligible fields of study are: business administration, economics, education, environmental management, international affairs, journalism and mass communication, law, library and information science, public administration, public health, and public policy.
Date(s) Application Is Due Jan 31.
Contact Grants Administrator; (202) 628-8188; fax: (202) 628-8189; email: muskie@irex.org
Internet http://www.irex.org/programs/muskie/index.asp
Sponsor International Research & Exchanges Board
2121 K Street, NW, Suite 700
Washington, DC 20037

IREX Eurasian Undergraduate Exchange Program Grants **2459**
Established by the US Congress in 1992 to foster democratization and economic development in Eurasia, the program was originally called the FREEDOM Support Act Undergraduate Program (FSAU). Key objectives are to: foster democratization and economic development; and promote cultural understanding. Project activities include: encouraging youth leadership; promoting community service in the United States and Eurasia; and supporting practical experience for professional development. IREX opened its first field office in Moscow, Russia and since has expanded its field presence to Armenia, Azerbaijan, Belarus, Georgia, Kazakhstan, Kyrgyzstan, Moldova, Turkmenistan, Tajikistan, Turkey, Ukraine, and Uzbekistan. Programs in Eurasia span academic exchanges, educational advising, alumni programming, independent media assistance and development, Internet training and access, professional training, NGO development, and partnership building.
Requirements Mid-level university faculty, researchers, scholars, and undergraduate students from the United States are eligible.
Date(s) Application Is Due Nov 6; Jan 31.
Contact Program Officers; (202) 628-8188; fax: (202) 628-8189; email: ugrad@irex.org
Internet http://www.irex.org/programs/ugrad/index.asp
Sponsor International Research & Exchanges Board
2121 K Street, NW, Suite 700
Washington, DC 20037

IREX Individual Advanced Research Opportunities Grants **2460**
The IARO program seeks to attract, select, and support in-depth field research by US students, scholars and experts in policy-relevant subject areas related to Southeast Europe and Eurasia, as well as to disseminate knowledge about these regions to a wide network of constituents in the United States and abroad. The IARO Program provides fellows with the means and support necessary to conduct incountry research on contemporary political, economic, historical, or cultural developments relevant to US foreign policy*. The IARO Program plays a vital role in supporting the emergence of a dedicated and knowledgeable cadre of US scholars and experts who can enrich the US understanding of developments in Southeast Europe and Eurasia. In addition to conducting their research, IARO fellows are asked to make themselves available as temporary consultants or experts to schools, local NGOs or the US Embassy in their host country. Fellows with grants of 4 months or less are asked to perform 10 hours of service during their grant period, and fellows with grants of 5 or more months are asked perform 20 hours. Grants will be awarded in EACH of the four categories: Master's Student--must be enrolled in a Master's program during the grant period; Predoctoral Student--must be enrolled in a PhD program during the grant period; Professional--must have one of the following degrees (MA, MS, MFA, MBA, MPA, MLIS, MPH, JD, MD) and must not currently be enrolled as a student; Postdoctoral Scholar--must hold a PhD by the application deadline.
Requirements Applicants must be US citizens who have a command of the host country language sufficient for the completion of their research. Normally, applicants are required to have a full-time affiliation with a college or university and to be faculty members or doctoral candidates who will have completed all requirements for the PhD except the dissertation by the time of participation.
Date(s) Application Is Due Nov 15.
Contact Program Officers; (202) 628-8188; fax: (202) 628-8189; email: iaro@irex.org
Internet http://www.irex.org/programs/iaro
Sponsor International Research & Exchanges Board
2121 K Street, NW, Suite 700
Washington, DC 20037

IREX International Leadership in Education Program Grants **2461**
The Program brings outstanding secondary teachers from the Near East, South Asia and Southeast Asia to the United States to further develop expertise in their subject areas, enhance their teaching skills, and increase their knowledge about the United States. ILEP is a program of the Bureau of Educational and Cultural Affairs of the US Department of State. Key issues and objectives are to: contribute to improving the quality of secondary education in participating countries; strengthen the ability of women and under-served populations to play a part in national development; and develop professional and personal relationships between American and international teachers. Project activities include: teacher training; providing leadership programs for women and under-served populations; and forming international partnerships for professional development and education,
Requirements Applicant must be secondary teachers from the Near East, South Asia and Southeast Asia
Contact Program Officer, (202) 628-8188; fax: (202) 628-8189; email: iep@irex.org
Internet http://www.irex.org/programs/iep/index.asp
Sponsor International Research & Exchanges Board
2121 K Street, NW, Suite 700
Washington, DC 20037

IREX MENA Media Emerging Leaders Fellowships **2462**
The Middle East and North Africa (MENA) program is open to media managers and supervisors based in the Middle East and North Africa with the desire to enhance

their media management skills and increase their exposure to alternate media business practices. Fellows will attend sessions on leadership skills and media management trends at Northwestern University's Media Management Center followed by a fellowship placement with a US media outlet. The key objective is to support independent media in the Middle East and North Africa.
Requirements Applicants must have at least ten years experience in either broadcast or print outlets in the MENA region and be proficient in English.
Contact Program Officer; (202) 628-8188; fax: (202) 628-8189; email: mena@irex.org
Internet http://www.irex.org/programs/MENAmedia/index.asp
Sponsor International Research & Exchanges Board
2121 K Street, NW, Suite 700
Washington, DC 20037

IREX Policy-Connect Collaborative Research Grants **2463**
The program provides fellowships to US scholars and professionals for overseas research on contemporary political, economic, historical, or cultural developments relevant to US foreign policy. Fellowships support collaborative teams of two or three US scholars and professionals for up to 12 months. The program seeks to attract, select, and support advanced research by US experts in policy-relevant subject areas related to Southeast Europe and Eurasia, facilitate collaboration among and between US and international scholars, and disseminate knowledge about Europe and Eurasia to a wide network of constituents in the United States and abroad. Upon completion of the project, scholars will be requested to present their research findings at a Policy Forum at the US Department of State and to write a short policy paper.
Requirements The principal investigator must be a US citizen or permanent resident. A PhD or equivalent terminal degree is required. Collaborative research programs involving international colleagues are strongly encouraged.
Amount $30,000 maximum
Date(s) Application Is Due Apr 1.
Contact Program Officers; (202) 628-8188; fax: (202) 628-8189; email: iaro@irex.org
Internet http://www.irex.org/programs/policy-connect/index.asp
Sponsor International Research & Exchange Board
2121 K Street, NW, Suite 700
Washington, DC 20037

IREX Regional Policy Symposium Grants **2464**
The Program provides U.S. students, scholars, and professionals with a forum to examine and discuss current policy research on the countries of Eurasia and Central and East Europe from multi-disciplinary and multi-regional approaches. The research ultimately results in the development and dissemination of policy recommendations to academic and policy communities. The program has three primary goals: to enable U.S. junior and senior scholars to work together in analyzing complex issues affecting the countries of Eurasia and Central and East Europe from multi-disciplinary and multi-regional approaches; to encourage the cross-fertilization of ideas and networking opportunities among scholars with similar regional interests; and to provide policymaking communities with knowledge of current research on evolving regions and valuable policy conclusions drawn from intensive interaction among scholars.
Date(s) Application Is Due Dec 15.
Contact Program Officers; (202) 628-8188; fax: (202) 628-8189; email: iaro@irex.org
Internet http://www.irex.org/programs/symp/index.asp
Sponsor International Research & Exchange Board
2121 K Street, NW, Suite 700
Washington, DC 20037

IREX Short-Term Travel Grants **2465**
Grants provide support for scholarly projects focusing on Central and Eastern Europe, Eurasia, and Mongolia in the humanities and social sciences disciplines. Projects should demonstrate academic merit and relevance for the American academic community studying these regions, as well as a positive impact on public, cultural, and historical knowledge of these regions through dissemination of research results. Funding is available for individual scholarly research visits to archives, libraries, museums, etc., or for conducting interviews; presentations at scholarly conferences focused on and located in Central and Eastern Europe or Eurasia; and collaborative projects such as joint publications or comparative surveys. The award provides; travel from the United States to the host country; a stipend to cover in-country costs for meals, lodging, and local transportation; and miscellaneous research expenses directly related to the project incidental expenses, such as conference registration fees, visa fees, and research expenses.
Requirements Applicants must be U.S. citizens or permanent residents (green card holder) of the U.S. for three consecutive years prior to application; submit a research proposal on a topic in one of the academic disciplines listed; and hold a PhD or other terminal degree.
Restrictions Applicants cannot be a current IREX employee or consultant or their immediate family members (spouses, parents, children, and siblings). Projects must be in the humanities and social science disciplines only. Travel may not exceed a total of 60 days. Individuals may apply for only one trip and one project per application deadline. IREX-funded project activity must be completed within one year of the application deadline.
Amount $5,000 maximum
Date(s) Application Is Due Feb 1.
Contact Program Officer, (202) 628-8188; fax: (202) 628-8189; email: stg@irex.org
Internet http://www.irex.org/programs/stg/index.asp
Sponsor International Research & Exchanges Board
2121 K Street, NW, Suite 700
Washington, DC 20037

IREX University Administration Support Program (UASP) **2466**
The Program benefits university administrators at select state universities in Russia by providing access to pertinent university management skills and models of administration. The Program is further designed to provide training to university administrators in the region while providing more concentrated funding to those university administrators who demonstrate they have the initiative, skills, and institutional support necessary to turn their institutions into models of administrative excellence. To this end, IREX implements a two-tiered program. First, fellowships in University Administration are offered that provide funding for senior level administrators to spend approximately 10 weeks at host universities in the United States. Second, after completion of their fellowships in the United States, the university administrators apply for small grants to jump-start reform projects at their home universities.
Contact Program Officer; (202) 628-8188; fax: (202) 628-8189; email: uasp@irex.org
Internet http://www.irex.org/programs/uasp/index.asp
Sponsor International Research & Exchanges Board
2121 K Street, NW, Suite 700
Washington, DC 20037

IREX US Embassy Policy Specialist (EPS) Program Grants **2467**
The Program (EPS) was established to support U.S. embassies and consulates overseas by providing policy specialists-in-residence. While serving at the embassy or consulate the specialists also conduct their own research. EPS fellows have served missions in: Baku, Azerbaijan; Bishkek, Kyrgyzstan; Dushanbe, Tajikistan; Ekaterinburg, Russia; and Vladivostok, Russia. EPS fellowships are one to two months. Grant length and dates are determined in consultation with the specific embassy or consulate. Examples of embassy service can include conducting field research, writing policy papers, consulting embassy staff, and assisting with grant panels.
Contact Program Officer; (202) 628-8188; fax: (202) 628-8189; email: eps@irex.org
Internet http://www.irex.org/programs/eps/index.asp
Sponsor International Research & Exchange Board
2121 K Street, NW, Suite 700
Washington, DC 20037

IRP Fellowships in International Journalism **2468**
The fellowships aim to strengthen the US public's understanding of key international topics by helping to educate early- and mid-career US journalists by providing them with access to leading international experts in the United States, and offering them opportunities to do reporting projects overseas. The program enables US journalists to study international issues in Washington, DC, at The Paul H. Nitze School of Advanced International Studies (SAIS) of The Johns Hopkins University before traveling abroad. During the program, journalists have access to some of the world's leading specialists in international issues at SAIS and other institutions in the nation's capital. As part of their four-month program, fellows travel for five weeks to the country or region of their choice. While overseas, journalists work on an important global story, which they discuss with other fellows on their return to Washington. Application and guidelines are available online.
Requirements Any US journalist with at least three years of professional journalistic experience is eligible to apply. The program is open to journalists from newspapers, magazines, wire services, radio, television, and on-line news organizations. Freelancers are also invited to apply.
Amount $2000 per month during the Washington stay
Date(s) Application Is Due Apr 1; Oct 1.
Contact International Reporting Project , (202) 663-7761; fax: (202) 663-7762; email: irp@jhu.edu
Internet http://www.pewfellowships.org/fellows/program/program1.htm
Sponsor Johns Hopkins University
1619 Massachusetts Ave, NW
Washington, DC 20036

Irvine Fellowships **2469**
The program is designed to attract faculty from historically underrepresented groups to teach in a liberal arts college setting. Of particular interest are the following areas: Asian studies, biological sciences, chemistry (analytical/environmental), child development, Chinese language/culture, economics (microeconomics), education (secondary/action research), English (19th century British/postcolonial), earth science, international relations, mathematics education, religious studies (South Asia and/or Islam), and theater arts (acting/directing). The fellowships are designed to allow scholarly time for writing, while gaining teaching experience. Fellows will teach three courses during the year. Fellows also are expected to work with other faculty to expand curricula that are inclusive of race, class, and gender; to present the substance of one's dissertation in a public lecture; or to serve as mentors to a diverse student population. Renewal for an additional year is possible, and the position may be converted to tenure-track in future years.
Requirements Applications should be either new PhDs or in the writing stage of the dissertation before beginning the position.

Amount $28,500 salary
Contact Susan Gotsch, (562) 907-4204; email: sgotsch@whittier.edu
Internet http://www.whittier.edu
Sponsor Whittier College
P.O. Box 634, 13406 E Philadelphia St
Whittier, CA 90608

Irvine Health Foundation Grants **2470**

The foundation supports IRS nonprofit organizations in support of projects and programs designed to meet the health care needs of Orange County, Ca, residents. Preference is given to activities addressing current unmet health care needs. Programs for youth, the elderly, and other groups also are supported. Types of support include challenge/matching grants, program grants, research grants, and seed money grants. There are no application deadlines; the board reviews requests ongoing.
Requirements Orange County, CA, nonprofit organizations are eligible.
Restrictions Grants are not awarded to individuals or for religious purposes, sporting activities, events, or endowments.
Contact Executive Director, (949) 253-2959; fax: (949) 253-2962; email: info@ihf.org
Internet http://www.ihf.org/grant/index.asp
Sponsor Irvine Health Foundation
18301 Von Karman Ave, Ste 440
Irvine, CA 92612

Irving and Rose Crown Scholarships and Fellowships in American History **2471**

These fellowships are awarded for a program of graduate study and research leading to the PhD degree in American History at Brandeis University. The primary goal of the program is to train historical scholars, teachers, and researchers. Full tuition is provided. Fellowships are normally renewable for four years; additional research grants are available for fellows.
Requirements Applicants must have a BA, MA, or professional training, preferably with a strong background in history, American studies, or related fields. Applicants must be accepted into the PhD program in American History at Brandeis University.
Amount $27,345 plus a cash stipend of $16,000
Contact Program Contact, Graduate Program in American History, (781) 736-2270; fax: (781) 736-2273; email: historia@brandeis.edu
Internet http://www.brandeis.edu/departments/history/grad/amst-crown.html
Sponsor Brandeis University - History Department
Dept of History, MS 036
Waltham, MA 02454-9110

Irving Langmuir Award in Chemical Physics **2472**

This award, sponsored by the General Electric Fund, the General Electric Corporate Research and Development Center and administered by the American Chemical Society, is presented in even-numbered years to recognize and encourage outstanding interdisciplinary research in chemistry and physics. (Selection and presentation is made by the Division of Chemical Physics of the American Physical Society in odd-numbered years.) A nominee must have made an outstanding contribution to chemical physics or physical chemistry within the 10 years preceding the year in which the award is made. Applications are accepted in odd-numbered years.
Requirements Any individual, except a member of the award committee, may submit one nomination or seconding letter for the award in any given year. Nominating documents consist of a letter of not more than 1000 words containing an evaluation of the nominee's accomplishments and a specific identification of the work to be recognized, a biographical sketch including date of birth, and a list of publications and patents authored by the nominee. The award is granted without restriction except that the recipient must be a resident of the United States and the monetary prize must be used in the United States or its possessions.
Restrictions Self-nominations are not accepted.
Amount $10,000 and allowance for traveling expenses to award meeting
Date(s) Application Is Due Feb 1.
Contact Awards Administrator, (202) 872-4408; fax: (202) 872-6317; email: awards@acs.org
Internet http://www.chemistry.org/portal/a/c/s/1/acsdisplay.html?DOC=awards%5Clangmuir.html
Sponsor American Chemical Society
1155 16th St NW
Washington, DC 20036

Irvington Institute Immunology Postdoctoral Fellowships **2473**

The institute will award up to 12 postdoctoral fellowships in immunology for three consecutive years of work in a US laboratory or hospital for the award period beginning January 1 or July 1. Fellowships support basic medical research in the prevention and treatment of AIDS, cancer, diabetes, allergies, lupus, rheumatoid arthritis, and other immune system diseases. These fellowships are available to students from foreign countries if they have the proper visas for their stay.
Requirements Medical doctors, PhDs, and MD/PhDs are encouraged to apply. Candidates with not more than three years' laboratory experience will receive priority. The institute does not have a citizenship requirement; however, applicants should indicate their citizenship and/or current visa status.
Restrictions A laboratory may qualify for only one fellow per year.
Amount $45,000 per year
Date(s) Application Is Due Jul 12.
Contact Fellowship Coordinator, (212) 576-1005; fax: 576-1006; email: irvingl@ix.netcom.com
Internet http://www.irvingtoninstitute.org/fellowships.html
Sponsor Irvington Institute for Immunological Research
245 Fifth Ave, Rm 2101
New York, NY 10016

ISA Hyland R. Johns Grant Program **2474**

This program provides funds to researchers for projects of interest and benefit to the arboricultural industry. Research must focus on the biology, management, and care of trees, and their relation to environmental, social, and economic benefits. The society encourages research partnerships to enhance industry involvement, increase interdisciplinary interaction, and provide broader funding potential. Write or fax the society for a list of priority areas. Phone calls will not be accepted.
Restrictions Grant funds cannot be used to pay overhead expenses.
Amount $7500-$25,000
Date(s) Application Is Due May 1.
Contact ISA Research Trust; (888) 472-8733 or (217) 355-9411; fax: (217) 355-9516; email: isa@isa-arbor.com
Internet http://www.treefund.org/GrantSumm.asp#Johns
Sponsor International Society of Arboriculture
P.O. Box 3129, 1400 W Anthony Dr
Champaign, IL 61826

ISA John Z. Duling Grants **2475**

The goal of the program is to provide seed money or partial support for research and technology transfer projects addressing topics that have the potential of benefiting the everyday work of arborists. Proposals in the following priority areas are more likely to be funded: root and soil management; planting and establishment; plant health care; and risk assessment and worker safety. Application information is available online.
Requirements Proposals must be submitted on the application form or an exact duplicate. No faxed or reduced copies of the original will be accepted. Applications sent electronically will not be accepted.
Restrictions Cannot be used to pay for overhead expenses or student tuition and fees.
Amount $7500 maximum
Contact Executive Director, TREE Fund, (630) 221-8127; fax: (630) 690-0702; email: treefund@treefund.org
Internet http://www.treefund.org/grants/Grants.aspx
Sponsor International Society of Arboriculture
711 East Roosevelt Road
Wheaton, IL 60187

ISI William E. Simon Fellowship for Noble Purposes **2476**

The fellowship is an unrestricted cash grant that will be awarded to those graduating college seniors who have demonstrated passion, dedication, a high capacity for self-direction, and originality in pursuit of a goal that will strengthen civil society. Examples of how recipients may use their award include: engage directly in the civic life of their community; help to create opportunity for others, including job creation; advance their expertise; and fund the ultimate realization of their noble purpose. Each year ISI will award three Fellowships for Noble Purpose. One top award and two additional fellowships will be awarded each year. Guidelines and application are available online.
Requirements Graduating college seniors who embody Mr. Simon's passion to make the most of their talents in such a way that they both realize their own capacities and contribute to larger causes beyond self are eligible.
Amount $40,000 top fellowship; $5000 fellowships
Date(s) Application Is Due Feb 1.
Contact Enza Loera, Fellowship Administrator, (800) 526-7022; email: simon@isi.org
Internet http://www.isi.org/programs/fellowships/simon.html
Sponsor Intercollegiate Studies Institute
P.O. Box 4431, 3901 Centerville Rd
Wilmington, DE 19807

Island Foundation Grants **2477**

Grants are awarded in the New England states for the support of arts and culture, civic and public affairs, community development, elementary and secondary education, environmental advocacy as it relates to alternatives in wastewater technology, and social services. Types of support include general operating budgets, matching funds, special projects, and research. Interested persons should request a copy of the foundation's annual report and guidelines before submitting their request.
Requirements Nonprofits in Maine, Massachusetts, and Rhode Island are eligible.
Restrictions Grants do not support individuals, international organizations, religious organizations, special events, benefit dinners, or political campaigns.
Amount $1.7 million total
Contact Julie Early, Executive Director, (508) 748-2809; fax: (508) 748-0991; email: islandfdn@earthlink.net
Sponsor Island Foundation
589 Mill Street
Marion, MA 02738

ISOA/Elan Research Program 2478

The objective of this program, which targets academia and the biotechnology industry, is to facilitate the discovery, development, and clinical evaluation of effective therapies for Alzheimer's disease. The goal is to catalyze and accelerate the development of innovative and effective treatments by funding the development of lead compounds through preclinical in-vitro and in-vivo evaluation, including pharmacology, toxicology, pharmacokinetics, formulation chemistry, and the conduct of preclinical proof-of-concept studies. One-year grants will be awarded. Proposals covering two years may be submitted, although the second year of funding will be contingent on progress of the completed work, the investigator's second-year work plan, and the numbers and quality of competing proposals. Application and guidelines are available online.
Requirements The principal investigator must hold an MD or PhD degree.
Amount $130,000 approximately
Date(s) Application Is Due Oct 14.
Contact Wendy Ramos, Grant and Database Manager, (212) 901-8005; fax: (212) 935-2408; email: wramos@aging-institute.org
Internet http://www.aging-institute.org
Sponsor Institute for the Study of Aging
1414 Avenue of the Americas, Ste 1502
New York, NY 10153

ISUD Jacobsen Prizes 2479

ISUD is a group of scholars and philosophers from many parts of the world who have joined together to discuss and debate leading questions concerning the theory and practice of global community. The Jacobsen Prizes recognize continuation of Jens A.B. Jacobsen's quest to look beyond the individual ego and seek universal meaning that can be shared by all. Submitted papers are eligible for the awards, which will be made during the Congress. All papers presented at the Congress wil be published in the ISUD bi-annual proceedings. Papers must be submitted by the listed deadline. Detailed information is contained on the Web site.
Requirements Participation in the Congresses, which take place every two years (odd-numbered years), is open to anyone with a philosophical bent and with the love of wisdom in his or her heart.
Amount $1500
Date(s) Application Is Due Nov 15.
Contact Dr. Daniel Shannon, Department of Philosophy, email: deshan@depauw.edu
Internet http://www.isud.org/papers/jacobsen.shtml
Sponsor International Society for Universal Dialogue
DePauw University, 212 Asbury Hall
Greencastle, IN46135 04011

Italian Academy for Advanced Studies in America Fellowships 2480

The program accepts applications at the postdoctoral and faculty level for fellowships in areas relating to the study of cultural identity, cultural transmission, and cultural memory, particularly--but not exclusively--with regard to Italy. Applications dealing with the scientific, sociological, and technological aspects of culture and memory are also encouraged. Special consideration will be given to projects in the neurosciences relevant to the academy's ongoing project in art and the neurosciences.
Requirements Complete applications include a cover letter, curriculum vita, a two- to five-page project statement, and two letters of reference.
Date(s) Application Is Due Dec 15.
Contact Elisabetta Assi, Assistant Director, (212) 854-2306; email: ea2146@columbia.edu
Internet http://www.italianacademy.columbia.edu/fellowships/fellowships.html
Sponsor Columbia University
1161 Amsterdam Ave, 6th Fl
New York, NY 10027

Italian History Prizes 2481

To encourage excellence in Italian history, the society in conjunction with the American Historical Association offers the Helen and Howard R. Marraro Prize for the best published book on Italian history and one prize for the best unpublished study (article- or dissertation-length). A double-spaced, typed manuscript in three copies must be submitted for the manuscript award, including name and address of author, brief vita, a short history of her/his interest in Italian history, and the date of completion of the manuscript. For the Marraro Prize, three copies of the book or article must be submitted.
Requirements Applicant must be a resident of the United States or Canada and be beginning a career in Italian history or, for the Marraro Prize, have published a work on Italian history.
Amount $200-$500
Date(s) Application Is Due May 15.
Contact Alan Reinerman, Executive Secretary, Department of History, Boston College, (617) 552-3814; email: alan.reinerman@bc.edu
Internet http://faculty.valenciacc.edu/ckillinger/sihs/AnnualAwards.htm
Sponsor Society of Italian Historical Studies
Boston College, Department of History
Chestnut Hill, MA 02167

Ittleson Foundation AIDS Grants 2482

The foundation is particularly interested in new model, pilot, and demonstration efforts: addressing the needs of underserved at-risk populations and especially those programs recognizing the overlap between such programs; responding to the challenges facing community-based AIDS service organizations and those addressing systemic change; providing meaningful school-based sex education; making treatment information accessible, available and easily understandable to those in need of it; or, addressing the psycho-social needs of those infected and affected by AIDS, especially adolescents.
Requirements Tax-exempt organizations may apply.
Restrictions The foundation generally does not provide funds for capital building projects, endowments, grants to individuals, scholarships or internships (except as part of a program), direct service programs (especially outside New York City), projects that are local in focus and unlikely to be replicated, continuing or general support, projects and organizations that are international in scope or purpose, or biomedical research.
Date(s) Application Is Due Sep 1.
Contact Anthony C. Wood, Executive Director; (212) 794-2008; fax: (212) 794-0351
Internet http://www.ittlesonfoundation.org/aids.html
Sponsor Ittleson Foundation
15 E. 67th Street, 5th Floor
New York, NY 10021

Ittleson Foundation Environment Grants 2483

The foundation supports innovative pilot, model and demonstration projects that will help move individuals, communities, and organizations from environmental awareness to environmental activism by changing attitudes and behaviors. This program seeks to encourage and nurture environmental action through: supporting the present generation of environmental activists, whether professionals or volunteers through education, training and other activities; educating and engaging the next generation of environmentalists with a special interest in supporting the training of those who are teaching that generation; strengthening the infrastructure of the environmental movement with a particular focus on efforts at the grassroots and statewide levels; activating new constituencies, particularly those focused on environmental equity issues.
Requirements Tax-exempt organizations may apply.
Restrictions The foundation generally does not provide funds for capital building projects, endowments, grants to individuals, scholarships or internships (except as part of a program), direct service programs (especially outside New York City), projects that are local in focus and unlikely to be replicated, continuing or general support, projects and organizations that are international in scope or purpose, or biomedical research.
Date(s) Application Is Due Sep 1.
Contact Anthony C. Wood, Executive Director; (212) 794-2008; fax: (212) 794-0351
Internet http://www.ittlesonfoundation.org/enviro.html
Sponsor Ittleson Foundation
15 E. 67th Street, 5th Floor
New York, NY 10021

Ittleson Foundation Mental Health Grants 2484

For this program, the foundation is interested in innovative, pilot, model and demonstration projects that are: fighting the stigma associated with mental illness and working to change the public's negative perception of people who have mental illness; utilizing new knowledge and current technological advances to improve programs and services for people who have mental illness; bringing the full benefits of this new knowledge and technology to those who presently do not have access to them; or, advancing preventative mental health efforts, especially those targeted to youth and adolescents, with a special focus on strategies that involve parents, teachers, and others in close contact with these populations.
Requirements Tax-exempt organizations may apply.
Restrictions The foundation generally does not provide funds for capital building projects, endowments, grants to individuals, scholarships or internships (except as part of a program), direct service programs (especially outside New York City), projects that are local in focus and unlikely to be replicated, continuing or general support, projects and organizations that are international in scope or purpose, or biomedical research.
Date(s) Application Is Due Sep 1.
Contact Anthony C. Wood, Executive Director; (212) 794-2008; fax: (212) 794-0351
Internet http://www.ittlesonfoundation.org/mental.html
Sponsor Ittleson Foundation
15 E. 67th Street, 5th Floor
New York, NY 10021

Ittleson Predoctoral Fellowship 2485

The fellowship is awarded for research in fields other than Western art to be held partly in residence at the National Gallery of Art, Center for Advanced Study in the Visual Arts, and partly elsewhere in the United States or abroad. The Ittleson fellow is expected to spend the second year of the fellowship at the center to complete the dissertation. Application must be made through the chair of the graduate department of art history or other appropriate department. Departments should limit nomination to one candidate. Fellowships begin September 1 and are not renewable.
Requirements Applicants must have completed their residence requirements and coursework for the PhD and general or preliminary examinations before the date of application and know two foreign languages related to the topic of the dissertation. Applicants must be either US citizens or enrolled in a university in the United States.

Amount $24,000 annually for two years
Date(s) Application Is Due Nov 15.
Contact Fellowships Program, Center for Advanced Study in Visual Arts, (202) 842-6482; fax: (202) 842-6733; email: advstudy@nga.gov
Internet http://www.nga.gov/resources/casvapre.htm
Sponsor National Gallery of Art
Fourth St and Constitution Ave NW
Washington, DC 20565

ITVS Research and Development/Commissioning Funding **2486**
TVS accepts proposals on an ongoing basis for production funding for projects that do not fit within the parameters of its standing initiatives (Open Call, LINCS and DDF), including limited series. ITVS also accepts proposals on an ongoing basis for projects in all genres in need of research and development funding. Examples of funding requests include travel, research, script development or development of a fundraising reel.
Contact Jonathan Archer, (415) 356-8383 ext 284; fax: (415) 356-8391; email: jonathan_archer@itvs.org
Internet http://www.itvs.org/producers/funding.html
Sponsor Independent Television Service
651 Brannan Street, Suite 410
San Francisco, CA 94107

IUCP Archives Program Fellowship **2487**
Grants support research in any discipline at Indiana University's Ruth Lilly Philanthropy Archives. To apply, submit a resume or vita and cover letter including the following information: name, contact information (including telephone and email address); title and brief description of the project; description of how the Philanthropy Archival collection will be utilized in the research project; dates and duration of the project; and amount requested and budget summary. Allowable expenses include round-trip travel, temporary lodging, food, photocopying, and other research expenses. Applications are accepted on an ongoing basis. Contact staff prior to proposal submission to ensure that the required research documents are available in the library.
Requirements Individual scholars and researchers are eligible.
Amount $4000 maximum
Contact Kathy Steinberg, (317) 684-8957; fax: (317) 684-8900; email: ksteinbe@iupui.edu
Internet http://www.philanthropy.iupui.edu/research.html
Sponsor Indiana University Center on Philanthropy
550 W North St, Ste 301
Indianapolis, IN 46202-3162

IUCP Dissertation Fellowship **2488**
One-year grants are awarded for doctoral research relating to issues facing philanthropy and nonprofit organizations. Participants are encouraged to obtain matching funds from their home institutions.
Requirements Applicants from Indiana institutions must be conducting dissertation research relevant to the center's priority research areas. Applicants from universities outside of Indiana may be asked to contact the Aspen Institute's Nonprofit Research Fund.
Amount $4000 maximum
Contact Kathy Steinberg, (317) 684-8957; email: ksteinbe@iupui.edu
Internet http://www.philanthropy.iupui.edu
Sponsor Indiana University Center on Philanthropy
550 W North St, Ste 301
Indianapolis, IN 46202-3272

IUCP Hearst Minority Fellowships **2489**
The fellowship is designed to provide members of minority groups the opportunity to engage in reflective thought and study as well as practical application of philanthropy. The fellowship is a nonrenewable 10-month appointment from August 15 to June 15. The fellow will devote a portion of time to formal study and a portion to the practice of philanthropy. The Center on Philanthropy will provide fellows a stipend and full tuition. The student is expected to pay the remaining tuition, housing, and living expenses, as well as other costs (books, insurance, fees, etc.). Application forms for the MA in philanthropic studies and the MPA program can be requested from the center. These applications are used to determine the fellowship recipient.
Requirements The fellowship is open to members of groups traditionally underrepresented in organized philanthropy who have bachelor's degrees or equivalent from another country in any academic field and are either recent graduates, scholars, active volunteers, or nonprofit practitioners. To be considered, a candidate must apply and be admitted to either the MA in philanthropic studies or the MPA in nonprofit management.
Amount $9000 for living and housing expenses.
Date(s) Application Is Due Feb 1.
Contact Hearst Minority Fellowships, (800) 854-1612; fax: (317) 684-8900; email: maphil@iupui.edu
Internet http://www.philanthropy.iupui.edu/hearst.html
Sponsor Indiana University Center on Philanthropy
550 W North St, Ste 301
Indianapolis, IN 46202-3162

IUCP Indiana Research Fund **2490**
Grants are awareded for research relating to issues facing philanthropy and nonprofit organizations. Priority will be given to well-designed projects consistent with the center's strategic emphasis on research and practice that may be translated into potential solutions for problems facing philanthropy, fund raising, and the nonprofit sector. Proposals involving collaboration among nonprofit practitioners, academic researchers, independent scholars, and policy analysts are welcome. Annual deadlines dates may vary; contact program staff for exact dates.
Requirements Grants will be awarded to faculty members affiliated with any of the branch campuses of Indiana University.
Amount $50,000 maximum
Contact Maggie Bowden, (317) 278-8984; email: mtbowden@iupui.edu
Internet http://www.philanthropy.iupui.edu/giving_opportunities.html
Sponsor Indiana University Center on Philanthropy
550 W North St, Ste 301
Indianapolis, IN 46202-3162

IUVSTA Prize for Science **2491**
The Prize is given for experimental and/or theoretical research in vacuum science, technique or its applications. The purpose is to recognize and encourage outstanding internationally-acclaimed research in the fields of interest to the IUVSTA. The award will normally be given to an individual; however, in exceptional cases involving team research, multiple awards may be given. The Prize consists of a cash award, a struck medal and a certificate setting forth the reasons for the award. The Prize will be conferred at intervals of not less than three years. Reasonable travel expenses of the recipient to the meeting at which the Prize is presented shall be agreed upon and reimbursed.
Requirements The nominee must have accomplished outstanding experimental and/or theoretical research in vacuum science, technique or its applications within the ten years preceding the year in which the award is made. Special consideration will be given to nominees currently engaged in an active career of research. Neither nominees nor nominators are required to be members of IUVSTA member societies.
Restrictions Current officers and members of the Executive Council and Standing Committees, as well as Division Officers of IUVSTA, are not eligible.
Date(s) Application Is Due Apr 2.
Contact Dr. Masatoshi Ono; fax: +81 44 366 6331; email: ono.m@funai-atri.co.jp
Internet http://www.iuvsta.org/prizeinfo.html
Sponsor International Union for Vacuum Science, Technique, and Applications
1-12 Minami-Wataridi-Cho
Kawasaki-shi, Kanagawa 210-0855
Japan

IUVSTA Prize for Technology **2492**
The purpose of the Award is to recognize and encourage outstanding internationally-acclaimed achievements in technology and instrumentation in the fields of interest to the IUVSTA. The award will normally be given to an individual; however, in exceptional cases involving team research, multiple awards may be given. The Prize consists of a cash award, a struck medal and a certificate setting forth the reasons for the award. The Prize will be conferred at intervals of not less than three years. Reasonable travel expenses of the recipient to the meeting at which the Prize is presented shall be agreed upon and reimbursed.
Requirements The nominee must have accomplished outstanding results in the area of technology and instrumentation within the ten years preceding the year in which the award is made. Special consideration will be given to nominees currently actively involved in this work. Neither nominees nor nominators are required to be members of IUVSTA member societies.
Restrictions Current officers and members of the Executive Council and Standing Committees, as well as Division Officers of IUVSTA, are not eligible.
Date(s) Application Is Due Apr 2.
Contact Dr. Masatoshi Ono; fax: +81 44 366 6331; email: ono.m@funai-atri.co.jp
Internet http://www.iuvsta.org/prizeinfo.html
Sponsor International Union for Vacuum Science, Technique, and Applications
1-12 Minami-Wataridi-Cho
Kawasaki-shi, Kanagawa 210-0855
Japan

IUVSTA Welch Foundation Scholarship **2493**
The scholarship is offered for a one-year period, starting in September, to a promising scholar who wishes to contribute to the study of vacuum science techniques or their application in any field. Because of the international nature of the scholarship, strong preference is given to applicants who propose study in a foreign lab in which they have not yet studied. Payment of the scholarship is in three installments totalling $15,000; one of $7500 at the beginning, another of $7000 after six months, and a third of $500 upon delivery of a final report after completion of work. The scholarship holder is encouraged to seek funds in addition to the scholarship, but should obtain authorization of the chairperson of the Welch Committee before accepting additional funds.
Requirements Candidates should have at least a bachelor's degree; a doctoral degree is preferred. Application should include a curriculum vita; a photocopy of, or attestation of, all diplomas; the name and address of laboratory chosen and a letter indicating that this laboratory's facilities will be available to the applicant; a 200-word abstract describing the proposed research; a declaration that the candidate will not violate any laws of

his/her own country during the tenure of the scholarship, as well as a declaration that the candidate will not violate any laws or engage in any political activity in the country where he/she intends working; and two recommendations from present or past professors or research directors. Additionally, candidates must produce satisfactory evidence of reasonable fluency either in the language of the country where he/she will work during the tenure of the scholarship or in English.
Restrictions If the candidate cannot begin work as scheduled, he or she may begin within three months after September 1. In the case of a delay of more than three months, another candidate may be chosen. The laboratory where the candidate wishes to work must approve any delay in the commencement of work.
Amount $15,000
Date(s) Application Is Due Apr 15.
Contact Dr. Frank R. Shepherd, Nortel Networks, 3 Grierson Lane, Ottawa ON K2W 1A6 Canada, (613) 763-3285; fax: (613) 763-2404; email: frank_shepherd@avs.org
Internet http://www.iuvsta.org/welchann.html
Sponsor International Union for Vacuum Science, Technique, and Applications
30 avenue de la Renaissance
Brussels B-1000
Belgium

IWMF Public Health Fellowship **2494**
The goals of the fellowship are to offer women newspaper editors and radio producers the opportunity to enhance their ability to cover public health issues, build their journalism skills, and learn first-hand about standards and practices in the US media. The six-month fellowship includes four months in the United States and two months in the fellows' home countries, where the fellows will implement a public health reporting project. Each applicant must clearly identify and describe a public health reporting project that she will focus on when she returns to her home country for that segment of the fellowship. Those demonstrating original approaches to covering HIV/AIDS will be given top consideration. The fellowship includes application costs for a US visa; round-trip economy airfare from the fellows' home countries to Washington, DC; round-trip economy airfare from Washington, DC, to the fellowship site and health insurance; and a fixed stipend to cover lodging, meals, and ground transportation during the US segment of the fellowship. For the home country segment, a fixed stipend will be provided to support the fellow and cover all costs associated with implementing her project. *Requirements* The fellowship is open to women journalists who are working in one of the following countries: Asia (China and Indonesia), West Africa (Benin, Burkina Faso, Cameroon, Cape Verde, Chad, Gambia, Ghana, Guinea, Guinea Bissau, Ivory Coast, Liberia, Mali, Mauritania, Niger, Nigeria, Senegal, Sierra Leone, and Togo), and Southern Africa (Angola, Botswana, Lesotho, Malawi, Mozambique, Namibia, Swaziland, Zambia, and Zimbabwe). A successful applicant will be dedicated to a career in journalism and have five or more years of full-time experience in the profession, with at least three of those years having been focused on public health journalism. She must be currently working as a newspaper editor or radio producer and show a strong commitment to sharing knowledge and skills with colleagues upon returning home. The fellow must also have excellent written and spoken English skills.
Date(s) Application Is Due Apr 15.
Contact Fellowship Administrator, (202) 496-1992; fax: (202) 496-1977; email: fellowship@iwmf.org
Internet http://iwmf.org/programs/8702
Sponsor International Women's Media Foundation
1625 K St NW, Ste 1275
Washington, DC 20006

Izaak Walton Killam Memorial Postdoctoral Fellowships at Dalhousie University **2495**
The postdoctoral fellowships are awarded annually at Dalhousie University to recently graduated scholars of superior academic research ability in any discipline. Awards are tenable for two years and include travel costs, a research grant, and a conference travel allowance. Guidelines and forms are available online.
Requirements Applicants must have recently completed a PhD (January 1 of last year) at a recognized university and have no current affiliation with Dalhousie University.
Restrictions Because these fellowships are intended to attract new scholars to Dalhousie, scholars already at Dalhousie and DalTech are not eligible to apply, including Dalhousie and DalTech PhDs, Dalhousie, DalTech or King's employees, and researchers using Dalhousie, DalTech, or King's facilities.
Amount $C40,000 plus travel allowance, $C3000 research allowance, and $C1000 conference travel grant
Date(s) Application Is Due Dec 15.
Contact Office of the Dean, Faculty of Graduate Studies, fax: (902) 494-8797; email: graduate.studies@dal.ca
Internet http://www.dalgrad.dal.ca/kpdf
Sponsor Dalhousie University
6299 South St
Halifax, NS B3H 4H6 Canada

Izaak Walton Killam Memorial Postdoctoral Fellowships at the University of British Columbia **2496**
These awards are offered to candidates who have shown superior ability in research and who possess doctorates or who are deemed to have similar qualifications. The candidate may pursue any field of research other than the arts. The basis of the award will be special distinction of intellect, with due regard for sound character and personal qualities. Subject to review at the end of the first year, Killam Memorial Postdoctoral Fellowships are awarded for two years. Fellowships are tenable at the University of British Columbia.
Requirements Applicants must have obtained the PhD no more than two academic years prior to the anticipated commencement date of the fellowship. The doctorate must be from a university other than The University of British Columbia. Application is open to citizens of any country.
Amount $C44,000 plus $6000 travel allowance
Date(s) Application Is Due Nov 15.
Contact Killam Secretary, Faculty of Graduate Studies, (604) 822-2848; fax: (604) 822-5802; email: graduate.awards@ubc.ca
Internet http://www.grad.ubc.ca/awards/index.asp?menu=015,000,000,000
Sponsor University of British Columbia
180-6371 Crescent Rd
Vancouver, BC V6T 1Z1 Canada

Izaak Walton Killam Memorial Predoctoral Fellowships at the University of British Columbia **2497**
These fellowships are awarded to highest ranked doctoral candidates in the university's graduate fellowships competitions. Approximately 25 awards are made each year. Applications are available on the Web site.
Requirements Applicants must be graduate students with a first-class standing in the last two years of full-time study. Students from any country and from all fields are eligible.
Amount $C25,000 plus $C1500 travel allowance
Contact Killam Secretary, Faculty of Graduate Studies, (604) 822-8501 or 822-0976; fax: (604) 822-5802; email: graduate.awards@ubc.ca
Internet http://www.grad.ubc.ca/awards/index.asp?menu=003,000,000,000
Sponsor University of British Columbia
180-6371 Crescent Rd
Vancouver, BC V6T 1Z2 Canada

Izaak Walton Killam Memorial Scholarships at Dalhousie University **2498**
These awards are offered in support of studies leading toward either a master's or doctoral degree. Supported by The Killam Trusts, the scholarships include stipends and funds to assist with transportation costs to Halifax. Scholars may perform instruction or demonstration duties at the discretion of the department, for which additional remuneration is given. Master's students may hold a Killam Scholarship for 12 months and PhD students for up to 36 months.
Requirements Eligibility is based on a first-class undergraduate degree in the field of study the student wishes to pursue. Candidates are not required to submit application forms but should apply to the Registrar for admission to graduate studies no later than the listed application deadline date. Killam scholars are selected on the basis of nominations made by departments. It is expected that nominees will also have applied for funding from relevant national or international agencies. Canadian students are eligible for nomination for the Killam Scholarships only if they have applied for the relevant national scholarship (NSERC, SSHRC, MRC, etc.).
Amount $C19,000 for the master's level; $C23,000 for the PhD level
Date(s) Application Is Due Apr 1; Aug 31; Dec 31.
Contact Margaret Wood, Killam Administrator; fax: (902) 494-2772; fax: (902) 494-8797; email: margaret.wood@dal.ca
Internet http://www.dalgrad.dal.ca/funding
Sponsor Dalhousie University
Henry Hicks Academic Administration Bldg, Rm 314
Halifax, NS B3H 4H6 Canada

Izaak Walton Killam Memorial Scholarships at the University of Calgary **2499**
Approximately nine awards are made annually to the top ranking students in the Open competition who are eligible to hold them. The scholarship has the highest monetary value of any of the university's awards ($20,100 per annum) and includes a research allowance. The awards are for two years, the second year being subject to satisfactory progress.
Requirements These scholarships are open for competition among PhD students who apply to the University of Calgary's Open Scholarship competition.
Amount $C20,100 per annum, plus $3000 research allowance
Date(s) Application Is Due Feb 1.
Contact Connie Busch, Faculty of Graduate Studies, (403) 220-5690; email: cbusch@ucalgary.ca
Internet http://www.ucalgary.ca/pubs/calendar/current/what/Awards/03GradAwards.htm#71
Sponsor University of Calgary
2500 University Dr NW, Earth Sciences Bldg, Rm 720
Calgary, AB T2N 1N4 Canada

Izumi Foundation Grants **2500**
The mission of the foundation is to alleviate human suffering through improved health care, especially the poorest and the most vulnerable members of society. The foundation's current geographic focus area is a select number of countries in Africa and Central and South America. Program interests include disease, disabilities, and inadequate health

care related to poverty. Within its expressed goals and designated geographic areas, the foundation seeks to support projects and programs that distribute medicines and vaccines, and provide direct services and care; provide interventions that encourage the most effective use of limited, local health care resources; address the underlying causes of disease and persistent health care problems; build health care capacity on the community level; provide cost-effective strategies for prevention; and advance health care partnerships and collaborations. The foundation does not accept unsolicited proposals. Potential applicants are asked to submit a letter of inquiry that does not exceed three pages in length. Letters of inquiry may be submitted any time during the year.
Requirements Organizations within the United States must have 501(c)3 tax-exempt status to be eligible to apply. Agencies and organizations outside of the United States will also be required to furnish documentation verifying their nonprofit status.
Restrictions The foundation does not fund medical research or other research-related activities; income generating, endowments, or fundraising activities; ongoing general operating expenses, indirect costs, or existing deficits; capital costs--the acquisition of land, buildings, or vehicles; direct support to individuals, scholarships, school fees, or clothing; or religious activities, media campaigns, or lobbying of any kind.
Amount $100,000 maximum
Contact Catherine Bryant, Program Officer, (617) 303-0345; fax: (617) 303-0339; email: cbryant@izumi.org
Internet http://www.izumi.org
Sponsor Izumi Foundation
One Financial Ctr, 28th Fl
Boston, MA 02111

J. Hall Taylor Medal **2501**
This medal is presented for distinguished service or eminent achievement in the field of codes and standards pertaining to the broad fields of piping and pressure vessels that are sponsored or undertaken by ASME. The scope shall include contributions to technical advancement and administration.
Amount $1000
Date(s) Application Is Due Nov 15.
Contact Gilda DiTullio, Manager, (212) 591-7736; fax: (212) 705-7739; email: ditulliog@asme.org or awards@asme.org
Internet http://www.asme.org/honors/ms71/saa/taylor.html
Sponsor American Society of Mechanical Engineers
3 Park Ave
New York, NY 10016

J. Waldo Smith Hydraulic Fellowship **2502**
The fellowship is restricted to research in the field of experimental hydraulics as distinguished from research concentrating on purely theoretical hydraulics. Emphasis is to be placed on practical experiments designed and executed for the purpose of advancing knowledge with respect to the laws of hydraulic flow, rather than to the type of research that proceeds on the theory of mathematical analysis based on assumptions of unknown validity. The purpose of the research is to test the assumptions that are currently made, and also to develop a better understanding of fluid flow. The fellowship is offered every third year (next in 2006) and runs for one full academic year. Administration is in part through the institution that invites cooperation through its engineering faculty. Application packets are available through the student chapter advisor or from ASCE.
Requirements Fellowships are awarded to graduate students, who are members of the society, who give promise of best fulfilling the ideals of the fellowship. There is a brief application form. Each application shall include a statement in general terms of the purposes for which the funds are expected to be used.
Amount $4000 per year, plus maximum of $1000 research equipment allowance
Date(s) Application Is Due Feb 9.
Contact Grants Coordinator, (703) 295-6342; fax: (703) 295-6343; email: student@asce.org
Internet http://www.asce.org/inside/stud_scholar.cfm
Sponsor American Society of Civil Engineers
1801 Alexander Bell Dr
Reston, VA 20191-4400

J.B. Reynolds Foundation **2503**
The foundation makes grants in the local Kansas City, MO, area. Grants are awarded for building and equipment, community development, medical research, social welfare, and the arts and humanities. Some support is given to colleges and universities. Additional types of support include general operating support, continuing support, annual campaigns, endowment funds, publications, and research. The board meets in April and December of each year to consider requests. All grants are awarded in December.
Requirements 501(c)3 organizations in the Kansas City, MO, area may apply.
Amount $700-$50,000 range
Contact Program Contact
Sponsor J.B. Reynolds Foundation
P.O. Box 219139
Kansas City, MO 64141-6139

J.H. Stewart Reid Memorial Fellowship for Doctoral Studies **2504**
This fellowship is awarded annually for doctoral study in a Canadian university in any field of study. Fellows must reapply for continuation.
Requirements Applicants must be Canadian citizens or have held permanent resident (landed immigrant) status for one year prior to application; must hold registration in a doctoral program at a Canadian university; must have completed comprehensive exams and have doctoral thesis proposal accepted by the listed deadline date of the year applying; must have a first-class academic record; and must not hold scholarships that exceed in total $25,000 inclusive of the J. H. Stewart Reid Memorial Fellowship Trust.
Amount $C5000 annually
Date(s) Application Is Due Apr 30.
Contact Johanne Smith, Awards Officer, (613) 820-2270; fax: (613) 820-7244; email: stewartreid@caut.ca
Internet http://stewartreid.caut.ca/English/policy.htm
Sponsor Canadian Association of University Teachers
2675 Queensview Dr
Ottawa, ON K2B 8K2 Canada

J.I. Staley Prize **2505**
This prize is awarded periodically to a living author for an outstanding book in the field of anthropology. The award is intended to acknowledge those innovative works that have gone beyond traditional frontiers in anthropology and given new dimensions to our understanding of the human species. By recognizing these publications and their authors, the prize helps to stimulate research and writing that steps outside the dominant schools of thought and crosses arbitrary boundaries between disciplines. To nominate a book, send a letter of nomination and solicit two additional scholars to do the same; a complete nomination requires three letters. Each letter of nomination should be a maximum of three pages, single-spaced, and should describe the book's innovative thinking; its use of two or more academic disciplines or of two or more subdisciplines of anthropology; its contribution to our understanding of humankind; and its impact within anthropology. Nomination forms are available on the Web site.
Requirements To be considered for the prize, a book must have been published at least two years but not more than eight years before the year of nomination. (Once a book has been nominated, it will stay in the pool of nominees until it passes the 10-year age limit.) Coauthored books may be nominated, but edited volumes may not. The nomination must clearly be a single book, even if it builds on prior work by the author or others.
Restrictions Authors and publishers may not nominate their own work.
Amount $10,000
Date(s) Application Is Due Oct 1.
Contact Staley Prize Coordinator, (505) 954-7201; fax: (505) 989-9809; email: staley@sarsf.org
Internet http://www.sarweb.org/staley/staley.htm
Sponsor School of American Research
P.O. Box 2188
Santa Fe, NM 87504-2188

J.S. Mill Fellowships in Economics for Exceptional Students **2506**
The fellowship assists students who are enrolled in the graduate program in economics at Washington University. Application materials may be obtained from the department.
Requirements Applicants must be admitted to the graduate program in the department of economics at Washington University.
Amount $16,000 maximum stipend plus full tuition
Date(s) Application Is Due Jan 15.
Contact Karen Rensing, Secretary, Department of Economics, (314) 935-5670; fax: (314) 935-4156; email: karenr@wuecona.wustl.edu or gradsec@wueconc.wustl.edu
Internet http://economics.wustl.edu/graduate/brochure/brochure.pdf
Sponsor Washington University
Campus Box 1208, 205 Eliot Hall
Saint Louis, MO 63130-4899

J.W. and Ida M. Jameson Foundation Grants **2507**
The foundation supports higher and theological education, hospitals, medical research, cultural programs, and Protestant and Catholic religion. Types of support include research and general operating budgets. Applicants should submit a proposal.
Requirements California nonprofits may submit applications for grant support.
Amount $5000-$50,000 range
Date(s) Application Is Due Feb 1.
Contact Les Hugn, President, (626) 355-6973
Sponsor J.W. and Ida M. Jameson Foundation
P.O. Box 397
Sierra Madre, CA 91025

J.W. Kieckhefer Foundation Grants **2508**
The foundation awards grants to support medical research; hospice; health; family planning; disabled; social services; higher, medical, and other education; youth; child welfare; conservation; community funds; public policy; and cultural programs. The grants are awarded for operating budgets, continuing support, annual campaigns, emergency funds, building funds, equipment, land acquisition, endowment funds, matching funds, research, publications, conferences and seminars, and special projects. Applications should be submitted between May and November. The board meets in November and December to consider requests.
Restrictions Grants are not awarded to individuals or for seed money, deficit financing, scholarships, or demonstration projects.

Amount $350-$100,000 range
Contact John Kieckhefer or Eugene Polk, Trustees, (928) 445-4010
Sponsor J.W. Kieckhefer Foundation
P.O. Box 1151, 116 E Gurley St
Prescott, AZ 86302

Jack Kent Cooke Foundation Graduate Scholarships **2509**
The program awards fellowships to outstanding students pursuing graduate or professional degrees. Scholars may use the award to attend any accredited graduate school in the United States or abroad. The award funds tuition and fees and will include a stipend based on reasonable expenses and demonstrated need. Scholarships are renewable each year for the duration of the graduate degree program, as long as the fellow continues to meet the eligibility requirements. Application materials are available online.
Requirements Candidates must be nominated by the Jack Kent Cooke Foundation Faculty Representative at their undergraduate institution (list available online).
Amount $50,000 maximum
Date(s) Application Is Due Apr 29.
Contact Graduate Scholarships, (800) 498-6478 or (703) 723-8000; fax: (703) 723-8030; email: jck@jackkentcookefoundation.org
Internet http://www.jackkentcookefoundation.org/jkcf_web/content.aspx?page=Grad
Sponsor Jack Kent Cooke Foundation
44115 Woodridge Pkwy, Ste 200
Lansdowne, VA 20176-5199

Jackson Foundation Grants Program **2510**
The Foundation was established to promote the welfare of the public of the City of Portland or the State of Oregon, or both. Projects located outside the Portland metropolitan area of statewide appeal, rather than local concern, are considered.
Requirements Grants are awarded to nonprofit 501(c)3 tax-exempt agencies located within the state of Oregon.
Restrictions Funding is not available for individuals or private businesses. Grants are generally not made to a K-12 school. Do not contact the Foundation by phone to check the status of an application.
Amount $1000-$25,000 average
Date(s) Application Is Due Mar 31; Jun 30; Sep 30; Dec 31.
Contact Program Contact, U.S. Bank, (503) 275-4414
Internet http://www.thejacksonfoundation.com
Sponsor Jackson Foundation
P.O. Box 3168
Portland, OR 97208

Jackson Laboratory Postdoctoral Research Training Program **2511**
Fellowships are intended for postdoctoral associateships at Jackson Laboratory allowing the fellows to participate in research into gene regulation, developmental genetics, hematology and immunology, and other fields of mammalian biology, with the purpose of the recipient receiving research training under the guidance of experienced researchers. The fellowships are awarded for one year, renewable for up to two years. Applications are accepted at any time.
Requirements Recent recipients of doctoral degrees in medicine, veterinary medicine, and the biological sciences are eligible to apply. Applicants may be of any nationality.
Contact Suzanne Serreze, Manager, Sponsored Training Programs, (207) 288-6420; fax: (207) 288-6079; email: sbs@jax.org
Internet http://www.jax.org/education/postdoc.html
Sponsor Jackson Laboratory
600 Main St
Bar Harbor, ME 04609-1500

Jacob and Charlotte Lehrman Foundation Grants **2512**
The foundation makes grants to establish scholarships and fellowships at institutions of learning and to foster research in medicine and science. Grants are also given for Jewish welfare funds, care of the aged and sick, the establishment of trade schools, the fostering of religious observance, recreation, and aid to refugees. Additional types of support include general operating grants and matching funds. The Foundation Board generally makes grants once a year, typically in October. The deadline for RFPs as well as proposals submitted from current grant recipients is April 1.
Requirements Grants are made primarily to organizations in the greater metropolitan Washington, DC, area.
Restrictions Grants are not made to individuals.
Amount $1000-$10,000 range
Date(s) Application Is Due Apr 1.
Contact Robert Lehrman, Vice President, (202) 338-8400; fax: (202) 338-8405; email: info@lehrmanfoundation.org
Internet http://www.lehrmanfoundation.org
Sponsor Jacob and Charlotte Lehrman Foundation
1027 33rd St NW, 2nd Fl
Washington, DC 20007

Jacob and Hilda Blaustein Foundation Grants **2513**
The Foundation promotes social justice and human rights through its five program areas: Jewish life; strengthening Israeli democracy; health and mental health; educational opportunity; and human rights. Support is provided to organizations in the United States and abroad. The Foundation supports organizations that promote systemic change; involve constituents in planning and decision-making; encourage volunteer and professional development; and engage in ongoing program evaluation. Application information is available online.
Requirements Nonprofit organizations are eligible to apply.
Restrictions Support is not provided for: grants or scholarships to individuals; unsolicited proposals for academic, scientific, or medical research; direct mail, annual giving, membership campaigns, fundraising and commemorative events. The Foundation rarely makes capital grants unless there is a prior relationship with the applicant organization.
Amount $5,000-$25,000
Contact Betsy Ringel, Executive Director, (410) 347-7103; fax: (410) 347-7210; email: info@blaufund.org
Internet http://www.blaufund.org/foundations/jacobandhilda_f.html
Sponsor Jacob and Hilda Blaustein Foundation
10 East Baltimore Street, Suite 1111
Baltimore, MD 21202

Jacob and Valeria Langeloth Foundation Grants **2514**
The Foundation's grantmaking program is centered on the concepts of health and well-being. The Foundation's purpose is to promote and support effective and creative programs, practices and policies related to healing from illness, accident, physical, social or emotional trauma and to extend the availability of programs that promote healing to underserved populations. The Foundation has established priority funding status for proposals that address caregiving, and correctional health care. Application information is available online.
Requirements The Foundation welcomes proposals from 501(c)(3) organizations that promote physical and emotional healing, especially to underserved populations, such as: community-based organizations, health care providers and research institutions.
Restrictions The Foundation will not consider proposals for annual or capital campaigns, for building or renovation projects, for budgetary relief, or preventive medicine. The Foundation does not support projects that focus on children or end-of-life issues. Neither will the Foundation make grants to individuals or for sectarian or religious purposes, or for political activities or lobbying. The Foundation will not fund any organization that discriminates on the basis of age, gender, national origin, race, or sexual preference.
Date(s) Application Is Due Feb 1; Aug 1.
Contact Scott Moyer, (212) 687-1133; fax: (212) 681-2628; email: smoyer@langeloth.org
Internet http://www.langeloth.org/apply.php
Sponsor Jacob and Valeria Langeloth Foundation
521 Fifth Avenue
New York, NY 10175-1699

Jacobs Research Funds Small Grants Program **2515**
Grants are given for anthropological research on living Native Americans on cultural, social, psychological, aesthetic, and linguistic problems. While the fund has a Pacific Northwest focus, research projects within Canada, Mexico, the rest of the continental United States, and Alaska are eligible. The fund emphasizes field research rather than the analysis of previously collected materials. Grant funds may cover fees for consultants, supplies (notebooks, audio- and videotapes, etc.), transportation to and from the field, and lodging in the field. Grants are made for a maximum of one year and are renewed only on the basis of a new application. Application forms are available upon request.
Requirements Grants are made to individuals. Applicants need not have completed degrees. Formal institutional affiliation is not required; however, in the absence of formal research training or institutional affiliation, cooperation with or supervision by an experienced research scholar is strongly recommended. Applications from Native Americans are encouraged.
Restrictions Projects in archaeology, physical anthropology, applied anthropology, and applied linguistics are not included in the program. Research on archive materials or museum collections is not ordinarily considered for funding. Funds are not provided for the salary of the researcher, major equipment, or living expenses.
Amount $1200
Date(s) Application Is Due Feb 15.
Contact Jacobs Research Funds Administrator, (360) 676-6981; fax: (360) 738-7409; email: museuminfo@cob.org
Internet http://www.whatcommuseum.org/pages/info/info.htm
Sponsor Whatcom Museum of History and Art
121 Prospect St
Bellingham, WA 98225

Jake Duerksen Memorial Scholarship **2516**
This scholarship is awarded annually to cover four months of graduate study based on the recipient's academic excellence. Students interested in the award should first apply to the Department of Biological Sciences.
Requirements The scholarship is open to full-time graduate students who have been enrolled in the Department of Biological Sciences for a minimum of one academic year.
Amount $C2000 maximum

Contact Connie Busch, Faculty of Graduate Studies, (403) 220-5690; email: cbusch@ucalgary.ca
Internet http://www.ucalgary.ca/pubs/calendar/current/What/Awards/03GradAwards.htm
Sponsor University of Calgary
2500 University Dr NW, Earth Sciences Bldg, Rm 720
Calgary, AB T2N 1N4 Canada

James Alexander Robertson Memorial Prize **2517**
This prize is awarded annually for an article appearing during the year preceding the award in one of the four consecutive issues (beginning with the August issue) of the Hispanic American Historical Review. The article selected for the award is to be one that, in the judgment of the prize committee, makes an outstanding contribution to Latin American historical literature. An honorable mention award (with no cash stipend) may be made for an additional distinguished article deemed worthy of the same by the prize committee.
Amount $500
Contact CLAH, (530) 752-3046; fax: (530) 752-8964; email: clah@ucdavis.edu
Internet http://www.h-net.org/~clah/about/index.html
Sponsor Conference on Latin American History
University of California at Davis, One Shields Ave
Davis, CA 95616

James and Sylvia Thayer Short -Term Research Fellowships **2518**
The short-term (one to three months) fellowships support researchers and scholars residing outside of the Los Angeles area to facilitate access to special collections materials. Located in the Arts, Louis M. Darling Biomedical, Music, and Charles E. Young Research libraries, these collections include primary resource materials across all disciplines. Application requirements include cover letter, curriculum vita, brief outline of research and specific collections to be used (two-page maximum), dates to be spent in residence, and three letters of recommendation. Annual deadline dates may vary; contact program staff for exact dates.
Requirements US citizens and foreign nationals engaged in graduate level, postdoctoral, or independent research are eligible.
Amount $500-$2500 per month
Date(s) Application Is Due Dec 31.
Contact Eunice MacGill, (310) 825-6940; (310) 825-0465; email: emacgill@library.ucla.edu
Internet http://www.library.ucla.edu/libraries/biomed/his/fellowships_prizes.html
Sponsor UCLA Arts Library
P.O. Box 951575
Los Angeles, CA 90095-1775

James Bradford Ames Fellowship **2519**
The fellowship was established to stimulate and support research of African American life and history on Nantucket Island including, but not limited to, the study of individual families, social life, occupations, the institution of slavery, and the interaction between African American and Cape Verdean communities. The studies may include those aspects that place Nantucket in a broader regional, national, and global perspective. The emphasis of the program is research, but the fund also may sponsor scholarly lectures, particularly as may allow for the presentation of research that has been funded in whole or in part by the Ames Fund.
Requirements ABD graduate students, full-time faculty, and professional staff in colleges and universities are invited to submit applications.
Amount $500-$2500
Date(s) Application Is Due Apr 15.
Contact Dr. Robert Johnson Jr., Department of African Studies, (617) 287-6794 or 287-6790; email: Robert.Johnson@umb.edu
Internet http://www.umb.edu/academic_programs/departments/africana_studies/scholarship/index.html
Sponsor University of Massachusetts Boston
100 Morrissey Blvd
Boston, MA 02125

James Flack Norris Award in Physical Organic Chemistry **2520**
This award, sponsored by The Northeastern Section of ACS and administered by the American Chemical Society, is given annually to encourage and reward outstanding contributions to physical organic chemistry. The award includes a certificate.
Requirements Any individual, except a member of the award committee, may submit one nomination or seconding letter for the award in any given year. Nominating documents consist of a letter of not more than 1000 words containing an evaluation of the nominee's accomplishments and a specific identification of the work to be recognized, a biographical sketch including date of birth, and a list of publications and patents authored by the nominee. Six copies of all items to be included in the nomination must be submitted.
Restrictions Self-nominations are not accepted.
Amount $5000
Date(s) Application Is Due Feb 1.
Contact Awards Administrator, (202) 872-4408; fax: (202) 872-6317; email: awards@acs.org
Internet http://www.chemistry.org/portal/a/c/s/1/acsdisplay.html?DOC=awards%5Cnorris.html
Sponsor American Chemical Society
1155 16th St NW
Washington, DC 20036

James Graham Brown Foundation Grants **2521**
The foundation supports nonprofit organizations in Kentucky, with emphasis on Louisville, in its areas of interest: higher education, civic organizations and social services, human service and health agencies, and economic development. Types of support include annual campaigns, building funds, capital campaigns, conferences and seminars, emergency funds, endowment funds, equipment, matching funds, professorships, operating budgets, renovation projects, research, scholarship funds, special projects, and land acquisition. There are no application deadlines; however, applications received after October 1 will be considered in the following calendar year. The board meets monthly, with funds disbursed December 31.
Requirements Nonprofit organizations in Kentucky may apply.
Restrictions Grants are not awarded to support private foundations, the performing arts, national organizations, political activities, elementary or secondary schools, or individuals.
Contact Dodie McKenzie, (502) 896-2440 or (866) 896-5423; fax: (502) 896-1774; email: dodie@jgbf.org
Internet http://www.jgbf.org
Sponsor James Graham Brown Foundation
4350 Brownsboro Rd, Ste 200
Louisville, KY 40207

James H. Cummings Foundation Grants **2522**
The grants are awarded exclusively for advancing medical science and research and education, and for charitable work among underprivileged boys and girls and aged and infirmed persons. The giving program is limited to the vicinity of the cities of Buffalo, NY; Hendersonville, NC; and Toronto, ON, Canada. The annual report includes application guidelines.
Requirements The giving program is limited to the vicinity of the cities of Buffalo, NY; Hendersonville, NC; and Toronto, ON, Canada.
Restrictions Grants are not awarded to individuals, nor for annual campaigns, program support, endowment funds, operating budgets, emergency funds, deficit financing, scholarships, fellowships, publications, conferences, or continuing support.
Amount $2000-$250,000 range
Contact William McFarland, Executive Director, (716) 874-0040; fax: (716) 874-0040; email: cummings.foundation@verizon.net
Sponsor James H. Cummings Foundation
1807 Elmwood Ave, Rm 112
Buffalo, NY 14207

James Harrison Steedman Memorial Fellowships in Architecture **2523**
This biennial fellowship permits well-qualified architectural graduates to benefit from nine months of travel and study of architecture in foreign countries. A design competition, to be completed during January after deadline date, determines the winner; fellowship will begin within nine months of receiving the award. Specific details about the award and application forms may be obtained from the university. Registration forms and a $50 application fee are due December 10; competition entries and research proposal are due January 24. Deadline dates may vary; contact the program office for exact dates.
Requirements The fellowships are open to architects who have worked for at least one year in an architect's office for a period of up to eight years after they have received their professional degrees from accredited schools. There are no citizenship requirements.
Amount $30,000
Date(s) Application Is Due Mar 12.
Contact Steedman Governing Committee, (314) 935-6293; fax: (314) 935-7656; email: shannonp@architecture.wustl.edu
Internet http://www.arch.wustl.edu/news_sc.lasso
Sponsor Washington University
Campus Box 1079, One Brookings Dr
Saint Louis, MO 63130-4899

James Harry Potter Gold Medal **2524**
The medal is awarded in recognition of eminent achievement or distinguished service in the appreciation of the science of thermodynamics in mechanical engineering. The basis of the award shall include contributions involving the teaching, appreciation, or utilization of thermodynamic principles in research, development, and design in mechanical engineering. Any individual member, group of members, or committee may nominate candidates for consideration. Award includes vermeil medal and certificate.
Amount $2000
Date(s) Application Is Due Feb 1.
Contact Gilda DiTullio, Manager, (212) 591-7736; fax: (212) 705-7739; email: awards@asme.org
Internet http://www.asme.org/honors/ms71/saa/potter.html
Sponsor American Society of Mechanical Engineers
3 Park Ave
New York, NY 10016

James J. and Angelia M. Harris Foundation Grants 2525

The foundation awards grants to eligible Georgia and North Carolina nonprofit organizations. Proposals in all areas will be considered. Types of support include annual campaigns, building construction/renovation, capital campaigns, challenge/matching grants, general operating support, program development, and scholarship funds. There are no application deadlines or forms. The board meets in May and November to consider requests. Letters of inquiry are due in April and October.

Requirements Nonprofit organizations in Clarke County, GA, and Mecklenburg County, NC, are eligible.

Amount $100-$100,000 average range

Contact Grants Administrator, (704) 364-6046

Sponsor James J. and Angelia M. Harris Foundation
P.O. Box 220427
Charlotte, NC 28222

James M. Collins Foundation Grants 2526

The foundation awards grants to Texas nonprofit organizations in its areas of interest, including arts, churches and religious organizations, healthcare and healthcare organizations, and higher education (primarily business education and medical education). Types of support include research grants, program support, and social services. There are no application deadlines or forms.

Requirements Texas nonprofit organizations are eligible.

Restrictions Individuals are not eligible.

Contact Grants Administrator

Sponsor James M. Collins Foundation
8115 Preston Rd, Ste 680
Dallas, TX 75225

James Marshall Public Policy Fellowship 2527

This fellowship is a two-year appointment representing SPSSI in approved policy and advocacy activities. The position is with the public policy office of the American Psychological Association (APA) in Washington, DC. The fellow will participate in supervised activities including using psychological research to analyze specific social policies and develop policy advocacy. In addition, the fellow will serve in various capacities including, but not limited to, serving on SPSSI committees and task forces; monitoring APA boards, committees, and/or task forces relevant to the fellow's main policy area; reporting to and attending SPSSI's semiannual council meetings; writing a public policy column for the SPSSI newsletter; and meeting regularly with the fellow oversight committee. Candidate is required to submit a detailed vita; a 1000-word biographical statement of past experience and interest in policy activities and/or social issues, career goals, and interest in the fellowship and its objectives; a 600-word briefing statement using social science data to inform legislators about a specific social issue; and three letters of reference. All application materials must be submitted in duplicate.

Requirements Applicant must hold a PhD or PsyD and either be a member of SPSSI and APA or be eligible to become a member. The selected fellow must join SPSSI before the appointment date. Candidates must demonstrate interest or involvement in the application of social science to social issues and policy and be interested in and knowledgeable about at least one current social issue such as homelessness, violence, adolescent pregnancy, child abuse, etc.

Amount $42,600 for first year, plus health and vacation benefits

Date(s) Application Is Due Mar 1.

Contact Dr. Shari Miles, (202) 675-6956; fax: (734) 662-5607; email: smiles@spssi.org

Internet http://www.spssi.org/jms.html

Sponsor Society for the Psychological Study of Social Issues
P.O. Box 1248
Ann Arbor, MI 48103

James Marston Fitch Charitable Trust Midcareer Grants 2528

The trust awards research grants to midcareer professionals who have an academic background, professional experience, and an established identity in one or more of the following fields: historic preservation, architecture, landscape architecture, urban design, environmental planning, architectural history, and the decorative arts. Proposals will be considered for the research and/or execution of the preservation-related projects in any of these fields. The foundation endeavors to establish new links between the academic and professional contingents primarily in the field of American historic preservation and to strengthen the connections between theory and practice in conservation technology.

Requirements Midcareer professionals with established backgrounds in historic preservation or related fields are eligible for grants. Candidate should have an advanced or professional degree and 10 years of professional experience in historic preservation or in related fields, such as architecture, landscape architecture, urban design, environmental planning, archaeology, architectural history, or the decorative arts.

Amount $10,000-$25,000

Date(s) Application Is Due Sep 8.

Contact Margaret Evans, Executive Director, (212) 252-6809; fax: (212) 471-9987; email: info@fitchfoundation.org

Internet http://www.fitchfoundation.org

Sponsor James Marston Fitch Charitable Trust
232 E 11th St
New York, NY 10003

James McKeen Cattell Fund Fellowships 2529

The nonrenewable fellowships advance the science of psychology and its useful applications by enabling faculty members to take a full year sabbatical leave for independent study and research. Annual deadline dates may vary; contact program staff for exact dates.

Requirements Eligibility is limited to residents of North America. The fellowships are intended for tenured faculty of a psychology department who are eligible for sabbatical leave. Matching institutions' support required.

Amount $32,000 maximum

Date(s) Application Is Due Dec 1.

Contact Dr. Christina Williams, Program Contact; email: williams@psych.duke.edu

Internet http://www.cattell.duke.edu

Sponsor James McKeen Cattell Fund
9 Flowers Dr, Box 90086, Duke University, Department of Psychological and Brain Sciences
Durham, NC 27708-0086

James N. Landis Medal 2530

The Landis Medal is given for outstanding personal performance related to designing, constructing, or managing the operation of major steam-powered electric stations using nuclear or fossil fuels, coupled with personal leadership in humanitarian pursuits, which may include committee activity, ASME section leadership, or the broad nontechnical professional activity of the nominee's engineering society. The award is presented preferably to a member of ASME, and includes stipend, bronze medal, and certificate.

Amount $7500 and expense supplement

Date(s) Application Is Due Feb 1.

Contact Gilda DiTullio, Manager, (212) 591-7736; fax: (212) 705-7739; email: awards@asme.org

Internet http://www.asme.org/honors/ms71/saa/landis.html

Sponsor American Society of Mechanical Engineers
3 Park Ave
New York, NY 10016

James R. Scobie Memorial Award for Preliminary Doctoral Research 2531

The award permits a short, exploratory research trip abroad to determine the feasibility of a PhD dissertation topic dealing with some facet of Latin American history. One or more travel grants will be awarded each year; the grant must be used during the summer following the award unless prior approval is received.

Requirements Applicant must submit a comprehensive research prospectus, including a preliminary bibliography; three letters of recommendation, one of which should attest to the language competence (Spanish or Portuguese) of the applicant; and a current curriculum vita.

Restrictions The award is not to be combined with a research grant for an extended stay.

Amount $1000 maximum

Date(s) Application Is Due Apr 1.

Contact CLAH, (530) 752-3046; fax: (530) 752-8964; email: clah@ucdavis.edu

Internet http://www.h-net.org/~clah/about/index.html

Sponsor Conference on Latin American History
University of California at Davis, One Shields Ave
Davis, CA 95616

James S. McDonnell Foundation Brain Cancer Research Collaborative Activity Awards 2532

The Foundation offers Collaborative Activity Awards to initiate interdisciplinary discussions on problems or issues, to help launch interdisciplinary research networks, or to fund communities of researchers/practitioners dedicated to developing new methods, tools, and applications of basic research to applied problems. All proposals submitted to the foundation must clearly link the experimental models and questions to human disease. Proposals primarily intending to characterize basic mechanisms of growth and development that may plausibly but are not yet known to be contributory to human brain cancer are not encouraged. Proposals testing molecules as possible treatment interventions should consider including tests designed to uncover unintended biological effects of such molecules that would disqualify future clinical usefulness. The Foundation is particularly interested in supporting novel research that will generate new knowledge leading to increased rates of survival and improve functional recovery for individuals with brain cancer.

Restrictions The Foundation does not fund: undergraduate tuition, stipends, scholarships, fellowships, research or travel expenses, or other educational expenses; graduate or postdoctoral stipends, scholarships, fellowships, research or travel expenses, or other educational expenses (exceptions include requests that qualify as allowable budget items as part of specific Research Award applications); expenses tied to projects whose explicit goal is the publication of a book or other bound volume (although publication of a book or special issue of a journal may be one goal or outcome of work funded by the Foundation); expenses tied to the establishment or day-to-day running of a journal or small press; scientific meetings or workshops other than those JSMF puts together or which are affiliated with Collaborative Activity Awards; ongoing operational support for university-based centers, programs, or institutes; professional society meetings or specific sessions at such meetings; charitable functions, museum exhibitions, or similar causes or events; or charitable donations to individuals and organizations.

Contact Cheryl Washington, Grants Manager, (314) 721-1532; fax: (314) 721-7421; email: washington@jmsf.org or info@jmsf.org
Internet http://www.jsmf.org/programs/bc/index.htm
Sponsor James S. McDonnell Foundation
1034 S. Brentwood Blvd., Suite 1850
Saint Louis, MO 63117

James S. McDonnell Foundation Brain, Mind, and Behavior Collaborative Activity Awards **2533**

The Foundation offers Collaborative Activity Awards to initiate interdisciplinary discussions on problems or issues, to help launch interdisciplinary research networks, or to fund communities of researchers/practitioners dedicated to developing new methods, tools, and applications of basic research to applied problems. The BMB Program supports research studying how neural systems are linked to and support cognitive functions and how cognitive systems are related to an organism's (preferably human) observable behavior. Funding is intended to help investigators pursue experiments designed to answer well-articulated questions. Applicants should keep in mind that the Foundation usually funds less than a dozen BMB research projects each year. Aspects of proposals appropriate to the program include, but are not limited to: characterizing the cognitive operations involved in performing a task; studying how the brain extracts and uses relevant information from complicated environments; examining how manipulations and/or perturbations at one spatial or temporal scale are meaningful at finer or coarser levels of organization (e.g. does a synaptic change account for a change in network function and vice versa?); re-examining common assumptions (such as the existence of critical periods in human learning); evaluating the usefulness of methodologies or improving the usefulness of methodologies commonly used in mind/brain research; or applying approaches and knowledge from cognitive psychology or cognitive science to important problems in education, training, or rehabilitation.
Restrictions The Foundation does not fund: undergraduate tuition, stipends, scholarships, fellowships, research or travel expenses, or other educational expenses; graduate or postdoctoral stipends, scholarships, fellowships, research or travel expenses, or other educational expenses (exceptions include requests that qualify as allowable budget items as part of specific Research Award applications); expenses tied to projects whose explicit goal is the publication of a book or other bound volume (although publication of a book or special issue of a journal may be one goal or outcome of work funded by the Foundation); expenses tied to the establishment or day-to-day running of a journal or small press; scientific meetings or workshops other than those JSMF puts together or which are affiliated with Collaborative Activity Awards; ongoing operational support for university-based centers, programs, or institutes; professional society meetings or specific sessions at such meetings; charitable functions, museum exhibitions, or similar causes or events; or charitable donations to individuals and organizations.
Contact Cheryl Washington, Grants Manager, (314) 721-1532; fax: (314) 721-7421; email: washington@jmsf.org or info@jmsf.org
Internet http://www.jsmf.org/programs/bmb/index.htm
Sponsor James S. McDonnell Foundation
1034 S. Brentwood Blvd., Suite 1850
Saint Louis, MO 63117

James S. McDonnell Foundation Complex Systems Collaborative Activity Awards **2534**

The Foundation offers Collaborative Activity Awards to initiate interdisciplinary discussions on problems or issues, to help launch interdisciplinary research networks, or to fund communities of researchers/practitioners dedicated to developing new methods, tools, and applications of basic research to applied problems. The Program supports scholarship and research directed toward the development of theoretical and mathematical tools that can be applied to the study of complex, nonlinear systems. It is anticipated that research funded in this program will address issues in fields such as biology, biodiversity, climate, demography, epidemiology, technological change, economic Complex Systems development, governance, or computation. While the program's emphasis is on the development and application of theoretical models used in these research fields and not on particular fields per se, JSMF is particularly interested in projects attempting to apply complex systems approaches to real world problems. Proposals attempting to apply tools and models to problems where such approaches are not yet considered usual or mainstream (for example, differentiating normal physiology from disease) are encouraged.
Restrictions The Foundation does not fund: undergraduate tuition, stipends, scholarships, fellowships, research or travel expenses, or other educational expenses; graduate or postdoctoral stipends, scholarships, fellowships, research or travel expenses, or other educational expenses (exceptions include requests that qualify as allowable budget items as part of specific Research Award applications); expenses tied to projects whose explicit goal is the publication of a book or other bound volume (although publication of a book or special issue of a journal may be one goal or outcome of work funded by the Foundation); expenses tied to the establishment or day-to-day running of a journal or small press; scientific meetings or workshops other than those JSMF puts together or which are affiliated with Collaborative Activity Awards; ongoing operational support for university-based centers, programs, or institutes; professional society meetings or specific sessions at such meetings; charitable functions, museum exhibitions, or similar causes or events; or charitable donations to individuals and organizations.
Contact Cheryl Washington, Grants Manager, (314) 721-1532; fax: (314) 721-7421; email: washington@jmsf.org or info@jmsf.org
Internet http://www.jsmf.org/programs/cs/index.htm
Sponsor James S. McDonnell Foundation
1034 S. Brentwood Blvd., Suite 1850
Saint Louis, MO 63117

James S. McDonnell Foundation Research Grants **2535**

The Awards are designed to support research projects with a high probability of generating new knowledge and insights. Projects submitted for funding consideration should be at an early, even preliminary stage of development that intend to break new ground or to challenge commonly-held assumptions. Projects submitted should be sufficiently novel, cross-disciplinary, or heterodox so that they have a strong likelihood of influencing the development of new ways of thinking about important problems. Awards provide adequate, flexible funding over a sufficient time period to allow investigators to pursue and develop innovative directions to their research programs. Funds can be expended over a minimum of 3 years or a maximum of 6 years. Smaller amounts of money expended over shorter amounts of time may be requested to help investigators pursue pilot projects or test the feasibility of an experimental approach. The applicant can apply the grant funds towards any research-based expense, including travel, equipment, and supplies. Funds can be used to support collaborative projects. A percentage of the funds can also be used to support small workshops organized by the applicant where the goal of the workshop is to gather expertise in support of the research objective.
Requirements Applications for grants are considered only from 501(c)3 organizations which are not private foundations. Applications from foreign organizations will be considered only if they provide written legal opinion that they qualify as tax-exempt under these sections of the US IRS code or if a qualifying American organization is authorized to receive funds for them under this code. Individuals also are eligible.
Amount $450,000 maximum
Date(s) Application Is Due Mar 12.
Contact Cheryl Washington, Grants Manager, (314) 721-1532; fax: (314) 721-7421; email: washington@jmsf.org or info@jmsf.org
Internet http://www.jsmf.org/apply/research/index.htm
Sponsor James S. McDonnell Foundation
1034 S. Brentwood Blvd., Suite 1850
Saint Louis, MO 63117

James S. McDonnell Foundation Scholar Awards **2536**

The Awards program derives from and is consistent with the foundation's commitment to supporting high quality research and scholarship leading to the generation of new knowledge and its responsible application. Currently, the Awards are only available in the Brain, Mind & Behavior program area, and provide largely unrestricted funding over a sufficient time period to allow investigators to pursue and develop new directions to their research programs. Applications must be submitted electronically via the JSMF website and are due on April 10, no later than 4:59 P.M. Central Time. The Foundation emphasizes that this is an international program for a limited number of awards.
Requirements Applications must be sponsored by a nonprofit institution as defined by Section 501(c)(3) of the United States Internal Revenue Tax Code. Eligible Scholar Award nominees must have completed all doctoral, postdoctoral, or fellowship training and hold an independent research position. Nominees in the earlier career stages are encouraged.
Restrictions Researchers with current grant support from JSMF are not eligible to apply for a Scholar Award until all prior JSMF grant funds have been fully expended and a final grant report has been received and approved by the foundation office.
Amount $600,000 to be expended over 6 years
Date(s) Application Is Due Apr 10.
Contact Cheryl Washington, Grants Manager, (314) 721-1532; fax: (314) 721-7421; email: washington@jmsf.org or info@jmsf.org
Internet http://www.jsmf.org/apply/scholar/index.htm
Sponsor James S. McDonnell Foundation
1034 S. Brentwood Blvd., Suite 1850
Saint Louis, MO 63117

James T. Grady-James H. Stack Award for Interpreting Chemistry for the Public **2537**

This award, sponsored and administered by the American Chemical Society, is given annually to recognize, encourage, and stimulate outstanding reporting directly to the public that materially increases the public's knowledge and understanding of chemistry, chemical engineering, and related fields. This information may have been disseminated through the press, radio, television, films, the lecture platform, or books or pamphlets for the lay public.
Requirements Any individual, except a member of the award committee, may submit one nomination or seconding letter for the award in any given year. The nominating documents consist of a letter of not more than 1000 words containing an evaluation of the nominee's accomplishments and a specific identification of the work to be recognized, a biographical sketch including date of birth, and a list of publications authored by the nominee.
Restrictions Application or self-nomination is not acceptable.
Amount $3000 and reimbursement of traveling expenses to award meeting
Date(s) Application Is Due Feb 1.
Contact Awards Administrator, (202) 452-2109 ; fax: (202) 776-8211; email: awards@acs.org

Internet http://www.chemistry.org/portal/a/c/s/1/acsdisplay.html?DOC=awards%5Cgrady-stack.html
Sponsor American Chemical Society
1155 16th St NW
Washington, DC 20036

Jane Beattie Memorial Scholarship **2538**

The purpose of the fund is to provide scholarships to subsidize travel to the U.S. for purposes of scholarly activity by a foreign scholar in the area of judgment and decision research, broadly defined. Attendance at the annual SJDM meetings is one example of an activity that would be appropriate for support, but by no means the only one. In most years, the Fund awards one or two scholarships in amounts of $400 - $700 each.
Requirements Applicants should be scholars living and working in a country other than the U.S. who will use the award to help pay for travel to the U.S. for scholarly activities associated with research in judgment and decision making. It is anticipated that most awards will be granted to faculty or graduate students at colleges and universities, especially recent and soon-to-be Ph.D.'s, but others will also be considered. Contact the sponsor for more details on the application process.
Restrictions U.S. Scholars are not eligible to apply.
Amount $400 - $700
Contact Joshua Klayman; University of Chicago Graduate School of Business; email: joshk@uchicago.edu
Internet http://www.sjdm.org/beattie.shtml
Sponsor Society for Judgment and Decision Making
c/o Bud Fennema, College of Business, Florida State University, P.O. Box 3061110
Tallahassee, FL 32306-1110

Jane Coffin Childs Memorial Fund for Medical Research Fellowships Fellowships **2539**

The fellowships are for furthering of research into the causes, origins, and treatment of cancer. The major effort of the fund, at this time, is directed toward the support of a fellowship program for the training of young men and women at the postdoctoral level for independent research in the same field. Stipend, child dependency allowance, travel for fellow and family, and an institutional allowance are provided. Fellowships are awarded for two to three years.
Requirements Applicants should not have more than one year of postdoctoral experience. They must either hold the MD degree or PhD degree in the field in which they propose to study. Applicants may be citizens of any country, but awards for foreign nationals will be made only for study in the United States. American citizens may hold fellowships either in the United States or in a foreign country.
Amount $41,000 first year, $42,000 second year, $44,000 third year; plus $1500 research allowance per year
Date(s) Application Is Due Feb 1.
Contact Kim Roberts, Administrative Director, (203) 785-4612; fax: (203) 785-3301; email: info@jccfund.org
Internet http://www.jccfund.org
Sponsor Jane Coffin Childs Memorial Fund for Medical Research
P.O. Box 208000, 333 Cedar St
New Haven, CT 06520

Japan Doctoral Fellowships **2540**

Fellowships are awarded to provide doctoral candidates in the social sciences and humanities with the opportunity to conduct dissertation research in Japan. Fellowships are for a duration of four to 12 months. Travel expenses for the fellow's family are not included. Requests for application forms must state the theme of the project to be conducted in Japan and the applicant's present position and citizenship. Letters of reference must be sent directly to the New York office.
Requirements Applicants must have completed all requirements for the PhD except the dissertation at the time the fellowship begins and have a functional knowledge of Japanese. Well-qualified candidates in political science, law, economics, business, and journalism are encouraged to apply. Candidates should be citizens or permanent residents of the United States; US citizens residing abroad are eligible and should apply through the foundation's overseas office or Japanese diplomatic mission in the country where they reside. Those residing in the United States who are not citizens or permanent residents should contact the Japan Foundation headquarters in Tokyo directly.
Restrictions Fellowships are not granted for improvement of proficiency in Japanese and may not be held concurrently with another major grant. Individuals in the fields of the physical, natural, medical, or engineering sciences are not eligible to apply.
Date(s) Application Is Due Nov 1.
Contact Doctoral Fellowships: (212) 489-0299; fax: (212) 489-0409; email: info@jfny.org
Internet http://www.jfny.org/jfny/arts.html#doc
Sponsor Japan Foundation in New York
152 W 57th St, 39th Fl
New York, NY 10019

Japan Foundation and Language Center Grants **2541**

The program comprises eight types of grants: audio-visual exchanges, exhibitions, fellowships, Japanese language, Japanese studies, performing arts, publication, and global partnerships. Check Web site for descriptions and eligibility criteria for specific grants.
Date(s) Application Is Due Dec 1.
Contact Masao Ito, Director, (213) 621-2267 ext 101; fax: (213) 621-2590; email: masao_ito@jflalc.org
Internet http://www.jflalc.org/?act=tpt&id=217
Sponsor Japan Foundation and Language Center in Los Angeles
333 S Grand Ave, Ste 2250
Los Angeles, CA 90071

Japan Foundation Center for Global Partnerships Grants **2542**

The center endeavors to deepen the dialogue between the United States and Japan and to contribute to a better world through US-Japan collaborative efforts addressing current issues of global and common concern. The program encompasses two types of exchanges: intellectual exchange, including collaborative research and dialogue projects in economics, security, sustainable development, civil society, and healthcare and aging; and grassroots exchange and education programs, including youth exchange, NP.O. exchange, public outreach, and projects of professional and curriculum development at the K-12 level. Application and deadline information are available online.
Requirements 501(c)3 tax-exempt organizations are eligible.
Contact Program Director, (212) 489-1255; fax: (212) 489-1344
Internet http://www.cgp.org
Sponsor Japan Foundation Center for Global Partnership
152 West 57th Street, 17th Floor
New York, NY 10019

Japan Foundation Center for Global Partnerships Travel Grants **2543**

The program supports travel to Japan in order to build networks between the Japanese and US nonprofit sectors. Through site visits and meetings with their counterparts in Japan, US nonprofit professionals and/or researchers committed to the sector exchange knowledge and expertise with the hope of forming a longer-term partnership. After returning to the United States, the individual(s) would share his/her experiences through a small event for the general public, nonprofit professionals from other organizations, and/or researchers. Examples of possible areas are disaster awareness, homelessness, HIV/AIDS, volunteerism, environment, and labor practices. Application guidelines are available online.
Requirements Interested individuals should apply through an affiliated US 501(c)3 nonprofit organizations.
Amount $5000 maximum
Date(s) Application Is Due Mar 1.
Contact Eva Heintzelman, (212) 489-1255; fax: (212) 489-1344; email: eva_heintzelman@cgp.org
Internet http://www.cgp.org
Sponsor Japan Foundation Center for Global Partnership
152 W 57th St, 17th Fl
New York, NY 10019

Japan Foundation Endowment Committee Grants **2544**

The foundation supports the academic study of Japanese studies within universities in the United Kingdom, including research in the fields of the arts and humanities, economic and international affairs, and law and human rights. Types of support include program development, grants to organizations, scholarships and fellowships, conferences, research publications, visits to Japan, and visits to the United Kingdom.
Requirements There are no restrictions on the nationality of grantees, although they must be based in the United Kingdom. All applications must be made by a member of staff. Grants are made formally to the institutions concerned which are required to administer the grants on behalf of the grant holder.
Restrictions Direct applications from individual students are not accepted and the committee does not fund coursework at any level, master's dissertations, or course development.
Amount @L5000 maximum typically
Contact Lynn Baird, Executive Secretary, c/o BAJS Secretariat, University of Esses, 01206 872543; fax: 01206 873965; email: jfec@bajs.org.uk
Internet http://66.102.7.104/search?q=cache:IRStLKnkkFcJ:www.keele.ac.uk/research/lpj/news/JapanFoundation051005.doc+Japan+Foundation+Endowment+Committee&hl=en
Sponsor Japan Foundation Endowment Committee
University of Sheffield, Fifth Court, Western Bank
Sheffield S10 2TN United Kingdom

Japan Foundation Visiting Professorship Grant Program **2545**

The program allows US academic institutions, independently or jointly with other institutions, to invite scholars or artists in residence from abroad (including Japan) to give courses in Japanese studies or Japanese arts at the graduate or undergraduate level. Visits range from one to 10 months. This program is meant to enhance established teaching programs by the contribution of a visiting scholar, not to replace regular instructors. Consortial applications are encouraged. Short-term lecture tours are also eligible. Payment is made directly to the applying institution. The fellowship covers round-trip airfare for the appointee and an amount not exceeding 75 percent of the other direct project costs.

Date(s) Application Is Due Nov 1.
Contact Research Fellowships, (212) 489-0299; fax: (212) 489-0409; email: info@jfny.org
Internet http://www.jfny.org/jfny/inst.html#vis
Sponsor Japan Foundation in New York
152 W 57th St, 39th Fl
New York, NY 10019

Japan Heart Foundation Grants **2546**
The foundation awards grants in Japan to individuals, organizations, and research institutes for research projects in the area of heart and blood vessel diseases.
Requirements Research institutes for research in the area of heart and blood vessel diseases, individuals, and organizations in Japan are eligible to apply.
Contact Grants Administrator, 81-3-3201-0810; fax: 81-3-3213-3920; email: info@jhf.or.jp
Internet http://www.jhf.or.jp
Sponsor Japan Heart Foundation
835-A, New Kokusai Bldg,3-4-1, Marunouchi
Chiyoda-ku, Tokyo 100-0005
Japan

Japan Research Fellowships **2547**
The fellowships give scholars, researchers, and professionals the opportunity to conduct research in Japan. All projects related substantially to Japan in the humanities and social sciences, including comparative research, are eligible. Research fellowships are awarded for periods of two to 12 months. A monthly stipend with a dependents' allowance, round-trip airfare, traveler's insurance, a departure allowance and a settling-in allowance, a research/cultural activities allowance, and enrollment fees are provided.
Requirements Scholars applying for research fellowships should hold academic positions in research institutions and have substantial experience in research, teaching, and writing in their respective fields of study.
Restrictions Projects focused on improving Japanese-language proficiency or on training or self-improvement in the performing arts, fine arts, crafts, the martial arts, or sports, or in the fields of the physical, medical, or engineering sciences will not be considered.
Date(s) Application Is Due Nov 1.
Contact Research Fellowships, (212) 489-0299; fax: (212) 489-0409; email: info@jfny.org
Internet http://www.jfny.org/jfny/arts.html#res
Sponsor Japan Foundation in New York
152 W 57th St, 39th Fl
New York, NY 10019

Japan Study Program Grants **2548**
The program comprises two subprograms. The Publication Assistance program provides financial assistance to publishers for the publication of books on or relating to Japan in the humanities, social sciences, and fine arts, in languages other than Japanese. The Translation Assistance program provides financial assistance to publishers for the translation of Japanese works of high quality on or relating to Japan in the humanities, social sciences, and fine arts. Contact the office for specific requirements of each subprogram.
Requirements Only publishers in the following states are eligible to apply: Alaska, Arizona, California, Colorado, Hawaii, Idaho, Montana, Nevada, New Mexico, Oregon, Utah, Washington, and Wyoming.
Restrictions Applications from authors, translators, or other individuals will not be accepted. Works in the natural sciences are not eligible.
Date(s) Application Is Due Dec 1.
Contact Mamiko Nakai, (213) 621-2267 ext 110; fax: (213) 621-2590; email: mamiko_nakai@jflalc.org
Internet http://www.jflalc.org/?act=tpt&id=229
Sponsor Japan Foundation and Language Center in Los Angeles
333 S Grand Ave, Ste 2250
Los Angeles, CA 90071

Japan-United States Friendship Commission Grants **2549**
The program promotes scholarly, cultural, and public affairs activities between Japan and the United States. Requests for support will be considered under six project areas: Japanese studies (for Americans), Study of the United States in Japan, the arts, policy-oriented research, public affairs/education, and infrastructure building. These areas have been chosen on the basis of the commission's considered judgment that both highly trained area specialists and a much broader public understanding and cultural involvement are essential to a stable foundation for the Japanese-American relationship in the years ahead. The commission provides support exclusively for institutional development; it does not provide support for individual training, research, or travel.
Requirements Programs supported are open to citizens and permanent residents of the United States or Japan without regard to race, creed, sex, disability, or national origin. Grants may be made to individual universities or local organizations but primarily in consideration of their contribution to national resources for understanding of the other country. Grants to individuals, under all programs, normally will be made through academic, professional, artistic, or other appropriate organizations that will examine, recommend, and in most instances, select the individuals to be supported financially by the commission. The commission, as a general rule, will work with nonprofit organizations in carrying out its programs.
Restrictions Projects not considered for support include language and area studies K-12, undergraduate and teenage exchanges, individual travel grants, university chairs or endowment funds; research, teaching, publications, and translations in mathematics, medicine, and the natural sciences; building construction, design, or maintenance costs; symphony or other strictly musical groups, solo performing artists, or amateur and university groups; or support for American museums for regular staff, acquisition of objects, or cataloging of existing collections. This award is granted twice a year.
Date(s) Application Is Due Mar 1; Aug 1.
Contact Eric Gangloff, Executive Director, (202) 418-9800; fax: (202) 418-9802; email: grants@jusfc.gov
Internet http://www.jusfc.gov/commissn/BrochureJan03.htm#_Japanese_Studies_in
Sponsor Japan-United States Friendship Commission
1120 Vermont Ave NW, Ste 800
Washington, DC 20005

Japanese Language Program Grants **2550**
The foundation offers a variety of grant programs and services to facilitate Japanese language teaching. Programs include: salary assistance for full-time Japanese language teachers; Japanese language research/conference/seminar grants; Japanese language teaching materials donation program; training programs for teachers of the Japanese language at the Japanese Language Institute, Urawa, Japan; assistance program for the development of Japanese language teaching resources; Japanese language education fellowship program; Japanese speech contest support program; and the Japanese language program for researchers and postgraduate students at the Japanese Language Institute, Kansai, Japan. Applications to each of the above programs are due December 1. Annual deadline dates may vary; contact program staff for exact dates.
Requirements Any educational, cultural, or public affairs nonprofit organization is eligible to apply.
Restrictions Programs planned for high school students are not applicable.
Date(s) Application Is Due Dec 1.
Contact Grants Administrator, (213) 621-2267; fax: (213) 621-2590; email: jflalc@jflalc.org
Internet http://www.jflalc.org
Sponsor Japan Foundation and Language Center in Los Angeles
333 S Grand Ave, Ste 2250
Los Angeles, CA 90071

Japanese Studies in the United States Research Grants **2551**
The goal of this program is to educate a broader stratum of American leadership with respect to Japan. The following project areas have been established: faculty research, library support, language training, and general education. Under its library support category, the commission also supports projects that help organize acquisitions of research materials on a national scale and help expand access to research materials in both printed and electronic format. In its support for language training, the commission will fund institutional activities that promise the greatest national or regional return. The commission will also consider collaborative research and general education projects in Japanese studies on a case-by-case basis. Potential applicants should consult with commission staff before submitting applications.
Requirements Citizens and permanent residents of the United States and Japan are eligible. Grants may be made to individual universities or local organizations. Awards made to individuals under all programs normally will be made through academic, professional, artistic, or other appropriate organizations that will examine, recommend, and, in most instances, select the individuals to be supported financially by the commission. This award is granted twice a year.
Date(s) Application Is Due Mar 1; Aug 1.
Contact Executive Director, (202) 418-9800; fax: (202) 418-9802; email: grants@jusfc.com
Internet http://www.jusfc.gov/commissn/BrochureJan03.htm#_Japanese_Studies_in
Sponsor Japan-United States Friendship Commission
1110 Vermont Ave NW, Ste 800
Washington, DC 20005

Japanese Studies Speakers and Panels Grants **2552**
The purpose of this program is to encourage scholarly study of Japan by disciplinary specialists such as political scientists, economists, geographers, musicologists, linguists, historians, and scientists, by providing financial support to organizers of panels at annual conventions of national scholarly organizations to bring Japan experts of any nationality and Japanese scholars to participate in those panels. Grants of up to $1500 are available to organizers of national conventions of a scholarly discipline to bring eminent speakers to address the convention on a Japanese topic. The person may be an academic figure, a public figure, a distinguished performer in the arts, or any person of distinction. The grant may cover domestic and international travel costs, two days' board and room, an honorarium ($500 maximum), and organizing costs. Additional grants for up to $1000 are available to cover travel within North America for up to four participants, per diem expenses limited to two nights' lodging, and administrative costs.
Requirements Applications for all programs must include the applicant's curriculum vita. Preference will be given to applications that come from the professional associations

where Japanese perspectives historically have been neglected (such as management and the history of science).
Restrictions Any airfare tickets purchased with funds from these grants must be secured in the United States, from American air carriers; grants may not be used to reimburse any expenses incurred in currencies other than the US dollar.
Amount $2500 maximum for any one panel; the daily expenses of lodging and/or food to be reimbursed per person will not exceed $100, and administrative costs are limited to $100.
Date(s) Application Is Due Feb 1; Oct 1.
Contact NEAC Grants, (313) 665-2490; email: postmaster@aasianst.org
Internet http://www.aasianst.org/grants/grants.htm#NEAC-JAPAN
Sponsor Northeast Asia Council/Association for Asian Studies
1021 E. Huron St
Ann Arbor, MI 48104

Japanese Studies United States Research Travel Grants 2553
These short-term grants, sponsored jointly by the Northeast Asia Council and the Association for Asian Studies, are open to those engaged in scholarly research on Japan who wish to use museum, library, or other archival materials located in the United States. A portion of the grant may be used for research materials, assistance, and reasonable subsistence costs. An application form is required.
Requirements Applicant must be a US citizen or permanent resident; grants are primarily for postdoctoral research, but PhD candidates are also eligible.
Restrictions Grants may not be used for overseas travel.
Amount $1500 maximum including $100 per diem
Date(s) Application Is Due Feb 1; Oct 1.
Contact NEAC Grants, (734) 665-2490; fax: (734) 665-3801; email: postmaster@aasianst.org
Internet http://www.aasianst.org/grants/grants.htm#NEAC-JAPAN
Sponsor Northeast Asia Council/Association for Asian Studies
1021 E Huron St
Ann Arbor, MI 48104

JDF Career Development Awards 2554
The program awards grants to applicants who have demonstrated superior scholarship and show the greatest promise for future achievement in diabetes research, including either clinically relevant research or basic research. The research plan should be suitable for a five-year project, and awardees must spend at least 75 percent of time and effort on the research project during the period of the award. Research may be conducted at foreign and domestic, for-profit and nonprofit, and public and private organizations such as universities, colleges, hospitals, laboratories, units of state and local governments, and eligible agencies of the federal government. Letters of reference are due two weeks before the application deadline, which are July 15 and January 16.
Requirements Candidates must have the doctoral degree or the equivalent from an accredited institution, with three to seven years of total professional postdoctoral clinical and/or research experience by the projected start of the award period. Candidate's institution must be a university, medical school, or comparable institution with strong, well-established research and training programs in the chosen area. Research may be conducted at foreign and domestic, for-profit and nonprofit, public and private laboratories; units of state and local governments; and eligible agencies of the federal government.
Restrictions Individuals holding academic positions of associate professor or professor at the time of the award are not eligible.
Amount $150,000 per year
Date(s) Application Is Due Jan 16; Jul 15.
Contact Grant Administrator, (212) 479-7565; fax: (212) 785-9595; email: fellowships@jdrf.org
Internet http://www.jdrf.org/index.cfm?page_id=103291
Sponsor Juvenile Diabetes Foundation International
120 Wall St, 19th Fl
New York, NY 10005-4001

Jeanne Humphrey Block Dissertation Award 2555
The grant assists dissertation research on the psychological development of women and girls for a doctoral student who is a woman. Proposals should focus on the sex and gender differences or some other developmental issue of particular concern to women or girls. Priority will be given to projects that draw on or contribute to the resources of the Murray Research Center. Research concerned with the life experiences of racially and ethnically diverse populations within the United States is encouraged.
Requirements Any female student currently enrolled in a doctoral program in a relevant field is eligible to apply. Dissertation proposals must be approved by an advisor or committee before the grant application is submitted.
Amount $5000 maximum
Date(s) Application Is Due Apr 1.
Contact Grants Program Administrator, Jeanne Humphrey Block Dissertation Awards Program, (617) 495-8140; fax: (617) 496-3993; email: mrc@radcliffe.com
Internet http://www.murray.harvard.edu/mra/index.jsp
Sponsor Radcliffe College Henry A. Murray Research Center
10 Garden St
Cambridge, MA 02138

Jefferson Science Fellows Program 2556
This program establishes a new model for engaging the American academic science, technology, and engineering communities in the formulation and implementation of US foreign policy. Each fellow will spend one year at the US Department of State for an on-site assignment in Washington, DC, that may also involve extended stays at US foreign embassies and/or missions. All JSF assignments will be designed in consultation with regional and/or functional bureaus within the US Department of State. Following the fellowship year, the fellow will return to his/her academic career, but will remain available to the US government as an experienced consultant for short-term projects over the following five years. Application and guidelines are available online.
Requirements Nominees and applicants must be US citizens and must hold a tenured faculty position at a US degree granting academic institution of higher learning. Nominations will be accepted from US academic institutions that have signed a JSF/MOU with the US Department of State.
Amount $50,000 stipend
Date(s) Application Is Due Dec 1.
Contact Fellowships Office, (202) 334-2872; fax: (202) 334-3419; email: jsf@nas.edu
Internet http://www7.nationalacademies.org/fellowships/Jefferson_Science_Fellows.html
Sponsor National Academies
500 Fifth Street NW, GR 322A
Washington, DC 20001

Jeffress Research Grants 2557
The trust supports research in chemical, medical, or other scientific fields through grants to nonprofit educational, charitable, scientific, literary, and research institutions in the Commonwealth of Virginia. Types of support include assistantships, fellowships, research grants, and program grants. Grants are awarded for one year, with possible renewal for two additional years. The deadline for receipt of applications for consideration at the May meeting is March 1; for the November meeting, September 1.
Requirements Tax-exempt institutions are eligible.
Amount $30,000 maximum first year; $10,000 maximum renewal per year for two years
Date(s) Application Is Due Mar 1; Sep 1.
Contact Dr. Richard Brandt, Advisor, Bank of America , Jeffress Memorial Trust, (804) 788-3698; fax: (804) 788-2700
Internet http://www.wm.edu/grants/OPPS/jeffress.htm
Sponsor Jeffress Memorial Trust
P.O. Box 26688
Richmond, VA 23261-6688

Jeffrey Campbell Graduate Fellow in Anthropology 2558
The university's Department of Anthropology invites applications for a fellowship in biological (physical) anthropology or paleoanthropology for next year's academic year. The successful candidate will be a specialist and qualified to teach in the area of human origins. The Campbell Fellow will receive a stipend per academic year with the possibility of additional funds for travel to conferences and professional meetings. The fellow will also be afforded office space and a personal computer. It is expected that fellows will reside at the university for one academic year and to teach one course per semester in an area of the candidate's research interest (in consultation with the department). Fellows will also present a research-based paper in the fellows' lecture series each year. Send a detailed letter of application, curriculum vita, three letters of reference, and a short (one to two pages) statement of pedagogy to the office. Guidelines are available online.
Requirements Applicants must have completed coursework and preliminary examinations for the PhD in anthropology. Candidates should be members of racial or ethnic groups historically underrepresented in higher education in the United States.
Restrictions Geographic area is open, except for South Asia.
Amount $28,500 stipend
Contact Dr. Alice Pomponio, Department of Anthropology, (315) 229-5797; email: apomponio@stlawu.edu
Internet http://web.stlawu.edu/resources/positions/faculty/fy%202005-2006/anthrojcgf0805.htm
Sponsor Saint Lawrence University
Department of Anthropology
Canton, NY 13617

JEHT Foundation Community Justice Grants 2559
JEHT stands for the core values that underlie the foundation's mission: Justice, Equality, Human dignity and Tolerance. The foundation's programs work to transform US criminal justice policies and practices; expand the role of international justice and the rule of law both at home and abroad; and democratize the electoral process in this country. The foundation also will consider limited support for issues or opportunities that fall within the broader scope of its programs but are not reflected in the primary program interests; issues that cut across one or more of the interest areas; internal capacity building for organizations that are already receiving funding from the foundation; external expertise for organizations that are already receiving funding from the foundation- (e.g., professional communications, technology, fundraising, or political consultants); and convenings within its primary interest areas that broaden knowledge in the field, promote cooperation and information-sharing, and link related fields to one another. There are no restrictions on the type of support as long as the organization's work is consistent with

the foundation's program interests and it is permissible under applicable US charities law. Grant amounts are determined based on the scope of the project, the size of the applicant's budget, the likelihood that other support can be raised, and the foundation's available financial resources in a given year. Letters of inquiry are accepted throughout the year; full proposals are by invitation. Information and guidelines are available online.
Requirements 501(c)3 are eligible. Organizations that can meet a 501(c)3 financial equivalency test will be considered.
Contact Grants Administrator, (212) 965-0400; fax: (212) 966-9606; email: info@jehtfoundation.org
Internet http://www.jehtfoundation.org/application/applicl_overview.html
Sponsor JEHT Foundation
120 Wooster St, 2nd Fl
New York, NY 10012

Jenifer Altman Foundation Grants **2560**
The foundation is a small foundation working for a socially just and ecologically sustainable future, innovative research and demonstration projects in mind-body health, and improved child care prospects for at-risk children. Small grants are made in two areas: initiatives concerning the impact of endocrine disrupting chemicals on human health and the preservation of the environment and initiatives supporting the global citizens' movement for a just and sustainable future in relation to international governmental decision-making forums. The foundation awards a few grants for innovative research and demonstration programs in mind-body health, especially those focused on cancer. Local initiatives that contribute to the quality of life in Bolinas, CA, are also of interest. Applicants should send a concept letter to determine if their projects align with the foundations areas of interest.
Requirements Creative and innovative nonprofits are eligible to apply for one-time grants.
Restrictions Grants are not made to individuals. The foundation rarely funds programs for the conservation of specific species or habitats and rarely funds research at universities on environmental issues. Grants are not made for civic programs, projects in other countries, or projects that are focused entirely on one city or region in the United States.
Amount $500-$50,000 range; $1500-$20,000 average
Contact Aditi Vaidya, Grants Administrator, (415) 561-2182; fax: (415) 561-6480; email: avaidya@jaf.org
Internet http://www.jaf.org/apply/index.html
Sponsor Jenifer Altman Foundation
P.O. Box 29209
San Francisco, CA 94129

Jeppson Memorial Fund for Brookfield **2561**
The Fund provides money to civic and community projects that help improve the lives of residents and enrich the cultural environment. The Fund provides support for: cultural or artistic performances; public seminars; festivals or exhibitions; services that help frail or vulnerable citizens, or that contribute to public health and safety; opportunities for educational enrichment; youth involvement in recreation, sports and the arts; and projects that foster community awareness and connections among different groups. Application information is available online.
Requirements Any nonprofit or civic organization that serves Brookfield may apply.
Restrictions Grant funds may not be used for expenses already incurred by the applicant. Fund awards are not intended to replace municipal funds.
Date(s) Application Is Due Jul 15.
Contact Joe Wlinikka-Lydon, (508) 755-0980; email: joewl@greaterworcester.org
Internet http://www.greaterworcester.org/grants/Jeppson.htm
Sponsor Greater Worcester Community Foundation
370 Main Street, Suite 650
Worcester, MA 01608-1738

Jessie Smith Noyes Foundation Grants **2562**
The foundation is committed to preventing damage to the natural systems upon which all life depends and to strengthening individuals and institutions committed to protecting natural systems and ensuring a sustainable society. The foundation makes grants primarily in the interrelated areas of environment and reproductive rights. The program components include toxics, sustainable agriculture (both with emphasis on southern and Rocky Mountain states), and US reproductive rights. In addition, a few grants are made in four areas of special concern: sustainable communities, US environmental justice, strengthening the US nonprofit sector, and environmental issues in the metropolitan New York region. Letters of inquiry are received at any time; proposals will be requested from the foundation after review.
Requirements 501(c)3 tax-exempt organizations are eligible.
Restrictions Normally, the foundation will not consider requests for direct service, endowments, loans or scholarships to individuals, capital construction funds, conferences, media events, production of media and TV programming, or general fund-raising drives. General research projects are not funded per se.
Contact Millie Buchanan, Program Officer, (212) 684-6577; fax: (212) 689-6549; email: noyes@noyes.org
Internet http://www.noyes.org
Sponsor Jessie Smith Noyes Foundation
6 E 39th St, 12th Fl
New York, NY 10016-0112

Jewish Education and Scholarships Program **2563**
The federation provides scholarships and special grants for all types of educational initiatives. The federation's dollars to congregations affiliated with its educational partners enable them to expand their programs, augmenting congregations' limited resources. In addition, federation financial incentive and scholarship programs, in partnership with congregations and families, enable parents to send their children to summer camps, as well as to participate in Israel Experience programs. Guidelines are available online.
Contact Education and Scholarships Program, (312) 346-6700
Internet http://juf.org/jewish_identity/ji_ed_fed.asp
Sponsor Jewish United Fund/Jewish Federation of Metropolitan Chicago
1 S Franklin St
Chicago, IL 60606-4594

Jewish Federation of Metropolitan Chicago Scholarships **2564**
Scholarship funds are available for Jewish college students. The scholarships support full-time students, predominantly those legally domiciled in the metropolitan Chicago area, who are identified as having promise for significant contributions in their chosen careers. Assistance is available for those in the helping professions, i.e., medicine, education, Jewish communal service, the rabbinate, social service, law, and communications at the University of Illinois (Champaign-Urbana).
Requirements Applicants must be Jewish; meet one or both of the following criteria--born and raised in either Cook County, Chicago metropolitan area or Northwest Indiana, or prior to starting professional education, worked full-time for at least 12 months in Cook County or Chicago metropolitan area; intend to remain in the Chicago metropolitan area after completing school; and be entering a professional postgraduate education program on a full-time basis (school acceptance is not required at time of scholarship application). Undergraduate applicants must be entering the junior or senior year of a professional education program that will allow them to pursue employment in their chosen helping professions at a bachelor's degree level.
Amount $500,000 total annually
Date(s) Application Is Due Feb 15.
Contact Program Administrator, (312) 673-3457; email: jvsscholarship@jvschicago.org
Internet http://www.jvschicago.org/scholarship
Sponsor Jewish Vocational Service
216 W. Jackson Blvd, Suite 700
Chicago, IL 60606

Jewish Foundation for Education of Women Scholarships **2565**
Scholarships are awarded to women pursuing undergraduate or graduate education. Requests for applications must be made in writing and specify whether aid is being sought for undergraduate or graduate studies. Financial assistance is offered every year depending on progress shown.
Requirements Eligible to apply are women who are permanent residents of the five boroughs of New York City, although schools attended may be located anywhere.
Restrictions No awards will be made for the pursuit of JD or MBA degrees. Scholarships will not be available for the upcoming school year.
Amount $5000 maximum
Date(s) Application Is Due Jun 1.
Contact Marge Goldwater, Executive Director, (212) 288-3931; fax: (212) 288-5798; email: fdnscholar@aol.com
Internet http://www.jfew.org
Sponsor Jewish Foundation for Education of Women
135 E 64 St.
New York, NY 10021

Jewish Foundation for Education of Women Scholarships for Emigres in the Health Professions **2566**
Scholarships are awarded to women emigres from the former Soviet Union for graduate and undergraduate education in medicine, dentistry, nursing, or pharmacy. Approximately 48 scholarships are awarded. Applications are available in late October.
Requirements Eligible to apply are women who are emigres from the former Soviet Union, live within a 50-mile radius of New York City, and demonstrate financial need.
Restrictions Pre-medical students are not eligible. Applications submitted directly from students are not accepted.
Amount $5000
Date(s) Application Is Due Jun 1.
Contact Marge Goldwater, Executive Director, (212) 288-3931; fax: (212) 288-5798; email: FdnScholar@aol.com
Internet http://www.jfew.org/programs.html#HP
Sponsor Jewish Foundation for Education of Women
135 East 64th Street
New York, NY 10021

Jewish Institute of Religion Graduate Fellowships and Scholarships **2567**
The Jewish Institute of Religion at Hebrew Union College awards graduate fellowships and tuition scholarships for MA and PhD studies in Bible, Semitics, History, Rabbinics, and Modern Jewish studies. Also, joint programs are offered with the University of Cincinnati in modern Hebrew, literature, and sociology.

Contact Graduate Study Admissions, (513) 221-1875, fax: (513) 221-0321
Internet http://www.huc.edu/admissions/aid.shtml
Sponsor Hebrew Union College
3101 Clifton Ave
Cincinnati, OH 45220-2488

Jewish Institutional Grants **2568**
The Memorial Foundation for Jewish Culture awards grants to universities and institutions for Jewish scholarship in such areas as the bible and semitics, Jewish history, Jewish philosophy and thought, Talmud, rabbinics and Jewish law, and general Jewish research; for Jewish educational and cultural programs; and for research and publication on the Holocaust. The amount awarded varies depending on the budget of the project; awards are limited to no more than 25 percent of the total cost excluding overhead. Application form must be requested in writing. Grants are made every two years, in even-numbered years. Applications are due February 28 in odd-numbered years.
Restrictions Grants are made only for team or collaborative projects of limited duration. Grants are not made to individuals.
Contact Dr. Jerry Hochbaum, Executive Vice President, (212) 425-6606; fax: (212) 425-6602; email: office@mfjc.org
Internet http://www.mfjc.org
Sponsor Memorial Foundation for Jewish Culture
50 Broadway, 34th Fl
New York, NY 10004

Jewish International Community Service Scholarships **2569**
Scholarships are awarded annually for professional training for careers in Jewish education, Jewish social service, the rabbinate, shehita, and milah. The recipients must commit themselves after their training to serve two to three years in a Jewishly deprived Diaspora community outside the United States, Canada, and Israel where such professional personnel are urgently needed. Recipient should also be knowledgeable in the language and culture of that country or be prepared to learn it. Scholarships are for one year, renewable up to a total of four years. Application forms are available upon written request.
Requirements Scholarships are open to any individual, regardless of country of origin, who is presently receiving or plans to undertake training in his/her chosen field in a recognized yeshiva, teacher training seminary, school of social work, university, or other educational institution. Application forms must be requested in writing.
Amount $1000-$3000 depending on the country in which the recipient is trained
Date(s) Application Is Due Nov 30.
Contact Dr. Jerry Hochbaum, Executive Vice President, (212) 425-6606; fax: (212) 425-6602; email: office@mfjc.org
Internet http://www.mfjc.org
Sponsor Memorial Foundation for Jewish Culture
50 Broadway, 34th Fl
New York, NY 10004

Jewish Post-Rabbinic Scholarships **2570**
These scholarships are awarded to newly ordained rabbis for advanced training leading to careers as judges on rabbinical courts, heads of institutions of higher learning, or other advanced religious leadership positions.
Requirements Eligible to apply are recently ordained rabbis enrolled in full-time graduate study in a rabbinical seminary, yeshiva, or other institution of higher Jewish learning. Application forms will be sent on written request from the individual (not the school).
Amount $2000-$6000
Contact Dr. Jerry Hochbaum, Executive Vice President, (212) 425-6606; fax: (212) 425-6602; email: office@mfjc.org
Internet http://www.mishpacha.com/mfjc.shtml
Sponsor Memorial Foundation for Jewish Culture
50 Broadway, 34th Fl
New York, NY 10004

Jewish Social Entrepreneurs Fellowships **2571**
The fellowship supports women and men who are developing projects that address current social issues in the Jewish community and the United States. Projects can be an idea in an advanced stage of planning, a young independent nonprofit organization, or an original transformative program within an existing organization. Selected programs can focus on a wide variety of social arenas, including education, social justice, the arts, technology, the environment, and spirituality. The fellowship provides seed capital, entrepreneurial training, mentorships, technical assistance, and Jewish learning. Each fellow is encouraged and supported in raising additional funds for his or her project. Guidelines and application forms are available online.
Requirements Jewish innovators between the ages of 21 and 35 are eligible.
Amount $30,000 per year; $5000 maximum self-directed learning grant
Contact Fellowship Administrator, (415) 777-4500; fax: (415) 777-4045; email: fellowship@joshuaventure.org
Internet http://www.joshuaventure.org
Sponsor Joshua Venture
28 Second St, Ste 500
San Francisco, CA 94105

Jewish Women's Foundation of New York Grants **2572**
The foundation provides support for unmet social, economic, and health needs of Jewish females in the New York metropolitan area and beyond. Strategic grants support cutting-edge projects that address Jewish education, training, and culture--projects related to education, training of educators, leadership development, ethics, spirituality, arts, sports, etc.; mental and physical health--projects involving genetics, self-esteem, violence prevention, issues concerning the end of life, and other areas that relate to women's health as a quality of life; and economic empowerment--projects that give women more independence, knowledge, competency, and responsibility for their economic situations. Grant requests may address innovative programs, services, and/or research. The projects primary target group must be Jewish females. The foundation expects to award three to four grants. The listed deadline is for concept letters; full proposals are by invitation.
Requirements 501(c)3 tax-exempt organizations in the New York metropolitan area (the five boroughs of New York City, Long Island and/or Westchester) are eligible.
Restrictions The foundation will not provide grants for scholarships, equipment, capital campaigns, or ongoing support for existing programs.
Amount $25,000 maximum
Date(s) Application Is Due Sep 30.
Contact Sherri Greenbach, Executive Director, (212) 836-1478; fax: (212) 836-1831
Internet http://www.jewishwomenny.org
Sponsor Jewish Women's Foundation of New York
130 E 59th St, Rm 563
New York, NY 10022

JFEW Scholarships for Emigres Training for Careers in Jewish Education **2573**
Scholarships are awarded to women emigres from the New Independent States for graduate education in the fields of rabbinical, cantorial, Jewish education, or Jewish studies. Approximately seven scholarships are awarded.
Requirements Eligible to apply are women who are emigres from the New Independent States who live within a 50-mile radius of New York City and demonstrate financial need.
Amount $5000 annually or $ 10,000-$20,000 one time grants
Contact Marge Goldwater, Executive Director, (212) 288-3931; fax: (212) 288-5798; email: FdnScholar@aol.com
Internet http://www.jfew.org/programs.html
Sponsor Jewish Foundation for Education of Women
135 E 64th St
New York, NY 10021

JFK Library Foundation Abba P. Schwartz Research Fellowship **2574**
The fellowship is intended to support a scholar in the preparation of a substantial work in the areas of immigration, naturalization, or refugee policy.
Requirements Scholars and students are invited to apply for support of their research and use of the archival, manuscript, and audiovisual holdings of the library.
Amount $3100
Date(s) Application Is Due Mar 15.
Contact Grant and Fellowship Coordinator, (617) 514-1600; fax: (617) 514-1652; email: kennedy.library@nara.gov
Internet http://www.jfklibrary.org/schwartz.htm
Sponsor John F. Kennedy Library Foundation
Columbia Point
Boston, MA 02125-3313

JFK Library Foundation Arthur M. Schlesinger Jr. Research Fellowship **2575**
The fellowship is intended to support scholars in the preparation of substantial works on the foreign policy of the Kennedy years, especially with regard to the western hemisphere, or on Kennedy domestic policy, especially with regard to racial justice and to the conservation of natural resources.
Requirements Proposals are invited from all sources, but preference will be given to those from applicants specializing in the areas indicated. Preference is also given to projects not supported by large grants from other institutions.
Amount $5000
Date(s) Application Is Due Aug 15.
Contact Grant and Fellowship Coordinator, (617) 514-1631; fax: (617) 514-1652; email: kennedy.library@nara.gov
Internet http://www.jfklibrary.org/schles.htm
Sponsor John F. Kennedy Library Foundation
Columbia Point
Boston, MA 02125-3313

JFK Library Foundation Hemingway Research Grants **2576**
Funds are awarded to help defray living, travel, and related costs incurred while doing research in the Hemingway Collection at the Kennedy Library. Applications are evaluated on the basis of expected utilization of the Hemingway Collection, the degree to which projects address research needs in Hemingway or related studies, and the qualifications of applicants. Preference is given to dissertation research by PhD candidates in newly opened or relatively unused portions of the collection. Applicants are advised to consult the catalog of the Ernest Hemingway Collection at the John F. Kennedy Library and to contact a member of the Kennedy Library staff for more information before applying.
Amount $200-$1000

Date(s) Application Is Due Nov 1.
Contact Grant and Fellowship Coordinator, (617) 514-1600; fax: (617) 514-1652; email: kennedy.library@nara.gov
Internet http://www.jfklibrary.org/ehgrants.htm
Sponsor John F. Kennedy Library Foundation
Columbia Point
Boston, MA 02125-3313

JFK Library Foundation Marjorie Kovler Research Fellowship **2577**
The fellowship is intended to support a scholar in the preparation of a substantial work in the area of foreign intelligence and the presidency, or a related topic. Application forms are available on the Web site.
Requirements Scholars and students are invited to apply for support of their research and use of the archival, manuscript, and audiovisual holdings of the library.
Amount $2500 maximum
Date(s) Application Is Due Mar 15.
Contact Grant and Fellowship Coordinator, (617) 514-1631; fax: (617) 514-1652; email: kennedy.library@nara.gov
Internet http://www.jfklibrary.org/kovler.htm
Sponsor John F. Kennedy Library Foundation
Columbia Point
Boston, MA 02125-3313

JFK Library Foundation Research Grants **2578**
The John F. Kennedy Library Foundation administers and funds programs on behalf of the Kennedy Library and Museum. Scholars and students are invited to apply for support of their research and use of the archival, manuscript, and audiovisual holdings of the library. Preference is given to dissertation research by PhD candidates working in newly opened or relatively unused collections, and to the work of recent PhD recipients who are expanding or revising their dissertations for publication, but all proposals are welcome and will receive careful consideration.
Amount $500-$2500
Date(s) Application Is Due Mar 15; Aug 15.
Contact Grant and Fellowship Coordinator, (617) 514-1600; fax: (617) 514-1652; email: library@kennedy.nara.gov
Internet http://www.jfklibrary.org/krg.htm
Sponsor John F. Kennedy Library Foundation
Columbia Point
Boston, MA 02125-3313

JFK Library Foundation Theodore C. Sorensen Research Fellowship **2579**
The fellowship is intended to support a scholar in the preparation of a substantial work in the areas of domestic policy, political journalism, polling, or press relations.
Requirements Scholars and students are invited to apply for support of their research and use of the archival, manuscript, and audiovisual holdings of the library.
Amount $3600
Date(s) Application Is Due Mar 15.
Contact Grant and Fellowship Coordinator, (617) 514-1600; fax: (617) 514-1652; email: kennedy.library@nara.gov
Internet http://www.jfklibrary.org/sorensen.htm
Sponsor John F. Kennedy Library Foundation
Columbia Point
Boston, MA 02125-3313

JHI International Fellows in Philanthropy Program **2580**
The program offers advanced study, research, and training to eight participants annually who are involved in studying or managing private nonprofit or philanthropic organizations outside the United States, or who are working as liaisons for nongovernmental organizations in the public or commercial sectors. Fellowships can be for either an academic year or a semester and are available at both the junior and senior levels. A high degree of English-language fluency is required.
Requirements Individuals studying nonprofit organizations or managing a nonprofit group outside the United States are eligible. Candidates are expected to have attained a university undergraduate degree and to be capable of carrying out independent research and inquiry.
Date(s) Application Is Due Feb 25.
Contact Lester Salamon, Program Director, (410) 516-5389; fax: (410) 516-8233; email: npmgt@jhu.edu
Internet http://www.jhu.edu/~philfellow
Sponsor Johns Hopkins Institute for Policy Studies
3400 N Charles St, Wyman Bldg, 5th Fl
Baltimore, MD 21218

JHMI Patrick C. Walsh Prostate Cancer Research Fund **2581**
Funding is available to support multidisciplinary research in prostate cancer through the Patrick C. Walsh Prostate Cancer Research Fund. Awards of $50,000 to $100,000 for up to 2 years are available to fund career development and developmental research programs (pilot projects). This fund will attract and support the best and brightest scientists throughout Johns Hopkins to join in an effort to defeat the number one cancer in men. 1) Awards will be for pilot projects, focused on prostate cancer, that develop a new research direction, explore an innovative idea, test an unconventional, but potentially important, new hypothesis, or ascertain the feasibility of a new research approach. These grants will be reviewed by a scientific advisory board which will award funding to projects that hold the most promise.
Requirements All faculty of the Johns Hopkins University may apply, whether or not they are members of the James Buchanan Brady Urological Institute or of the Sidney Kimmel Comprehensive Cancer Center. However, an investigator may hold only one pilot project award at a time.
Amount $50,000-$100,000
Date(s) Application Is Due Jan 8.
Contact Angela Sciuto, Sponsored Projects Officer, (410) 614-0257; email: asciuto2@jhmi.edu
Internet http://prostatecancerprogram.onc.jhmi.edu/
Sponsor Johns Hopkins Medical Institute
733 N. Broadway, Suite 117
Baltimore, MD 21205

JILA Visiting Fellowships and Postdoctoral Research Associateships **2582**
One-year postdoctoral research associateships are intended to provide advanced research training in the years immediately after the PhD degree. These research associateships are generally renewable for a second year. Visiting fellowships are awarded for independent research and study, usually to those with extensive research experience. For those in doubt as to which type of appointment is more suitable, the institute advises application for a research associateship. If all materials for the completed application are received by November 1, the applicant may request to be considered for both the visiting fellowship program and the postdoctoral research associateship program. Transportation to Boulder may be paid for the appointee and his/her spouse and minor children, and an allowance for shipment of personal effects and an allowance for appropriate professional travel within the United States during the period of the appointment are usually made available.
Date(s) Application Is Due Nov 1.
Contact Secretary, Visiting Scientists Program, (303) 492-7796; fax: (303) 492-5235; email: jilavf@jila.colorado.edu
Internet http://jilawww.colorado.edu/www/programs/pd.html
Sponsor Joint Institute for Laboratory Astrophysics (JILA)
University of Colorado, 440 UCB
Boulder, CO 80309-0440

JM Foundation Grants **2583**
The foundation awards grants to eligible nonprofit organizations in its areas of interest, including education and research that fosters market-based policy solutions; developing state and national organizations that promote free enterprise, entrepreneurship, and private initiative; and identifying and educating young leaders. Types of support include internships, matching/challenge grants, program grants, publication, research grants, seed grants, and technical assistance. The foundation's board of directors meets bi-annually, usually in May and October. There are no formal proposal deadlines. Inquiries and proposals are processed on an ongoing basis.
Requirements Public charities, including 501(c)3, 509(a)1, and 170(b)l(a)(vi) nonprofit organizations, are eligible.
Restrictions Grants do not support individuals, the arts, government agencies, public schools, and international agencies; or requests for operating expenses, annual fundraising campaigns, capital campaigns, equipment, endowment funds, and loans.
Contact Carl Helstrom, Executive Director, (212) 687-7735; fax: (212) 697-5495
Internet http://fdncenter.org/grantmaker/jm-milbank
Sponsor JM Foundation
654 Madison Ave, Ste 1605
New York, NY 10021

JMO American Institutions Grants **2584**
Grants promote understanding of the moral, cultural, and institutional foundations of free government. Under this program the foundation supports studies of and research on the American Constitution, the operation of American political institutions and the moral and cultural principles underlying these institutions, economics, foreign policy, and security studies. Financial support is awarded for research, institutional support, fellowships, professorships, lectures, conferences/seminars, books, scholarly journals and journals of opinion, and sometimes television and radio programs.
Requirements A 501(c)3 nonprofit may apply by submitting a concise written proposal describing the project and grant request and offering background on the organization and its current sources of funding.
Restrictions Grants are not awarded to support endowments or capital campaigns.
Amount $5000-$600,000
Contact William Voegeli, Program Officer, (212) 661-2670; fax: (212) 661-5917; email: wvoegeli@jmof.org
Internet http://www.jmof.org/grant_programs.html
Sponsor John M. Olin Foundation
330 Madison Ave, 22nd Fl
New York, NY 10017

JMO Law and Legal System Grants **2585**
Grants are given to deepen the understanding of the American judicial system and to preserve the rule of law as the bedrock of American constitutional government.

The foundation supports public interest law and studies related to the judicial system, jurisprudence, and the relationship between law and economics. Financial support is awarded for research, institutional support, fellowships, professorships, lectures, conferences/seminars, books, scholarly journals and journals of opinion, and sometimes for television and radio programs.
Requirements A 501(c)3 nonprofit may apply by submitting a concise written proposal describing the project and grant request and offering background on the organization and its current sources of funding.
Contact Caroline Hemphill, Program Officer, (212) 661-2670; fax: (212) 661-5917; email: chemphill@jmof.org or inquiry@jmof.org
Internet http://www.jmof.org/grant_programs.html
Sponsor John M. Olin Foundation
330 Madison Ave, 22nd Fl
New York, NY 10017

JMO Public Policy Research Grants **2586**
Grants support research on the formulation, implementation, and evaluation of public policy in the social and economic fields. Grants are made in such areas as regulatory policy, tax policy, fiscal policy, monetary policy, and welfare policy. The larger grants are made to graduate schools at universities in these areas. Financial support is awarded for research, institutional support, fellowships, professorships, lectures, conferences/seminars, books, scholarly journals and journals of opinion, and sometimes for radio and television programs.
Requirements A 501(c)3 nonprofit may apply by submitting a concise written proposal describing the project and grant request and offering background on the organization and its current sources of funding.
Restrictions Grants do not support endowments, building campaigns, annual giving programs, or individuals.
Amount $20,000-$300,000
Contact Caroline Hemphill, Program Officer, (212) 661-2670; fax: (212) 661-5917; email: chemphill@jmof.org or inquiry@jmof.org
Internet http://www.jmof.org/grant_programs.html
Sponsor John M. Olin Foundation
330 Madison Ave, 22nd Fl
New York, NY 10017

JMO Strategic and International Studies Grants **2587**
Grants support projects that address the relationship between American institutions and the international context in which they operate. Such projects include studies of national security affairs, strategic issues, American foreign policy, and the international economy. Financial support is awarded for research, institutional support, fellowships, professorships, lectures, conferences/seminars, books, scholarly journals and journals of opinion, and sometimes for television and radio programs.
Requirements A 501(c)3 nonprofit may apply by submitting a concise written proposal describing the project and grant request and offering background on the organization and its current sources of funding.
Amount $10,000-$300,000
Contact Caroline Hemphill, Program Officer, (212) 661-2670; fax: (212) 661-5917; email: chemphill@jmof.org or inquiry@jmof.org
Internet http://www.jmof.org/grant_programs.html
Sponsor John M. Olin Foundation
330 Madison Ave, 22nd Fl
New York, NY 10017

Joan B. Kroc Institute for International Peace Studies Rockefeller Foundation Visiting Fellowships **2588**
The fellowships support research that explores the complex role of religion in contemporary conflicts, ranging from the legitimation or sacralization of violence, to participation in conflict mediation and reconciliation, to the advocacy and practice of nonviolent resistance as a religious imperative. Research focuses on the relationship between religious ethics, human rights, and attitudes of tolerance and intolerance toward the other; religious roles in conflict resolution, including conflict within and between religious traditions; and the contributions of religious actors to postconflict reconciliation, justice, and peacebuilding. The program seeks to include research by scholars and practitioners with expertise in Hindu, Muslim, Jewish, Buddhist, Sikh, or Christian traditions and movements. Projects that consider program themes from the perspective of a public intellectual are particularly encouraged. Guidelines are available online.
Requirements Senior and junior scholars in the humanities and social sciences, as well as religious leaders and peacebuilding practitioners, of any nationality are eligible.
Amount $35,000 minimum per year
Date(s) Application Is Due Nov 15.
Contact Rashied Omar, Program Coordinator, (574) 631-7740; fax: (574) 631-6973; email: omar.1@nd.edu
Internet http://www.nd.edu/~krocinst/visiting_fellows/rockvf0607.html
Sponsor University of Notre Dame
P.O. Box 639
Notre Dame, IN 46556-0639

Joan B. Kroc Institute for International Peace Studies Visiting Fellows Program **2589**
The institute brings together outstanding scholars to conduct peace-related research, broadly defined. Themes include the peacemaking role of international norms, policies, and institutions; approaches to the study and resolution of violence; and the quest for social, economic, and environmental justice. Fellows conduct research and write in their areas of interest, for a semester or a year, while interacting with institute faculty and staff, and with Kroc faculty fellows in the broader Notre Dame community. Fellows are provided an office, library access, communications links, document retrieval services, and housing. Guidelines are available online.
Requirements Applications at the predoctoral, postdoctoral, and senior scholar level will be considered.
Amount $20,000 maximum per semester, junior fellows; $25,000 maximum per semester, senior fellows
Date(s) Application Is Due Nov 1.
Contact Dr. Martha Merritt, Associate Director, (574) 631-7695; email: mmerritt@nd.edu
Internet http://www.nd.edu/~krocinst/visiting_fellows/visfell0607.html
Sponsor University of Notre Dame
P.O. Box 639, 100 Hesburgh Center for International Studies
Notre Dame, IN 46556

Joan Cahalin Robinson Prize **2590**
This prize is awarded annually for the best paper presented at the SHOT annual meeting by a historian under 30 years of age or by a person past 30 who is an accredited graduate student or candidate for a higher degree and who is presenting his or her first paper at a SHOT annual meeting. Candidates for the award are judged not only on the quality of the historical research and scholarship demonstrated in the written papers submitted to the Robinson Prize Committee before the meeting, but also on the effectiveness of their oral presentations. A certificate is included with the prize. Annual deadline dates may vary; contact program staff for exact dates.
Amount $350
Date(s) Application Is Due Mar 15; Jul 1.
Contact Program Contact, (515) 294-8469 ; fax: (515) 294-6390; email: shot@jhu.edu
Internet http://shot.jhu.edu/Awards/Awards_Main_Page.htm
Sponsor Society for the History of Technology
618 Ross Hall, History, ISU
Ames, IA 50011

Joan's Legacy Lung Cancer Research Grants **2591**
Joan's Legacy invites grant applications for institutional research that studies lung cancer. The foundation is particularly interested in the genetic basis and biology of bronchoalveolar carcinoma as well as novel therapeutic approaches for the treatment of this disease. This funding is intended primarily as seed money for promising new work. It is not for supporting research where funding has either lapsed or has been previously disapproved. Preference will be given to applications where indirect costs are minimal or nonexistent. Grants are awarded for one or two years. Funding for promising research may be extended further at the discretion of the medical committee. Application and guidelines are available online.
Amount $50,000 per year
Date(s) Application Is Due Jul 1.
Contact Grants Administrator, (212) 627-5500; fax: (917) 661-7811
Internet http://www.joanslegacy.org/grant_app.html
Sponsor Joan Scarangello Foundation to Conquer Lung Cancer
27 Union Square W, Ste 205
New York, NY 10003

Joe W. and Dorothy Dorsett Brown Foundation Grants **2592**
The foundation awards grants to nonprofit organizations in Louisiana and the Gulf Coast of Mississippi. Areas of interest include medical research; housing for the homeless; support for organizations who care for the sick, hungry or helpless; religious and educational institutions; and organizations and groups concerned with improving the local community. Types of support include operating budgets, research, and student aid. The foundation also supports Service Learning, a learn-by-doing approach to the curriculum. Students receive practical, hands-on experience in the subject matter studied by meeting identified community needs through active participation. The listed deadline date is for Service Learning grants.
Requirements Louisiana and Mississippi nonprofit organizations, with a focus on South Louisiana, the New Orleans area, and the Mississippi Gulf Coast, are eligible. Service Learning grant applications are available yearly to sixth through 12th grades in the following parishes: Orleans, Jefferson, Plaquemines, Saint Bernard, Saint Charles, Tangipahoa, Saint James, Saint John, Saint Tammany, and Washington.
Amount $5000-$25,000 average
Date(s) Application Is Due Sep 30.
Contact Beth Buscher, (504) 834-3433; email: BethBuscher@thebrownfoundation.org
Internet http://www.thebrownfoundation.org
Sponsor Joe W. and Dorothy Dorsett Brown Foundation
320 Hammond Hwy, Ste 500
Metairie, LA 70005

Subject Index

NOTE: Numbers refer to entry numbers

Biology, Reproductive

Biology, Structural

Biology, Systematic

Biomass Fuels

Biomaterials

Biomechanics

Biomedical Education

Biomedical Engineering

Biomedical Research

Biomedicine

Biometry

Biophysics

Canadian Studies

Cancer/Carcinogenesis

Carbohydrates

Carbon Dioxide

Cardiology

Cardiovascular Diseases

Chemistry Education

Chemistry, Analytical

Chemistry, Colloid

Chemistry, Environmental

Chemistry, Inorganic

Education Reform

Educational Planning/Policy

Egypt

Elderly

Embryology

Emergency Preparedness

Emergency Programs

Emergency Services

Emission Control

Employment/Unemployment Studies

Endangered Language

Endocrinology

Energy

Engineering Administration/Management

Engineering Design

Engineering Education

Environmental Health see also Occupational Health & Safety; Radiation Effects

Environmental Law

Environmental Planning/Policy

Environmental Studies

Enzymes

Epidemiology

Genetics

Genetics, Molecular

Higher Education Administration

Higher Education Studies

Higher Education, Private

HIV *see also* **AIDS**

International Trade & Finance

Internet *see also* **Networking (Computers)**

Interstellar Studies

Interventions

Inventions

Investments & Securities

Ionized Gases

Iran

Lipids

Literacy

Literary Arts

Literary Criticism

Literary Magazines

Literature

Medical Ethics

Medical Informatics

Mental Health

Mental Retardation

Mentoring Programs

Minority Education

Minority Education

Minority Employment

Minority Health

Minority Schools

Minority/Woman-Owned Business

Missouri

Modern Languages

Moldova

Molecular Probes

Mongolia

Montana

Morocco

Morphology

Physics Education

Physics, Applied

Physics, Atomic

Physics, Computational

Physics, Fluid

Physics, High Energy

Physics, Molecular

Physics, Nuclear

Physics, Optical

Physics, Particle

Physics, Plasma

Preventive Medicine

Primary Care Services

Primatology

Print Media

Printing

Printmaking

Prion Disease

Prison Reform

Public Planning/Policy

Religious Programs

Religious Studies

Science & Technology

Science & Technology, History of

Social Sciences Education

Social Security

Social Services

Social Services Delivery

Social Stratification/Mobility

Social Work

Program Type Index

Building Construction and/or Renovation

Curriculum Development/Teacher Training

Citizenship Instruction

Cultural Outreach

Centers: Rsch/Demonstration/Service

Consulting/Visiting Personnel

Demonstration Grants

Development (Institutional/Departmental)

Dissertation/Thesis Research Support

Exhibitions, Collections, Performances, Video/Film Production

Environmental Programs

Educational Programs

Fellowships

Faculty/Professional Development

Graduate Assistantships

General Operating Support

International Exchange Programs

International Grants

Materials/Equipment Acquisition (Computers, Books, Videos, etc.)

Publishing/Editing/Translating

Preservation/Restoration

Scholarships

Symposiums, Conferences, Workshops, Seminars

Service Delivery Programs

Technical Assistance

Travel Grants

Training Programs/Internships

Vocational Education

Geographic Index

Note: This index lists grants for which applicants must be residents of or located in a specific geographic area. Numbers refer to entry numbers.

United States

Canada

Outside U.S. and Canada

Africa

Argentina

Asia

Australia